# Modern Macroeconomics

*In loving memory of Brian's parents, Joseph and Margaret Snowdon, and Howard's father, Philip M. Vane*

# Modern Macroeconomics

## Its Origins, Development and Current State

Brian Snowdon

*Principal Lecturer in Economics in the Newcastle Business School, Northumbria University, Newcastle upon Tyne, UK*

Howard R. Vane

*Professor of Economics in the School of Accounting, Finance and Economics, Liverpool John Moores University, Liverpool, UK*

**Edward Elgar**
Cheltenham, UK • Northampton, MA, USA

Published by
Edward Elgar Publishing Limited
Glensanda House
Montpellier Parade
Cheltenham
Glos GL50 1UA
UK

Edward Elgar Publishing, Inc.
136 West Street
Suite 202
Northampton
Massachusetts 01060
USA

Paperback edition reprinted 2006


A catalogue record for this book
is available from the British Library


ISBN 1 84376 394 X (cased)
      1 84542 208 2 (paperback)

Typeset by Manton Typesetters, Louth, Lincolnshire, UK.
Printed and bound in Great Britain by MPG Books Ltd, Bodmin, Cornwall.

# Contents

*List of figures*                                                          x
*List of tables*                                                         xiii
*Preface*                                                                xiv
*Acknowledgements*                                                      xvii

**1    Understanding modern macroeconomics**                               **1**
1.1   Macroeconomic issues and ideas                                       1
1.2   The role of economic theory and controversy                         3
1.3   Objectives, instruments and the role of government                  7
1.4   The Great Depression                                                9
1.5   Keynes and the birth of macroeconomics                             13
1.6   The rise and fall of the Keynesian consensus                       15
1.7   Theoretical schizophrenia and the neoclassical synthesis           21
1.8   Schools of thought in macroeconomics after Keynes                  24
1.9   The new political macroeconomics                                   29
1.10  The renaissance of economic growth research                        32

**2    Keynes v. the 'old' classical model**                               **36**
2.1   Introduction                                                        36
2.2   Classical macroeconomics                                            37
2.3   Employment and output determination                                 38
2.4   Say's Law                                                           45
2.5   The quantity theory of money                                        50
2.6   Keynes's *General Theory*                                           54
2.7   Interpreting the *General Theory*                                   57
2.8   Keynes's main propositions                                          58
2.9   Keynes's analysis of the labour market                             65
2.10  Keynes's rejection of Say's Law                                    69
2.11  Keynes and the quantity theory of money                            69
2.12  Three important interpretations of Keynes                          70
2.13  The 'new' Keynes scholarship                                        75
2.14  Causes and consequences of the Great Depression                    76
2.15  How to pay for the war                                             82
2.16  Keynes and international macroeconomics                             83

2.17   Keynes's legacy and the classical revival                     85
*Interview with* Robert Skidelsky                                    91

**3      The orthodox Keynesian school                             101**
3.1    Introduction                                                 101
3.2    The orthodox Keynesian school                                102
3.3    The IS–LM model for a closed economy                         102
3.4    Underemployment equilibrium in the Keynesian model           114
3.5    The IS–LM model for an open economy                          123
3.6    The Phillips curve and orthodox Keynesian economics          135
3.7    The central propositions of orthodox Keynesian economics     144
*Interview with* James Tobin                                        148

**4      The orthodox monetarist school                           163**
4.1    Introduction                                                 163
4.2    The quantity theory of money approach                        165
4.3    The expectations-augmented Phillips curve analysis           174
4.4    The monetary approach to balance of payments theory and
       exchange rate determination                                  187
4.5    The orthodox monetarist school and stabilization policy      192
*Interview with* Milton Friedman                                    198

**5      The new classical school                                 219**
5.1    Introduction                                                 219
5.2    The influence of Robert E. Lucas Jr                          220
5.3    The structure of new classical models                        223
5.4    Equilibrium business cycle theory                            236
5.5    The policy implications of the new classical approach        242
5.6    An assessment                                                267
*Interview with* Robert E. Lucas Jr                                 272

**6      The real business cycle school                           294**
6.1    Introduction: the demise of new classical macroeconomics
       mark I                                                       294
6.2    The transition from monetary to real equilibrium business
       cycle theory                                                 295
6.3    Real business cycle theory in historical perspective         297
6.4    Cycles versus random walks                                   300
6.5    Supply-side shocks                                           303
6.6    Business cycles: main features and stylized facts            304
6.7    Real business cycle theory                                   307
6.8    The structure of a real business cycle model                 309

| 6.9 | Technology shocks | 313 |
| 6.10 | A real business cycle aggregate demand and supply model | 315 |
| 6.11 | Calibrating the model | 320 |
| 6.12 | Real business cycle theory and the neutrality of money | 322 |
| 6.13 | Measuring technology shocks: the Solow residual | 325 |
| 6.14 | Real business cycle theory and the stylized facts | 326 |
| 6.15 | The policy implications of real business cycle theory | 330 |
| 6.16 | Criticisms of real business cycle theory | 332 |
| 6.17 | Great Depressions: a real business cycle view | 336 |
| 6.18 | An assessment | 338 |
| *Interview with* Edward C. Prescott | | 344 |

| **7** | **The new Keynesian school** | **357** |
| 7.1 | The fall and rise of Keynesian economics | 357 |
| 7.2 | A Keynesian resurgence | 358 |
| 7.3 | New Keynesian economics | 361 |
| 7.4 | Core propositions and features of new Keynesian economics | 363 |
| 7.5 | Nominal rigidities | 366 |
| 7.6 | Dornbusch's overshooting model | 376 |
| 7.7 | Real rigidities | 378 |
| 7.8 | New Keynesian business cycle theory | 396 |
| 7.9 | Hysteresis and the NAIRU | 401 |
| 7.10 | New Keynesian economics and the stylized facts | 408 |
| 7.11 | Policy implications | 409 |
| 7.12 | Keynesian economics without the *LM* curve | 423 |
| 7.13 | Criticisms of new Keynesian economics | 428 |
| 7.14 | An assessment of new Keynesian economics | 431 |
| *Interview with* N. Gregory Mankiw | | 433 |

| **8** | **The Post Keynesian school** | **451** |
| | *Paul Davidson* | |
| 8.1 | Introduction | 451 |
| 8.2 | The significance of the principle of effective demand | 453 |
| 8.3 | Taxonomy | 454 |
| 8.4 | Keynes's taxonomic attack on Say's Law | 455 |
| 8.5 | Can relative price changes induce $D_2$ to fill the gap? | 457 |
| 8.6 | Investment spending, liquidity, and the non-neutrality of money axiom | 459 |
| 8.7 | What type of an economic system is 'irrational' enough to use money contracts? | 461 |
| 8.8 | Information, decisions and uncertainty | 463 |
| 8.9 | Classifying decision-making environments | 464 |

| | | |
|---|---|---|
| 8.10 | Keynesian uncertainty, money and explicit money contracts | 468 |
| 8.11 | Conclusions | 472 |

**9**     **The Austrian school**     **474**
*Roger W. Garrison*

| | | |
|---|---|---|
| 9.1 | The Mengerian vision | 474 |
| 9.2 | The intertemporal structure of capital | 475 |
| 9.3 | Saving and economic growth | 479 |
| 9.4 | The saving–investment nexus | 482 |
| 9.5 | The market for loanable funds | 489 |
| 9.6 | Full employment and the production possibilities frontier | 492 |
| 9.7 | The capital-based macroeconomic framework | 496 |
| 9.8 | Saving-induced capital restructuring | 498 |
| 9.9 | Keynes's paradox of thrift revisited | 501 |
| 9.10 | The Austrian theory of the business cycle | 503 |
| 9.11 | A Keynesian downturn in the Austrian framework | 509 |
| 9.12 | Inflation and deflation in the Austrian theory | 513 |
| 9.13 | Policy and reform | 515 |

**10**     **The new political macroeconomics**     **517**

| | | |
|---|---|---|
| 10.1 | Introduction: political distortions and macroeconomic performance | 517 |
| 10.2 | Political influences on policy choice | 518 |
| 10.3 | The role of government | 521 |
| 10.4 | Politicians and stabilization policy | 523 |
| 10.5 | Alternative approaches to the 'political business cycle': an overview | 525 |
| 10.6 | The Nordhaus opportunistic model | 526 |
| 10.7 | The Hibbs partisan model | 532 |
| 10.8 | The decline and renaissance of opportunistic and partisan models | 535 |
| 10.9 | Rational political business cycles | 537 |
| 10.10 | Rational partisan theory | 538 |
| 10.11 | Opportunistic and partisan behaviour: a synthesis | 545 |
| 10.12 | Politics, time inconsistency, credibility and reputation | 546 |
| 10.13 | Policy implications of politico-economic models: an independent central bank? | 549 |
| 10.14 | The political economy of debt and deficits | 554 |
| 10.15 | Political and economic instability: are they related? | 555 |
| 10.16 | The political economy of economic growth | 556 |
| 10.17 | Political barriers to economic growth | 562 |
| 10.18 | The size of nations | 564 |

10.19   Conclusion                                                           565
*Interview with* Alberto Alesina                                             567


**11       The renaissance of economic growth research             579**
11.1     Introduction                                                       579
11.2     The 'Great Divergence'                                             580
11.3     In praise of economic history                                      584
11.4     Back to the long run                                               585
11.5     Why is economic growth so important?                              589
11.6     Modern economic growth in historical perspective                  593
11.7     The stylized facts of growth                                      595
11.8     Proximate v. fundamental sources of growth                        596
11.9     The Harrod–Domar model                                            598
11.10    The Solow neoclassical growth model                               602
11.11    Accounting for the sources of economic growth                     612
11.12    The convergence debate                                            614
11.13    Beyond the Solow model                                            622
11.14    Endogenous growth: constant returns to capital accumulation       625
11.15    Endogenous growth: the economics of ideas                         627
11.16    An augmented Solow model: a neoclassical revival?                 632
11.17    Focusing on the fundamental causes of growth                      633
11.18    Institutions and economic growth                                  635
11.19    Trade and economic growth                                         647
11.20    Geography and growth                                              652
11.21    Growth in history: in search of a unified theory                  654
11.22    The ideal conditions for growth and development:
         rediscovering old truths                                          657
*Interview with* Robert M. Solow                                           660
*Interview with* Paul M. Romer                                             673


**12       Conclusions and reflections                             695**
12.1     Introduction                                                       695
12.2     Twentieth-century developments in macroeconomics:
         evolution or revolution?                                          696
12.3     Is there a consensus on key macroeconomic issues?                 703

*Bibliography*                                                             708
*Author index*                                                            791
*Subject index*                                                           803

# Figures

| | | |
|---|---|---|
| 1.1 | Unemployment in the US and UK economies over the course of the twentieth century | 2 |
| 1.2 | Inflation in the US and UK economies over the course of the twentieth century | 3 |
| 2.1 | The aggregate production function (a) and the marginal product of labour (b) | 40 |
| 2.2 | Output and employment determination in the classical model | 43 |
| 2.3 | The classical interest rate mechanism and Say's Law | 48 |
| 2.4 | The determination of the price level in the classical model | 53 |
| 2.5 | The determination of output and employment | 64 |
| 2.6 | Keynes and involuntary unemployment | 67 |
| 2.7 | Aggregate demand failure in the US economy, 1929–33 | 78 |
| 3.1 | Demand for speculative balances | 105 |
| 3.2 | The generalized IS–LM model | 105 |
| 3.3 | Expansionary fiscal policy | 107 |
| 3.4 | Expansionary monetary policy | 108 |
| 3.5 | The government budget constraint and bond-financed fiscal expansion | 111 |
| 3.6 | The general case with the Keynes effect | 115 |
| 3.7 | The liquidity trap case | 117 |
| 3.8 | The interest-inelastic investment case | 119 |
| 3.9 | The Mundell–Fleming/Keynesian model | 127 |
| 3.10 | Fiscal expansion under imperfect capital mobility | 128 |
| 3.11 | Monetary expansion under imperfect capital mobility | 129 |
| 3.12 | Fiscal expansion under (a) and (b) imperfect and (c) perfect capital mobility | 131 |
| 3.13 | Monetary expansion under (a) imperfect and (b) perfect capital mobility | 134 |
| 3.14 | The Phillips curve | 136 |
| 3.15 | The relationship between wage change and excess demand for labour | 138 |
| 3.16 | The relationship between excess demand for labour and unemployment | 139 |
| 3.17 | The relationship between excess demand for labour, vacancy and unemployment rates | 141 |

3.18   The link between the Keynesian model and wage and price
       inflation                                                        143
4.1    The evolution of orthodox monetarism                             164
4.2    The classical case                                               172
4.3    The Keynesian case                                               172
4.4    The expectations-augmented Phillips curve                        177
4.5    The trade-off between inflation and unemployment                 179
4.6    The output–employment costs of reducing inflation                183
5.1    The structure of new classical models                            224
5.2    The welfare implications of equilibrium in a competitive
       market                                                           231
5.3    The effects of anticipated and unanticipated changes in the
       money supply on the level of output and the price level          243
5.4    Consistent and optimal equilibrium                               253
5.5    Game played between the monetary authorities and wage
       negotiators                                                      255
5.6    The relationship between average inflation and central bank
       independence                                                     261
5.7    The evolution of new classical macroeconomics                    269
6.1    The path of output in the 'trend-reverting' case                 302
6.2    The path of output where shocks have a permanent influence       302
6.3    Output and employment fluctuations due to a technology
       shock                                                            314
6.4    The IS–LM model with flexible prices                             315
6.5    The real business cycle aggregate demand and supply model        316
6.6    The impact of a technology shock                                 318
6.7    The impact of a government expenditure shock                     319
6.8    The impact of temporary and permanent technology shocks in
       the real business cycle model                                    320
6.9    The annual growth rates of technology and output in the USA,
       1955–85                                                          327
6.10   Supply shocks and the price level                                329
7.1    Nominal wage contracts, rational expectations and monetary
       policy                                                           368
7.2    Price adjustment under monopolistic competition                  373
7.3    Menu costs v. price adjustment                                   374
7.4    Near rationality                                                 375
7.5    The efficiency wage and the Solow condition                      386
7.6    Involuntary unemployment in the efficiency wage model            387
7.7    The shirking model                                               391
7.8    The impact of an aggregate demand shock in the new
       Keynesian model                                                  397

7.9    The risk-based aggregate supply curve                              400
7.10   Standardized unemployment rates for North America (USA
       and Canada) and OECD Europe, 1972–98                               402
7.11   The 'natural rate' view of the relationship between actual
       unemployment and equilibrium unemployment                         404
7.12   The hysteresis view of a 'time-varying' NAIRU                      406
7.13   Bank of England inflation report fan chart for February 2004:
       forecast of CPI inflation at constant nominal interest rates of
       4.0 per cent                                                       417
7.14   UK inflation and inflation expectations, October 1991–
       October 2003                                                       418
7.15   Derivation of the *AD* curve                                       425
7.16   Adjusting to long-run equilibrium in the AD–IA model              427
9.1    The intertemporal structure of production                         476
9.2    A possible temporal pattern of consumable output                  480
9.3    Intertemporal capital restructuring                               481
9.4    Time discount and derived demand                                  488
9.5    The loanable funds market                                         490
9.6    The production possibilities frontier                             495
9.7    A capital-based macroeconomic framework                           496
9.8    Saving-induced economic growth                                    498
9.9    A saving-induced recession                                        502
9.10   A policy-induced boom and bust                                     505
9.11   An investment-led collapse into recession                         511
10.1   Influences on policy choice                                        520
10.2   A politico-economic model                                         524
10.3   The Nordhaus political business cycle model                       529
10.4   The long-run solution in the Nordhaus model                       530
10.5   The Hibbs partisan model                                          533
10.6   How inequality may adversely affect growth                        561
11.1   The impact on per capita income of differential growth rates      591
11.2   The great divergence                                              591
11.3   The neoclassical aggregate production function                    605
11.4   The Solow growth model                                            608
11.5   Technological progress                                            610
11.6   Transition dynamics                                               618
11.7   Conditional convergence                                           619
11.8   Proximate and fundamental sources of growth                       634

# Tables

| | | |
|---|---|---|
| 1.1 | The Great Depression | 12 |
| 1.2 | Growth of per capita GDP, world and major regions, 1820–1998 | 18 |
| 1.3 | Growth rates (GDP), 1820–1998 | 18 |
| 1.4 | Unemployment rates, 1964–2002 | 19 |
| 1.5 | Inflation rates, 1964–2002 | 20 |
| 2.1 | US GDP, prices and unemployment: 1929–33 | 78 |
| 2.2 | Keynes and the international economic system, 1944 | 85 |
| 2.3 | Most-cited macroeconomists: 1920–30 | 86 |
| 2.4 | Most-cited macroeconomists: 1931–5 | 86 |
| 2.5 | Most-cited macroeconomists: 1936–9 | 87 |
| 2.6 | Most-cited macroeconomists: 1940–44 | 87 |
| 5.1 | Citation counts: 1966–97 | 221 |
| 5.2 | Central bank independence and economic performance | 260 |
| 6.1 | The 'stylized facts' of the business cycle | 306 |
| 7.1 | NAIRU estimates for the G7 countries and the euro area | 402 |
| 7.2 | Evidence on reasons for price stickiness | 428 |
| 10.1 | Politico-economic models of aggregate fluctuations | 526 |
| 10.2 | Partisan influence on macroeconomic outcomes, USA, 1948–2001 | 534 |
| 10.3 | Rates of growth of GDP in real terms | 543 |
| 10.4 | Alternative politico-economic models | 547 |
| 10.5 | Selected indicators of governance: 20 sub-Saharan African countries | 559 |
| 11.1 | Level and rate of growth of GDP per capita: world and major regions, 0–1998 AD | 581 |
| 11.2 | Three indicators of living standards: 40 countries | 583 |
| 11.3 | The cumulative impact of differential growth rates | 590 |
| 11.4 | A tale of two Koreas | 639 |
| 11.5 | Growth rates of per capita GDP (%): the two Koreas | 640 |
| 12.1 | Some areas of agreement and disagreement in macroeconomics | 702 |

# Preface

Over the last ten years we have collaborated in co-writing and/or editing five books on macroeconomics. The first of this series of books, *A Modern Guide to Macroeconomics: An Introduction to Competing Schools of Thought*, was published by Edward Elgar in 1994, while our most recent joint venture, *An Encyclopedia of Macroeconomics*, was published by Edward Elgar in 2002. During the course of co-writing and editing the *Encyclopedia of Macroeconomics* a number of eminent economists, who contributed to the project, asked if we had any plans to write a second edition of the *Modern Guide to Macroeconomics*, a book which has received widespread critical acclaim and been translated into French (Ediscience, 1997), Chinese (Commercial Press, 1998), Italian (Etas Libri, 1998), and Polish (Polish Scientific Publishers, 1998). Initially we intended to produce a second edition of the *Modern Guide to Macroeconomics* involving amendments to each chapter, as well as updating the data and references. However, as the project unfolded we decided that the *Modern Guide to Macroeconomics* required an *extensive* rewrite, not only involving major amendments to each chapter, but also requiring the addition of two new chapters surveying the burgeoning literature on the 'new political macroeconomics' and the 'new growth' literature. As a result of these extensive changes we decided that the current book was sufficiently different to warrant a new title, which reflects its theme and contents. In writing *Modern Macroeconomics: Its Origins, Development and Current State* we have also been kindly aided by two eminent scholars in their respective fields, Professor Paul Davidson who contributed Chapter 8 on the Post Keynesian school and Professor Roger Garrison who contributed Chapter 9 on the Austrian school.

The main aim of our new book, as reflected in its title, is to consider the origins, development and current state of modern macroeconomics in a manner appropriate for *intermediate* undergraduates taking courses in macroeconomics. As such we have assumed that such students will already have a firm grasp of basic economic principles and be familiar with introductory macroeconomic theories and models as developed, for example, in textbooks such as those by Abel and Bernanke (2001), Blanchard (2003), or Mankiw (2003). This book should, however, also prove useful to students taking other undergraduate economics courses, most notably in the history of economic thought, as well as economic history. For the benefit of intermediate undergraduates we have marked with an asterisk those references in the bibliography that are particularly recommended for further reading. In providing extensive referencing the book should also prove to be a useful introductory guide to the research literature for postgraduate students in their preliminary year of study.

While the book is written so as to allow students on a range of degree courses to read individual chapters in isolation, according to their interests and needs, in line with the *Modern Guide to Macroeconomics* the book follows a structured direction tracing the origins and development of modern macroeconomics in historical perspective. In a book of this nature it is obviously impossible to cover every area. We have therefore aimed to highlight what we consider to have been the major issues that emerged following the birth of macroeconomics in the 1930s.

Following the introductory chapter on understanding macroeconomics, Chapter 2 considers the debate between Keynes and the old classical model before tracing the development of the orthodox Keynesian school (Chapter 3), the orthodox monetarist school (Chapter 4), the new classical school (Chapter 5), the real business cycle school (Chapter 6), the new Keynesian school (Chapter 7), the Post Keynesian school (Chapter 8) and the Austrian school (Chapter 9). Readers familiar with a *Modern Guide to Macroeconomics* will recognize our chosen approach, namely to discuss the central tenets underlying, and the policy implications of, these main competing schools of thought in macroeconomics as they evolved in historical perspective. In doing so we have taken the opportunity to include in Chapters 2–7 more recent references and, more importantly, to assess the impact these schools have had on the current state of macroeconomics. We have also introduced much new material compared to the equivalently titled chapters in a *Modern Guide to Macroeconomics*. To give two examples: in Chapter 2, section 2.14, we have introduced a discussion of the causes and consequences of the Great Depression, while in Chapter 3, section 3.5, we discuss the effectiveness of fiscal and monetary policy for stabilization purposes when the Keynesian IS–LM model is extended to an open economy. In this book the Post Keynesian and Austrian schools command individual chapters (each written by leading scholars in the area), rather than the single chapter approach used in the *Modern Guide to Macroeconomics*. Furthermore, to reflect important developments that have taken place in macroeconomics over the final decades of the twentieth century we have introduced two entirely new chapters. In Chapter 10 we consider what has come to be known as the 'new political macroeconomics', while in Chapter 11 we discuss the renaissance of research into the area of 'economic growth'. It is hoped that these changes will be welcomed by reviewers and readers alike.

In line with the *Modern Guide to Macroeconomics*, to help bring the subject matter alive and capture the imagination of the reader, we have included at the end of certain chapters interviews with world-renowned scholars who are experts in their field of study. We are extremely grateful to (listed in the order in which the interviews appear in the book): Robert Skidelsky (a leading authority on Keynes and the interwar period); the late James Tobin (the 1981 Nobel Memorial Laureate, who was one of America's most prominent and distinguished Keynesian economists); Milton Friedman (the 1976 Nobel Memorial Laureate, who is widely recognized as the founding father of monetarism); Robert E. Lucas Jr (the 1995 Nobel Memorial Laureate, who is widely acknowledged as the leading figure in the development of new classical macroeconomics); Edward Prescott (widely acknowledged as a leading advocate of the real business cycle approach to economic fluctuations); Greg Mankiw (a leading exponent of the new Keynesian school of macroeconomics); Alberto Alesina (a leading contributor to the literature on the new political macroeconomics); and Robert Solow (the 1987 Nobel Memorial Laureate) and Paul Romer, who have made very influential contributions to the field of economic growth. Their illuminating and contrasting answers demonstrate that modern macroeconomics is both an exciting and controversial subject. As an aside the reader may wonder why we have not included interviews at the end of Chapter 8 on the Post Keynesian school and Chapter 9 on the Austrian school. The reason for this is that these two chapters have been written by Paul Davidson, a leading world authority on Post Keynesian economics, and Roger Garrison, a leading world authority on Austrian economics – the two people we would have chosen to interview if they hadn't kindly agreed to write Chapters 8 and 9 respectively.

Thus, for the potential reviewer or prospective buyer it should be clear that this book is far more than a second edition of the *Modern Guide to Macroeconomics*. It is a new book which we hope successfully conveys the importance of the issues under discussion. As Keynes recognized, the ideas of economists are more powerful than is commonly understood. In this book we have attempted to show why this is the case by tracing the development and interaction of key events and ideas as they occurred during the twentieth century and into the new millennium.

Brian Snowdon
Howard R. Vane

# Acknowledgements

The authors would like to thank the following who have kindly given their permission to reproduce previously published material, namely:

The NIESR to reproduce Figures 1.1 and 1.2 from the article by A. Britton, 'Macroeconomics and History', in the *National Institute Economic Review*, January 2002.

The Ohio State University Press to reproduce Figure 5.6 and Table 5.2 from the article by A. Alesina and L.H. Summers, 'Central Bank Independence and Macroeconomic Performance: Some Comparative Evidence', *Journal of Money, Credit and Banking*, May 1993.

The OECD to reproduce Tables 1.2 and 11.1 from the book by A. Maddison, *The World Economy: A Millennial Perspective*, copyright 2001, OECD.

Palgrave Macmillan to reproduce Tables 2.3–2.6 from the book by P. Deutscher, *R.G. Hawtrey and the Development of Macroeconomics*, 1990, Macmillan.

Pearson Education, Inc. publishing as Pearson Addison Wesley to reproduce Table 6.1 from the book by A.B. Abel and B.S. Bernanke, *Macroeconomics*, 4th edn., p. 288, copyright 2001, Pearson Education.

The International Honor Society in Economics to reproduce the interview with Greg Mankiw which appears as part of a fuller article by the authors, 'New Keynesian Economics Today: The Empire Strikes Back', in *The American Economist*, Spring 1995.

MCB University Press to reproduce the interview with Milton Friedman which appears as part of a fuller article by the authors, 'Modern Macroeconomics and Its Evolution from a Monetarist Perspective: An Interview with Professor Milton Friedman', in the *Journal of Economic Studies*, 1997.

Routledge to reproduce the interview with Robert E. Lucas Jr which appears as part of a fuller article by the authors, 'Transforming Macroeconomics: An Interview with Robert E. Lucas Jr.', in the *Journal of Economic Methodology*, June 1998.

The International Honor Society on Economics to reproduce the interview with Alberto Alesina which appears as part of a fuller article by the authors, 'The New Political Macroeconomics', in *The American Economist*, Spring 1999.

NTC Economic and Financial Publishing, Washington, DC, USA and Henley-on Thames, UK to reproduce the interview with James Tobin which appears as part of a fuller article by the authors, 'James Tobin, 1918–2002: An "Unreconstructed Old Keynesian" Who Wouldn't Quit', in *World Economics*, July–September 2002.

The authors also wish to thank Professor Paul Romer for permission to use their interview with him, the copyright on which is held by Professor Romer.

# 1. Understanding modern macroeconomics

> Economic knowledge is historically determined ... what we know today about the economic system is not something we discovered this morning but is the sum of all our insights, discoveries and false starts in the past. Without Pigou there would be no Keynes; without Keynes no Friedman; without Friedman no Lucas; without Lucas no ... (Blaug, 1991a, pp. x–xi)

## 1.1 Macroeconomics Issues and Ideas

Macroeconomics is concerned with the structure, performance and behaviour of the economy as a whole. The prime concern of macroeconomists is to analyse and attempt to understand the underlying determinants of the main aggregate trends in the economy with respect to the total output of goods and services (GDP), unemployment, inflation and international transactions. In particular, macroeconomic analysis seeks to explain the cause and impact of short-run fluctuations in GDP (the business cycle), and the major determinants of the long-run path of GDP (economic growth). Obviously the subject matter of macroeconomics is of crucial importance because in one way or another macroeconomic events have an important influence on the lives and welfare of all of us. It is difficult to overstate just how important satisfactory macroeconomic performance is for the well-being of the citizens of any country. An economy that has successful macroeconomic management should experience low unemployment and inflation, and steady and sustained economic growth. In contrast, in a country where there is macroeconomic mismanagement, we will observe an adverse impact on the living standards and employment opportunities of the citizens of that country. In extreme circumstances the consequences of macroeconomic instability have been devastating. For example, the catastrophic political and economic consequences of failing to maintain macroeconomic stability among the major industrial nations during the period 1918–33 ignited a chain of events that contributed to the outbreak of the Second World War, with disastrous consequences for both humanity and the world economy.

Because macroeconomic performance and policies are closely connected, the major macroeconomic issues are also the subject of constant media attention and inevitably play a central role in political debate. The influence of the

economic performance of the economy on political events is particularly
important and pertinent in liberal democracies during election campaigns.
Research has confirmed that in the post-war period the outcome of elections
has in many cases been affected by the performance of the economy as
measured by three main macroeconomic indicators – inflation, unemployment and economic growth. While there are obviously many non-economic
factors that influence the 'happiness' of voters, it is certainly the case that
economic variables such as employment and income growth are an important
explanatory factor in voting behaviour. Furthermore, ideological conflict often revolves around important macroeconomic issues (see, for example, Frey
and Schneider, 1988; Alesina and Roubini with Cohen, 1997; Drazen, 2000a).

To get some idea of how two major economies have performed with respect
to unemployment and inflation consider Figures 1.1 and Figure 1.2. Here we
can clearly see that the pathologies of high unemployment and inflation occasionally take on proportions that are well above the norm. Figure 1.1 traces the
path of unemployment in the US and UK economies for the twentieth century.
The impact of the Great Depression (1929–33) on unemployment is dramatically illustrated for both countries although the increase in unemployment in
the USA was much more dramatic than in the UK, where unemployment was
already high before 1929 (see section 1.4 below and Chapter 2).

*Source*:   Britton (2002).

*Figure 1.1   Unemployment in the US and UK economies over the course of
the twentieth century*

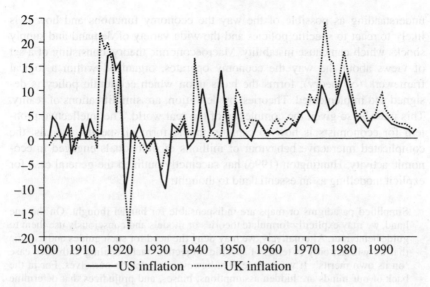

Source: Britton (2002).

*Figure 1.2 Inflation in the US and UK economies over the course of the twentieth century*

Figure 1.2 shows how inflation has varied in the US and the UK economies throughout the twentieth century. Notable features here include: the dramatic increase in inflation associated with the two world wars (1914–18, 1939–45) and the Korean War (1950–53); the deflations of the early 1920s and 1930s; and the 'Great Inflation' of the 1970s (Taylor, 1992a). As DeLong (1997) notes, 'the 1970s are America's only peacetime outburst of inflation'.

Several questions confront economists with respect to these exceptional episodes: were they due to specific large shocks, the failure of adjustment mechanisms, the result of policy errors, or some combination of all three? Finding answers to these questions is important because the contemporary conduct of stabilization policy must reflect the lessons of history and the theoretical and empirical research findings of economists.

## 1.2 The Role of Economic Theory and Controversy

An understanding by government policy makers of the factors which determine the long-run growth of an economy and the short-run fluctuations that constitute the business cycle is essential in order to design and implement economic policies which have the potential vastly to improve economic welfare. The primary aim of macroeconomic research is to develop as comprehensive an understanding as possible of the way the economy functions and how it is likely to react to specific policies and the wide variety of demand and supply shocks which can cause instability. Macroeconomic theory, consisting of a set of views about the way the economy operates, organized within a logical framework (or theory), forms the basis upon which economic policy is designed and implemented. Theories, by definition, are simplifications of reality. This must be so given the complexity of the real world. The intellectual problem for economists is how to capture, in the form of specific models, the complicated interactive behaviour of millions of individuals engaged in economic activity. Huntington (1996) has succinctly outlined the general case for explicit modelling as an essential aid to thought:

> Simplified paradigms or maps are indispensable for human thought. On the one hand, we may explicitly formulate theories or models and consciously use them to guide behaviour. Alternatively, we may deny the need for such guides and assume that we will act only in terms of specific 'objective' facts, dealing with each case 'on its own merits'. If we assume this, however, we delude ourselves. For in the back of our minds are hidden assumptions, biases, and prejudices that determine how we perceive reality, what facts we look at, and how we judge their importance and merits.

Accordingly, explicit or implicit models are necessary to make sense of a very complex world. By definition economic theories and specific models act as the laboratories we otherwise lack in the social sciences. They help economists decide what are the important factors that need to be analysed when they run thought experiments about the causes and consequences of various economic phenomena. A successful theory will enable economists to make better predictions about the consequences of alternative courses of action thereby indicating the policy regime most likely to achieve society's chosen objectives.

The design of coherent economic policies aimed at achieving an acceptable rate of economic growth and reduced aggregate instability depends then on the availability of internally consistent theoretical models of the economy which can explain satisfactorily the behaviour of the main macro variables and are not rejected by the available empirical evidence. Such models provide an organizing framework for reviewing the development and improvement of institutions and policies capable of generating reasonable macroeconomic stability and growth. However, throughout the twentieth century, economists have often differed, sometimes substantially, over what is to be regarded as the 'correct' model of the economy. As a result, prolonged disagreements and controversies have frequently characterized the history of macroeconomic thought (Woodford, 2000).

The knowledge that macroeconomists have today about the way that economies function is the result of a prolonged research effort often involving intense controversy and an ever-increasing data bank of experience. As Blanchard (1997a) points out:

> Macroeconomics is not an exact science but an applied one where ideas, theories, and models are constantly evaluated against the facts, and often modified or rejected ... Macroeconomics is thus the result of a sustained process of construction, of an interaction between ideas and events. What macroeconomists believe today is the result of an evolutionary process in which they have eliminated those ideas that failed and kept those that appear to explain reality well.

Taking a long-term perspective, our current understanding of macroeconomics, at the beginning of the twenty-first century, is nothing more than yet another chapter in the history of economic thought. However, it is important to recognize from the outset that the evolution of economists' thinking on macroeconomics has been far from smooth. So much so that many economists are not averse to making frequent use of terminology such as 'revolution' and 'counter-revolution' when discussing the history of macroeconomics. The dramatic decline of the Keynesian conventional wisdom in the early 1970s resulted from both the empirical failings of 'old Keynesianism' and the increasing success of critiques ('counter-revolutions') mounted by monetarist and new classical economists (Johnson, 1971; Tobin, 1981, 1996; Blaug, 1997; Snowdon and Vane, 1996, 1997a, 1997b).

In our view, any adequate account of the current state of macroeconomics needs to explore the rise and fall of the old ideas and the state of the new within a comparative and historical context (see Britton, 2002). This book examines, compares and evaluates the evolution of the major rival stories comprising contemporary macroeconomic thought. We would maintain that the coexistence of alternative explanations and views is a sign of strength rather than weakness, since it permits mutual gains from intellectual trade and thereby improved understanding. It was John Stuart Mill who recognized, almost one hundred and fifty years ago, that all parties gain from the comparative interplay of ideas. Alternative ideas not only help prevent complacency, where 'teachers and learners go to sleep at their post as soon as there is no enemy in the field' (Mill, 1982, p. 105), but they also provide a vehicle for improved understanding whereby the effort to comprehend alternative views forces economists to re-evaluate their own views. Controversy and dialogue have been, and will continue to be, a major engine for the accumulation of new knowledge and progress in macroeconomics. We would therefore endorse Mill's plea for continued dialogue (in this case within macroeconomics) between the alternative frameworks and suggest that all economists have something to learn from each other. The macroeconomic problems that economists address and endeavour to solve are often shared.

That there is a wide variety of schools of thought in economics in general, and macroeconomics in particular, should not surprise us given the intrinsic difficulty and importance of the issues under investigation. While there are 'strong incentives in academia to differentiate products' (Blanchard and Fischer, 1989), there is no doubt that much of the controversy in macroeconomics runs deep. Of course, it is true that economists disagree on many issues, but they seem to do so more frequently, vociferously, and at greater length, in macroeconomics. In his discussion of why there is much controversy in macroeconomics Mayer (1994) identifies seven sources, namely, limited knowledge about how the economy works, the ever-widening range of issues that economists investigate, the need to take into account wider influences, such as political factors, and differences in the 'metaphysical cores, value judgements, social empathies and methodologies' of various economists. Knut Wicksell's (1958, pp. 51–2) contention that within economics 'the state of war seems to persist and remain permanent' seems most appropriate for contemporary macroeconomics. To a large extent this reflects the importance of the issues which macroeconomists deal with, but it also supports the findings of previous surveys of economists which revealed a tendency for consensus to be stronger on microeconomic compared to macroeconomic propositions (see, for example, Alston et al., 1992).

It is certainly true that in specific periods during the twentieth century the contemporary state of macroeconomic theory had the appearance of a battlefield, with regiments of economists grouped under different banners. However, it is our view that economists should always resist the temptation to embrace, in an unquestioning way, a one-sided or restrictive consensus 'because the right answers are unlikely to come from any pure economic dogma' (Deane, 1983). In addition, the very nature of scientific research dictates that disagreements and debate are most vocal at the frontier, as they should be, and, as Robert E. Lucas Jr argues (see interview at the end of Chapter 5), the responsibility of professional economists is 'to create new knowledge by pushing research into new, and hence necessarily controversial, territory. Consensus can be reached on specific issues, but consensus for a research area as a whole is equivalent to stagnation, irrelevance and death.' Furthermore, as Milton Friedman observes (see interview at the end of Chapter 4), 'science in general advances primarily by unsuccessful experiments that clear the ground'.

Macroeconomics has witnessed considerable progress since its birth in the 1930s. More specifically, any Rip Van Winkle economist who had fallen asleep in 1965, when the 'old Keynesian' paradigm was at its peak, would surely be impressed on waking up at the beginning of the twenty-first century and surveying the enormous changes that have taken place in the macroeconomics literature.

## 1.3 Objectives, Instruments and the Role of Government

In our historical journey we will see that macroeconomics has experienced periods of crisis. There is no denying the significant conflicts of opinion that exist between the different schools of thought, and this was especially evident during the 1970s and 1980s. However, it should also be noted that economists tend to disagree more over theoretical issues, empirical evidence and the choice of policy instruments than they do over the ultimate objectives of policy. In the opening statement of what turned out to be one of the most influential articles written in the post-war period, Friedman (1968a) gave emphasis to this very issue:

> There is wide agreement about the major goals of economic policy: high employment, stable prices, and rapid growth. There is less agreement that these goals are mutually compatible or, among those who regard them as incompatible, about the terms at which they can and should be substituted for one another. There is least agreement about the role that various instruments of policy can and should play in achieving the several goals.

The choice of appropriate instruments in order to achieve the 'major goals' of economic policy will depend on a detailed analysis of the causes of specific macroeconomic problems. Here we encounter two main intellectual traditions in macroeconomics which we can define broadly as the classical and Keynesian approaches. It is when we examine how policy objectives are interconnected and how different economists view the role and effectiveness of markets in coordinating economic activity that we find the fundamental question that underlies disagreements between economists on matters of policy, namely, what is the proper role of government in the economy? The extent and form of government intervention in the economy was a major concern of Adam Smith (1776) in the *Wealth of Nations*, and the rejection of uncontrolled *laissez-faire* by Keynes is well documented. During the twentieth century the really big questions in macroeconomics revolved around this issue. Mankiw (1989) identifies the classical approach as one 'emphasising the optimization of private actors' and 'the efficiency of unfettered markets'. On the other hand, the Keynesian school 'believes that understanding economic fluctuations requires not just the intricacies of general equilibrium, but also appreciating the possibility of market failure'. Obviously there is room for a more extensive role for government in the Keynesian vision. In a radio broadcast in 1934, Keynes presented a talk entitled 'Poverty and Plenty: is the economic system self-adjusting?' In it he distinguished between two warring factions of economists:

> On the one side are those that believe that the existing economic system is, in the long run, a self-adjusting system, though with creaks and groans and jerks and

interrupted by time lags, outside interference and mistakes ... On the other side of the gulf are those that reject the idea that the existing economic system is, in any significant sense, self-adjusting. The strength of the self-adjusting school depends on it having behind it almost the whole body of organised economic thinking of the last hundred years ... Thus, if the heretics on the other side of the gulf are to demolish the forces of nineteenth-century orthodoxy ... they must attack them in their citadel ... Now I range myself with the heretics. (Keynes, 1973a, Vol. XIII, pp. 485–92)

Despite the development of more sophisticated and quantitatively powerful techniques during the past half-century, these two basic views identified by Keynes have persisted. Witness the opening comments of Stanley Fischer in a survey of developments in macroeconomics published in the late 1980s:

> One view and school of thought, associated with Keynes, Keynesians and new Keynesians, is that the private economy is subject to co-ordination failures that can produce excessive levels of unemployment and excessive fluctuations in real activity. The other view, attributed to classical economists, and espoused by monetarists and equilibrium business cycle theorists, is that the private economy reaches as good an equilibrium as is possible given government policy. (Fischer, 1988, p. 294)

It appears that many contemporary debates bear an uncanny resemblance to those that took place between Keynes and his critics in the 1930s. Recently, Kasper (2002) has argued that in the USA, the 1970s witnessed a strong revival in macroeconomic policy debates of a presumption in favour of *laissez-faire*, a clear case of 'back to the future'.

In this book we are primarily concerned with an examination of the intellectual influences that have shaped the development of macroeconomic theory and the conduct of macroeconomic policy in the period since the publication of Keynes's (1936) *General Theory of Employment, Interest and Money*. The first 25 years following the end of the Second World War were halcyon days for Keynesian macroeconomics. The new generation of macroeconomists generally accepted Keynes's central message that a *laissez-faire* capitalist economy could possess equilibria characterized by excessive involuntary unemployment. The main policy message to come out of the *General Theory* was that active government intervention in order to regulate aggregate demand was necessary, indeed unavoidable, if a satisfactory level of aggregate output and employment were to be maintained. Although, as Skidelsky (1996a) points out, Keynes does not deal explicitly with the Great Depression in the *General Theory*, it is certain that this major work was written as a direct response to the cataclysmic events unfolding across the capitalist economies after 1929.

## 1.4 The Great Depression

The lessons from the history of economic thought teach us that one of the main driving forces behind the evolution of new ideas is the march of events. While theoretical ideas can help us understand historical events, it is also true that 'the outcome of historical events often challenges theorists and overturns theories, leading to the evolution of new theories' (Gordon, 2000a, p. 580). The Great Depression gave birth to modern macroeconomics as surely as accelerating inflation in the late 1960s and early 1970s facilitated the monetarist counter-revolution (see Johnson, 1971). It is also important to note that many of the most famous economists of the twentieth century, such as Milton Friedman, James Tobin and Paul Samuelson, were inspired to study economics in the first place as a direct result of their personal experiences during this period (see Parker, 2002).

While Laidler (1991, 1999) has reminded us that there is an extensive literature analysing the causes and consequences of economic fluctuations and monetary instability prior to the 1930s, the story of modern macroeconomics undoubtedly begins with the Great Depression. Before 1936, macroeconomics consisted of an 'intellectual witch's brew: many ingredients, some of them exotic, many insights, but also a great deal of confusion' (Blanchard, 2000). For more than 70 years economists have attempted to provide a coherent explanation of how the world economy suffered such a catastrophe. Bernanke (1995) has even gone so far as to argue that 'to understand the Great Depression is the Holy Grail of macroeconomics'.

Although Keynes was a staunch defender of the capitalist system against all known alternative forms of economic organization, he also believed that it had some outstanding and potentially fatal weaknesses. Not only did it give rise to an 'arbitrary and inequitable distribution of income'; it also undoubtedly failed 'to provide for full employment' (Keynes, 1936, p. 372). During Keynes's most productive era as an economist (1919–37) he was to witness at first hand the capitalist system's greatest crisis of the twentieth century, the Great Depression. To Keynes, it was in the determination of the total volume of employment and GDP that capitalism was failing, not in its capacity to allocate resources efficiently. While Keynes did not believe that the capitalist market system was violently unstable, he observed that it 'seems capable of remaining in a chronic condition of sub-normal activity for a considerable period without any marked tendency towards recovery or towards complete collapse' (Keynes, 1936, p. 249). This is what others have interpreted as Keynes's argument that involuntary unemployment can persist as a equilibrium phenomenon. From this perspective, Keynes concluded that capitalism needed to be purged of its defects and abuses if it was to survive the ideological onslaught it was undergoing during the interwar period from the totalitarian alternatives on offer in both fascist Germany and communist Soviet Union.

Although a determination to oppose and overturn the terms of the Versailles peace settlement was an important factor in the growing influence of the Nazis throughout the 1920s, there seems little doubt that their final rise to power in Germany was also very closely linked to economic conditions. Had economic policy in the USA and Europe been different after 1929, 'one can well imagine that the horrors of Naziism and the Second World War might have been avoided' (Eichengreen and Temin, 2002). In Mundell's (2000) assessment, 'had the major central banks pursued policies of price stability instead of adhering to the gold standard, there would have been no great Depression, no Nazi revolution, and no World War II'.

During the 1930s the world entered a 'Dark Valley' and Europe became the world's 'Dark Continent' (Mazower, 1998; Brendon, 2000). The interwar period witnessed an era of intense political competition between the three rival ideologies of liberal democracy, fascism and communism. Following the Versailles Treaty (1919) democracy was established across Europe but during the 1930s was almost everywhere in retreat. By 1940 it was 'virtually extinct'. The failures of economic management in the capitalist world during the Great Depression allowed totalitarianism and extreme nationalism to flourish and the world economy began to disintegrate. As Brendon (2000) comments, 'if the lights went out in 1914, if the blinds came down in 1939, the lights were progressively dimmed after 1929'. The Great Depression was 'the economic equivalent of Armageddon' and the 'worst peacetime crisis to afflict humanity since the Black Death'. The crisis of capitalism discredited democracy and the old liberal order, leading many to conclude that 'if *laissez-faire* caused chaos, authoritarianism would impose order'. The interwar economic catastrophe helped to consolidate Mussolini's hold on power in Italy, gave Hitler the opportunity in January 1933 to gain political control in Germany, and plunged Japan into years of 'economic depression, political turmoil and military strife'. By 1939, after three years of civil war in Spain, Franco established yet another fascist dictatorship in Western Europe.

The famous Wall Street Crash of 1929 heralded one of the most dramatic and catastrophic periods in the economic history of the industrialized capitalist economies. In a single week from 23 to 29 October the Dow Jones Industrial Average fell 29.5 per cent, with 'vertical' price drops on 'Black Thursday' (24 October) and 'Black Tuesday' (29 October). Controversy exists over the causes of the stock market crash and its connection with the Great Depression in the economic activity which followed (see the interviews with Bernanke and Romer in Snowdon, 2002a). It is important to remember that during the 1920s the US economy, unlike many European economies, was enjoying growing prosperity during the 'roaring twenties' boom. Rostow's

(1960) 'age of high mass consumption' seemed to be at hand. The optimism visible in the stock market throughout the mid to late 1920s was reflected in a speech by Herbert Hoover to a Stanford University audience in November 1928. In accepting the Republican Presidential nomination he uttered these 'famous last words':

> We in America today are nearer to the final triumph over poverty than ever before in the history of any land. The poorhouse is vanishing from among us. We have not yet reached the goal, but, given a chance to go forward with the policies of the last eight years, we shall soon with the help of God be in sight of the day when poverty will be banished from this nation. (See Heilbroner, 1989)

In the decade following Hoover's speech the US economy (along with the other major industrial market economies) was to experience the worst economic crisis in its history, to such an extent that many began to wonder if capitalism and democracy could survive. In the US economy the cyclical peak of economic activity occurred in August 1929 and a decline in GDP had already begun when the stock market crash ended the 1920s bull market. Given that the crash came on top of an emerging recession, it was inevitable that a severe contraction of output would take place in the 1929–30 period. But this early part of the contraction was well within the range of previous business cycle experience. It was in the second phase of the contraction, generally agreed to be between early 1931 and March 1933, that the depression became 'Great' (Dornbusch et al., 2004). Therefore, the question which has captured the research interests of economists is: 'How did the severe recession of 1929–30 turn into the Great Depression of 1931–33?' The vast majority of economists now agree that the catastrophic collapse of output and employment after 1930 was in large part due to a series of policy errors made by the fiscal and monetary authorities in a number of industrial economies, especially the USA, where the reduction in economic activity was greater than elsewhere (see Bernanke, 2000, and Chapter 2).

The extent and magnitude of the depression can be appreciated by referring to the data contained in Table 1.1, which records the timing and extent of the collapse of industrial production for the major capitalist market economies between 1929 and 1933.

The most severe downturn was in the USA, which experienced a 46.8 per cent decline in industrial production and a 28 per cent decline in GDP. Despite rapid growth after 1933 (with the exception of 1938), output remained substantially below normal until about 1942. The behaviour of unemployment in the USA during this period is consistent with the movement of GDP. In the USA, unemployment, which was 3.2 per cent in 1929, rose to a peak of 25.2 per cent in 1933, averaged 18 per cent in the 1930s and never fell below 10 per cent until 1941 (Gordon, 2000a). The economy had

Table 1.1   The Great Depression

| Country | Depression began* | Recovery begins* | Industrial production** % decline |
|---|---|---|---|
| USA | 1929 (3) | 1933 (2) | 46.8 |
| UK | 1930 (1) | 1931 (4) | 16.2 |
| Germany | 1928 (1) | 1932 (3) | 41.8 |
| France | 1930 (2) | 1932 (3) | 31.3 |
| Italy | 1929 (3) | 1933 (1) | 33.0 |
| Belgium | 1929 (3) | 1932 (4) | 30.6 |
| Netherlands | 1929 (4) | 1933 (2) | 37.4 |
| Denmark | 1930 (4) | 1933 (2) | 16.5 |
| Sweden | 1930 (2) | 1932 (3) | 10.3 |
| Czechoslovakia | 1929 (4) | 1932 (3) | 40.4 |
| Poland | 1929 (1) | 1933 (2) | 46.6 |
| Canada | 1929 (2) | 1933 (2) | 42.4 |
| Argentina | 1929 (2) | 1932 (1) | 17.0 |
| Brazil | 1928 (3) | 1931 (4) | 7.0 |
| Japan | 1930 (1) | 1932 (3) | 8.5 |

Notes:
*   Year; quarter in parentheses.
**  Peak-to-trough decline.

Source:   C. Romer (2004).

fallen so far below capacity (which continued to expand as the result of technological improvements, investment in human capital and rapid labour force growth) that, despite a 47 per cent increase in output between 1933 and 1937, unemployment failed to fall below 9 per cent and, following the impact of the 1938 recession, was still almost 10 per cent when the USA entered the Second World War in December 1941 (see Lee and Passell, 1979; C. Romer, 1992). Events in Europe were also disastrous and closely connected to US developments. The most severe recessions outside the USA were in Canada, Germany, France, Italy, the Netherlands, Belgium, Czechoslovakia and Poland, with the Scandinavian countries, the UK and Japan less severely affected. Accompanying the decline in economic activity was an alarming rise in unemployment and a collapse of commodity and wholesale prices (see Aldcroft, 1993).

How can we explain such a massive and catastrophic decline in aggregate economic activity? Before the 1930s the dominant view in what we now call macroeconomics was the 'old' classical approach the origins of which go back more than two centuries. In 1776, Adam Smith's celebrated *An Inquiry into the Nature and Causes of the Wealth of Nations* was published, in which he set forth the invisible-hand theorem. The main idea here is that the profit- and utility-maximizing behaviour of rational economic agents operating under competitive conditions will, via the 'invisible-hand' mechanism, translate the activities of millions of individuals into a social optimum. Following Smith, political economy had an underlying bias towards *laissez-faire,* and the classical vision of macroeconomics found its most famous expression in the dictum 'supply creates its own demand'. This view, popularly known as Say's Law, denies the possibility of general overproduction or underproduction. With the notable exception of Malthus, Marx and a few other heretics, this view dominated both classical and early neoclassical (post-1870) contributions to macroeconomic theory (see Baumol, 1999; Backhouse, 2002, and Chapter 2). While Friedman argues that during the Great Depression expansionary monetary policies were recommended by economists at Chicago, economists looking to the prevailing conventional wisdom contained in the work of the classical economists could not find a coherent plausible answer to the causes of such a deep and prolonged decline in economic activity (see Friedman interview at the end of Chapter 4 and Parker, 2002).

### 1.5  Keynes and the Birth of Macroeconomics

Although it is important to remember that economists before Keynes discussed what we now call macroeconomic issues such as business cycles, inflation, unemployment and growth, as we have already noted, the birth of modern macroeconomics as a coherent and systematic approach to aggregate economic phenomena can be traced back to the publication in February 1936 of Keynes's book *The General Theory of Employment, Interest and Money.* In a letter written on 1 January 1935 to a friend, the writer George Bernard Shaw, Keynes speculated that 'I believe myself to be writing a book on economic theory which will largely revolutionise – not, I suppose, at once but in the course of the next ten years – the way the world thinks about economic problems'. That Keynes's bold prediction should be so accurately borne out is both a comment on his own self-confidence and a reflection of the inadequacy of classical economic analysis to provide an acceptable and convincing explanation of the prevailing economic situation in the early 1930s. Keynes recognized that the drastic economic situation confronting the capitalist system in the 1930s threatened its very survival and was symptomatic of a fundamental flaw in the operation of the price mechanism as a coordinating device.

To confront this problem Keynes needed to challenge the classical economists from within their citadel. The flaw, as he saw it, lay in the existing classical theory whose teaching Keynes regarded as not only 'misleading' but 'disastrous' if applied to the real-world problems facing the capitalist economies during the interwar period. For Keynes, capitalism was not terminally ill but unstable. His objective was to modify the rules of the game within the capitalist system in order to preserve and strengthen it. He wanted full employment to be the norm rather than the exception and his would be a conservative revolution. As Galbraith (1977) has noted, Keynes never sought to change the world out of personal dissatisfaction: 'for him the world was excellent'. Although the republic of Keynes's political imagination lay on the 'extreme left of celestial space', he was no socialist. Despite the prompting of George Bernard Shaw, Keynes remained notoriously blind to Marx. In his opinion, *Das Kapital* contained nothing but 'dreary out of date academic controversialising' which added up to nothing more than complicated *hocus pocus*. At one of Keynes's Political Economy Club meetings he admitted to having read Marx in the same spirit as reading a detective story. He had hoped to find some clue to an idea but had never succeeded in doing so (see Skidelsky, 1992, pp. 514–23). But Keynes's contempt for Marxist analysis did not stop those on the right of the political spectrum from regarding his message as dangerously radical. For Keynes the ultimate political problem was how to combine economic efficiency, social justice and individual freedom. But questions of equity were always secondary to questions of efficiency, stability and growth. His solution to the economic malaise that was sweeping the capitalist economies in the early 1930s was to accept 'a large extension of the traditional functions of government'. But as Keynes (1926) argued in *The End of Laissez-Faire*, if the government is to be effective it should not concern itself with 'those activities which private individuals are already fulfilling' but attend to 'those functions which fall outside the private sphere of the individual, to those decisions which are made by no one if the state does not make them' (Keynes, 1972, Vol. IX, p. 291).

The most plausible explanation of the Great Depression is one involving a massive decline in aggregate demand. Both Patinkin (1982) and Tobin (1997) have argued forcefully that Keynes's major discovery in the *General Theory* was the 'Principle of Effective Demand' (see also Chapter 8). According to the classical macroeconomic system, a downward shift of aggregate (effective) demand will bring into play corrective forces involving falling prices so that the final impact of a reduction in aggregate demand will be a lower price level with real output and employment quickly returning to their full employment levels. In the classical world self-correcting market forces, operating via the price mechanism, restore equilibrium without the help of government intervention. While it could be argued that the US economy behaved in a way consistent with the classical model during the 1920s, it certainly did not in the decade after 1929. The classical model could not adequately account for either the length or depth of the economic decline experienced by the major economies of the world. Indeed those economists belonging to the Mises–Hayek–Robbins–Schumpeter Austrian school of thought (see Chapter 9) believed that the depression should be allowed to run its course, since such an occurrence was the inevitable result of overinvestment during the artificially created boom. In their view the Great Depression was not a problem which policy makers should concern themselves with and intervention in the form of a stimulus to aggregate demand would only make things worse. The choice was between depression now or, if governments intervened inappropriately, even worse depression in the future.

The current consensus views the behaviour of economies during this period as consistent with an explanation which focuses on aggregate demand deficiency. However, this deficient aggregate demand explanation is one that a well-trained classical economist, brought up on Say's Law of markets and slogans of equilibrium, would find hard to either understand or accept. Indeed, explanations of the Great Depression that downplay the role of aggregate demand and instead emphasize the importance of supply-side factors have recently made a comeback (see Cole and Ohanian, 1999, 2002a). For those economists determined to find an explanation for the economic catastrophe which had befallen the economic systems of the Western world, the Great Depression had a depressing impact on their enthusiasm for *laissez-faire* capitalism.

## 1.6 The Rise and Fall of the Keynesian Consensus

The elimination of mass unemployment during the Second World War had a profound influence on the spread and influence of Keynesian ideas concerning the responsibility of government for maintaining full employment. In the UK, William Beveridge's *Full Employment in a Free Society* was published in 1944 and in the same year the government also committed itself to the maintenance of a 'high and stable level of employment' in a White Paper on *Employment Policy*. In the USA, the Employment Act of 1946 dedicated the Federal Government to the pursuit of 'maximum employment, production and purchasing power'. These commitments in both the UK and the USA were of great symbolic significance although they lacked specific discussion of how such objectives were to be attained. In the case of the UK, Keynes thought that the Beveridge target of an average level of unemployment of 3 per cent was far too optimistic although there was 'no harm in trying' (see Hutchison, 1977). Nevertheless the post-war prosperity enjoyed in the advanced economies was assumed to be in large part the direct result of Keynesian stabilization policies. In the words of Tobin who, until his death in 2002, was the USA's most prominent Keynesian economist:

A strong case has been made for the success of Keynesian policies. Virtually all advanced democratic capitalist societies adopted, in varying degrees, Keynesian strategies of demand management after World War Two. The period, certainly between 1950 and 1973, was one of unparalleled prosperity, growth, expansion of world trade, and stability. During this 'Golden Age' inflation and unemployment were low, the business cycle was tamed. (Tobin, 1987)

In a similar vein, Stewart (1986) has also argued that:

the common sense conclusion is that Britain and other Western countries had full employment for a quarter of a century after the war because their governments were committed to full employment, and knew how to secure it; and they knew how to secure it because Keynes had told them how.

It is also the case that before the 1980s it was conventional wisdom that real output had been more stable in the USA 'under conscious policies of built-in and discretionary stabilisation adopted since 1946 and particularly since 1961' compared to the period before the Second World War (Tobin, 1980a). This was one of the most widely held empirical generalizations about the US economy (Burns, 1959; Bailey, 1978). However, Christina Romer, in a series of very influential papers, challenged the conventional macroeconomic wisdom that for the US economy, the period after 1945 had been more stable than the pre-Great Depression period (see C. Romer, 1986a, 1986b, 1986c, 1989, 1994). Romer's thesis, expressed in her 1986 papers, is that the business cycle in the pre-Great Depression period was only slightly more severe than the instability experienced after 1945. In a close examination of data relating to unemployment, industrial production and GNP, Romer discovered that the methods used in the construction of the historical data led to systematic biases in the results. These biases exaggerated the pre-Great Depression data relating to cyclical movements. Thus the conventional assessment of the historical record of instability that paints a picture of substantial reductions in volatility is in reality a popular, but mistaken, view, based on a 'figment of the data'. By creating post-1945 data that are consistent with pre-1945 data Romer was able to show that both booms and recessions are more severe after 1945 than is shown in the conventional data. Romer also constructed new GNP data for the pre-1916 era and found that cyclical fluctuations are much less severe in the new data series than the original Kuznets estimates. Thus Romer concludes that there is in fact little evidence that the pre-1929 US economy was much more volatile than the post-1945 economy. Of course this same analysis also implies that the Great Depression was an event of 'unprecedented magnitude' well out of line with what went before as well as after. As Romer (1986b) writes, 'rather than being the worst of many, very severe pre-war depressions, the Great Depression stands out as the unprecedented collapse of a relatively stable pre-war economy'. In other words, the

Great Depression was not the norm for capitalism but a truly unique event. Although initially critical of Romer's findings, DeLong now accepts that Romer's critique is correct (DeLong and Summers, 1986; DeLong, 2001; see also the DeLong and Romer interviews in Snowdon, 2002a).

In a recent paper Romer (1999) has surveyed the facts about short-run fluctuations relating to US data since the late nineteenth century. There she concludes that although the volatility of real macroeconomic indicators and average severity of recessions has declined only slightly between the pre-1916 and post-1945 periods, there is strong evidence that recessions have become less frequent and more uniform. The impact of stabilization policies has been to prolong post-1945 expansions and prevent severe economic downturns. However, there are also examples of policy-induced booms (for example 1962–9 and 1970–73) and recessions (for example 1980–82) since 1945 and this is what 'explains why the economy has remained volatile in the post-war era'.

Even if we accept the conventional view that the post-war economy has been much more stable than the pre-1914 era, not everyone would agree that there was a Keynesian revolution in economic policy (the opposing views are well represented in Stein, 1969; Robinson, 1972; Tomlinson, 1984; Booth, 1985; Salant, 1988; Laidler, 1999). Some authors have also questioned whether it was the traditional Keynesian emphasis on fiscal policy that made the difference to economic performance in the period after 1945 (Matthews, 1968). What is not in doubt is that from the end of the Second World War until 1973 the industrial market economies enjoyed a 'Golden Age' of unparalleled prosperity. Maddison (1979, 1980) has identified several special characteristics which contributed to this period of exceptional economic performance:

1. increased liberalization of international trade and transactions;
2. favourable circumstances and policies which contributed to producing low inflation in conditions of very buoyant aggregate demand;
3. active government promotion of buoyant domestic demand;
4. a backlog of growth possibilities following the end of the Second World War.

As Table 1.2 indicates, growth of per capita GDP in Western Europe, which averaged 4.08 per cent during the period 1950–73, was unprecedented. Although Crafts and Toniolo (1996) view the 'Golden Age' as a 'distinctly European phenomenon', it should be noted that the growth miracle also extended to the centrally planned economies: Latin America, Asia and Africa. During this same period growth of per capita GDP in Japan was nothing less than exceptional, averaging 8.05 per cent. Table 1.3 presents data on growth

*Table 1.2   Growth of per capita GDP, world and major regions, 1820–1998 (annual average compound growth rates)*

| Region | 1820–70 | 1870–1913 | 1913–50 | 1950–73 | 1973–98 |
|---|---|---|---|---|---|
| Western Europe | 0.95 | 1.32 | 0.76 | 4.08 | 1.78 |
| Western offshoots* | 1.42 | 1.81 | 1.55 | 2.44 | 1.94 |
| Japan | 0.19 | 1.48 | 0.89 | 8.05 | 2.34 |
| Asia (excluding Japan) | –0.11 | 0.38 | –0.02 | 2.92 | 3.54 |
| Latin America | 0.10 | 1.81 | 1.42 | 2.52 | 0.99 |
| Eastern Europe and former USSR | 0.64 | 1.15 | 1.50 | 3.49 | –1.10 |
| Africa | 0.12 | 0.64 | 1.02 | 2.07 | 0.01 |
| World | 0.53 | 1.30 | 0.91 | 2.93 | 1.33 |

*Source*:   Maddison (2001), Table 3-1a.

*Table 1.3   Growth rates (GDP), 1820–1998*

| Country | 1820–70 | 1870–1913 | 1913–50 | 1950–73 | 1973–98 |
|---|---|---|---|---|---|
| France | 1.27 | 1.63 | 1.15 | 5.05 | 2.10 |
| Germany | 2.01 | 2.83 | 0.30 | 5.68 | 1.76 |
| Italy | 1.24 | 1.94 | 1.49 | 5.64 | 2.28 |
| UK | 2.05 | 1.90 | 1.19 | 2.93 | 2.00 |
| USA | 4.20 | 3.94 | 2.84 | 3.93 | 2.99 |
| Canada | 4.44 | 4.02 | 2.94 | 4.98 | 2.80 |
| Japan | 0.41 | 2.44 | 2.21 | 9.29 | 2.97 |

*Source*:   Adapted from Maddison (2001).

rates of GDP for the G7 for the same five sub-periods over the period 1820–1998. The table further demonstrates the historically high growth performance achieved during the period 1950–73, especially in France, Germany, Italy and Japan (see Chapter 11).

Whatever the causes, this 'Golden Age' came to an end after 1973 and the economic problems of the 1970s brought the Keynesian bandwagon to an abrupt (but temporary) halt. The acceleration of inflation, rising unemployment and a slowdown in economic growth (see Tables 1.3–1.5) during the 1970s were attributed, by Keynesian critics, to the misguided expansionary policies carried out in the name of Keynes. Taking the 1960–2002 period as a

*Table 1.4   Unemployment rates, 1964–2002*

|      | USA  | Canada | Japan | France | Germany | Italy | UK   |
|------|------|--------|-------|--------|---------|-------|------|
| 1964 | 5.0  | 4.3    | 1.1   | 1.4    | 0.4     | 4.3   | 2.6  |
| 1965 | 4.4  | 3.6    | 1.2   | 1.5    | 0.3     | 5.3   | 2.3  |
| 1966 | 3.6  | 3.3    | 1.3   | 1.8    | 0.2     | 5.7   | 2.2  |
| 1967 | 3.7  | 3.8    | 1.3   | 1.9    | 1.3     | 5.3   | 3.3  |
| 1968 | 3.5  | 4.4    | 1.2   | 2.7    | 1.5     | 5.6   | 3.1  |
| 1969 | 3.4  | 4.4    | 1.1   | 2.3    | 0.9     | 5.6   | 2.9  |
| 1970 | 4.8  | 5.6    | 1.1   | 2.5    | 0.8     | 5.3   | 3.0  |
| 1971 | 5.8  | 6.1    | 1.2   | 2.7    | 0.9     | 5.3   | 3.6  |
| 1972 | 5.5  | 6.2    | 1.4   | 2.8    | 0.8     | 6.3   | 4.0  |
| 1973 | 4.8  | 5.5    | 1.3   | 2.7    | 0.8     | 6.2   | 3.0  |
| 1974 | 5.5  | 5.3    | 1.4   | 2.8    | 1.6     | 5.3   | 2.9  |
| 1975 | 8.3  | 6.9    | 1.9   | 4.0    | 3.6     | 5.8   | 4.3  |
| 1976 | 7.6  | 7.1    | 2.0   | 4.4    | 3.7     | 6.6   | 5.6  |
| 1977 | 6.9  | 8.1    | 2.0   | 4.9    | 3.6     | 7.0   | 6.0  |
| 1978 | 6.1  | 8.4    | 2.2   | 4.7    | 3.0     | 5.3   | 5.7  |
| 1979 | 5.8  | 7.5    | 2.1   | 5.3    | 2.7     | 5.8   | 4.7  |
| 1980 | 7.2  | 7.5    | 2.0   | 5.8    | 2.6     | 5.6   | 6.2  |
| 1981 | 7.6  | 7.6    | 2.2   | 7.0    | 4.0     | 6.2   | 9.7  |
| 1982 | 9.7  | 11.0   | 2.4   | 7.7    | 5.7     | 6.8   | 11.1 |
| 1983 | 9.6  | 11.9   | 2.7   | 8.1    | 6.9     | 7.7   | 11.1 |
| 1984 | 7.5  | 11.3   | 2.7   | 9.4    | 7.1     | 7.9   | 10.9 |
| 1985 | 7.2  | 10.7   | 2.6   | 9.8    | 7.2     | 8.1   | 11.2 |
| 1986 | 7.0  | 9.6    | 2.8   | 9.9    | 6.5     | 8.9   | 11.2 |
| 1987 | 6.2  | 8.8    | 2.8   | 10.1   | 6.3     | 9.6   | 10.3 |
| 1988 | 5.5  | 7.8    | 2.5   | 9.6    | 6.2     | 9.7   | 8.5  |
| 1989 | 5.3  | 7.5    | 2.3   | 9.1    | 5.6     | 9.7   | 7.1  |
| 1990 | 5.6  | 8.1    | 2.1   | 8.6    | 4.8     | 8.9   | 6.9  |
| 1991 | 6.8  | 10.3   | 2.1   | 9.1    | 4.2     | 8.5   | 8.6  |
| 1992 | 7.5  | 11.2   | 2.2   | 10.0   | 6.4     | 8.7   | 9.7  |
| 1993 | 6.9  | 11.4   | 2.5   | 11.3   | 7.7     | 10.1  | 9.9  |
| 1994 | 6.1  | 10.4   | 2.9   | 11.8   | 8.2     | 11.0  | 9.2  |
| 1995 | 5.6  | 9.4    | 3.1   | 11.4   | 8.0     | 11.5  | 8.5  |
| 1996 | 5.4  | 9.6    | 3.4   | 11.9   | 8.7     | 11.5  | 8.0  |
| 1997 | 4.9  | 9.1    | 3.4   | 11.8   | 9.7     | 11.6  | 6.9  |
| 1998 | 4.5  | 8.3    | 4.1   | 11.4   | 9.1     | 11.7  | 6.2  |
| 1999 | 4.2  | 7.6    | 4.7   | 10.7   | 8.4     | 11.3  | 5.9  |
| 2000 | 4.0  | 6.8    | 4.7   | 9.3    | 7.8     | 10.4  | 5.4  |
| 2001 | 4.7  | 7.2    | 5.0   | 8.5    | 7.8     | 9.4   | 5.0  |
| 2002 | 5.8  | 7.7    | 5.4   | 8.7    | 8.2     | 9.0   | 5.1  |

*Notes*:   Standardized unemployment rates (percentage of total labour force up to 1977, there-after percentage of civilian labour force).

*Source*:   OECD, *Economic Outlook*, various issues.

*Modern macroeconomics*

*Table 1.5   Inflation rates, 1964–2002*

|      | USA  | Canada | Japan | France | Germany | Italy | UK   |
|------|------|--------|-------|--------|---------|-------|------|
| 1964 | 1.3  | 1.8    | 3.8   | 3.2    | 2.4     | 5.9   | 3.2  |
| 1965 | 1.6  | 2.5    | 6.6   | 2.7    | 3.2     | 4.5   | 4.8  |
| 1966 | 3.0  | 3.7    | 5.1   | 2.6    | 3.6     | 2.2   | 3.9  |
| 1967 | 2.8  | 3.6    | 4.0   | 2.8    | 1.6     | 1.6   | 2.4  |
| 1968 | 4.2  | 4.1    | 5.4   | 4.6    | 1.6     | 1.5   | 4.7  |
| 1969 | 5.4  | 4.5    | 5.2   | 6.0    | 1.9     | 2.4   | 5.5  |
| 1970 | 5.9  | 3.4    | 7.7   | 5.9    | 3.4     | 5.0   | 6.4  |
| 1971 | 4.3  | 2.8    | 6.4   | 5.4    | 5.2     | 4.9   | 9.4  |
| 1972 | 3.3  | 4.8    | 4.8   | 6.1    | 5.5     | 5.8   | 7.1  |
| 1973 | 6.2  | 7.6    | 11.6  | 7.4    | 7.0     | 10.8  | 9.2  |
| 1974 | 11.0 | 10.8   | 23.2  | 13.6   | 7.0     | 19.0  | 15.9 |
| 1975 | 9.2  | 10.8   | 11.9  | 11.8   | 5.9     | 17.2  | 24.1 |
| 1976 | 5.8  | 7.6    | 9.4   | 9.6    | 4.3     | 16.7  | 16.7 |
| 1977 | 6.5  | 8.0    | 8.2   | 9.5    | 3.7     | 18.5  | 15.9 |
| 1978 | 7.6  | 8.9    | 4.2   | 9.3    | 2.7     | 12.1  | 8.2  |
| 1979 | 11.2 | 9.1    | 3.7   | 10.6   | 4.1     | 14.8  | 13.4 |
| 1980 | 13.5 | 10.2   | 7.8   | 13.5   | 5.4     | 21.2  | 18.1 |
| 1981 | 10.4 | 12.5   | 4.9   | 13.3   | 6.3     | 19.6  | 11.9 |
| 1982 | 6.2  | 10.8   | 2.7   | 12.1   | 5.3     | 16.5  | 8.7  |
| 1983 | 3.2  | 5.9    | 1.9   | 9.5    | 3.3     | 14.7  | 4.6  |
| 1984 | 4.3  | 4.4    | 2.3   | 7.7    | 2.4     | 10.8  | 5.0  |
| 1985 | 3.6  | 4.0    | 2.0   | 5.8    | 2.2     | 9.2   | 6.1  |
| 1986 | 1.9  | 4.2    | 0.6   | 2.6    | −0.1    | 5.8   | 3.4  |
| 1987 | 3.7  | 4.4    | 0.1   | 3.3    | 0.2     | 4.7   | 4.2  |
| 1988 | 4.1  | 4.0    | 0.7   | 2.7    | 1.3     | 5.1   | 4.9  |
| 1989 | 4.8  | 5.0    | 2.3   | 3.5    | 2.8     | 6.3   | 7.8  |
| 1990 | 5.4  | 4.8    | 3.1   | 3.4    | 2.7     | 6.4   | 9.5  |
| 1991 | 4.3  | 5.6    | 3.2   | 3.2    | 3.5     | 6.3   | 5.9  |
| 1992 | 3.0  | 1.5    | 1.7   | 2.4    | 1.7     | 5.2   | 3.7  |
| 1993 | 3.0  | 1.8    | 1.3   | 2.1    | 5.1     | 4.5   | 1.6  |
| 1994 | 2.6  | 0.2    | 0.7   | 1.7    | 4.4     | 4.1   | 2.5  |
| 1995 | 2.8  | 2.2    | −0.1  | 1.8    | 2.8     | 5.2   | 3.4  |
| 1996 | 2.9  | 1.6    | 0.1   | 2.0    | 1.7     | 4.0   | 2.5  |
| 1997 | 2.3  | 1.6    | 1.7   | 1.2    | 1.4     | 2.0   | 3.1  |
| 1998 | 1.6  | 1.0    | 0.7   | 0.7    | 1.9     | 2.0   | 3.4  |
| 1999 | 2.2  | 1.7    | −0.3  | 0.5    | 0.9     | 1.7   | 1.6  |
| 2000 | 3.4  | 2.8    | −0.7  | 1.7    | 0.6     | 2.5   | 2.9  |
| 2001 | 2.8  | 2.5    | −0.7  | 1.6    | 2.0     | 2.8   | 1.8  |
| 2002 | 1.6  | 2.3    | −0.9  | 1.9    | 1.3     | 2.5   | 1.6  |

*Notes*:   Percentage change over previous year of consumer prices (calculated from indexes).

*Source*:   International Monetary Fund, *International Financial Statistics*, various issues.

whole, on average in the 'Golden Age' both unemployment and inflation were low. In the period 1983–93, inflation came down but unemployment remained stubbornly high in many countries, especially in Western Europe where high unemployment has been attributed by some economists to hysteresis effects and/or various labour market rigidities (see Chapter 7). In the most recent period, 1994–2002, inflation was low but unemployment remained high in Western Europe while it declined in the USA. But only in the period 1973–83 do we see the simultaneous combination of high unemployment and high inflation, i.e. stagflation. To the critics of Keynesianism stagflation was an inevitable legacy of the 'Golden Age' of demand management (Friedman, 1975; Bruno and Sachs, 1985; DeLong, 1997; see also Cairncross and Cairncross, 1992, for a discussion of the legacy of the 1960s).

### 1.7 Theoretical Schizophrenia and the Neoclassical Synthesis

We can only speculate on what Keynes would have made of the Keynesian policies carried out in his name. What we can see more clearly, with the benefit of hindsight and experience, is that at the theoretical level Keynesian economics created schizophrenia in the way that economics was taught, with courses in microeconomics typically concentrating on issues relating to allocation, production and distribution (questions of efficiency and equity) and courses in macroeconomics focusing on problems associated with the level and the long-term trend of aggregate output and employment, and the rate of inflation (questions of growth and stability). The Keynesian propositions of market failure and involuntary unemployment expounded within macroeconomics did not rest easily alongside the Walrasian theory of general competitive equilibrium, where the actions of rational optimizing individuals ensure that all markets, including the labour market, are cleared by flexible prices. In the Walrasian model, which dominated microeconomics, lapses from full employment cannot occur. Although Paul Samuelson and others attempted to reconcile these two strands of economics, producing a 'neoclassical synthesis', Keynesian macroeconomics and orthodox neoclassical microeconomics integrated about as well as oil and water. During the 'Golden Age' this problem could be ignored. By 1973, with accelerating inflation, it could not. As Greenwald and Stiglitz (1987) have argued, from this point there were two ways in which the two subdisciplines could be reconciled. Either macro theory could be adapted to orthodox neoclassical micro theory (the new classical approach) or micro theory could be adapted to macro theory (the new Keynesian approach). As we shall see, these attempts at reconciliation have been a dominating influence on macroeconomic theorizing during the past three decades.

Keynes himself had contributed to this dichotomy because he saw 'no reason to suppose that the existing system seriously misemploys the factors

of production which are in use ... It is in determining the volume, not the
direction, of actual employment that the existing system has broken down'
(Keynes, 1936, p. 379). In other words, the apparent inability of the capitalist
system to provide for full employment was the main blemish on an economic
system which Keynes otherwise held in high regard. Once this major defect
was remedied and full employment restored, 'the classical theory comes into
its own again from this point onwards' and there 'is no objection to be raised
against classical analysis of the manner in which private self-interest will
determine what in particular is produced, in what proportions the factors of
production will be combined to produce it, and how the value of the final
product will be distributed between them' (Keynes, 1936, pp. 378–9). Thus
Keynes can be viewed as attempting to reconcile two opposing views of a
capitalist market economy. First, we have the classical–neoclassical view
which extols the efficiency of the price mechanism in solving the fundamental allocation and production problems which arise from the scarcity of
resources. Second, we have Keynes's iconoclastic vision which highlights the
shortcomings of the invisible hand, at least with respect to the general level
of output and employment. Keynes was optimistic that this later problem
could be solved with limited government intervention, and capitalism could
be saved from itself.

The synthesis of the ideas of the classical economists with those of Keynes
dominated mainstream economics at least until the early 1970s. The standard
textbook approach to macroeconomics from the period following the Second
World War until the early 1970s relied heavily on the interpretation of the
*General Theory* provided by Hicks (1937) and modified by the contributions
of Modigliani (1944), Patinkin (1956) and Tobin (1958). Samuelson's best-
selling textbook popularized the synthesis of Keynesian and classical ideas,
making them accessible to a wide readership and successive generations of
students. It was Samuelson who introduced the label 'neoclassical synthesis'
into the literature in the third edition of *Economics*, in 1955. This synthesis of
classical and Keynesian ideas became the standard approach to macroeconomic analysis, both in textbooks and in professional discussion (see Chapter
3). The orthodox Keynesian model provided the foundation for the large-
scale macroeconometric models developed by Lawrence Klein and also those
associated with the Cowles Commission. Such models were used for forecasting purposes and to enable economists to assess the likely impact on the
economy of alternative economic policies. Lucas and Sargent (1978) have
attributed the 'dominant scientific position' that orthodox Keynesian economics attained by 1960 to the fact that it 'lent itself so readily to the formulation
of explicit econometric models'. As far as macroeconomics was concerned,
for the majority of researchers in the 1960s, the 'Keynesian model was the
only game in town' (Barro, 1989a).

The orthodox Keynesian argument that government intervention, in the form of activist monetary and fiscal policies, could correct the aggregate instability exhibited by market economies also influenced political decision makers. At least up until the mid-1970s both Labour and Conservative parties in the UK adhered to orthodox Keynesian principles. In the USA it was not until the early 1960s that the Keynesian approach (known as the 'New Economics') was adopted with any real enthusiasm (Tobin, 1987; Perry and Tobin, 2000). The Council of Economic Advisers (CEA) appointed by President Kennedy was dominated by Keynesian economists. Chaired by Walter Heller, the CEA also included James Tobin and Robert Solow while Paul Samuelson served as an unofficial adviser (see Snowdon and Vane, 2002a). In 1971 even President Nixon had declared that 'we are all Keynesians now!' However, by the 1980s, US economic policy was very different from that prevailing during the Kennedy–Johnson era (see Feldstein, 1992).

Before the 1970s the Keynesian approach gave emphasis to demand-side factors. Keynes had reversed Say's Law, and Keynesianism, based on the IS–LM interpretation of Keynes, was the established orthodoxy in macroeconomics (see Chapter 3 and Patinkin, 1990a, for a discussion of the IS–LM interpretation of Keynes). Initially Keynesianism was associated with fiscalism but by the late 1960s the importance of monetary factors was widely recognized by Keynesians (see Tobin, 1987, 1996; Buiter, 2003a). The most important Keynesian development during this period was the incorporation of the Phillips curve into the prevailing macroeconomic model (see Phillips, 1958; Lipsey, 1978; Chapter 3). By the early 1960s the IS–LM model was being used to explain the determination of output and employment, while the Phillips curve enabled the policy maker to predict the rate of inflation which would result from different target levels of unemployment. The simultaneous increase in both unemployment and inflation (shown in Tables 1.4 and 1.5) in the major industrial economies in the early 1970s proved fatal to the more simplistic versions of 'hydraulic' Keynesianism and prepared the way for the monetarist and new classical counter-revolutions (see Johnson, 1971; Bleaney, 1985; Colander, 1988). The 1970s witnessed a significant renaissance of the pre-Keynesian belief that the market economy is capable of achieving macroeconomic stability and rapid growth providing the visible (and palsied) hand of government is prevented from conducting activist discretionary fiscal and monetary policies. The stagflation of the 1970s gave increasing credibility and influence to those economists who had for many years warned that Keynesian macroeconomic policies were both over-ambitious and, more importantly, predicated on theories that were fundamentally flawed (see Friedman, 1968a; Hayek, 1978; Buchanan et al., 1978; Lucas and Sargent, 1978; Romer and Romer, 1997).

The demise of the neoclassical synthesis mainstream position signalled the beginning of a period when the dominance of Keynesian macroeconomics came to an end and, as we have seen, the breakdown of this consensus position was due to both empirical and theoretical flaws (see Mankiw, 1990). For the more extreme critics of Keynesianism the task facing the new generation of macroeconomic theorists was to 'sort through the wreckage determining which features of that remarkable intellectual event called the Keynesian revolution can be salvaged and put to good use and which others must be discarded' (Lucas and Sargent, 1978).

## 1.8   Schools of Thought in Macroeconomics After Keynes

According to Johnson (1971), 'by far the most helpful circumstance for the rapid propagation of a new revolutionary theory is the existence of an established orthodoxy which is clearly inconsistent with the most salient facts of reality'. As we have seen, the inability of the classical model to account adequately for the collapse of output and employment in the 1930s paved the way for the Keynesian revolution. During the 1950s and 1960s the neoclassical synthesis became the accepted wisdom for the majority of economists (see Chapter 3). The work of Nobel Memorial Laureates James Tobin, Lawrence Klein, Robert Solow, Franco Modigliani, James Meade, John Hicks and Paul Samuelson dominated the Keynesian school and provided intellectual support for the view that government intervention in the form of demand management can significantly improve the performance of the economy. The 'New Economics' adopted by the Kennedy administration in 1961 demonstrated the influence of Keynesian thinking and the 1962 *Economic Report of the President* explicitly advocated stabilization policies with the objective of keeping 'overall demand in step with the basic production potential of the economy'.

During the 1970s this Keynesian approach increasingly came under attack and was subjected to the force of two 'counter-revolutionary' approaches, namely monetarism and new classical macroeconomics. Both of these approaches are underpinned by the belief that there is no need for activist stabilization policy. The new classical school in particular supports the view that the authorities cannot, and therefore should not, attempt to stabilize fluctuations in output and employment through the use of activist demand management policies (Lucas, 1981a).

As we shall discuss in Chapter 4, in the orthodox monetarist view there is no need for activist stabilization policy (except in extreme circumstances) given the belief that capitalist economies are inherently stable, unless disturbed by erratic monetary growth. Monetarists hold that when subjected to some disturbance the economy will return, fairly quickly, to the neighbourhood of the 'natural' level of output and employment. Given this view they question the need for stabilization policy involving the 'fine-tuning' of aggregate demand. Even if there were a need, monetarists argue that the authorities can't stabilize fluctuations in output and employment due to the problems associated with stabilization policy. These problems include those posed by the length of the inside lag associated with fiscal policy, the long and variable outside time lags associated with monetary policy and uncertainty over what precise value to attribute to the natural rate of unemployment. In consequence monetarists argue that the authorities shouldn't be given discretion to vary the strength of fiscal and monetary policy as and when they see fit, fearing that they could do more harm than good. Instead, monetarists advocate that the monetary authorities should be bound by rules.

With hindsight two publications were particularly influential in cementing the foundations for the monetarist counter-revolution. First there is Friedman and Schwartz's (1963) monumental study, *A Monetary History of the United States, 1867–1960*. This influential volume presents persuasive evidence in support of the monetarist view that changes in the money supply play a largely independent role in cyclical fluctuations. Second is Friedman's (1968a) *American Economic Review* article on 'The Role of Monetary Policy' in which he put forward the natural rate hypothesis and the view that there is no long-run trade-off between inflation and unemployment. The influence of Friedman's article was greatly enhanced because it anticipated the events of the 1970s and, in particular, predicted accelerating inflation as a consequence of the repeated use of expansionary monetary policy geared to over-optimistic employment targets.

During the 1970s a second counter-revolution took place associated with new classical macroeconomics. This approach, which cast further doubt on whether traditional Keynesian aggregate demand management policies can be used to stabilize the economy, is often seen as synonymous with the work of one of Friedman's former University of Chicago students, the 1995 Nobel Memorial Laureate, Robert E. Lucas Jr. Other leading advocates of the new classical monetary approach to analysing economic fluctuations during the 1970s include Thomas Sargent, Neil Wallace, Robert Barro, Edward Prescott and Patrick Minford (see Hoover, 1988; Snowdon et al., 1994).

As we will discuss in Chapter 5, by combining the rational expectations hypothesis (first put forward by John Muth in the context of microeconomics in the early 1960s), the assumption that markets continuously clear, and Friedman's natural rate hypothesis, Lucas was able to demonstrate in his 1972 *Journal of Economic Theory* paper on 'Expectations and the Neutrality of Money' how a short-run equilibrium relationship between inflation and unemployment (Phillips curve) will result if inflation is unanticipated due to incomplete information.

In line with the monetarist school, new classical economists believe that the economy is inherently stable, unless disturbed by erratic monetary growth, and that when subjected to some disturbance will quickly return to its natural level of output and employment. However, in the new classical approach it is unanticipated monetary shocks that are the dominant cause of business cycles. The new classical case against discretionary policy activism, and in favour of rules, is based on a different set of arguments to those advanced by monetarists. Three insights in particular underlie the new classical approach. First, the policy ineffectiveness proposition (Sargent and Wallace, 1975, 1976) implies that only random or arbitrary monetary policy actions undertaken by the authorities can have short-run real effects because they cannot be anticipated by rational economic agents. Given that such actions will only increase the variation of output and employment around their natural levels, increasing uncertainty in the economy, the proposition provides an argument against discretionary policy activism in favour of rules (see Chapter 5, section 5.5.1). Second, Lucas's (1976) critique of economic policy evaluation undermines confidence that traditional Keynesian-style macroeconometric models can be used to accurately predict the consequences of various policy changes on key macroeconomic variables (see Chapter 5, section 5.5.6). Third, Kydland and Prescott's (1977) analysis of dynamic time inconsistency, which implies that economic performance can be improved if discretionary powers are taken away from the authorities, provides another argument in the case for monetary policy being conducted by rules rather than discretion (see Chapter 5, section 5.5.3).

Following the demise of the monetary-surprise version of new classical macroeconomics in the early 1980s a second phase of equilibrium theorizing was initiated by the seminal contribution of Kydland and Prescott (1982) which, following Long and Plosser (1983), has come to be referred to as real business cycle theory. As we shall discuss in Chapter 6, modern equilibrium business cycle theory starts with the view that 'growth and fluctuations are not distinct phenomena to be studied with separate data and analytical tools' (Cooley and Prescott, 1995). Proponents of this approach view economic fluctuations as being predominantly caused by persistent real (supply-side) shocks, rather than unanticipated monetary (demand-side) shocks, to the economy. The focus of these real shocks involves large random fluctuations in the rate of technological progress that result in fluctuations in relative prices to which rational economic agents optimally respond by altering their supply of labour and consumption. Perhaps the most controversial feature of this approach is the claim that fluctuations in output and employment are Pareto-efficient responses to real technology shocks to the aggregate production function. This implies that observed fluctuations in output are viewed as fluctuations in the natural rate of output, not deviations of output from a smooth deterministic trend. As such the government should not attempt to reduce these fluctuations through stabilization policy, not only because such attempts are unlikely to achieve their desired objective but also because reducing instability would reduce welfare (Prescott, 1986).

The real business cycle approach conflicts with both the conventional Keynesian analysis as well as monetarist and new classical monetary equilibrium theorizing where equilibrium is identified with a stable trend for the natural (full employment) growth path. In the Keynesian approach departures from full employment are viewed as disequilibrium situations where societal welfare is below potential and government has a role to correct this macroeconomic market failure using fiscal and monetary policy. In sharp contrast the 'bold conjecture' of real business cycle theorists is that each stage of the business cycle, boom and slump, is an equilibrium. 'Slumps represent an undesired, undesirable, and unavoidable shift in the constraints that people face; but, given these constraints, markets react efficiently and people succeed in achieving the best outcomes that circumstances permit ... every stage of the business cycle is a Pareto efficient equilibrium' (Hartley et al., 1998). Needless to say, the real business cycle approach has proved to be highly controversial and has been subjected to a number of criticisms, not least the problem of identifying negative technological shocks that cause recessions. In Chapter 6 we shall examine these criticisms and appraise the contribution that real business cycle theorists have made to modern macroeconomics.

The new classical equilibrium approach to explaining economic fluctuations has in turn been challenged by a revitalized group of new Keynesian theorists who prefer to adapt micro to macro theory rather than accept the new classical approach of adapting macro theory to orthodox neoclassical market-clearing microfoundations. Important figures here include George Akerlof, Janet Yellen, Olivier Blanchard, Gregory Mankiw, Edmund Phelps, David Romer, Joseph Stiglitz and Ben Bernanke (see Gordon, 1989; Mankiw and Romer, 1991). As we will discuss in Chapter 7, new Keynesian models have incorporated the rational expectations hypothesis, the assumption that markets may fail to clear, due to wage and price stickiness, and Friedman's natural rate hypothesis. According to proponents of new Keynesian economics there is a need for stabilization policy as capitalist economies are subjected to both demand- and supply-side shocks which cause inefficient fluctuations in output and employment. Not only will capitalist economies fail to rapidly self-equilibrate, but where the actual rate of unemployment remains above the natural rate for a prolonged period, the natural rate (or what new Keynesians prefer to refer to as NAIRU – non-accelerating inflation rate of unemployment) may well increase due to 'hysteresis' effects. As governments can improve macroeconomic performance, if they are given discretion to do so, we also explore in Chapter 7 the new Keynesian approach to monetary policy as set out by Clarida et al. (1999) and Bernanke et al. (1999).

Finally we can identify two further groups or schools of thought. The Post Keynesian school is descended from some of Keynes's more radical contemporaries and disciples, deriving its inspiration and distinctive approach from the writings of Joan Robinson, Nicholas Kaldor, Michal Kalecki, George Shackle and Piero Sraffa. Modern advocates of this approach include Jan Kregel, Victoria Chick, Hyman Minsky and Paul Davidson, the author of Chapter 8 which discusses the Post Keynesian school. There is also a school of thought that has its intellectual roots in the work of Ludwig von Mises and Nobel Memorial Laureate Friedrich von Hayek which has inspired a distinctly Austrian approach to economic analysis and in particular to the explanation of business cycle phenomena. Modern advocates of the Austrian approach include Israel Kirzner, Karen Vaughn and Roger Garrison, the author of Chapter 9 which discusses the Austrian school.

To recap, we identify the following schools of thought that have made a significant contribution to the evolution of twentieth-century macroeconomics: (i) the orthodox Keynesian school (Chapter 3), (ii) the orthodox monetarist school (Chapter 4), (iii) the new classical school (Chapter 5), (iv) the real business cycle school (Chapter 6), (v) the new Keynesian school (Chapter 7), (vi) the Post Keynesian school (Chapter 8) and (vii) the Austrian school (Chapter 9). No doubt other economists would choose a different classification, and some have done so (see Cross, 1982a; Phelps, 1990). For example, Gerrard (1996) argues that a unifying theme in the evolution of modern macroeconomics has been an 'ever-evolving classical Keynesian debate' involving contributions from various schools of thought that can be differentiated and classified as orthodox, new or radical. The two 'orthodox' schools, 'IS–LM Keynesianism' and 'neoclassical monetarism', dominated macroeconomic theory in the period up to the mid-1970s. Since then three new schools have been highly influential. The new classical, real business cycle and new Keynesian schools place emphasis on issues relating to aggregate supply in contrast to the orthodox schools which focused their research primarily on the factors determining aggregate demand and the consequences of demand-management policies. In particular, the new schools share Lucas's view that macroeconomic models should be based on solid microeconomic foundations (Hoover, 1988, 1992). The 'radical' schools, both Post Keynesian and Austrian, are critical of mainstream analysis, whether it be orthodox or new.

We are acutely aware of the dangers of categorizing particular economists in ways which are bound to oversimplify the sophistication and breadth of their own views. Many economists dislike being labelled or linked to any specific research programme or school, including some of those economists listed above. As Hoover (1988) has observed in a similar enterprise, 'Any economist is described most fully by a vector of characteristics' and any definition will 'emphasise some elements of this vector, while playing down related ones'. It is also the case that during the last decade of the twentieth century, macroeconomics began to evolve into what Goodfriend and King (1997) have called a 'New Neoclassical Synthesis'. The central elements of this new synthesis involve both new classical and new Keynesian elements, namely:

1. the need for macroeconomic models to take into account intertemporal optimization;
2. the widespread use of the rational expectations hypothesis;
3. recognition of the importance of imperfect competition in goods, labour and credit markets;
4. incorporating costly price adjustment into macroeconomic models.

Therefore, one important development arising from the vociferous debates of the 1970s and 1980s is that there is now more of a consensus on what constitutes a 'core of practical macroeconomics' than was the case 25 years ago (see Blanchard, 1997b, 2000; Blinder, 1997a; Eichenbaum, 1997; Solow, 1997; Taylor, 1997b).

With these caveats in mind we will examine in Chapters 3–9 the competing schools of macroeconomic thought identified above. We also include interviews with some of the economists who are generally recognized as being leading representatives of each group and/or prominent in the development of macroeconomic analysis in the post-war period. In discussing these various schools of thought it is important to remember that the work of Keynes remains the 'main single point of reference, either positive or negative, for all the schools of macroeconomics'. Therefore, it is hardly surprising that all the schools define themselves in relation to the ideas originally put forward by Keynes in his *General Theory,* 'either as a development of some version of his thought or as a restoration of some version of pre-Keynesian classical thought' (Vercelli, 1991, p. 3).

Before considering the central tenets and policy implications of these main schools of thought we also need to highlight two other important changes that have taken place in macroeconomics during the final decades of the twentieth century. First, in section 1.9 we outline the development of what has come to be known as the new political macroeconomics. The second key change of emphasis during the last 20 years, reviewed in section 1.10, has been the renaissance of growth theory and empirics.

## 1.9 The New Political Macroeconomics

During the past two decades research into the various forms of interaction between politics and macroeconomics has become a major growth area giving rise to a field known as the 'new political macroeconomics' (Alesina,

1995; Alt and Alesina, 1996; Alesina and Rosenthal, 1995; Alesina et al. 1997; Drazen, 2000a). This research area has developed at the interface of macroeconomics, social choice theory and game theory. Of particular interest to macroeconomists is the influence that political factors have on such issues as business cycles, inflation, unemployment, growth, budget deficits and the conduct and implementation of stabilization policies (Snowdon and Vane, 1999a).

As we will discuss in Chapter 10, modern politico-economic models, initially developed in the 1970s by Nordhaus (1975), Hibbs (1977) and Frey and Schneider (1978a), view the government as an endogenous component of the political and economic system. The conventional normative approach, in sharp contrast, regards the policy maker as a 'benevolent social planner' whose only objective is to maximize social welfare. The normative approach is concerned with how policy makers should act rather than how they do act.

Alesina (1994) has highlighted two general political forces that are always likely to play a crucial distorting role in the economy. The first factor is the incumbent policy maker's desire to retain power, which acts as an incentive to 'opportunistic' behaviour. Second, society is polarized and this inevitably gives rise to some degree of social conflict. As a result ideological considerations will manifest themselves in the form of 'partisan' behaviour and actions.

Nordhaus's model predicts self-interested opportunistic behaviour, irrespective of party allegiance, before an election. When these political motivations are mixed with myopic non-rational behaviour of voters and non-rational expectations of economic agents, a political business cycle is generated which ultimately leads to a higher rate of inflation in a democracy than is optimal. In the Hibbs model 'left'-inclined politicians have a greater aversion to unemployment than inflation, and 'right'-inclined politicians have the opposite preference. The Hibbs model therefore predicts a systematic difference in policy choices and outcomes in line with the partisan preferences of the incumbent politicians.

Both of these models were undermined by the rational expectations revolution. By the mid-1970s models which continued to use adaptive expectations or were reliant on a long-run stable Phillips curve trade-off were coming in for heavy criticism. The scope for opportunistic or ideological behaviour seemed to be extremely limited in a world dominated by rational 'forward-looking' voters and economic agents who could not be systematically fooled. However, after a period of relative neglect a second phase of politico-economic models emerged in the mid-1980s. These models capture the insights emanating from and including the rational expectations hypothesis in macroeconomic models. Economists such as Rogoff and Sibert (1988) have developed 'rational opportunistic' models, and Alesina has been prominent in developing the 'rational partisan' theory of aggregate instability (Alesina, 1987, 1988; Alesina and

Sachs, 1988). These models show that while the scope for opportunistic or idcological behaviour is more limited in a rational expectations setting, the impact of political distortions on macroeconomic policy making is still present given the presence of imperfect information and uncertainty over the outcome of elections (Alesina and Roubini, 1992). As such this work points towards the need for greater transparency in the conduct of fiscal policy and the introduction of central bank independence for the conduct of monetary policy (Alesina and Summers, 1993; Alesina and Gatti, 1995; Alesina and Perotti 1996a; Snowdon, 1997).

More recently several economists have extended the reach of the new political macroeconomics and this has involved research into the origin and persistence of rising fiscal deficits and debt ratios, the political economy of growth, the optimal size of nations, the economic and political risk involved with membership of fiscal unions and the political constraints on economic growth (Alesina and Perotti, 1996b, 1997a; Alesina et al., 1996; Alesina and Spolare, 1997, 2003; Alesina and Perotti, 1998; Acemoglu and Robinson, 2000a, 2003). With respect to achieving a reduction in the fiscal deficit/GDP ratio, Alesina's research has indicated that successful fiscal adjustment is highly correlated with the composition of spending cuts. Unsuccessful adjustments are associated with cuts in public investment expenditures whereas in successful cases more than half the expenditure cuts are in government wages and transfer payments (Alesina et al., 1997). In addition, because fiscal policy is increasingly about redistribution in the OECD countries, increases in labour taxation to finance an increase in transfers are likely to induce wage pressure, raise labour costs and reduce competitiveness (Alesina and Perotti, 1997b). Research into the optimal size of nations has indicated an important link between trade liberalization and political separatism. In a world dominated by trade restrictions, large political units make sense because the size of a market is determined by political boundaries. If free trade prevails relatively small homogeneous political jurisdictions can prosper and benefit from the global marketplace (Alesina and Spolare, 2003). Work on the implications of fiscal unions has also indicated the potential disadvantages of larger units. While larger jurisdictions can achieve benefits in the form of a centralized redistribution system, 'these benefits may be offset (partially or completely) by the increase in the diversity and, thus, in potential conflicts of interests among the citizens of larger jurisdictions' (Alesina and Perotti, 1998).

In recent years the 'politicisation of growth theory' (Hibbs, 2001) has led to a burgeoning of research into the impact on economic growth of politics, policy, and institutional arrangements. Daron Acemoglu and his co-authors have made a highly influential contribution to the debate relating to the 'deeper' institutional determinants of economic growth and the role of political distortions as barriers to progress (see Acemoglu, 2003a; Snowdon, 2004c). Acemoglu's recent research highlights the importance of 'political barriers to development'. This work focuses on attitudes to change in hierarchical societies. Economists recognize that economic growth is a necessary condition for the elimination of poverty and sustainable increases in living standards. Furthermore, technological change and innovation are key factors in promoting growth. So why do political élites deliberately block the adoption of institutions and policies that would help to eliminate economic backwardness? Acemoglu and Robinson (2000a, 2003) argue that superior institutions and technologies are resisted because they may reduce the political power of the élite. Moreover, the absence of strong institutions allows autocratic rulers to adopt political strategies that are highly effective at defusing any opposition to their regime. As a result economic growth and development stagnate.

## 1.10 The Renaissance of Economic Growth Research

There is no doubt that one very important consequence arising from the work of Keynes was that it led to a shift of emphasis from the classical long-run issue of economic growth to the shorter-run issue of aggregate instability. As Tobin (1997) emphasizes, Keynesian economics does not pretend to apply to the long-run issues of growth and development. This is in sharp contrast to the work of Adam Smith, David Ricardo and the other classical economists who sought to understand the nature and causes of the 'Wealth of Nations' rather than focus on the issue of short-run instability. This should hardly surprise us given the rapid self-equilibrating properties of the classical macroeconomic model (see Chapter 2).

Even small differences in growth rates of per capita income, if sustained over long periods of time, lead to significant differences in relative living standards between nations. The importance of economic growth as a basis for improvements in human welfare cannot be overstated because the impact of even small differentials in growth rates, when compounded over time, are striking (see Chapter 11). Barro and Sala-i-Martin (1995) provide a simple but illuminating example of the long-term consequences of growth differentials. They note that the US economy grew by an annual average of 1.75 per cent over the period 1870–1990 thereby raising real GDP per capita from $2244 in 1870 to $18 258 in 1990 (measured in 1985 dollars). If growth over the same period had been 0.75 per cent, real GDP per capita in 1990 would have been $5519 rather than $18 258. If, on the other hand, growth had been 2.75 per cent, then real GDP per capita in the USA by 1990 would have been $60 841. Note how this amazing difference in outcomes arises from relatively small variations in the growth rate. David Romer (1996) has also expressed the same point succinctly as follows: 'the welfare implications of long-run growth swamp any possible effects of the short-run fluctuations that macr-oeconomics traditionally focuses on'. In reviewing the differential growth performances of countries such as India, Egypt, the 'Asian Tigers', Japan and the USA, and the consequences of these differentials for living standards, Lucas (1988) comments that 'the consequences for human welfare involved in questions like these are simply staggering. Once one starts to think about them, it is hard to think about anything else.' For some economists, such as Prescott (1996), the renewed interest in growth over the last 20 years stems from their belief that business cycle fluctuations 'are not costly to society' and that it is more important for economists to worry about 'increasing the rate of increase in economy-wide productivity and not smoothing business fluctuations'. This position had been publicly expressed earlier by Lucas in May 1985 when delivering his Yrjo Jahnsson lectures. There he argued that post-1945 economic stability had been a relatively 'minor problem' especially in comparison 'to the costs of modestly reduced rates of growth' (Lucas, 1987). More recently, Lucas (2003) has repeated this message using US performance over the last 50 years as a benchmark. Lucas argues that 'the potential for welfare gains from better long-run, supply-side policies exceeds by far the potential from further improvements in short-run demand management'.

Given the significant adverse impact that poor growth performance has on economic welfare and the resultant importance attached to growth by economists, it is perhaps surprising that the research effort in this field has been cyclical. Although growth issues were a major concern of the classical economists, during the period 1870–1945 economists' research was heavily influenced by the 'marginalist revolution' and was therefore predominantly micro-oriented, being directed towards issues relating to the efficient allocation of given resources (Blaug, 1997). For a quarter of a century after 1929–33, issues relating to the Great Depression and Keynes's response to that event dominated discussion in macroeconomics.

As we shall discuss in Chapter 11, in the post-1945 period there have been three waves of interest in growth theory (Solow, 1994). The first wave focused on the neo-Keynesian work of Harrod (1939, 1948) and Domar (1947). In the mid-1950s the development of the neoclassical growth model by Solow (1956) and Swan (1956) stimulated a second more lasting and substantial wave of interest, which, after a period of relative neglect between 1970 and 1986, has been reignited (Mankiw et al., 1992). Between 1970 and 1985 macroeconomic research was dominated by theoretical issues relating to the degeneration of the orthodox Keynesian model, new equilibrium theories of the business cycle, supply shocks, stagflation, and the impact of rational expectations on macroeconomic modelling and policy formulation. Although empirical growth-accounting research continued (for example

Denison, 1974), research on the theoretical front in this field 'effectively died' in the 1970–85 period because economists had run out of ideas.

The third wave, initiated by the research of Paul Romer and Robert Lucas, led to the development of endogenous growth theory, which emerged in response to theoretical and empirical deficiencies in the neoclassical model. During the 1980s several factors led to a reawakening of theoretical research into the growth process and new directions in empirical work also began to develop. On the theoretical front Paul Romer (1986) began to publish material relating to his 1983 University of Chicago PhD thesis. In the same year, 1986, Baumol and Abramovitz each published highly influential papers relating to the issue of 'catch-up and convergence'. These contributions were soon followed by the publication of Lucas's 1985 Marshall lectures given at the University of Cambridge (Lucas, 1987). This work inspired the development of a 'new' breed of endogenous growth models and generated renewed interest in empirical and theoretical questions relating to long-run development (P.M. Romer, 1994a; Barro, 1997; Aghion and Howitt, 1998; Jones, 2001a). Another important influence was the growing awareness that the data suggested that there had been a slowdown in productivity growth in the post-1973 period in the major OECD economies (P.M. Romer, 1987a).

In the eighteenth and nineteenth centuries growth had been largely confined to a small number of countries (Pritchett, 1997; Maddison, 2001). The dramatic improvement in living standards that has taken place in the advanced industrial economies since the Industrial Revolution is now spreading to other parts of the world. However, this diffusion has been highly uneven and in some cases negligible. The result of this long period of uneven growth is a pattern of income per capita differentials between the richest and poorest countries of the world that almost defies comprehension. Much of the motivation behind recent research into economic growth derives from concern about the origin and persistence of these enormous cross-country inequalities in income per capita. The origin of this 'Great Divergence' in living standards has always been a major source of controversy among economic historians (Pomeranz, 2000). Recently, this issue has also captured the imagination of economists interested in providing a unified theory of growth. Such a theory should account for both the 'Malthusian growth regime' witnessed throughout history before the eighteenth century, and the 'modern growth regime' that subsequently prevailed in those countries that have experienced an 'Industrial Revolution' (see Galor and Weil, 2000). To sum up, the analysis of economic growth has once more become an active and vibrant research area, central to contemporary macroeconomics (Klenow and Rodriguez-Clare, 1997a) and will be discussed more fully in Chapter 11.

In the following chapters we will return to these issues, which over the years have been an important source of controversy. But first we will begin our tour of twentieth-century developments in macroeconomics with a review of the essential features of the stylized 'old' classical model which Keynes attacked in his *General Theory*. The important 'Keynes versus the classics' debate sets the scene for subsequent chapters of this book.

# 2. Keynes v. the 'old' classical model

This book is chiefly addressed to my fellow economists ... its main purpose is to deal with difficult questions of theory, and only in the second place with the application of this theory to practice ... if my explanations are right, it is my fellow economists, not the general public, whom I must first convince. (Keynes, 1936, pp. v–vi)

## 2.1 Introduction

In order to better understand current controversies within macroeconomics it is necessary to trace their origin back to the 'Keynes v. Classics' debate which began in the 1930s and has continued in various forms ever since. For example, during the 1980s the two schools of thought at the centre of the mainstream debate were represented by the new classical (real) equilibrium business cycle theorists and the new Keynesian school. The former carry on the tradition of the classical economists and emphasize the optimizing power of economic agents acting within a framework of free market forces. The latter 'believe that understanding economic fluctuations requires not just studying the intricacies of general equilibrium, but also appreciating the possibility of market failure on a grand scale' (Mankiw, 1989; see Chapters 6 and 7).

Classical economics is that body of thought which existed prior to the publication of Keynes's (1936) *General Theory*. For Keynes the classical school not only included Adam Smith, David Ricardo and John Stuart Mill, but also 'the *followers* of Ricardo, those, that is to say, who adopted and perfected the theory of Ricardian economics' (Keynes, 1936, p. 3). Keynes was therefore at odds with the conventional history of economic thought classification, particularly with his inclusion of both Alfred Marshall and Arthur Cecil Pigou within the classical school. However, given that most of the theoretical advances which distinguish the neoclassical from the classical period had been in microeconomic analysis, Keynes perhaps felt justified in regarding the macroeconomic ideas of the 1776–1936 period, such as they existed, as being reasonably homogeneous in terms of their broad message. This placed great faith in the natural market adjustment mechanisms as a means of maintaining full employment equilibrium.

Before moving on to examine the main strands of macroeconomic thought associated with the classical economists, the reader should be aware that, prior to the publication of the *General Theory*, there was no single unified or formalized theory of aggregate employment, and substantial differences existed between economists on the nature and origin of the business cycle (see Haberler, 1963). The structure of classical macroeconomics mainly emerged after 1936 and did so largely in response to Keynes's own theory in order that comparisons could be made. Here we take the conventional approach of presenting a somewhat artificial summary of classical macroeconomics, a body of thought that in reality was extremely complex and diverse (see O'Brien, 1975).

Although no single classical economist ever held all the ideas presented below, there are certain strands of thought running through the pre-Keynes literature which permit us to characterize classical theory as a coherent story with clearly identifiable building-blocks. To do so will be analytically useful, even if 'historically somewhat inaccurate' (see Ackley, 1966, p. 109). Even an 'Aunt Sally' version of the classical theory can, by comparison, help us better understand post-1936 developments in macroeconomic theory. We accept that, whilst the major presentations of the 'Keynes v. Classics' debate consist of ahistorical fictions – especially those of Hicks (1937) and Leijonhufvud (1968) – and serve as straw men, they aid our understanding by overtly simplifying both the Keynes and the classics positions.

## 2.2 Classical Macroeconomics

Classical economists were well aware that a capitalist market economy could deviate from its equilibrium level of output and employment. However, they believed that such disturbances would be temporary and very short-lived. Their collective view was that the market mechanism would operate relatively quickly and efficiently to restore full employment equilibrium. If the classical economic analysis was correct, then government intervention, in the form of activist stabilization policies, would be neither necessary nor desirable. Indeed, such policies were more than likely to create greater instability. As we shall see later, modern champions of the old classical view (that is, new classical equilibrium business cycle theorists) share this faith in the optimizing power of market forces and the potential for active government intervention to create havoc rather than harmony. It follows that the classical writers gave little attention to either the factors which determine aggregate demand or the policies which could be used to stabilize aggregate demand in order to promote full employment. For the classical economists full employment was the normal state of affairs. That Keynes should attack such ideas in the 1930s should come as no surprise given the mass unemployment experienced in all the major capitalist economies of that era. But how did the classical economists reach such an optimistic conclusion? In what follows we will present a 'stylized' version of the classical model which seeks to explain the determinants of an economy's level of real output ($Y$), real ($W/P$) and nominal ($W$) wages, the price level ($P$) and the real rate of interest ($r$) (see Ackley, 1966). In this stylized model it is assumed that:

1. all economic agents (firms and households) are rational and aim to maximize their profits or utility; furthermore, they do not suffer from money illusion;
2. all markets are perfectly competitive, so that agents decide how much to buy and sell on the basis of a given set of prices which are perfectly flexible;
3. all agents have perfect knowledge of market conditions and prices before engaging in trade;
4. trade only takes place when market-clearing prices have been established in all markets, this being ensured by a fictional Walrasian auctioneer whose presence prevents false trading;
5. agents have stable expectations.

These assumptions ensure that in the classical model, markets, including the labour market, always clear. To see how the classical model explains the determination of the crucial macro variables, we will follow their approach and divide the economy into two sectors: a real sector and a monetary sector. To simplify the analysis we will also assume a closed economy, that is, no foreign trade sector.

In examining the behaviour of the real and monetary sectors we need to consider the following three components of the model: (i) the classical theory of employment and output determination, (ii) Say's Law of markets, and (iii) the quantity theory of money. The first two components show how the equilibrium values of the real variables in the model are determined exclusively in the labour and commodity markets. The third component explains how the nominal variables in the system are determined. Thus in the classical model there is a dichotomy. The real and monetary sectors are separated. As a result, changes in the quantity of money will not affect the equilibrium values of the real variables in the model. With the real variables invariant to changes in the quantity of money, the classical economists argued that the quantity of money was neutral.

## 2.3 Employment and Output Determination

The classical neutrality proposition implies that the level of real output will be independent of the quantity of money in the economy. We now consider what determines real output. A key component of the classical model is the short-run production function. In general terms at the micro level a production function expresses the maximum amount of output that a firm can produce from any given amounts of factor inputs. The more inputs of labour ($L$) and capital ($K$) that a firm uses, the greater will be the output produced (providing the inputs are used effectively). However, in the short run, it is assumed that the only variable input is labour. The amount of capital input and the state of technology are taken as constant. When we consider the economy as a whole the quantity of aggregate output ($GDP = Y$) will also depend on the amount of inputs used and how efficiently they are used. This relationship, known as the short-run aggregate production function, can be written in the following form:

$$Y = AF(K, L) \tag{2.1}$$

where (1) $Y$ = real output per period,
      (2) $K$ = the quantity of capital inputs used per period,
      (3) $L$ = the quantity of labour inputs used per period,
      (4) $A$ = an index of total factor productivity, and
      (5) $F$ = a function which relates real output to the inputs of $K$ and $L$.

The symbol $A$ represents an autonomous growth factor which captures the impact of improvements in technology and any other influences which raise the overall effectiveness of an economy's use of its factors of production. Equation (2.1) simply tells us that aggregate output will depend on the amount of labour employed, given the existing capital stock, technology and organization of inputs. This relationship is expressed graphically in panel (a) of Figure 2.1.

The short-run aggregate production function displays certain properties. Three points are worth noting. First, for given values of $A$ and $K$ there is a positive relationship between employment ($L$) and output ($Y$), shown as a movement along the production function from, for example, point $a$ to $b$. Second, the production function exhibits diminishing returns to the variable input, labour. This is indicated by the slope of the production function ($\Delta Y/\Delta L$) which declines as employment increases. Successive increases in the amount of labour employed yield less and less additional output. Since $\Delta Y/\Delta L$ measures the marginal product of labour (MPL), we can see by the slope of the production function that an increase in employment is associated with a declining marginal product of labour. This is illustrated in panel (b) of Figure 2.1, where $D_L$ shows the MPL to be both positive and diminishing (MPL declines as employment expands from $L_0$ to $L_1$; that is, $MPL_a > MPL_b$). Third, the production function will shift upwards if the capital input is increased and/or there is an increase in the productivity of the inputs represented by an increase in the value of $A$ (for example, a technological improvement). Such

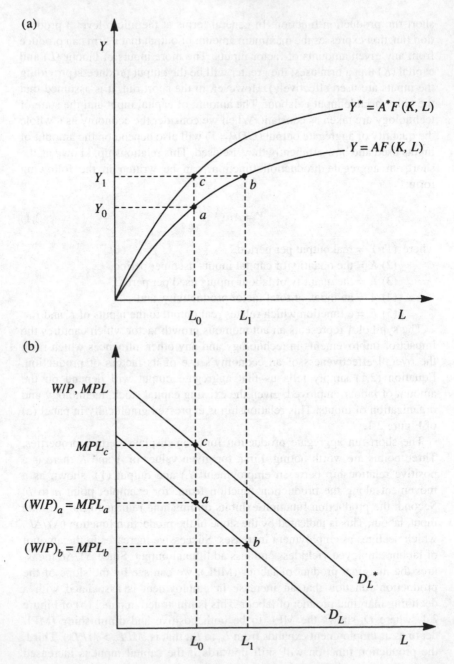

*Figure 2.1    The aggregate production function (a) and the marginal product of labour (b)*

a change is shown in panel (a) of Figure 2.1 by a shift in the production function from $Y$ to $Y^*$ caused by $A$ increasing to $A^*$. In panel (b) the impact of the upward shift of the production function causes the MPL schedule to shift up from $D_L$ to $D_L^*$. Note that following such a change the productivity of labour increases ($L_0$ amount of labour employed can now produce $Y_1$ rather than $Y_0$ amount of output). We will see in Chapter 6 that such production function shifts play a crucial role in the most recent new classical real business cycle theories (see Plosser, 1989).

Although equation (2.1) and Figure 2.1 tell us a great deal about the relationship between an economy's output and the inputs used, they tell us nothing about how much labour will actually be employed in any particular time period. To see how the aggregate level of employment is determined in the classical model, we must examine the classical economists' model of the labour market. We first consider how much labour a profit-maximizing firm will employ. The well-known condition for profit maximization is that a firm should set its marginal revenue ($MR_i$) equal to the marginal cost of production ($MC_i$). For a perfectly competitive firm, $MR_i = P_i$, the output price of firm $_i$. We can therefore write the profit-maximizing rule as equation (2.2):

$$P_i = MC_i \tag{2.2}$$

If a firm hires labour within a competitive labour market, a money wage equal to $W_i$ must be paid to each extra worker. The additional cost of hiring an extra unit of labour will be $W_i \Delta L_i$. The extra revenue generated by an additional worker is the extra output produced ($\Delta Q_i$) multiplied by the price of the firm's product ($P_i$). The additional revenue is therefore $P_i \Delta Q_i$. It pays for a profit-maximizing firm to hire labour as long as $W_i \Delta L_i < P_i \Delta Q_i$. To maximize profits requires satisfaction of the following condition:

$$P_i \Delta Q_i = W_i \Delta L_i \tag{2.3}$$

This is equivalent to:

$$\frac{\Delta Q_i}{\Delta L_i} = \frac{W_i}{P_i} \tag{2.4}$$

Since $\Delta Q_i / \Delta L_i$ is the marginal product of labour, a firm should hire labour until the marginal product of labour equals the real wage rate. This condition is simply another way of expressing equation (2.2). Since $MC_i$ is the cost of the additional worker ($W_i$) divided by the extra output produced by that worker ($MPL_i$) we can write this relationship as:

$$MC_i = \frac{W_i}{MPL_i} \qquad (2.5)$$

Combining (2.5) and (2.2) yields equation (2.6):

$$P_i = \frac{W_i}{MPL_i} = MC_i \qquad (2.6)$$

Because the MPL is a declining function of the amount of labour employed, owing to the influence of diminishing returns, the MPL curve is downward-sloping (see panel (b) of Figure 2.1). Since we have shown that profits will be maximized when a firm equates the $MPL_i$ with $W_i/P_i$, the marginal product curve is equivalent to the firm's demand curve for labour ($D_{Li}$). Equation (2.7) expresses this relationship:

$$D_{Li} = D_{Li}(W_i / P_i) \qquad (2.7)$$

This relationship tells us that a firm's demand for labour will be an inverse function of the real wage: the lower the real wage the more labour will be profitably employed.

In the above analysis we considered the behaviour of an individual firm. The same reasoning can be applied to the economy as a whole. Since the individual firm's demand for labour is an inverse function of the real wage, by aggregating such functions over all the firms in an economy we arrive at the classical postulate that the *aggregate* demand for labour is also an inverse function of the real wage. In this case $W$ represents the economy-wide average money wage and $P$ represents the general price level. In panel (b) of Figure 2.1 this relationship is shown as $D_L$. When the real wage is reduced from $(W/P)_a$ to $(W/P)_b$, employment expands from $L_0$ to $L_1$. The aggregate labour demand function is expressed in equation (2.8):

$$D_L = D_L(W / P) \qquad (2.8)$$

So far we have been considering the factors which determine the demand for labour. We now need to consider the supply side of the labour market. It is assumed in the classical model that households aim to maximize their utility. The market supply of labour is therefore a positive function of the real wage rate and is given by equation (2.9); this is shown in panel (b) of Figure 2.2 as $S_L$.

$$S_L = S_L(W / P) \qquad (2.9)$$

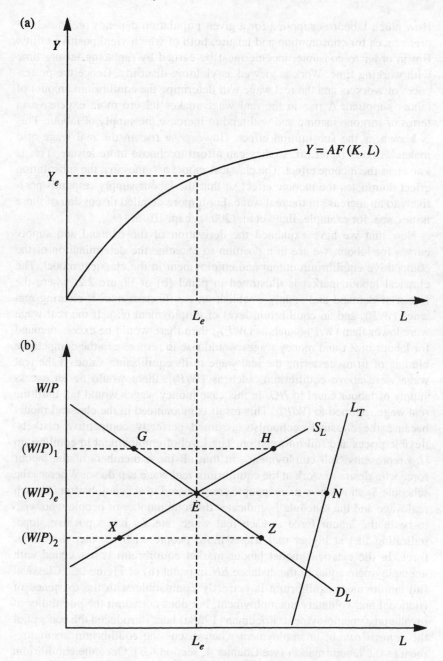

*Figure 2.2   Output and employment determination in the classical model*

How much labour is supplied for a given population depends on household preferences for consumption and leisure, both of which yield positive utility. But in order to consume, income must be earned by replacing leisure time with working time. Work is viewed as yielding disutility. Hence the preferences of workers and the real wage will determine the equilibrium amount of labour supplied. A rise in the real wage makes leisure more expensive in terms of forgone income and will tend to increase the supply of labour. This is known as the substitution effect. However, a rise in the real wage also makes workers better off, so they can afford to choose more leisure. This is known as the income effect. The classical model assumes that the substitution effect dominates the income effect so that the labour supply responds positively to an increase in the real wage. For a more detailed discussion of these issues, see, for example, Begg et al. (2003, chap. 10).

Now that we have explained the derivation of the demand and supply curves for labour, we are in a position to examine the determination of the competitive equilibrium output and employment in the classical model. The classical labour market is illustrated in panel (b) of Figure 2.2, where the forces of demand and supply establish an equilibrium market-clearing real wage $(W/P)_e$ and an equilibrium level of employment $(L_e)$. If the real wage were lower than $(W/P)_e$, such as $(W/P)_2$, then there would be excess demand for labour of $ZX$ and money wages would rise in response to the competitive bidding of firms, restoring the real wage to its equilibrium value. If the real wage were above equilibrium, such as $(W/P)_1$, there would be an excess supply of labour equal to $HG$. In this case money wages would fall until the real wage returned to $(W/P)_e$. This result is guaranteed in the classical model because the classical economists assumed perfectly competitive markets, flexible prices and full information. The level of employment in equilibrium $(L_e)$ represents 'full employment', in that all those members of the labour force who desire to work at the equilibrium real wage can do so. Whereas the schedule $S_L$ shows how many people are prepared to accept job offers at each real wage and the schedule $L_T$ indicates the total number of people who wish to be in the labour force at each real wage rate. $L_T$ has a positive slope, indicating that at higher real wages more people wish to enter the labour force. In the classical model labour market equilibrium is associated with unemployment equal to the distance $EN$ in panel (b) of Figure 2.2. Classical full employment equilibrium is perfectly compatible with the existence of frictional and voluntary unemployment, but does not admit the possibility of involuntary unemployment. Friedman (1968a) later introduced the concept of the *natural rate* of unemployment when discussing equilibrium unemployment in the labour market (see Chapter 4, section 4.3). Once the equilibrium level of employment is determined in the labour market, the level of output is determined by the position of the aggregate production function. By referring to panel (a) of Figure 2.2, we can see that $L_e$ amount of employment will produce $Y_e$ level of output.

So far the simple stylized model we have reproduced here has enabled us to see how the classical economists explained the determination of the equilibrium level of real output, employment and real wages as well as the equilibrium level of unemployment. Changes in the equilibrium values of the above variables can obviously come about if the labour demand curve shifts and/or the labour supply curve shifts. For example, an upward shift of the production function due to technological change would move the labour demand curve to the right. Providing the labour supply curve has a positive slope, this will lead to an increase in employment, output and the real wage. Population growth, by shifting the labour supply curve to the right, would increase employment and output but lower the real wage. Readers should verify this for themselves.

We have seen in the analysis above that competition in the labour market ensures full employment in the classical model. At the equilibrium real wage no person who wishes to work at that real wage is without employment. In this sense 'the classical postulates do not admit the possibility of involuntary unemployment' (Keynes, 1936, p. 6). However, the classical economists were perfectly aware that persistent unemployment in excess of the equilibrium level was possible if artificial restrictions were placed on the equilibrating function of real wages. If real wages are held above equilibrium (such as $(W/P)_1$, in panel (b) of Figure 2.2) by trade union monopoly power or minimum wage legislation, then obviously everyone who wishes to work at the 'distorted' real wage will not be able to do so. For classical economists the solution to such 'classical unemployment' was simple and obvious. Real wages should be reduced by cutting the money wage.

Keynes regarded the equilibrium outcome depicted in Figure 2.2 as a 'special case' which was not typical of the 'economic society in which we actually live' (Keynes, 1936, p. 3). The full employment equilibrium of the classical model was a special case because it corresponded to a situation where aggregate demand was just sufficient to absorb the level of output produced. Keynes objected that there was no guarantee that aggregate demand would be at such a level. The classical economists denied the possibility of a deficiency of aggregate demand by appealing to 'Say's Law' which is 'equivalent to the proposition that there is no obstacle to full employment' (Keynes, 1936, p. 26). It is to this proposition that we now turn.

## 2.4 Say's Law

In 1803, Jean-Baptiste Say's *Treatise of Political Economy* was published. The simplest version of the law associated with this economist is that labour will only offer itself for employment in order to obtain income which is then used to purchase the output produced. In his own words, Say puts forward the proposition in the following way.

> A product is no sooner created, than it, *from that instant*, affords a market for other products to the full extent of its own value ... the mere circumstance of the creation of one product immediately opens a vent for other products. (Say, 1821)

In other words, because the act of production simultaneously creates income and purchasing power, there could be no impediment to full employment caused by a deficiency of aggregate demand. The dictum 'supply creates its own demand' captures the essence of Say's Law, which aimed to characterize the essential feature of exchange within a specialized economy. That the act of supply created an equivalent demand seemed obvious to the classical writers. The law does not deny the possibility that a misallocation of resources can occur and that a glut of certain commodities can develop, but this problem would be temporary and no such excess supply could occur for goods as a whole. For more detailed and sophisticated discussions of Say's contribution, see Sowell (1972); Baumol (1977, 1999); and Backhouse (2002).

Say's Law was originally set forth in the context of a barter economy where, by definition, the act of supplying one good unavoidably implies the demand for some other good. In general, classical economists, notably Ricardo and Mill, gave support to Say's Law, which they believed also held true for a monetary exchange economy. Money was nothing more than a convenient medium of exchange which enabled market participants to avoid the awkwardness and inconvenience of barter. If Say's Law applies to a money-using economy, then the implication is that a market is guaranteed for whatever level of output is produced, although market forces will obviously lead to changes in the composition of aggregate output. If aggregate demand and aggregate supply are always guaranteed equality, then money is nothing more than a 'veil' covering the underlying real forces in the economy.

At this point it is important to distinguish between two versions of Say's Law. According to Trevithick (1992) the *weak* version is taken to imply that each act of production and supply necessarily involves the creation of an equivalent demand for output in general. But this version of Say's Law does not guarantee that the output produced will be consistent with full employment. It merely states that whatever level of aggregate output happens to be forthcoming will find a market. This weak version of Say's Law applies to both depressed and buoyant levels of output. The strong version of Say's Law states that in a competitive market economy there will be an automatic tendency for full employment to be established (see panel (b) of Figure 2.2). Since the strong version of Say's Law implies an equality of aggregate demand and supply which is consistent with labour market equilibrium, it is equivalent to the proposition that there is no obstacle to the achievement of full employment in terms of a deficiency of aggregate demand. To see how the classical economists justified their belief that aggregate spending in the economy will always be sufficient to purchase the full employment level of output, we need to examine their ideas relating to investment, saving and the rate of interest.

The classical theory of interest rate determination plays a crucial role in ensuring that a deficiency of aggregate demand does not occur. If we imagine an economy consisting of two sectors, firms and households, we can write down the following equation, which tells us that in equilibrium aggregate expenditure ($E$) must equal aggregate output ($Y$).

$$E = C(r) + I(r) = Y \qquad (2.10)$$

Furthermore, aggregate expenditure consists of two components: investment expenditure ($I$) which arises from firms and consumption expenditure ($C$) which arises from households. The planned demand for goods ($E$) is the sum of the planned demand for consumption goods plus the planned demand for investment goods. In the classical model the demand for both types of goods is a function of the interest rate ($r$). Since households do not automatically spend all of their income, we can also write down equation (2.11):

$$Y - C(r) = S(r) \qquad (2.11)$$

Combining (2.10) and (2.11) yields the equilibrium condition given by (2.12):

$$S(r) = I(r) \qquad (2.12)$$

We can see from (2.11) that in the classical model saving ($S$) is also a function of the interest rate. The higher the rate of interest the more willing will savers be to replace present consumption with future consumption. Hence the classical economists viewed the interest rate as a real reward for abstinence or thrift. The flow of saving therefore represents a supply of loanable funds in the capital market. Since household saving responds positively to the rate of interest ($\Delta S/\Delta r > 0$), household consumption must be negatively related to the rate of interest ($\Delta C/\Delta r < 0$). Investment expenditure on capital goods is negatively related to the rate of interest in the classical model ($\Delta I/\Delta r < 0$) and represents a demand for loanable funds in the capital market. Investment spending by firms can only be justified if the expected rate of return from the expenditure is greater than, or at least equal to, the cost of acquiring the funds used to purchase the capital goods. The higher the rate of interest, the higher the explicit (and implicit) cost of the funds used to purchase the capital goods. We can therefore represent business expenditure ($I$) as a declining function of the interest rate. The relationship between investment, saving and the interest rate in the classical model is shown in panel (a) of Figure 2.3. The twin forces of productivity and thrift determine the real rate of interest, and variations in the interest rate act as an equilibrating force which maintains equality between the demand for and supply of loanable funds, ensuring that aggregate demand is never deficient. By referring to Figure 2.3 we can see how important flexibility in the interest rate was to the classical equilibration process. In panel (a) we represent the classical theory of interest rate determination, with the interest rate on the vertical axis

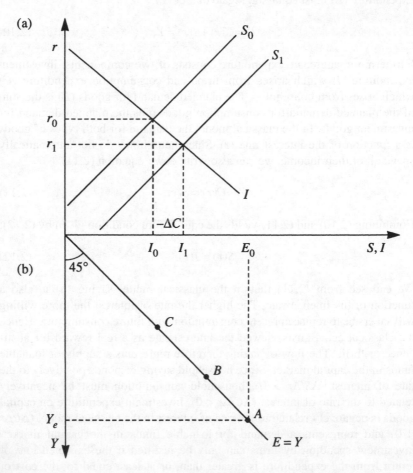

*Figure 2.3   The classical interest rate mechanism and Say's Law*

and the flows of saving and investment measured on the horizontal axis. In panel (b) real output is measured on the vertical axis with the overall demand for commodities $(C + I)$ measured on the horizontal axis. From Figure 2.2 we know that competition in the labour market will yield an equilibrium real wage and level of employment which, when combined with the production function, give a level of full employment output of $Y_e$. Panel (b) of Figure 2.3 indicates that aggregate expenditures of an amount equal to $E_0$ are necessary to purchase the output of $Y_e$. Since output and demand are identical at all points along the 45° line, any point such as $B$ and $C$ is consistent with the weak version of Say's Law. Point $A$ in panel (b) corresponds to the strong version of Say's Law. Not only are aggregate expenditure and output in equality, $Y_e$ corresponds to the level of output associated with full employment labour market equilibrium.

We can best see the importance of interest rate flexibility in this model by asking what would happen if households suddenly decided to save more (consume less). This is represented in panel (a) of Figure 2.3 by a rightward shift of the saving function from $S_0$ to $S_1$. The initial excess supply of loanable funds would lead to a fall in the rate of interest from $r_0$ to $r_1$. This would encourage an increase in investment expenditure from $I_0$ to $I_1$. Since $E_0 - I_0$ equals consumption expenditure, it is clear that the rise in investment expenditure, $I_1 - I_0$, exactly offsets the fall in consumption expenditure equal to $-\Delta C$ in the diagram. Aggregate expenditure would remain at $E_0$, although its composition would change.

Even though in the classical model the decisions to save and invest can be carried out by different sets of people, the rate of interest will change so as to reconcile the desires to save and invest. In Keynesian theory divergences between $S$ and $I$ cause a quantity response. In the case of an increase in saving, the Keynesian model predicts a decline in aggregate spending, output and employment; that is, Keynes's paradox of thrift. The classical model, armed with Say's Law, flexible wages, prices and the interest rate, can experience changes in the structure of final demand but no prolonged demand deficiency and involuntary unemployment. A remarkable result.

Not all the classical economists accepted Say's Law and its implications. Robert Thomas Malthus argued that a general glut of commodities was possible. Whereas Ricardo, Mill and the followers of Say believed that the conditions of supply determine aggregate output, Malthus, anticipating Keynes, gave emphasis to demand as the determining factor (see Dorfman, 1989). But 'Ricardo conquered England as completely as the Holy Inquisition conquered Spain' (Keynes, 1936, p. 32). For Keynes the completeness of the Ricardian victory was something of a curiosity and a mystery. For this reason he gave high praise to Malthus for anticipating his own ideas with respect to a general deficiency of aggregate demand (see Keynes, 1936, pp. 362–71).

Although Ricardo appeared to be stone deaf to what Malthus was saying, part of the disagreement had its origin in the time horizon adopted by each writer. Ricardo had his eyes fixed firmly on the long run, whereas Malthus, like Keynes, was more concerned with the short run.

In our discussion of the classical model so far we have concentrated on the real sector. The operation of the labour and capital markets, buttressed by Say's Law, provided the classical economists with a theoretical system capable of explaining the determination of the real variables in the system. But what determines the price level in the classical model? The final component that explains the determination of the price level and the other nominal values in the classical economists' system is the quantity theory of money.

## 2.5   The Quantity Theory of Money

The hallmark of classical macroeconomic theory is the separation of real and nominal variables. This classical dichotomy enables us to examine the behaviour of the real variables in the economic system while ignoring the nominal variables. In the stylized classical model we have developed, the quantity of money is irrelevant for the determination of the real variables. Long-run money neutrality is a crucial property of the classical model.

To explain the determination of the nominal variables in the system, the classical economists subscribed to the quantity theory of money. A long line of famous economists have either contributed to the development of this theory or have been associated with its policy prescriptions. The list includes Cantillon, Hume, Ricardo, Mill, Marshall, Fisher, Pigou, Hayek and even Keynes. More recently the quantity theory of money has been associated with the development of monetarism and the work of Milton Friedman, perhaps the most influential economist in the past quarter-century. Although the term 'monetarism' did not emerge until 1968 (see Brunner, 1968), its main core proposition, the quantity theory of money, was well established in classical macroeconomics following the publication of David Hume's influential essay, *Of Money*, in 1752. Indeed, Mayer (1980) has argued that the salient date for the birth of monetarist ideas was 1752, since most of the fundamental propositions which characterize monetarism date back to Hume's essay. Here we will present only a short exposition of the quantity theory in order to complete the classical scheme. For a more detailed discussion, see Laidler (1991).

The dominant macroeconomic theory prior to the 1930s was the quantity theory of money. Two highly influential versions of the quantity theory can be identified in the literature. The first version, associated with Marshall and Pigou, is known as the Cambridge cash-balance approach. The second version is associated with Irving Fisher.

The Cambridge economists drew a clear distinction in their version of the quantity theory between the demand for money (*Md*) and the supply of money (*M*). The demand for money was primarily determined by the need to conduct transactions which will have a positive relationship to the money value of aggregate expenditure. Since the latter is equal to money national income we can represent the Cambridge money demand function as equation (2.13):

$$Md = kPY \tag{2.13}$$

where *Md* is the demand to hold nominal money balances, and *k* is the fraction of the annual value of money national income (*PY*) that agents (firms and households) wish to hold. The reader should be aware that the Cambridge monetary approach did recognize that *k* could vary in the short run (see Laidler, 1993) but, in the stylized presentation we consider in equation (2.13), the coefficient *k* is assumed to be constant. As it stands, the Cambridge equation is a theory of the demand for money. In order to explain the price level we must introduce the supply of money. If we assume that the supply of money is determined by the monetary authorities (that is, *M* is exogenous), then we can write the condition for monetary equilibrium as equation (2.14):

$$M = Md \tag{2.14}$$

Substituting (2.14) into (2.13) we obtain (2.15):

$$M = kPY \tag{2.15}$$

To obtain the quantity theory result that changes in the quantity of money have no real effects in the long run but will determine the price level, we simply need to remember from our earlier discussion that *Y* is predetermined at its full employment value by the production function and the operation of a competitive labour market. With *k* and *Y* constant, *M* determines *P*. If the money market is initially in equilibrium, then an increase in the money supply creates disequilibrium (*M* > *Md*). Since the values of *Y* and *k* are fixed, equilibrium in the money market can only be restored if the price level rises. The reason why prices rise in the classical model is that, if households and firms find themselves holding more money than they desire, the excess money balances are used to purchase goods and services. Since the supply of goods and services is constrained by the predetermined full employment level of output, excess demand in the goods market causes the general price level to rise in proportion to the initial increase in the money supply.

The second approach uses the income version of Fisher's equation of exchange. This relationship is given by equation (2.16):

$$MV = PY \qquad (2.16)$$

where $V$ is the income velocity of circulation of money and represents the average number of times a unit of money is used in the course of conducting final transactions which constitute nominal GDP. Since $V$ can be defined as the reciprocal of $k$, the constancy of $V$ can be justified because institutional factors which determine the frequency of the transactions carried out by agents are likely to change slowly over time. That $V$ is the reciprocal of $k$ can be seen by comparing (2.15) with (2.16) and noting that both $V$ and $1/k$ equal $PY/M$. That the price level is dependent on the nominal money supply is clearly brought out if we examine equation (2.17), which rearranges (2.16):

$$P = MV/Y \qquad (2.17)$$

With $V$ and $Y$ constant, it is easy to see that $P$ depends on $M$ and that $\Delta M$ equals $\Delta P$.

To see how the price level is determined in the classical model and how real output, real wages and employment are invariant to the quantity of money, consider Figure 2.4. In quadrants (a) and (b) we reproduce Figure 2.2. Here a competitive labour market generates equilibrium employment of $L_0$ and an equilibrium real wage of $W_0/P_0$. From the production function we can see that full employment in this model leads to an output of $Y_0$. In quadrant (c) we have the classical aggregate demand ($AD$) and aggregate supply ($AS$) functions. The $AS$ function is perfectly inelastic, indicating that real output is invariant to the general price level. The classical $AD$ curve is derived from equation (2.16). With a constant supply of money (for example, $M_0$) and $V$ constant, a higher price level must be associated with a lower level of real output. $AD_0(M_0)$ shows how, for a given money supply, $MV$ can be split up among an infinite number of combinations of $P$ and $Y$. Since we have assumed $V$ is fixed, the nominal value of all transactions in the economy is determined by the supply of money. With higher prices each transaction requires more units of currency and therefore the quantity of goods and services that can be bought must fall. Since the $AD$ curve is drawn for a given quantity of money, an increase in the money supply will shift the $AD$ curve to the right, as shown by $AD_1(M_1)$. Finally, in quadrant (d) we show the relationship between the real wage and the price level for a given nominal wage. If the nominal wage is $W_0$ then a higher price level will reduce the real wage.

Let us assume that the initial equilibrium values in the model associated with the quantity of money $M_0$ are $Y_0$, $W_0/P_0$, and $L_0$. Suppose the monetary

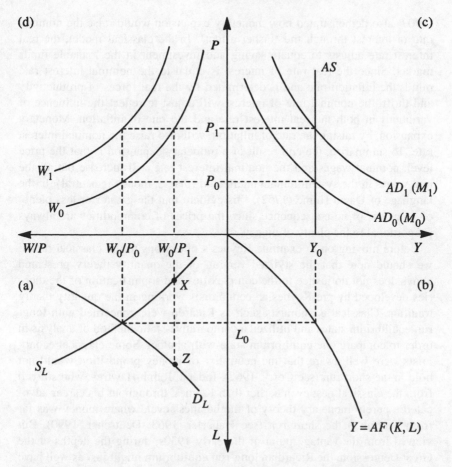

*Figure 2.4 The determination of the price level in the classical model*

authorities increase the supply of money to $M_1$ in an attempt to increase real output and employment. We can see that such a policy will be completely ineffectual in the classical model. The increase in the quantity of money, by creating disequilibrium in the money market ($Md < M$), will lead to an increase in the demand for goods and services. Since $Y$ is constrained at $Y_0$ by labour market equilibrium employment ($L_0$), prices rise to $P_1$. For a given nominal wage of $W_0$, an increase in the price level lowers the real wage and creates disequilibrium in the labour market. An excess demand for labour of $ZX$ emerges at a real wage of $W_0/P_1$. Competitive bidding by employers will drive the nominal wage up until it reaches a value of $W_1$, which restores the real wage to its equilibrium value (that is, $W_0/P_0 = W_1/P_1$). Irving Fisher

(1907) also demonstrated how monetary expansion would raise the nominal rate of interest through the 'Fisher effect'. In the classical model, the real interest rate adjusts to equate saving and investment in the loanable funds market. Since the real rate of interest is equal to the nominal interest rate minus the inflation rate and is determined by the real forces of productivity and thrift, the nominal rate of interest will adjust to reflect the influence of variations in both the real interest rate and the rate of inflation. Monetary expansion, by raising the rate of inflation, will also raise the nominal interest rate. To summarize, the end result of a monetary expansion is that the price level, nominal wages and the nominal interest rate will increase but all the real values in the system remain unaffected (that is, money is neutral). In the language of David Hume (1752), ''tis evident that the greater or less plenty of money is of no consequence since the prices of commodities are always proportional to the plenty of money'.

Before moving on to examine Keynes's objections to the classical model we should note that the stylized version of the quantity theory presented above does not do justice to the complexities and sophistication of the theories developed by pre-Keynesian economists working in the quantity theory tradition. Classical economists such as Ricardo were concerned with long-run equilibrium states and utilized a comparative-static method of analysis in order to compare one equilibrium state with another. Some classical economists were well aware that the neutrality of money proposition would not hold in the short run (see Corry, 1962). Indeed, Ralph Hawtrey, who strayed from the classical nest even earlier than Keynes, throughout his career advocated a purely monetary theory of the business cycle where money was far from neutral in the short run (see Haberler, 1963; Deutscher, 1990). But viewed from the vantage point of the early 1930s, during the depths of the Great Depression, the Ricardian long-run equilibrium might just as well have been located on Mars. In his *Tract on Monetary Reform* (1923), Keynes declared, 'In the long run we are all dead. Economists set themselves too easy, too useless a task if in tempestuous seasons they can only tell us that when the storm is long past the ocean is flat again.' We now turn to consider Keynes's objections to classical theory, which culminated in the publication of his most influential book in 1936.

## 2.6   Keynes's *General Theory*

Keynes's contribution to economic theory remains a matter of considerable debate, despite almost seventy years having gone by since the publication of the *General Theory*, in February 1936. Few economists would challenge Samuelson's (1988) view that Keynes's influence on the course of economics has been 'the most significant event in twentieth-century economic science' or that macroeconomics was his creation. Opponents are convinced that Keynes was fundamentally mistaken (Hayek, 1983; see also the Friedman and Lucas interviews at the end of Chapters 4 and 5 respectively). Keynesians themselves are divided between those who, like Keynes, regard the policy implications of the *General Theory* as being moderately conservative (Tobin, 1987), and others who see Keynes's *magnum opus* as representing a revolutionary break from mainstream classical and neoclassical doctrines (Robinson, 1971; Davidson, 1994, and Chapter 8). That the *General Theory* has had a profound influence on the development of macroeconomics and the conduct of macroeconomic policy making, for good or ill, is beyond question.

Keynes was essentially an applied economist brought up in the Cambridge tradition of Alfred Marshall, where the attraction of economics lay in the prospect it held out to its practitioners for making the world a better place. But for Keynes to write the *General Theory* involved a 'long struggle to escape ... from habitual modes of thought and expression'. The old ideas from which Keynes sought to escape were the *laissez-faire* doctrines associated with the liberal tradition of nineteenth-century classical economics. Following Adam Smith, political economy had an underlying bias towards *laissez-faire*. The classical economists, with some exceptions, were preoccupied with government failure. In their view the state should confine its activities to ensuring a peaceful, competitive environment within which citizens could pursue their individual objectives as fully as possible. Only the evils of monopoly power or too much state involvement in economic affairs could prevent the price mechanism from yielding maximum national output, given the constraint of scarce but fully employed resources. In contrast to this orthodoxy, the most revolutionary aspect of Keynes's work, which we can detect in his writings from the mid-1920s onwards, was his clear and unambiguous message that with regard to the general level of employment and output there was no 'invisible hand' channelling self-interest into some social optimum. Although Keynes's iconoclastic vision emerges time and time again in his critiques of UK government policy during the 1920s, many of his policy recommendations lacked the theoretical structure from which they could logically be derived. For example, in 1929 Keynes was arguing forcefully for government programmes to expand demand via deficit financing in full support of Lloyd George's Liberal programme of recovery (see Keynes, 1929). But he was doing so without a theory of effective demand and a multiplier mechanism which are so important to the argument (see Keynes, 1972, Vol. IX).

In order effectively to confront the existing classical orthodoxy head-on, Keynes needed to provide an alternative theory. With the onset of the Great Depression we find Keynes retreating 'into his ivory tower at King's to engage, at age forty-eight, in a supreme intellectual effort to save Western civilisation from the engulfing tide of barbarism which economic collapse was bringing about' (Skidelsky, 1992, p. xxvii). Keynes was acutely aware of the extreme fragility of world capitalism at this point in world history.

> The authoritarian state systems of today seem to solve the problem of unemploy-ment at the expense of efficiency and freedom. It is certain that the world will not much longer tolerate the unemployment which, apart from brief intervals of excitement, is associated ... and, in my opinion, inevitably associated ... with present-day capitalistic individualism. But it may be possible by a right analysis of the problem to cure the disease whilst preserving efficiency and freedom. (Keynes, 1936, p. 381)

We therefore find Keynes from 1931 onwards groping towards his *General Theory*, a book that, unlike many of his earlier writings, was addressed to his fellow economists.

By late 1932, and certainly no later than early 1933, the initial vision or 'grey fuzzy woolly monster' in his mind was beginning to appear in his Cambridge lectures (see Skidelsky, 1992; Patinkin, 1993). To his critics the *General Theory* has remained a 'monster'. Lucas, a leading modern critic of Keynesianism, finds it a book 'he can't read' which is 'carelessly written' and represents a 'political response to the Depression' (see Klamer, 1984). Even Samuelson, one of Keynes's earliest converts, describes the book as 'poorly organised' and 'badly written'. But for Samuelson 'it is a work of genius' which, because of its obscurity and polemical character, will remain a long-run influence on the development of economics (Samuelson, 1946). Galbraith (1977), reaching a similar conclusion, sees the ambiguity contained in the *General Theory* as a feature guaranteed to win converts, for:

> When understanding is achieved after much effort, readers hold tenaciously to their belief. The pain, they wish to think, was worthwhile. And if there are enough contradictions and ambiguities, as there are also in the Bible and Marx, the reader can always find something he wants to believe. This too wins disciples.

It is hardly surprising that it was mainly the younger generation of econo-mists at Cambridge UK and Cambridge USA that took quickly to the new ideas. Whereas economists over the age of 50 were on the whole immune from Keynes's message, the *General Theory* 'caught most economists under the age of thirty-five with the unexpected virulence of a disease first attacking and decimating an isolated tribe of South Sea islanders' (Samuelson, 1946). That change in economics comes with the changing generations also played an important role some forty years later when the rise of new classical economics infected mainly the younger generation of economists, so much so that Keynesians appeared to be threatened with extinction (see Colander, 1988; Blinder, 1988b).

## 2.7 Interpreting the *General Theory*

One of the great problems in discussing the content of the *General Theory* is that, being a highly complex, controversial and influential book, it has enabled economists of widely different persuasions to find statements within it which support their own vision of Keynes's essential message. The Keynesiology literature, already vast, continues to grow exponentially! The diverse range of views is a source of confusion and enlightenment. E. Roy Weintraub (1979), for example, has a chapter entitled 'The 4,827th re-examination of Keynes's system'! To get some idea of the contrasting theoretical interpretations of the *General Theory* the reader should consult Hicks (1937), Modigliani (1944, 2003), Klein (1947), Patinkin (1956, 1976, 1990b), Leijonhufvud (1968), Davidson (1978, 1994), Chick (1983), Coddington (1983), Kahn (1984) and Meltzer (1988). The papers collected in the edited volumes by Cunningham Wood (1983) give some idea of the critiques and developments which emerged after 1936. To understand the development of Keynes's contributions in the wider context of his life and philosophy, the reader should consult the excellent biographies of Keynes by Harrod (1951), Moggridge (1992) and Skidelsky (1983, 1992 and 2000). *The Collected Writings of John Maynard Keynes*, edited by Donald Moggridge, runs to 30 volumes!

There is no definitive interpretation of Keynes which commands universal support; nor could there ever be, given the non-mathematical style of the book. The turbulence Keynes has caused in economics continues and the *General Theory* remains a text which is 'not yet fully mined' (Phelps, 1990; see also Akerlof's Nobel Memorial Lecture, 2002). One of the reasons for this is that the very issue with which Keynes was concerned, namely the effectiveness of market forces in generating a stable full employment equilibrium without active government intervention, is still at the centre of economic debate (the same issue relating to government v. market failure lies at the heart of controversy elsewhere in economics – see Snowdon, 2001b).

Bill Gerrard (1991) attempts to analyse the reasons why different interpretations occur. These include confusions generated by Keynes himself due to 'technical incompetence', 'stylistic difficulties', 'inconsistencies' and 'mistakes'. Other possible sources of confusion are 'reader-generated' and result from 'selective reading', 'inappropriate framing' and 'reliance on secondary sources'. A further problem arises in the sheer quantity of material which Keynes produced in addition to the *General Theory*; for example, some contributors have shifted emphasis towards Keynes's earlier and neglected philosophical papers (O'Donnell, 1989). Gerrard concludes that the achievement of Keynes's *General Theory* is mainly in 'its ability to generate a diversity of research programmes' reflecting a number of possible ways of looking at the macroeconomy. In short, Gerrard suggests that we should stop worrying about multiple interpretations, since this confirms the fertility of Keynes's work and its 'reference power'.

Since we cannot hope to do justice to the wide variety of interpretations of Keynes, here we will present a conventional account of some of the main arguments associated with the *General Theory*.

## 2.8  Keynes's Main Propositions

In the *General Theory* Keynes sets out to 'discover what determines at any time the national income of a given system and (which is almost the same thing) the amount of its employment' (Keynes, 1936, p. 247). In the framework he constructs, 'the national income depends on the volume of employment'. In developing his theory Keynes also attempted to show that macroeconomic equilibrium is consistent with involuntary unemployment. The theoretical novelty and central proposition of the book is the principle of effective demand, together with the equilibrating role of changes in output rather than prices. The emphasis given to quantity rather than price adjustment in the *General Theory* is in sharp contrast to the classical model and Keynes's own earlier work contained in his *Treatise on Money* (1930), where discrepancies between saving and investment decisions cause the price level to oscillate.

The development of the building-blocks that were eventually to form the core ideas of Keynes's *General Theory* began to emerge several years before its construction. As noted above, in 1929 Keynes was arguing in support of government programmes to expand aggregate demand via deficit financing. In his famous pamphlet co-authored with Hubert Henderson (1929) Keynes argued the case for public works programmes in support of Lloyd George's 1929 election pledge to the nation to reduce unemployment 'in the course of a single year to normal proportions' (see Skidelsky, 1992). However, Keynes and Henderson were unable to convincingly rebuff the orthodox 'Treasury dogma', expressed by the Chancellor of the Exchequer in 1929 as 'whatever might be the political or social advantages, very little additional employment can, in fact, and as a general rule, be created by State borrowing and State expenditure'. Implicit in Keynes and Henderson's arguments in favour of public works programmes to reduce unemployment was the idea of demand-determined output and the concept of an employment multiplier.

The principle of effective demand states that in a closed economy with spare capacity the level of output (and hence employment) is determined by aggregate planned expenditure, which consists of two components, consumption expenditure from the household sector ($C$) and investment expenditure from firms ($I$). In the *General Theory* there is no explicit analysis of the effects of variations in spending stimulated either directly by government expenditure or indirectly via changes in taxation. Hence in the *General Theory* there are two sectors (households and firms), and planned expenditure is given by equation (2.18):

$$E = C + I \qquad (2.18)$$

The reader will recall that in the classical model, consumption, saving and investment are all functions of the interest rate – see equations (2.10) and (2.11). In Keynes's model, consumption expenditure is endogenous and essentially passive, depending as it does on income rather than the interest rate. Keynes's theory of the consumption function develops this relationship.

Investment expenditure depends on the expected profitability of investment and the interest rate which represents the cost of borrowing funds. Keynes called expected profits the 'marginal efficiency of capital'. Thus, unavoidably, in Keynes's model employment becomes dependent on an unstable factor, investment expenditure, which is liable to wide and sudden fluctuations. The dependence of output and employment on investment would not be so important if investment expenditure were stable from year to year. Unfortunately the investment decision is a difficult one because machinery and buildings are bought now to produce goods that will be sold in a future that is inevitably uncertain. Expectations about future levels of demand and costs are involved in the calculation, allowing hopes and fears, as well as hard facts, to influence the decision. Given the volatility of expectations, often driven by 'animal spirits', the expected profitability of capital must also be highly unstable. That investment decisions could be influenced by tides of irrational optimism and pessimism, causing large swings in the state of business confidence, led Keynes to question the efficacy of interest rate adjustments as a way of influencing the volume of investment. Expectations of the future profitability of investment are far more important than the rate of interest in linking the future with the present because: 'given the psychology of the public, the level of output and employment as a whole depends on the amount of investment', and 'it is those factors which determine the rate of investment which are most unreliable, since it is they which are influenced by our views of the future about which we know so little' (Keynes, 1937).

The 'extreme precariousness' of a firm's knowledge concerning the prospective yield of an investment decision lies at the heart of Keynes's explanation of the business cycle. In his analysis of instability, 'violent fluctuations' in the marginal efficiency of capital form the shocks which shift *real* aggregate demand; that is, the main source of economic fluctuations comes from the real side of the economy, as described by the *IS* curve; see Chapter 3, section 3.3.1. From his analysis of the consumption function Keynes developed the concept of the marginal propensity to consume which plays a crucial role in determining the size of the multiplier. Because of the multiplier any distur-bance to investment expenditure will have a magnified impact on aggregate output. This can be shown quite easily as follows. Letting $c$ equal the mar-ginal propensity to consume ($\Delta C/\Delta Y$) and $a$ equal autonomous consumption, we can write the behavioural equation for consumption as (2.19):

$$C = a + cY \tag{2.19}$$

Remember in Keynes's model the amount of aggregate consumption is (mainly) dependent on the amount of aggregate income. Substituting (2.19) into (2.18) we get the equilibrium condition given by (2.20):

$$Y = a + cY + I \tag{2.20}$$

Since $Y - cY = a + I$ and $Y - cY = Y(1 - c)$, we obtain the familiar reduced-form equation (2.21):

$$Y = (a + I)/(1 - c) \tag{2.21}$$

where $1/1 - c$ represents the multiplier. Letting $\kappa$ symbolize the multiplier, we can rewrite equation (2.21) as $Y = (a + I)\kappa$. It follows that for a given change in investment expenditure ($\Delta I$):

$$\Delta Y = \Delta I \kappa \tag{2.22}$$

Equation (2.22) tells us that income (output) changes by a multiple of the change in investment expenditure. Keynes defines the investment multiplier ($\kappa$) as the ratio of a change in income to a change in autonomous expenditure which brought it about: 'when there is an increment of aggregate investment, income will increase by an amount which is $\kappa$ times the increment in invest-ment' (Keynes, 1936, p. 115).

   *Ceteris paribus* the multiplier will be larger the smaller the marginal pro-pensity to save. Therefore the size of the multiplier will depend on the value of $c$, and $1 > c > 0$. The multiplier effect shows that for an autonomous demand shift ($\Delta I$) income will initially rise by an equivalent amount. But this rise in income in turn raises consumption by $c\Delta I$. The second-round increase in income again raises expenditure by $c(c\Delta I)$, which further raises expendi-ture and income. So what we have here is an infinite geometric series such that the full effect of an autonomous change in demand on output is given by (2.23):

$$\Delta Y = \Delta I + c\Delta I + c^2\Delta I + = \Delta I(1 + c + c^2 + c^3 + \ldots) \tag{2.23}$$

and $(1 + c + c^2 + c^3 + ...) = 1/1 - c$. Throughout the above analysis it is assumed that we are talking about an economy with spare capacity where firms are able to respond to extra demand by producing more output. Since more output requires more labour input, the output multiplier implies an employment multiplier (Kahn, 1931). Hence an increase in autonomous spending raises output and employment. Starting from a position of less than full employment, suppose there occurs an increase in the amount of autonomous investment undertaken in the economy. The increase in investment spending will result in an increase in employment in firms producing capital goods. Newly employed workers in capital-goods industries will spend some of their income on consumption goods and save the rest. The rise in demand for consumer goods will in turn lead to increased employment in consumer-goods industries and result in further rounds of expenditure. In consequence an initial rise in autonomous investment produces a more than proportionate rise in income. The same multiplier process will apply following a change not only in investment expenditure but also in autonomous consumer expenditure. In terms of Samuelson's famous Keynesian cross model, a larger multiplier will show up as a steeper aggregate expenditure schedule, and vice versa (see Pearce and Hoover, 1995). Within the Keynesian IS–LM model the multiplier affects the slope of the IS curve. The IS curve will be flatter the larger the value of the multiplier, and vice versa (see Chapter 3).

Keynes was well aware of the various factors that could limit the size of the multiplier effect of his proposed public expenditure programmes, including the effect of 'increasing the rate of interest' unless 'the monetary authority take steps to the contrary' thus crowding out 'investment in other directions', the potential for an adverse effect on 'confidence', and the leakage of expenditures into both taxation and imports in an open economy such as the UK (see Keynes, 1936, pp. 119–20). In the case of a fully employed economy, Keynes recognized that any increase in investment will 'set up a tendency in money-prices to rise without limit, irrespective of the marginal propensity to consume'.

Although the concept of the multiplier is most associated with Keynes and his *General Theory*, the concept made its first influential appearance in a memorandum from Richard Kahn to the Economic Advisory Council during the summer of 1930. Kahn's more formal presentation appeared in his famous 1931 paper published in the *Economic Journal*. This article analysed the impact of an increase in government investment expenditure on employment assuming that: (1) the economy had spare capacity, (2) there was monetary policy accommodation, and (3) money wages remained stable. Kahn's article was written as a response to the Treasury's 'crowding-out' objections to loan-financed public works expenditures as a method of reducing unemployment. The following year Jens Warming (1932) criticized, refined and extended Kahn's analysis. It was Warming who first brought the idea of a consumption function into the multiplier literature (see Skidelsky, 1992, p. 451). The first coherent presentation of the multiplier by Keynes was in a series of four articles published in *The Times* in March 1933, entitled 'The Means to Prosperity', followed by an article in the *New Statesman* in April entitled 'The Multiplier'. However, the idea of the multiplier met with considerable resistance in orthodox financial circles and among fellow economists wedded to the classical tradition. By 1933, Keynes was attributing this opposition to the multiplier concept to

> the fact that all our ideas about economics ... are, whether we are conscious of it or not, soaked with theoretical pre-suppositions which are only applicable to a society which is in equilibrium, with all its productive capacity already employed. Many people are trying to solve the problem of unemployment with a theory which is based on the assumption that there is no unemployment ... these ideas, perfectly valid in their proper setting, are inapplicable to present circumstances. (Quoted by Meltzer, 1988, p. 137; see also Dimand, 1988, for an excellent survey of the development of the multiplier in this period)

There is no doubt that the multiplier process plays a key role in Keynesian economics. In Patinkin's (1976) view the development of the multiplier represented a 'major step towards the *General Theory*' and Skidelsky (1992) describes the concept of the multiplier as 'the most notorious piece of Keynesian magic'. We should also note that the multiplier came to play a key role in the early post-war Keynesian approach to business cycles. Following an initial increase in autonomous investment, the rise in income due to the multiplier process will be reinforced by an increase in new investment, via the 'accelerator' mechanism, which will in turn have a further multiplier effect on income and so on. Combining the so-called multiplier–accelerator model with an analysis of 'ceilings' and 'floors' allows exponents of the Keynesian approach to business cycles to account for both upper and lower turning points in the cycle.

Keynes's explanation of interest rate determination also marked a break with his classical predecessors. Keynes rejected the idea that the interest rate was determined by the real forces of thrift and the marginal productivity of capital. In the *General Theory* the interest rate is a purely monetary phenomenon determined by the liquidity preference (demand for money) of the public in conjunction with the supply of money determined by the monetary authorities. To the transactions motive for holding money, Keynes added the precautionary and speculative motives, the last being sensitive to the rate of interest (see Chapter 3, section 3.3.2). Keynes rejected the classical notion that interest was the reward for postponed current consumption. For him the rate of interest is the reward for parting with liquidity or not hoarding for a specified period. In a world characterized by uncertainty there will always be a speculative motive to hold cash in preference to other financial assets (such as bonds), and in Keynes's view 'liquidity preference' will always exert a more powerful influence on the rate of interest than saving decisions. By introducing the speculative motive into the money demand function, Keynes made the rate of interest dependent on the state of confidence as well as the money supply (see Chapter 3). If liquidity preference can vary, this undermines the classical postulate relating to the stability of the money demand function. This in turn implies that the velocity of circulation of money is liable to vary.

The basic structure of Keynes's theory of effective demand can be understood with reference to Figure 2.5. From this the reader can see that the dependence of aggregate output and employment on aggregate expenditure $(C + I)$ creates the potential for instability, since investment expenditure is typically unstable owing to the influence of business expectations relating to an uncertain future. An uncertain future also creates the desire for liquidity, so that variations in the demand for money as well as changes in the money supply can influence output and employment. Therefore in Keynes's model the classical proposition that the quantity of money is neutral is rejected. An increase in the money supply, by reducing the rate of interest, can stimulate aggregate spending via an increase in investment and the subsequent multiplier effect – see equation (2.22). The relationship can be depicted as follows:

$$+\Delta M \to -\Delta r \to +\Delta I \to \Delta Y, +\Delta L \qquad (2.23)$$

It should now be obvious why the title of Keynes's book is *The General Theory of Employment, Interest and Money*. For Keynes it was *General* because full employment was a special case and the characteristics of this special case assumed by classical theory 'happen not to be those of the economic society in which we actually live' (Keynes, 1936, p. 3). However, Keynes recognized that the power of monetary policy may be limited, particularly in a deep recession, and there 'may be several slips between the cup and the lip' (Keynes, 1936, p. 173). Should monetary policy prove to be weak or ineffective, aggregate expenditure could be stimulated directly via government expenditure or indirectly via tax changes which stimulate consumer spending by raising household disposable income. In the concluding notes of the *General Theory* we get some hints on Keynes's policy conclusions: 'The State will have to exercise a guiding influence on the propensity to consume partly through its scheme of taxation, partly by fixing the rate of interest, and partly, perhaps, in other ways' (Keynes, 1936, p. 378).

But what are the 'other ways'? In Keynes's view, because of the chronic tendency for the propensity to save to exceed the inducement to invest, the key to reducing aggregate instability was to find ways of stabilizing investment

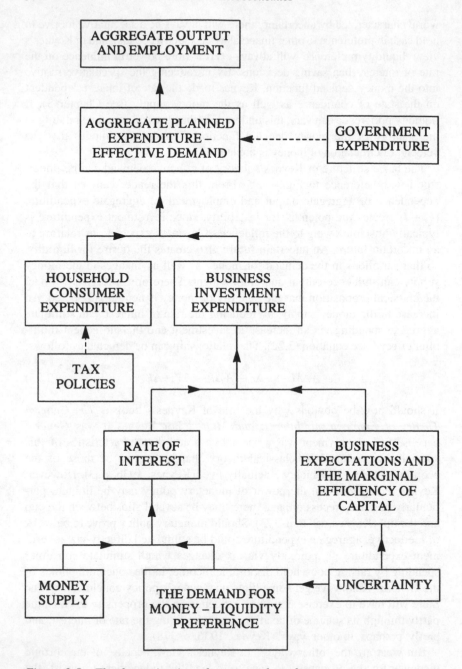

*Figure 2.5    The determination of output and employment*

expenditure at a level sufficient to absorb the full employment level of savings. Keynes's suggestion that 'a somewhat comprehensive socialisation of investment' would prove the 'only means of securing an approximation to full employment' is open to a wide variety of interpretations (see Meltzer, 1988). That Keynes saw his theory as having 'moderately conservative' implications and at the same time implying a 'large extension of the traditional functions of government' is a perfect example of the kind of ambiguity found in the *General Theory* which has allowed for considerable variation of interpretation in subsequent work.

In our discussion of the classical model we drew attention to three main aspects of their work: the theory of employment and output determination, Say's Law of markets and the quantity theory of money. We can now briefly examine how Keynes rejected the basic ideas relating to each of these foundations of classical economics.

## 2.9 Keynes's Analysis of the Labour Market

We have already seen (section 2.3) that full employment is guaranteed in the classical model providing that competition prevails in the labour market, and prices and wages are perfectly flexible (see Figures 2.2 and 2.4). In sharp contrast, Keynes did not accept that the labour market worked in a way that would always ensure market clearing. Involuntary unemployment is likely to be a feature of the labour market if money wages are rigid. But Keynes went further than this and argued that flexibility of nominal wages would be unlikely to generate powerful enough forces which could lead the economy back to full employment. Let us examine each of these cases.

### 2.9.1 Rigidity of nominal wages
In the *General Theory*, to begin with, Keynes assumes that the money wage is 'constant' in order to 'facilitate the exposition' while noting that the 'essential character of the argument is precisely the same whether or not money-wages are liable to change' (Keynes, 1936, p. 27). We can see the impact of a negative demand shock on real output and employment in the case of nominal wage rigidity by referring to Figure 2.6. Suppose an economy which is initially in equilibrium at full employment ($L_e$ and $Y_F$) experiences a fall in aggregate demand illustrated by a shift of the $AD$ curve from $AD_0$ to $AD_1$. If prices are flexible but nominal wages are rigid, the economy moves from $e_0$ to $e_1$ in panel (b). With nominal wage rigidity the aggregate supply curve becomes $W_0AS$. With a fall in the price level to $P_1$, and nominal wages remaining at $W_0$, the real wage increases to $W_0/P_1$ in panel (a). At this real wage the supply of labour ($L_d$) exceeds the demand for labour ($L_c$) and involuntary unemployment of $cd$ emerges.

According to Keynes (1936, p. 15) workers are involuntarily unemployed if 'in the event of a small rise in the price of wage-goods relatively to the money-wage, both the aggregate supply of labour willing to work for the current money-wage and the aggregate demand for it at that wage would be greater than the existing volume of employment'. This makes sense when we remember that the labour supply curve indicates the maximum amount of labour supplied at each real wage. Since $L_e - L_c$ part of the involuntarily unemployed workers are prepared to work for the equilibrium real wage $W_0/P_0$ a fall in the real wage from $W_0/P_1$ to $W_0/P_0$ is acceptable to them since they would have been prepared to work for a lower real wage, as indicated by the supply curve for labour between $b$ and $e$. A fall in the real wage will also induce profit-maximizing firms to demand more labour.

But how can the real wage be reduced? There are basically two ways. Either money wages must fall relative to the price level, or the price level must rise relative to the nominal wage. Keynes favoured the latter, and advocated expansions of aggregate demand in order to exert upward pressure on the price level. In terms of Figure 2.6, panel (b), policies are required which will shift $AD$ from $AD_1$ to $AD_0$. The rise in the price level from $P_1$ to $P_0$ reduces the real wage back to its equilibrium level of $W_0/P_0$ and involuntary unemployment is eliminated. Keynes rejected the alternative policy of wage cutting as a method of stimulating employment on both practical and theoretical grounds. The practical reason was that in a democracy characterized by decentralized wage bargaining wage reductions are only likely to occur after 'wasteful and disastrous struggles', producing an end result which is not justifiable on any criterion of social justice or economic expediency (see Chapters 3 and 19 of the *General Theory*). Keynes also argued that workers will not resist real wage reductions brought about by an increase in the general price level, since this will leave relative real wages unchanged and this is a major concern of workers. We should note that this does not imply money illusion on the part of workers. The resistance to money wage cuts and acceptance of reductions in the real wage via a general rise in the cost of living has the advantage of preserving the existing structure of relativities (see Trevithick, 1975; Keynes, 1936, p. 14). In any case, since labour can only bargain over money wages and the price level is outside their control, there is no way in which labour as a whole can reduce its real wage by revising money wage bargains with entrepreneurs (Keynes, 1936, p. 13). But Keynes went further in his objections to nominal wage cutting than these practical issues. He rejected wage and price flexibility as a reliable method of restoring equilibrium on theoretical grounds also. Indeed, in many circumstances extreme flexibility of the nominal wage in a monetary economy would in all probability make the situation worse.

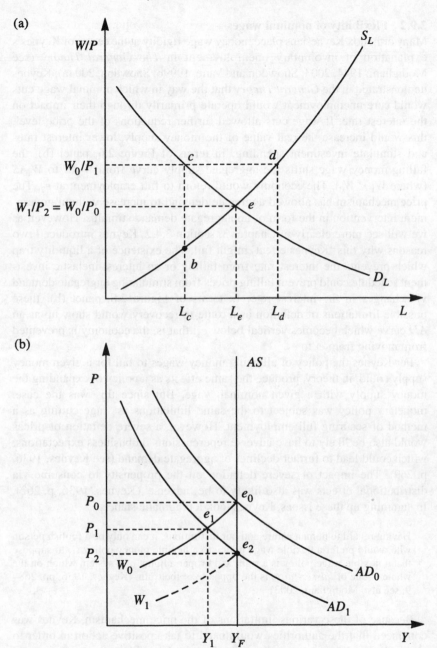

*Figure 2.6    Keynes and involuntary unemployment*

**2.9.2   Flexibility of nominal wages**

Many orthodox Keynesians place money wage rigidity at the centre of Keynes's explanation of involuntary unemployment in *The General Theory* (see Modigliani, 1944, 2003; Snowdon and Vane, 1999b; Snowdon, 2004a). Keynes demonstrated in the *General Theory* that the way in which nominal wage cuts would cure unemployment would operate primarily through their impact on the interest rate. If wage cuts allowed further reductions of the price level, this would increase the real value of the money supply, lower interest rates and stimulate investment spending. In terms of Figure 2.6, panel (b), the falling money wage shifts the aggregate supply curve from $W_0AS$ to $W_1AS$ (where $W_1 < W_0$). The economy would return to full employment at $e_2$. The price mechanism has allowed aggregate demand to increase without government intervention in the form of an aggregate demand stimulus. However, as we will see more clearly in Chapter 3, section 3.4.2, Keynes introduced two reasons why this 'Keynes effect' might fail. The existence of a liquidity trap which prevents the interest rate from falling or an interest-inelastic investment schedule could prevent falling prices from stimulating aggregate demand via changes in the interest rate. In terms of Figure 2.6, panel (b), these possible limitations of deflation as a route to recovery would show up as an *AD* curve which becomes vertical below $e_1$; that is, the economy is prevented from moving from $e_1$ to $e_2$.

For Keynes the policy of allowing money wages to fall for a given money supply could, in theory, produce the same effects as a policy of expanding the money supply with a given nominal wage. But since this was the case, monetary policy was subject to the same limitations as wage cutting as a method of securing full employment. However, a severe deflation of prices would also be likely to have adverse repercussions on business expectations, which could lead to further declines of aggregate demand (see Keynes, 1936, p. 269). The impact of severe deflation on the propensity to consume via distributional effects was also likely to be 'adverse' (Keynes, 1936, p. 262). In summing up these issues, Keynes took a pragmatic stance.

> Having regard to human nature and our institutions, it can only be a foolish person who would prefer a flexible wage policy to a flexible money policy ... to suppose that a flexible wage policy is a right and proper adjunct of a system which on the whole is one of *laissez-faire*, is the opposite of the truth. (Keynes, 1936, pp. 268–9; see also Modigliani, 2003)

Because of these various limitations of the price mechanism, Keynes was convinced that the authorities would need to take positive action in order to eliminate involuntary unemployment. Unless they did so the system could find itself caught in a situation of underemployment equilibrium, by which he meant the tendency of market economies to remain in a chronic condition of subnormal activity for a considerable period 'without any marked tendency either towards recovery or towards complete collapse' (Keynes, 1936, p. 249).

## 2.10 Keynes's Rejection of Say's Law

Say's Law, if accepted, makes macroeconomic demand management policies redundant. We have seen earlier that in the classical model a decision to refrain from current consumption is equivalent to a decision to consume more in the future. This decision therefore automatically implies that resources need to be diverted to the production of investment goods which will be needed to provide the flow of future consumption goods. An increase in saving automatically becomes an increase in investment expenditure via adjustment of the interest rate. In the classical model, saving is in effect just another form of spending. The principles underlying Say's Law raised their head during discussions relating to anti-depression economic policy during the interwar period. Ralph Hawtrey, a strong advocate of the 'Treasury View', argued forcefully that public works programmes would be useless since such expenditures would simply 'crowd out' an equivalent amount of private spending. Such views only make sense in the context of a fully employed economy (Deutscher, 1990).

A principal objective of writing the *General Theory* was to provide a theoretical refutation of Say's Law, something Malthus over a century earlier had tried and failed to do. In Keynes's model output and employment are determined by effective demand, and the operation of the labour market cannot guarantee full employment. The interest rate is determined in the money market rather than by saving and investment decisions. Variations in the marginal efficiency of investment bring about variations in real output via the multiplier effect and as a result saving adjusts to investment through changes in income. Hence in Keynes's model any inequality between planned investment and planned saving leads to quantity adjustments rather than equilibrating adjustments of the rate of interest. By demonstrating the flaws inherent in wage and price flexibility as a method of returning the economy to full employment following a negative demand shock, Keynes effectively reversed Say's Law. In Keynes's world of underemployment equilibrium, demand creates supply!

## 2.11 Keynes and the Quantity Theory of Money

In the classical model a monetary impulse has no real effects on the economy. Money is neutral. Since the quantity of real output is predetermined by the combined impact of a competitive labour market and Say's Law, any change in the quantity of money can only affect the general price level. By rejecting

both Say's Law and the classical model of the labour market, Keynes's theory
no longer assumes that real output is predetermined at its full employment
level. In Chapter 21 of the *General Theory*, Keynes discusses the various
possibilities. If the aggregate supply curve is perfectly elastic, then a change
in effective demand brought about by an increase in the quantity of money
will cause output and employment to increase with no effect on the price
level until full employment is reached. However, in the normal course of
events, an increase in effective demand will 'spend itself partly in increasing
the quantity of employment and partly in raising the level of prices' (Keynes,
1936, p. 296). In other words, the supply response of the economy in Keynes's
model can be represented by an aggregate supply function such as $W_0AS$ in
Figure 2.6, panel (b). Therefore for monetary expansions carried out when $Y$
$< Y_F$, both output and the price level will rise. Once the aggregate volume of
output corresponding to full employment is established, Keynes accepted that
'the classical theory comes into its own again' and monetary expansions will
produce 'true inflation' (Keynes, 1936, pp. 378, 303). A further complication
in Keynes's model is that the linkage between a change in the quantity of
money and a change in effective demand is indirect, coming as it does via its
influence on interest rates, investment and the size of the multiplier. We
should also note that, once Keynes had introduced the theory of liquidity
preference, the possibility that the demand for money function might shift
about unpredictably, causing velocity to vary, implies that changes in $M$ may
be offset by changes in $V$ in the opposite direction. With $Y$ and $V$ no longer
assumed constant in the equation $MV = PY$, it is clear that changes in the
quantity of money may cause $V$, $P$ or $Y$ to vary. The neutrality of money is no
longer guaranteed.

## 2.12   Three Important Interpretations of Keynes

In the vast literature relating to Keynes's contribution since 1936 we can
identify three distinct interpretations which command varying degrees of
support (see Snowdon and Vane, 1997a). Coddington (1983) identifies three
interpretations, namely: (i) the 'hydraulic' interpretation, (ii) the 'fundamentalist' interpretation, and (iii) the modified general equilibrium approach.

### 2.12.1   The 'hydraulic' interpretation
This is the orthodox interpretation of Keynes initiated and inspired by Hicks
(1937), Modigliani (1944), Klein (1947), Samuelson (1948) and Hansen
(1953). The IS–LM model formed the backbone of theorizing within this
approach and it dominated thinking in the emerging neoclassical synthesis
during the 1950s and 1960s. Samuelson's famous textbook, *Economics*, first
published in 1948, played a very important role here, popularizing Keynes

with the aid of the 45° Keynesian cross diagram. Following Modigliani's contribution, Keynesian economics was seen to be the economics of wage and price rigidities. The destabilizing impact of unstable expectations was played down in this approach. Although Keynesians such as Modigliani and Tobin worked on improving the microfoundations of Keynes's model, a major weakness of hydraulic Keynesianism was the lack of a convincing reason for wage and price rigidities based on rational behaviour. The ideas associated with this hydraulic variety of Keynesianism are developed in Chapter 3, while the more recent attempts by new Keynesian theorists to rectify the theoretical shortcomings of the neoclassical synthesis model are examined in Chapter 7.

### 2.12.2 The 'fundamentalist' interpretation

This interpretation of the *General Theory* regards Keynes's work as a frontal assault on neoclassical orthodoxy. Fundamentalists regard the influence of unstable expectations due to uncertainty as a key feature of Keynes's work, particularly as expressed in Chapters 12 and 17 of the *General Theory*, where he discusses 'The State of Long-Term Expectations' and 'The Essential Properties of Interest and Money'. Fundamentalists also point to Keynes's (1937) *Quarterly Journal of Economics* article entitled 'The General Theory of Employment', which Keynes wrote in response to his critics, as evidence that the problems of decision making under conditions of uncertainty lay at the heart of his system. The key figures in this school include George Shackle (1967, 1974) and Joan Robinson (1962), although a very early statement can be found in Townshend (1937). Fundamentalists reject the hydraulic interpretation as a 'bastardization' of Keynes's contribution. The ideas and development of this Post Keynesian school are explored in Chapter 8.

### 2.12.3 The modified general equilibrium approach

Coddington (1983) refers to this view as 'reconstituted reductionism' (reductionists are those economists whose method of analysis consists of 'analysing markets on the basis of the choices made by individual traders'; see Coddington, 1983, p. 92). This approach initially received stimulus from Patinkin's (1956) suggestion that Keynesian economics is the economics of unemployment disequilibrium and that involuntary unemployment should be viewed as a problem of dynamic disequilibrium. In Patinkin's analysis, involuntary unemployment can exist in a perfectly competitive economy with flexible wages and prices. The emphasis given by Patinkin to the speed with which markets are able to absorb and rectify shocks shifted attention away from the degree of price and wage flexibility to the issue of coordination. This line of enquiry was followed by Clower (1965) and Leijonhufvud (1968), who developed a modified general equilibrium approach along Walrasian lines in order to make sense of coordination problems which inevitably emerge in a market economy operating without the fictional 'auctioneer'. If the hydraulic interpretation played down Keynes's contribution as a theorist, the reconstituted, reductionist approach attempts to rehabilitate the *General Theory* as a pioneering exercise in disequilibrium dynamics.

Clower's reinterpretation of the *General Theory* suggests that Keynes's revolt was against the Walrasian general equilibrium tradition within neoclassical economics. In the Walrasian paradigm all markets continuously clear thanks to the work of the fictional auctioneer. Building on the insights of Patinkin (1956), Clower's work emphasizes the dynamic disequilibrium nature of Keynes's work. Clower argues that Keynes's objective was to kill off the auctioneer myth in order to raise the profile of information and intertemporal coordination difficulties within real economies. The cumulative declines in output in Keynes's *General Theory* result from massive coordination failures as agents respond to wrong (false) price signals. Once the assumption of instantaneously adjusted prices is abandoned there is no longer any guarantee that a decentralized price system will coordinate economic activity at full employment. Once again the classical model is shown to be a 'special case', and Keynes's theory the more 'general' theory. Clower has continued to be highly critical of all the mainstream macro schools for not taking market processes seriously. To do so involves recognizing that markets and monetary institutions are created by firms, individuals and governments. In Clower's view, in order to really understand market processes economists need to create a 'Post Walrasian Macroeconomics' based on Marshallian rather than Walrasian microfoundations (Clower and Howitt, 1996; Colander, 1996). While Keynes had a profound influence on the development of macroeconomics, his anti-formalist approach was swept away by the 'Walrasian formalism' of mainstream theorists in the post-1945 period (Backhouse, 1997a).

In the 1970s several economists inspired by Clower's insights went on to develop neo-Keynesian quantity-constrained models (Barro and Grossman, 1976; Malinvaud, 1977). This work served to remind economists that conventional Keynesian models lacked solid microfoundations (Barro, 1979). This was a theme the new classical economists were to exploit throughout the 1970s but in a very different way from that favoured by Clower. During the 1970s the new classical approach prospered while the neo-Keynesian models gradually fell out of favour, not least because high inflation made fix-price models appear 'unrealistic' (Backhouse, 1995).

In the mid to late 1960s, Axel Leijonhufvud also provided an influential and provocative interpretation of Keynes's *General Theory*. His dissertation thesis, *On Keynesian Economics and the Economics of Keynes*, was an instantaneous success when published in 1968 and became the subject of intense debate and controversy given its novel analysis of Keynes's most influential contribution. Leijonhufvud elaborates upon the Clower theme by building an 'economics of Keynes' that is distinct from the Walrasian Keynesianism that characterizes the mainstream neoclassical synthesis interpretation. Leijonhufvud, following Patinkin (1948), provides a neo-Walrasian interpretation of Keynes which focuses on the process and implications of disequilibrium trading and coordination failure. In doing so, Leijonhufvud shows how Keynes's (1936, p. 15) concept of 'involuntary unemployment' emerges as a dynamic disequilibrium phenomenon. In Leijonhufvud's reinterpretation of the *General Theory*, Keynes's main innovation is seen to be his attempt at providing a coherent and systematic analysis of how a predominantly private enterprise market economy reacts, responds and adjusts in the short run to aggregate demand shocks when price and wage adjustments are less than perfectly flexible. The Walrasian assumptions of instantaneous price and wage flexibility and complete information are nothing more than a fiction. Leijonhufvud therefore argues that Keynes provided a more *General Theory* where the incomplete information of agents prevents the economic system from moving quickly and smoothly to a new equilibrium following an aggregate demand shock. Leijonhufvud's reinterpretation of Keynes attempts to show that the content of the *General Theory* is consistent with a choice-theoretic framework providing the key assumption, that agents have complete information when trading, is abandoned. There is no need to resort to imposing institutional rigidities (such as rigid nominal wages) on the price mechanism to generate Keynesian outcomes. This is a direct refutation of the 'Keynesian Gospel According to Modigliani' (2003). The late Nobel Memorial Laureate Franco Modigliani (2003) continued to maintain that 'the essence of Keynesian economics is wage rigidity. That is Keynes' (see the interview with Modigliani in Snowdon and Vane, 1999b, and Chapter 3).

Leijonhufvud suggests that the neoclassical synthesis interpretation of Keynes provides an incoherent theoretical basis for a Keynesian revolution. He argues that Keynes recognized the difficulties experienced, within decentralized market economies, of finding the appropriate market-clearing price vector. In Keynes's vision, the initial response to shocks on the system is via quantity adjustment rather than price adjustment, with the relative speed of adjustment of the latter tending to lag behind the former (a reversal of the Walrasian approach). In the absence of the fictional 'Walrasian auctioneer', the key issue focuses on the control mechanisms and relates to the generation and dissemination of information. According to Leijonhufvud, the information and coordination deficiencies lead to deviation-amplifying (positive feedback) processes, such as the multiplier, which were played down by the Walrasian synthesis which highlighted the deviation-counteracting (negative feedback) mechanisms.

Leijonhufvud argues that the neoclassical synthesis totally misunderstands and misinterprets Keynes (Leijonhufvud, 1981; Snowdon, 2004a). The orthodox Keynesian story highlights elements that play no real part in the argument of the *General Theory* (but a significant part in the work of the Keynesians) – such as the claims that wages are rigid; that the liquidity trap exists in actuality; and that investment is interest-inelastic. Leijonhufvud controversially maintains that none of these essential Keynesian building blocks is to be found in the economics of Keynes (see Chapter 3).

After the initial enthusiasm and wide interest that Leijonhufvud's interpretation of Keynes aroused during the 1970s, the younger generation of economists were soon caught up in the excitement created by the 'rational expectations' revolution inspired by Robert Lucas (see Chapter 5). Interest in Keynes and Keynesian economics began to wane. By his own admission Leijonhufvud (1993) 'drifted out of the professional mainstream from the mid-1970s onwards, as intertemporal optimisation became all the rage'. As Leijonhufvud (1998a) recalls, 'macroeconomics seemed to have taken a turn very similar to the movies: more and more simple-minded plots but ever more mind-boggling special effects. One would like to look forward to a macroeconomics whose plots will give more insight into the human condition.' While the younger generation of new classical economists was everywhere pronouncing the end of the Keynesian era and embracing rational expectations and equilibrium theories of the business cycle, Leijonhufvud has continued to argue that Keynesian economics has a future. Leijonhufvud (1992) suggests two main reasons for such optimism. First, the coordination problem is too important an issue to be kept indefinitely off economists' research agenda. 'Will the market system "automatically" coordinate economic activities? Always? Never? Sometimes very well, but sometimes pretty badly? If the latter, under what conditions, and with what institutional structures, will it do well or do badly?' Leijonhufvud regards these questions as *the* central ones in macroeconomics. Second, Leijonhufvud believes that sooner or later economists must open up their theoretical structures to allow results from other behavioural sciences to be utilized in economic analysis. When that happens, 'the "unbounded rationality" postulate will have to go'.

In his Nobel Memorial Lecture, George Akerlof (2002) also presents a strong case for strengthening macroeconomic theory by incorporating assumptions that take account of behaviour such as 'cognitive bias, reciprocity, fairness, herding and social status'. By doing so Akerlof argues that macroeconomics will 'no longer suffer from the "ad hockery" of the neoclassical synthesis which had overridden the emphasis in the *General Theory* on the role of psychological and sociological factors'. Since in Akerlof's view Keynes's *General Theory* 'was the greatest contribution to behavioural economics before the present era', it would seem that economists need to rediscover the 'wild side' of macroeconomic behaviour in order to begin the construction of 'a not too rational macroeconomics' (Leijonhufvud, 1993).

The interested reader is referred to Chapter 3, section 3.5 (and references therein) of Snowdon, et al. (1994), for a more detailed discussion of the work of Clower, Leijonhufvud and Malinvaud.

## 2.13 The 'New' Keynes Scholarship

During the 1980s there was a growth of interest in the early Keynes in order to better understand the later Keynes of the *General Theory*. There is an increasing recognition and acceptance that Keynes's philosophical and methodological framework had a significant influence upon his economic analysis as well as his politics. Whilst much has been written about the alleged content of Keynes's economics, very little has dealt with Keynes's method and philosophy. Littleboy and Mehta (1983) argue that 'The great stimulus to macroeconomic theory provided by Keynes is well recognised but much less is said about his views on scientific methodology', and Lawson and Pesaran (1985, p. 1) concede that 'Keynes's methodological contribution has been neglected generally'. The only major exception to the charge, until the contributions of, for example, Carabelli (1988), Fitzgibbons (1988) and O'Donnell (1989), was the latter's earlier study, (O'Donnell, 1982) which endeavoured to provide a serious extended analysis of the connection between Keynes's philosophy and his economics. The more recent attempts to explore the methodological and philosophical foundations of Keynes's political economy have been termed 'the new Keynes scholarship' by Skidelsky (1992, pp. 82–9).

The main aim of the new scholarship is to highlight the need to recognize that Keynes's economics has a strong philosophical base and to provide a detailed examination of Keynes's rich and elaborate treatment of uncertainty, knowledge, ignorance and probability. The new scholarship also gives prime importance to Keynes's lifelong fascination with the problem of decision making under conditions of uncertainty. Carabelli (1988) has argued that the general epistemological premises of Keynes's method have been generally overlooked, even though they were systematically presented, albeit in a very refined state, in his *A Treatise on Probability* (1921). Fitzgibbons (1988) maintains that economists have been guilty of suppressing Keynes's philosophy because of its lack of systematization and anti-modernist stance. For Fitzgibbons, Keynes provided a radical alternative to long-run thinking firmly based on the temporary nature of the short run. It is argued that the *General Theory* is centred upon a radical economics of uncertainty organized around 'animal spirits' and creative impulses, alongside the constant threat of economic breakdown: within such a world, money has a rationale and impact on the real side of the economy. Keynes is seen to be concerned with the problems of economic indeterminacy and the abandonment of equilibrium. Likewise Carabelli has placed stress on Keynes's focus on the close relation between time and change and the need to analyse and attend to the problems of the short period. O'Donnell (1982, pp. 222–9) attempted to reconcile the long-period and short-period interpretations of Keynes by acknowledging Keynes's interest in both periods, but with greater emphasis being placed on the latter. In O'Donnell's interpretation of Keynes, a universal role for uncertainty and expectations regardless of the period dimension has to be granted.

Although the new scholarship has increased awareness of the linkages between Keynes's philosophy and his economics, it can be argued that, in locating the core of Keynes's method in *A Treatise on Probability*, a work which largely pre-dates much of his serious and scholarly economic writing, authors such as Carabelli fail to consider adequately the reciprocal influence of the economic upon the philosophical and their interaction and continued development. Nevertheless the new scholarship does add weight to the 'fundamentalist' Keynesian position that Keynes's ideas on uncertainty were central to his vision (see Shackle, 1974; Davidson, 1978, 1994; and Chapter 8).

However, throughout this book we take the view that, more than anything else, it was the experience of the Great Depression that drove Keynes to write his most important book on economic theory, *The General Theory of Employment, Interest and Money*. Within that book Keynes placed a great deal of emphasis on the role of expectations and uncertainty in his explanation of aggregate instability (see section 2.8 above).

### 2.14   Causes and Consequences of the Great Depression

The Great Depression was the most significant economic catastrophe of modern times to affect capitalist market economies and even today most economists regard the 1930s worldwide slump, and the consequences of that catastrophe, as one, if not *the* most important single macroeconomic event of the twentieth century. The political and economic significance of this event is reflected in the continuous outpouring of research on this traumatic historical event (see Temin, 1976, 1989; Bernanke, 1983, 1995, 2000; Eichengreen, 1992a; 1992b; C. Romer, 1992, 1993; Bordo et al., 1998; Hall and Ferguson, 1998; Wheeler, 1998; Krugman, 1999; Cole and Ohanian, 1999, 2002a; Prescott, 1999; James, 2001). It is easy to see why the interwar period in general, and the Great Depression in particular, continue to exert such an attraction to economists and economic historians:

1.   the events of this period contributed significantly to the outbreak of the Second World War which changed the political and economic world forever;

2.  the Great Depression was by far the most severe economic downturn experienced by the world's industrialized capitalist economies in the twentieth century and the nature of the causes and consequences of the worldwide slump in economic activity are still hotly debated;

3.  it is generally recognized that the Great Depression gave Keynes (1936) the necessary impetus to write the *General Theory*, a book that marks the birth of macroeconomics. According to Skidelsky (1996a), 'the *General Theory* could not have been published ten years earlier. That particular indictment of classical economics and, indeed, of the way the economy behaved needed the great slump to crystallise it';

4.  the Great Depression is frequently used by macroeconomists to test their models of aggregate fluctuations, while the whole interwar period provides an invaluable data set for macroeconomic researchers;

5.  there are always some commentators who periodically ask the question 'could such an event ever happen again?';

6.  finally, after the 1930s experience the role of government in all market economies increased considerably, leading to a fundamental and lasting change in the relationship between the government and the private sector. As a result, economic institutions at the end of the twentieth century were very different from those in place in 1929. It is therefore with considerable justification that Bordo et al. (1998) describe the Great Depression as the 'defining moment' in the development of the US economy during the twentieth century. In the macroeconomic sphere the modern approach to stabilization policy evolved out of the experience of the 'great contraction' of the 1930s (DeLong, 1996, 1998).

Economists have generally concluded that the proximate causes of the Great Depression involved the interaction of several factors leading to a drastic decline in aggregate demand (see Fackler and Parker, 1994; Snowdon and Vane 1999b; Sandilands, 2002). The data in Table 2.1 reveal convincing evidence of a huge aggregate demand shock given the strong procyclical movement of the price level, that is, the price level falling as GDP declines. Note also the dramatic increase in unemployment.

Bernanke and Carey's data also show that in the great majority of countries there was a countercyclical movement of the real wage. This pattern would emerge in response to an aggregate demand shock in countries where price deflation exceeded nominal wage deflation. Hence the evidence 'for a non-vertical aggregate supply curve in the Depression era is strong' (Bernanke and Carey, 1996). In Figure 2.7 we illustrate the situation for the US economy in the period 1929–33 using the familiar AD–AS framework. The dramatic decline in aggregate demand is shown by the leftward shift of the *AD* curve during this period. Note that a combination of a falling price level and GDP

*Table 2.1   US GDP, prices and unemployment: 1929–33*

| Year | Real GDP[a] $ billions | Price level[b] | Unemployment % |
|------|------------------------|----------------|----------------|
| 1929 | 103.1 | 100.0 | 3.2 |
| 1930 | 94.0 | 96.8 | 8.9 |
| 1931 | 86.7 | 88.0 | 16.3 |
| 1932 | 75.2 | 77.6 | 24.1 |
| 1933 | 73.7 | 76.0 | 25.2 |

*Notes:*
a   Measured at 1929 prices.
b   GDP deflator, 1929 = 100.

*Source:*   Adapted from Gordon (2000a).

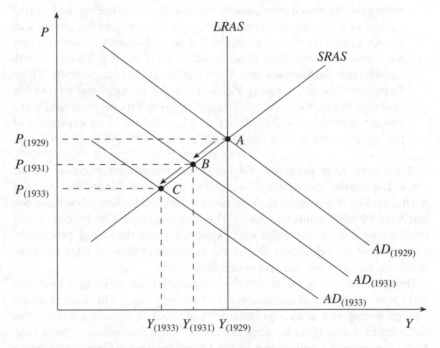

*Figure 2.7   Aggregate demand failure in the US economy, 1929–33*

could not arise from a negative supply shock (leftward shift of the *AS* curves)
which would reduce GDP and raise the price level.

In the debate relating to the causes of the Great Depression in the USA five main hypotheses have been put forward, the first four of which focus on the causes of the dramatic decline in aggregate demand:

1.  *The non-monetary/non-financial hypothesis.* Here the focus is on the impact of the decline in consumer and investment spending as well as the adverse effect on exports of the Smoot–Hawley Tariff introduced in 1930 (see Temin, 1976; C. Romer, 1990; Crucini and Kahn, 1996); in chapter 22 of the *General Theory*, Keynes argued that 'the trade cycle is best regarded as being occasioned by a cyclical change in the marginal efficiency of capital, though complicated and often aggravated by associated changes in other significant short-period variables of the economic system', thus the 'predominant' determination of slumps is a 'sudden collapse in the marginal efficiency of capital'.

2.  *The monetary hypothesis* of Friedman and Schwartz (1963) attributes the huge decline in GDP mainly to an unprecedented decline in the *nominal* money supply, especially following the succession of bank failures beginning in 1930, which the Fed failed to counter by using expansionary monetary policies. This prevented the deflation of prices from increasing the *real* money supply which via the 'Keynes effect' would have acted as a stabilizing mechanism on aggregate demand. An alternative monetary hypothesis, initially put forward by Fisher (1933b), focuses on the impact of the debt-deflation process on the solvency of the banking system.

3.  *The non-monetary/financial hypothesis* associated in particular with the seminal paper of Bernanke (1983). Bernanke's credit view takes the Fisher debt-deflation story as its starting point. Because many banks failed during the slump, this led to a breakdown in the financial system and with it the network of knowledge and information that banks possess about existing and potential customers. Many borrowers were thus denied available credit even though their financial credentials were sound (see also Bernanke and James, 1991).

4.  *The Bernanke–Eichengreen–Temin Gold Standard hypothesis.* In looking for what made the depression a 'Great' international event it is necessary to look beyond the domestic mechanisms at work within the USA. 'The Great Depression did not begin in 1929. The chickens that came home to roost following the Wall Street crash had been hatching for many years. An adequate analysis must place the post-1929 Depression in the context of the economic developments preceding it' (Eichengreen, 1992a).

5.  *The non-monetary neoclassical real business cycle hypothesis.* This very recent (and very controversial) contribution is associated in particular with the work of Cole and Ohanian (1999, 2002a) and Prescott (1999, 2002). This approach highlights the impact of real shocks to the economy

arising from 'changes in economic institutions that lowered the normal
or steady state market hours per person over 16' (Prescott, 1999; see also
Chapter 6).

With respect to those explanations that emphasize the decline in aggregate
demand, much of the recent research on the Great Depression has moved
away from the traditional emphasis placed on events within the USA and
focuses instead on the international monetary system operating during the
interwar period. Because the Great Depression was such an enormous *international* macroeconomic event it requires an explanation that can account for
the international transmission of the depression worldwide. According to
Bernanke (1995), 'substantial progress' has been made towards understanding the causes of the Great Depression and much research during the last 20
years has concentrated on the operation of the international Gold Standard
during the period after its restoration in the 1920s (see Choudri and Kochin,
1980; Eichengreen and Sachs, 1985; Eichengreen, 1992a, 1992b; Eichengreen
and Temin, 2000, 2002; Hamilton, 1988; Temin, 1989, 1993; Bernanke,
1993, 1995, 2000; Bernanke and James, 1991; Bernanke and Carey, 1996;
James, 2001).

The heyday of the Gold Standard was in the 40-year period before the First
World War. The balance of payments equilibrating mechanism operated via
what used to be known as the 'price specie flow mechanism'. Deficit countries would experience an outflow of gold while surplus countries would
receive gold inflows. Since a country's money supply was linked to the
supply of gold, deficit countries would experience a deflation of prices as the
quantity of money declined while surplus countries would experience inflation. This process would make the exports of the deficit country more
competitive and vice versa, thus restoring equilibrium to the international
payments imbalances. These were the 'rules of the game'. The whole mechanism was underpinned by a belief in the classical quantity theory of money
and the assumption that markets would clear quickly enough to restore full
employment following a deflationary impulse. This system worked reasonably well before the First World War. However, the First World War created
huge imbalances in the pattern of international settlements that continued to
undermine the international economic system throughout the 1920s. In particular the war 'transformed the United States from a net foreign debtor to a
creditor nation' and 'unleashed a westward flow of reparations and war-debt
repayments ... the stability of the inter-war gold standard itself, therefore,
hinged on the continued willingness of the United States to recycle its balance of payments surpluses' (Eichengreen, 1992a).

To both Temin (1989) and Eichengreen the war represented a huge shock
to the Gold Standard and the attempt to restore the system at the old pre-war

parities during the 1920s was doomed to disaster. In 1928, in response to fears that the US economy was overheating, the Fed tightened monetary policy and the USA reduced its flow of lending to Europe and Latin America. As central banks began to experience a loss of reserves due to payments deficits, they responded in line with the requirements of the Gold Standard and also tightened their monetary policies. And so the deflationary process was already well under way at the international level by the summer of 1929, and well before the stock market crashed so dramatically in October. Eichengreen and Temin (2000) argue that once the international economic downturn was under way it was the 'ideology, mentalité and rhetoric of the gold standard that led policy makers to take actions that only accentuated economic distress in the 1930s. Central bankers continued to kick the world economy while it was down until it lost consciousness.' Thus the ultimate cause of the Great Depression was the strains that the First World War imposed on the Gold Standard, followed by its reintroduction in a very different world during the 1920s. No longer would it be relatively easy, as it had been before 1914, to engineer wage cuts via deflation and unemployment in order to restore international competitiveness. The internal politics of capitalist economies had been transformed by the war, and the working classes were increasingly hostile to the use of monetary policies that were geared towards maintenance of the exchange rate rather than giving greater priority to employment targets. Hence the recession, which visibly began in 1929, was a disaster waiting to happen.

The Gold Standard mentalité constrained the mindset of the policy makers and 'shaped their notions of the possible'. Under the regime of the Gold Standard, countries are prevented from devaluing their currencies to stimulate exports, and expansionary monetary policies on a unilateral basis are also ruled out because they would undermine the stability of a country's exchange rate. Unless the governments of Gold Standard countries could organize a coordinated reflation, the only option for countries experiencing a drain on their gold reserves was monetary contraction and deflation. But as Eichengreen (1992a) points out, political disputes, the rise of protectionism, and incompatible conceptual frameworks proved to be an 'insurmountable barrier' to international cooperation. And so the recession, which began in 1929, was converted into the Great Depression by the universal adoption of perverse policies designed to maintain and preserve the Gold Standard. As Bernanke and Carey (1996) argue, by taking into account the impact on economic policy of a 'structurally flawed and poorly managed international gold standard', economists can at last explain the 'aggregate demand puzzle of the Depression', that is, why so many countries experienced a simultaneous decline in aggregate demand. It was the economic policy actions of the gold bloc countries that accentuated rather than alleviated the worldwide slump in economic activity. Incredibly, in the midst of the Great Depression, central bankers were still worried about inflation, the equivalent of 'crying fire in Noah's flood'! In order to restore the US economy to health, President Herbert Hoover was advised by Treasury Secretary Andrew Mellon to 'liquidate labour, liquidate stocks, liquidate the farmers, liquidate real estate ... purge the rottenness out of the system' and as a result 'people will work harder, and live a more moral life' (quoted by Eichengreen and Temin, 2000). Ultimately these policies destroyed the very structure they were intended to preserve.

During the 1930s, one by one countries abandoned the Gold Standard and devalued their currencies. Once they had shed their 'golden fetters', policy makers were able to adopt expansionary monetary policies and reflate their economies (the UK left the Gold Standard in the autumn of 1931, the USA in March 1933, Germany in August/September 1931; and France in 1936). Thus, while Friedman and Schwartz (1963) and others have rightly criticized the Fed for not adopting more expansionary monetary policies in 1931, Eichengreen (1992b) argues that, given the constraints imposed by the Gold Standard, it is 'hard to see what else could have been done by a central bank committed to defending the fixed price of gold'. Research has shown that economic recovery in the USA was largely the result of monetary expansion (C. Romer, 1992) and also that those countries that were quickest to abandon their golden fetters and adopt expansionary monetary policies were the first to recover (Choudri and Kochin, 1980; Eichengreen and Sachs, 1985).

The Bernanke–Eichengreen–Temin hypothesis that the constraint imposed by the Gold Standard prevented the use of expansionary monetary policies has not gone unchallenged. Bordo et al. (2002a) argue that while this argument is valid for small open economies, it does not apply to the USA, which 'held massive gold reserves' and was 'not constrained from using expansionary policy to offset banking panics'. Unfortunately, by the time the more stable democracies had abandoned their 'golden fetters' and begun to recover, the desperate economic conditions in Germany had helped to facilitate Hitler's rise to power. Thus, it can be argued that the most catastrophic result of the disastrous choices made by economic policy makers during the interwar period was the slaughter of humanity witnessed during 1939–45 (Eichengreen and Temin, 2002).

## 2.15   How to Pay for the War

According to Skidelsky (2000), from 1937 onwards Keynes began to devote his attention to the problems posed by rearmament in an economy as it 'neared full employment'. In a fully employed economy, room has to be created for the necessary increase in war production involved with rearmament. This could only be engineered by reducing the consumption component of aggregate demand given the need to maintain exports and investment expenditures. To achieve this objective, Keynes, in his *How to Pay for the War* (1940), advocated wartime fiscal restraint. This pamphlet is described by Vines (2003, p. 343) as a 'marvellous piece of applied economics' even if his plan was only partially adopted (Keynes believed that an alternative system of universal rationing amounted to 'Bolshevism'; see Skidelsky, 2000, p. 68). Keynes's analysis involved comparing aggregate demand, including war expenditures, with potential aggregate supply. Keynes (see Skidelsky, 2000, p. 84) defined the 'inflationary gap' as 'the amount of purchasing power which has to be withdrawn either by taxation or primary saving ... in order that the remaining purchasing power should be equal to the available supplies on the market at the existing level of prices'. The aim of fiscal restraint (forced saving) was to eliminate the 'inflationary gap' by reducing consumption. It should be noted that Keynes's proposal reveals his great faith in the price mechanism rather than bureaucratic control as the most efficient allocation mechanism even if at the macro level there was likely to be market failure requiring aggregate demand management.

An important side effect of Keynes's discussions in the Treasury after the outbreak of the Second World War was that it became increasingly obvious that there was an urgent need to develop and improve national income accounting calculations and procedures, and also there developed an increasing acceptance of the need for demand management both in depressions and booms. For Skidlesky (2000) the idea of demand management is Keynes's most important intellectual legacy. It also shows that Keynes was not an out-and-out expansionist. For Keynes, the need for demand management was symmetrical if both inflation and depressions were to be avoided. As Skidelsky (2000) makes clear, Keynes was always prepared to warn of the dangers posed by inflation. We should also remember that in the *General Theory* (1936, pp. 295–6) Keynes makes it clear that once full employment is achieved, 'the wage unit and prices will increase in exact proportion to the increase in effective demand', and we are back to the world where the classical model is relevant. But for Keynes (1936, p. 3) the classical world is a 'special case' and not the 'general case' of the 'society in which we actually live'.

## 2.16 Keynes and International Macroeconomics

Although Keynes is widely recognized as the economist who more than any other helped to create macroeconomics, according to Vines (2003), the final volume of Robert Skidelsky's magnificent biography of Keynes makes it clear that he also played a key role in the development of modern international macroeconomics. In 1945 the international economic system was in a complete shambles and it has taken over 50 years to rebuild the global economic system. In July 1944 representatives from 45 countries met at Bretton Woods in New Hampshire, USA, to discuss the post-war establishment of major international institutions whose purpose would be to facilitate international cooperation and increasing international economic integration and development, thereby improving the stability of the world economy. A major concern of the Bretton Woods delegates was to help prevent a recurrence of the disastrous events and consequences of economic mismanagement that had occurred during the interwar years. The outcome of the meeting was the creation of what John Maynard Keynes labelled the 'Bretton Woods twins', the International Monetary Fund (IMF) and the International Bank for Reconstruction and Development (IBRD), now known as the World Bank. While the main objective of the World Bank is to focus on long-term economic development and poverty reduction issues, the main objective of the IMF, as originally set out in its Articles of Agreement (Charter), is the short-run stabilization of the international monetary system. In December 1945, the IMF officially came into existence when 29 countries joined, and it finally began financial operations on 1 March 1947. The World Bank began formal operations on 25 June 1946. In addition, the General Agreement on Tariffs and Trade (GATT) was established in 1947, with the main purpose to promote trade liberalization by encouraging and facilitating the lowering of trade barriers. In a series of eight negotiating rounds before the current Doha Round, GATT succeeded in significantly cutting tariffs and reducing other barriers to trade. The GATT was never established as a formal institution but was set up as an interim device which would operate until the establishment of an international trade organization (ITO). In 1995 this was finally achieved with the establishment of the World Trade Organization (WTO).

Skidelsky describes Keynes as a 'joint author', along with Harry Dexter White, of the Bretton Woods international monetary system. Vines (2003, p. 339) goes further and argues that Keynes 'came to an extraordinary clear understanding of how pieces of the global economy interact, driven by policies of autonomous nations'. Keynes's work on British war finance and his quest to 'save Britain from financial ruin at the hands of the US at the end of the war' pushed him towards a sophisticated understanding of the emerging post-war international economic system. By 1945 Britain's economic and financial position was catastrophic. In response to this crisis Keynes's work during the last few years of his life created international macroeconomics and this contribution is 'as important as *any* of Keynes's achievements as an economist' (Vines, 2003, p. 339). Keynes's wartime work builds on his earlier contributions to international finance contained in *Indian Currency and Finance* (1913), *A Tract on Monetary Reform* (1923), *The Economic Consequences of the Peace* (1919), *The Economic Consequences of Mr. Churchill* (1925), and *A Treatise on Money* (1930).

Unlike the *General Theory*, which has a closed economy setting, Keynes's earlier work highlighted the workings of the international monetary system. Vines goes so far as to claim that 'Keynes invented' the two-country version of what later became the Mundell–Fleming IS–LM–BP model (see Chapter 3, section 3.5).

Keynes's extraordinary vision of the emerging shape of the international economic system had already crystallized by 1944. Vines relates a personal discussion he had with Nobel Memorial Laureate James Meade in which Meade recalled witnessing Keynes sketching out 'on the back of an envelope' something similar to Table 2.2 as his vision of the future.

*Table 2.2   Keynes and the international economic system, 1944*

| Objective | Instruments | Responsible authority |
|---|---|---|
| Full employment | Demand management (mainly fiscal) | National governments |
| Balance of payments adjustment | Pegged but adjustable exchange rates | International Monetary Fund |
| Promotion of international trade | Tariff reductions etc. | International Trade Organization |
| Economic development | Official international lending | World Bank |

*Source*:   Vines (2003).

While the GATT rather than an international trade organization was established in 1947, the vision contained in Table 2.2 is a remarkably accurate picture of what came to be known as the 'Bretton Woods system'.

## 2.17   Keynes's Legacy and the Classical Revival

Although the word 'macroeconomics' does not make its appearance in the economics literature until De Wolff's 1941 article in the *Economic Journal*, it was John Maynard Keynes who first pulled together in a single formal framework all the real and monetary variables necessary to investigate macroeconomic phenomena (Blanchard, 2000; Woodford, 2000). The dominance of Keynes in the emerging field of macroeconomics before his death in 1946 is clearly illustrated in the data on citations for the period 1920–44 contained in Tables 2.3–2.6.

*Table 2.3    Most-cited macroeconomists: 1920–30*

| Rank | Name | Number of citations |
|------|------|---------------------|
| 1 | Irving Fisher | 30 |
| 2 | W.C. Mitchell | 24 |
| 3 | A.C. Pigou | 21 |
| 4 | Alfred Marshall | 15 |
| 5 | W.S. Jevons | 13 |
| 6 | R.G. Hawtrey | 11 |
|   | D.H. Robertson | 11 |
| 8 | H.L. Moore | 10 |
|   | Carl Snyder | 10 |
| 10 | J.M. Keynes | 9 |

*Source*:   Deutscher (1990).

*Table 2.4    Most-cited macroeconomists: 1931–5*

| Rank | Name | Number of citations |
|------|------|---------------------|
| 1 | J.M. Keynes | 66 |
| 2 | D.H. Robertson | 44 |
| 3 | F. von Hayek | 33 |
| 4 | R.G. Hawtrey | 30 |
|   | I. Fisher | 30 |
| 6 | G. Cassel | 22 |
| 7 | A.C. Pigou | 20 |
| 8 | K. Wicksell | 17 |
| 9 | A. Hansen | 14 |
| 10 | A. Marshall | 13 |

*Source*:   Deutscher (1990).

The outstanding feature of this information is the extent to which Keynes came to dominate 'macroeconomics' by the mid-1930s. However, as we will see in the remaining chapters, the development of macroeconomics since 1936 has been a process of evolution overlain with periodic counter-revolutions and, as a result, in the 30 years after his death in 1946, 'Keynes's reputation soared and then crashed'. To a large extent, this change of fortune is related to the over-enthusiastic application of 'Keynesian' expansionary policies. Skidelsky (2000) concludes his third and final volume of his biography of Keynes by

*Table 2.5     Most-cited macroeconomists: 1936–9*

| Rank | Name | Number of citations |
|---|---|---|
| 1 | J. M. Keynes | 125 |
| 2 | D. H. Robertson | 48 |
| 3 | J. Hicks | 33 |
| 4 | A.C. Pigou | 31 |
| 5 | Roy Harrod | 27 |
| 6 | R.G. Hawtrey | 25 |
| 7 | F.von Hayek | 24 |
|  | G. Haberler | 24 |
| 9 | Joan Robinson | 20 |
| 10 | J.M. Clark | 18 |

*Source*:   Deutscher (1990).

*Table 2.6     Most-cited macroeconomists: 1940–44*

| Rank | Name | Number of citations |
|---|---|---|
| 1 | J.M. Keynes | 59 |
| 2 | J. Hicks | 30 |
| 3 | G. Haberler | 24 |
| 4 | D.H. Robertson | 22 |
| 5 | R.G. Hawtrey | 20 |
| 6 | M. Kalecki | 18 |
|  | J. Schumpeter | 18 |
| 8 | A. Hansen | 17 |
|  | N. Kaldor | 17 |
| 10 | S. Kuznets | 16 |
|  | A. Lerner | 16 |

*Source*:   Deutscher (1990).

highlighting four important elements in 'the Keynesian mindset' that prevailed during the 'Golden Age' from about 1950 until the early 1970s:

1. economies are viewed as 'sticky, not fluid', so they adjust to shocks relatively slowly;
2. there is a powerful political-economy argument that liberal democracies will not tolerate for long high and persistent levels of unemployment

such as those experienced during the interwar period of the twentieth century; so while 'in the long run we are all dead', in the short run, high unemployment may lead to revolution;

3. investment opportunities may flag in rich societies leading to secular stagnation;

4. many Keynesians professed a serious faith in statistical forecasting.

While Keynes certainly adhered to the first three of these elements, he was always 'deeply sceptical' of 'Joy through Statistics'. His followers exhibited less restraint. The long shadow cast by the experience of the Great Depression combined with a fear of secular stagnation was sufficient to fuel the case for frequent stimulation of aggregate demand and also led to the neglect of important supply-side considerations (see DeLong, 1998). While Keynes (1936, p. 16) was well aware that there were other sources of unemployment than demand deficiency, he understandably paid little attention to these in the *General Theory*. While Keynes understood that much of interwar British unemployment had a large structural component, to try to explain the simultaneous international outbreak of increasing rates of unemployment across the major capitalist economies after 1929 in terms of changing structural or frictional factors seemed completely implausible to him. The expected secular stagnation via a lack of investment opportunities also failed to materialize. As Abramovitz (1986, 1990) notes, a large backlog of unexploited technological opportunities arising from the interwar stagnation and failure of Western European industrialized countries to adopt the American system of mass production manufacturing, provided enormous scope for 'catch-up'. As a result capital investment had a high marginal productivity and the West experienced a long boom during the Golden Age.

Jeffrey Sachs (1999) has also argued that the impression given by the more extreme enthusiasts of demand management, that the Great Depression might somehow represent the normal functioning of market economies, turned out to be wrong. As discussed in section 2.14, we now know that the Great Depression was exceptional and largely the result of a perverse policy response. Sachs writes:

> The importance of the Great Depression in economic history is probably on a par with the First World War in political history. The Great Depression taught many lessons, most of them wrong. Keynes, the greatest political economist of the century, made a grave mistake when he titled his text *The General Theory of Employment, Interest and Money*. He left the impression that the Great Depression was a 'general' situation of market economies, not a one-time fluke of grotesque proportions. He failed to make clear that it occurred because of the international gold standard, a monetary arrangement that Keynes had heatedly attacked and abhorred, but strangely under-emphasised in the *General Theory*. In any event, the

Great Depression left the world deeply sceptical about the self-organising market system. It took decades to revive robust confidence in market economies.

So, from this perspective, Keynes's *General Theory* was 'not quite as general as he believed' (Skidelsky, 2000, p. 499).

Throughout the period after 1936 there have been numerous developments and contributions which reflect a hostile response to Keynes's *General Theory* and have ultimately contributed to a classical revival. The influence of Friedman and the monetarist counter-revolution represented a major challenge to the more simplistic versions and policy conclusions associated with hydraulic Keynesianism. In Friedman's (1983) opinion, 'While the *General Theory* is a great book, I do not regard it as his best ... I have been led to reject it ... because I believe that it has been contradicted by the evidence.'

In Chapter 4 we examine the important challenge to the Keynesian orthodoxy posed by monetarist analysis. Following this we examine the emergence of the new classical school, which launched a much more fundamental attack against Keynesianism during the 1970s. To many, this critique represents the most important challenge to date for the Keynesian conventional wisdom. For Lucas and Sargent, it is a simple matter of 'fact' that the predictions of Keynesian models were 'wildly incorrect' and based on a doctrine which is 'fundamentally flawed'. The 'spectacular failure' of Keynesian models in the 1970s has led to more attention and respect being accorded to 'the theoretical casualties of the Keynesian revolution, to the ideas of Keynes's contemporaries and of *earlier economists whose thinking has been regarded for years as outmoded*' (Lucas and Sargent, 1978, emphasis added).

Charles Plosser, a leading advocate of the new classical real business cycle approach to macroeconomic fluctuations, is also of the view that the Keynesian model is fundamentally flawed. In his opinion, 'the underpinnings of our understanding of economic fluctuations are likely to be found somewhere other than a suitably modified version of the Keynesian model' (Plosser, 1989). Minford and Peel (1983), in commenting on the impact of rational expectations on macroeconomics, feel that 'It has turned a body of knowledge – macroeconomics based on the neo-Keynesian or neo-classical systems of the late 1960s – upside down; virtually every topic ... has been found to be in need of rethinking'. In Chapters 5 and 6 we examine the development of the new classical ideas particularly associated with Lucas, Sargent, Barro, Prescott, Kydland and Plosser.

From the Austrian viewpoint, Friedrich von Hayek throughout his life remained a stern critic of Keynes and Keynesians. In Hayek's own words, Keynes was 'wholly wrong in the scientific work for which he is chiefly known' (Hayek, 1983). The powerful Austrian critique associated with the work of Hayek and his followers is reviewed in Chapter 9.

Although we do not deal with the 'public choice' perspective as a specific school, the perspective offered by Buchanan and Wagner (1978) is worth noting, given the influence such ideas have had on popular opinion. Buchanan and Wagner accuse Keynes of 'Intellectual error of monumental proportions' and assert that Keynesian economics 'has turned politicians loose; it has destroyed the effective constraint on politicians' ordinary appetites to spend and spend without the apparent necessity to tax' (see Chapter 10).

Only a great economist could stir up such reactions. In writing to Roy Harrod in 1935, Keynes made it clear that his attack on the classical economists in his forthcoming book was quite deliberate because he wanted 'to force the classicals to make a rejoiner'. His objective was, 'so to speak, to raise a dust' (see Skidelsky, 1992, p. 534). We can only conclude that in this objective Keynes was spectacularly successful!

In subsequent chapters as well as the interviews we will explore the reasons why economists have reached such a wide variety of conclusions.

# ROBERT SKIDELSKY

Robert Skidelsky was born in 1939 in China and graduated in 1960 from Jesus College, Oxford, where he also obtained his MA and DPhil, in 1961 and 1967, respectively. He was a research fellow at Nuffield College, Oxford (1965–8) and at the British Academy (1968–70), Associate Professor of History at Johns Hopkins University (1970–76), Head of Department of History, Philosophy and European Studies, Polytechnic of North London (1976–8), Professor of International Studies, University of Warwick (1978–90) and is currently Professor of Political Economy, University of Warwick (since 1990). He was made a life peer in 1991.

Professor Skidelsky is one of the leading authorities on Keynes and the interwar period. Among his best-known books are: *Politicians and the Slump* (Macmillan, 1967); *The End of the Keynesian Era* (editor) (Macmillan, 1977); *John Maynard Keynes, Vol. 1: Hopes Betrayed, 1883–1920* (Macmillan, 1983); *John Maynard Keynes, Vol. 2: The Economist as Saviour, 1920–1937* (Macmillan, 1992); *Keynes* (Oxford University Press, 1996); and *John Maynard Keynes, Vol. 3: Fighting for Britain 1937–46* (Macmillan, 2000).

His articles include: 'Keynes's Political Legacy' and 'Some Aspects of Keynes the Man', in O.F. Hamouda and J.N. Smithin (eds), *Keynes and Public Policy After Fifty Years, Vol. 1: Economics and Policy* (New York University Press, 1988); 'Keynes and the State', in D. Helm (ed.), *The Economic Borders of the State* (Oxford University Press, 1989); and 'The Influence of the Great Depression on Keynes's *General Theory*', *History of Economics Review*, Winter–Summer, 1996.

Together with Peter Wynarczyk (formerly Principal Lecturer in Economics at Northumbria University), we interviewed Professor Skidelsky in his office at Warwick University on 9 March 1993.

*Why did you decide to write a biography of Keynes?*
It evolved out of my earlier historical work relating to the interwar years. Keynes was a major presence in my previous books and a major source of inspiration for my view of that period. I thought he was an interesting person and I had better write about him. I came to that conclusion after reading the biography by Roy Harrod in which I thought there were things which were left too vague and unclear.

*Does your interpretation of Keynes's life and work differ in any fundamental way from that offered by Harrod and Moggridge?*
I am more historically minded. That may be the major difference. There are historical ways of thinking about phenomena and economic ways of thinking about them. Now I do not think you must draw a very sharp divide but economists tend to be generalizers and historians tend to concentrate on the idiosyncratic and unexpected. Historians make better biographers, on balance, than economists. For many economists, evidence is simply data rather than being history – the stuff of illumination. They treat history like statisticians. That is not a very illuminating approach to understanding a man's life or work.

*Why are there so many varied interpretations of Keynes's* General Theory? *Does this demonstrate the strength or weakness of the book?*
Probably the main reason is that Keynes was a fertile rather than a systematic thinker. He was much better over the short essay than over the treatise. His mind was always brimming with ideas, and he could not really stick to one line for any length of time. Too many things kept coming in. The second reason is that there was, in all his work, a strong polemical element. He wanted very much to do things. You have to sort out the polemics from the theory and it is not always very clear where one begins and the other ends. Keynes would always overemphasize one part of an argument in order to clinch a policy conclusion. The third reason is that Keynes operated on many different levels. You can pick and choose which level you find most attractive. That is why there are these different interpretations.

*Do you see this multidimensional picture as a strength?*

Yes, because, in the end, fertility is what lasts, not rigour. Rigour is for its own time, fertility is for all time.

*What elements of Marshall did Keynes reject and which did he retain in his intellectual journey from* The Tract *to the* General Theory*?*
The most obvious thing is that he took from Marshall his particular method of dealing with time. He made a clear distinction, in many of his writings, between the short period and the long period – that came straight out of Marshall. But one must not take that too rigidly because Keynes retained a fairly open mind about the analytic method he would use till quite late in the writing of the *General Theory* – whether to use a short period equilibrium framework or to use a disequilibrium framework. Secondly, he probably never deviated much from Marshall's theory of the firm and he always, rather illogically, accepted Marshall's perfect competition models, despite Marshall's acceptance of increasing returns. Keynes never thought much beyond that, which is why he was really very uninterested in the imperfect competition revolution. I always found that fascinating, paradoxical and odd. The evidence is that although he was a great admirer of Piero Sraffa, he never took on board that element of the Cambridge revolution starting with Sraffa's [1926] article leading through to Joan Robinson's [1933] contribution. This was partly because he remained very Marshallian on the supply side of microeconomics and perhaps as confused as Marshall was on one or two of these issues. Keynes believed in a third-generation theory of the firm and tended to assume that firms decayed naturally before they established any serious monopolistic position in the market. The third influence was the idea that you should not take wants as given and that there were higher-value wants. But, unlike Marshall, he thought that these higher-value wants were derived from philosophy rather than from evolution. Fourthly, Keynes took from Marshall the cash-balances version of the quantity theory of money. He always thought about the quantity theory in that way and not in the Fisher way. That's how he got into the *Treatise on Money* and beyond that into the *General Theory*. These legacies of Marshall were enormously important.

*How would you characterize Keynes's methodological stance?*
I think Keynes was only weakly verificationist. He would not have much favoured the view that hypotheses can be verified by tests of one kind or another – certainly not hypotheses in the social or moral sciences. In fact that was the root cause of his opposition to econometrics. He thought that the most important thing about a theory is that it must be fertile and atuned to one's intuitions. He thought data were very important in forming these intuitions: you should not ignore the real world. You should be a vigilant observer, this was one of the economist's most important tasks, but it was raw

stuff, it was not doctored or predigested. The kind of stuff modern economists look at is all pre-done, the curves are already there. Keynes hated
economic data presented as graphs – that is why he never used graphs in any
of his writings, and the one diagram contained in the *General Theory* was
provided by Harrod. He always wanted the actual figures. The figures were
not to verify hypotheses; they were to indicate the sort of limits of the
validity of our intuitions. If the figures were totally contrary to your intuitions
then probably your intuition is wrong – but it was a rough and ready kind of
testing: nothing that could claim to be verificationist theory. What he would
have said about Popper's falsifiability method I do not know. He may have
been more interested in that.

*Given your detailed biographical work on Keynes, were there any real sur-
prises which you unearthed in your research?*
The surprises, if at all, arise from the historical treatment itself, by embedding
Keynes's ideas very carefully in historical and biographical situations, including values and, therefore, paying greater attention to the more ephemeral
writings. It is usually there that one can see the mind in action and at the edge
of things. I find his lectures from the period 1931–3 to be much more interesting, in a way, than the *General Theory* itself, because you can see the whole
thing raw. You can actually see more clearly what was going into it. When he
was writing his *Treatise on Probability*, he wrote to Lytton Strachey and said, 'I
am now turning my stuff into a more formal treatise and everything original
that I have thought is going to be snuffed out in the course of doing it because
that is what academic life is like.' Now that is not quite true; of course, the
*General Theory* was thought to be a revolutionary book when it came out. But I
think some of the raw energy that went into the creation of it was lost.

*You have written that 'Keynes's inspiration was radical, his purpose con-
servative' – how did Keynes reconcile these conflicting forces?*
Well, the best answer to that was given by Galbraith, who said people who
are radical in monetary matters are usually social conservatives. In other
words, there is a certain kind of therapy for an economy which is non-
structural, which serves the purpose of preserving the existing structures.
That does not give rise to a problem, in my mind. If you think of some of the
competing radicalisms of Keynes's time, particularly Marxism, you do see
that Keynes's theory was, by comparison with that, very conservative about
the social order, and deliberately so. He said, time and again, if you do not
accept my modest remedies you will be faced with having to accept much
more disagreeable ones sooner or later. I do not think his theory was simply
instrumental to preserving the existing social order but he had that as an aim
in his mind. He also really did believe that, with some small changes in the

way things were run, you could avoid the worst of business fluctuations and stabilize the economy. You could do this by improvements in economic science. So in terms of economic theory he was eventually very radical, but in terms of the concluding notes of the *General Theory* he maintains that his theory is moderately conservative.

*What exactly did Keynes mean when he talked about the 'socialisation of investment'?*

Keynes was a political operator and it was one of those phrases tossed out to the Labour Party. That phrase comes out of the 1920s when he was talking about the growth of socialistic institutions in the womb of capitalism. By the late 1920s he was really arguing that a large part of private enterprise was not properly private any longer; it was, in some sense, socialized because its managers paid more attention to stability than short-run profit maximization. Once firms reached a certain size they also started developing public motives and responsibilities and they tended to be run by people who are much more like civil servants and dons than old-style thrusting Schumpeterian entrepreneurs. So I think the socialization of investment minimally meant simply a growing tendency for investment criteria to be social, arising from the natural evolution of the capitalist system. I think Galbraith has something of the same thought in his *New Industrial State* [1967].

*How would you account for the very rapid spread of Keynesian ideas, especially in the USA?*

Well, did they spread very rapidly in the USA? Within academia you find a very patchy picture if you look at the USA as a whole. Harvard, yes, certainly. The Harvard–Washington nexus has been very well explored. Once Keynesianism could take a tax remission form rather than a public spending form, then, of course, you got quite a lot of conservative business support. You could always give it a supply-side justification. That is why you had a Reagan version of Keynes in the 1980s. There was a much more modest built-in stabilizers version in the 1940s and 1950s. I personally think Keynes had more effect on Roosevelt's New Deal than he has latterly been given credit for, especially in the first phase of the New Deal, the pre-*General Theory* phase. But, as in Britain, Keynesianism really arrived in connection with wartime finance.

*Would you draw a clear separation between the work of Keynes and the contributions of Keynesians? In particular, what is your view of the IS–LM interpretation?*

You always have to draw a distinction between the work of an original pioneer and that of his followers. The fertility, innocence and sharpness of the original version is modified and made acceptable for the ordinary business of life. Keynes was always quite careful to have a portion of his theory that could be modelled, even though he did not particularly spend much time modelling it himself. It was left for others to do that, not only Hicks, but Harrod and Meade; the whole thing was reduced to a set of simultaneous equations, an approach which was not true to Keynes's own spirit. He was much more a chain equation person, being far more interested in chains of causation, and trying to work those out. Hicks emptied the *General Theory* of its real bite, he generalized and increased its acceptability, whilst laying the basis for the neoclassical synthesis. It was a very important PR job but I do not think it captured the essence of what Keynes was trying to say. In fact, Hicks conceded this. The interesting point is Keynes's reaction to Hicks's interpretation. Here I do differ somewhat from Don Patinkin, who has always argued that Keynes accepted the Hicks version as an entirely accurate representation of his theory. That Keynes never criticized it is perfectly true. My own feeling is that Keynes, although it sounds odd to say this, never grasped the significance of it and never thought it particularly interesting. He never reacted to it, that is the important point. It is not that he said that this is marvellous or awful, he just never reacted and that is puzzling. He was a punctilious correspondent. Hicks sent it to him, yet he did not reply for six months, and then said 'I have got nothing to say about this', apart from one or two points which seemed rather unimportant. But it does seem to me he thought Hicks was not a very interesting thinker. He said Hicks had got a good beta plus mind. That was a mistake. There was something about Hicks Keynes did not respond to – in exactly the same way Kaldor never did. Kaldor once said to me that Hicks was not a great economist because 'a great economist has to be a pamphleteer – Hicks is a judge, he weighs up everything and takes a middle view. That is not the tradition of Adam Smith at all. Keynes was in that tradition, I, Kaldor, am in that tradition, Hicks is not.' There was some lack of sympathy between Keynes and Hicks which meant that Keynes tended to ignore anything which Hicks did.

*Did Keynes give the classics a rough deal in the* General Theory*?*
Yes. He set up an Aunt Sally. No classical economist ever believed in the things Keynes claimed that classical economics stood for and none of his associates did really. Neither Robertson, Hawtrey nor Hayek were classical economists. The only classical economist was someone like Pigou. Keynes was quite deliberate. He said the things he was describing as classical economics were not what the economists of his day actually believed in, but the things they would need to believe to make sense of what they were saying. Keynes was challenging them to make their premises consistent with their conclusions.

*If the* General Theory *had been written in 1926, could the economic disaster experienced in the 1930s have been avoided?*
No, I do not think that the *General Theory* could have been published ten years earlier. That particular indictment of classical economics and, indeed, of the way the economy behaved needed the great slump to crystallize it. Keynes's books were very good reflections of the experience of the different decades. The *Treatise on Money* sums up the 1920s and had nothing to do with the great slump. It is an open economy model where one country is not doing very well. The *General Theory* is a book about a world slump and, therefore, there is no escape except through the government. But your question, in addition, seems to be asking: if people had been equipped with better theory, would they have had better policy? You needed not only the better theory but also the better theory *to be accepted*, and that is very different. My hunch is that all theories of a Keynesian type, paradoxically, start to wilt a bit if things get very, very bad. They are most acceptable when they are least needed. In other words, everyone was Keynesian in the 1950s and 1960s when there was no pressure. As soon as the pressure starts you find that orthodoxy has a habit of coming back and here is a psychological puzzle: when people are under great stress and there is a great increase in nervousness, then people do cling to the oldest of their verities, not the newfangled ones.

*Do you think too much has been made of the Pigou effect as a way of diminishing Keynes's theoretical contribution? Did he not anticipate but reject this idea himself?*
In the 1920s it came under the rubric of 'induced lacking' which Keynes added to Dennis Robertson's *Banking Policy and the Price Level* [1926]. This is where you increase your saving in order to restore the real value of your cash balances eroded by inflation, and that is an equilibrating mechanism, and Keynes suggested this real-balance effect to Robertson. Why did Keynes not see it working in reverse, in a situation of deflation? I think the answer is that he was not thinking along those equilibrium lines. I know Presley [1986] makes out the case that he was, but I did not find his argument persuasive. In the case of the Pigou effect, why did not Keynes admit it as a sort of theoretical possibility and then simply discount it as irrelevant or very weak? I do not know. Keynes was greatly concerned about the consequences of a community becoming increasingly impoverished, rather than mechanical adjustments of balances.

*To what extent was there a Keynesian revolution in the UK and USA in the post-Second World War period? Do you think Keynes would have approved of the policies so often carried out in his name?*

It is hard to say that there was not a revolution. Some commentators have doubted whether there was. It still seems to me that if you commit yourself to maintain a high and stable level of employment you are saying something new, and governments had not said that before. How much you intend to do about it is another matter. But once you have produced a form of words, even politicians are somewhat constrained by them. And, of course, they would only have made that pledge, had they had a somewhat different model of the economy than they had before the war, and some experience of Keynesian fiscal management, which came in the Second World War. So there was a worldwide Keynesian revolution which was obviously different in different countries. Everyone took what they wanted from Keynes and added it to their own traditions.

*How fundamental are the 'presuppositions of Harvey Road' to Keynes the political economist? Surely the contributions made by the public choice school and from the political business cycle literature have shown Keynes to have been politically naive?*
No, I would not accept that. You cannot really say that someone was naive unless they lived through the relevant period and failed to register the findings of that period. It is not the right word to use about Keynes and I think his political views would have developed had he lived through the 1960s and 1970s. The assumptions that he made at the time probably fitted the facts of the time rather better than they fitted the facts of later times.

*Other than Keynes, who in your view has had the most important influence on the post-*General Theory *development of macroeconomics?*
Undoubtedly Friedman. Both as a challenger to Keynes and as a leader of thought in his own right. The Friedmanite challenge to Keynes also led into the rational expectations revolution. It is very, very important to understand that Friedman is a macroeconomist and shares many of Keynes's presuppositions of the role of macroeconomics in stabilizing economies. Friedman has always given high praise to Keynes's *Tract on Monetary Reform*. The other great economist of the twentieth century was Hayek, but Hayek disbelieved in macroeconomics; he did not believe it to be a valid science because he was a methodological individualist of a very extreme kind.

*Given Keynes's emphasis upon the importance of expectations in the* General Theory, *what do you think he would have made of the rational expectations hypothesis and the new classical models developed by Lucas and others?*
Again, it is terribly difficult, because you are really asking a question about Keynes's epistemology and that takes you into his *Treatise on Probability* and how you talk about the rationality of beliefs. There are flashes of rational

expectations in Keynes – you could tell a rational expectations story about the instantaneous multiplier if you wanted to, since you expect or anticipate all of the effects immediately – but on the whole, surely, his leading idea was uncertain expectations.

*David Laidler* [1992b] *has drawn attention to the low standards of historical scholarship amongst economists. As a historian and an economist would you agree with this view?*
Yes, I think so, partly for the reasons I have outlined earlier. Economists are not very good historians and I believe this comes out particularly in connection with Keynesian studies which emphasize or pay exclusive attention to a single book – the *General Theory* – and which show a lack of interest as to how it fits into the whole of his thought and the history of the time. One of the few economists who understood that was Axel Leijonhufvud [1968], who took the *Treatise on Money* seriously and tried to build up a picture of Keynesian theory that was halfway between the *Treatise on Money* and the *General Theory*. That was a very interesting exercise. The new scholarship has taken seriously the problem of linking Keynes's later economic writings to his earlier philosophical writing, but this approach is curiously unhistorical. They do not, for example, see the *Treatise on Probability* as a work of before 1914, which is what a historian would instinctively see it as, and root it there. These new scholars simply set it side by side with the *General Theory* and explore the differences and similarities. That is not history.

*Which non-economic elements most influenced Keynes's economics?*
I would have thought there were three key non-economic elements. First, the classics, which he studied at school, and his sense of the classical world and its methods. There are lots of classical and fairy-tale allusions in his writings. Second, theology. A lot of his language, and the way he used it, was quite theological. After all, economics was theology's successor and retains many of its characteristics. Third, the arts. What is economic activity for? This comes out especially in essays like 'Economic Possibilities for our Grand-children' [1930]. Aesthetics influenced his view of the role of economics.

*The vehement opposition to the UK's membership of the ERM expressed by leading British monetarists such as Alan Walters and Patrick Minford bears an uncanny resemblance to Keynes's attack upon Churchill in the 1920s. Are the two episodes similar?*
The two episodes are similar in many ways. In both cases the pound was overvalued and insufficient attention was paid to the adjustment process. Keynes's opposition to the Gold Standard was based upon the argument of the *Tract on Monetary Reform*, which is very monetarist. It has to do with the

lag system in the adjustment to new sets of prices or exchange rates. But I do
not think that Keynes was ever a currency floater in the 1970s monetarist
sense. He wanted a managed system, and remember he was one of the main
architects of the Bretton Woods system. In a world in which there were no
controls on capital and where you had a financial system that was much more
deregulated than it was even in Keynes's day, one may conjecture whether he
would have thought that we cannot win the game against speculators; hence
the attempt to maintain fixed exchange rates is doomed to failure.

*Despite the crisis in Keynesianism, widely recognized in the 1970s, such
ideas are now experiencing something of a resurgence. How do you account
for this? Do you see an emerging consensus, perhaps, where Keynesianism
again has a focal point in macroeconomics?*
Well, yes. Keynes said two things that seem to me of permanent value and
must be part of anyone's thinking about the way economies work. Firstly, he
emphasized uncertainty leading to volatility. Speculation is the balancer of
economies and the way it balances is through extreme volatility in other
markets. Secondly, he emphasized repercussions on income, output and prices,
rather than prices alone. These two things are very important and any modern
understanding of the way economies work must bear them in mind. If you
believe economies are volatile, that recessions are sufficiently severe and that
their effects do not go away automatically, then that dictates some role for
government. Other economists say that government should not play very
much of a role, just follow a few rules. This is where the real debate is and I
am on Keynes's side. That does not mean that we shall exactly follow Keynes's
own prescriptions. Times change and his policies would have changed with
them.

*If Keynes had still been alive in 1969, do you think he would have received
the first Nobel Prize in Economics?*
Ah [*laughter*]. Well, all one can say is yes [*further laughter*].

# 3. The orthodox Keynesian school

> The Keynesian revolution was the most significant event in 20th-century economic science. (Samuelson, 1988)

## 3.1 Introduction

In the decade or so following the publication of the *General Theory* economists engaged in the Keynes v. Classics debate sought to clarify the arguments of Keynes and the counter-arguments of his critics. For example, a major theme of Modigliani's (1944) paper was to show that, except for the case of extreme wage rigidity, Keynes's system did allow for a restoration of full employment equilibrium via price flexibility, aside for some special limiting cases. However, by the mid-1950s Samuelson (1955) declared a truce. He argued that 90 per cent of American economists had ceased to be anti- or pro-Keynesian but were now committed to a 'neoclassical synthesis' where it was generally accepted that neoclassical microeconomics and Keynesian macroeconomics could sit alongside each other. The classical/neoclassical model remained relevant for microeconomic issues and the long-run analysis of growth, but orthodox Keynesian macroeconomics provided the most useful framework for analysing short-run aggregate phenomena. This historical compromise remained the dominant paradigm in economics until the 1970s.

The main purpose of this chapter is fourfold: first, to review one highly influential orthodox Keynesian interpretation of Keynes's (1936) *General Theory*, namely the Hicksian IS–LM model for a closed economy, before considering more fully the theoretical debate on underemployment equilibrium in the context of that model (sections 3.3–3.4); second, to consider the effectiveness of fiscal and monetary policy for stabilization purposes when the model is extended to an open economy (section 3.5); third, to discuss the original Phillips curve analysis and comment on the importance of the Phillips curve to orthodox Keynesian analysis (section 3.6); and finally, in the light of this discussion, to summarize the central propositions of orthodox Keynesian economics (section 3.7).

The reader should be aware that throughout this and subsequent chapters two recurrent and interrelated issues arise, concerning (i) the controversy over the self-equilibrating properties of the economy and (ii) the role for interventionist government policies. We begin our discussion with the early orthodox Keynesian approach to these central issues within macroeconomics.

## 3.2  The Orthodox Keynesian School

For the early post-war years the central distinguishing beliefs within the orthodox Keynesian school can be listed as follows:

1.  The economy is inherently unstable and is subject to erratic shocks. These shocks are attributed primarily to changes in the marginal efficiency of investment following a change in the state of business confidence, or what Keynes referred to as a change in investors' 'animal spirits' (see Chapter 2, section 2.8).
2.  Left to its own devices the economy can take a long time to return to the neighbourhood of full employment after being subjected to some disturbance; that is, the economy is not rapidly self-equilibrating.
3.  The aggregate level of output and employment is essentially determined by aggregate demand and the authorities can intervene to influence the level of aggregate 'effective' demand to ensure a more rapid return to full employment.
4.  In the conduct of stabilization policy, fiscal as opposed to monetary policy is generally preferred as the effects of fiscal policy measures are considered to be more direct, predictable and faster acting on aggregate demand than those of monetary policy. These beliefs found expression in the orthodox Keynesian model, known as the IS–LM model, to which we now turn.

## 3.3  The IS–LM Model for a Closed Economy

The orthodox Keynesian model which has had such an important bearing on the development of macroeconomics, right through to the present day, initially stemmed from Hicks's (1937) famous article entitled 'Mr. Keynes and the "Classics": A Suggested Interpretation'. This Hicksian model was subsequently elaborated upon by Modigliani (1944) and was popularized in the USA by Hansen (1949, 1953). Indeed, over the next half-century the Hicksian IS–LM model became the established model for macroeconomic theorizing and it had a tremendous influence on the direction of macroeconomic policy right up to the mid-1960s.

It is assumed that most readers will at least be familiar with the derivation of the IS–LM model, so that in what follows initially we merely review the main features of the model for a closed economy, in particular the way the model integrates real and monetary factors in determining aggregate demand

and therefore the level of output and employment. Those readers who are unfamiliar with the derivation of the model (or the extension of the model to an open economy) should refer to any standard macroeconomics text, such as Dornbusch et al. (2004). We begin our review with the goods market and the *IS* curve.

### 3.3.1  The goods market and the *IS* curve

Equilibrium in the goods market occurs where the aggregate demand for and aggregate supply of goods are equal. In the orthodox Keynesian model the level of output and employment is assumed to be determined entirely by aggregate demand; that is, supply constraints are ignored. In a closed economy aggregate demand comprises the sum of consumption, government expenditure and investment. In order to simplify the analysis, consumption expenditure is held to depend positively on disposable income, government expenditure is taken as being exogenously determined, while investment is treated as being inversely related to the rate of interest, a variable determined within the model by the interaction of the goods and money markets.

The *IS* curve traces out a locus of combinations of interest rates and income associated with equilibrium in the goods market. The *IS* curve derives its name from the equilibrium condition in the goods market where, in a closed economy with no government sector, investment (*I*) equals savings (*S*). Given the assumption that investment is inversely related to the rate of interest, the *IS* curve is downward-sloping (see Figure 3.2). *Ceteris paribus*, as the rate of interest falls, investment increases, resulting in a higher level of income. The slope of the *IS* curve depends on the interest elasticity of investment expenditure and the value of the multiplier (see Chapter 2, section 2.8). The *IS* curve will be steeper (flatter) the less (more) investment responds to a change in the rate of interest and the smaller (greater) is the value of the multiplier. For example, *ceteris paribus*, the less investment increases for a given fall in the rate of interest, the less income will increase, generating a steeper *IS* curve. Similarly, the smaller the value of the multiplier, the less income will increase following a given increase in investment, and hence the steeper the *IS* curve will be. In the limiting (extreme Keynesian) case where investment is perfectly interest-inelastic, the *IS* curve will be vertical.

Finally, it is important to remember that the *IS* curve is drawn for a given level of government expenditure, taxation and expectations, so that expansionary fiscal policy (that is, an increase in government expenditure and/or a reduction in taxation, or a more optimistic business outlook) shifts the *IS* curve outwards to the right, and vice versa. For example, an increase in government expenditure will be associated with a higher level of income at any given level of the rate of interest, the outward shift of the *IS* curve being equal to the increase in government expenditure times the value of the multiplier. We now turn to the money market and the *LM* curve.

### 3.3.2 The money market and the *LM* curve

Equilibrium in the money market occurs where the demand for and supply of money are equal. The money supply is assumed to be exogenously determined by the authorities. Within the model three main motives for holding money are identified: the transactions, the precautionary and the speculative motives. The demand for transactions and precautionary balances is assumed to vary positively with income. The demand for speculative or idle balances depends on the current level of the rate of interest relative to the normal rate of interest. By assuming that different people have different expectations about the future course of the rate of interest, it is possible to postulate that the demand for speculative balances will vary inversely with the rate of interest (see Figure 3.1). The higher the current level of the rate of interest (relative to the level regarded as normal), the greater the number of individuals who expect future reductions in the rate of interest (and therefore rising bond prices) and the less speculative balances demanded, and vice versa. Of particular importance is the theoretical possibility that, at low interest rates, which would be expected to prevail in conditions of underemployment equilibrium, the demand for money could become perfectly elastic with respect to the rate of interest. This is illustrated by the horizontal section of the curve at $r^*$ in Figure 3.1. At $r^*$ expectations converge as everyone expects that the only future course of the rate of interest is upwards, so that the demand for money becomes perfectly interest-elastic: the so-called 'liquidity trap'. With regard to the liquidity trap, it is interesting to note that Keynes put it forward only as a theoretical possibility and even commented that he was not aware of it ever having been operative in practice (see Keynes, 1936, p. 207). Nevertheless, as we will discuss in section 3.4.2, it became especially important to the analysis of underemployment equilibrium in the orthodox Keynesian model.

The *LM* curve traces out a locus of combinations of interest rates and income associated with equilibrium in the money market. The *LM* curve derives its name from the equilibrium condition in the money market where the demand for money, or what Keynes called liquidity preference (*L*), equals the supply of money (*M*). Given the assumption that the demand for money is positively/negatively related to income/interest rate, the *LM* curve is upward-sloping (see Figure 3.2). *Ceteris paribus*, as income rises the transactions and precautionary demand for money increase, which, given the supply of money, necessitates a higher rate of interest to reduce the speculative demand for money and maintain equilibrium in the money market. The slope of the *LM* curve depends on the income elasticity and the interest elasticity of the demand for money. The *LM* curve will be steeper (flatter) the higher (smaller) the income elasticity and

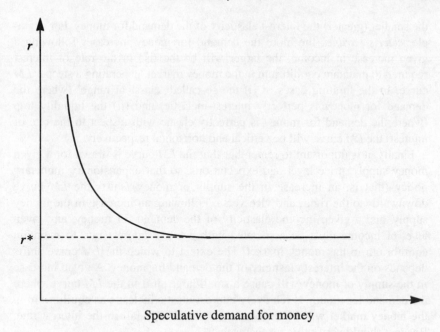

**Speculative demand for money**

*Figure 3.1    Demand for speculative balances*

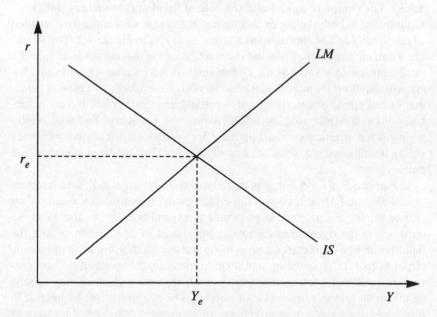

*Figure 3.2    The generalized IS–LM model*

the smaller (greater) the interest elasticity of the demand for money. For example, *ceteris paribus*, the more the demand for money increases following a given increase in income, the larger will be the rise in the rate of interest required to maintain equilibrium in the money market, generating a steeper *LM* curve. In the limiting cases of (i) the so-called 'classical range' (where the demand for money is perfectly interest-inelastic) and (ii) the liquidity trap (where the demand for money is perfectly elastic with respect to the rate of interest) the *LM* curve will be vertical and horizontal respectively.

Finally, it is important to remember that the *LM* curve is drawn for a given money supply, price level and expectations, so that expansionary monetary policy (that is, an increase in the supply of money) shifts the *LM* curve downwards to the right, and vice versa. Following an increase in the money supply, and a given income elasticity of the demand for money, any given level of income must be associated with a lower interest rate to maintain equilibrium in the money market. The extent to which the *LM* curve shifts depends on the interest elasticity of the demand for money. A given increase in the supply of money will cause a small/large shift in the *LM* curve where the demand for money is relatively interest-elastic/inelastic as equilibrium in the money market will be restored by a small/large fall in the interest rate. Readers should verify this for themselves.

### 3.3.3 The complete model and the role of fiscal and monetary policy

Equilibrium in both the goods and money markets is simultaneously attained where the *IS* and *LM* curves intersect, that is, at $r_e Y_e$ in Figure 3.2. Two points are worth emphasizing. First, the intersection of the two curves in Figure 3.2 represents the *only* value of the rate of interest and income which is consistent with equilibrium in both markets. Second, if the level of income is below that of full employment, then both fiscal and monetary policy have a potentially important role to play in stabilizing the economy. We now briefly review what determines the relative effectiveness of fiscal and monetary policy in influencing aggregate demand and therefore the level of output and employment.

In Figure 3.3, the economy is initially in equilibrium at $r_0 Y_0$ (the intersection of $IS_0$ and *LM*) at less than full employment. Expansionary fiscal policy (for example, an increase in government expenditure) shifts the *IS* curve outwards to the right, from $IS_0$ to $IS_1$, and results in an increase in both the equilibrium rate of interest (from $r_0$ to $r_1$) and the equilibrium level of income (from $Y_0$ to $Y_1$). As spending and income increase, the transactions and precautionary demand for money increase, which, with a fixed money supply, results in an increase in the rate of interest. The rise in the rate of interest in turn leads to a reduction in private sector investment spending, the extent of which depends on the interest elasticity of investment. Readers should verify

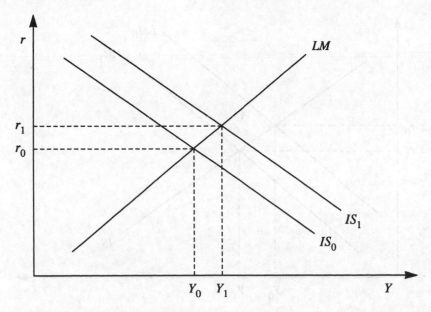

*Figure 3.3   Expansionary fiscal policy*

for themselves that fiscal policy will be more effective in influencing aggregate demand and therefore the level of output and employment (i) the more interest-elastic is the demand for money; that is, the flatter is the *LM* curve, and (ii) the less interest-elastic is investment; that is, the steeper is the *IS* curve. In the limiting cases of (i) a vertical *LM* curve (classical range) fiscal expansion will have no effect on income, as the rise in the rate of interest will reduce private investment by an amount identical to the increase in government expenditure; that is, complete (100 per cent) crowding out or the so-called 'Treasury View'; and (ii) a horizontal *LM* curve (liquidity trap) fiscal expansion will result in the full multiplier effect of the simple Keynesian 45° or cross model.

In Figure 3.4, the economy is again initially in equilibrium at $r_0Y_0$ (the intersection of $LM_0$ and $IS$) at less than full employment. Expansionary monetary policy shifts the *LM* curve downwards to the right, from $LM_0$ to $LM_1$, and results in a fall in the equilibrium rate of interest (from $r_0$ to $r_1$) and an increase in the equilibrium level of income (from $Y_0$ to $Y_1$). Within the orthodox Keynesian transmission mechanism the strength of monetary policy depends on (i) the degree to which the rate of interest falls following an increase in the money supply; (ii) the degree to which investment responds to a fall in the rate of interest; and (iii) the size of the multiplier. Readers should verify for themselves that monetary policy will be more effective in influenc-

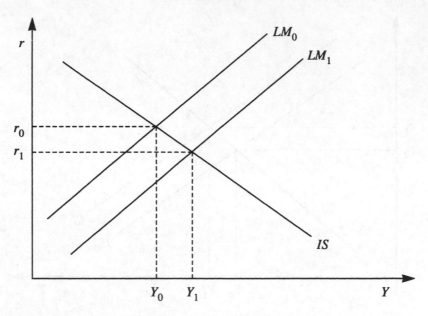

*Figure 3.4   Expansionary monetary policy*

ing aggregate demand and therefore the level of output and employment (i) the more interest-inelastic is the demand for money; that is, the steeper is the *LM* curve, and (ii) the more interest-elastic is investment; that is, the flatter is the *IS* curve. In the limiting (extreme Keynesian) cases of either (i) a horizontal *LM* curve (liquidity trap) or (ii) a vertical *IS* curve (that is, where investment is completely interest-inelastic) the transmission mechanism breaks down and monetary policy will have no effect on the level of income.

From the above discussion it should be evident that, while both fiscal and monetary policy can, in normal circumstances, be used to influence the level of output and employment, the relative effectiveness of these two policy instruments depends on the structural parameters of the model, that is, the relative slopes of the *IS* and *LM* curves. Within the orthodox Keynesian approach, the demand for money has traditionally been viewed as being highly responsive to changes in the rate of interest (generating a relatively flat *LM* curve), while investment has been taken as being fairly unresponsive to changes in the rate of interest (generating a relatively steep *IS* curve). Indeed, there was early empirical support for orthodox Keynesianism associated with the elasticities of the *IS* and *LM* curves, with Klein referring to its 'solid empirical basis' (see Klein, 1968, pp. 65–6, pp. 71–2) – a basis, we hasten to add, which became increasingly questionable in the early 1960s. In these circumstances disturbances from the real side of the economy (that is, stochastic shifts in the *IS* curve) tend to dominate changes in income. Furthermore, fiscal policy is generally preferred as it is relatively powerful, while monetary policy is relatively weak. At this point the reader should note that by the end of the 1950s the belief in the efficacy of fiscal policy relative to monetary policy was much stronger among British as compared to American Keynesians.

This analysis can also be summarized in algebraic terms. In what follows it is assumed that the price level is fixed when the economy is at less than full employment. Aggregate real expenditure (*E*) is equal to an autonomous component (*A*), a component dependent on real income (*cY*) and an interest-sensitive component (*ar*).

$$E = A + cY - ar \tag{3.1}$$

Equilibrium in the goods market occurs where the aggregate demand for and aggregate supply of goods are equal.

$$E = Y \tag{3.2}$$

Turning to the money market, the demand for real money balances (*M/P*) has a component dependent on real income (*mY*) and an interest-sensitive component (*br*).

$$\frac{M}{P} = mY - br \tag{3.3}$$

The supply of nominal money balances is assumed to be exogenously determined ($\overline{M}_s$). Equilibrium in the money market occurs where the demand for and supply of money are equal.

$$\frac{M}{P} = \frac{\overline{M}_s}{P} \tag{3.4}$$

Rearranging these relationships and solving the system for *Y* gives:

$$Y = \frac{1}{1 - \left(c - \frac{a}{b}m\right)} A + \frac{1}{m + \frac{b}{a}(1 - c)} \frac{\overline{M}_s}{P} \tag{3.5}$$

Within this framework, orthodox Keynesians can be characterized as low *a* and high *b* people. Reference to equation (3.5) reveals that, where the ratio *a/b* is small, (i) disturbances from the real side of the economy tend to dominate changes in income, and (ii) fiscal policy is relatively powerful with the autonomous expenditure multiplier tending to $1/1 - c$, while monetary policy is relatively weak with the money multiplier tending to zero. These central distinguishing beliefs of orthodox Keynesians were noted earlier, in section 3.2.

The orthodox Keynesian faith in the effectiveness of fiscal policy has been challenged by, among others, monetarists who typically argue that in the long run 'pure' fiscal expansion (that is, expansion without any accommodating changes in the money supply) will result in the crowding out or replacement of components of private expenditure with relatively minor effects on aggregate demand, the level of income and employment. A number of reasons as to why crowding out can occur in the IS–LM framework have been put forward in the literature, which do not rely on the demand for money being perfectly interest-inelastic (a vertically sloped *LM* curve), including expectations and wealth effects (see Carlson and Spencer, 1975). In what follows we outline the Keynesian response which reasserted the importance of fiscal policy (see Blinder and Solow, 1973) focusing on the wealth effects of a bond-financed increase in government expenditure. This analysis involves an extended version of the Keynesian IS–LM model incorporating the government budget constraint.

The top panel of Figure 3.5 depicts the conventional IS–LM model and the lower panel the government budget position determined by the relationship between government expenditure ($G$), which is assumed to be independent of income, and tax receipts ($T$), which are endogenous to the level of income. At $Y_0$ (the intersection of $IS_0$ and *LM*) both the goods and money markets are in equilibrium and the government budget is balanced ($G_0 = T$); that is, a stable equilibrium position prevails. Suppose the authorities now seek to raise the level of income and employment by increasing their expenditure. An increase in government expenditure shifts the *IS* curve outwards to the right, from $IS_0$ to $IS_1$, and the government expenditure function downwards, from $G_0$ to $G_1$. At $Y_1$ (the intersection of $IS_1$ and *LM*) there is a budget deficit equal to *AB*. As long as the deficit persists, the authorities will have to issue more bonds, which will lead to an increase in private sector wealth (owing to increased bond holdings) and an increase in private consumption expenditure and the demand for money. If the wealth effect on consumption (which shifts the *IS* curve further outwards to the right, as indicated by the arrows) outweighs that on the demand for money (which shifts the *LM* curve upwards to the left), then in the long run bond-financed fiscal expansion will result in income increasing to $Y_2$, where the deficit will be removed; that is, crowding out will be absent. Furthermore, if increased interest payments arising from bond finance are taken into account (shifting the government expenditure function downwards beyond $G_1$), income will have to rise above $Y_2$ in order to balance the government budget. It is evident therefore that incorporating wealth

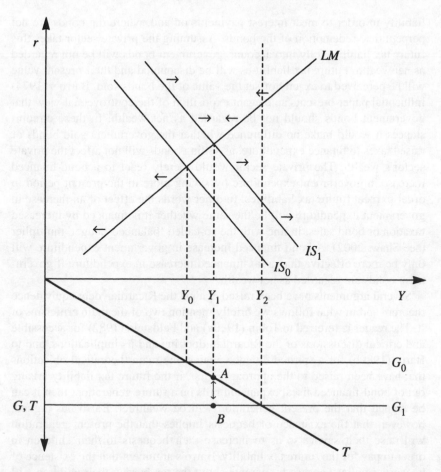

*Figure 3.5   The government budget constraint and bond-financed fiscal expansion*

effects and the government budget constraint into the IS–LM model makes a bond-financed increase in government expenditure potentially very effective in raising the level of income and employment.

One particular objection to the predictions of this analysis concerning the efficacy of fiscal policy worth commenting on is that which derives from what has come to be known as the Ricardian debt equivalence theorem (see, for example, Buchanan, 1976; Dimand, 2002a). In short, this theorem states that the burden of government expenditure on the private sector is equivalent whether it is financed by an increase in taxation or by bond sales. The sale of government bonds places a burden on the private sector involving a future tax liability in order to meet interest payments on and, where the bonds are not perpetuities, redemption of the bonds. Assuming the private sector takes this future tax liability fully into account, government bonds will be not regarded as net wealth. Future tax liabilities will be discounted and their present value will be perceived to exactly offset the value of the bonds sold. Barro's (1974) influential paper presents an elegant exposition of the controversial view that government bonds should not be regarded as net wealth. In these circumstances it would make no difference whether the government sold bonds or raised taxes to finance expenditure, as selling bonds will not affect the private sector's wealth. The private sector would merely react to a bond-financed increase in government expenditure by saving more in the present period in order to meet future tax liabilities. In other words the effect of an increase in government expenditure will be the same whether it is financed by increased taxation or bond sales, in line with the so-called 'balanced-budget' multiplier (see Shaw, 2002). A bond-financed increase in government expenditure will only be more effective than a tax-financed increase in expenditure if government bonds are regarded as net wealth.

Several arguments have been raised against the Ricardian debt equivalence theorem and in what follows we briefly mention two of the main criticisms of it. The reader is referred to Tobin (1980a) and Feldstein (1982) for accessible and critical discussions of the Ricardian doctrine and its implications, and to Barro (1989b) for a spirited defence against the main theoretical objections that have been raised to the approach. First, if the future tax liability arising out of bond-financed fiscal expansion falls on a future generation, then it can be argued that the present generation will be wealthier. Barro has argued, however, that the existence of bequests implies that the present generation will raise their saving so as to increase their bequests to their children in order to pay for the future tax liability. Barro's argument that the existence of bequests implies concern by parents about the tax burden their children will face has itself been subjected to a number of criticisms. For example, it is open to debate as to whether or not all parents will be so far-sighted, or concerned enough, to take into account the expected tax liability of their children. Second, given imperfect capital markets, government bonds may be regarded as net wealth. The rate of interest the government pays on bonds establishes the magnitude of the future tax liability. If, as a result of the government having more favourable access to capital markets than individuals, the rate of interest is less than the discount rate appropriate to the private sector when estimating the present value of the future tax liability, government bonds will be regarded as net wealth. In this situation a bond-financed increase in government expenditure will increase private sector wealth and consumption, and be more expansionary that a tax-financed increase in government expenditure.

Before moving on and making use of the IS–LM framework to discuss the Keynes v. Classics debate on the issue of 'underemployment equilibrium', we should note that over the years the IS–LM model has stirred up a considerable amount of controversy. Reflecting on the theoretical developments of the early post-war period, Modigliani (1986) has identified the 'Keynesian system' as resting on four building-blocks: the consumption function; the investment function; the demand for and supply of money; and the mechanisms for determining the movement of prices and wages. Following Hicks's (1937) effort to model the first three of Modigliani's 'building blocks', other major contributions to our understanding were made in the 1940s and 1950s by Keynesian economists, including those by Modigliani (1944), Modigliani and Brumberg (1954), Patinkin (1956), Phillips (1958) and Tobin (1958). By the early 1960s, following the publication of Phillips's (1958) influential article, the mainstream macroeconomic model was one which could be described as a Hicks (1937)–Hansen (1949) IS–LM model, augmented by a Phillips curve relationship. The MPS–FMP macroeconometric model (based on an extended IS–LM model) constructed by Modigliani and his associates in the 1960s is probably the best practical example of the consensus position during this era (Beaud and Dostaler, 1997; Blaug, 1997).

While a majority of economists (see, for example, Patinkin, 1990a; and the Tobin interview at the end of this chapter) accepted the Hicksian inspired IS–LM model as an accurate representation of the essence of Keynes's thinking in the *General Theory*, a vocal minority of 'Keynesians' view the IS–LM model as a distortion or 'bastardization' of Keynes's ideas (see Leijonhufvud, 1968; Robinson, 1975; Davidson, 1994). Interestingly, Dimand (2004) has recently shown, using evidence from Keynes's lecture notes compiled by Rymes (1989) that Keynes himself used a similar IS–LM type of general equilibrium system of equations to express his new ideas in his lectures during Michaelmas Term of 1933 as well as a 1934 draft of the *General Theory*. Monetarists such as Friedman, Brunner and Meltzer also 'dislike' the IS–LM framework. Bordo and Schwartz (2003) attribute this negative view to the model's narrow definition of investment and its narrow view of monetary influences. Nevertheless, even if the IS–LM model no longer forms the foundation of graduate macro courses (now dominated by dynamic general equilibrium theorizing), as it did until the mid-1970s, the model still forms a major input into most mainstream intermediate macroeconomics textbooks such as Blanchard (2003), Dornbusch et al. (2004), Gordon (2000a) and Mankiw (2003). Readers interested in recent controversies and discussions surrounding the origin, development and persistence of the IS–LM model should consult King (1993), Young (1987), Young and Zilberfarb (2000), Young and Darity (2004), Barens and Caspari (1999), De Vroey (2000), Backhouse (2004), Colander (2004), Dimand (2004), and Snowdon (2004a).

We now turn to consider the Keynesian belief that the economy can take a long time to return to full employment after being subjected to some disturbance. This involves a discussion of the debate on underemployment equilibrium and in what follows we examine the circumstances under which the IS–LM model will fail to self-equilibrate at full employment.

## 3.4   Underemployment Equilibrium in the Keynesian Model

### 3 4.1   The general case

Within the IS–LM model the existence of underemployment equilibrium can be attributed to the existence of 'rigidities' in the system, especially two key prices, the money wage and the interest rate. We begin with that of the 'Keynesian' assumption of downward rigidity in money wages. This case can be illustrated using the four-quadrant diagram of Figure 3.6. Quadrant (a) depicts the standard IS–LM model. Quadrant (c) shows the short-run production function where, with the capital stock and technology taken as given, the level of output/income ($Y$) depends on the level of employment ($L$) – see Chapter 2, section 2.3. Quadrant (d) depicts the labour market in which it is assumed that the demand for/supply of labour is negatively/positively related to real wages ($W/P$). Finally, quadrant (b) shows, via a 45° line, equality between the two axes, both of which depict income. The inclusion of this quadrant allows us to see more easily the implications of a particular equilibrium level of income, established in the goods and money markets in quadrant (a), for the level of employment shown in quadrant (d). In other words, in what follows the reader should always start in quadrant (a) and move in an anti-clockwise direction to trace the implications of the level of income (determined by aggregate demand) in terms of the level of employment in quadrant (d).

Suppose the economy is initially at point $E_0$, that is, the intersection of $LM_0$ and $IS$ in quadrant (a). While both the goods and money markets are in equilibrium, the income level of $Y_0$ is below the full employment income level $Y_F$. Reference to quadrant (d) reveals that with a fixed money wage (set exogenously) and a price level consistent with equilibrium in the money market (that is, the curve $LM_0$), the resultant level of real wages $(W/P)_0$ is inconsistent with the labour market clearing. In other words there is no guarantee that the demand-determined level of employment ($L_0$) will be at full employment ($L_F$). The excess supply of labour has no effect on the money wage, so that it is possible for the economy to remain at less than full employment equilibrium with persistent unemployment. We now consider what effect combining the IS–LM model with the classical assumption of flexible prices *and* money wages has on the theoretical possibility of underemployment equilibrium.

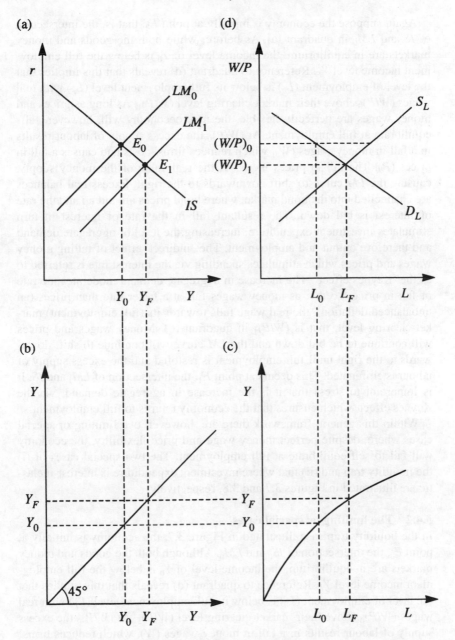

*Figure 3.6   The general case with the Keynes effect*

Again suppose the economy is initially at point $E_0$, that is, the intersection of *IS* and $LM_0$ in quadrant (a). As before, while both the goods and money markets are in equilibrium, the income level of $Y_0$ is below the full employment income level $Y_F$. Reference to quadrant (d) reveals that this implies that the level of employment ($L_0$) is below its full employment level ($L_F$) with real wages $(W/P)_0$ above their market-clearing level $(W/P)_1$. As long as prices and money wages are perfectly flexible, the macroeconomy will, however, self-equilibrate at full employment. At $(W/P)_0$ the excess supply of labour results in a fall in money wages ($W$), which reduces firms' costs and causes a fall in prices ($P$). The fall in prices increases the real value of the money supply, causing the *LM* curve to shift downwards to the right. Excess real balances are channelled into the bond market where bond prices are bid up and the rate of interest is bid down. The resultant fall in the rate of interest in turn stimulates investment expenditure, increasing the level of aggregate demand and therefore output and employment. The 'indirect' effect of falling money wages and prices which stimulates spending via the interest rate is referred to as the 'Keynes effect'. The increase in aggregate demand moderates the rate of fall in prices so that as money wages fall at a faster rate than prices (an unbalanced deflation), the real wage falls towards its (full employment) market-clearing level, that is $(W/P)_1$ in quadrant (d). Money wages and prices will continue to be bid down and the *LM* curve will continue to shift downwards to the right until full employment is restored and the excess supply of labour is eliminated. This occurs at point $E_1$, the intersection of $LM_1$ and *IS*. It is important to stress that it is the increase in aggregate demand, via the Keynes effect, which ensures that the economy returns to full employment.

Within this general framework there are, however, two limiting or special cases where, despite perfect money wage and price flexibility, the economy will fail to self-equilibrate at full employment. The two special cases of (i) the liquidity trap and (ii) that where investment expenditure is interest-inelastic are illustrated in Figures 3.7 and 3.8, respectively.

### 3.4.2   The limiting or special cases

In the liquidity trap case illustrated in Figure 3.7, the economy is initially at point $E_0$, the intersection of $IS_0$ and $LM_0$. Although both the goods and money markets are in equilibrium, the income level of $Y_0$ is below the full employment income level $Y_F$. Reference to quadrant (d) reveals that this implies that the level of employment ($L_0$) is below its full employment level ($L_F$) with real wages $(W/P)_0$ above their market-clearing level $(W/P)_1$. At $(W/P)_0$ the excess supply of labour results in a fall in money wages ($W$), which reduces firms' costs and causes a fall in prices. Although the fall in prices increases the real value of the money supply (which shifts the *LM* curve outwards, from $LM_0$ to $LM_1$), the increased real balances are entirely absorbed into idle or specula-

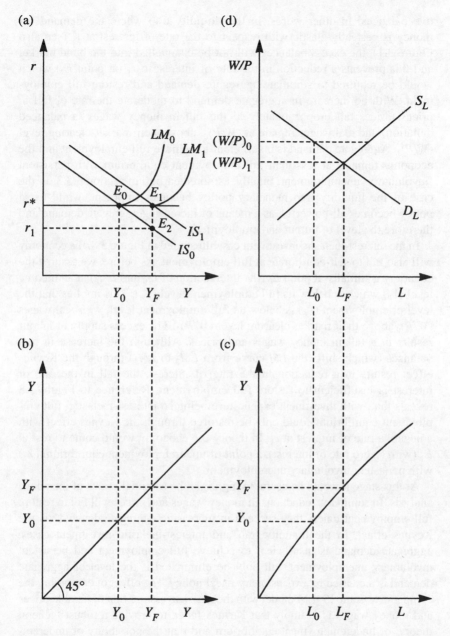

*Figure 3.7   The liquidity trap case*

tive balances. In other words, in the liquidity trap where the demand for money is perfectly elastic with respect to the rate of interest at $r^*$ (see also Figure 3.1), the excess balances will not be channelled into the bond market and this prevents a reduction in the rate of interest to $r_1$ (at point $E_2$) which would be required to stimulate aggregate demand and restore full employment. With no increase in aggregate demand to moderate the rate of fall in prices, prices fall proportionately to the fall in money wages (a balanced deflation) and real wages remain at $(W/P)_0$, above their market-clearing level $(W/P)_1$. Aggregate demand is insufficient to achieve full employment and the economy remains at less than full employment equilibrium with persistent 'involuntary' unemployment. Finally, as noted earlier, in section 3.3.3, in the case of the liquidity trap monetary policy becomes impotent, while fiscal policy becomes all-powerful, as a means of increasing aggregate demand and therefore the level of output and employment.

In the interest-inelastic investment case illustrated in Figure 3.8, the economy will also fail to self-equilibrate at full employment. As before, we assume the economy is initially at point $E_0$ (the intersection of $IS_0$ and $LM_0$) at an income level $(Y_0)$ which is below its full employment level $(Y_F)$. This implies that the level of employment $(L_0)$ is below its full employment level, with real wages $(W/P)_0$ above their market-clearing level $(W/P)_2$. The excess supply of labour results in a fall in money wages and prices. Although the increase in real balances (which shifts the $LM$ curve from $LM_0$ to $LM_1$) through the Keynes effect results in a reduction in the rate of interest, the fall in the rate of interest is insufficient to restore full employment. Reference to Figure 3.8 reveals that, with investment expenditure being so interest-inelastic, full employment equilibrium could only be restored through the Keynes effect with a negative rate of interest at $r_1$. In theory the economy would come to rest at $E_1$ (with a zero rate of interest), a point of underemployment equilibrium $(Y_1)$ with persistent involuntary unemployment.

At this stage it would be useful to highlight the essential points of the above analysis. In summary, reductions in money wages and prices will fail to restore full employment unless they succeed in increasing aggregate demand via the Keynes effect. In the liquidity trap and interest-inelastic investment cases, aggregate demand is insufficient to achieve full employment and persistent involuntary unemployment will only be eliminated if the level of aggregate demand is increased by expansionary fiscal policy. The effect of combining the comparative-static IS–LM model with the classical assumption of flexible prices and money wages is to imply that Keynes failed to provide a robust 'general theory' of underemployment equilibrium and that the possibility of underemployment equilibrium rests on two highly limiting/special cases.

The above equilibrium analysis, which owes much to the work of Modigliani, implies, as we have seen, that it is possible for the economy to

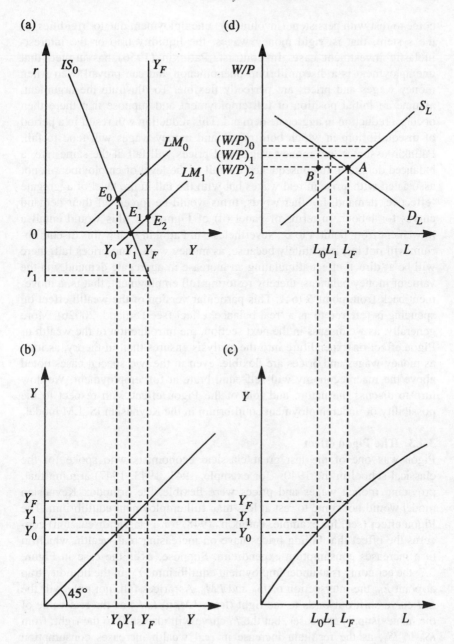

*Figure 3.8   The interest-inelastic investment case*

come to rest with persistent (involuntary) unemployment due to 'rigidities' in the system, that is, rigid money wages, the liquidity trap or the interest-inelastic investment case. In contrast, Patinkin (1956) has argued that unemployment is a disequilibrium phenomenon and can prevail even when money wages and prices are perfectly flexible. To illustrate the argument, assume an initial position of full employment and suppose that there then occurs a reduction in aggregate demand. This reduction will result in a period of disequilibrium in which both prices and money wages will tend to fall. Patinkin assumes that money wages and prices will fall at the same rate: a balanced deflation. In consequence the fall in the level of employment is not associated with a rise in real wages but with the fall in the level of aggregate 'effective' demand. In other words, firms would be forced off their demand curves for labour. In terms of panel (d) of Figure 3.8, this would entail a movement from point $A$ to $B$. Nevertheless, in Patinkin's view this disequilibrium will not last indefinitely because, as money wages and prices fall, there will be a 'direct' effect stimulating an increase in aggregate demand, via the value of money balances, thereby restoring full employment, that is, a movement back from point $B$ to $A$. This particular version of the wealth effect on spending is referred to as a 'real balance' effect (see Dimand, 2002b). More generally, as we discuss in the next section, the introduction of the wealth or Pigou effect on expenditure into the analysis ensures that, in theory, as long as money wages and prices are flexible, even in the two special cases noted above the macroeconomy will self-equilibrate at full employment. We now turn to discuss the nature and role of the Pigou effect with respect to the possibility of underemployment equilibrium in the Keynesian IS–LM model.

### 3.4.3   The Pigou effect

Pigou was one of the last great classical economists who spoke for the classical school in the 1940s (for example, 1941, 1943, 1947) arguing that, providing money wages and prices were flexible, the orthodox Keynesian model would not come to rest at less than full employment equilibrium. The Pigou effect (see, for example, Patinkin, 1948, for a classic discussion) concerns the effect that falling prices have on increasing real wealth, which in turn increases consumption expenditure. Suppose, as is the case in Figure 3.7, the economy is at underemployment equilibrium ($Y_0$) in the liquidity trap at point $E_0$, the intersection of $IS_0$ and $LM_0$. As prices fall, not only will the LM curve shift outwards to the right (from $LM_0$ to $LM_1$) as the real value of the money supply increases, but the IS curve will also shift to the right, from $IS_0$ to $IS_1$, as the resultant increase in real wealth increases consumption expenditure. In theory the economy cannot settle at underemployment equilibrium but will automatically adjust until full employment is achieved at point $E_1$, the intersection of $IS_1$ and $LM_1$. The reader should verify that, once the Pigou or wealth effect on expenditure is incorporated into the analysis, in the special interest-inelastic investment case illustrated in Figure 3.8 the economy will automatically adjust to restore full employment, at point $E_2$. The importance of the Pigou effect at the theoretical level has been neatly summarized by Johnson (1964, p. 239): 'the Pigou effect finally disposes of the Keynesian contention that underemployment equilibrium does not depend on the assumption of wage rigidity. It does.'

Over the years a number of reservations have been put forward which question whether, in practice, the Pigou or wealth effect will ensure a quick return to full employment (see, for example, Tobin, 1980a). In what follows we consider two of the main criticisms of the effect. First, dynamic considerations may invalidate the Pigou effect as a rapid self-equilibrating mechanism. For example, if individuals expect a further future fall in prices, they may postpone consumption, causing unemployment to rise. At the same time, if firms expect a recession to continue, they may postpone their investment plans, again causing unemployment to rise. Furthermore, in a deep recession bankruptcies are likely to increase, reducing expenditure still further (see, for example, Fisher, 1933b). In terms of the diagrammatic analysis we have been considering, falling prices may cause the *IS* curve to shift to the left, driving the economy further away from full employment equilibrium. In these circumstances expansionary fiscal policy would ensure a more rapid return to full employment.

Second, we need to consider briefly the debate on which assets constitute 'net' wealth. Net wealth can be defined as total wealth less outstanding liabilities. In the Keynesian model wealth can be held in money and bonds. Consider first money, which is widely accepted as comprising currency plus bank deposits. Outside money can be defined as currency, plus bank deposits which are matched by banks' holdings of cash reserves or reserves at the central bank. Outside money may be considered as net wealth to the private sector as there is no offsetting private sector liability. In contrast, inside money can be defined as bank deposits which are created by lending to the private sector. As these bank deposits are matched by a corresponding private sector liability (bank loans), it can be argued that inside money cannot be regarded as net wealth. It is worth noting that the argument that inside money does not constitute net wealth has been challenged by, among others, Pesek and Saving (1967) and Johnson (1969). While this is an interesting debate within monetary economics, it goes beyond what is required for our purposes. Suffice it to say that, if one accepts the argument that only outside money unambiguously constitutes net wealth, the wealth effect of falling prices on consumption expenditure is greatly diminished. Next, as noted earlier, in section 3.3.3, there is debate over whether government bonds can be regarded as net wealth. It could be argued that the private sector will realize that, following a fall in prices, the increase in the real value of government debt outstanding will necessitate future increases in taxes to meet the increased value of interest payments on, and redemption of, government bonds. If the rise in the present value of future tax liabilities exactly offsets the increase in the real value of government debt outstanding there would be no wealth-induced shift in the *IS* curve. Again, while this view is not one that is universally accepted, it does nevertheless cast doubt on the self-equilibrating properties of the economy via the Pigou effect. The empirical evidence for the strength of the Pigou effect shows it to be extremely weak. For example, both Glahe (1973, pp. 213–14) for the USA and Morgan (1978, pp. 55–7) for the UK found that the Pigou effect was not strong enough to restore full employment in the interwar period, with actual price level falls taking place alongside a decline in expenditure and output. Furthermore, on reasonable assumptions, Stiglitz (1992) has shown that, if prices were to fall by 10 per cent per year, then *ceteris paribus* 'to increase consumption by 25 per cent would take roughly 400 years' and 'it is hard to see even under the most optimistic view, the quantitative significance of the real balance effect for short-run macroeconomic analysis'. Given such doubts, orthodox Keynesians prescribe expansionary fiscal policy to ensure a more rapid return to full employment.

Finally it is interesting to quote Pigou (1947), who suggested that the 'puzzles we have been considering ... are academic exercises, of some slight use perhaps for clarifying thought, but with very little chance of ever being posed on the chequer board of actual life'.

### 3.4.4 The neoclassical synthesis

From the discussion of sections 3.4.1–3.4.3 it will be apparent that, if money wages and prices are flexible, the Keynesian IS–LM model can in theory, via the Pigou or wealth effect, automatically adjust to achieve full employment, the main prediction of classical economics. In terms of pure analytical theory, Pigou was said to have won the intellectual battle, establishing a triumph for classical theory. Some writers (for example, Wilson, 1980; Presley, 1986; Bridel, 1987) have suggested that Keynes anticipated the wealth effect but rejected it on theoretical and practical grounds. Notwithstanding this neglected point, Keynesians regarded themselves as having won the policy debate in that the process of adjustment via the Pigou effect might be so slow that interventionist policies (notably expansionary fiscal policy) would be required to ensure a more rapid return to full employment. During the late 1950s and early 1960s a consensus view emerged, the so-called 'neoclassical synthesis' (see Fletcher, 2002), in which the *General Theory* was seen as a special case of a more general classical theory (that is, the case where downward money wage rigidity prevents the classical automatic adjustment to full employment), while the need was recognized for Keynesian interventionist policies to ensure a more rapid return to full employment.

## 3.5 The IS–LM Model for an Open Economy

Having discussed the Keynesian approach to stabilization policy in the context of the IS–LM model for a closed economy (sections 3.2–3.4), we next consider the use of fiscal and monetary policy for stabilization purposes in an open economy using a model first developed by Robert Mundell and Marcus Fleming at the start of the 1960s (see Mundell, 1963; Fleming, 1962). As we will discuss, the effects of a change in fiscal and monetary policy depend on the degree of capital mobility and the type of exchange rate regime in existence. We begin with a review of the main changes we need to incorporate in extending the IS–LM model to an open economy.

### 3.5.1 The goods market and the *IS* curve

As in the case of a closed economy, equilibrium in the goods market occurs where the aggregate demand for and aggregate supply of goods are equal. In an open economy aggregate demand is composed of not only the sum of consumption, investment and government expenditure, but also 'net' exports, that is, exports minus imports $(X - Im)$. Exports are assumed to be a function of: (i) income in the rest of the world; (ii) the price of a country's goods *relative* to those produced by competitors abroad, which may be defined as $eP_D/P_F$, where $e$ is the exchange rate expressing domestic currency in terms of foreign currency, $P_D$ is the price of domestic goods in terms of domestic currency and $P_F$ is the price of foreign goods in terms of foreign currency; and (iii) other factors such as tastes, quality of the goods, delivery dates and so on. Imports are assumed to be determined by the same factors that influence exports (since one country's exports are another country's imports) with the exception that the income variable relevant to imports is domestic income. As domestic income rises, *ceteris paribus*, aggregate demand will increase and some portion of this increase in demand will be met by imported goods; that is, the marginal propensity to import is greater than zero.

As discussed in section 3.3.1, the *IS* curve traces out a locus of combinations of interest rates and income associated with equilibrium in the goods market. The open economy *IS* curve is downward-sloping but is steeper than in the case of a closed economy because of the additional leakage of imports which increase as domestic income increases, thereby reducing the size of the multiplier. In addition to the factors which affect the position of the *IS* curve in a closed economy, a change in any of the variables which affect 'net' exports will cause the *IS* curve to shift. For example, an increase in exports due to a rise in world income will be associated with a higher level of domestic income, at any given level of the rate of interest, causing the *IS* curve to shift outwards to the right. Similarly, *ceteris paribus*, net exports will increase if: (i) the exchange rate falls (that is, depreciates or is devalued) providing the Marshall–Lerner conditions are fulfilled, namely that starting from an initial balanced trade position and also assuming infinite price elasticities of supply for imports and exports, the sum of the price elasticities of demand for imports and exports is greater than unity (see De Vanssay, 2002); (ii) the foreign price level rises; and (iii) the domestic price level falls. In each of these cases the *IS* curve would shift outwards to the right, as before, the magnitude of the shift being equal to the size of the shock times the multiplier. Conversely a change in the opposite direction in any one of these variables will shift the *IS* curve to the left.

### 3.5.2   The money market and the *LM* curve

The open economy *LM* curve is exactly the same as in the case of a closed economy with one important extension. In an open economy operating a fixed exchange rate the domestic money supply will be altered by balance of payments deficits/surpluses (that is, the net balance on the combined current and capital accounts) unless the authorities are able to sterilize or neutralize the effects of the balance of payments deficits/surpluses on the domestic money supply. Under a regime of fixed exchange rates the authorities are committed to buy and sell foreign exchange for the home currency at a fixed price. For example, in the case of a balance of payments surplus residents will sell foreign currency to the authorities for domestic currency at a fixed exchange rate. *Ceteris paribus*, a balance of payments surplus will result in an increase in both the authorities' foreign exchange reserves and the domestic money supply, thereby shifting the *LM* curve downwards to the right. Conversely, a balance of payments deficit will result in a fall in both the authorities' foreign exchange reserves and the domestic money supply, thereby shifting the *LM* curve upwards to the left. In contrast, under a regime of flexible exchange rates the exchange rate adjusts to clear the foreign exchange market (that is, the central monetary authorities do not intervene in the foreign exchange market) so that the sum of the current and capital accounts is always zero. In consequence the *LM* curve is independent of external factors and the determinants of the position of the *LM* curve are the same as those discussed earlier in section 3.3.2.

To complete the IS–LM model for an open economy we next turn to consider overall balance of payments equilibrium and the *BP* curve.

### 3.5.3   The overall balance of payments and the *BP* curve

Early Keynesian analysis of the balance of payments (see Dimand, 2002c) focused on the determination of the current account and how government policy could improve the balance of payments on it (in particular the conditions under which devaluation would be successful in doing just this). The late 1950s/early 1960s witnessed a period of increasingly liberalized trade and capital movements and, as noted earlier, Mundell and Fleming extended the Keynesian model of an open economy to include capital flows. At the onset of this discussion it is important to note that we assume we are dealing with a small open economy in the sense that changes within the domestic economy of that country and its macroeconomic policies have an insignificant effect on the rest of the world.

Overall balance of payments equilibrium requires that the sum of the current and capital accounts of the balance of payments is zero. As noted earlier, imports are a function of domestic income and relative prices (of domestic and foreign goods), while exports are a function of world income and relative prices. *Ceteris paribus*, as domestic income rises, imports increase and the balance of payments on the current account worsens. With static expectations about exchange rate changes, net capital flows are a function of the differential between domestic and foreign interest rates. *Ceteris paribus*, as the domestic interest rate rises, domestic assets become more attractive and the capital account of the balance of payments improves due to the resulting inward flow of funds.

The *BP* curve (see Figure 3.9) traces out a locus of combinations of domestic interest rates and income levels that yield an overall zero balance of payments position on the combined current and capital accounts. The *BP* curve is positively sloped because if balance of payments equilibrium is to be maintained (that is, a zero overall balance) then increases (decreases) in the level of domestic income which worsen (improve) the current account have to be accompanied by increases (decreases) in the domestic rate of interest which improve (worsen) the capital account. Points above and to the left of the *BP* curve are associated with an overall balance of payments surplus since, given the level of income, the domestic rate of interest is higher than that necessary to produce an overall zero balance of payments position. Conversely, points below and to the right of the *BP* curve indicate an overall balance of payments deficit since, given the level of income, the domestic rate of interest is lower than that necessary to produce an overall zero balance of payments position.

The slope of the *BP* curve depends on the marginal propensity to import and the interest elasticity of international capital flows. *Ceteris paribus*, the *BP* curve will be flatter (steeper) the smaller (larger) is the marginal propensity to import and the more (less) interest-elastic are capital flows. For example, the more sensitive capital flows are to changes in domestic interest rates, the smaller will be the rise in the domestic interest rate required to maintain a zero overall balance of payments equilibrium for a given increase in income, and hence the flatter will be the *BP* curve. The *BP* curve shown in Figure 3.9 represents a situation of imperfect capital mobility since the domestic rate of interest can depart from that ruling in the rest of the world. With respect to the interest elasticity of international capital movements it is important to note that in the two limiting cases of perfect capital mobility and complete capital immobility the *BP* curve would become horizontal and vertical respectively. For example, in the case of perfect capital mobility the *BP* curve will be horizontal; that is, the domestic rate of interest will be tied to the rate ruling in the rest of the world. If the domestic rate of interest were to rise above the given world rate there would be an infinite capital inflow, and vice versa.

The *BP* curve is drawn for given levels of the world income, interest rate and price level; the exchange rate; and the domestic price level. If any of these variables should change, then the *BP* curve would shift. For example, anything that results in an increase in exports and/or a decrease in imports (such as a rise in world income; a fall in the exchange rate; a rise in the foreign price level; or a fall in the domestic price level) will cause the *BP* curve to shift downwards to the right, and vice versa. In other words, at any given level of domestic income an improvement in the current account will require a lower domestic rate of interest to maintain a zero overall balance of payments position via capital account effects.

### 3.5.4   The complete model and the effects of a change in fiscal and monetary policy

We are now in a position to consider the full IS–LM model for a small open economy. Equilibrium in the goods and money markets, and in the balance of payments, occurs at the triple intersection of the *IS*, *LM* and *BP* curves indicated in Figure 3.9. In what follows we analyse the effects of a change in fiscal and monetary policy on: (i) the level of income and the balance of payments in a fixed exchange rate regime, and (ii) the level of income and the exchange rate in a flexible exchange rate regime.

Under a regime of fixed exchange rates, while fiscal expansion will result in an increase in income, it may lead to either an improvement or a deterioration in the overall balance of payments position, and vice versa. The effects of fiscal expansion on the level of income and the balance of payments are illustrated in the two panels of Figure 3.10. In panel (a) the *LM* curve is steeper than the *BP* curve, while in panel (b) the converse is true. In both panels of Figure 3.10 the economy is initially operating at point $A$, the triple intersection of the three curves $IS_0$, *LM* and *BP* with equilibrium in the goods and money markets, and in the balance of payments, at $r_0 Y_0$. Expansionary fiscal policy shifts the *IS* curve outwards to the right from $IS_0$ to $IS_1$ and results in an increase in the domestic rate of interest from $r_0$ to $r_1$ (improving the capital account) and an increase in income from $Y_0$ to $Y_1$ (worsening the

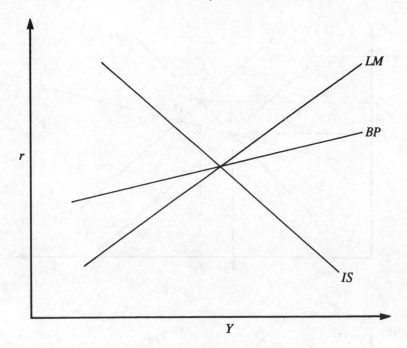

*Figure 3.9    The Mundell–Fleming/Keynesian model*

current account). As can be seen from both panels of Figure 3.10, the net outcome on the overall balance of payments position depends on the relative slopes of the *LM* and *BP* curves (that is, the structural parameters underlying the model). In panel (a) the net outcome is an overall balance of payments surplus at point *B* (that is, the curves $IS_1$ and *LM* intersect at a point above the *BP* curve), while in panel (b) it is one of an overall balance of payments deficit (that is, the curves $IS_1$ and *LM* intersect at point *B* below the *BP* curve). Expansionary fiscal policy is more likely to lead to an improvement in the overall balance of payments position: (i) the smaller is the marginal propensity to import and the more interest-elastic are capital flows (that is, the flatter the slope of the *BP* curve) and (ii) the greater is the income elasticity and the smaller is the interest elasticity of the demand for money (that is, the steeper the slope of the *LM* curve), and vice versa. In practice the *LM* curve is likely to be steeper than the *BP* curve due to the interest elasticity of the demand for money being less than that for capital flows. This view tends to be backed up by available empirical evidence and will be adopted in the discussion that follows on long-run equilibrium.

At this point it is important to stress that in analysing the consequences for the balance of payments of a change in fiscal policy under fixed exchange

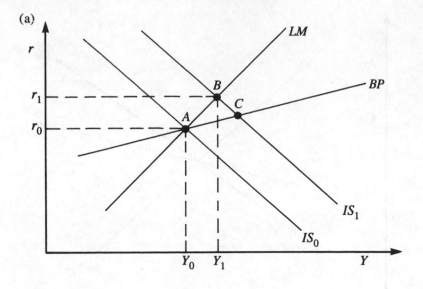

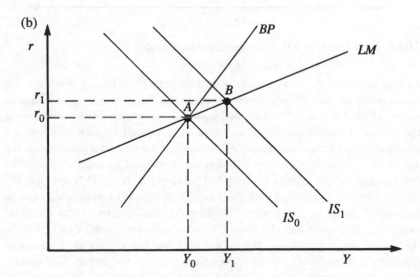

*Figure 3.10    Fiscal expansion under imperfect capital mobility*

rates the Keynesian approach assumes that the authorities can, in the short run, sterilize the effects of a balance of payments surplus or deficit on the money stock. The results we have been analysing necessarily relate to the short run because in the long run it becomes increasingly difficult to sterilize the effects of a persistent surplus or deficit on the money stock. Long-run equilibrium requires a zero balance on the balance of payments, otherwise the domestic money supply changes in the manner discussed in section 3.5.2. As such the balance of payments surplus at point *B* in panel (a) of Figure 3.10 will cause an expansion of the domestic money supply following intervention by the authorities to maintain the fixed exchange rate. This causes the *LM* curve to shift downwards to the right and long-run equilibrium will occur at point *C*, where the balance of payments is zero and the goods and monetary markets are in equilibrium.

In contrast to fiscal expansion under a regime of fixed exchange rates, with imperfect capital mobility, monetary expansion will always lead to a deterioration in the balance of payments, and vice versa, regardless of whether or not the *LM* curve is steeper than the *BP* curve. This is illustrated in Figure 3.11, where the economy is initially operating at point *A*, the triple intersection of the three curves *IS*, $LM_0$ and *BP*, with equilibrium in the goods and money markets, and in the balance of payments. Expansionary monetary policy shifts the *LM* curve from $LM_0$ to $LM_1$ and results in a reduction in the domestic rate of interest from $r_0$ to $r_1$ (worsening the capital account) and an increase in the level of income from $Y_0$ to $Y_1$ (worsening the current account).

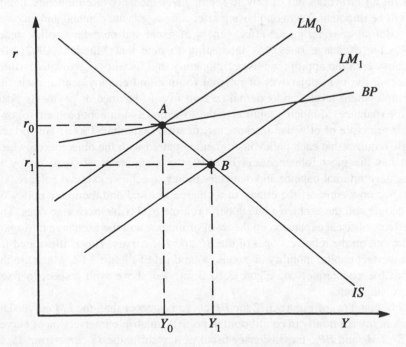

*Figure 3.11   Monetary expansion under imperfect capital mobility*

With adverse interest and income effects on the capital and current accounts respectively, the overall balance of payments is unambiguously in deficit at point *B* (that is, the curves *IS* and $LM_1$ intersect at a point below the *BP* curve).

In a similar manner to that discussed for expansionary fiscal policy, point *B* cannot be a long-run equilibrium. The implied balance of payments deficit causes a contraction in the money supply, shifting the *LM* curve backwards. The long-run adjustment process will cease at point *A* where the *LM* curve has returned to its original position. In other words, in the absence of sterilization, monetary policy is completely ineffective as far as influencing the level of income is concerned. This assumes that the domestic country is small relative to the rest of the world so that expansion of its money supply has a negligible effect on the world money supply.

Readers should verify for themselves that, for a small open economy operating under a regime of fixed exchange rates, in the limiting case of perfect capital mobility, the equilibrium level of domestic income is in the long run established at the intersection of the *IS* and 'horizontal' *BP* curves. In this situation fiscal policy becomes all-powerful (that is, fiscal expansion results in the full multiplier effect of the simple Keynesian 45° or cross model with no crowding out of private sector investment), while monetary policy will be impotent, having no lasting effects on aggregate demand and income.

Before considering the effectiveness of fiscal and monetary policy under flexible exchange rates it is interesting to note that Mundell (1962) also considered the appropriate use of monetary and fiscal policy to successfully secure the twin objectives of internal (output and employment at their full employment levels) and external (a zero overall balance of payments position) balance. Mundell's solution to the so-called assignment problem follows his principle of effective market classification (Mundell, 1960). This principle requires that each policy instrument is paired with the objective on which it has the most influence and involves the assignment of fiscal policy to achieve internal balance and monetary policy to achieve external balance.

We now consider the effects of a change in fiscal and monetary policy on income and the exchange rate under a regime of flexible exchange rates. The effects of fiscal expansion on the level of income and the exchange rate again depend on the relative slopes of the *BP* and *LM* curves. This is illustrated for imperfect capital mobility in panels (a) and (b) of Figure 3.12, which are the flexible counterparts of Figure 3.10 discussed above with respect to fixed exchange rates.

In panel (a) of Figure 3.12 the *BP* curve is steeper than the *LM* curve. The economy is initially in equilibrium at point *A*, the triple intersection of curves $IS_0$, $LM_0$ and $BP_0$. Expansionary fiscal policy shifts the *IS* curve from $IS_0$ to $IS_1$. As we have discussed above, under fixed exchange rates fiscal expansion

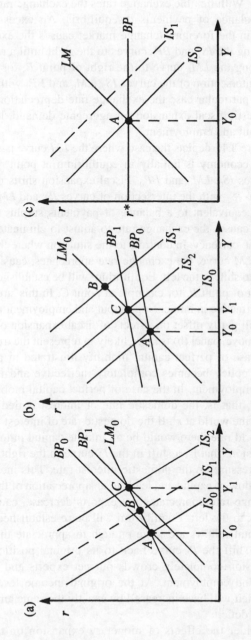

*Figure 3.12  Fiscal expansion under (a) and (b) imperfect and (c) perfect capital mobility*

*Modern macroeconomics*

would result in a balance of payments deficit (that is, $IS_1$ and $LM_0$ intersect at point $B$ below $BP_0$). With flexible exchange rates the exchange rate adjusts to correct potential balance of payments disequilibria. An excess supply of domestic currency in the foreign exchange market causes the exchange rate to depreciate, shifting the $IS_1$ and $BP_0$ curves to the right until a new equilibrium is reached along the $LM_0$ curve to the right of point $B$, for example at point $C$, the triple intersection of the curves $IS_2$, $LM_0$ and $BP_1$ with an income level of $Y_1$. In this particular case the exchange rate depreciation reinforces the effects of domestic fiscal expansion on aggregate demand, leading to a higher level of output and employment.

Panel (b) of Figure 3.12 depicts the case where the $LM$ curve is steeper than the $BP$ curve. The economy is initially in equilibrium at point $A$, the triple intersection of curves $IS_0$, $LM_0$ and $BP_0$. Fiscal expansion shifts the $IS$ curve outwards from $IS_0$ to $IS_1$ with the intersection of curves $IS_1$ and $LM_0$ at point $B$ above $BP_0$. This is equivalent to a balance of payments surplus under fixed exchange rates and causes the exchange rate to adjust to eliminate the excess demand for domestic currency. In contrast to the situation where the $BP$ curve is steeper than the $LM$ curve, the exchange rate appreciates, causing both the $IS_1$ and $BP_0$ curves to shift to the left. Equilibrium will be established along the $LM$ curve to the left of point $B$, for example at point $C$. In this situation fiscal policy will be less effective in influencing output and employment as exchange rate appreciation will partly offset the effects of fiscal expansion on aggregate demand. As noted above, panel (b) is more likely to represent the true situation.

In the limiting case of perfect capital mobility illustrated in panel (c) of Figure 3.12, fiscal policy becomes completely ineffective and is unable to affect output and employment. In the case of perfect capital mobility the $BP$ curve is horizontal; that is, the domestic rate of interest is tied to the rate ruling in the rest of the world at $r^*$. If the domestic rate of interest were to rise above the given world rate there would be an infinite capital inflow, and vice versa. Fiscal expansion (that is, a shift in the $IS$ curve to the right from $IS_0$ to $IS_1$) puts upward pressure on the domestic interest rate. This incipient pressure results in an inflow of capital and leads to an appreciation of the exchange rate. As the exchange rate appreciates net exports decrease, causing the $IS$ curve to move back to the left. Equilibrium will be re-established at point $A$ only when the capital inflows are large enough to appreciate the exchange rate sufficiently to shift the $IS$ curve back to its original position. In other words fiscal expansion completely crowds out net exports and there is no change in output and employment. At the original income level of $Y_0$ the current account deficit will have increased by exactly the same amount as the government budget deficit.

Finally we consider the effects of monetary expansion on the level of income and the exchange rate under imperfect and perfect capital mobility.

The case of imperfect capital mobility is illustrated in panel (a) of Figure 3.13. The economy is initially in equilibrium at point $A$, the triple intersection of curves $IS_0$, $LM_0$ and $BP_0$. Monetary expansion shifts the $LM$ curve from $LM_0$ to $LM_1$. Under fixed exchange rates this would result in a balance of payments deficit. With flexible exchange rates the exchange rate depreciates to maintain balance of payments equilibrium and both the $BP$ and $IS$ curves shift to the right until a new equilibrium is established along the curve $LM_1$ to the right of point $B$, such as point $C$, the triple intersection of curves $IS_1$, $LM_1$ and $BP_1$. The effect of monetary expansion is reinforced by exchange rate depreciation, leading to a higher level of income. In the limiting case of perfect capital mobility illustrated in panel (b) monetary expansion (which shifts the $LM$ curve from $LM_0$ to $LM_1$) will put downward pressure on the domestic interest rate. This incipient pressure results in capital outflows and a depreciation of the exchange rate, causing the $IS$ curve to shift to the right (from $IS_0$ to $IS_1$) until a new equilibrium is established at point $C$, the triple intersection of curves $LM_1$, $IS_1$ and $BP$ at the given world interest rate $r^*$ and a new income level $Y_1$. In this limiting case monetary policy is completely effective and contrasts with the position of fiscal policy discussed above.

In summary, under a regime of fixed exchange rates with imperfect capital mobility, while fiscal expansion will result in an increase in income, its effects on the overall balance of payments (assuming sterilization takes place) are ambiguous (depending on the relative slopes of the $LM$ and $BP$ curves). In contrast, there is no ambiguity following a change in monetary policy. Monetary expansion will result in an increase in income and always lead to a deterioration in the balance of payments. However, in the absence of sterilization, monetary policy is completely ineffective in influencing the level of income. Furthermore, in the limiting case of perfect capital mobility fiscal policy becomes all-powerful, while monetary policy will be impotent, having no lasting effects on aggregate demand and the level of income. Under a regime of flexible exchange rates, with imperfect capital mobility, while fiscal expansion will result in an increase in income, it could (depending on the relative slopes of the $LM$ and $BP$ curves) cause the exchange rate to depreciate or appreciate, thereby reinforcing or partly offsetting the effect of fiscal expansion on aggregate demand and income. In contrast, monetary expansion results in an increase in income, with the effects of monetary expansion on aggregate demand and income being reinforced by exchange rate depreciation. In the limiting case of perfect capital mobility fiscal policy becomes impotent and is unable to affect output and employment, while monetary policy becomes all-powerful.

In concluding our discussion it is important to note that there are a number of limitations of the above IS–LM model for an open economy. These limita-

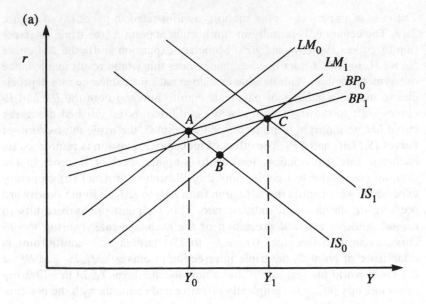

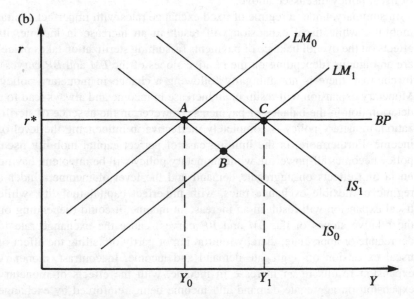

*Figure 3.13    Monetary expansion under (a) imperfect and (b) perfect capital mobility*

tions include: restrictive assumptions (for example fixed wages and prices, and static expectations about exchange rate changes); specification of the capital account (where net capital flows between countries depend solely on the differential between domestic and foreign interest rates) which is inconsistent with portfolio theory where perpetual capital flows require continuous interest changes; the implicit assumption that a country is able to match a continuous deficit on the current account with a surplus on the capital account whereas, in reality, the nature of the balance of payments objective is likely to be much more precise than just overall balance of payments equilibrium; and adopting comparative statics rather than considering the dynamics of adjustment following a disturbance (see Ugur, 2002). For a discussion of the origin and subsequent refinements of the Mundell–Fleming model the reader is referred to Frenkel and Razin (1987); Mundell (2001); Obstfeld (2001); Rogoff (2002); Broughton (2003).

Having analysed the effectiveness of fiscal and monetary policy in the context of the fixed-price Keynesian models of both a closed and open economy we next discuss the original Phillips curve analysis and comment on the importance of the curve to orthodox Keynesian economics.

## 3.6 The Phillips Curve and Orthodox Keynesian Economics

The Phillips curve is concerned with the controversy over the relationship between inflation and unemployment and is one of the most famous relationships in macroeconomics (see Smithin, 2002). It should be noted that the first statistical study investigating the relationship between unemployment and inflation was carried out by Irving Fisher in 1926 (see Fisher, 1973). However, the curve that bears A.W. Phillips's name was derived from a *statistical* investigation published in 1958 into the relationship between unemployment ($U$) and the rate of change of *money* wages ($\dot{W}$) in the UK over the period 1861–1957. As depicted in Figure 3.14, the estimated average relationship was found to be non-linear and inverse. For example, at an unemployment level of approximately 5.5 per cent, the rate of change of money wages was zero per cent, while at an unemployment level of approximately 2.5 per cent the rate of change of money wages was 2.0 per cent.

Remarkably, Phillips found that the data for the period 1948–57 fitted very closely to the curve fitted for the earlier period, 1861–1913, given by equation (3.6).

$$\dot{W} = -0.9 + 9.638(U)^{-1.394} \tag{3.6}$$

To some, this finding suggested the possible existence of a *stable long-run* negative relationship between wage inflation and unemployment.

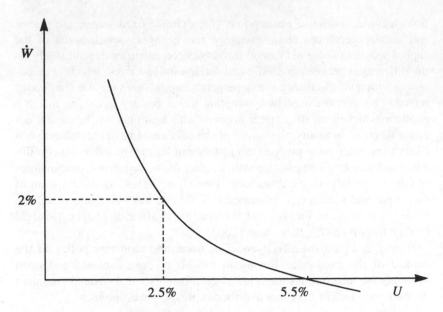

*Figure 3.14   The Phillips curve*

Although the original Phillips paper (1958) was an empirical investigation into the relationship between money wage inflation and unemployment, Phillips opens his paper with an outline sketch of the underlying theoretical reasoning that could be used to explain why we might expect to observe a negative relationship between these two variables. He opens with these words:

> When the demand for a commodity or service is high relative to the supply of it we expect the price to rise, the rate of rise being greater the greater the excess demand. Conversely, when the demand is low relative to the supply we expect the price to fall, the rate of fall being greater the greater the deficiency of demand. It seems plausible that this principle should operate as one of the factors determining the rate of change of money wage rates.

Following Phillips's pioneering work, there developed two strands to the literature, one theoretical, the other empirical. On the *empirical* front, economists were interested to establish whether a stable relationship between inflation and unemployment prevailed in other market economies (for a discussion of the empirical literature, see Santomero and Seater, 1978). As far as the simultaneous achievement of low inflation and low unemployment was concerned, the discovery of a possible stable trade-off between these two objectives implied a policy dilemma, one which might be overcome if the curve could be shifted to the left by appropriate economic policies. However, the design of effective policies to achieve this objective would first necessitate a coherent *theoretical* explanation of the economic forces which lay behind the relationship.

The first major attempt to provide a robust theoretical underpinning to the curve was provided by Lipsey (1960) through the combination of two postulated relationships: (i) a positive linear relationship between the rate of increase in money wages and the excess demand for labour ($X_L$), and (ii) a negative non-linear relationship between excess demand and unemployment. These postulated relationships are given in equations (3.7) and (3.8).

$$\dot{W} = \alpha(X_L) = \alpha[(D_L - S_L)/S_L] \tag{3.7}$$

$$X_L = \beta(U) \tag{3.8}$$

where $D_L$ is the demand for labour, $S_L$ is the supply of labour, $\alpha$ is a positive coefficient of wage flexibility, and $\beta$ is a variable negative parameter such that when $X_L \to 0$, $U = U^*$ and $U^* > 0$; and when $X_L \to \infty$, $U \to 0$. By combining these two postulated relationships, Lipsey was able to provide an economic rationale for Phillips's observed non-linear inverse relationship between the rate of change of money wages and unemployment shown in Figure 3.14.

The relationship between wage change and excess demand for labour is illustrated in Figure 3.15. Panel (a) shows that at any wage rate below $W_e$, wages will rise as a result of excess demand in the labour market. Panel (b) shows that the rate of increase in money wage rates will be greater the larger the excess demand for labour. For example, at a wage rate $W_1$ in panel (a) there is an excess demand for labour of $aa$. This excess demand is equal to $0a$ in panel (b) and results in a rate of increase in money wage rates of $\dot{W}_1$. The relationship between excess demand for labour and unemployment is illustrated in Figure 3.16. Even when the labour market clears (that is to say, there is neither excess demand nor excess supply) there will be some positive amount of unemployment due to frictions in the labour market as people change jobs and search for new employment, that is, $0e$ in Figure 3.16. Lipsey argued that, although unemployment would fall in response to positive excess demand (for example, jobs become easier to find as vacancies increase), unemployment would only asymptotically approach zero. In other words, steadily increasing excess demand would be accompanied by increasingly smaller reductions in unemployment.

In summary, Lipsey's rationale suggests that, in its simplest form, the rate of change of money wages depends on the degree of excess demand (or supply) in the labour market as proxied by the level of unemployment. This can be expressed by the equation:

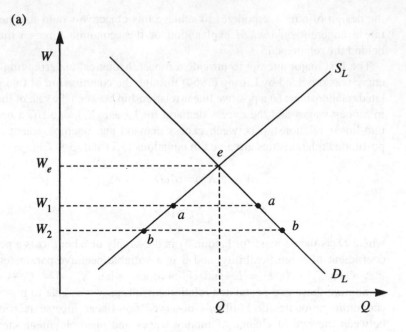

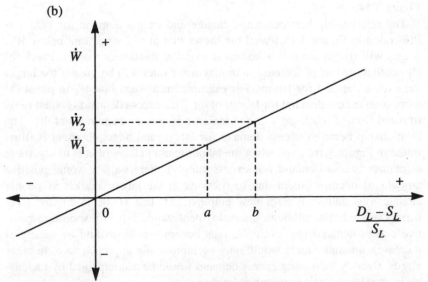

*Figure 3.15   The relationship between wage change and excess demand for labour*

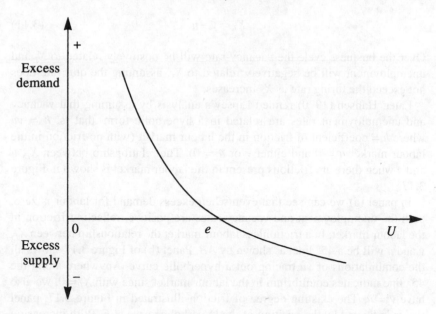

*Figure 3.16   The relationship between excess demand for labour and unemployment*

$$\dot{W} = f(U) \qquad (3.9)$$

Referring back to Phillips's opening statement in his 1958 paper, it is clear that he viewed the high correlation between money wage inflation and unemployment as strong evidence in favour of the 'demand pull' explanation of inflation.

In Lipsey's model, due to labour market frictions, equilibrium in the labour market occurs when $U = U^* > 0$ (see Lipsey, 1960, pp. 470–71). When $U = U^*$, the number of job vacancies ($V$) is equal to the number of unemployed who are actively seeking work. Since $S_L$ equals the total number employed ($E$) and unemployed ($E + U$), and $D_L$ equals the total number of vacancies ($V$) plus the number employed ($V + E$), we can express the *proportional* excess demand for labour as follows:

$$X_L = [(D_L - S_L)/S_L] = [(V - U)/(E + U)] \qquad (3.10)$$

Letting $v = V/S_L$ and $u = U/S_L$, we can express the excess demand for labour in terms of variables that can be measured, that is the vacancy rate ($v$) and the unemployment rate ($u$).

$$X_L = v - u \tag{3.11}$$

Over the business cycle the vacancy rate will be positively related to $X_L$ and unemployment will be negatively related to $X_L$, assuming the quit rate does not exceed the hiring rate as $X_L$ increases.

Later, Hansen (1970) refined Lipsey's analysis by assuming that vacancy and unemployment rates are related in a hyperbolic form, that is, $h = vu$ where $h$ = coefficient of friction in the labour market (with no friction in the labour market $h = 0$ and either $v$ or $u = 0$). The relationship between $X_L$, $u$ and $v$ when there are frictions present in the labour market is shown in Figure 3.17.

In panel (a) we can see that even when excess demand for labour is zero, both the unemployment and vacancy rates are positive, reflecting friction in the labour market. In a frictionless labour market the relationship between $X_L$, $v$ and $u$ will be a 45° line, as shown by $AB$. Panel (b) of Figure 3.17 shows all the combinations of $vu$ tracing out a hyperbolic curve. Anywhere along the 45° line indicates equilibrium in the labour market since with $X_L = 0$, we also have $v = u$. The existing degree of friction illustrated in Figure 3.17, panel (b), is indicated by the position of the hyperbolic curve at $F$. With increasing friction in the labour market this curve will shift out. In turn this will cause the Phillips curve to shift to the right since the level of unemployment consistent with $X_L = 0$ increases as labour market friction increases. There is strong evidence, for example, that such a shift occurred in the UK economy in the late 1960s and early 1970s (Gujarati, 1972; see also Taylor, 1972).

Given Hansen's refinements, the Phillips relationship can now be expressed in the following form:

$$\dot{W} = \alpha(h/u - u) + w^* = \alpha h/u - \alpha u + w^* \tag{3.12}$$

where $w^*$ is exogenously determined wage inflation (for example, brought about by trade union power). In (3.12) we can see that the slope of the Phillips curve is dependent on the coefficient of wage flexibility, $\alpha$, and the position of the Phillips curve will be influenced by $w^*$ and also the degree of friction in the labour market, $h$. The more inflexible the labour market the higher the degree of friction, and the higher will wage inflation be for any given level of unemployment (see Rothschild, 1971; Frisch, 1977; Lipsey, 1978).

During the 1960s the Phillips (1958) curve was quickly taken on board as an integral part of the then-dominant orthodox Keynesian paradigm, not least because it was interpreted by many orthodox Keynesians as implying a stable long-run trade-off which provided the authorities a menu of possible inflation–unemployment combinations for policy choice. Within academia the

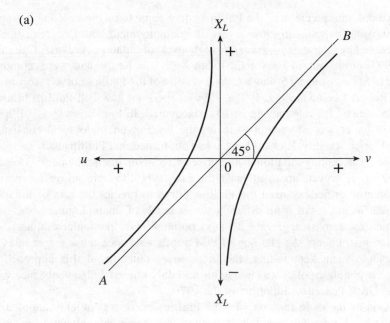

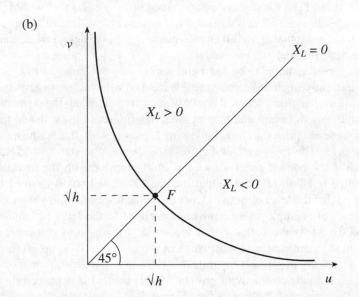

*Figure 3.17   The relationship between excess demand for labour, vacancy and unemployment rates*

textbook interpretation of the Phillips curve came to be presented as a proposition that *permanently* low levels of unemployment could be realistically achieved by tolerating *permanently* high levels of inflation. As James Galbraith (1997) points out, in 1968 mainstream American Keynesians were 'committed to Samuelson and Solow's (1960) version of the Phillips curve'. According to Robert Leeson (1994a, 1997a, 1999), this is not how Bill Phillips himself ever viewed the relationship he had discovered. In Leeson's view, Phillips's 1958 paper was an attempt to locate the level of unemployment consistent with price stability. Richard Lipsey has confirmed that Phillips had 'no tolerance for accepting inflation as the price of reducing unemployment' (Leeson, 1997a). However, up to at least the late 1960s the prevailing Keynesian economic orthodoxy used the Phillips curve to predict the rate of inflation which would result from different target levels of unemployment being attained by activist aggregate demand policies, with particular emphasis on fiscal instruments. As DeLong (1998) points out, once those target rates of unemployment kept falling, the inflationary outcome of this approach to macroeconomic policy was inevitable and duly arrived with a vengeance with the 'Great Peacetime Inflation' of the 1970s.

One of the main reasons why the Phillips curve was quickly adopted by orthodox Keynesians was that it seemed to provide an explanation of inflation which was missing in the then-prevailing macroeconomic model. The reader will recall from the discussion contained in section 3.3 that within the IS–LM model the price level is assumed to be fixed at less than full employment, with the result that up to full employment, changes in aggregate demand affect the level of real income and employment. Up to full employment money wages are assumed to be fixed and unresponsive to changes in aggregate demand. Only when full employment is reached will changes in aggregate demand affect the price level. The Phillips curve allowed the orthodox Keynesian theory of output and employment determination to be linked to a theory of wage and price inflation. Following Lipsey (1978), this is illustrated in Figure 3.18. The top panel of Figure 3.18 depicts the standard IS–LM model, while the bottom panel shows the Phillips curve with the modified axes of price inflation ($\dot{P}$) and output/income ($Y$). Panel (b) is derived by assuming (i) that the level of output depends on the level of employment and that the level of unemployment is inversely related to the level of employment, and (ii) a hypothesis that prices are set by a mark-up to unit costs of production, the main component of which is wages. Put in its simplest form, the mark-up pricing hypothesis suggests that price inflation depends on money wage inflation minus productivity growth. In this context it is interesting to note that the estimated Phillips curve (Figure 3.14) showed that an unemployment level of approximately 2.5 per cent was compatible with stable prices because at this level of unemployment the rate of change of money

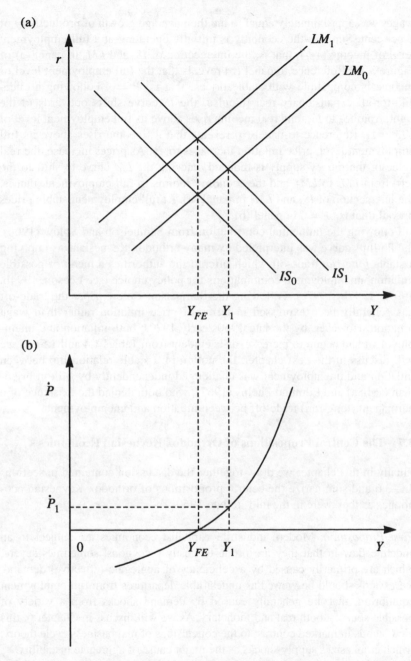

*Figure 3.18   The link between the Keynesian model and wage and price
inflation*

wages was approximately equal to the then average growth of productivity of 2 per cent. Suppose the economy is initially operating at a full employment level of income ($Y_{FE}$), that is, the intersection of $IS_0$ and $LM_0$ in panel (a) of Figure 3.18. Reference to panel (b) reveals that the full employment level of income is compatible with stable prices; that is, $\dot{P} = 0$. Following a once-and-for-all expansionary real impulse, the *IS* curve shifts outwards to the right, from $IS_0$ to $IS_1$, and real income rises above its full employment level of $Y_{FE}$ to $Y_1$. Reference to panel (b) reveals that as income rises above its full employment level, price inflation increases to $\dot{P}_1$. As prices increase, the real value of the money supply is reduced, causing the *LM* curve to shift to the left, from $LM_0$ to $LM_1$, and the economy returns to full employment, that is, the intersection of $IS_1$ and $LM_1$ in panel (a). At full employment stable prices prevail, that is, $\dot{P} = 0$ in panel (b).

Following the influential contribution from Samuelson and Solow (1960), the Phillips curve was interpreted by many orthodox Keynesians as implying a stable *long-run* trade-off which offered the authorities a menu of possible inflation–unemployment combinations for policy choice (see Leeson, 1994b, 1997a, 1997b, 1997c). Following the Samuelson–Solow paper the trade-off has generally been expressed in terms of price inflation rather than wage inflation. However, by the late 1960s/early 1970s, both inflation and unemployment had begun to increase, as is evident from Tables 1.4 and 1.5. As we will discuss in the next chapter, the notion of a stable relationship between inflation and unemployment was challenged independently by Milton Friedman (1968a) and Edmund Phelps (1967), who both denied the existence of a permanent (long-run) trade-off between inflation and unemployment.

### 3.7   The Central Propositions of Orthodox Keynesian Economics

Finally in this chapter we draw together the discussion contained in sections 3.2–3.6 and summarize the central propositions of orthodox Keynesian economics as they were in the mid- to late 1960s.

*First Proposition*: Modern industrial capitalist economies are subject to an endemic flaw in that they are prone to costly recessions, sometimes severe, which are primarily caused by a deficiency of aggregate (effective) demand. Recessions should be viewed as undesirable departures from full employment equilibrium that are generally caused by demand shocks from a variety of possible sources, both real and monetary. As we will discuss in Chapter 6, this view stands in marked contrast to the conclusions of real business cycle theory, which emphasizes supply shocks as the major cause of aggregate instability.

*Second Proposition*: Orthodox Keynesians believe that an economy can be in either of two regimes. In the Keynesian regime aggregate economic activity is demand-constrained. In the classical regime output is supply constrained and in this situation supply creates its own demand (Say's Law). The 'old' Keynesian view is that the economy can be in either regime at different points in time. In contrast, new classical economists, such as Robert Lucas and Edward Prescott, model the economy as if it were always in a supply-constrained regime. In the Keynesian demand-constrained regime employment and output will respond positively to additional real demand from whatever source.

*Third Proposition*: Unemployment of labour is a major feature of the Keynesian regime and a major part of that unemployment is involuntary in that it consists of people without work who are prepared to work at wages that employed workers of comparable skills are currently earning (see for example, Solow, 1980; Blinder, 1988a). As we will discuss in subsequent chapters, this contrasts sharply with the view of many monetarist, new classical and real business cycle economists who view unemployment as a voluntary phenomenon (Lucas, 1978a).

*Fourth Proposition*: 'A market economy is subject to fluctuations in aggregate output, unemployment and prices, which need to be corrected, can be corrected, and therefore should be corrected' (Modigliani, 1977, 1986). The discretionary and coordinated use of both fiscal and monetary policy has an important role to play in stabilizing the economy. These macroeconomic instruments should be dedicated to real economic goals such as real output and employment. By the mid-1960s the early 'hydraulic' Keynesian emphasis on fiscal policy had been considerably modified among Keynesian thinkers, particularly Modigliani and Tobin in the USA (see Snowdon and Vane, 1999b). However, supporters of the 'New Economics' in the USA were labelled as 'fiscalists' to distinguish them from 'monetarists'. But, as Solow and Tobin (1988) point out, 'The dichotomy was quite inaccurate. Long before 1960 the neo-Keynesian neoclassical synthesis recognised monetary measures as co-equal to fiscal measures in stabilisation of aggregate demand' (see Buiter, 2003a).

*Fifth Proposition*: In modern industrial economies prices and wages are not perfectly flexible and therefore changes in aggregate demand, anticipated or unanticipated, will have their greatest impact in the short run on real output and employment rather than on nominal variables. Given nominal price rigidities the short-run aggregate supply curve has a positive slope, at least until the economy reaches the supply-constrained full employment equilibrium.

*Sixth Proposition*: Business cycles represent fluctuations in output, which are undesirable deviations below the full employment equilibrium trend path of output. Business cycles are not symmetrical fluctuations around the trend.

*Seventh Proposition*: The policy makers who control fiscal and monetary policy face a non-linear trade-off between inflation and unemployment in the short run. Initially, in the 1960s, many Keynesians thought that this trade-off relationship was relatively stable and Solow and Tobin (1988) admit that in the early 1960s they 'may have banked too heavily on the stability of the Phillips curve indicated by post-war data through 1961' (see Leeson, 1999).

*Eighth Proposition*: More controversial and less unanimous, some Keynesians, including Tobin, did on occasions support the temporary use of incomes policies ('Guideposts') as an additional policy instrument necessary to obtain the simultaneous achievement of full employment and price stability (Solow, 1966; Tobin, 1977). The enthusiasm for such policies has always been much greater among European Keynesians than their US counterparts, especially in the 1960s and early 1970s.

*Ninth Proposition*: Keynesian macroeconomics is concerned with the short-run problems of instability and does not pretend to apply to the long-run issues of growth and development. The separation of short-run demand fluctuations from long-run supply trends is a key feature of the neoclassical synthesis. However, stabilization policy that combines tight fiscal policy with easy monetary policy will 'bring about an output mix heavier on investment and capital formation, and lighter on consumption'. This mix will therefore be more conducive to the growth of an economy's long-run growth of potential output (see Tobin, 1987, pp. 142–67, Tobin, 2001). 'Taming the business cycle and maintaining full employment were the first priorities of macroeconomic policy. But this should be done in ways that promote more rapid growth in the economy's capacity to produce' (Tobin, 1996, p. 45).

The orthodox Keynesians reached the peak of their influence in the mid-1960s. In the UK Frank Paish (1968) concluded that on the basis of Phillips's data, if unemployment were held at around 2.5 per cent, then there would be a good chance of achieving price stability. In the USA, reflecting on the experience of 20 years of the Employment Act of 1946, the 1966 *Annual Report of the Council of Economic Advisers* concluded on the following optimistic note with respect to the effectiveness of Keynesian demand management policies (emphasis added):

> Twenty years of experience have demonstrated our ability to avoid ruinous inflations and severe depressions. It is now within our capabilities to set more ambitious goals. We strive to avoid recurrent recessions, *to keep unemployment far below rates of the past decade*, to maintain essential price stability at full employment, to move toward the Great Society, and, indeed, to make full prosperity the normal state of the American economy. It is a tribute to our success under the Employment Act that *we now have not only the economic understanding* but also the will and determination to use economic policy as an effective tool for progress.

As we now know, this statement turned out to be far too optimistic with respect to the knowledge that economists had about macroeconomics and the ability to target the economy toward increasingly lower unemployment targets (see DeLong, 1996, 1997, 1998).

Does this mean that Keynesian economics is dead (Tobin, 1977)? Certainly not. Paul Krugman (1999) has warned economists that the 1990s have witnessed 'The Return of Depression Economics'. Krugman's argument is that 'for the first time in two generations, failures on the demand side of the economy – insufficient private spending to make use of available productive capacity – have become the clear and present limitation on prosperity for a large part of the world'. Krugman sets out to remind economists not to be complacent about the possibility of economic depression and deflation, particularly in view of what happened in the Japanese, Asian Tiger and several European economies during the 1990s. DeLong (1999a, 1999b, 1999c) has also emphasized that the business cycle and threat of deflation are far from dead. Several economists have argued that the Japanese economy appears to be caught in a 'liquidity trap' (Krugman, 1998). Krugman (1999) writes:

> Even now, many economists still think of recessions as a minor issue, their study as a faintly disreputable subject; the trendy work has all been concerned with technological progress and long-run growth. These are fine important questions, and in the long run they are what really matters ... Meanwhile, in the short run the world is lurching from crisis to crisis, all of them crucially involving the problem of generating sufficient demand ... Once again, the question of how to keep demand adequate to make use of the economy's capacity has become crucial. Depression economics is back.

So even given that there were significant deficiencies in the orthodox Keynesian framework that required new thinking, the issues that concerned Keynes have not disappeared.

In the next chapter we discuss the development of the orthodox monetarist school which, over the period of the mid-1950s to the early 1970s, highlighted a number of weaknesses both at the theoretical and empirical levels of the then-prevailing orthodox Keynesian framework.

## JAMES TOBIN (1918–2002)

*Photograph courtesy of T. Charles Erickson,*
*Yale University, Office of Public Information*

James Tobin was born in 1918 in Champaign, Illinois and obtained his BA, MA and PhD from Harvard University in 1939, 1940 and 1947, respectively. He began teaching while a graduate student at Harvard University in 1946. In 1950, he moved to Yale University where he remained, until his death in 2002, as Professor of Economics, with the exception of one and a half years in Washington as a member of President Kennedy's Council of Economic Advisers (1961–2), and academic leaves including a year as Visiting Professor at the University of Nairobi Institute for Development Studies in Kenya (1972–3).

James Tobin was one of America's most prominent and distinguished Keynesian economists. He was a longstanding advocate of Keynesian stabilization policies and a leading critic of monetarism and the new classical equilibrium approach. He made fundamental contributions to monetary and macroeconomic theory as well as important contributions to the links between cyclical fluctuations and economic growth. In 1981 he was awarded the Nobel Memorial Prize in Economics: 'For his analysis of financial markets and their relations to expenditure decisions, employment, production and prices.'

Among his best-known books are: *National Economic Policy* (Yale University Press, 1966); *Essays in Economics: Macroeconomics* (Markham, 1971; North-Holland, 1974); *The New Economics One Decade Older* (Princeton

University Press, 1974); *Essays in Economics: Consumption and Econometrics* (North-Holland, 1975); *Asset Accumulation and Economic Activity* (Basil Blackwell, 1980); *Policies for Prosperity: Essays in a Keynesian Mode* (Harvester Wheatsheaf, 1987) edited by Peter Jackson; and *Full Employment and Growth: Further Keynesian Essays on Policy* (Edward Elgar, 1996).

Among the numerous articles he wrote, the best-known include: 'The Interest-Elasticity of Transactions Demand for Cash', *Review of Economics and Statistics* (1956); 'Liquidity Preference as Behaviour Towards Risk', *Review of Economic Studies* (1958); 'Money and Economic Growth', *Econometrica* (1965); 'A General Equilibrium Approach to Monetary Theory', *Journal of Money, Credit, and Banking* (1969); 'Money and Income: Post Hoc, Ergo Propter Hoc', *Quarterly Journal of Economics* (1970); 'Inflation and Unemployment', *American Economic Review* (1972); 'How Dead is Keynes?', *Economic Inquiry* (1977); 'Are New Classical Models Plausible Enough to Guide Policy?', *Journal of Money, Credit, and Banking* (1980); and 'The Monetarist Counter-Revolution: An Appraisal', *Economic Journal* (1981).

We interviewed Professor Tobin in his office on 17 February 1993 and subsequently corresponded in January/February 1998.

## Keynes and Keynesian Economics

*You began your study of economics at Harvard the very year that the* General Theory *was published. What attracted you to economics?*
It was an unbelievably happy combination of a subject that promised to save the world and was fascinating from an intellectual puzzle-solving point of view. I was also very much worried about the Great Depression and had every reason to think that the massive failure of our economies was the key to many other of the world's ills, political as well as economic.

*The* General Theory *is a very difficult book and reflects Keynes's 'long struggle to escape' previous ideas. What were your first impressions of the* General Theory?
I didn't know enough to know it was a difficult book, which I had no business reading. I was 19 years old. My tutor at Harvard, who had been in England for a year, just said at our first one-on-one tutorial meeting 'Why don't you and I read this new book I've heard about for our tutorial this year?' I didn't know any better so I read it, and I didn't feel it was that difficult. One of the exciting things, of course, for a 19-year-old was the sense of intellectual revolution, overturning the obsolete wisdom encrusted in the past, especially when the new theory was on the side of promising to do something constructive about the main problems that concerned me and people of my generation.

*Skidelsky [1992] in his biography of Keynes [Volume 2] has argued that 'Keynes's inspiration was radical but his purpose conservative'. How did Keynes reconcile these two opposing forces?*
I think that what Skidelsky says is essentially right. Compare Keynes's remedies for the problems of the world at the time to those of Marxians and Spengler's *Decline of the West* – all those apocalyptic warnings of the death of capitalism, because capitalism can't ever succeed. Keynes comes along and says that the basic problem is not really the organization of the economy but rather the way that aggregate demand is controlled. Keynes had no great complaint about the way the economy allocates the resources that it does employ, just that it doesn't employ them all.

*It only took about twelve years for the* General Theory *to capture the hearts and minds of the vast majority of the economics profession. Why did Keynes's ideas spread so quickly?*
Well, because it did look as if they would work to remedy the problems of the Great Depression. There was a lot of anxiety in all countries that after the Second World War we would revert to the depression conditions of the pre-war period. Keynes's ideas looked like a pretty good way to avoid that possibility. In the USA, consider the spending for mobilization even before we got in the war, and what it did to GNP and employment. That was a dramatic living vindication of Keynes's ideas.

*You are widely recognized as being America's most distinguished Keynesian economist. Are you happy with the label Keynesian and what does being a Keynesian mean to you?*
If you'd asked me that, let's say 25 years ago, I would have said that I don't like any label and that I'm just an economist working on problems that I happen to be interested in; macroeconomic problems, monetary–fiscal policy and all those things. There appeared to be a considerable practical consensus about these matters. A lot of my work had been fixing up Keynes in various ways where I found theoretical problems or a lack of 'micro foundations'. In fact the first thing I wrote and got published [in 1941] was a piece of anti-Keynesian theory on his problem of the relation of money wage and employment. So at that time I would have said let's not label people, let's just do our work. After the counter-revolutions, when all these schools and labels arose, I certainly would be proud to be regarded as a Keynesian, considering the alternatives [*laughter*].

*What are the fundamental propositions which Keynesians adhere to?*
One way to put it is to say that there is a two-regime model of the economy. Sometimes the economy is in a classical situation where markets are clearing

(demand equals supply) and the economy's ability to produce output is supply-constrained. You can't produce any more because there are essentially no idle resources (I exaggerate to simplify). Therefore the constraint on output is *capacity*. That capacity constraint results in a price and income structure that equalizes demand and supply at those prices. At other times the economy is in a Keynesian situation in which the constraint on actual output is *demand* – aggregate spending. Extra output would be produced if there were extra aggregate real demand, and the inputs to make it are available at real returns which won't exceed what the factors of production could earn by their productivity if they were employed. That situation obtains lots of the time, not always, and there are then demand-increasing policies that will eliminate the social waste involved. That I think is the distinction. Whereas for the real business cycle theorists (like Ed Prescott) and new classical guys (like Robert Barro) you are always supply-constrained. There is just one regime, and the observed cyclical fluctuations are fluctuations in voluntary willingness to be employed.

*Some interpretations of the neoclassical synthesis which emerged in the late 1950s and early 1960s suggest that the* General Theory *represents a special case of a more general classical model. What is your view on that particular interpretation?*
I wouldn't interpret it that way. Rather there was a consensus on the two-regime model just mentioned. I thought there was also a normative consensus, in the sense that you shouldn't regard any output that you get from putting unemployed resources to work as free, because you have alternative ways of putting unemployed resources to work. The same classical opportunity cost considerations that determine allocation of resources in a classical equilibrium determine the allocation of resources as among different ways of returning to that supply-constrained regime. So I think in that sense there is no excuse for wasteful projects to increase employment, like digging holes in the ground, because you can arrange to employ people by investments or other projects that are socially beneficial. In that sense the classical opportunity cost considerations apply in either regime. But that's only if you're prepared to do something to get out of the wasteful situation that you're in.

*Has too much been made of the Pigou effect as a way of diminishing Keynes's contribution to economic theory?*
Of course. I've said that all the time in print. It's a very slender reed on which to assert the efficacy of self-adjusting mechanisms. For one thing the accounting aggregation of credits and debts doesn't necessarily imply behavioural netting out of credits and debts. I believe that the effects of deflation on aggregate demand can be perverse if debtors have a bigger propensity to

spend from wealth than creditors do – a reasonable expectation. Then there's the whole issue of how you get to the lower price level from where you are. The immaculate conception effect of getting there suggests there's no real time involved – it's just the static comparison of one price level to another price level. As Keynes himself observed, although he didn't make of it a point of theoretical principle, the process of deflation – or disinflation for that matter – involves an increase in the real interest rate and certainly produces perverse effects.

*Do you think that if Keynes had still been alive in 1969 (aged 86) he would have been awarded the first Nobel Prize in economics?*
Very likely. He would have got my vote. As for Keynes versus Tinbergen and Frisch, the actual recipients, I don't know. The prize says for economic *science*. In some senses they might have been considered to have made identifiable innovations more similar to those of Nobel-winning natural scientists. But JMK would have been an early award-winner.

*How do you feel about your award of the Nobel Prize in 1981? What do you consider to be your most important contributions to macroeconomics?*
I never thought I was going to get it. I was interested in straightening out macroeconomics and the neoclassical synthesis as I understood them, in generalizing monetary models to take account of the variety of assets, in portfolio theory and its macroeconomic implications – that's what I was trying to do.

*Why do you think there are so many conflicting interpretations of the* General Theory*?*
Well, I suppose one reason is that the book is ambiguous in many ways and has a number of strands that could be cited to support different messages. They allow people a variety of views about the world, in particular, on the one hand, since people interpret the *General Theory* as a kind of general equilibrium model of the determination of output, employment and interest rates that could be used in both of the two regimes I referred to above. That's what J.R. Hicks was doing in his famous article. On the other hand you have Chapter 12 on long-run expectations, which suggests that maybe there is not an investment function at all. In the Hicks general equilibrium model you have got to have an investment function. The second approach, stressing the conventionality of expectations and animal spirits, may be seen as opening the way to a different kind of model. This would be supported by Keynes's own tentative advocacy of the socialization of investment, his suspicion that maybe investment wouldn't be adequately stabilized by monetary and fiscal policy, his feeling that you need some central planning to get it right. I guess

those ambiguities allow us to interpret it one way or the other. Of course, some people hoped to extract from Keynes a much more radical position with regard to the social and political institutions than he had explicitly expressed. I have in mind Mrs Robinson and others who claim to be the true heirs of Keynes. I never could get that excited about this kind of battle over Keynes's mantle, so to speak. The central part of the book, the central core of the modelling, is on the other side, Hicks's side, in my opinion. Certainly that's in practice the model that has been taught and has influenced policy making and macroeconomic theorizing for more than 50 years.

*Do you think teaching the IS–LM model is still an important part of an undergraduate's understanding of the macro economy given the criticisms of the IS–LM model by people like Robinson, Clower and Leijonhufvud?*
Yes I think the IS–LM model is the tool of first resort. If you're faced with a problem of interpretation of the economy – policy or events – probably the most useful first thing you can do is to try to see how to look at it in these terms. Since students are in that position, yes they need to know it. It's not the end of the matter by any means. I don't say that it's enough. I doubt if Keynes or Hicks would have thought it enough. But it's a start and lots of times it's exactly right.

## Critiques of Keynesianism

*Would you accept that many of the theoretical changes made in the 1970s, and inspired by people like Lucas, were the inevitable consequence of defects in the Keynesian model?*
No I wouldn't accept that. I do think the idea of model-consistent expectations is a good idea. It would be a bad feature of any equilibrium model that people chronically perpetuate mistaken expectations about variables, mistaken in the sense that they are different from those that the model persistently creates itself. But I think that applying that idea to dynamic situations where learning is going on and people can have a lot of different opinions about the world is carrying it too far.

*How important do you think it is for macroeconomics to have neoclassical choice-theoretic foundations?*
Well, I think it's important for the behavioural equations of a macroeconomic model not to contradict choice-theoretic considerations, to be in principle consistent with them. But I think the stronger version of 'micro foundations' is a methodological mistake, one that has produced a tremendous amount of mischief. I refer to the now orthodox requirement of postulating representative agents whose optimizations generate 'macroeconomic' behavioural

equations. That is a considerable sacrifice of the essence of much of macroeconomics. Suppose you have a lot of different types of agents, who are all maximizing. Then it's their aggregation into a behavioural equation that you want for a macro model. That aggregation won't necessarily be the solution for any single agent. To insist that it must be seems to me very wrong-headed. It has put us on the wrong track in macroeconomics or what passes for macroeconomics.

*In the late 1960s you had a considerable debate with Friedman who at one stage argued that the main differences between macroeconomists were over empirical matters. Surely the 1970s demonstrated that there were some fundamental theoretical differences between macroeconomists?*
What Friedman was saying was disingenuous. He had a theory of the demand for money which put a lot of variables in the demand function including various interest rates, and yet his monetary policy propositions were based on the assumption that interest rates were not in the function. He asserted empirical results that he was unique in finding – that the interest elasticity of the demand for money was negligible. When he was really stuck by the weight of evidence, he then wrote that the question of the size of interest elasticity of the demand for money had nothing to do with anything. The only way one could make sense of that particular proposition was that you were going to be at full employment anyway, no matter what the stock of money was, and so the interest rate would have to be what was consistent with the demand and supply of savings at full employment. But that was a complete evasion of the original issues of our debate. He had never before said that monetary policy would have *no* effects on real variables. He said they have a lot of effects on real variables. He had some kind of Phillips curve (although he didn't call it that) in his mind, and even when he invented the natural rate he still did. He didn't deny that monetary policy would have some effects on real output during cyclical fluctuations – so he was caught between being a true new classical economist, in which case he was going to have to say that money doesn't ever matter, or being a pragmatic monetarist, where he didn't have a good theoretical or empirical basis for what he had been saying.

*What exactly is the difference between Friedman's concept of the natural rate of unemployment and NAIRU – the non-accelerating inflation rate of unemployment? Is there some important difference between these two concepts?*
I don't think there is a big practical difference. Maybe what was in the mind of Modigliani when he started that acronym was that Friedman said that the natural rate was the amount of unemployment that was the solution to Walrasian general equilibrium equations – a proposition that neither he nor anybody else ever proved as far as I know – complete speculation. I mean, why would

Walrasian equations have any unemployment at all in their solution? [*laughter*]. That identification of the natural rate doesn't make any sense, and it's certainly not true. When Modigliani and others started talking about NAIRU, they were talking more about a pragmatic empirical idea.

*At the end of the day politicians make economic policy. The public choice school, as well as the work of your colleague William Nordhaus on political business cycles, suggests that politicians may actually use economic policy for their own gain. Do you think that Keynes was perhaps naive in thinking that we could hand over policy making to politicians and they would follow the advice of economists?*

I won't quote the last paragraph of the *General Theory*, which says that in the long run ideas matter. I think that's true, but I think my point would be a little different. If we are advising government officials, politicians, voters, it's not for us economists to play games with them. It's not for Keynes to say, I am not going to suppress the *General Theory* and not tell the House of Commons, the Labour Party, the Tories, whomever, that it would be possible to reduce unemployment by public works expenditure. If I am giving advice to them about war finance – or whatever else my advice will be not to do bad things – I am not going to decide myself that they are so evil and irresponsible that I don't give them advice about what actions will do what. I don't think that Jim Buchanan has, or I have, the right to withhold advice from Presidents of the United States or Members of Congress or the electorate on the grounds that if they knew what we know, they would misuse it. I don't think that is for us to decide.

*You have said that good papers in economics contain surprises and stimulate further work. On this criterion the 1970s contributions of people like Lucas, Sargent, Wallace and Barro were good. Do you feel that new classical macroeconomics has changed macroeconomics for the better?*

In some respects I think Lucas's ideas about policies being anticipated by actors, so you can't be sure that behaviour will stay put when you change policy, is an important idea, one we have to worry about. I don't think it is as important an idea as he seemed to think it was. I thought his ingenious explanation of how you can have observations that look like Phillips curves yet have none of the operational policy implications of the curve – that was neat. However, I think it turned out not to be a good idea. It didn't survive because of the implausible notion that people are confused about what the money supply is. If they're confused, why don't we publish the money supply data every Friday afternoon – which in the USA we do of course and have been doing for a long time. I observe that the new classicals no longer pay any attention to this misperception story. They have become much more extreme. Barro's [1974] paper was provocative and stimulated a lot of theoretical and empirical work. I had a paper in my Jahnsson lectures [Tobin, 1980a] that gave, I don't know, say 15 reasons why Barro's neutrality proposition doesn't work, and I think there have been numerous articles since on each of them.

*We have seen a lot of contributions recently from what are called new Keynesian economists. What is the central difference between your view of Keynesian economics and the new Keynesian contributions? Is it that they accept rational expectations and a lot of monetarist ideas?*
Yes, they accept rational expectations. Moreover they accept the methodology of choice-theoretic foundations and representative agents, much more than I would. They accept market clearing, except as it is modified by imperfect competition, much more than I would. They regard their task as to give a rationale for the alleged rigidity of money wages and money prices, a rationale that allows nominal shocks to create real consequences. I think that was *not* Keynes's idea. Keynes was primarily concerned not with nominal demand shocks but real demand shocks, which would create problems even if prices were flexible. They have said that all they are going to do is show how it is rational for nominal prices to be inflexible and derive unemployment results from that. I don't find it extremely convincing – and I'm sure Keynes wouldn't have – that the whole effective demand problem is that there are real costs of changing nominal prices on the menu at the restaurant. I think Keynes would have laughed at the idea that menu costs are a big enough resource-using problem to cause the Great Depression or any other substantial losses of economic activity. It's not credible. If I had a copyright on who could use the term Keynesian I wouldn't allow them to use it [*laughter*].

*What do you think of the real business cycle approach?*
That's really the enemy at the other extreme of macroeconomics. Real business cycle theory suggests that society is a moving equilibrium responding continuously to technological–productivity–supply shocks all the time, and that the economy is doing the best job possible in responding to them. It's those benign responses that generate the fluctuations we call business cycles. There isn't any unemployment in the Keynesian sense. There are simply intertemporal substitutions of employment now and employment later, which are rational responses to the stochastic environment in which people live. I don't see any credibility to the idea that people are doing a lot of intertemporal substitution as to how much they want to work. To interpret the rise in unemployment in this country from 5.7 per cent in 1978 to 11 per cent in 1982 as a desire on the part of workers to take leisure in preparation for working when real wages will be higher – that is ridiculous (*laughter*).

*Should we take Lucas's [1978a] advice and abandon the concept of involuntary unemployment?*
Certainly not. Any time that you don't have supply and demand equal at existing prices then there is involuntary something. Some people would like to supply more, or some people might like to demand more, at those prices but are not able to do so. The only way you can say that everything must be voluntary is to assume market clearing all the time – that at every moment in time the economy is in market-clearing equilibrium.

*In new classical models full employment is equated with actual unemployment. How should we define full employment?*
I would define it, as Keynes did, in a classical way at the point where people are on the supply curve for labour, getting all the work they are willing to accept at real wages that employers can and will pay for them. Keynes himself allows for intersectoral flux and frictional unemployment, but essentially I wouldn't define equilibrium full employment any differently from a classical model.

*There seems to be more consensus amongst economists on microeconomic issues than macroeconomic issues. Why do you think this is the case?*
Let's go back to what Keynes said. He didn't have any big reservations about the way the market economy allocates the resources it does employ. I think myself, and many microeconomists and economists in general would say, that Keynes gave away too much. He should have recognized more externalities in the ordinary market allocation of resources, and he should have worried more about the possible social wastes of monopolistic competition than he did. In many areas of microeconomics like rent control and minimum wages, choice-theoretic opportunity-cost methodology is being used the way we are trained to use it. That's the secret that we know, and sociologists and other social scientists don't know. We are a more scientific discipline, but I don't think that all is well in those respects. What rational expectations has done to macroeconomics is what game theory has been doing to microeconomics. Game theory has the problem that it leads to multiple solutions all the time, so it doesn't seem to get results. It's got the same fascination for people looking for ways to use their mathematical and puzzle-solving prowess as rational expectations has, and that comes at the expense of more pragmatic, and empirical, and institutional industrial organization studies. So, I am not so sure that all is well in microeconomics either. A lot of good policy work continues in more applied areas.

*Do you see any signs of an emerging consensus in macroeconomics?*
It may be coming, but I don't see it. There is still great conflict.

**Economic Policy**

*When in office Mrs Thatcher repeatedly stated that in her view inflation was
the most important target for macroeconomic policy. How do you react to this
view?*
Well, that's substituting a subordinate target for a real target. To the extent
that inflation is damaging to real standards of living now or in the future, then
inflation is something to worry about. But you could easily make greater
sacrifices of real output and real consumption in the name of inflation than
the benefits of reducing inflation are worth.

*Structural budget deficits have been a feature of the US economy in the 1980s
and indeed at the moment there is a lot of talk of the problem of growing
budget deficits. Are budget deficits damaging? Do you think that the structural budget deficit of the US economy is a real problem, and what should be
done about it?*
Well, again you have to keep your eye on the ball and not confuse ends and
means. When you think about the objectives to which fiscal policy may be
relevant, it is the growth of our capacity to provide higher standards of living
to people in the future. For the USA we are talking about a deficit that is in
dollars, a debt that is in the currency that we print. It's not a debt in sterling,
in yen, or anything else. It's largely an internally held debt and when you
think about international wealth balance sheets it's not important whether
foreigners hold our federal public debt, or hold other assets. There is a
burden, however, in that the public debt diverts some private wealth that
could be placed in privately owned productive capital to holding government
paper that was generated to finance private or collective consumption. In that
sense deficits which increase the debt have been using savings that could
have been used for productive investments in capital that would have raised
real wages that our grandchildren would earn. But that doesn't mean we need
a deficit reduction this year, when the economy is in a slump. Today GDP is
not supply-constrained; the amount of investment in the economy is not
constrained by the supply of saving. In fact deficit reduction in a weak
economy would be counterproductive, reduce GDP, reduce investment. We
would be doing not as well for our children and their children as we would if
we did some spending on public investment or cut taxes in ways that stimulate private investment. All this is terribly mixed up in the political discussion
about deficits. I have been one of the principal opponents of the kind of fiscal
policy that the Reagan and Bush Administrations ran for 12 years. And at the
same time, to rush into a blind policy of deficit reduction that begins too
soon, before we are out of the slump – I wouldn't do that either. It all gets
back to trying to suit the medicine to the circumstances of the patient.

*Are you still an advocate of incomes policies? Some Keynesians like Alan Blinder have little enthusiasm for such policies, whereas you seem to think that incomes policy has a role to play in addition to demand management.*
Well I thought incomes policy did have a role in the 1970s, and especially in the disinflation that was going to take place beginning in 1979. I think we could have done that disinflation with less loss in output and employment if we'd used some kind of incomes policy then. Right now, I'm not very excited about incomes policy. One thing that has come out well in the 1980s, partly a matter of good fortune, is that we haven't had any more oil shocks. Wage pressures are also very moderate. In 1979/80 there were very few economists who would have said it was possible to get unemployment down to almost 5 per cent in 1988 and have virtually no inflationary consequences. I wouldn't have said that ten years earlier – yet it happened. We don't have an inflation problem right now. If it comes back, then incomes policy may be a possible thing to do, but I wouldn't muddy the waters and get excited about it right now.

*Why has Keynesian economics experienced something of a restoration in the last decade?*
Well, it's because you have had Keynesian problems for the last five years. Keynesian economics got a bum rap in the 1970s. I see it all the time. People say 'Why do you want to go back to the failed policies of the 1970s and the late 1960s?' Keynesian policies were thought to be responsible for inflation and stagflation – people never mention, or erase from the memory, the oil shocks and the Vietnam War. Now we are back to a more normal environment and the new classical ideas are not so appealing to a new generation of economists, who have grown up subsequent to the high tides of the counter-revolutions.

*If you were advising Clinton about the economic strategy to be pursued over the next four years, what are the important things you think he should do?*
Well, that's a tricky thing for reasons we already discussed. The problem he has right now is to pep up the economy and the recovery. The economy is doing a little better than it was six months ago, but it is still not doing great. At the same time there is all this pressure to do something about the federal deficit. He is trying to do both. Since one really requires more deficit while the other requires less deficit, it's rather difficult. I'm afraid the stimulus he is going to give is not very big, and it's not going to last long enough. There is going to be a deficit-increasing phase of his programme this year and maybe next year [1994] his budget is going to be deficit-neutral. Thereafter tax increases and cuts in entitlements and other outlays are going to be phased in, so eventually for the fiscal year 1997 he will be able to say that he will have

done what he said. He is asking for both these things at once. It's sort of like saying we're going to have to perform some surgery on this patient but right now the patient is a little weak, so we'll have to build the patient up first. There are two difficulties. One is that the dual approach is a rather subtle point to explain – why we do one thing now when we are going to do the opposite later. In fact, he hasn't even explained it yet.

*Maybe he doesn't understand it.*
Oh he does, this is a smart guy. This is as smart a politician as I have ever met – he understands it.

## Additional Questions Answered by Correspondence January/February 1998

*In your 1995 paper 'The Natural Rate as New Classical Economics' you suggested that Friedman's [1968a] paper 'The Role of Monetary Policy' is 'very likely the most influential paper ever published in an economics journal'. In what important ways did that paper change macroeconomics and do you regard the natural rate hypothesis as part of the 'core' of mainstream macroeconomics?*
Perhaps that was hyperbole, but the article was certainly very influential in the profession and, in its implications for policy all over the world, far beyond. If, as I argued in my 1995 paper, the article was a giant step towards new classical macro and real business cycle theory, then the initial impact of the Friedman paper was greatly multiplied. If those doctrines are now the core of mainstream macroeconomics, then the natural rate idea is likewise. While this may be true of academic macro theory, I think it is not true of practical macro as used in government policy and business practice. There the NAIRU is the preferred concept, and as I have argued in the 1995 paper and elsewhere it is not the same as the natural rate. Both concepts have suffered from the empirical surprises of the last few years, when previous estimates of the NAIRU turned out to be wrong. Moreover, the idea that there is a vertical Phillips curve in the long run has lost ground relative to my own idea that a trade-off persists at low rates of inflation, a proposition recently supported by Akerlof, Dickens and Perry [1996] in *Brookings Papers*.

*The US economy currently [January 1998] has an unemployment rate of 4.7 per cent and an inflation rate of just over 2 per cent. Given that most estimates of the natural rate of unemployment for the US economy are around 6 per cent, how would you account for this current situation?*
Indicators of labour market tightness other than the unemployment rate suggest that labour markets are considerably less tight than the unemployment

rate itself would suggest, given the experience since the mid-1970s. Vacancies (proxied in the USA by help-wanted indexes) are more plentiful, quitting jobs less frequent relative to losing jobs, and persons counted as out of labour force more available for work. The Beveridge curve seems to have shifted back to its location in the 1950s and 1960s. Other factors include the decline in trade union membership and power *vis-à-vis* private business employers, the increased acceptability of downsizing employment to improve the bottom line and stock prices, even at the expense of long-time employees, import competition, yes, but especially domestic competition, and of course the absence of supply shocks, which has more to do with the stagflation of the 1970s than new classicals want to remember. It very well may be possible to reduce unemployment to 4 per cent, the target of the Kennedy administration in the 1960s, while keeping inflation below 3.5 per cent.

*Although unemployment in the US and UK economies is relatively low at the moment, the average rate of unemployment in the European Union economies is relatively high. How can we explain the considerable unemployment differentials that exist at the moment between the USA and countries such as France and Germany? Do you think that EMU is likely to exacerbate the unemployment problem in Europe?*

I am incorrigible. I still believe that wilfully bad macro policy is responsible for much of the excess unemployment in Europe. It can't be that the natural rate keeps rising along with the actual rate, from single to double digits. The Europeans conclude that if they don't see significant deflation at whatever actual U-rate, then that rate must be equal to or less than the natural rate, so that any expansionary monetary or fiscal policy will cause inflation to increase. But it may be that the short-run Phillips curve is pretty flat, so that this inference is not justified. Anyway they never try the experiment of expansionary policy. I can believe that there are more structural obstacles to reducing unemployment in continental Europe than in America and Britain. I can believe that Thatcher's bashing of labour unions helped, although I didn't see UK wages and prices tumbling when sterling was pegged to the DM. I think some of the structural problems on the continent reflect hysteresis. The governments and central banks never tried to recover from the 1979–82 recessions, unlike the USA, so the cyclical unemployment achieved by those recessions became 'structural'. Whatever the nature and cause, European unemployment is a disgrace and should be within the power of European governments to correct in some way, rather than complain about, as if it has been imposed on them by the USA.

I don't expect EMU to change the unemployment situation much either way. If anything, it will get worse. EU members haven't done much under the EMS to improve their own macro outcomes. But to the extent they have done anything individually, they won't have any macro policy tools once they are in EMU. Nor will the new central bank act differently from the Bundesbank, and the Union has no fisc with which to conduct fiscal policy.

*Do you feel that there has been any move towards greater consensus in macroeconomics since we last talked to you in 1993?*
Maybe there's more consensus in macro theory, in the sense that Keynesian theory is just ignored and graduate students don't learn anything about it. Maybe there's more consensus in practical macroeconomics, because it can't help having large Keynesian elements and because mechanical monetarism is dead.

*Many prominent macroeconomists (for example Barro and Sala-i-Martin, 1995; Lucas, 1987) have argued that the part of macroeconomics that really matters is growth. Do you agree with this view and have the endogenous growth theories of the past decade improved our understanding of growth processes?*
Yes, without doubt increasing the productivity, health and life expectancy of billions of people in poor and underdeveloped countries throughout the world adds more utility than reducing the unemployment in Western Europe by three or four points. I don't think the macroeconomists studying growth have answers on how to do that. Aggregate demand problems are a luxury available to advanced industrial capitalist countries. The basic problem of poor countries is poverty of supply. It's possible that aggregate demand shortage – the social disorganization of unnecessary poverty in the midst of potential plenty in the Great Depression – is no longer a high-priority problem because macroeconomics solved it, not because it never was a problem and the macro theory and policy it evoked was wrong. The fact that there are few auto accidents at intersections doesn't suggest that traffic lights are unnecessary. Barro and Lucas, it seems to me, trashed demand-oriented macroeconomics and then left the field, saying it's not interesting anyway. The endogenous growth theories, which interestingly enough rely on externalities of one kind or another to overcome diminishing returns, are intriguing but not as yet convincing to me.

# 4. The orthodox monetarist school

> the drastic change that has occurred in economic theory has not been the result of ideological warfare. It has not resulted from divergent political beliefs or aims. It has responded almost entirely to the force of events: brute experience proved far more potent than the strongest of political or ideological preferences. (Friedman, 1977, p. 470)

## 4.1 Introduction

During the 1950s and up to at least the mid- to late 1960s Keynesian economics, which came to be epitomized by the Hicks–Hansen IS–LM model, was the dominant force in the development of macroeconomics in terms of both theorizing and policy prescriptions. As one leading critic of Keynesian economics has admitted, in the late 1960s the Keynesian model 'seemed to be the only game in town in terms of macroeconomics' (see Barro, 1984). A central theme of Keynes's *General Theory* is the contention that capitalist market economies are inherently unstable and can come to rest at less than full employment equilibrium for prolonged periods of time. This instability was, in Keynes's view, predominantly the result of fluctuations in aggregate demand. In the mid- to late 1940s and the 1950s the then-prevailing Keynesian orthodoxy emphasized real disturbances (notably fluctuations in investment and autonomous consumption) as the main cause of fluctuations in money or nominal income, predominantly in the form of changes in real income. To the early Keynesians, the Great Depression had resulted from a sharp fall in the level of investment with the associated severe unemployment reflecting a state of deficient aggregate demand. This contrasted with the earlier quantity theory of money (QTM) tradition that viewed changes in the money stock as the predominant, though not the only, factor explaining changes in money income.

During the 1950s and 1960s, Milton Friedman, more than any other economist, was responsible for reviving the fortunes of the quantity theory of money. In 1968 Karl Brunner famously gave the label of 'monetarism' to the ideas of those economists, particularly Friedman, who adhered to the quantity theory of money. The quantity theory of money is the central plank to monetarism and this idea is, according to Mark Blaug, 'the oldest surviving theory in economics' Blaug et al. (1995). In a reasonably coherent form, the quantity theory of

*Modern macroeconomics*

money stretches back over at least 300 years to John Locke's *Some Considerations of the Consequences of the Lowering of Interest and Raising the Value of Money* published in 1692 (see Eltis, 1995). However, David Hume's classic essay, *Of Money*, published in 1752, is widely recognized as perhaps the most sophisticated early statement of the quantity theory of money. According to Mayer (1980), most of the fundamental propositions of monetarism date back to this essay. Thereafter, the quantity theory of money was accepted and developed throughout the nineteenth and early twentieth centuries by many notable economists, including David Ricardo, Alfred Marshall, Irving Fisher and, at least up until 1930, Keynes himself. As Blaug notes, 'Keynes began by loving it but ended up by hating it' (see Blaug et al., 1995).

The main purpose of this chapter is twofold. First, to trace the historical development of orthodox monetarism (see Figure 4.1) beginning with the quantity theory of money approach (section 4.2) as it evolved from the mid-1950s to the mid-1960s; through to the expectations-augmented Phillips curve analysis (section 4.3) which was absorbed into monetarist analysis after the mid- to late 1960s; finally to the monetary approach to balance of payments theory and exchange rate determination (section 4.4) which was incorporated into monetarist analysis in the early 1970s. Second, in the light of this discussion, to summarize the central distinguishing beliefs commonly held within the orthodox monetarist school, especially with respect to the role and

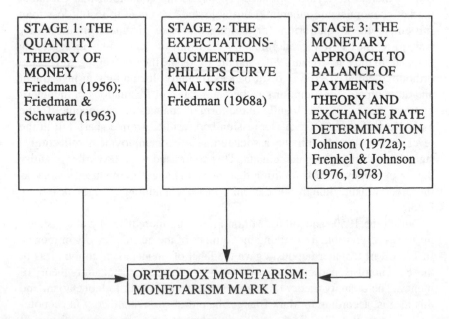

*Figure 4.1   The evolution of orthodox monetarism*

conduct of stabilization policy (section 4.5) and to reflect on what remains today of the monetarist counter-revolution.

Before examining the QTM approach to macroeconomic analysis we should note the key role played by Friedman in what came to be known as the 'monetarist counter-revolution' (see Johnson, 1971; Snowdon and Vane, 1996, 1997b). Unlike the majority of economists, Friedman is well known outside academic circles, a characteristic he shares with Keynes. Together with Keynes, Friedman has probably influenced macroeconomic theory and policy making more than any other economist in the twentieth century. This can be attributed not only to the quality and quantity of his research output, but also to his artistry and rhetoric in promoting a cause. In recognition of his academic work, Friedman was awarded the Nobel Memorial Prize in Economics in 1976 for 'his achievements in the fields of consumption analysis, monetary history and theory, and for his demonstration of the complexity of stabilisation policy'. There is no doubt that Friedman's monetary analysis and his demonstration of the limitations and dangers of discretionary stabilization policies in a dynamic and uncertain world have influenced a whole generation of eminent macroeconomists, most notably Robert Lucas Jr, who freely admits his intellectual debt to his former teacher whom he describes as a 'superb economist' (Klamer, 1984). Particularly influential to the generation of economists educated in the USA since the early 1960s was the publication of the Friedman and Schwartz (1963) volume *A Monetary History of the United States* which for Lucas (1994b) played an important, 'perhaps decisive', role in the 1960s debate over stabilization policy. In reflecting on the longevity of this 'classic' text Lucas has commented that it would be the first book in his suitcase if he is ever invited to Washington 'for some reason other than viewing cherry blossoms'. According to Lucas, Friedman was also 'by far' his 'most important teacher', suggesting that he is sure that he has read everything that Friedman has ever written (see Lucas, 1994a). In this chapter we shall explore many of Friedman's achievements.

## 4.2 The Quantity Theory of Money Approach

The first stage in the development of orthodox monetarism can be traced from the mid-1950s to the mid-1960s, and involved an attempt to re-establish the quantity theory of money approach to macroeconomic analysis, which had been usurped by the Keynesian revolution. Within the quantity theory of money approach (see also Chapter 2, section 2.5) changes in the money stock are regarded as the predominant, though not the only, factor explaining changes in money or nominal income (see Laidler, 1991).

Orthodox Keynesian analysis (see Chapter 3, section 3.3) emphasized real disturbances (notably fluctuations in investment and autonomous consumption) as the main cause of fluctuations in money income, predominantly in the form of changes in real income. In terms of the stylized quantity theory outlined in Chapter 2, section 2.5, Keynes's *General Theory* was interpreted as implying that in conditions of underemployment (which could prevail for protracted periods) income velocity ($V$) would be highly unstable and would passively adapt to whatever changes occurred independently in the money supply ($M$) or money income ($PY$). In these circumstances money was regarded as being relatively unimportant. For example, in the two extreme cases of the liquidity and investment traps, money does not matter inasmuch as monetary policy would be completely ineffective in influencing economic activity. In the liquidity trap case, an increase in the money supply would be exactly and completely offset by an opposite change in velocity. The increase in the money supply would be absorbed entirely into idle/speculative balances at an unchanged rate of interest and level of income. In the investment trap case, where investment is completely interest-inelastic, an increase in the money supply would again have no effect on the level of real income. The money supply would be powerless to influence real income because investment is insensitive to interest rate changes. Velocity would fall as the demand for money increased relative to an unchanged level of income. Readers should verify for themselves that, in either of these two extreme Keynesian cases where money does not matter, any change in autonomous consumption, investment or government expenditure would result in the full multiplier effect of the simple Keynesian cross or 45° model. Under such conditions, although the quantity theory relationship (equation 2.16) would be valid, orthodox Keynesians argued it would be useless in terms of monetary policy prescription.

### 4.2.1 The quantity theory as a theory of the demand for money

It was against this orthodox Keynesian background that Milton Friedman sought to maintain and re-establish across the profession what he regarded as the oral tradition of the University of Chicago, namely the quantity theory of money approach to macroeconomic analysis (for a criticism of this interpretation, see Patinkin, 1969). Although the traditional quantity theory is a body of doctrine concerned with the relationship between the money supply and the general price level, Friedman (1956) initially presented his restatement of the quantity theory of money as a theory of the demand for money, rather than a theory of the general price level or money income.

Friedman postulated that the demand for money (like the demand for any asset) yields a flow of services to the holder and depends on three main factors: (i) the wealth constraint, which determines the maximum amount of money that can be held; (ii) the return or yield on money in relation to the return on other financial and real assets in which wealth can be held; and (iii) the asset-holder's tastes and preferences. The way total wealth is allocated between various forms depends on the relative rates of return on the various assets. These assets include not just money and bonds but also equities and physical goods. In equilibrium wealth will be allocated between assets such that marginal rates of return are equal. Although Patinkin (1969) has suggested that Friedman's restatement should be regarded as an extension of Keynesian analysis, there are three important differences worth highlighting. First, Friedman's analysis of the demand for money can be regarded as an application of his permanent income theory of consumption to the demand for a particular asset. Second, he introduced the expected rate of inflation as a potentially important variable into the demand for money function. Third, he asserted that the demand for money was a stable function of a limited number of variables.

A simplified version of Friedman's demand function for real money balances can be written in the following form:

$$\frac{M_d}{P} = f(Y^P; r, \dot{P}^e; u) \tag{4.1}$$

where $Y^P$ represents permanent income, which is used as a proxy for wealth, the budget constraint;

$r$  represents the return on financial assets,

$\dot{P}^e$ represents the expected rate of inflation; and

$u$  represents individuals' tastes and preferences.

This analysis predicts that, *ceteris paribus*, the demand for money will be greater (i) the higher the level of wealth; (ii) the lower the yield on other assets; (iii) the lower the expected rate of inflation, and vice versa. Utility-maximizing individuals will reallocate wealth between different assets whenever marginal rates of return are not equal. This portfolio adjustment process is central to the monetarist specification of the transmission mechanism whereby changes in the stock of money affect the real sector. This can be illustrated by examining the effects of an increase in the money supply brought about by open market operations by the monetary authorities. An initial equilibrium is assumed where wealth is allocated between financial and real assets such that marginal rates of return are equal. Following open market purchases of bonds by the monetary authorities, the public's money holdings will increase. Given that the marginal return on any asset diminishes as holdings of it increase, the marginal rate of return on money holdings will in consequence fall. As excess money balances are exchanged for financial and real assets (such as consumer durables), their prices will be bid up until portfolio equilibrium is re-established when once again all assets are willingly held and marginal rates of return are equal. In contrast to orthodox

Keynesian analysis, monetarists argue that money is a substitute for a wide range of real and financial assets, and that no single asset or group of assets can be considered a close substitute for money. A much broader range of assets and associated expenditures is emphasized and in consequence monetarists attribute a much stronger and more direct effect on aggregate spending to monetary impulses.

### 4.2.2  The quantity theory and changes in money income: empirical evidence

The assertion that there exists a stable functional relationship (behaviour) between the demand for real balances and a limited number of variables that determine it lies at the heart of the modern quantity theory of money approach to macroeconomic analysis. If the demand for money function is stable, then velocity will also be stable, changing in a predictable manner if any of the limited number of variables in the demand for money function should change. Friedman (1968b, p. 434) has postulated the QTM as

> the empirical generalisation that changes in desired real balances (in the demand for money) tend to proceed slowly and gradually or to be the result of events set in train by prior changes in supply, whereas, in contrast, substantial changes in the supply of nominal balances can and frequently do occur independently of any changes in demand. The conclusion is that substantial changes in prices or nominal income are almost invariably the result of changes in the nominal supply of money.

In this section we discuss various empirical evidence put forward in support of the quantity theory of money approach to macroeconomic analysis, beginning with the demand for money function. Constraints of space preclude a detailed discussion of the empirical evidence on the demand for money. Nevertheless two points are worth highlighting. First, although Friedman (1959) in his early empirical work on the demand for money claimed to have found that the interest rate was insignificant, virtually all studies undertaken thereafter have found the interest rate to be an important variable in the function. Indeed, in a subsequent paper Friedman (1966) acknowledged this. Buiter (2003a) recounts that Tobin, in his long debate with Friedman, 'convinced most of the profession that the demand for money has an economically and statistically significant interest rate-responsiveness' (that is, the LM curve is not perfectly inelastic). This argument was a crucial part of Tobin's case in support of discretionary fiscal policy having a role to play in stabilization policy. Furthermore, in the 1950s and 1960s there also appeared little evidence that the interest elasticity of the money demand increased as the rate of interest fell, as the liquidity trap requires. This means that both the extreme quantity theory and Keynesian cases of vertical and horizontal *LM* curves, respectively, could be ruled out. The static IS–LM model can, however, still be used to illustrate the quantity theory approach to macroeconomic analysis if both the real rate of interest and real income are determined by real, not monetary, forces and the economy automatically tends towards full employment (see Friedman, 1968a). Second, although the belief in a stable demand for money function was well supported by empirical evidence up to the early 1970s, since then a number of studies, both in the USA and other economies, have found evidence of apparent instability of the demand for money. In the USA, for example, there occurred a marked break in the trend of the velocity of the narrow monetary aggregate, M1, in the early 1980s and subsequent breaks in the velocities of the broader monetary aggregates, M2 and M3, in the early 1990s. A number of possible explanations have been put forward to explain this apparent instability, including institutional change within the financial system which took place in the 1970s and 1980s. The reader is referred to Laidler (1993) for a detailed and very accessible discussion of the empirical evidence on the demand for money, and the continuing controversy over the question of the stability of the demand for money function.

Friedman (1958) sought to re-establish an important independent role for money through a study of time series data comparing rates of monetary growth with turning points in the level of economic activity for the USA. On the average of 18 non-war cycles since 1870, he found that peaks (troughs) in the rate of change of the money supply had preceded peaks (troughs) in the level of economic activity by an average of 16 (12) months. Friedman concluded that this provided strong suggestive evidence of an influence running from money to business. Friedman's study was subsequently criticized by Culbertson (1960, 1961) and by Kareken and Solow (1963) on both methodological and statistical grounds. First, the question was raised as to whether the timing evidence justified the inference of a causal relationship running from money to economic activity (see also Kaldor, 1970a; Sims, 1972). Second, statistical objections to Friedman's procedure were raised in that he had not compared like with like. When Kareken and Solow reran the tests with Friedman's data using rates of change for both money and economic activity, they found no uniform lead of monetary changes over changes in the level of economic activity. Later, the issue of money to income causality was famously taken up by Tobin (1970), who challenged the reliability of the timing (leads and lags) evidence accumulated by Friedman and other monetarists. Using an 'Ultra Keynesian' model Tobin demonstrated how the timing evidence could just as easily be interpreted in support of the Keynesian position on business cycles and instability. Tobin accused Friedman of falling foul of the *'Post Hoc Ergo Propter Hoc'* fallacy. He also went further by criticizing Friedman for not having an explicit theoretical foundation linking cause and effect on which to base his monetarist claims. The claim was frequently made that much of Friedman's work was 'measurement without theory' and that monetarism remained too much a 'black box'. As Hoover (2001a, 2001b) has recently reminded economists, correlation can never prove causation. This problem of 'causality in macroeconomics' has led to, and will continue to lead to, endless arguments and controversy in empirical macroeconomics (see also Friedman, 1970b; Davidson and Weintraub, 1973; Romer and Romer, 1994a, 1994b; Hoover and Perez, 1994; Hammond, 1996).

In 1963, Friedman and Schwartz (1963) presented more persuasive evidence to support the monetarist belief that changes in the stock of money play a largely independent role in cyclical fluctuations. In their influential study of the *Monetary History of the United States, 1867–1960*, they found that, while the stock of money had tended to rise during both cyclical expansions and contractions, the *rate of growth* of the money supply had been slower during contractions than during expansions in the level of economic activity. Within the period examined, the only times when there was an appreciable *absolute* fall in the money stock were also the six periods of major economic contraction identified: 1873–9, 1893–4, 1907–8, 1920–21, 1929–33 and 1937–8. Furthermore, from studying the historical circumstances underlying the changes that occurred in the money supply during these major recessions, Friedman and Schwartz argued that the factors producing monetary contraction were mainly independent of contemporary or prior changes in money income and prices. In other words, monetary changes were seen as the cause, rather than the consequence, of major recessions. For example, Friedman and Schwartz argued that the absolute decline in the money stock which took place during both 1920–21 and 1937–8 was a consequence of highly restrictive policy actions undertaken by the Federal Reserve System: for example, reserve requirements were doubled in 1936 and early 1937. These actions were themselves followed by sharp declines in the money stock, which were in turn followed by a period of severe economic contraction.

Even more controversial was the reinterpretation of the Great Depression as demonstrating the potency of monetary change and monetary policy. Friedman and Schwartz argued that an initial mild decline in the money stock from 1929 to 1930 was converted into a sharp decline by a wave of bank failures which started in late 1930 (see also Bernanke, 1983). Bank failures produced an increase in both the currency-to-deposit ratio, owing to the public's loss of faith in the banks' ability to redeem their deposits, and the reserve-to-deposit ratio, owing to the banks' loss of faith in the public's willingness to maintain their deposits with them. In Friedman and Schwartz's view, the consequent decline in the money stock was further intensified by the Federal Reserve System's restrictive action of raising the discount rate in October 1931, which in turn led to further bank failures. In this interpretation the depression only became great as a consequence of the failure of the Federal Reserve to prevent the dramatic decline in the money stock – between October 1929 and June 1933, the money stock fell by about a third. By adopting alternative policies the Federal Reserve System, they argued, could have prevented the banking collapse and the resulting fall in the money stock and severe economic contraction. Friedman and Schwartz further justified their view that changes in the stock of money play a largely independent role in cyclical fluctuations from the evidence that cyclical movements in money had much the same relationship (both in timing and amplitude) as cyclical movements in business activity, even under substantially different monetary arrangements that had prevailed in the USA over the period 1867–1960 (for further discussion of these issues, see Temin, 1976; Romer and Romer, 1989; Romer, 1992; Hammond, 1996).

A more intense exchange was triggered by the publication of the study undertaken by Friedman and Meiselman (1963) for the Commission on Money and Credit. Although the ensuing Friedman–Meiselman debate occupied economists for a lengthy period of time, the debate itself is now generally regarded as largely only of interest to students of the history of economic thought. In brief, Friedman and Meiselman attempted to estimate how much of the variation in consumption (a proxy variable for income) could be explained by changes in (i) the money supply, in line with the quantity theory approach, and (ii) autonomous expenditure (investment), in line with Keynesian analysis. Using two test equations (one using money and the other autonomous expenditure as the independent variable) for US data over the period 1897–1958, they found that, apart from one sub-period dominated by the Great Depression, the money equation gave much the better explanation. These results were subsequently challenged, most notably by De Prano and Mayer (1965) and Ando and Modigliani (1965), who showed that a change in the definition of autonomous expenditure improved the performance of the autonomous expenditure equation.

On reflection it is fair to say that these tests were ill devised to discriminate between the quantity theory of money and the Keynesian view, so that they failed to establish whether it was changes in the supply of money or autonomous expenditure that were causing changes in income. This can be illustrated by reference to the IS–LM model for a closed economy. In general, within the Hicksian IS–LM framework, monetary and fiscal multipliers each depend on both the consumption function and the liquidity preference function. Equally good results can be obtained using the two equations when income determination is either purely classical or Keynesian. The classical case is illustrated in Figure 4.2, where the demand for money is independent of the rate of interest. The economy is initially in equilibrium at a less than full employment income level of $Y_0$ and a rate of interest $r_0$, that is, the intersec-

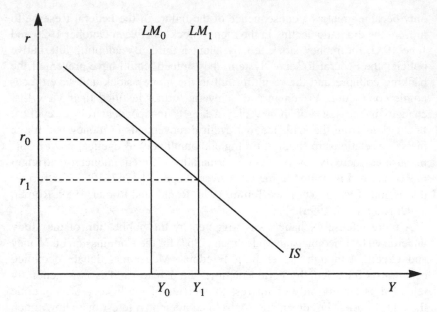

*Figure 4.2    The classical case*

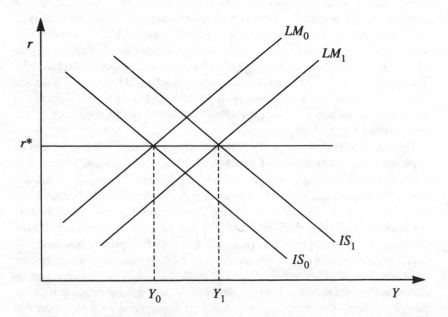

*Figure 4.3    The Keynesian case*

tion of $LM_0$ and $IS$. An increase in the money supply (which shifts the $LM$ curve from $LM_0$ to $LM_1$) would result in a lower rate of interest ($r_1$) and a higher level of income ($Y_1$). As the interest rate falls, investment expenditure is stimulated, which in turn, through the multiplier, affects consumption and income. In the classical case, empirical studies would uncover a stable relationship between autonomous expenditure and the level of income, even though the direction of causation would run from money to income.

The Keynesian case is illustrated in Figure 4.3. The economy is initially in equilibrium at an income level of $Y_0$ and a rate of interest of $r^*$, that is, the intersection of $IS_0$ and $LM_0$. Following an expansionary real impulse (which shifts the $IS$ curve outwards to the right, from $IS_0$ to $IS_1$), the authorities could stabilize the interest rate at $r^*$ by expanding the money supply (shifting the $LM$ curve downwards to the right, from $LM_0$ to $LM_1$). In the Keynesian case, empirical studies would uncover a stable relationship between the money supply and the level of income, even though in this particular case the direction of causation would run from income to money. In conclusion, what the Friedman–Meiselman tests appeared to demonstrate was that (i) the marginal propensity to consume had been relatively stable and (ii) contrary to the extreme Keynesian view, the economy had not been in a liquidity or investment trap because if it had the tests would not have found such good fits for the money equation.

### 4.2.3  An assessment

At this point it would be useful to draw together the material presented in this section and summarize the central tenets that proponents of the quantity theory of money approach to macroeconomic analysis generally adhered to by the mid-1960s (see Mayer, 1978; Vane and Thompson, 1979; Purvis, 1980; Laidler, 1981). The central distinguishing beliefs at that time could be listed as follows:

1. Changes in the money stock are the predominant factor explaining changes in money income.
2. In the face of a stable demand for money, most of the observed instability in the economy could be attributed to fluctuations in the money supply induced by the monetary authorities.
3. The authorities can control the money supply if they choose to do so and when that control is exercised the path of money income will be different from a situation where the money supply is endogenous.
4. The lag between changes in the money stock and changes in money income is long and variable, so that attempts to use discretionary monetary policy to fine-tune the economy could turn out to be destabilizing.
5. The money supply should be allowed to grow at a fixed rate in line with the underlying growth of output to ensure long-term price stability.

The Keynesian–monetarist debate, relating to the importance of changes in the money stock as the predominant factor explaining changes in money income, reached a climax in 1970, when Friedman, in response to his critics, attempted to set forth his 'Theoretical Framework for Monetary Analysis'. Until the publication of Friedman's 1970 paper there existed no *explicit, formal* and *coherent* statement of the theoretical structure underlying monetarist pronouncements. In opening up the monetarist 'black box' for theoretical scrutiny, Friedman intended to demonstrate that 'the basic differences among economists are empirical not theoretical'. His theoretical statement turned out to be a generalized IS–LM model which helped to place the monetarist approach *within* the mainstream position (see Friedman, 1970a, 1972; Tobin, 1972b; Gordon, 1974). This debate represented the 'final big battle between Friedman and his Keynesian critics' before the rational expectations revolution and new classical economics 'swept both Keynesianism and monetarism from center stage' (see Hammond, 1996). According to Tobin (1981), the central issue for both macroeconomic theory and policy is the supply response of the economy to monetary impulses. The division of such impulses between prices and quantities was referred to by Friedman as 'the missing equation'. In Tobin's view, Friedman's solution to this problem 'was not different in spirit from the wage/price/output mechanisms of mainstream eclectic Keynesian theory and econometrics' (Tobin, 1981, p. 36).

In retrospect we can now see that Friedman's debate with his critics demonstrated that their differences were more quantitative than qualitative, and contributed towards an emerging synthesis of monetarist and Keynesian ideas. This emerging synthesis, or theoretical accord, was to establish that the Keynesian-dominated macroeconomics of the 1950s had understated (but not neglected) the importance of monetary impulses in generating economic instability (see Laidler, 1992a). This was perhaps especially true in the UK in the period culminating in the Radcliffe *Report* (1959) on the working of the monetary system in the UK. According to Samuelson, a leading US Keynesian, 'the contrast between British and American Keynesianism had become dramatic' by 1959 because many of Keynes's admirers in Britain 'were still frozen in the Model T version of his system' (see Samuelson, 1983, 1988; Johnson, 1978).

### 4.3   The Expectations-augmented Phillips Curve Analysis

The second stage in the development of orthodox monetarism came with a more precise analysis of the way the effects of changes in the rate of monetary expansion are divided between real and nominal magnitudes. This analysis involved the independent contributions made by Friedman (1968a) and Phelps (1967, 1968) to the Phillips curve literature (see Chapter 3, section 3.6). The notion of a stable relationship between inflation and unemployment was challenged by Friedman and Phelps, who both denied the existence of a permanent (long-run) trade-off between inflation and unemployment (Phelps's analysis originated from a non-monetarist perspective; see Cross, 1995). The problem with the original specification of the Phillips curve is that the rate of change of money wages is determined quite independently of the rate of inflation. This in turn implies that workers are irrational and suffer from complete money illusion, in that they base their labour supply decisions on the level of money wages quite independently of what is happening to prices. In what follows we focus on the highly influential arguments put forward by Friedman (1968a) in his 1967 Presidential Address to the American Economic Association. Before doing so we should recognize just how important Friedman's paper proved to be for the development of macroeconomics after 1968. While *A Monetary History* has undoubtedly been Friedman's most influential book in the macroeconomics sphere, his 1967 Presidential Address published as 'The Role of Monetary Policy' has certainly been his most influential article. In 1981 Robert Gordon described this paper as probably the most influential article written in macroeconomics in the previous 20 years. James Tobin (1995), one of Friedman's most eloquent, effective and long-standing critics, went even further, describing the 1968 paper as 'very likely the most influential article *ever* published in an economics journal' (emphasis added). Paul Krugman (1994a) describes Friedman's paper as 'one of the decisive intellectual achievements of post-war economics' and both Mark Blaug (1997) and Robert Skideksky (1996b) view it as 'easily the most influential paper on macroeconomics published in the post-war era'. Between 1968 and 1997 Friedman's paper has approximately 924 citation counts recorded by the Social Sciences Citation Index and it continues to be one of the most heavily cited papers in economics (see Snowdon and Vane, 1998). Friedman's utilization of Wicksell's concept of the 'natural rate' in the context of unemployment was in rhetorical terms a 'masterpiece of marketing' (see Dixon, 1995), just as the application of the term 'rational' to the expectations hypothesis turned out to be in the rise of new classical economics during the 1970s. The impact of Professor Friedman's work forced Keynesians to restate and remake their case for policy activism even before that case was further undermined by the penetrating theoretical critiques of Professor Lucas and other leading new classical economists.

### 4.3.1 The expectations-augmented Phillips curve

The prevailing Keynesian view of the Phillips curve was overturned by new ideas hatched during the 1960s and events in the 1970s (Mankiw, 1990). A central component of the new thinking involved Friedman's critique of the trade-off interpretation of the Phillips curve. This was first provided by Friedman (1966) in his debate with Solow (1966) over wage and price guideposts and had even been outlined much earlier in conversation with Richard Lipsey in 1960 (Leeson, 1997a). However, the argument was developed more fully in his famous 1967 Presidential Address. According to Friedman, the original Phillips curve which related the rate of change of money wages to unemployment was misspecified. Although money wages are set in negotiations, both employers and employees are interested in real, not money, wages. Since wage bargains are negotiated for discrete time periods, what affects the anticipated real wage is the rate of inflation expected to exist throughout the period of the contract. Friedman argued that the Phillips curve should be set in terms of the rate of change of real wages. He therefore augmented the basic Phillips curve with the anticipated or expected rate of inflation as an additional variable determining the rate of change of money wages. The expectations-augmented Phillips curve can be expressed mathematically by the equation:

$$\dot{W} = f(U) + \dot{P}^e \tag{4.2}$$

Equation (4.2) shows that the rate of money wage increase is equal to a component determined by the state of excess demand (as proxied by the level of unemployment) plus the expected rate of inflation.

Introducing the expected rate of inflation as an additional variable to excess demand which determines the rate of change of money wages implies that, instead of one unique Phillips curve, there will be a family of Phillips curves, each associated with a different expected rate of inflation. Two such curves are illustrated in Figure 4.4. Suppose the economy is initially in equilibrium at point $A$ along the short-run Phillips curve ($SRPC_1$) with unemployment at $U_N$, its natural level (see below) and with a zero rate of increase of money wages. For simplification purposes in this, and subsequent, analysis we assume a zero growth in productivity so that with a zero rate of money wage increase the price level would also be constant and the expected rate of inflation would be zero; that is, $\dot{W} = \dot{P} = \dot{P}^e = 0$ per cent. Now imagine the authorities reduce unemployment from $U_N$ to $U_1$ by expanding aggregate demand through monetary expansion. Excess demand in goods and labour markets would result in upward pressure on prices and money wages, with commodity prices typically adjusting more rapidly than wages. Having recently experienced a period of price stability ($\dot{P}^e = 0$), workers would misinterpret their money wage increases as real wage increases and supply more labour; that is, they would suffer from temporary money illusion. Real wages would, however, actually fall and, as firms demanded more labour, unemployment would fall, with money wages rising at a rate of $\dot{W}_1$, that is, point $B$ on the short-run Phillips curve ($SRPC_1$). As workers started slowly to adapt their inflation expectations in the light of the actual rate of inflation experienced ($\dot{P} = \dot{W}_1$), they would realize that, although their money wages had risen, their real wages had fallen, and they would press for increased money wages, shifting the short-run Phillips curve upwards from $SRPC_1$ to $SRPC_2$. Money wages would rise at a rate of $\dot{W}_1$ plus the expected rate of inflation. Firms would lay off workers as real wages rose and unemployment would increase until, at point $C$, real wages were restored to their original level, with unemployment at its natural level. This means that, once the actual rate of inflation is completely anticipated ($\dot{P}_1 = \dot{P}^e$) in wage bargains ($\dot{W}_1 = \dot{P}^e$, that is to say there is no money illusion), there will be no long-run trade-off between unemployment and wage inflation. It follows that if there is no excess demand (that is, the economy is operating at the natural rate of unemployment), then the rate of increase of money wages will equal the expected rate of inflation and only in the special case where the expected rate of inflation is zero will wage inflation be zero, that is, at point $A$ in Figure 4.4. By joining points such as $A$ and $C$ together, a long-run vertical Phillips curve is obtained at the natural rate of unemployment ($U_N$). At $U_N$ the rate of increase in money wages is exactly equal to the rate of increase in prices, so that the real wage is constant. In consequence there will be no disturbance in the labour market. At the natural rate the labour market is in a state of equilibrium and the actual and expected rates of inflation are equal; that is, inflation is fully anticipated.

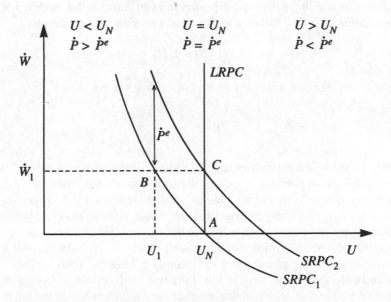

*Figure 4.4   The expectations-augmented Phillips curve*

Friedman's analysis helped reconcile the classical proposition with respect to the long-run neutrality of money (see Chapter 2, section 2.5), while still allowing money to have real effects in the short run.

Following Friedman's attack on the Phillips curve numerous empirical studies of the expectations-augmented Phillips curve were undertaken using the type of equation:

$$\dot{W} = f(U) + \beta \dot{P}^e \qquad (4.3)$$

Estimated values for $\beta$ of unity imply no long-run trade-off. Conversely estimates of $\beta$ of less than unity, but greater than zero, imply a long-run trade-off but one which is less favourable than in the short run. This can be demonstrated algebraically in the following manner. Assuming a zero growth in productivity so that $\dot{W} = \dot{P}$, equation (4.3) can be written as:

$$\dot{P} = f(U) + \beta \dot{P}^e \qquad (4.4)$$

Rearranging equation (4.4) we obtain:

$$\dot{P} - \beta \dot{P}^e = f(U) \qquad (4.5)$$

Starting from a position of equilibrium where unemployment equals $U^*$ (see Figure 4.5) and the actual and expected rates of inflation are both equal to zero (that is, $\dot{P} = \dot{P}^e$), equation (4.5) can be factorized and written as:

$$\dot{P}(1 - \beta) = f(U) \qquad (4.6)$$

Finally, dividing both sides of equation (4.6) by $1 - \beta$, we obtain

$$\dot{P} = \frac{f(U)}{1 - \beta} \qquad (4.7)$$

Now imagine the authorities initially reduce unemployment below $U^*$ (see Figure 4.5) by expanding aggregate demand through monetary expansion. From equation (4.7) we can see that, as illustrated in Figure 4.5, (i) estimated values for $\beta$ of zero imply both a stable short- and long-run trade-off between inflation and unemployment in line with the original Phillips curve; (ii) estimates of $\beta$ of unity imply no long-run trade-off; and (iii) estimates of $\beta$ of less than unity, but greater than zero, imply a long-run trade-off but one which is less favourable than in the short run. Early evidence from a wide range of studies that sought to test whether the coefficient ($\beta$) on the inflation expectations term is equal to one proved far from clear-cut. In consequence,

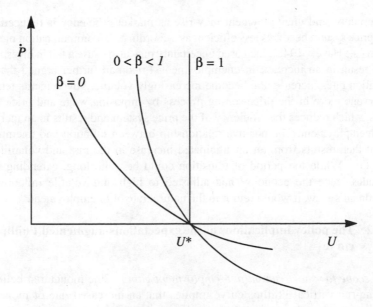

*Figure 4.5   The trade-off between inflation and unemployment*

during the early 1970s, the subject of the possible existence of a long-run vertical Phillips curve became a controversial issue in the monetarist–Keynesian debate. While there was a body of evidence that monetarists could draw on to justify their belief that β equals unity, so that there would be no trade-off between unemployment and inflation in the long run, there was insufficient evidence to convince all the sceptics. However, according to one prominent American Keynesian economist, 'by 1972 the "vertical-in-the-long-run" view of the Phillips curve had won the day' (Blinder, 1992a). The reader is referred to Santomero and Seater (1978) for a very readable review of the vast literature on the Phillips curve up to 1978. By the mid- to late 1970s, the majority of mainstream Keynesians (especially in the USA) had come to accept that the long-run Phillips curve is vertical. There is, however, still considerable controversy on the time it takes for the economy to return to the long-run solution following a disturbance.

Before turning to discuss the policy implications of the expectations-augmented Phillips curve, it is worth mentioning that in his Nobel Memorial Lecture Friedman (1977) offered an explanation for the existence of a positively sloped Phillips curve for a period of several years, which is compatible with a vertical long-run Phillips curve at the natural rate of unemployment. Friedman noted that inflation rates tend to become increasingly volatile at higher rates of inflation. Increased volatility of inflation results in greater uncertainty, and unemployment may rise as market efficiency is reduced and the price system becomes less efficient as a coordinating/communication mechanism (see Hayek, 1948). Increased uncertainty may also cause a fall in investment and result in an increase in unemployment. Friedman further argued that, as inflation rates increase and become increasingly volatile, governments tend to intervene more in the price-setting process by imposing wage and price controls, which reduces the efficiency of the price system and results in an increase in unemployment. The positive relationship between inflation and unemployment then results from an unanticipated increase in the rate and volatility of inflation. While the period of transition could be quite long, extending over decades, once the economy had adjusted to high and volatile inflation, in Friedman's view, it would return to the natural rate of unemployment.

### 4.3.2  The policy implications of the expectations-augmented Phillips curve

*The scope for short-run output–employment gains*   The monetarist belief in a long-run vertical Phillips curve implies that an increased rate of monetary expansion can reduce unemployment below the natural rate only because the resulting inflation is unexpected. As we have discussed, as soon as inflation is fully anticipated it will be incorporated into wage bargains and unemployment will return to the natural rate. The assumption underlying orthodox monetarist analysis is that expected inflation adjusts to actual inflation only gradually, in line with the so-called 'adaptive' or error-learning expectations hypothesis. Interestingly, it seems that Friedman was profoundly influenced by 'Phillips's adaptive inflationary expectations formula' (Leeson, 1999). The adaptive expectations equation implicit in Friedman's analysis of the Phillips curve, and used in *Studies in the Quantity Theory of Money* (1956), appears to have been developed by Friedman in conjunction with Philip Cagan following a discussion he had with Phillips which took place on a park bench somewhere in London in May 1952 (Leeson, 1994b, 1997a). In fact Friedman was so impressed with Phillips as an economist that he twice (in 1955 and 1960) tried to persuade him to move to the University of Chicago (Hammond, 1996).

The main idea behind the adaptive expectations hypothesis is that economic agents adapt their inflation expectations in the light of past inflation rates and that they learn from their errors. Workers are assumed to adjust their inflation expectations by a fraction of the last error made: that is, the difference between the actual rate of inflation and the expected rate of inflation. This can be expressed by the equation:

$$\dot{P}_t^e - \dot{P}_{t-1}^e = \alpha(\dot{P}_t - \dot{P}_{t-1}^e) \tag{4.8}$$

where $\alpha$ is a constant fraction. By repeated back substitution expected inflation can be shown to be a geometrically weighted average of past actual inflation rates with greater importance attached to more recent experience of inflation:

$$\dot{P}_t^e = \alpha\dot{P}_t + \alpha(1-\alpha)\dot{P}_{t-1}\ldots\alpha(1-\alpha)^n\dot{P}_{t-n} \qquad (4.9)$$

In this 'backward-looking' model, expectations of inflation are based solely on past actual inflation rates. The existence of a gap in time between an increase in the actual rate of inflation and an increase in the expected rate permits a temporary reduction in unemployment below the natural rate. Once inflation is fully anticipated, the economy returns to its natural rate of unemployment but with a higher equilibrium rate of wage and price inflation equal to the rate of monetary growth. As we will discuss in Chapter 5, section 5.5.1, if expectations are formed according to the rational expectations hypothesis and economic agents have access to the same information as the authorities, then the expected rate of inflation will rise immediately in response to an increased rate of monetary expansion. In the case where there was no lag between an increase in the actual and expected rate of inflation the authorities would be powerless to influence output and employment even in the short run.

*The accelerationist hypothesis*   A second important policy implication of the belief in a vertical long-run Phillips curve concerns the so-called 'accelerationist' hypothesis. This hypothesis implies that any attempt to maintain unemployment permanently below the natural rate would result in accelerating inflation and require the authorities to increase continuously the rate of monetary expansion. Reference to Figure 4.4 reveals that, if unemployment were held permanently at $U_1$ (that is, below the natural rate $U_N$), the continued existence of excess demand in the labour market would lead to a higher actual rate of inflation than expected. As the actual rate of inflation increased, people would revise their inflation expectations upwards (that is, shifting the short-run Phillips curve upwards), which would in turn lead to a higher actual rate of inflation and so on, leading to hyperinflation. In other words, in order to maintain unemployment below the natural rate, real wages would have to be kept below their equilibrium level. For this to happen actual prices would have to rise at a faster rate than money wages. In such a situation employees would revise their expectations of inflation upwards and press for higher money wage increases, which would in turn lead to a higher actual rate of inflation. The end result would be accelerating inflation which would necessitate continuous increases in the rate of monetary expansion to validate the continuously rising rate of inflation. Conversely, if unemployment is held permanently above the natural rate, accelerating deflation will occur. Where unemployment is held permanently above the natural rate, the continued existence of excess supply in the labour market will lead to a lower actual rate of inflation than expected. In this situation people will revise their inflation expectations downwards (that is, the short-run Phillips curve will shift downwards), which will in turn lead to a lower actual rate of inflation and so on. It follows from this analysis that the natural rate is the only level of unemployment at which a constant rate of inflation may be maintained. In other words, in long-run equilibrium with the economy at the natural rate of unemployment, the rate of monetary expansion will determine the rate of inflation (assuming a constant growth of output and velocity) in line with the quantity theory of money approach to macroeconomic analysis.

Undoubtedly the influence of Friedman's (1968a) paper was greatly enhanced because he anticipated the acceleration of inflation that occurred during the 1970s as a consequence of the repeated use of expansionary monetary policy geared to an over-optimistic employment target. The failure of inflation to slow down in both the US and UK economies in 1970–71, despite rising unemployment and the subsequent simultaneous existence of high unemployment and high inflation (so-called stagflation) in many countries, following the first adverse OPEC oil price (supply) shock in 1973–4, destroyed the idea that there might be a permanent long-run trade-off between inflation and unemployment. Lucas (1981b) regards the Friedman–Phelps model and the verification of its predictions as providing 'as clear cut an experimental distinction as macroeconomics is ever likely to see'. In the philosophy of science literature Imre Lakatos (1978) makes the prediction of novel facts the *sole* criterion by which theories should be judged, a view shared by Friedman (1953a). While Blaug (1991b, 1992) has argued that the principal novel fact of the *General Theory* was the prediction that the size of the instantaneous multiplier is greater than one, he also argues that the prediction of novel facts emanating from Friedman's 1968 paper were enough to make Mark I monetarism a progressive research programme during the 1960s and early 1970s. As Backhouse (1995) notes, 'the novel facts predicted by Phelps and Friedman were dramatically corroborated by the events of the early 1970s'.

*The output–employment costs of reducing inflation*   Friedman (1970c) has suggested that 'inflation is always and everywhere a monetary phenomenon in the sense that it can be produced only by a more rapid increase in the quantity of money than in output'. Given the orthodox monetarist belief that inflation is essentially a monetary phenomenon propagated by excessive monetary growth, monetarists argue that inflation can only be reduced by slowing down the rate of growth of the money supply. Reducing the rate of monetary expansion results in an increase in the level of unemployment. The policy dilemma the authorities face is that, the more rapidly they seek to reduce

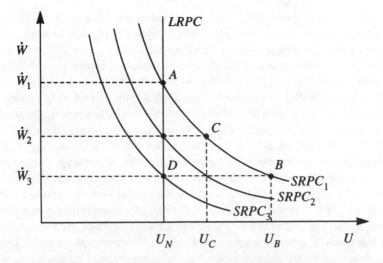

*Figure 4.6 The output–employment costs of reducing inflation*

inflation through monetary contraction, the higher will be the costs in terms of unemployment. Recognition of this fact has led some orthodox monetarists (such as David Laidler) to advocate a gradual adjustment process whereby the rate of monetary expansion is slowly brought down to its desired level in order to minimize the output–employment costs of reducing inflation. The costs of the alternative policy options of gradualism versus cold turkey are illustrated in Figure 4.6.

In Figure 4.6 we assume the economy is initially operating at point *A*, the intersection of the short-run Phillips curve ($SRPC_1$) and the long-run vertical Phillips curve (*LRPC*). The initial starting position is then both a short- and long-run equilibrium situation where the economy is experiencing a constant rate of wage and price inflation which is fully anticipated (that is, $\dot{W}_1 = \dot{P} = \dot{P}^e$) and unemployment is at the natural rate ($U_N$). Now suppose that this rate of inflation is too high for the authorities' liking and that they wish to reduce the rate of inflation by lowering the rate of monetary expansion and move to position *D* on the long-run vertical Phillips curve. Consider two alternative policy options open to the authorities to move to their preferred position at point *D*. One (cold turkey) option would be to reduce *dramatically* the rate of monetary expansion and raise unemployment to $U_B$, so that wage and price inflation quickly fell to $\dot{W}_3$; that is, an initial movement along $SRPC_1$ from point *A* to *B*. The initial cost of this option would be a relatively large increase in unemployment, from $U_N$ to $U_B$. As the actual rate of inflation fell below the expected rate, expectations of future rates of inflation would be revised in a downward direction. The short-run Phillips curve would shift downwards and a new short- and long-run equilibrium would eventually be achieved at point $D$, the intersection of $SRPC_3$ and $LRPC$ where $\dot{W}_3 = \dot{P} = \dot{P}^e$ with unemployment at $U_N$. Another (gradual) policy option open to the authorities would be to begin with a much smaller reduction in the rate of monetary expansion and initially increase unemployment to, say, $U_C$ so that wage and price inflation fell to $\dot{W}_2$, that is, an initial movement along $SRPC_1$ from point $A$ to $C$. Compared to the cold turkey option, this gradual option would involve a much smaller initial increase in unemployment, from $U_N$ to $U_C$. As the actual rate of inflation fell below the expected rate (but to a much lesser extent than in the first option), expectations would be revised downwards. The short-run Phillips curve would move downwards as the economy adjusted to a new lower rate of inflation. The short-run Phillips curve ($SRPC_2$) would be associated with an expected rate of inflation of $\dot{W}_2$. A further reduction in the rate of monetary expansion would further reduce the rate of inflation until the inflation target of $\dot{W}_3$ was achieved. The transition to point $D$ on the $LRPC$ would, however, take a much longer time span than under the first policy option. Such a policy entails living with inflation for quite long periods of time and has led some economists to advocate supplementary policy measures to accompany the gradual adjustment process to a lower rate of inflation. Before we consider the potential scope for such supplementary measures as indexation and prices and incomes policy, we should stress the importance of the credibility of any anti-inflation strategy (this issue is discussed more fully in Chapter 5, section 5.5.3). If the public believes that the authorities are committed to contractionary monetary policies to reduce inflation, economic agents will adjust their inflation expectations downwards more quickly, thereby reducing the output–employment costs associated with the adjustment process.

Some monetarists (for example Friedman, 1974) have suggested that some form of indexation would be a useful supplementary policy measure to accompany the gradual adjustment process to a lower rate of inflation. It is claimed that indexation would reduce not only the cost of unanticipated inflation incurred through arbitrary redistribution of income and wealth, but also the output–employment costs that are associated with a reduction in the rate of monetary expansion. With indexation, money wage increases would automatically decline as inflation decreased, thereby removing the danger that employers would be committed, under existing contracts, to excessive money wage increases when inflation fell. In other words, with indexation wage increases would be less rapid and unemployment would therefore rise by a smaller amount. Further some economists (for example Tobin, 1977, 1981; Trevithick and Stevenson, 1977) have suggested that a prices and incomes policy could have a role to play, as a temporary and supplementary policy measure to monetary contraction, to assist the transition to a lower rate of inflation by reducing inflationary expectations. In terms of Figure 4.6, to the extent that a prices and incomes policy succeeded in reducing inflationary expectations, the short-run Phillips curves would shift downwards more quickly. This in turn would enable adjustment to a lower rate of inflation to be achieved both more quickly and at a lower cost in terms of the extent and duration of unemployment that accompanies monetary contraction. However, one of the problems of using prices and incomes policy is that, even if the policy initially succeeds in reducing inflationary expectations, once the policy begins to break down or is ended, inflationary expectations may be revised upwards. As a result the short-run Phillips curve will shift upwards, thereby offsetting the initial benefit of the policy in terms of lower unemployment and wage inflation. For example, Henry and Ormerod (1978) concluded that:

> Whilst some incomes policies have reduced the rate of wage inflation during the period in which they operated, this reduction has only been temporary. Wage increases in the period immediately following the ending of policies were higher than they would otherwise have been, and these increases match losses incurred during the operation of the incomes policy.

In summary, within the orthodox monetarist approach the output–employment costs associated with monetary contraction depend upon three main factors: first, whether the authorities pursue a rapid or gradual reduction in the rate of monetary expansion; second, the extent of institutional adaptations – for example, whether or not wage contracts are indexed; and third, the speed with which economic agents adjust their inflationary expectations downwards.

The monetarist view that inflation can only be reduced by slowing down the rate of growth of the money supply had an important bearing on the course of macroeconomic policy pursued both in the USA (see Brimmer, 1983) and in the UK during the early 1980s. For example, in the UK the Conservative government elected into office in 1979 sought, as part of its medium-term financial strategy, to reduce progressively the rate of monetary growth (with pre-announced target ranges for four years ahead) in order to achieve its overriding economic policy objective of permanently reducing the rate of inflation. Furthermore, the orthodox monetarist contention that inflation cannot be reduced without output–employment costs appears to have been borne out by the recessions experienced in the US and UK economies in 1981–2 and 1980–81, respectively (see Chapter 5, section 5.5.2). For well-written and highly accessible accounts of the background to, and execution and effects of what the media dubbed 'Thatcher's monetarist experiment', the interested reader is referred to Keegan (1984) and Smith (1987).

*The role and conduct of monetary policy* The belief in a long-run vertical Phillips curve and that aggregate-demand management policies can only affect the level of output and employment in the short run has important implications for the role and conduct of monetary policy. Before discussing the rationale for Friedman's policy prescription for a fixed monetary growth rule, it is important to stress that, even if the long-run Phillips curve is vertical, arguments justifying discretionary monetary intervention to stabilize the economy in the short run can be made on the grounds of either the potential to identify and respond to economic disturbances or the length of time required for the economy to return to the natural rate following a disturbance. Friedman's policy prescription for a fixed rate of monetary growth (combined with a floating exchange rate), in line with the trend/long-run growth rate of the economy, is based on a number of arguments. These arguments include the beliefs that: (i) if the authorities expand the money supply at a steady rate over time the economy will tend to settle down at the natural rate of unemployment with a steady rate of inflation, that is, at a point along the long-run vertical Phillips curve; (ii) the adoption of a monetary rule would remove the greatest source of instability in the economy; that is, unless disturbed by erratic monetary growth, advanced capitalist economies are inherently stable around the natural rate of unemployment; (iii) in the present state of economic knowledge, discretionary monetary policy could turn out to be destabilizing and make matters worse rather than better, owing to the long and variable lags associated with monetary policy; and (iv) because of ignorance of the natural rate itself (which may change over time), the government should not aim at a target unemployment rate for fear of the consequences noted earlier, most notably accelerating inflation.

We finally consider the implication of the belief in a natural rate of unemployment for employment policy.

*The natural rate of unemployment and supply-side policies*   As we have discussed earlier, the natural rate of unemployment is associated with equilibrium in the labour market and hence in the structure of real wage rates. Friedman (1968a) has defined the natural rate as:

> the level that would be ground out by the Walrasian system of general equilibrium equations provided there is embedded in them the actual structural characteristics of the labor and commodity markets, including market imperfections, stochastic variability in demands and supplies, the cost of gathering information about job vacancies and labor availabilities, the costs of mobility and so on.

What this approach implies is that, if governments wish to reduce the natural rate of unemployment in order to achieve higher output and employment levels, they should pursue supply-management policies that are designed to improve the structure and functioning of the labour market and industry, rather than demand-management policies. Examples of the wide range of (often highly controversial) supply-side policies which were pursued over the 1980s both in the UK (see for example Vane, 1992) and elsewhere include measures designed to increase: (i) the incentive to work, for example through reductions in marginal income tax rates and reductions in unemployment and social security benefits; (ii) the flexibility of wages and working practices, for example by curtailing trade union power; (iii) the occupational and geographical mobility of labour, for example in the former case through greater provision of government retraining schemes; and (iv) the efficiency of markets for goods and services, for example by privatization.

Following the Friedman–Phelps papers the concept of the natural rate of unemployment has remained controversial (see Tobin, 1972a, 1995; Cross, 1995). It has also been defined in a large variety of ways. As Rogerson (1997) shows, the natural rate has been equated with 'long run = frictional = average = equilibrium = normal = full employment = steady state = lowest sustainable = efficient = Hodrick–Prescott trend = natural'. Such definitional problems have led sceptics such as Solow (1998) to describe the 'doctrine' of the natural rate to be 'as soft as a grape'. When discussing the relationship between unemployment and inflation many economists prefer to use the 'NAIRU' concept (non-accelerating inflation rate of unemployment), a term first introduced by Modigliani and Papademos (1975) as 'NIRU' (non-inflationary rate of unemployment). While the majority of economists would probably admit that it is 'hard to think about macroeconomic policy without the concept of NAIRU' (Stiglitz, 1997), others remain unconvinced that the natural rate concept is helpful (J. Galbraith, 1997; Arestis and Sawyer, 1998; Akerlof, 2002).

## 4.4 The Monetary Approach to Balance of Payments Theory and Exchange Rate Determination

The third stage in the development of orthodox monetarism came in the 1970s, with the incorporation of the monetary approach to balance of payments theory and exchange rate determination into monetarist analysis. Until the collapse of the Bretton Woods system of fixed exchange rates against the United States dollar in 1971, the US economy could be treated as a reasonably close approximation to a closed economy. The monetary approach was particularly important in that it made monetarist analysis, which had been implicitly developed in this closed economy context, relevant to open economies such as the UK.

### 4.4.1 The monetary approach to the balance of payments under fixed exchange rates

During the 1970s, a large number of different monetary models of the balance of payments appeared in the literature. However, common to all monetary models is the view that the balance of payments is essentially a monetary phenomenon. As we will discuss, the approach concentrates primarily on the money market in which the relationship between the stock demand for and supply of money is regarded as the main determinant of balance of payments flows. Furthermore, despite different specifications, in most of the monetary models of the balance of payments four key assumptions are generally made. First, the demand for money is a stable function of a limited number of variables. Second, in the long run output and employment tend towards their full employment or natural levels. Third, the authorities cannot sterilize or neutralize the monetary impact of balance of payments deficits/surpluses on the domestic money supply in the long run. Fourth, after due allowance for tariffs and transport costs, arbitrage will ensure that the prices of similar traded goods will tend to be equalized in the long run.

The most influential contributions to the development of the monetary approach to balance of payments theory have been made by Johnson (1972a) and Frenkel and Johnson (1976). Following Johnson (1972a) we now consider a simple monetary model of the balance of payments for a small open economy. Within this model it is assumed that: (i) real income is fixed at its full employment or natural level; (ii) the law of one price holds in both commodity and financial markets, and (iii) both the domestic price level and interest rate are pegged to world levels.

The demand for real balances depends on real income and the rate of interest.

$$M_d = Pf(Y, r) \tag{4.10}$$

The supply of money is equal to domestic credit (that is, money created domestically) plus money associated with changes in international reserves.

$$M_s = D + R \tag{4.11}$$

In money market equilibrium, $M_d$ must be equal to $M_s$ so that:

$$M_d = D + R \tag{4.12}$$

or

$$R = M_d - D \tag{4.13}$$

Assuming the system is initially in equilibrium, we now examine the consequence of a once-and-for-all increase in domestic credit ($D$) by the authorities. Since the arguments in the demand for money function (equation 4.10) are all exogenously given, the demand for money cannot adjust to the increase in domestic credit. Individuals will get rid of their excess money balances by buying foreign goods and securities, generating a balance of payments deficit. Under a regime of fixed exchange rates, the authorities are committed to sell foreign exchange for the home currency to cover a balance of payments deficit, which results in a loss of international reserves (*R*). The loss of international reserves would reverse the initial increase in the money supply, owing to an increase in domestic credit, and the money supply would continue to fall until the balance of payments deficit was eliminated. The system will return to equilibrium when the money supply returns to its original level, with the increase in domestic credit being matched by an equal reduction in foreign exchange reserves (equation 4.11). In short, any discrepancy between actual and desired money balances results in a balance of payments deficit/ surplus which in turn provides the mechanism whereby the discrepancy is eliminated. In equilibrium actual and desired money balances are again in balance and there will be no changes in international reserves; that is, the balance of payments is self-correcting.

The analysis can also be conducted in dynamic terms. To illustrate the predictions of the approach, we again simplify the analysis, this time by assuming that the small open economy experiences continuous real income growth while world (and hence domestic) prices and interest rates are constant. In this case the balance of payments position would reflect the relationship between the growth of money demand and the growth of domestic credit. A country will experience a persistent balance of payments deficit, and will in consequence be continually losing international reserves, whenever domestic credit expansion is greater than the growth in the demand for money balances (owing to real income growth). Clearly the level of foreign exchange reserves provides a limit to the duration of time a country can finance a persistent balance of payments deficit. Conversely a country will experience a persistent balance of payments surplus whenever the authorities fail to expand domestic credit in line with the growth in the demand for money balances. While a country might aim to achieve a balance of payments surplus in order to build up depleted international reserves in the short run, in the long run it would be irrational for a country to pursue a policy of achieving a continuous balance of payments surplus, thereby continually acquiring international reserves.

### 4.4.2   The policy implications of the monetary approach under fixed exchange rates

*Automatic adjustment and the power of expenditure switching policies*   The monetary approach predicts that there is an automatic adjustment mechanism that operates, without discretionary government policy, to correct balance of payments disequilibria. As we have discussed, any discrepancy between actual and desired real balances results in balance of payments disequilibria as people try to get rid of or acquire real money balances through international markets for goods and securities. The adjustment process operates through balance of payments flows and continues until the discrepancy between actual and desired real money balances has been eliminated. Closely linked to the belief in an automatic adjustment mechanism is the prediction that expenditure-switching policies will only temporarily improve the balance of payments if they induce an increase in the demand for money by raising domestic prices. For example, devaluation would raise the domestic price level, which would in turn reduce the level of real money balances below their equilibrium level. Reference to equation (4.12) reveals that, assuming there is no increase in domestic credit, the system will return to equilibrium once the money supply has increased, through a balance of payments surplus and an associated increase in the level of foreign exchange reserves, to meet the increased demand for money.

*The power of monetary policy*  From the above analysis it will be apparent that, in the case of a small country maintaining a fixed exchange rate with the rest of the world, the country's money supply becomes an endogenous variable. *Ceteris paribus*, a balance of payments deficit leads to a reduction in a country's foreign exchange reserves and the domestic money supply, and vice versa. In other words, where the authorities are committed to buy and sell foreign exchange for the home currency at a fixed price, changes in the money supply can arise not only from domestic sources (that is, domestic credit) but also from balance of payments intervention policy to maintain a fixed exchange rate. Reference to equation (4.11) reveals that domestic monetary policy only determines the division of the country's money supply between domestic credit and foreign exchange reserves, not the money supply itself. *Ceteris paribus*, any increase in domestic credit will be matched by an equal reduction in foreign exchange reserves, with no effect on the money supply. Monetary policy, in a small open economy, is completely impotent to influence any variable, other than foreign exchange reserves, in the long run. For an open economy operating under fixed exchange rates, the rate of growth of the money supply ($\dot{M}$) will equal domestic credit expansion ($\dot{D}$) plus the rate of change of foreign exchange reserves ($\dot{R}$), reflecting the balance of payments position. Domestic monetary expansion will have no influence on the domestic rate of inflation, interest rates or the rate of growth of output. Monetary expansion by a large country relative to the rest of the world can, however, influence the rate of world monetary expansion and world inflation.

*Inflation as an international monetary phenomenon* In a world of fixed exchange rates, inflation is viewed as an international monetary phenomenon which can be explained by an excess-demand expectations model. Excess demand depends on world, rather than domestic, monetary expansion. An increase in the world rate of monetary expansion (due to rapid monetary expansion by either a large country or a number of small countries simultaneously) would create excess demand and result in inflationary pressure throughout the world economy. In this context it is interesting to note that monetarists have argued that the acceleration of inflation that occurred in Western economies in the late 1960s was primarily the consequence of an increase in the rate of monetary expansion in the USA to finance increased spending on the Vietnam War (see, for example, Johnson, 1972b; Laidler, 1976). Under the regime of fixed exchange rates that existed up to 1971, it is claimed that the inflationary pressure initiated in the USA was transmitted to other Western economies via changes in their domestic money supplies originating from the US balance of payments deficit. In practice the USA determined monetary conditions for the rest of the world. This situation eventually proved unacceptable to other countries and helped lead to the breakdown of the Bretton Woods system.

### 4.4.3 The monetary approach to exchange rate determination

The monetary approach to exchange rate determination is a direct application of the monetary approach to the balance of payments to the case of flexible exchange rates (see Frenkel and Johnson, 1978). Under a system of perfectly flexible exchange rates, the exchange rate adjusts to clear the foreign exchange market so that the balance of payments is always zero. In the absence of balance of payments deficits/surpluses there are no international reserves changes, so that domestic credit expansion is the only source of monetary expansion. In contrast to a regime of fixed exchange rates where, *ceteris paribus*, an increase in domestic credit leads to a balance of payments deficit and a loss of international reserves, under flexible exchange rates it leads to a depreciation in the nominal exchange rate and an increase in the domestic price level. In the flexible exchange rate case of the monetary approach, 'the proximate determinants of exchange rates ... are the demand for and supply of various national monies' (Mussa, 1976).

The monetary approach to exchange rate determination can be illustrated using the simple monetary model first introduced in section 4.4.1. Assuming the system is initially in equilibrium, we again examine the consequence of a once-and-for-all increase in the domestic money supply (that is, domestic credit) by the authorities which disturbs the initial money market equilibrium. Reference to equation (4.10) reveals that, with real income fixed at its full employment or natural level, and the domestic rate of interest pegged to the world rate, the excess supply of money can only be eliminated by an increase in the domestic price level. The discrepancy between actual and desired money balances results in an increased demand for foreign goods and securities and a corresponding excess supply of domestic currency on the foreign exchange market, which causes the domestic currency to depreciate. The depreciation in the domestic currency results in an increase in the domestic price level, which in turn leads to an increased demand for money balances, and money market equilibrium is restored when actual and desired money balances are again in balance. In this simple monetary model, the nominal exchange rate depreciates in proportion to the increase in the money supply. In other words the exchange rate is determined by relative money supplies. For example, in a two-country world, *ceteris paribus* there would be no change in the (real) exchange rate if both countries increased their money supplies together by the same amount.

The analysis can also be conducted in dynamic terms using slightly more complicated monetary models which allow for differential real income growth and differential inflation experience (due to different rates of monetary expansion). These models predict that the rate of change of the exchange rate depends on relative rates of monetary expansion and real income growth. Two examples will suffice. First, *ceteris paribus*, if domestic real income growth is lower than in the rest of the world, the exchange rate will depreciate, and vice versa. Second, *ceteris paribus*, if the domestic rate of monetary expansion is greater than in the rest of the world, the exchange rate will depreciate, and vice versa. In other words the monetary approach predicts that, *ceteris paribus*, a slowly growing country or a rapidly inflating country will experience a depreciating exchange rate, and vice versa. The important policy implication that derives from this approach is that exchange rate flexibility is a necessary, but not a sufficient, condition for the control of the domestic rate of inflation via control of the domestic rate of monetary expansion. In the case of perfectly flexible exchange rates, the domestic rate of inflation is held to be determined by the domestic rate of monetary expansion relative to the domestic growth of real income.

### 4.5   The Orthodox Monetarist School and Stabilization Policy

In conclusion it would be useful to assess the development of orthodox monetarism and how this school influenced the ongoing debate on the role and conduct of stabilization policy. The development of orthodox monetarism can be appraised in a positive light, given that it displayed both theoretical and empirical progress over the period of the mid-1950s to the early 1970s (see, for example, Cross, 1982a, 1982b). The reformulation of the quantity theory of money approach (QTM), the addition of the expectations-augmented Phillips curve analysis (EAPC), using the adaptive expectations hypothesis (AEH), and the incorporation of the monetary approach to the balance of payments theory and exchange rate determination (MTBE), generated a large amount of real-world correspondence and empirical support (see Laidler, 1976). We can therefore summarize the main characteristics of orthodox monetarism (OM) as:

$$OM = QTM + EAPC + AEH + MTBE$$

In contrast to orthodox monetarism, towards the close of this period, in the early 1970s, the orthodox Keynesian position was looking increasingly degenerative given (i) its failure to explain theoretically the breakdown of the Phillips curve relationship and (ii) its willingness to retreat increasingly into non-economic explanations of accelerating inflation and rising unemployment (see for example, Jackson et al., 1972).

We can draw together the discussion contained in sections 4.2–4.4 and seek to summarize the central distinguishing beliefs within the orthodox monetarist school of thought (see also Brunner, 1970; Friedman, 1970c; Mayer, 1978; Vane and Thompson, 1979; Purvis, 1980; Laidler, 1981, 1982; Chrystal, 1990). These beliefs can be listed as follows:

1. Changes in the money stock are the predominant, though not the only, factor explaining changes in money income.
2. The economy is inherently stable, unless disturbed by erratic monetary growth, and when subjected to some disturbance, will return fairly rapidly to the neighbourhood of long-run equilibrium at the natural rate of unemployment.
3. There is no trade-off between unemployment and inflation in the long run; that is, the long-run Phillips curve is vertical at the natural rate of unemployment.
4. Inflation and the balance of payments are essentially monetary phenomena.
5. In the conduct of economic policy the authorities should follow some rule for monetary aggregates to ensure long-run price stability, with fiscal policy assigned to its traditional roles of influencing the distribution of income and wealth, and the allocation of resources. In the former case, Laidler (1993, p. 187) has argued that the authorities must be prepared to adapt the behaviour of the supply of whatever monetary aggregate they chose to control (that is, in response to shifts in the demand for money resulting from, for example, institutional change) rather than pursue a rigid (legislated) growth rule for a chosen monetary aggregate as suggested by Friedman.

The monetarist aversion to activist stabilization policy, both monetary and fiscal policy (and prices and incomes policy), which derives both from the interrelated theoretical propositions and from empirical evidence discussed in sections 4.2–4.4, is the central issue which distinguishes orthodox monetarists from Keynesians.

Throughout the period 1950–80, a key feature of the Keynesian–monetarist debate related to disagreement over the most effective way of managing aggregate demand so as to limit the social and economic waste associated with instability and also over the question of whether it was desirable for governments to try to 'fine-tune' the economy using counter-cyclical policies. In this debate Friedman was one of the earliest critics of activist discretionary policies. Initially he focused on some of the practical aspects of implementing such policies. As early as 1948 Friedman noted that 'Proposals for the control of the cycle thus tend to be developed almost as if there were no other objectives and as if it made no difference within what framework cyclical fluctuations take place'. He also drew attention to the problem of *time lags* which in his view would in all likelihood 'intensify rather than mitigate cyclical fluctuations'. Friedman distinguished between three types of time lag: the recognition lag, the action lag, and the effect lag. These inside and outside lags, by delaying the impact of policy actions, would constitute the equivalent of an 'additional random disturbance'. While Friedman argued that monetary policy has powerful effects and could be implemented relatively quickly, its effects were subject to a long outside lag. Discretionary fiscal adjustments, particularly in a political system like that of the USA, could not realistically be implemented quickly. In principle, *accurate* forecasts could help to overcome this problem by enabling the authorities to adjust monetary and fiscal policy in anticipation of business cycle trends. However, poor forecasts would in all probability increase the destabilizing impact of aggregate demand management. As Mankiw (2003) emphasizes, 'the Great Depression and the (US) recession of 1982 show that many of the most dramatic economic events are unpredictable. Although private and public decision-makers have little choice but to rely on economic forecasts, they must always keep in mind that these forecasts come with a large margin of error'. These considerations led Friedman to conclude that activist demand management policies are more likely to destabilize than stabilize a decentralized market economy.

Another important contribution made by Friedman, not directly related to his theoretical and empirical work on monetary economics, but with important implications for stabilization policy, is his book *A Theory of the Consumption Function*, published in 1957. An important assumption in the orthodox Keynesian theory of fiscal policy is that the fiscal authorities can stimulate aggregate demand by boosting consumption expenditure via tax cuts that raise disposable income (or vice versa). This presumes that current consumption is largely a function of current disposable income. Friedman argued that current income ($Y$) has two components, a temporary component ($Y_T$) and a permanent component ($Y_P$). Since people regard $Y_P$ as their average income and $Y_T$ as a deviation from average income, they base their consumption decisions on the permanent component. Changes in $Y$ brought about by tax-induced changes in $Y_T$ will be seen as transitory and have little effect on current consumption ($C$) plans. So in Friedman's model we have:

$$Y = Y_T + Y_P \qquad\qquad (4.14)$$

$$C = \alpha Y_P \qquad\qquad (4.15)$$

If consumption is proportional to permanent income, this obviously reduces the power of tax-induced changes in aggregate demand. This further weakens the Keynesian case for activist fiscal policy.

Friedman has also always been very sympathetic to the public choice literature that suggested that structural deficits, with damaging effects on national saving and hence long-run growth, would be the likely result of discretionary fiscal policy operating within a democracy (see Buchanan and Wagner, 1978). Politicians may also deliberately create instability when they have discretion since within a democracy they may be tempted to manipulate the economy for political profit as suggested in the political business cycle literature (Alesina and Roubini with Cohen, 1997; see Chapter 10).

Although theoretical and empirical developments in economics facilitated the development, by Klein, Goldberger, Modigliani and others, of the highly aggregative simultaneous-equation macroeconometric models used for forecasting purposes, many economists remained unconvinced that such forecasts could overcome the problems imposed by the problem of time lags and the wider political constraints. Friedman concluded that governments had neither the knowledge nor the information required to conduct fine-tuning forms of discretionary policy in an uncertain world and advocated instead that the monetary authorities adopt a passive form of monetary rule whereby the growth in a specified monetary aggregate be predetermined at some stated known ($k$ per cent) rate (Friedman, 1968a, 1972). While Friedman (1960) argued that such a rule would promote greater stability, 'some uncertainty and instability would remain', because 'uncertainty and instability are unavoidable concomitants of progress and change. They are one face of a coin of which the other is freedom.' DeLong (1997) also concludes that it is 'difficult to argue that "discretionary" fiscal policy has played any stabilising role at all in the post-World war II period' in the US economy. However, it is generally accepted that automatic stabilizers have an important role to play in mitigating the impact of economic shocks. The debate over the role and conduct of stabilization policy as it stood in the 1970s is neatly summarized in the following passage, taken from Modigliani's (1977) Presidential Address to the American Economic Association:

> Nonmonetarists accept what I regard to be the fundamental practical message of *The General Theory*: that a private enterprise economy using an intangible money *needs* to be stabilized, *can* be stabilized, and therefore *should* be stabilized by appropriate monetary and fiscal policies. Monetarists by contrast take the view that there is no serious need to stabilize the economy; that even if there were a need, it could not be done, for stabilization policies would be more likely to increase than decrease instability.

Despite its considerable achievements, by the late 1970s/early 1980s, monetarism was no longer regarded as the main rival to Keynesianism within academia. This role was now taken up at the theoretical level during the 1970s by developments in macroeconomics associated with the new classical school. These developments cast further doubt on whether traditional stabilization policies can be used to improve the overall performance of the economy. However, monetarism was exercising a significant influence on the policies of the Thatcher government in the UK (in the period 1979–85) and the Fed in the USA (in the period 1979–81). Of particular significance to the demise of monetarist influence was the sharp decline in trend velocity in the 1980s in the USA and elsewhere. The deep recession experienced in the USA in 1982 has been attributed partly to the large and unexpected decline in velocity (B.M. Friedman, 1988; Modigliani, 1988a; Poole 1988). If velocity is highly volatile, the case for a constant growth rate monetary rule as advocated by Friedman is completely discredited. Therefore, there is no question that the collapse of the stable demand for money function in the early 1980s proved to be very damaging to monetarism. As a result monetarism was 'badly wounded' both within academia and among policy makers (Blinder, 1987) and subsequently 'hard core monetarism has largely disappeared' (Pierce, 1995). One important result of the unpredictability of the velocity of circulation of monetary aggregates has been the widespread use of the short-term nominal interest rate as the primary instrument of monetary policy (see Bain and Howells, 2003). In recent years activist Taylor-type monetary-feedback rules have been 'the only game in town' with respect to the conduct of monetary policy. As Buiter notes, 'Friedman's prescription of a constant growth rate for some monetary aggregate is completely out of favour today with both economic theorists and monetary policy makers, and has been for at least a couple of decades' (see Buiter, 2003a and Chapter 7).

Finally, it is worth reflecting on what remains today of the monetarist counter-revolution. As a result of the 'Great Peacetime Inflation' in the 1970s many key monetarist insights were absorbed within mainstream models (see, for example, Blinder, 1988b; Romer and Romer, 1989; Mayer, 1997; DeLong, 2000). According to DeLong, the key aspects of monetarist thinking that now form a crucial part of mainstream thinking in macroeconomics are the natural rate of unemployment hypothesis, the analysis of fluctuations as movements about trend rather than deviations below potential, the acceptance that under normal circumstances monetary policy is 'a more potent and useful tool' for stabilization than fiscal policy, the consideration of macroeconomic policy within a rules-based framework, and the recognition of the limited possibilities for success of stabilization policies. Therefore, although within academia monetarism is no longer the influential force it was in the late 1960s and early 1970s (as evidenced by, for example, the increasing scarcity of journal articles and conference papers on monetarism), its apparent demise can, in large part, be attributed to the fact that a significant number of the insights of 'moderate' monetarism have been absorbed into mainstream macroeconomics. Indeed, two leading contributors to the new Keynesian literature, Greg Mankiw and David Romer (1991), have suggested that new Keynesian economics could just as easily be labelled 'new monetarist economics' (see Chapter 7 for a discussion of the new Keynesian school).

Monetarism has therefore made several important and lasting contributions to modern macroeconomics. First, the expectations-augmented Phillips curve analysis, the view that the long-run Phillips curve is vertical and that money is neutral in the long run are all now widely accepted and form an integral part of mainstream macroeconomics. Second, a majority of economists and central banks emphasize the rate of growth of the money supply when it comes to explaining and combating inflation over the long run. Third, it is now widely accepted by economists that central banks should focus on controlling inflation as their *primary* goal of monetary policy. Interestingly, since the 1990s inflation targeting has been adopted in a number of countries (see Mishkin, 2002a and Chapter 7). What has not survived the monetarist counter-revolution is the 'hard core' belief once put forward by a number of leading monetarists that the authorities should pursue a non-contingent 'fixed' rate of monetary growth in their conduct of monetary policy. Evidence of money demand instability (and a break in the trend of velocity, with velocity becoming more erratic), especially since the early 1980s in the USA and elsewhere, has undermined the case for a fixed monetary growth rate rule. Finally, perhaps the most important and lasting contribution of monetarism has been to persuade many economists to accept the idea that the potential of *activist discretionary* fiscal and monetary *policy* is much more limited than conceived prior to the monetarist counter-revolution.

# MILTON FRIEDMAN

Milton Friedman was born in 1912 in New York City and graduated from Rutgers University with a BA in 1932, before obtaining his MA from the University of Chicago in 1933 and his PhD from Columbia University in 1946. Between 1946 and 1977 (when he retired) he taught at the University of Chicago and he has lectured at universities throughout the world. He is currently a Senior Research Fellow at the Hoover Institution (on War, Revolution and Peace) at Stanford University, California. Along with John Maynard Keynes he is arguably the most famous economist of the twentieth century. Professor Friedman is widely recognized as the founding father of monetarism and an untiring advocate of free markets in a wide variety of contexts. He has made major contributions to such areas as methodology; the consumption function; international economics; monetary theory, history and policy; business cycles and inflation. In 1976 he was awarded the Nobel Memorial Prize in Economics: 'For his achievements in the fields of consumption analysis, monetary history and theory and for his demonstration of the complexity of stabilization policy'.

Among his best-known books are: *Essays in Positive Economics* (University of Chicago Press, 1953); *Studies in the Quantity Theory of Money* (University of Chicago Press, 1956); *A Theory of the Consumption Function* (Princeton University Press, 1957); *Capitalism and Freedom* (University of Chicago Press, 1962); *A Monetary History of the United States, 1867–1960*

(Princeton University Press, 1963), co-authored with Anna Schwartz; *Free to Choose* (Harcourt Brace Jovanovich, 1980), co-authored with his wife Rose Friedman; *Monetary Trends in the United States and the United Kingdom* (University of Chicago Press, 1982), co-authored with Anna Schwartz; and *Monetarist Economics* (Basil Blackwell, 1991).

Among the numerous articles he has written, the best-known include: 'The Methodology of Positive Economics' and 'The Case for Flexible Exchange Rates' in *Essays in Positive Economics* (University of Chicago Press, 1953); 'The Quantity Theory of Money: A Restatement', in *Studies in the Quantity Theory of Money* (ed. M. Friedman) (University of Chicago Press, 1956); 'The Role of Monetary Policy', *American Economic Review* (1968a) – his presidential address to the American Economic Association; 'A Theoretical Framework for Monetary Analysis', *Journal of Political Economy* (1970a); and 'Inflation and Unemployment', *Journal of Political Economy* (1977) – his Nobel Lecture.

We interviewed Professor Friedman in his study at his apartment in San Francisco on 8 January 1996, while attending the annual conference of the American Economic Association.

## Background Information

*What first attracted you to study economics and become an economist?*
I graduated from college in 1932. As a college student I had majored jointly in economics and mathematics and when I graduated I was offered two postgraduate scholarships. At that time there weren't any such things as our current generous fellowships; graduate scholarships consisted of somebody offering to pay for your tuition, period. I was offered one in mathematics at Brown and one in economics at Chicago. Now put yourself in 1932 with a quarter of the population unemployed. What was the important urgent problem? It was obviously economics and so there was never any hesitation on my part to study economics. When I first started in college I was very ignorant about these matters because I grew up in a rather low-income family which had no particular understanding of the broader world. I was very much interested in and pretty good at mathematics. So I looked around to see if there was any way I could earn a living by mathematics. The only way I could find before I went to college was to become an actuary, and so my original ambition when entering college was to become an actuary. I did take some of the actuarial exams in my first two years at college, but I never continued after that.

## Keynes's *General Theory* and Keynesian Economics

*When you were a graduate student at Chicago, what interpretation did your*
*teachers put forward to explain the Great Depression?*
Well that's a very interesting question because I have believed for a long time
that the fundamental difference between my approach to Keynes and Abba
Lerner's approach to Keynes, to take a particular example, is due to what our
professors taught us. I started graduate school in the fall of 1932 when the
Depression wasn't over by any means. My teachers, who were Jacob Viner,
Frank Knight and Lloyd Mints, taught us that what was going on was a
disastrous mistake by the Federal Reserve in reducing the money supply. It
was not a natural catastrophe, it was not something that had to happen, it was
not something which had to be allowed to run its course. There were things
which should be done. Jacob Viner, from whom I took my first course in pure
economic theory as a graduate, had given a talk in Minnesota in which he
very specifically called for expansive policy on the part of the Federal Reserve and the government. Therefore the Keynesian revolution didn't come as
a sudden light from the dark showing what you could do about a situation
that nobody else seemed to know how to do anything about.

*Can you recall when you first read the* General Theory *[1936] and what your*
*impressions were of the book?*
I can't really answer that; I don't recall. I may be able to tell you if I look in
my original copy of the *General Theory* as I sometimes had a habit of
marking in my books the date when I bought them and how much money I
paid for them. Yes, here it is. I bought it in 1938 and paid $1.80 cents for it
[*laughter*]. That's probably when I first read it but I can't remember my
impressions, it's a long, long time ago, but I do remember that in the early
1940s I wrote a book review in which I was very critical of the Keynesian
analysis contained in the book that I reviewed.

*Why do you think Keynes's* General Theory *captured the minds of such a*
*large percentage of the economics profession in such a relatively short period*
*of around a decade following its publication in 1936?*
I don't think there is any problem in explaining that at all. If you took the
economics profession as a whole, what I have described as the teaching at
Chicago was very much an exception. The bulk of the teaching in schools of
economics went more nearly along the lines of a Mises–Hayek view. If you
take the London School of Economics, that's where the contrast with Abba
Lerner was most obvious because he, and most of the people who were
studying economics, were taught that the Depression was a necessary purgative for the economy to cure the ills that had been produced by the prior

expansion. That's a terribly dismal approach. Then all of a sudden out of the blue comes this attractive doctrine from Cambridge, Keynes's *General Theory*, by a man who already has an enormous reputation primarily because of *The Economic Consequences of the Peace* [1919]. He says: look, we know how to solve these problems and there is a very simple way. Given a hypothesis which tells you why we got into this trouble you would surely grasp at that when the only alternative you had was the dismal Austrian view [*laughter*].

*How important was Paul Samuelson's [1948] introductory textbook and Alvin Hansen's [1953] intermediate textbook in contributing to the spread of Keynesian economics?*
They were very important. I think Hansen was really important in the USA; I can't say about the rest of the world, partly because he had undergone such a sharp conversion. If you look at his early work before Keynes, it was strictly along the Mises–Hayek line. Hansen was very much a believer that this was a necessary purgative but then he suddenly saw the light and he became a convinced exponent of Keynesianism. He was at Harvard at the time, whereas he had been at Minneapolis when he expressed the earlier view. He was a very good teacher, a very nice human being. He had a great deal of influence, I don't have any doubt at all. Samuelson's influence comes later. Unless I'm mistaken, Hansen converted by 1938 or 1939 but Samuelson's elementary text only came after the war so he was a much later influence. Hansen was extremely important because of his effect on the people at Harvard. There was a very good group of economists at Harvard who played a significant role at the Federal Reserve, the Treasury and in Washington who were recruited during the war. So I think Hansen had a very important influence.

*A prominent real business cycle theorist, Charles Plosser [1994] has suggested that in the absence of John Hicks's IS–LM framework Keynes's* General Theory *would have been much less influential. Do you agree with this view?*
I believe that there is a great deal to that because later Samuelson was able to use his cross diagram that came entirely out of Hicks's IS–LM framework. I think that's a correct observation.

*If Keynes had lived to have been awarded the Nobel Prize in Economics, what do you think the citation would have been?*
It depends on when it would have been awarded. If it had been awarded at the beginning in 1969 the citation would undoubtedly have been 'the man who showed us how to get out of depressions and how to pursue a policy that would lead to reasonably full and stable employment'. But if the citation had been in 1989, let's say, I think it would have been written differently. It would have said 'an economist whose continued work beginning with his *Treatise*

*on Probability* [1921], and right on through, has had a major influence on the course of the economics profession'. But you know that's just conjecture, who knows what it would have been? [*laughter*]. Let me make clear my own view about Keynes. I believe that he was a great economist, one of the great economists of our time and that the *General Theory* is a remarkable intellectual achievement. We had a phenomenon that needed an explanation. How could you have widespread unemployment in the midst of an economy with such large productive capacity? That was a phenomenon in search of an explanation and he produced an explanation for it which, in my opinion, was the right kind of explanation. What you need to do is to have a very simple theory that gets at the fundamentals. No theory is successful if it's extremely complicated and difficult, because most phenomena are driven by a very few central forces. What a good theory does is to simplify; it pulls out the central forces and gets rid of the rest. So Keynes's *General Theory* was the right kind of theory. Science in general advances primarily by unsuccessful experiments that clear the ground and I regard the *General Theory* as having been an unsuccessful experiment. It was the right kind of a theory; it had content because it enabled you to make predictions, but when you made those predictions they were not confirmed and as a result I regard it as an unsuccessful experiment.

*What do you think has been the main contribution that the new Keynesian literature has made to the development of macroeconomics?*
Well, I'm not going to comment on that because I really haven't followed it carefully enough. Since our *Monetary Trends* [Friedman and Schwartz, 1982] came out and particularly since my book on *Money Mischief* [1992] came out I really haven't been doing any work on issues like that. In the past three or four years I have rather been working on my wife's and my memoirs.

## Monetarism

*Do you regard your [1956] restatement of the quantity theory of money as a more sophisticated elaboration of the Keynesian theory of liquidity preference?*
Not at all. I regarded it, as I said then, as a continuation of the general monetary theory that I had been taught as a student before Keynes's theory came out. One component of it is consistent with liquidity preference analysis. But if you are asking me whether at the time that was my motivation, or my understanding of it, I have to say no.

*Do you view your restatement then as a distinct break with Keynesian analysis?*
No. I didn't look at it in that way at all. I was just trying to set down what I thought was a reformulation of the quantity theory of money. Remember

Keynes was a quantity theorist. Look at his *Monetary Reform* [1923], for example, which I believe is one of his best books, a much under-appreciated and more useful book than the *General Theory*. Unlike the *General Theory* it was not an attempt to construct a new theory. It involved an application of the existing theory to a set of interesting phenomena, the immediate post-war inflations. It's a very good piece of work, which is straight quantity theory, and I was a quantity theorist. So if you ask in what way was Keynes's liquidity preference theory different from the quantity theory that he had adopted in his *Monetary Reform*, it was different only in the idea of having a liquidity trap. That was the only essential different idea. In my reformulation I don't have a liquidity trap, a liquidity trap is possible but that's not a part of the analysis.

*Although the belief in a stable demand for money function was well supported by empirical evidence up to the early 1970s, since then a number of studies have found evidence of apparent instability. Does this undermine the case for a fixed monetary growth rule?*
Yes and no. If you have a stable money demand function that's not the same as saying that it's never going to shift, never going to be affected by anything else. Let's take the case of the USA which I know best. If you take the period after the Second World War to let's say 1980, you have a very stable money demand function and it doesn't matter whether you use the base, M1, M2 or M3, you'll get essentially the same result. In the early 1980s there was a series of structural changes in the system, in particular the payment of interest on demand deposits which had the effect of changing the money demand function, particularly for the base and M1. There's a period of about five years when it is very hard to know what's going on because of these structural shifts. Then from about 1985 on the earlier demand function with M2 is re-established, but not with M1 or the base; they are very unstable. If you plot, as I have done, the rate of change of these various aggregates year over year against year over year changes in inflation two years later, up to 1980 it doesn't matter, they are all pretty good. After 1980 M1 and the base go haywire completely. On the other hand the relationship with M2 stays pretty much the same. So there is a real problem there because if, as many people were (I was not), you were thinking in terms of M1 as the major monetary aggregate it would have been a mistake to have continued this steady rate of growth. But if you had continued a steady rate of growth of M2 you would have been all right.

*How do you react to Robert Lucas's [1994b] suggestion that the 1970s were a time of prosperity for the Friedman and Schwartz [1963] volume* The Monetary History of the United States, *while the 1980s must be viewed as a*

*time of mild recession? Has this been due to the influence of real business cycle theorists?*
I'm not sure how to answer that. I really have never looked at the history of the volume itself in terms of prosperity or recession [*laughter*]. There were three reviews in all on what was the thirtieth anniversary of the volume. I must say that the review I like best is the one by Jeffrey Miron because it emphasized what I think is really important and is relevant, not merely to monetary issues but to the economics profession as a whole, namely the importance of testing your theories on historical and empirical material. It seems to me that in many ways one of the contributions of the *Monetary History* was methodological. I don't mean it didn't make a substantive contribution, but there was also a methodological contribution and Miron emphasized that, if I remember rightly, in his review. But now to your question. There is the problem of keeping science distinct from politics. The 1980s was the Reagan period. I was known as a close adviser to Reagan. The academic community was almost wholly anti-Reagan, although that was probably less true of economics than it was of any other academic discipline you can name. I'm talking here about the social sciences and the humanities, not the natural sciences. I may be entirely wrong on this, I hope I am, but I believe that the fact that I was connected with the Reagan administration had something to do with the desire on the part of the economics profession to separate themselves from my work. There's one other thing that has to be said. The interesting thing in any science, whether it's economics or mathematics or anything else, is not repeating the past but going ahead to new things. Every science every ten or twenty years has to have a new fad or it goes dead. I think that the emphasis on real business cycle theory did provide a new fad for a while which has had a great deal of influence on the work that economists have done.

*Would you agree that your [1968a] paper on 'The Role of Monetary Policy' has perhaps turned out to be your most influential paper?*
As to that, I don't doubt that it had a great deal of influence. But when you talk about comparisons it is hard for me to decide between that and 'The Methodology of Positive Economics' [1953a] which had as much influence in a different direction, not on the substance but on the methodology.

*How far do you think that the influence of your [1968a] paper was greatly enhanced because it anticipated the events of the 1970s and in particular predicted accelerating inflation?*
On that I don't think there is any doubt whatsoever. It was a major reason for the shift in attitude. As I said earlier, the right kind of a theory is one that makes predictions that are capable of being contradicted. The Keynesian theory made a prediction that was capable of being contradicted and it was

contradicted. The theory I was describing also made predictions; in this case it made predictions that we would experience accelerating inflation and it was not contradicted.

*In the same year as your Presidential Address to the American Economic Association, Edmund Phelps in his [1967]* Economica *article also denied the existence of a long-run trade-off between inflation and unemployment. Are there are significant differences between your Phillips curve analysis and that of Edmund Phelps?*
There are enormous similarities and tremendous overlaps. The main difference is that I was looking at it from the monetary side whereas Edmund Phelps was looking at it from the labour market side. But the theories are the same, the statements are the same, there is no difference there.

*Is there any significant difference between your definition of the natural rate of unemployment and Keynes's definition of full employment?*
That's a tough one. His definition of full employment is simply a situation in which there is no unsatisfied employee, in which anybody who is willing to work for the current wage has a job. I think I'm quoting it reasonably correctly. My definition of the natural rate of unemployment is that rate at which demand and supply are equal so there is no excess supply or demand and in which people's expectations are satisfied. I think both of these are related to Wicksell's natural rate of interest. I don't think there is much difference between us.

*In your [1968a] paper on 'The Role of Monetary Policy' you highlighted the implications of introducing inflationary expectations into the Phillips curve. Since then adaptive expectations has gone out of fashion following what could be described as a rational expectations revolution. Which hypothesis do you favour as a way of modelling how economic agents form such expectations?*
I'm not sure how to answer that. The theoretical principle has always been the same, that what matters is what the expectations are and that they play a very important role. That's an old idea, that's not anything new. I'm sure you can find it in Marshall. I know you can find it in Schumpeter. In fact you can find it everywhere. The adaptive expectations approach was simply a way to try to make that empirically observable and in many cases it seemed to work. The most obvious case was Philip Cagan's [1956] study of hyperinflation in Germany and other European countries and there adaptive expectations worked up to the point at which you had reform. Then it didn't work at all. The best studies along that line were Tom Sargent's [1982] later studies about the effect of the monetary reforms.

Rational expectations, Bob Lucas's approach, in a way is obvious and well known. Everybody knew in the past that a rational man would not base his expectations simply on what had happened in the past. If there was a major change or any significant changes in public policy, he would also look at what he knew about that. The contribution of Lucas was partly to give that notion a name and I don't think you want to underestimate the importance of naming things. You know nobody can take everything into their head at one time, as Marshall used to say; you can't do it. You have to have ways of simplifying things and showing how things fit together. Bob Lucas's real contribution was showing how you might be able to mathematize and empirically design studies that would give you some way to get an empirical counterpart of the hypothetical and unmeasurable rational expectation. That was his real contribution.

I have always had great difficulties with the basic notion that there is some sense in which you can say expectations are correct or not correct. Let me explain what I mean. At the moment it is perfectly rational to suppose that there will be a major inflation some time in the next 20 years. There have been lots of major inflations. Suppose I have an expectation that there is a 10 per cent chance of there being a major inflation and no major inflation occurs. All along I have been betting that there might be a major inflation and I have been buying real assets, rather than nominal assets, in order to protect myself. If a major inflation doesn't occur, in what sense can you say I was wrong? There was always a chance. In a way the probability of anything happening *ex post* is always one. How do I judge whether someone's so-called rational expectations were correct? You might say that you have to get a distribution of what happened. Do I have to take 1000 years, 100 years, 50 years? What is the right basis? Moreover, every rational expectation notion recognizes that in advance what you have is a probability distribution, not a single point, and that gets to the question of whether there is such a thing as objective probability. The only probability notion I can make sense of is personal probability in the spirit of Savage and others. Keynes's degree of belief is in the same family. In fact I believe that Keynes's contribution in his *Probability* book has been underrated and overlooked. The whole Bayesian movement today in statistics, which has had a great deal of influence on statistical methods, is based on the idea of personal probability, of degree of belief. It is based on the kind of idea that Keynes was putting forward in his [1921] *Treatise on Probability* volume.

*Should we worry about moderate rates of inflation when the evidence seems to suggest that they don't have strong effects on real variables?*
No, we should not worry about moderate inflation except as a breeder of larger inflation, and that's a big exception [*laughter*]. My summary of the

evidence on that, and I really can't pretend this is authoritative because I haven't followed the research in that area for the past few years, is that there is a short-term relation between unexpected inflation and unemployment. But there is no long-term relation and even the short-term relation is very weak. The main case that I cite on the long-term relation is the USA from 1879 to 1896 and from 1896 to 1913. From 1879 to 1896 prices fell at about 3 per cent per year, not regularly of course but on the average, and from 1896 to 1913 they rose at about 3 per cent per year. Yet the rate of real growth is roughly the same in the two periods.

*Over the years monetarism has often been associated with conservative politics. Is this alleged association inevitable?*
The alleged association is not inevitable. Karl Marx was a quantity theorist. The Bank of China (communist China) is monetarist. Moreover, I am not myself a conservative. I am a liberal in the classical sense or, in the terminology that has become common in the USA, a libertarian in philosophy. In any event, monetarism properly interpreted is an objective set of propositions about the relation between monetary magnitudes and other economic variables. Conservative, radical, communist, socialist, any ruling authorities can only achieve their objectives if they can predict what the consequences of their actions will be. A correct body of monetarist propositions is as necessary to authorities of one stripe as of another.

**New Classical Macroeconomics**

*It can be argued that one of the most difficult things in economics is to create a new vision. Is this one of the most important features of Robert Lucas's impact?*
No, because I think that vision was present in a way before. Everybody knew that you ought to be forward-looking. What he did was to develop a method whereby you could make that vision operational. Once I got together some quotations on expectations. One particularly good one from Schumpeter just stated out and out the notion of rational expectations in the sense of the vision, but it wasn't operational. I think Lucas's big contribution was to make it operational. Everybody understood that people behaved on the basis of what they anticipated in the future and the question is how you approximate that. Of course the real start of rational expectations was John Muth's [1961] piece in *Econometrica*.

*Why do you think new classical macroeconomics proved to be so attractive to the younger generation of economists in the USA?*
The policy ineffectiveness proposition was very popular for a while but it's another one of those theories which is the right kind of a theory but is

contradicted by its predictions. Nobody in the face of the experience of the early 1980s can believe the policy ineffectiveness proposition is a valid prediction of what will happen in the short term. The 1980–82 recession completely contradicted it. I don't know how popular the approach was. It was popular with a small group. The beauty of it is that it brings you back to a pure theoretical analysis. It's not sort of besmirched by any complexities, any complications, any friction, anything else [*laughter*]. It hangs together as a theoretical matter if people correctly anticipate the future, but the situation will be wholly different if they don't.

*Kevin Hoover [1984] has drawn a methodological distinction between your work as a Marshallian and that of Robert Lucas as a Walrasian. Is that distinction valid?*
There is a great deal to that. On the whole I believe that is probably true. I have always distinguished between the Marshallian approach and the Walrasian approach. I have always been personally a Marshallian. That doesn't mean that the Walrasian approach is not a useful or appropriate approach. People's temperaments and attitudes are different, I guess. I yield to no one in my admiration for Marshall as an economist, but he had real flaws as an individual. The way he treated his wife was disgraceful. We found out about it way back in the 1950s when we spent a year at Cambridge in 1952–3. We spent a lot of time at the Marshall library and read a good deal of the Marshall documents. It seemed that Mary Paley, his wife, was a very able, competent woman. I won't go into that story; it will take us too long.

*How important has the Kydland–Prescott time inconsistency argument been in the rules v. discretion debate?*
That has been quite influential in the debate and is a very nice and entirely valid point.

*Since the demise of the monetary-surprise version of new classical macroeconomics in the early 1980s the new classical approach has been revitalized by real business cycle theory. Has this, in your opinion, been a fruitful line of research?*
I have some hesitancy in answering that question because I have not followed or investigated that literature as much as I should in order to give a considered answer. I don't believe that there is a business cycle; it is a misleading concept. The notion of a business cycle is something of a regularly recurring phenomenon that is internally driven by the mechanics of the system. I don't believe there is a business cycle in that sense. I believe that there is a system that has certain response mechanisms and that system is subject over time to external random forces (some large, some small) that play on it and it adapts

to those forces. The adaptation process has certain regularities that in a way go back to the basic Slutsky idea of an accumulation of random forces. Some of those forces are unquestionably real and in so far as the real business cycle people emphasize that the disturbances come from outside, that's all to the good. On the other hand the mechanism that reacts to the real disturbances is largely monetary, and by underplaying the monetary role in the process the so-called real business cycle theory has not been very helpful. You probably know my own little piece on what I call the 'plucking model' in *Economic Inquiry* [1993]. It was written many years earlier in an annual report of the National Bureau of Economic Research and it's also in the collection of papers contained in *The Optimum Quantity of Money* [1969] though I modified it a little for the *Inquiry* version, but not much. To quote: 'consider an elastic string stretched taut between two points on the underside of a rigid horizontal board and glued lightly to the board. Let the string be plucked at a number of points chosen more or less at random with a force that varies at random, and then held down at the lowest point reached. The result will be to produce a succession of apparent cycles in the string whose amplitudes depend on the force used in plucking the string' and so on. For me personally I find that a much more useful model than the model of a self-generating cycle.

*With the growth in the popularity of real business cycle models in the 1980s many new classical macroeconomists have turned to the calibration method rather than conventional econometric techniques to test the performance of their models. How do you view the calibration method?*
I believe that it is evading the issue. It isn't enough to show that the characteristics of the time series can be duplicated in a model. If the model has any meaning it is going to make predictions about things that can be observed and contradicted. You can match any set of data precisely with a least squares regression if you have enough variables in it.

## Methodological and General Issues

*You commented earlier that your [1953a] essay on the 'Methodology of Positive Economics' has been one of your most influential papers. Did you in any way anticipate the controversy that your paper would subsequently generate?*
No.

*Is the philosophy of science and formal methodology an area that still interests you?*
It was an area that interested me at the time but after I wrote that paper I decided I really would rather do economics than tell people how to do

economics. I found out that my views were very similar to Karl Popper's and I followed his writings in a sort of a vague way, but not very seriously. One of the major reasons why that article led to so much controversy is that I decided early on that I wasn't going to answer attacks on it [*laughter*]. I am serious. If you want to get controversy about one of your articles, write something which will be attacked and then don't answer the attackers because it opens a field day.

*Why do you think there is more consensus among economists over micro-economic issues compared to macroeconomic issues?*
Primarily because there has not been in the microeconomic area anything comparable to the Keynesian revolution in the macroeconomic area. For a time it looked as if the imperfect competition developments of Chamberlin and Robinson would play the same role in the microeconomic area, but they turned out to be more readily absorbed in the traditional classical body of microeconomic theory as presented in Marshall's *Principles*. A second reason, indeed the one that gave rise to the Keynesian revolution, was that the issues of employment/unemployment and business cycles became major political issues.

*How important do you think it is for macroeconomic models to have choice-theoretic microfoundations?*
It is less important for macroeconomic models to have choice-theoretic microfoundations than it is for them to have empirical implications that can be subjected to refutation. Choice-theoretic microfoundations may provide hypotheses for improving macroeconomic models, but the key macroeconomic models have been of long standing and have had a great deal of success without the more recent emphasis on choice-theoretic microfoundations.

*Do you think that attempts to try to understand the reasons for wage and price rigidities are a fruitful line of research?*
I don't believe that you can tell people what is a fruitful line of research. Everything is a fruitful line of research. I remember very well when I was advising doctoral students about their theses, they would come in and say well, a lot's been done on that subject. There is no subject on which there isn't more to be done, building on what's gone before. I don't have any doubt that there are wage rigidities because obviously there are; it's a fact of life, it's hard to deny it. The question is whether they are important or not, in what ways they are important and in what kind of phenomena are they important. As I said before, the essence of a successful theory is that it extracts the key elements from the whole host of attendant circumstances. So I wouldn't want

to discourage anybody from doing research in that area. Moreover I wouldn't want to discourage anybody from doing research in any area. What people have to do is to do things that interest them, follow up their own insights and their own ideas.

*Robert Lucas [1994a, p. 226] has argued that 'Professional economists are primarily scholars ... [whose] responsibility is to create new knowledge by pushing research into new, and hence necessarily controversial, territory'. Where do you see macroeconomic research heading?*
Economists are scholars but they are going to be influenced by developments in the world around them. There is no doubt that the great interest in business cycles was partly a consequence of the phenomenon of the Great Depression. We have in the world today the most striking phenomena: on the one hand there is the worldwide technological revolution, and on the other hand there is the political revolution – the collapse of the Soviet Union and the independence of its satellites. Both influences have had one common effect – what has been called the globalization of the economy, a term I hate. Both revolutions have led to a situation in which a producer can produce a product anywhere in the world, sell it anywhere in the world, use resources located anywhere in the world and be himself located anywhere in the world. So it is no longer meaningful to talk about the domestic content of things. Is a car made in America when parts of it come from Japan and parts come from another country? That's always been true, but it's a much more important phenomenon today. In addition there are also issues relating to the so-called underdeveloped or backward countries which are now coming into the modern stream for the first time. Those are phenomena of major importance and they need to be discussed and analysed. It is appropriate that economists should move to see how they can understand those phenomena and what can contribute to those phenomena. I have no doubt that this will be a major focus of research over the coming years.

*In your [1991]* Economic Journal *paper you drew attention to major improvements in the 'engine of analysis' but seemed to suggest that the quality of much economic research had declined. Can you elaborate on this view?*
I don't believe I was saying that. What I would say is that economics has become increasingly an arcane branch of mathematics rather than dealing with real economic problems. There is no doubt that that has happened. I believe that economics has gone much too far in that direction, but there is a correction on the way. Take the *Economic Journal*. It has introduced a section on current controversies which is a real departure from the kind of thing it had before. There is no doubt that it's become harder for anybody to keep up with the literature, except in his or her own special field, and I believe that's a very bad feature of the developments in economics. In that sense, what you

said about the decline and deterioration in economic research is true. But the engine of analysis as a technical, theoretical structure has certainly improved over the period a great deal.

*Why do you think the leadership in macroeconomic research passed from the UK to the USA after the Second World War?*
The answer is simple. If you have too strong an orthodoxy you are not going to have any leadership. What happened was that Britain was a leader in the 1930s, no question. But that became solidified into a rock of orthodox opinion which was not going to be a breeding ground for leading the future. Of course this is a complicated question because it is all tied up with the change in the role of Britain as a whole in the world as a result of the Second World War. The First World War reduced the influence of Britain a great deal as a world leader and the Second went further. But I think fundamentally the problem was that the leadership in economics at Cambridge, England became hardened into an orthodoxy, which is not a good breeding ground for revolutionary or innovative work.

**Economic Policy**

*Some economists, perhaps most, would argue that the fundamental difference between monetarists and Keynesians is not so much their respective views on the influence of the money supply but their differing views on the equilibrating powers of the market mechanism. Whereas monetarists have faith in the equilibrating tendencies of market forces, Keynesians argue that there is substantial market failure requiring some sort of activist intervention at the macro level. Would you agree with this view?*
I do not agree with this view. There are monetarists of all kinds, some who stress market failure and some who do not. All economists – monetarists, Keynesians, or what-not – recognize that there is such a thing as market failure. I believe that what really distinguishes economists is not whether they recognize market failure, but how much importance they attach to government failure, especially when government seeks to remedy what are said to be market failures. That difference in turn is related to the time perspective that economists bring to various issues. Speaking for myself, I do not believe that I have more faith in the equilibrating tendencies of market forces than most Keynesians, but I have far less faith than most economists, whether Keynesians or monetarists, in the ability of government to offset market failure without making matters worse.

*You have argued [*American Economic Review, *1968a] that most disagreements appear not to be concerned with the major goals of economic policy but*

*rather are over the choice of appropriate instruments to achieve the goals. In the light of your work on the consumption function and monetary economics in general, what role do you see for fiscal policy in a macroeconomic context?*
None. I believe that fiscal policy will contribute most if it doesn't try to offset short-term movements in the economy. I'm expressing a minority view here but it's my belief that fiscal policy is not an effective instrument for controlling short-term movements in the economy. One of the things I have tried to do over the years is to find cases where fiscal policy is going in one direction and monetary policy is going in the opposite. In every case the actual course of events follows monetary policy. I have never found a case in which fiscal policy dominated monetary policy and I suggest to you as a test to find a counter-example. There are two possible explanations for that. One which I believe to be true is that the Keynesian view that a government deficit is stimulating is simply wrong. A deficit is not stimulating because it has to be financed, and the negative effects of financing it counterbalance the positive effects, if there are any, on spending. But that may not be the reason because there is the other reason: it is much harder to adjust fiscal policy in a sensitive short-term way than it is to adjust monetary policy. So I don't believe that there is any role for fiscal policy in the short term. There is an enormous role for fiscal policy in terms of the long-term allocation of resources among different uses and that is where the argument needs to be.

*Are you saying that even in the case of the 1930s you would not have advocated expansionary fiscal policy?*
It wasn't fiscal policy, it was monetary policy that dominated. There was nothing you could do with fiscal policy that was going to offset a decline of a third in the quantity of money. Let me show you a current example. Take Japan right now. They are wasting their time and money in trying to have an expansive fiscal policy without an expansive monetary policy. I'm exaggerating a little about Japan because in the last year or so, mostly since the appointment of the new Head of the Bank of Japan, they have been starting to follow an expansive monetary policy. I believe that Japan is going to show a considerable degree of improvement and that they will start to come back up. It's a very interesting phenomenon because the behaviour of the Japanese central bank in the past five years duplicates the behaviour of the Federal Reserve after 1929.

*Persistent high unemployment has been a feature of European economies since the early 1980s. A variety of explanations has been put forward including hysteresis theories. How do you explain such persistent unemployment?*
I believe it is a consequence of the extensive welfare state and rigidities in the system. I have just read a very interesting working paper of the Federal

Reserve Bank of Chicago co-written by Lars Ljungqvist and Tom Sargent [1998]. I agree with their conclusion. They start out by saying one obvious explanation is the welfare state arrangements and the change in the incentives that people have. But then an obvious answer to that is why didn't that have the same effect on unemployment earlier. Their explanation is that the earlier period was a more nearly stationary period in which it was not necessary to make rapid and extensive dynamic adjustments to the changes in circumstances. But in the last ten or twenty years, what with the technological revolution and the political revolution, it has been necessary to make major changes and the European system is rigid. It's OK if everything goes along smoothly but it's not very good at adapting to major dynamic change. It seems to me that that makes a great deal of sense. You might ask the question why is it that the USA hasn't had the same experience. I'm not sure that my answer now will be valid in the future because we have been going in the same direction although we haven't gone nearly as far. We have a much more flexible wage system. It's much easier to fire people although it is getting harder and harder to hire people. There are more and more disincentives to employers to hire people because of affirmative action and all the rules and regulations involved. But still we are better off than the European economies.

*In another highly influential paper published in 1953[b], only nine years after the establishment of the Bretton Woods fixed exchange rates system, you presented the case for flexible exchange rates. In the light of experience since the breakdown of the system in the early 1970s, how do you respond to the issue of variability or instability, which critics of flexible exchange rates have highlighted?*

The variability has been much larger than I would have expected. I don't have any doubt about that, but there are two propositions. Number one, the reason for the high variability is the highly variable forces that have been playing upon the international market which derive in my opinion from the fact that beginning in 1971 the world had a monetary system that had no predecessor, no precedent whatsoever. For the first time in the history of the world no current major currency, or minor currency for that matter, in the world was linked to a commodity, however indirectly. To begin with, everybody was sailing on an uncharted sea and on that uncharted sea some went one way and some went another. So you had a much wider variability in the rates of inflation in different countries than you were accustomed to and that led to a greater variability in exchange rates. The second proposition is that the variability in exchange rates was a good thing. If you had tried to maintain fixed exchange rates under those conditions it would have required major interferences in the freedom of trade among various countries. So that while the variability of exchange rates was much greater than I would have anticipated,

I believe it was a necessary reaction, maybe overreaction, to what was going on and that if you look at the experience over that time it did not have any serious negative effects. I don't doubt that any exchange rate adjustment is going to be overdone. If you need a large change it's going to be too large and then it's going to come back again because of the influence of (a) expectations and (b) speculation. But I don't believe you have any examples of destabilizing speculation. The speculators have on the whole performed a positive function. The European Exchange Rate Mechanism was fundamentally unstable and in so far as the speculators broke it in September 1992, earlier than otherwise, it was a desirable thing. Britain made a great mistake by linking its currency to the Exchange Rate Mechanism; it should never have done that and it paid dearly for doing so.

*What are your views on the desirability of forming a single currency in Europe?*
There are two different questions, the desirability and the possibility. I believe that it is an impossible thing to do and this is something that I have been saying over and over again everywhere. It seems to me that you must distinguish between a unified currency and currencies linked by a fixed exchange rate. You can only have a unified currency if you have only one central bank, one locus of authority. I cannot believe that you are going to be willing to close down the Bank of England, that France is going to be willing to close down the Bank of France and so on. So it seems to me political unification has to come first. How many times do we have to see the same phenomenon repeat itself? After the war there was the Bretton Woods system and it broke down, in the 1970s the 'Snake' broke down and so on. How many times do you have to repeat an experience before you realize that there must be some real problem in having fixed exchange rates among countries that are independent? The period of the nineteenth century, which is always pointed to, can be distinguished from the current period in a very simple way. Government spending of the major countries in the pre-1913 period was around 10 per cent of the national income. A system that could operate when governments were spending 10 per cent of the national income cannot operate when governments are spending 50 per cent of the national income. There is a sense in which a single currency is desirable, but what does it mean to say something unachievable is desirable?

*It is interesting that you say political unification is needed before economic union, as many critics in Britain suspect that monetary union is being used as a way of moving towards political union.*
I don't doubt that. I don't doubt that the Germans and the French are trying to do that, but I don't believe that they will succeed.

*Macroeconomics is not a laboratory science; we learn from events. What did we learn from the so-called 'monetarist experiments' in the USA and UK at the start of the 1980s?*

You have got to distinguish between two different things. The so-called monetarist experiment was in 1979 when Volcker [Fed Chairman] announced that he was going to take the quantity of money and not the interest rate as his guide. But he didn't do it! If you look at the monetary aggregates, they were more variable during the Volcker period than at any previous time in history. So he did not follow a monetarist course. On the other hand if you eliminate the perturbations and you look at the general direction over the period from 1980 to 1995 in every country in the world aggregate, monetary growth has come way down and with it has come inflation. So I think that the experiment in all of the countries of the world has been enormously confirmatory of the proposition that inflation is a monetary phenomenon.

*Why do governments create inflation?*

They create inflation in order to get the revenue from it, and the reason it has come down is not because governments have become more noble but because you can't get much revenue out of it. I gave a talk at the Bank of Japan in 1985, on which I based the last chapter of my book *Money Mischief* [1992]. I entitled it 'Monetary policy in a fiat world'. To quote, 'inflation has become less attractive as a political option. Given that the voting public is very sensitive to inflation it may currently be politically profitable to establish monetary arrangements that will make the present irredeemable paper standard an exception to Fisher's generalization'. In Fisher's *Purchasing Power of Money* [1911] he says that every attempt at a paper money standard has been a disaster. How do governments get money from inflation? Number one, there is the direct value of the high-powered money base. That's a very small source, it's trivial. Much more important are two other sources. One is that if your tax system is expressed in nominal terms, inflation raises taxes without anyone having to vote for higher taxes. The second is that if you have been able to issue securities at an interest rate that is lower than the rate of inflation, you can expropriate those securities. The expropriation of past debt plus the automatic increases in taxes were undoubtedly the major source of revenue for the USA from the inflations of the 1970s. There is no doubt about that. I remember having breakfast on some occasion with the then Senator Long from Louisiana who was on the Finance Committee. He said, you know we never could have passed these rates of tax on current incomes if it hadn't been that they were automatically brought up there by inflation. It would have been politically impossible. The adjustment of tax rates for inflation, indexing the tax rates, has eliminated one source of revenue. The fact that bond markets have become so much more sensitive to inflation has eliminated the second. So how much revenue can you now get out of inflation? It isn't worth inflating. If you have inflation in the future, my prediction is that it will only be as an attempt for full employment purposes and not as a way to raise revenue. That's why I'm pretty confident that there will not be a major inflation in the future.

*Do you think that disinflation can ever be achieved without significant real output/employment costs?*
I doubt it very much. That's why you don't want to let inflation get started – because it's so hard to bring it down.

## Personal Information

*What importance do you personally attach to being awarded the Nobel Prize in Economics?*
Obviously it is extremely rewarding. However, when I first learned of the award from a reporter in a parking lot in Detroit who stuck a microphone in my face and asked, 'Do you regard this as the high point of your career?', I answered, 'I care more what my successors fifty years from now will think about my professional work than I do about the judgement of seven people from Sweden who happen to be serving on the Nobel Committee.' I do not mean to denigrate the Nobel Committee. They have been doing a very conscientious and good job on the whole, but at the same time what really matters to a scientist is the long-run effect of his work on his science.

*The number of books and refereed articles you have had published is prodigious.*
I don't know what it is. It is very large, yes.

*How have you found the time to write so much and has this impinged on your family and social life?*
[*Laughter*] No. For much of our married life and the first part when we were at Chicago in particular, we typically spent three solid months in the country at our second home in New Hampshire to begin with and later on in Vermont. Then later on I split my life 50–50: we spent six months a year in Chicago and six months a year in Vermont. Almost all of my writing was done in Vermont or in New Hampshire, relatively little during the actual school year. I managed pretty much to keep down outside activities. I didn't go away from Vermont or New Hampshire to make speeches or to address committee meetings or hearings. There were occasional exceptions but for the most part I made it an absolute rule. When I look at my remaining diaries from that period I am shocked by how full the pages are when I am in Chicago and how

empty they are when I'm up in Vermont or New Hampshire [*laughter*]. So
that's the only reason I was able to write as much as I did.

*Do you find it ironic that many of your views, once the subject of intense
debate and controversy, are now firmly embedded as part of the established
mainstream orthodoxy in macroeconomics?*
I find it very satisfying but not ironic at all. Why should it be ironic? New
ideas have to fight a battle to get accepted. If you are against the conventional
wisdom, the course of reaction from your critics is very simple. The first
reaction is that it's all a bunch of nonsense, it's just so extreme it can't
possibly be right. The second reaction is, well, you know, there is something
to it. The third reaction is it gets embedded in the theory and nobody talks
about it any more.

*Don't you need to be thick skinned and have great strength of conviction in
your views in such circumstances?*
I don't think the question is one of having a thick skin. I think the question is
one of belief in what you are doing. Conviction is strong. I have never been
bothered by intellectual attacks; that hasn't been a problem. I've always had
very good personal relations with people whose views are different from
mine. With very very rare exceptions, I never had any personal problems.
Paul Samuelson and I, for example, are good personal friends.

*Have you any as yet unfulfilled academic ambitions?*
No I don't think so. My main ambition now is to get our memoirs finished.
We've been working on them too long. Over the last year and a half I've had
health problems which have slowed down our progress on our memoirs.

*One final question. John Burton [1981] has described you as the Adam Smith
of the twentieth century. Is that a description you would be happy to have?*
[*Laughter.*] Sure, I'd be happy to have that. Adam Smith was the great father
of modern economics, there's no question. I'd regard it as a great compliment
to be regarded in that way. But I believe that view is based not on my
scientific work but on my outside activities propagandizing for free markets.

# 5. The new classical school

existing Keynesian macroeconometric models are incapable of providing reliable guidance in formulating monetary, fiscal and other types of policy. This conclusion is based in part on the spectacular recent failure of these models, and in part on their lack of a sound theoretical or econometric basis ... on the latter ground, there is no hope that minor or even major modification of these models will lead to significant improvement in their reliability. (Lucas and Sargent, 1978)

## 5.1 Introduction

During the early 1970s there was a significant renaissance of the belief that a market economy is capable of achieving macroeconomic stability, providing that the visible hand of government is prevented from conducting misguided discretionary fiscal and monetary policies. In particular the 'Great Inflation' of the 1970s provided increasing credibility and influence to those economists who had warned that Keynesian activism was both over-ambitious and, more importantly, predicated on theories that were fundamentally flawed. To the Keynesian critics the events of the Great Depression together with Keynes's theoretical contribution had mistakenly left the world 'deeply sceptical about self-organising market systems' (Sachs, 1999). As we have seen in Chapters 3 and 4, the orthodox Keynesian insistence that relatively low levels of unemployment are achievable via the use of expansionary aggregate demand policies was vigorously challenged by Milton Friedman, who launched a monetarist 'counter-revolution' against policy activism during the 1950s and 1960s. During the 1970s another group of economists provided a much more damaging critique of Keynesian economics. Their main argument against Keynes and the Keynesians was that they had failed to explore the full implications of *endogenously* formed expectations on the behaviour of economic agents. Moreover, these critics insisted that the only acceptable way to incorporate expectations into macroeconomic models was to adopt some variant of John Muth's (1961) 'rational expectations hypothesis'.

Following Thomas Sargent's (1979) contribution, rational expectationists, who also adhered to the principle of equilibrium theorizing, became known collectively as the new classical school. As the label infers, the new classical school has sought to restore classical modes of equilibrium analysis by assuming continuous market clearing within a framework of competitive markets.

*219*

The assumption of market clearing, which implies perfectly and instantaneously flexible prices, represents the most controversial aspect of new classical theorizing. According to Hoover (1992), the incorporation of this assumption represents the classical element in their thinking, namely a firm conviction 'that the economy should be modelled as an economic equilibrium'. Thus, to new classical theorists, 'the ultimate macroeconomics is a fully specified general equilibrium microeconomics'. As Hoover notes, this approach implies not only the revival of classical modes of thought but also 'the euthanasia of macroeconomics'!

## 5.2 The Influence of Robert E. Lucas Jr

Professor Robert E. Lucas Jr is widely acknowledged as the originator and central figure in the development of the new classical approach to macroeconomics and has been described by Michael Parkin (1992) as 'the leading macro mountaineer of our generation'. In recognition of Lucas's seminal research in macroeconomics, in October 1995 the Royal Swedish Academy of Sciences announced its decision to award him the Nobel Memorial Prize in Economics 'for having developed and applied the hypothesis of rational expectations, and thereby having transformed macroeconomic analysis and deepened our understanding of economic policy'. The award of this prestigious prize to Lucas came as no surprise to economists since, without doubt, his important contributions have made him the most influential macroeconomist during the last quarter of the twentieth century (see Fischer, 1996a; Hall, 1996; Svensson, 1996; Hoover, 1988, 1992, 1999; Snowdon and Vane, 1998). While some commentators see Lucas's contributions to business cycle analysis as 'part of the natural progress of economics' (Chari, 1998), or as 'part of the steady accumulation of knowledge' (Blanchard, 2000), others make frequent reference to 'revolution' or counter-revolution when discussing the influence of Lucas's contributions to macroeconomics (Tobin, 1996; Snowdon and Vane, 1999b; Woodford, 2000).

Although Lucas made explicit use of the rational expectations hypothesis in analysing optimal investment policy as early as 1965, it was not until he began to wrestle with aggregate supply issues, within a Walrasian general equilibrium framework, that the real significance of this hypothesis for macroeconomics became clear (Fischer, 1996a). While the Lucas and Rapping (1969) paper is perhaps the first 'new classical' paper in spirit, because of its emphasis on the equilibrium (voluntary) nature of unemployment and its utilization of the intertemporal labour substitution hypothesis (see Hoover, 1988 and Chapter 6), it was the series of papers written by Lucas and published in the period 1972–8 that established the analytical base of the rational expectations equilibrium approach to research into aggregate economic fluctuations (business cycles). Collectively these papers had an immense influence on the direction of macroeconomic research during the last quarter of the twentieth century. One objective measure or indication of the impact/influence that certain papers have on the development of macroeconomics is provided by citation counts as recorded by the Social Science Citations Index. In Table 5.1 citation counts are provided for the three most heavily cited papers written by Lucas (1972a, 1973, 1976) in the area of mainstream macroeconomics, together with one example taken from the field of economic growth (Lucas, 1988). In order to help place the influence of these papers in context we also provide information on citation counts for three other well-known and heavily cited papers, namely those by Friedman (1968a) and Kydland and Prescott (1977, 1982).

*Table 5.1   Citation counts: 1966–97*

| Article | 1966–70 | 1971–75 | 1976–80 | 1981–97 | Total | Average citations per year since publication |
|---|---|---|---|---|---|---|
| Friedman (1968a) | 30 | 148 | 238 | 508 | 924 | 31 |
| Kydland and Prescott (1977) | – | – | 25 | 499 | 524 | 25 |
| Kydland and Prescott (1982) | – | – | – | 443 | 443 | 28 |
| Lucas (1972a) | – | 12 | 112 | 503 | 627 | 24 |
| Lucas (1973) | – | 10 | 122 | 583 | 715 | 29 |
| Lucas (1976) | – | – | 105 | 654 | 759 | 35 |
| Lucas (1988) | – | – | – | 568 | 568 | 57 |

*Source*:   Snowdon and Vane (1998).

As Table 5.1 suggests, the influence of Lucas has been tremendously important for the direction of macroeconomics since 1970. However, other influential American exponents of new classical macroeconomics during the 1970s included Thomas Sargent, Robert Barro, Edward Prescott and Neil Wallace. In the UK the new classical approach, in particular the need to incorporate the rational expectations hypothesis into macroeconomic analysis, was mainly championed by Patrick Minford (see interviews with Professors Barro and Minford in Snowdon et al., 1994).

Building on the insights developed by Milton Friedman (1968a) and Edmund Phelps (1968) concerning the neglect of endogenous expectations in Keynesian macro models, the work of Lucas (1972a, 1972b, 1973, 1975, 1976) was crucial in introducing macroeconomists to Muth's (1961) rational expectations hypothesis, together with its enormous implications for theoretical and empirical work (Lucas, 1981a). In particular, with the introduction of rational expectations the standard Keynesian models seemed unable to deliver their traditional policy conclusions. It soon became apparent that what Alan Blinder refers to as the 'Lucasian revolution' represented a much more powerful and potentially damaging challenge to the Keynesian mainstream than the monetarist critique, which was of longer standing (see Snowdon, 2001a). Lucas recalls that he was 'raised as a monetarist in the 1960s' and that Friedman 'has been an enormous influence'. Indeed, during the 1990s, Lucas still thought of himself as a 'monetarist' (Lucas, 1994b; Snowdon and Vane, 1998). But while orthodox monetarism presented itself as an alternative to the standard Keynesian model, it did not constitute a radical theoretical challenge to it (see Laidler, 1986). Thus while the mark I 1970s version of new classical macroeconomics initially evolved out of monetarist macroeconomics, and incorporates certain elements of that approach (such as the monetarist explanation of inflation), it is clear that new classical economics should be regarded as a separate school of thought from orthodox monetarism. While the new classical school during the 1970s was undoubtedly 'monetarist' in terms of its policy prescriptions, according to Hoover (1984) the more radical tone to new classical conclusions stems from key theoretical differences between Lucas and Friedman, and the roots of this theoretical divide are methodological: while Friedman is a Marshallian, Lucas is a Walrasian. Despite their methodological differences, De Vroey (2001) is undoubtedly correct in arguing that 'Friedman and Lucas have probably been the most influential economists of the second half of the twentieth century: between them they were able to throw the Keynesian paradigm off its pedestal'. In his review of Tobin's (1980a) book, *Asset Accumulation and Economic Activity: Reflections on Contemporary Macroeconomic Theory*, Lucas (1981b) declared that:

> Keynesian orthodoxy or the neoclassical synthesis *is* in deep trouble, the deepest kind of trouble in which an applied body of theory can find itself. It appears to be giving seriously wrong answers to the most basic questions of macroeconomic policy.

Why and how Lucas and other new classical economists came to this negative view of Keynesian economics during the 1970s is the main theme of this chapter.

In the remainder of this chapter we have four main objectives. First, to discuss the central theoretical propositions which underlie new classical models (section 5.3). Second, in the light of this discussion, to consider the new classical theory of the business cycle (section 5.4). Third, to examine the main policy implications that derive from the new classical approach to macroeconomics (section 5.5). Finally (section 5.6) we assess the impact that the new classical school has had on the development of macroeconomics.

## 5.3 The Structure of New Classical Models

The new classical school emerged as a distinctive group during the 1970s and, as we have already noted, the key figure in this development was Robert E. Lucas Jr. However, the roots of the new classical research tradition are diverse. For example, the emphasis in early new classical models on information and expectations provides a link to the Austrian tradition best represented by the work of Hayek (see Chapter 9). The distinction made by Lucas between impulse (shocks) and propagation mechanisms when analysing business cycles has its origins in the pioneering research of Frisch (1933). The important role given to monetary disturbances in generating aggregate instability is solidly in the classical and Friedmanite monetarist traditions; indeed, Tobin (1981) refers to the early new classical contributions as 'monetarism mark II'. The work of Phelps et al. (1970) on the *Microfoundations of Employment and Inflation Theory* inspired Lucas to utilize the insights gleaned from Phelps's use of the 'island parable' and search theory to analyse labour market dynamics. Finally the methodological approach of Lucas is heavily influenced by the general equilibrium tradition of Walras, Hicks, Arrow and Debreu (see Zijp, 1993; Beaud and Dostaler, 1997).

The new classical approach as it evolved in the early 1970s exhibited several important features:

1.  a strong emphasis on underpinning macroeconomic theorizing with neo-classical choice-theoretic microfoundations within a Walrasian general equilibrium framework;
2.  the adoption of the key neoclassical assumption that all economic agents are rational; that is, agents are continuous optimizers subject to the constraints that they face, firms maximize profits and labour and households maximize utility;
3.  agents do not suffer from money illusion and therefore only real magnitudes (relative prices) matter for optimizing decisions;
4.  complete and continuous wage and price flexibility ensure that markets continuously clear as agents exhaust all mutually beneficial gains from trade, leaving no unexploited profitable opportunities.

Given these assumptions, changes in the quantity of money should be neutral and real magnitudes will be independent of nominal magnitudes. However, empirical evidence shows that there are positive correlations (at least in the short run) between real GDP and the nominal price level (an upward-sloping aggregate supply curve), between changes in the nominal money supply and real GDP, and negative correlations between inflation and unemployment (a Phillips curve); that is, empirically money does not appear to be neutral in the short run. Solving this puzzle between the neutrality of money predicted by classical/neoclassical theory and empirical evidence showing non-neutralities would be a considerable intellectual achievement (Zijp, 1993, refers to this as the 'Lucas problem'). Lucas's (1972a) seminal paper, 'Expectations and the Neutrality of Money', was just such an achievement. Lucas's key insight was to change the classical assumption that economic agents have perfect information to an assumption that agents have imperfect information.

We can sum up the main elements of the early new classical approach to macroeconomics as the joint acceptance of three main sub-hypotheses involving (i) the rational expectations hypothesis; (ii) the assumption of continuous market clearing; and (iii) the Lucas ('surprise') aggregate supply hypothesis. In the discussion of these hypotheses individually in what follows, the reader should bear in mind that although new classicists accept all three hypotheses (see Figure 5.1), it is possible for economists of different persuasions to support the rational expectations hypothesis without necessarily accepting all three together (see Chapter 7).

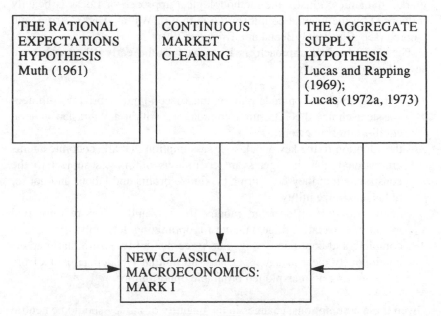

*Figure 5.1   The structure of new classical models*

### 5.3.1 The rational expectations hypothesis

One of the central tenets underlying new classical macroeconomics is the rational expectations hypothesis (REH) associated with the work of John Muth (1961) initially in the context of microeconomics. It is, however, interesting to note that Keuzenkamp (1991) has suggested that Tinbergen was a precursor to Muth, having presented a model of rational expectations nearly 30 years earlier. We should also note that it was Alan Walters (1971) who first applied the idea of what he called 'consistent expectations' to macroeconomics. However, it was John Muth's (1961) seminal paper that proved to be most influential on the research of the young new classical Turks during the early 1970s. In his seminal article, Muth suggested 'that expectations since they are informed predictions of future events are essentially the same as the predictions of the relevant economic theory'.

Expectations, which are subjective, are fundamental to the behaviour of economic agents and all economic activities have an informational/expectational dimension. For example, expectations of the future value of economic variables will clearly influence demand and supply decisions. As Carter and Maddock (1984) note, 'since virtually all economic decisions involve taking actions now for uncertain rewards in the future, expectations of the future are crucial in decision making'. An obvious example where expectations of inflation will influence behaviour concerns wage negotiations between trade unions and employers. Should a trade union negotiator underestimate the rate of inflation prevailing over the period of the negotiated wage contract, then workers are likely to find that they have suffered a nominal wage increase, but a real wage cut.

An expectation of the future value of some key economic variable need not be confined to a single predicted value but can more realistically take the form of a probability distribution of outcomes. Therefore, there are two key questions facing macroeconomists with respect to incorporating expectations into macroeconomic models:

1. how do individuals acquire, process and make use of information in order to form expectations of key variables?
2. what form of expectations hypothesis should we use in macroeconomic models?

During the 1970s, the rational expectations hypothesis replaced the adaptive expectations hypothesis as the dominant way of modelling endogenous expectations (in his *General Theory*, published in 1936, Keynes had stressed the importance of expectations for understanding macroeconomic instability, but in Keynes's theory expectations were exogenous, being driven by 'animal spirits'; see Chapter 8 and Keynes, 1937). One great appeal of the rational expectations hypothesis is that alternative (non-rational) hypotheses of expectations formation involve systematic errors, a situation that does not sit comfortably with the rational calculating agents that populate orthodox neo-classical models.

The rational expectations hypothesis has over the years been presented in the literature in a number of different forms and versions (see Redman, 1992). At the outset it is important to note the distinction between weak and strong versions of the hypothesis. The main idea behind the weak version of the hypothesis is that, in forming forecasts or expectations about the future value of a variable, rational economic agents will make the best (most efficient) use of all publicly available information about the factors which they believe determine that variable. In other words, expectations are assumed to be formed 'rationally' in line with utility-maximizing behaviour on the part of individual economic agents. For example, if economic agents believe that the rate of inflation is determined by the rate of monetary expansion, they will make the best use of all publicly available information on rates of monetary expansion in forming their expectations of future rates of inflation. The strong version of the rational expectations hypothesis is captured in the above quotation taken from Muth's (1961) article and it is the Muthian version that has been taken up by leading exponents of the new classical school and incorporated into their macroeconomic models. In the Muthian 'strong' version, economic agents' subjective expectations of economic variables will coincide with the true or objective mathematical conditional expectations of those variables. Using the example of economic agents' expectations of inflation ($\dot{P}_t^e$), the rational expectations hypothesis may be expressed algebraically in the following way:

$$\dot{P}_t^e = E(\dot{P}_t \mid \Omega_{t-1}) \tag{5.1}$$

where $\dot{P}_t$ is the actual rate of inflation; $E(\dot{P}_t \mid \Omega_{t-1})$ is the rational expectation of the rate of inflation subject to the information available up to the previous period ($\Omega_{t-1}$). It is important to emphasize that rational expectations does not mean that agents can foresee the future exactly. Rational expectations is not the same as perfect foresight. In order to form a rational expectation of inflation, agents will need to take into account what they believe to be the 'correct' macroeconomic model of the economy. Agents will make errors in their forecasts, since available information will be incomplete. Indeed, this is an essential element of Lucas's monetary surprise model – see sections 5.3.3 and 5.5.1. However, such forecast errors will be unrelated to the information set at the time the expectation (for example of inflation) was formed. With rational expectations, agents' expectations of economic variables on average will be correct, that is, will equal their true value. Furthermore, the hypoth-

esis implies that agents will not form expectations which are systematically
wrong (biased) over time. If expectations were systematically wrong, agents
would, it is held, learn from their mistakes and change the way they formed
expectations, thereby eliminating systematic errors. More formally, the strong
version of the rational expectations hypothesis implies that:

$$\dot{P}_t^e = \dot{P}_t + \varepsilon_t \tag{5.2}$$

where $\dot{P}_t^e$ = expected rate of inflation from $t$ to $t + 1$; $\dot{P}_t$ = actual rate of
inflation from $t$ to $t + 1$; and $\varepsilon_t$ = random error term, which (i) has a mean of
zero, and (ii) is uncorrelated with the information set available at the time
when expectations are formed, otherwise economic agents would not be fully
exploiting all available information. In summary, the forecasting errors from
rationally formed expectations will (i) be essentially random with a mean of
zero; (ii) be unrelated to those made in previous periods, revealing no discernible pattern: that is, they will be serially uncorrelated over time; and (iii)
have the lowest variance compared to any other forecasting method. In other
words, rational expectations is the most accurate and efficient form of expectations formation.

The rational expectations hypothesis contrasts with the adaptive expectations
hypothesis initially used by orthodox monetarists in their explanation of expectations-augmented Phillips curve (see Chapter 4, section 4). In the adaptive
expectations hypothesis, economic agents base their expectations of future
values of a variable (such as inflation) only on past values of the variable
concerned. One of the main problems with this 'backward-looking' approach to
forming expectations is that, until the variable being predicted is stable for a
considerable period of time, expectations formed of it will be repeatedly wrong.
For example, following the discussion of Chapter 4, section 4.3.2, on the
accelerationist hypothesis, if unemployment is held below the natural rate,
inflation will accelerate and inflation expectations will be biased in a downward
direction. This problem results from (i) the assumption that economic agents
only partially adjust their expectations by a fraction of the last error made; and
(ii) the failure of agents to take into consideration additional information available to them other than past values of the variable concerned, despite making
repeated errors. In contrast, in the 'forward-looking' approach, rational expectations are based on the use of all publicly available information, with the
crucial implication of the strong version of the hypothesis being that economic
agents will not form expectations which are systematically wrong over time;
that is, such expectations will be unbiased.

A number of criticisms have been raised against the rational expectations
hypothesis and we now consider three common ones. The first of these
concerns the costs (in time, effort and money) of acquiring and processing all

publicly available information in order to forecast the future value of a variable, such as inflation. It is important to note that the weak version of the hypothesis does not require, as some critics have suggested, that economic agents actually use 'all' publicly available information. Given the costs involved in acquiring and processing information, it is unlikely that agents would ever use all publicly available information. What proponents of the weak version of the hypothesis suggest is that 'rational' economic agents will have an incentive to make the 'best' use of all publicly available information in forming their expectations. In other words, agents will have an incentive to use information up to the point where the marginal benefit (in terms of improved accuracy of the variable being forecast) equals the marginal cost (in terms of acquiring and processing all publicly available information). In this case, expectations would be less efficient than they would be if all available information were used. Furthermore, the weak version of the hypothesis does not require, as some critics have suggested, that all individual agents directly acquire and process available information personally. Economic agents can derive information indirectly from, for example, published forecasts and commentaries in the news media. Given that forecasts frequently differ, the problem then arises of discerning which is the 'correct' view.

A far more serious objection concerns the problem of how agents actually acquire knowledge of the 'correct' model of the economy, given that economists themselves display considerable disagreement over this. The issue of whether individual agents operating in decentralized markets will be able to 'learn' the true model of the economy has been the subject of considerable debate (see, for example, Frydman and Phelps, 1983; Evans and Honkapohja, 1999). With regard to this particular criticism, it is important to note that the strong version of the hypothesis does not require that economic agents actually know the correct model of the economy. What the hypothesis implies is that rational agents will not form expectations which are systematically wrong over time. In other words, expectations, it is suggested, will resemble those formed 'as if' agents did know the correct model to the extent that they will be unbiased and randomly distributed over time. Critics of the hypothesis are not, however, convinced by arguments such as these and suggest that, owing to such problems as the costs of acquiring and processing all available information, and uncertainty over which is the correct model, it 'is' possible for agents to form expectations which are systematically wrong. There is some evidence that agents do make systematic errors in expectations (see, for example, Lovell, 1986).

A third important criticism, associated in particular with the Post Keynesian school, relates to the problems of expectations formation in a world of fundamental uncertainty. To Keynesian fundamentalists, a major achievement of Keynes was to place the problem of uncertainty at the centre stage of macroeconomics. In the Post Keynesian vision, the world is *non-ergodic*; that is, each historical event is unique and non-repetitive. In such situations the rules of probability do not apply. We are in a world of 'kaleidic' change and fundamental discontinuities (Shackle, 1974). Accordingly, Post Keynesians argue that it is important to follow both Keynes (1921) and Knight (1933) and distinguish between situations involving risk and situations involving uncertainty. In situations of risk the probability distribution is known. In contrast, in situations of uncertainty there is no possibility of formulating any meaningful probability distribution. Because the rational expectations hypothesis assumes that economic agents can formulate probability distributions of outcomes of various economic changes and situations, it belongs to the world of risk. In new classical models the problem of fundamental uncertainty is ignored since Lucas (1977) interprets business cycles as repeated instances of essentially similar events. Hence, in Lucas's ergodic world, meaningful probability distributions of outcomes can be gauged by intelligent and rational economic agents. Unfortunately, according to Post Keynesians, the real world is one characterized by fundamental uncertainty and this means that conclusions built on models using the rational expectations hypothesis are useless. Likewise, the Austrian school are also very critical of the rational expectations hypothesis (see Snowdon et al., 1994, and Chapters 8 and 9).

The various influences on expectations have recently been investigated by the Bank of England (2003). Reporting the results of a recent 'inflation attitudes survey' the Bank of England finds the following interesting results:

1.   disaggregating the data reveals that different people and groups have different attitudes to inflation;
2.   the expectations of 'professional' groups cluster around the mean expectation;
3.   younger respondents have lower expectations of inflation than older respondents;
4.   mortgage holders have lower inflation expectations than respondents who rent accommodation;
5.   people in the south of Britain have higher expectations of inflation than those living in the north; and
6.   lifetime experience of inflation influences expectations of inflation.

Thus expectations of inflation are influenced by age, geographical location, education and occupation, and housing status. Clearly those old enough to have lived through the 'Great Inflation' of the 1970s have not been entirely able to remove that experience from their judgement.

Notwithstanding these criticisms, during the 1970s there was undoubtedly a 'rational expectations revolution' in macroeconomics (Taylor, 1989; Hoover, 1992). However, it should be noted that Muth's idea was not immediately taken up by macroeconomists, maybe because during the 1960s the orthodox Keynesian model was 'the only game in town'. It took almost ten years before Lucas, Sargent and other leading new classical economists began to incorporate the hypothesis into their macroeconomic models.

Evidence of this lag can be gleaned from citation counts for Muth's (1961) paper. In an interesting comparison of the relative influence of Muth's paper with that of Axel Leijonhufvud's (1968) famous book, *On Keynesian Economics and the Economics of Keynes* (see Chapter 2), Backhouse (1995) has shown how during the 1970s and 1980s citations of Muth's paper exploded while citations of Leijonhufvud's book declined as interest in Keynesian economics waned (see Snowdon, 2004a). While Leijonhufvud's book had an immediate impact, but ultimately failed to transform macroeconomics in the direction of coordination failure stressed by Leijonhufvud, in contrast, Muth's paper got off to a slow start but ultimately played a key role in transforming macroeconomics (see Leijonhufvud, 1992, 1993, 1998a, 1998b on the need for macroeconomics to reconsider, among many other things, the coordination question in macroeconomics).

One final point is worth making. The use of the word 'rational' in the presentation of the hypothesis proved to be an important 'rhetorical' weapon in the battle to win the minds of macroeconomists during the 1970s. As Barro (1984) has pointed out:

> One of the cleverest features of the rational expectations revolution was the application of the term 'rational'. Thereby, the opponents of this approach were forced into the defensive position of either being irrational or of modelling others as irrational, neither of which are comfortable positions for an economist.

For a more detailed discussion of the rational expectations hypothesis and its application in macroeconomics, the reader is referred to Begg (1982); Carter and Maddock (1984); Shaw (1984); Attfield et al. (1985); Redman (1992); Sheffrin (1996); and Minford (1997). On the use of rhetoric in new classical economics, see Backhouse (1997a).

### 5.3.2 Continuous market clearing

A second key assumption in new classical models is that all markets in the economy continuously clear, in line with the Walrasian tradition. At each point of time all observed outcomes are viewed as 'market-clearing', and are the result of the optimal demand and supply responses of economic agents to their perceptions of prices. As a result the economy is viewed as being in a continuous state of (short- and long-run) equilibrium. New classical models are in consequence often referred to as 'equilibrium' models, where equilibrium is interpreted to mean that all economic agents within a market economy have made choices that optimize their objectives subject to the constraints that they face.

In market-clearing models economic agents (workers, consumers and firms) are 'price takers'; that is, they take the market price as given and have no market power that could be used to influence price. Firms are operating within a market structure known as 'perfect competition'. In such a market structure firms can only decide on their optimal (profit-maximizing) output (determined where marginal revenue = marginal cost) given the market-determined price. In the absence of externalities the competitive equilibrium, with market prices determined by the forces of demand and supply, is Pareto-optimal and leads to the maximization of total surplus (the sum of producer and consumer surplus). In Figure 5.2(a) we can see that a competitive market-clearing equilibrium ($P^*$, $Q^*$) maximizes the total of consumer and producer surplus (equal to area $BCE$) whereas non-market-clearing prices (output), such as $P_1(Q_1)$ or $P_2(Q_2)$, indicated in Figure 5.2(b), result in a welfare loss indicated by the areas $FEI$ and $GEH$ respectively (see Dixon, 1997).

In Figure 5.2(a) all the mutual gains from trade have been exhausted by economic agents and there are 'no dollar bills left on the sidewalk' (see Barro, 1979). It is important to note that the position of supply and demand curves, and hence market-clearing prices and equilibrium output, will be influenced by the expectations of economic agents. Since even rationally

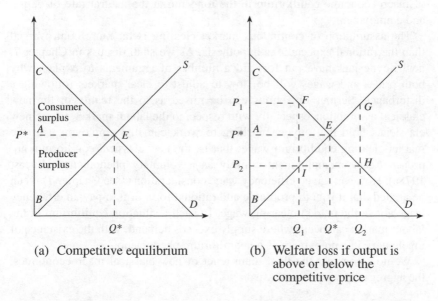

(a) Competitive equilibrium

(b) Welfare loss if output is above or below the competitive price

*Figure 5.2   The welfare implications of equilibrium in a competitive market*

formed expectations can turn out to be wrong due to incomplete information, this means that, at least until agents acquire more accurate information, a currently observed market-clearing equilibrium will differ from a full information equilibrium. Nevertheless, since agents are doing the best they can with the information they have acquired, they are seen to be in a state of equilibrium at all times, as illustrated below.

## RATIONALITY ⇒ OPTIMIZATION ⇒ EQUILIBRIUM

The assumption of continuous market clearing is the most critical and controversial assumption underlying new classical analysis and is highly contentious, as it implies that prices are free to adjust instantaneously to clear markets (see Tobin, 1993, 1996). The assumption stands in bold contrast to the approach adopted in both orthodox Keynesian and monetarist models. As we have discussed in the two previous chapters, orthodox Keynesians and monetarists disagree about the time it takes for markets to clear. Keynesian models incorporate the assumption that markets may fail to clear because of the slow adjustment of prices, so that the economy is viewed as being in a possible state of continuous disequilibrium. In contrast, orthodox monetarist models incorporate the assumption that prices adjust fairly rapidly to clear markets and, while accepting that the economy may be in disequilibrium in the short run, monetarists assume that the economy will automatically return to a state of macroeconomic equilibrium in the long run at the natural rate of output and employment.

The assumption of continuous market clearing is far more controversial than the rational expectations hypothesis. As we shall discuss in Chapter 7, new Keynesians have put forward a number of arguments to explain why both prices and wages will be slow to adjust to clear markets following a disturbance. Serious objections can be raised as to the reality of the new classical assumption, especially with respect to the labour market, where new classicists hold that anyone wishing to work can find employment at the market-clearing equilibrium wage; that is, the new classical equilibrium approach treats unemployment entirely as a voluntary phenomenon (Lucas, 1978a). However, given efficiency wage considerations (see Chapter 7) it can be argued that it is both profitable and rational for a firm to pay an efficiency wage above the market-clearing wage. In such a situation equilibrium in the labour market can occur where supply exceeds demand, with the existence of involuntary unemployment as an equilibrium phenomenon.

We now consider the final main tenet of new classical macroeconomics, the aggregate supply hypothesis.

### 5.3.3 The aggregate supply hypothesis

As with the rational expectations hypothesis, various explanations of the aggregate supply hypothesis can be found in the literature. Having said this, two main approaches to aggregate supply can be identified. Underlying these approaches are two orthodox microeconomic assumptions: (i) rational decisions taken by workers and firms reflect optimizing behaviour on their part; and (ii) the supply of labour/output by workers/firms depends upon relative prices.

The first new classical approach to aggregate supply focuses on the supply of labour and derives from the work of Lucas and Rapping (1969). This analysis is discussed more fully in Chapter 6 and in what follows we merely outline the essence of the approach. During any period, workers have to decide how much time to allocate between work and leisure. Workers, it is assumed, have some notion of the normal or expected average real wage. If the current real wage is above the normal real wage, workers will have an incentive to work more (take less leisure time) in the current period in the anticipation of taking more leisure (working less) in the future, when the real wage is expected to be lower. Conversely, if the current real wage is below the norm, workers will have an incentive to take more leisure (work less) in the current period in the anticipation of working more (taking less leisure) in the future, when the real wage is expected to be higher. The supply of labour is postulated, therefore, to respond to perceived temporary changes in the real wage. This behavioural response of substituting current leisure for future leisure and vice versa is referred to as 'intertemporal substitution'. Within the intertemporal substitution model, changes in employment are explained in terms of the 'voluntary' choices of workers who change their supply of labour in response to perceived temporary changes in the real wage.

The second new classical approach to aggregate supply again derives from the highly influential work of Lucas (1972a, 1973). In what follows we illustrate the spirit of Lucas's arguments by focusing on the goods market and the supply decisions of firms. An important element of Lucas's analysis concerns the structure of the information set available to producers. It is assumed that, while a firm knows the current price of its own goods, the general price level for other markets only becomes known with a time lag. When a firm experiences a rise in the current market price of its output it has to decide whether the change in price reflects (i) a real shift in demand towards its product, in which case the firm should respond (rationally) to the increase in the price of its output relative to the price of other goods by increasing its output, or (ii) merely a nominal increase in demand across all markets, producing a general increase in prices which would not require a supply response. Firms are faced by what is referred to as a 'signal extraction' problem, in that they have to distinguish between relative and absolute price changes. Indeed, the greater the variability of the general price level, the more difficult it will be for a producer to extract a correct signal and the smaller the supply response is likely to be to any given change in prices (see Lucas, 1973).

The analysis of the behaviour of individual agents in terms of the supply of both labour and goods has led to what is referred to as the Lucas 'surprise' supply function, the simplest from of which is given by equation (5.3):

$$Y_t = Y_{N_t} + \alpha[P_t - P_t^e], \quad \alpha > 0 \qquad (5.3)$$

Since in new classical models expectations are formed rationally, we can replace (5.3) with (5.4):

$$Y_t = Y_{N_t} + \alpha[P_t - E(P_t \mid \Omega_{t-1})] \qquad (5.4)$$

Equation (5.4) states that output ($Y_t$) deviates from its natural level ($Y_{N_t}$) only in response to deviations of the actual price level ($P_t$) from its (rational) expected value [$E(P_t \mid \Omega_{t-1})$], that is, in response to an unexpected (surprise) increase in the price level. For example, when the actual price level turns out to be greater than expected, individual agents are 'surprised' and mistake the increase for an increase in the relative price of their own output, resulting in an increase in the supply of output and employment in the economy. In the absence of price surprises, output will be at its natural level. For any given expectation of the price level, the aggregate supply curve will slope upwards in *P–Y* space, and the greater the value of $\alpha$, the more elastic will be the 'surprise' aggregate supply curve and the bigger will be the impact on real variables of an unanticipated rise in the general price level (see Figure 5.3 and section 5.5.1).

An alternative specification of the Lucas surprise function states that output only deviates from its natural level in response to a deviation of actual from expected inflation (that is, in response to errors in inflation expectations):

$$Y_t = Y_{N_t} + \alpha[\dot{P}_t - E(\dot{P}_t \mid \Omega_{t-1})] + \varepsilon_t \qquad (5.5)$$

In equation (5.5) $\dot{P}_t$ is the actual rate of inflation, $E(\dot{P}_t \mid \Omega_{t-1})$ is the rational expectation of rate of inflation subject to the information available up to the previous period, and $\varepsilon_t$ is a random error process. According to Lucas, countries where inflation has been relatively stable should show greater supply response to an inflationary impulse and vice versa. In his famous empirical paper, Lucas (1973) confirmed that:

In a stable price country like the United States ... policies which increase nominal income tend to have a large initial effect on real output, together with a small positive effect on the rate of inflation ... In contrast, in a volatile price county like Argentina, nominal income changes are associated with equal, contemporaneous price movements with no discernible effect on real output.

Equation (5.4) can be reformulated to include a lagged output term ($Y_{t-1} - Y_{N_{t-1}}$) and this version was used by Lucas (1973) in his empirical work to deal with the problem of persistence (serial correlation) in the movement of economic aggregates. The surprise aggregate supply function now takes the form shown in equation (5.6):

$$Y_t = Y_{N_t} + \alpha[P_t - E(P_t \mid \Omega_{t-1})] + \beta(Y_{t-1} - Y_{N_{t-1}}) + \varepsilon_t \qquad (5.6)$$

By invoking 'Okun's law' (Okun, 1962), that is, that there is a stable and predictable negative relationship between unemployment and GDP, the Lucas surprise aggregate supply equation can be seen as simply an alternative representation of the rational expectations-augmented Phillips curve shown in equation (5.7):

$$\dot{P}_t = E(\dot{P}_t \mid \Omega_{t-1}) - \varphi(U_t - U_{N_t}), \quad \varphi > 0 \qquad (5.7)$$

where $U_t$ is the current rate of unemployment, and $U_{N_t}$ is the natural rate of unemployment. Rearranging (5.7), we get equation (5.8):

$$U_t = U_{N_t} - 1/\varphi[\dot{P}_t - E(\dot{P}_t \mid \Omega_{t-1})] \qquad (5.8)$$

In this formulation an inflation surprise leads to a temporary reduction of unemployment below the natural rate. In equations (5.6) and (5.8) a real variable is linked to a nominal variable. But, as Lucas demonstrated, the classical dichotomy only breaks down when a change in the nominal variable is a 'surprise'. Indeed, Lucas himself regards the finding that anticipated and unanticipated changes in monetary growth have very different effects, as the key idea in post-war macroeconomics (Snowdon and Vane, 1998). Furthermore, Lucas (1996) notes that this distinction between anticipated and unanticipated monetary changes is a feature of all rational expectations-style models developed during the 1970s to explain the monetary non-neutrality exhibited in short-run trade-offs.

## 5.4 Equilibrium Business Cycle Theory

Before Keynes's (1936) *General Theory* many economists were actively engaged in business cycle research (see Haberler, 1963). However, one of the important consequences of the Keynesian revolution was the redirection of macroeconomic research towards questions relating to the level of output at a point in time, rather than the dynamic evolution of the economy over time. Nevertheless, within mainstream macroeconomics, before the 1970s, the main approach to the analysis of business cycles after 1945 was provided by Keynesians and monetarists (see Mullineux, 1984). During the 1970s a new approach to the study of aggregate fluctuations was initiated by Lucas, who advocated an equilibrium approach to business cycle modelling (Kim, 1988). Lucas's equilibrium theory was a significant departure from Keynesian business cycle analysis where fluctuations of GDP were viewed as disequilibrium phenomena. Keynesian macroeconomic models are typically characterized by various rigidities and frictions that inhibit wage and price flexibility. Consequently, in the short run, markets fail to clear and GDP can depart significantly from its potential level for extended periods of time. Milton Friedman also criticized Keynesian models for their downplaying of the importance of monetary disturbances as a major source of aggregate instability. The Friedman and Schwartz (1963) study proved to be highly influential to a whole generation of economists. In particular Friedman and Schwartz argued that the Great Depression was 'a tragic testimonial to the importance of monetary factors'. While Lucas was very much influenced by Friedman's monetarist ideas, he preferred to utilize a Walrasian research methodology rather than build on Friedman's Marshallian approach when analysing business cycles (see Hoover, 1984).

The foundations of Lucas's approach to business cycle modelling can be found in his seminal *Journal of Economic Theory* paper (Lucas, 1972a), where his objective is clearly stated in the opening paragraphs:

> This paper provides a simple example of an economy in which equilibrium prices and quantities exhibit what may be the central feature of the modern business cycle: a systematic relation between the rate of change of nominal prices (inflation) and the level of real output. The relationship, essentially a variant of the well-known Phillips curve, is derived within a framework from which all forms of 'money illusion' are rigorously excluded: all prices are market clearing, all agents behave optimally in light of their objectives and expectations, and expectations are formed optimally ... In the framework presented, price movement results from a *relative demand shift* or a *nominal (monetary)* one. This hedging behaviour results in the nonneutrality of money, or broadly speaking a Phillips curve, similar in nature to that we observe in reality. At the same time, classical results on the long-run neutrality of money, or independence of real and nominal magnitudes, continue to hold.

Lucas demonstrated that within this Walrasian framework, monetary changes have real consequences, but 'only because agents cannot discriminate perfectly between monetary and real demand shifts' so 'there is no usable trade-off between inflation and real output'. In Lucas's 1972 model 'the Phillips curve emerges not as an unexplained empirical fact, but as a central feature of the solution to a general equilibrium system'.

Building on this insight, Lucas proceeded to develop an equilibrium approach to the analysis of aggregate fluctuations. Lucas (1975) defines business cycles as the serially correlated movements about trend of real output that 'are not explainable by movements in the availability of factors of production'. Associated with fluctuations in GDP are co-movements among different aggregative time series, such as prices, consumption, business profits, investment, monetary aggregates, productivity and interest rates (see Abel and Bernanke, 2001). Such are the regularities that Lucas (1977) declares that 'with respect to the qualitative behaviour of co-movements among series, *business cycles are all alike*' (the Great Depression being an exception). To Lucas the 'recurrent character of business cycles is of central importance'. As Lucas (1977) explains:

> Insofar as business cycles can be viewed as repeated instances of essentially similar events, it will be reasonable to treat agents as reacting to cyclical changes as 'risk', or to assume their expectations are *rational*, that they have fairly stable arrangements for collecting and processing information, and that they utilise this information in forecasting the future in a stable way, free of systematic and easily correctable biases.

Building on his path-breaking 1972 and 1973 papers, Lucas (1975, 1977) provides a 'new classical' monetarist explanation of the business cycle as an equilibrium phenomenon. As Kevin Hoover (1988) observes, 'to explain the related movements of macroeconomic aggregates and prices without recourse to the notion of disequilibrium is the desideratum of new classical research on the theory of business cycles'. As Lucas (1975) puts it, 'the central problem in macroeconomics' is to find a theoretical framework where monetary disturbances can cause real output fluctuations which at the same time does not imply 'the existence of persistent, recurrent, unexploited profit opportunities' such as occur in Keynesian models characterised by price rigidities and non-rational expectations.

Hayek (1933) had set forth a research agenda where 'the crucial problem of Trade Cycle Theory' was to produce a solution that would allow 'incorporation of cyclical phenomena into the system of economic equilibrium theory, with which they are in apparent contradiction'. By equilibrium theory Hayek meant that which had been 'most perfectly expressed by the Lausanne School of theoretical economics'. While Keynesian economists regarded the quest for an equilibrium theory of the business cycle as unattainable, it is one of Lucas's most notable achievements to demonstrate that it is possible to develop an equilibrium account of aggregate instability. Although initially Lucas claimed some affinity, via the notion of equilibrium theorizing, with the work of Hayek on business cycles, it is now clear that new classical and Austrian theories of the business cycle are very different. While the Austrian theory views business cycles as an equilibrating *process*, in new classical models the business cycle is viewed as a 'continuum of equilibrium' (Kim, 1988; see also Chapter 9; Lucas, 1977; Hoover, 1984, 1988; Zijp, 1993).

Lucas's monetary equilibrium business cycle theory (MEBCT) incorporates Muth's (1961) rational expectations hypothesis, Friedman's (1968a) natural rate hypothesis, and Walrasian general equilibrium methodology. With continuous market clearing due to complete wage and price flexibility the fluctuations in the MEBCT are described as competitive equilibria. But how can monetary disturbances create fluctuations in such a world? In the stylized classical model where agents have perfect information, changes in the money supply should be strictly neutral, that is, have no impact on real variables such as real GDP and employment. However, the leading and procyclical behaviour of money observed empirically by researchers such as Friedman and Schwartz (1963), and more recently by Romer and Romer (1989), suggests that money is non-neutral (ignoring the possibility of reverse causation). The intellectual challenge facing Lucas was to account for the non-neutrality of money in a world inhabited by rational profit-maximizing agents and where all markets continuously clear. His main innovation was to extend the classical model so as to allow agents to have 'imperfect information'. As a result Lucas's MEBCT has come to be popularly known as the 'misperceptions theory', although the idea of instability being the result of monetary-induced misperceptions is also a major feature of Friedman's (1968a) analysis of the Phillips curve. In Lucas's (1975) pioneering attempt to build a MEBCT his model is characterized by: prices and quantities determined in competitive equilibrium; agents with rational expectations; and imperfect information, 'not only in the sense that the future is unknown, but also in the sense that no agent is perfectly informed as to the current state of the economy'.

The hypothesis that aggregate supply depends upon relative prices is central to the new classical explanation of fluctuations in output and employment. In new classical analysis, unanticipated aggregate demand shocks (resulting mainly from unanticipated changes in the money supply) which affect the whole economy cause errors in (rationally formed) price expectations and result in output and employment deviating from their long-run (full information) equilibrium (natural) levels. These errors are made by both workers and firms who have incomplete/imperfect information, so that they mistake general price changes for relative price changes and react by changing the supply of labour and output, respectively.

In neoclassical microeconomic theory the supply curve of an individual producer in a competitive market slopes upward, indicating that the supplier will produce more in response to a rise in price. However, this profit-maximizing response is a reaction of producers to a rise in their relative price. Therefore, individual suppliers need to know what is happening to the general price level in order to make a rational calculation of whether it is profitable to expand production in response to an increase in the nominal price of the good they supply. If all prices are rising due to inflation, suppliers should not increase production in response to a rise in price of their good because it does not represent a relative (real) price increase. And yet the data reveal that aggregate output increases as the general price level increases; that is, the short-run aggregate supply curve slopes upwards in *P–Y* space. This must mean that the aggregate response of thousands of individual suppliers to a rise in the general price level is positive and yet profit-maximizing individuals should not be reacting in this way. How can that be? Rational agents should only respond to real variables and their behaviour should be invariant to nominal variables. The answer provided by Lucas relates to agents (workers, households, firms) having imperfect information about their relative prices (Lucas, 1972a). If agents have been used to a world of price stability, they will tend to interpret an increase in the supply price of the good (or service) they produce as a relative price increase and produce more in response. Therefore an unexpected or unanticipated increase in the price level will surprise agents and they will misinterpret the information they observe with respect to the rise in price of their good and produce more. Agents have what Lucas (1977) refers to as a 'signal extraction problem', and if all agents make the same error we will observe an aggregate increase in output correlated with an increase in the general price level. Since Lucas's model is 'monetarist', the increase in the general price level is caused by a prior increase in the money supply and we therefore observe a positive money-to-output correlation, that is, the non-neutrality of money.

Consider, for example, an economy which is initially in a position where output and employment are at their natural levels. Suppose an unanticipated monetary disturbance occurs which leads to an increase in the general price level, and hence individual prices, in all markets ('islands') throughout the economy. As noted above, firms are assumed to have information only on prices in the limited number of markets in which they trade. If individual firms interpret the increase in the price of their goods as an increase in the relative price of their output, they will react by increasing their output. Workers are also assumed to have incomplete information. If workers mistakenly perceive an increase in money wages (relative to their expected value) as an increase in real wages, they will respond by increasing the supply of labour (Lucas and Rapping, 1969). In contrast to Friedman's model (see Chapter 4), where workers are fooled, Lucas's model does not rely on any asymmetry of information between workers and firms. Both firms and workers are inclined to make expectational errors and respond positively to misperceived global price increases by increasing the supply of output and labour, respectively. As a result aggregate output and employment will rise temporarily above their natural levels. Once agents realize that there has been no change in relative prices, output and employment return to their long-run (full information) equilibrium (natural) levels.

The Lucas model emphasizes monetary shocks as the main cause of aggregate instability and the whole story is based on a confusion on the part of agents between relative and general price movements (Dore, 1993; Arnold, 2002). In the MEBCT, the supply of output at any given time ($Y_t$) has both a permanent (secular) component ($Y_{N_t}$) and a cyclical component ($Yc_t$) as shown in equation (5.9):

$$Y_t = Y_{N_t} + Yc_t \tag{5.9}$$

The permanent component of GDP reflects the underlying growth of the economy and follows the trend line given by (5.10):

$$Y_{N_t} = \lambda + \phi_t \tag{5.10}$$

The cyclical component is dependent on the price surprise together with the previous period's deviation of output from its natural rate, as shown in equation (5.11):

$$Yc_t = \alpha[P_t - E(P_t \mid \Omega_{t-1})] + \beta(Y_{t-1} - Y_{N_{t-1}}) \tag{5.11}$$

The lagged output term in (5.11) is to recognize that deviations in output from the trend will be more than transitory due to the influence of a variety of propagation mechanisms, and the coefficient $\beta > 0$ determines the speed with which output returns to its natural rate after a shock. Because the combination of the rational expectations hypothesis and the surprise supply function implies that output and employment will fluctuate randomly around their natural levels, further assumptions are required to explain why during the business cycle output and employment remain persistently above (upswing) or below (downswing) their trend values for a succession of time periods. The observed serially correlated movements in output and employment (that is, where output and employment levels in any one time period are correlated with their preceding values) have been explained in the literature in a number of ways. These explanations (propagation mechanisms) include reference to lagged output, investment accelerator effects, information lags and the durability of capital goods, the existence of contracts inhibiting immediate adjustment and adjustment costs (see Zijp, 1993). For example, in the field of employment firms face costs both in hiring and in firing labour: costs associated with interviewing and training new employees, making redundancy payments and so on. In consequence their optimal response may be to adjust their employment and output levels gradually over a period of time following some unanticipated shock.

By combining equations (5.9), (5.10) and (5.11) we get the Lucas aggregate supply relationship given by equation (5.12):

$$Y_t = \lambda + \phi_t + \alpha[P_t - E(P_t \mid \Omega_{t-1})] + \beta(Y_{t-1} - Y_{N_{t-1}}) + \varepsilon_t \qquad (5.12)$$

where $\varepsilon_t$ is a random error process.

Although the actions of agents in Lucas's model turn out *ex post* to be nonoptimal, they are in a rational expectations equilibrium doing the best they can given the (imperfect or incomplete) information they have acquired. As Lucas (1973) demonstrated, this implies that monetary disturbances (random shocks) are likely to have a much bigger impact on real variables in countries where price stability has been the norm. In countries where agents are used to inflation, monetary disturbances are unlikely to impact in any significant way on real variables. Let $\theta$ represent the fraction of total individual price variance due to relative price variation. Thus the larger is $\theta$, the more any observed variability in prices is attributed by economic agents to a real shock (that is, a change in relative price) and the less it is attributed to purely inflationary (nominal) movements of the general price level. We can therefore modify equation (5.12) and present the Lucas aggregate supply curve in a form similar to how it appeared in his 1973 paper 'Some International Evidence on Output–Inflation Trade-Offs':

$$Y_t = \lambda + \phi_t + \theta\alpha[P_t - E(P_t \mid \Omega_{t-1})] + \beta(Y_{t-1} - Y_{N_{t-1}}) + \varepsilon_t \qquad (5.13)$$

According to (5.13) an unanticipated monetary disturbance that takes place in a country where agents are expecting price stability will lead to a significant real output disturbance. In (5.13) we observe that output ($Y_t$) has:

1. a permanent component = $\lambda + \phi_t$;
2. a component related to the impact of a price surprise = $\theta\alpha[P_t - E(P_t \mid \Omega_{t-1})]$;
3. a component related to last period's deviation of output from permanent output = $\beta(Y_{t-1} - Y_{N_{t-1}})$; and
4. a random component = $\varepsilon_t$.

Thus, in the Lucas model business cycles are generated by exogenous monetary demand shocks that transmit imperfect price signals to economic agents who, in a world of imperfect information, respond to price increases by increasing supply. The greater is the general price variability (the lower the variation in price attributed to relative price variation), the lower will be the cyclical response of output to a monetary disturbance, and vice versa. A major policy implication of the MEBCT is that a benign monetary policy would eliminate a large source of aggregate instability. Thus new classical economists come down on the side of rules in the 'rules versus discretion' debate over the conduct of stabilization policy.

We now turn to consider the main policy implications of the new classical approach to macroeconomics in more detail.

## 5.5   The Policy Implications of the New Classical Approach

The combination of the rational expectations, continuous market-clearing and aggregate supply hypotheses produces a number of important policy conclusions. In what follows we discuss the main policy implications of the new classical approach, namely (i) the policy ineffectiveness proposition; (ii) the output–employment costs of reducing inflation; (iii) dynamic time inconsistency, credibility and monetary rules; (iv) central bank independence; (v) the role of microeconomic policies to increase aggregate supply; and (vi) the Lucas critique of econometric policy evaluation.

We begin with a discussion of the strong policy conclusion that fully anticipated changes in monetary policy will be ineffective in influencing the level of output and employment even in the short run, that is, the superneutrality of money.

### 5.5.1   The policy ineffectiveness proposition
The new classical policy ineffectiveness proposition was first presented in two influential papers by Sargent and Wallace (1975, 1976). The proposition can best be illustrated using the aggregate demand/supply model shown in Figure 5.3. Those readers unfamiliar with the derivation of this model should refer to any standard macroeconomics text, such as Mankiw (2003). In Figure 5.3, the economy is initially operating at point $A$, the triple intersection of $AD_0$, $SRAS_0$ and $LRAS$. At point $A$, in line with equation (5.3), the price level $(P_0)$ is fully anticipated (that is, the actual and expected price levels coincide) and output and employment are at their long-run (full information) equilibrium (natural) levels. Suppose the authorities announce that they intend to increase the money supply. Rational economic agents would take this information into account in forming their expectations and fully anticipate the effects of the increase in the money supply on the general price level, so that

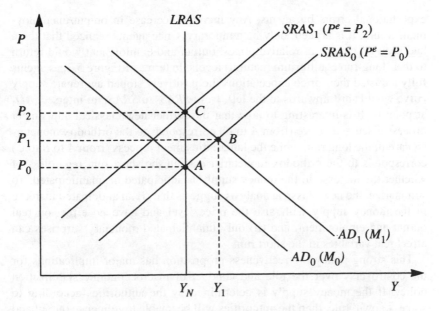

*Figure 5.3    The effects of anticipated and unanticipated changes in the money supply on the level of output and the price level*

output and employment would remain unchanged at their natural levels. The rightward shift of the aggregate demand curve from $AD_0$ to $AD_1$ would be offset by an upward shift to the left of the positively sloped aggregate supply curve from $SRAS_0$ to $SRAS_1$, as money wages were increased following an immediate upward revision of price expectations. In this case the economy would move straight from point $A$ to $C$, remaining on the vertical long-run aggregate supply curve with no change in output and employment even in the short run; that is, money is super-neutral.

In contrast, suppose the authorities surprise economic agents by increasing the money supply without announcing their intentions. In this situation firms and workers with incomplete information would misperceive the resultant increase in the general price level as an increase in relative prices and react by increasing the supply of output and labour. In other words, workers and firms would mistakenly perceive this as a real (as opposed to a nominal) increase in the demand for their services/goods and respond by increasing the supply of labour/output. In terms of Figure 5.3, the aggregate demand curve would shift to the right from $AD_0$ to $AD_1$ to intersect the positively sloped aggregate supply curve $SRAS_0$ at point $B$. In line with equation (5.3), output ($Y_1$) would deviate from its natural level ($Y_N$) as a consequence of deviations of the price level ($P_1$) from its expected level ($P_0$), that is, as the result of expectational errors by agents. Any increase/decrease in output/unemployment would, it is argued, only be temporary. Once agents realized that there had been no change in relative prices, output and employment would return to their long-run equilibrium (natural) levels. In terms of Figure 5.3, as agents fully adjusted their price expectations the positively sloped aggregate supply curve would shift upwards to the left, from $SRAS_0$ to $SRAS_1$, to intersect $AD_1$ at point $C$. It is interesting to note that the former new classical adjustment process discussed above (from $A$ to $C$) corresponds to the orthodox monetarist case in the long run, while the latter adjustment process (from $A$ to $B$ to $C$) corresponds to the orthodox monetarist case in the short run, regardless of whether the increase in the money supply is anticipated or unanticipated. To summarize, the new classical analysis suggests that (i) an anticipated increase in the money supply will raise the price level and have no effect on real output and employment, and (ii) only unanticipated monetary surprises can affect real variables in the short run.

This strong policy ineffectiveness proposition has major implications for the controversy over the role and conduct of macroeconomic stabilization policy. If the money supply is determined by the authorities according to some 'known' rule, then the authorities will be unable to influence output and employment even in the short run by pursuing a systematic monetary policy as it can be anticipated by agents. For example, the authorities might adopt a monetary rule which allows for a given fixed rate of monetary growth of 6 per cent per annum. In forming their expectations of inflation, rational economic agents would include the anticipated effects of the 6 per cent expansion of the money supply. Consequently the systematic component (that is, 6 per cent) of the monetary rule would have no effect on real variables. If, in practice, the money supply grew at a rate of 8 per cent per annum, the non-systematic (unanticipated) component of monetary expansion (that is, 2 per cent per annum) would cause output and employment to rise temporarily above their long-run equilibrium (natural) levels, owing to errors in inflation expectations. Alternatively the authorities might allow the money supply to be determined by a feedback rule (for example, in response to changes in unemployment and output). Again changes in the rate of monetary growth which arise from a known feedback rule will be anticipated by agents, making the feedback policy rule ineffective. Only departures from a known monetary rule (such as policy errors made by the monetary authorities or unforeseen changes in policy) which are unanticipated will influence output.

The policy ineffectiveness proposition can be expressed algebraically in the following way (see Gordon, 1976). We begin by rewriting the Friedman–Phelps equation in modified linear form as:

$$\dot{P}_t = \dot{P}_t^e - \phi(U_t - U_{N_t}) + \phi\theta S_t \qquad (5.14)$$

where $\theta S_t$ represents an 'exogenous' supply shock (with zero mean) and $U_t - U_{N_t}$ represents the deviation of unemployment from its natural rate. Equation (5.14) can be rewritten as:

$$U_t = U_{N_t} - 1/\phi(\dot{P}_t - \dot{P}_t^e) + \theta S_t \qquad (5.15)$$

The structural relationship between inflation $\dot{P}_t$ and the rate of monetary growth $\dot{M}_t$ is given by:

$$\dot{P}_t = \dot{M}_t + \theta D_t \qquad (5.16)$$

where $\theta D_t$ represents 'unpredictable' demand shocks (such as shocks from the private sector) which also have a zero mean. If $\dot{M}_t^e$ is the expected rate of growth of the money supply, the rational expectation of inflation will be:

$$\dot{P}_t^e = \dot{M}_t^e \qquad (5.17)$$

Suppose a Keynesian-inspired monetary authority attempts to control monetary growth so that it grows at some constant rate ($\lambda_0$) plus some proportion ($\lambda_1$) of the previous period's deviation of unemployment from its natural rate. In this case the actual rate of monetary growth will be:

$$\dot{M}_t = \lambda_0 + \lambda_1(U_{t-1} - U_{N_{t-1}}) + \theta \dot{M}_t \qquad (5.18)$$

where $\theta \dot{M}_t$ signifies a random or unanticipated element in monetary growth. Equation (5.18) indicates that the monetary authorities are operating a systematic feedback monetary rule which can be predicted by rational economic agents as it becomes part of their information set ($\Omega_{t-1}$) in equation (5.1). Rational economic agents will therefore have expectations of inflation based on the expected rate of monetary growth, shown in equation (5.19).

$$\dot{M}_t^e = \lambda_0 + \lambda_1(U_{t-1} - U_{N_{t-1}}) \qquad (5.19)$$

By subtracting (5.19) from (5.18) we obtain:

$$\dot{M}_t - \dot{M}_t^e = \theta \dot{M}_t \qquad (5.20)$$

Subtracting (5.17) from (5.16) and substituting from (5.20) we derive equation (5.21):

$$\dot{P}_t - \dot{P}_t^e = \theta \dot{M}_t + \theta D_t \qquad (5.21)$$

Finally substituting (5.21) into (5.15) gives us:

$$U_t = U_{N_t} - 1/\theta(\theta \dot{M}_t + \theta D_t) + \theta S_t \tag{5.22}$$

The important point to notice about equation (5.22) is that the systematic component of monetary growth, $(\lambda_0 + \lambda_1(U_{t-1} - U_{N_{t-1}}))$, which the government was attempting to use in order to prevent unemployment from deviating from its natural rate, does not enter into it. The only component of equation (5.22) that the monetary authorities can influence directly is $\theta \dot{M}_t$, the random component of monetary growth. Therefore equation (5.22) tells us that, in a Sargent and Wallace world, unemployment can deviate from its natural rate as the result of unpredictable demand $(\theta D_t)$ and supply $(\theta S_t)$ shocks or *unanticipated* monetary surprises $(\theta \dot{M}_t)$. Any systematic feedback monetary rule, by becoming part of economic agents' information set, cannot cause inflation to deviate from its expected rate. Only departures from a known monetary rule (such as policy errors made by the monetary authorities or unforeseen changes in policy) which are unanticipated will influence output and employment.

In summary, the approach predicts that, as rational economic agents will take into account any known monetary rule in forming their expectations, the authorities will be unable to influence output and employment even in the short run by pursuing a systematic monetary policy. Furthermore, any attempt to affect output and employment by random or non-systematic monetary policy will, it is argued, only increase the variation of output and employment around their natural levels. It can be seen, therefore, that the argument advanced by new classicists against policy activism is subtly different from those put forward by orthodox monetarists (see Chapter 4, section 4.3.2 on the role and conduct of monetary policy).

The policy ineffectiveness proposition that only unanticipated monetary surprises have real output effects (or what is sometimes referred to as the 'anticipated–unanticipated money debate') has been the subject of a number of empirical studies. Early work, in particular the seminal papers by Barro (1977a, 1978), seemed to support the proposition. Using annual data for the US economy over the period 1941–76, Barro used a two-stage method in first estimating anticipated and unanticipated money growth before regressing output and unemployment on unanticipated money growth. In general, Barro's studies provided support for the view that, while output and unemployment are significantly affected by unanticipated money growth, anticipated money growth has no real effects. However, subsequent studies, most notably by Mishkin (1982) and Gordon (1982a), found evidence to suggest that both unanticipated and anticipated monetary policy affect output and employment. Overall, while the empirical evidence is mixed, it does not appear to support the view that systematic monetary policy has no real effects. Moreover, as Buiter (1980) pointed out, theoretical models can be constructed where even fully anticipated changes in the rate of monetary growth can have real affects by altering the rate inflation and hence the rate of return on money balances that have a zero nominal rate of return. This in turn will affect the rate of capital accumulation by changing the equilibrium portfolio composition. It also goes without saying that fully anticipated fiscal changes, such as changes in tax rates that alter labour supply and saving behaviour, will have real effects. 'Clearly fiscal policy is non-neutral in even the most classical of systems' (Buiter, 1980). In non-market-clearing models, where prices are fixed, anticipated changes in monetary policy will have real effects via the normal IS–LM–AD–AS mechanisms. In response to the Sargent and Wallace papers, Fischer (1977), Phelps and Taylor (1977) and Taylor (1980) produced models incorporating multi-period wage contracts and rational expectations where monetary policy is non-neutral (see Chapter 7).

In addition, many Keynesians find this whole approach misguided, preferring instead to explore the possibility that non market clearance can be compatible with maximising behaviour on the part of all market participants (Akerlof, 1979). In addition, the idea of stimulating aggregate demand when the economy is already in (full employment) equilibrium would have been anathema to Keynes. Why would such a policy ever be considered necessary? As Frank Hahn (1982, p. 75) has commented, 'Keynesians were concerned with the problem of pushing the economy to its natural rate, not beyond it. If the economy is there already, we can all go home.'

### 5.5.2 The real costs of disinflation

The second main policy implication of the new classical approach concerns the output–employment costs of reducing inflation. New classical economists share the monetarist view that inflation is essentially a monetary phenomenon propagated by excessive monetary growth. However, substantial disagreement exists between economists over the real costs of disinflation. Here we will compare the new classical view with that of Keynesians and monetarists.

The amount of lost output that an economy endures in order to reduce inflation is known as the 'sacrifice ratio'. In Keynesian models the sacrifice ratio tends to be large, even if agents have rational expectations, owing to the sluggish response of prices and wages to reductions in aggregate demand. Given gradual price adjustment, a deflationary impulse will inevitably lead to significant real losses which can be prolonged by hysteresis effects, that is, where a recession causes the natural rate of unemployment to increase (see Cross, 1988; Gordon, 1988; and Chapter 7). Some Keynesians have advocated the temporary use of incomes policy as a supplementary policy measure to accompany monetary restraint as a way of increasing the efficiency of disinflation policies (see, for example, Lipsey, 1981). It should also be noted that Post Keynesian economists regard incomes policy as a crucial permanent anti-inflationary weapon. Monetary disinflation alone will tend to produce a permanently higher level of unemployment in Post Keynesian models (see Cornwall, 1984).

The orthodox monetarist view, discussed in Chapter 4, section 4.3.2, is that unemployment will rise following monetary contraction, the extent and duration of which depend on the degree of monetary contraction, the extent of institutional adaptations and how quickly people adjust downwards their expectations of future rates of inflation. The critical factor here is the responsiveness of expectations to the change of monetary regime and this in turn implies that the credibility and reputation of the monetary authority will play a crucial role in determining the sacrifice ratio.

In contrast to both the Keynesian and monetarist models, the new classical approach implies that announced/anticipated changes in monetary policy will have no effect on the level of output and employment even in the short run, provided the policy is credible. An announced monetary contraction which is believed will cause rational agents immediately to revise downwards their inflation expectations. The monetary authorities can in principle reduce the rate of inflation without the associated output and employment costs predicted by Keynesian and monetarist analysis; that is, the sacriflce ratio is zero! As one critic has noted, 'in a Sargent–Wallace world the Fed could eliminate inflation simply by announcing that henceforth it would expand the money supply at a rate compatible with price stability' (Gordon, 1978, p. 338). In terms of Figure 4.6, the rate of inflation could be reduced from *A* to *D* without any increase in unemployment. In such circumstances there is no necessity to follow a policy of gradual monetary contraction advocated by orthodox monetarists. Given the absence of output–employment costs, new classicists argue that the authorities might just as well announce a dramatic reduction in the rate of monetary expansion to reduce inflation to their preferred target rate.

With respect to the output–employment costs of reducing inflation, it is interesting to note briefly the *prima facie* evidence provided by the Reagan (USA) and Thatcher (UK) deflations in the early 1980s. Following the restrictive monetary policy pursued in both economies during this period, both the US economy (1981–2) and the UK economy (1980–81) experienced deep recessions. Between 1979 and 1983, inflation fell from 11.2 per cent to 3.2 per cent in the US economy and from 13.4 per cent to 4.6 per cent in the UK economy, while over the same period unemployment rose from 5.8 per cent to 9.6 per cent in the USA and from 4.7 to 11.1 per cent in the UK (see Tables 1.4 and 1.5). In commenting on the UK experience, Matthews and Minford (1987) attribute the severity of the recession in this period primarily to adverse external and supply-side shocks. However, the monetary disinflation initiated by the Thatcher government was also a factor. This disinflation was unintentionally severe and as a result 'expectations were quite unprepared for it'. Because initially the Thatcher government had a credibility problem, the 'accidental shock treatment' produced painful effects on output and employment. An important influence on credibility in new classical models is the growth path of government debt. New classical economists insist that in order to engineer a disinflation without experiencing a severe sacrifice ratio, a fiscal strategy is required which is compatible with the announced monetary policy, otherwise agents with rational expectations will expect a policy reversal ('U-turn') in the future. As Matthews and Minford (1987) point out, 'A key feature of the Thatcher anti-inflation strategy was a parallel reduction in government budget deficits.' This 'Medium Term Financial Strategy' was aimed at creating long-run credibility (see also Minford et al., 1980; Sargent and Wallace, 1981; Sargent, 1993, 1999).

In the USA a 'monetary policy experiment' was conducted between October 1979 and the summer of 1982. This Volcker disinflation was also associated with a severe recession, although the influence of the second oil shock must also have been a contributory factor. In commenting on this case, Milton Friedman (1984) has argued that the relevant economic agents did not have any widespread belief in the new disinflationary policy announced by the Fed in October 1979. In a similar vein, Poole (1988) has observed that 'a recession may be necessary to provide the evidence that the central bank is serious'. For a discussion of the US 'monetarist experiment', the reader is referred to Brimmer (1983) and B. Friedman (1988). Useful surveys relating to the issue of disinflation are provided by Dalziel (1991), Ball (1991, 1994) and Chadha et al. (1992).

From the above discussion it is clear that, for painless disinflation to occur, the public must believe that the monetary authority is prepared to carry through its announced monetary contraction. If policy announcements lack credibility, inflationary expectations will not fall sufficiently to prevent the economy from experiencing output–employment costs. Initially the arguments relating to the importance of credibility were forcefully presented by Fellner (1976, 1979). A second line of argument, closely related to the need for policy credibility, is that associated with the problem of dynamic time inconsistency. This matter was first raised in the seminal paper of Kydland and Prescott (1977) and we next examine the policy implications of this influential theory.

### 5.5.3 Dynamic time inconsistency, credibility and monetary rules

The 'hard core' monetarist case for a constant monetary growth rate rule was well articulated by Milton Friedman during the 1950s and 1960s. Friedman's case is based on a number of arguments, including the informational constraints facing policy makers; problems associated with time lags and forecasting; uncertainty with respect to the size of fiscal and monetary policy multipliers; the inflationary consequences of reducing unemployment below the natural rate; and a basic distrust of the political process compared to market forces. The Lucas–Sargent–Wallace policy ineffectiveness proposition calls into question the power of anticipated monetary policy to influence real variables, adding further weight to Friedman's attack on discretionary policies. While the Walrasian theoretical framework of the new classical economists differed markedly from Friedman's Marshallian approach, the policy conclusions of Lucas, Sargent and Wallace were 'monetarist' in that their models provided further ammunition against the Keynesian case for activist discretionary stabilization policies. For example, in his highly theoretical paper, 'Expectations and the Neutrality of Money', Lucas (1972a) demonstrates the optimality of Friedman's $k$ per cent rule.

In 1977, Kydland and Prescott provided a reformulation of the case against discretionary policies by developing an analytically rigorous new classical model where the policy maker is engaged in a strategic dynamic game with sophisticated forward-looking private sector agents. In this setting, discretionary monetary policy leads to an equilibrium outcome involving an 'inflation bias'. As Ball (1995) notes, models based on dynamic consistency problems have now become the leading theories of moderate inflation.

The theory of economic policy which Kydland and Prescott attack in their paper is that which evolved during the 1950s and 1960s. The conventional approach, inspired by Tinbergen (1952), consists of three crucial steps. First, the policy maker must specify the targets or goals of economic policy (for example, low inflation and unemployment). Second, given this social welfare function which the policy maker is attempting to maximize, a set of instruments (monetary and fiscal) is chosen which will be used to achieve the targets. Finally, the policy maker must make use of an economic model so that the instruments may be set at their optimal values. This normative approach to economic policy is concerned with how policy makers should act and, within the context of optimal control theory, economists sought to identify the optimal policy in order to reach the best outcome, given the decision takers' preferences (see Chow, 1975). Kydland and Prescott argue that there is 'no way' that 'optimal control theory can be made applicable to economic planning when expectations are rational'. Although optimal control theory had proved to be very useful in the physical sciences, Kydland and Prescott deny that the control of social systems can be viewed in the same way. Within social systems there are intelligent agents who will attempt to anticipate policy actions. As a result, in dynamic economic systems where policy makers are involved with a sequence of actions over a period of time, 'discretionary policy, namely the selection of that decision which is best, given the current situation, does not result in the social objective function being maximised' (Kydland and Prescott, 1977, p. 463). This apparent paradox results because 'economic planning is not a game against nature but, rather, a game against rational economic agents'. This argument has very important implications both for the conduct of monetary policy and for the institutional structure most likely to generate credibility with respect to the stated objective of low inflation.

The fundamental insight provided by Kydland and Prescott relating to the evaluation of macroeconomic policy is that when economic agents are for-ward-looking the policy problem emerges as a dynamic game between intelligent players – the government (or monetary authorities) and the private sector (see Blackburn, 1987). Suppose a government formulates what it con-siders to be an optimal policy which is then announced to private agents. If this policy is believed, then in subsequent periods sticking to the announced policy may not remain optimal since, in the new situation, the government finds that it has an incentive to renege or cheat on its previously announced optimal policy. The difference between *ex ante* and *ex post* optimality is known as 'time inconsistency'. As Blackburn (1992) notes, an optimal policy computed at time $t$ is time-inconsistent if reoptimization at $t + n$ implies a different optimal policy. Kydland and Prescott demonstrate how time-incon-sistent policies will significantly weaken the credibility of announced policies.

The demonstration that optimal plans are time-inconsistent is best illus-trated in the macroeconomic context by examining a strategic game played between the monetary authorities and private economic agents, utilizing the Lucas monetary surprise version of the Phillips curve trade-off between inflation and unemployment to show how a consistent equilibrium will in-volve an inflationary bias. In the Kydland and Prescott model discretionary policies are incapable of achieving an optimal equilibrium. In what follows we assume that the monetary authorities can control the rate of inflation perfectly, that markets clear continuously and that economic agents have rational expectations. Equation (5.23) indicates that unemployment can be reduced by a positive inflation surprise:

$$U_t = U_{N_t} + \psi(\dot{P}_t^e - \dot{P}_t) \tag{5.23}$$

Equation (5.23) represents the constraint facing the policy maker. Here, as before, $U_t$ is unemployment in time period $t$, $U_{N_t}$ is the natural rate of unem-ployment, $\psi$ is a positive constant, $\dot{P}_t^e$ is the expected and $\dot{P}_t$ the actual rate of inflation in time period $t$. Kydland and Prescott assume that expectations are rational as given by equation (5.24):

$$\dot{P}_t^e = E(\dot{P}_t \mid \Omega_{t-1}) \tag{5.24}$$

where, as before, $\dot{P}_t$ is the actual rate of inflation; $E(\dot{P}_t \mid \Omega_{t-1})$ is the rational expectation of the rate of inflation subject to the information available up to the previous period ($\Omega_{t-1}$). Kydland and Prescott then specify that there is some social objective function ($S$) which rationalizes the policy choice and is of the form shown in equation (5.25):

$$S = S(\dot{P}_t, U_t), \text{ where } S'(\dot{P}_t) < 0, \text{ and } S'(U_t) < 0 \tag{5.25}$$

The social objective function (5.25) indicates that inflation and unemployment are 'bads' since a reduction in either or both increases social welfare. A consistent policy will seek to maximize (5.25) subject to the Phillips curve constraint given by equation (5.23). Figure 5.4 illustrates the Phillips curve trade-off for two expected rates of inflation, $\dot{P}_{to}^e$ and $\dot{P}_{tc}^e$. The contours of the social objective function are indicated by the indifference curves $S_1 S_2 S_3$ and $S_4$. Given that inflation and unemployment are 'bads', $S_1 > S_2 > S_3 > S_4$, and the form of the indifference curves implies that the 'socially preferred' rate of inflation is zero. In Figure 5.4, all points on the vertical axis are potential equilibrium positions, since at points $O$ and $C$ unemployment is at the natural rate (that is, $U_t = U_{N_t}$) and agents are correctly forecasting inflation (that is, $\dot{P}_t^e = \dot{P}_t$). The indifference curves indicate that the optimal position (consistent equilibrium) is at point $O$ where a combination of $\dot{P}_t$ = zero and $U_t = U_{N_t}$ prevails. While the monetary authorities in this model can determine the rate of inflation, the position of the Phillips curves in Figure 5.4 will depend on the inflationary expectations of private economic agents. In this situation a time-consistent equilibrium is achieved where the indifference curve $S_3$ is at a tangent to the Phillips curve passing through point $C$. Since $C$ lies on $S_3$, it is clear that the time-consistent equilibrium is sub-optimal. Let us see how such a situation can arise in the context of a dynamic game played out between policy makers and private agents.

In a dynamic game, each player chooses a strategy which indicates how they will behave as information is received during the game. The strategy chosen by a particular player will depend on their perception of the strategies likely to be followed by the other participants, as well as how they expect other participants to be influenced by their own strategy. In a dynamic game, each player will seek to maximize their own objective function, subject to their perception of the strategies adopted by other players. The situation where the game is between the government (monetary authorities) and private agents is an example of a non-cooperative 'Stackelberg' game. Stackelberg games have a hierarchical structure, with the dominant player acting as leader and the remaining participants reacting to the strategy of the leader. In the

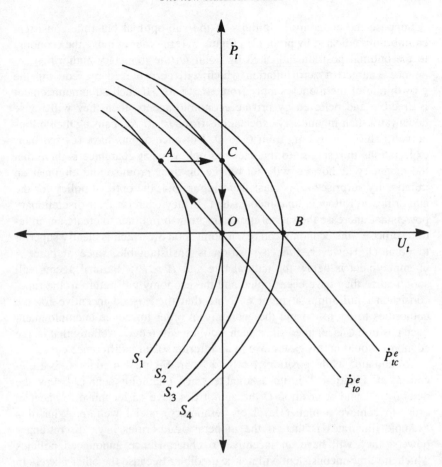

*Figure 5.4    Consistent and optimal equilibrium*

monetary policy game discussed by Kydland and Prescott, the government is the dominant player. When the government decides on its optimal policy it will take into account the likely reaction of the 'followers' (private agents). In a Stackelberg game, unless there is a precommitment from the leader with respect to the announced policy, the optimal policy will be dynamically inconsistent because the government can improve its own pay-off by cheating. Since the private sector players understand this, the time-consistent equilibrium will be a 'Nash' equilibrium. In such a situation each player correctly perceives that they are doing the best they can, given the actions of the other players, with the leader relinquishing the dominant role (for a non-technical discussion of game theory, see Davis, 1983).

Suppose the economy is initially at the sub-optimal but time-consistent equilibrium indicated by point $C$ in Figure 5.4. In order to move the economy to the optimal position indicated by point $O$, the monetary authorities announce a target of zero inflation which will be achieved by reducing the growth rate of the money supply from $\dot{M}_c$ to $\dot{M}_o$. If such an announcement is credible and believed by private economic agents, then they will revise downwards their inflationary expectations from $\dot{P}_{tc}^e$ to $\dot{P}_{to}^e$, causing the Phillips curve to shift downwards from $C$ to $O$. But once agents have revised their expectations in response to the declared policy, what guarantee is there that the monetary authorities will not renege on their promise and engineer an inflationary surprise? As is clear from Figure 5.4, the optimal policy for the authorities to follow is time-inconsistent. If they exercise their discretionary powers and increase the rate of monetary growth in order to create an 'inflation surprise', the economy can reach point $A$ on $S_1$, which is clearly superior to point $O$. However, such a position is unsustainable, since at point $A$ unemployment is below the natural rate and $\dot{P}_t > \dot{P}_t^e$. Rational agents will soon realize they have been fooled and the economy will return to the time-consistent equilibrium at point $C$. Note that there is no incentive for the authorities to try to expand the economy in order to reduce unemployment once position $C$ is attained since such a policy will reduce welfare; that is, the economy would in this case move to an inferior social indifference curve.

To sum up, while position $A > O > C$ in Figure 5.4, only $C$ is time-consistent. Position $A$ is unsustainable since unemployment is below the natural rate, and at position $O$ the authorities have an incentive to cheat in order to achieve a higher level of (temporary) social welfare. What this example illustrates is that, if the monetary authorities have discretionary powers, they will have an incentive to cheat. Hence announced policies which are time-inconsistent will not be credible. Because the other players in the inflation game know the authorities' objective function, they will not adjust their inflationary expectations in response to announcements which lack credibility and in the absence of binding rules the economy will not be able to reach the optimal but time-inconsistent position indicated by point $O$. The non-cooperative Nash equilibrium indicated by point $C$ demonstrates that discretionary policy produces a sub-optimal outcome exhibiting an inflationary bias. Because rational agents can anticipate the strategy of monetary authorities which possess discretionary powers, they will anticipate inflation of $\dot{P}_{tc}^e$. Hence policy makers must also supply inflation equal to that expected by the private sector in order to prevent a squeeze on output. An optimal policy which lacks credibility because of time inconsistency will therefore be neither optimal nor feasible. Discretionary policies which emphasize selecting the best policy given the existing situation will lead to a consistent, but sub-optimal, outcome. The only way to achieve the optimal position, $O$, is for

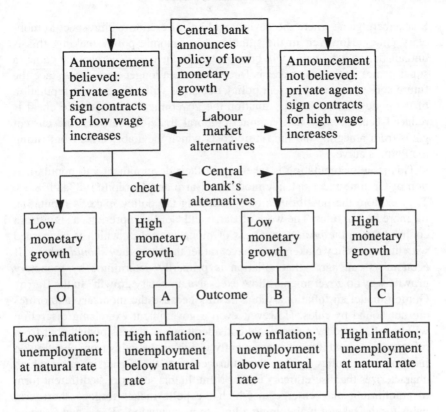

*Figure 5.5  Game played between the monetary authorities and wage negotiators*

the monetary authorities to pre-commit to a non-contingent monetary rule consistent with price stability.

The various outcomes which can arise in the game played between the monetary authorities and wage negotiators has been neatly captured by Taylor (1985). Figure 5.5, which is adapted from Taylor (1985), shows the four possible outcomes in a non-cooperative game between private agents and the central bank. The time-consistent outcome is shown by C, whereas the optimal outcome of low inflation with unemployment at the natural rate is shown by O. The temptation for a government to stimulate the economy because of time inconsistency is indicated by outcome A, whereas the decision not to validate a high rate of expected inflation and high wage increases will produce a recession and is indicated by outcome B.

The credibility problem identified by Kydland and Prescott arises most clearly in the situation of a one-shot full information non-cooperative

Stackelberg game where the government has discretion with respect to monetary policy. However, in the situation of economic policy making, this is
unrealistic since the game will be repeated. In the case of a repeated game (a
super-game) the policy maker is forced to take a longer-term view since the
future consequences of current policy decisions will influence the reputation
of the policy maker. In this situation the government's incentive to cheat is
reduced because they face an intertemporal trade-off between the current
gains from reneging and the future costs which inevitably arise from riding
the Phillips curve.

This issue of reputation is taken up in their development and populariza-
tion of the time-inconsistency model by Barro and Gordon (1983a, 1983b).
They explore the possibilities of substituting the policy maker's reputation
for more formal rules. The work of Barro and Gordon represents a significant
contribution to the *positive* analysis of monetary policy which is concerned
with the way policy makers *do* behave, rather than how they *should* behave. If
economists can agree that inflation is primarily determined by monetary
growth, why do governments allow excessive monetary growth? In the Barro–
Gordon model an inflationary bias results because the monetary authorities
are not bound by rules. However, even a government exercising discretion
will be influenced by reputational considerations if it faces punishment from
private agents, and it must consequently weigh up the gains from cheating on
its announced policy against the future costs of the higher inflation which
characterizes the discretionary equilibrium. In this scenario, 'a different form
of equilibrium may emerge in which the policymaker forgoes short-term
gains for the sake of maintaining a long-term reputation' (Barro and Gordon,
1983b). Given this intertemporal trade-off between current gains (in terms of
lower unemployment and higher output) and the future costs, the equilibrium
of this game will depend on the discount rate of the policy maker. The higher
the discount rate, the closer the equilibrium solution is to the time-consistent
equilibrium of the Kydland–Prescott model (point *C* in Figure 5.4). If the
discount rate is low, the equilibrium position will be closer to the optimal
zero inflation pre-commitment outcome. Note that it is the presence of pre-
commitment that distinguishes a monetary regime based on rules compared
to one based on discretion.

One problem with the above analysis is that private agents do not know
what type of government behaviour they face since they have incomplete
information (see Driffill, 1988). Given uncertainty with respect to government intentions, private agents will carefully analyse various signals in the
form of policy actions and announcements. In this scenario it is difficult for
private agents to distinguish 'hard-nosed' (zero-inflation) administrations from
'wet' (high-inflation) administrations, since 'wets' have an incentive to masquerade as 'hard-nosed'. But as Blackburn (1992) has observed, agents 'extract

information about the government's identity by watching what it does, knowing full well that what they do observe may be nothing more than the dissembling actions of an impostor'. Backus and Driffill (1985) have extended the Barro and Gordon framework to take into account uncertainty on the part of the private sector with respect to the true intentions of the policy maker. Given this uncertainty, a dry, hard-nosed government will inevitably face a high sacrifice ratio if it initiates disinflationary policies and engages in a game of 'chicken' with wage negotiators. For detailed surveys of the issues discussed in this section, the reader should consult Barro (1986), Persson (1988), Blackburn and Christensen (1989) and Fischer (1990).

More recently Svensson (1997a) has shown how inflation targeting has emerged as a strategy designed to eliminate the inflation bias inherent in discretionary monetary policies. The time-inconsistency literature pioneered by Kydland and Prescott and Barro and Gordon assumes that monetary authorities with discretion will attempt to achieve an implicit employment target by reducing unemployment below the natural rate, which they deem to be inefficiently high. This problem has led economists to search for credible monetary frameworks to help solve the inflation bias problem. However, the 'first-best' solution is to correct the supply-side distortions that are causing the natural rate of unemployment to be higher than the monetary authorities desire, that is, tackle the problem at source. If this solution is for some reason politically infeasible (strong trade unions), a second-best solution involves a commitment to a monetary policy rule or assigning the monetary authorities an employment target equal to the natural rate. If none of these solutions is feasible, then policy will be discretionary and the economy will display an inflation bias relative to the second-best equilibrium. Svensson classes the discretionary (time-inconsistent) outcome as a fourth-best solution. Improvements on the fourth-best outcome can be achieved by 'modifying central bank preferences' via delegation of monetary policy to a 'conservative central banker' (Rogoff, 1985) or by adopting optimal central bank contracts (Walsh, 1993, 1995a). Svensson argues that inflation targeting can move an economy close to a second-best solution.

### 5.5.4 Central bank independence
The debate relating to central bank independence (CBI) has been very much influenced by new classical thinking, especially with respect to inflationary expectations, time inconsistency, reputation and credibility. If we accept the Kydland–Prescott argument that discretionary policies lead to an inflation bias, then it is clearly necessary to establish some institutional foundation that will constrain discretionary actions. Many economists are persuaded that some form of CBI will provide the necessary restraint. The theoretical case for CBI relates to the general acceptance of the natural rate hypothesis that in

the long run the rate of inflation is independent of the level of unemployment and that discretionary policies are likely to lead to an inflation bias. Hence with no long-run exploitable trade-off, far-sighted monetary authorities ought to select a position on the long-run Phillips curve consistent with a low sustainable rate of inflation (a point near to $O$ in Figure 5.4). The dynamic inconsistency theories of inflation initiated by Kydland and Prescott and developed by Barro and Gordon, and Backus and Driffill, provide an explanation of why excessive (moderate) inflation will be the likely outcome of a monetary regime where long-term commitments are precluded. Such discretionary regimes contrast sharply with monetary regimes such as the Gold Standard, where the underlying rules of the game revolve around a pre-commitment to price stability. The emphasis of these models on the importance of institutions and rules for maintaining price stability provides a strong case for the establishment of independent central banks whose discretion is constrained by explicit anti-inflation objectives acting as a pre-commitment device. Since the problem of credibility has its source in the discretionary powers of the monetary authorities with respect to the conduct of monetary policy, this could be overcome by transferring the responsibility for anti-inflationary policy to a non-political independent central bank. In addition, an independent central bank will benefit from a 'credibility bonus', whereby disinflationary policies can be accomplished at a low 'sacrifice ratio' (Cukierman, 1992; Goodhart, 1994a, 1994b).

In the debate over CBI it is important to make a distinction between 'goal independence' and 'instrument independence' (see Fischer, 1995a, 1995b). The former implies that the central bank sets its own objectives (that is, political independence), while the latter refers to independence with respect to the various levers of monetary policy (that is, economic independence). The recently (May 1997) created 'independent' Bank of England has instrument independence only. Initially, an inflation target of 2.5 per cent was set by government, which formed the Bank's explicitly stated monetary policy objective. Therefore, in the UK, the decisions relating to goals remain in the political sphere (Bean, 1998; Budd, 1998).

As noted above, Svensson (1997a) argues that the inflation bias associated with the time-inconsistency problem can be improved upon by 'modifying central bank preferences' via delegation of monetary policy to a 'conservative central banker' (for example Alan Greenspan) as suggested by Rogoff (1985) or by adopting optimal central bank contracts, as suggested by Walsh (1993, 1995a). Rogoff's conservative central banker has both *goal* and *instrument* independence and is best represented by the German Bundesbank, which before European Monetary Union remained the most independent central bank in Europe (Tavelli et al., 1998). In Rogoff's model an inflation-averse conservative central banker is appointed who places a higher relative weight on the control of inflation than does society in general (for example President Jimmy Carter's appointment of Paul Volcker as Chairman of the Fed in 1979). This is meant to ensure that the excessive inflation associated with the time-inconsistency problem is kept low in circumstances where it would otherwise be difficult to establish a pre-commitment to low inflation. Overall, lower average inflation and higher output variability are predicted from this model (Waller and Walsh, 1996). However, the research of Alesina and Summers (1993) shows that only the first of these two predictions appears in cross-sectional data. In contrast, Hutchison and Walsh (1998), in a recent study of the experience of New Zealand, find that central bank reform appears to have increased the short-run output–inflation trade-off. In Rogoff's model the conservative central banker reacts less to supply shocks than someone who shared society's preferences, indicating a potential trade-off between flexibility and commitment. In response to this problem Lohmann (1992) suggests that the design of the central bank institution should involve the granting of partial independence to a conservative central banker who places more weight on inflation than the policy maker, but 'the policymaker retains the option to over-ride the central bank's decisions at some strictly positive but finite cost'. Such a clause has been built into the Bank of England Act (1998), where the following reserve power is set out: 'The Treasury, after consultation with the Governor of the Bank, may by order give the Bank directions with respect to monetary policy if they are satisfied that the directions are required in the public interest and by extreme economic circumstances.' It remains to be seen if such powers are ever used.

The contracting model, associated with Walsh (1993, 1995a, 1998), utilizes a principal–agent framework and emphasizes the *accountability* of the central bank. In Walsh's contracting approach the central bank has instrument independence but no goal independence. The central bank's rewards and penalties are based on its achievements with respect to inflation control. The Reserve Bank of New Zealand resembles this principal–agent type model. An important issue in the contracting approach is the optimal length of contract for a central banker (Muscatelli, 1998). Long terms of appointment will reduce the role of electoral surprises as explained in Alesina's partisan model (see Chapter 10). But terms of office that are too long may be costly if societal preferences are subject to frequent shifts. Waller and Walsh (1996) argue that the optimal term length 'must balance the advantages in reducing election effects with the need to ensure that the preferences reflected in monetary policy are those of the voting public'.

The empirical case for CBI is linked to cross-country evidence which shows that for advanced industrial countries there is a negative relationship between CBI and inflation. During the last 15 years a considerable amount of research has been carried out which has examined the relationship between central bank independence and economic performance (see Grilli et al., 1991; Bernanke and Mishkin, 1992; Alesina and Summers, 1993; Eijffinger and Schaling, 1993; Bleaney, 1996; Eijffinger, 2002a, 2002b). The central difficulty recognized by researchers into the economic impact of central bank independence is the problem of constructing an index of independence. Alesina and Summers (1993) identify the ability of the central bank to select its policy objectives without the influence of government, the selection procedure of the governor of the central bank, the ability to use monetary instruments without restrictions and the requirement of the central bank to finance fiscal deficits as key indicators that can be used to construct a measure of central bank independence. Using a composite index derived from Parkin and Bade (1982a) and Grilli et al. (1991), Alesina and Summers examined the correlation between an index of independence and some major economic indicators. Table 5.2 indicates that, 'while central bank independence promotes price stability, it has no measurable impact on real economic performance' (Alesina and Summers, 1993, p. 151).

*Table 5.2    Central bank independence and economic performance*

| Country | Average index of central bank independence | Average inflation 1955–88 | Average unemployment rate 1958–88 | Average real GNP growth 1955–87 |
|---|---|---|---|---|
| Spain | 1.5 | 8.5 | n/a | 4.2 |
| New Zealand | 1 | 7.6 | n/a | 3.0 |
| Australia | 2.0 | 6.4 | 4.7 | 4.0 |
| Italy | 1.75 | 7.3 | 7.0 | 4.0 |
| United Kingdom | 2 | 6.7 | 5.3 | 2.4 |
| France | 2 | 6.1 | 4.2 | 3.9 |
| Denmark | 2.5 | 6.5 | 6.1 | 3.3 |
| Belgium | 2 | 4.1 | 8.0 | 3.1 |
| Norway | 2 | 6.1 | 2.1 | 4.0 |
| Sweden | 2 | 6.1 | 2.1 | 2.9 |
| Canada | 2.5 | 4.5 | 7.0 | 4.1 |
| Netherlands | 2.5 | 4.2 | 5.1 | 3.4 |
| Japan | 2.5 | 4.9 | 1.8 | 6.7 |
| United States | 3.5 | 4.1 | 6.0 | 3.0 |
| Germany | 4 | 3.0 | 3.6 | 3.4 |
| Switzerland | 4 | 3.2 | n/a | 2.7 |

*Source*:   Alesina and Summers (1993).

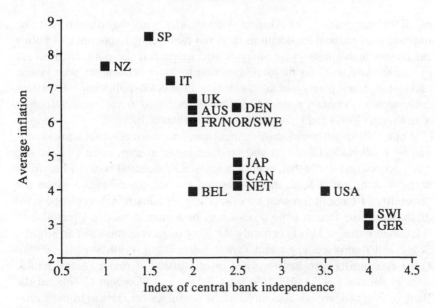

*Source*: Alesina and Summers (1993).

*Figure 5.6*    *The relationship between average inflation and central bank*
            *independence*

The 'near perfect' negative correlation between inflation and central bank independence is clearly visible in Figure 5.6. However, as Alesina and Summers recognize, correlation does not prove causation, and the excellent anti-inflationary performance of Germany may have more to do with the public aversion to inflation following the disastrous experience of the hyperinflation in 1923 than the existence of an independent central bank. In this case the independent central bank could be an effect of the German public aversion to inflation rather than a cause of low inflation. Indeed, the reputation established by the German Bundesbank for maintaining low inflation was one important reason given by the UK government for joining the ERM in October 1990. The participation of the UK in such a regime, where monetary policy is determined by an anti-inflationary central bank which has an established reputation and credibility, was intended to tie the hands of domestic policy makers and help lower inflationary expectations (see Alogoskoufis et al., 1992).

Considerable research has also been conducted into the role played by politics in influencing economic performance. The 'political business cycle' or 'monetary politics' literature also suggests that CBI would help reduce the problem of political distortions in macroeconomic policy making. What is now known as the 'new political macroeconomics' has been heavily influenced by the research of Alberto Alesina. His work has shown that the imposition of rational expectations does not remove the importance of political factors in business cycle analysis and in general the political business cycle literature provides more ammunition to those economists who favour taking monetary policy out of the hands of elected politicians. Excellent surveys of the monetary politics literature can be found in Alesina and Roubini with Cohen (1997) and Drazen (2000a); see Chapter 10.

While CBI might avoid the dynamic time-inconsistency problems identified by Kydland and Prescott and produce lower average rates of inflation, many economists doubt that, overall, a rules-bound central bank will perform better than a central bank that is allowed to exercise discretion given the possibility of large unforeseen shocks. A central bank which could exercise discretion in the face of large shocks may be a more attractive alternative to rule-based policies. This is certainly the view of Keynesians such as Stiglitz, Solow and Tobin (see Solow and Taylor, 1998; Tobin, 1998; Stiglitz, 1999a). Other economists who have worked on the inside of major central banks, such as Blinder (1997b, 1998) at the US Fed, and Goodhart (1994a) at the Bank of England, are not convinced of the usefulness or realism of the game-theoretic approach to central bank behaviour. The research of Bernanke and Mishkin also confirms that 'Central banks never and nowhere adhere to strict, ironclad rules for monetary growth' (Bernanke and Mishkin, 1992, p. 186).

One of the most important theoretical objections to CBI is the potential for conflict that it generates between the monetary and fiscal authorities (Doyle and Weale, 1994; Nordhaus, 1994). It is recognized that the separation of fiscal and monetary management can lead to coordination problems which can undermine credibility. In countries where this has led to conflict (such as the USA in the period 1979–82) large fiscal deficits and high real interest rates have resulted. This monetary/fiscal mix is not conducive to growth and, during the early period of Reaganomics in the USA, came in for severe criticism from many economists (Blanchard, 1986; Modigliani, 1988b; and Tobin, 1987). The tight-monetary easy-fiscal mix is hardly a surprising combination given the predominant motivations that drive the Fed and the US Treasury. Whereas independent central banks tend to emphasize monetary austerity and low inflation, the fiscal authorities (politicians) know that increased government expenditure and reduced taxes are the 'meat, potatoes and gravy of politics' (Nordhaus, 1994). To the critics CBI is no panacea. In particular, to say that inflation should be the primary goal of the central bank is very different from making inflation the sole goal of monetary policy in all circumstances (Akhtar, 1995; Carvalho, 1995/6; Minford, 1997; Forder, 1998; Posen, 1998). As Blackburn (1992) concludes, 'the credibility of monetary policy does not depend upon monetary policy alone but also upon the macroeconomic programme in its entirety'.

## 5.5.5 Microeconomic policies to increase aggregate supply

The next policy implication of the new classical approach we consider concerns what policies the authorities should pursue if they wish to increase output/reduce unemployment permanently (the role of monetary policy is not to try to reduce unemployment permanently but to keep inflation low and stable). As we have already seen, microeconomic policies to reduce distortions in the labour market have been recommended as the 'first-best' solution to the inflation bias problem identified by Kydland and Prescott (1977). Unemployment is regarded as an equilibrium outcome reflecting the optimal decisions of workers who substitute work/leisure in response to movements in current and expected future real wages. The labour market continuously clears, so that anyone wanting to work at the current real wage can do so. Those who are unemployed voluntarily choose not to work at the current real wage (Lucas, 1978a). Changes in output and employment are held to reflect the equilibrium supply decisions of firms and workers, given their perceptions of relative prices. It follows from this view that the appropriate policy measures to increase output/reduce unemployment are those that increase the microeconomic incentives for firms and workers to supply more output and labour (examples of the wide range of often highly controversial supply-side policies which have been pursued over recent years can be found in Chapter 4, section 4.3.2; see also Minford et al., 1985; Minford, 1991). The importance of supply-side reforms has recently been taken up by Lucas. In his Presidential Address to the American Economic Association in January 2003, Lucas focused on 'Macroeconomic Priorities' (Lucas, 2003). In an analysis using US performance over the last 50 years as a benchmark, Lucas concluded that the potential for welfare gains from better long-run, supply-side policies far exceeds the potential gains to be had from further improvements in short-run stabilization policies.

To some economists the unemployment problem in Europe is not fundamentally a monetary policy issue but a suppy-side problem, often referred to as 'Eurosclerosis'. During the 1950s and 1960s the European 'welfare state' OECD economies experienced lower unemployment on average than that experienced in the USA. Since around 1980 this experience has been reversed. Many economists have attributed the poor labour market performance in Europe to various institutional changes which have adversely affected the flexibility of the labour market, in particular measures relating to the amount and duration of unemployment benefit, housing policies which limit mobility, minimum wage legislation, job protection legislation which increases hiring and firing costs, the 'tax wedge' between the cost of labour to firms (production wage) and the net income to workers (consumption wage), and 'insider' power (Siebert, 1997; Nickell, 1997). In the face of an increasingly turbulent economic environment, economies require ongoing restructuring. Ljungqvist and Sargent (1998) argue that the generous entitlement programmes in the European OECD welfare states have generated 'a virtual time bomb waiting to explode'. That explosion arrives when large economic shocks occur more frequently. The welfare state programmes hinder the necessary restructuring of the economy and this shows up as high and prolonged rates of unemployment.

While accepting the validity of some of the supply-side arguments, Solow (1998) and Modigliani (1996) see a significant part of the rise in European unemployment as having its origin in the tight anti-inflationary monetary policies which have been a characteristic of the past two decades. The solution to the unemployment problem in Europe therefore requires micro-oriented supply-side policies combined with more expansionary aggregate demand policies.

### 5.5.6   The Lucas critique of econometric policy evaluation

The final implication of the new classical approach for the formulation of macroeconomic policy concerns what is popularly known as the 'Lucas critique', after the title of Lucas's seminal paper in which the proposition first appeared. Lucas (1976) attacked the established practice of using large-scale macroeconometric models to evaluate the consequences of alternative policy scenarios, given that such policy simulations are based on the assumption that the parameters of the model remain unchanged when there is a change in policy. The Keynesian macroeconometric models developed during the 1950s and 1960s consisted of 'systems of equations' involving endogenous variables and exogenous variables. Such models, following Koopmans (1949), contain four types of equation referred to as 'structural equations', namely:

1.   identities, equations that are true by definition;
2.   equations that embody institutional rules, such as tax schedules;
3.   equations that specify the technological constraints, such as production functions;
4.   behavioural equations that describe the way in which individuals or groups will respond to the economic environment; for example, wage adjustment, consumption, investment and money demand functions.

A good example of this type of 'system of equation' model is the famous FMP model (named after the Federal Reserve–MIT–University of Pennsylvania model) constructed in the USA by Ando and Modigliani. Such models were used for forecasting purposes and to test the likely impact of stochastic or random shocks. The model builders used historical data to estimate the model, and then utilized the model to analyse the likely consequences of alternative policies. The typical Keynesian model of the 1960s/early 1970s was based on the IS–LM–AD–AS framework combined with a Phillips curve relationship. Obviously the behaviour of this type of model will, among other things, depend on the estimated value of the coefficients of the variables in the model. For example, such models typically include a consumption function as one of the key relationships. Suppose the consumption function takes the following simple form: $C = \alpha + \beta(Y - T)$. That is, consumption is proportional to disposable (after tax) income $(Y - T)$. However, in this simple Keynesian consumption function the parameters $(\alpha, \beta)$ will depend on the optimal decisions that economic agents made in the past relating to how much to consume and save given their utility function; that is, these parameters were formed during an earlier optimization process directly influenced by the particular policy regime prevailing at the time. Lucas argues that we cannot use equations such as this to construct models for predictive purposes because their parameters will typically alter as the optimal (consumption) responses of rational utility-maximizing economic agents to the policy changes work their way through the model. The parameters of large-scale macro-econometric models may not remain constant (invariant) in the face of policy changes, since economic agents may adjust their expectations and behaviour to the new environment (Sargent, 1999, refers to this as the problem of 'drifting coefficients'). Expectations play a crucial role in the economy because of the way in which they influence the behaviour of consumers, firms, investors, workers and all other economic agents. Moreover, the expectations of economic agents depend on many things, including the economic policies being pursued by the government. If expectations are assumed to be rational, economic agents adjust their expectations when governments change their economic policies. Macroeconometric models should thus take into account the fact that any change in policy will systematically alter the structure of the macroeconometric model. Private sector structural behavioural relationships are non-invariant when the government policy changes. Thus, estimating the effect of a policy change requires knowing how economic agents' expectations will change in response to the policy change. Lucas (1976) argued that the traditional (Keynesian-dominated) methods of policy evaluation do not adequately take into account the impact of policy on expectations. Therefore, Lucas questioned the use of such models, arguing that:

> given that the structure of an econometric model consists of optimal decision rules of economic agents, and that optimal decision rules vary systematically with changes in the structure of series relevant to the decision maker, it follows that any change in policy will systematically alter the structure of econometric models.

In other words, the parameters of large-scale macroeconometric models are unlikely to remain constant in the face of policy changes, since rational economic agents may adjust their behaviour to the new environment. Because the estimated equations in most existing Keynesian-style macroeconometric models do not change with alternative policies, any advice given from policy simulations is likely to be misleading. When trying to predict the impact on the economy of a change in policy it is a mistake, according to Lucas, to take as given the relations estimated from past data.

This weakness of Keynesian-style macroeconometric models was particularly exposed during the 1970s as inflation accelerated and unemployment increased. The experiences of the 1950s and 1960s had led some policy makers and economic theorists to believe that there was a stable long-run trade-off between inflation and unemployment. However, once policy makers, influenced by this idea, shifted the policy regime and allowed unemployment to fall and inflation to rise, the Phillips curve shifted as the expectations of economic agents responded to the experience of higher inflation. Thus the predictions of orthodox Keynesian models turned out to be 'wildly incorrect' and a 'spectacular failure', being based on a doctrine that was 'fundamentally flawed' (Lucas and Sargent, 1978). Lucas's rational expectations version of the Friedman–Phelps natural rate theory implies that policy makers cannot base policy on the apparent existence of any short-run Phillips curve trade-off. The monetary authorities should aim to achieve low inflation, which has significant welfare gains (see Sargent, 1999; Lucas, 2000a, 2003).

The Lucas critique has profound implications for the formulation of macroeconomic policy. Since policy makers cannot predict the effects of new and different economic policies on the parameters of their models, simulations using existing models cannot in turn be used to predict the consequences of alternative policy regimes. In Lucas's view the invariability of parameters in a model to policy changes cannot be guaranteed in Keynesian-type disequilibrium models. In contrast, the advantage of equilibrium theorizing is that, by focusing attention on individuals' objectives and constraints, it is much more likely that the resulting model will consist entirely of structural relations which are invariant to changes in policy. Lucas identified the treatment of expectations as a major defect of the standard large-scale macroeconometric models. With rational expectations, agents will react quickly to announced policy changes. The underprediction of inflation during the late 1960s and early 1970s seemed to confirm Lucas's argument. In 1978 Lucas and Sargent famously declared that 'existing Keynesian macroeconometric models are incapable of providing reliable guidance in formulating monetary, fiscal and other types of policy'.

The Lucas critique implies that the building of macroeconometric models needs to be wholly reconsidered so that the equations are structural or behavioural in nature. Lucas and Sargent (1978) claim that equilibrium models are free of the difficulties associated with the existing Keynesian macroeconometric models and can account for the main quantitative features of business cycles. Ultimately the influence of the Lucas critique contributed to the methodological approach adopted in the 1980s by modern new classical theorists of the business cycle, namely 'Real Business Cycle' theory (see Figure 5.7). Such models attempt to derive behavioural relationships within a dynamic optimization setting.

With respect to macroeconomic stabilization policy, the Lucas critique also 'directs attention to the necessity of thinking of policy as a choice of stable "rules of the game", well understood by economic agents. Only in such a setting will economic theory help us to predict the actions agents will choose to take' (Lucas and Sargent, 1978).

However, some economists, such as Alan Blinder, believe that the 'Lucas critique' had a negative impact on progress in macroeconomics (see Snowdon, 2001a). In addition, direct tests of the Lucas critique have not provided strong support for the proposition that policy changes lead to shifts of the coefficients on behavioural equations (see Hoover, 1995a). Blanchard (1984) has shown that 'there is no evidence of a major shift of the Phillips curve' during the change of policy regime adopted during the Volcker disinflation. Other economists have pointed out that the Volcker disinflation involved a lower sacrifice ratio than would have been expected before October 1979, when the policy was implemented (see Sargent, 1999). Finally, it should be noted that even the structural parameters of new classical 'equilibrium' models may not be invariant to policy changes if economic agents' tastes and technology change following a shift in the rules of economic policy. In practice it would seem that the significance of the Lucas critique depends upon the stability of the parameters of a model following the particular policy change under consideration.

## 5.6 An Assessment

The contributions made by leading new classicists such as Lucas, Barro, Sargent and Wallace dominated macroeconomics discussion throughout the 1970s, particularly in the USA. In particular the business cycle research of Lucas during the 1970s had an enormous methodological impact on how macroeconomists conducted research and looked at the world (Lucas, 1980a, 1981a; Hoover, 1992, 1999; Chapter 6). For example, although the idea that all unemployment should be viewed as voluntary remains controversial, economists after the 'Lucasian revolution' have been much less willing to accept uncritically Keynes's idea of 'involuntary unemployment' (see Solow, 1980; Blinder, 1988a; Snowdon and Vane, 1999b).

However, by the close of the 1970s, several weaknesses of the new classical equilibrium approach were becoming apparent. These deficiencies were mainly the consequence of utilizing the twin assumptions of continuous market clearing and imperfect information. By 1982 the monetary version of new classical equilibrium models had reached both a theoretical and empirical impasse. For example, on the theoretical front the implausibility of the assumption relating to information confusion was widely recognized (Okun, 1980; Tobin, 1980b). With sticky prices ruled out on methodological grounds, new classical models were left without an acceptable explanation of business cycles involving money-to-output causality. Furthermore, the doubts cast by Sims (1980) on the causal role of money in money–output correlations raised questions with respect to monetary explanations of the business cycle. On the empirical front, despite some early success, the evidence in support of the proposition that anticipated money was neutral did not prove to be robust (see Barro, 1977a, 1978, 1989a). According to Gordon (1989) the influence of the first phase of new classical theorizing peaked in the period 1976–8. Gordon also dates the downfall of this phase 'precisely at 8.59 a.m. EDT on Friday 13th October, 1978, at Bald Peak, New Hampshire' for it was here that Robert Barro and Mark Rush (1980) began their presentation 'of an empirical test of the policy-ineffectiveness proposition on quarterly US post-war data that was not only severely criticised by three discussants, but also contained dubious results that seemed questionable even to the authors' (see Hoover, 1992, Vol. 1). Thus the early 1980s witnessed the demise of the mark I (monetary surprise) version of the new classical approach in large part due to the implausibility of supposed information gaps relating to aggregate price level and money supply data, and the failure of empirical tests to provide strong support for the policy ineffectiveness proposition (Barro, 1989a). The depth of the recessions in both the USA and the UK in the 1980–82 period following the Reagan and Thatcher deflations provided the critics with further ammunition. As a consequence of these difficulties the monetary surprise model has come to be widely regarded as inappropriate for modern information-rich industrial economies.

Meanwhile Stanley Fischer (1977) and Edmund Phelps and John Taylor (1977) had already shown that nominal disturbances were capable of producing real effects in models incorporating rational expectations providing the assumption of continuously clearing markets was abandoned. While accepting the rational expectations hypothesis was a necessary condition of being a new classicist, it was certainly not sufficient. Following the embryonic new Keynesian contributions it was quickly realized that the rational expectations hypothesis was also not a sufficient condition for policy ineffectiveness. As a result the policy-ineffectiveness proposition was left 'to die neglected and unmourned' and 'Into this vacuum stepped Edward Prescott from Minnesota, who has picked up the frayed new classical banner with his real business cycle theory' (Gordon, 1989). Thus Lucas's MEBCT has been replaced since the early 1980s by new classical real business cycle models emphasizing technological shocks (Stadler, 1994), new Keynesian models emphasizing monetary disturbances (Gordon, 1990), and new neoclassical synthesis models combining insights from both approaches (see Lucas, 1987; Goodfriend and King, 1997; Blanchard, 2000).

Economists sympathetic to the new classical approach (such as Finn Kydland and Edward Prescott) have developed a mark II version of the new classical model, known as real equilibrium business cycle theory (REBCT, see Figure 5.7). While proponents of the REBCT approach have abandoned the monetary surprise approach to explaining business cycles, they have retained components of the equilibrium approach and the propagation mechanisms (such as adjustment costs) used in mark I versions. Responding to the Lucas critique was also a major driving force behind the development of REBCT (see Ryan and Mullineux, 1997).

Despite the controversy that surrounds the approach, new classical economics has had a significant impact on the development of macroeconomics over the last decade and a half. This impact can be seen in a number of areas.

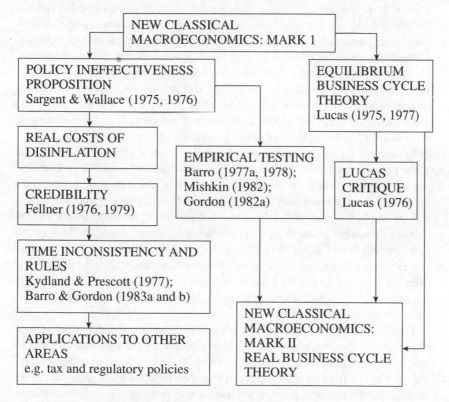

*Figure 5.7   The evolution of new classical macroeconomics*

First, it has led to much greater attention being paid to the way that expectations are modelled, resulting in a so-called 'rational expectations revolution' in macroeconomics (Taylor, 1989). For example, the rational expectations hypothesis has been widely adopted by new Keynesians and researchers in the area of the 'new political macroeconomics (see Chapters 7 and 10). It also formed a crucial input to Dornbusch's (1976) exchange rate overshooting model (see Chapter 7). Second, the insight of rational expectations that a change in policy will almost certainly influence expectations (which in turn is likely to influence the behaviour of economic agents) is now fairly widely accepted. This in turn has led economists to reconsider the role and conduct of macroeconomic stabilization policy. In particular, the modern emphasis on 'policy rules' when discussing the stabilizing role of monetary policy has been heavily influenced by the idea of rational expectations.

Much of the controversy that surrounds new classical macroeconomics is directed, not at the rational expectations hypothesis *per se*, but at the policy implications that derive from the structure of new classical models. In this context it is interesting to note that Keynesian-like disequilibrium models (where markets do not clear continuously) but which allow agents to have rational expectations, as well as incorporating the natural rate hypothesis, still predict a role for demand management policies to stabilize the economy. If, in the face of random shocks to aggregate demand, the government is able to adjust its policies more quickly than the private sector can renegotiate money wages, then there is still a role for aggregate demand management to stabilize the economy and offset fluctuations in output and employment around their natural levels. As Buiter (1980) summed it up, 'in virtually all economically interesting models there will be real consequences of monetary and fiscal policy–anticipated or unanticipated. This makes the cost–benefit analysis of feasible policy intervention the focus of the practical economist's concern.' There should therefore be no presumption that 'a government that sits on its hands and determines the behaviour of its instruments by the simplest possible fixed rules is guaranteed to bring about the best of all possible worlds'. Furthermore, given the gradual adjustment of prices and wages in new Keynesian models, any policy of monetary disinflation, even if credible and anticipated by rational agents, will lead to a substantial recession in terms of output and employment, with hysteresis effects raising the natural rate of unemployment (see Chapter 7).

Finally, in trying to come to an overall assessment of the impact of new classical macroeconomics on the debate concerning the role and conduct of macroeconomic stabilization policy, three conclusions seem to suggest themselves. First, it is fairly widely agreed that the conditions necessary to render macroeconomic stabilization policy completely powerless to influence output and employment in the short run are unlikely to hold. Having said this, the possibility that economic agents will anticipate the effects of changes in economic policy does imply that the authorities' scope to stabilize the economy is reduced. Second, new classical macroeconomics has strengthened the case for using aggregate supply policies to stimulate output and employment. Lastly, new Keynesians have been forced to respond to the challenge of new classical macroeconomics and in doing so, in particular explaining why wages and prices tend to adjust only gradually, have provided a more sound micro-theoretical base to justify interventionist policies (both demand and supply management policies) to stabilize the economy.

Before discussing new Keynesian economics we first examine in the next chapter the evolution of the Mark II version of new classical economics, that is, real business cycle theory.

# ROBERT E. LUCAS JR

Permission to reprint from the University of
Chicago
Credit: Lloyd De Grane

Robert Lucas was born in 1937 in Yakima, Washington and obtained his BA (History) and PhD from the University of Chicago in 1959 and 1964 respectively. He was a lecturer at the University of Chicago (1962–3), Assistant Professor (1963–7), Associate Professor (1967–70) and Professor of Economics (1970–74) at Carnegie-Mellon University, Ford Foundation Visiting Research Professor (1974–5) and Professor (1975–80) at the University of Chicago. Since 1980 he has been John Dewey Distinguished Service Professor of Economics at the University of Chicago.

Best known for his equilibrium approach to macroeconomic analysis, and his application of rational expectations to the analysis of macroeconomic policy, Robert Lucas is widely acknowledged as being the leading figure in the development of new classical macroeconomics. In addition to his highly influential work on macroeconomic modelling and policy evaluation, he has made a number of important contributions to other research fields including, more recently, economic growth. In 1995 he was awarded the Nobel Memorial Prize in Economics: 'For having developed and applied the hypothesis of rational expectations, and thereby having transformed macroeconomic analysis and deepened our understanding of economic policy'.

Among his best-known books are: *Studies in Business Cycle Theory* (Basil Blackwell, 1981); *Rational Expectations and Econometric Practice* (University of Minnesota Press, 1981), co-edited with Thomas Sargent; *Models of*

*Business Cycles* (Basil Blackwell, 1987); *Recursive Methods in Economic Dynamics* (Harvard University Press, 1989), co-authored with Nancy Stokey and Edward Prescott; and *Lectures on Economic Growth* (Harvard University Press, 2002).

Among the numerous articles he has written, the best-known include: 'Expectations and the Neutrality of Money', *Journal of Economic Theory* (1972a); 'Some International Evidence on Output–Inflation Tradeoffs', *American Economic Review* (1973); 'Econometric Policy Evaluation: A Critique' in *The Phillips Curve and Labor Markets* (North-Holland, 1976); 'On the Mechanics of Economic Development', *Journal of Monetary Economics* (1988); 'Nobel Lecture: Monetary Neutrality', *Journal of Political Economy* (1996); and 'Macroeconomic Priorities', *American Economic Review* (2003).

We interviewed Professor Lucas in New Orleans, in his hotel room, on 3 January 1997 while attending the annual conference of the American Economic Association.

## Background Information

*As an undergraduate you studied history at the University of Chicago and you also started graduate school as a student of history at Berkeley. Why did you decide to switch to study economics as a postgraduate student back at Chicago?*
I was getting more interested in economics and economic history as a history student. The work of Henri Pirenne, the Belgian historian, who stressed economic forces influenced me. When I was at Berkeley I started taking some economic history classes and even attended an economics course. That is when I first learned what a technical field economics is and how impossible it would be to pick it up as an amateur. I decided then that I wanted to switch to economics. I didn't have any hope of financial support at Berkeley to study economics so that was what led me back to Chicago.

*Did you find the techniques and tools used by economists difficult to master when you did make the switch?*
Sure, but it was exciting for me. I had no idea that people were using mathematics for social science questions before I got into economics. Once I became aware of that I enjoyed it enormously.

*Was mathematics a strong subject for you when you were in high school?*
In high school it was and in college I took a little bit, but dropped out. I was not interested in hard science. I wasn't really motivated to keep going in

maths, but when I learned how maths was being used in economics it rekindled my interest in the field.

*Which economists have had the most influence on your own work?*
Dozens and dozens of people. Samuelson's *Foundations* was a big influence when I started graduate school. His book was just a bible for my generation of economists. Friedman was a great teacher, really an unusual teacher. Anyone from Chicago will tell you that.

*In what respect? Was it his ability to communicate complex ideas?*
That's a hard question to answer. I think it was the breadth of problems he showed that you could address with economic reasoning. That's what Friedman emphasized. No single problem was analysed all that deeply but the range of problems included everything. So we got the impression, and rightly so, that we were getting a powerful piece of equipment for dealing with any problem that came up in human affairs.

*To what extent did the work of the Austrians (Hayek and so on) influence your ideas?*
I once thought of myself as a kind of Austrian, but Kevin Hoover's book persuaded me that this was just a result of my misreading of Hayek and others.

*David Laidler [1992b] has drawn attention to what he described as 'the appalling low standards of historical scholarship amongst economists'. Is it important for an economist to be a competent historian?*
No. It is important that some economists be competent historians, just as it is important that some economists be competent mathematicians, competent sociologists, and so on. But there is neither a need nor a possibility for everyone to be good at everything. Like Stephen Dedalus, none of us will ever be more than a shy guest at the feast of the world's culture.

**Keynes's *General Theory* and Keynesian Economics**

*You were born in 1937. The Great Depression was a huge influence on economists such as Friedman, Samuelson and Tobin in stimulating their interest in economics in the first place. Do you regard the Great Depression as the premier macroeconomic event of the twentieth century?*
I think that economic growth, and particularly the diffusion of economic growth to what we used to call the Third World, is *the* major macroeconomic event of the twentieth century. But the Great Depression is a good second. I was too young to know what was going on at the time, but the Depression

was the main influence on my parents. They became politically aware during the 1930s. Politics and economics were issues that were always talked about in my house when I was growing up.

*How important do you think historical events are for theoretical developments? For example it is generally recognized that the Great Depression led to the* General Theory.
Absolutely.

*Do you think they are crucial?*
Yes, I like that example.

*What about the influence of increasing inflation in the 1970s? Do you think that event played the same kind of role in the move away from Keynesian economics, just as the Great Depression led to the development of Keynesian economics?*
The main ideas that are associated with rational expectations were developed by the early 1970s, so the importance of the inflation that occurred was that it confirmed some of these theoretical ideas. In a way the timing couldn't have been better. We were arguing that there was no stable Phillips curve relating unemployment and inflation. You could go either way on that question given the available post-war data up to the early 1970s, but by the end of the 1970s it was all over.

*How do you view Keynes as a macroeconomist?*
I suppose Keynes, via Hicks, Modigliani and Samuelson, was the founder of macroeconomics, so one has to view him as a leading figure in the field!

*Robert Solow [1986] has described the* General Theory *as 'the most influential work of economics of the twentieth century, and Keynes as the most important economist'. Yet the impression one gets from your various comments on Keynes is that you find the* General Theory *almost incomprehensible. You certainly don't seem to regard it in the same light as Solow.*
If you look through Solow's collected writings for evidence of intellectual indebtedness, evidence that scholars look for – citations and transfer of ideas – you would find almost no influence of Keynes. So I think such comments are somewhat disingenuous, unless he is thinking simply of ideology. Of course Keynes is an extremely important figure in twentieth-century history, but I think his major influence was ideological. The Depression followed soon after the Russian revolution, and there was a lot of idealism about socialism as a way of resolving economic problems, especially as the Soviet Union had no depression. Keynes went to great

lengths to disassociate himself from the rest of the economics profession in the *General Theory*, making almost no references to mainstream economists in the entire book, compared to the *Treatise on Money* which is full of references to mainstream economists. The message of the *General Theory*, in which he emphasized the seriousness of depressions, is that they can be solved within the context of a liberal democracy without having to resort to centralized planning. That was a highly important message which certainly sustained defenders of democracy in countries like yours and mine that maintained it. It helped to organize the entire world after the war and was the flag around which liberal democracies rallied. The *General Theory* was an unusually important book in that sense. Maybe more important than economic theory. But that seems to be a different question from that of the influence of Keynes's theoretical ideas on the way we practise economics, which I think is now very slight.

*Should students of macroeconomics still read the* General Theory*?*
No.

*Had Keynes still been living in 1969, do you think he would have been awarded the first Nobel Prize in Economics? Would he have received your vote?*
I thought Joan Robinson would get the first one, so my credentials as a Nobel forecaster have been dubious from the start. But certainly Keynes would have got one early on. Since I am not a member of the Swedish Academy, I do not have a vote to cast.

*Do you find it puzzling that both Keynes and Marshall started off as mathematicians and yet both of them in terms of their methodology seemed to downplay the use of mathematics in economics, not regarding it as an important way of setting down economic ideas? Why do you think they turned away from what was becoming a major trend in economic science?*
When Marshall was educated, and even when Keynes was educated, England was a mathematical backwater. If they had been educated in France, Germany or Russia, working with people like Kolmogorov, Borel or Cantor, they would have thought differently. Walras, Pareto and Slutzky thought differently. The people who were giving birth to mathematical economics were mainly on the continent at that time.

*Is it your view that the traditional approach of distinguishing between short-run and long-run forces in macroeconomics has been misconceived and counterproductive? Did Keynes send everyone off down the wrong track?*

The short-run–long-run distinction is Marshall's, not Keynes's. Indeed, Keynes is quite explicit in the *General Theory* that he thinks that permanent stagnation can result from demand deficiencies. Samuelson's neoclassical synthesis reclaimed the long run for neoclassical analysis, at least here in the USA. Now Samuelson's students – my whole generation – are trying to get the short run back, too! It's hard going, I know, but Samuelson already did the easy part, and we have to make a living somehow.

The 1930s sent all of us off on the wrong track, starting with Keynes. Even today, 50 years after the Depression ended, public figures talk about every little wiggle in the GNP figures as though it were the end of capitalism. If Keynes were alive today, he would take pride in his role in setting up the system that permitted the recovery of Europe and the Japanese miracle, and he would be excited about the prospects for integrating the second and third worlds into the world economy. I think he would be as impatient with the overemphasis on short-term fine-tuning as I am.

## Monetarism

*What were the major factors which contributed to the rise of monetarism both in academia and policy circles during the 1970s?*
It is hard for me to say because I was raised as a monetarist in the 1960s [*laughter*].

*Well, in the UK circumstances were very different, monetarist ideas came as much more of a shock to many British economists who were steeped in what Coddington [1976] has labelled 'hydraulic Keynesianism' and Samuelson [1983] has referred to as the 'Model T' version of Keynes's system.*
Our leading Keynesian theorists, people like Tobin and Modigliani, always had a role for money in their models and the models that I learnt as a graduate student. Isn't it true that in England monetarism is used as a much broader label for the whole Thatcher programme?

*The UK media has certainly tended to think of supply-side economics and monetarism as being the same. Sometimes any belief in the market mechanism and* laissez-faire *philosophy is also classified as being a part of monetarism.*
You can take the various elements separately and mix them any way you like.

*Do you see Friedman as almost single-handedly having engineering a monetarist counter-revolution?*
Friedman has been an enormous influence. It is hard to say what would have happened without him.

*We know from our own experience as undergraduate students of economics in
the late 1960s in Britain that Friedman was often portrayed as some sort of
strange crank in Chicago.*
Well, that was the way people tried to deal with him here too in a way, but not
successfully.

*Moving on to Friedman's 1968a AER article. In 1981 Robert Gordon de-
scribed it as probably the most influential article written in macroeconomics
in the previous 20 years, while more recently James Tobin [1995] has gone
much further when he described it as 'very likely the most influential article
ever published in an economics journal'. What importance do you attach to
that particular article?*
It had a huge influence on me. Leonard Rapping and I were doing econometric work on Phillips curves in those days and that paper hit us right when we
were trying to formulate our ideas. Our models were inconsistent with Friedman's reasoning and yet we couldn't see anything wrong with his reasoning.
It was a real scientific tension of trying to take two incompatible points of
view and see what adjustments you can make to end up in a coherent position. Edmund Phelps was pursuing similar ideas. Phelps spelled out the
theory a little more clearly than Friedman did and he had an enormous
influence on me as well.

*Was this with respect to the need for microfoundations?*
Yes. I always think of the proposition that there is no long-run Phillips trade-
off as the Friedman–Phelps proposition.

*What do you feel remains of the monetarist counter-revolution today?*
It has gone in so many different directions. Rational expectations macroeconomics has gone in many different directions. There is real business cycle
theory which assigns no importance to monetary forces. This work has been
hugely influential, on me as well as on others, although I still think of myself
as a monetarist. Then there are those whom Sargent calls fiscalists, people
who think that government deficits are crucial events for the determination of
inflation and whether they are financed by bond issues or money issues is
secondary, or maybe not relevant at all. Then there are old-fashioned monetarists, which is where I would class myself, with people like Friedman and
Allan Meltzer. One of the things that people are coming to agree on, although
not too many come right out and say it, is that econometrically it seems to be
hard to account for more than a quarter to a third of US real variability in the
post-war period to monetary forces, no matter how you look at the data.
People from very different points of view have come up with that as a kind of
upper bound. I used to think that monetary shocks were 90 per cent of the

story in real variability and I still think they are the central story in the 1930s. But there is no way to get monetary shocks to account for more than about a quarter of real variability in the post-war era. At least, no one has found a way of doing it.

*One of the consensus propositions now is that monetary forces cause inflation, certainly in the long term. That still leaves open the question, if we know what causes inflation, why do governments insist on increasing the money supply too rapidly? What are the forces which lie behind monetary expansions?*

Well, to be fair, since the 1970s the advanced capitalist countries have what I would regard as a fantastic record on inflation. Every central bank has shifted its focus exclusively, or almost exclusively, on price stability. They have done a great job. I like the idea of going from 3 per cent to 0, but the big thing is going from 13 per cent to 3. Everyone would agree with that. So the record in the advanced countries has just been tremendous, although there are a few outliers in some Latin America countries where inflation is still a persistent problem. Chile, though, has dealt with inflation forcefully and they have had a solid record for ten years. Country after country is coming around to deal with inflation by restricting money growth. But there is still ignorance and there is always going to be a temptation to generate surprise inflation in order to default on obligations.

*Do you think that Democratic governments will tend to generate in the long term more inflation than Republican governments because of their greater announced commitment to employment targets?*

Easy money and tight money have been an issue in the USA since the nineteenth century. I guess it is a pretty good generalization that the Republicans on the whole have been a tight money party.

*According to Alberto Alesina's [1989] rational partisan model it should generally be better.*

I think of Nixon and Ford as having been fairly inept at monetary policy (*laughter*).

*Alan Blinder [1986, 1988b, 1992b] has argued that during the 1970s American Keynesianism absorbed the Friedman–Phelps proposition and that after allowing for the effects of the OPEC supply shock, a modified Keynesian model was quite capable of explaining the 1970s macroeconomic phenomena. Do you think he is wrong?*

The direct effect of the OPEC shock was minor in my opinion. I like to be more explicit about which models are being discussed and what properties are being boasted about. I don't know what 'modified Keynesian model' Alan is referring to.

*In his view the expectations-augmented Phillips curve had become part of mainstream macroeconomics by the mid-1970s and by then Keynesianism had become 'less crude', having absorbed some of Friedman's monetarist arguments. However, rational expectations models remained controversial.*
I don't know how you would separate those two. But again I don't know whether Alan is referring to some body of research, or whether he just means to say that he thinks he is pretty much on top of things [*laughter*].

## New Classical Macroeconomics

*Did you regard your work and that of your associates in developing new classical macroeconomics as having created a separate school of thought from monetarism?*
I don't like the collective, me and my associates [*laughter*]. I am responsible for my work just as Sargent, Barro and Prescott are responsible for their own work. When you are in the middle of doing research, it's a paper-by-paper, problem-by-problem kind of thing. You don't say 'I am a school and here is what my school is going to do'. These labels get pasted on after the fact; they don't play much of a role. My most influential paper on 'Expectations and the Neutrality of Money' [1972a] came out of a conference that Phelps organized where Rapping and I were invited to talk about our Phillips curve work. Phelps convinced us that we needed some kind of general equilibrium setting. Rapping and I were just focusing on labour supply decisions. Phelps kept on insisting that these labour suppliers are situated in some economy, and that you have to consider what the whole general equilibrium looks like, not just what the labour supply decision looks like. That's what motivated me. I didn't think of it as being monetarist but I didn't think of it as a new school either.

*Do you regard the new classical approach as having resulted in a revolution in macroeconomic thought?*
Sargent once wrote that you can interpret any scientific development as continuous evolution or discontinuous revolution, at your pleasure. For myself, I do not have any romantic associations with the term 'revolution'. To me, it connotes lying, theft and murder, so I would prefer not to be known as a revolutionary.

*One of the policy implications of new classical analysis is that there will be no trade-off between inflation and unemployment even in the short run fol-*

*lowing announced anticipated monetary expansion. How do you now view this policy ineffectiveness proposition in the light of the disinflationary experience of both the UK and the US economies in the early 1980s?*

It is nearly impossible to tell what was and was not anticipated in any particular episode, so the 1980s did not offer a crucial test of anything. Sargent's two essays on disinflation in his book *Rational Expectations and Inflation* [1993] provide the best analysis of this issue, and a serious discussion of what is meant by an 'anticipated' policy change.

*The early 1980s witnessed the demise of your monetary surprise version of the new classical model. On reflection, how do you view this work and what do you think remains of that first phase of the new classical revolution?*

I discuss this in my Nobel lecture [1996]. My models stress the distinction between anticipated and unanticipated inflation and I arrived at that distinction through an information-processing model. But other people have arrived at the same distinction by thinking about contracts. There are many ways to motivate that distinction. At the time I guess I thought my way of looking at it was just a lot better than other people's ways of looking at it [*laughter*]. Now they all seem pretty similar to me. I think this distinction between anticipated and unanticipated money, and how different their effects are, is the key idea in post-war macro. I would like to see it embodied in better theoretical models. I hope it doesn't get forgotten or lost.

*What do you regard as being the most serious criticisms that have been raised in the literature against new classical equilibrium models?*

To me the most interesting debates are not about classes of models but about particular models. For example, Mehra and Prescott's [1985] paper on 'The Equity Premium' highlighted the failure of any neoclassical model that we know about to account for the enormous differential between the return on equity and the return on bonds. Now they certainly didn't view this fact as a failure of neoclassical economics as a body of thought, but on the other hand it is undeniably a failure of a *particular* neoclassical model. I think that is a much more fruitful way to proceed. I think general discussions, especially by non-economists, of whether the system is in equilibrium or not are almost entirely nonsense. You can't look out of this window and ask whether New Orleans is in equilibrium. What does that mean? [*laughter*]. Equilibrium is just a property of the way we look at things, not a property of reality.

*Many critics of new classical macroeconomics have argued that there is a lack of available supporting evidence of strong intertemporal labour substitution effects. How do you react to this line of criticism?*

I'm not at all sympathetic to it. I don't know what you mean by the 'available evidence'. The degree of intertemporal substitution of labour assumed in real business cycle models is *selected* to generate employment fluctuations of the magnitude we observe, which is to say, to be consistent with some of the 'available evidence'. Economists who have used survey data on individuals have been unsuccessful in explaining employment fluctuations at the individual level – we just haven't learned anything about preferences from their work. This is a disappointment, but no good purpose is served by reinterpreting this failure as though it were a successful attempt to estimate something.

*Do you consider your 1972* Journal of Economic Theory *paper on 'Expectations and the Neutrality of Money' to be your most influential paper?*
It seems to be, or maybe the paper on policy evaluation [1976].

*How important do you think the 'Lucas critique' has been?*
I think it has been tremendously important, but it is fading. It used to be that you could hold that up, like a cross to a vampire, and defeat people simply by saying 'Lucas critique'. People have gotten tired of that and I think that is fair enough. If you want to criticize work effectively you have to get into it and criticize its details. But I think it is basic that you can't get economic conclusions without putting in some economic theories, some economic structure.

*Your 1978 paper with Thomas Sargent 'After Keynesian Macroeconomics' seemed to be pronouncing the death of Keynesian macroeconomics. Do you now think that this was perhaps premature given its revival in the form of new Keynesian economics?*
Well, the label 'Keynesian' is a flag a lot of people salute, so it's not going to lie around unused. Of course Sargent and I were talking about a particular set of models which we were completely clear about.

*You were talking about 1960s-style Keynesian models?*
The Wharton model, the Michigan model, the MPS model, models which existed and were in some sense Keynesian. If a completely different class of models comes up which people like to call Keynesian, of course our criticisms can't apply. You can't write a paper in 1978 criticizing work done in 1988 [*laughter*].

*That [1978] paper contains a lot of powerful rhetorical statements. Were you conscious of this at the time of writing?*
Yes. We were invited to a conference sponsored by the Boston Fed. In a way it was like being in the enemy camp and we were trying to make a statement that we weren't going to be assimilated.

**Real Business Cycle Theory**

*In your 1980 paper 'Methods and Problems in Business Cycle Theory' you seem to be anticipating in some respects the next decade's work. You appear to be asking for the kind of methodological approach which Kydland and Prescott were about to take up. Were you aware of what they were doing at the time?*
Yes. But I wasn't anticipating their work.

*But your statements in that paper seem to be calling for the kind of methodology that they have used.*
Well, Prescott and I have been very close for years and we talk about everything. But if you're asking whether at the time I wrote that paper I had an idea that you could get some sort of satisfactory performance out of a macroeconomic model in which the only disturbances were productivity shocks, then the answer is no. I was as surprised as everybody else when Kydland and Prescott showed that was possible [*laughter*].

*Is it fair to say that you, Friedman, Tobin and other leading macroeconomists up until 1980 tended to think of a long-run smooth trend around which there are fluctuations?*
Yes.

*Basically differences of opinion concerned what caused these fluctuations and what you could do about them. Then Kydland and Prescott [1982] came along and changed that way of thinking.*
Well, they talk about business cycles in terms of deviations from trend as well. The difference is that Friedman, Tobin and I would think of the sources of the trend as being entirely from the supply side and the fluctuations about trend as being induced by monetary shocks. Of course we would think of very different kinds of theoretical models to deal with the long-run and the short-run issues. Kydland and Prescott took the sources that we think of as long term to see how well they would do for these short-term movements. The surprising thing was how well it worked. I am still mostly on the side of Friedman and Tobin, but there is no question that our thinking has changed a lot on the basis of this work.

*In an article in* Oxford Economic Papers *Kevin Hoover [1995b] has suggested that 'the calibration methodology, to date, lacks any discipline as stern as that imposed by econometric methods ... and above all, it is not clear on what standards competing, but contradictory models are to be compared and adjudicated'. Does this pose a problem?*

Yes, but it is not a problem that's resolved by Neyman–Pearson statistics. There the whole formalism is for testing models that are nested. It has always been a philosophical issue to compare non-nested models. It's not something that Kydland and Prescott introduced. I think Kydland and Prescott are in part responding to the sterility of Neyman–Pearson statistical methods. These methods just don't answer the questions that we want to answer. Maybe they do for studying the results of agricultural experiments, or something like that, but not for dealing with economics.

*Would you agree with the view that a major contribution of the real business cycle approach has been to raise fundamental questions about the meaning, significance and characteristics of economic fluctuations?*
I think that is true of any influential macroeconomics. I don't think that statement isolates a unique contribution of real business cycle theory.

*In commenting on recent developments in new classical economics Gregory Mankiw [1989] has argued that although real business cycle theory has 'served the important function of stimulating and provoking scientific debate, it will [he predicts] ultimately be discarded as an explanation of observed fluctuations'. What are your predictions for the future development of macroeconomics?*
I agree with Mankiw, but I don't think he understands the implication of his observation. We are now seeing models in the style of Kydland and Prescott with nominal rigidities, imperfect credit markets, and many other features that people thinking of themselves as Keynesians have emphasized. The difference is that within an explicit equilibrium framework we can begin to work out the quantitative implications of these features, not just illustrate them with textbook diagrams.

### New Keynesian Economics

*When we interviewed Gregory Mankiw in 1993 [see Snowdon and Vane, 1995] he suggested that 'the theoretical challenge of Lucas and his followers has been met' and that Keynesian economics is now 'well founded on microeconomic models'. Do you think that new Keynesians such as Mankiw have created firm microeconomic foundations for Keynesian models?*
There are some interesting theoretical models by people who call themselves 'new Keynesians'. I don't know who first threw out this challenge but I would think it was Patinkin. When I was a student this idea of microfoundations for Keynesian models was already on everyone's agenda and I thought of Patinkin as the leading exponent of that idea.

Keynesian models in the 1960s, and this is what excited people like Sargent and me, were operational in the sense that you could quantify the effects of various policy changes by simulating these models. You could find out what would happen if you balanced the budget every year, or if you increased the money supply, or changed fiscal policy. That was what was exciting. They were operational, quantitative models that addressed important policy questions. Now in that sense new Keynesian models are not quantitative, are not fitted to data; there are no realistic dynamics in them. They are not used to address any policy conclusions. What are the principal policy conclusions of 'new Keynesian economics'? Ask Greg Mankiw that question the next time you interview him [*laughter*]. I don't even ask that they prove interesting policy conclusions, just that they attempt some. Everyone knows that Friedman said we ought to expand the money supply by 4 per cent per year. Old Keynesians had similar ideas about what we ought to do with the budget deficit, and what they thought the effects of it would be. New Keynesian economics doesn't seem to make contact with the questions that got us interested in macroeconomics in the first place.

*In Europe, where currently unemployment is a much bigger problem compared to the USA, some new Keynesian work has tried to explain this phenomenon in terms of hysteresis effects. This work implies that Friedman [1968a] was wrong when he argued that aggregate demand disturbances cannot affect the natural rate. So in that sense some new Keynesian economists are trying to address the problem of unemployment, suggesting that aggregate demand management still has a role to play.*
When Friedman wrote his 1968 article the average rate of unemployment in the USA was something like 4.8 per cent and the system always seemed to return to about that level. Since then the natural rate has drifted all over the place. It looked much more like a constant of nature back in those days than it does now. Everyone would have to agree with that. That is not a theory but an observation about what has happened. Now in Europe the drift upwards has been much more striking. Unemployment is a hugely important problem. But I don't want to call anyone who notes that that is a problem a Keynesian. Ljungqvist and Sargent (1998) have done some very exciting work on this, trying to make the connections between the European welfare state and unemployment rates. I don't know whether they have got it right or not.

*That has also been a theme of Patrick Minford et al.'s [1985] work in the UK.* It is a tough theme to defend though, because the welfare state has been in place for 30 years more or less in its present form in most European countries.

*Perhaps the best way is to identify changes within the incentive structure rather than the level of benefits.*

Yes, that is what you have got to do. Ljungqvist and Sargent try to address that issue as well.

### General and Methodological Issues

*Do you think it is healthy to subject students to a breadth of perspectives at the undergraduate level?*
I don't know. I teach introductory macro and I want my students to see specific, necessarily pretty simple, models and to compare their predictions to US data. I want them to see for themselves rather than just be told about it. Now that does give a narrowness to their training. But the alternative of giving them a catalogue of schools and noting what each says without giving students any sense of how economic reasoning is used to try to account for the facts is not very attractive either. Maybe there is a better way to do it.

*Have you ever thought of writing a basic introductory textbook?*
I have thought a lot about it, but it would be hard to do. I sat down once with my course notes, to see how far the notes I had been using over the years were from a textbook, and it was a long long way [*laughter*]. So I have never done it.

*Is the philosophy of science and formal methodology an area that interests you?*
Yes. I don't read very much in the area but I like to think about it.

*You acknowledge that Friedman has had a great influence on you, yet his methodological approach is completely different to your own approach to macroeconomics. Why did his methodological approach not appeal to you?*
I like mathematics and general equilibrium theory. Friedman didn't. I think that he missed the boat [*laughter*].

*His methodological approach seems more in keeping with Keynes and Marshall.*
He describes himself as a Marshallian, although I don't know quite what that means. Whatever it is, it's not what I think of myself as.

*Would you agree that the appropriate criterion for establishing the fruitfulness of a theory is the degree of empirical corroboration attained by its predictions?*
Something like that. Yes.

*You are Friedmanite on that issue of methodology?*

I am certainly a Friedmanite. The problem with that statement is that not all empirical corroborations are equal. There are some crucial things that a theory has to account for and if it doesn't we don't care how well it does on other dimensions.

*Do you think that it is crucial for macroeconomic models to have neoclassical choice-theoretic microfoundations?*
No. It depends on the purposes you want the model to serve. For short-term forecasting, for example, the Wharton model does very well with little in the way of theoretical foundations, and Sims, Litterman and others have had pretty good success with purely statistical extrapolation methods that involve no economics at all. But if one wants to know how behaviour is likely to change under some change in policy, it is necessary to model the way people make choices. If you see me driving north on Clark Street, you will have good (though not perfect) predictive success by guessing that I will still be going north on the same street a few minutes later. But if you want to predict how I will respond if Clark Street is closed off, you have to have some idea of where I am going and what my alternative routes are – of the nature of my decision problem.

*Why do you think there is more consensus among economists over micro-economic issues compared to macroeconomic issues?*
What is the microeconomic consensus you are referring to? Does it just mean that microeconomists agree on the Slutsky equation, or other purely mathematical propositions? Macroeconomists all take derivatives in the same way, too. On matters of application and policy, microeconomists disagree as vehemently as macroeconomists – neither side in an antitrust action has any difficulty finding expert witnesses.

I think there is a tremendous amount of consensus on macroeconomic issues today. But there is much that we don't know, and so – necessarily – a lot to argue about.

*Do you see any signs of an emerging consensus in macroeconomics, and if so, what form will it take?*
When a macroeconomic consensus is reached on an issue (as it has been, say, on the monetary sources of inflation) the issue passes off the stage of professional debate, and we argue about something else. Professional economists are primarily scholars, not policy managers. Our responsibility is to create new knowledge by pushing research into new, and hence necessarily controversial, territory. Consensus can be reached on specific issues, but consensus for a research area as a whole is equivalent to stagnation, irrelevance and death.

*In what areas, other than the monetary sources of inflation, do you think there is now a consensus in macro? Do you think, for example, that there is a majority of economists who are now anti fine-tuning?*
Yes. Fine-tuning certainly has come down a few pegs. Paul Krugman has been doing a lot of very effective writing attacking non-economists writing about economic matters. Paul is speaking for the whole profession in a very effective way and addressing the most important questions in social science. Economists have a lot of areas of agreement, partly due to the fact that we look at numbers. If somebody says the world is breeding itself into starvation, we look at numbers and see that per capita incomes are rising in the world. It seems to be that on a lot of questions there is a huge amount of consensus among economists. More and more we are focusing on technology, supply-side, long-run issues. Those are the big issues for us now, not on depression prevention.

## Economic Growth

*In their recent book on economic growth Robert Barro and Xavier Sala-i-Martin [1995] express the view that 'economic growth is the part of macroeconomics that really matters'. In your Yrjo Jahnsson lectures [1987] you seem to be saying something similar, that macroeconomists have spent too much time on stabilization and neglected growth, which is a far more important issue for macroeconomics to look at.*
Yes. That is becoming the consensus view. David Romer's new textbook, which we use in our first-year graduate macro course at Chicago, begins with growth. Romer would call himself a new Keynesian and he is perfectly entitled to call himself that. But his book shows a shift in emphasis towards long-run growth questions. Quite rightly, I think.

*So it's back to the classics and the grand issues of the long run?*
Yes. OK [*laughter*].

*What in your view was the stimulus to the new endogenous growth economics? Was it the lack of convergence which people were observing empirically between rich and poor countries, apart from maybe a 'convergence club'?*
No. What is new about the new growth theory is the idea that what we ought to be trying to do is get a single neoclassical model that can account for rich and poor countries alike in the same terms. This contrasts with the view that we had in the 1960s that there was one theory for the advanced countries and some other model was needed for the Third World. The whole presumption in the 1960s was that some explicit policy, perhaps based on the Russian model, was needed to promote development in poor countries.

We didn't think of economic growth as something that just happened through market forces.

*What do you see as being the important policy implications of the work that has been done so far on endogenous growth? Some economists have interpreted the work as suggesting that there is a more positive role for government than, say, was the case with the Solow model.*
Yes. An implication of the Solow model was that the long-term growth rate of an economy was dictated by technological change and there wasn't anything we could do about it. Some of the endogenous growth models have the property that the long-term growth rate is endogenously determined and that changes in the tax structure, for example, can influence what that growth rate is. We can now use these new models to analyse the growth effects of changes in tax policy. That is something we couldn't do before. But these effects I think are pretty small. Even where you have a model where growth rates can be changed by policy the effects seem to be pretty modest.

*What in your view is the reason why the 'Tiger' economies of South East Asia have been so successful? While the Tiger economies have been catching up with the West with 8 or 9 per cent growth rates, in Africa the 1980s was almost a completely lost decade as far as economic growth was concerned.*
Well, you know Africa has had awful politics.

*Do you think African countries generally lack the necessary institutional framework required for successful development?*
No. There has been much too much socialist influence. The common feature of countries like Taiwan, Korea and Japan is that they have had some kind of conservative, pro-market, pro-business, economic policies. I mean I wouldn't exactly call them free trade because Japan and Korea at least are very mercantilist in their trade policies, which I don't approve of. But it is better than socialism and import substitution by a long, long way.

*While they have been outward-looking, some development economists would argue that within many of the South East Asian Tiger economies there has been quite a lot of government intervention. As such they see it as being an example of successful government intervention.*
Right. That is how everybody in Japan and Korea sees it [*laughter*].

*You don't see it that way?*
Even Chicago Korean students think that the Korean growth rates have been engineered by government manipulation. I don't agree with that view. I don't see any evidence for that at all. But it is hard to refute. There is no question

that governments have been extremely active in doing things that they think promote economic growth.

## Economic Policy

*In your 1978* AER *paper on 'Unemployment Policy' you suggested that macroeconomic analysis would make better progress if the concept of involuntary unemployment were abandoned. Many economists, for example Kevin Hoover [1988, 1995c], have criticized you for this and question whether you can regard unemployment as simply voluntary.*
There is both an involuntary and a voluntary element in any kind of unemployment. Take anybody who is looking for a job. At the end of the day if they haven't found one, they are unhappy about it. They did not choose to find one in some sense. Everyone wishes he has better options than he does. But there is also obviously a voluntary element in unemployment when there are all these jobs around. When we are unemployed it is because we think we can do better.

*I suppose this is something that bothers Europeans more because aggregate unemployment is much more of an issue in Europe. It doesn't seem to be as much of an issue in the USA.*
It should be.

*Many European economies including Germany, France and Italy are currently experiencing unemployment rates in excess of 10 per cent.*
Well, if you go into the neighbourhoods within a mile of my university you will find 50 per cent unemployment rates. So it is an issue here too.

*The Bank of England is less independent than the German Bundesbank. Do you see that as a possible reason why Britain's inflation performance has been less successful than that of Germany?*
I don't know, it could be. I don't feel I have much understanding of the political sources of differences in monetary policy across countries.

*Economic policy doesn't seem to have been guided by new classical theoretical developments in the same way as it has by Keynesianism and monetarism. Why has its impact been less influential in economic policy making?*
Why do you say that? We have talked about the increasing focus of central bankers on inflation and the de-emphasis of everybody on fine-tuning. That is an important trend in the last 20 years in the USA and Europe, and to my mind a very healthy one.

*Would this not have come about in any case as a result of Friedman's influence, without rational expectations and equilibrium theorizing?*
Maybe.

*Have you ever been invited to be an economic adviser in Washington? Is that a role you see for yourself?*
No.

*You once made a comment [Lucas, 1981c] that 'as an advice-giving profession we are in way over our heads'. Is that the reason you haven't considered such a role more seriously?*
No. Not at all. I believe economists ought to run everything [*laughter*].

*So did Keynes.*
I know. I don't think I personally have any particular talent or liking for that kind of role. But I am glad that other people like John Taylor or Larry Summers do. For example, I think that the whole reason the Clinton health insurance reform fell on its face was that not enough economists were involved. I like economics and I think economics is hugely relevant on almost any issue of national policy. The more good economists are involved the happier I am. But I don't personally feel drawn to doing it.

*What are your views on European Monetary Union?*
Again I don't know enough about the politics, which has to be central.

*Does it make economic sense to you?*
Well, it's an issue in inventory theory. The cost of dealing with multiple currencies is that if you are doing business in Europe you, or people you hire to help you, have to have stocks of inventories of a lot of different currencies because payments are coming due in a lot of different currencies. The inventory cost of holding money is the interest foregone you could have earned by holding interest-bearing assets. If you have a common currency you can consolidate your cash inventories so that there is a saving involved. That is a very modest saving, but it is positive. But obviously multiple currencies are not inconsistent with a huge amount of prosperity. If you can consolidate, all the better, but those purely economic gains are pretty modest. If you don't trust somebody else to run your monetary policy, maybe you want to oppose monetary union. For myself, I would be happy to turn my monetary policy over to the Germans any day [*laughter*].

**Personal Information**

*When we interviewed Milton Friedman [see Snowdon and Vane, 1997b] he commented that he had experienced three reactions to many of his views, to quote: 'the first reaction is that it's all a bunch of nonsense, the second reaction is that there is something to it and the third reaction is that it gets embedded in the theory and nobody talks about it anymore'. How well does this parallel with new and controversial ideas you have fought to get accepted?*

A little bit. But you know Milton is like Keynes. He goes directly to the public, to the voters, with ideas. The reactions he is talking about are the reactions of non-economists, of politicians, of a huge range of people, to the changes in policies he is advocating. My career hasn't really taken that form. My influence has been very much more inside the profession and for that matter on a technical subset of the profession. In so far as I have had any influence on the larger world you can't really identify it because my influence is contained with the influence of many others. How do you tell my influence from Tom Sargent's influence? Nobody other than professional economists would even have heard of me. No one in the US Congress is going to say 'I favour Lucas's policy'. The reply would be, 'who is Lucas?'! [*laughter*].

*Turning to the award of the Nobel Prize. When we interviewed James Tobin in 1993 and asked him how he felt about being awarded the Prize his reaction was somewhat defensive along the lines that he didn't ask for it; the Swedish Academy gave it to him. In correspondence we asked Milton Friedman a similar question and he acknowledged that it was extremely rewarding. He also told us that he first learned of the award from a reporter who stuck a microphone in his face when he was in a parking lot in Detroit. We were wondering what importance you attach to having been awarded the Nobel Prize.*

Oh, it was a tremendous thing for me. I don't know what else I can say. I don't know what Jim could possibly have had in mind. He was certainly pleased when it happened and he certainly merited the award. Reporters will ask you, and this annoys me too after a while, 'what did you do to deserve this prize?' They should look up what the Swedish Academy said on the Internet. I don't want to have to defend it. If that is what Jim meant, then I have been through the same thing and I am just as irritated by it as he is.

*What issues or areas are you currently working on?*

I'm thinking about monetary policy again, actually. In particular all central banks now want to talk about the interest rate as being the immediate variable they manipulate. I don't get it and yet their record on controlling inflation is pretty good. Talking in terms of interest rate targets as opposed to monetary targets seems to me just the wrong way to think about it, but if so, why does it work so well?

*Finally, is there any question that you would have liked to have been asked in this interview?*
I don't know [*laughter*]. Your questions are interesting to me. You guys are economists and it's a lot more fun being interviewed by an economist than being interviewed by a journalist who is completely ignorant of economics [*laughter*].

# 6.   The real business cycle school

If these theories are correct, they imply that the macroeconomics developed in the wake of the Keynesian revolution is well confined to the ashbin of history. (Summers, 1986)

## 6.1   Introduction: The Demise of New Classical Macroeconomics Mark I

The dramatic statement by Lawrence Summers concerning real business cycle theory is no exaggeration. The reason has to do with the striking implications of developments in business cycle theory associated with the real business cycle school that initially took place in the early 1980s. We have already seen in the previous two chapters how the influence of both monetarism and new classical economics called into question the desirability and effectiveness of activist discretionary stabilization policies. Such policies were founded on the belief that aggregate demand shocks were the main source of aggregate instability. But rather than advocate the persistent use of expansionary aggregate demand policies in an attempt to achieve some target rate of (full) employment, both Friedman and Lucas advocated the use of supply-side policies in order to achieve employment goals (Friedman, 1968a; Lucas, 1978a, 1990a). During the 1960s and 1970s, both Friedman and Lucas, in their explanation of business cycles, emphasized monetary shocks as the primary impulse mechanism driving the cycle. The real business cycle theorists have gone much further in their analysis of the supply side. In the model developed during the early 1980s by Kydland and Prescott (1982) a purely supply-side explanation of the business cycle is provided. This paper marked the launch of a 'mark II' version of new classical macroeconomics. Indeed, the research of Kydland and Prescott represented a serious challenge to *all* previous mainstream accounts of the business cycle that focused on aggregate demand shocks, in particular those that emphasized monetary shocks.

Particularly shocking to conventional wisdom is the bold conjecture advanced by real business cycle theorists that each stage of the business cycle (peak, recession, trough and recovery) is an equilibrium! As Hartley et al. (1998) point out, 'to common sense, economic booms are good and slumps are bad'. This 'common sense' vision was captured in the neoclassical synthesis period with the assumption that 'full employment' represented equilibrium and that recessions were periods of welfare-reducing disequilibrium implying market failure and the need for stabilization policy. Real business cycle theorists reject this market failure view. While recessions are not desired by economic agents, they represent the aggregate outcome of responses to unavoidable shifts in the constraints that agents face. Given these constraints, agents react optimally and market outcomes displaying aggregate fluctuations are efficient. There is no need for economists to resort to disequilibrium analysis, coordination failure, price stickiness, monetary and financial shocks, and notions such as fundamental uncertainty to explain aggregate instability. Rather, theorists can make use of the basic neoclassical growth model to understand the business cycle once allowance is made for randomness in the rate of technological progress (the neoclassical growth model is discussed in Chapter 11). In this setting, the business cycle emerges as the aggregate outcome of maximizing decisions made by all the agents populating an economy.

## 6.2 The Transition from Monetary to Real Equilibrium Business Cycle Theory

As we have seen in Chapter 5, the dominant new classical theory of the business cycle during the period 1972–82 was the monetary surprise model (MEBCT) initially developed by Lucas (1975, 1977). Since the early 1980s the leading new classical explanation of aggregate instability has focused on real rather than monetary shocks, and after the contribution of Long and Plosser (1983) became known as real (equilibrium) business cycle theory (REBCT). The best-known advocates or contributors to this approach are Edward Prescott of the University of Minnesota, Finn Kydland of Carnegie-Mellon University, Charles Plosser, John Long and Alan Stockman of the University of Rochester, Robert King of Boston University, Sergio Rebelo of Northwestern University and Robert Barro of Harvard University (see interviews with Robert Barro and Charles Plosser in Snowdon et al. 1994).

In the early 1980s, in response to recognized weaknesses in the MEBCT some new classical theorists sought to provide a rigorous equilibrium account of the business cycle which is both free from the theoretical flaws of earlier new classical models and would, at the same time, be empirically robust. The result has been the development of REBCT, which replaces the *impulse* mechanism of the earlier models (that is, unanticipated monetary shocks) with supply-side shocks in the form of random changes in technology. The *propagation* mechanisms of the earlier new classical models are, however, retained and developed. Ironically it was Tobin (1980b) who was one of the first to recognize this unlikely escape route for equilibrium theorists. In criticizing the monetary misperception stories of Lucas, Tobin noted that the 'real equilibrium of a full information model could move around, driven by fluctuations in natural endowments, technologies and tastes' and, if such fluctuations were seriously persistent random processes, the observations generated 'may look like business cycles'. Meanwhile, around 1980, Kydland and Prescott were working on just such a model and two years after Tobin made his comments *Econometrica* published Kydland and Prescott's paper containing their prototype non-monetary equilibrium model.

Before moving on to consider real business cycle theory in more detail, it is interesting to note the reaction to this second phase of equilibrium theorizing of two of the leading pioneers of the new classical mark I approach. In Robert Lucas's view, Kydland and Prescott have taken macroeconomic modelling 'into new territory' (Lucas, 1987). However, Lucas's initial reaction to REBCT was to suggest that the exclusive focus of such models on real as opposed to monetary considerations was 'a mistake' and argued the case for a 'hybrid' model as a fruitful way forward. Nevertheless Lucas warmly approved of the methodology adopted by real business cycle theorists who have followed his own earlier recommendation that an understanding of business cycles is best achieved 'by constructing a *model* in the most literal sense: a fully articulated artificial economy which behaves through time so as to imitate closely the time series behaviour of actual economies' (Lucas, 1977). Such artificial economic systems can serve as laboratories 'in which policies that would be prohibitively expensive to experiment with in actual economies can be tested out at much lower cost' (Lucas, 1980a). This is exactly what real business cycle theorists established as their research agenda during the 1980s, and Lucas's (1980a) paper is the reference point for the modern era of equilibrium theorizing. As Williamson (1996) points out, 'in Lucas one finds a projection for future research methodology which is remarkably close to the real business cycle program'.

By 1996 Lucas admitted that 'monetary shocks just aren't that important. That's the view that I've been driven to. There is no question that's a retreat in my views' (see Gordon, 2000a, p. 555). Meanwhile Lucas has put forward the view several times that he considers the business cycle to be a relatively 'minor' problem, at least at the level experienced since 1945 (Lucas, 1987, 2003). In his view it is far more important to understand the process of economic growth if we are really interested in raising living standards, rather than trying to devise ever more intricate stabilization policies in order to remove the residual amount of business cycle risk (see Lucas, 1988, 1993, 2002, 2003, and Chapter 11).

By the late 1980s Robert Barro (1989a, 1989c) also declared that the emphasis given by new classical economists during the 1970s to explaining the non-neutrality of money was 'misplaced' because the 'new classical approach does not do very well in accounting for an important role for money in business fluctuations'. By the mid-1980s, Barro regarded the contributions of real business cycle theorists as 'especially promising' and representing 'real progress' (Barro, 1984). Furthermore, his own work had provided a bridge between the mark I and mark II versions of new classical macroeconomics (see Barro, 1981). In any case the lack of robust empirical success of the earlier models does not invalidate the achievements of the new classical theorists in the 1970s which in Barro's view led to 'superior methods of theoretical and empirical analysis' (Barro, 1984).

The three main new classical achievements identified by Barro (1989a) are (i) the application of equilibrium modelling to macroeconomic analysis, (ii) the adoption and promotion of the rational expectations hypothesis, and (iii) the application of game theory to policy making and evaluation. The first two contributions satisfy the objectives of building macro models on choice-theoretic microfoundations, as well as providing an analytical framework which can better withstand the Lucas (1976) critique. The third area relating to dynamic games has drawn out the importance in policy analysis of the roles of commitment, credibility and reputation as well as clarifying the distinction between rules and discretion. The insights gained relating to the time inconsistency of policy have now been applied to a wide variety of areas other than the conduct of monetary policy. Although Barro remains enthusiastic about real business cycle theory, he, like Lucas, began to redirect his research work in the late 1980s primarily towards issues related to economic growth (see Barro, 1991, 1997; Barro and Sala-i-Martin, 1995).

For detailed surveys of the evolution and development of REBCT, the reader is referred to Walsh (1986), Rush (1987), Kim (1988), Plosser (1989), Mullineux and Dickinson (1992), McCallum (1992), Danthine and Donaldson (1993), Stadler (1994), Williamson (1996), Ryan and Mullineux (1997), Snowdon and Vane (1997a), Hartley et al. (1998), Arnold (2002), and Kehoe and Prescott (2002).

## 6.3 Real Business Cycle Theory in Historical Perspective

Real business cycle theory, as developed by its modern proponents, is built on the assumption that there are large random fluctuations in the rate of technological progress. These supply-side shocks to the production function generate fluctuations in aggregate output and employment as rational individuals respond to the altered structure of relative prices by changing their labour supply and consumption decisions. While this development is in large part a response to the demise of the earlier monetary misperception models and Lucas's call to construct 'artificial economies', it also represents a general revival of interest in the supply side of the macro equation.

The idea that business cycles might be driven by real rather than monetary forces is certainly not an entirely new idea. The real business cycle models inspired by Kydland and Prescott's (1982) seminal paper belong to a long line of analysis which was prominent in the literature before Keynes's (1936) *General Theory* (see Haberler, 1963, for a superb survey of the interwar business cycle literature). Whereas some economists such as Ralph Hawtrey held to the extreme monetary interpretation of the business cycle, the work of others, in particular Dennis Robertson, Joseph Schumpeter and Knut Wicksell, emphasized real forces as the engine behind business fluctuations (see Deutscher, 1990; Goodhart and Presley, 1991; T. Caporale, 1993). While the work of Robertson was not as dismissive of monetary forces as modern real business cycle theory, according to Goodhart and Presley there is a great deal of similarity between the emphasis given by Robertson to technological change and the recent work of the equilibrium theorists. Technological change also played a pivotal role in Joseph Schumpeter's analysis of the short-run instability and long-run dynamics of capitalist development. Since the intro-duction of new technology influences the long-run growth of productivity as well as causing short-run disequilibrating effects, Schumpeter, like modern real business cycle theorists, viewed cycles and growth as inseparably inter-related (see Schumpeter, 1939). Caporale (1993) argues that Knut Wicksell was also an early expositor of real business cycle theory. Caporale shows that Wicksell attributed 'trade cycles to *real* causes independent of movements in commodity prices'. To Wicksell the main cause of the trade cycle is a supply-side shock that raises the natural rate of interest above the loan rate of interest. This is equivalent to a reduction in the loan rate of interest since the banking system will typically fail to adjust the loan rate immediately to reflect the new natural rate. Loan market disequilibrium acting as a propaga-tion mechanism leads to endogenous money creation by the banking system in response to entrepreneurs' demand for loans to finance investment. The investment boom, by distorting the time structure of production, thereby creates inflationary pressures. Eventually the money rate of interest catches up with the natural rate and the boom comes to an end. While this story had a major influence on later Swedish and Austrian monetary theories of the trade cycle, Caporale highlights how the Wicksell trade cycle story begins with a real shock to the marginal product of capital. Wicksell's real shocks plus endogenous money account of the trade cycle is therefore remarkably similar to the modern versions of REBCT provided by, for example, King and Plosser (1984); see below, section 6.12.

Following the publication of Keynes's (1936) *General Theory*, models of the business cycle were constructed which emphasized the interaction of the multiplier–accelerator mechanism (Samuelson, 1939; Hicks, 1950; Trigg, 2002). These models were also 'real' in that they viewed fluctuations as being driven by *real* aggregate demand, mainly unstable investment expenditures, with monetary factors downgraded and supply-side phenomena providing the constraints which give rise to business cycle turning points (see Laidler, 1992a). Whatever their merits, multiplier–accelerator models ceased to be a focus of active research by the early 1960s. To a large extent this reflected the impact of the Keynesian revolution, which shifted the focus of macroeconomic analysis away from business cycle phenomena to the development of methods and policies which could improve macroeconomic performance. Such was the confidence of some economists that the business cycle was no longer a major problem that by 1969 some were even considering the question: 'Is the Business Cycle Obsolete?' (Bronfenbrenner, 1969). Similar conjectures about 'The End of the Business Cycle' appeared during the late 1990s, often framed in terms of discussions of the 'new economy'; see, for example, Weber (1997). We have already seen that during the 1970s and 1980s the business cycle returned with a vengeance (relative to the norm for instability post 1945) and how dissatisfaction with Keynesian models led to monetarist and new classical counter-revolutions.

The most recent developments in business cycle research inspired by equilibrium theorists during the 1980s have proved to be a challenge to *all* the earlier models relying on aggregate demand fluctuations as the main source of instability. Hence real business cycle theory is not only a competitor to the 'old' Keynesian macroeconomics of the neoclassical synthesis period but also represents a serious challenge to all monetarist and early MEBCT new classical models.

In addition to the above influences, the transition from monetary to real theories of the business cycle was further stimulated by two other important developments. First, the supply shocks associated with the two OPEC oil price increases during the 1970s made macroeconomists more aware of the importance of supply-side factors in explaining macroeconomic instability (Blinder, 1979). These events, together with the apparent failure of the demand-oriented Keynesian model to account adequately for rising unemployment accompanied by accelerating inflation, forced all macroeconomists to devote increasing research effort to the construction of macroeconomic theories where the supply side has coherent microfoundations (see Chapter 7). Second, the seminal work of Nelson and Plosser (1982) suggested that real shocks may be far more important than monetary shocks in explaining the path of aggregate output over time. Nelson and Plosser argue that the evidence is consistent with the proposition that output follows a path, which could best be described as a 'random walk'.

Before examining the contribution of Nelson and Plosser in more detail it is important to note that the desire of both Keynesian and new classical economists to build better microfoundations for the supply side of their models should not be confused with the emergence during the late 1970s and 1980s of a distinctive 'supply-side school' of economists, particularly in the USA during the presidency of Ronald Reagan. Writing in the mid-1980s, Feldstein distinguished between 'traditional supply-siders' and the 'new supply-side economics' (Feldstein, 1986). Traditional supply-siders base their analysis on mainstream neoclassical economic analysis and emphasize the efficiency of markets, the importance of incentives for economic growth, and the possibility of government failure. A large consensus of economists would subscribe to this form of supply-side economics, including Keynesians, monetarists and new classicists (see Friedman, 1968a; Tobin, 1987; Lucas, 1990a). In contrast, the new supply-siders, such as Arthur Laffer, Jude Wanniski and President Reagan himself, made 'extravagant claims' relating to the impact of tax cuts and deregulation on the rate of economic growth. While supply-siders claimed that the incentive effects of the Reagan tax cuts were responsible for the US recovery after 1982, Tobin (1987) argued that Reagan's policies amounted to 'Keynesian medicine, demand tonics masquerading as supply-side nostrums, serendipitously administered by anti-Keynesian doctors'. For discussions of 'Reaganomics' and the influence of 'new supply-siders' during the 1980s see Samuelson (1984); Blanchard (1986); Feldstein (1986); Levacic (1988); Modigliani (1988b); Roberts (1989); and Minford (1991).

### 6.4 Cycles versus Random Walks

During the 1970s, with the rebirth of interest in business cycle research, economists became more involved with the statistical properties of economic time series. One of the main problems in this work is to separate trend from cycle. The conventional approach has been to imagine that the economy evolves along a path reflecting an underlying trend rate of growth described by Solow's neoclassical model (Solow, 1956). This approach assumes that the long-run trend component of GNP is smooth, with short-run fluctuations about trend being primarily determined by demand shocks. This conventional wisdom was accepted by Keynesian, monetarist and new classical economists alike until the early 1980s. The demand-shock models of all three groups interpret output deviations from trend as temporary. If business cycles are temporary events, then recessions create no long-run adverse effects on GDP. However, whereas Keynesians feel that such deviations could be severe and prolonged and therefore justify the need for corrective action, monetarists, and especially new classical economists, reject the need for activist stabilization policy, having greater faith in the equilibrating power of market forces and rules-based monetary policy.

In 1982, Nelson and Plosser published an important paper which challenged this conventional wisdom. Their research into macroeconomic time series led them to conclude that 'macroeconomic models that focus on monetary disturbances as a source of purely transitory fluctuations may never be successful in explaining a large fraction of output variation and that stochastic variation due to real factors is an essential element of any model of macroeconomic fluctuations'. If real factors are behind aggregate fluctuations, then business cycles should not be viewed as temporary events. Recessions may well have permanent effects on GDP. The much-discussed 'productivity slowdown' after 1973 represents one such example (see Fischer et al., 1988). Abel and Bernanke (2001) note that GDP in the USA remained below the levels consistent with the 1947–73 trend throughout the 1980s and 1990s. In an analysis of the UK economy in the interwar period Solomou (1996) finds that the shock of the First World War, and further shocks in the immediate post-war period, had a permanent effect on the path of equilibrium output.

Nelson and Plosser reached their important conclusion because in their research into US data they were unable to reject the hypothesis that GNP follows a random walk. How does this conclusion differ from the conventional approach? The view that reversible cyclical fluctuations can account for most of the short-term movements of real GNP can be represented by equation (6.1):

$$Y_t = g_t + bY_{t-1} + z_t \tag{6.1}$$

where $t$ represents time, $g$ and $b$ are constants and $z$ represents random shocks which have a zero mean. In equation (6.1) $g_t$ represents the underlying average growth rate of GNP which describes the deterministic trend. Suppose there is some shock to $z_t$ that causes output to rise above trend at time $t$. We assume that the shock lasts one period only. Since $Y_t$ depends on $Y_{t-1}$, the shock will be transmitted forward in time, generating serial correlation. But since in the traditional approach $0 < b < 1$, the impact of the shock on output will eventually die out and output will return to its trend rate of growth. In this case output is said to be 'trend-reverting' or 'trend-stationary' (see Blanchard and Fischer, 1989).

The impact of a shock on the path of income in the trend-stationary case is illustrated in Figure 6.1, where we assume an expansionary monetary shock occurs at time $t_1$. Notice that $Y$ eventually reverts to its trend path and therefore this case is consistent with the natural rate hypothesis, which states that deviations from the natural level of output caused by unanticipated monetary shocks will be temporary.

In contrast to the above, Nelson and Plosser argue that most of the changes in GNP that we observe are permanent, in that there is no tendency for output to revert to its former trend following a shock. In this case GNP is said to

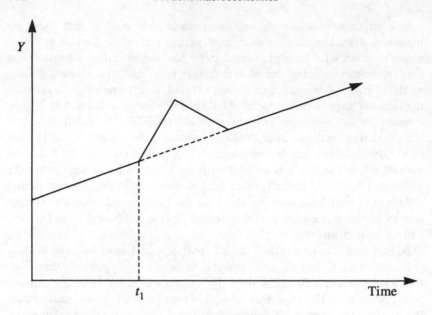

*Figure 6.1    The path of output in the 'trend-reverting' case*

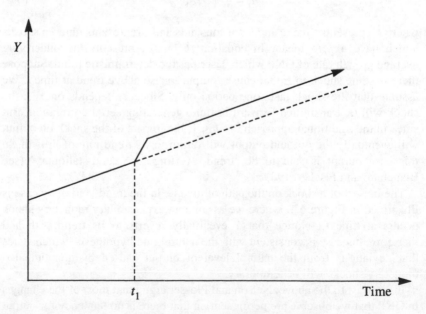

*Figure 6.2    The path of output where shocks have a permanent influence*

evolve as a statistical process known as a random walk. Equation (6.2) shows a random walk with drift for GNP:

$$Y_t = g_t + Y_{t-1} + z_t \tag{6.2}$$

In equation (6.2) $g_t$ reflects the 'drift' of output and, with $Y_t$ also being dependent on $Y_{t-1}$, any shock to $z_t$ will raise output permanently. Suppose a shock raises the level of output at time $t_1$ in Figure 6.2. Since output in the next period is determined by output in period $t_1$, the rise in output persists in every future period. In the case of a random walk with drift, output is said to have a 'unit root'; that is, the coefficient on the lagged output term in equation (6.2) is set equal to unity, $b = 1$. The identification of unit roots is assumed to be a manifestation of shocks to the production function.

These findings of Nelson and Plosser have radical implications for business cycle theory. If shocks to productivity growth due to technological change are frequent and random, then the path of output following a random walk will exhibit features that resemble a business cycle. In this case, however, the observed fluctuations in GNP are fluctuations in the natural (trend) rate of output, not deviations of output from a smooth deterministic trend. What looks like output fluctuating around a smooth trend is in fact fluctuations in the natural rate of output induced by a series of permanent shocks, with each permanent productivity shock determining a new growth path. Whereas, following Solow's seminal work, economists have traditionally separated the analysis of growth from the analysis of fluctuations, the work of Nelson and Plosser suggests that the economic forces determining the trend are not different from those causing fluctuations. Since permanent changes in GNP cannot result from monetary shocks in a new classical world because of the neutrality proposition, the main forces causing instability must be real shocks. Nelson and Plosser interpret their findings as placing limits on the importance of monetary theories of the business cycle and that real disturbances are likely to be a much more important source of output fluctuations. If there are important interactions between the process of growth and business cycles, the conventional practice of separating growth theory from the analysis of fluctuations is illegitimate. By ending the distinction between trend and cycle, real business cycle theorists began to integrate the theory of growth and fluctuations (see King et al., 1988a, 1988b; Plosser, 1989).

## 6.5 Supply-side Shocks

Cyclical instability can arise because of shocks to aggregate demand or shocks to aggregate supply, or some combination of the two. On the demand side, the shocks may originate from instability in some component of the *IS* curve, as stressed by Keynes and most of the earlier Keynesian models, or they may originate from instability on the monetary side, as described by the *LM* curve and emphasized by monetarists. On the supply side, we can imagine a variety of shocks which could result in significant changes in productivity:

1. Unfavourable developments in the physical environment which adversely affect agricultural output. This type of shock would include natural disasters such as earthquakes, drought and floods.
2. Significant changes in the price of energy, such as the oil price 'hikes' of 1973 and 1979 and the subsequent reduction in 1986. James Hamilton (1983, 1996) has argued that most US recessions since 1945 have been preceded by energy price increases.
3. War, political upheaval, or labour unrest which disrupts the existing performance and structure of the economy, as with the disruption experienced in the former Yugoslavia and Soviet Union, and more recently in Iraq, or the strikes and labour unrest in the UK during the 1970s and 1984.
4. Government regulations, such as import quotas, which damage incentives and divert entrepreneurial talent towards rent-seeking activities.
5. Productivity shocks generated by changes in the quality of the capital and labour inputs, new management practices, the development of new products and the introduction of new techniques of production.

While some or all of the above will be important at specific points in time and space, it is the fifth category, which we can broadly define as 'technological shocks', which we can expect under normal circumstances to be the driving force on the supply side over the longer term for advanced industrial economies. It should not be forgotten that politically stable economies, which are normally free from natural disasters, are still characterized by aggregate fluctuations.

Before examining the main features of REBCT we will first review the main features and 'stylized facts' that characterize fluctuations in aggregate economic activity (business cycles).

### 6.6 Business Cycles: Main Features and Stylized Facts

As we noted earlier, the main objective of macroeconomic analysis is to provide coherent and robust explanations of aggregate movements of output, employment and the price level, in both the short run and the long run. We have also drawn attention to the major research programmes, or schools of thought which attempt to explain such movements, that emerged following the publication of Keynes's (1936) *General Theory* (Snowdon and Vane,

1997a). Any assessment of a particular theory must take into account its ability to explain the main features and 'stylized facts' which characterize macroeconomic instability (see Greenwald and Stiglitz, 1988).

By 'stylized facts' we mean the broad regularities that have been identified in the statistical property of economic time series. The identification of the major 'stylized facts' relating to business cycle phenomena is a legitimate field of enquiry in its own right (see Zarnowitz, 1992a, 1992b). In the USA the National Bureau of Economic Research, founded in 1920, pioneered research into business cycle phenomena, the landmark work being *Measuring Business Cycles* by Arthur Burns and Wesley Mitchell, published in 1946. In this book Burns and Mitchell provide their classic definition of business cycles:

> Business cycles are a type of fluctuation found in the aggregate economic activity of nations that organise their work mainly in business enterprises. A cycle consists of expansions occurring at about the same time in many economic activities, followed by similarly general recessions, contractions, and revivals which merge into the expansion phase of the next cycle; this sequence of changes is recurrent but not periodic, in duration business cycles vary from more than one year to ten or twelve years.

The identification by Burns and Mitchell and subsequent research of co-movements of economic variables behaving in a predictable way over the course of the business cycle led Lucas (1977) to claim that 'with respect to the qualitative behaviour of co-movements among series (economic variables) *business cycles are all alike*'. This is an attractive characteristic for the economic theorist because 'it suggests the possibility of a unified explanation of business cycles grounded in the general laws governing market economies, rather than in political or institutional characteristics specific to particular countries or periods' (Lucas, 1977, p. 10). Although many economists would not go this far, it is obvious that theoretical explanations of business cycle phenomena must be generally guided by the identified statistical properties of the co-movements of deviations from trend of the various economic aggregates with those of real GDP. The co-movement of many important economic variables in a predictable way is an important feature of business cycles. While business cycles are not periodic (that is, they vary in their length and do not occur at predictable intervals), they are recurrent (that is, they repeatedly occur in industrial economies). How well a particular theory is capable of accounting for the major stylized facts of the business cycle will be a principal means of evaluating that theory. As Abel and Bernanke (2001, p. 284) have argued, 'to be successful, a theory of the business cycle must explain the cyclical behaviour of not just a few variables, such as output and employment, but of a wide range of key economic variables'.

Business cycles have been a major feature of industrialized economies for the last 150 years. The textbook description of a typical business cycle highlights the phases of a business cycle, from trough through the expansionary phase to peak, followed by a turning point leading to a recessionary phase where aggregate economic activity contracts. Within this general cyclical pattern, what are the key business cycle 'stylized facts' which any viable macroeconomic theory must confront? Here we present only a brief summary of the research findings (for a more detailed discussion see Lucas, 1981a;

*Table 6.1   The 'stylized facts' of the business cycle*

| Variable | Direction | Timing |
|---|---|---|
| **Production** | | |
| Industrial production* | Procyclical | Coincident |
| **Expenditure** | | |
| Consumption | Procyclical | Coincident |
| Business fixed investment | Procyclical | Coincident |
| Residential investment | Procyclical | Leading |
| Inventory investment ** | Procyclical | Leading |
| Government purchases | Procyclical | Undesignated |
| **Labour market variables** | | |
| Employment | Procyclical | Coincident |
| Unemployment | Countercyclical | No clear pattern |
| Average labour productivity | Procyclical | Leading |
| Real wage | Procyclical | Undesignated |
| **Money supply and inflation** | | |
| Money supply | Procyclical | Leading |
| Inflation | Procyclical | Lagging |
| **Financial variables** | | |
| Stock prices | Procyclical | Leading |
| Nominal interest rates | Procyclical | Lagging |
| Real interest rates | Acyclical | Undesignated |

*Notes*:
\*    Durable goods industries are more volatile than non-durable goods and services.
\*\*   Investment expenditures are more volatile than consumption expenditures.

*Source*:   Abel and Bernanke (2001, p. 288).

Blanchard and Fischer, 1989; Zarnowitz, 1992a; Danthine and Donaldson, 1993; Simkins, 1994; Els, 1995; Abel and Bernanke, 2001; Ryan, 2002).

Within macroeconomics there is a great deal of controversy about the causes of aggregate fluctuations in economic activity. However, according to Abel and Bernanke (2001), there is a reasonable amount of agreement about the basic empirical business cycle facts. Even though no two business cycles are identical, they do tend to have many features in common. The main 'stylized facts', as summarized by Abel and Bernanke, are classified according to both direction and timing relative to the movement of GDP. With respect to the direction of movement, variables that move in the same direction (display positive correlation) as GDP are procyclical; variables that move in the opposite direction (display negative correlation) to GDP are countercyclical; variables that display no clear pattern (display zero correlation) are acyclical. With respect to timing, variables that move ahead of GDP are leading variables; variables that follow GDP are lagging variables; and variables that move at the same time as GDP are coincident variables.

Table 6.1 indicates that the main stylized facts, as set out by Abel and Bernanke (2001), show that output movements tend to be correlated across all sectors of the economy, and that industrial production, consumption and investment are procyclical and coincident. Government purchases also tend to be procyclical. Investment is much more volatile over the course of the business cycle than consumption, although spending on consumer durables is strongly procyclical. Employment is procyclical and unemployment countercyclical. The real wage and average labour productivity are procyclical, although the real wage is only slightly procyclical. The money supply and stock prices are procyclical and lead the cycle. Inflation (and by implication the price level) and nominal interest rates are procyclical and lagging while the real interest rate is acyclical. As we shall see, this 'agreement' about the stylized facts has implications for our assessment of the competing theories. However, deciding what are the 'facts' is certainly not uncontroversial (see Ryan and Mullineux, 1997; Ryan, 2002).

## 6.7 Real Business Cycle Theory

The modern new classical research programme starts from the position that 'growth and fluctuations are not distinct phenomena to be studied with separate data and different analytical tools' (Cooley, 1995). The REBCT research programme was initiated by Kydland and Prescott (1982), who in effect took up the challenge posed by Lucas (1980a) to build an artificial imitation economy capable of imitating the main features of actual economies. The artificial economy consists of optimizing agents acting in a frictionless perfectly competitive environment that is subject to repeated shocks to productivity. Although the second phase of new classical macroeconomics has switched emphasis away from monetary explanations of the business cycle, the more recently developed equilibrium models have retained and refined the other new classical building blocks.

Following Frisch (1933) and Lucas (1975, 1977), real business cycle theorists distinguish between *impulse* and *propagation* mechanisms. An impulse mechanism is the initial shock which causes a variable to deviate from its steady state value. A propagation mechanism consists of those forces which carry the effects of the shock forward through time and cause the deviation from the steady state to persist. The more recent brand of new classical equilibrium theories have the following general features (Stadler, 1994):

1.  REBCT utilizes a representative agent framework where the agent/household/firm aims to maximize their utility or profits, subject to prevailing resource constraints.
2.  Agents form expectations rationally and do not suffer informational asymmetries. While expected prices are equal to actual prices, agents may still face a signal extraction problem in deciding whether or not a particular productivity shock is temporary or permanent.
3.  Price flexibility ensures continuous market clearing so that equilibrium always prevails. There are no frictions or transaction costs.
4.  Fluctuations in aggregate output and employment are driven by large random changes in the available production technology. Exogenous shocks to technology act as the impulse mechanism in these models.
5.  A variety of propagation mechanisms carry forward the impact of the initial impulse. These include the effect of consumption smoothing, lags in the investment process ('time to build'), and intertemporal labour substitution.
6.  Fluctuations in employment reflect voluntary changes in the number of hours people choose to work. Work and leisure are assumed to be highly substitutable over time.
7.  Monetary policy is irrelevant, having no influence on real variables, that is, money is neutral.
8.  The distinction between the short run and the long run in the analysis of economic fluctuations and trends is abandoned.

It can be seen from the above that the major changes from MEBCT are with respect to: (i) the dominant impulse factor, with technological shocks replacing monetary shocks; (ii) the abandonment of the emphasis given to imperfect information as regards the general price level which played such a crucial role in the earlier monetary misperception models inspired by Lucas; and (iii) the breaking down of the short-run/long-run dichotomy in macroeconomic analysis by integrating the theory of growth with the theory of fluctuations. The lack of clear supporting evidence from econometric work on the causal role of money in economic fluctuations was generally interpreted as providing a strong case for shifting the direction of research towards models where real forces play a crucial role. As we have already seen, this case was further strengthened by the findings of Nelson and Plosser (1982) that most macroeconomic time series are better described as a random walk, rather than as fluctuations or deviations from deterministic trends. Real business cycle theorists also claim that their theories provide a better explanation of the 'stylized facts' which characterize aggregate fluctuations. Indeed, they have challenged much of the conventional wisdom with respect to what are the stylized facts (see section 6.14 below).

## 6.8 The Structure of a Real Business Cycle Model

In the typical real business cycle model, aggregate output of a single good, which can be used for both consumption or investment purposes, is produced according to a constant returns to scale neoclassical production function shown by equation (6.3):

$$Y_t = A_t F(K_t, L_t) \qquad (6.3)$$

where $K_t$ is the capital stock, $L_t$ is the labour input, and $A_t$ represents a stochastic productivity shift factor (shocks to technology or total factor productivity = TFP). The evolution of the technology parameter, $A_t$, is random and takes the form shown in equation (6.4):

$$A_{t+1} = \rho A_t + \varepsilon_{t+1}, \quad \text{where } 0 < \rho < 1, \qquad (6.4)$$

Here $\rho$ is large but less than 1, and $\varepsilon$ is a random disturbance to technology. Equation (6.4) tells us that the level of technology in any given period depends on the level prevailing in the previous period plus a random disturbance (Kydland and Prescott, 1996). In real business cycle models it is usually assumed that the typical economy is populated by identical individuals. This allows group behaviour to be explained by the behaviour of a representative agent (Plosser, 1989; Hartley, 1997). The representative agent's utility function takes the general form given by (6.5):

$$U_t = f(C_t, Le_t), \text{ where } f'(C_t) > 0, \text{ and } f'(Le_t) > 0 \qquad (6.5)$$

Here $C_t$ is units of consumption and $Le_t$ hours of leisure for our representative agent. It is assumed that the objective function of the representative agent

(Robinson Crusoe) is to maximize the expected discounted sum of their current and future utility over an infinite time horizon. This maximization problem is given by equation (6.6):

$$U_t = \max E_t \left\{ \sum_{j=0}^{\infty} \beta^{t+j} u \left[ C_{t+j}, 1 - L_{t-j} \right] | \Omega_t \right\}, \quad 1 > \beta > 0 \qquad (6.6)$$

where $C_t$ is the representative agent's level of consumption, $L_t$ is the number of hours of work, $1 - L_t$ is the hours of leisure consumed, $E_t \{\cdot\}$ is the mathematical expectations operator, $\Omega_t$ is the information set on which expectations are based, and $\beta$ is the representative agent's discount factor. Equation (6.6) provides a specification of a representative agent's willingness to substitute consumption for leisure. Thus the choice problem for the representative agent is how to maximize their lifetime (infinite) utility subject to resource constraints shown in equations (6.7) and (6.8):

$$C_t + I_t, \leq A_t F(K_t, L_t) \qquad (6.7)$$

$$L_t + Le_t \leq 1 \qquad (6.8)$$

Equation (6.7) indicates that the total amount of consumption ($C_t$) plus investment ($I_t$) cannot exceed production ($Y_t$), and equation (6.8) limits the total number of hours available to a maximum of 1. The evolution of the capital stock depends on current investment (= saving) and the rate of depreciation, $\delta$, as given in equation (6.9):

$$K_{t+1} = (1 - \delta)K_t + I_t \qquad (6.9)$$

In this setting a disturbance to the productivity shift factor $A_t$ (technological shock) will result in a dynamic response from the utility-maximizing representative agent such that we will observe variations in output, hours worked, consumption and investment over many periods.

To illustrate how a 'business cycle' can occur in a world without money or financial institutions, let us take the extreme case of Robinson Crusoe on a desert island. Suppose an exogenous shock occurs (a change in $A_t$ in equation 6.3), raising Robinson Crusoe's productivity. In this particular example we can think in terms of an unusual improvement in the weather compared to what Crusoe has been used to over the previous years. With the same number of hours worked Crusoe can now produce much more output given the more favourable weather. Because Crusoe is concerned about consumption in the future as well as the present (see equation 6.6), it is likely that he will choose to reduce current leisure and work more hours in the current period; that is, Crusoe will engage in intertemporal labour substitution.

The incentive to save and work longer hours will be especially strong if Crusoe believes the shock (better-than-normal weather) is likely to be short-lived. Because some of the increase in output is saved and invested, according to equation (6.9), the capital stock will be higher in the next period, and all future periods. This means that the impact of even a temporary shock on output is carried forward into the future. Moreover, the response of the representative agent to the economic shock is optimal, so that Crusoe's economy exhibits dynamic Pareto efficiency. When the weather returns to normal the following year Crusoe reverts to his normal working pattern and output declines, although it is now higher than was the case before the shock. Remember, Crusoe now has a higher capital stock due to the accumulation that took place during the previous year. As Plosser (1989) argues, the outcomes we observe in response to a shock are ones *chosen* by the representative agent. Therefore the social planner should in no way attempt to enforce a different outcome via interventionist policies. Note that throughout this hypothetical example we have just witnessed a fluctuation of output (a business cycle) on Crusoe's island induced entirely by a supply-side shock and Crusoe's optimal response to that shock. At no time did money or financial variables play any part.

In the Crusoe story we noted how our representative agent engaged in intertemporal labour substitution when the price of leisure increased (in terms of lost potential current output) due to more favourable weather. According to real business cycle theorists, the large response of the labour supply to small changes in the real wage, resulting from the intertemporal substitution of labour, acts as a powerful propagation mechanism. According to this hypothesis, first introduced by Lucas and Rapping (1969), households shift their labour supply over time, being more willing to work when real wages are temporarily high and working fewer hours when real wages are temporarily low. Why should this be the case?

Since the aggregate supply of labour depends on the labour supply decisions of individuals, we need to consider the various factors which influence the amount of labour individuals choose to supply. The benefits of current employment relate primarily (but obviously not entirely) to the income earned which allows the individual worker to consume goods and services. In order to earn income, workers will need to allocate less of their time to leisure, a term used to encapsulate all non-income-producing activities. The utility function for the representative worker indicates that consumption and leisure both yield utility. But in making their labour supply decisions workers will consider future as well as current consumption and leisure. In taking into account the future when deciding how much labour to supply in the current period, workers will need to consider how much the current real wage offers are above or below the norm. The substitution effect of a higher real wage offer will tend to increase the quantity of labour supplied. However, since higher real wages also make workers feel wealthier, this will tend to suppress the supply of labour. This wealth or income effect works in the opposite direction to the substitution effect. The impact of an increase in the current real wage on the amount of labour supplied will clearly depend on which of the above effects predominates. Real business cycle theorists distinguish between permanent and temporary changes in the real wage in order to analyse how rational maximizing individuals respond over time to changes in their economic circumstances that are brought about by technological shocks. The intertemporal labour substitution hypothesis suggests two things. First, if a technological shock is transitory, so that the current above-normal real wage offers are temporary, workers will 'make hay while the sun shines' and substitute work for current leisure. Less work will be offered in the future when the real wage is expected to be lower and hence the decision to supply more labour now is also a decision to consume more leisure in the future and less leisure now. Therefore real business cycle theory predicts a large supply response from temporary changes in the real wage. Permanent technological shocks, by raising the future real wage, induce wealth effects which will tend to lower the current labour supply.

Second, some theorists have stressed the importance of real interest rates on labour supply in flexible price models (see Barro, 1981, 1993). An increase in the real interest rate encourages households to supply more labour in the current period, since the value of income earned from working today relative to tomorrow has risen. This effect would show up as a shift of the labour supply curve to the right.

We can therefore express the general form of the labour supply function in the real business cycle model as equation (6.10), where $r$ = real interest rate:

$$S_L = S_L(W/P, r) \qquad (6.10)$$

The appropriate intertemporal relative price (IRP) is given by (6.11):

$$IRP = (1 + r)(W/P)_1/(W/P)_2 \qquad (6.11)$$

According to (6.11) any shocks to the economy that cause either the real interest rate to rise or the current real wage $(W/P)_1$ to be temporarily high relative to the future real wage $(W/P)_2$, will increase labour supply and hence employment.

## 6.9 Technology shocks

Although some versions of real business cycle theory allow for real demand shocks, such as changes in preferences or government expenditures, to act as the impulse mechanism, these models are more typically driven by exogenous productivity shocks. These stochastic fluctuations in factor productivity are the result of large random variations in the rate of technological change. The conventional Solow neoclassical growth model postulates that the growth of output per worker over prolonged periods depends on technological progress which is assumed to take place smoothly over time. Real business cycle theorists reject this view and emphasize the erratic nature of technological change which they regard as the major cause of changes in aggregate output.

To see how aggregate output and employment vary in a real business cycle model, consider Figure 6.3. Panel (a) of Figure 6.3 illustrates the impact of a beneficial technology shock, which shifts the production function from $Y$ to $Y^*$. The impact of this shift on the marginal product of labour and hence the demand for labour is shown in panel (b). By increasing the demand for labour a productivity shock raises employment as well as output. How much employment expands will depend on the elasticity of labour supply with respect to the current real wage. The 'stylized facts' of the business cycle indicate that small procyclical variations in the real wage are associated with large procyclical variations of employment. Thus a crucial requirement for real business cycle theory to be consistent with these facts is for the labour supply schedule to be highly elastic with respect to the real wage, as indicated in panel (b) by $S_{L2}$. In this case a technology shock will cause output to expand from $Y_0$ to $Y_2$ with the real wage increasing from $(W/P)_a$ to $(W/P)_c$, and employment increasing from $L_0$ to $L_2$. If the labour supply schedule is relatively inelastic, as shown by $S_{L1}$, large variations of the real wage and small changes in employment would result from a technology shock. However, this does not fit the stylized facts.

It is clear that, in order for real business cycle theories to explain the substantial variations in employment observed during aggregate fluctuations, there must be significant intertemporal substitution of leisure. Since in these models it is assumed that prices and wages are completely flexible, the labour market is always in equilibrium. In such a framework workers *choose* unemployment or employment in accordance with their preferences and the opportunities that are available. To many economists, especially to those with a Keynesian orientation, this explanation of labour market phenomena remains unconvincing (Mankiw, 1989; Tobin, 1996).

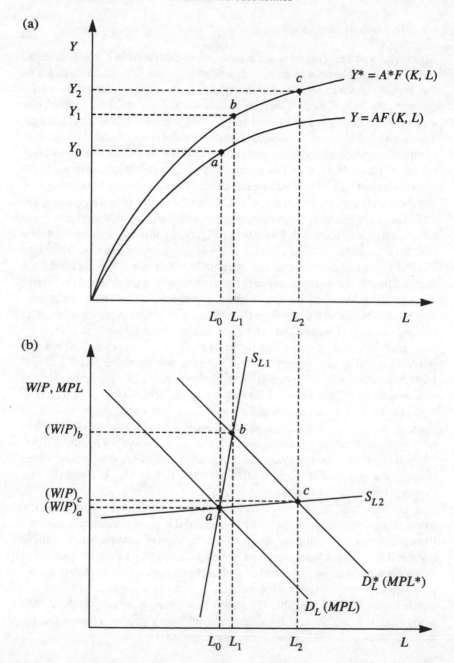

*Figure 6.3    Output and employment fluctuations due to a technology shock*

## 6.10 A Real Business Cycle Aggregate Demand and Supply Model

The model presented above to illustrate the impact of a technology shock is incomplete because it neglects the impact of supply shocks on the real rate of interest. In this section we present a more complete 'real aggregate demand and supply' model to illustrate the impact of technology shocks that does include the influence of changes in the real interest rate on the supply of labour as specified in the intertemporal labour substitution hypothesis. However, in this example we will ignore the impact that a technology shock may have on real aggregate demand via wealth effects.

In a world of rational expectations, perfect price flexibility and full information relating to the money supply, the neutrality of money is guaranteed. Since nominal variables do not influence real variables, output and employment are entirely determined by the real forces which underlie the production function and supply of factors of production. An IS–LM model which conforms to such a world is shown in Figure 6.4. The *IS* curve shows that real aggregate demand (*RAD*) is a declining function of the real interest rate. The *LM/P* curve will always shift so as to intersect the *IS* curve at the full employment level of output, providing prices are perfectly flexible. The position of the real aggregate supply curve (*RAS*) is determined by the position of the production function and the willingness of workers to supply labour (see Figure 6.3). A technology

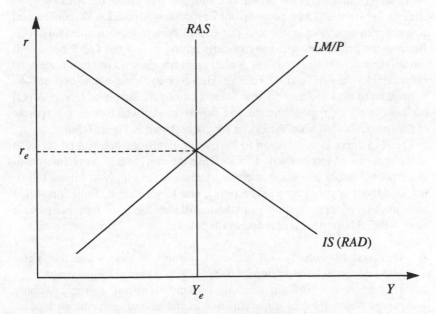

*Figure 6.4   The IS–LM model with flexible prices*

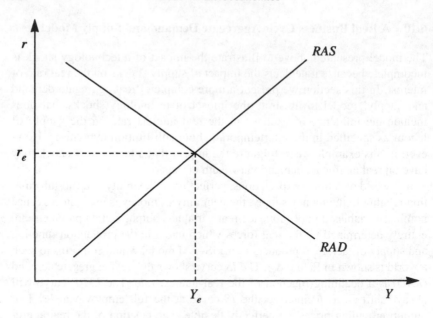

*Figure 6.5   The real business cycle aggregate demand and supply model*

improvement that shifts the production function will cause the *RAS* curve to
shift to the right and any point on *RAS* represents a position of equilibrium
(full) employment; that is, the *RAS* curve is a labour market equilibrium curve.
Because the price level will automatically adjust so that the *LM/P* curve will
always intersect the *RAD* curve at the full employment level of output, we need
only consider the *RAD* and *RAS* curves. However, in Figure 6.4 no account has
been taken of the impact of the real interest rate on the supply of labour. A real
business cycle aggregate demand and supply model which does incorporate
real interest rate effects on the labour supply is shown in Figure 6.5.

   The *RAS* curve is now shown to have a positive slope because an increase
in the real rate of interest will also increase the current real wage relative to
the expected future real wage, thereby increasing the supply of labour (shifting the labour supply curve to the right), and hence output. Equation (6.11)
indicates that the current supply of labour will increase if the real interest rate
rises. Several important points are worth noting:

1.   This model is entirely real, since the quantity of money and the aggre-
     gate price level have no impact on aggregate output or employment.
2.   The distinction between the long-run and short-run aggregate supply
     curves which play an important role in monetarist, early new classical
     and new Keynesian models is abandoned.

3. The RAS schedule traces out a range of equilibrium positions which are all consistent with 'full employment'.
4. The assumption of price flexibility allows the real interest rate to equilibrate the goods market, so that $RAD = RAS$.
5. In explaining fluctuations in output, real business cycle theorists have emphasized shifts of the $RAS$ curve due to technological shocks (see Kydland and Prescott, 1982; Plosser, 1989).
6. Some equilibrium theorists have shown that real aggregate demand shocks can also be important during some periods as an explanation of aggregate fluctuations. For example, Barro has shown how a temporary increase in government expenditure can cause output to expand (see Barro, 1993, chap. 12). He concludes that 'variations in government purchases play a major role during wartime but not in peacetime business fluctuations' (see below, Figure 6.7).

In Figure 6.6 we illustrate the impact of a favourable technology shock, taking into account the impact of such a shock on real output ($Y$), the real rate of interest ($r$), and the real wage ($W/P$). In Figure 6.6 we re-label the $RAD$ and $RAS$ curves as $Cd$ and $Ys$ respectively. The initial equilibrium position is at point $a$ in all four quadrants of Figure 6.6. A favourable technology shock shifts the $Ys$ curve from $Ys_1$ to $Ys_2$ in quadrant (d) and the production function up from $AF(K,L)$ to $A^*F(K,L)$ in quadrant (b). A favourable technology shock increases the marginal productivity of labour, thereby shifting the labour demand curve ($D_L$) to the right in quadrant (a); that is, from $D_{L1}$ to $D_{L2}$. However, the labour supply curve also shifts from $S_{L1}$ to $S_{L2}$ in quadrant (a), this decrease in labour supply being a rational intertemporal response to the fall in the real interest rate (from $r_1$ to $r_2$). The new equilibrium taking into account all of these effects is given by point $b$ in all four quadrants of Figure 6.6. Thus a favourable technology shock increases real output (from $Y_1$ to $Y_2$), lowers the real rate of interest (from $r_1$ to $r_2$), increases labour productivity and the real wage (from $(W/P)_1$ to $(W/P)_2$). That is, the real wage and labour productivity are procyclical, as the stylized facts suggest.

Figure 6.7 shows the likely impact of an increase in government purchases. As before the initial equilibrium position is at point $a$ in all four quadrants of Figure 6.7. An increase in government purchases shifts the real aggregate demand curve from $Cd_1$ to $Cd_2$. In this case real output increases (from $Y_1$ to $Y_2$), the real rate of interest rises (from $r_1$ to $r_2$) and the real wage falls (from $(W/P)_1$ to $(W/P)_2$) in response to an increase in labour supply, with the labour supply curve shifting from $S_{L1}$ to $S_{L2}$ in quadrant (a). The new equilibrium taking into account all of these effects is given by point $b$ in all four quadrants of Figure 6.7. In the old classical model aggregate supply is perfectly inelastic, as in Figure 6.4, and an increase in government purchases has no

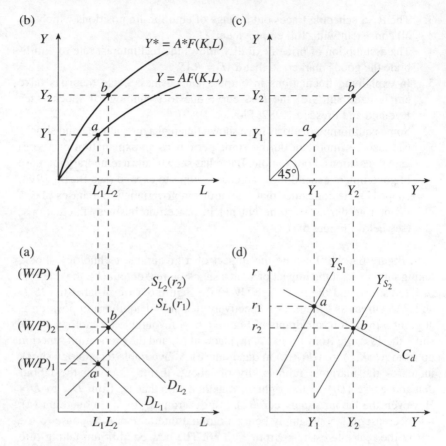

*Figure 6.6   The impact of a technology shock*

effect on real output. In contrast, in REBCT, an increase in government purchases leads to an increase in real output because the induced rise in the real rate of interest encourages an increase in labour supply, thereby increasing employment and real output.

Finally, we can use the *Cd–Ys* model to examine the impact of temporary v. permanent technology shocks. In this case we simply reproduce the *Cd–Ys* diagram on its own, but we also allow for possible wealth effects on the *Cd* curve.

Figure 6.8 represents the basic market-clearing diagram which is central to the modern new classical equilibrium approach to macroeconomic analysis. Following Barro (1993), the market-clearing condition is given by (6.12):

$$Cd(r, \ldots) = Ys(r, \ldots) \qquad (6.12)$$

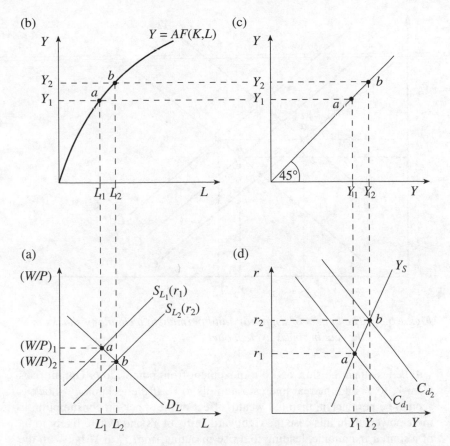

*Figure 6.7  The impact of a government expenditure shock*

In equation (6.12) variables omitted and indicated by ... include the various wealth and substitution effects which result from shocks to the production function or government expenditure and so on. The response of *Cd* and *Ys* to changes in the real rate of interest is illustrated by movements *along* the aggregate demand and supply curves. The *Cd* and *Ys* curves will *shift* if any of the other variables which influence *Cd* and *Ys* change, as with a shock to the production function or an increase in government expenditure.

To see how a technology shock will influence aggregate output in this model, consider Figure 6.8, where, starting from point *a*, we assume a beneficial technology change takes place of the type considered in Figure 6.3. Such a shock will clearly shift the *Ys* curve to the right from $Ys_1$ to $Ys^*$. If the technology shock is seen to be temporary, the impact on consumer demand of the wealth effect is likely to be small and the resultant rightward shift of *Cd*

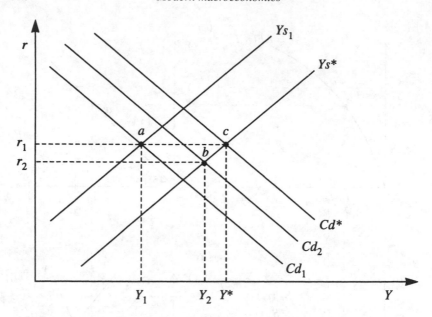

*Figure 6.8    The impact of temporary and permanent technology shocks in
the real business cycle model*

will be less than the shift of $Ys$: a movement from point $a$ to $b$. Output rises
from $Y_1$ to $Y_2$ and the real interest rate falls to $r_2$. If the technology shock is
seen to be permanent, then the wealth effect of the shock on consumption is
more powerful. In this case the rightward shifts of $Ys$ and $Cd$ are likely to be
of a similar magnitude, leading to a rise in output from $Y_1$ to $Y^*$ but with the
real interest rate remaining at $r_1$: a movement from point $a$ to $c$. According to
Barro, this model does reasonably well in accounting for the stylized facts of
business fluctuations. For a detailed discussion of these issues, see Barro
(1993), especially pp. 232–41.

## 6.11   Calibrating the Model

It was Kydland and Prescott (1982) who first demonstrated that a general
equilibrium real business cycle model, driven by exogenous technological
shocks, was capable of generating time series data that possessed the statistical properties of US business cycles over the period 1950–79. However,
real business cycle theorists have not generally attempted to provide models capable of conventional econometric testing but have instead tended to
focus on providing numerical examples of a more general theory of
fluctuations. In order to examine the quantitative implications of their mod-

els, real business cycle theorists have developed a method known as 'calibration' or 'computational experiments'. Cooley (1997) defines calibration as 'a strategy for finding numerical values for the parameters of artificial economies' and involves a 'symbiotic relationship between theory and measurement'. The calibration strategy consists of the following steps (see Kydland and Prescott, 1982, 1991, 1996; Plosser, 1989; Backhouse, 1997b; Abel and Bernanke, 2001):

1. Pose a question relating to a specific issue of concern, for example an important policy issue such as 'What is the quantitative nature of fluctuations caused by technology shocks?'
2. Use a 'well-tested' theory, where 'theory' is interpreted as a specific set of instructions about how to build the imitation economy.
3. Construct a model economy and select functional forms. Kydland and Prescott (1982) utilize the basic stochastic neoclassical growth model as the cornerstone of their model.
4. Provide specific algebraic forms of the functions used to represent production and consumption decisions. For example, a specific Cobb–Douglas production function is used by Plosser (1989).
5. Calibrate the model economy using data from pre-existing microeconomic studies and knowledge of the 'stylized facts'. Where no information exists select values for parameters so that the model is capable of mimicking the real-world behaviour of variables.
6. The calibration exercise then involves simulating the effect of subjecting the model to a series of random technology shocks using a computer.
7. The impact that these shocks have on the key macroeconomic variables is then traced out so that the results can be compared with the actual behaviour of the main macroeconomic time series.
8. Run the experiment and compare the equilibrium path of the model economy with the behaviour of the actual economy. Use these types of simulations to answer questions relating to the important issues initially identified under (1).

In their seminal 1982 paper Kydland and Prescott use the neoclassical growth model and follow the calibration/simulation procedure to see if the model can explain aggregate fluctuations when the model economy is subject to technology shocks. As Prescott (1986) recalls, 'the finding that when uncertainty in the rate of technological change is incorporated into the growth model it displays business cycle phenomena was both dramatic and unanticipated'. The simulations carried out by Kydland, Prescott and Plosser produced some impressive results in that their models are able to mimic an actual economy with respect to some important time series data. These simulations indicate that a competitive economy hit by repeated technology shocks can exhibit the kind of fluctuations that are actually observed.

On the negative side, one of the problems with calibration is that it currently does not provide a method that allows one to judge between the performance of real and other (for example Keynesian) business cycle models. As Hoover (1995b) notes, 'the calibration methodology, to date, lacks any discipline as stern as that imposed by econometric methods … Above all, it is not clear on what standards competing, but contradictory, models are to be compared and adjudicated.' Nevertheless calibration has provided an important new contribution to the methodology of empirical macroeconomic research. While initially the calibration methodology was focused on business cycle research, more recently calibrated models have been used to investigate issues in public finance, economic growth, industry, firm and plant dynamics and questions related to the choice of economic policy (Cooley, 1997). For more detailed discussions and critiques of the calibration methodology see Kydland and Prescott (1991, 1996); Summers (1991a); Quah (1995); Hoover (1995b); Wickens (1995); Hansen and Heckman (1996); Sims (1996); Cooley (1997); Hartley et al. (1998).

### 6.12 Real Business Cycle Theory and the Neutrality of Money

Real business cycle theorists claim that recent research relating to the stylized facts of the business cycle support the general predictions of 'real' as opposed to 'monetary' theories of fluctuations. But, as we noted earlier, the correlation between money and output is an accepted stylized fact. How do real business cycle theories deal with the apparent causal influence of money?

Monetary neutrality is an important property of real business cycle models. In such models neutrality applies to the short run as well as the long run. In the late 1970s, leading representatives from the other major schools of thought, such as Tobin, Friedman and Lucas, all agreed that the rate of growth of the money supply has real effects on the economy and plays an important role in any explanation of output fluctuations. There was of course considerable disagreement on the nature and strength of the relationship between money and output and on the relative power of monetary and fiscal policy, but economists of all persuasions took it for granted that monetary phenomena were crucial to business cycle research. The accepted business cycle stylized fact that money and output exhibit positive correlation, with money leading output, was taken by many as strong evidence of causality running from money to output (Sims, 1972). The research of Friedman and Schwartz (1963, 1982) added further weight to the monetarist claim that monetary instability lies at the heart of real instability. However, the well-established positive association between money and aggregate output may simply indicate that the money supply is responding to economic activity rather than the reverse. In such a situation money is endogenous and the money-to-output correlations that we observe are evidence of reverse causation; that is, expectations of future output expansion lead to current increases in the money supply. According to real business cycle theories, the demand for money expands during business expansions and elicits an accommodating response from the money supply, especially if the monetary authorities are targeting interest rates (see Barro, 1993, chap. 18). The impetus to downgrade the causal role of money was also given support from the evidence emerging from vector autoregression analysis which indicated that, once interest rates were included among the variables in the estimated system, money ceased to have strong predictive power. The contributions from Sims (1980, 1983) and Litterman and Weiss (1985) provided important evidence which advocates of the real business cycle approach point to in support of their preference for a non-monetary approach to business cycle modelling (see also Eichenbaum and Singleton, 1986).

Initially real business cycle models were constructed without monetary features. Kydland and Prescott (1982) originally set out to construct a model which included only real variables but which could then be extended to take into account nominal variables. But after building their real model Kydland and Prescott concluded that the addition of a monetary sector may not be necessary since business cycles can be explained almost entirely by real quantities (see Prescott, 1986). Although the Long and Plosser (1983) model contains no monetary sector, King and Plosser (1984) explain the historical association between money and output as reflecting an endogenous response of money to output. Building on the work of Black (1987) and Fama (1980), King and Plosser reject the orthodox monetarist interpretation of money-to-output causality. In their model, 'monetary services are privately produced intermediate goods whose quantities rise and fall with real economic developments'. King and Plosser view the financial industry as providing a flow of accounting services that help to facilitate market transactions. By grafting a financial sector on to a general equilibrium model of production and consumption, King and Plosser show how a positive correlation between real production, credit and transaction services will arise with the timing paths in these co-movements dependent on the source of the variation in real output. Their model implies that the volume of *inside* money (bank deposits) will vary positively with output. Furthermore, the fact that financial services can be produced more rapidly than the final product means that an expansion of financial services is likely to occur before the expansion of output. The stock of bank deposits is therefore highly correlated with output and a leading indicator in the business cycle.

The money–output correlation noted above corresponds with the evidence presented by Friedman and Schwartz (1963) but from an entirely different perspective. Whereas in monetarist models exogenous changes in the quantity of money play an important role in causing movements in output, King and Plosser stress the endogenous response of deposits to planned movements in output. In effect the output of the financial sector moves in line with the output of other sectors. However, by the end of the 1980s, despite the progress made by REBCT in explaining the money–output correlation, Plosser's (1989) view was that 'the role of money in an equilibrium theory of growth and fluctuations is not well understood and thus remains an open issue'.

Paradoxically the REBCT argument that money is endogenous is also a major proposition of the Post Keynesian school (see Kaldor, 1970a; Davidson, 1994). For example, with respect to this very issue of money-to-output causality, Joan Robinson (1971) suggested that the correlations could be explained 'in quantity theory terms if the equation were read right-handed. Thus we might suggest that a marked rise in the level of activity is likely to be preceded by an increase in the supply of money.' In an unholy alliance, both Post Keynesian and real business cycle theorists appear to agree with Robinson that the quantity theory equation ($MV = PY$) should be read in causal terms from right to left. Orthodox Keynesians have also raised the issue of timing in questioning money-to-output causality. Tobin (1970) showed how an ultra-Keynesian model could be constructed where the money supply is an endogenous response to income changes. In this model changes in real economic activity are preceded by expansions of the money supply as firms borrow funds from the banking sector in order to finance their planned expansions. Tobin demonstrated that to infer from the timing evidence that changes in the money supply are causing changes in real economic activity was to fall foul of the *post hoc ergo propter hoc* (after this therefore because of this) fallacy. However, although Tobin used this argument to challenge what he considered to be the exaggerated claims of monetarists relating to the power of monetary forces, he certainly did not conclude that money does not matter for business fluctuations (see also Cagan, 1993).

Kydland and Prescott (1990) have questioned the whole basis of this debate on timing and causality by rejecting one of the 'established' stylized facts of the business cycle relating to monetary aggregates. They argue that 'there is no evidence that either the monetary base or M1 leads the cycle although some economists still believe this monetary myth'. Clearly such claims represent a serious challenge to conventional views concerning the role of money. This 'blasphemy' has been rejected by Keynesian and monetarist economists alike who, as a result of real business cycle analysis, have been thrown into an alliance which would have seemed unthinkable during the intense debates that took place between Tobin and Friedman during the 1960s and early 1970s. (For a defence of the earlier Friedman and Schwartz research, see Schwartz, 1992.)

## 6.13 Measuring Technology Shocks: The Solow Residual

If technology shocks are the primary cause of business cycles, then it is important to identify and measure the rate of technological progress. Given the
structure of real business cycle models, the key parameter is the variance of the
technology shock. Prescott (1986) suggests that Solow's method of measuring
this variance is an acceptable and reasonable approach. Solow's (1957) technique was to define technological change as changes in aggregate output minus
the sum of the weighted contributions of the labour and capital inputs. In short,
the Solow residual measures that part of a change in aggregate output which
cannot be explained by changes in the measurable quantities of capital and
labour inputs. The derivation of the Solow residual can be shown as follows.
The aggregate production function in equation (6.13) shows that output ($Y$) is
dependent on the inputs of capital ($K$), labour ($L$) and the currently available
technology ($A$) which acts as an index of total factor productivity:

$$Y = AF(K,L) \tag{6.13}$$

Output will change if $A$, $K$ or $L$ change. One specific type of production
function frequently used in empirical studies relating to growth accounting is
the Cobb–Douglas production function, which is written as follows:

$$Y = AK^\delta L^{1-\delta}, \quad \text{where } 0 < \delta < 1 \tag{6.14}$$

In equation (6.14) the exponent on the capital stock $\delta$ measures the elasticity of
output with respect to capital and the exponent on the labour input $(1 - \delta)$
measures the elasticity of output with respect to labour. The weights $\delta$ and $1 - \delta$
measure the income shares of capital and labour, respectively (see Dornbusch
et al., 2004, pp. 54–8 for a simple derivation). Since these weights sum to unity
this indicates that this is a constant returns to scale production function. Hence
an equal percentage increase in both factor inputs ($K$ and $L$) will increase $Y$ by
the same percentage. By rearranging equation (6.14) we can represent the
productivity index which we need to measure as equation (6.15):

$$\text{Solow residual} = A = \frac{Y}{K^\delta L^{1-\delta}} \tag{6.15}$$

Because there is no direct way of measuring $A$, it has to be estimated as a
residual. Data relating to output and the capital and labour inputs are available. Estimates of $\delta$ and hence $1 - \delta$ can be acquired from historical data.
Since the growth rate of the product of the inputs will be the growth rate of $A$
plus the growth rate of $K^\delta$ plus the growth rate of $L^{1-\delta}$, equation (6.15) can be

rewritten as (6.16), which is the basic growth accounting equation that has been used in numerous empirical studies of the sources of economic growth (see Denison, 1985; Maddison, 1987).

$$\frac{\Delta Y}{Y} = \frac{\Delta A}{A} + \delta \frac{\Delta K}{K} + (1 - \delta)\frac{\Delta L}{L} \qquad (6.16)$$

Equation (6.16) is simply the Cobb–Douglas production function written in a form representing rates of change. It shows that the growth of output ($\Delta Y/Y$) depends on the contribution of changes in total factor productivity ($\Delta A/A$), changes in the weighted contribution of capital ($\delta \Delta K/K$) and changes in the weighted contribution of labour $(1 - \delta)(\Delta L/L)$. By writing down equation (6.15) in terms of rates of change or by rearranging equation (6.16), which amounts to the same thing, we can obtain an equation from which the growth of total factor productivity (technology change) can be estimated as a residual. This is shown in equation (6.17).

$$\frac{\Delta A}{A} = \frac{\Delta Y}{Y} - \left[\delta \frac{\Delta K}{K} + (1 - \delta)\frac{\Delta L}{L}\right] \qquad (6.17)$$

In equation (6.17) the Solow residual equals $\Delta A/A$. Real business cycle theorists have used estimates of the Solow residual as a measure of technological progress. Prescott's (1986) analysis suggests that 'the process on the percentage change in the technology process is a random walk with drift plus some serially uncorrelated measurement error'. Plosser (1989) also argues that 'it seems acceptable to view the level of productivity as a random walk'. Figure 6.9 reproduces Plosser's estimates for the annual growth rates of technology and output for the period 1955–85 in the USA. These findings appear to support the real business cycle view that aggregate fluctuations are induced, in the main, by technological disturbances. In a later study, Kydland and Prescott (1991) found that about 70 per cent of the variance in US output in the post-war period can be accounted for by variations in the Solow residual. We will consider criticisms of the work in this area in section 6.16 below. In particular, Keynesians offer an alternative explanation of the observed procyclical behaviour of productivity.

## 6.14 Real Business Cycle Theory and the Stylized Facts

The rapidly expanding business cycle literature during the 1980s provoked considerable controversy and discussion with respect to the ability of different macroeconomic models to explain the 'stylized facts'. As Danthine and Donaldson (1993) point out, the real business cycle programme 'has forced

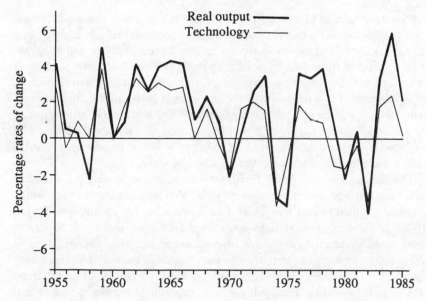

*Source*:   Plosser (1989).

*Figure 6.9    The annual growth rates of technology and output in the USA, 1955–85*

theorists to recognise how incomplete our knowledge of business cycle phenomena actually was', and a major achievement of this literature has been to 'free us to reconsider what we know about the business cycle'. Research in this area has called into question much of the conventional wisdom with respect to what are the established stylized facts. Controversy also exists over which model of the business cycle best explains the agreed stylized facts. For a detailed discussion of this debate, the reader is referred to Greenwald and Stiglitz (1988), Kydland and Prescott (1990), Hoover (1991), Blackburn and Ravn (1992), Smith (1992), Zarnowitz (1992b), Danthine and Donaldson (1993); Judd and Trehan (1995); Ryan and Mullineux (1997); and Ryan (2002). Here we will briefly discuss the controversy relating to the cyclical behaviour of real wages and prices.

In both orthodox Keynesian and monetarist macroeconomic theories where aggregate demand disturbances drive the business cycle, the real wage is predicted to be countercyclical. In Keynes's *General Theory* (1936, p. 17) an expansion of employment is associated with a decline in the real wage and the Keynesian models of the neoclassical synthesis era also assume that the economy is operating along the aggregate labour demand curve, so that the real wage must vary countercyclically.

Referring back to Figure 2.6 panel (b) in Chapter 2, we can see that for a given money wage $W_0$ the real wage must vary countercyclically as aggregate demand declines and the economy moves into a recession. The fall in aggregate demand is illustrated by a shift of the $AD$ curve from $AD_0$ to $AD_1$. If prices are flexible but nominal wages are rigid, the economy moves from $e_0$ to $e_1$ in panel (b). With a fall in the price level to $P_1$, and nominal wages remaining at $W_0$, the real wage increases to $W_0/P_1$ in panel (a) of Figure 2.6. At this real wage the supply of labour $(L_d)$ exceeds the demand for labour $(L_c)$ and involuntary unemployment of $cd$ emerges. With the money wage fixed, a falling price level implies a countercyclical real wage.

The theories associated with Friedman's monetarism, as well as some early new classical and new Keynesian models, also incorporate features which imply a countercyclical real wage (see Fischer, 1977; Phelps and Taylor, 1977). In Gordon's (1993) view, apart from the big oil shocks of the 1970s, there is no systematic movement of real wages but, if anything, 'there is slight tendency of prices to rise more than wages in booms, implying counter-cyclical real wages'. However, Kydland and Prescott (1990) find that the real wage behaves in a 'reasonably strong' procyclical manner, a finding that is consistent with shifts of the production function. The current consensus is that the real wage is mildly procyclical, and this poses problems for both traditional monetary explanations of the business cycle and real business cycle theory (see Fischer, 1988; Brandolini, 1995; Abraham and Haltiwanger, 1995; Snowdon and Vane, 1995). If the real wage is moderately procyclical, then shocks to the production function can significantly influence employment only if the labour supply curve is highly elastic (see panel (b) of Figure 6.3). However, the empirical evidence does not offer strong support for the significant intertemporal substitution required for real business cycles to mimic the large variations in employment which characterize business cycles (see Mankiw et al., 1985; Altonji, 1986; Nickell, 1990).

While the behaviour of the real wage over the cycle has been controversial ever since Dunlop (1938) and Tarshis (1939) debated this issue with Keynes (1939a), the assumption that prices (and inflation) are generally procyclical was accepted by economists of varying persuasions. The procyclical behaviour of prices is a fundamental feature of Keynesian, monetarist and the monetary misperception version of new classical models (Lucas, 1977). Mankiw (1989) has argued that, in the absence of recognizable supply shocks, such as the OPEC oil price rises in the 1970s, the procyclical behaviour of the inflation rate is a 'well documented fact'. Lucas (1977, 1981a) also lists the procyclical nature of prices and inflation as a basic stylized fact. In sharp contrast to these views, Kydland and Prescott (1990) show that, in the USA during the period 1954–89, 'the price level has displayed a clear *counter-cyclical* pattern'. This leads them to the following controversial conclusion:

'We caution that any theory in which procyclical prices figure crucially in accounting for postwar business cycle fluctuations is doomed to failure.' This conclusion is supported by Cooley and Ohanian (1991) and also in a study of UK data by Blackburn and Ravn (1992), who describe the conventional wisdom with respect to the procyclical behaviour of the price level as 'a fiction'. In their view the traditional presumption that prices are procyclical is overwhelmingly contradicted by the evidence and they interpret their findings as posing a 'serious challenge' for monetary explanations of the business cycle. The evidence presented by Backus and Kehoe (1992), Smith (1992) and Ravn and Sola (1995) is also supportive of the real business cycle view. (For a defence of the conventional view, see Chadha and Prasad, 1993.)

To see why evidence of a countercyclical price level is supportive of real business cycle models, consider Figure 6.10. Here we utilize the conventional aggregate demand and supply framework with the price level on the vertical axis. Because prices and wages are perfectly flexible, the aggregate supply curve (AS) is completely inelastic with respect to the price level (although it will shift to the right if technology improves or the real rate of interest increases, leading to an increase in labour supply and employment; see Jansen et al., 1994). The economy is initially operating at the intersection of AD and $AS_0$. If the economy is hit by a negative supply shock which shifts the AS curve from $AS_0$ to $AS_2$, the equilibrium level of output falls from $Y_0$ to $Y_2$ for a

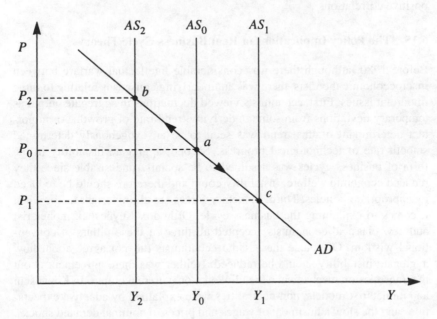

*Figure 6.10   Supply shocks and the price level*

given money supply. Aggregate demand and supply are brought into equilibrium by a rise in the price level from $P_0$ to $P_2$. A favourable supply shock which shifts the $AS$ curve from $AS_0$ to $AS_1$ will lead to a fall in the price level for a given money supply. The equilibrium positions $a$, $b$ and $c$ indicate that the price level will be countercyclical if real disturbances cause an aggregate supply curve to shift along a given aggregate demand curve. Referring back to panel (b) of Figure (2.6), it is clear that fluctuations brought about by shifts of the aggregate demand curve generate observations of a procyclical price level. Keynesians argue that the countercyclical behaviour of the price level following the clearly observable oil shocks of the 1970s does not present a problem for the conventional aggregate demand and supply model and that such effects had already been incorporated into their models by 1975 (see Gordon, 1975; Phelps, 1978; Blinder, 1988b). What Keynesians object to is the suggestion that the business cycle is *predominantly* caused by supply shocks. The consensus view that prices are sometimes procyclical and sometimes countercyclical indicates to an eclectic observer that both demand and supply shocks are important in different periods. Judd and Trehan (1995) also show that this debate is further complicated by the fact that the observed correlations between prices and output in response to various shocks reflect complex dynamic responses, and it is 'not difficult to find plausible patterns that associate either a demand or a supply shock with either negative or positive correlations'.

## 6.15 The Policy Implications of Real Business Cycle Theory

Before 1980, although there was considerable intellectual warfare between macroeconomic theorists, there was an underlying consensus relating to three important issues. First, economists viewed fluctuations in aggregate output as temporary deviations from some underlying trend rate of growth. An important determinant of this trend was seen to be an exogenously determined smooth rate of technological progress. Second, aggregate instability in the form of business cycles was assumed to be socially undesirable since they reduced economic welfare. Instability could and therefore should be reduced by appropriate policies. Third, monetary forces are an important factor when it comes to explaining the business cycle. Orthodox Keynesian, monetarist and new classical economists accepted all three of these pillars of conventional wisdom. Of course these same economists did not agree about how aggregate instability should be reduced. Neither was there agreement about the transmission mechanism which linked money to real output. In Keynesian and monetarist models, non-neutralities were explained by adaptive expectations and the slow adjustment of wages and prices to nominal demand shocks. In the new classical market-clearing models of the 1970s, non-neutralities were explained as a consequence of agents having imperfect information. When it came to policy discussions about how to stabilize the economy, monetarists and new classical economists favoured a fixed ($k$ per cent) monetary growth rate rule, whereas Keynesian economists argued in favour of discretion (see Modigliani, 1986; Tobin, 1996). The main impact of the first wave of new classical theory on policy analysis was to provide a more robust theoretical case against activism (see Kydland and Prescott, 1977). The political business cycle literature also questioned whether politicians could be trusted to use stabilization policy in order to reduce fluctuations, rather than as a means for maximizing their own interests (see Nordhaus, 1975 and Chapter 10).

During the 1980s everything changed. The work of Nelson and Plosser (1982) and Kydland and Prescott (1982) caused economists to start asking the question, 'Is there a business cycle?' Real business cycle theorists find the use of the term 'business cycle' unfortunate (Prescott, 1986) because it suggests there is a phenomenon to explain that is independent of the forces determining economic growth. Real business cycle theorists, by providing an integrated approach to growth and fluctuations, have shown that large fluctuations in output and employment over relatively short time periods are 'what standard neoclassical theory predicts'. Indeed, it 'would be a puzzle if the economy did not display large fluctuations in output and employment' (Prescott, 1986). Since instability is the outcome of rational economic agents responding optimally to changes in the economic environment, observed fluctuations should *not* be viewed as welfare-reducing deviations from some ideal trend path of output. In a competitive theory of fluctuations the equilibria are Pareto-optimal (see Long and Plosser, 1983; Plosser, 1989). The idea that the government should in any way attempt to reduce these fluctuations is therefore anathema to real business cycle theorists. Such policies are almost certain to reduce welfare. As Prescott (1986) has argued, 'the policy implication of this research is that costly efforts at stabilisation are likely to be counter-productive. Economic fluctuations are optimal responses to uncertainty in the rate of technological progress.' Business cycles trace out a path of GDP that reflects random fluctuations in technology. This turns conventional thinking about economic fluctuations completely on its head. If fluctuations are Pareto-efficient responses to shocks to the production function largely resulting from technological change, then monetary factors are no longer relevant in order to explain such instability; nor can monetary policy have any real effects. Money is neutral. Since workers can decide how much they want to work, observed unemployment is always voluntary. Indeed, the observed fluctuating path of GNP is nothing more than a continuously moving equilibrium. In real business cycle theory there can be no meaning to a stated government objective such as 'full employment' because the economy is already there! Of course the real business cycle view is that the government can do a great deal of harm if it creates various distortions through its taxing and spending policies. However, as we have already noted, in real business cycle models a temporary increase in government purchases will increase output and employment because the labour supply increases in response to the higher real interest rate brought about by higher (real) aggregate demand.

If technological change is the key factor in determining both growth and fluctuations, we certainly need to develop a better understanding of the factors which determine the rate of technological progress, including institutional structures and arrangements (see Chapter 11). To real business cycle theorists the emphasis given by Keynesian and monetarist economists to the issue of stabilization has been a costly mistake. In a dynamic world instability is as desirable as it is inevitable.

Finally, Chatterjee (1999) has pointed out that the emergence of REBCT is a legacy of successful countercyclical policies in the post-Second World War period. These policies, by successfully reducing the volatility of GDP due to aggregate demand disturbances compared to earlier periods, has allowed the impact of technological disturbances to emerge as a dominant source of modern business cycles.

### 6.16   Criticisms of Real Business Cycle Theory

In this section we will review some of the more important criticisms of real business cycle theory. For critical surveys of the literature, the reader is referred to Summers (1986), Hoover (1988), Sheffrin (1989), Mankiw (1989), McCallum (1989), Phelps (1990), Eichenbaum (1991), Stadler (1994), and Hartley et al. (1997, 1998).

The conventional neoclassical analysis of labour supply highlights two opposing effects of an increase in the real wage. A higher real wage induces an increase in labour supply through the substitution effect, but at the same time a higher real wage also has an income effect that induces a worker to consume more leisure. In real business cycle models the substitution effect must be very powerful compared to the income effect if these models are to plausibly explain large variations of employment induced by technology shocks. But, as we have already noted, the available micro evidence relating to the intertemporal elasticity of substitution in labour supply indicates a weak response to transitory wage changes. If the wage elasticity of labour supply is low, then technological shocks that shift the labour demand curve (see Figure 6.3) will produce large variability of real wages and lower variability of employment. However, the variations in employment observed over the business cycle seem to be too large to be accounted for by intertemporal substitution. In addition, Mankiw (1989) has argued that the real interest rate is not a significant consideration in labour supply decisions. How, for example, can agents be expected to accurately predict future interest rates and real wages in order to engage in intertemporal substitution?

A second major criticism of real business cycle theory relates to the reliance of these models on mainly unobservable technology shocks. Many economists doubt whether the technology shocks required in order to generate business cycle phenomena are either large enough or frequent enough. In these models large movements in output require significant aggregate disturbances to technology. Muellbauer (1997) argues that the kind of technological volatility implied by REBCT is 'quite implausible' for three reasons, namely: (i) technological diffusion tends to be slow; (ii) aggregation of diffusion processes tends to produce a smooth outcome in aggregate; and (iii) the technical regress required to produce recessions cannot be given plausible microfoundations. In relation to this issue, Summers (1986) rejects Prescott's use of variations in the Solow residual as evidence of significant shocks to technology. Large variations in the Solow residual can be explained as the outcome of 'off the production function behaviour' in the form of labour hoarding. Whereas real business cycle theorists interpret procyclical labour productivity as evidence of shifts in the production function, the traditional Keynesian explanation attributes this stylized fact to the quasi-fixity of the labour input. The reason why productivity falls in recessions is that firms retain more workers than they need, owing to short-run adjustment costs. In such circumstances it will pay firms to smooth the labour input over the cycle, which implies the hoarding of labour in a cyclical downturn. This explains why the percentage reduction in output typically exceeds the percentage reduction in the labour input during a recession. As the economy recovers, firms utilize their labour more intensively, so that output increases by a larger percentage than the labour input.

In general many economists explain the procyclical movement of the Solow residual by highlighting the underutilization of both capital and labour during periods of recession. Following Abel and Bernanke (2001), we can illustrate this idea by rewriting the production function given by (6.13) and (6.14) as (6.18):

$$Y = AF(\mu_K K, \mu_L L) = A(\mu_K K)^\delta (\mu_L L)^{1-\delta} \qquad (6.18)$$

where $\mu_K$ represents the underutilization rate of the capital input, and $\mu_L$ represents the underutilization rate of labour input. Substituting (6.18) for $Y$ in (6.15) we obtain a new expression (6.19) for the Solow residual that recognizes that the capital and labour inputs may be underutilized.

$$\text{Solow residual} = A(\mu_K K)^\delta (\mu_L L)^{1-\delta} / K^\delta L^{1-\delta} = A\mu_K^\delta \mu_L^{1-\delta} \qquad (6.19)$$

Equation (6.19) shows that the Solow residual can vary even if technology remains constant. If the utilization rates of capital and labour inputs are procyclical, as the empirical evidence suggests is the case, then we will observe a procyclical Solow residual that reflects this influence (for discussions of this issue see Fay and Medoff, 1985; Rotemberg and Summers, 1990; Bernanke and Parkinson, 1991; Burnside et al., 1995; Braun and Evans, 1998; Millard et al., 1997).

A third line of criticism relates to the idea of recessions being periods of technological regress. As Mankiw (1989, p. 85) notes, 'recessions are important events; they receive widespread attention from the policy-makers and the media. There is, however, no discussion of declines in the available technology. If society suffered some important adverse technological shock we would be aware of it.' In response to this line of criticism, Hansen and Prescott (1993) have widened the interpretation of technological shocks so that any 'changes in the production functions, or, more generally, the production possibility sets of the profit centres' can be regarded as a potential source of disturbance. In their analysis of the 1990–91 recession in the USA, they suggest that changes to the legal and institutional framework can alter the incentives to adopt certain technologies; for example, a barrage of government regulations could act as a negative technology shock. However, as Muellbauer (1997) points out, the severe recession in the UK in the early 1990s is easily explained as the consequence of a 'massive' rise in interest rates in 1988–9, an associated collapse of property prices, and UK membership, at an overvalued exchange rate, of the ERM after October 1990. Few of these influences play a role in REBCT.

An important fourth criticism relates to the issue of unemployment. In real business cycle models unemployment is either entirely absent or is voluntary. Critics find this argument unconvincing and point to the experience of the Great Depression, where 'it defies credulity to account for movements on this scale by pointing to intertemporal substitution and productivity shocks' (Summers, 1986). Carlin and Soskice (1990) argue that a large proportion of the European unemployment throughout the 1980s was involuntary and this represents an important stylized fact which cannot be explained within a new classical framework. Tobin (1980b) also questioned the general approach of new classical economists to treat all unemployment as voluntary. The critics point out that the pattern of labour market flows is inconsistent with equilibrium theorizing. If we could explain unemployment as the result of voluntary choice of economic agents, then we would not observe the well-established procyclical movement of vacancy rates and voluntary quits. Recessions are not periods where we observe an increase in rate of voluntary quits! In Blinder's view, the challenge posed by high unemployment during the 1980s was not met by either policy makers or economists. In a comment obviously directed at real business cycle theorists, Blinder (1988b) notes that 'we will not contribute much toward alleviating unemployment while we fiddle around with theories of Pareto optimal recessions – an avocation that might be called Nero-Classical Economics'. Although the intersectoral shifts model associated with Lilien (1982) introduces unemployment into a model where technology shocks motivate the need to reallocate resources across sectors, the critics regard the neglect of unemployment in real business cycle theory as a major weakness (see Hoover, 1988).

A fifth objection to real business cycle theory relates to the neutrality of money and the irrelevance of monetary policy for real outcomes. It is a matter of some irony that these models emerged in the early 1980s when in both the USA and the UK the monetary disinflations initiated by Volcker and Thatcher were followed by deep recessions in both countries. The 1990–92 economic downturn in the UK also appears to have been the direct consequence of another dose of monetary disinflation. In response to this line of criticism, real business cycle theorists point out that the recessions experienced in the early 1980s were preceded by a second major oil shock in 1979. However, the majority of economists remain unconvinced that money is neutral in the short run (see Romer and Romer, 1989, 1994a, 1994b; Blanchard, 1990a; Ball, 1994; and Chapter 7).

A sixth line of criticism relates to the important finding by Nelson and Plosser that it is hard to reject the view that real GNP is as persistent as a random walk with drift. This finding appeared to lend support to the idea that fluctuations are caused by supply-side shocks. The work of Nelson and Plosser (1982) showed that aggregate output does not appear to be trend-reverting. If fluctuations were trend-reverting, then a temporary deviation of output from its natural rate would not change a forecaster's estimate of output in ten years' time. Campbell and Mankiw (1987, 1989), Stock and Watson (1988) and Durlauf (1989) have confirmed the findings of Nelson and Plosser. As a result, the persistence of shocks is now regarded as a 'stylised fact' (see Durlauf, 1989, p. 71). However, Campbell, Mankiw and Durlauf do not accept that the discovery of a near unit root in the GNP series is clear evidence of real shocks, or that explanations of fluctuations based on demand disturbances should be abandoned. Aggregate demand could have permanent effects if technological innovation is affected by the business cycle or if hysteresis effects are important (see Chapter 7). Durlauf has shown how, in the presence of coordination failures, substantial persistence in real activity can result from aggregate demand shocks. This implies that demand-side policies can have long-lasting effects on output. Stadler (1990) has also shown how the introduction of endogenous technological change fundamentally alters the properties of both real and monetary theories of the business cycle. REBCT does not provide any deep microeconomic foundations to explain technologi-

cal change and innovative activity. But the plausible dependence of technological progress on economic factors such as demand conditions, research
and development expenditures and 'learning by doing' effects (Arrow, 1962)
implies that changes on the supply side of the economy are not independent
of changes on the demand side. Hence an unanticipated increase in nominal
aggregate demand can induce technology changes on the supply side which
permanently increase output. In such a model the natural rate of unemployment will depend on the history of aggregate demand as well as supply-side
factors. A purely monetary model of the business cycle where technology is
endogenous can also account for the Nelson and Plosser finding that output
appears to follow a random walk.

A seventh criticism relates to the pervasive use of the representative agent
construct in real business cycle theory. Real business cycle theorists sidestep
the aggregation problems inherent in macroeconomic analysis by using a
representative agent whose choices are assumed to coincide with the aggregate choices of millions of heterogeneous individuals. Such models therefore
avoid the problems associated with asymmetric information, exchange and
coordination. To many economists the most important questions in macroeconomic theory relate to problems associated with coordination and
heterogeneity. If the coordination question and the associated possibility of
exchange failures lie at the heart of economic fluctuations, then to by-pass the
problem by assuming that an economy is populated only by Robinson Crusoe
is an unacceptable research strategy for many economists (see Summers,
1986; Kirman, 1992; Leijonhufvud, 1992, 1998a; Akerlof, 2002; Snowdon,
2004a).

A final important criticism relates to the lack of robust empirical testing
(see Fair, 1992; Laidler, 1992a; Hartley et al., 1998). As far as the stylized
facts are concerned, both new Keynesian and real business cycle theories can
account for a broad pattern of time series co-movements (see Greenwald and
Stiglitz, 1988). In an assessment of the empirical plausibility of real business
cycle theory, Eichenbaum (1991) finds the evidence put forward by its proponents as 'too fragile to be believable'.

### 6.17 Great Depressions: A Real Business Cycle View

As noted above, REBCT has been criticized for its lack of plausibility with
respect to explaining the Great Depression. However, during recent years
several economists have begun to investigate economic depressions using
neoclassical growth theory.

Cole and Ohanian (1999) were the first economists to study the Great
Depression from this perspective and they attempt to account not only for the
downturn in GDP in the period 1929–33, but also seek to explain the recov-

ery of output between 1934 and 1939. In their analysis they do not deny the contribution of real and monetary aggregate demand shocks in initiating the Great Depression. However, conventional models predict a rapid recovery from such shocks after 1933 given the expansionary monetary policies adopted after abandoning the Gold Standard constraint, the elimination of bank failures and deflation, and the significant rise in total factor productivity. Given these changes, output should have returned to trend by 1936, but US output remained up to 30 per cent below trend throughout the 1930s. Cole and Ohanian argue that the weak recovery process was mainly due to the adverse consequences of New Deal policies, particularly policies related to the National Industrial Recovery Act (NIRA) of 1933. The NIRA, by suspending anti-trust laws in over 500 sectors of the US economy, encouraged cartelization and reductions in price competition. Firms were also encouraged to grant large pay increases for incumbent workers. Cole and Ohanian claim that it was the impact of NIRA that depressed employment and output during the recovery, thereby lengthening the Great Depression. Prescott (1999) provides a similar perspective for the US economy, arguing that the Great Depression was 'largely the result of changes in economic institutions that lowered the normal steady-state market hours per person over 16'. Thus, for Prescott, the Keynesian explanation of the slump is upside down. A collapse of investment did not cause the decline in employment. Rather employment declined as a result of changes in industrial and labour market policies that lowered employment! (see also Chari et al., 2002). While arguing that a liquidity preference shock rather than technology shocks played an important role in the contraction phase of the Great Depression in the USA (providing support for the Friedman and Schwartz argument that a more accommodative monetary policy by the US Federal Reserve could have greatly reduced the severity of the Great Depression), Christiano et al. (2004) also agree with the Cole and Ohanian view that the recovery of employment in the USA during the 1930s was adversely affected by President Roosevelt's 'New Deal' policies.

In a subsequent paper, Cole and Ohanian (2002b) focus on why both the US and UK Great Depressions lasted so long, with output and consumption in both economies some 25 per cent below trend for over ten years. Such a duration in both countries cannot be 'plausibly explained by deflation or other financial shocks'. Instead, Cole and Ohanian focus on the negative impact of the NIRA (1933) and the NLRA (National Labour Relations Act, 1935) in the USA, both of which distorted the efficient working of markets by increasing monopoly power. In the case of the UK, their analysis follows the lead given in earlier research by Benjamin and Kochin (1979) that a generous increase in unemployment benefits lengthened the Great Depression.

This new approach to explaining depressions has not convinced the majority of economists, who mainly continue to highlight the importance of aggregate demand shocks and monetary and financial factors in their explanations of the Great Depression (see Chapter 2). Nevertheless, Prescott's (2002) Ely Lecture focused on using supply-side explanations of 'Prosperity and Depression' for the interwar experience of the USA, UK and Germany, the recent depression in France and the post-war record of Japan. In each case the most important factor causing output to be below trend is supply-side, rather than demand-side in origin (see also Kehoe and Prescott, 2002). Crucial to the maintenance of prosperity are policies that focus on enhancing total factor productivity. Given this perspective, Prescott recommends supply-side policies that will:

1. promote the establishment of an efficient financial sector to allocate scarce investment funds;
2. enhance competition, both domestic and international; and
3. promote international integration, including the establishment of trading clubs such as the EU.

### 6.18   An Assessment

In his Yrjo Jahnsson lectures, given in 1978, James Tobin noted that 'there is no economic business cycle theory, new or old, involved in assuming that waves of economic activity simply mirror waves in underlying technology and taste' (Tobin, 1980a, p. 37). This state of affairs was to change dramatically during the 1980s when, following the widespread rejection of the monetary misperception version of equilibrium theory, real business cycle models proliferated. The research initiated by Nelson and Plosser provided substantial support for the view that shocks to aggregate output tend to have long-lasting effects. Output does not appear to revert to a deterministic trend. This finding has had a profound influence on business cycle research, in that it suggests that much of the disturbance to aggregate output that we witness is caused by supply-side influences. By demonstrating that equilibrium models are not inconsistent with aggregate instability, real business cycle theorists have challenged the conventional wisdom and forced theorists on all sides to recognize just how deficient our knowledge is of business cycle phenomena. The real business cycle approach has therefore performed a useful function in raising profound questions relating to the meaning, significance and characteristics of economic fluctuations. We have seen in this chapter how REBCT is a continuation of the research programme, stimulated in the modern era by Lucas, that aims to explore the general equilibrium intertemporal characteristics of macroeconomics (Wickens, 1995). In doing so, REBCT has integrated the theory of growth and fluctuations and irreversibly changed the direction of business cycle research. New insights have been gained, along with innovative modelling techniques.

More than 30 years ago, Harry Johnson (1971), in his lecture to the 1970 meeting of the American Economic Association, attempted to provide reasons for the rapid propagation of the Keynesian revolution in order to better understand the monetarist counter-revolution which during the late 1960s and early 1970s had begun to fill the intellectual vacuum created by the retreat of the Keynesian orthodoxy in the face of accelerating inflation. In Johnson's highly perceptive article, attention was drawn to the shared characteristics of both the Keynesian revolution and the monetarist counter-revolution which appear important in explaining the success of these developments. According to Johnson, there are two types of factor which can help explain the rapid acceptance and propagation of new ideas among professional economists. The first factor relates to the 'objective social situation in which the new theory was produced'. The second important factor encompasses the 'internal scientific characteristics of the new theory'. We would argue that these factors can help in understanding the rapid propagation of new classical ideas, both the MEBCT and the REBCT (see Snowdon and Vane, 1996).

Although an established orthodoxy, such as trend-reverting cycles, which is in apparent contradiction to the 'most salient facts of reality' is the 'most helpful circumstance for the rapid propagation of a new and revolutionary theory', Johnson also identified five internal scientific characteristics which in his view were crucial because it was these aspects of the new theory which appealed to the younger generation of economists. In summary, the five main characteristics Johnson identified involved:

1. 'a central attack, on theoretically persuasive grounds, on the central proposition of the orthodoxy of the time';
2. 'the production of an apparently new theory that nevertheless absorbed all that was valid in the existing theory';
3. a new theory having an 'appropriate degree of difficulty to understand' that would 'challenge the intellectual interest of younger colleagues and students';
4. 'a new more appealing methodology' than that prevailing;
5. 'the advancement of a new and important empirical relationship suitable for determined estimation' by econometricians.

To what extent have these five internal scientific characteristics played an important role in explaining the success of new classical macroeconomics, in particular the REBCT?

The first characteristic (that is, an attack on a central proposition of the established orthodoxy) can be straightforwardly identified in REBCT. Before 1980 the established consensus regarded business cycles as socially undesirable. In sharp contrast, the main policy implication of real business cycle theory is that because the existence of fluctuations in aggregate output does not imply the failure of markets to clear, the government should refrain from any attempt to reduce such fluctuations not only because such policies are unlikely to achieve their desired objective, but also because reducing instability would reduce welfare!

The application of Johnson's second internal characteristic (that is, the ability of a new theory to absorb as much as possible of the valid components of the existing orthodox theory) can also be applied to REBCT, which has pioneered the use of the orthodox neoclassical growth model as a framework for the quantitative analysis of aggregate fluctuations as well as absorbing much of the methodology advocated by Lucas in the 1970s.

Johnson's third characteristic (that is, an intellectually challenging new theory with appeal to the younger generation of economists) is one that again can be readily applied to REBCT. There is no question that the new classical revolution pushed macroeconomic theory into new, more abstract directions involving the introduction of techniques not found in the 'kit bags of the older economists' (Blinder, 1988b). Being better trained mathematically, the younger generation has been able to absorb the new techniques, such as calibration, giving them a 'heavy competitive edge' over the 'older' economists.

Turning to the fourth characteristic (that is, a new methodology), the REBCT programme has wholeheartedly embraced a methodological framework involving a formal general equilibrium approach. Responding to the 'Lucas critique' has fostered an emphasis on a return to first principles in the quest to establish sound microfoundations for general equilibrium macroeconomic models. Since real business cycle methodology is in principle ideologically neutral, it has the capability of fostering models with enormous diversity.

The fifth characteristic (concerning a 'new and important empirical relationship' for estimation) is more difficult to apply to REBCT developments. Rather than attempting to provide models capable of conventional econometric testing, real business cycle theorists have instead developed the 'calibration method' in which the simulated results of their specific models (when hit by random shocks) in terms of key macroeconomic variables are compared with the actual behaviour of the economy. Unfortunately calibration does not provide a method that allows one to judge between the performance of real and other (for example Keynesian) business cycle models.

From the above discussion it should be evident that while Johnson put forward five main 'internal' characteristics to help explain the success of the Keynesian revolution and monetarist counter-revolution, the first four of these same characteristics also help in understanding why REBCT has made such an important impact on the development of macroeconomics since the early

1980s. In assessing whether or not REBCT has constituted a 'fashion' or a 'revolution' in macroeconomics, Kirschner and Rhee (1996) conclude from their statistical analysis of the spread of scientific research that data on publications and researchers in the REBCT field exhibit 'mini-revolution' characteristics.

A distinguishing feature of the early REBCT is the downplaying of monetary influences as a major cause of business cycles. Instead random shocks to technology play the major role in creating disturbances, and the desire of economic agents for consumption smoothing and 'time to build' constraints acts as a major propagation mechanism leading to persistence. While the early REBCT models had too narrow a focus, more recent work has also begun to add monetary and financial variables into the model, as well as to extend this line of research to include government and open economy influences (see Mendoza, 1991; Backus et al., 1992; Hess and Shin, 1997). Going further and adding market imperfections to REBCT will provide a bridge between new classical and new Keynesian approaches to business cycle research (Wickens, 1995). We should also note that the real business cycle approach has furthered the cause of those economists who insist that macro models need to be based on a firmer microeconomic base. This in turn has strengthened the general move to improve our understanding of the supply side. If anyone seriously questioned it before, no one now doubts that macroeconomics is about demand and supply and their interaction. As Blinder (1987b) notes, 'events in the 1970s and 1980s demonstrated to Keynesian and new classical economists alike that Marshall's celebrated scissors also come in a giant economy size'.

While recognizing the achievements of the real business research programme, the critics remain convinced that this approach has serious deficiencies. A majority of economists believe that the short-run aggregate demand disturbances that arise from monetary policy can have significant real effects because of the nominal price and wage rigidities which characterize actual economies (see Chapter 7). This important line of criticism challenges the new classical assumption that markets continuously clear, even in a recession. If markets do not clear quickly and the world is characterized by both aggregate demand and aggregate supply disturbances, the actual fluctuations that we observe will consist of a stochastic trend around which output deviates as the result of demand shocks. This view is well represented by Blanchard and Quah (1989) where they 'interpret fluctuations in GNP and unemployment as due to two types of disturbances: disturbances that have a permanent effect on output and disturbances that do not. We interpret the first as supply disturbances, the second as demand disturbances.' Clearly the role of stabilization policy in such a world is immensely complicated, even if we accept that demand disturbances are important. How, for example, can a government make the requisite distinction between demand and supply shocks, especially when such shocks are not independent but interdependent? (see Friedman, 1992).

Further support for keeping an open mind on the causes of aggregate instability is provided by G.M. Caporale (1993). In an investigation of business cycles in the UK, France, Finland, Italy, Norway, Sweden and West Germany, Caporale found that that neither demand nor supply shocks alone could account for economic fluctuations. Recent empirical research by Temin (1998) also finds a variety of causes responsible for US business cycles. Temin suggests a four-way classification of the causes of US business cycles over the twentieth century, namely Domestic Real, Domestic Monetary, Foreign Real and Foreign Monetary. According to Temin's data it appears that domestic causes far outweigh foreign shocks (16.5 v. 7.5), and real disturbances dominate monetary disturbances (13.5 v. 10.5). The real domestic shocks are diverse and include all manner of real demand disturbance. Temin concludes that 'all four types of shock have acted as a source of the American business cycle' and the dominant conclusion of his enquiry is that 'the sources of instability are not homogeneous'. In his study of large recessions in the twentieth century, Dow (1998) discusses three major findings. First, major recessions and growth slowdowns are mainly due to aggregate demand shocks. Second, these demand shocks can be identified, for example, the 1979–82 recession in the UK was largely the result of a decline in exports brought about by an appreciation of the exchange rate in response to the new monetary and fiscal regime under Prime Minister Margaret Thatcher. Third, recessions are not predictable given economists' present state of knowledge.

A balanced conclusion from the above discussion would seem to point towards the advantage of taking an eclectic approach when analysing the causes of business cycles. There is no evidence that the business cycle is dead or that governments now have the ability and knowledge to offset the various shocks that buffet every economy. While governments can never hope to eliminate the business cycle, they should have the knowledge and capacity to avert another Great Depression or Great Inflation.

In a recent assessment of the contribution of REBCT to twentieth-century macroeconomics (see Snowdon, 2004a), Axel Leijonhufvud commented:

> I think the legacy of Ed Prescott's work will be in terms of the analytical machinery available to technically minded economists, although those techniques are not always appropriate and you cannot always apply them. In particular, you cannot meaningfully run these dynamic stochastic general equilibrium models across the great catastrophes of history and hope for enlightenment.

Even taking into account these important deficiencies, there is no doubt that the REBCT research programme has been 'extremely influential' and current work in the field is 'a far cry' from the initial representative agent competitive (and unique) equilibrium model constructed by Kydland and Prescott in the early 1980s (Williamson, 1996). However, while noting that new and controversial ideas are often the most fruitful, even when false, Hartley et al. (1998) conclude that 'real business cycle models are bold conjectures in the Popperian mould and that, on the preponderance of the evidence, they are refuted'. However, for those economists who reject the real business cycle view that stabilization policy has no role to play, there remains the theoretical difficulty of explaining in a coherent way why markets fail to clear.

Beginning in the late 1970s, and continuing thereafter, many economists have taken up this challenge of attempting to explain why the adjustment of prices and wages in many markets is sluggish. 'The rationality of rigidities' theme is a major feature of the research of new Keynesian economists and it is to this work that we turn in the next chapter.

# EDWARD C. PRESCOTT

Edward Prescott was born in 1940 in Glens Falls, New York and obtained his BA (Maths) from Swarthmore College in 1962, his MS (Operations Research) from Case Institute of Technology in 1963 and his PhD from Carnegie-Mellon University in 1967. He was Assistant Professor of Economics at the University of Pennsylvania (1966–71), Assistant Professor (1971–2), Associate Professor (1972–5) and Professor of Economics (1975–80) at Carnegie-Mellon University, and Regents' Professor at the University of Minnesota (1980–2003). Since 2003 he has been Professor of Economics at Arizona State University.

Professor Prescott is best known for his highly influential work on the implications of rational expectations in a variety of contexts and more recently the development of stochastic dynamic general equilibrium theory. He is widely acknowledged as a leading advocate of the real business cycle approach to economic fluctuations. In 2004 he was awarded, with Finn Kydland, the Nobel Memorial Prize in Economics for 'contributions to dynamic macroeconomics: the time consistency of economic policy and the driving forces behind business cycles'. Among his best-known books are: *Recursive Methods in Economic Dynamics* (Harvard University Press, 1989), co-authored with Nancy Stokey and Robert E. Lucas Jr, and *Barriers to Riches* (MIT Press, 2000), co-authored with Stephen Parente. His most widely read articles include: 'Investment Under Uncertainty', *Econometrica*

(1971), co-authored with Robert E. Lucas Jr; 'Rules Rather Than Discretion: The Inconsistency of Optimal Plans', *Journal of Political Economy* (1977), co-authored with Finn Kydland; 'Time to Build and Aggregate Fluctuations', *Econometrica* (1982), co-authored with Finn Kydland; 'Theory Ahead of Business Cycle Measurement', *Federal Reserve Bank of Minneapolis Quarterly Review* (1986); 'Business Cycles: Real Facts and a Monetary Myth', *Federal Reserve Bank of Minneapolis Quarterly Review* (1990), co-authored with Finn Kydland; 'The Computational Experiment: An Econometric Tool', *Journal of Economic Perspectives* (1996), co-authored with Finn Kydland; and 'Prosperity and Depression', *American Economic Review* (2002).

We interviewed Professor Prescott in Chicago, in his hotel room, on 3 January 1998, while attending the annual conference of the American Economic Association.

## Background Information

*Where and when did you first study economics?*
I first studied economics as a graduate student at Carnegie-Mellon in 1963, which was then the Carnegie Institute of Technology. As an undergraduate I initially started out as a physics major – back then it was the *Sputnik* era and that was the glamorous field. I had two boring laboratory courses, which I didn't enjoy, so I transferred into math.

*What was it about economics that attracted you?*
Having transferred from physics to math I first considered doing applied math – I got my degree in operations research. Then I went to an interdisciplinary programme and it seemed to me that the smartest, most interesting people were doing economics. Bob Lucas was a new assistant professor when I arrived at Carnegie-Mellon. My mentor, though, was Mike Lovell, a wonderful person.

*Apart from Bob Lucas and Mike Lovell, did any of your other teachers stand out as being particularly influential or inspirational?*
Sure. Morie De Groot, a great Bayesian statistician.

*With respect to your own research which economists have had the greatest influence?*
I would say Bob Lucas. Also Finn Kydland, who was a student of mine – perhaps my two most important papers were written with Finn [Kydland and Prescott, 1977, 1982].

*For over 20 years you have had a very productive relationship with Finn Kydland. When did you first meet him?*
My first position after leaving Carnegie-Mellon was at the University of Pennsylvania. When I came back to Carnegie-Mellon Finn was an advanced graduate student there, ready to work on research. We had a very small economics programme with approximately seven faculty members and seven students. It was a good programme where students worked quite closely with faculty members. Bob Lucas and I had a number of joint students – unlike Bob I didn't scare the students [*laughter*].

## Development of Macroeconomics

*You have already mentioned that Bob Lucas was very influential on your own thinking. Which other economists do you regard as being the most influential macroeconomists since Keynes?*
Well, if you define growth as being part of macroeconomics Bob Solow has to be up there. Peter Diamond, Tom Sargent and Neil Wallace have also been very influential.

*What about Milton Friedman?*
Well, I know Bob Lucas regards Friedman as being incredibly influential to the research programme in the monetary area. Friedman's work certainly influenced people interested in the monetary side of things – Neil Wallace, for example, was one of Friedman's students. But I'm more biased towards Neil Wallace's programme, which is to lay down theoretical foundations for money. Friedman's work in the monetary field with Anna Schwartz [1963] is largely empirically orientated. Now when Friedman talked about the natural rate – where the unit of account doesn't matter – that is serious theory. But Friedman never accepted the dynamic equilibrium paradigm or the extension of economic theory to dynamic stochastic environments.

*You were a graduate student at a time when Keynesianism 'seemed to be the only game in town in terms of macroeconomics' [Barro, 1994]. Were you ever persuaded by the Keynesian model? Were you ever a Keynesian in those days?*
Well, in my dissertation I used a Keynesian model of business cycle fluctuations. Given that the parameters are unknown, I thought that maybe you could apply optimal statistical decision theory to better stabilize the economy. Then I went to the University of Pennsylvania. Larry Klein was there – a really fine scholar. He provided support for me as an assistant professor, which was much appreciated. I also had an association with the Wharton Economic Forecasting group. However, after writing the paper on 'Invest-

ment under Uncertainty' with Bob Lucas [*Econometrica*, 1971], plus reading his 1972 *Journal of Economic Theory* paper on 'Expectations and the Neutrality of Money', I decided I was not a Keynesian [*big smile*]. I actually stopped teaching macro after that for ten years, until I moved to Minnesota in the spring of 1981, by which time I thought I understood the subject well enough to teach it.

## Business Cycles

*The study of business cycles has itself gone through a series of cycles. Business cycle research flourished from the 1920s to the 1940s, waned during the 1950s and 1960s, before witnessing a revival of interest during the 1970s. What were the main factors which were important in regenerating interest in business cycle research in the 1970s?*
There were two factors responsible for regenerating interest in business cycles. First, Lucas beautifully defined the problem. Why do market economies experience recurrent fluctuations of output and employment about trend? Second, economic theory was extended to the study of dynamic stochastic economic environments. These tools are needed to derive the implications of theory for business cycle fluctuations. Actually the interest in business cycles was always there, but economists couldn't do anything without the needed tools. I guess this puts me in the camp which believes that economics is a tool-driven science – absent the needed tools we are stymied.

*Following your work with Finn Kydland in the early 1980s there has been considerable re-examination of what are the stylized facts of the business cycle. What do you think are the most important stylized facts of the business cycle that any good theory needs to explain?*
Business cycle-type fluctuations are just what dynamic economic theory predicts. In the 1970s everybody thought the impulse or shock had to be money and were searching for a propagation mechanism. In our 1982 *Econometrica* paper, 'Time to Build and Aggregate Fluctuations', Finn and I loaded a lot of stuff into our model economy in order to get propagation. We found that a prediction of economic theory is that technology shocks will give rise to business cycle fluctuations of the nature observed. The magnitude of the fluctuations and persistence of deviations from trend match observations. The facts that investment is three times more volatile than output, and consumption one-half as volatile, also match, as does the fact that most business cycle variation in output is accounted for by variation in the labour input. This is a remarkable success. The theory used, namely neoclassical growth theory, was not developed to account for business cycles. It was developed to account for growth.

*Were you surprised that you were able to construct a model economy which generated fluctuations which closely resembled actual experience in the USA?*
Yes. At that stage we were still searching for the model to fit the data, as opposed to using the theory to answer the question – we had not really tied down the size of the technology shock and found that the intertemporal elasticity of labour supply had to be high. In a different context I wrote a paper with another one of my students, Raj Mehra [Mehra and Prescott, 1985] in which we tried to use basic theory to account for the difference in the average returns on stock and equity. We thought that existing theory would work beforehand – the finance people told us that it would [*laughter*]. We actually found that existing theory could only account for a tiny part of the huge difference.

*How do you react to the criticism that there is a lack of available supporting evidence of strong intertemporal labour substitution effects?*
Gary Hansen [1985] and Richard Rogerson's [1988] key theoretical development on labour indivisibility is central to this. The margin that they use is the number of people who work, not the number of hours of those that do work. This results in the stand-in or representative household being very willing to intertemporally substitute even though individuals are not that willing. Labour economists using micro data found that the association between hours worked and compensation per hour was weak for full-time workers. Based on these observations they concluded that the labour supply elasticity is small. These early studies ignore two important features of reality. The first is that most of the variation in labour supply is in the number working – not in the length of the workweek. The second important feature of reality ignored in these early studies is that wages increase with experience. This suggests that part of individuals' compensation is this valuable experience. Estimates of labour supply are high when this feature of reality is taken into account. The evidence in favour of high intertemporal labour supply elasticity has become overwhelming. Macro and micro labour economics have been unified.

*Many prominent economists such as Milton Friedman [see Snowdon and Vane, 1997b], Greg Mankiw [1989] and Lawrence Summers [1986] have been highly critical of real business cycle models as an explanation of aggregate fluctuations. What do you regard as being the most serious criticisms that have been raised in the literature against RBC models?*
I don't think you criticize models – maybe the theory. A nice example is where the Solow growth model was used heavily in public finance – some of its predictions were confirmed, so we now have a little bit more confidence in that structure and what public finance people say about the consequences of

different tax policies. Bob Lucas [1987] says technology shocks seem awfully big and that is the feature he is most bothered by. When you look at how much total factor productivity changes over five-year periods and you assume that changes are independent, the quarterly changes have to be big. The difference between total factor productivity in the USA and India is at least 400 per cent. This is a lot bigger than if in say a two-year period the shocks are such that productivity growth is a couple of per cent below or above average. This is enough to give rise to a recession or boom. Other factors are also influential – tax rates matter for labour supply and I'm not going to rule out preference shocks either. I can't forecast what social attitudes will be, I don't think anybody can – for example, whether or not the female labour participation rate will go up.

*In your 1986 Federal Reserve Bank of Minneapolis paper, 'Theory Ahead of Business Cycle Measurement', you concluded that attention should be focused on 'determinants of the average rate of technological advance'. What in your view are the main factors that determine the average rate at which technology advances?*
The determinants of total factor productivity is *the* question in economics. If we knew why total factor productivity in the USA was four times bigger than in India, I am sure India would immediately take the appropriate actions and be as rich as the USA [*laughter*]. Of course the general rise throughout the world has to be related to what Paul Romer talks about – increasing returns and the increase in the stock of usable knowledge. But there is a lot more to total factor productivity, particularly when you look at the relative levels across countries or different experiences over time. For example, the Philippines and Korea were very similar in 1960 but are quite different today.

*How important are institutions?*
Very. The legal system matters and matters a lot, particularly the commercial code and the property rights systems. Societies give protection to certain groups of specialized factor suppliers – they protect the *status quo*. For example, why in India do you see highly educated bank workers manually entering numbers into ledgers? In the last few years I have been reading quite a lot about these types of issues. However, there seem to be more questions than answers [*laughter*].

*When it comes to the issue of technological change, are you a fan of Schumpeter's work?*
The old Schumpeter, but not the new [*laughter*]. The new suggests that we need monopolies – what the poor countries need is more competition, not more monopolies.

*In your 1991* Economic Theory *paper, co-authored with Finn Kydland, you estimated that just over two-thirds of post-war US fluctuations can be attributed to technology shocks. A number of authors have introduced several modifications of the model economy, for example Cho and Cooley [1995]. How robust is the estimate of the contribution of technology shocks to aggregate fluctuations to such modifications?*

The challenge to that number has come from two places. First, the size of the estimate of the intertemporal elasticity of labour supply. Second, are technology shocks as large as we estimated them to be? You can have lots of other factors and they need not be orthogonal – there could be some moving in opposite directions that offset each other or some moving in the same direction that amplify each other. Are the shocks that big? Marty Eichenbaum [1991] tried to push them down and came up with a 0.005 number for the standard deviation of the total factor productivity shocks. My number is 0.007. I point out to Marty that Ian Fleming's secret agent 005 is dead. Agent 007 survives [*laughter*].

*How do you view the more recent development of introducing nominal rigidities, imperfect credit markets and other Keynesian-style features into RBC models?*

I like the methodology of making a theory quantitative. Introducing monopolistic competition with sticky prices has been an attempt to come up with a good mechanism for the monetary side. I don't think it has paid off as much as people had hoped, but it is a good thing to explore.

*The new classical monetary-surprise models developed in the 1970s by Lucas, Sargent, Wallace and others were very influential. When did you first begin to lose faith in that particular approach?*

In our 1982 paper Finn and I were pretty careful – what we said was that in the post-war period if the only shocks had been technology shocks, then the economy would have been 70 per cent as volatile. When you look back at some of Friedman and Schwartz's [1963] data, particularly from the 1890s and early 1900s, there were financial crises and associated large declines in real output. It is only recently that I have become disillusioned with monetary explanations. One of the main reasons for this is that a lot of smart people have searched for good monetary transmission mechanisms but they haven't been that successful in coming up with one – it's hard to get persistence out of monetary surprises.

*How do you now view your 1977* Journal of Political Economy *paper, co-authored with Finn Kydland, in which monetary surprises, if they can be achieved, have real effects?*

Finn and I wanted to make the point about the inconsistency of optimal plans in the setting of a more real environment. The pressure to use this simple example came from the editor – given the attention that paper has subsequently received, I guess his call was right [*laughter*].

*What do you regard to be the essential connecting thread between the monetary-surprise models developed in the 1970s and the real business cycle models developed in the 1980s?*
The methodology – Bob Lucas is the master of methodology, as well as defining problems. I guess when Finn and I undertook the research for our 1982 piece we didn't realize it was going to be an important paper. *Ex post* we see it as being an important paper – we certainly learnt a lot from writing it and it did influence Bob Lucas in his thinking about methodology. That paper pushed the profession into trying to make macroeconomic theory more quantitative – to say how big things are. There are so many factors out there – most of them we have got to abstract from, the world is too complex otherwise – we want to know which factors are little and which are significant.

*Turning to one of the stylized facts of the business cycle, does the evidence suggest that the price level and inflation are procyclical or countercyclical?*
Finn and I [Kydland and Prescott, 1990] found that in the USA prices since the Second World War have been countercyclical, but that in the interwar period they were procyclical. Now if you go to inflation you are taking the derivative of the price level and things get more complex. The lack of a strong uniform regular pattern has led me to be a little suspicious of the importance of the monetary facts – but further research could change my opinion.

*What is your current view on the relationship between the behaviour of the money supply and the business cycle?*
Is it OK to talk about hunches? [*laughter*]. My guess is that monetary and fiscal policies are really tied together – there is just one government with a budget constraint. In theory, at least, you can arrange to have a fiscal authority with a budget constraint and an independent monetary authority – in reality some countries do have a high degree of independence of their central bank. Now I've experimented with some simple closed economy models which unfortunately get awfully complicated, very fast [*laughter*]. In some of those models government policy changes do have real consequences – the government 'multipliers' are very different from those in the standard RBC model. Monetary and fiscal policy are not independent – there is a complex interaction between monetary and fiscal policy with respect to debt management, money supply and government expenditure. So I think that there is a

rich class of models to be studied and as we get better tools we are going to learn more.

*One of the main features of Keynesianism has always been the high priority given by its advocates to the problem of unemployment. Equilibrium business cycle theory seems to treat unemployment as a secondary issue. How do you think about unemployment?*
When I think about employment it is easy because you can go out and measure it – you see how many hours people work and how many people work. The problem with unemployment is that it is not a well-defined concept. When I look at the experience of European economies like France and Spain, I see unemployment as something to do with the arrangements that these societies set up. Unemployment, particularly among the young, is a social problem. Lars Ljungqvist and Tom Sargent [1998] are doing some very interesting work on this question and that is something I want to study more.

*Given that your work has provided an integrated approach to the theory of growth and fluctuations, should we perhaps abandon the term 'business cycle' when we refer to aggregate economic fluctuations?*
Business cycles are in large part fluctuations due to variations in how many hours people work. Is that good language or not? I think I'll leave that for you to decide [*laughter*]. I'm sympathetic to what your question implies, but I can't think of any better language right now.

## Methodology

*You are known as a leading real business cycle theorist. Are you happy with that label?*
I tend to see RBC theory more as a methodology – dynamic applied general equilibrium modelling has been a big step forward. Applied analyses that people are doing now are so much better than they used to be. So in so far as I am associated with that, and have helped get that started, I am happy with that label.

*Do you regard your work as having resulted in a revolution in macroeconomics?*
No – I have just followed the logic of the discipline. There has been no real dramatic change, only an extension, to dynamic economics – it takes time to figure things out and develop new tools. People are always looking for the revolutions – maybe some day some revolution will come along, but I don't think I'll sit around and wait for it [*laughter*].

*What role have calibration exercises played in the development of real business cycle models?*
I think of the model as something to use to measure something. Given the posed question, we typically want our model economy to match reality on certain dimensions. With a thermometer you want it to register correctly when you put it in ice and in boiling water. In the past economists have tried to find *the* model and that has held them back. Today people don't take the data as gospel; they look at how the data are collected. So it has forced people to learn a lot more about government statistics on the economy.

*How important was Lucas's [1980a] paper on 'Methods and Problems in Business Cycle Theory' in your development of the calibration approach?*
It's hard to recall exactly – I saw his vision more clearly later on. Back then I kept thinking of trying to find the model, as opposed to thinking of economic theory in terms of a set of instructions for constructing a model to answer a particular question. There never is a right or wrong model – the issue is whether a model is good for the purpose it is being used.

*Kevin Hoover [1995b] has suggested that 'the calibration methodology, to date, lacks any discipline as stern as that imposed by econometric methods'. What happens if you have a Keynesian and a real business cycle model which both perform well? How do you choose between the two?*
Well, let's suppose you work within a Keynesian theoretical framework and it provides guidance to construct models, and you use those models and they work well – that's success, by definition. There was a vision that neoclassical foundations would eventually be provided for Keynesian models but in the Keynesian programme theory doesn't provide much discipline in constructing the structure. A lot of the choice of equations came down to an empirical matter – theory was used to restrict these equations, some coefficients being zero. You notice Keynesians talk about equations. Within the applied general equilibrium approach we don't talk about equations – we always talk about production functions, utility functions or people's ability and willingness to substitute. We are not trying to follow the physicist in discovering the laws of motion of the economy, unlike Keynesians and monetarists. Keynesian approaches were tried and put to a real test, and to quote Bob Lucas and Tom Sargent [1978], in the 1970s Keynesian macroeconometric models experienced 'econometric failure on a grand scale'.

*To what extent is the question of whether the computational experiment should be regarded as an econometric tool an issue of semantics?*
It is pure semantics. Ragnar Frisch wanted to make neoclassical economics quantitative – he talked about quantitative theoretical economics and quanti-

tative empirical economics, and their unification. The modern narrow definition of econometrics only focuses on the empirical side.

*Lawrence Summers [1991a] in a paper on 'The Scientific Illusion in Empiri-
cal Macroeconomics' has argued along the lines that formal econometric
work has had little impact on the growth of economic knowledge, whereas the
informal pragmatic approach of people like Friedman and Schwartz [1963]
has had a significant effect. Are you sympathetic to Summers's view?*
In some ways I'm sympathetic, in others I'm unsympathetic – I think I'll
hedge (*laughter*). With regard to representing our knowledge in terms of the
likelihood of different things being true, so that as we get more observations
over time we zero in on the truth, it doesn't seem to work that way.

## Growth and Development

*Since the mid-1980s many eminent economists have turned their attention to
the issue of economic growth. Are we any closer to explaining why there has
been a lack of convergence between rich and poor countries?*
The new growth and development literature, which was touched off by Paul
Romer [1986] and Bob Lucas [1988], is very exciting. We now know that
standards of living were more or less constant from the beginning of civiliza-
tion until the industrial revolution; then something changed. When I compare
countries in the East (China, India, Japan and so on) with those in the West
they were about the same in 1800 in terms of per capita GDP – by 1950 the
West was almost ten times richer, now it is only about four times richer. So I
do see signs of convergence. Divergence occurred when modern economic
growth started. In China, for example, the peasants were equally well off in
AD 2 as they were in 1950 – today they are a lot better off. The process of
modern economic growth started earlier in Japan – even so, they didn't do all
that well until the post-war period. Japan's relative position to England or the
USA in 1870 was about the same as it was in 1937. Even per capita income
growth in Africa is now taking place at the same rate as in the rich countries –
they should be growing much faster and I expect that they soon will start to
catch up. Furthermore, when you look at countries like India, Pakistan,
Indonesia and the Philippines, they are now growing faster than the rich
industrial countries. So I believe that there will be a lot of convergence over
the next 50 years, in the same way that there has been a lot of convergence
over the last 50 years – it all depends upon how you look at the data.

*The endogenous growth literature has led to a reopening of the debate relat-
ing to the role of government in promoting economic growth. What role do
you see for the government?*

My interest is in the problem of the poor countries, like India. In those countries it is important to let things happen and not protect the *status quo*. For example, there are some bizarre licensing practices in India. Once things start happening, they can happen pretty fast and there can be rapid development.

*How do you account for the revival of interest in development economics?*
People pushed the paradigm as far as the old tools would allow it to go. Now a new generation has come along and has sought to advance it a little bit further. Exciting theoretical developments as well new data sets are key to the revival of interest. People like Kravis, and more recently Summers and Heston [1991], have done a major service to the profession by providing new data.

## General

*If you were asked to teach macroeconomics to intermediate undergraduates, how would you go about the task?*
Basically I concentrate on the Solow growth model, with factors paid their marginal product and consider the two key decisions: consumption–saving and labour–leisure. In discussing monetary issues I follow some basic simple intertemporal model with people holding assets – Neil Wallace and his students have developed some pretty good material that can be used. The hard thing about teaching macro to undergraduates is that the textbooks are not that good – there is a need for a Paul Samuelson. Samuelson is an artist; he brought undergraduates pretty well up to the level of the state of knowledge in the profession. Now there is a big gap.

*Most of your work has involved research which has pushed back the frontiers of knowledge in economics. Have you ever thought about writing a basic principles of economics textbook or an intermediate macro textbook?*
Writing this type of book requires a special talent – if I had this talent I would give it some serious thought. I don't [*laughter*].

*Have you ever been asked to be an economic adviser in Washington?*
No [*laughter*]. I get too excited – you have to be calm and have the right style. You also have to be a good actor as well as being a good economist. So again I've never been tempted – maybe if I had the ability I might have been asked.

*Are you optimistic about the future of macroeconomics?*
Yes – I think a lot of progress has been made and will continue to be made.

*What issues or areas are you currently working on?*

I always work on a variety of issues in the hope that one will break [*laughter*]. I've recently completed a couple of papers [Parente and Prescott, 1997; Prescott, 1998]. One paper is on economic development for a monograph on barriers to riches – I use game theory to construct an explicit model economy where a particular set of monopoly rights can give rise to large differences in total factor productivity. The other paper is on financial economics, considering why there occurs such a big jump in the value of firms associated with mergers. I also want to look more fully at the issue of the relationship and interaction between monetary and fiscal policy I hinted at earlier.

# 7. The new Keynesian school

It is time to put Keynes to rest in the economists' Hall of Fame, where he certainly belongs, and to proceed with integrating the most relevant contributions by Keynes and his early and late followers with other strands of macroeconomic theory. (Lindbeck, 1998)

## 7.1 The Fall and Rise of Keynesian Economics

Dennis Robertson, one of Keynes's most articulate critics, once wrote that 'high brow opinion is like the hunted hare; if you stand in the same place, or nearly the same place, it can be relied upon to come around to you in a circle' (Robertson, 1956). Good examples that illustrate Robertson's observation have been provided by the revival of both classical and Keynesian ideas in their 'new' guise. In Chapters 5 and 6 we have seen how classical ideas have been given new form through the technically impressive and imaginative contributions inspired, in particular, by Robert Lucas and Edward Prescott. In this chapter we survey how Keynesian economics has also undergone a 'renaissance' during the last 20 years.

We have seen in the previous chapters how the orthodox Keynesian model associated with the neoclassical synthesis came under attack during the 1970s. It soon became apparent to the Keynesian mainstream that the new classical critique represented a much more powerful and potentially damaging challenge than the one launched by the monetarists, which was of longer standing. Although orthodox monetarism presented itself as an alternative to the standard Keynesian model, it did not constitute a radical theoretical challenge to it (see Laidler, 1986). While Lucas's new classical monetary theory of aggregate instability had its roots in Friedman's monetarism, the new classical real business cycle school represents a challenge to Keynesianism, monetarism and Lucas's monetary explanations of the business cycle. The poor performance of Keynesian wage and price adjustment equations, during the 'Great Inflation' of the 1970s, based on the idea of a stable Phillips curve, made it imperative for Keynesians to modify their models so as to take into account both the influence of inflationary expectations and the impact of supply shocks. This was duly done and once the Phillips curve was suitably modified, it performed 'remarkably well' (Blinder, 1986; Snowdon, 2001a). The important work of Gordon (1972, 1975), Phelps (1968, 1972, 1978) and

Blinder (1979), all of whom are 'Keynesians', was particularly useful in creating the necessary groundwork which has subsequently allowed the Keynesian model to adapt and evolve in a way that enabled monetarist influences to be absorbed within the existing framework (Mayer, 1997; DeLong, 2000). Moreover, this transition towards a synthesis of ideas did not require any fundamental change in the way economists viewed the economic machine. For example, Gordon (1997) argues that his 'resolutely Keynesian' model of inflation, introduced in the mid-1970s and based on inertia, demand and supply shocks, within an expectations-augmented Phillips curve framework, performs very well in explaining the behaviour of output, unemployment and inflation during the 'Great Inflation' period. By introducing supply shocks into the Phillips curve framework, Gordon's 'triangle' model proved capable of explaining the positive correlation between inflation and unemployment observed during the 1970s. Meanwhile, debate continues on the relative importance of demand and supply shocks as causes of the 'Great Inflation' (see Bernanke et al., 1997; Barsky and Kilian, 2001).

Despite these positive developments within Keynesian economics, by 1978 Lucas and Sargent were contemplating life 'After Keynesian Macroeconomics'. In their view the Keynesian model could not be patched up. The problems were much more fundamental, and related in particular to: (i) inadequate microfoundations which assume non-market clearing; and (ii) the incorporation in both Keynesian and monetarist models of a hypothesis concerning the formation of expectations which was inconsistent with maximizing behaviour, that is, the use of an adaptive rather than rational expectations hypothesis. In an article entitled 'The Death of Keynesian Economics: Issues and Ideas', Lucas (1980b) went so far as to claim that 'people even take offence if referred to as Keynesians. At research seminars people don't take Keynesian theorising seriously anymore; the audience starts to whisper and giggle to one another' (cited in Mankiw, 1992). In a similar vein, Blinder (1988b) has confirmed that 'by about 1980, it was hard to find an American academic macroeconomist under the age of 40 who professed to be a Keynesian. That was an astonishing intellectual turnabout in less than a decade, an intellectual revolution for sure.' By this time the USA's most distinguished 'old' Keynesian economist had already posed the question, 'How Dead is Keynes'? (see Tobin, 1977). When Paul Samuelson was asked whether Keynes was dead he replied, 'Yes, Keynes is dead; and so are Einstein and Newton' (see Samuelson, 1988).

## 7.2 A Keynesian Resurgence

Lucas's obituary of Keynesian economics can now be seen to have been premature because Robert Barro's 'bad guys' have made a comeback (Barro,

1989a). By the mid-1980s Howitt (1986) was commenting on 'The Keynesian Recovery', and Blinder was discussing 'Keynes After Lucas' (1986) and 'The Fall and Rise of Keynesian Economics' (1988b). By the early 1990s Blinder had announced that 'A Keynesian Restoration is Here' (1992b), Mankiw (1992) proclaimed that Keynesian economics had been 'reincarnated' and Thirlwall (1993) enthusiastically discussed the 'Keynesian Renaissance'. While in the late 1980s the Keynesian promised land was not yet in sight, Blinder (1988a) believed that 'we may at long last be emerging from the arid desert and looking over the Jordan'.

In answering his own (1977) question about the 'death' of Keynesian economics, Tobin (1987) later provided an unequivocal answer in his essay, 'The Future of Keynesian Economics':

> One reason Keynesian economics has a future is that rival theories of economic fluctuations do not ... I hazard the prediction that neither of the two species of business cycle theory offered by new classical macroeconomics will be regarded as serious and credible explanations of economic fluctuations a few years from now. Whatever cycle theory emerges in a new synthesis will have important Keynesian elements ... Yes, Keynesian economics has a future because it is essential to the explanation and understanding of a host of observations and experiences past and present, that alternative macroeconomic approaches do not illuminate.

Tobin (1996) was particularly critical of the 'elegant fantasies' of the 'Robinson Crusoe macroeconomics' of real business cycle theory because it ignores the coordination question in macroeconomics (see Chapter 6). To economists such as Akerlof, Stiglitz, Tobin and Leijonhufvud, an essential task for macroeconomic theory is to explain in what circumstances the invisible hand does, and does not, efficiently coordinate the economic behaviour of numerous diverse agents. Leijonhufvud (1992) has succinctly summed up this issue:

> The co-ordination question, simply stated, is this: Will the market system 'automatically' co-ordinate economic activities? Always? Never? Sometimes very well, but sometimes pretty badly? If the latter, under what conditions, and with what institutional structures, will it do well or do badly? I regard these questions as the central and basic ones in macroeconomics.

Certainly the persistence of high unemployment in Europe during the 1980s and 1990s also called into question the plausibility of equilibrium explanations of the business cycle while also providing increasing 'credibility to Keynesian theory and policy' (Tobin, 1989; Arestis and Sawyer, 1998).

We have seen in Chapter 5 and 6 how new classical macroeconomists resolved the tension between neoclassical microeconomics and Keynesian macroeconomics by abandoning the latter. An alternative approach to this problem has been put forward by those economists who feel that the neoclassical synthesis contained some fundamental truths and that, suitably modified, Keynesian economics could once again dominate macroeconomics. The central analytical message of the orthodox Keynesian school comprised the following main propositions (Greenwald and Stiglitz, 1987, 1993a; Tobin, 1996; Lindbeck, 1998):

1. an unregulated market economy will experience 'prolonged' periods of excess supply of output and labour in contradiction to 'Say's Law' of markets; that is, in Keynes's terminology, market economies will exhibit 'unemployment equilibrium';
2. aggregate macroeconomic instability (business cycles) are mainly caused by aggregate demand disturbances;
3. 'money matters' most of the time, although in very deep recessions monetary policy may be ineffective (Blanchard, 1990a; Krugman, 1998);
4. government intervention in the form of stabilization policy has the potential to improve macroeconomic stability and economic welfare.

While 'new' Keynesian economists would agree with these 'old' Keynesian propositions, we shall see that the new Keynesian models are very different in many aspects from their distant (1960s) cousins. While new Keynesians disagree with the new classical explanations of instability, they do share two new classical methodological premises. First, macroeconomic theories require solid microeconomic foundations. Second, macroeconomic models are best constructed within a general equilibrium framework. However, as Greenwald and Stiglitz (1993a) point out, real business cycle theorists adopt microfoundations that describe a world of perfect information, perfect competition, zero transactions costs, and the existence of a complete set of markets. Problems associated with asymmetric information, heterogeneous agents and imperfect and incomplete markets are assumed away. The essence of the new Keynesian approach is to recognize the importance of a whole variety of real-world imperfections (Stiglitz, 2000; 2002). By rebuilding the microfoundations of Keynesian economics utilizing the findings of modern microeconomic theory, new Keynesian theorists have established a research programme aimed at rectifying the theoretical flaws which permeated the supply side of the 'old' Keynesian model (see Snowdon and Vane, 1995). Because the typical market economy is riddled with numerous imperfections, aggregate supply does respond to changes in aggregate demand.

For a detailed and critical discussion of the new Keynesian literature, we refer the reader to McCallum (1986); Greenwald and Stiglitz (1987, 1993a); Rotemberg (1987); Fischer (1988); Barro (1989a); Blanchard (1990a); Gordon

(1990); Phelps (1990); Colander et al. (1992); Hargreaves-Heap (1992, 2002); Stiglitz (1992); King (1993); D. Romer (1993); Tobin (1993); Davidson (1994); Dixon (1997); Snowdon and Vane (1997a); Lindbeck (1998). Most of the important papers are collected in the twin volumes edited by Mankiw and Romer (1991), who also provide an excellent tour of the early literature in their introductory survey.

## 7.3 New Keynesian Economics

Although the term 'new Keynesian' was first used by Parkin and Bade in 1982 in their textbook on modern macroeconomics (1982b), it is clear that this line of thought had been conceived in the 1970s during the first phase of the new classical revolution. The burgeoning new Keynesian literature since then has been primarily concerned with the 'search for rigorous and convincing models of wage and/or price stickiness based on maximising behaviour and rational expectations' (Gordon, 1990). New Keynesian economics developed in response to the perceived theoretical crisis within Keynesian economics which had been exposed by Lucas during the 1970s. The paramount task facing Keynesian theorists is to remedy the theoretical flaws and inconsistencies in the old Keynesian model. Therefore, new Keynesian theorists aim to construct a coherent theory of aggregate supply where wage and price rigidities can be rationalized.

Both the old and new versions of classical economics assume continuous market clearing and in such a world the economy can never be constrained by a lack of effective demand. To many economists the hallmark of Keynesian economics is the absence of continuous market clearing. In both the old (neoclassical synthesis) and new versions of Keynesian models the failure of prices to change quickly enough to clear markets implies that demand and supply shocks will lead to substantial real effects on an economy's output and employment. In a Keynesian world, deviations of output and employment from their equilibrium values can be substantial and prolonged, and are certainly interpreted as damaging to economic welfare. As Gordon (1993) points out, 'the appeal of Keynesian economics stems from the evident unhappiness of workers and firms during recessions and depressions. Workers and firms *do not act as if they were making a voluntary choice to cut production and hours worked.*' New Keynesians argue that a theory of the business cycle based on the failure of markets to clear is more realistic than the new classical or real business cycle alternatives. The essential difference between the old and new versions of Keynesian economics is that the models associated with the neoclassical synthesis tended to assume nominal rigidities, while the attraction of the new Keynesian approach is that it attempts to provide acceptable microfoundations to explain the phenomena of wage and price stickiness.

The reader should be aware that new Keynesian economists are an extremely heterogeneous group, so much so that the use of the term 'school' is more convenient than appropriate. Nevertheless, economists who have made significant contributions to the new Keynesian literature, even if some of them may object to the label 'new Keynesian', include Gregory Mankiw and Lawrence Summers (Harvard); Olivier Blanchard (MIT), Stanley Fischer (Citigroup, and formerly at MIT); Bruce Greenwald, Edmund Phelps and Joseph Stiglitz (Columbia); Ben Bernanke (Princeton); Laurence Ball (Johns Hopkins); George Akerlof, Janet Yellen and David Romer (Berkeley); Robert Hall and John Taylor (Stanford); Dennis Snower (Birkbeck, London) and Assar Lindbeck (Stockholm). The proximity of US new Keynesians to the east and west coasts inspired Robert Hall to classify these economists under the general heading of 'Saltwater' economists. By a strange coincidence new classical economists tend to be associated with 'Freshwater' academic institutions: Chicago, Rochester, Minnesota and Carnegie-Mellon (see Blanchard, 1990b; Snowdon and Vane, 1999b; Snowdon, 2002a).

At this point it should be noted that some writers have also identified a 'European' brand of macroeconomic analysis which has also been called 'new Keynesian'. The European variant emphasizes imperfect competition in the labour market as well as the product market, reflecting the higher unionization rates which characterize European economies (Hargreaves-Heap, 1992). The appropriateness of a bargaining approach to wage determination, as a microfoundation to Keynesian macroeconomics, is much more contentious in the USA, where a minority of workers belong to a union. The use of the imperfect competition macro model to examine the problem of unemployment is best represented in the work of Richard Layard, Stephen Nickell and Richard Jackman (LSE), Wendy Carlin (University College, London) and David Soskice (Duke). These economists provide the most comprehensive introduction to the European brand of new Keynesianism (see Layard et al., 1991, 1994; Carlin and Soskice, 1990). There is of course considerable overlap between the two brands of new Keynesianism, especially when it comes to the issue of real wage rigidity (see section 7.7.3). Economists such as Bénassy, Drèze, Grandmont and Malinvaud have also developed general equilibrium models where non-market-clearing and price-making agents give such models Keynesian features. In a survey of this literature Bénassy (1993) suggests that 'it would certainly be worthwhile to integrate the most relevant new Keynesian insights' into this general equilibrium approach.

At the beginning of the 1980s, three alternative explanations of the business cycle were on offer within mainstream economics (there were others outside the mainstream such as Austrian, Post Keynesian and Marxian; see Chapters 8 and 9, and Snowdon and Vane, 2002b). The mainstream alternatives were (i) flexible price, monetary misperception equilibrium business cycle theories developed and advocated by Lucas (see Chapter 5); (ii) sticky price expectational models emphasizing some element of wage and price rigidity (for example, Fischer, 1977; Phelps and Taylor, 1977; Taylor, 1980); and (iii) real business cycle models which increasingly became the main flagship of the new classical equilibrium theorists during the 1980s (see Chapter 6). By the mid-1980s the 'Saltwater–Freshwater' debate was essentially between the sticky price and real business cycle varieties, given the demise of the new classical monetary models. However, a major concern of new Keynesian theorists has been to explain how nominal rigidities arise from optimizing behaviour. Ball et al. (1988) consider the decline of Keynesian economics during the 1970s to have been mainly due to the failure to solve this theoretical problem.

In the remainder of this chapter we will examine the main elements of the very diverse new Keynesian literature. First we identify the essential characteristics of what is commonly understood to be the new Keynesian approach.

### 7.4 Core Propositions and Features of New Keynesian Economics

New Keynesian economics emerged mainly as a response to the theoretical crisis facing Keynesian economics that emerged during the 1970s. In their brief survey of new Keynesian economics Mankiw and Romer (1991) define new Keynesian economics with reference to the answer a particular theory gives to the following pair of questions:

Question 1    Does the theory violate the classical dichotomy? That is, is money non-neutral?

Question 2    Does the theory assume that real market imperfections in the economy are crucial for understanding economic fluctuations?

Of the mainstream schools only new Keynesians answer both questions in the affirmative. Non-neutralities arise from sticky prices, and market imperfections explain this behaviour of prices. Thus, according to Mankiw and Romer, it is the 'interaction of nominal and real imperfections' that distinguishes new Keynesian economics from the other research programmes in macroeconomics. In contrast, the early real business cycle models gave a negative response to both questions.

The disequilibrium Keynesian models of the 1970s (for example, Barro and Grossman, 1976) imposed wage and price rigidities on a Walrasian system, whereas more traditional Keynesian and monetarist models did not regard the explanation of nominal rigidities as a priority. The latter two groups tend to regard empirical evidence as being far more important than theoretical purity; for example, speaking from a monetarist perspective, Laidler

(1992b) has argued emphatically that 'better and more explicit micro-foundations do not guarantee more accurate empirical predictions about the outcome of any macropolicy experiment'. However, as Mankiw and Romer (1991) highlight, new Keynesians are not protagonists in the old 1960s-style monetarist–Keynesian debate. This is for two reasons. First, there is no unified new Keynesian view of the role of fiscal policy although new Keynesians do give much greater weight to the stabilizing role of monetary policy compared to the old Keynesian view (see Mankiw, 2002, and Chapters 3 and 4). For this reason Mankiw and Romer argue that much of new Keynesian economics could just as easily be renamed 'new monetarist economics' (see also DeLong, 2000). Second, new Keynesians do not hold a unified view on the desirability and feasibility of activist (discretionary) stabilization policy. While most new Keynesians accept the thrust of Friedman's critique relating to the problems that arise from uncertainty, time lags and the potential for political distortions of policy, they also reject the 'hard core' monetarist argument relating to the need for a strict monetary growth rate rule. Their views relating to Friedman's natural rate hypothesis also vary from extreme scepticism to *modified* acceptance in terms of a 'time-varying NAIRU' (see Gordon, 1997, 1998; Galbraith, 1997; Stiglitz, 1997; Phelps and Zoega, 1998; Mankiw, 2001; Akerlof, 2002; Ball and Mankiw, 2002; Mankiw and Reis, 2002).

During the 1980s new Keynesian developments had a distinctly non-empirical flavour. Those younger-generation economists seeking to strengthen the Keynesian model did so primarily by developing and improving the microfoundations of 'Fort Keynes' which had come under theoretical attack (see Blinder, 1992a). This is recognized by Mankiw and Romer (1991), who note that the reconstruction of Keynesian economics has 'been part of a revolution in microeconomics'. Those Keynesian commanders who allocated scarce research resources to the theoretical, rather than empirical, front in defence of 'Fort Keynes' did so because they felt that the modified Keynesian model incorporating both the Phelps–Friedman expectations-augmented Phillips curve and the impact of supply shocks was sufficiently resilient to hold its own on the empirical front. Once the theoretical defences had been reinforced, resources could gradually be reallocated to the empirical front in order to test the new Keynesian models.

A crucial difference between new classical and new Keynesian models arises with regard to price-setting behaviour. In contrast to the price takers who inhabit new classical models, new Keynesian models assume price-making monopolistic, rather than perfectly competitive, firms (Dixon, 1997). Although the theory of monopolistic competition had been developed independently by Robinson (1933) and Chamberlin (1933) before the publication of Keynes's *General Theory*, it is only recently that mainstream Keynesian theorists have begun seriously to incorporate imperfect competition into non-market-clearing models. In this matter Post Keynesians were first off the mark (see Chapter 8, and Dixon and Rankin, 1994).

Most new Keynesian models assume that expectations are formed rationally. This is clearly one area where the new classical revolution of the 1970s has had a profound effect on macroeconomists in general. However, some prominent Keynesians (Blinder, 1987b; Phelps, 1992), as well as some economists within the orthodox monetarist school (Laidler, 1992b) remain critical of the theoretical foundations and question the empirical support for the rational expectations hypothesis. Hence, although the incorporation of rational expectations in new Keynesian models is the norm, this need not always be the case.

Although new Keynesian economists share an interest in improving the supply side of Keynesian models, they hold a wide diversity of views relating to policy issues such as the debate over the importance of discretion, rather than rules, in the conduct of fiscal and monetary policy. New Keynesians regard both supply and demand shocks as potential sources of instability (see Blanchard and Quah, 1989) but part company with real business cycle theorists particularly when it comes to an assessment of a market economy's capacity to absorb such shocks so that equilibrium (full employment) is maintained. Many new Keynesians (but not all) also share Keynes's view that involuntary unemployment is both possible and likely.

New Keynesian economists inhabit a brave new theoretical world characterized by imperfect competition, incomplete markets, heterogeneous labour and asymmetric information, and where agents are frequently concerned with fairness. As a result the 'real' macro world, as seen through new Keynesian eyes, is characterized by the possibility of coordination failures and macroeconomic externalities. One problem with new Keynesian developments is that the research programme has proved to be so 'article-laden' (Colander, 1988) that there is no single unified new Keynesian model; rather there is a multiplicity of explanations of wage and price rigidities and their macroeconomic consequences. Different elements within the new Keynesian school emphasize various aspects and causes of market imperfections and their macroeconomic effects. However, the numerous explanations are not mutually exclusive and often complement each other. In short, as Leslie's (1993) comment captures so well, 'New Keynesianism throws bucketfuls of grit into the smooth-running neoclassical paradigms.'

Because the literature reviewed here is so wide-ranging, it is convenient to divide the explanations of rigidities between those that focus on *nominal* rigidities and those that focus on *real* rigidities. A nominal rigidity occurs if something prevents the nominal price level from adjusting so as exactly to mimic nominal demand disturbances. A real rigidity occurs if some factor prevents real wages from adjusting or there is stickiness of one wage relative to another, or of one price relative to another (see Gordon, 1990). First we shall examine the impact of nominal rigidities.

## 7.5  Nominal Rigidities

Both orthodox and new Keynesian approaches assume that prices adjust slowly following a disturbance. But, unlike the Keynesian cross or IS–LM approaches, which arbitrarily assume fixed nominal wages and prices, the new Keynesian approach seeks to provide a microeconomic underpinning for the slow adjustment of both wages and prices. In line with the choice-theoretical framework of new classical analysis, the new Keynesian approach assumes that workers and firms are rational utility and profit maximizers, respectively.

As we have seen, new classicists adopt the flexible price auction model and apply this to the analysis of transactions conducted in all markets, including the labour market. In contrast, new Keynesians argue that it is important to utilize the Hicksian (1974) distinction between markets which are essentially fix-price, predominantly the labour market and a large section of the goods market, and markets which are flex-price, predominantly financial and commodity markets. In fix-price markets price setting is the norm, with price and wage inertia a reality. In order to generate monetary non-neutrality (real effects) Keynesian models rely on the failure of nominal wages and prices to adjust promptly to their new market-clearing levels following an aggregate demand disturbance. Keynesians have traditionally concentrated their attention on the labour market and nominal wage stickiness in order to explain the tendency of market economies to depart from full employment equilibrium. However, it is important to note that for any given path of nominal aggregate demand it is price, not wage, stickiness which is necessary to generate fluctuations in real output. Providing profits are sufficiently flexible, nominal prices could adjust to exactly mimic changes in nominal aggregate demand, leaving real output unaffected (see Gordon, 1990).

Nevertheless the first wave of new Keynesian reaction to the new classical critique concentrated on nominal wage rigidity.

### 7.5.1  Nominal wage rigidity
In traditional Keynesian models the price level is prevented from falling to restore equilibrium by the failure of money wages (costs) to adjust (see Figure 2.6). In the new classical models developed by Lucas, Sargent, Wallace and Barro during the 1970s, any anticipated monetary disturbance will cause an immediate jump of nominal wages and prices to their new equilibrium values, so preserving output and employment. In such a world, systematic monetary policy is ineffective. Initially it was widely believed that this new classical policy ineffective proposition was a direct implication of incorpo-

rating the rational expectations hypothesis into macroeconomic models. Fischer (1977) and Phelps and Taylor (1977) showed that nominal disturbances were capable of producing real effects in models incorporating rational expectations, providing the assumption of continuously clearing markets was dropped (see also Buiter, 1980). Following these contributions it became clear to everyone that the rational expectations hypothesis did not imply the end of Keynesian economics. The crucial feature of new classical models was shown to be the assumption of continuous market clearing, that is, perfect and instantaneous wage and price flexibility. But, as Phelps (1985) reminds us, it is often through the rejection of a theoretically interesting model that a science progresses and 'even if dead wrong, the new classical macroeconomics is still important because it demands Keynesians to fortify their theoretical structure or reconstruct it'.

The early Keynesian attempts to fortify their theoretical structure concentrated on nominal wage rigidities and the models developed by Fischer (1977) and Taylor (1980) introduced nominal inertia in the form of long-term wage contracts. In developed economies wages are not determined in spot markets but tend to be set for an agreed period in the form of an explicit (or implicit) contract. The existence of these long-term contracts can generate sufficient nominal wage rigidity for monetary policy to regain its effectiveness. It should be noted, however, that neither Fischer nor Phelps and Taylor pretend to have a rigorous microfoundation for their price- and wage-setting assumptions. Instead they take it for granted that there is a 'revealed preference' for long-term wage contracts reflecting the perceived disadvantages that accompany too frequent adjustments to wages and prices (for an innovative attempt to explain nominal wage inflexibility, see Laing, 1993).

Fischer's analysis has the following main features and involves the construction of a model similar to the Lucas–Sargent–Wallace policy ineffectiveness models discussed in Chapter 5. The output supply equation is the standard rational expectations Lucas 'surprise' function (7.1), where $\dot{P}_t$ and $\dot{P}_t^e$ are the actual and expected rates of inflation respectively:

$$Y_t = Y_{N_t} + \alpha(\dot{P}_t - \dot{P}_t^e), \quad \alpha > 0 \tag{7.1}$$

Fischer assumes that inflation expectations are formed rationally, $\dot{P}_t^e = E(\dot{P}_t \mid \Omega_{t-1})$, so we can write (7.1) as (7.2):

$$Y_t = Y_{N_t} + \alpha[\dot{P}_t - E(\dot{P}_t \mid \Omega_{t-1})] \tag{7.2}$$

Fischer's model abstracts from growth, so wage negotiators are assumed to aim for constancy of the real wage by setting nominal wage increases equal to expected inflation. This is given by (7.3):

$$\dot{W}_t = E(\dot{P}_t \mid \Omega_{t-1}) \tag{7.3}$$

Substituting (7.3) into (7.2) yields equation (7.4), which shows that aggregate supply is a decreasing function of the real wage (note this implies a countercyclical real wage).

$$Y_t = Y_{N_t} + \alpha[\dot{P}_t - \dot{W}_t], \text{ and } \alpha > 0 \tag{7.4}$$

For the multi-period contract nominal wage increases are fixed at $\dot{W}_t = \dot{W}_t^*$. Fischer (1977) makes the 'empirically reasonable' assumption that economic agents negotiate contracts in nominal terms for 'periods longer than the time it takes the monetary authority to react to changing economic circumstances'. Because the monetary authorities can change the money supply (and hence inflation) more frequently than overlapping labour contracts are renegotiated, monetary policy can have real effects in the short run although it will remain neutral in the long run.

The argument presented by Fischer can be understood with reference to Figure 7.1. The economy is initially operating at point *A*. Suppose in the current period an unexpected nominal demand shock occurs (such as a fall in velocity) which shifts the aggregate demand curve from $AD_0$ to $AD_1$. If prices

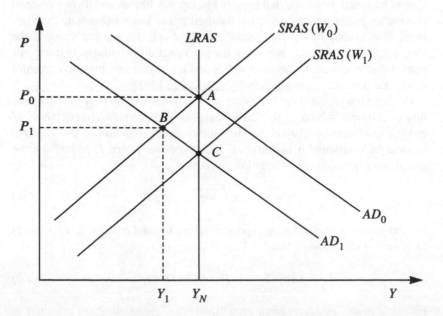

*Figure 7.1   Nominal wage contracts, rational expectations and monetary policy*

are flexible but nominal wages are temporarily rigid (and set $= W_0$) as the result of contracts negotiated in the previous period and which extend beyond the current period, the economy will move to point $B$, with real output falling from $Y_N$ to $Y_1$. With flexible wages and prices the short-run aggregate supply curve would shift down to the right from $SRAS$ $(W_0)$ to $SRAS$ $(W_1)$, to re-establish the natural rate level of output at point $C$. However, the existence of long-term nominal wage contracts prevents this and provides the monetary authorities with an opportunity to expand the money supply which, even if anticipated, shifts the $AD$ curve to the right and re-establishes equilibrium at point $A$. Providing the authorities are free to react to exogenous shocks at every time period, while workers are not, there is scope for demand management to stabilize the economy even if agents have rational expectations. In effect, if the monetary authorities can react to nominal demand shocks more quickly than the private sector can renegotiate nominal wages, there is scope for discretionary intervention. The fixed nominal wage gives the monetary authorities a handle on the real wage rate and hence employment and output. The non-neutrality of money in the Fischer model is not due to an unanticipated monetary surprise. Anticipated monetary policy has real effects because it is based on information that only becomes available after the contract has been made.

Wage contracts are an important feature in all major industrial market economies. However, there are significant differences between countries with respect to both contract duration and the timing of contract renegotiations. For example, in Japan nominal wage contracts typically last for one year and expire simultaneously. The synchronized renegotiation of contracts (the *shunto* system) in Japan is consistent with greater macroeconomic stability than is the case in the US economy, which has a system of non-synchronized over-lapping (staggered) contracts, many of which last for three years (see Gordon, 1982b; Hall and Taylor, 1997). In the UK contracts are overlapping but are typically shorter than in the USA, usually lasting for one year. When contracts are staggered, nominal wages will exhibit more inertia in the face of shocks than would be the case if existing contracts were renegotiated in a synchronized way so as to accommodate new information. Taylor (1980) demonstrated that if workers are concerned with their nominal wage relative to others, then staggered contracting will allow the impact of monetary policy on real variables to persist well beyond the length of the contracting period. Taylor (1992b) has shown that the responsiveness of wages to supply and demand conditions is much greater in Japan than in the USA, Canada and other major European countries, and this accounts for the more stable macroeconomic performance in Japan during the 1970s and early 1980s.

An immediate question arises from the above discussion. Why are long-term wage agreements formed if they increase macroeconomic instability?

According to Phelps (1985, 1990) there are private advantages to both firms
and workers from entering into long-term wage contracts:

1. Wage negotiations are costly in time for both workers and firms. Research must be carried out with respect to the structure of wage relativities
   both within and outside the negotiating organization. In addition, forecasts are required with respect to the likely future paths of key variables
   such as productivity, inflation, demand, profits and prices. The longer the
   period of the contract, the less frequently are such transaction costs
   incurred and in any case management will always tend to prefer a pre-set
   schedule for dealing with the complex issues associated with pay negotiations.
2. There always exists the potential for such negotiations to break down,
   with workers feeling that they may need to resort to strike action in order
   to strengthen their bargaining position. Such disruption is costly to both
   firms and workers.
3. It will not be an optimal strategy for a firm to 'jump' its wage rates to the
   new 'ultimate' equilibrium following a negative demand stock because if
   other firms do not do likewise the firm will have reduced its relative
   wage, which would be likely to increase labour turnover, which is costly
   to the firm.

Thus the responsiveness of wage rates during a recession does not follow the
new classical 'precision drill process'; rather we observe a 'ragged, disor-
derly retreat' as new information becomes available (Phelps, 1985, p. 564).

Another important question raised by this discussion relates to the absence
of indexing. Why are labour contracts not indexed to the rate of inflation?
Full cost of living agreements (COLAs) are simply too risky for firms (see
Gordon, 2003). The danger for firms is that not all shocks are nominal
demand shocks. If a firm agreed to index its wage rates to the rate of inflation,
then supply shocks, such as occurred in the 1970s, would drive up the price
level and with it a firm's wage costs, so preventing the necessary fall in real
wages implied by the energy shock.

Finally, we should also note that the staggering of wage contracts does
have some microeconomic purpose even if it causes macroeconomic problems. In a world where firms have imperfect knowledge of the current economic
situation, they can gain vital information by observing the prices and wages
set by other firms. According to Hall and Taylor (1997), staggered wage
setting provides useful information to both firms and workers about the
changing structure of wages and prices. In a decentralized system without
staggering, 'tremendous variability' would be introduced into the system.
Ball and Cecchetti (1988) show how imperfect information can make stag-

gered price and wage setting socially optimal by helping firms set prices closer to full information levels, leading to efficiency gains which outweigh the costs of price level inertia. Thus staggered price adjustment can arise from rational economic behaviour. In contrast, the case of wage setting in a synchronized system would seem to require some degree of active participation from the government.

### 7.5.2 Nominal price rigidity

Keynesian models based on nominal wage contracting soon came in for considerable criticism (see Barro, 1977b). Critics pointed out that the existence of such contracts is not explained from solid microeconomic principles. A further problem relates to the countercyclical path of the real wage in models with nominal wage contracts. In Fischer's model, a monetary expansion increases employment by lowering the real wage. Yet, as we have seen, the stylized facts of the business cycle do not provide strong support for this implication since real wages appear to be mildly procyclical (see Mankiw, 1990). Indeed, it was this issue that persuaded Mankiw (1991) that sticky nominal wage models made little sense. A combination of price-taking firms, neoclassical production technology and sticky nominal wages implies that aggregate demand contractions will be associated with a rise in the real wage, that is, real wages move countercyclically. As Mankiw notes, if this were the case then recessions would be 'quite popular'. While many people will be laid off, most people who remain employed will enjoy a higher real wage! 'If high real wages accompanied low employment as the *General Theory* and my Professors has taught me, then most households would welcome economic downturns'. So 'it was thinking about the real wage puzzle that originally got me interested in thinking about imperfections in goods markets, and eventually, about monopolistically competitive firms facing menu costs' (Mankiw, 1991, pp. 129–30).

As a result of these and other criticisms, some economists sympathetic to the Keynesian view that business cycles can be caused by fluctuations of aggregate demand switched their attention to nominal rigidities in the goods market, rather than continue with research into nominal wage inertia (Andersen, 1994). Indeed, the term 'new Keynesian' emerged in the mid-1980s as a description of those new theories that attempted to provide more solid microfoundations for the phenomenon of nominal price rigidity (see Rotemberg, 1987). From this standpoint, the 'fundamental new idea behind new Keynesian models is that of imperfect competition' (Ibid.). This is the crucial innovation which differentiates new Keynesians from Keynes, orthodox Keynesians, monetarists and new classicals.

If the process of changing prices were a costless exercise and if the failure to adjust prices involved substantial changes in a firm's profitability we would certainly expect to observe a high degree of nominal price flexibility. A firm operating under conditions of perfect competition is a price taker, and prices change automatically to clear markets as demand and supply conditions change. Since each firm can sell as much output as it likes at the going market price, a perfectly competitive firm which attempted to charge a price above the market-clearing level would have zero sales. There is also no profit incentive to reduce price independently, given that the firm's demand curve is perfectly elastic at the prevailing market price. Thus in this world of perfect price flexibility it makes no sense to talk of the individual firm having a pricing decision.

When firms operate in imperfectly competitive markets a firm's profits will vary differentially with changes in its own price because its sales will not fall to zero if it marginally increases price. Price reductions by such a firm will increase sales but also result in less revenue per unit sold. In such circumstances any divergence of price from the optimum will only produce 'second-order' reductions of profits. Hence the presence of even small costs to price adjustment can generate considerable aggregate nominal price rigidity. This observation, due to Akerlof and Yellen (1985a), Mankiw (1985) and Parkin (1986), is referred to by Rotemberg (1987) as the 'PAYM insight'.

The PAYM insight makes a simple but powerful point. The private cost of nominal rigidities to the individual firm is much smaller than the macroeconomic consequences of such rigidities. A key ingredient of the PAYM insight is the presence of frictions or barriers to price adjustment known as 'menu costs'. These menu costs include the physical costs of resetting prices, such as the printing of new price lists and catalogues, as well as expensive management time used up in the supervision and renegotiation of purchase and sales contracts with suppliers and customers. To illustrate how small menu costs can produce large macroeconomic fluctuations, we will review the arguments made by Mankiw and by Akerlof and Yellen.

In imperfectly competitive markets a firm's demand will depend on (i) its relative price and (ii) aggregate demand. Suppose following a decline in aggregate demand the demand curve facing an imperfectly competitive firm shifts to the left. A shift of the demand curve to the left can significantly reduce a firm's profits. However, faced with this new demand curve, the firm may gain little by changing its price. The firm would prefer that the demand curve had not shifted but, given the new situation, it can only choose some point on the new demand curve. This decline in demand is illustrated in Figure 7.2 by the shift of demand from $D_0$ to $D_1$. Before the decline in demand the profit-maximizing price and output are $P_0$ and $Q_0$, since marginal revenue ($MR_0$) is equal to marginal cost ($MC_0$) at point $X$. For convenience we assume that marginal cost does not vary with output over the range shown. Following the decline in demand, the firm suffers a significant reduction in its profits. Before the reduction in demand, profits are indicated in

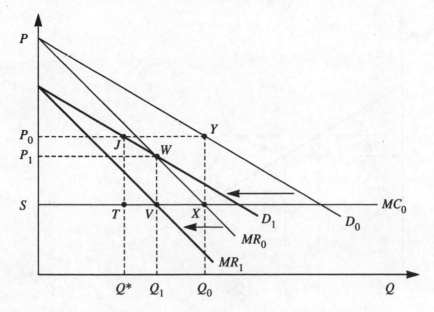

*Figure 7.2   Price adjustment under monopolistic competition*

Figure 7.2 by the area $SP_0YX$. If the firm does not initially reduce its price following the decline in demand, profits fall to the area indicated by $SP_0JT$. Because this firm is a 'price maker' it must decide whether or not to reduce price to the new profit-maximizing point indicated by $W$ on the new demand curve $D_1$. The new profit-maximizing level of output is determined where $MR_1 = MC_0$. With a level of output of $Q_1$, the firm would make profits of $SP_1$ $WV$. If there were no adjustment costs associated with changing price, a profit-maximizing firm would reduce its price from $P_0$ to $P_1$. However, if a firm faces non-trivial 'menu costs' of $z$, the firm may decide to leave price at $P_0$; that is, the firm moves from point $Y$ to point $J$ in Figure 7.2.

Figure 7.3 indicates the consequences of the firm's decision. By reducing price from $P_0$ to $P_1$ the firm would increase its profits by $B - A$. There is no incentive for a profit-maximizing firm to reduce price if $z > B - A$. The loss to society of producing an output of $Q^*$ rather than $Q_1$ is indicated by $B + C$, which represents the loss of total surplus. If following a reduction of demand $B + C > z > B - A$, then the firm will not cut its price even though doing so would be socially optimal. The flatter the $MC$ schedule, the smaller are the menu costs necessary to validate a firm's decision to leave the price unchanged. Readers should confirm for themselves that the incentive to lower prices is therefore greater the more marginal cost falls when output declines (see Gordon, 1990; D. Romer, 2001).

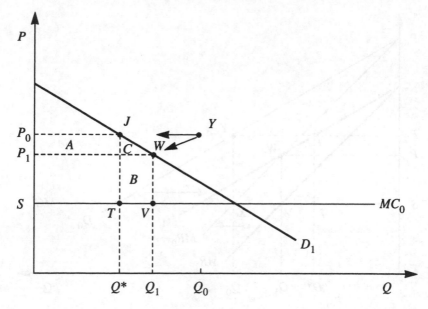

*Figure 7.3   Menu costs v. price adjustment*

In the Akerlof and Yellen (1985a, 1985b) model, inertial wage-price be-haviour by firms 'may be near rational'. Firms that behave sub-optimally in their price-setting behaviour may suffer losses but they are likely to be second order (small). The idea of near rationality is illustrated in Figure 7.4. As before, the profit-maximizing price following a decline in demand is indicated by $P_1$. The reduction in profits $(\pi_1 - \pi^*)$ that results from failure to reduce price from $P_0$ to $P_1$ is small (second order) even without taking into account menu costs (that is, in Figure 7.3, $B - A$ is small). Akerlof and Yellen (1985a) also demonstrate that, when imperfect competition in the product market is combined with efficiency wages in the labour market, aggregate demand disturbances will lead to cyclical fluctuations (see Akerlof, 2002).

Although the firm may optimally choose to maintain price at $P_0$, the impact of their decision, if repeated by all firms, can have significant macroeconomic effects. Blanchard and Kiyotaki (1987), in their interpretation of the PAYM insight, show that the macroeconomic effects of nominal price rigidity differ from the private costs because price rigidity generates an aggregate demand externality. Society would be considerably better off if all firms cut their prices, but the private incentives to do so are absent. As before, assume that a firm's demand curve has shifted left as a result of a decline in aggregate demand. If firms did not face menu costs, then profit-maximizing behaviour would dictate that all firms lowered their prices; that is, in terms of Figures

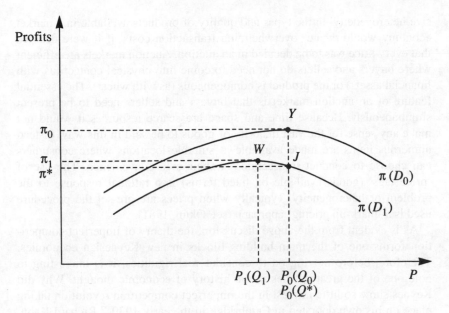

*Figure 7.4   Near rationality*

7.2 and 7.3, each firm would move from $Y$ to $W$. Because all firms are lowering their prices, each firm will find the cost of its inputs are falling, including money wages. Hence each firm will find that its marginal cost curve begins to shift down. This allows firms to reduce prices further. In Figure 7.3, as $MC_0$ shifts down, output will expand. Since all firms are engaged in further price reductions, input prices will fall again, producing another reduction of $MC$. Since this process of price deflation will increase real money balances, thereby lowering interest rates, aggregate demand will increase. This will shift the demand curves facing each firm to the right, so that output will return to $Q_0$.

If the presence of menu costs and/or near rational behaviour causes nominal price rigidity, shocks to nominal aggregate demand will cause large fluctuations in output and welfare. Since such fluctuations are inefficient, this indicates that stabilization policy is desirable. Obviously if money wages are rigid (because of contracts) the marginal cost curve will be sticky, thus reinforcing the impact of menu costs in producing price rigidities.

We noted earlier that there are several private advantages to be gained by both firms and workers from entering into long-term wage contracts. Many of these advantages also apply to long-term agreements between firms with respect to product prices. Pre-set prices not only reduce uncertainty but also economize on the use of scarce resources. Gordon (1981) argues that 'persuasive heterogeneity' in the types and quality of products available in a market economy would create 'overwhelming transaction costs' if it were decided that every price was to be decided in an auction. Auction markets are efficient where buyers and sellers do not need to come into physical contact (as with financial assets) or the product is homogeneous (as with wheat). The essential feature of an auction market is that buyers and sellers need to be present simultaneously. Because time and space are scarce resources it would not make any sense for the vast majority of goods to be sold in this way. Instead numerous items are made available at suitable locations where consumers can choose to conduct transactions at their own convenience. The use of 'price tags' (goods available on fixed terms) is a rational response to the problem of heterogeneity. Typically when prices are pre-set the procedure used is a 'mark-up pricing' approach (see Okun, 1981).

As is evident from the above discussion, the theory of imperfect competition forms one of the main building-blocks in new Keynesian economics. Therefore, before moving on to consider real rigidities, it is interesting to note one of the great puzzles in the history of economic thought. Why did Keynes show so little interest in the imperfect competition revolution taking place on his own doorstep in Cambridge in the early 1930s? Richard Kahn, author of the famous 1931 multiplier article and colleague of Keynes, was fully conversant with the theory of imperfect competition well before Joan Robinson's famous book was published on the subject in 1933. Given that Keynes, Kahn and Robinson shared the same Cambridge academic environment during the period when the *General Theory* was being written, it is remarkable that Keynes adopted the classical/neoclassical assumption of a perfectly competitive product market which Kahn (1929) had already argued was unsound for short-period analysis (see Marris, 1991)! As Dixon (1997) notes, 'had Kahn and Keynes been able to work together, or Keynes and Robinson, the *General Theory* might have been very different'. In contrast to the orthodox Keynesian school, and inspired by the work of Michal Kalecki, Post Keynesians have always stressed the importance of price-fixing firms in their models (Arestis, 1997).

## 7.6 Dornbusch's Overshooting Model

As we have already seen, the sticky-price rational expectations models put forward by Fischer (1977) and Phelps and Taylor (1977) analyse the role of monetary policy in the context of a closed economy. Before considering the importance of real rigidities in new Keynesian analysis we briefly examine Dornbusch's (1976) sticky-price rational expectations model of a small open economy. This exchange rate 'overshooting' model has been described by Kenneth Rogoff (2002) 'as one of the most influential papers written in the field of International Economics since World War II', a paper which Rogoff suggests 'marks the birth of modern international macroeconomics'.

Before discussing the main predictions of Dornbusch's model it is helpful to place the model in the context of earlier discussion of aspects of international macroeconomics. In Chapter 3, section 3.5.4 we discussed how in the fixed price (IS–LM–BP) Mundell–Fleming model of an open economy operating under a regime of flexible exchange rates monetary expansion results in an increase in income, with the effects of monetary expansion on aggregate demand and income being reinforced by exchange rate depreciation. Furthermore, in the limiting case of perfect capital mobility monetary policy becomes 'all-powerful'. In contrast, in Chapter 4, section 4.4.3 we considered how in the monetary approach to exchange rate determination, where real income is exogenously given at its natural level, monetary expansion leads to a depreciation in the exchange rate and an increase in the domestic price level. In what follows we outline the essence of Dornbusch's (1976) sticky-price rational expectations model in which monetary expansion causes the exchange rate to depreciate (with short-run overshooting) with no change in real output.

In his model Dornbusch made a number of assumptions, the most important of which are that:

1. goods markets are slow to adjust compared to asset markets and exchange rates; that is, goods prices are sticky;
2. movements in the exchange rate are consistent with rational expectations;
3. with perfect capital mobility, the domestic rate of interest of a small open economy must equal the world interest rate (which is given exogenously), plus the expected rate of depreciation of the domestic currency; that is, expected exchange rate changes have to be compensated by the interest rate differential between domestic and foreign assets; and
4. the demand for real money balances depends on the domestic interest rate (determined where equilibrium occurs in the domestic money market) and real income, which is fixed.

Given these assumptions, what effect will monetary expansion have on the exchange rate? In the short run with fixed prices and a given level of real income an increase in the (real) money supply results in a fall in the domestic interest rate, thereby maintaining equilibrium in the domestic money market. The fall in the domestic interest rate means that, with the foreign interest rate fixed exogenously (due to the small-country assumption), the domestic currency must be expected to appreciate. While short-run equilibrium requires an expected appreciation of the domestic currency, long-run equilibrium requires a depreciation of the exchange rate. In other words, since long-run equilibrium requires a depreciation of the domestic currency (compared to its initial level), the exchange rate depreciates too far (that is, in the short run it overshoots), so that it can be expected to appreciate back to its long-run equilibrium level. Such short-run exchange rate overshooting is fully consistent with rational expectations because the exchange rate follows the path it is expected to follow.

A number of points are worth noting with respect to the above analysis. First, the source of exchange rate overshooting in the Dornbusch model lies in goods prices being relatively sticky in the short run. In other words, the crucial assumption made in the model is that asset markets and exchange rates adjust more quickly than do goods markets. Second, the rate at which the exchange rate adjusts back to its long-run equilibrium level depends on the speed at which the price level adjusts to the increase in the money stock. Finally, in the long run, monetary expansion results in an equi-proportionate increase in prices and depreciation in the exchange rate.

## 7.7   Real Rigidities

One important criticism of the menu cost literature noted by Ball et al. (1988) is that models with nominal frictions can in theory produce large nominal rigidities but 'do so for implausible parameter values'. However, Ball and Romer (1990) demonstrated that substantial nominal rigidities can result from a combination of real rigidities and small frictions to nominal adjustment. Indeed, Mankiw and Romer (1991) identify the interaction between nominal and real imperfections as 'a distinguishing feature of the new Keynesian economies'.

If all nominal prices in an economy were completely and instantaneously flexible, a purely nominal shock would leave the real equilibrium of an economy unchanged. As Ball and Romer (1990) note, 'Real rigidity does not imply nominal rigidity: without an independent source of nominal stickiness prices adjust fully to nominal shocks regardless of the extent of real rigidities.' However, rigidity of real prices and wages will magnify the non-neutralities which result from small nominal frictions. The importance of this point can be seen by considering the impact of a decline in the money supply. Suppose initially that the presence of menu costs deters firms from reducing their prices in response to this nominal disturbance. With the price level unchanged real output will decline. Each monopolistically competitive firm will find that its demand curve has shifted to the left. Because each firm is producing less output, the effective demand for labour declines (see Abel and Bernanke, 2001). If labour supply is relatively inelastic, the shift of labour demand implied by the decline in output will cause a large fall in real wages; that is, the nominal wage rate declines to bring this about (see Ball et al., 1988; Gordon, 1990; D. Romer, 1993). This decline in the real wage rate implies a decline in marginal cost, a decline which will be strongly reinforced if the marginal product of labour rises sharply as the labour input decreases. As is evident from Figure 7.2, an upward-sloping marginal cost curve would greatly increase the incentive to reduce price and would 'swamp any plausible barriers to nominal adjustment' unless the elasticity of demand at the existing price falls as the firm's demand curve shifts to the left. The greater the decline in the elasticity of demand at the existing price as output falls, the more the marginal revenue curve facing a firm shifts to the left and the less incentive there is for a firm to reduce its price.

David Romer (1993) sums up the essence of this issue as follows: 'Thus if the classical dichotomy is to fail, it must be that marginal cost does not fall sharply in response to a demand-driven output contraction, or that marginal revenue does fall sharply, or some combination of the two.' Real price rigidity is high the greater is the cyclical sensitivity of the elasticity of demand and the smaller is the cyclical sensitivity of marginal cost. Hence nominal shocks have large real consequences the greater the degree of real rigidity (see D. Romer, 2001).

The points discussed above can be more easily understood by referring to the familiar mark-up pricing equation facing a profit-maximizing monopolistically competitive firm (see Pindyck and Rubinfeld, 1998, p. 340). Profit maximization requires that the firm produces that level of output where marginal revenue (*MR*) equals cost (*MC*). Marginal revenue can be expressed in the form shown by equation (7.5):

$$MR = P + P(1/\eta) \tag{7.5}$$

where $P$ is the firm's price and $\eta$ is the price elasticity of demand. Profit maximization therefore requires that:

$$P + P(1/\eta) = MC \tag{7.6}$$

By rearranging equation (7.6) we get equation (7.7):

$$\frac{P - MC}{P} = -1/\eta \tag{7.7}$$

This equation can also be rearranged so as to express price as a mark-up on marginal cost. The mark-up equation is given by (7.8):

$$P = MC\frac{1}{1+1/\eta} \qquad (7.8)$$

Since marginal cost is the nominal wage ($W$) divided by the marginal product of labour ($MPL$), we finally get equation (7.9):

$$P = \frac{W}{MPL}\left(\frac{1}{1+1/\eta}\right) \qquad (7.9)$$

The term inside the brackets represents the mark-up, the size of which varies *inversely* with the elasticity of demand (remember $\eta$ is negative). Equation (7.9) indicates that $P$ will not fall when $MC$ declines if the mark-up rises sufficiently to offset this decline (see Stiglitz, 1984). If the elasticity of demand does not decline, then equation (7.9) also indicates that the incentive to change price will be small in the presence of menu costs if $MPL$ does not rise strongly as the labour input is reduced (see Hall, 1991). Rotemberg and Woodford (1991) suggest that desired mark-ups over marginal cost fall during a boom because it becomes increasingly difficult to maintain oligopolistic collusion; that is, industries become more competitive in periods of high economic activity. During recessions implicit collusion increases, leading to a countercyclical mark-up that acts as a real rigidity, magnifying the impact on nominal rigidity of relatively small menu costs (D. Romer, 2001).

### 7.7.1 Other sources of real price rigidity

We have already noted that mild sensitivity of marginal cost to variations in output and procyclical elasticity of demand (implying a countercyclical mark-up) will contribute towards real price rigidity. The new Keynesian literature has also identified several other potential sources of real price rigidity.

*Thick market externalities* In the real world buyers and sellers are not brought together without incurring search costs. Consumers must spend time searching the market for the goods they desire and firms advertise in order to attract customers. Workers and employers must also spend time and resources searching the market. When markets are thick during periods of high economic activity it seems plausible that search costs will be lower than is the case in a thin market characterized by a low level of trading activity (see Diamond, 1982). It may also be the case that people are much more willing to participate in thick markets where a lot of trade is taking place and this leads to strategic complementary; that is, the optimal level of activity of one firm depends on the activity of other firms. If these thick market externalities help to shift the marginal cost curve up in recessions and down in booms, then this will contribute to real price rigidity.

*Customer markets* The distinction between auction and customer markets has been developed by Okun (1975, 1981). The crucial characteristic of a customer market is a low frequency of search relative to the frequency of purchase (McDonald, 1992). Most products are sold through a process of shopping and, providing the costs of searching the market are non-trivial, the buyer will always have imperfect (limited) information concerning the lowest price in the marketplace. Because of the search costs associated with the shopping process, sellers have some monopoly power even though there may be a large number of firms in the market, each selling a similar product. Since a large number of customers make repetitive purchases it is in the interests of any firm to discourage its customers from searching the market in order to find a better deal. Firms are therefore discouraged from frequently changing their prices, a practice which will provide an incentive for customers to look elsewhere. Whereas an increase in price will be noticed immediately by customers, a decrease in price will produce a much smaller initial response as it takes time for this new information to reach the buyers at other firms. This difference in the response rates of customers to price increases and decreases, and the desire of a firm to hold on to its regular customers, will tend to produce relative price stickiness (see Phelps, 1985, for an excellent discussion of customer markets).

*Price rigidity and the input–output table* Gordon (1981, 1990) has drawn attention to the complexity of decision making in a world where, typically, thousands of firms buy thousands of components containing thousands of ingredients from numerous other firms, many of which may reside overseas. 'Once decentralisation and multiplicity of supplier–producer relationships are recognised, no single firm can perform an action that would eliminate the aggregate business cycle' (Gordon, 1981, p. 525).

Because a firm is linked to thousands of other firms via a complex input–output table, it is impossible for it to know the identity of all the other agents linked together in the web of supplier–producer relationships. Because of this complexity there is no certainty that marginal revenue and marginal cost will move in tandem following an aggregate demand shock. There is no certainty for an individual firm that, following a decline in aggregate demand, its marginal cost will move in proportion to the decline in demand for its products. Many of its suppliers may be firms in other countries facing different aggregate demand conditions. To reduce price in these circumstances is more likely to produce bankruptcy for the particular firm than it is to contribute to the elimination of the business cycle because a typical firm will be subject to both local and aggregate demand shocks as well as local and aggregate cost shocks. As Gordon (1990) argues, in such a world no firm would be likely to take the risk of nominal GNP indexation that would inhibit its freedom and flexibility of action in responding to the wide variety of shocks which can influence the position of its marginal revenue and cost curves. Since indexation is undesirable when there is substantial independence of marginal cost and aggregate demand, Gordon's input–output theory not only provides an explanation of real price rigidity but also translates into a theory of nominal rigidity. The fundamental reason for the gradual adjustment of prices is that this represents the safest course of action for firms operating in an uncertain world where information is inevitably imperfect.

Clearly the informational requirements necessary for rational pricing behaviour in every period are enormous for price-setting firms. Not only do they need to know the position and shape of their demand and cost curves; they also need to predict the pricing behaviour of all the other firms in the input–output table. Since the firm's demand and cost curves are influenced by aggregate demand, it is also necessary for firms to predict the value of all the relevant macro variables that influence aggregate demand. In short, the decision makers within monopolistically competitive firms need to be first-class general equilibrium theorists with perfect information! Given these complications, the tendency of firms to follow simple mark-up pricing rules may be close to optimal. The incentive to follow such rules is reinforced if other firms do likewise, since this ensures that a firm will maintain its relative price, which will tend to minimize its losses (see Naish, 1993). Another simple rule which a firm can follow in a complex input–output world is to wait until other firms raise or lower their price before initiating a change. This produces *staggering* in price setting, which implies that the price level will take longer to adjust to an aggregate demand shock.

*Capital market imperfections*   An important obstacle to firms seeking external finance is the problem of asymmetric information between borrowers and lenders; that is, borrowers are much better informed about the viability and quality of their investment projects than lenders. One consequence of this will be that external finance will be more expensive to a firm than internal finance. During booms when firms are making higher profits there are more internal funds to finance various projects. Hence during recessions the cost of finance rises as the result of a greater reliance on external sources. If the cost of capital is countercyclical, this too will tend to make a firm's costs rise during a recession (see Bernanke and Gertler, 1989; D. Romer, 1993).

*Judging quality by price*   Stiglitz (1987) has emphasized another reason why firms may be reluctant to reduce price when faced with a decline in demand. In markets where customers have imperfect information about the characteristics of the products which they wish to buy, the price may be used as a quality signal. By lowering price a firm runs the risk that its customers (or potential customers) may interpret this action as a signal indicating a deterioration of quality.

Having examined several potential sources of real rigidity in the product market, we will now turn to real rigidities in the labour market. If real wages are rigid in the face of demand disturbances, this substantially reduces a firm's incentive to vary its price as a response to such disturbances.

### 7.7.2 Real wage rigidity

Economists have been much better at explaining the consequences of nominal wage rigidity than they have at providing a generally acceptable theoretical explanation of the causes of such inertia. Nominal rigidities allow fluctuations of aggregate demand to have real effects and contribute to a non-market-clearing explanation of business cycles. However, Keynesian economists are also concerned to explain the persistently high levels of unemployment that have been a major feature of the labour markets of the major industrial countries since the early 1970s and particularly in Europe during the 1980s (see Table 1.4). In new classical monetary and real business cycle models all agents are price takers. Perfect and instantaneous price and wage flexibility ensures that the labour market always clears at a Walrasian market-clearing real wage. In a new Keynesian world, where price makers predominate, an equilibrium real wage can emerge which differs from the market-clearing real wage. Stiglitz (1987) defines a market equilibrium as 'a state where no agents have an incentive to change their behaviour' and in new Keynesian models of real wage rigidity equilibrium may not be characterized by market clearing; that is, demand equals supply. Models involving real wage rigidity are capable of generating involuntary unemployment in long-run equilibrium, in contrast to new classical models where, with everyone on their labour supply function, unemployment in equilibrium is a voluntary phenomenon. Whereas Lucas (1978a) argues for the abandonment of the idea that a large part of unemployment is involuntary, Solow (1980) believes that 'what looks like involuntary unemployment is involuntary unemployment' (see also Hahn, 1987; Blinder, 1988a).

New Keynesian explanations of real wage rigidity fall into three main groups: (i) implicit contract theories; (ii) efficiency wage theories; and (iii) insider–outsider theories. Since new Keynesian theorists have been mainly associated with the second and third of these, we will provide only a brief comment on implicit contract theory. The reader should consult Rosen (1985) and Timbrell (1989), who provide comprehensive surveys of the implicit contract literature. It should also be noted that Phelps (1990, 1994) treats theories of real wage rigidity as a separate category from new Keynesian theory, belonging instead to what he calls the 'Structuralist school'.

*Implicit contract models*    The original implicit (non-union) contract models were provided by Bailey (1974), D.F. Gordon (1974) and Azariadis (1975). Following the development of the natural rate hypothesis (Friedman, 1968a; Phelps, 1968), economists devoted more attention to modelling labour market behaviour as the outcome of maximizing behaviour. The main contribution of the 'new' microeconomics literature (Phelps et al., 1970) was to explain why the natural rate of unemployment was positive. However, there appears to be much less turnover in the labour market than search theory implies. Furthermore, wages frequently diverge from marginal productivities. Implicit contract theory seeks to understand what it is that forms the 'economic glue' that keeps workers and firms together in long-term relationships since such arrangements, rather than the Walrasian auctioneer, dominate the labour market. Because firms seek to maintain the loyalty of their workforce they find it necessary to enter into unwritten (implicit) understandings with their workers. This 'invisible handshake' provides each worker with assurances concerning the terms of the working relationship under a variety of working circumstances. The models of Bailey, Gordon and Azariadis examine the consequences of optimal labour contracts established between risk-neutral firms and risk-averse workers. In these circumstances the wage rate not only represents payment for labour services but also serves as an insurance against the risk of variable income in the face of shocks. A constant real wage smooths the individual worker's consumption stream and firms provide this 'insurance' since they are in a better position than workers to weather economic fluctuations, given their better access to capital and insurance markets. Because firms provide stable wages over time, workers, for their part, accept a real wage which is lower on average than the highly varying rates that would be dictated by market forces.

A major problem with this approach is that it predicts work sharing rather than lay-offs when the economic climate deteriorates. The theory also fails to explain why the firm does not pay lower wages to new recruits. In attempting to remedy these and other weaknesses of this explanation of real wage rigidity, new Keynesian economists have developed efficiency wage and insider–outsider models of wage inertia (see Manning, 1995).

*Efficiency wage models*    Any acceptable account of involuntary unemployment must explain why unemployed workers are unable to bid down wages to a level that will generate full employment. Efficiency wage theories suggest that it is not in a firm's interest to lower real wages because the productivity (effort or efficiency) of workers is not independent of the wage, rather real wages and worker effort are interdependent, at least over some meaningful range. Efficiency wage theory, described by Gordon (1990) as the 'rage of the 80s', is surveyed by Yellen (1984), Akerlof and Yellen (1986), Katz (1986,

1988), Haley (1990), and Weiss (1991); see also Akerlof (1979, 2002), and Stiglitz (2002).

Solow (1979) provides the basic structure of efficiency wage models. In Solow's model, wage stickiness is in the employer's interest because wage cutting would lower productivity and raise costs. Because the wage enters a firm's short-run production function in a labour-augmenting way, a cost-minimizing firm will favour real wage rigidity. This can be demonstrated as follows (see Yellen, 1984; Katz, 1988). Assume an economy with identical perfectly competitive firms, each of which has a production function of the form shown in equation (7.10):

$$Q = AF[e(w)L], e'(w) > 0 \qquad (7.10)$$

Here $Q$ is the firm's output, $A$ represents a productivity shift factor, $e$ is effort per worker, $w$ is the real wage and $L$ is the labour input. Effort is assumed to be an increasing function of the real wage and all workers are assumed to be identical. The firm aims to maximize its profits ($\pi$), which are given by equation (7.11):

$$\pi = AF[e(w)L] - wL \qquad (7.11)$$

Since effort enters the profit equation as $e(w)$, a cut in the real wage below that which generates maximum worker effort will lower the firm's profits. If the firm can hire all the labour it desires at the wage it offers, it will maximize its profits by offering an efficiency wage of $w^*$ which satisfies two conditions. The first condition is that the elasticity of effort with respect to the wage is unity. Restated, this means that the firm should set a wage which will minimize labour costs per efficiency unit of labour. This is illustrated in Figure 7.5. In panel (a) the effort curve indicated by $E$ shows the relationship between the effort of workers and the real wage. The higher the real wage, the greater the effort of workers. Initially there is a region of increasing returns where increases in the real wage rate elicit a more than proportionate increase in worker effort (productivity). Effort per pound (dollar) of real wage is measured by $e/w$. This ratio is maximized at point $M$, where $0X$ is tangential to the effort function. Since the slope of the effort curve ($e/w$) is the inverse of wage costs per efficiency unit ($w/e$), as the slope of $E$ increases the wage cost per efficiency unit falls and vice versa. The relationship between $w/e$ and $w$ is shown in panel (b) of Figure 7.5. Since $e/w$ is maximized at $M$ with an efficiency wage of $w^*$, the wage cost per efficiency unit also reaches a minimum at a real wage of $w^*$ (see Stiglitz, 1987, p. 5).

The second condition for profit maximization is that the firm should hire labour up to the point where its marginal product is equal to the efficiency

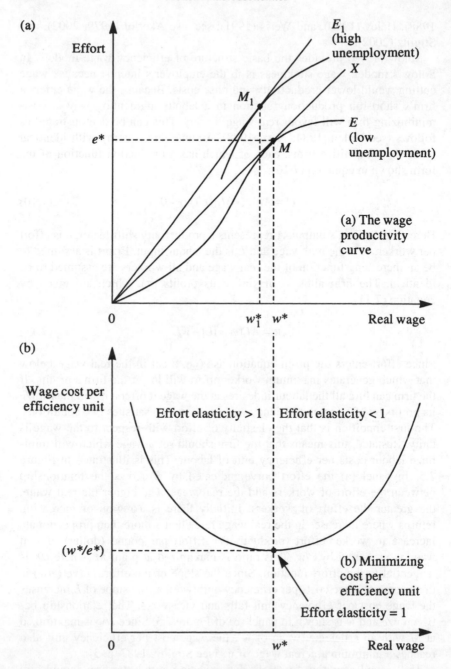

*Figure 7.5    The efficiency wage and the Solow condition*

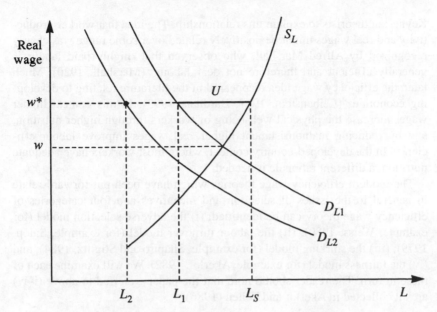

*Figure 7.6   Involuntary unemployment in the efficiency wage model*

wage. If the aggregate demand for labour at $w^*$ is less than the aggregate supply of labour, then the market equilibrium will entail involuntary unemployment. Since the optimal wage rate $w^*$ does not depend on either the level of employment or the productivity shift parameter $(A)$, a shock which shifts the aggregate demand for labour will lead to a change in employment but no change in the rigid real (efficiency) wage. These points are illustrated in Figure 7.6. Here $D_{L1}$ shows the marginal product of labour for a given level of effort $(e^*)$. If the efficiency wage exceeds the market-clearing wage $(w)$, then the market equilibrium is consistent with involuntary unemployment shown by $U$. If a shock shifts the labour demand curve to $D_{L2}$, then involuntary unemployment will increase, since the efficiency wage remains at $w^*$. Only if the market-clearing (Walrasian) wage exceeds the efficiency wage will involuntary unemployment be absent (see Abel and Bernanke, 2001). With $w > w^*$ firms would be forced to pay the market-clearing wage but, for reasons discussed in the following section, $w^*$ is always likely to be greater than the market-clearing wage. If an increase in unemployment influences the effort of employed workers, then the effort curve will shift up, which lowers the wage at which $e/w$ is maximized. This possibility is illustrated in Figure 7.5 by a shift of the effort curve from $E$ to $E_1$. The $e/w$ ratio is now maximized at $M_1$, with a new efficiency wage of $w_1^*$.

So far we have assumed that effort is positively related to the real wage rate. Now we must examine the reasons that have been advanced by new

Keynesian theorists to explain this relationship. The idea that worker productivity and real wages might be positively related over some range was clearly recognized by Alfred Marshall, who observed that 'highly paid labour is generally efficient and therefore not dear labour' (Marshall, 1920). Much later, the efficiency wage idea reappeared in the literature relating to developing economies (Leibenstein, 1957; Bardhan, 1993). In this context higher wages increase the physical well-being of workers through higher nutrition, and by reducing malnourishment higher real wages improve labour efficiency. In the developed-country context, where most workers have adequate nutrition, a different rationale is needed.

The modern efficiency wage theories which have been put forward relate in general to the issues of selection and incentives and four categories of efficiency wage theory can be identified: (i) the adverse selection model (for example, Weiss, 1980); (ii) the labour turnover model (for example, Salop, 1979); (iii) the shirking model (for example, Shapiro and Stiglitz, 1984); and (iv) the fairness model (for example, Akerlof, 1982). We will examine each of these in turn. The reader should note that the papers referred to above (i–iv) are all collected in Akerlof and Yellen (1986).

*The adverse selection model*   In the adverse selection model, firms that offer higher wages will attract the best workers. Because the labour market is populated by heterogeneous individuals, firms have imperfect information about the productivity characteristics of job applicants; the labour market is an excellent example of a market where asymmetric information predominates. When there is asymmetric information one party to a transaction has more information than the other party. In this case workers have more information about their own abilities, honesty and commitment than employers before they are hired and will attempt to send signals to potential employers that convey information about their qualities, such as educational qualifications, previous employment record and current wage if employed (see Spence, 1974, for a discussion of job market signalling). Because of the non-trivial hiring and firing costs firms prefer not to hire workers and then find they need to fire those with low productivity. The firm may also need to invest considerable resources in training new employees before it becomes clear that they are not up to scratch. One way of avoiding this problem is for the firm to send a signal to the labour market in the form of offers of high wages. In the model presented by Weiss (1980) the wage offered by a firm influences both the number and quality of job applicants. If workers' abilities are closely connected to their reservation wage, then higher wage offers will attract the most productive job applicants and any applicant who offers to work for less than the efficiency wage will be regarded as a potential 'lemon'. Firms will also be reluctant to lower wage rates even if faced with an excess supply of labour wishing to work at the prevailing wage offer because this would in all likelihood induce the most productive workers to quit voluntarily. As a result of these influences an underemployment equilibrium is attained. To avoid adverse selection problems firms will attempt to introduce screening devices, but these measures involve costs, as will the continuous monitoring of workers after they have been appointed.

*The labour turnover model*  A second reason why firms may offer an efficiency wage in excess of the market-clearing wage is to reduce costly labour turnover. This approach received inspiration from the pioneering work of Phelps (1968) and Phelps et al. (1970) in the development of explanations of the natural rate of unemployment and search behaviour. The idea here is that workers' willingness to quit a job will be significantly reduced if a firm pays above the going rate. With quitting rates a decreasing function of the real wage, firms have an incentive to pay an efficiency wage to reduce costly labour turnover. In the model developed by Salop (1979), labour market equilibrium entails involuntary unemployment since all firms need to raise their wages to deter workers from quitting. In situations where unemployment increases, the wage premium necessary to deter labour turnover will fall.

*The shirking model*  In most occupations labour contracts are incomplete, which allows workers to exercise discretion with respect to their effort levels. Because contracts cannot specify every aspect of a worker's performance and duties there is 'effort discretion' (see Leibenstein, 1979, for a similar approach). Since the collection of information relating to the productivity of individual workers and the continual monitoring of workers is very costly to the firm, the payment of an efficiency wage in excess of the market-clearing equilibrium wage can act as an incentive which will deter the worker from shirking. Such behaviour may be particularly difficult to detect and monitor when teamwork characterizes the workplace.

The possibility that workers may vary their effort is a further example of the type of problem that can arise when there is an informational asymmetry present. Workers know more about their effort levels than do their employers. This asymmetry creates a 'principal–agent' problem. An agency relationship develops whenever there is a relationship between economic actors and the welfare of one person depends on the actions of the other party; that is, when the welfare of the principal is influenced by the action (or inaction) of the agent. In the labour market case the principal is the owner of an enterprise and the managers and other workers are the agents. One way of reducing the problem of shirking in this context is to pay an efficiency wage.

The threat of dismissal is not an effective deterrent in a labour market where workers can quickly find a new job at the same wage rate. However, if a firm pays a wage in excess of that available elsewhere, or if there is unemployment, workers have an incentive not to shirk, since there is now a real cost to being fired and shirking becomes more risky for each worker. In the Shapiro–Stiglitz (1984) model, the payment of an efficiency wage acts as a disincentive to shirking, and involuntary unemployment in equilibrium is an outcome of the problems firms face when monitoring is imperfect: 'With imperfect monitoring and full employment workers will choose to shirk.' By being paid more than the going rate, workers now face a real penalty if they are caught shirking. But, as Shapiro and Stiglitz (1984) note, 'if it pays one firm to raise its wage it will pay all firms to raise their wages'. Since a rise in the general level of real wages raises unemployment, even if all firms pay the same efficiency wage, workers again have an incentive not to shirk because if caught they will now face the possibility of prolonged unemployment. The 'reserve army' of the unemployed act as a disincentive device. Hence the effort (productivity) of the worker hired by the $i$th firm, $e_i$, is a function of the wage it pays, $w_i$, the wage paid by all other firms, $w_{-i}$, and the rate of unemployment, $u$. This is shown in equation (7.12):

$$e_i = e_i(w_i, w_{-i}, u) \tag{7.12}$$

When all firms pay the same wages ($w_i = w_{-i}$) shirking depends positively on the level of employment. The no-shirking constraint (*NSC*) indicates the minimum wage at each level of employment below which shirking will occur, and is shown in Figure 7.7. In Figure 7.7 the market-clearing wage is $w$. However, as is evident from the diagram, no shirking is inconsistent with full employment. As an incentive not to shirk, a firm must offer an efficiency wage greater than $w$. With all firms offering a wage of $w^*$, workers are deterred from shirking by the risk of becoming unemployed. The diagram also shows that the need to pay a wage greater than $w$ decreases as unemployment increases and that the efficiency wage $w^*$ and level of employment $L_0$ are associated with an equilibrium level of involuntary unemployment indicated by $L_F - L_0$. As the *NSC* will always lie above and to the left of the labour supply curve, there will always be some involuntary unemployment in equilibrium.

The *NSC* will shift to the left if the firm reduces its monitoring intensity and/or the government increases unemployment benefit. In each case the wage necessary to deter shirking at each level of employment is higher. A change in the *NSC* brought about by either of the above reasons is shown in Figure 7.7 as a shift of *NSC* from $NSC_0$ to $NSC_1$. The equilibrium following this shift is indicated by $E_1$, showing that the model predicts an increase in the efficiency wage and an increase in the equilibrium rate of involuntary unemployment as a result of these changes.

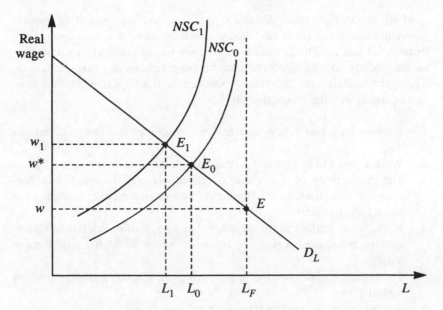

*Figure 7.7  The shirking model*

*The fairness model*  In recent years several economists have examined the adverse effects of 'unfair wages' and wage cuts on worker effort via the impact such cuts will have on the morale of the workforce. Sociological models stress such factors as the importance of wage relativities, status, relative deprivation, loyalty, trust and equity. In a series of papers, Akerlof (1982, 1984) and Akerlof and Yellen (1987, 1988, 1990) responded to Solow's (1979, 1980) 'piece of home-made sociology' and developed models where feelings about equity and fairness act as a deterrent to firms to offer too low wages in the labour market. Thurow (1983), Blinder (1988a) and Solow (1990) have also indicated that this socioeconomic line of enquiry could prove fruitful as an explanation of persistent unemployment. Recently, in his Nobel Memorial Lecture, George Akerlof (2002) presented a strong case for strengthening macroeconomic theory by incorporating assumptions that take account of behaviour such as 'cognitive bias, reciprocity, fairness, herding and social status'. By doing so Akerlof argues that macroeconomics will 'no longer suffer from the "*ad hockery*" of the neoclassical synthesis which had overridden the emphasis in the *General Theory* on the role of psychological and sociological factors'. Since in Akerlof's view Keynes's *General Theory* 'was the greatest contribution to behavioural economics before the present era', it would seem that economists need to rediscover the 'wild side' of macroeconomic behaviour in order to begin the construction of 'a not too rational macroeconomics' (Leijonhufvud, 1993).

Many economists share Akerlof's concerns and are critical of models where the labour market is modelled in much the same way as a commodity or financial market. The flexible price–auction model employed by new classical economists does not seem to resemble observed labour market behaviour. There are fundamental differences between labour inputs and other non-human inputs into the production process:

1. Workers have preferences and feelings; machines and raw materials do not.
2. Workers need to be motivated; machines do not.
3. The productivity of a machine is reasonably well known before purchase, so that problems of asymmetric information relating to quality are much less significant.
4. Workers can strike and 'break down' because of ill health (stress and so on); machines can break down but never strike for higher pay or more holidays.
5. The human capital assets of a firm are more illiquid and risky than its capital assets.
6. Workers normally require training; machines do not.
7. Human capital cannot be separated from its owner; non-human capital can.
8. Workers' utility functions are interdependent, not independent.

Because of these crucial differences, worker productivity is a discretionary variable; the effort or output of a worker is not given in advance and fixed for the future, irrespective of changes which take place in working conditions (see also Leibenstein, 1979). A machine does not get angry when its price fluctuates, nor does it feel upset if it is switched off. In contrast, workers are not indifferent to their price, nor are they unmoved by becoming unemployed against their will. For these and other reasons, the notion of fairness would seem to be an important factor in determining outcomes in the labour market. As Solow (1990) has argued, 'The most elementary reason for thinking that the concept of fairness, and beliefs about what is fair and what is not, play an important part in labour market behaviour is that we talk about them all the time.' The words 'fair' and 'unfair' have even been used by neoclassical economists at university departmental meetings!

The first formal model to bring in sociological elements as an explanation of efficiency wages was the seminal paper by Akerlof (1982), where issues relating to fairness lie at the centre of the argument. According to Akerlof, the willing cooperation of workers is something that must usually be obtained by the firm because labour contracts are incomplete and teamwork is frequently the norm. The essence of Akerlof's gift exchange model is neatly summed up in the phrase 'A fair day's work for a fair day's pay'. Everyday observation suggests that people have an innate psychological need to feel fairly treated, otherwise their morale is adversely affected. In Akerlof's model, workers' effort is a positive function of their morale and a major influence on their morale is the remuneration they receive for a given work standard which is regarded as the norm. If a firm pays its workers a wage above the going market rate, workers will respond by raising their group work norms, providing the firm with a *gift* of higher productivity in *exchange* for the higher wage.

In subsequent work Akerlof and Yellen (1990) have developed what they call the 'fair wage–effort hypothesis', which is derived from equity theory. In the workplace personal contact and potentially conflicting relationships within a team of workers are unavoidable. As a result issues relating to fairness are never far away. Since there is no absolute measure of fairness, people measure their treatment by reference to other individuals within their own group. Fairness is measured by making comparisons with workers similarly situated (inside and outside the firm). Thus an individual worker's utility function can be summarized as equation (7.13):

$$U = U(w/\overline{\omega}, e, u) \tag{7.13}$$

The utility of this worker ($U$) is dependent on the real wage ($w$) relative to the perceived 'fair' wage ($\overline{\omega}$), the worker's effort ($e$) and the unemployment rate ($u$). Assuming the worker wishes to maximize this function, the effort expended will depend on the relationship between $w$ and $\overline{\omega}$ for a given level of unemployment. Workers who feel unfairly treated ($w < \overline{\omega}$) will adjust their effort accordingly. 'The ability of workers to exercise control over their effort, and their willingness to do so in response to grievances, underlies the fair wage–effort hypothesis' (Akerlof and Yellen, 1990, p. 262). Just as firms face a no-shirking constraint in the Shapiro–Stiglitz model, they face a 'fair wage constraint' in the fairness version of the efficiency wage model. Since the fair wage exceeds the market-clearing wage, this framework generates an equilibrium with involuntary unemployment.

The essence of this innovative approach to explaining real wage rigidity is that the morale of a firm's human capital can easily be damaged if workers perceive that they are being unfairly treated. Firms that attach importance to their reputation as an employer and that wish to generate high morale and loyalty from their workforce will tend to pay efficiency wages which are perceived as fair.

It appears that American entrepreneur Henry Ford shared Marshall's insight that 'highly paid labour is generally efficient and therefore not dear labour'. In the autumn of 1908, Henry Ford launched the production of the

famous Model T Ford. During the period 1908–14, he pioneered the introduction of mass production techniques that characterized the 'American System
of Manufactures' (Rosenberg, 1994). The assembly line production methods
introduced by Ford required relatively unskilled workers rather than the
skilled craftsmen he had previously needed to assemble automobiles one by
one. The first moving assembly lines began operation in April 1913 but
unfortunately for Ford, the introduction of these mass production techniques
drastically changed the working environment and led to a massive and costly
increase in absenteeism and the turnover of workers. In 1913 the annual
turnover of workers at Ford was 370 per cent and daily absenteeism was 10
per cent. In January 1914 Ford responded to this problem by introducing a
payment system of $5 for an eight-hour day for male workers over the age of
22 who had been with the company for at least six months. Previously these
same workers had been working a nine-hour day for $2.34. For a given level
of worker productivity an increase in the wage paid was certain to increase
unit labour costs and, to contemporary observers, Ford's policy seemed to
imply a certain reduction in the firm's profits. However, the result of Ford's
new wage policy was a dramatic reduction in absenteeism (down 75 per
cent), reduced turnover (down 87 per cent), a massive improvement in productivity (30 per cent), a reduction in the price of the Model T Ford, and an
increase in profits. It appears that Ford was one of the first entrepreneurs to
apply efficiency wage theory. Later, Henry Ford described the decision to pay
his workers $5 per day as 'one of the finest cost cutting moves we ever made'
(see Meyer, 1981; Raff and Summers, 1987). There is no evidence that Ford
was experiencing trouble recruiting workers before 1914 or that the new
wage policy was introduced to attract more highly skilled workers. The most
plausible rationale for the policy is the favourable impact that it was expected
to have on workers' effort, turnover and absenteeism rates, and worker morale. Raff and Summers (1987) conclude that the introduction by Ford of
'supracompetitive' wages did yield 'substantial productivity benefits and
profits' and that this case study 'strongly supports' the relevance of several
efficiency wage theories.

*Insider–outsider models* Why don't unemployed workers offer to work for
lower wages than those currently paid to employed workers? If they did so,
wages would be bid down and employment would increase. There appears to
be an unwritten eleventh commandment: 'Thou shalt not permit job theft by
underbidding and stealing the jobs of thy comrades.' The insider–outsider
theory also attempts to explain why wage rigidity persists in the face of
involuntary unemployment (see Ball, 1990, and Sanfey, 1995 for reviews).

The insider–outsider approach to real wage rigidity was developed during
the 1980s in a series of contributions by Lindbeck and Snower (1985, 1986,

1988a, 1988b). In this model the insiders are the incumbent employees and the outsiders are the unemployed workers. Whereas in efficiency wage models it is firms that decide to pay a wage higher than the market-clearing wage, in the insider–outsider approach the focus shifts to the power of the insiders who at least partially determine wage and employment decisions. No direct effects of wages on productivity are assumed.

Where does the insider power come from? According to Lindbeck and Snower, insider power arises as a result of turnover costs (Vetter and Andersen, 1994). These include hiring and firing costs such as those associated with costs of searching the labour market, advertising and screening, negotiating conditions of employment, mandatory severance pay and litigation costs. Other important costs are production-related and arise from the need to train new employees. In addition to these well-known turnover costs, Lindbeck and Snower (1988a) also emphasize a more novel form of cost – the insider's ability and incentive to cooperate with or harass new workers coming from the ranks of the outsiders. If insiders feel that their position is threatened by outsiders, they can refuse to cooperate with and train new workers, as well as make life at work thoroughly unpleasant. By raising the disutility of work, this causes the outsiders' reservation wage to rise, making it less attractive for the firm to employ them. To the extent that cooperation and harassment activities lie within the control of workers, they can have a significant influence on turnover costs by their own behaviour.

Because firms with high rates of turnover offer both a lack of job security and few opportunities for advancement, workers have little or no incentive to build reputations with their employers. Low motivation damages productivity and this represents yet another cost of high labour turnover.

Because it is costly to exchange a firm's current employees for unemployed outsiders, the insiders have leverage which they can use to extract a share of the economic rent generated by turnover costs (the firm has an incentive to pay something to avoid costly turnover). Lindbeck and Snower assume that workers have sufficient bargaining power to extract some of this rent during wage negotiations. Although unions are not necessary for insider power, they enhance it with their ability to threaten strikes and work-to-rule forms of non-cooperation (For a discussion of union bargaining models and unemployment, see McDonald and Solow, 1981; Nickell, 1990; Layard *et al.*, 1991.)

Although the insider–outsider theory was originally put forward as an explanation of involuntary unemployment, it also generates some other important predictions (see Lindbeck and Snower, 1988b). First, insider–outsider theory implies that pronounced aggregate shocks which shift the demand for labour may have persistent effects on wages, employment and unemployment. In countries with large labour turnover costs and powerful unions, this 'effect persistence' will be significant. Second, in cases where the shocks are mild, firms with high turnover costs have an incentive to hoard labour, and this reduces employment variability. Third, the insider–outsider model can provide a rationale for many features associated with 'dual labour markets'. Fourth, this model has implications for the *composition* of unemployment. Lindbeck and Snower (1988b) argue that 'unemployment rates will be comparatively high for people with comparatively little stability in their work records'. This offers an explanation for the relatively high unemployment rates which are frequently typical among the young, the female population and various minority groups.

While the insider–outsider theory and efficiency wage theories provide different explanations of involuntary unemployment, they are not incompatible but complementary models, since the amount of involuntary unemployment 'may depend on what firms are willing to give and what workers are able to get' (Lindbeck and Snower, 1985).

## 7.8 New Keynesian Business Cycle Theory

New Keynesian economists accept that the source of shocks which generate aggregate disturbances can arise from the supply side or the demand side. However, new Keynesians argue that there are frictions and imperfections within the economy which will amplify these shocks so that large fluctuations in real output and employment result. The important issue for new Keynesians is not so much the source of the shocks but how the economy responds to them.

Within new Keynesian economics there have been two strands of research relating to the issue of aggregate fluctuations. The predominant approach has emphasized the importance of nominal rigidities. The second approach follows Keynes (1936) and Tobin (1975), and explores the potentially destabilizing impact of wage and price flexibility. We will examine each in turn. Consider Figure 7.8. In panel (a) we illustrate the impact of a decline in the money supply which shifts aggregate demand from $AD_0$ to $AD_1$. If a combination of menu costs and real rigidities makes the price level rigid at $P_0$, the decline in aggregate demand will move the economy from point $E_0$ to point $E_1$ in panel (a). The decline in output reduces the effective demand for labour. In panel (c) the effective labour demand curve ($D_{Le}$) shows how much labour is necessary to produce different levels of output. As the diagram shows, $L_1$ amount of labour is required to produce $Y_1$ amount of output. With prices and the real wage fixed at $P_0$ and $w_0$, respectively, firms move off the notional demand curve for labour, $D_L$, operating instead along their effective labour demand curve indicated by $NKL_1$ in panel (d). At the rigid real wage of $w_0$, firms would like to hire $L_0$ workers,

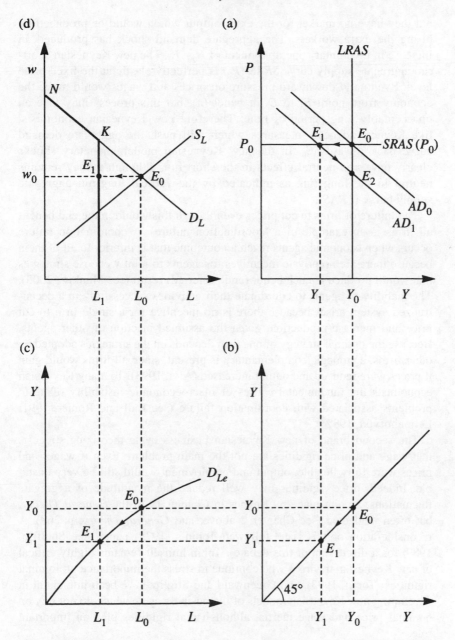

*Figure 7.8   The impact of an aggregate demand shock in the new Keynesian model*

but they have no market for the extra output which would be produced by hiring the extra workers. The aggregate demand shock has produced an increase in involuntary unemployment of $L_0 - L_1$. The new Keynesian short-run aggregate supply curve $SRAS$ $(P_0)$ is perfectly elastic at the fixed price level. Eventually downward pressure on prices and wages would move the economy from point $E_1$ to $E_2$ in panel (a), but this process may take an unacceptably long period of time. Therefore new Keynesian economists, like Keynes, advocate measures which will push the aggregate demand curve back towards $E_0$. In the new Keynesian model, monetary shocks clearly have non-neutral effects in the short run, although money remains neutral in the long run, as indicated by the vertical long-run aggregate supply curve ($LRAS$).

The failure of firms to cut prices even though this would in the end benefit all firms is an example of a 'coordination failure'. A coordination failure occurs when economic agents reach an outcome that is inferior to all of them because there are no private incentives for agents to jointly choose strategies that would produce a much better (and preferred) result (see Mankiw, 2003). The inability of agents to coordinate their activities successfully in a decentralized system arises because there is no incentive for a single firm to cut price and increase production, given the assumed inaction of other agents. Because the optimal strategy of one firm depends on the strategies adopted by other firms, a strategic complementary is present, since all firms would gain if prices were reduced and output increased (Alvi, 1993). To many Keynesian economists the fundamental causes of macroeconomic instability relate to problems associated with coordination failure (see Ball and Romer, 1991; Leijonhufvud, 1992).

The second brand of new Keynesian business cycle theorizing suggests that wage and price rigidities are not the main problem. Even if wages and prices were fully flexible, output and employment would still be very unstable. Indeed, price rigidities may well reduce the magnitude of aggregate fluctuations, a point made by Keynes in Chapter 19 of the *General Theory*, but often neglected (see Chapter 2 above, and *General Theory*, p. 269). A reconsideration of this issue followed Tobin's (1975) paper (see Sheffrin, 1989, for a discussion of this debate). Tobin himself remains highly critical of new Keynesian theorists who continue to stress the importance of nominal rigidities (Tobin, 1993), and Greenwald and Stiglitz have been influential in developing new Keynesian models of the business cycle which do not rely on nominal price and wage inertia, although real rigidities play an important role.

In the Greenwald and Stiglitz model (1993a, 1993b) firms are assumed to be risk-averse. Financial market imperfections generated by asymmetric information constrain many firms from access to equity finance. Equity-rationed firms can only partially diversify out of the risks they face. Their resultant dependence on debt rather than new equity issues makes firms more vulnerable to bankruptcy, especially during a recession when the demand curve facing most firms shifts to the left. Faced with such a situation, a risk-averse equity-constrained firm prefers to reduce its output because the uncertainties associated with price flexibility are much greater than those from quantity adjustment. As Stiglitz (1999b) argues, 'the problem of price-wage setting should be approached within a standard dynamic portfolio model, one that takes into account the risks associated with each decision, the non-reversibilities, as well as the adjustment costs associated with both prices and quantities'.

Greenwald and Stiglitz argue that, as a firm produces more, the probability of bankruptcy increases, and since bankruptcy imposes costs these will be taken into account in firms' production decisions. The marginal bankruptcy cost measures the expected extra costs which result from bankruptcy. During a recession the marginal bankruptcy risk increases and risk-averse firms react to this by reducing the amount of output they are prepared to produce at each price (given wages). Any change in a firm's net worth position or in their perception of the risk they face will have a negative impact on their willingness to produce and shifts the resultant risk-based aggregate supply curve to the left. As a result, demand-induced recessions are likely to induce leftward shifts of the aggregate supply curve. Such a combination of events could leave the price level unchanged, even though in this model there are no frictions preventing adjustment. Indeed, price flexibility, by creating more uncertainty, would in all likelihood make the situation worse. In the Greenwald–Stiglitz model aggregate supply and aggregate demand are interdependent and 'the dichotomy between "demand" and "supply" side shocks may be, at best, misleading' (Greenwald and Stiglitz, 1993b, p. 103; Stiglitz, 1999b).

In Figure 7.9 we illustrate the impact of an aggregate demand shock which induces the aggregate supply curve to shift to the left. The price level remains at $P_0$, even though output falls from $Y_0$ to $Y_1$. A shift of the aggregate supply curve to the left as the result of an increase in perceived risk will also shift the demand curve of labour to the left. If real wages are influenced by efficiency wage considerations, involuntary unemployment increases without any significant change in the real wage.

In addition to the above influences, new Keynesians have also examined the consequences of credit market imperfections which lead risk-averse lenders to respond to recessions by shifting their portfolio towards safer activities. This behaviour can magnify an economic shock by raising the real costs of intermediation. The resulting credit squeeze can convert a recession into a depression as many equity-constrained borrowers find credit expensive or difficult to

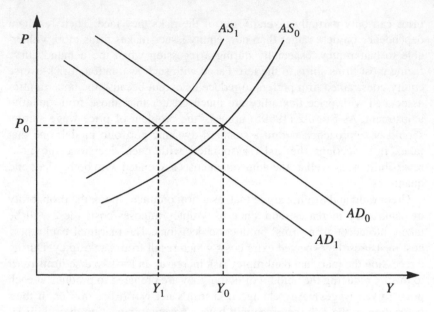

*Figure 7.9    The risk-based aggregate supply curve*

obtain, and bankruptcy results. Because high interest rates can increase the probability of default, risk-averse financial institutions frequently resort to credit rationing. Whereas the traditional approach to analysing the monetary transmission mechanism focuses on the interest rate and exchange rate channels, the new paradigm emphasizes the various factors that influence the ability of financial institutions to evaluate the 'creditworthiness' of potential borrowers in a world of imperfect information. Indeed, in the new paradigm, banks are viewed as risk-averse firms that are constantly engaged in a process of screening and monitoring customers. In a well-known paper, Bernanke (1983) argues that the severity of the Great Depression was in large part due to the breakdown of the economy's credit facilities, rather than a decline in the money supply (see Jaffe and Stiglitz, 1990, and Bernanke and Gertler, 1995, for surveys of the literature on credit rationing; see also Stiglitz and Greenwald, 2003, who champion what they call 'the new paradigm' in monetary economics).

Some new Keynesians have also incorporated the impact of technology shocks into their models. For example, Ireland (2004) explores the link between the 'current generation of new Keynesian models and the previous generation of real business cycle models'. To identify what is driving aggregate instability, Ireland's model combines technology shocks with shocks to household preferences, firm's desired mark-ups, and the central bank's monetary policy rule. Ireland finds that monetary shocks are a major source of real GDP instability, particularly before 1980. Technology shocks play only a 'modest role', accounting for less than half of the observed instability of output in the post-1980 period.

## 7.9 Hysteresis and the NAIRU

Since the early 1970s the natural rate of unemployment 'seems to have taken a wild ride' in OECD countries. For OECD countries in general, unemployment in the 1980s and 90s was higher than during the 'Golden Age' of the 1950–73 period. The steadily rising unemployment rates appear to have their origins in the two OPEC oil price shocks in 1973 and 1979 respectively (Phelps and Zoega, 1998) and in the case of the European OECD countries, unemployment that averaged 1.7 per cent in the early 1960s rose to 11 per cent by the mid-1990s. This high average also hides the large dispersion of unemployment rates across the European countries (Blanchard and Wolfers, 2000). Gordon's (1997, 1998) estimates show that the US natural rate of unemployment has also varied during this same period although the long-run unemployment repercussions of the 1980s recessions appear to have been much more persistent in Europe than in the USA. Figure 7.10 shows the standardized unemployment rates for the USA and OECD Europe for the period 1972–98. While unemployment in OECD Europe was less than US unemployment until the early 1980s, since then European unemployment has remained stubbornly high while it has fallen in the USA.

While the problem of inflation was a major policy concern during the 1970s and early 1980s, by the mid-1980s economists were once again turning their attention to the problem of unemployment, in particular the rise in the estimated NAIRU (see Bean et al., 1986; Fitoussi and Phelps, 1988; Summers, 1990; Layard et al., 1991, 1994; Bean, 1994; Cross, 1995; Nickell, 1997, 1998; Siebert, 1997; Katz and Krueger, 1999; Blanchard and Wolfers, 2000; Fitoussi et al., 2000; Hall, 2003).

While estimates of the NAIRU are obviously subject to uncertainty given the broad range of determinants, recent OECD estimates shown in Table 7.1 indicate the much superior performance of the US economy compared to the euro area and G7 countries.

During the late 1960s, Friedman and Phelps independently put forward expectations-augmented models of the Phillips curve. In Friedman's model the market-clearing rate of unemployment is called the natural rate of unemployment and is associated with a stable rate of inflation. As we noted in Chapter 4, many economists (especially those sympathetic to Keynesianism) prefer to use the 'NAIRU' concept (non-accelerating inflation rate of unemployment), rather than 'natural rate' when discussing long-run unemployment. The NAIRU terminology was first introduced by Modigliani and Papademos

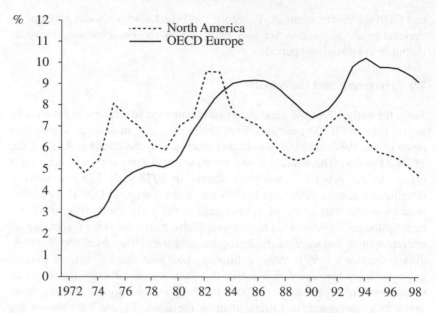

*Source*: 'Labour market performance and the OECD jobs strategy', OECD, June 1999, www.oecd.org.

*Figure 7.10    Standardized unemployment rates for North America (USA and Canada) and OECD Europe, 1972–98*

*Table 7.1    NAIRU estimates for the G7 countries and the euro area*

| Country/area | 1980 | 1985 | 1990 | 1995 | 1999 |
|---|---|---|---|---|---|
| Canada | 8.9 | 10.1 | 9.0 | 8.8 | 7.7 |
| France | 5.8 | 6.5 | 9.3 | 10.3 | 9.5 |
| Germany | 3.3 | 4.4 | 5.3 | 6.7 | 6.9 |
| Italy | 6.8 | 7.8 | 9.1 | 10.0 | 10.4 |
| Japan | 1.9 | 2.7 | 2.2 | 2.9 | 4.0 |
| UK | 4.4 | 8.1 | 8.6 | 6.9 | 7.0 |
| USA | 6.1 | 5.6 | 5.4 | 5.3 | 5.2 |
| Euro area | 5.5 | 7.1 | 8.8 | 9.2 | 8.8 |

*Source*: 'Revised OECD Measures of Structural Unemployment', OECD, December 2000.

(1975) as 'NIRU' (non-inflationary rate of unemployment), defined as 'a rate such that, as long as unemployment is above it, inflation can be expected to decline'. The NAIRU acronym was introduced by James Tobin (1980c) and has since been used to describe estimates of the natural rate of unemployment (see Cross et al., 1993; Cross, 1995). However, according to King (1999):

> the natural rate of unemployment and the NAIRU are quite different concepts. The former describes a real equilibrium determined by the structural characteristics of the labour and product markets – the grinding out of Friedman's Walrasian general equilibrium system (modified, if necessary, by non-Walrasian features of labour markets such as imperfect competition, search behaviour and efficiency wages). It exists independently of the inflation rate. In contrast, the latter, as well as being affected by these structural characteristics, is also affected by the gradual adjustment of the economy to past economic shocks that determine the path of inflation. Because it is defined as the unemployment rate at which there is no immediate pressure for a change in the inflation rate, it is a reduced form – not a structural – variable.

Therefore, the NAIRU concept takes into account inertia in the system which allows a protracted response of the economy to various economic shocks.

Another way to distinguish between these concepts relates to their microfoundations. Friedman's natural rate is a market-clearing concept, whereas the NAIRU is that rate of unemployment which generates consistency between the *target* real wage of workers and the *feasible* real wage determined by labour productivity and the size of a firm's mark-up. Since the NAIRU is determined by the balance of power between workers and firms, the microfoundations of the NAIRU relate to theories of imperfect competition in the labour and product markets (see Carlin and Soskice, 1990; Layard et al., 1991). However, while recognizing these differences between the concepts of the natural rate and the NAIRU, Ball and Mankiw (2002) argue that NAIRU is 'approximately a synonym for the natural rate of unemployment'. Therefore, in the discussion that follows we will assume that the two concepts can be used interchangeably.

According to Friedman's natural rate hypothesis, fluctuations of aggregate demand cannot exercise any influence over the natural rate of unemployment, which is determined by real supply-side influences. The conventional natural rate view allows monetary and other demand shocks to shift aggregate demand, thereby influencing the actual rate of unemployment in the short run. But, as inflationary expectations adjust, unemployment returns to its long-run equilibrium (natural) value. In new classical models, if the change in aggregate demand is unanticipated, the combined effect of perfectly flexible prices and rational expectations ensures that unemployment will quickly return to its natural rate.

This conventional view is illustrated in Figure 7.11, where the natural rate of unemployment ($U_N$) is given by point $A$. Any decline in aggregate demand will increase the actual rate of unemployment temporarily to point $B$, while an expansion of aggregate demand will lower actual unemployment and will

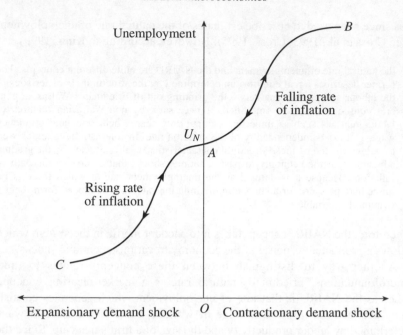

*Figure 7.11   The 'natural rate' view of the relationship between actual
              unemployment and equilibrium unemployment*

move the economy temporarily to point *C*. However, in the long run, unemployment returns to the natural rate of unemployment at point *A*.

The dramatic rise in unemployment rates, particularly in Europe during the 1980s, suggested that this conventional view of the natural rate of unemployment (or NAIRU) must be wrong. It seems that the NAIRU must have risen, and estimates made by econometricians, such as those presented in Table 7.1, confirm this view. Several explanations have been put forward to explain these higher levels of unemployment. One view explains it as a result of specific policy changes that have reduced the flexibility of the labour market; more powerful trade unions, higher unemployment compensation and longer duration of benefits, minimum wage laws, excessive regulations, employment protection, and higher taxation are, or have been, favourite candidates (see Minford, 1991; Nickell, 1997; Siebert, 1997; Ljungqvist and Sargent, 1998; Fitoussi et al., 2000; Roed and Zhang, 2003). However, while some of these factors may account for rising unemployment in the 1970s, many economists do not believe that they offer a complete explanation of the unemployment experienced in the 1980s and 1990s (union power, for example, has been significantly reduced in the UK and has never been a major factor in the US economy).

The simultaneous rise in the actual and equilibrium rates of unemployment has led some new Keynesian economists to explore a second explanation which allows aggregate demand to influence the natural rate (or NAIRU). Models which embody the idea that the natural rate depends on the history of the equilibrium rate are called 'hysteresis' theories. It was Phelps (1972) who first suggested that the natural rate equilibrium will be partly influenced by the path taken to reach equilibrium. Phelps called this path dependence 'hysteresis', a term borrowed from physics, where it is used to describe the lagging of magnetic induction behind the source of magnetism (see Cross, 1995).

In hysteresis models the natural rate of unemployment will increase if the actual rate of unemployment in the previous period exceeds the former time period's natural rate (Hargreaves-Heap, 1980). This can be expressed as follows:

$$U_{Nt} = U_{Nt-1} + a(U_{t-1} - U_{Nt-1}) + b_t \qquad (7.14)$$

In equation (7.14) $U_{Nt}$ is the natural rate of unemployment at time $t$, $U_{Nt-1}$ is the previous period's natural rate of unemployment, $U_{t-1}$ is the previous period's actual rate of unemployment and $b_t$ captures other influences on the natural rate such as unemployment compensation. If we assume $b_t = 0$, then equation (7.14) can be rearranged as (7.15):

$$U_{Nt} - U_{Nt-1} = a(U_{t-1} - U_{Nt-1}) \qquad (7.15)$$

From equation (7.15) it can be seen that $U_{Nt} > U_{Nt-1}$ if $U_{t-1} > U_{Nt-1}$. In other words, the shifting actual rate of unemployment acts like a magnet, pulling the natural rate of unemployment in the same direction. Thus while it may be reasonable to argue that aggregate demand does not affect $U_N$ in the short run, it is likely that prolonged periods of abnormally high or low economic activity will shift the natural rate of unemployment.

The impact of hysteresis is illustrated in Figure 7.12. The initial equilibrium unemployment rate is represented by point $A$. If the economy is subject to a negative aggregate demand shock, output falls and unemployment rises to point $B$. When the economy recovers from recession, the unemployment rate does not return to point $A$. Instead, because of hysteresis effects, the new NAIRU is at point $C$. If the economy is now subject to a positive aggregate demand shock, unemployment falls to point $D$. When the economy returns to equilibrium the NAIRU has now fallen to point $E$. A further recession traces out a path for this economy through points $F$ to $G$. In other words, the NAIRU is influenced by the actual rate of unemployment which itself is determined mainly by aggregate demand.

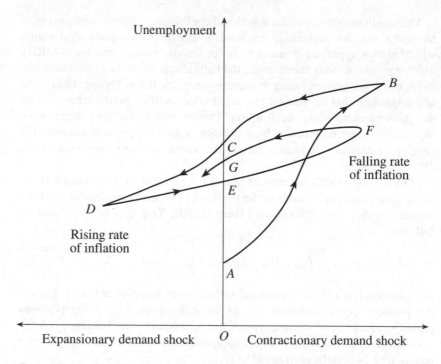

*Figure 7.12   The hysteresis view of a 'time-varying' NAIRU*

Theories of hysteresis fall into two main categories, namely duration theories and insider–outsider theories. Duration theories point out that, when $U_t >$ $U_{Nt}$, the problem of structural unemployment is exacerbated because the unemployed suffer a depreciation of their human capital (skills) and as a result become increasingly unemployable. A high rate of unemployment also tends to generate an increasing number of long-term unemployed who exercise little influence on wage bargaining, which also raises the NAIRU. Insider–outsider theories emphasize the power of insiders which prevents the downward adjustment of wages in the face of high unemployment. As a result, outsiders are unable to price their way back into jobs following a rise in unemployment (see Blanchard and Summers, 1986, 1988). If hysteresis effects are important, the sacrifice ratio associated with disinflation and recessions is much greater than is suggested by the original natural rate hypothesis, since high unemployment will tend to persist (for an extended discussion of the issues raised in this section, the reader is referred to Cross, 1988; Cross et al., 1993, Layard et al., 1991; Blanchard and Katz, 1997; Gordon, 2003).

Another distinctive approach to explaining movements in the equilibrium rate of unemployment over time has been developed by Edmund Phelps and his co-researchers. In a series of books and papers Phelps has sought to construct an endogenous theory of the natural rate of unemployment where 'the equilibrium path of unemployment is driven by the natural rate that is a *variable* of the system rather than a constant or a forcing function of time ... hence a moving-natural-rate theory holds the solution to the mystery of what is behind the *shifts* and *long swings* of the unemployment rate' (Phelps, 1994; see also Fitoussi and Phelps, 1988; Phelps and Zoega, 1998; Phelps, 2000). While in Friedman's natural rate model equilibrium unemployment can change due to supply-side influences, in Phelps's dynamic intertemporal non-monetary equilibrium model it is real demand shocks that are 'the great movers and shakers of the economy's equilibrium path', although real supply (energy) shocks also play an important role. Phelps (1990, 1994) classifies his approach to explaining unemployment as both 'modern' and 'structuralist', although it does contain both neoclassical (the role of real interest rates determined in the capital market), Austrian (the effect of the rate of interest on the supply of output) and new Keynesian elements (asymmetric information and efficiency wages). Phelps highlights the impact on the path of the equilibrium unemployment rate of real influences such as technology, preferences, social values and institutions. As Phelps (1994) recalls, by the 1980s he had decided that any chance of accounting for the major swings in economic activity since the war would require:

> abandoning the simplification of a natural rate unemployment rate invariant to non-monetary (not just monetary) macro shocks in favour of models making the equilibrium rate an endogenous variable determined by a variety of non-monetary forces ... the longer booms and slumps ... must be explained largely as *displacements of the equilibrium path of unemployment itself*, not as deviations of unemployment around an impervious equilibrium path.

In looking for the causes of what Fitoussi et al. (2000) call 'the great slump', that is, the upward shift of equilibrium unemployment rates in the 1980s, the chief suspects identified are five OECD-wide real shocks to business profitability and worker's incentives (see Phelps, 1994), namely:

1. reduced expectations of productivity growth, hence increased effective cost of capital;
2. an increase in the expected real interest rate which also raises the effective cost of capital;
3. an increase in services from workers private assets (see Phelps, 2000);
4. an increase in social entitlements relative to after-tax real wages resulting from the 1970s productivity slowdown and expansion of the welfare state;
5. the two OPEC oil price shocks in 1973 and 1979.

In the Phelps (1994) model the main driving force behind the rise of the NAIRU is the increase in real interest rates that occurred across the OECD countries after the mid-1970s and on into the 1980s (Blanchard and Wolfers, 2000). The rise in world real interest rates, to a large extent induced by US fiscal expansion in the early 1980s, lowered incentives to accumulate capital, and, for a given real wage, led to a reduction of labour demand. The high real interest rate which induced an appreciation of the US dollar (real depreciation of European currencies) during this period also led to an increase in European price mark-ups (firms do not lower their export prices in proportion to the depreciation) and, in consequence, this led to a reduction in labour demand and a rise in the equilibrium rate of unemployment. For example, Phelps and Zoega (1998, p. 788) find a very strong correlation between the world real rate of interest and UK unemployment for the period 1975–95. Note that in contrast to real business cycle models, where changes in the real interest rate influence the supply of labour through the intertemporal labour substitution hypothesis, in Phelps's model changes in the real interest affect the demand for labour (for a critique see Madsen, 1998).

While the impact of real shocks as an explanation of increases in the broad evolution of European unemployment is persuasive, Blanchard and Wolfers (2000) argue that 'there is insufficient heterogeneity in these shocks to explain cross-country differences … Adverse shocks can potentially explain the general increase in unemployment. Differences in institutions can potentially explain differences in outcomes across countries.' Therefore, a more convincing story of the evolution of the NAIRU in Europe must involve the interaction of observable real shocks combined with a recognition of the institutional diversity present across European countries (see Nickell, 1997; and Layard and Nickell, 1998).

## 7.10   New Keynesian Economics and the Stylized Facts

The new Keynesian model is relatively successful in explaining many of the business cycle stylized facts (see Abel and Bernanke, 2001):

1. new Keynesian analysis is consistent with the procyclical behaviour of employment as well as procyclical consumption, investment and government expenditures and productivity (see Chapter 6 for a discussion of procyclical productivity);
2. the non-neutrality of money in new Keynesian models is consistent with the stylized fact that money is procyclical and leading;
3. more controversial (see Chapter 6) is the new Keynesian prediction that inflation will tend to be procyclical and lagging. Procyclical inflation is consistent with new Keynesian models which emphasize aggregate de-

mand disturbances. However, this stylized fact has in recent years been challenged (see Kydland and Prescott, 1990, and Chapter 6);

4. new Keynesian models, unlike the old Keynesian models, do not imply a countercyclical real wage. When sticky nominal prices are introduced, the real wage in new Keynesian models can be procyclical or acyclical (see Mankiw, 1990). If the efficiency wage is sensitive to the rate of unemployment, then real wages will tend to be mildly procyclical in such models (see Shapiro and Stiglitz, 1984).

Greenwald and Stiglitz (1988) in their survey of macroeconomic theories conclude that no model successfully explains all the data, but the new Keynesian model does better than either the traditional Keynesian or real business cycle alternatives. For those economists who see involuntary unemployment as a stylized fact in need of explanation, the new Keynesian models rooted in imperfect competition are 'impressively better' than the new classical or real business cycle alternatives (Carlin and Soskice, 1990).

## 7.11 Policy Implications

Following the contributions of Fischer (1977), Phelps and Taylor (1977), it was clear that the new classical conclusion that government demand management policy was ineffective did not depend on the assumption of rational expectations but rather on the assumption of instantaneous market clearing. In new Keynesian models which emphasize sticky prices, money is no longer neutral and policy effectiveness is, at least in principle, re-established. Since in the Greenwald–Stiglitz model greater price flexibility exacerbates the problems of economic fluctuations, new Keynesians have also demonstrated the potential role for corrective demand management policies even if prices are flexible (but not instantaneously so). In a world where firms set prices and wages in an uncoordinated way, and where they are uncertain of the consequences of their actions, it is not surprising that considerable inertia with respect to prices and wages results.

In a market economy endogenous forces can frequently amplify the disturbing impact of exogenous shocks. While new Keynesians tend to be more concerned with the way an economy responds to shocks than with the source of the shocks, experience during the past quarter-century has confirmed that economies can be disturbed from the supply side as well as the demand side. Indeed, as Benjamin Friedman (1992) has observed, it is often practically and conceptually difficult to draw a clear distinction between what is and what is not the focal point of any disturbance. Because in new Keynesian models fluctuations are irregular and unpredictable, new Keynesians are not enthusiastic supporters of government attempts to 'fine-tune' the macroeconomy. Many new Keynesians (such as Mankiw) accept the monetarist criticisms relating to old-style Keynesianism as well as several of the criticisms raised by new classical economists, such as those related to dynamic consistency (see Chapter 5). There is no unified new Keynesian view on the extent of discretionary fiscal and monetary action that a government may take in response to aggregate fluctuations (see Solow and Taylor, 1998). However, most new Keynesians do see a need for activist government action of some form because of market failure, especially in the case of a deep recession. For example, Taylor (2000a) argues that while fiscal policy should normally be used to achieve long-term objectives such as economic growth, there is a strong case for the explicit use of fiscal expansionary policy in 'unusual situations such as when nominal interest rates hit a lower bound of zero'.

Because of uncertainty with respect to the kinds of problems an economy may confront in the future, new Keynesians do not support the fixed-rules approach to monetary policy advocated by Friedman (1968a) and new classical equilibrium theorists such as Lucas, Sargent, Wallace, Barro, Kydland and Prescott during the 1970s. If the monetarists and new classicists successfully undermined the case for fine-tuning, new Keynesians have certainly championed the case for what Lindbeck (1992) has referred to as 'coarse-tuning' – policies designed to offset or avoid serious macro-level problems.

Here it is interesting to recall Leijonhufvud's (1973, 1981) idea that market economies operate reasonably well within certain limits. Leijonhufvud argues that

> The system is likely to behave differently for large than for moderate displacements from the 'full coordination' time path. Within some range from the path (referred to as the corridor for brevity), the system's homeostatic mechanisms work well, and deviation counteracting tendencies increase in strength.

However, Leijonhufvud argues that outside 'the corridor' these equilibrating tendencies are much weaker and the market system is increasingly vulnerable to effective demand failures. More recently Krugman (1998, 1999) has also reminded economists about the dangers of 'Depression Economics' and the potential for a liquidity trap (see Buiter, 2003b).

Echoing this concern, new Keynesian analysis provides theoretical support for policy intervention, especially in the case of huge shocks which lead to persistence, because the adjustment process in market economies works too slowly. An increasing consensus of economists now support the case for some form of constrained discretion in the form of an activist rule. Indeed, during the last decade of the twentieth century, macroeconomics began to evolve into what Goodfriend and King (1997) have called a 'New Neoclassical Synthesis'. The central elements of this new synthesis involve:

1. the need for macroeconomic models to take into account intertemporal optimization;
2. the widespread use of the rational expectations hypothesis;
3. recognition of the importance of imperfect competition in goods, labour and credit markets;
4. incorporating costly price adjustment into macroeconomic models.

Clearly this new consensus has a distinctly new Keynesian flavour. Indeed, Gali (2002) refers to the new generation of small-scale monetary business cycle models as either 'new Keynesian' or 'new Neoclassical Synthesis' models. This 'new paradigm' integrates Keynesian elements such as nominal rigidities and imperfect competition into a real business cycle dynamic general equilibrium framework.

According to Goodfriend and King, the 'New Neoclassical Synthesis' models suggest four major conclusions about the role of monetary policy. First, monetary policy has persistent effects on real variables due to gradual price adjustment. Second, there is 'little' long-run trade-off between real and nominal variables. Third, inflation has significant welfare costs due to its distorting impact on economic performance. Fourth, in understanding the effects of monetary policy, it is important to take into account the credibility of policy. This implies that monetary policy is best conducted within a rules-based framework, with central banks adopting a regime of inflation targeting (Muscatelli and Trecroci, 2000). As Goodfriend and King note, these ideas relating to monetary policy 'are consistent with the public statements of central bankers from a wide range of countries' (see, for example Gordon Brown, 1997, 2001, and the 'core properties' of the Bank of England's macroeconometric model, Bank of England, 1999; Treasury, 1999).

### 7.11.1 Costs of inflation

An important element of the growing consensus in macroeconomics is that low and stable inflation is conducive to growth, stability and the efficient functioning of market economies (Fischer, 1993; Taylor, 1996, 1998a, 1998b). The consensus view is that inflation has real economic costs, especially unanticipated inflation. The costs of anticipated inflation include 'shoe leather' costs, menu costs and the costs created by distortions in a non-indexed tax system. The costs of unanticipated inflation include distortions to the distribution of income, distortions to the price mechanism causing efficiency losses, and losses due to increased uncertainty which lowers investment and reduces economic growth. Also important are the costs of disinflation (the 'sacrifice ratio'), especially if hysteresis effects are present (Ball, 1999; Cross, 2002). Leijonhufvud also argues that during non-trivial inflation the principal–agent problems in the economy, particularly in the government sector, become impossible of solution. This is because nominal auditing and bookkeeping are the only methods invented for principals to control agents in various situations. For example, Leijonhufvud highlights the problems that arise when the national budget for the coming year becomes meaningless when 'money twelve months hence is of totally unknown purchasing power'. In such situations government departments cannot be held responsible for not adhering to their budgets since the government has lost overall control. 'It is not just a case of the private sector not being able to predict what the monetary authorities are going to do, the monetary authorities themselves have no idea what the rate of money creation will be next month because of constantly shifting, intense political pressures' (Snowdon, 2004a; see also Heymann and Leijonhufvud, 1995). Other significant costs arise if governments choose to suppress inflation, leading to distortions to the price mechanism and further significant efficiency losses. Shiller (1997) has also shown that inflation is extremely unpopular among the general public although 'people have definite opinions about the mechanisms and consequences of inflation and these opinions differ ... strikingly between the general public and economists'. To a large extent these differences seem to depend on the finding of Diamond et al. (1997) that 'money illusion seems to be widespread among economic agents'.

While the impact of inflation rates of less than 20 per cent on the rate of economic growth may be small, it is important to note that small variations in growth rates have dramatic effects on living standards over relatively short historical periods (see Chapter 11, and Fischer, 1993; Barro, 1995; Ghosh and Phillips, 1998; Feldstein, 1999; Temple, 2000; Kirshner, 2001). Ramey and Ramey (1995) also present evidence from a sample of 95 countries that volatility and growth are related; that is, more stable economies normally grow faster. Given that macroeconomic stability and economic growth are positively related (Fischer, 1993), achieving low and stable inflation will be conducive to *sustained* growth. For example, Taylor, in a series of papers, argues that US growth since the early 1980s (the 'Great Boom') was sustained due to lower volatility induced by improved monetary policy (Taylor, 1996, 1997a, 1997b, 1998a, 1998b, 1999).

Recently, Romer and Romer (1999) and Easterly and Fischer (2001) have presented evidence showing that inflation damages the well-being of the poorest groups in society. The Romers find that high inflation and macroeconomic instability are 'correlated with less rapid growth of average income and lower equality'. They therefore conclude that a low-inflation economic environment is likely to result in higher income for the poor over time due to its favourable effects on long-run growth and income equality, both of which are adversely affected by high and variable inflation. Although expansionary monetary policies can induce a boom and thus reduce poverty, these effects are only temporary. As Friedman (1968a) and Phelps (1968) demonstrated many years ago, expansionary monetary policy cannot create a permanent boom. Thus 'the typical package of reforms that brings about low inflation and macroeconomic stability will also generate improved conditions for the poor and more rapid growth for all' (Romer and Romer, 1999).

### 7.11.2 Monetary regimes and inflation targeting

If a consensus of economists agree that inflation is damaging to economic welfare, it remains to be decided how best to control inflation. Since it is now widely accepted that the primary long-run goal of monetary policy is to control inflation and create reasonable price stability, the clear task for economists is to decide on the exact form of monetary regime to adopt in order to achieve this goal. Monetary regimes are characterized by the use of a specific nominal anchor. Mishkin (1999) defines a nominal anchor as 'a constraint on the value of domestic money' or more broadly as 'a constraint on discretionary policy that helps weaken the time-inconsistency problem'. This helps to solve the inflation bias problem inherent with the use of discretionary demand management policies (Kydland and Prescott, 1977). In practice, during the last 50 years, we can distinguish four types of monetary regime that have operated in market economies; first, exchange rate targeting, for example the UK, 1990–92; second, monetary targeting, for example the UK, 1976–87; third, explicit inflation targeting, for example the UK, 1992 to date; fourth, implicit inflation targeting, for example the USA, in recent years (see Mishkin, 1999; Goodfriend, 2004). While each of these monetary regimes has advantages and disadvantages, in recent years an increasing number of countries have begun to adopt inflation targeting in various forms, combined with an accountable and more transparent independent central bank (see Alesina and Summers, 1993; Fischer, 1995a, 1995b, 1996b; Green, 1996; Bernanke and Mishkin, 1992, 1997; Bernanke and Woodford, 1997; Bernanke et al., 1999; King, 1997a, 1997b; Snowdon, 1997; Svensson, 1997a, 1997b, 1999, 2000; Artis et al., 1998; Haldane, 1998; Vickers, 1998; Mishkin, 1999, 2000a, 2000b, 2002; Gartner, 2000; Muscatelli and Trecroci, 2000; Piga, 2000; Britton, 2002; Geraats, 2002; Bernanke and Woodford, 2004; see also the interview with Bernanke in Snowdon, 2002a, 2002b).

Following Svensson (1997a, 1997b) and Mishkin (2002), we can view inflation targeting as a monetary regime that encompasses six main elements:

1. the public announcement of medium-term numerical targets for inflation;
2. a firm institutional commitment to price stability (usually a low and stable rate of inflation around 2–3 per cent) as the primary goal of monetary policy; the government, representing society, assigns a loss function to the central bank;

3.   an 'information-inclusive strategy' where many variables are used for deciding the setting of policy variables;
4.   greater transparency and openness in the implementation of monetary policy so as to facilitate better communication with the public; inflation targets are much easier to understand than exchange rate or monetary targets;
5.   increased accountability of the central bank with respect to achieving its inflation objectives; the inflation target provides an *ex post* indicator of monetary policy performance; also, by estimating inflationary expectations relative to the inflation target, it is possible to get a measure of the credibility of the policy;
6.   because the use of inflation targeting as a nominal anchor involves comparing the announced target for inflation with the inflation forecast as the basis for making monetary policy decisions, Svensson (1997b) has pointed out that 'inflation targeting implies inflation *forecast* targeting' and 'the central bank's inflation forecast becomes the intermediate target'.

The successful adoption of an inflation targeting regime also has certain other key prerequisites. The credibility of inflation targeting as a strategy will obviously be greatly enhanced by having a sound financial system where the central bank has complete instrument independence in order to meet its inflation objectives (see Berger et al., 2001; Piga, 2000). To this end the Bank of England was granted operational independence in May, 1997 (Brown, 1997). It is also crucial that central banks in inflation targeting countries should be free of fiscal dominance. It is highly unlikely that countries with persistent and large fiscal deficits will be able to credibly implement a successful inflation targeting strategy. This may be a particular problem for many developing and transition economies (Mishkin, 2000a). Successful inflation targeting also requires the adoption of a floating exchange rate regime to ensure that the country adopting this strategy maintains independence for its monetary policy. The well-known open economy policy trilemma shows that a country cannot simultaneously maintain open capital markets + fixed exchange rates + an independent monetary policy oriented towards domestic objectives. A government can choose any two of these but not all three simultaneously! If a government wants to target monetary policy towards domestic considerations such as an inflation target, either capital mobility or the exchange rate target will have to be abandoned (see Obstfeld, 1998; Obstfeld and Taylor, 1998; Snowdon, 2004b).

As we noted in Chapter 5, Svensson (1997a) has shown how inflation targeting has emerged as a strategy designed to eliminate the inflation bias inherent in discretionary monetary policies. While Friedman and Kuttner (1996) interpret inflation targeting as a form of monetary rule, Bernanke and

Mishkin (1997) prefer to view it as a monetary regime that subjects the central bank to a form of 'constrained discretion'. Bernanke and Mishkin see inflation targeting as a framework for monetary policy rather than a rigid policy rule. In practice all countries that have adopted inflation targeting have also built an element of flexibility into the target. This flexible approach is supported by Mervyn King (2004), who was appointed Governor of the Bank of England following the retirement of Eddie George in June 2003. King identifies the 'core of the monetary policy problem' as being 'uncertainty about future social decisions resulting from the impossibility and the undesirability of committing successors to any given monetary policy strategy'. These problems make any form of fixed rule undesirable even if it were possible to commit to one because, as King (2004) argues,

> The exercise of some discretion is desirable in order that we may learn. The most cogent argument against the adoption of a fixed monetary policy rule is that no rule is likely to remain optimal for long ... So we would not want to embed any rule deeply into our decision making structure ... Instead, we delegate the power of decision to an institution that will implement policy period by period exercising constrained discretion.

The need for flexibility due to uncertainty is also emphasized by Alan Greenspan, who became Chaiman of the US Federal Reserve in August 1987 (he is due to retire in June 2008). The Federal Reserve's experiences over the post-war era make it clear that 'uncertainty is not just a pervasive feature of the monetary policy landscape; it is the defining characteristic of that landscape' (Greenspan, 2004). Furthermore:

> Given our inevitably incomplete knowledge about key structural aspects of an ever-changing economy and the sometimes symmetric costs or benefits of particular outcomes, a central bank needs to consider not only the most likely future path for the economy but also the distribution of possible outcomes about that path. The decision-makers then need to reach a judgement about the probabilities, costs, and benefits of the various possible outcomes under alternative choices for policy.

Clearly the setting of interest rates is as much 'art as science' (Cecchetti, 2000). The need for flexibility can in part be illustrated by considering a conventional form of the loss function ($L_t$) assigned to central bankers given by equation (7.16).

$$L_t = \frac{1}{2}[\dot{P}_t - \dot{P}*)^2 + \phi(Y_t - Y*)^2], \quad \phi > 0 \qquad (7.16)$$

In this quadratic social loss function $\dot{P}_t$ is the rate of inflation at time period $t$, $\dot{P}^*$ is the inflation target, $Y_t$ is aggregate output at time $t$, and $Y^*$ represents the natural rate or target rate of output. The parameter φ is the relative weight given to stabilizing the output gap. For strict inflation targeting φ = 0, whereas with flexible inflation targeting φ > 0. As Svenssson (1997a) notes, 'no central bank with an explicit inflation target seems to behave as if it wishes to achieve the target at all cost'. Setting φ = 0 would be the policy stance adopted by those who Mervyn King (1997b) describes as 'inflation nutters'. Thus all countries that have introduced inflation targeting have built an element of flexibility into the target (Allsopp and Vines, 2000).

What should be the numerical value of the inflation target? Alan Greenspan, currently the most powerful monetary policy maker in the world, has reputedly defined price stability as a situation where people cease to take inflation into account in their decisions. More specifically, Bernanke et al. (1999) come down in favour of a positive value for the inflation target in the range 1–3 per cent. This is supported by Summers (1991b, 1996), Akerlof et al. (1996), and Fischer (1996b). One of the main lessons of the Great Depression, and one that has been repeated in much milder form in Japan during the last decade, is that it is of paramount importance that policy makers ensure that economies avoid deflation (Buiter, 2003b; Eggertsson and Woodford, 2003; Svensson, 2003a). Because the nominal interest rate has a lower bound of zero, any general deflation of prices will cause an extremely damaging increase in real interest rates. Cechetti (1998) argues that the message for inflation targeting strategies is clear, 'be wary of targets that imply a significant chance of deflation'. It would therefore seem unwise to follow Feldstein's (1999) recommendation to set a zero inflation target. Akerlof et al. (1996) also support a positive inflation target to allow for relative price changes. If nominal wages are rigid downwards, then an alternative way of engineering a fall in real wages in order to stimulate employment is to raise the general price level via inflation relative to sticky nominal wages. With a flexible and positive inflation target this option is available for the central bank.

Following the UK's departure from the ERM in September 1992 it became imperative to put in place a new nominal anchor to control inflation. During the post-1945 period we can identify five monetary regimes adopted by the UK monetary authorities, namely, a fixed (adjustable peg) exchange rate regime, 1948–71; a floating exchange rate regime with no nominal anchor, 1971–6; monetary targets, 1976–87; exchange rate targeting ('shadowing the Deutchmark' followed by membership of the ERM), 1987–92; and finally inflation targeting, 1992 to date (Balls and O'Donnell, 2002). The credibility of the inflation targeting regime was substantially improved in May 1997 when the Bank of England was given operational independence. This decision, taken by the 'New Labour' government, was designed to enhance the administration's anti-inflation credibility by removing the suspicion that ideological or short-term electoral considerations would in future influence the conduct of stabilization policy (see Chapter 10).

The current UK monetary policy framework encompasses the following main features:

1.  *A symmetrical inflation target.* The targets or goals of policy are set by the Chancellor of the Exchequer.
2.  *Monthly monetary policy meetings* by a nine-member Monetary Policy Committee (MPC) of 'experts'. To date, current and past membership of the MPC has included many distinguished economists, including Mervyn King, Charles Bean, Steven Nickell, Charles Goodhart, Willem Buiter, Alan Budd, John Vickers, Sushil Wadhami, DeAnne Julius, Christopher Allsopp, Kate Barker and Eddie George.
3.  *Instrument independence* for the central bank. The MPC has responsibility for setting interest rates with the central objective of publication of MPC minutes.
4.  Publication of a quarterly *Inflation Report* which sets forth the Bank of England's inflation and GDP forecasts. The Bank of England's inflation forecast is published in the form of a probability distribution presented in the form of a 'fan chart' (see Figure 7.13). The Bank's current objective is to achieve an inflation target of 2 per cent, as measured by the 12-month increase in the consumer prices index (CPI). This target was

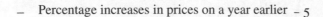

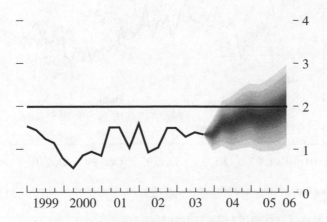

*Figure 7.13   Bank of England inflation report fan chart for February 2004: forecast of CPI inflation at constant nominal interest rates of 4.0 per cent*

announced on 10 December 2003. Previously the inflation target was 2.5 per cent based on RPIX inflation (the retail prices index excluding mortgage interest payments).

5. *An open letter system.* Should inflation deviate from target by more than 1 per cent in either direction, the Governor of the Bank of England, on behalf of the MPC, must write an open letter to the Chancellor explaining the reasons for the deviation of inflation from target, an accommodative approach when confronted by large supply shocks to ease the adverse output and employment consequences in such circumstances (Budd, 1998; Bean, 1998; Treasury, 1999; Eijffinger, 2002b).

Since 1992 the inflation performance of the UK economy has been very impressive, especially when compared to earlier periods such as the 1970s

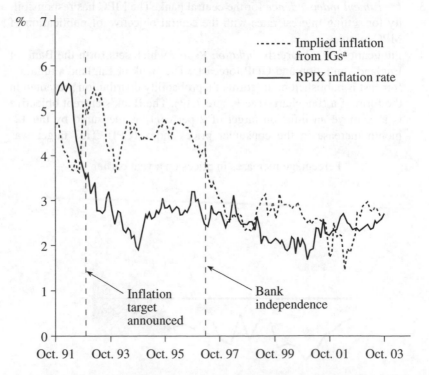

*Note*:    [a] Implied average expectations from 5 to 10 years ahead, derived from index-linked gilts.

*Source*:    Bank of England, www.bankofengland.co.uk.

*Figure 7.14    UK inflation and inflation expectations, October 1991–
October 2003*

and 1980s when inflation was high and volatile. Figure 7.14 clearly illustrates the dramatic improvement in the UK's inflation performance since 1992, especially compared to earlier periods (see King, 2004).

While it is too early to tell if this monetary arrangement can deliver lower inflation and greater economic stability over the longer term, especially in a more turbulent world than that witnessed during the 1990s, the evidence from recent years at least gives some cause for optimism, a case of 'so far so good' (see Treasury, 1999; Balls and O'Donnell, 2002). However, Ball and Sheridan (2003) argue that there is no evidence that inflation targeting has improved economic performance as measured by inflation, output growth and interest rates. They present evidence that non-inflation-targeting countries have also experienced a decline in inflation during the same period as the inflation targeters, suggesting perhaps that better inflation performance may have been the result of other factors. For example, Rogoff (2003), in noting the fall in global inflation since the early 1980s, identifies the interaction of globalization, privatization and deregulation as important factors, along with better policies and institutions, as major factors contributing to disinflation.

### 7.11.3 A new Keynesian approach to monetary policy

In two influential papers, Clarida et al. (1999, 2000) set out what they consider to be some important lessons that economists have learned about the conduct of monetary policy. Economists' research in this field points towards some useful general principles about optimal policy. They identify their approach as new Keynesian because in their model nominal price rigidities allow monetary policy to have non-neutral effects on real variables in the short run, there is a positive short-run relationship between output and inflation (that is, a Phillips curve), and the *ex ante* real interest rate is negatively related to output (that is, an IS function).

In their analysis of US monetary policy in the period 1960–96 Clarida et al. (2000) show that there is a 'significant difference in the way that monetary policy was conducted pre-and post-1979', being relatively well managed after 1979 compared to the earlier period. The key difference between the two periods is the magnitude and speed of response of the Federal Reserve to expected inflation. Under the respective chairmanships of William M. Martin, G. William Miller and Arthur Burns, the Fed was 'highly accommodative'. In contrast, in the years of Paul Volcker and Alan Greenspan, the Fed was much more 'proactive toward controlling inflation' (see Romer and Romer, 2002, 2004).

Clarida et al. (2000) conduct their investigation by specifying a baseline policy reaction function of the form given by (7.17):

$$r_t^* = r* + \beta[E(\dot{P}_{t,k} \mid \Omega_t) - \dot{P}*] + \gamma E[y_{t,q} \mid \Omega_t] \qquad (7.17)$$

Here $r_t^*$ represents the target rate for the Federal Funds (FF) nominal interest rate; $\dot{P}_{t,k}$ is the rate of inflation between time periods $t$ and $t + k$; $\dot{P}^*$ is the inflation target; $y_{t,q}$ measures the average deviation between actual GDP and the target level of GDP (the output gap) between time periods $t$ and $t + q$; E is the expectations operator; $\Omega_t$ is the information set available to the policy maker at the time the interest rate is set; and $r^*$ is the 'desired' nominal FF rate when both $\dot{P}$ and $y$ are at their target levels. For a central bank with a quadratic loss function, such as the one given by equation (7.16), this form of policy reaction function (rule) is appropriate in a new Keynesian setting. The policy rule given by (7.17) differs from the well-known 'Taylor rule' in that it is forward-looking (see Taylor, 1993, 1998a). Taylor proposed a rule where the Fed reacts to lagged output and inflation whereas (7.17) suggests that the Fed set the FF rate according to their expectation of the future values of inflation and output gap. The Taylor rule is equivalent to a 'special case' of equation (7.17) where lagged values of inflation and the output gap provide sufficient information for forecasting future inflation. First recommended at the 1992 Carnegie-Rochester Conference, Taylor's (1993) policy formula is given by (7.18):

$$r = \dot{P} + g(y) + h(\dot{P} - \dot{P}^*) + r^* \tag{7.18}$$

where $y$ is real GDP measured as the percentage deviation from potential GDP; $r$ is the short-term nominal rate of interest in percentage points; $\dot{P}$ is the rate of inflation and $\dot{P}^*$ the target rate of inflation; $r^*$ is the 'implicit real interest rate in the central bank's reaction function'; and the parameters $g$, $h$, $\dot{P}^*$ and $r^*$ all have a positive value. With this rule short-term nominal interest rates will rise if output and/or inflation are above their target values and nominal rates will fall when either is below their target value. For a critique of Taylor rules see Svensson (2003b).

In the case of (7.17) the policy maker is able to take into account a broad selection of information about the future path of the economy. In standard macroeconomic models aggregate demand responds negatively to the *real* rate of interest; that is, higher real rates dampen economic activity and lower real rates stimulate economic activity. From equation (7.17) we can derive the 'implied rule' for the target (*ex ante*) real rate of interest, $rr_t^*$. This is given by equation (7.19):

$$rr_t^* = rr^* + (\beta - 1)[E(\dot{P}_{t,k} \mid \Omega_t) - \dot{P}^*] + \gamma E[y_{t,q} \mid \Omega_t] \tag{7.19}$$

Here, $rr_t^* \equiv r_t - [E(\dot{P}_{t,k} \mid \Omega_t) - \dot{P}^*]$, and $rr^* \equiv r^* - \dot{P}^*$ is the long-run equilibrium real rate of interest. According to (7.19) the real rate target will respond to changes in the Fed's expectations about future output and inflation. However, as Clarida et al. point out, the sign of the response of $rr_i^*$ to expected changes in output and inflation will depend on the respective values of the coefficients $\beta$ and $\gamma$. Providing that $\beta > 1$ and $\gamma > 0$, then the interest rate rule will tend be stabilizing. If $\beta \leq 1$ and $\gamma \leq 0$, then interest rate rules 'are likely to be destabilising, or, at best, accommodative of shocks'. With $\beta < 1$, an increase in expected inflation leads to a decline in the real interest rate, which in turn stimulates aggregate demand thereby exacerbating inflation. During the mid-1970s, the real interest rate in the USA was negative even though inflation was above 10 per cent.

By building on this basic framework, Clarida et al. (2000), in their examination of the conduct of monetary policy in the period 1960–96, find that

> the Federal reserve was highly accommodative in the pre-Volcker years: on average, it let the real short-term interest rate decline as anticipated inflation rose. While it raised the nominal rate, it did so by less than the increase in expected inflation. On the other hand, during the Volcker–Greenspan era the Federal Reserve adopted a proactive stance toward controlling inflation: it systematically raised real as well as nominal short-term interest rates in response to higher expected inflation.

During the 1970s, despite accelerating inflation, the FF nominal rate tracked the rate of inflation but for much of the period this led to a zero or negative *ex post* real rate. There was a visible change in the conduct of monetary policy after 1979 when, following the Volcker disinflation via tight monetary policy, the real rate for most of the 1980s became positive. In recognition of the lag in monetary policy's impact on economic activity, the new monetary regime involved a pre-emptive response to the build-up of inflationary pressures. As a result of this marked change in the Fed's policy, inflation was successfully reduced although as a consequence of the disinflation the USA suffered its worst recession since the Great Depression. Unemployment rose from 5.7 per cent in the second quarter of 1979 to 10.7 per cent in the fourth quarter of 1982 (Gordon, 2003).

In their analysis of the change of policy regime at the Fed, Clarida et al. compare the FF rate with the estimated target forward (FWD) value for the interest rate under the 'Volcker–Greenspan' rule for the whole period. According to Clarida et al. the estimated rule 'does a good job' of capturing the broad movements of the FF rate for the post-1979 sample period.

There seems little doubt that the lower inflation experienced during the past two decades owes a great deal to the more anti-inflationary monetary stance taken by the Fed and other central banks around the world. DeLong (1997) suggests that the inferior monetary policy regime of the pre-Volcker period may have been due to the Fed believing that the natural rate of unemployment was lower than it actually was during the 1970s. Clarida et al. (2000) suggest another possibility. At that time 'neither the Fed nor the economics profession understood the dynamics of inflation very well. Indeed it was not until the mid-to-late 1970s that intermediate textbooks began emphasising the absence of a long-run trade-off between inflation and output. The ideas that expectations matter in generating inflation and that credibility is important in policymaking were simply not well established during that era' (see also Taylor, 1997a; Mayer, 1999; Romer and Romer, 2004). To understand the historical perform-ance of an economy over time it would seem imperative to have an understanding of the policy maker's knowledge during the time period under investigation. Since a great deal of policy makers' knowledge is derived from the research findings of economists, the state of economists' knowledge at each point in history must always be taken into consideration when assessing economic performance (Romer and Romer, 2002). Although it is a very important task of economists to analyse and be critical of past policy errors, we should remember that, as with all things, it is easy to be wise after the event.

While a consensus among new Keynesian economists would support the new Keynesian style of monetary policy outlined above, there remain doubt-ers. For example, Stiglitz (1993, pp. 1069–70) prefers a more flexible approach to policy making and argues:

> Changing economic circumstances require changes in economic policy, and it is impossible to prescribe ahead of time what policies would be appropriate ... The reality is that no government can stand idly by as 10, 15, or 20 percent of its workers face unemployment ... new Keynesian economists also believe that it is virtually impossible to design rules that are appropriate in the face of a rapidly changing economy.

### 7.11.4  Other policy implications

For those new Keynesians who have been developing various explanations of real wage rigidity, a number of policy conclusions emerge which are aimed specifically at reducing highly persistent unemployment (Manning, 1995; Nickell, 1997, 1998). The work of Lindbeck and Snower (1988b) suggests that institutional reforms are necessary in order to reduce the power of the insiders and make outsiders more attractive to employers. Theoretically con-ceivable power-reducing policies include:

1.  a softening of job security legislation in order to reduce the hiring and firing (turnover) costs of labour; and
2.  reform of industrial relations in order to lessen the likelihood of strikes.

Policies that would help to 'enfranchise' the outsiders would include:

1.  retraining outsiders in order to improve their human capital and marginal product;

2.    policies which improve labour mobility; for example, a better-functioning housing market;
3.    profit-sharing arrangements which bring greater flexibility to wages;
4.    redesigning of the unemployment compensation system so as to encourage job search.

Weitzman (1985) has forcefully argued the case for profit-sharing schemes on the basis that they offer a decentralized, automatic and market incentive approach to encourage wage flexibility, which would lessen the impact of macroeconomic shocks. Weitzman points to the experience of Japan, Korea and Taiwan with their flexible payment systems which have enabled these economies in the past to ride out the business cycle with relatively high output and employment levels (see Layard et al., 1991, for a critique).

The distorting impact of the unemployment compensation system on unemployment is recognized by many new Keynesian economists. A system which provides compensation for an indefinite duration without any obligation for unemployed workers to accept jobs offered seems most likely to disenfranchise the outsiders and raise efficiency wages in order to reduce shirking (Shapiro and Stiglitz, 1984). In the shirking model the equilibrium level of involuntary unemployment will be increased if the amount of unemployment benefit is raised. Layard et al. (1991) also favour reform of the unemployment compensation system (see Atkinson and Micklewright, 1991, for a survey of the literature).

Some new Keynesians (particularly the European branch) favour some form of incomes policy to modify the adverse impact of an uncoordinated wage bargaining system; for example, Layard et al. (1991) argue that 'if unemployment is above the long-run NAIRU and there is hysteresis, a temporary incomes policy is an excellent way of helping unemployment return to the NAIRU more quickly' (see also Galbraith, 1997). However, such policies remain extremely contentious and most new Keynesians (for example, Mankiw) do not feel that incomes policies have a useful role to play.

## 7.12    Keynesian Economics Without the *LM* Curve

The modern approach to stabilization policy outlined in section 7.11 above is now reflected in the ideas taught to students of economics, even at the principles level (see D. Romer, 2000; Taylor, 2000b, 2001). The following simple model is consistent with the macroeconomic models that are currently used in practice by the US Federal Reserve and the Bank of England (see Bank of England, 1999; Taylor, 1999; Clarida et al., 2000). Following Taylor (2000b), the model consists of three basic relationships. First, a negative relationship between the *real* rate of interest and GDP of the following form:

$$y = -ar + \mu \qquad (7.20)$$

where $y$ measures real GDP relative to potential GDP, $r$ is the real rate of interest, $\mu$ is a shift term which, for example, captures the influence of exogenous changes to exports and government expenditures and so on. A higher real rate of interest depresses total demand in an economy by reducing consumption and investment expenditures, and also net exports via exchange rate appreciation in open economies with floating exchange rates. This relationship is 'analogous' to the *IS* curve of conventional textbook IS–LM analysis. The second key element in the model is a positive relationship between inflation and the real rate of interest of the form:

$$r = b\dot{P} + v \qquad (7.21)$$

where $\dot{P}$ is the rate of inflation and $v$ is a shift term. This relationship, which closely mirrors current practice at leading central banks, indicates that when inflation rises the monetary authorities will act to raise the short-term nominal interest rate sufficient to raise the real rate of interest. As Taylor (2000b) and D. Romer (2000) both point out, central banks no longer target monetary aggregates but follow a simple real interest rate rule. The third key relationship underlying the modern monetary policy model is a 'Phillips curve' type relationship between inflation and GDP of the form:

$$\dot{P} = \dot{P}_{t-1} + cy_{t-1} + w \qquad (7.22)$$

where $w$ is a shift term. As equation (7.22) indicates, inflation will increase with a lag when actual GDP is greater than potential GDP ($y > y^*$) and vice versa. The lag in the response of inflation to the deviation of actual GDP from potential GDP reflects the staggered price-setting behaviour of firms with market power inducing nominal stickiness. While this aspect indicates the new Keynesian flavour of this model, the relationship also allows for expectations of inflation to influence the actual rate.

From these three simple relationships we can construct a graphical illustration of the modern approach to stabilization policy. Combining equations (7.20) and (7.21) yields the following equation:

$$y = -ab\dot{P} + \mu - av \qquad (7.23)$$

Equation (7.23) indicates a negatively sloped relationship between inflation and real GDP, which both Taylor and Romer call an aggregate demand (*AD*) curve. Figure 7.15 illustrates the derivation of the aggregate demand curve.

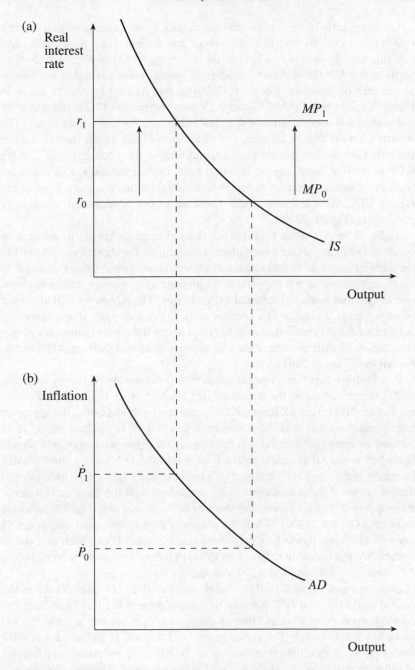

*Figure 7.15   Derivation of the AD curve*

For simplicity, if we assume that the central bank's choice of real interest rate depends entirely on its inflation objective, the monetary policy (*MP*) real rate rule can be shown as a horizontal line in panel (a) of Figure 7.15, with shifts of the *MP* curve determined by the central bank's reaction to changes in the rate of inflation. Equation (7.20) is represented by the *IS* curve in Figure 7.15. In panel (b) of Figure 7.15 we see equation (7.23) illustrated by a downward-sloping aggregate demand curve in inflation–output space. The intuition here is that as inflation rises the central bank raises the real rate of interest, thereby dampening total expenditure in the economy and causing GDP to decline. Similarly, as inflation falls, the central bank will lower the real rate of interest, thereby stimulating total expenditure in the economy and raising GDP. We can think of this response as the central bank's *monetary policy rule* (Taylor, 2000b).

Shifts of the *AD* curve would result from exogenous shocks to the various components to aggregate expenditure, for example the *AD* curve will shift to the right in response to an increase in government expenditure, a decrease in taxes, an increase in net exports, or an increase in consumer and/or business confidence that leads to increased expenditures. The *AD* curve will also shift in response to a change in monetary policy. For example, if the monetary authorities decide that inflation is too high under the current monetary policy rule, they will shift the rule, raise real interest rates and shift the *AD* curve to the left (see Taylor, 2001).

The Phillips curve or inflation adjustment relationship, given by equation (7.22), is represented by the horizontal line labelled $IA_0$ in Figure 7.16. Following Taylor (2000b) and D. Romer (2000), this can be thought of as the aggregate supply component of the model, assuming first that the immediate impact of an increase in aggregate demand will fall entirely on aggregate output, and second that when actual GDP equals potential or 'natural' GDP ($y = y^*$), inflation will be steady, but when $y > y^*$, inflation will increase and when $y < y^*$, inflation will decline. Both of these assumptions are consistent with the empirical evidence and supported by new Keynesian theories of wage and price stickiness in the short run (Gordon, 1990). When the economy is at its potential output the *IA* line will also shift upwards in response to supply-side shocks such as a rise in commodity prices and in response to shifts in inflationary expectations. Figure 7.16 illustrates the complete AD–IA model.

Long-run equilibrium in this model requires that *AD* intersect *IA* at the natural rate of output ($y^*$). Assume that the economy is initially in long-run equilibrium at point $E_{LR\,0}$ and that an exogenous demand shock shifts the *AD* curve from $AD_0$ to $AD_1$. The initial impact of this shift is an increase in GDP from $y^*$ to $y_1$, with inflation remaining at $\dot{P}_0$. Since $y_1 > y^*$, over time the rate of inflation will increase, shifting the *IA* curve upwards. The central bank will respond to this increase in inflation by raising the real rate of interest, shown

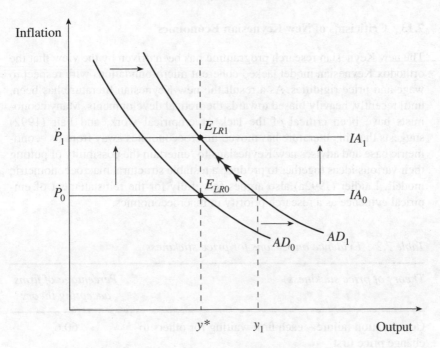

*Figure 7.16   Adjusting to long-run equilibrium in the AD-IA model*

by an upward shift of the *MP* curve in the *IS–MP* diagram (Figure 7.15). The *IA* curve continues to shift upwards until the *AD* and *IA* curves intersect at the potential level of output $y^*$, that is, where $AD_1$ and $IA_1$ intersect. The economy is now at a new long-run equilibrium shown by $E_{LR1}$, but with a higher steady rate of inflation of $\dot{P_1}$. The central bank has responded to the demand shock by increasing the real rate of interest from $r_0$ to $r_1$. If the central bank decides that the new steady rate of inflation is too high (that is, above its inflation target), then it would have to take steps to shift the *AD* curve to the left by changing its monetary policy rule. This would lead to a recession ($y < y^*$) and declining inflation. As the *IA* curve shifts down, the central bank will reduce real interest rates, stimulating demand, and the economy will return to $y^*$ at a lower steady rate of inflation.

The simple model described above gives a reasonably accurate portrayal of how monetary policy is now conducted. In Taylor's (2000b) view this theory 'fits the data well and explains policy decisions and impacts in a realistic way'. Whether this approach eventually becomes popularly known as 'new Keynesian' (Clarida et al., 2000; Gali, 2002) or as 'new neoclassical synthesis' (Goodfriend and King, 1997) remains to be seen. David Romer (2000) simply calls it 'Keynesian macroeconomics without the LM curve'.

**7.13　Criticisms of New Keynesian Economics**

The new Keynesian research programme has been driven by the view that the orthodox Keynesian model lacked coherent microfoundations with respect to wage and price rigidities. As a result the new Keynesian literature has been, until recently, heavily biased towards theoretical developments. Many economists have been critical of the lack of empirical work, and Fair (1992) suggests that this literature has moved macroeconomics away from its econometric base and advises new Keynesians to 'entertain the possibility of putting their various ideas together to produce a testable structural macroeconometric model'. Laidler (1992a) also argues forcefully for the reinstatement of empirical evidence as a research priority in macroeconomics.

*Table 7.2　Evidence on reasons for price stickiness*

| *Theory of price stickiness* | *Percentage of firms accepting theory* |
|---|---|
| Coordination failure – each firm waiting for others to change price first | 60.6 |
| Cost-based pricing with lags | 55.5 |
| Preference for varying product attributes other than price | 54.8 |
| Implicit contracts – fairness to customers necessitates stable prices | 50.4 |
| Explicit nominal contracts | 35.7 |
| Costly price adjustment – menu costs | 30.0 |
| Procyclical elasticity – demand curves become more inelastic as they shift to the left | 29.7 |
| Psychological significance of pricing points | 24.0 |
| Preference for varying inventories rather than change price | 20.9 |
| Constant marginal cost and constant mark-ups | 19.7 |
| Bureaucratic delays | 13.6 |
| Judging quality by price – fear that customers will interpret reductions in price as a reduction in quality | 10.0 |

*Source*:　Adapted from Blinder (1994).

In response, new Keynesians can point to the non-orthodox but interesting and innovative research by Blinder (1991, 1994) into the pricing behaviour of firms, the empirical work related to testing the efficiency wage hypothesis (for example, Drago and Heywood, 1992; Capelli and Chauvin, 1991) and the influential paper by Ball et al. (1988) testing menu cost models using cross-country data. In seeking an answer to the important question 'Why are prices sticky?', Blinder's research utilizes the data collected from interviews to discriminate between alternative explanations of price stickiness, which is regarded as a stylized fact by Keynesian economists (see Carlton, 1986, for evidence on price rigidities). Blinder's results, reproduced in Table 7.2, give some support to Keynesian explanations which emphasize coordination failures, cost-plus pricing, preference for changing product attributes other than price, and implicit contracts.

In an interview (Snowdon, 2001a) Blinder summarized his findings on price stickiness in the following way:

> of the twelve theories tested, many of the ones which come out best have a Keynesian flavour. When you list the twelve theories in the order that the respondents liked and agreed with them, the first is co-ordination failure – which is a very Keynesian idea. The second relates to the simple mark-up pricing model, which I might say is a very British-Keynesian idea. Some of the reasons given for price stickiness are not Keynesian at all. For example, non-price competition during a recession. The Okun (1981) implicit contract idea is also very Keynesian ... if you look at the top five reasons given by firms as to why prices are sticky, four of them look distinctly Keynesian in character ... To the extent that you are prepared to believe survey results, and some people won't, I think this research strikes several blows in favour of Keynesian ideas.

Similar work by Bhaskar et al. (1993), utilizing data collected in the UK during the 1980s, confirms that most firms tend not to increase prices in booms or reduce them in recessions, but quantity adjustment responses via variations in hours, shift work, inventories or customer rationing are 'overwhelmingly important'.

A second major problem with the new Keynesian literature is that it has yielded numerous elegant theories which are often unrelated (Gordon, 1990). This makes the pulling together of these ideas in order to produce a testable new Keynesian model all the more difficult. New Keynesians have themselves recognized this problem, with Blanchard (1992) reflecting that 'we have constructed too many monsters' with 'few interesting results'. The fascination with constructing a 'bewildering array' of theories with their 'quasi religious' adherence to microfoundations has become a disease. Because there are too many reasons for wage and price inertia, no agreement exists on which source of rigidity is the most important (for a critique of efficiency wage theory, see Katz, 1986; Weiss, 1991).

A third line of criticism also relates to the menu cost literature. Critics doubt that the small costs of price adjustment can possibly account for major contractions of output and employment (Barro, 1989a). Caplin and Spulber (1987) also cast doubt on the menu cost result by showing that, although menu costs may be important to an individual firm, this influence can disappear in the aggregate. In response to these criticisms, new Keynesians argue that the emerging literature which incorporates real rigidities widens the scope for nominal rigidities to have an impact on output and employment (see Ball and Romer, 1990; D. Romer, 2001). A further weakness of models incorporating small costs of changing prices is that they generate multiple equilibria. Rotemberg (1987) suggests that 'if many things can happen the models are more difficult to reject' and 'when there are multiple equilibria it is impossible to know how the economy will react to any particular government policy'. Golosov and Lucas (2003) also highlight that in calibration exercises their menu cost model is consistent with the fact that 'even large disinflations have small real effects if credibly carried out'.

A fourth criticism of new Keynesian economics relates to the emphasis it gives to deriving rigidities from microfoundations. Tobin (1993) denies that Keynesian macroeconomics 'asserts or requires' nominal and/or price rigidity. In Tobin's view, wage and price flexibility would, in all likelihood, exacerbate a recession and he supports Keynes's (1936) intuition that rigidity of nominal wages will act as a stabilizing influence in the face of aggregate demand shocks. Tobin also reminds the new Keynesians that Keynes had a 'theoretically impeccable' and 'empirically realistic' explanation of nominal wage rigidity based on workers' concern with wage relativities. Since a nominal wage cut will be viewed by each group of workers as a relative real wage reduction (because workers have no guarantee in a decentralized system of knowing what wage cuts other groups of workers are accepting), it will be resisted by rational workers. Summers (1988) has taken up this neglected issue and suggests relative wage influences give rise to significant coordination problems. Greenwald and Stiglitz (1993b) have also developed a strand of new Keynesian theorizing which highlights the destabilizing impact of price flexibility.

A fifth criticism relates to the acceptance by many new Keynesians of the rational expectations hypothesis. Phelps (1992) regards the rational expectations hypothesis as 'unsatisfactory' and Blinder (1992a) notes that the empirical evidence in its favour is 'at best weak and at worst damning'. Until someone comes up with a better idea, it seems unlikely that this line of criticism will lead to the abandonment of the rational expectations hypothesis in macroeconomics. However, with respect to the formation of expectations Leijonhufvud is enthusiastic about recent research into 'Learning' (see Evans and Honkapohja, 2001; Snowdon, 2004a).

A sixth problem identified with new Keynesian economics relates to the continued acceptance by the 'new' school of the 'old' IS–LM model as the best way of understanding the determinants of aggregate demand. King (1993) argues that the IS–LM model has 'no greater prospect of being a viable analytical vehicle for macroeconomics in the 1990s than the Ford Pinto has of being a sporty, reliable car for the 1990s'. The basic problem identified by King is that, in order to use the IS–LM model as an analytical tool, economists must essentially ignore expectations, but 'we now know that this simplification eliminates key determinants of aggregate demand' (King, 1993). King advises macroeconomists and policy makers to ignore new Keynesian advertising because, despite the new packaging, the new product is as unsound as the original one (however, see section 7.12 above).

Finally, Paul Davidson (1994) has been very critical of new Keynesian analysis, claiming that 'there is no Keynesian beef in new Keynesianism'. From Davidson's Post Keynesian perspective, new Keynesians pay no attention to crucial aspects of Keynes's monetary theory (see Chapter 8). However, Mankiw (1992) does not regard consistency between new Keynesian analysis and the *General Theory*, which he describes as 'an obscure book', as an important issue.

### 7.14 An Assessment of New Keynesian Economics

How successful have new Keynesian economists been in their quest to develop coherent microfoundations for sticky price models? Barro's (1989a) main conclusion regarding new Keynesian economics (for which he uses the acronym NUKE) was that, although some of these ideas may prove to be useful as elements in real business cycle models, NUKE models have 'not been successful in rehabilitating the Keynesian approach'. In sharp contrast, Mankiw and Romer (1991, p. 15) concluded that 'The new classical argument that the Keynesian assumption of nominal rigidities was incapable of being given theoretical foundations has been refuted.'

Keynesian economics has displayed a remarkable resilience during the past 30 years, given the strength of the theoretical counter-revolutions launched against its essential doctrines, particularly during the period 1968–82. This resilience can be attributed to the capacity of Keynesian analysis to adapt to both theoretical innovations and new empirical findings (see Shaw, 1988; Lindbeck, 1998; Gali, 2002). Not only has Keynesian economics proved capable of absorbing the natural rate hypothesis and expectations-augmented Phillips curve; it has also managed to accommodate the rational expectations hypothesis and build on the insights and methodology of the real business cycle school (Ireland, 2004). This fundamental metamorphosis continues, with new Keynesian theorists rebuilding and refining the foundations of

Keynesian economics in line with modern developments in microeconomic and macroeconomic theory. By emphasizing a variety of imperfections in the labour, product and capital markets, new Keynesian economics is viewed by its advocates as an 'exciting' and 'dynamic research programme' (Stiglitz, 1992). To the critics, new Keynesians have achieved little more than reintroduce 'old wine in new bottles'.

In his assessment of new Keynesian economics, Lindbeck (1998) argues that the current 'sophisticated structure of macroeconomic theory' has arisen through numerous contributions from many different strands of economic analysis. As this process continues and involves the closer integration of real business cycle analysis with new Keynesian frictions, 'traditional labels' on macroeconomic theories, such as new Keynesian, new classical and real business cycle, will 'probably become increasingly irrelevant'.

In his Nobel Memorial Lecture, 'Behavioural Macroeconomics and Macroeconomic Behaviour', Akerlof (2002) provides a significant critique of new classical models and a spirited defence of Keynesian economics broadly defined. Akerlof argues that the behavioural assumptions of the new classical models are so 'primitive' that they lead to an outright denial of several important macroeconomic phenomena. These include denying 'the existence of involuntary unemployment', denying that monetary policy, even if anticipated, does impact on real variables such as output and employment, and ignoring the fact that deflation fails to accelerate when unemployment and output are above their natural rates, as predicted by new classical models. Akerlof agrees with Lucas that the orthodox Keynesian models of the neoclassical synthesis era were in need of coherent microfoundations. However, the orthodox neoclassical microfoundations adopted by the new classical school ignored, and continue largely to ignore, the tremendous progress that has been made by economists in modelling the impact of asymmetric information, imperfect competition and adopting assumptions 'grounded in psychological and sociological observation'. Akerlof believes that future progress in macroeconomics depends on building a 'behavioural macroeconomics' in the spirit of Keynes (see also Stiglitz, 2000, 2002). It remains to be seen if a 'Keynesian economics' will proceed in the direction recommended by Akerlof.

# N. GREGORY MANKIW

Gregory Mankiw was born in 1958 in Trenton, New Jersey and graduated from Princeton University in 1980 before obtaining his PhD in economics from the Massachusetts Institute of Technology in 1984. Since 1985 he has been teaching at Harvard University, where he is Professor of Economics.

Gregory Mankiw is best known for his work on price adjustment, the determinants of consumer spending and the theory and empirics of economic growth. He is widely recognized as a leading exponent of the new Keynesian school of macroeconomics. His best-known books include: *New Keynesian Economics. Vol. 1, Imperfect Competition and Sticky Prices* (MIT Press, 1991), co-edited with David Romer; *New Keynesian Economics, Vol. 2, Co-ordination Failures and Real Rigidities* (MIT Press, 1991), co-edited with David Romer; *Monetary Policy* (University of Chicago Press, 1994); and *Macroeconomics*, 5th edn (Worth Publishers, 2003).

Professor Mankiw's best-known articles include: 'Intertemporal Substitution in Macroeconomics', *Quarterly Journal of Economics* (1985), co-authored with Julio Rotemberg and Laurence Summers; 'Small Menu Costs and Large Business Cycles: A Macroeconomic Model of Monopoly', *Quarterly Journal of Economics* (1985); 'The New Keynesian Economics and the Output–Inflation Trade-off', *Brookings Papers on Economic Activity* (1988), co-authored with Lawrence Ball and David Romer; 'Real Business Cycles: A New Keynesian Perspective', *Journal of Economic Perspectives* (1989); 'A Contribution to the

Empirics of Economic Growth', *Quarterly Journal of Economics* (1992), co-authored with David Romer and David Weil; 'The Growth of Nations', *Brookings Papers on Economic Activity* (1995); and 'The Inexorable and Mysterious Trade-off Between Inflation and Unemployment', *Economic Journal* (2001).

We interviewed Professor Mankiw in his office at Harvard University on 18 February 1993 and subsequently corresponded in February/March 1998.

## General Issues

*Why do you think we have so much controversy in macroeconomics compared to microeconomics?*
That is a hard question. It is certainly true that there is more agreement among microeconomists as to how they approach things. That is, most microeconomists start off with utility and profit maximization as the underlying motives and go on from there. Macroeconomics is in some ways harder since you are dealing with the whole economy; the field therefore requires more simplifying assumptions to make anything manageable, to make the problem simpler than it really is in the world. I think there is disagreement as to which simplifying assumptions are the most natural or the most useful.

*How important do you think it is for macroeconomics to have neoclassical choice-theoretic foundations?*
Well it is certainly true that all macro phenomena are the aggregate of many micro phenomena; in that sense macroeconomics is inevitably founded on microeconomics. Yet I am not sure that all macroeconomics necessarily has to start off with microeconomic building-blocks. To give an analogy, all of biology is in some sense the aggregate of particle physics, because all biological creatures are made up of particles. That doesn't mean that the natural place to start in building biology is to start with particle physics and aggregate up. Instead I would probably start with theory at the level of the organism or the cell, not the level of the sub-atomic particle. We have a lot of models like the IS–LM model that are very useful for studying the macroeconomy, even though those models don't start off with the individual unit and build up from there.

*Which papers or books do you feel have had the biggest impact on the development of macroeconomics over the last 25 years?*
The biggest impact has undoubtedly come from Lucas. He put the cracks into the Keynesian consensus that existed in the 1960s. He really pulled macroeconomics apart by proposing new and intriguing new ideas. The disagreements today among macroeconomists have largely arisen from the critiques of

Lucas and of his followers. As you know, I don't agree with Lucas's solutions, but I take the problems that he pointed out very seriously. A lot of the work that I and other new Keynesians have done is a response to the problems he pointed out in the old Keynesian ideas.

*To some extent you've answered our next question. Where did you draw inspiration for your own work?*
It's been a combination of influences. Part comes from the older generation of macroeconomists. I view much of the work I do as building on the work of Tobin, Modigliani and Friedman. I see a great deal of truth in the views they were pushing. I also take the problems that Lucas pointed out very seriously. A lot of new Keynesian work is trying to reformulate the 1960s Friedman–Tobin view of the world. What is now called the neoclassical synthesis had a large element of truth in it. On the other hand, it had problems, and Lucas pointed out those problems very forcefully. We need to fix those problems and address the concerns of Lucas while still maintaining the element of truth in the neoclassical synthesis.

## Keynes and the *General Theory*

*One interpretation of the neoclassical synthesis which emerged at the end of the 1950s suggested that the* General Theory *was a special case of a more general classical model. Would you agree with that interpretation?*
I would say that the classical model and the Keynesian model make different assumptions about adjustment of prices. I think of the classical model as being the model that assumes complete price flexibility, and therefore describes a horizon over which it is plausible to make such an assumption. Probably a period of years, rather than a period of months. The Keynesian model applies over a horizon where wages and prices are relatively inflexible or sluggish. Both models are special cases of a more general model which allows a varying degree of flexibility and sluggishness in prices depending on the horizon we want to study. When we study the effect of policies over a quarter or a decade, we want to make different assumptions about the degree of flexibility of prices.

*Why do you think there are so many conflicting interpretations of the* General Theory*?*
There are a great many conflicting interpretations because Keynes had a lot of different ideas. The ideas don't necessarily have to be packaged all together, so some people grab on to one set of ideas and say that this is really what is central to what Keynes was saying, and other people grab on to another set of ideas. The question is, when we look at the market imperfec-

tion that we call the business cycle, which set of general ideas from the *General Theory* is the most important? There is so much in the *General Theory* that it is hard to comprehend it all at once. Some is very important, but some is not particularly important. Disagreements come by choosing different pieces of Keynes's world view and emphasizing those.

*Do you think that, if Keynes had still been living in 1969, he would have received the first Nobel Prize in Economics?*
Oh, undoubtedly. I think there are a few very very important economists of the century, and there is no question that Keynes has got to be on anybody's shortlist.

## New Classical Macroeconomics

*Do you regard new classical macroeconomics as a separate school of thought from monetarism?*
I think so. My impression is that monetarism is a school of thought that says fluctuations in the money supply are the primary cause of fluctuations in aggregate demand and in aggregate income, whereas new classicism is a particular theory as to why fluctuations in aggregate demand might matter through an unanticipated price surprise. This price surprise view proposed by Lucas is, I think, the next step after monetarism. More recently, new classical economists have turned their attention to real business cycle theory, which is the antithesis of monetarism.

*Do you think that overall the new classical contributions have had a beneficial effect on the development of macroeconomics?*
Debate is healthy, and the new Keynesian school arose largely in response to the new classical school. In that sense it is a debate leading to greater truths, and it has been helpful. Many of the specific contributions, especially real business cycle theory, are probably not going to survive the test of time. The literature on the time inconsistency of policy is a contribution that will survive and has probably been one of the most important contributions to policy analysis in the past two decades.

*How important is the rational expectations hypothesis?*
It is important in the sense that it has now become the working hypothesis of all practising macroeconomists. Economists routinely assume that people are rational when they make decisions: they maximize utility, they rationally maximize profits, and so on. It would be peculiar for us to assume that people are rational except when they come to form expectations and then they act irrationally. I don't think the rational expectations hypothesis is important in

the sense of having all the sweeping implications, as was at first believed. At first people thought that it had all sorts of properties about policy being ineffective.

*Isn't that more to do with the market-clearing assumption?*
Exactly. People have come to realize that it is other assumptions, like the market-clearing assumption, that are really important and that rational expectations in itself doesn't have implications as sweeping as once thought.

*You have questioned the argument that the disinflation experience of the early 1980s both in the USA and in Britain provided decisive evidence against the new classical claim of painless disinflation. Is that because the deflation was unanticipated?*
There are two new classical views. The first is the price surprise theory of Lucas. The second is the real business cycle theory. This second view says that money anticipated or unanticipated doesn't matter. My view of that is that it is completely at variance with the evidence. Larry Ball has a paper that shows systematically for a large number of countries that whenever you have a major disinflation it is associated with a period of low output and high unemployment [see Ball, 1994]. So I think that the evidence is completely clear on that. The evidence is more favourable to early new classical theory. You're right that to a large extent the disinflation was unanticipated even in the USA, where Volcker said he was going to disinflate. I don't think people believed he was going to disinflate as fast as he did. Most measures of expectations of inflation did not come down until after the recession was well under way. I am sympathetic to the view that credibility is one determinant of how costly a disinflation will be.

## Keynesianism and the New Keynesians

*Do you regard yourself as a Keynesian?*
I do, but I'm always nervous about the term because Keynesian can mean different things to different people, just as different people will read the *General Theory* and pull out different elements as being important. People use the word Keynesian in so many different ways that recently I have actually tried to avoid using the term at all, on the grounds that it is more confusing than illuminating. I think of myself as a Keynesian in the sense of believing that the business cycle represents some sort of market imperfection on a grand scale. Milton Friedman was also a Keynesian in that sense. My own views emerged as much from Milton Friedman as they have from John Maynard Keynes. Some people take the word Keynesian as meaning a belief in fine-tuning the economy so that the government controls every wiggle of

ups and downs. Other people take it as a belief that deficit spending is not a bad thing. I don't subscribe to either of those views. I think that the broad theme of the *General Theory* is that the business cycle is something that we really need to worry about because it is a sign of a market imperfection. In that way I am a Keynesian, but as I said before, so is Milton Friedman.

*Was the breakdown of the Phillips curve fatal for orthodox Keynesianism?*
It highlighted the absence of a good theory of aggregate supply. What orthodox Keynesians had was a pretty good theory of aggregate demand. The IS–LM model has held up pretty well as a general structure for thinking about how aggregate demand is determined. The problem is once you've got aggregate demand – a downward-sloping curve in P–Y space – you still need a good story for the aggregate supply curve. The Phillips curve came out of nowhere. It is really just an empirical description of what was true in the data without any particular good theories as to why it should look that way, how it would change in response to policy, and what might make it unstable. So we never had a good theory of that, and the breakdown of the Phillips curve made that very apparent and provided room for the more general critique that Lucas put forward. The deficiency on the supply side was always a weakness, but it wasn't given attention until the Phillips curve broke down.

*What would you summarize as being the central propositions of new Keynesian macroeconomics?*
The central propositions are largely theoretical rather than policy-oriented. New Keynesians accept the view of the world summarized by the neoclassical synthesis: the economy can deviate in the short term from its equilibrium level, and monetary and fiscal policy have important influences on real economic activity. New Keynesians are saying that the neoclassical synthesis is not as flawed as Lucas and others have argued. The purpose of the new Keynesian school has been largely to fix those theoretical problems raised by Lucas and also to accept Lucas's argument that we need models supported by better microeconomic foundations.

*So you wouldn't subscribe to arguments in favour of incomes policies advocated by Post Keynesians?*
No, not at all. When the government gets in the business of setting wages and prices it is not very good at it. The setting of wages and prices should be left to free markets.

*So you are no Galbraithian?*
Absolutely not [*laughter*].

*How important is the theory of imperfect competition to new Keynesian macroeconomics?*
A large part of new Keynesian economics is trying to explain why firms set and adjust prices over time in the way that they do. Firms in a perfectly competitive environment don't have any choice over what their prices are going to be. Competitive firms are price takers. If you want to even talk about firms setting prices you have to talk about firms that have some ability to do so, and those are firms that have some market power: they are imperfectly competitive. So I think imperfect competition is central to thinking about price setting and therefore central to new Keynesian economics.

*This is strange, because if you think of the 1930s, you had Keynes and Joan Robinson at Cambridge. Joan Robinson developed the theory of imperfect competition and Keynes developed his* General Theory. *Why did it take so long to bring these two ideas together?*
I don't think that Keynes was as worried about building his model based on microfoundations as we are today. Joan Robinson was building the microeconomics that would later prove to be very useful for addressing the macroeconomics of Keynes. Keynes, not having read Robert Lucas yet, wasn't worried about building the microeconomics of aggregate supply [*laughter*].

*In a sense haven't the Post Keynesians been ahead of you here? People like Paul Davidson have for years taken imperfect competition as their microfoundation. So are the new Keynesians simply catching up on what the Post Keynesians did a while ago?*
They have a broad theme of imperfect competition, but the details are not very similar. My impression is that the new Keynesian economics is much more in line with the neoclassical synthesis than with the Post Keynesians.

*You will obviously be very familiar with Alan Blinder's recent surveys. Are they supporting the new Keynesian views? [See Blinder, 1991.]*
Alan is providing a way of judging a variety of different new Keynesian views. There are a lot of new theories about wage and price rigidities. He is trying to sort out which is right and wrong using a fairly novel perspective of asking firms how they set wages and prices. This is terrific work, but what we are going to learn in the end is still unclear. He is still producing the papers and we haven't seen all the results yet. The goal is to provide one way of deciding which theories we like and which we don't. It's a very exciting project.

*An important distinction seems to be made by new Keynesians between real rigidities and nominal rigidities. Why is it important to make this distinction?*

The reason is that a real rigidity, which is a rigidity in a relative price, is not a reason for monetary non-neutrality. Unions, for example, could set rigid real wages away from equilibrium. A rigid real wage is not going to provide any reason to believe that money is not neutral, since it does not create any nominal lever for money to work on. It would cause unemployment, but not monetary non-neutrality. To get monetary non-neutrality, which is a central challenge for macro theorists, you need some nominal rigidity, such as sticky prices. Having said that, there does seem to be a variety of real rigidities in the world – unions setting wages above equilibrium levels, for example. The question is whether nominal and real rigidities interact. One of the big themes of this literature, mainly due to Larry Ball and David Romer, is that real and nominal rigidities seem to reinforce each other. The real rigidity is actually going to make the nominal rigidity much more important than it would be otherwise.

*Critics of the menu cost literature have suggested that this is a small peg on which to hang an explanation of the business cycle. How can small menu costs have such large real effects on the macroeconomy? [See Barro, 1989a.]* It is clear that menu costs are quite small. Firms don't bear huge costs when they change their prices. Yet it is also clear that recessions are very costly events. The question is whether these relatively small menu costs can be a key part of understanding this relatively costly business cycle. This literature shows that price adjustments by firms have external effects. When a firm decides to keep prices sticky, this could well be costly for the economy in a way that is not costly for the firm that is making the decision.

*How do efficiency wage and insider–outsider theories fit into new Keynesian thinking?*
Both of these theories provide a particular explanation for real rigidities, such as why real wages don't move to the equilibrium level in labour markets. As I said before, real rigidities and nominal rigidities can complement each other. That is, the insider–outsider and efficiency wage explanations for rigid real wages in some senses complement the menu cost story of rigid prices.

*Is the idea of hysteresis crucial to new Keynesian macroeconomics?*
Actually I don't think of it as being crucial. It is an interesting idea that a recession can have long-lived effects on the economy and leave permanent scars after the initial cause of the recession has gone. For example, the high unemployment in Europe in the 1980s persisted far longer than anyone could explain with standard models. But if this idea turned out to be wrong it would not bring down our theories. This has been an interesting, but relatively separate, question.

*Do you see the concept of NAIRU, and Friedman's natural rate, as being the same idea or are they different?*
I have always thought of them as being basically the same. Most new Keynesian models involve some sort of natural rate; in that sense Milton Friedman has won the debate. Most new Keynesians believe in the natural rate hypothesis except for a small group of people working with hysteresis. The natural rate hypothesis is pretty well entrenched.

*What about the concept of full employment? It was difficult to think of doing macroeconomics 15–20 years ago without the concept of full employment being central. What do we do about issues like involuntary unemployment? Lucas suggests that we should abandon this concept, what are your views on this? (See Lucas, 1978)*
I think there is involuntary unemployment. Part of the new Keynesian literature has come up with models of the labour market to explain why involuntary unemployment exists, why real wages don't adjust to equilibrate labour markets. There is a lot of truth to the efficiency wage theories and the insider–outsider theories, for example.

*Do new Keynesians think of full employment as the natural rate?*
I avoid the term full employment because it suggests that the natural rate is in some sense desirable. I think there is some natural rate which is the long-run unemployment rate that the economy tends to, that can't be influenced by monetary policy in the long run. That doesn't mean that it is immutable in response to any policy intervention. There are things that have been done to the labour market that either increase or decrease the natural rate, things like the minimum wage, unemployment insurance laws, labour training policies. There are all sorts of things that the government can do to change the natural rate. I don't like calling it full employment because good labour market policies might well raise employment beyond that level.

*How important do you think it is to take into account fairness when you are looking at the labour market? We are thinking here of the work of George Akerlof, Janet Yellen and Robert Solow, who have stressed the idea of fairness. Doesn't this work suggest that perhaps new Keynesians should start looking more closely at the psychology and sociology literature? [See Akerlof and Yellen, 1990; Solow, 1990.]*
Some of the papers that they have written have been extremely interesting. I don't think there is a lot of compelling evidence yet that we need to abandon neoclassical assumptions. I'm not doing so yet in my work, but I'm certainly happy to read the work of others who are doing so [*laughter*].

*In your recent edited volumes of collected papers on new Keynesian econom-*
*ics you say that 'new Keynesian macroeconomics could just as easily be*
*labelled new monetarist economics'. What exactly did you mean? [See Mankiw*
*and Romer, 1991.]*
The challenge raised by the real business cycle school is the question of
whether money is neutral and, if not, why not? Twenty years ago when
Friedman and Tobin were debating, there were some things they agreed on.
They agreed on the proposition that the Federal Reserve was an important
player in the economy, that what it did really mattered. The real business
cycle school has challenged that by writing down models without any real
effects of monetary policy. What the new Keynesian models have tried to do
is establish why money is not neutral, what microeconomic imperfections are
necessary to explain monetary non-neutrality at the macro level. In this sense,
these models are trying to support both traditional Keynesian and monetarist
views.

*Would you agree with Stanley Fischer that the views of Friedman, Brunner*
*and Meltzer are closer to those of Keynesians than they are to equilibrium*
*business cycle theorists? [See Fischer, 1988.]*
Oh yes absolutely. The essence of real business cycle models is the absence
of any role for the Federal Reserve, whereas I think Brunner, Meltzer and
Friedman would agree with Tobin that the Fed is very important. None of
them would ever argue that money is neutral in the way that real business
cycle theorists have.

*James Tobin has suggested that good papers in economics contain surprises.*
*What surprises have new Keynesian papers uncovered? [See Tobin, 1988.]*
One of the big surprises is that one can go much further with menu cost
models than people had once thought. A lot of people used to see these
models as a silly way of thinking about price rigidity. What the new literature
is trying to do is to say no, maybe we should take menu cost models seriously. I think the complementarity between real and nominal rigidities is a
surprise. As I mentioned earlier, one of the disappointing features so far of
the new Keynesian literature is that it hasn't been as empirical as I would
have liked. That is a problem being remedied right now in some research.
Ultimately that is where the literature should go. More empirical work is
needed.

*Peter Howitt has talked about a Keynesian recovery, Alan Blinder about a*
*Keynesian restoration; you seem to prefer the term reincarnation. Is there*
*something important in the different terms used? [See Howitt, 1990; Blinder,*
*1992b and Mankiw, 1992.]*

I chose the term reincarnation because it means rebirth into another body. While there are many similarities between new and old Keynesian economics, there are also a lot of differences as well, and I wanted to emphasize that. In some senses the spirit of Keynes has been brought back, but it doesn't look like the old Keynes. In fact Keynes might not recognize the new Keynesians as Keynesians at all. In general, people might not recognize themselves after they have been reincarnated. So that is why I used the term reincarnation [*laughter*].

*Would you say that your work is, with respect to Keynes, faithful in spirit, but critical in detail?*
I think that is fair. It tries to go beyond Keynes in a sense of taking microfoundations more seriously. Alan Blinder wrote a paper 'Keynes after Lucas' and I think that title pretty much describes new Keynesians. It takes some of Keynes's ideas seriously, and it also takes some of the critiques of Lucas seriously as well. [See Blinder, 1986.]

*Do you think Keynes would have been a new Keynesian?*
I don't know; I think Keynes was a very unpredictable fellow. I guess he would see some things in it he would like, and some things in it he wouldn't.

**Real Business Cycle Theory**

*You've recently argued that real business cycle theory has served an important function in stimulating and provoking scientific debate, but you predict that the approach will eventually be discarded. What are your main objections to real business cycle theory? What are the weaknesses, theoretical, empirical, or both?*
My objections are mainly empirical. Theoretically they are very elegant models, and that is a large part of their appeal. They are very parsimonious models. But when I look at the real world I see the same things that Milton Friedman and James Tobin do, which is a very powerful Federal Reserve board in the USA or the Bank of England in the UK. There is a lot of evidence across countries that periods of disinflation are periods of low output and high unemployment. Those effects are completely absent in real business cycle models. I think the central driving forces for the business cycle that those models highlight – technology shocks – aren't very important.

*Isn't the procyclical behaviour of the real wage a strong feature of these theories? How do new Keynesians explain the movement of real wages over the business cycle?*
The theories do predict procyclical wages. Although I've not looked at the models carefully on this question, my understanding is that they predict very

procyclical, real wages. While it is true that real wages are procyclical, my reading of the evidence is that they are only mildly procyclical. Therefore, the fact that these theories predict very procyclical real wages, and the data show that they are only mildly procyclical, makes it hard to reconcile this model with the evidence. I think the real wage evidence is not hard to explain. If you believe in a world where wages and prices are sluggish over time, the cyclical behaviour of the real wage is really a question of whether wages or prices are more sluggish. The fact that real wages are roughly acyclical, maybe slightly procyclical, is some indication to me that wages and prices are simply equally sticky. This is consistent with Alan Blinder's evidence, which says that prices change on average once a year, and we know a lot of wages change on average once a year. So I think that explanation is consistent with much of the evidence.

*How do we explain procyclical productivity? Some Keynesians seem to suggest that it is due to labour hoarding.*
The procyclical behaviour of productivity is a puzzle for people who don't believe in technology shocks. The traditional explanation for why productivity is procyclical is labour hoarding. In recessions firms keep on workers they don't really need so that they can have the workers still available when the next boom comes, and that tends to give the appearance of procyclical productivity. These theories make a lot of sense to me. I know I work my secretary harder when I have more work to be done; therefore her productivity is procyclical. I know I work harder when there is more work to be done [*laughter*]. I think there is a great deal of casual evidence that labour hoarding and procyclical effort are important.

## Macroeconomic Policy

*One of the central ideas of Keynesian economics is that an increase in aggregate demand will stimulate the economy. Under what circumstances do you think a government should actually stimulate demand?*
There are a couple of questions. First, when should it act? Second, how should it act? That is, should it use monetary or fiscal policy? On the first question, one should stimulate aggregate demand when it is too low to maintain full employment – that is, when you observe very high unemployment or when there is reason to believe that unemployment is going to rise. The policy implications of many new Keynesian theories really go back to the policy implications of the neoclassical synthesis of the 1960s. Some of the limitations on policy that were then debated are still relevant today. Even if you accept everything that new Keynesians say about prices being sluggish and so on, there is still the question of how good the government is at

responding in a timely fashion to the shocks. In that debate, I side to a large extent with Milton Friedman. The government is very bad at recognizing shocks in a timely fashion, and when they do respond to shocks they often do so quite late and counterproductively. So while I see the business cycle as a sign of market failure, I also think that it is a kind of market failure that a government is very limited in its ability to fix. If we have a very deep persistent recession, certainly something along the lines of the Great Depression, there is room for the government to do something. For the relatively minor wiggles that we have experienced in the post-war economy, it is not clear that the government can do much better than it has.

*Do you think Keynes was politically naive in thinking that politicians would be advised by technocrats and take the correct action? We are thinking here of the public choice literature and the political business cycle literature. Can we actually trust politicians once they have their hands on the fiscal and monetary levers to use them in the right way?*
I think that this is a serious concern, but there are many ways of fixing that problem. For example, there is a large literature showing that countries with more independent central banks have lower inflation on average. With less independence in the central bank, there is more political pressure and therefore a greater possibility of following a policy of inflating too much. There are ways around the political problem, like making independent central banks, which to some extent are staffed by technocrats. For that reason an independent central bank would be better at fine-tuning the economy, to the extent we fine-tune it at all, compared to fiscal policy which is always run by politicians.

*You've said that the literature on time inconsistency has provided a persuasive case for a commitment to some sort of rule for monetary policy; do you also support fiscal rules?*
Fiscal rules have to be well crafted. A balanced budget amendment that is too strict could be a disaster. At certain times, like recessions and wars, it is appropriate to run budget deficits. So any fiscal rule has to take into account those special situations where budget deficits are the appropriate policy response. A fiscal rule by itself wouldn't be a bad idea, but it has to be well crafted and so far I haven't seen one that is.

*Isn't one of the problems with devising rules that if the economy is hit by an unforeseen shock, then the government has to renege on that rule and take some discretionary action? It is difficult to think of a rule which really would be binding?*
There are two parts to the question. First, how might you make the rule binding? Second, do you want to make the rule binding? One way to make

the rule binding is reputational. Many rules are rules just because long tradition has established them as rules and people don't want to break the tradition. Another more legalistic way of imposing rules is by writing them into the constitution. I think the harder question you raise is do you want to make rules binding? The question is whether you can write a rule that works well even in response to unforeseen events. If it becomes too costly to be tied by the rule, people will stop abiding by it. What we want to do is write down a rule that will be good in response to normal kinds of shocks. That is, you don't know what the shocks are going to be, but you know what kind of shocks are possible. You've got oil shocks, monetary demand shocks and so on. You write down a rule that is good in response to the kind of shocks you expect the economy to experience, based on the shocks experienced in the past. Therefore, unless something completely unforeseeable happens, you stick by the rule.

*Leijonhufvud once argued that the economy can be thought of as travelling along a corridor. As long as it stays in the corridor, leave it alone, but if it gets out of the corridor into a severe recession, that is the time for intervention. Is that what you are saying? [See Leijonhufvud, 1981.]*
Well no, because recessions are reasonably foreseeable. Although you don't know when a recession is going to occur, you know that one will occur eventually. A recession is one of the contingencies that you want your rule to deal with. So I don't think a recession *per se* is one of those extraordinary events that make you want to break the rule. A recession is something you can plan for in advance. I'm talking about an event that not only can you not predict when it is going to happen, but you have never even thought that it might happen. For example, before 1973 people never imagined an OPEC supply shock. The whole idea of OPEC never even crossed anybody's mind. This is the type of situation where you might want to rethink the rule. Now that we know what OPEC is capable of, we can write down a rule that takes this into account.

*What is the role of fiscal policy in new Keynesian macroeconomics?*
To a large extent new Keynesian economics has been about the theory of aggregate supply and why it is that prices adjust slowly. It has been relatively neutral on the question of what determines aggregate demand, in particular whether monetary or fiscal levers are most useful. As I mentioned a moment ago, I am sceptical personally about the usefulness of fiscal policy in fine-tuning the economy because, at least in the USA, the Congress acts very slowly. Even as we are doing this interview [18 February 1993] the Congress is debating a fiscal stimulus, even though the recovery has been going on for about a year now. By the time this fiscal stimulus actually has an effect on the

economy, my guess is that we will be pretty close to the natural rate again. This is a perfect example of how the lags can be very long in fiscal policy. Monetary policy is a more useful tool for stabilizing aggregate demand.

### Do budget deficits matter?

I think they matter a lot. The way they matter is not for short-run macroeconomic reasons but for long-run reasons – reasons that are best described not by Keynesian models but by growth models. The evidence as I see it is that large budget deficits reduce national saving. And the lesson from growth theory and growth experience across countries is that low saving leads to low growth. That is a big problem for the USA today.

### If you were advising President Clinton about macroeconomic policy for the next three or four years, what would be the kinds of policies you feel are necessary?

My reaction to President Clinton's speech [17 February 1993] is that I don't think we need the fiscal stimulus that he is proposing. Recovery is already on its way. It wasn't a very deep recession to start off with, so I'm not terribly shocked that there is a mild recovery. It will take the fiscal stimulus a while to get people employed. I am happy that he is worried about the budget deficit, as low national saving is an important macro problem in the long term in the USA. Yet I am disappointed that he is putting so much emphasis on tax increases rather than spending cuts. That is really a view not so much about macroeconomics as about the size of government. I am also disappointed that he is giving no attention to the low rate of private saving in the USA. I would recommend tax reforms to remove the present disincentives toward saving. So I give him a mixed review.

## Current and Future Progress in Macroeconomics

### Much research in the 1980s, your own included, was directed at providing more rigorous microeconomic foundations for the central elements of Keynesian economics. Taking an overview of the last decade, how successful do you think that research has been in providing a more substantial microfoundation for Keynesian economics?

It has been successful at the theoretical level in the sense that one can now say that Keynesian economics, the economics of wage and price rigidities, is well founded on microeconomic models. There are now several microeconomic models that people can pull off the shelf. The theoretical challenge of Lucas and his followers has been met. It is less clear whether this line of research is going to be successful as an empirical matter. That is, to what extent does it yield new insights to help understand actual economic fluctuations? Does it give us new ways to look at data and policies? The jury is still out on that one. There is a small empirical literature, but I can probably count the number of empirical papers on the fingers of two hands. I hope it is a growth area, but so far the literature has not been as empirically orientated as I would like.

*Do you think there is some truth to the view that at the moment we have too many theories?*
Yes, I have a lot of sympathy with that view. There is too big a premium for coming up with clever theories in the profession. Yet I don't know of any way to solve this problem. Obviously I believe the things I believe, and I can't tell people that they should believe what I believe, just because there are too many theories [*laughter*]. It would be nice if macroeconomists reached a consensus and they could do more work on details and less work on creating brand new theories of the business cycle. Until we reach a consensus, there is no way to enforce that by fiat.

*Do you see any signs of an emerging consensus in macroeconomics?*
That is a good question. I change my mind on that a lot, depending on what conference I go to [*laughter*]. There are certainly groups within the profession that are agreeing with each other. There is much agreement among new Keynesian people like Olivier Blanchard, Larry Ball, David Romer, George Akerlof, Alan Blinder and so on. Whether we as a group are coming to agreement with some of the real business cycle group is hard to say. I'm delighted that some of the people who previously worked closely with the real business cycle models are now trying to incorporate monetary effects into those models. That provides a hope that somewhere down the line the new Keynesian models and the real business cycle models are going to merge to some grand synthesis that incorporates the strengths of both approaches. That hasn't happened yet; that is just a hope.

## Additional Questions Answered by Correspondence: February/March 1988

*When we last talked with you in February 1993 you were somewhat hopeful that 'somewhere down the line the new Keynesian models and the real business cycle models are going to merge to some grand synthesis that incorporates the strengths of both approaches'. Have developments in macroeconomic research during the last five years moved in the direction of more consensus, as you had hoped?*
To some extent, yes. Increasingly, there are economists (such as Bob King, Julio Rotemberg and Mike Woodford) trying to integrate the insights of the

new Keynesian and real business cycle literatures. Not surprisingly, this raises a host of difficult technical issues. We have long known that dynamic sticky price models are hard to solve except in some special cases. But some progress has been made.

*Your new* Principles of Economics *textbook [Mankiw, 1997] has generated a great deal of interest and comment. For example, in his* Wall Street Journal *review of your book [October 1997] Mark Skousen interprets your overall message to be that 'classical economics is now the "general theory" and Keynesian economics to be the "special" case'. Skousen also writes that 'virtually the entire book is devoted to classical economics leaving the Keynesian model as an afterthought in the end chapters'. Is this an accurate view of the balance of the book and your own current position?*
I have been delighted about the response to my new textbook. Some of the commentary, such as the Skousen op-ed piece in the *Wall Street Journal* exaggerated what my book does, and the *Journal* published a letter I wrote responding to that article. In the book, I try to present a balance between Keynesian and classical ideas. The Keynesian analysis is developed over three full chapters, which explain and apply the model of aggregate demand and aggregate supply. That is perhaps less coverage than in many traditional texts, but in no sense is Keynesian economics treated as a mere 'after-thought'. I begin with classical ideas – including long-run growth, the quantity theory of money and so on – but by the end of the book the student is fully acquainted with the importance and role of Keynesian theory.

*In our previous interview you commented that the 'natural rate hypothesis is pretty well entrenched' and that 'most new Keynesians believe in the natural rate hypothesis'. How do you account for the remarkably low combination of inflation and unemployment currently being experienced in the US economy?*
It seems increasingly clear that the natural rate of unemployment has fallen in the USA. At one level, that is not terribly shocking, since in principle there is no reason to think the natural rate must be constant. Various changes in the labour market can alter the natural rate. But I have not yet seen a good explanation of the decline, which is somewhat troubling. Some people might react by rejecting the whole natural rate framework, but I am not ready to do so. In part, I remain committed to the natural rate model because I have not seen a good alternative to it.

*Your research interests in recent years have been more focused on economic growth than the short-run issues of aggregate fluctuations. Unlike Paul Romer and other endogenous growth theorists, you provide a spirited defence of a modified Solow model in your [1995] 'Growth of Nations' paper. What is your assessment of the progress that has been made in this burgeoning research area?*

The growth literature has been a very positive development for the economics profession. After all, long-run growth is at least as important for human welfare as the business cycle, so it's great that the issue is being studied seriously again. In my new principles textbook, as well as in my intermediate macro text, I introduce the topic of long-run growth quite early. This is in large part a reflection of the research trend started by Paul Romer and others.

On the question of what progress has been made, I remain somewhat ambivalent. There are now many theoretical models of growth and more empirical studies than we have data points. Yet it is hard to find important questions that we can now answer with confidence that we couldn't answer before. Adam Smith once said that 'little else is requisite to carry a state to the highest degree of opulence from the lowest barbarism, but peace, easy taxes, and tolerable administration of justice'. That still seems like the best policy advice. In that sense, we haven't made much progress in 200 years. On the other hand, perhaps we better understand why Smith's instincts were right ones, and that is progress.

*What are the main differences between your view of technological progress and Paul Romer's?*

I don't disagree with Paul Romer about technological progress. It comes mainly from the creation of ideas that are largely but not completely public goods. Both of us would agree that this explains why most nations are richer than they were a century ago.

Where Romer and I seem to disagree is whether this old insight is important for understanding cross-country differences. I have argued that much of the international variation in living standards can be explained by the differences in the quantities of human and physical capital. As I understand Paul Romer's view, he is sceptical of this possibility. He argues that differences in knowledge across countries are important; in essence, he claims that different countries have access to different sets of blueprints. One problem in testing these two theories is that physical capital and human capital (schooling) can be measured and evaluated, which is what I tried to do in my [1992] *Quarterly Journal of Economics* paper with David Romer and David Weil, while the 'ideas' that Paul Romer emphasizes are harder to measure. I am sure that there is some truth in both the 'capital view' and the 'ideas view' and that other things – trade policy, property rights and so on – matter as well. The relative importance of these different factors is ultimately an empirical question that is very hard to answer conclusively.

# 8. The Post Keynesian school

## Paul Davidson*

human decisions affecting the future, whether personal or political or economic, cannot depend on strict mathematical expectation, since the basis for making such calculations does not exist ... it is our innate urge to activity which makes the wheels go round, our rational selves choosing between the alternatives as best we are able, calculating where we can, but often falling back for our motive on whim or sentiment or chance. (Keynes, 1936, pp. 162–3)

## 8.1 Introduction

A heterogeneous group of economists, united solely by their rejection of the neoclassical synthesis, often claim the same name to their approach to macroeconomic modelling, namely Post Keynesian economics. Unfortunately many of these heterogeneous models are merely variants of orthodox classical theory and are not based on the theoretical revolution that underlies Keynes's (1936) *General Theory*. Consequently classifying many of these diverse economists (for example Michal Kalecki, Piero Sraffa and his neo-Ricardian followers), who still cling to variants of classical economics as Post Keynesian economists, merely obfuscates the difference between Keynes (and those Post Keynesians who use Keynes's analytical model) and mainstream macroeconomists who are really putting forth twenty-first-century versions of classical analytical theory. A consistent, precise definition of Post Keynesian economics will be presented in the next section.

While Lawrence Klein (1947) described Keynes's analysis as representing a 'revolution' in economic theory, many economists claim that mainstream developments in 'Keynesian' macroeconomics have turned out to be 'a road to nowhere'. The development of the 'hydraulic' Keynesian model, by economists such as Hicks, Samuelson, Modigliani and Tobin, represents a 'retreat back inside the orthodox citadel' (see also Gerrard, 1988; Coddington, 1976). Even worse, the failure of orthodox Keynesian analysis and policy prescriptions fuelled the monetarist and new classical 'counter-revolutions'. Furthermore,

* Paul Davidson, Holly Chair of Excellence in Political Economy, Emeritus, University of Tennessee, Knoxville, Tennessee (USA), is Editor of the *Journal of Post Keynesian Economics*.

the 'new' Keynesian research programme, which emerged as a response to the critiques of the neoclassical synthesis by the new classical school, contains no 'Keynesian beef' (Davidson, 1994). In the light of these developments, from a Post Keynesian perspective, the 'Keynesian revolution', in the sense of representing a successful and radical break with classical thinking, never took off.

According to Holt (1997), most economists who call themselves Post Keynesians have traditionally been divided into two broad groups, namely the 'European' and the 'American' camps. The 'European', or Cambridge UK, group includes the body of work associated with economists such as Geoff Harcourt, Richard Kahn, Nicholas Kaldor, Michal Kalecki, Joan Robinson and Piero Sraffa. Throughout the 1950s and 1960s some of Keynes's former Cambridge colleagues, in particular Joan Robinson, consistently and repeatedly highlighted what they interpreted as the misinterpretation of Keynes's main insights by leading mainstream ('bastard') Keynesian thinkers (Robinson, 1972). The second broad camp identified by Holt includes the work of economists such as Victoria Chick, Alfred Eichner, Jan Kregel, Hyman Minsky, Basil Moore, George Shackle, Sidney Weintraub and Paul Davidson. Although Holt labels this latter group as 'American', it is the style and emphasis of analysis, rather than nationality, that matters in deciding who is in which broad group. For example, George Shackle is English and Victoria Chick, though born in America, has spent most of her professional career in England.

As a broad generalization Holt's 'European' group, like all classical economists, has emphasized the behaviour and functioning of the real economy while ignoring, or at least downplaying, monetary and financial implications. Some but not all in Holt's American grouping have typically concentrated their attention on the impact of uncertainty, and monetary and financial influences, on the economy (see Hamouda and Harcourt, 1988; Chick, 1995; Davidson, 1991, 1996, 2002; Arestis and Sawyer, 1998).

Although Eichner and Kregel (1975) have argued that Post Keynesian economics represented a coherent alternative school of thought to mainstream macroeconomic analysis, controversy still surrounds this claim (Coddington, 1976, and Patinkin, 1990b, have provided excellent surveys of the various interpretations of Keynes's *General Theory*; see also Arestis, 1996; Walters and Young, 1997; and Snowdon and Vane, 1997a). In fact, there is some basis for this lack of a coherent view because many who claim to be Post Keynesians among Holt's European group and at least one in the American group utilize variants of a classical model rather than Keynes's financial and monetary analytical approach. Accordingly, in the remainder of this chapter, rather than survey the complete body of work created by this heterogeneous group of economists all wanting to display the label of Post Keynesians, I argue that only those analytical models that adopt Keynes's principle of effective demand and recognize the importance liquidity preference plays in the *General Theory* (Keynes, 1936) *are entitled to use the appellation of Post Keynesians.* The main thrust of this argument implies that the true theoretical legacy of Keynes cannot be found within any branch of mainstream Keynesianism, old or new.

## 8.2 The Significance of the Principle of Effective Demand

Post Keynesian economics accepts Keynes's (1936, chap. 2) 'Principle of Effective Demand' as the basis for all macroeconomic theory that is applicable to an entrepreneurial economy. Keynes was primarily a monetary theorist. The words money, currency and monetary appear in the titles of most of his major volumes in economics. Post Keynesian theory evolves from Keynes's revolutionary approach to analysing a money-using, entrepreneur economy.

Addressing the *General Theory* chiefly to his 'fellow economists' (Keynes, 1936, p. v), Keynes insisted that:

> the postulates of the classical theory are applicable to a special case only and not to the general case ... Moreover, the characteristics of the special case assumed by the classical theory happen not to be those of the economic society in which we actually live, with the result that its teaching is misleading and disastrous if we attempt to apply it to the facts of experience. (Keynes, 1936, p. 3)

Elsewhere I (Davidson, 1984) have argued that all variants of mainstream macroeconomic theory, whether it be rational expectations (new classical) theory, monetarism (old classical theory), old (neoclassical synthesis) Keynesian or new Keynesian theory, are founded on three fundamental classical postulates and, as Keynes specifically noted:

> the classical theory is only applicable to full employment, [and therefore] it is fallacious to apply it to the problems of involuntary unemployment. ... The classical theorists resemble Euclidean geometers in a non-Euclidean world, discovering that in experience straight lines apparently parallel often meet, rebuke the lines for not keeping straight – as the only remedy for the unfortunate collisions that are occurring. Yet in truth there is no remedy except to throw over the axiom of parallels and to work out a non-Euclidean geometry. Something similar is required today in economics. (Keynes, 1936, p. 16)

Keynes's principle of effective demand basically overturned three restrictive classical postulates. Once freed of these postulates, Keynes (1936, p. 26) could logically demonstrate why Say's Law is not a 'true law' when we model an economy which possesses real-world characteristics; and until we get our theory to accurately mirror and apply to the 'facts of experience', there is little hope of getting our policies right. That message is just as relevant today.

To throw over an axiom is to reject what the faithful believe are 'universal truths'. Keynes's revolution in economic theory was therefore truly a revolt since it aimed at rejecting basic mainstream axioms in order to develop a logical foundation for a non-Say's Law model more closely related to the real world in which we happen to live. In the light of Keynes's analogy to geometry, Post Keynesian theory might be called non-Euclidean economics!

The restrictive classical axioms rejected by Keynes in his revolutionary logical analysis were (i) the gross substitution axiom, (ii) the neutrality of money axiom and (iii) the axiom of an ergodic economic world. The characteristics of the real world which Keynes believed could be modelled only by overthrowing these axioms are:

1.  money matters in the long and short run; that is money and liquidity preference are not neutral, they affect real decision making;
2.  the economic system is moving through calendar time from an irrevocable past to an uncertain future. Important decisions involving production, investment and consumption activities are, therefore, often taken in an uncertain environment;
3.  forward contracts in money terms are a human institution developed to efficiently organize time-consuming production and exchange processes. The money-wage contract is the most ubiquitous of these contracts. Modern production economies are on a money-wage contract based system, or what Keynes called an 'entrepreneur system'; and
4.  unemployment, rather than full employment, is a common *laissez-faire* situation in a market-oriented, monetary production economy.

## 8.3   Taxonomy

A precise taxonomy is a necessary precondition for all scientific enquiry. All too often, common words used in economics have a multitude of connotations. Consequently, many of the arguments among economists often involve semantic obfuscation where participants are using the same words to connote different meanings or, even worse, the same participant uses the same word to suggest different concepts at various points of their argument. Nowhere is this more obvious than in the use of the word 'money' in economic discussions. To avoid such semantic confusion, it is necessary to provide a dictionary of oft-used, and misused, words up front to explain exactly what the concept denotes. For example, how many economists have carefully read and comprehended Keynes's definitional Chapter 6 and its Appendix in his *General Theory*? Similarly, how many have worked through Chapters 1 and 2 of Friedman's (1957) *Theory of the Consumption Function* and realized that Friedman defines saving (p. 11) to include the purchase of new durable goods including clothing and so on while, for Keynes, saving involves the decision *not* to purchase durables or non-durables by households? Harrod (1951, pp. 463–4), with typical lucidity, highlighted the essential nature of Keynes's revolution when he wrote:

> Classification in economics, as in biology, is crucial to the scientific structure ... The real defect in the classical system was that it deflected attention from what most needed attention. It was Keynes' extraordinarily powerful intuitive sense of what was important that convinced him that the old classification was inadequate. It was his highly developed logical capacity that enabled him to construct a new classification of his own.

### 8.4   Keynes's Taxonomic Attack on Say's Law

When Keynes became convinced that the vocabulary of orthodox economics was not sufficient to explain why an economy might become mired in unemployment, he developed an expanded classification and new definitions to demonstrate that Say's Law 'is not the true law relating the aggregate demand and supply functions ... [and hence] there is a vitally important chapter of economic theory which remains to be written and without which all discussions concerning the volume of aggregate employment are futile' (Keynes, 1936, p. 26).

Keynes's *General Theory* is developed via an aggregate supply–aggregate demand function analysis to achieve a point of effective demand (Keynes, 1936, pp. 25–6). The aggregate supply function (Z) relates entrepreneurs' expected sales proceeds with the level of employment (N) entrepreneurs will hire for any volume of expected sales receipts. This aggregate supply (Z) function indicates that the higher entrepreneurs' sales expectations, the more workers they will hire. The aggregate demand function relates buyers' desired expenditure flows with any given level of employment (see Davidson, 1994).

Say's Law specifies that all expenditure (aggregate demand) on the products of industry is equal to the total costs of aggregate production (aggregate supply) including gross profits. Letting D symbolize aggregate demand and Z aggregate supply, if:

$$D = f_d(N) \tag{8.1}$$

and

$$Z = f_z(N) \tag{8.2}$$

then Say's Law asserts that:

$$f_d(N) = f_z(N) \tag{8.3}$$

'for *all* values of $N$, i.e. for all values of output and employment' (Keynes, 1936, pp. 25–6). In other words, in an economy subject to Say's Law, all costs of production are always recouped by the sale of output. There is never a lack of effective demand. The aggregate demand and aggregate supply curves coincide. In a Say's Law economy, there is no obstacle to full employment.

The aggregate demand and supply functions will be coincident only if money is neutral, everything is a good substitute for everything else (gross substitution) and the future can be reliably predicted in terms of probabilities (the ergodic axiom).

To challenge the applicability of Say's Law to the real world in which we live, Keynes had to develop a model where the aggregate demand and aggregate supply functions, $f_d(N)$ and $f_z(N)$, were not coincident. Since Keynes accepted the normal firm short-run flow-supply function developed in Marshallian economics as the micro-basis for the aggregate supply function, he could therefore differentiate his approach only via the concept of aggregate demand. Keynes divided aggregate demand into two classes, that is,

$$D = D_1 + D_2 \tag{8.4}$$

where:

$$D_1 = f_1(N) \tag{8.5}$$

and

$$D_2 \quad f_2(N) \tag{8.6}$$

$D_1$ represents *all* expenditures which 'depend on the level of aggregate income and, therefore, on the level of employment $N$' (Keynes, 1936, p. 28). $D_2$, therefore, represents all other expenditures which are *not* related to income. Even if $D_2$ is related to aggregate income (that is, $D_2 = f_2(N)$ so long as $f_1(N) + f_2(N) \quad f_z(N)$ for all values of $N$, then Say's Law is not applicable.

Explicit recognition of the possibility of two classes of demand expenditures must make Keynes's analysis a more general theory than the orthodox theory since the latter recognizes only a single demand class. Classical theory is 'a special case' (Keynes, 1936, p. 8) where:

$$D_2 = 0 \tag{8.7}$$

and

$$D_1 = f_1(N) = f_z(N) = Z \qquad (8.8)$$

for all values of $N$.

By proclaiming a 'fundamental psychological law' associated with 'the detailed facts of experience' where the marginal propensity to consume was always less than unity (Keynes, 1936, p. 96), by decree, Keynes declared that $f_1(N)$ would never coincide with $f_z(N)$ in the real world, even if $D_2 = 0$. Say's Law could not be applicable to 'the facts of experience'.

## 8.5   Can Relative Price Changes Induce $D_2$ to Fill the Gap?

Keynes's primary level of attack on classical theory involved the expansion of demand into two distinct classes with different determinants. Keynes's claim that the classical demand relationship, where all spending was related and equal to income, is required to validate Say's Law and this classically assumed demand relationship was not compatible with 'the facts of experience'.

The next step required Keynes to demonstrate that a change in relative prices via a gross substitution effect could not resurrect Say's Law. In classical theory, all income earned in any accounting period is divided – on the basis of *time preference* – between spending income on currently produced consumption goods and services and spending on current investment goods that will be used to produce goods for future consumption. In other words, all income earned in this period is always spent on the current products of industry. In Keynes's analysis, however, *time preference* determines how much of current income is spent on currently produced consumption goods and how much is *not spent on consumption goods but is instead saved by purchasing liquid assets*. Accordingly, in Keynes's system, there is a second decision step, *liquidity preference*, where the income earner determines in what liquid assets should his/her saved income be stored in order to be used to transfer purchasing power of saving to a future time period. Since *all* liquid assets have certain essential properties (Keynes, 1936, chap. 17) – namely they are non-producible and non-substitutable for the products of industry, the demand for liquid assets does not *per se* create a demand for the products of industry.

Keynes developed his theory of liquidity preference in order to demonstrate that any explanation of involuntary unemployment required specifying 'The Essential Properties of Interest and Money' (Keynes, 1936, chap. 17), which differentiates his theory from old classical, new classical, old Keynesian and new Keynesian theory, that is, from all mainstream macroeconomic theories not only in Keynes's time but in mainstream economics of the twenty-first century.

These essential properties are:

1.  the elasticity of productivity of all liquid assets including money was zero or negligible; and
2.  the elasticity of substitution between liquid assets (including money) and reproducible goods was zero or negligible.

The zero elasticity of productivity of money means that when the demand for money (liquidity) increases, entrepreneurs cannot hire labour to produce more money to meet this change in demand for a non-reproducible (in the private sector) good. In other words, a zero elasticity of productivity means that money does not grow on trees! In classical theory, on the other hand, money is either a reproducible commodity or the existence of money does not affect, in any way, the demand for producible goods and services; that is, money is neutral (by assumption). In many neoclassical textbook models, peanuts are the money commodity or numeraire. Peanuts may not grow on trees, but they do grow on the roots of bushes. The supply of peanuts can easily be augmented by the hiring of additional workers by private sector entrepreneurs.

The zero elasticity of substitution ensures that the portion of income that is not spent on consumption producibles will find, in Frank Hahn's terminology, 'resting places' in the demand for non-producibles. Some forty years after Keynes, Hahn rediscovered Keynes's point that Say's Law would be violated and involuntary unemployment could occur whenever there are 'resting places for savings in other than reproducible assets' (Hahn, 1977, p. 31). The existence of non-reproducible goods that would be demanded for stores of new 'savings' means that all income earned by engaging in the production of goods is not, in the short or long run, necessarily spent on products producible by labour.

If the gross substitution axiom were applicable, however, any new savings would increase the price of non-producibles (whose supply curve is, by definition, perfectly inelastic). This relative price rise in non-producibles would, under the gross substitution axiom, induce savers to substitute reproducible durables for non-producibles in their wealth holdings and therefore non-producibles could not be ultimate resting places for savings. As the price of non-reproducibles rose the demand for these non-producibles would spill over into a demand for producible goods (see Davidson, 1972, 1977, 1980). Thus the acceptance of the gross substitution axiom denies the logical possibility of involuntary unemployment as long as all prices are perfectly flexible. To overthrow the axiom of gross substitution in an intertemporal context is truly heretical. It changes the entire perspective as to what is meant by 'rational' or 'optimal' savings, as to why people save or what they save. For example, it would deny the life cycle hypothesis. Indeed, Danziger et al. (1982–3) have shown that the facts regarding consumption spending by the elderly are incompatible with the notion of intertemporal gross substitution of consumption plans which underlie both life cycle models and overlapping generation models currently so popular in mainstream macroeconomic theory. In the absence of a universal axiom of gross substitution, however, income effects (for example the Keynesian multiplier) predominate and can swamp any hypothetical classical substitution effects. Just as in non-Euclidean geometry lines that are apparently parallel often crash into each other, in the Keynes–Post Keynesian non-Euclidean economic world, an increased demand for 'savings', even if it raises the relative price of non-producibles, will not spill over into a demand for producible goods.

## 8.6  Investment Spending, Liquidity, and the Non-neutrality of Money Axiom

Keynes's theory implies that agents who planned to buy producible goods in the current period need not have earned income currently or previously in order to exercise this demand $(D_2)$ in an entrepreneurial, money-using economic system. This means that spending for $D_2$, which we normally associate with the demand for reproducible fixed and working capital goods, is not constrained by either actual income or inherited endowments. $D_2$ is constrained in a money-creating banking system solely by the expected future monetary (not real) cash inflow (Keynes, 1936, chap. 17). In a world where money is created only if someone goes into debt (borrows) in order to purchase goods, then real investment spending will be undertaken as long as the purchase of newly produced capital goods is expected to generate a future cash inflow (net of operating expenses) whose discounted present value equals or exceeds the money cash outflow (the supply price) currently needed to purchase the asset.

For the $D_2$ component of aggregate demand not to be constrained by actual income, therefore, agents must have the ability to finance investment by borrowing from a banking system which can create money. This Post Keynesian financing mechanism where increases in the nominal quantity of money are used to finance increased demand for producible goods, resulting in increasing employment levels, means that money cannot be neutral. Hahn (1982, p. 44) describes the money neutrality axiom as one where

> The objectives of agents that determine their actions and plans do not depend on any nominal magnitudes. Agents care only about 'real' things such as goods ...

leisure and effort. We know this as the axiom of the absence of money illusion, which it seems impossible to abandon in any sensible sense.

To reject the neutrality axiom does not require assuming that agents suffer from a money illusion. It only means that 'money is not neutral' (Keynes, 1973b, p. 411); money matters in both the short run and the long run, in affecting the equilibrium level of employment and real output. As Keynes (1973b, pp. 408–9) put it:

> The theory which I desiderate would deal ... with an economy in which money plays a part of its own and affects motives and decisions, and is, in short, one of the operative factors in the situation, so that the course of events cannot be predicted in either the long period or in the short, without a knowledge of the behaviour of money between the first state and the last. And it is this which we ought to mean when we speak of a monetary economy.

Once we recognize that money is a real phenomenon, that money matters, then neutrality must be rejected. Keynes (1936, p. 142) believed that the 'real rate of interest' concept of Irving Fisher was a logical confusion. In a monetary economy, moving through calendar time towards an uncertain (statistically unpredictable) future, there is no such thing as a forward-looking real rate of interest. In an entrepreneur economy the only objective for a firm is to end the production process by liquidating its working capital in order to end up with more money than it started with (Keynes, 1979, p. 82). Moreover, money has an impact on the real sector in both the short and long run. Thus money is a real phenomenon. This is just the reverse of what classical theory and modern mainstream theory teach us. In orthodox macroeconomic theory the rate of interest is a real (technologically determined) factor while money (at least in the long run for both Friedman and Tobin) does not affect the real output flow. This reversal of the importance or the significance of money and interest rates for real and monetary phenomena between the orthodox and Keynes's theory is the result of Keynes's rejection of a neoclassical universal truth – the axiom of neutral money. Arrow and Hahn (1971, pp. 356–7) implicitly recognized that money matters when they wrote:

> The terms in which contracts are made matter. In particular, if money is the good in terms of which contracts are made, then the prices of goods in terms of money are of special significance. This is not the case if we consider an economy without a past or future ... *if a serious monetary theory* comes to be written, the fact that contracts are made in terms of money will be of considerable importance. (Italics added)

Moreover, Arrow and Hahn (1971, p. 361) demonstrate that, if contracts are made in terms of money (so that money affects real decisions) in an economy moving along in calendar time with a past and a future, then all existence theorems demonstrating a classical full employment equilibrium result are jeopardized. The existence of money contracts – a characteristic of the world in which we live – implies that there need never exist, in the long run or the short run, any rational expectations equilibrium or general equilibrium market-clearing price vector.

## 8.7 What Type of an Economic System is 'Irrational' Enough to use Money Contracts?

A fundamental axiom of neoclassical theory is the neutrality of money. Hence economic agents in a neoclassical world are presumed to make decisions based solely on 'real' valuations; they do not suffer from any 'money illusion'. Thus in a 'rational' classical world, all contracts should be made in real terms and are always enforceable in real terms.

The economy in which we live, on the other hand, utilizes money contracts – not real contracts – to seal production and exchange agreements among self-interested individuals. The ubiquitous use of money contracts has always presented a dilemma to neoclassical theory. Logically consistent mainstream classical theorists must view the universal use of money contracts by modern economies as irrational, since such agreements, fixing payments in nominal terms, can impede the self-interest optimizing pursuit of real incomes by economic decision makers. Hence mainstream economists tend to explain the existence of money contracts by using non-economic reasons such as social customs, invisible handshakes and so on – societal institutional constraints which limit price signalling and hence limit adjustments for the optimal use of resources to the long run. For Post Keynesians, on the other hand, binding nominal contractual commitments are a sensible method for dealing with true uncertainty regarding future outcomes whenever economic activities span a long duration of calendar time.

In order to understand why there is this fundamental difference in viewpoints regarding the use of money contracts, one must distinguish between a money-using entrepreneur economy and a cooperative (barter) economy. The distinction between a cooperative economy and an entrepreneur economy was developed by Keynes in an early draft of the *General Theory* (see Keynes, 1979, pp. 76–83). A cooperative economy is defined as one where production is organized such that each input owner is rewarded for its real contribution to the process by a predetermined share of the aggregate physical output produced. Examples of cooperative economic systems include monasteries, nunneries, prisons, or even an Israeli kibbutz. In each of these cooperative economies, a central authority or a predetermined set of rules governs both the production and payments in terms of real goods distributed to the inputs. There is never any involuntary unemployment of monks, nuns, prisoners, or workers on a kibbutz. Say's Law prevails. This is the world of classical analysis.

An entrepreneur economy, on the other hand, is a system that has two distinctly different characteristics. First, production is organized by 'a class of entrepreneurs who hire the factors of production for money and look to their recoupment from selling the output for money' (Keynes, 1979, p. 77). Second, there is no automatic mechanism which guarantees that all the money paid out to inputs in the production process will be spent on the products of industry. Hence entrepreneurs can never be sure that they can recoup all the money costs of production. As Keynes (1979, p. 78) pointed out, 'it is obvious on these definitions that it is in an entrepreneur economy that we actually live to-day'. In an entrepreneur economy, by definition, Say's Law cannot be applicable.

In our entrepreneur economy, market-oriented managers of business firms organize the production process on a forward-money contract basis; that is, they hire inputs and purchase raw materials for the production process by entering into contractual agreements to pay money sums for delivery of specific materials and services at exact future dates. These managers of production processes expect to recoup these money outlays by selling the resulting output for money on either a spot or forward contracting basis. When we speak of 'the bottom line' in our economy we are essentially indicating that entrepreneurs are motivated by pursuing cash inflow from sales that will equal or exceed the money outflows spent on production costs.

In an entrepreneurial economic system, the earning of income (as defined by Keynes above) is directly associated with the existence of these money contracts which permit entrepreneurs to 'control' both the sequencing of inputs into production activities and the cash outflows of firms. These contractual money payments give the recipient claims on the products of industry. The reader should recall that in some economic discourse, the term income is not only associated with current output, but also with a welfare aspect as measured by the current services available to the community. Since some services available to the community in any period will flow from pre-existing durables, the use of the income term in its welfare garb is not compatible with the use of income as the value of current output, except if all the goods produced are always non-durable. Since the term 'income' is associated with contributions to the production of current output in the economy, therefore aggregate income is equal to the money receipts arising from the contractual sale of services and current products. (Profits occupy a sort of halfway house, since they are not directly determined by factor-hire contracts. Instead they are the residual due to the difference between the contractually determined receipts on the sale of products and the contractual costs of the hired factors of production.) Income-in-kind payments should be conceived of as the combination of two separate contractual transactions, namely money income payments to factor owners from the employer, with a simultaneous purchase commitment of goods by the factor owner to the employer.

Although Keynes defined the economy that we live in on the basis of the use of monetary contracts for hire and sale, this definition does not *per se* explain the existence and ubiquitous use of this human institution. In order to provide an explanation for the widespread use of money contracts, we must delve into how entrepreneurs make decisions, and recognize the difference between risk and uncertainty – a difference that is essential to Keynes's analysis of involuntary unemployment.

## 8.8 Information, Decisions and Uncertainty

Mainstream perspectives involving uncertainty presume that expectations are based on either (i) a statistical analysis of past data, with market signals providing information about immutable objective probabilities, or (ii) a subjective perception of these probabilities founded on the axioms of expected utility theory. In the mainstream perspective on uncertainty, probabilistic risk and uncertainty are synonymous.

Post Keynesians (Davidson, 1978, 1982–3) have developed a different perspective about uncertainty, where probability distributions are not the basis for comprehending real-world behaviour under uncertainty. According to this analysis, there are many important situations where 'true' uncertainty exists regarding future consequences of today's choices. In these cases of true uncertainty, today's decision makers believe that no expenditure of current resources can provide reliable statistical or intuitive clues regarding future prospects. In terms of the theory of stochastic processes, such an uncertain future would be the result of a non-ergodic stochastic system that makes predicting future outcomes on the basis of past or current probability distributions obtained from market data unreliable.

Given this Post Keynesian perspective on uncertainty, decision makers may, in an uncertain environment, either avoid choosing between alternatives because they 'haven't got a clue' about the future, *or* follow their 'animal spirits' for positive action in a 'damn the torpedoes, full speed ahead' approach. This perspective on uncertainty provides a more general theory explaining long-run decisions regarding liquidity demands and investment decisions, the existence of long-period underemployment equilibrium, the long-run non-neutrality of money, and the unique and important role Keynes assigned to nominal contracts and especially the money-wage contract.

### 8.9   Classifying Decision-making Environments

Time is a device that prevents everything from happening at once. In every real-world choice, the prospective pay-off associated with any action is necessarily separated by some period of calendar time from the moment of choice. The production of commodities requires considerable time; the consumption of capital goods and consumer durables needs even more. Because of this fundamental fact of elapsing time, all economic decisions can be conceived of as occurring under one of the following mutually exclusive environments:

### 1.   The objective probability environment
Decision makers believe that the past is a statistically reliable guide to the future. This is the rational expectations hypothesis, where knowledge regarding future consequences of today's decisions involves a confluence of subjective and objective probabilities.

### 2.   The subjective probability environment
In the individual's mind, subjective (or what Savage, 1954, calls personal) probabilities regarding future prospects at the moment of choice govern future outcomes. These subjective probabilities need not coincide with objective distributions, even if well-defined objective distributions happen to exist.

### 3.   The true uncertainty environment
Regardless of whether objective relative frequencies can be shown to have existed in the past and/or subjective probabilities exist today, the economic agent believes that during the time between the moment of choice and the pay-off, unforeseeable changes will occur. The decision maker believes that *no* information regarding future prospects exists today and therefore the future is not calculable. This is uncertainty (or ignorance about future consequences) in the sense of Keynes (1937, p. 113). Keynes wrote that by uncertainty he did 'not mean merely to distinguish what is known for certain from what is only probable. The game of roulette is not subject, in this sense to uncertainty ... The sense in which I am using the term is that ... there is no scientific basis on which to form any calculable probability whatever. We simply do not know'. Moreover, Keynes (1937, p. 122) added 'the hypothesis of a calculable future leads to a wrong interpretation of the principles of behaviour'. The longer the lapse between choice and consequence, the more likely individuals are to suspect that they must decide in an environment of true uncertainty.

*The objective probability environment and true uncertainty*   Keynes (1936, pp. 148–50, 161) claimed that some future consequences could have no probability ratios assigned to them. Of course, as a computational matter, mechanical use of formulas permits one to calculate a value for an arithmetic mean, standard deviation, and so on, of any data set collected over time. The question is what meaning the values calculated in this way should carry. If economists do not possess, never have possessed, and conceptually never will possess an ensemble of macroeconomic worlds, then it can be logically argued that objective probability structures do not even fleetingly exist, and a distribution function of probabilities cannot be defined. The application of the mathematical theory of stochastic processes to macroeconomic phenomena would be therefore highly questionable, if not invalid in principle. Hicks (1979, p. 129) reached a similar judgement and wrote:

> I am bold enough to conclude, from these considerations, that the usefulness of 'statistical' or 'stochastic' methods in economics is a good deal less than is now conventionally supposed. We have no business to turn to them automatically; we should always ask ourselves, before we apply them, whether they are appropriate to the problem at hand. Very often they are not.

Clearly, the objective probability environment associated with the rational expectations hypothesis involves a very different conception. In the context of forming macroeconomic expectations, it holds that time averages calculated from past data will converge with the time average of any future realization. Knowledge about the future involves projecting averages based on the past and/or current realizations to forthcoming events. The future is merely the statistical reflection of the past and economic actions are in some sense timeless. There can be no ignorance of upcoming events for those who believe the past provides reliable statistical information (price signals) regarding the future, and this knowledge can be obtained if only one is willing to spend the resources to examine past market data.

For the rational expectations hypothesis to provide a theory of expectational formation without persistent errors, not only must the subjective and objective distribution functions be equal at any given point of time, but these functions must be derived from what are called ergodic stochastic processes. By definition, an ergodic stochastic process simply means that averages calculated from past observations cannot be persistently different from the time average of future outcomes. In the ergodic circumstances of objective probability distributions, probability is knowledge, not uncertainty! Non-stationarity is a sufficient, but not a necessary, condition for non-ergodicity. Some economists have suggested that the economy is a non-stationary process moving through historical time and societal actions can permanently alter economic prospects. Indeed, Keynes's (1939b, p. 308) famous criticism of Tinbergen's econometric methodology was that economic time series are not stationary for 'the economic environment is not homogeneous over a period of time (perhaps because non-statistical factors are relevant)'.

However, at least some economic processes may be such that expectations based on past distribution functions differ persistently from the time average that will be generated as the future unfolds and becomes historical fact. In these circumstances, sensible economic agents will disregard available market information regarding relative frequencies, for the future is not statistically calculable from past data and hence is truly uncertain. Or as Hicks (1977, p. vii) succinctly put it, 'One must assume that the people in one's models do not know what is going to happen, and know that they do not know just what is going to happen'. In conditions of true uncertainty, people often realize they just don't have a clue!

Whenever economists talk about 'structural breaks' or 'changes in regime', they are implicitly admitting that the economy is, at least at that stage, not operating under the assumptions that allow the objective probability to hold. For example, Robert Solow has argued that there is an interaction of historical–societal circumstances and economic events. In describing 'the sort of discipline economics *ought* to be', Solow (1985, p. 328) has written: 'Unfortunately, economics is a social science' and therefore 'the end product of economic analysis is ... contingent on society's circumstances – on historical context ... For better or worse, however, economics has gone down a different path'.

The possibility of true uncertainty indicates that while objective probabilities and the rational expectations hypothesis may be a reasonable approximation in some areas where actions are routine, it cannot be seen as a general theory of choice. Moreover, if the entire economy were encompassed by the objective probability environment, there would be no role for money; that is, money would be neutral! In all Arrow–Debreu type systems where perfect knowledge about the future is provided by a complete set of spot and forward markets, all payments are made at the initial instant at market-clearing prices. No money is needed, since in essence goods trade for goods.

*The subjective probability environment and true uncertainty*   In the subjective probability environment, the concept of probability can be interpreted either in terms of degrees of conviction (Savage, 1954, p. 30), or as relative frequencies (von Neumann and Morgenstern, 1953). In either case, the underlying assumptions are less stringent than in the objective probability environment; for example, the Savage framework does not rely on a theory of stochastic processes. However, true Keynesian uncertainty will still exist when the decision maker either does not have a clue as to any basis for making such subjective calculations, or recognizes the inapplicability of today's calculations for future pay-offs.

This environment of ignorance regarding future outcomes provides the basis of a more general theory of choice, which can be explained in the language of expected utility theorists. In expected utility theory, 'a *prospect* is defined as a list of *consequences* with an associated list of probabilities, one for each consequence, such that these probabilities sum to unity. Consequences are to be understood to be *mutually exclusive* possibilities: thus a prospect comprises an exhaustive list of the possible consequences of a particular course of action ... [and] An individual's preferences are defined over the set of all conceivable prospects' (Sugden, 1987, p. 2). Using these definitions, an environment of true uncertainty (that is, one which is non-ergodic) occurs whenever an individual cannot specify and/or order a complete set of prospects regarding the future, either because: (i) the decision maker cannot conceive of a complete list of consequences that will occur in the future; or (ii) the decision maker cannot assign probabilities to all consequences because 'the evidence is insufficient to establish a probability' so that possible consequences 'are not even orderable' (Hicks, 1979, pp. 113, 115).

A related but somewhat different set of conditions that will lead to true uncertainty can be derived from Savage's observation (1954, pp. 11–13) that his integration of personal probabilities into expected utility theory 'makes no formal reference to time. In particular, the concept of an event as here formulated is timeless'. Savage develops an ordering axiom of expected utility theory, which explicitly requires 'that the individual should have a preference ordering over the set of all conceivable prospects' (Sugden, 1987, p. 2) and that the ordering be timeless. Hence, even if a decision maker can conceive of a complete set of prospects if the pay-off is instantaneous, as long as he or she fears that tomorrow's prospects can differ in some unknown way, then the decision maker will be unable to order tomorrow's pay-off completely, Savage's ordering axiom is violated, and Keynes's uncertainty concept prevails.

Interestingly enough, Savage recognized (although many of his followers have not) that his analytical structure is not a general theory; it does not deal with true uncertainty. Savage (1954, p. 15) admits that 'a person may not know the consequences of the acts open to him in each state of the world. He might be ... ignorant'. However, Savage then states that such ignorance is merely the manifestation of 'an incomplete analysis of the possible states'. Ignorance regarding the future can be defined away by accepting the 'obvious solution' of assuming that the specification of these timeless states of the world can be expanded to cover all possible cases. Savage (1954, p. 16) admits that this 'all possible states' specification presumption when 'carried to its logical extreme ... is utterly ridiculous ... because the task implied in making such a decision is not even remotely resembled by human possibility'.

By making this admission, Savage necessarily restricts his theory of choice to 'small world' states (Savage, 1954, pp. 82–6) in which axioms of expected utility theory apply, and hence he writes: '[T]his theory is practical [only] in suitably limited domains ... At the same time, the behavior of people is often at variance with the theory ... The main use I would make of [expected utility postulates] ... is normative, to police my own decisions for consistency' (Savage, 1954, p. 20). Any monetary theory that does not recognize the possibility of non-ergodic uncertainty cannot provide a non-neutral role for money and hence is logically incompatible with Post Keynesian monetary theory. In a Keynesian 'large world' as opposed to Savage's small one, decision makers may be unable to meet the axioms of expected utility theory and instead adopt 'haven't a clue' behaviour one time and 'damn the torpedoes' behaviour at another, even if this implies that they make arbitrary and inconsistent choices when exposed to the same stimulus over time.

## 8.10	Keynesian Uncertainty, Money and Explicit Money Contracts

Individuals in the real world must decide whether past experience provides a useful guide to the future. Should one presume that economic processes are uniform and consistent so that events are determined, either by ergodic stochastic processes or at least by specified and completely ordered prospects? Can the agent completely dismiss any fear of tragedy during the time between choice and outcome? Does the agent believe he or she is ignorant regarding the future? No rule can be specified in advance regarding how individuals decide whether they are in an objective, a subjective, or a true uncertainty environment. However, their perception will make a difference to their behaviour.

Keynes laid great stress on the distinction between uncertainty and probability, especially in relation to decisions involving the accumulation of wealth and the possession of liquidity. The essence of his *General Theory* involves liquidity preferences and animal spirits dominating real expenditure choices. Money plays a unique role in 'ruling the roost' among all assets (Keynes, 1936, p. 223) and it is non-neutral in both the short and long run (Keynes, 1973a, pp. 408–11). These claims, as Keynes made clear in his 1937 restatement (Keynes, 1973b, pp. 112, 114) of where he saw his general theory 'most clearly departing from previous theory', rested on the clear distinction between the 'probability calculus' and conditions of uncertainty when 'there is no scientific basis to form any calculable probability whatever. We simply do not know.'

Liquidity and animal spirits are the driving forces behind Keynes's analysis of long-period underemployment equilibrium, even in a world of flexible prices. Neither objective nor subjective probabilities suffice to understand the role of non-neutral money and monetary policy in Keynes's underemployment equilibrium analysis. It is not surprising, therefore, that unemployment still plagues most twenty-first-century economies, since most economists still formulate policy guidelines which are only applicable to a limited domain where agents choose 'as if' they had specific and completely ordered knowledge about the future outcomes of their actions.

In Davidson (1978, 1982), I have shown that the existence of the societal institution of legally enforceable forward contracts denominated in nominal (not real!) terms creates a monetary environment that is not neutral, even in the long run. These legal arrangements permit agents to protect themselves to some extent against the unpredictable consequences of current decisions to commit real resources towards production and investment activities of long duration. Legal enforcement of fixed money contracts permits each party in a contract to have sensible expectations that if the other party does not fulfil its contractual obligation, the injured party is entitled to just compensation and hence will not suffer a pecuniary loss. Tobin (1985, pp. 108–9) has written that the existence of money 'has always been an awkward problem for neoclassical general equilibrium theory … [and] the alleged neutrality of money … The application of this neutrality proposition to actual real world monetary policies is a prime example of the fallacy of misplaced concreteness.' Tobin then associates Keynes's rejection of money neutrality presumption with Keynes's emphasis on 'the essential unpredictability, even in a probabilistic sense' of the future (Tobin, 1985, pp. 112–13).

The social institution of money and the law of fixed money contracts enables entrepreneurs and households to form sensible expectations regarding cash flows (but not necessarily real outcomes) over time and hence cope with the otherwise unknowable future. Contractual obligations fixed in nominal terms provide assurance to the contracting parties that despite uncertainty, they can at least determine future consequences in terms of cash flows. Entering into fixed purchase and hiring contracts of long duration limits nominal liabilities to what the entrepreneur believes his or her liquidity position (often buttressed by credit commitments from a banker) can survive. Entrepreneurs feeling the animal urge to action in the face of uncertainty will not make any significant decisions involving real resource commitments until they are sure of their liquidity position, so that they can meet their contractual (transaction demand) cash outlays. Fixed forward money contracts allow entrepreneurs (and households) to find an efficient sequence for the use of and payment for resources in time-consuming production and exchange processes.

Money, in an entrepreneur economy, is defined as the 'means of contractual settlement'. This implies that in the Post Keynesian monetary theory, the civil law of contracts determines what is money in any law-abiding society.

In the first page of text in his *Treatise on Money*, Keynes (1930a, Vol. 1, p. 3) reminds us that money comes into existence in association with contracts! The possession of money, or any liquid asset (Davidson, 1982, p. 34), provides liquidity (a liquid asset is one that is resaleable for money on a well-organized, orderly spot market). Liquidity is defined as the ability to meet one's nominal contractual obligations when they come due. In an uncertain world where liabilities are specified in terms of money, the holding of money is a valuable choice (Keynes, 1936, pp. 236–7). Further, the banking system's ability to create 'real bills' to provide the liquidity to finance increases in production flows is an essential expansionary element in the operation of a (non-neutral) money production economy. If tight money policies prevent some entrepreneurs from obtaining sufficient additional bank money commitments at reasonable pecuniary cost, when managers (in the aggregate) wish to expand their production flows (and the liquidity preference of the public is unchanged), then some entrepreneurs will not be able to meet their potential additional contractual payroll and materials-purchase obligations before the additional output is produced and then profitably sold. Accordingly, without the creation of additional bank money, entrepreneurs will not be willing to sign additional hiring and material supply contracts and long-run employment growth is stymied, even when entrepreneurs feel that future effective demand is sufficient to warrant expansion. A shortage of money can hold up the expansion of real output, despite expected profits!

Liquid assets also provide a safe haven for not committing one's monetary claims on resources when the threat of uncertainty becomes great, as in Keynes's discussion of precautionary and speculative motives. Keynes (1936) claimed that the attribute of liquidity is only associated with durables that possess 'essential properties so that they are neither readily produced by labour in the private sector nor easily substitutable, *for liquidity purposes*, with goods produced by labour'.

When agents' fear of the uncertain future increases their aggregate demand for 'waiting' (even in the long run), agents will divert their earned income claims from the purchase of the current products of industry to demanding additional liquidity. Consequently, effective demand for labour in the private sector declines. Only in an unpredictable (non-ergodic) environment does it make sense to defer expenditures in this way, as opposed to spending all one's earnings on the various products of industry being traded in free markets.

This liquidity argument may appear to be similar to the view of general equilibrium theorists like Grandmont and Laroque (1976), who stress an option demand for money. However, in their model and many others, money has an option value only because of very unrealistic assumptions elsewhere in the model. For example, Grandmont and Laroque (1976) assume that (i) all producible goods are non-storable; (ii) no financial system exists, which means no borrowing and no spot markets for reselling securities; and (iii) fiat money is the only durable and hence the only possible store of value which can be carried over to the future. Of course, if durable producible and productive goods existed (as they do in the real world) and outcomes associated with holding producible durables were completely orderable, flexible spot and forward prices would reflect the multiperiod consumption plans of individuals and no 'optimizing' agent would hold fiat money as a store of value. Say's Law would be applicable, and the nominal quantity of money would be neutral. Hence Grandmont and Laroque can achieve 'temporary' Keynesian equilibrium via an option demand for money to hold over time only under the most inane of circumstances. By contrast, Keynes allowed the demand to hold money as a long-run store of value to coexist with the existence of productive durables.

Another approach to liquidity is that of Kreps, whose analysis of 'waiting' (Kreps, 1988, p. 142) presumes that at some earlier future date each agent will receive 'information about which state prevails' at a later future pay-off date. Accordingly, waiting to receive information is only a short-run phenomenon; long-run waiting behaviour is not optimal in the Kreps analysis – unless the information is never received! The option to wait is normally associated with a 'preference for flexibility' until sufficient information is obtained. Although Kreps does not draw this implication, his framework implies that if agents never receive the needed information and thus remain in a state of true uncertainty, they will wait forever.

Keynes (1936, p. 210), on the other hand, insisted that decisions not to buy products – to save – did '*not* necessitate a decision to have dinner or to buy a pair of boots a week hence or a year hence or to consume any specified thing at any specified date … It is not a substitution of future consumption demand for current consumption demand – it is a net diminution of such demand.' In other words, neither Kreps's waiting option nor the Grandmont and Laroque option demand for money explain Keynes's argument that there may be no intertemporal substitution. In the long run, people may still want to stay liquid and hence a long-run unemployment equilibrium can exist.

This argument has empirical support. Danziger et al. (1982–3, p. 210) analysed microdata on consumption and incomes of the elderly and have shown that 'the elderly do not dissave to finance their consumption at retirement … they spend less on consumption goods and services (save significantly more) than the non-elderly at all levels of income. Moreover, the oldest of the elderly save the most at given levels of income.' These facts suggest that as life becomes more truly uncertain with age, the elderly 'wait' more without making a decision to spend their earned claims on resources. This behaviour is irrational according to the life cycle hypothesis, inconsistent with the Grandmont–Laroque option demand for waiting, and not compatible with

Kreps's 'waiting' – unless one is willing to admit that even in the long run 'information about which state will prevail' may not exist, and these economic decisions are made under a state of Keynesian uncertainty.

Probabilistic analysis of waiting and option value recognize only a need to postpone spending over time. However, only Keynesian uncertainty provides a basis for a long-run demand for liquidity and the possibility of long-run underemployment equilibrium.

## 8.11 Conclusions

The fundamental building blocks of Post Keynesian theory are: (i) the non-neutrality of money; (ii) the existence of non-ergodic uncertainty in some important decision-making aspects of economic life; and (iii) the denial of the ubiquitousness of the gross substitution axiom. One way that humans have coped with having to make decisions where pay-offs will occur in the unforeseen and possibly unforeseeable future is via the development of the law of contracts by civilized societies, and the use of money as a chartalist means of discharging contracts. The abolition of slavery makes the enforcement of real contracts for human labour illegal. Accordingly, civilized society has decided not to permit 'real contracting' no matter how efficient it can be proved to be in neoclassical economics.

Keynes's revolutionary analysis, where money is never neutral and liquidity matters, is a general theory of an economy where the complete unpredictability of the future may have important economic consequences. By contrast, neoclassical optimization requires restrictive fundamental postulates regarding uncertainty and hence expectations regarding future consequences that Keynes's analysis does not. The analyst must therefore choose which system is more relevant for analysing the economic problem under study.

For many routine decisions, assuming the uniformity and consistency of nature over time (that is, assuming ergodicity) may be, by the definition of routine, a useful simplification for handling the problem at hand. For problems involving investment and liquidity decisions where large unforeseeable changes over long periods of calendar time cannot be ruled out, the Keynesian uncertainty model is more applicable. To presume a universe of discoverable regularities which can be expected to continue into the future and where the neutrality of money is therefore central (Lucas, 1981b, p. 561) will provide a misleading analogy for developing macro policies for monetary, production economies whenever money really matters and affects production decisions in the real economy.

Economists should be careful not to claim more for their discipline than they can deliver. The belief that in '*some* circumstances' the world is probabilistic (Lucas and Sargent, 1981, pp. xi–xii), or that future prospects can be completely ordered, will tend to lead to the argument that individuals in free markets will not make persistent errors and will tend to know better than the government how to judge the future. Basing general rules on these particular assumptions can result in disastrous policy advice for governmental officials facing situations where many economic decision makers feel unable to draw conclusions about the future from the past.

However, if economists can recognize and identify when these (non-ergodic) economic conditions of true uncertainty are likely to be prevalent, government can play a role in improving the economic performance of markets. Economists should strive to design institutional devices which can produce legal constraints on the infinite universe of events which could otherwise occur as the economic process moves through historical time. For example, governments can set up financial safety nets to prevent, or at least offset, disastrous consequences that might occur, and also provide monetary incentives to encourage individuals to take civilized actions which are determined by democratic processes to be in the social interest (Davidson and Davidson, 1988). Where private institutions do not exist, or need buttressing against winds of true uncertainty, government should develop economic institutions which attempt to reduce uncertainties by limiting the possible consequences of private actions to those that are compatible with full employment and reasonable price stability.

# 9.   The Austrian school

## Roger W. Garrison*

Mr. Keynes's aggregates conceal the most fundamental mechanisms of change.
(Hayek, 1931)

## 9.1   The Mengerian Vision

The Austrian school is best known for its microeconomics and, in particular,
for its role in the marginalist revolution. In the early 1870s, Carl Menger,
along with French economist Léon Walras and English economist William
Stanley Jevons, reoriented value theory by calling attention to the marginal
unit of a good as key to our understanding the determination of the good's
market price. With marginality central to the analysis, microeconomics was
forever changed. It is less widely recognized, however, that a viable macroeconomic construction also arises quite naturally out of the marginalist
revolution in the context of Menger's vision of a capital-using market economy.

Modern macroeconomics makes a distinction between factor markets (inputs) and product markets (outputs). Intermediate inputs and outputs are
rarely in play. By contrast, the economics of the Austrian school features a
production process – a sequence of activities in which the outputs associated
with some activities feed in as inputs to subsequent activities. The eventual
yield of consumable output constitutes the end of the sequence. Menger
(1981 [1871]) set out the theory in terms of 'orders of goods', the first, or
lowest, order constituting consumer goods and second, third and higher orders constituting producers' goods increasingly remote in time from goods of
the lowest order. Eugen von Böhm-Bawerk (1959 [1889]) introduced the
similar notion of 'maturity classes' to capture this temporal element in the
economy's production process. He stressed the point that an increase in the
economy's growth rate must entail an increase in activity in the earlier maturity classes relative to (concurrent) activity in the later maturity classes.

*   Roger W. Garrison, Professor of Economics at Auburn University, Auburn, Alabama (USA),
    is the author of *Time and Money: The Macroeconomics of Capital Structure* (London:
    Routledge, 2001). He gratefully acknowledges helpful suggestions offered by Lane Boyte
    and Sven Thommesen during the preparation of this chapter.

Böhm-Bawerk was possibly the first economist to insist that propositions about the macroeconomy have firm microeconomic foundations. In an 1895 essay, he wrote that 'One cannot eschew studying the microcosm if one wants to understand properly the macrocosm of a developed economy' (Hennings, 1997, p. 74). Ludwig von Mises (1953 [1912]), who is generally credited for using marginal utility analysis to account for the value of money, was also the first to recognize the significance of credit creation in the context of a decentralized, time-consuming production process. The capital theory originated by Menger and the theory of money and credit set out by Mises were developed by Friedrich Hayek (1967 [1935]) into the Austrian theory of the business cycle. Lionel Robbins (1971 [1934]) and Murray Rothbard (1963) applied the theory to the interwar episode of boom and bust. Eventually, the insights of these and other Austrians gave rise to a full-fledged capital-based macroeconomics (Horwitz, 2000 and Garrison, 2001; see also Littlechild, 1990).

## 9.2   The Intertemporal Structure of Capital

Hayek greatly simplified the Austrian vision of a capital-using economy by modelling the economy's production activities as a sequence of inputs and a point output. Each element in the sequence is designated a 'stage of production', the number of stages posited being largely a matter of pedagogical convenience. This simple construction was first introduced as a bar chart with the individual bars arrayed temporally, their (equal) widths representing increments of production time. The length of the final bar represents the value of consumable output; the attenuated lengths of the preceding bars represent the values of the goods in process at the various stages of production.

Figure 9.1 shows ten stages of production arrayed from left to right. (In the original Hayekian rendition, five stages were arrayed from top to bottom.) The specific number of stages is not intended to quantify any actual, empirically established detail about the economy's production process but rather to capture our general understanding that in many instances the (intermediate) output of one stage is used as an input to a subsequent stage. That is, vertical integration – and, certainly, complete vertical integration – is not the norm. Hayek's 'stages' do not translate cleanly into 'firms' or 'industries'. Some vertically integrated activities may be carried out within a single firm. An oil company, for example, may be engaged in exploring, extracting, refining, distributing and retailing. A paper manufacturer, for another example, may be supplying paper for blueprints and for greeting cards, thus operating simultaneously in different stages. And there are obvious deviations from the strict one-way temporal sequence: coal may be used in the production of steel while steel is used in the production of coal.

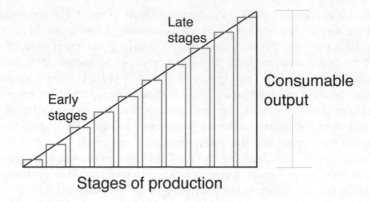

*Figure 9.1    The intertemporal structure of production*

(This is the supposedly telling counter-example offered by Frank Knight in his critical introduction to the English translation of Menger's *Principles*.) Still, as with all simple models, this Austrian model of the capital structure is notable not for its many sins of omission but rather for the essential truths that are captured by its construction.

Means are employed to achieve ends, and those means are temporally prior to the corresponding ends. Production moves forward through time. Valuation, however, emanates in the reverse direction. That is, the anticipated value of an end attaches itself to the means capable of achieving that end. This is Menger's Law. The demand for the factors of production and hence for the outputs of the intermediate stages of production is a derived demand. The direction of valuation is implicit in Menger's designation of consumption goods as 'goods of the *first* order'. The market values of goods of the second, third and higher orders are ultimately derived from the anticipated value of the first-order goods. But even with the doctrine of derived demand fully in play, those values entail a systematic time discount consistent with the temporal remoteness of higher-order goods.

The Austrian vision puts the entrepreneur in a key role. At a minimum, the entrepreneur operating in some particular stage of production must anticipate the demand for his own output, assessing the profitability of his activities with due attention to the cost of borrowed funds. Longer-run planning may require gauging the strength of demand several stages forward, including ultimately the demand for the consumable output. Speculative activities may consist in part in the movement of resources – in response to a change in credit conditions – from one stage to another and possibly in the creation of new stages of production that are of a higher order than the highest order of the existing stages. The increasing 'roundaboutness', to use Böhm-Bawerk's term, and the increasing significance of the time element in the production process, are characteristic of developing (and developed) capitalist economies.

The attention to the temporal structure of production suggests that the time element is an important variable in our understanding of how a decentralized economy works to coordinate production activities with consumer preferences and hence in our understanding of what might go wrong with the coordinating mechanisms. The use of multiple stages of production gives full play to marginalist thinking. Austrian macro is micro-friendly. The pattern of resource allocation can be modified in systematic ways, changing the temporal profile of production activities. A marginal decrease in late-stage activities coupled with a marginal increase in early-stage activities has important implications for the economy's overall growth rate. Significantly, a related pattern of marginal changes gives rise to boom and bust. Changes in the intertemporal pattern of resource allocation have a claim on our attention, according to the Austrians, even if these marginal changes cancel one another out in some conventional macroeconomic aggregate such as investment spending (in all stages) or total spending (by both consumers and the investment community).

The pattern of resource allocation associated with intertemporal equilibrium exhibits a certain uniformity in terms of the value differentials that separate the stages of production. The difference in the value of the output of one stage and the value of the output of the next stage reflects, among other things, the general terms of intertemporal exchange, expressed summarily as the market rate of interest. With a given rate of interest, excessive stage-to-stage value differentials would present themselves as profit opportunities which could be exploited only by reallocating resources toward the earlier stages of production. In the limit, when all such profit opportunities have been competed away, the relative prices of inputs used in the various stages are brought into line with the equilibrium rate of interest. A summary graphical rendering of the intertemporal capital structure takes the form of a triangle encasing the sequence of stages that constitute such an intertemporal equilibrium. The Hayekian triangle in Figure 9.1 keeps the many complexities of capital theory at bay while keeping in play the overall time element in the production process.

The extreme level of simplification warrants some discussion. First, we note that the triangle's hypotenuse, which tracks the value of the yet-to-be completed consumables, rises linearly from no value at all to the full market value of the consumables. Yet we know that the interest rate is expressed in percentage terms and, starting from some initial input value, allows for compounding. Clearly – and contrary to the Hayekian triangle – such percentage value differentials imply that the cumulative value should be tracked by a curve that rises exponentially from some initial value to some final value.

Here, linearity wins out on the grounds of its being simpler in construction yet adequate to the task. It is also true to Hayek's original formulation. We need to recognize, however, that the triangle would be inadequate for dealing with any issue for which the compounding effect is critical. Ambiguities about the precise relationship between the interest rate and the overall degree of roundaboutness arise when the effects of compound interest are factored in. These and related ambiguities concerning capital intensity lay at the heart of the Cambridge capital controversy (see Harcourt, 1972), a protracted and, ultimately, sterile debate that attracted much attention a few decades ago. But for dealing with the business cycle and related macroeconomic issues, the triangle, simple as it is, does just fine.

Second, the horizontal leg of the triangle, which invites us to imagine a sequence of unit time intervals, does not translate readily into calendar time. In application, an early stage of production consists only partly in goods in process – pine saplings that mature over time into lumber or wine that undergoes an ageing process. Earliness is also implicit in durable capital goods or even in human capital. These factors of production are categorized as early-stage because they will have a yield over an extended future. The heterogeneity of capital warns against trying to create a single metric, such as some average period of production, or to quantify in some other way the production time for the macroeconomy. Still, many early-stage activities and late-stage activities are readily discernible. Inventory management at retail is a late-stage activity. Product development is an early-stage activity. Increases in the time dimension of the economy's capital structure might take the form of shifting resources from relatively late to relatively early stages, of creating capital goods of greater durability, or of simply changing the mix of goods produced in favour of those involving more time-consuming (but higher-yielding) production processes.

Third, the vertical leg of the Hayekian triangle, which represents the value of consumable output, implies that consumption occurs at a single point in time at the end of the production process. This is not to deny the existence of consumer durables. But expanding the intertemporal aspect of the macro-economy to include consumption time would complicate matters without adding much to the analysis. The triangle focuses attention on the particulars of production and on aspects of the market process that lose much of their relevance once the goods are in the hands of the consumer. The notion of 'stages of consumption' would be contrived if not meaningless.

In application there is a fine line – in Austrian theory as in more conventional theory – between an investment good and a consumer durable. Residential housing, whether or not owner-occupied, is universally categorized as investment, the rental value (actual or implicit) of its services qualifying as consumption. Owner-driven automobiles, however, despite their considerable durability and implicit lease value, are categorized as consumption goods. Instances can be imagined in which a consumable (for example a light truck purchased new for non-commercial use) is later sold into an early stage of production (for example as a work truck). But as a general rule, goods delivered into the hands of consumers stay in the hands of consumers. Attention to these and related matters may be necessary in particular applications of the Austrian theory, but the theory itself is based on the vision of a multi-stage production process that yields a consumable output.

In its simplest interpretation, Figure 9.1 represents a no-growth economy. Gross investment, financed by saving, is just enough to offset capital depreciation. With given tastes and technology, the macroeconomy settles into an intertemporal equilibrium and produces consumption goods at an unchanging rate. More typically, saving and gross investment exceed capital depreciation, allowing the economy to grow at every margin. If we can assume for the moment an unchanging rate of interest, the growth can be represented by a triangle of increasing size, its general shape remaining the same.

The pay-off to Hayekian triangulation, however, comes from allowing for changes in the triangle's shape. More conventional macroeconomic constructions make the implicit assumption of structural fixity or structural irrelevance. In the Austrian theory, changes in saving behaviour have implications for the allocation of resources within the economy's capital structure. In turn, the changing shape of the triangle affects the time profile of consumable output. The natural focus of the analysis is on intertemporal coordination and possible causes of intertemporal discoordiantion.

## 9.3  Saving and Economic Growth

We tend to think of economies as experiencing some ongoing rate of growth. The growth rate will be positive, negative, or zero, depending upon the relationship between saving and capital depreciation. In a stationary, or no-growth, economy, saving finances just enough investment to offset capital depreciation. Consumable output is constant over time, as depicted in the first two periods in Figure 9.2.

If saving is in excess of capital depreciation, the economy grows. The volume of consumable output rises over time, as depicted in the last three periods of Figure 9.2. The output of each of the stages of production increases as well. The economy grows at every margin, allowing even for a continual increase in the number of stages. During a period of secular growth, the Hayekian triangle increases in size but not – or not necessarily – in shape.

An interesting question, one whose answer serves as a prelude to the Austrian analysis of business cycles, concerns the transition from no growth to a positive rate of growth – or, for that matter, from some initial growth rate to a

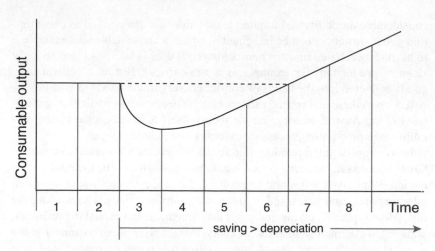

*Figure 9.2   A possible temporal pattern of consumable output*

higher growth rate. What must be true about the time profile of consumable output during the transition? Let's assume that there has been no change in the state of technology or in the general availability of resources. We assume, though, that people's intertemporal preferences change if favour of future consumption. If confronted with the simple choice between no growth and growth, people would surely prefer the latter. The choice, however, is never quite that simple. The memorable acronym introduced by science-fiction writer Robert Heinlein (1966) applies. TANSTAAFL: 'There ain't no such thing as a free lunch'. Modifying the acronym to fit the application, we recognize that TANSTAFG. Free growth is not available for the asking, either.

The relevant trade-off is that between consumable output in the near future and consumable output in the more remote future. Are people willing to forgo some current and near-term consumption in order to enjoy increasing consumption over an extended period? It is the forgoing of current and near-term consumption, after all, that frees up the resources with which to expand the economy's productive capacity and make increasing future consumption possible. In Figure 9.2 the hypothesized preference change occurs at the end of the second period. In light of this change, the output of consumption goods during the third period needs to be reduced. The freed-up resources can be employed in earlier stages of production. So altered, the capital structure will eventually begin yielding consumables at an increased rate, matching the initial output level at the end of the sixth period (in this particular example) and exceeding it in the subsequent periods.

The market economy, in the judgement of the Austrians, is capable of tailoring intertemporal production activities to match intertemporal consump-

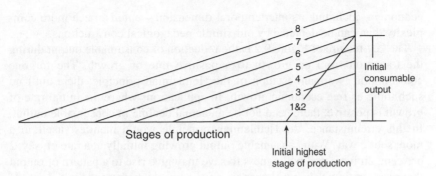

Figure 9.3 *Intertemporal capital restructuring*

tion preferences. The temporal pattern of consumable output shown in Figure 9.2 requires a capital restructuring, as can be depicted by a change in the Hayekian triangle's shape. Figure 9.3 shows the general nature of the required change. The no-growth periods 1 and 2, which pre-date the preference change, are depicted by the triangle having a relatively short intertemporal capital structure. Beginning with the preference change at the end of period 2, consumption falls, reaching a minimum at the end of period 3. The freed-up resources can be allocated to the early stages of production and to the creation of still earlier stages, enhancing the ability of the economy to produce consumable output in the future. The reduced near-term yield of consumable output and the increased number of stages of production are depicted by the triangle 3, the smallest of the reshaped triangles.

As goods in process begin to move through the restructured sequence of stages, the output of consumables begins to rise, and with saving now in excess of capital depreciation, expansion continues in each of the stages of production. The economy experiences a positive secular growth rate, as shown by the triangles 4 through 8, triangle 6 having the same consumable output as the initial no-growth triangle. Yet to be discussed are the market mechanisms that actually bring about this capital restructuring. At this point, the focus is on the correspondence between the intertemporal capital restructuring shown in Figure 9.3 and the temporal pattern of consumable output shown in Figure 9.2.

The attention here to a one-time simple preference change resulting in a transition from a no-growth economy to an economy experiencing a positive secular growth rate finds justification in analytical and heuristic convenience. More complex preference changes can easily be imagined. Actual changes in intertemporal preferences may themselves be gradual, and the preferred time profile of consumables is undoubtedly not as simply described as is the intertemporal pattern in Figure 9.2. This is only to say that a decentralized economy – including its intertemporal dimension – entails much more complexity than can be depicted by our simple pedagogical constructions.

The key feature of Figure 9.2 is the reduction of consumable output during the transition from no growth to a positive rate of growth. The forgone consumption is a manifestation of the Heinleinian principle: there ain't no such thing as free economic growth. In applications where the initial rate of growth is positive, there need not be an actual decline in consumable output. In this circumstance, the Heinleinian principle would manifest itself in a more subtle way. With consumable output growing initially at a rate of, say, 2 per cent, an increased willingness to save may give rise to a pattern of output that rises continuously but at changing rates – possibly from the initial rate of 2 per cent to 1 per cent and then subsequently to 3 per cent. During the transition period, in which the growth rate is only 1 per cent, people are forgoing consumable output that they could have enjoyed had they not decided to increase their saving.

The explicit recognition of the opportunity costs associated with saving-induced growth underlies a general proscription relevant to policy making. In short, the Austrians are not cheerleaders for growth. Many introductory and intermediate texts introduce the subject matter of macroeconomics with a short list of policy goals. Invariably, a prominent entry on the list is rapid economic growth. But is there any basis for including a high growth rate as a goal for policy makers to achieve? What is needed, according to the Austrians, are institutional arrangements that allow the growth rate of consumable output to be consistent with people's willingness to save. Production plans need to be consistent with consumption preferences. But that consistency may entail a low growth rate, no growth, or – in unusual circumstances – even a negative growth rate. The growth rate itself is nothing but a summary description of people's willingness to forgo consumption in the near future in order to enjoy increased consumption in the more remote future. Macroeconomists should not adopt 'rapid growth' as one of their goals any more than microeconomists should adopt 'plenty of vegetables' as one of theirs.

Still, there are key macroeconomic issues in play here. Achieving the right growth rate in macroeconomics has its parallel in microeconomics in achieving the right quantity of vegetables. As discussed in the following two sections, both of these goals are achieved if the relevant supply and demand schedules accurately reflect the fundamentals – the preferences and constraints that govern the respective market activities.

## 9.4   The Saving–Investment Nexus

Is there a market mechanism that allows people to actually make the trade-offs discussed in the previous section? This is a critical question – one that lies at the heart of macroeconomic debate and one whose answers separate the different schools of thought. The question can be posed in a way that highlights the macroeconomic concerns: is there a market mechanism that brings saving and investment in line with one another without at the same time having perverse effects (for example widespread resource idleness) on the macroeconomy? The alternative answers have clear implications for the viability of market economies and for the proper role of the policy maker.

### 9.4.1 A detour through monetarism

Some macroeconomists would answer the critical question in the affirmative, taking the market's allocation of resources to the production of consumption goods and the production of investment goods, the latter financed by saving, to be on a par with the market's allocation of resources to the production of fruits and the production of vegetables. In other words, within the overall output aggregate, the allocation issue – whether among narrowly defined goods (peaches and potatoes) or among broad-based sub-aggregates (consumption and investment) – is largely the province of microeconomics.

Macroeconomics, in this view, should focus on the overall output aggregate itself as it relates to other macroeconomic variables, such as the general price level and the money supply. These macroeconomic variables, symbolized as $Q$, $P$ and $M$, come together in the familiar equation of exchange:

$$MV = PQ \qquad (9.1)$$

This equation, of course, was ground zero for the monetarist counter-revolution against the Keynesianism of the 1950s (see Chapter 4). The velocity of money, $V$, is defined by the equation itself, and before the early 1980s its empirically demonstrated near-constancy in different countries and in different time periods established a strong relationship between the money supply and some index of output prices. What is commonly known as the quantity theory of money is more descriptively called the quantity-of-money theory of the price level.

The monetarists argued that the long-run consequence of a change in the money supply is an equiproportional change in the general level of prices – a consequence tempered only by ongoing secular changes in real output and in the velocity of money. Allowances were made for short-run variations in real output. That is, overall output $Q$ may rise and then fall while $P$ is adjusting to an increased $M$. However, the monetarists paid little attention to the relative movements of the major sub-aggregates (consumption and investment) during the adjustment process and no attention at all to the sub-aggregates (stages of production) that make up aggregate investment. Whether dealing with long-run secular growth or with short-run money-induced movements in real output, the focus was on the summary output variable $Q$. Whatever change is occurring within the output aggregate – as might be tracked by the Austrians in terms of the Hayekian triangle – was taken to be irrelevant to the greater issues of macroeconomics.

### 9.4.2   The saving–investment perversity of Keynesianism

It was Keynesian economics, of course, that the monetarist counter-revolution was intended to counter. But on the issue of a saving–investment nexus, the counter could be more accurately described as a cover-up. In his *General Theory* Keynes (1936, p. 21) had explicitly faulted his predecessors and contemporaries for 'fallaciously supposing that there is a nexus which unites decisions to abstain from present consumption with decisions to provide for future consumption'. According to Keynes, there is no simple and effective way of coordinating these two decisions. Rather, the mechanisms that do eventually bring saving into line with investment are indirect and perverse. The saving–investment perversity, in fact, is central to the Keynesian vision of the macroeconomy (see Leijonhufvud, 1968).

The equation of exchange can be rewritten in a way that uncovers the issues on which the Keynesian revolution was based. Aggregate output $Q$ consists of the output of consumption goods plus the output of investment goods. That is, $Q = Q_C + Q_I$, the $Q_I$ reckoned as the 'final' output of investment goods – so as to avoid double counting. The equation of exchange, then, can be rewritten as:

$$MV = P(Q_C + Q_I) \tag{9.2}$$

emphasizing that the problem as seen by Keynes (the volatility of $Q_I$ and its impact on all other macroeconomic magnitudes) is a problem that is simply not addressed by the monetarists. Rather, replacing the Keynesian $Q_C + Q_I$ with the monetarist $Q$ served only to cover up the primary locus of perversity. The question of just how the output of investment goods gets squared with preferred trade-off between current consumption and future consumption is not answered by the monetarists – nor is it even asked.

In the Keynesian vision, which will be dealt with at some length in section 9.11, movements in the investment aggregate impinge in the first instance on incomes, which in turn impinge on consumption spending. That is, $Q_C$ and $Q_I$ move in the same direction, the movements in $Q_I$ being unpredictable and the corresponding same-direction movements in $Q_C$ being amplified by the familiar Keynesian multiplier (see Chapter 2). Similarly, autonomous changes in current consumption, if any, would tend to affect profit expectations and hence cause investment spending to change in the same direction. Here, the principle of derived demand is in play. With the two major sub-aggregates moving up and down together (though at different rates), the Keynesian theory precludes by construction any possibility of there being a trade-off of the sort emphasized by the Austrians. Further, considerations of durable capital and the so-called investment accelerator imply the absence of a generally binding supply-side constraint. There is simply no scope in the Keynesian vision for investment to rise *at the expense of* current consumption. Similarly, market participants willing to forgo current consumption (that is, to save) in order to be able to enjoy greater future consumption would find their efforts foiled by the market mechanisms that link saving and investment. Rather than stimulating investment, increased saving would impinge on overall spending and hence on overall income. This perverse negative income effect, which Keynes identified as the paradox of thrift, is discussed at length in section 9.9.

### 9.4.3 Austrian disaggregation

The Austrian perspective on Keynesianism and monetarism in the context of the equation of exchange is revealing. Keynesianism adopts a level of aggregation that suggests a potential problem – one of dividing resources appropriately between consumption and investment – but without allowing for a non-perverse market solution to that problem. Monetarism, as well as most strands of new classicism, increases the level of aggregation, obscuring this central issue and hence relegating the problem as well as its solution to the realm of microeconomics. Pre-dating both monetarism and Keynesianism, the Austrians were inclined to work at a lower level of aggregation than either of these schools, one in which both the problem and a potentially viable market solution could be identified.

Again, the equation of exchange can serve as the common denominator of the different schools of thought. For the Austrians, the investment aggregate in the Keynesian rendition must be disaggregated so as to bring the stages of production into play. $Q_C$ is consumable output, or goods of the first order – to use Menger's terminology. Investments distributed across the nine preceding stages are identified as $Q_2$ through $Q_{10}$. The equation of exchange thus becomes:

$$MV = P(Q_C + Q_2 + Q_3 + Q_4 + Q_5 + Q_6 + Q_7 + Q_8 + Q_9 + Q_{10}) \quad (9.3)$$

Just as $Q_I$ is reckoned as 'final' output in conventional macroeconomic theorizing, the second- and higher-order goods ($Q_2$ through $Q_{10}$) in equation (9.3) are similarly reckoned so as to maintain the integrity of the equation of exchange. Double counting is thus avoided, and the sum of the output magnitudes (in equations 9.2 and 9.3) is equal to total output and, equivalently, to total income. But with the Austrian disaggregation, the focus of the analysis is on the relative movements among the $Q$s as well as on their sum.

In the Keynesian construction, it might well seem implausible that an increase in saving and a corresponding decrease in spending on $Q_C$ could cause $Q_I$ to increase. If business firms are having problems selling out of their current inventories, they are unlikely to be inspired to commit additional resources to an expanded capacity and hence to the further overstocking of these inventories. The doctrine of derived demand suggests that the demand for productive capacity will mirror the demand for output. In the Austrian construction, the doctrine of derived demand is tempered by considerations of time discount. The multiple stages of production allow for enough degrees of freedom for the consequences of a fall in consumer spending to be described in terms of a change in the pattern of investment spending rather than exclusively in terms of an opposing movement in an all-inclusive investment aggregate. The story of how the market can plausibly work can be squared with the doctrine of derived demand, but as told by the Austrians, the story is not dominated by it. The analysis draws on microeconomics as well as macroeconomics and, as indicated earlier, the main character is the entrepreneur.

### 9.4.4   Derived demand and time discount

An increase in saving sends two market signals to the business community. Both must come into play if a change in intertemporal preferences is to get translated successfully into corresponding changes in the economy's multistage production process. Changes in output prices together with changes in the interest rate have consequences that affect the various stages of production differentially. A non-perverse reallocation of resources in the face of increased saving hinges critically on two principles: the principle of derived demand and the principle of time discount. It is worth noting here that perceived perversities in the saving–investment nexus of market economies stem from an implicit denial of the second-mentioned principle. If derived demand is taken to be the only principle in play, then it follows almost trivially that the market cannot adapt to an increase in saving.

Increased saving means reduced current demand for consumer goods. (Of course, for a growing economy in which both saving and consumption are increasing, we would have to think in terms of changes in the relative rates of increase. More rapidly increasing saving means a less rapidly increasing demand for consumer goods.) A decrease in the demand for goods of the first order – again, Menger's terminology – has straightforward implications for the demand for goods of the second order. The demand for coffee beans moves with the demand for coffee. Menger's Law prevails. More generally, the demand for inputs that are in close temporal proximity to the consumable output moves with the demand for that output. The demand for goods of the second order is a derived demand. Under strict *ceteris paribus* conditions, which would entail no change in the rate of interest, derived demand would be the whole story.

The more favourable credit conditions brought about by the increase in saving is the basis for the rest of the story. A lower interest rate allows businesses to carry inventories more cheaply. But how important is this change in supply conditions? In gauging the relative changes in the demands for goods of the first order and goods of the second order (coffee and coffee beans), the time-discount effect is weak. Inventories of coffee beans are held for only a short period of time, and consequently, the time-discount effect – in this case, the reduced costs of carrying inventory – is trivial compared to the derived-demand effect. The demand for coffee beans falls *almost* as much as the demand for coffee. The strength of the time-discount effect is greater – and increasingly greater – for the higher orders of goods. Consider, say, a tenth-order good in the form of durable capital equipment. Testing facilities and laboratory fixtures devoted to product development are good examples. More favourable credit conditions could easily tip the scales toward creating or expanding such a facility. In early stages of production, the time-discount effect can more than offset the derived-demand effect.

Considerations of time discount draw resources into early stages of production. Further, in gauging the profitability of early-stage activities, the derived-demand effect itself can be augmenting rather than offsetting. Here, the entrepreneurial element comes into play in a special way. What counts as the relevant derived demand is not based on the current demand for goods of the first order but rather on the anticipated demand at some future point in time – a demand that may well be strengthened precisely because of the accumulation of savings. The increased saving need not be taken as an indication that the demand for consumables is *permanently* reduced. Rather, savers are saving up for something. And entrepreneurs who best anticipate just what they will be inclined to buy with their increased buying power stand to profit from the intertemporal shift in spending.

The interplay between derived demand and time discount accounts for the change in the pattern of resource allocation brought about by an increase in saving. A judgement might be made that this account saddles the entrepreneurs with a greater burden than they can bear. Yet those same entrepreneurial skills were already in play in maintaining the intertemporal capital structure before the increase in saving. That is, even in the absence of a change in intertemporal preferences, market conditions throughout the economy are continuously changing in every other respect – changes in tastes, in technology, in resource availabilities. Entrepreneurs must continuously adapt to those changes, while maintaining the temporal progression from early-stage to late-stage activities. An increase in saving simply requires that they make use of those same skills – but under marginally changed credit conditions. A more

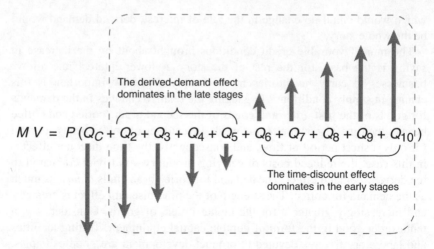

$$MV = P(Q_C + Q_2 + Q_3 + Q_4 + Q_5 + Q_6 + Q_7 + Q_8 + Q_9 + Q_{10})$$

The derived-demand effect dominates in the late stages

The time-discount effect dominates in the early stages

*Figure 9.4   Time discount and derived demand*

plausible judgement would be that an economy unable to adapt to a change in saving preferences is most likely unable to maintain a tolerable degree of economic coordination even in the absence of such changes.

Figure 9.4 reproduces the equation of exchange with the investment sector disaggregated into nine stages of production. The arrows indicate the direction and relative magnitude of the change in the output quantities brought about by an increase in saving. The reduction in the output of first-order goods $(Q_C)$ is echoed in the reduction in the output of second-through-fifth-order goods $(Q_2, Q_3, Q_4$ and $Q_5)$, the magnitude of the reduction attenuated by the time-discount effect for the increasingly higher orders of goods. Starting (in this illustration) with sixth-order goods, the time-discount more than offsets the derived-demand effect. There are increases in the output levels of the sixth and earlier stages of production $(Q_6, Q_7, Q_8, Q_9$ and $Q_{10})$, the time-discount effect becoming more dominant with increasingly higher-order goods.

The increased saving frees up resources, which are then allocated to the different stages of production in a pattern governed by the more favourable credit conditions. Grouping $Q_2$ through $Q_{10}$ together in Figure 9.4, we see that overall investment rises as the current demand for consumable output $(Q_C)$ falls. Contrary to Keynes's paradox of thrift, consumption and investment can move in opposite directions. Attention to the intertemporal pattern of investment allows us to resolve the paradox and to show how changes in investment can be consistent with changes in saving behaviour. The wholesale neglect of the pattern of investment underlay an early judgement by Hayek (1931) that 'Mr. Keynes's aggregates conceal the most fundamental mechanisms of change'. It is significant that those fundamental mechanisms are set into motion by the supply and demand for loanable funds – because it was loanable funds theory, a staple in the pre-Keynesians' toolkit, that Keynes specifically jettisoned.

## 9.5 The Market for Loanable Funds

Loanable funds theory has an honourable history. Over the years and across several schools of thought, theorizing abstractly in terms of 'loans' was simply a way of recognizing that the mechanisms of supply and demand govern the intertemporal allocation of resources. The macroeconomic implications of loanable funds theory are best seen by focusing on the resources themselves rather than on any particular financial instrument that allows the allocator – the entrepreneur – to take command of the resources.

People produce output in a wide variety of forms. With their incomes they engage in consumption spending, laying claim to most but not all of the output that they have collectively produced. The part of income not so spent, that is, their saving, bears a strong and systematic relationship to the part of the output that is not currently consumed. These unconsumed resources can be made available for increasing the economy's productive capacity. In a market economy, there are a number of different financial instruments (bank deposits, passbook accounts, bonds and equity shares) that transfer command over the unconsumed resources to the business community.

The term 'loanable funds', then, refers summarily to all the ways that the investment community takes command of the unconsumed resources. Further, *taking* command has to include retaining command – in the case of the undistributed earnings of the business community. Here, the business firm, in order to expand its own productive capacity, is forgoing some market rate of return on its retained earnings, a rate that it could have obtained through the financial sector. For macroeconomic relevance, however, loanable funds exclude consumer loans. Income earned by one individual and spent on consumption either by that individual or – through saving and the consumer loan market – by another individual is not the focus of loanable funds theorizing.

With loanable funds broadly defined to capture the variety of ways that real investments can be financed, the corresponding interest rate that equilibrates this market must be understood in terms that are similarly broad. A full-bodied theory of finance would have to allow for many interest rates, the variations among them being attributable to differences in risk, liquidity and time to maturity. But for getting at the fundamental relationships among the variables of capital-based macroeconomics (output, consumption, saving, investment, and even the intertemporal pattern of resource allocation), a summary rate is adequate. As will be noted in subsequent sections, some

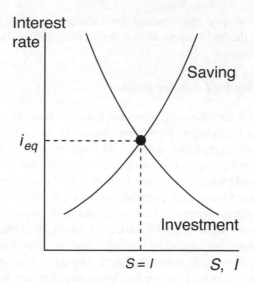

*Figure 9.5   The loanable funds market*

considerations that account for a variation among different interest rates may exacerbate the effects of a change in the summary rate, while other considerations may ameliorate those effects. But in any case, the fundamental differences that separate capital-based macroeconomics from other schools of macroeconomics do not hinge in any important or first-order way on relative movements of different rates of return within the financial sector.

Figure 9.5 represents the simple analytics of the loanable funds market. The supply of loanable funds is, for the most part, saving out of current income. In real terms, it is that part of current output not consumed. The demand for loanable funds reflects the eagerness of the business community to use that saving to take command of the unconsumed resources. These two macroeconomically relevant magnitudes of saving and investment are not definitionally the same thing but rather are brought into balance by equilibrating movements in the broadly conceived rate of interest.

To feature the supply and demand for loanable funds in this way is only to suggest that in a market economy the interest rate is the fundamental mechanism through which intertemporal coordination is achieved. Simply put, the interest rate allocates resources over time. There need be no claim here that this Marshallian mechanism works as cleanly and as swiftly as the supply and demand for fish at Billingsgate. Because of the elements of time and uncertainty inherent in the intertemporal dimension of the loanable funds market, the interest rate signal can be subject to interpretation.

What if some income is neither spent on consumption nor offered as funds for lending? That is, what if people – unexpectedly and on an economy-wide basis – prefer to add to their cash holdings? The increased demand for cash holdings would constitute saving in the sense of income not consumed but would not constitute saving in the sense of an increase in the supply of loanable funds. One important consequence of the Keynesian revolution was to elevate considerations of liquidity preferences to the point of dwarfing considerations of intertemporal preferences. The rate of interest was thought to be dominated by changes in the demand for money. Even in the counter-revolutionary contributions of the monetarists, the interest rate was featured on the left-hand side of the equation of exchange – as a parameter that affects the demand for money – and not on the right-hand side as a key allocating mechanism working within the output aggregate. (It is precisely because of this left-handedness of its treatment of the interest rate that Milton Friedman's restatement of the quantity theory is taken by some scholars as a contribution in the Keynesian tradition; see Garrison, 1992.)

The attention to the loanable funds market as depicted in Figure 9.5 reflects the judgement of the Austrians that the rate of interest, though hidden from view in the monetarists' equation of exchange, is quintessentially a key right-hand-side variable. The interest rate's primary role in a market economy is that of allocating investable resources in accordance with saving behaviour. There is no denying that the interest rate can, on occasion, play a role on the left-hand side of the equation of exchange – as a minor determinant of money demand or as a short-run consequence of hoarding behaviour. Still, these monetarist and Keynesian concerns are subordinate ones in the Austrians' judgement. An exogenous change in money demand is rarely if ever the source of a macroeconomic disruption. (Here, the Austrians fall in with the monetarists.) And an occasional dramatic change in liquidity preference is more likely to be a consequence of an economy-wide intertemporal coordination failure than a cause of it. (Here, even Keynes agreed that in the context of business cycles the scramble for liquidity is a secondary phenomenon. His concern about the 'fetish of liquidity', a wholly unfounded concern in the Austrians' view, was spelled out in the context of long-term secular unemployment.)

Figure 9.5 (the loanable funds market) and Figure 9.1 (the Hayekian triangle) tell the same story but at two different levels of aggregation. Figure 9.5 shows how much of the economy's resources are available for investment purposes. Figure 9.1 shows just how those resources are allocated throughout the sequence of stages. A change in the interest rate, say, a reduction brought about by an increase in saving, has systematic consequences that can be depicted in both figures. The interest rate governs both the amount of investable resources and the general pattern of allocation of those resources. A rightward shift in the supply of loanable funds would move the market along its demand curve, reducing the interest rate to reflect the increased availability of investable resources. At the same time, that reduced rate on interest would give a competitive edge to early-stage investment activities. Resources available for the expansion of long-term projects come in part from the overall increase in unconsumed resources and in part from a transfer of resources from late-stage activities, where lower investment demand reflects the lower demand for current and near-term output.

The effects of increased saving at both levels of aggregation are explicit in Figure 9.4 and implicit in Figure 9.5. The change in the pattern of resource allocation is depicted as the systematic changes in the direction and magnitude of the stage-by-stage output levels. The increase in unconsumed resources is depicted by the reduction in the output of goods of the first order and in the corresponding increase in the output of second-through-tenth-order goods. And all this is implied by a rightward shift in the supply of loanable funds: more unconsumed resources are being allocated on the basis of lower interest rate.

What is missing in the discussion at this point is any explicit recognition of an overall resource constraint. Scarcity is implicit in the notion that, for a given period, output magnitudes as depicted in Figures 9.3 and 9.4 move differentially, with some increasing and others decreasing. Early-stage activities are expanded at the expense of current consumption and late-stage activities. The overall resource constraint can be made explicit by the introduction of a production possibilities frontier that makes the two-way distinction between current consumption, which is already depicted as the vertical leg of the Hayekian triangle, and investment, which is already being tracked along the horizontal axis of the loanable funds diagram. A fully employed economy can be represented as an economy producing on its production possibilities frontier.

## 9.6   Full Employment and the Production Possibilities Frontier

The existence of an overall resource constraint is inherent in the concept of full employment. A fully employed economy is one in which the supply-side constraints are binding. The full employment of labour and other factors of production gets us full-employment output and full-employment income. This much is accepted by all schools of macroeconomic thought. But what constitutes unemployment in the macroeconomically relevant sense? And what can we make of the conventionally defined categories of frictional, structural and cyclical components of unemployment? These are the issues that separate the Austrians from other schools.

For Keynes, unemployment was to be gauged with reference to some 'going wage', which itself came into being during a period when the economy was suffering from no macroeconomic maladies. In subsequent periods the economy's actual state of macroeconomic health is determined, in the Keynesian way of thinking, by comparing the quantity of labour demanded at the going wage with the quantity of labour offered in supply. If these two quantities (demanded and supplied) are the same, then labour (along with all other resources) is fully employed. If, under less favourable market conditions, the quantity demanded is deficient relative to the quantity offered in supply at the previously established going wage, the discrepancy stands as a measure of cyclical unemployment.

Central to this Keynesian reckoning was the idea that the going wage kept going even after the market conditions that underlay it were gone. It was in this context that Keynes (1936, p. 15) used the term 'involuntary unemployment', the involuntariness deriving from the idea that the workers have fallen victim to the institutions of capitalism – institutions that do not allow for some uniform adjustment in the overall level of wages. Involuntary unemployment is used here to mean cyclical unemployment. Here, we should acknowledge Keynes's belief, not shared by modern Keynesians, that ongoing secular unemployment of the involuntary variety is inherent in the nature of the market system.

Both Keynes and modern Keynesians allow for some unemployment even in the absence of involuntary unemployment, that is, even when the economy is not in recession. In a healthy economy, the unemployed consist of new entrants into the labour force who haven't yet accepted a job offer as well as members of the labour force who are between jobs. Modern textbooks commonly make the distinction between frictional unemployment, meaning simply that in a market economy job applicants and job openings are not matched up infinitely fast, and structural unemployment, meaning that there are significant mismatches between applicants and openings, such as to require costly retraining and/or relocation.

Though the difference between frictional and structural unemployment is a substantive one, the ultimate purpose of this unemployment taxonomy is to make a sharp distinction between these components of unemployment and the remaining component, which alone is a measure of the economy's departure from its overall, macroeconomically relevant supply-side constraints. As a rule of thumb, the frictional–structural unemployment may be 5–6 per cent of the labour force. Hence a measured unemployment in a market economy of, say, 8 per cent would suggest that the economy is in recession and that the cyclical component of the measured unemployment, that is, the unemployment attributable to recessionary conditions, is 2–3 per cent.

This well-known taxonomy of unemployment (frictional, structural and cyclical) is spelled out here to facilitate an important contrast between the Austrians' reckoning of unemployment and this more conventional reckoning. Capital-based macroeconomics features the intertemporal structure of production. And, as will be seen in section 9.10 below, business cycles entail a distortion of the structure, a misallocation of labour and other resources among the stages of production. Hence, cyclical unemployment – or, at least, an essential part of it – is a special case of structural unemployment. The Austrians depart from convention, then, in their judgement that structural unemployment and cyclical unemployment are not mutually exclusive categories.

A second feature of the Austrian's reckoning of employment levels – and of resource constraints generally – is illuminated by considering the monetarists' notion of the natural rate of unemployment (see Chapter 4). Rather than emphasize the different categories of unemployment as discussed above, the monetarists make the two-way distinction between the rate of unemployment that would 'naturally' exist even in a healthy market economy and rates of unemployment that are in excess of this natural rate. (Milton Friedman coined the term 'natural rate of unemployment' to emphasize its kinship with the 'natural rate of interest', a similarly defined term introduced by Swedish economist Knut Wicksell; see Leijonhufvud, 1981.) The difference here between the monetarists and the Keynesians is terminological rather than substantive. The natural rate of unemployment is in the range of 5–6 per cent. And an economy that is experiencing the natural rate of unemployment is said to be fully employed; see Dixon (1995).

Consistent with this reckoning, an economy experiencing the natural rate of unemployment can be said to be on its production possibility frontier. The frontier, then, can allow for deviations in either direction. That is, an economy in recession would be represented by a point inside its frontier, and an overheated economy, one in which the unemployment rate has been pushed temporarily below the natural rate, would be represented by a point beyond its frontier. This is only to say that the frontier itself is defined in terms of sustainable levels of output and not in terms of some short-run maximal level of output.

Figure 9.6 depicts a wholly private economy's production possibilities frontier in terms of sustainable combinations of consumable output and investment. This economy is experiencing full employment, its unemployment rate being no more than 5–6 per cent. The vertical axis keeps track of consumables in a way that conforms to final-stage output as represented by the vertical leg of the Hayekian triangle. The horizontal axis keeps track of gross investment. Hence, if capital depreciation just happened to be equal to gross investment, the economy would be experiencing no economic growth. Typically, depreciation will be something less than gross investment, and the economy will enjoy a positive growth rate, the frontier itself expanding outward from period to period. In the unlikely case in which gross investment

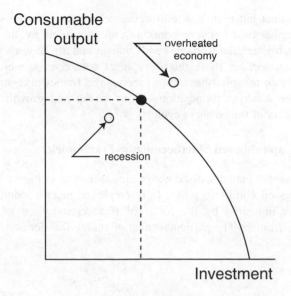

*Figure 9.6   The production possibilities frontier*

falls short of depreciation, of course, the economy would be in economic decline, the frontier shifting inward from period to period.

As one of its critical features, capital-based macroeconomics allows for movements *along* the frontier in one direction or the other in response to changes in intertemporal preferences. A clockwise movement would represent the sacrifice of current consumption in favour of additional investment. The initial reduction of consumable output would eventually be offset and then more than offset as the frontier itself shifts outward at an accelerated rate. The time path of consumable output would be that depicted in Figure 9.2. A counterclockwise movement would represent a sacrifice in the opposite direction. The initial increase in consumable output would carry the cost of a decrease in the economy's growth rate and possibly even a negative growth rate.

Significantly, these possible clockwise and counterclockwise movements are the sort of movements precluded by construction in Keynesian theorizing, as will be shown in sections 9.9 and 9.11, and ignored in monetarist theorizing, owing to the level of aggregation that characterizes the equation of exchange. A major focus of Austrian theorizing is on the market mechanisms that allow for such movements – and on policy actions that lead to a disruption of these mechanisms. Macroeconomic health entails more than an unemployment rate that stays within the range of 5–6 per cent. It also entails a growth rate that is consistent with intertemporal preferences.

Three distinct but mutually reinforcing perspectives on the key relationships of capital-based macroeconomics are provided by the production possibilities frontier, the loanable funds market and the Hayekian triangle. In the following section, these three graphical components, which come together to create a capital-based macroeconomic framework, provide a firm basis for the Austrian propositions about saving and growth and for the Austrian theory of the business cycle.

## 9.7   The Capital-based Macroeconomic Framework

The three components discussed above are assembled in Figure 9.7 to depict an intertemporal equilibrium in a fully employed macroeconomy. Full employment is indicated by the locus of this economy on its production possibilities frontier. The particular location on the frontier is determined by

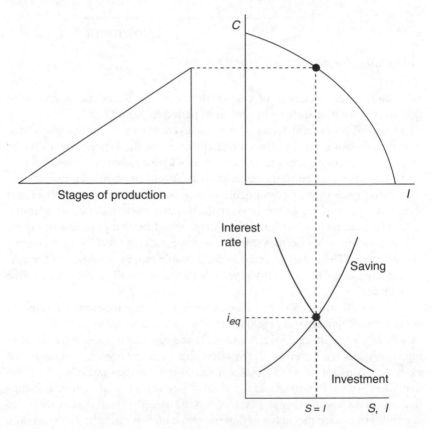

*Figure 9.7   A capital-based macroeconomic framework*

the loanable funds market, in which the rate of interest reflects the saving preferences of market participants. The corresponding consumption preferences are accommodated by the output of the final stage of production in the Hayekian triangle. Resources are being allocated among the stages of production on the basis of the cost of investment funds, such that the rate of return in the real sector, as reflected in the slope of the triangle's hypotenuse, corresponds to the rate of return in the financial sector, as depicted by the market-clearing interest rate in the loanable funds market. Figure 9.7 and subsequent figures are adapted from Garrison (2001).

For an economy in a macroeconomic equilibrium as just described, the rates of return (in both the real and the financial sectors) can be summarily described as 'the natural rate of interest'. Parametric changes, such as a change in saving preferences, can change the natural rate. For instance, increased saving preferences will cause the market-clearing rate of interest to be lower and the slope of the triangle's hypotenuse to be a shallower one. The capital-based macroeconomic framework is designed to show (i) how market forces establish a new natural rate in response to some parametric change and (ii) how the economy reacts to policies aimed at maintaining an interest rate in the financial sector that is inconsistent with – typically below – the natural rate. Uses of these analytics to deal with other macroeconomic issues, such as deficit finance and tax reform, are demonstrated in Garrison (2001); some extensions of Austrian business cycle theory are suggested by Cochran (2001).

In its simplest interpretation, Figure 9.7 depicts a steady-state, no-growth economy. There is no *net* investment. The positive level of saving and investment shown in the loanable funds market is just enough to offset capital depreciation. As capital goods wear out and are replaced, the Hayekian triangle is maintained from period to period in terms of both size and shape. This is the circumstance that corresponds to the first two periods of Figure 9.2. If, as is ordinarily the case, investment exceeds capital depreciation, the economy experiences secular growth in all its dimensions. The production possibilities frontier shifts outward, both the supply and demand for loanable funds shift rightward, and the Hayekian triangle changes in size but not – or, at least, not necessarily – in shape. This is the circumstance that corresponds to the last several periods of Figure 9.2. It should be noted that secular growth in which there is no change in the shape of the Hayekian triangle presupposes that the supply of loanable funds and the demand for loanable funds shift rightward to the very same extent, such that there is no change in the rate of interest. Ordinarily, we would think of the increased income and wealth that economic growth makes possible as being accompanied by an expanding time horizon and hence by an increased inclination to save. Factoring in increased saving preferences would allow for a reduction in the rate of interest and a change in the shape as well as of the size of the Hayekian triangle.

## 9.8   Saving-induced Capital Restructuring

Suppose that in circumstances of a no-growth economy and a natural rate of interest of $i_{eq}$, people become more thrifty. The increased saving is depicted in Figure 9.8 as a rightward shift in the supply of loanable funds (from $S$ to $S'$). With the resulting downward pressure on the interest rate, the loanable funds market is brought back into equilibrium. The natural rate of interest falls from $i_{eq}$ to $i'_{eq}$. The reduced cost of borrowing motivates the business community to expand investment activities. Increased saving, of course, *means* reduced consumption. But the reduced consumption is offset by the increased investment, allowing the economy to stay on its production possibility frontier. The clockwise movement along the frontier in the direction of increased investment is consistent with the hypothesized change in intertemporal preferences.

The corresponding changes in the Hayekian triangle follow straightforwardly. The currently reduced demand for consumable output (which

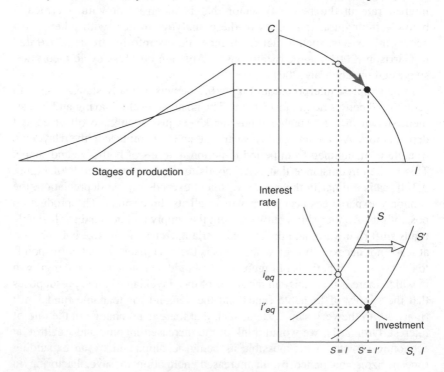

*Figure 9.8   Saving-induced economic growth*

depresses investment) is accompanied by reduced borrowing costs (which stimulate investment). The effects of these changes in market conditions were discussed in section 9.4.4 above in terms of 'derived demand' and 'time discount'. The derived-demand effect dominates in the late stages; the time-discount effect dominates in the early stages. Input prices are bid down in the late stages (reflecting the low demand for current and near-term output) and are bid up in the early stages (reflecting the low borrowing costs). The changes in relative prices draw resources out of the late stages and into the early stages. Further, stages of production temporally more remote from final consumption than had existed before will have yields that are attractive in the light of the low borrowing costs. In the absence of any further changes in saving preferences or in any other data, the new intertemporal equilibrium will entail a rate of return in the real sector (consisting of all the stages) that matches the low rate of interest in the financial sector. The general pattern of resource reallocation is depicted as a shallower slope of the triangle's hypotenuse.

In discussing in more concrete terms the nature of these saving-induced reallocations, the relevant distinction is not between labour and capital but rather between resources of both kinds that are (relatively) non-specific and resources of both kinds that are (relatively) specific. Non-specific capital, such as building materials that can be used for building either retail outlets or research facilities, will move out of comparatively late stages and into early ones in response to relatively small price differentials. Specific capital, such as mining equipment or amusement park attractions, may enjoy a capital gain (in the first instance) or suffer a capital loss (in the second). Similarly, non-specific labour will migrate in the direction of the early stages in response to small wage-rate differentials, while workers who are wedded to particular stages may experience increased – or reduced – wage rates. Note that the focus on the allocation of resources among the stages of production in re-sponse to changes in relative prices and wages warns against theorizing in terms of the wage rate.

Once the capital restructuring is complete and the earliest saving-induced investments work their way through the stages of production, the output of consumables will increase, eventually exceeding the output that characterized the initial no-growth economy. If we understand the saving that gave rise to the capital restructuring not as a permanent reduction in consumption but rather as an increased demand for future consumption, then we see that the reallocations are consistent with the preference change that gave rise to them. Further, we see that the clockwise movement along the production possibili-ties frontier, followed by an outward expansion of the frontier itself, traces out a temporal pattern of consumption that is wholly consistent with the pattern depicted in Figure 9.2. By forgoing consumption in the near term, people's saving behaviour allows the economy to make the transition from a no-growth economy to an economy experiencing secular growth.

Two qualifications will help to put in perspective this account of the market's reaction to an increase in saving. First, the assumption of an initial no-growth economy was made purely for pedagogical reasons. In this setting the changes brought about by an increase in saving are isolated from any other ongoing changes, such as those associated with secular growth. The demand for inputs falls in some stages and rises in others. Some stages lose resources; others gain them. In application, however, where there is already ongoing secular growth, these same relative effects are expressed not in terms of absolute decreases and increases but rather in terms of increases at a relatively slow rate and increases at a relative rapid rate. The market is simply doing the same things it did before the increase in saving – except for its doing them under conditions of moderated consumption demand marginally more favourable credit conditions. As suggested earlier, the plausibility of the market being able to accommodate itself to the increase in saving is about the same as the plausibility that it could function reasonably well during the period of secular growth.

Second, and relatedly, the substantial one-time shift in the supply of loanable funds shown in Figure 9.8 is not intended to suggest that saving behaviour sometimes changes that dramatically. Like adopting the assumption of no-growth, hypothesizing a dramatic change serves a purely pedagogical purpose. In teaching the basics of supply and demand, professors draw a substantially shifted curve on the blackboard so that students in the back row can see it. There is no implication here that actual changes in saving preferences tend to be dramatic ones or that saving is in some sense unstable. Quite the contrary: in light of the complexities of the capital structure and the nature of the market mechanisms that keep it in line with saving preferences, the message should be that even small and gradual changes in saving preference need to be accommodated by the appropriate movements of resources among the stages of production. As in microeconomics, Austrian macroeconomics is about marginal adjustments to parametric changes.

Because of the explicit temporal element in the capital structure, any inter-stage misallocations can be cumulative. The avoidance of such misallocations requires the interest rate to tell the truth about intertemporal preferences. The consequences of a falsified interest rate (cumulative intertemporal mis-allocations followed by a crisis) are the subject of section 9.10. But it the following section we consider the Keynesian view of increased saving in the context of our capital-based macroeconomic framework.

## 9.9 Keynes's Paradox of Thrift Revisited

It is instructive to compare the Austrians' treatment of increased saving and consequent market adjustments with Keynes's treatment of these issues. There are two important differences. First, pre-empting any extended analysis of changes in saving preferences was Keynes's judgement that such changes are unlikely to occur. Second, any increase in thriftiness, should such a preference change actually occur, would in his reckoning have perverse consequences for the economy.

Saving, in Keynes's theory, is a residual. It's what's left over after people do their consumption spending, which itself is dependent only (or predominantly) upon incomes. In the Keynesian framework, the rate of interest has no effect (or only a negligible effect) on saving behaviour. Hence an extended analysis of a change in saving preferences was largely uncalled for. Keynes's analysis of the interest rate is carried out in terms of the supply and demand for money (that is, cash balances) and not in terms of the supply and demand for loanable funds. And to the extent that Keynes did deal with loanable funds – or, more pointedly, investment funds – his focus was on the other side of the loanable funds market. The demand for investment funds, in his view, is subject to dramatic shifts owing to the uncertainties inherent in investment decisions. A comparison of Keynesian and Austrian theories of the business cycles, the Keynesian theory featuring a collapse in investment demand, will be the subject of section 9.11.

Keynes's judgement that saving behaviour is not subject to change was accompanied by some degree of relief that this was the case. He argued that an increase in saving would send the economy into recession. This is Keynes's celebrated 'paradox of thrift'. If people try to save more out of a given income, they will find themselves saving no more than before but saving that unchanged amount out of a reduced income. That is, in their effort to increase their saving rate, $S/Y$, by increasing the numerator of that ratio, they set a market process in motion that increases the saving rate by reducing the ratio's denominator. What is the essence of this market process that produces results so different from those envisioned by the Austrians? In summary terms, the Austrian story about derived demand and time discount becomes, in Keynesian translation, a story about derived demand alone.

The market adjustments envisioned by Keynes can be revealingly depicted as an alternative sequence to the one shown in Figure 9.8. In Figure 9.9 the same initial conditions of full employment are assumed. But in the spirit of Keynes, the loanable funds market is drawn with relatively inelastic saving and investment schedules. The initial saving schedule is labelled $S(Y_0)$ to indicate that people are saving out of an initial level of income of $Y_0$. As in the Austrian story, we show an increase in thriftiness by a rightward shift of the

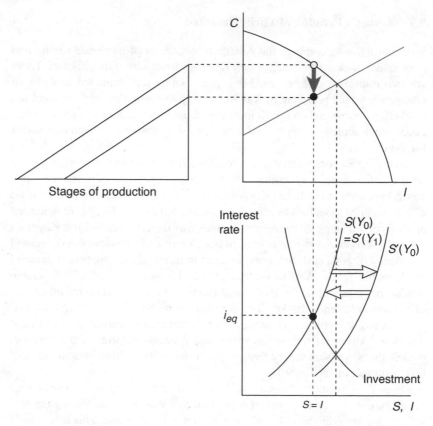

*Figure 9.9    A saving-induced recession*

supply of loanable funds – from $S(Y_0)$ to $S'(Y_0)$. And, as before, there is downward pressure on the interest rate. But in the Keynesian story, the market process that might otherwise restore an equilibrium relationship between saving and investment is cut short by a dominating income effect. More saving means less consumption spending. And less consumption spending means lower incomes for those who sell these consumer goods. It also means reduced demand for the inputs with which to produce the consumables, that is, a reduced demand in factor markets, generally.

The economy spirals downward as spending and incomes fall in multiple rounds. With reduced incomes, saving is also reduced. As the process plays itself out, the saving schedule shifts leftward from $S'(Y_0)$ to $S'(Y_1)$, where $Y_1 < Y_0$. The negative income effect fully offsets the positive increased-thrift effect. Both saving and investment are the same as before the preference change. But with reduced consumer spending and no change – and certainly no increase –

in investment spending, the economy has fallen inside the production possibilities frontier. (In Figure 9.9 the upward-sloping line that intersects the frontier suggests that the level of consumption in the thrift-depressed economy is lower than it would have been had intertemporal coordination somehow been achieved without the lapse from full employment. The parameters of this upward-sloping 'demand constraint' will be identified in section 9.11.)

The Hayekian triangle changes in size but not in shape. Note that even if Keynes were to allow for the allocation of resources within the capital structure to be achieved by changes in the interest rate, no thrift-induced reallocation would take place – since (abstracting from possible changes in liquidity preferences, which would only compound the perversities) the interest rate does not change.

To isolate the consequences of increased thriftiness, it is assumed that investment spending does not change at all. But, of course, if the recessionary conditions dampen profit expectations in the business community, investment spending will actually fall, exacerbating the problems caused by the increased thriftiness.

The paradoxical – and perverse – consequences of an increase in thriftiness are seen by Keynes as the unavoidable outcome of the market process. In his own words, 'Every such attempt to save more by reducing consumption will so affect incomes that the attempt necessarily defeats itself' (Keynes, 1936, p. 84). The economy simply cannot move along its production possibilities frontier, and savers who push in that direction will cause the economy to sink into recession. Keynes's paradox of thrift stands as a summary denial that a market economy has the capability of achieving and maintaining an intertemporal equilibrium in the face of changing saving preferences. Relative change in resource allocations within the capital structure are no part of the story. Again, the wholesale neglect of all such structural changes is what Hayek (1931) had in mind when he remarked that 'Mr. Keynes's aggregates conceal the most fundamental mechanisms of change'.

## 9.10 The Austrian Theory of the Business Cycle

The previous two sections provide a stark contrast between Austrian and Keynesian views. They show how an increase in saving can move the economy along its production possibilities frontier, allowing for an increase in the economy's rate of economic growth (the Austrian view), and how an increase in saving necessarily throws the economy off its frontier and into recession (the Keynesian view). Simply put, markets work in one view and don't work in the other.

For the Austrians, the idea that markets work is not axiomatic. There is no claim that markets are always guided only by the underlying economic realities – no matter what institutional arrangements are in place and no matter what macroeconomic policies are pursued. In fact, the Austrian theory of the business cycle is a theory about a policy-induced departure – first in one direction and then in the other – from the economy's production possibilities frontier.

For Keynes, increased saving leads to recession. This proposition, however, did not transform his paradox of thrift into an excess-saving theory of recessions. As already indicated, Keynes believed that saving preferences were not likely to change. The recession-inducing changes, in his view, were almost always spontaneous changes on the demand side of the loanable funds market.

Keynes and Hayek were critical of one another's efforts to explain recessions, but their assessments of one another's books generated more heat than light and failed to produce a head-to-head comparison of the contrasting views. Despite all the interpreting, reinterpreting and reconstructing of Keynesian ideas over the last three-quarters of a century, it is instructive to compare (in this and the following sections) the Austrian and (original) Keynesian views on the nature and causes of business cycles (see Garrison, 1989, 1991, 2002).

According to the Austrians, the market is capable of allocating resources in conformity with intertemporal preferences on the basis of a market-determined (natural) rate of interest. It follows, then, almost as a corollary that an interest rate substantially influenced by extra-market forces will lead to an intertemporal misallocation of resources. This latter proposition is the essence of the Austrian theory of business cycles. The cyclical quality of the departures from the economy's production possibilities frontier derives from the self-correcting properties of a market economy. Misallocations are followed by reallocations. Note that the market is not judged to be so efficient as to prevent from the outset all policy-induced misallocations. As Hayek (1945) has taught us, it cannot allocate resources in accordance with the 'real factors' (consumer preferences, technological possibilities and resource availabilities) except on the basis of information conveyed by market signals, including, importantly, the rate of interest. It is movements in the interest rate, along with the corresponding movements in input prices and output prices, that give clues to the business community about what those real factors are and about how they may have changed.

The Austrian theory of the business cycle is a theory of boom and bust with special attention to the extra-market forces that initiate the boom and the market's own self-correcting forces that turn boom into bust. We have already seen that increased saving lowers the rate of interest and gives rise to a genuine boom, one in which no self-correction is called for. The economy simply grows at a more rapid rate. By contrast, a falsified interest rate that mimics the loan market conditions of a genuine boom but is not accompanied by the requisite savings gives rise to an artificial boom, one whose artificiality is eventually revealed by the market's reaction to excessively future-oriented production activities in conditions of insufficient saving.

As with the graphical depiction of saving and growth, the analytics of boom and bust is begun with an assumed no-growth economy in an intertemporal equilibrium. The initial (market-determined) rate of interest ($i_{eq}$ in Figure 9.10) also qualifies as the natural rate of interest. An artificial boom is initiated by the injection of new money through credit markets. The central bank adopts an interest rate target below the rate of interest that otherwise would have prevailed. Its operational target rate, of course, is much more narrowly defined than the broadly conceived market rates shown in the diagram. The central bank achieves its interest rate target by augmenting the supply of loanable funds with newly created credit. The Federal Reserve's Open Market Committee buys securities in sufficient volume so as to drive the Federal Funds rate down to the chosen target. With this action, market rates generally are brought down to a similar extent – although, of course, some more so than others. The fact that long-term rates tend not to fall as

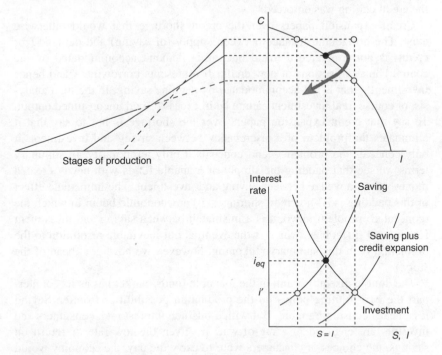

*Figure 9.10   A policy-induced boom and bust*

much as short-term rates may mitigate – but cannot eliminate – the general effects of the credit expansion. Further, these general effects are independent of which particular policy tool the Federal Reserve employs. Credit expansions brought about by a reduction in the discount rate (now called the primary credit rate) or by a reduction in reserve requirements could be similarly described. All of the institutionally distinct monetary tools are macroeconomically equivalent: they are all means of lending money into existence and hence have their initial effect on interest rates.

For comparison, the central bank's augmentation of credit depicted in Figure 9.10 is set to match the actual shift in the supply of saving depicted in Figure 9.8. Rather than create a new equilibrium interest rate and a corresponding equality of saving and investment as was the case in a saving-induced expansion, the credit expansion creates a double disequilibrium at a sub-natural interest rate. Savers save less, while borrowers borrow more. Note that if this low interest rate were created by the imposition of an interest rate ceiling, the situation would be different. With a legislated ceiling, borrowing would be saving-constrained. The horizontal distance at the ceiling rate between supply and demand would represent a frustrated demand for credit. A credit shortage would be immediately apparent and would persist as long as the credit ceiling was enforced.

Credit expansion papers over the credit shortage that would otherwise exist. The horizontal distance between supply (of saving) and demand (for credit) is not frustrated demand but rather demand accommodated by the central bank's injections of new credit. It represents borrowing – and hence investment – that is not accommodated by genuine saving. In the final analysis, of course, real investment cannot be in excess of real unconsumed output. To say that credit expansion papers over the shortage is not to say that it eliminates the problem of a discrepancy between saving and investment. It only conceals the problem – and conceals it only temporarily. In summary terms we see that padding the supply of loanable funds with newly created money drives a wedge between saving and investment. The immediate effect of this padding is (i) no credit shortage, (ii) an economic boom in which the (concealed) problem inherent is a mismatch between saving and investment festers, and (iii) a bust, which is the eventual but inevitable resolution to the problem. (With this summary reckoning, however, we have got ahead of the story.)

The double disequilibrium in the loanable funds market has as its counterpart the two limiting points on the production possibilities frontier. Saving less means consuming more. But with a falsified interest rate, consumers and investors are engaged in a tug-of-war. If, given the low rate or return on savings, the choices of consumers were to carry the day, the economy would move counterclockwise along the frontier to the consumers' limiting point.

Similarly, if, with artificially cheap credit, the decisions of investors were to carry the day, the economy would move clockwise along the frontier to the investors' limiting point. Of course, neither set of participants in this tug-of-war is wholly victorious. But both consumer choices and investment decisions have their separate – and conflicting – real consequences. Graphically, the participants are pulling at right angles to one another – the consumers pulling upward in the direction of more consumption, the investors pulling rightward in the direction of more investment. Their combined effect is a movement of the economy beyond the frontier in the direction of a 'virtual' disequilibrium point that is defined by the two limiting points.

Having defined the production possibilities frontier in terms of sustainable levels of output, we can allow for the economy to move beyond the frontier – but only on a temporary basis. People are drawn into the labour force in numbers that cannot be sustained indefinitely. Additional members of households may take a job because of the unusually favourable labour market conditions. Some workers may work overtime. Others may delay retirement or forgo vacations. Maintenance routines that interrupt production activities may be postponed. These are the aspects of the boom that allow the economy to produce temporarily beyond the production possibilities frontier. However, the increasingly binding real resource constraints will keep the economy from actually reaching the virtual disequilibrium point – hence the 'virtual' quality of that point. The general nature of the path traced out by the economy – its rotation in the clockwise direction – will become evident once we consider the corresponding changes in the economy's structure of production.

The wedge driven between saving and investment in the loanable funds market and the tug-of-war that pulls the economy beyond its production possibility frontier manifests itself in the economy's capital structure as clashing triangles. In the case of a saving-induced capital restructuring, the derived-demand effect and the time-discount effect work together to reallocate resources toward the earlier stages – a reallocation that is depicted by a change in the shape of the Hayekian triangle. In the case of credit expansion, the two effects work in opposition to one another. The time-discount effect, which is strongest in the early stages, attracts resources to long-term projects. Low interest rates stimulate the creation of durable capital goods, product development and other activities whose ultimate pay-off is in the distant future. The excessive allocations to long-term projects are called 'malinvestment' in the Austrian literature. The derived-demand effect, which is strongest in the late stages, draws resources in the opposite direction so as to satisfy the increased demand for consumer goods. The Hayekian triangle is being pulled at both ends against the middle. Skousen (1990) identifies this same internal conflict in terms of an early-stage 'aggregate supply vector' and a late-stage 'aggregate demand vector'.

During the boom, resource allocations among the various stages are being affected in both absolute and relative terms. As explained above, the economy is producing generally at levels of output that cannot be sustained indefinitely. And at the same time that the overall output levels are higher, the pattern of output is skewed in both directions – toward the earliest stages and toward the latest stages. Middle stages experience a relative decline and some of them an absolute decline. While this characterization of the boom is gleaned from Hayek (1967 [1935]) and Mises (1953 [1912] and 1966), there remain some fundamental doctrinal differences (both terminological and substantive) in the alternative expositions offered by these early developers of capital-based macroeconomics (Garrison, 2004).

Richard Strigl (2000 [1934]), writing without reference to the Hayekian triangle, provided an account of boom and bust consistent with the one offered here. In his account, production activities are divided into three broadly conceived categories: current production of consumables (late stage), capital maintenance (middle stage), and new ventures (early stage). Policy-induced boom conditions tend to favour current production and new ventures at the expense of capital maintenance. The economic atmosphere has a 'make hay while the sun shines' quality about it, and the economy seems to be characterized by prosperity and rapid economic growth. However, the under-maintenance of existing capital (the sparse allocations to the middle stages) distinguishes the policy-induced boom from genuine, sustainable, saving-induced economic growth.

In time, but before the new ventures (the early-stage activities) have come to full fruition, the under-maintained capital (the attenuated middle-stage outputs) must impinge negatively on consumable output. This is the essence of intertemporal discoordination. The relative or even absolute reduction of consumable output is dubbed 'forced saving' in the Austrian literature. That is, the pattern of early-stage investment reflects a higher level of saving than was forthcoming on a voluntary basis. The push beyond the production possibilities frontier towards the virtual disequilibrium point is cut short by the lack of genuine saving. The downward rotation of the economy's adjustment path in Figure 9.10 reflects the forced saving.

The forced saving is but one aspect – and not necessarily the first observed aspect – of the self-reversing process that is characteristic of an artificial boom. Increasingly binding resource constraints drive up the prices of consumables as well as the prices of inputs needed to support the new ventures. The rate of interest rises as overextended businesses bid for additional funding. Distress borrowing (not shown in Figure 9.10) is a feature of a faltering boom.

Many of the new ventures and early-stage activities generally are now recognized as unprofitable. Some are seen through to completion in order to minimize losses. Others are liquidated. The beginning of the liquidation phase of the business cycle is depicted in Figure 9.10 by the economy's adjustment path turning back towards the production possibilities frontier.

As boom turns to bust, much of the unemployment is associated with liquidations in the early stages of production. Too much capital and labour have been committed to new ventures. The liquidations release these factors of production, most of which can be reabsorbed – though, of course, not instantaneously – elsewhere in the structure of production. For the Austrians, this particular instance of structural unemployment is not something distinct from cyclical unemployment. Quite to the contrary: the cyclical unemployment that marks the beginning of the downturn has a characteristically structural quality about it.

Under the most favourable conditions, the bust could be followed by a recovery in which the structural maladjustments induced by the credit expansion are corrected by the ordinary market forces. The structurally unemployed resources are reabsorbed where they are most needed, and the economy returns to a point on its production possibilities frontier. But because of the economy-wide nature of the intertemporal disequilibrium, the negative income effect of the unemployment may initially propel the economy deeper into depression rather than back to the frontier. This secondary, or compounding, aspect of the downturn is likely to be all the more severe if the general operation of markets is countered by macroeconomic policies aimed at preventing liquidation and at reigniting the boom.

The following section puts the Austrian theory in perspective by using the capital-based analytics to depict the Keynesian view of economy-wide downturns. For Keynes, the negative income effect that can compound the problem of a discoordinated capital structure becomes the whole problem, the origins of which are shrouded in the cloud of uncertainty inherent in investment activities.

## 9.11  A Keynesian Downturn in the Austrian Framework

The level of aggregation that characterizes the Keynesian framework precludes any treatment of boom and bust as an instance of intertemporal discoordination. Structural changes in the economy as might be depicted by a change in the shape of the Hayekian triangle are no part of the analysis. The triangle can change only in size, increasing with economic growth (but, in light of the paradox of thrift, not with saving-induced growth) and decreasing with occasional lapses from full employment.

The interest rate plays no role in allocating resources among the stages of production and only a minor role in determining the overall level of investment. Hence investment is treated as a simple aggregate, with the demand for investment funds taken to be unstable and highly interest-inelastic. Further, to the extent that investment is self-financing, such that increased investment leads to increased income, which in turn leads to increased saving, the two curves (saving and investment) shift together and hence the particular interest elasticity of investment is irrelevant.

Straightforwardly, the circular-flow equation (the equality of income and expenditure as an equilibrium condition) together with a simple consumption function imply a positively sloped, linear relationship between investment and consumption. Consider a wholly private economy in which income and expenditures are in balance:

$$Y = C + I \qquad\qquad (9.4)$$

Consumer behaviour is described by the conventional linear consumption equation:

$$C = c_0 + mpc\, Y \qquad\qquad (9.5)$$

where $c_0$ is the autonomous component of consumption spending and *mpc* is the marginal propensity to consume. Combining these two equations so as to eliminate the income variable gives us the relationship between consumption and investment for an economy in a circular-flow equilibrium.

$$C = c_0/mps + (mpc/mps)\, I \qquad\qquad (9.6)$$

where *mps*, of course, is simply the marginal propensity to save: $mps = 1 - mpc$. This upward-sloping linear relationship was clearly recognized by Keynes (1937, pp. 220–21) and can be called the Keynesian demand constraint. It has an intuitive interpretation that follows straightforwardly from our understanding of the investment multiplier and the marginal propensity to consume. The slope of this line is simply the marginal propensity (*mpc*) times the multiplier (1/*mps*). Suppose the *mpc* is 0.80, implying an *mps* of 0.20 and a multiplier of 5. An increase in investment spending of $100, then, would cause income to spiral up by $500, which would boost consumption spending by $400. This same result follows directly from the slope of the demand constraint (*mpc/mps* = 0.80/0.20 = 4): an increase in investment of $100 increases consumption by $400.

The Keynesian demand constraint appears in Figure 9.11, sharing axes with the production possibilities frontier. In Keynesian expositions, however, the downward-sloping supply constraint plays a very limited role. When the multiplier theory is put through its paces, the frontier serves only to mark the boundary between real changes in the spending magnitudes (below the fron-

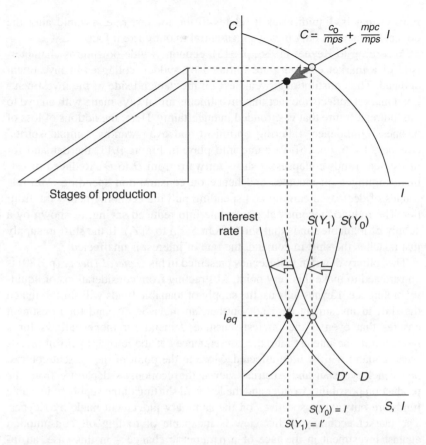

$$C = \frac{c_0}{mps} + \frac{mpc}{mps}\,I$$

*Figure 9.11   An investment-led collapse into recession*

tier) and nominal changes in the spending magnitudes (beyond the frontier). Significantly, the economy is precluded by the demand constraint from moving *along* the frontier.

The constraint itself is as stable as the consumption function – as is clear from its sharing parameters with that function. Hence the point of intersection of the constraint and the frontier is the only possible point of full employment. (In the earlier Figure 9.9, which illustrates the paradox of thrift, the demand constraint shifts downward, reflecting an increase in saving – and hence a decrease in the consumption function's intercept parameter $c_0$. It was precisely because of his belief that this parameter was *not* subject to change that Keynes was not particularly concerned about the implications of increased saving.) Finally, we can note that a more comprehensive rendering of the Keynesian relationships – one that takes into account the demand for money (that is, liquidity) as it relates to the interest rate – would alter the demand constraint only in ways inessential to our current focus.

According to Keynes (1936, p. 315), economy-wide downturns character-istic of a market economy are initiated by sudden collapses in investment demand. The constitutional weakness on the demand side of the investment-good market reflects the fact that investments are always made with an eye to the future, a future that is shrouded in uncertainty. Here, the notions of loss of business confidence, faltering optimism and even waning 'animal spirits' (Keynes, 1936, pp. 161–2) come into play. In Figure 9.11, the demand for investment funds collapses: it shifts leftward from $D$ to $D'$. Reduced invest-ment impinges on incomes and hence on consumption spending. Multiple rounds of decreased earning and spending pull the economy below the fron-tier. The reduced incomes also translate into reduced saving, as shown by a supply of loanable funds that shifts from $S(Y_0)$ to $S(Y_1)$. If the shift in supply just matches the shift in demand, the rate of interest is unaffected.

The solitary diagram that Keynes presented in his *General Theory* (p. 180) is constructed to make this very point. Abstracting from considerations of liquid-ity preference, Keynes tells us, the supply of loanable funds will shift to match the shift in investment demand. Further, an inelastic demand for investment ensures that even if the interest-sensitive demand for money allows for a reduction in the interest rate, the consequences of the leftward shift in invest-ment demand will be little affected. More to the point of the present contrast between Keynesian and Austrian views, the economy's departure from the production possibility frontier and the leftward shifting of the supply of loanable funds are but two perspectives on the summary judgement made by Keynes. The market economy in his view is incapable of trading off consumption against investment in the face of a parametric change – in this case, an in-creased aversion to the uncertainties associated with investment activities. The economy cannot move along its production possibilities frontier.

The reduction in demands all around is depicted by a shrunken Hayekian triangle. With an unchanged rate of interest, there can be no time-discount effect. Hence an untempered derived-demand effect reduces the triangle's size without changing its shape. But even if, following Keynes, we were to allow for a change in the rate of interest, the change would be in the wrong direction, compounding the economic collapse. A scramble for liquidity would increase the interest rate, with consequences (not shown in Figure 9.11) of further reduced investment, further reduced incomes, further reduced con-sumption and further reduced saving.

The Austrians would be on weak grounds if they were to deny even the possibility of a self-aggravating downward spiral. Markets are at their best in making marginal adjustments in the face of small or gradual parametric changes. A dramatic loss of confidence by the business community may well send the economy into a downward spiral. Axel Leijonhufvud (1981) discusses price and quantity movements relative to their equilibrium levels in terms of a 'corridor'. Price or quantity deviations from equilibrium that remain within the corridor are self-correcting; more dramatic deviations that take prices or quantities outside the corridor can be self-aggravating.

The Austrians are on firmer grounds in questioning the notion that such widespread losses of confidence are inherent in market economies and are to be attributed to psychological factors that rule the investment community. Business people's confidence may instead be shaken by economy-wide intertemporal discoordination, which itself is attributable to a prior credit expansion and its consequent falsification of interest rates. If this is the case, then Keynes's theory of the downturn is no more than an elaboration of the secondary contraction that was already a part of the Austrian theory of boom and bust.

## 9.12   Inflation and Deflation in the Austrian Theory

The Austrian theory of the business cycle is an account of the credit-induced, unsustainable boom. The 'fundamental mechanisms' mentioned in Hayek's assessment of Keynesian constructions are the market forces (time discount and derived demand) that keep production plans aligned with intertemporal preferences and that can malfunction when the rate of interest is falsified by credit expansion. Artificial booms contain the seeds of their own undoing – hence their fundamental unsustainability.

The reader may well have noticed that the Austrian theory does not feature the general rise in prices and wages that may be experienced during a credit-induced boom. Neither price and wage inflation nor the potential misperceptions of the inflation rate are fundamental to the theory. The focus instead is on the misallocation of resources during the period of artificially cheap credit. Intertemporal discoordination can occur on an economy-wide basis, according the Austrians, even during a period of overall price-level stability. In fact, it is during just such periods that the conflict between producers and consumers is likely to be hidden until market conditions in the various stages of production eventually reveal the boom's unsustainability. The problem that festers during the boom is likely to go undetected, all the more so if macroeconomists – and financial markets – take an unchanging price level to the hallmark of macroeconomic health.

Showing the particulars of saving-induced growth (Figure 9.8) and of credit-induced booms (Figure 9.10) made use of the simplifying assumption that we begin with a no-growth economy. In application, of course, we have to allow for some ongoing economic growth – and possibly for some fairly high real growth rate. In a rapidly growing economy, credit expansion may be seen by policy makers as simply 'enabling' growth or possibly as 'fostering' growth. The Austrians take a different view: credit expansion fosters a little more growth than can be supported by real saving. The upward pressure on prices attributable to credit expansion may just offset the downward pressure on prices attributable to the underlying real growth. Thinking in terms of the equation of exchange, we can say that increases in $M$ may just about match increases in $Q$, such that $P$ remains fairly constant. While the monetarists would see this price-level stability as evidence of a successful and commendable application of the monetarist rule, the Austrians would see price-level constancy during a period of real economic growth as a warning sign. The monetary rule does not rule out credit-induced intertemporal discoordination.

The contrast here between monetarist and Austrian views sheds light on the issue of the respective theories' applicability. For the monetarists who rely on Phillips curve analysis (and for new classicists who set out a monetary misperception theory of the business cycle), booms that lead to busts must be characterized by inflation. The differential perceptions of inflation experienced by employers and employees (in the case of Phillips curve analysis) and the general misperceptions of inflation (in the case of new classical theory) have as a strict prerequisite that there must actually be some inflation to perceive differentially or to misperceive (see Chapters 4 and 5). These theories, then, cannot apply to the boom and bust during the interwar period or to the more recent expansion of the 1990s. In these key cyclical episodes, the inflation rate was nil (in the former case) and very mild (in the latter). The inflation-dependent theories apply only to the less dramatic cyclical variations dating from the late 1960s and extending into the late 1980s. The ability of the Austrian theory to account for the downturns in 1929 and 2001 would seem to add to this theory's credibility.

The Austrian literature does contain much discussion about inflation. But in connection with business cycle theory, the strong long-run relationship between the quantity of money and the overall price level serves to answer a secondary question about the sustainability of the credit-induced boom. Once the artificial boom is under way, can the bust be avoided by further credit expansion? The Austrian answer is that there may be some scope for postponing the market correction, but only by worsening the root problem of intertemporal discoordination and hence increasing the severity of the eventual downturn. In the long run, credit is not a viable substitute for saving. Further, attempts to prolong the boom through continued increases in credit can fuel an asset bubble. (Think of the stock market orgy in the late 1920s and the 'irrational exuberance' in the late 1990s.) And, ultimately, increasingly dramatic injections of credit can set off an accelerating inflation (hyperinflation) that robs money of its utility.

Deflation, like inflation, is a secondary issue in the Austrian literature. Growth-induced deflation, that is, the decline in some overall price index that accompanies increases in real output, is considered a non-problem. Price reductions occur wherever supply and demand conditions warrant. Here, the microeconomic forces that govern individual markets are fully in play.

Deflation caused by a severe monetary contraction is another matter. Strong downward pressures on prices in general put undue burdens on market mechanisms. Unless, implausibly, all prices and wages adjust instantaneously to the lower money supply, output levels will fall. Monetary contraction could be the root cause of a downturn – as, for instance, it seems to have been in the 1936–7 episode in the USA. The Federal Reserve, failing to understand the significance of the excess reserves held by commercial banks, dramatically increased reserve requirements, causing the money supply to plummet as banks rebuilt their cushion of free reserves. But what caused the money supply to fall at the end of the 1920s boom? The monetarists attribute the monetary contraction to the inherent ineptness of the central bank or to the central bank's (ill-conceived?) attempt to end the speculative orgy in the stock market, an orgy that itself goes unexplained.

In the context of Austrian business cycle theory, the collapse in the money supply is a complicating factor rather than the root cause of the downturn. In 1929, when the economy was in the final throes of a credit-induced boom, the Federal Reserve, uncertain about just what to do and hampered by internal conflict, allowed the money supply to collapse. The negative monetary growth during the period 1929 to 1933 helps to account for the unprecedented depth of the depression. But like Keynes's focus on the loss of business confidence, the monetarists' focus on the collapse of the money supply diverts attention from the underlying maladjustments in the economy that preceded – and necessitated – the downturn.

## 9.13  Policy and Reform

The political attractiveness of the policy prescriptions based on the Keynesian theory (spending programmes, tax cuts, deficit finance and monetary expansion) and the absence of a comparable list of politically attractive policy prescriptions associated with the Austrian theory go a long way in accounting for the decisive victory in the 1930s of Keynesianism over Austrianism. Over the following decades, however, the cumulative effects of the excesses of Keynesian policy (debt monetization and double-digit inflation) eventually caused monetarism to be seen as the more responsible alternative. Endorsing monetarism – though not actually institutionalizing the monetary rule – became politically viable.

Although credit expansion was curtailed in the 1980s, there was never a sustained period of steady monetary growth at a pre-announced low rate. Further, monetary reforms enacted in that same period blurred the distinction between money and other highly liquid assets, making the implementation of the monetary rule all but impossible. The very definition of money became problematic, and the once-stable demand for money (as tracked by 'velocity' in the equation of exchange) itself became unstable. By default, the Federal Reserve reverted to managing interest rates, expanding credit to whatever extent was necessary to achieve its chosen target rate. With a pro-active central bank dominating credit markets, the natural rate of interest is a strictly non-observable rate, but to the extent that the central bank is sensitive to political considerations, the managed rate is more often than not below the natural rate.

The Austrians' policy advice to the central bank consists of prevention rather than cure: do not engage in credit expansion – not even if ongoing economic growth is causing some index of output prices to fall. Abiding by this imperative is not only politically difficult but also technically difficult, because the central bank cannot know what the natural rate of interest is and how it might be changing. The difficulties (both political and technical) of the central bank's avoiding a credit-induced boom suggest that what is needed is fundamental reform rather than policy prescription. Late in his career, Hayek recommended the *Denationalisation of Money* (1976). Subsequent writings by contemporary Austrians – Lawrence H. White (1989) and George Selgin (1988) – have made the case that a thoroughly decentralized banking system, one in which the market rate of interest is an unbiased approximation of the natural rate, may be the ultimate solution to the problem of boom and bust.

# 10. The new political macroeconomics

Most economists have now come to the realization that good economic advice requires an understanding of the political economy of the situation. (Rodrik, 1996)

## 10.1 Introduction: Political Distortions and Macroeconomic Performance

The relationship between the economy and the political system has always attracted the interest of economists since it is obvious that politics will influence the choice of economic policies and consequently economic performance. During the last quarter of the twentieth century research into the various forms of interaction between politics and macroeconomics has become a major growth area, giving rise to a field known as 'the new political macroeconomics', a research area which has developed at the interface of macroeconomics, social choice theory and game theory. This burgeoning field makes specific use of the modern technical apparatus of economic analysis to investigate numerous key public policy issues. Of particular interest to macroeconomists is the influence that the interaction of political and economic factors has on such issues as business cycles, inflation, unemployment, the conduct and implementation of stabilization policies, the relationship between dictatorship, democracy, inequality and economic growth, instability and conflict, the origin of persistent budget deficits, international integration and the size of nations. Major contributions to this field of activity, both in terms of theoretical analysis and empirical investigation, have come from the research of economists such as Daron Acemoglu, Alberto Alesina, Alan Drazen, Bruno Frey, Douglass Hibbs, William Nordhaus, Douglass North, Mancur Olson, Kenneth Rogoff, Fredrich Schneider, and Andrei Shleifer (see Willett, 1988; Persson and Tabellini, 1990; Alesina and Rosenthal, 1995; Keech, 1995; Alesina and Roubini with Cohen, 1997; Drazen, 2000a, 2000b; Gartner, 2000; Olson, 2000; Hibbs, 2001; Besley and Case, 2003; Acemoglu and Robinson, 2005).

In this chapter we will examine some of the progress that has been made with regard to the development of the 'new political macroeconomics'.

## 10.2  Political Influences on Policy Choice

Keynes (1926) believed that capitalism 'can probably be made more efficient for attaining economic ends than any alternative yet in sight'. However, for that to be the case would necessarily involve an extension of government intervention in the economy. Classical economists did not deny that fluctuations in aggregate economic activity could occur, but they firmly believed that the self-correcting forces of the price mechanism would prevail and restore the system to full employment within an acceptable time period. By the mid-1920s Keynes was already expressing his disillusionment with this classical *laissez-faire* philosophy which presented a vision of capitalist market economies where order and stability were the norm. For Keynes the wise management of capitalism was defended as the only practicable means of 'avoiding the destruction of existing economic forms in their entirety'. Hence the orthodox Keynesian view evolved out of the catastrophic experience of the Great Depression and suggested that market economies are inherently unstable. Such instability generates welfare-reducing fluctuations in aggregate output and employment (see Chapters 1–3). As a result, 'old' Keynesians argue that this instability can and should be corrected by discretionary monetary and fiscal policies (see Modigliani, 1977; Tobin, 1996). Implicit in this orthodox Keynesian view is the assumption that governments actually desire stability.

Michal Kalecki (1943) was one of the first economists to challenge this rather naive assumption by presenting a Marxo-Keynesian model where a partisan government, acting on behalf of capitalist interests, deliberately creates politically induced recessions in order to reduce the threat to profits resulting from the enhanced bargaining power of workers. This increased bargaining power is acquired as a direct result of prolonged full employment. In Kalecki's model it is the dominance of capitalists' interests which, by generating an unrepresentative political mechanism, causes the political business cycle (see Feiwel, 1974). Akerman (1947), anticipating later developments, suggested that the electoral cycle, by influencing economic policies, would also contribute to aggregate instability. This of course runs counter to traditional Keynesian models which treat the government as exogenous to the circular flow of income and in which politicians are assumed to act in the interests of society. According to Harrod (1951), Keynes was very much an élitist who assumed that economic policy should be formulated and implemented by enlightened people drawn from an intellectual aristocracy. These 'presuppositions of Harvey road' imply that Keynes thought that economic policies would always be enacted in the public interest. This benevolent dictator image of government acting as a platonic guardian of social welfare has increasingly been questioned by economists. In particular the work of public choice economists has called into question the assumption that elected politicians will always pursue policies aimed at maximizing net social benefit (see Buchanan et al., 1978). During the early days of the Keynesian revolution Joseph Schumpeter also recognized that, since capitalist democracies are inhabited by politicians who compete for votes, this will inevitably influence policy decisions and outcomes (see Schumpeter, 1939, 1942). For example, from a public choice perspective Keynesian economics is seen to have fundamentally weakened the fiscal constitutions of industrial democracies by giving respectability to the idea that budget deficits should be accepted as a method of reducing the risk of recessions. Buchanan et al. (1978) argue that such a philosophy, operating within a democratic system where politicians are constantly in search of electoral favour, inevitably leads to an asymmetry in the application of Keynesian policies. Because voters do not understand that the government faces an intertemporal budget constraint, they underestimate the future tax liabilities of debt-financed expenditure programmes, that is, voters suffer from 'fiscal illusion' (see Alesina and Perotti, 1995a). Instead of balancing the budget over the cycle (as Keynes intended), in accordance with Abba Lerner's (1944) principle of functional finance, stabilization policies become asymmetric as the manipulation of the economy for electoral purposes generates a persistent bias towards deficits. A deficit bias can also result from strategic behaviour whereby a current government attempts to influence the policies of future governments by manipulating the debt (Alesina, 1988).

Given these considerations, it would seem that macroeconomists ought to consider the possibility that elected politicians may engage in 'economic manipulation for political profit' (Wagner, 1977). In the neoclassical political economy literature government is no longer viewed as exogenous; rather it is (at least) partially endogenous and policies will reflect the various interests in society (Colander, 1984). This is certainly not a new insight, as is evident from the following comment taken from Alexis de Tocqueville's famous discussion of *Democracy in America* (1835):

> It is impossible to consider the ordinary course of affairs in the United States without perceiving that the desire to be re-elected is the chief aim of the President ... and that especially as [the election] approaches, his personal interest takes the place of his interest in the public good.

Although Keynes had an extremely low opinion of most politicians, in the context of his era it never really crossed his mind to view the political process as a marketplace for votes. What Keynes had in mind was what can be described as a linear model of the policy-making process whereby the role of the economist is to offer advice, predictions and prescriptions, based on sound economic analysis, to role-oriented politicians responsible for policy making. In turn, it is assumed that that because politicians are looking for

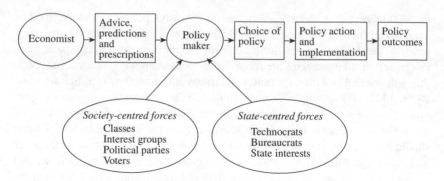

*Source*:   Adapted from Meier (1995).

*Figure 10.1   Influences on policy choice*

efficient solutions to major economic problems, they will automatically take the necessary actions to maximize social welfare by following the impartial and well-informed advice provided by their economic advisers. The traditional economists view of the policy-making process is illustrated in the upper part of Figure 10.1.

The conventional approach to the analysis of policy making traditionally adopted the approach of Tinbergen (1952) and Theil (1956). For example, in the traditional optimizing approach pioneered by Theil the policy maker is modelled as a 'benevolent social planner' whose only concern is to maximize social welfare. Thus the conventional normative approach to the analysis of economic policy treats the government as exogenous to the economy. Its only interest is in steering the economy towards the best possible outcome. Economic policy analysis is reduced to a technical exercise in maximization subject to constraint.

From a new political economy perspective policy makers will be heavily influenced by powerful societal and state-centred forces rather than acting impartially on the advice of economists. Therefore the theoretical insights and policy advice based on those insights that economists can offer are mediated through a political system that reflects a balance of conflicting interests that inevitably arise in a country consisting of heterogeneous individuals. In the society-centred approach, various groups exert pressure on the policy maker to 'supply' policies that will benefit them directly or indirectly. While neo-Marxists typically focus on class struggle and the power of the capitalist class, the new political economy literature highlights the influence of interest groups (for example farmers), political parties and voters. In the state-centred approach, emphasis on the role of technocrats is equivalent to accepting the 'benevolent dictator' assumption. In contrast, the new political economy literature focuses on the impact that bureaucrats and state interests exert on the policy maker.

The traditional approach to the policy-making process adopted by economists was neatly summarized by Tony Killick (1976) many years ago, in a critique of 'The Possibilities of Developent Planning':

> Economists have adopted a rational actor model of politics. This would have us see governments as composed of publicly-spirited, knowledgeable, and role-oriented politicians: clear and united in their objectives; choosing those policies which will achieve optimal results for the national interest; willing and able to go beyond a short-term point of view. Governments are stable, in largely undifferentiated societies; wielding a centralized concentration of power and a relatively unquestioned authority; generally capable of achieving the results they desire from a given policy decision.

In reality, societies are often fragmented and heterogeneous, especially if there are significant religious, ethnic, linguistic and geographical divides compounded by extreme inequalities of income and wealth. As a result governments will frequently be preoccupied with conflict management, representing particular rather than general interests, responding to a constantly shifting balance of preferences. In such a world concepts such as the 'national interest' and 'social welfare function' have little operational meaning. 'Decision making in the face of major social divisions becomes a balancing act rather than a search for optima; a process of conflict resolution in which social tranquility and the maintenance of power is a basic concern rather than the maximization of the rate of growth' (Killick, 1976).

In modelling politico-economic relationships the new political macroeconomics views the government as standing at the centre of the interaction between political and economic forces. Once this endogenous view of government is adopted, the welfare-maximizing approach to economic policy formulation associated with the normative approach 'is no longer logically possible' (see Frey, 1978). Incumbent politicians are responsible for the choice and implementation of economic policy, and their behaviour will clearly be shaped by the various institutional constraints that make up the political system. Accordingly, a politico-economic approach to the analysis of macroeconomic phenomena and policy highlights the incentives which confront politicians and influences their policy choices.

## 10.3 The Role of Government

What governments do, or do not do, will obviously have an important impact on economic growth and stability. Fiscal, monetary and exchange rate policies, along with policies towards international trade, competition, regulation, the labour market, education, technology, healthcare and the provision of key institutions such as property rights, all have a profound influence on economic performance. During the nineteenth century the economic role of government, as measured by government expenditure as a percentage of GDP, was around 10 per cent. By 1996 the government expenditure/GDP ratio had risen to an average of 45 per cent in developed OECD countries (see Tanzi and Schuknecht, 2000). This expanding role of government activity in all countries during the twentieth century reflects the influence of several factors, in particular:

1.  the impact of two world wars;
2.  the Great Depression and subsequent Keynesian revolution;
3.  the initial post-1945 influence of the Soviet state-led model of development;
4.  rising military expenditures associated with the cold war and global ideological competition between the USA and the USSR;
5.  the influence of socialist/humanitarian thinking and a growing concern for greater equity via income redistribution;
6.  the rise of welfare state capitalism;
7.  the general recognition by economists of a wider range of important market failures beyond those initially identified by Adam Smith, particularly widespread distortions created by externalities, imperfect information and the problems of aggregate instability (Stiglitz, 2000, 2002).

At the beginning of the twentieth century the role of the state in the economic sphere was minimal. However, over the past one hundred years we have witnessed a dramatic change in the balance of economists' vision of the appropriate role of government in economic affairs. For the first 75 years of the twentieth century the role of the state expanded but during the last quarter of the twentieth century there has been a marked change in economists' thinking on the desirability of this trend. This change, in large part, reflects the fact that over the past 25 years there has been an unmistakable convergence of beliefs among economists in the power of a market economy to deliver rising living standards compared to any known alternative.

What should be the role of government in an economy? This important question has been debated throughout history and permeates all important public policy issues. The current borders of the state have been mainly determined by historical events combined with developments in economic analysis that recognized the importance of both market failure and government failure.

While the 1950s and 1960s represent the high-water mark of economists' belief in the capacity of governments to correct market failures, the 1970s and 1980s witnessed increasing scepticism about the expanding role for government and saw a return of economists' faith in markets. Among economists there was a growing recognition of various forms of government failure. The state was doing much more, but doing it less well. Even in the case where a government is attempting to act as a benevolent social planner and intervenes to correct market failures, it must do so via the use of agents (bureaucrats) who actually implement the strategy. Because these agents are likely to be self-interested and difficult to monitor, government interventions invariably provide opportunities for rent-seeking behaviour and corruption. From the 1970s onwards, the debate on market failure versus government failure gathered momentum and became a key feature of the economics literature. Many economists, influenced by the critiques of economists such as Peter Bauer, Milton Friedman, James Buchanan, Friedrich von Hayek, Robert Lucas Jr and Anne Krueger, began to accept that the state was trying to do too much. In many countries this had deleterious effects on the efficient functioning of markets, economic growth and stability. The idea of government acting as a 'benevolent social guardian' and the dubious assumption that state agencies are populated by 'selfless bureaucrats' had been severely eroded by experience. This does not imply that capitalism is a perfect system, that markets always work efficiently, or that there is not an important role for government. But it does mean that throughout the world 'governments have come to plan less, to own less, and to regulate less, allowing instead the frontiers of the market to expand' (Yergin and Stanislaw, 1999). Markets and effective accountable government are complementary (see World Bank, 1997; Snowdon, 2001b; Stiglitz, 2002).

## 10.4 Politicians and Stabilization Policy

This 'Downsian' view of politicians indicates that government should be viewed as endogenous in macroeconomic models (see Downs, 1957). According to Frey (1978), the traditional Keynesian circular flow model needs to be modified to take account of self-interested government behaviour. The politico-economic system resulting from this modification is illustrated in Figure 10.2. There is no doubt that following the Keynesian revolution voters have increasingly held governments responsible for the state of the economy. But in choosing to whom they will delegate decision-making power, voters are faced with a *principal–agent* problem since the agent (government) may have different preferences which it can conceal from the imperfectly informed voters.

As is evident from Figure 10.2, in the politico-economic circular flow model politicians are seen to be driven by a balance of both ideological and re-election considerations. Voters evaluate politicians on the basis of how

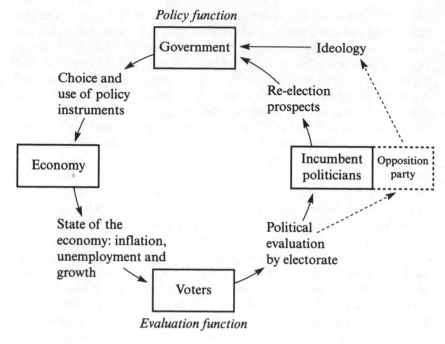

*Source*:   Adapted from Frey (1978).

*Figure 10.2   A politico-economic model*

successful they have been in achieving desirable economic goals such as high
employment, low inflation and rapid growth of real disposable incomes. The
state of the economy in the immediate pre-election period is crucial and
politicians are obviously aware that in order to survive in government it is
preferable to have a buoyant economy. If economic conditions are unfavourable, voters may well choose to elect the opposition party and the incumbents
lose office. Meanwhile the opposition party makes attractive promises to the
electorate (recall, for example, George Bush Sr's famous 1988 pre-election
pledge. 'Read my lips, no new taxes'). Hence economic conditions influence
election results and the incentive to get elected directly influences the choice
and use of macroeconomic policies.

   Politicians are also driven by partisan considerations, but ideological programmes cannot be implemented unless parties first of all win or maintain
power. During the past 25 years a considerable amount of empirical work has
been undertaken to test the importance of key macroeconomic variables
(such as inflation, unemployment and the growth of disposable income) for
the popularity of governments. This work indicates that such macroeconomic

variables are statistically significant and have an important influence on election outcomes (see Kramer, 1971; Tufte, 1975, 1978; Mosley, 1978; Fair, 1988; Schneider and Frey, 1988). Given that incumbent politicians occupy a position similar to that of a monopolist with respect to the supply of policies, it is hardly surprising that they may often succumb to temptation and use discretionary policies in order to maximize their re-election prospects.

During the past 20 years or so economists have produced a rich array of politico-economic models which incorporate many of these considerations. The interdependence between the economy and the polity is now a well-established area of research for economists interested in identifying the underlying causes of aggregate instability. This research has attempted to answer a number of interesting questions, for example:

1.  how important are economic factors in influencing voter choice? (Frey and Schneider, 1978a, 1978b);
2.  do opportunistic politicians manipulate the economy for political profit? (Nordhaus, 1975);
3.  do ideological (partisan) considerations lead to political parties producing a differentiated product? (Hibbs, 1977);
4.  can political cycles exist in a world of rational non-myopic voters and economic agents? (Alesina, 1987; Rogoff and Sibert, 1988);
5.  does the empirical evidence provide support for politico-economic models? (Alesina and Roubini with Cohen, 1997);
6.  what are the policy implications of such models? (Alesina, 1989; Drazen, 2000a).

In what follows we shall show how economists have attempted to answer these and other questions.

## 10.5 Alternative Approaches to the 'Political Business Cycle': An Overview

In the theoretical literature on the political business cycle, which has developed since the mid-1970s, we can distinguish four main approaches which have evolved in two separate phases. The assumptions underlying these four different approaches are summarized in Table 10.1 (see Alesina, 1988). During the first phase, in the mid- to late 1970s, Nordhaus (1975) reawakened interest in this area by developing an opportunistic model of the political business cycle. This was followed by Hibbs (1977), who emphasized ideological rather than office-motivated considerations. However, both the Nordhaus and Hibbs models (the 'old' political macroeconomics) were swept aside somewhat during the so-called rational expectations revolution which

*Table 10.1    Politico-economic models of aggregate fluctuations*

|                                          | *Assumptions about voters and economic agents* | |
| --- | --- | --- |
| *Assumptions about politicians* | *Non-rational behaviour, non-rational expectations* | *Rational behaviour, rational expectations* |
| Non-Partisan opportunistic politicians | Nordhaus (1975) | Rogoff and Sibert (1988) |
| Partisan ideological politicians | Hibbs (1977) | Alesina (1987) |

*Source*:   Alesina (1988).

dominated macroeconomic discussions during the mid- to late 1970s (see Chapter 5). After a period of relative neglect a second phase of politico-economic models emerged in the mid-1980s and research in this area has continued to flourish ever since. Due to the influence of new classical theorists these new models incorporate the assumption of rational economic agents and voters. While economists such as Rogoff and Sibert (1988) developed rational opportunistic models, Alesina (1987) produced a rational partisan theory (the 'new' political macroeconomics).

In what follows we shall examine all four of these approaches (plus the hybrid model of Frey and Schneider, 1978a, 1978b), each of which attempts to endogenize the influence of political behaviour on the macroeconomy.

## 10.6    The Nordhaus Opportunistic Model

The modern literature on political business cycles was stimulated by the seminal paper of Nordhaus (1975). In the electoral model popularized by Nordhaus the party in power 'chooses economic policies during its incumbency which maximize its plurality at the next election'. Since voters are influenced by a government's macroeconomic performance before an election, politicians will be tempted to manipulate policy instruments so that policy outcomes are most favourable around the election period. The important consequence of such behaviour is that policies are implemented in democracies which are biased against future generations (see also Lindbeck, 1976; MacRae, 1977). Thus while elections and electoral competition are necessary to increase the accountability of government, they are also likely to introduce potentially damaging distortions into the policy-making process. In producing this result Nordhaus makes a number of important assumptions, namely:

N1    The political system contains two parties between which there has been complete policy convergence as predicted by the median voter theorem of Downs (1957).

N2    Both parties are interested in maximizing political profit rather than engaging in ideological programmes. Only election outcomes matter to these *opportunistic* non-partisan politicians.

N3    The timing of elections is exogenously fixed.

N4    Individual voters are identical and have aggregate unemployment ($U_t$) and inflation ($\dot{P}_t$) in their preference functions and low inflation and unemployment rates are preferred. Policy makers are fully informed of voters' preferences but have no specific preferences with respect to inflation and unemployment.

N5    Voters make political choices based on the past performance of incumbent politicians in managing the economy during their term of office. Not only are voters *retrospective* in their voting behaviour (they have no foresight); they also have a decaying memory (a high discount rate on past economic performance), that is, they are *myopic*.

N6    The macroeconomic system can be described by an expectations-augmented Phillips curve where the short-run trade-off is less favourable than the long-run trade-off. Voters are ignorant of the macroeconomic framework.

N7    Expectations of inflation ($\dot{P}_t^e$) are formed adaptively, that is, agents are backward-looking.

N8    Policy makers can control the level of unemployment by manipulating aggregate demand via fiscal and monetary policies.

Nordhaus assumes (N4) that policy decisions will be based on the observed aggregate voting function ($V_t$) which reflects individual preferences; this is described by equation (10.1):

$$V_t = g(U_t, \dot{P}_t), \text{ where } g'(U_t) < 0, \text{ and } g'(\dot{P}_t) < 0 \qquad (10.1)$$

In equation (10.1) votes are a decreasing function of $\dot{P}$ and $U$. Figure 10.3 shows the contours (iso-vote lines) of the aggregate voting function ($V_1$, $V_2$ and so on), which indicate the percentage of votes acquired by the incumbents for a given policy outcome. Since inflation and unemployment are 'bads', $V_1 > V_2 > V_3 > V_4$. Voters prefer any point on $V_1$ to any point on $V_2$ but are indifferent between points on the same contour. Governments seeking to win elections will endeavour to manipulate the economy towards the highest feasible vote contour so as to coincide with the election period.

The macroeconomic framework adopted by Nordhaus involves an expectations-augmented Phillips curve framework summarized by equations (10.2)–(10.5).

Expectations-augmented Phillips curve:

$$\dot{P}_t = f(U_t) + \lambda \dot{P}_t^e \qquad (10.2)$$

Adaptive expectations hypothesis:

$$\dot{P}_t^e - \dot{P}_{t-1}^e = \alpha[\dot{P}_{t-1} - \dot{P}_{t-1}^e], \text{ and } \alpha > 0 \qquad (10.3)$$

Equilibrium condition:

$$\dot{P}_t = \dot{P}_t^e \qquad (10.4)$$

Long-run Phillips curve trade-off:

$$\dot{P}_t = \frac{f(U)}{(1-\lambda)} \qquad (10.5)$$

Nordhaus assumes that $1 > \lambda > 0$ which yields a long-run Phillips curve which is less favourable (steeper) than the short-run relationship. In Figure 10.3 the short-run curves are indicated by $S_G$, $S_W$ and $S_M$ and the position of each curve depends on the expected rate of inflation. The long-run Phillips curve is labelled *LRPC*. If the $\lambda$ coefficient is unity, the Phillips curve becomes a vertical line at the natural rate of unemployment (see Friedman, 1968a). However, as Nordhaus (1975, p. 176) notes, 'a vertical long-run Phillips curve makes no difference in principle' to the substantial conclusions of the model.

### 10.6.1 Optimal inflation and unemployment

Given assumption N4, the social welfare function (*W*) of the policy makers will be the discounted value of the aggregate voting function. In the absence of political constraints a social planner will seek to maximize the welfare function given by equation (10.6) subject to the macroeconomic constraints given by equations (10.2)–(10.5):

$$W = \int_0^\infty g(U_t, \dot{P}_t)_e^{-rt} \, dt \qquad (10.6)$$

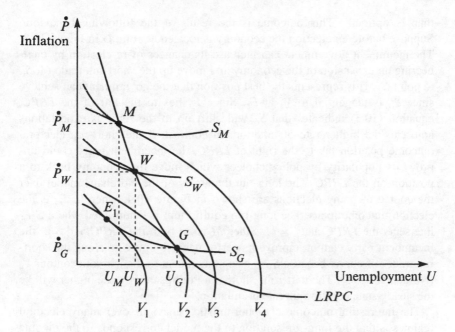

*Figure 10.3   The Nordhaus political business cycle model*

There are several possible outcomes depending on the policy makers' choice of discount rate ($r$). Where future generations are given the same weight as the current generation ($r = 0$), the outcome is indicated by $G$ in Figure 10.3. Here the *LRPC* is at a tangent to the aggregate voting function ($V_2$) and this represents the best sustainable combination of inflation and unemployment. Nordhaus calls this outcome the 'golden rule' policy solution, which involves inflation = $\dot{P}_G$ and unemployment = $U_G$. Where the policy makers care only about the current generation (infinite discount rates are applied) a 'purely myopic' policy results in an outcome indicated in Figure 10.3 by point $M$, where $S_M$ is at a tangent to $V_4$. In other words, 'myopic' policies which ignore the welfare of future generations lead to higher inflation ($\dot{P}_M$) and lower unemployment ($U_M$) than golden rule policies (Nordhaus, 1975). Where the policy maker cares about both generations ($\infty > r > 0$), an outcome Nordhaus refers to as the 'general welfare optimum' ($W$) results. In this case $U = U_W$ and $\dot{P} = \dot{P}_W$.

### 10.6.2   Long-run implications of the Nordhaus model

Where incumbent politicians are concerned about their re-election prospects, the Nordhaus model predicts that 'democratic systems will choose a policy on the long-run trade-off that has lower unemployment and higher inflation than is optimal'. This outcome is the result of the following behaviour. Suppose before an election the economy is located at point $G$ in Figure 10.3. The incumbent government can increase its chances of re-election by engineering an expansion of the economy and move up the short-run trade-off $S_G$ to point $E_1$. This represents the best position that the government can achieve since $S_G$ is tangential to $V_1$ at $E_1$. Since $E_1$ lies to the left of the *LRPC*, equation (10.3) indicates that $S_G$ will shift up to the right as expectations adjust to the higher rate of inflation. In contrast, if the short-run electoral outcome position lay to the right of *LRPC*, the incumbent party could improve its popularity by policy choices which move the economy back to a position on the *LRPC*. The long-run dynamics of the Nordhaus model over the course of many elections are shown in Figure 10.4, where $E_0 E_0$ is the election outcome locus. The long-run equilibrium is determined where $E_0 E_0$ intersects the *LRPC* at $E^* = M$. Since $M$ is on both the *LRPC* and $S_M$, 'the incumbent party cannot improve its performance by moving along the short-run trade-off curve' because $S_M$ is also at a tangent to the iso-vote contour $V_4$ (Nordhaus, 1975). The flatter the short-run Phillips curves, the higher will be the steady state equilibrium rate of inflation.

The interesting outcome of opportunistic behaviour over many electoral regimes is that the long-run solution to the model corresponds to the myopic position $M$. Thus democratic systems are predicted to produce a steady state equilibrium with higher inflation and lower unemployment than is optimal,

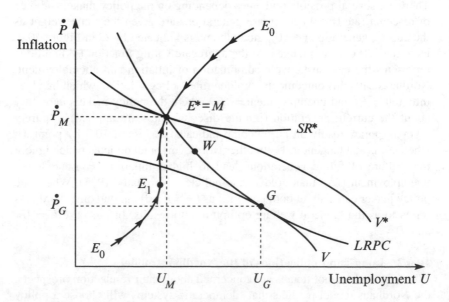

*Figure 10.4   The long-run solution in the Nordhaus model*

that is, an inflation bias (with $\lambda = 1$ and a vertical Phillips curve, the outcome involves an inflation bias only).

### 10.6.3 Short-run outcomes: the 'political business cycle'

In his analysis of short-run behaviour, Nordhaus introduces the possibility that voters have a 'decaying memory' (assumption N5). Voters place more weight on recent events than distant events from the past. In this case equation (10.1) is replaced by (10.7), where $T$ is the length of the electoral period and $z$ is the decay rate of voters' memories:

$$V_T = \int_0^T g(U_t, \dot{P}_t)_e^{zt}\, dt \qquad (10.7)$$

The modified vote function (10.7) indicates that although voters hold the government responsible for inflation and unemployment in the current period, their decaying memory provides the incumbents with the opportunity to systematically fool the electorate. A typical short-run political business cycle would progress as follows. As before, suppose the economy is initially located at point $G$ in Figure 10.3 in the period immediately preceding an election. By expanding aggregate demand the government can lower unemployment and achieve a position such as $E_1$, which will generate more votes than is possible at $G$ (that is, $V_1 > V_2$). The cost of this manoeuvre is a (delayed) acceleration of inflation ($S_G$ eventually shifts up to the right as expectations adjust). However, this cost tends to arise after the election has already been won. Even if inflation accelerates just before the election, with adaptive expectations it will take time for economic agents and voters to realize that inflation has increased. Having caused higher inflation, the government now needs to reduce it. Therefore, immediately following an election victory the government will deflate aggregate demand which, by increasing unemployment, will eventually reduce inflationary expectations, thereby shifting the short-run Phillips curve back towards $S_G$. Because voters have a decaying memory, this strategy can be repeated at the next election: recent events are 'more poignant' than 'ancient ills'. Hence the government can benefit from opportunistic behaviour which deliberately destabilizes the economy to produce a politically induced business cycle. This outcome is clearly at odds with the basic Keynesian notion that a major objective of government is to stabilize the economy.

The Nordhaus model gives clear predictions about the pattern of unemployment and inflation during the electoral cycle. In the first half of an electoral period unemployment should be rising, GDP falling and inflation (eventually) falling. In the run-up to an election, the second half of the electoral period should be characterized by falling unemployment and rising GDP. In the immediate post-electoral period inflation rises and a recession sets in. Nordhaus tested this hypothesis for nine countries over the period

1947–72 and concluded that 'given both casual and formal evidence of economic behaviour, and the historical record in the countries examined, it is clear that a political business cycle is a significant factor in the operation of *some* capitalist economies' (Nordhaus, 1975, emphasis added). Later, Nordhaus (1989) argued that there can be no monocausal explanation of the political influences on economic cycles, but in his view the impact of ideological considerations remained secondary to opportunistic behaviour.

Perhaps the best example of opportunistic behaviour was observed towards the end of the first term of Richard Nixon's Presidency in the USA. The deliberately induced 1970–71 recession was quickly reversed by expansionary policies in the run-up to the 1972 election. According to Tufte (1978), Nixon ensured that all social security recipients received a letter in the period just before the 1972 presidential election. With each letter was a cheque containing a social security benefits increase of 20 per cent. Apparently Nixon was concerned that his defeat by Kennedy in 1960 was due to the failure of President Eisenhower to reflate the economy. It is therefore hardly surprising that Richard Nixon has been described by Rogoff (1988) as the 'all time hero of political business cycles'.

Given the potentially serious nature of this phenomenon, Nordhaus suggested a number of possible remedies which included increasing the information available to voters and entrusting monetary policy to an independent central bank (see section 10.13).

## 10.7   The Hibbs Partisan Model

In the Nordhaus model there is policy convergence in that all governments behave in the same opportunistic way, and all voters are assumed to have identical preferences over inflation and unemployment. An alternative approach is to view voters and politicians as *ideological* or *partisan*. Politicians view winning elections as a means of putting into action their partisan programme and heterogeneous voters will clearly have different preferences over inflation and unemployment. Hibbs (1977) examined the post-war patterns of economic policies and outcomes in 12 advanced capitalist democracies for the period 1945–69 in order to test the proposition that left- and right-wing governments have different preferences with respect to the trade-off between inflation and unemployment. In particular, Hibbs argues that his evidence supports the proposition that left-wing governments prefer a lower $U$, higher $P$ outcome than right-wing governments. We can represent this difference in preferences in terms of differences in loss functions. Equations (10.8) and (10.9) show the loss (cost) functions in terms of unemployment and inflation for two parties, a right-wing party = $C_R$, and a left-wing party = $C_L$ (see Alesina, 1987).

$$C_R = \frac{(U_R - U_R^*)^2}{2} + \phi_R \frac{(\dot{P}_t - \dot{P}_R^*)^2}{2} \tag{10.8}$$

$$C_L = \frac{(U_L - U_L^*)^2}{2} + \phi_L \frac{(\dot{P}_t - \dot{P}_L^*)^2}{2} \tag{10.9}$$

Here $U_R^*$ and $\dot{P}_R^*$ are the unemployment and inflation targets of the right wing party and $\phi_R$ is the relative weight placed on deviations of inflation from target $(\dot{P}_t - \dot{P}_R^*)$ relative to deviations of unemployment from target $(U_R - U_R^*)$. The partisan differences can be summed up as follows.

$$U_L^* \leq U_R^*$$

$$\dot{P}_L^* \geq \dot{P}_R^*$$

$$\phi_L \leq \phi_R$$

Partisan effects are further illustrated in Figure 10.5, where *RR* and *LL* indicate the respective preferences of right- and left-wing politicians. Given the assumption of a stable exploitable Phillips curve trade-off, left-wing governments will choose a combination of $\dot{P}_L$ and $U_L$, indicated by point $L^*$, and right-wing governments will choose a combination of $\dot{P}_R$ and $U_R$, indicated by point $R^*$.

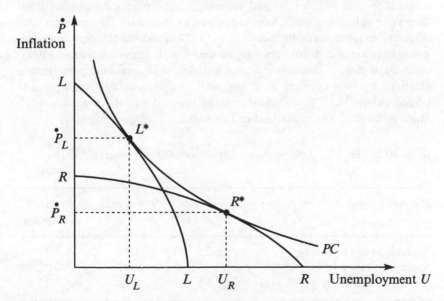

*Figure 10.5   The Hibbs partisan model*

According to Hibbs, 'different unemployment/inflation outcomes have important class-linked effects on the distribution of national income'. The revealed preference of policy makers reflects the interests of the social groups who typically provide support for different parties. Since macroeconomic policies have distributional consequences, Hibbs rejects Nordhaus's assumption (N1) of policy convergence. According to Hibbs, the empirical evidence supports the partisan view that 'a relatively low unemployment–high inflation macroeconomic configuration is associated with substantial relative and absolute improvements in the economic well-being of the poor'. Because tight labour markets tend to generate income-equalizing effects, we should expect left-wing governments to favour a point on the Phillips curve trade-off indicated by $L^*$. Right-wing parties view inflation as more damaging to their constituency of upper middle-class voters and choose a position such as $R^*$.

According to Hibbs, the empirical evidence supports the ideological view of macroeconomic policy making. The differing interests of various occupational groups is reflected in the policy preferences of left- and right-wing political parties. In an examination of 12 Western European and North American countries over the period 1945–69 Hibbs found strong support for the proposition that the mean inflation rate is higher and the mean unemployment rate lower, the greater the percentage of years that labour/socialist parties have been in office. In addition to the static aggregated evidence, Hibbs also found that the time series evidence for the USA and the UK supports the proposition that Democratic and Labour administrations have usually reduced unemployment while Republican and Conservative governments have tended to increase unemployment. Hibbs (1987) also reports significant partisan effects on the distribution of income and Bartels and Brady (2003) conclude that the 'consistent partisan differences in economic performance identified by Hibbs remain alive and well two decades later' and partisan influences have had a 'profound influence on the workings of the US economy'. These influences are summarized in Table 10.2.

*Table 10.2   Partisan influence on macroeconomic outcomes, USA, 1948–2001*

| Macroeconomic outcomes | Republican presidents | Democratic presidents | Partisan difference |
|---|---|---|---|
| Average unemployment (%) | 6.35 | 4.84 | 1.51 |
| Average inflation (%) | 3.95 | 3.97 | −0.02 |
| Average annual GDP growth (%) | 2.86 | 4.08 | −1.22 |

*Source*:   Adapted from Bartels and Brady (2003).

Hence there is evidence supporting the Hibbs model that systematic differences exist in the policy choices and outcomes of partisan governments. Hibbs argues that this is in line with the subjective preferences of the class-based political constituencies of right- and left-wing political parties.

## 10.8 The Decline and Renaissance of Opportunistic and Partisan Models

The 1970s were a turbulent time for the capitalist democracies as the 'Golden Age' of low inflation, low unemployment and above average growth came to an end. The stagflation crisis of the 1970s also brought to an end the Keynesian consensus which had dominated macroeconomic theory and policy making in the quarter-century following the Second World War. In the wake of the monetarist counter-revolution, Lucas inspired a rational expectations revolution in macroeconomics. By the mid-1970s models which continued to use the adaptive expectations hypothesis were coming in for heavy criticism from new classical theorists, as the hypothesis implies that economic agents can make systematic errors. In market-clearing models with rational expectations the assumption that economic agents are forward-looking makes it more difficult for the policy maker to manipulate real economic activity. There is no exploitable short-run Phillips curve which policy makers can use. Pre-election monetary expansions, for example, will fail to surprise rational agents because such a manoeuvre will be expected.

The rational expectations hypothesis also implies that voters will be forward-looking and will not be systematically fooled in equilibrium. According to Alesina (1988), 'the theoretical literature on political business cycles made essentially no progress' after the contributions of Nordhaus (1975), Lindbeck (1976) and MacRae (1977) because of the 'devastating' effect of the rational expectations critique. The Nordhaus model involves an exploitable short-run Phillips curve trade-off combined with myopic voters. Once the rational expectations hypothesis is introduced, however, voters can be expected to recognize the incentives politicians have to manipulate the economy for electoral profit. Given that US presidential elections are held on a regular four-year basis, it is difficult to believe that rational voters and economic agents would allow themselves to be systematically duped by the macroeconomic manipulations of self-interested politicians. Moreover, it is difficult to reconcile the predictions of the Nordhaus model with situations where monetary policy is conducted by an independent central bank, unless government can in some way pressurize the central bank to accommodate the incumbent government's preferred monetary policy (on this see Havrilesky, 1993; Woolley, 1994). However, Blinder, in discussing this issue, denies that political pressure was an issue during his period as Vice Chairman at the US Federal

Reserve, 1994–6. In his experience the political influence on monetary policy was 'trivial, next to zero', although he agrees that this was not the case during the Richard Nixon–Arthur Burns era (see Snowdon, 2001a).

The Hibbs model also has major theoretical shortcomings, especially with respect to the stability of the Phillips curve trade-off implicit in his analysis. Remarkably, Hibbs makes no mention of the expectations-augmented Phillips curve in his 1977 paper even though the Friedman–Phelps theory was a decade old and by then a well-established idea, even among Keynesians (see Gordon, 1975, 1976; Blinder, 1988b, 1992a; Laidler, 1992a). The assumption of rationality also has implications for the Hibbs model. Since the output and employment effects of expansionary and contractionary demand management policies are only transitory in new classical models, the identification of partisan influences on macroeconomic outcomes will be harder to detect (see Alesina, 1989). Alt (1985) concluded that partisan effects are not permanent but occur temporarily after a change of government.

In addition to the theoretical shortcomings of the early political business cycle literature, the Nordhaus model also failed to attract strong empirical support, with the econometric literature yielding inconclusive results (see Mullineux et al., 1993). While McCallum (1978) rejected the implications of the Nordhaus model for US data, Paldam (1979) could only find weak evidence of a political business cycle in OECD countries. Later studies, such as those conducted by Hibbs (1987), Alesina (1988, 1989), Alesina and Roubini (1992), Alesina and Roubini with Cohen (1997) and Drazen (2000a, 2000b), also find little evidence of a political business cycle in data on unemployment and GNP growth for the US and other OECD economies. This also applies where the timing of elections is endogenous (see Alesina et al., 1993). More favourable results for the Nordhaus model are reported by Soh (1986), Nordhaus (1989), Haynes and Stone (1990) and Tufte (1978), who found some evidence of pre-election manipulation of fiscal and monetary policy for the USA. In addition, Drazen (2000a) distinguishes between empirical predictions that focus on policy outcomes (inflation, unemployment, growth) and those that focus on policy instruments (taxes, government expenditure interest rates) and concludes that 'the evidence for opportunistic manipulation of macroeconomic policies is stronger than for macroeconomic outcomes'. With respect to policy outcomes there is more support for the opportunistic political business cycle theory coming from post-electoral inflation behaviour than can be found in the pre-electoral movement of real GDP and unemployment. Drazen also concludes that the evidence in favour of opportunistic manipulation of policy instruments is much stronger for fiscal policy than it is for monetary policy.

A significant problem for partisan theories in general is the argument and evidence presented by Easterly and Fischer (2001) that low inflation helps the poor more than the rich. Inflation acts as a financial tax that hits the poor disproportionately because they tend to hold more of their wealth in cash relative to their income than the rich, whereas the rich are more likely to have access to various financial instruments that allow them to hedge against inflation. In addition the poor obviously depend more on minimum wages and state-determined income payments that are not always indexed to protect against the effects of inflation (see Snowdon, 2004b). Easterly and Fischer present evidence drawn from an international poll of over 30 000 respondents from 38 countries and the responses indicate that the poor themselves are more strongly averse to inflation than those with higher incomes. This undermines a key assumption of Hibbs's model that the rich are more inflation-averse than the poor.

By the mid-1980s the politico-economic literature had reached a new ebb. Zarnowitz (1985), in his survey of business cycle research, devotes one footnote to the idea of an electoral cycle and refers critically to the 'strong' and 'questionable' assumptions of such models as well as the lack of supporting evidence. The same neglect is also a feature of Gordon's (1986) edited survey of *The American Business Cycle*.

Following a period of relative neglect, the literature on the relationship between politics and the macroeconomy underwent a significant revival since the mid-1980s (see Willet, 1988). Economists responded to the rational expectations critique by producing a new generation of rational politico-economic models. Like the first phase in the 1970s, the second phase of politico-economic models consisted of opportunistic and partisan versions of the interaction between politics and the macroeconomy. In the next two sections we examine the main features of rational political business cycle models and the rational partisan theory.

## 10.9 Rational Political Business Cycles

Recent work in the political business cycle tradition has shown that some of the insights of Nordhaus (1975) can survive even in a model with rational expectations, providing there is asymmetric information between voters and policy makers. In other words, voters need not be myopic in order for politicians to generate political business cycles. Optimal policies are only likely in a world of political competition when there is unanimity about social objectives and symmetric information between agents, voters and politicians. Since these conditions are unlikely ever to hold, politicians have the opportunity to follow non-optimal policies. Providing there is some element of imperfect information, so that forward-looking voters are not fully informed about some characteristics of the political and economic environment, incumbents have the opportunity of creating 'a temporary illusion of prosperity' (Alesina, 1989) in order to gain favour with the electorate.

In the rational opportunistic models proposed by Cukierman and Meltzer (1986), Rogoff and Sibert (1988), Rogoff (1990) and Persson and Tabellini (1990), electoral cycles are created in policy variables such as government spending, taxes and monetary growth, and such cycles are made possible by temporary information asymmetries. Although rational voters aim to choose politicians who they believe can deliver the highest utility, they lack information on the competence of different policy makers. Voters acquire information on competence by observing outcomes. Therefore before elections the incumbents engage in a 'signalling process' which aims to persuade voters that the politicians in power are competent. Such signalling is always observed in the UK during the Chancellor of the Exchequer's annual budget speech, especially just before an election.

Rogoff and Sibert define competence as the ability to reduce waste in the budget process; that is, competent governments can produce more public goods and transfers for a given amount of tax revenue. Incumbents have the potential to create a temporary fiscal boost (or fail to impose necessary tax increases), which is popular with voters. Because the budgetary process is so complicated the inevitable post-election tax increases needed to finance the pre-election boost are not foreseen even by rational voters, due to their incomplete information. Rather than generating a regular inflation–unemployment cycle as in the Nordhaus model, rational political business cycle theories predict the manipulation of various policy instruments before and after the election. The temptation of incumbents to cut taxes and increase spending before an election in order to appear competent clearly generates departures from optimality. Hence opportunistic behaviour survives in rational opportunistic models, although such models give rise to a different set of empirical predictions compared to the original Nordhaus model. In particular, because of rational expectations, any cycles resulting from the manipulation of monetary and fiscal policies will be predicted to be less regular and of shorter duration.

Finally, we should note that developing-country governments appear to behave in a similar way to their counterparts in richer countries. In a study of 35 developing countries Schuknecht (1996) found 'considerable evidence' in favour of election-generated fiscal policy cycles although the opportunities for self-interested political behaviour are less in more open economies.

## 10.10 Rational Partisan Theory

As noted earlier, Hibbs (1977), in his partisan theory of macroeconomic policy choices, argued that parties of the left will systematically select combinations of unemployment and inflation which differ from those preferred by right-wing parties. Following the rational expectations revolution, theorists questioned the ability of policy makers to influence real economic activity using aggregate demand management policies. Alesina, in a series of publications, has shown that the partisan theory of political business cycles can survive in models incorporating rational expectations providing (i) voters are uncertain about election outcomes, and (ii) uncontingent labour contracts are signed for discrete periods and are not subject to renegotiation after the election result is declared (see Alesina, 1987, 1988, 1989). In Alesina's model economic agents cannot enter into state-contingent nominal wage contracts that provide insurance against electoral risk. Central to the rational partisan theory is the idea that the political systems of many industrial democracies are polarized. Alesina rejects the traditional view of politicians' behaviour associated with Downs (1957) that vote-maximizing politicians in a two-party system will generate a convergence of policies, as both parties choose the policies favoured by the median voter (see also Minford and Peel, 1982). In the partisan theory politicians are ideological and adopt different policies when in power. 'There is no presumption that in a multi-party system with self-interested politicians one should observe policy convergence' (Alesina, 1989). In the case of the USA, empirical work has shown that although the degree of polarization has varied throughout American history, the Republican and Democratic parties have never fully converged (Alesina and Rosenthal, 1995). This in part reflects the fact that a presidential candidate has to appeal to the median voter in his/her own party in order to win the nomination. 'Since the platform adopted in the primary is a constraint on the choice of platform for the presidential elections, even self-interested politicians may have to choose polarized policies' (Alesina, 1989). Alesina follows Wittman (1977) and Hibbs (1977) and emphasizes the ideological preferences of politicians who aim to please their supporters by implementing policies which are likely to lead to a redistribution of income in their favour. Hence the rational partisan theory shows how parties follow different macroeconomic strategies because of their impact on the redistribution of income. It is assumed that voters are well aware of these ideological differences between the parties. In this framework macroeconomic policies create short-run aggregate disturbances because rational voters are uncertain about election results. When Republicans or Conservatives are elected, economic agents are confronted in the period immediately following the election with a deflationary shock, that is, inflation is lower than expected. When Democratic and Socialist governments are elected, the opposite occurs. There is a larger than expected 'inflation surprise'. It is the combination of election outcome uncertainty combined with ideological differences between the two parties that leads to aggregate instability in Alesina's model. If a common macroeconomic policy could be agreed between the two political parties aggregate fluctuations would be reduced.

The 'eclectic' macroeconomic framework adopted by Alesina is based on Fischer's (1977) well-known rational expectations model which includes a labour market where nominal wage contracts are signed and extend for considerable time periods (see Chapter 7). The 'neutrality' result or 'policy ineffectiveness proposition' associated with Lucas (1972a) and Sargent and Wallace (1975) depends on perfect (instantaneous) wage and price flexibility as well as agents having rational expectations (see Chapter 5). Fischer (1977) demonstrated that the crucial assumption for new classical results is instantaneous market clearing. With nominal wage contracts, an element of price stickiness is introduced into the model and in a non-market-clearing setting policy effectiveness is restored with monetary policy having real effects on aggregate output and employment. When ideological politicians use monetary policy in such a setting a rational partisan business cycle is generated.

How does this come about? Consider equations (10.10)–(10.13) below.

$$y_t = \beta[\dot{P}_t - \dot{W}_t] + y_{N_t}, \text{ and } \beta > 0 \qquad (10.10)$$

Ignoring capital accumulation, equation (10.10) shows that the rate of output growth ($y_t$) depends on the natural rate of growth of output ($y_{N_t}$) and positively on the difference between the rate of inflation ($\dot{P}_t$), and nominal wage growth ($\dot{W}_t$), that is, the path of real wages. (By Okun's Law unemployment and output are assumed to be inversely related and the natural rate of output growth is that which is compatible with the natural rate of unemployment.) Alesina uses output growth rather than the level of output since this is the variable that empirical research uses to capture partisan effects on the economy. If we assume that non-indexed nominal wage contracts lasting one period (for example, two years) are drawn up with the objective of maintaining a real wage consistent with natural output growth, we derive equation (10.11), which shows that nominal wage growth is set equal to the current expected rate of inflation ($\dot{P}_t^e$):

$$\dot{W}_t = \dot{P}_t^e \qquad (10.11)$$

Unlike the situation in the Nordhaus and Hibbs models, agents form their expectations rationally. The rational expectations hypothesis is given in equation (10.12):

$$\dot{P}_t^e = E[\dot{P}_t \mid I_{t-1}] \qquad (10.12)$$

Here $E$ is the mathematical expectations operator and $I_{t-1}$ indicates the information which has been accumulated by economic agents up to the end of time period $t-1$. By combining (10.10) and (10.11) we arrive at equation

(10.13), which tells us that output growth will deviate from its natural rate if there is an inflation surprise, that is, an unexpected change in monetary policy:

$$y_t = \beta[\dot{P}_t - \dot{P}_t^e] + y_{N_t} \tag{10.13}$$

In rational partisan models it is assumed that the incumbent politicians have the ability to control the rate of inflation by monetary policy. Since party preferences with respect to the extent of aversion to inflation differ, with the right being assumed to be more averse than the left, an election which brings about a change of government will lead to an inflation surprise, causing output to deviate from its natural growth path. Agents have rational expectations but are uncertain about forthcoming election results. Because agents sign nominal wage contracts before the election result is known, the rate of inflation forthcoming after the election can differ from the rational expectation of inflation formed by wage negotiators in the pre-election period. Consider the following possible sequence of events. Suppose the current administration is a party of the left (Democrats in the USA, Labour in the UK). Following Hibbs (1977), we can assume that left-wing governments have a reputation for wanting to lower unemployment. Wage negotiators, if they assume that the incumbents will win the election, will sign nominal wage contracts which have built into them a high expected rate of inflation. Even if the right-wing party looks like winning the election, risk-averse negotiators will probably sign contracts involving inflation expectations higher than would have been the case if agents knew for certain that the right would win. If a Conservative (inflation-averse) government replaces the left-wing incumbents, they will begin to tighten monetary policy in order to reduce inflation, thus creating a surprise which has not been built into the wage contracts. As a result, following an election victory by a Republican or Conservative party, the Alesina rational partisan theory predicts a recession in output growth and a rise in unemployment as inflation declines. The opposite sequence of events would follow a change in government from right to left (Maloney et al., 2003). In the period following an election, left-wing governments expand the economy and reduce unemployment. Eventually, when inflationary expectations adjust to the new situation, output growth returns to the natural rate but the economy is locked into an equilibrium with high inflation. The election of parties of the left will, according to Alesina's model, be followed by a cyclical pattern which is the opposite of that predicted by the Nordhaus model. In both cases expectations are assumed to adjust to the actual rate of inflation in the second half of a term of office, and from equation (10. 13) we can see that output growth will settle back to its natural rate for both right- and left-wing governments during this period of the electoral cycle. Since there are no election surprises in the second half of an administration's term of office, real variables settle down to their natural rates. However, because left-wing governments will be locked into a high-inflation equilibrium in Alesina's model, they may feel obliged to fight inflation before the next election. President Carter found himself in such a situation in 1979–80.

We can now summarize the predictions of the rational partisan theory of the business cycle:

A1    A change to a Conservative or Republican government will be followed by a recession and rising unemployment. Once inflationary expectations have been reduced, output growth returns to its natural rate. Inflation is low as the next election approaches.

A2    A change to a Labour or Democratic government will be followed by an acceleration of inflation as the economy expands more rapidly. Unemployment will initially fall. Once inflationary expectations adjust, output growth returns to its natural rate but inflation remains high. Should a government of the left attempt to fight inflation in the run-up to the next election, it will create a recession.

A3    The stronger the ideological convictions of the two parties, the greater will be the disturbance to output and employment following a change of policy regime after an election.

A4    Unlike the Hibbs model, the rational partisan theory predicts that differences in unemployment and growth resulting from changes in government will only be a temporary phenomenon.

### 10.10.1 Empirical evidence for rational partisan cycles

A considerable amount of empirical work has been done in recent years to test the rational partisan theory (see Alesina and Sachs, 1988; Alesina, 1989; Alesina and Roubini, 1992; Alesina and Rosenthal, 1995). These studies have found supporting evidence for temporary partisan effects on output and employment and long-run partisan effects on the rate of inflation as predicted. For the USA systematic differences have been found to occur in the first half, but not the second half, of a large number of administrations. This evidence is reported in Table 10.3. Although the rational partisan theory of Alesina and the political business cycle model of Nordhaus (1975) give similar predictions for Republican and Conservative administrations, the data in Table 10.3 do not show, on average, evidence of opportunistic behaviour. In line with the predictions of the Alesina model, 'Every Republican administration in the post-World War II period except Reagan's second one has started with a recession. No recessions have occurred at the beginning of Democratic administrations' (Alesina, 1995). The deep recessions in the US and UK economies following the elections of President Reagan and Prime Minister

*Table 10.3    Rates of growth of GDP in real terms*

| | Year | | | |
|---|---|---|---|---|
| | *First* | *Second* | *Third* | *Fourth* |
| *Democratic administrations* | | | | |
| Truman | 0.0 | 8.5 | 10.3 | 3.9 |
| Kennedy/Johnson | 2.6 | 5.3 | 4.1 | 5.3 |
| Johnson | 5.8 | 5.8 | 2.9 | 4.1 |
| Carter | 4.7 | 5.3 | 2.5 | -0.2[a] |
| Average | 3.3 | 6.2 | 5.0 | 3.3 |
| Average first/second halves | 4.8 | | 4.1 | |
| *Republican administrations* | | | | |
| Eisenhower I | 4.0 | -1.3 | 5.6 | 2.1 |
| Eisenhower II | 1.7 | -0.8 | 5.8 | 2.2 |
| Nixon | 2.4 | -0.3 | 2.8 | 5.0 |
| Nixon/Ford | 5.2 | -0.5 | -1.3[a] | 4.9 |
| Reagan I | 1.9 | -2.5 | 3.6 | 6.8 |
| Reagan II | 3.4 | 2.7 | 3.4 | 4.5 |
| Bush | 2.5 | 0.9 | -0.7 | – |
| Average | 3.0 | -0.3 | 2.7 | 4.3 |
| Average first/second halves | 1.4 | | 3.5 | |

*Note*:    [a] Oil shocks.

*Source*:    Economic Report of the President, 1992 (cited in Alesina, 1995).

Thatcher conform very well to predictions A1 and A3 above. Prediction A2 fits very well the experience in France in the period 1981–3. During the early part of the French Socialist administration of Mitterand, expansionary policies were pursued initially, even though many other major economies were in recession. Both President Mitterand and President Carter in the USA ended their administrations trying to fight inflation, although it should be recognized that the second OPEC oil-price shock complicates matters in the case of the Carter administration.

Alesina concludes that the more recent rational versions of politico-economic models of cycles have been much more successful empirically than the earlier models of Nordhaus and Hibbs. In particular, 'partisan effects' appear to be 'quite strong' while 'opportunistic effects' appear to be 'small in magnitude' and seem to affect only certain policy instruments, particularly fiscal variables (see Alesina, 1995). It is also well documented that during the Reagan and Thatcher administrations the income distribution consequences of the micro and macro policies were 'particularly partisan'. Inequality increased under both administrations (see Alesina, 1989).

### 10.10.2   Criticisms of the rational partisan theory

There are a number of important weaknesses in the rational partisan theory. First of all, if the cyclical effects are due to the signing of wage contracts before an election, then one obvious solution is to delay the signing of contracts until the election result is known. This solution is, of course, not as applicable where the timing of elections is fixed endogenously. However, in the USA wage contracts are staggered and overlapping, which means that at least a significant proportion of wage contracts will inevitably go over the election date. A second important criticism is that, in line with other models which assume nominal wage rigidity, the Alesina model implies a counter-cyclical real wage which is at odds with the stylized facts of the business cycle. For theoretical purists a third criticism relates to the lack of firm microeconomic foundations in such models to explain the mechanism of nominal wage contracting. Alesina (1995) describes this as the 'Achilles heel' of the rational partisan theory. A fourth line of criticism originates from the most recent generation of equilibrium business cycle theories. According to real business cycle theorists, monetary policy cannot be used to produce real effects on output and employment, although they agree that monetary growth determines the rate of inflation. In real business cycle models aggregate fluctuations are determined mainly by shocks to the production function, and such shocks are endemic. The pre-electoral behaviour of politicians and post-electoral monetary surprises are largely irrelevant. A benign monetary policy would not bring to an end aggregate fluctuations (see Chapter 6). A fifth criticism relates to hysteresis effects. If the natural rate properties of rational partisan models do not hold due to persistence effects following an aggregate demand disturbance, the political business cycle may be turned 'upside down' (see Gartner, 1996). A sixth criticism relates to the empirical evidence. In an extensive survey Carmignani (2003) concludes that monetary policy is not the source of political cycles in real variables (see also Drazen, 2000a, 2000b). Finally, some theorists argue that partisan and opportunistic models are not incompatible and a more complete model should incorporate both influences (see Frey and Schneider, 1978a, 1978b; Schultz, 1995). It is to this latter criticism that we now turn.

## 10.11   Opportunistic and Partisan Behaviour: A Synthesis

We have seen in our earlier discussion that opportunistic theories of the political business cycle assume that politicians are only office-motivated. Their macroeconomic policies are designed to win elections. Partisan theories stress ideological considerations and reject the assumption made in opportunistic theories that all parties will follow the same policies. Partisan theory rejects policy convergence. An alternative hypothesis is to follow the suggestion of Frey and Schneider (1978a, 1978b) that political parties behave in an opportunistic way when their chances of re-election are perceived to be low. Governments can use independent surveys to assess their popularity. When a party is 'popular' and confident of winning the next election, it can afford to indulge in ideological policies. Frey and Schneider (1978a) suggest that 'a government's lead over the opposition is determined by both the *state of the economy* and the *election cycle*'. This latter feature is the tendency of the incumbents to become less popular between elections (see also Alesina and Rosenthal, 1995). Incumbent politicians want to be re-elected in order to implement their ideological programmes, but may face an incentive structure which varies at each election. Because the temptation to use opportunistic policies is strongest when governments do not feel confident they can win the next election, opportunistic behaviour will be an increasing function of the incumbents' political insecurity. Such an approach can account for the lack of systematic evidence in support of opportunistic behaviour. Where political security is an important factor opportunistic policy manipulations should be observed before some elections but not all (see Schultz, 1995).

When considering the use of policy manipulations which have as their objective the maximization of re-election prospects, incumbents need to consider the marginal benefits and marginal costs of such policies. The marginal benefits of opportunistic behaviour, in the form of extra votes, are greatest when the government has a large popularity deficit. However, policy manipulations also generate extra costs to the incumbents in the form of loss of reputation, and this could damage long-term partisan support (see Schultz, 1995). Schultz argues that 'by engineering a pre-election boom, governments already open themselves up to charges of irresponsibility and opportunism'. However, 'when governments feel insecure in the current election, they can ill afford the luxury of being far-sighted and hence they discount the future quite heavily'. From these observations Schultz formulates the following hypothesis: '*The degree to which the government manipulates the economy prior to an election will be negatively correlated with its lead in public opinion polls at the time.*' Given the potential costs of policy manipulations, it is also the case that governments should only respond to popularity deficits close to the next election. Schultz tested this hypothesis for the manipulation of UK government transfer payments, which have significant and instantaneous effects on real disposable income. Schultz found that, with the exception of the October 1974 election, there is a clearly discernible negative correlation between growth of real transfers and the pre-election poll lead of the incumbents. These results are suggestive. The strength of the political business cycle effect in generating opportunistic behaviour will differ from one election to the next 'because the government's incentives also differ from one election to the next' (Schultz, 1995). Clearly more research is needed in this area. Table 10.4 summarizes the main features of the five main politico-economic models of aggregate fluctuations.

In his survey of what economists have learned from 25 years of research into the political business cycle, Drazen (2000b) concludes with a 'clear message' that:

> monetary surprises are an unconvincing force for political cycles, either opportunistic or partisan; research should concentrate on fiscal policy as the driving force, especially for opportunistic cycles. Political monetary cycles are more likely the effect of accommodation of fiscal impulses, that is, are passive while fiscal policy is active in trying to affect election outcomes.

## 10.12  Politics, Time Inconsistency, Credibility and Reputation

Following the incorporation of the rational expectations hypothesis into macroeconomic models, the theoretical literature on economic policy has been dominated by the game-theoretic approach. Policy makers are seen to be engaged in a complicated dynamic game with private sector economic agents (who are also voters). This literature was stimulated by the seminal paper of Kydland and Prescott (1977), who raised the general problem of *time inconsistency* of policy (see Chapter 5). According to Kydland and Prescott, governments that are free from rules (pre-commitment) so that they can use discretionary policies will be unable to persuade rational agents that they will stick to low-inflation policies. Agents know that if they lower their inflation expectations the government will have an incentive to cheat and, by creating an inflation surprise, increase employment temporarily. However, because rational agents are aware of the policy makers' incentives, the time-consistent policy involves an inflationary bias. If a government has discretion, low-inflation declarations are time-inconsistent and are not credible. Therefore a credible policy announcement can be defined as one which is time-consistent. Solutions to the time-inconsistency problem include contractual arrangements, delegation of decisions and institutional and legal constraints (see Drazen, 2000a).

As we have already seen, in industrial democracies subject to regular democratic elections, politicians have an incentive to deviate from optimal

*Table 10.4   Alternative politico-economic models*

| Politico-economic model | Main assumptions | Predictions |
|---|---|---|
| Non-rational opportunistic business cycle theory (Nordhaus, 1975) | Expectations-augmented Phillips curve. Politicians only care about re-election. Agents are myopic and have non-rational expectations. | All governments, both left and right, behave the same. Output will increase and unemployment will fall before an election. Inflation will accelerate as the election approaches but will peak and be observed by voters after the election. |
| Strong partisan theory (Hibbs, 1977) | Exploitable Phillips curve trade-off. Policy makers and voters are ideological and non-rational. Left-of-centre parties have a strong aversion to unemployment relative to inflation. Right-of-centre parties have a strong aversion to inflation relative to unemployment. | Governments of different ideological persuasions will have different macroeconomic objectives with respect to inflation and unemployment. Governments of the right will tend to have persistently higher unemployment and less inflation than governments of the left. |
| Rational opportunistic theory (Rogoff and Sibert, 1988) | Short-run Phillips curve trade-off. Agents have rational expectations, but imperfect information. Voters elect the party that they expect to perform best. Politicians care only about re-election. | All governments behave the same. Monetary growth and fiscal expansions before elections. |
| Rational partisan theory (Alesina, 1987) | Short-run Phillips curve trade-off. Agents have rational expectations, but election outcome uncertain. Left-of-centre parties have a strong aversion to unemployment relative to inflation. Right-of-centre parties have a strong aversion to inflation relative to unemployment. | Left-of-centre governments produce an inflation bias compared to right-of-centre governments. Output is above (below) the natural rate at the beginning of a left- (right-) of-centre government. The partisan effect of monetary policy on real variables is temporary. |
| Weak partisan theory. Opportunistic–partisan synthesis. (Frey and Schneider, 1978a) | Politicians alternate between partisan and opportunistic behaviour. Actual behaviour of politicians depends on their 'popularity surplus' in the polls. | If incumbent's popularity is in deficit (below some critical level) prior to an election, the incumbent switches from partisan to opportunistic behaviour. Incumbents with a popularity surplus behave ideologically. |

*Source:*   Adapted from Edwards (1994).

547

policies and create an inflation surprise. In the Nordhaus model there is an incentive to expand the economy before an election in order to gain votes. This is possible in the Nordhaus model because the policy makers never lose credibility due to the assumption of non-rational economic agents and myopic voters. In models with rational expectations and forward-looking voters, policy makers are under pressure to establish their credibility and reputation (see Blackburn and Christensen, 1989). By reputation in this context economists are referring to 'the actions that policymakers are *expected* to take' (Drazen, 2000a). In a game-theoretic context the reputation of a player will depend on the way they have played and reacted to events in the past. Rational agents will only believe politicians who make *ex ante* policy announcements which are also optimal to implement *ex post*. However, rational agents have imperfect information about the real motives of politicians as opposed to their pre-election promises. Therefore private sector agents will need to analyse carefully the various signals that politicians give out. In this scenario it may be difficult for voters to distinguish 'hard-nosed' (inflation-averse) from 'wet' (inflation-prone) politicians since the latter will always have an incentive to masquerade as 'hard-nosed' (see Backus and Driffill, 1985).

Alesina (1987) has shown that the prediction of the median voter theorem, that in a two-party system there will be policy convergence, is time-inconsistent. In the period before an election both parties find it in their interest to announce convergent policies on the assumption that this will appeal to the median voter. Ideological issues take back stage in order to maximize re-election prospects. However, because there is no mechanism for holding an elected government to its promises, these announced convergent policies must be time-inconsistent. After the election the influence of partisan considerations will predominate as the elected politicians re-optimize and follow a programme which best fits their ideological stance. Thus the time-consistent equilibrium involves no policy convergence and the two parties 'follow their most preferred policy' (Alesina and Tabellini, 1988). This inevitably creates too much volatility in policy making which, in turn, causes politically induced business cycles.

It follows from the above analysis that only those pre-election announcements and promises which are consistent with a party's ideology should be taken seriously by voters. Once elected, politicians will tend to follow a more partisan strategy. This may prove to be a particular problem for parties of the left that declare themselves to be 'tough on inflation'. Given the underlying assumptions of the Hibbs (1977) and Alesina (1987) models that politicians on the left give a high priority to reducing unemployment, voters may well look with suspicion at pronouncements claiming an aversion to inflation. Inflation-prone parties have an incentive to masquerade as 'hard-nosed' on this objective. Rational voters are likely to interpret such signalling as the 'dissembling actions of an impostor' (Blackburn, 1992). An implication of this is that 'a low inflation policy announced by a government concerned with unemployment would not be credible; indeed if expected inflation was low, this government would create an inflation surprise in order to reduce unemployment' (Alesina, 1989).

These issues were very pertinent in the UK in the run-up to the 1997 election. The 'New' Labour Party, led by Tony Blair, declared that it intended to be 'tough on inflation' and that it also aimed to achieve much lower unemployment. In terms of Alesina's model, the statement on inflation is clearly time-inconsistent. However, to give credibility to its anti-inflation rhetoric, on winning the 1997 election, new Labour immediately granted operational independence to the Bank of England (see Snowdon, 1997).

## 10.13 Policy Implications of Politico-Economic Models: An Independent Central Bank?

In introducing 'The New Monetary Policy Framework' for the UK economy on 6 May 1997, which established 'operational independence' for the Bank of England, Chancellor Gordon Brown, in an official statement, provided the following rationale for the government's strategy (Brown, 1997, emphasis added):

> We will only build a fully credible framework for monetary policy if the long-term needs of the economy, not short-term political considerations guide monetary decision-making. *We must remove the suspicion that short-term party political considerations are influencing the setting of interest rates.*

Chancellor Brown's decision to grant much greater independence to the Bank of England had its origins in a 1992 Fabian Society paper entitled 'Euro Monetarism', written by Ed Balls, Brown's economic adviser. As a former student of Larry Summers at Harvard, Balls was familiar with the empirical work on central bank independence produced by Alesina and Summers (1993). In a visit to the USA in March 1997, Shadow Chancellor Brown and his economic adviser met both Alan Greenspan and Larry Summers. And so was born the strategy to go for immediate greater central bank independence if elected.

The general debate on the relative merits of rules versus discretion in the conduct of fiscal and monetary policy was given a new stimulus by the research surveyed in Chapters 5 and 7. Since the non-optimal use of monetary and fiscal instruments lies at the heart of the various strands of the political business cycle literature, most of this work points towards the desirability of establishing a policy regime which curtails the incentives policy makers have to engage in destabilizing policies. The new classical contributions of Kydland and Prescott (1977) and Barro and Gordon (1983a), which highlighted time-inconsistency, credibility and reputational issues, have provided extra weight to the case for monetary rules associated with the work of Friedman (1968a). The politico-economic literature has also shown how strong partisan or opportunistic behaviour can generate a non-optimal outcome for aggregate variables. However, in order to make policy rules credible, some sort of enforcement mechanism is required. For this reason many economists in recent years have argued in favour of institutional reform involving the establishment of an independent central bank (see Goodhart, 1994a, 1994b). The assumption lying behind this argument is that such an institution (at least in principle) is capable of conducting monetary policy in a manner free from opportunistic and partisan influences. In addition, fiscal policy will also be subject to a harder budget constraint, providing the independent central bank is not obliged to monetize deficits (see Alesina and Perotti, 1995a). Greater central bank independence was also one of the objectives contained in the Maastricht Treaty, which sought to bring about some fundamental changes in national banking legislation in anticipation of European monetary union (see Walsh, 1995a, 1995b).

The case for central bank independence is usually framed in terms of the inflation bias present in the conduct of monetary policies. Such an inflation bias is evident from the relatively high rates of inflation experienced in industrial countries in the 1970s and early 1980s. Because a majority of economists emphasize monetary growth as the underlying cause of sustained inflation (see Lucas, 1996), it follows that prolonged differences in countries' rates of inflation result from variations in their rates of monetary expansion. Any plausible explanation of these 'stylized facts' must therefore include an understanding of central bank behaviour (Walsh, 1993). In particular, we need to identify the reasons why monetary policy is conducted in a way that creates a positive average rate of inflation which is higher than desirable. There are several reasons why monetary authorities may generate inflation. These include political pressures to lower unemployment in order to influence re-election prospects, partisan effects as emphasized by Hibbs and Alesina, dynamic inconsistency influences and motivations related to the financing of deficits. The last is particularly important in economies with inefficient or underdeveloped fiscal systems (see Cukierman, 1994).

The theoretical case for central bank independence in industrial democracies relates to a general acceptance that the long-run Phillips curve is vertical at the natural rate of unemployment. This implies that although monetary policy is non-neutral in the short run, it has little effect on real variables such as unemployment and output in the long run. With no exploitable long-run trade-off, far-sighted monetary authorities ought to select a position on the vertical Phillips curve consistent with a sustainable objective of price stability (see Goodhart, 1994b; Cukierman, 1994).

The empirical *case* for central bank independence is linked to cross-country evidence which shows that for advanced industrial countries there is a clear negative relationship between central bank independence and inflation (see Grilli et al., 1991; Cukierman, 1992; Alesina and Summers, 1993; Eijffinger and Keulen, 1995; Eijffinger, 2002a). It should be noted, however, that this negative correlation does not prove causation and fails to hold for a larger sample of countries which includes those from the developing world (see Jenkins, 1996). Poor countries with shallow financial markets and unsustainable budget deficits are unlikely to solve their inflation problems by relying on the creation of an independent central bank (Mas, 1995). However, at least as far as advanced industrial democracies are concerned, the theoretical and empirical work suggests that monetary constitutions should be designed to ensure a high degree of central bank autonomy.

Although the success of the independent German Bundesbank in delivering low inflation over a long period of time inspired other countries to follow its example, it is also clear that some important problems emerge with the measurement, form and consequences of central bank independence. First, the whole question of independence is one of degree. Although before May 1997 the Federal Reserve had much more independence than the Bank of England, it is clear that legal independence does not (and cannot) completely remove the influence of 'monetary politics' (see Mayer, 1990; Havrilesky, 1993; Woolley, 1994). For example, Chappell et al. (1993) show how partisan influences on the conduct of monetary policy can arise through presidential appointments to the Board of Governors of the Federal Reserve. Through these 'political' appointments and other forms of presidential signalling (moral suasion) the Federal Reserve's monetary policy making can never be totally independent of political pressures. Nevertheless, considerable research effort has been made in recent years to measure the extent of central bank independence in a large number of countries (see Cukierman, 1992; Eijffinger and Keulen, 1995; Healey, 1996). According to Cukierman, four sets of indices can be used to identify the degree of independence of a central bank: (i) legal indices; (ii) questionnaire-based indices; (iii) the turnover of central bank governors; and (iv) the political vulnerability of the bank. However, such studies and their implications have come in for considerable criticism (see Jenkins, 1996).

In discussing the form of central bank independence, Fischer (1995a, 1995b) introduces the distinction between 'goal independence' and 'instrument independence'. The former implies that the central bank sets its own policy objectives (that is, political independence) while the latter refers to independence with respect to the various levers of monetary policy (that is, economic independence). Using this framework the Bank of England was granted instrument (economic) independence but not goal (political) independence in May 1997. The distinction between goal and instrument independence can be used to illustrate the difference between the two main models of independent central banks which have been developed in the theoretical literature. The first model is based on Rogoff's (1985) 'conservative central banker'. In this model an inflation-averse conservative central banker is appointed who ensures that inflation is kept low in circumstances where it would otherwise be difficult to establish a pre-commitment to low inflation. Rogoff's inflation-averse central banker has both goal and instrument independence. The result is lower average inflation but higher output variability. The second model, associated with Walsh (1995b), utilizes a principal–agent framework and emphasizes the accountability of the central bank. In Walsh's contracting approach the central bank has instrument independence but no goal independence, and the central bank's rewards and penalties are based on its achievements with respect to inflation control. However as Walsh (1995a) notes:

> An inflation-based contract, combined with central bank independence in the actual implementation of policy, achieves optimal policy outcomes only if the central bank shares social values in trading off unemployment and inflation. When the central bank does not share society's preferences, the optimal contract is no longer a simple function of inflation; more complicated incentives must be generated to ensure that the central bank maintains low average inflation while still engaging in appropriate stabilization policies.

While the New Zealand Federal Reserve Bank, which was set up following the 1990 reforms, resembles the principal–agent model, the German Bundesbank, before EMU, comes close to the conservative central banker of the Rogoff model. In Fischer's (1995a) view, the important conclusion to emerge from this literature is that 'a central bank *should* have instrument independence, but *should not* have goal independence'.

In recent years many countries have set about reforming the institutions of monetary policy. Such countries include those of the former 'Eastern bloc' of communist economies as well as those from Latin America and Western Europe. Most have adopted some variant of the principal–agent approach whereby the central bank is contracted to achieve clearly defined goals, provided with the instruments to achieve these desired objectives, and held accountable for deviating from the chosen path (see Bernanke and Mishkin, 1992; Walsh 1995a). In the New Zealand model the central bank governor is accountable to the finance minister. This contrasts with the German Bundesbank, which was held accountable to the public. In both Canada and the UK, emphasis has been placed on inflation targeting. Failure to meet inflation targets involves a loss of reputation for the central bank. In the case of the UK, the approach adopted since 1992 has involved inflation targeting combined (since May 1997) with operational independence for the Bank of England (see Chapter 7).

One of the main theoretical objections to central bank independence is the potential for conflict that this gives rise to between the monetary and fiscal authorities (see Doyle and Weale, 1994). An extensive discussion of the problems faced by policy makers in countries where monetary and fiscal policies are carried out independently is provided by Nordhaus (1994). In countries where this has led to conflict (for example in the USA during the period 1979–82) large fiscal deficits and high real interest rates have frequently resulted. According to Nordhaus this leads to a long-run rate of growth which is too low. The tight monetary–easy fiscal mix is hardly surprising given the predominant motivations driving the 'Fed' and the 'Treasury' in the USA. Whereas independent central banks emphasize monetary austerity and low stable rates of inflation, the fiscal authorities know that increased government expenditure and reduced taxes are the 'meat, potatoes and gravy of politics' (Nordhaus, 1994). In this scenario the economy is likely to be locked into a 'high-deficit equilibrium'. Self-interested politicians are unlikely to engage in deficit reduction for fear of losing electoral support. These coordination problems which a non-cooperative fiscal–monetary game generates arise inevitably from a context where the fiscal and monetary authorities have different tastes with respect to inflation. At the end of the day these problems raise a fundamental issue. Should a group of unelected individuals be allowed to make choices on the use of important policy instruments which will have significant repercussions for the citizens of a country? In short, does the existence of an independent central bank threaten democracy (see Stiglitz, 1999a)? What is clear is that independence without democratic accountability is unacceptable (Eijffinger, 2002b).

There is now an extensive literature related to the issue of central bank independence. The academic literature has pointed to the various reasons why industrial democracies have developed an inflation bias in which governments are allowed discretion in the operation of fiscal and monetary policies. In contrast to Rogoff (1985), Alesina and Summers (1993) point to the empirical evidence which, for advanced industrial countries, shows that inflation is negatively correlated with the degree of central bank independence without this having significant adverse effects on real growth and employment in the long run. Central bank independence seems to offer a 'free lunch'! However, this issue is made more complicated by the causes of output variability. Alesina and Gatti (1995) distinguish between two types of variability which can contribute to aggregate instability. The first is economic variability resulting from different types of exogenous shocks to aggregate demand and/or supply. The second type is political or policy-induced and has been the subject of this chapter. Rogoff's conservative central banker does not react much to 'economic shocks'. However, Alesina and Gatti (1995) argue that an independent central bank will reduce policy-induced output variability. Hence the 'overall effect of independence on output induced variability is, thus, ambiguous'. It follows that in cases where policy-induced variability exceeds that resulting from exogenous shocks, a more independent central bank can reduce inflation and the variance of output, a result consistent with the Alesina and Summers (1993) data. To the critics, central bank independence is no panacea and the Alesina–Summers correlations do not prove causation (Posen, 1995). In addition, the numerous domestic and international policy coordination problems which independence can give rise to could outweigh the potential benefits. In the face of powerful 'economic' shocks a conservative and independent central bank may not be superior to an elected government.

## 10.14   The Political Economy of Debt and Deficits

During the mid-1970s several OECD countries accumulated large public debts. This rise in the debt/GNP ratios during peacetime among a group of relatively homogeneous economies is unprecedented and difficult to reconcile with the neoclassical approach to optimal fiscal policy represented by the 'tax smoothing' theory. While countries such as Greece, Italy and Ireland had accumulated public debt ratios in excess of 95 per cent in 1990, other countries such as Germany, France and the UK had debt ratios in 1990 of less than 50 per cent (Alesina and Perotti, 1995b).

In order to explain the variance of country experience and the timing of the emergence of these rising debt ratios, Alesina and Perotti (1995b) argue that an understanding of politico-institutional factors is 'crucial'. In explaining such wide differences Alesina and Perotti conclude that the two most significant factors are:

1. the various rules and regulations which surround the budget process; and
2. the structure of government; that is, does the electoral system tend to generate coalitions or single party governments?

In the face of large economic shocks weak coalition governments are prone to delaying necessary fiscal adjustments. While a 'social planner' would react quickly to an economic shock, in the real world of partisan and opportunistic politics a 'war of attrition' may develop which delays the necessary fiscal adjustment (see Alesina and Drazen, 1991). Persson and Tabellini (2004) have investigated the relationship between electoral rules, the form of government and fiscal outcomes. Their main findings are that: (i) majoritarian elections lead to smaller government and smaller welfare programmes than elections based on proportional representation; and (ii) presidential democracies lead to smaller governments than parliamentary democracies.

Research by Alesina and Perotti (1996b, 1997a) also indicates that the 'composition' of a fiscal adjustment matters for its success in terms of its sustainability and macroeconomic outcome. Two types of adjustment are identified: Type 1 fiscal adjustments rely on expenditure cuts, reductions in transfers and public sector wages and employment; Type 2 adjustments depend mainly on broad-based tax increases and cuts in public investment. Alesina and Perotti (1997a) find that Type 1 adjustments 'induce more lasting consolidation of the budget and are more expansionary while Type 2 adjustments are soon reversed by further deterioration of the budget and have contractionary consequences for the economy'. Hence any fiscal adjustment that 'avoids dealing with the problems of social security, welfare programs and inflated government bureaucracies is doomed to failure' (see Alesina, 2000). Type 1 adjustments are also likely to have a more beneficial effect on 'competitiveness' (unit labour costs) than policies which rely on distortionary increases in taxation (see Alesina and Perotti, 1997b).

## 10.15 Political and Economic Instability: Are They Related?

A further related area of research in the politico-economic sphere concerns the relationship between political and economic stability (see Carmignani, 2003). There are good reasons to believe that economic performance will suffer if a country is politically unstable. Frequent riots, politically motivated violence and revolution inevitably have a negative impact on a country's economic performance. As Keynes always highlighted, uncertainty has a depressing effect on investment and productive entrepreneurship.

Alesina's partisan theory predicts that instability will increase the greater the partisan effects because widely divergent policies create uncertainty and destabilize expectations. It is also unlikely that reputational considerations will be important to a government which feels that it has little chance of being re-elected. In this situation an incumbent has an 'incentive to follow particularly shortsighted policies, since it is not concerned with a future in which it is likely to be out of office' (Alesina, 1989).

A further destabilizing influence on policy arising from political instability derives from the inability of fragile coalition governments to carry through the tough but necessary economic policies crucial for long-run stability. Alesina (1989) finds a positive correlation between an index of political instability and Okun's misery index (inflation + unemployment) for the period 1973–86. An exception in his 20-country sample is the UK, which managed to combine relatively poor economic performance during this period despite having a high degree of political stability. In Alesina and Drazen's (1991) analysis of why necessary stabilization policies are frequently delayed, they consider a situation where two parties with different ideologies engage in a war of attrition as they each attempt to pass on the burden of fiscal reform to the other party's supporters. The resultant delay and government inaction in the reform process leads to debt accumulation and crisis before one of the parties is forced to accept a larger share of the fiscal burden. As Drazen (2000a) notes, 'the failure to adopt socially beneficial economic reforms or their adoption only after long delays is a leading example of the divergence between the simple textbook models of economic policymaking and real world experience'.

Considerable cross-country evidence now exists which indicates that seigniorage (the inflation tax) is positively related to the degree of political instability. In a study of 79 developed and developing countries for the period 1971–82, Cukierman et al. (1992) found evidence in support of their hypothesis that 'more unstable countries rely relatively more on seigniorage to finance the government budget than do stable and homogenous societies'. These conclusions are also supported by Edwards (1994), who found that the incentive to use inflationary finance is closely related to the volatility of the political system. In the extreme, hyperinflation may erupt (see Capie, 1991; Siklos, 1995; Fischer et al., 2002).

### 10.16  The Political Economy of Economic Growth

One of the most important adverse effects of political instability is its negative impact on economic growth. In Chapter 11 we discuss several strands in the new growth literature that focus on the deeper determinants of growth, including politics and institutions. Drazen (2000a) argues that the political economy of growth literature is a natural extension of the research on the political economy of income redistribution and in this chapter we review some recent research into the links between inequality, economic growth, dictatorship and democracy (see Alesina and Perotti, 1994; Alesina and Rodrik, 1994; Persson and Tabellini, 1994; Alesina and Perotti, 1996c; Benabou, 1996; Deininger and Squire, 1996; Aghion et al., 1999; Barro, 2000; Forbes, 2000; Lundberg and Squire, 2003).

In exploring the connection between inequality and economic growth we first of all need to distinguish between the 'old' view and the 'new' view. The old view dominated thinking in development economics throughout the 1960s and 1970s and is captured in the work of economists such as Arthur Lewis (1954) and Richard Nelson (1956). The old view is dominated by 'capital fundamentalism'; that is, capital accumulation is the key to economic growth. Capital fundamentalism is associated in particular with the wide acceptance

and use of the Harrod–Domar growth model within the development literature and development institutions such as the World Bank (see Easterly, 1999,
2001a, and Chapter 11). In order to foster high rates of accumulation, in the
absence of substantial inflows of foreign capital, a country must generate the
necessary resources through high rates of domestic saving. It was assumed
that inequality of income would produce this result since the rich were
assumed to have a higher propensity to save than the poor (see Kaldor, 1955).
This view is encapsulated in the following statement by Harry Johnson (1958):

> There is likely to be a conflict between rapid growth and an equitable distribution
> of income; and a poor country anxious to develop would be probably well advised
> not to worry too much about the distribution of income.

Another reason why inequality may lead to faster growth is linked to the idea
of investment indivisibilities, that is, the setting up of new industries frequently involves very large sunk costs. Meeting these costs in poorly developed
countries with inadequate financial markets requires the concentration of
wealth. Finally, it was also argued that without adequate incentives, investment rates would remain insufficient to generate sustained growth

That there was a trade-off between growth and equity dominated early post-
Second World War development thinking. In addition, the 'Kuznets hypothesis'
suggested that as countries develop, inequality will initially increase before
declining (see Kuznets, 1955). Hence the relationship between inequality and
GDP per capita shows up in both time series and cross-sectional data as an
inverted U-shaped relationship. Barro's (2000) empirical results confirm that
the Kuznets curve remains a 'clear empirical regularity'.

As economic development spread across the world during the latter half of
the twentieth century it became clear that there was an increasing number of
successful development stories where outstanding rates of economic growth
were achieved without those countries exhibiting high degrees of income
inequality, namely the Asian Tigers. In addition many countries, for example
in Latin America, with high inequality had a poor record of economic growth.
Hence, during the last decade there has been a change in thinking on this
issue. Several economists have begun to emphasize the potential adverse
impact of inequality on growth, an idea that had already been propounded by
Gunnar Myrdal (1973). Aghion et al. (1999) conclude that the old view that
inequality is necessary for capital accumulation and that redistribution damages growth 'is at odds with the empirical evidence'.

Various mechanisms have been suggested as possible causes of a negative
association between inequality and subsequent growth performance (see Alesina
and Perotti, 1994). The credit market channel highlights the limited access to
finance that the poor have in order to invest in human capital formation. Since
in this environment most people have to rely on their own resources to finance

education, a reduction in inequality could increase the rate of human capital formation and economic growth. A second 'fiscal' channel highlights the distortions and disincentive effects of taxation introduced under political pressure to reduce high inequality. Redistribution of income, by raising the tax burden on potential investors, reduces investment and consequently economic growth (Alesina and Rodrik, 1994; Persson and Tabellini, 1994). A third channel suggests that high inequality leads to a larger number of agents engaging in rent seeking, corruption and criminal activities. These activities threaten property rights and the incentive to invest. Glaeser et al. (2003) develop a model where inequality adversely influences economic outcomes by threatening property rights due to the subversion of legal, political and regulatory institutions by a rich, powerful élite. The answer to this problem is not to replace 'King John redistribution' with 'Robin Hood distribution', that is, not to replace an old corrupt oligarchy with a bureaucratic socialist oligarchy. Rather, the solution lies in institutional reform. According to Olson (2000), there are two key requirements for any society to prosper: first, the establishment of secure and well-defined individual rights with respect to private property and impartial enforcement of contracts, as capitalism is first and foremost a legal system; and second, the 'absence of predation of any kind'. The empirical evidence suggests that there 'is no society in the post-war world that has fully met the two foregoing conditions'. But clearly some economies have come much closer to the ideal than others and this is generally reflected in their long-term economic performance (Olson, 1996). Gyimah-Brempong's (2002) empirical analysis of corruption, economic growth and inequality in Africa finds that corruption is positively related to income inequality and hurts the poor more than the rich. To understand the political roots of economic success is a crucial research area for social scientists because, as Table 10.5 indicates, sub-Saharan Africa's 'Subjective indictors of governance' make depressing reading. Fajnzylber et al. (2002) have also shown that violent crime is positively correlated to inequality and their results are robust after controlling for the overall level of poverty. Furthermore, Alesina and Perotti (1996c) show that inequality promotes social and political unrest and the threat of violence and revolution reduces growth-enhancing activities. These conclusions are empirically 'quite solid' (see also Alesina et al., 1996).

Albert Hirschman (1973) also drew attention to the impact of inequality on growth via what he labelled 'the tunnel effect', which consists of the following basic propositions:

1.  in the early stages of development and growth there is a high tolerance for growing inequalities;
2.  this tolerance erodes through time if the low income groups fail to benefit from the growth process;

*Table 10.5    Selected indicators of governance: 20 sub-Saharan African countries[a]*

| Country and year of independence[b] | Voice and accountability[c] -2.5-2.5 | Rule of law[c] -2.5-2.5 | Government effectiveness[c] -2.5-2.5 | Corruption index[c] -2.5-2.5 |
|---|---|---|---|---|
| Angola 1975 | -1.26 | -1.49 | -1.31 | -1.14 |
| Burkino Faso 1960 | -0.26 | -0.79 | -0.02 | -0.93 |
| Cameroon 1960 | -0.82 | -0.40 | 2.0 | -1.11 |
| Côte d'Ivoire 1960 | -1.19 | -0.54 | -0.81 | -0.71 |
| Ethiopia 1941 | -0.85 | -0.24 | -1.01 | -0.40 |
| Ghana 1957 | 0.02 | -0.08 | -0.06 | -0.28 |
| Kenya 1963 | -0.68 | -1.21 | -0.76 | -1.11 |
| Madagascar 1960 | 0.28 | -0.68 | -0.35 | -0.93 |
| Malawi 1964 | -0.14 | -0.36 | -0.77 | 0.10 |
| Mali 1960 | 0.32 | -0.66 | -1.44 | -0.41 |
| Mozambique 1975 | -0.22 | -0.32 | -0.49 | 0.10 |
| Niger 1960 | 0.11 | -1.17 | -1.16 | -1.09 |
| Nigeria 1960 | -0.44 | -1.13 | -1.00 | -1.05 |
| Senegal 1960 | 0.12 | -0.13 | 0.16 | -0.39 |
| South Africa 1934 | 1.17 | -0.05 | 0.25 | 0.35 |
| Sudan 1956 | -1.53 | -1.04 | -1.34 | -1.24 |
| Tanzania 1961 | -0.07 | 0.16 | -0.43 | -0.92 |
| Uganda 1962 | -0.79 | -0.65 | -0.32 | -0.92 |
| Zaire 1960 | -1.70 | -2.09 | -1.38 | -1.24 |
| Zimbabwe 1965 | -0.90 | -0.94 | -1.03 | -1.08 |

*Notes*:
[a]    UNDP, *Human Development Report,* 2002.
[b]    *Chambers Political Systems of the World*, Edinburgh: Chambers.
[c]    UNDP (2002). In the scoring range -2.5-2.5, higher is better. The highest scores for each category are:
      Switzerland for Voice and accountability (1.73);
      Switzerland for Rule of law (1.91);
      Singapore for Government effectiveness (2.16);
      Finland for the Corruption index (2.25).
      The UK scores 1.46, 1.61, 1.77 and 1.86 respectively for each category.

3.    in the long run persistent and growing inequalities in a developing country are likely to lead to 'development disasters' as internal tensions, fuelled by inequality, lead to political instability.

Hirschman argues that individuals assess their individual welfare in relative terms, that is, by comparing their own income with that of others. Even if the poor make some modest gains in terms of real income, the fact that other groups make spectacular progress will lead to feelings of relative deprivation. Hirschman uses the analogy of motorists stuck in a traffic jam in a two-lane tunnel, both lanes heading in the same direction. If the traffic is stationary in both lanes, drivers will initially show patience in the hope that soon the blockage will be removed. If the one lane of traffic then begins to move, those who are not yet moving initially have their hopes raised. Soon they to expect to be on their way. So initially the 'tunnel effect' is strong and the drivers who are not moving wait patiently for their turn to move. But if one lane of traffic continues to move, and at an ever-increasing pace, while the other lane remains blocked, very soon the drivers in the static lane will become furious at the injustice they are being subjected to and they will be prepared to engage in 'foul play', dangerous acts of driving and maybe even in severe violence (road rage) towards the drivers in the unblocked lane. In other words, as long as the 'tunnel effect' lasts, everyone feels better off even though it involves increased inequality. But once the 'tunnel effect' wears off there is potential for revolution and demand for political change. That change may take place with or without violent disruption. This seems to be an accurate description of the experience of several developing countries.

A fourth channel is one that derives from Murphy et al.'s (1989b) reinvigorated version of the 'Big Push' theory. Here the idea is that successful industrialization requires a large market in terms of domestic demand in order to make increasing-returns technologies profitable. A high degree of income inequality, by suppressing domestic demand, inhibits the development of an economic environment conducive to facilitating a 'Big Push' on economic development.

The various mechanisms whereby inequality impacts on economic growth are illustrated in Figure 10.6. As Alesina and Perotti (1996c) recognize, some of these channels work in opposing directions. The distortionary effect of taxes on the incentive to invest operating through the fiscal channel will tend to reduce growth, but at the same time may also reduce social tensions and thereby reduce the threat of political instability. 'Therefore the net effect of redistributive policies on growth has to weigh the costs of distortionary taxation against the benefits of reduced social tensions'.

Is there any way of linking the old view to the new view of the impact of inequality on growth? In an interview Acemoglu suggests the following possibility (see Snowdon, 2004c):

> One way of linking the 'old inequality is good for growth' story with the newer stories that 'inequality is bad for growth' is as follows. Think of a model where in the early stages of development, by giving resources and political power to the same group, this leads to higher rates of investment. But suppose also, that in a dynamic world these people who are rich and powerful are no longer the ones

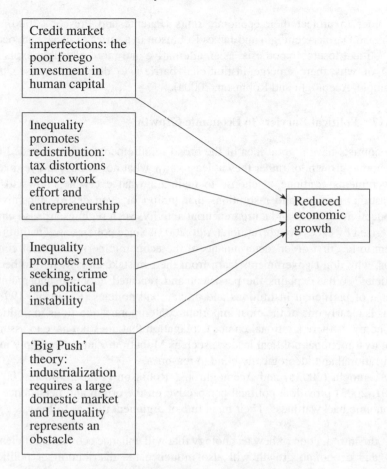

*Figure 10.6   How inequality may adversely affect growth*

who can take advantage of the changing economic opportunities. The entrenched groups with political power become an unproductive oligarchy resistant to change. They utilise their economic and political power to block the entry of new more dynamic groups of people. This reverses the relationship between inequality and growth. The high inequality countries are those that begin to stagnate. Of course this is conjecture squared [*laughter*]. But it is a story that is consistent with the history of the Caribbean economy.

It is becoming increasingly clear from economists' research that institutional failures frequently prevent a country from adopting the most productive technologies. Some economists have suggested an 'economic losers' hypothesis' whereby powerful interest groups resist the adoption of new technology in order to protect their economic rents (Parente and Prescott, 2000). In contrast, Daron Acemoglu and James Robinson in a series of papers advocate a 'political losers' hypothesis' as an alternative and more plausible explanation of why there emerge institutional barriers to development (see, for example, Acemoglu and Robinson, 2000a).

## 10.17   Political Barriers to Economic Growth

Economists have a good idea of the broad requirements that are needed for economic growth, or rather they at least know what not to do! And yet many governments continue to choose to maintain what everyone knows to be disastrous policies and institutions that inhibit or even destroy incentives, productivity growth and entrepreneurial activity. Such regimes are also characterized by excessive corruption (Aidt, 2003). Since policies and institutions seem to be 'first-order' determinants of the economic performance of countries, why don't governments learn from their mistakes and switch to better policies? What explains the persistent and repeated adoption and maintenance of inefficient institutions and proven bad policies (Robinson, 1998)? This is clearly one of the most important contemporary questions in political economy. Is there a rational choice explanation that does not have to assume that dysfunctional political leaders, such as Mobutu in Zaire, are simply mad or irrational and ideologically blind to reason?

Acemoglu (2003b) and Acemoglu and Robinson (2000a, 2000b, 2000c, 2001, 2003) provide a political perspective on the origin and persistence of economic backwardness. Their main line of argument runs as follows:

1.  the introduction of new technology that will enhance economic efficiency and economic growth will also influence the distribution of political power;
2.  groups who feel that their political power will be eroded as a result of the introduction of new technology will deliberately block such change even if it is to the overall benefit of society;
3.  although new technology will increase future output, and hence the revenue of the politically powerful groups, the incumbent élite also fear that new technology will enhance the power of competing groups thereby threatening the future of the élite;
4.  therefore there is a trade-off facing any élite between the potential rents that can be earned from allowing technological progress and the threat to the élite's monopoly of political power;
5.  serious commitment problems prevent the élite from supporting growth-enhancing technological, institutional and policy changes and then redistributing a part of the gains to themselves;

6. external threats may shock an élite into accepting change, for example, the programme of 'defensive modernization' adopted in Japan in the late nineteenth century following the Meiji restoration in 1868.

Using this framework, Acemoglu and Robinson examine the history of political change and industrialization in the USA, Britain, Germany, Austria-Hungary (the Hapsburg Empire), and Russia. They argue that where political élites are subject to competition they are forced to accept change or be replaced. Where an élite is deeply entrenched they are also likely to accept change more readily. However, where an élite is insecure they will block change. In the case of both Russia and Austria-Hungary unconstrained absolute monarchies resisted the forces of industrialization because they feared that this would lead to a loss of political power. In contrast, in the USA, where political competition is guaranteed by the constitution and the opportunity to extract rents is restricted by the separation of powers, change was encouraged and promoted. In Britain, where the landed aristocracy that made up the élite were 'sufficiently entrenched', incremental political change accompanied the Industrial Revolution. A similar story characterizes the German experience in the latter part of the nineteenth century.

Many of the worst cases of development failure have involved countries that have suffered from the personal rule of 'kleptocrats' who use their political power as a means to control assets and expropriate the wealth of their citizens on a massive scale, usually for their own (their families' and their close supporters') consumption and glorification. The best-known kleptocratic regimes include those of Trujillo (Dominican Republic, 1930–61), the Duvaliers (Haiti, 1957–86), Mobutu (Zaire, 1965–97), Amin (Uganda, 1971–9), the Somozas (Nicaragua, 1936–79) and Marcos (the Philippines, 1965–86). As Acemoglu et al. (2003b) point out, one of the most puzzling features of kleptocracies is their longevity. Why don't the oppressed majority overthrow the kleptocrat? Acemoglu et al. suggest that this longevity is the result of 'weakly institutionalised polities' that allow the kleptocrat to operate a 'divide and rule strategy'. The kleptocrat is able to survive by intensifying the collective action problem, thereby destroying the coalition against him by bribing the pivotal groups (Bates, 1981, 2001). In turn, the feasibility of a divide and rule strategy is enhanced if the kleptocrat has easy access to natural resource rents (oil, diamonds, copper and so on) and foreign aid flows (see Easterly, 2003; Sala-i-Martin and Subramanian, 2003). Kleptocractic regimes are also more likely to appear in low-income per capita countries where bribes are more attractive to pivotal groups.

Where ethnic diversity is a feature of a country, the kleptocrat will use this as a basis for divide and rule, with certain ethnic groups receiving bribes in order to buy off their opposition. Mauro (1995) links political instability to ethno-linguistic fractionalization and the impact that this has on the quality of institutions. Easterly and Levine (1997) also trace much of sub-Saharan Africa's poor economic performance to political instability related to ethnic diversity (see also Collier, 2001; Alesina et al., 2003).

## 10.18 The Size of Nations

Since the late 1990s several economists have been using the tools of modern economic analysis to explore the determinants of the size of nations (see Alesina and Spolare, 1997, 2003; Bolton and Roland, 1997; Alesina et al., 2000, 2005). Although historians and other social scientists have studied this issue, economists 'have remained on the sidelines'. Of particular interest to economists is the observation of Alesina et al. (2005) that there has been a dramatic increase in the number of nations since the end of the Second World War. In 1948 there were 74 countries, 89 in 1950, and 192 in 2001. They also note that the world 'now comprises a large number of relatively small countries: in 1995, 87 of the countries of the world had a population of less than 5 million, 58 had a population of less than 2.5 million, and 35 less than 500 thousands'. The proliferation of countries has also led to too many separate currencies (Alesina and Barro, 2002; Alesina et al., 2002). During this same period the second age of globalization has emerged and the share of international trade in world GDP has 'increased dramatically' (Snowdon, 2002a, 2003c). Is there a connection? Alesina et al. (2005) make the following important points:

1.  political borders are made by humans and are not exogenous geographical features;
2.  economists should think of the equilibrium size of nations (measured by total population) 'as emerging from a trade-off between the benefits of size and the *costs* of preference heterogeneity in the population';
3.  the main benefits of size are as follows: economies of scale with respect to the production of public goods such as defence, maintenance of law and order, public health and so on; greater safety from foreign aggression; internalization of cross-regional externalities; better income insurance to regions subject to specific shocks; transfers of income across regions to achieve greater equity among the overall population; a larger internal market increases the potential for greater specialization, as noted by Adam Smith;
4.  in a world of free trade, country size, as measured by population, is no longer a determinant of market size;
5.  it therefore follows that 'the benefits of country size decline as international economic integration increases';

6. the benefits of international economic integration increase the smaller is a country;
7. economic integration and political disintegration are positively correlated;
8. the costs of size include administrative and congestion costs, but much more important are problems associated with the heterogeneity of preferences of individuals, which obviously increase with the size of a nation;
9. using ethno-linguistic fractionalization as a proxy for heterogeneity of preferences economists have found that ethnic diversity is inversely correlated with economic performance, the quality of governance, and economic and political freedom (see Alesina et al., 2003);
10. as international economic integration increases, the trade-off between the benefits of size of a nation and the costs in terms of heterogeneity of preferences shifts in favour of small nations.

This work has important implication for the future of the European Union (EU). EU enlargement clearly increases the heterogeneity of preferences and economic integration lowers the benefits of country size, thereby reducing the costs of independence for small countries. As Alesina et al. (2005) note, 'many have argued that Europe will (and perhaps should) become a collection of regions loosely connected within a European confederation of independent regions'.

Research by economists on the determinants of the size of nations is in its infancy. However, many interesting relationships remain to be explored, including the interconnection between international integration, democracy, the size of nations and international conflict.

## 10.19 Conclusion

Since the late 1980s there has been a major revival of political economy utilizing the tools of modern economic analysis. A common theme running throughout this 'new political economy' is the need to integrate the political process into mainstream economics. In the mid- to late 1970s the seminal contribution of Nordhaus (1975) reawakened interest in the idea of political business cycles, an idea which can be traced back to the work of Schumpeter and Kalecki. However, for a period following the rational expectations revolution, interest in politico-economic models lost momentum. The theoretical shortcomings and inconclusive empirical results of the non-rational opportunistic and partisan models led to a temporary demise of this line of research. On the empirical front Alt and Chrystal (1983) declared that 'no one could read the political business cycle literature without being struck by the lack of supporting evidence'. While interest in the politico-economic approach ebbed, new classical theorists were busy following through the policy implications of rational expectations market-clearing models. The emphasis in these models on policy ineffectiveness and rationality was initially interpreted as being inconsistent with politically motivated policy manipulations. Nevertheless, new rational politico-economic models have been successfully developed which incorporate features such as asymmetric/imperfect information, non-contingent nominal wage contracts and uncertainty over election results. The policy-making process does not consist of a benevolent dictator taking advice from economists in order to maximize social welfare; rather it consists of a complex game played out by various competing groups whose interests do not coincide.

While the importance given to political influences in causing aggregate instability in industrial democracies remains highly controversial, few commentators would challenge the view that politicians, faced with a regular election cycle, will tend to develop short time horizons. The desire to be re-elected or regain office may lead politicians to pursue or promise an economic policy package which creates aggregate economic instability. If this line of argument is accepted, then it follows that what is needed is an institutional framework which creates an environment conducive to the more frequent implementation of sustainable economic policies geared to longer-term objectives. The dilemma faced in industrial democracies is how to constrain the over-zealous short-term discretionary actions of politicians through institutional reform without threatening the basic principles of democratic government. Trying to find a solution to this dilemma will ensure that the relationship between economic and electoral cycles will remain a rich and fertile area of research for macroeconomists.

Not only have economists enhanced our understanding of aggregate instability by adding a political dimension to their models; they have also explored the deeper determinants of growth miracles and disasters. In doing so they have highlighted the important constraint on economic growth imposed by 'bad' institutions and policies. Recent research has explored the interaction of politics and economics, yielding new insights into the political economy of economic growth and development, and the impact of international economic integration on the size of nations. These are certainly areas where much more research is required (see Chapter 11).

Just as economic forces cannot be ignored by political scientists, the message coming from the research discussed in this chapter is that economists interested in positive models of economic policy 'cannot and should not ignore the political arena' (Alesina, 1988).

# ALBERTO ALESINA

Alberto Alesina was born in 1957 in Broni, Italy and obtained his Laurea from the Università Bocconi, Milan in 1981 and his PhD from Harvard University in 1986. His main posts have included: Assistant Professor of Economics at Carnegie-Mellon University (1986–8); Assistant Professor of Economics and Government (1988–90) and Associate Professor of Political Economy (1990–93) at Harvard University. Since 1993 he has been Professor of Economics and Government at Harvard University.

Professor Alesina is best known for his contributions, in terms of both theoretical analysis and empirical investigation, to the various forms of interaction between politics and macroeconomics; and his influential work on politico-economic cycles, the origin and implications of fiscal deficits, and the relationship between political stability and economic growth. Among his best-known books are: *Partisan Politics, Divided Government and the Economy* (Cambridge University Press, 1995), co-authored with H. Rosenthal; *Political Cycles and the Macroeconomy* (MIT Press, 1997), co-authored with N. Roubini; and *The Size of Nations* (MIT Press, 2002), co-authored with E. Spolare. His most widely read articles include: 'Macroeconomic Policy in a Two-Party System as a Repeated Game', *Quarterly Journal of Economics* (1987); 'Political Cycles in OECD Economies', *Review of Economic Studies* (1992), co-authored with N. Roubini; 'Central Bank Independence and Macroeconomic Performance: Some Comparative Evidence', *Journal of Money,*

*Credit, and Banking* (1993), co-authored with L. Summers; 'Distributive Politics and Economic Growth', *Quarterly Journal of Economics* (1994), co-authored with D. Rodrik; and 'The Political Economy of the Budget Surplus in the US' , *Journal of Economic Perspectives* (2000).

We corresponded with Professor Alesina in March/April 1997.

## Background Information

*How did you become interested in economics and where did you study as an undergraduate and postgraduate student?*
In high school I was very interested in socio-political problems. I thought that economics was the most rigorous of the social sciences. As an undergraduate I studied at Università Bocconi in Milan, Italy [1976–81] and took both my Masters degree and PhD at Harvard University [1982–6].

*Which papers and/or books have influenced your research interests?*
I have been much more influenced by 'facts' rather than by specific papers or books and have always been very interested in the policy-making process. The basic fact which has always impressed me is how different actual policy making is from the predictions of models which assume social planners and a representative consumer. I always noted how in politics discourse is about redistributive conflicts while in most macroeconomic models distributive issues are absent.

*Is there any aspect of the Italian economy and/or political system that stimulated your interest in the link between economics and politics?*
Yes: the inability of government after government in Italy to address serious fiscal problems has been an important influence. More generally, thinking about Italy made me wonder about the relationship between political fragmentation and economic performance.

*Do you regard yourself as belonging to any identifiable school of thought in macroeconomics?*
No.

## Keynes and Keynesianism

*Was Keynes naive in assuming that economic policy should be, and would be, carried out in the public interest?*
If we can characterize Keynes's view as such, I would say *yes*, although I think that your question oversimplifies his view.

*In Roy Harrod's 1951 biography of Keynes he argued that Keynes tended to think of important decisions being taken by 'intelligent people' and gave little consideration to the political constraints placed on this vision by 'interfering democracy'.*

If one reads beyond the *General Theory*, for instance the pamphlet *How To Pay For The War*, I think that one can see that Keynes was aware of the subtleties of policy making. I agree that in his main scientific work he did not consider the effects of political distortions on policy making. You can't expect everything from the same economist. He did quite a lot as it is!

*Do you think that Keynesian economics, with its emphasis on discretionary fiscal policy, has fundamentally weakened the fiscal constitutions of Western industrial democracies?*

No. In my opinion this point has been overemphasized. Italy, for instance, has accumulated a very large debt for several reasons. The adoption of Keynesian policies is not one of them.

*Have Italy's fiscal problems stemmed from its political system?*

Yes, from its fragmented political system, over-powerful unions, lack of a strong party committed to fiscal discipline and an overextended and entrenched bureaucracy.

*Why are some countries more prone to budget deficits than others? Why is deficit reduction such an intractable problem?*

In my paper with Roberto Perotti [1995a] we conclude that it is difficult to explain these large cross-country differences using economic arguments alone. Politico-institutional factors are crucial to understanding budget deficits in particular, and fiscal policy in general. While the economies of the OECD countries are relatively similar, their institutions, such as electoral laws, party structure, budget laws, central banks, degree of centralization, political stability and social polarization, are quite different. In a companion paper examining fiscal adjustments in OECD countries [Alesina and Perotti, 1995b] we find that coalition governments are almost always unsuccessful in their adjustment attempts, being unable to maintain a tough fiscal stance because of conflicts among coalition members. We also find that a successful fiscal adjustment is best started during a period of relatively high growth, does not raise taxes, but rather cuts transfer programme and government wages and employment. Politicians and their advisers must stop thinking of just about everything on the expenditure side of the government budget as untouchable.

*What do you regard as being the most important contribution made by Keynes to our understanding of macroeconomic phenomena?*

The idea that aggregate demand policy matters because of lack of complete price flexibility.

## The Political Business Cycle

*Prior to Michal Kalecki [1943] were there other economists who anticipated the possibility of a political business cycle?*
Not that I know of.

*To what extent could the deep UK recession of 1979–82 be viewed as being politically induced? For example, it can be argued that the then Prime Minister, Margaret Thatcher, used high unemployment in order to restore the health of British capitalism, a development consistent with Kalecki's model.*
Thatcher's recession was the result of the need for disinflation. I am not sure that unemployment is needed 'in order to restore the health of capitalism'. Unemployment is in part a cyclical phenomenon, in part the result of supply-side rigidities. This latter influence is particularly strong in the European economies.

*How important are macroeconomic variables for voting behaviour?*
In the USA, the rate of GNP growth is extremely important, inflation and unemployment somewhat less so. In other countries the evidence is less clear cut, in part due to differences in the electoral systems. In general, the state of the economy is very important for elections but how this effect manifests itself may vary dramatically from one country to another.

*Nordhaus's [1975] model is intuitively very appealing. What do you regard to be its main strengths and weaknesses?*
Its main strength is that it makes a simple powerful point which is easily testable. Its main weaknesses are that it is based on the assumption of extremely naive behaviour, and also has very weak empirical support.

*How can voters (principals) ensure that their agents (the politicians) refrain from opportunistic behaviour which creates economic inefficiencies?*
Mainly with the threat of voting them out of office.

## Non-Rational Partisan Theory

*What do you regard to be the important contributions of Hibbs [1977] to the development of politico-economic models?*
Hibbs played an important role by introducing ideological–partisan differences and moved attention away from models in which it was assumed that all politicians have identical motivations.

*How strong is the evidence that inflation is more harmful to higher income than lower income groups?*
The evidence on this is not very strong. How harmful inflation is depends on the level of inflation and various institutional arrangements, such as indexation.

*For the post-war period as a whole, is the empirical evidence supportive of the partisan view that left-of-centre governments favour and achieve lower unemployment than right-of-centre governments? Have left-of-centre administrations also been associated with higher inflation than right of centre administrations?*
To some extent yes. However, the success of left-wing governments in reducing unemployment has only been temporary. After taking into account structural breaks such as the break in exchange rate regime in the early 1970s, the oil shocks and so on, it is true that left-of-centre governments have been associated with higher inflation than those right of centre.

## Rational Expectations and Business Cycle Models

*Do you attribute the decline of interest in politico-economic explanations of the business cycle between the late 1970s and mid-1980s to theoretical developments associated with Robert Lucas and the rational expectations revolution or was empirical failure a more important factor?*
I think that the 'rational expectations revolution' was a much more important contributing factor to the decline of interest in such models. Furthermore, empirical 'failures' have not stopped economists investigating this matter further in the 1990s.

*An important criticism of democratic markets is that voters are, in most cases, uninformed. For each voter the benefits of gaining more information will be outweighed by the costs. In this world of imperfect information is it not inevitable that politicians will engage in opportunistic fiscal behaviour prior to elections?*
To some extent this is the case, but I would not overemphasize this point for several reasons. First, if this were the main explanation for budget deficits, it should apply (more or less) to every democracy. Thus one should not observe such large differences in fiscal policies in OECD democracies. Second, large deviations from efficient policies, such as huge deficits in election years, are easily observable, if not by the individual voter, then certainly by the press. Third, I do not know of any conclusive evidence which shows that larger deficits favour the re-election of an incumbent. I think that in practice what happens all the time is that in election years fiscal favours may not be very

large, and may therefore be hard to detect. Nevertheless, the political benefits may be quite significant. Let me add on this point that I am not a great fan of models of politics where imperfect information is the critical factor. I personally think that conflict of interest is much more important than asymmetric information.

*In 1988 George Bush told the American electorate: 'Read my lips, no new taxes'. Each year in the UK the Chancellor of the Exchequer in his budget speech emphasizes the competence of the administration in managing fiscal affairs. Do you regard these examples as typical of the kind of political behaviour predicted by the Rogoff–Sibert [1988] class of rational opportunistic models?*
With the caveats discussed in the previous answer, I think that Rogoff and Sibert have a good point. Their model is also much more consistent with the empirical evidence than the original Nordhaus model. My empirical research on the subject is quite supportive of their model. This research is included in Alesina and Roubini, with Cohen (1997): *Political Cycles and the Macroeconomy*, MIT Press.

*What role does 'fiscal illusion' play in politico-economic models?*
I think that this concept is oversold. Explanations of excessive fiscal deficits based on fiscal illusion are not totally convincing because they imply a systematic bias in the errors made by the electorate concerning their estimation of the costs and benefits of taxes and spending. Fiscal illusion is also unable to explain the timing of the deficit problem in OECD economies or the cross-country differences in budget deficits. I prefer models based on rational behaviour and expectations.

**Rational Partisan Theories**

*How strong is the evidence against the median voter theorem?*
It depends. For large elections I would not use it: in fact, its key implication is that when in office all the parties do the same thing. This is clearly inconsistent with the evidence even of predominantly two-party systems that exist in countries such as the UK and the USA. In multi-party systems the median voter theorem proves to be even less applicable. Therefore, for macroeconomic and macropolitical research I would not use it. On the other hand, if I want to study voting behaviour on one issue in a committee of five people, then the median voter theorem is a good start!

*In the UK Tony Blair's 'New Labour Party' has been moving closer to the position adopted by the Conservative Party on many economic issues. For*

*example, on 20 January 1997 the Shadow Chancellor of the Exchequer,
Gordon Brown, promised the electorate that 'New Labour' would not increase tax rates if elected. On 21 January 1997 Tony Blair promised not to
reverse the Conservative Party's industrial relations legislation of the 1980s.
Does this imply that polarization is less important than it used to be?*
In the case of the UK we shall have to wait and see! However, on the more
general issue of increasing party convergence, in *Political Cycles and the
Macroeconomy* [1997] we conclude that 'the idea that political parties are
becoming more alike when it comes to macroeconomic management is somewhat exaggerated'. Our view is that while the macroeconomic problems of the
1970s and early 1980s 'have probably made politicians on both sides of the
political spectrum more cautious in terms of macroeconomic management,
they have not completely eliminated ideological differences'. Furthermore, we
also point out that 'both left-wing and right-wing governments in the next
decade will have to face issues of fiscal retrenchment' and that 'partisan conflicts
are very likely to explode on how to achieve this goal'.

*In your rational partisan models [1987, 1989] you appear to adopt an
eclectic approach to your theoretical framework based on a variant of the
'monetary surprise' rational expectations model associated with Fischer
[1977]. Lucas and other new classical theorists now appear to attach more
importance to real shocks as an explanation of post-war macroeconomic
fluctuations. Does this not undermine the basis of models based on monetary
shocks?*
I do not like the view that macroeconomic fluctuations are due to either
supply or demand shocks. First, an economy can be subjected to both types
of shock. Second, real business cycle models have certainly not been an
empirical success. The rational partisan theory does not imply that real shocks
do not exist. In fact in empirical testing one may want to control for supply
shocks.

*What are the essential predictions of the rational partisan theory and have
they been supported by empirical work?*
The basic idea of the model is that, given the sluggishness in wage adjustments, changes in the inflation rate associated with changes in government
create temporary deviations of real economic activity from its natural level.
At the beginning of a right-wing government output growth is below its
natural level and unemployment is above its natural level. The opposite is
predicted for left-wing governments. After expectations, prices and wages
adjust, output and employment return to their natural level and the level of
economic activity should be independent of the party in office. However, the
rate of inflation should remain higher throughout the term of a left-wing

government. These implications of rational partisan theory are consistent with the empirical evidence particularly for a subset of countries with bipartisan systems or with clearly identifiable movements from left to right and vice versa. The rational partisan theory is less applicable, and in fact tends to fail in countries with large coalition governments with frequent government collapses.

*In the UK the Conservative Party gained power in the four elections between 1979 and 1992. President Clinton has also been re-elected. What does the rational partisan theory predict will be the effect of the repeated re-election of a particular party?*
Strictly speaking, it depends on how unexpected is the re-election. If the Conservative Party had been sure to win in the previous four elections, not much should have happened to the economy. Inflation should have continued to remain low and growth (*ceteris paribus*) should have been stable. President Clinton was probably less sure of being re-elected. In this case the model predicts that growth should slightly increase in the USA.

*What is likely to happen according to your model if a left-of-centre party gains office at the peak of an economic expansion?*
According to the model, the left-of-centre party will do as much as possible to avoid a recession, including increasing inflation. If we speak of the UK in 1997, one has to consider other issues which may influence the outcome, such as European Monetary Union. This kind of issue is clearly not considered in the model.

*What are the main policy implications of your model for the conduct of macroeconomic policy and the design of political institutions?*
The model in its stripped-down version is 'positive' rather than 'normative', thus it does not have any direct policy implications. However, the model can be used in a normative direction. Let me give a couple of examples to illustrate the point. First, the model suggests that independent central banks, by insulating monetary policy from partisan influences, can reduce the extent of both monetary and real variability. This point is formally derived in my paper with Roberta Gatti [1995]. Second, as for political institutions, the model points towards a trade-off. Proportional electoral systems which result in coalition governments lead to 'compromise' and policy moderation. This reduces partisan fluctuations and polarization, but may induce deadlocks in policy making, particularly with respect to fiscal issues. Majoritarian systems leading to two-party systems have the opposite feature, namely more policy polarization but no policy deadlocks. Extreme versions of the two systems are unlikely to be optimal although I regard the

risk of excessive 'governing by coalition' to be a particularly significant problem in the European context.

*Which is likely to create the most instability: exogenous or endogenous timing of elections?*
Endogenous elections undoubtedly generate more frequent elections. Whether that creates more or less instability is less obvious. Italy is a perfect example. One may argue that in the post-war period Italy has been very unstable because it has had numerous government changes and many early elections. On the other hand, one may argue that at least until the early 1990s nothing much ever changed, because the same parties and individuals were always in office.

*What are the main weaknesses of the rational partisan theory?*
I guess I am not the right person to ask that particular question, but elsewhere [1995] I have pointed out that the Achilles' heel of the rational partisan theory is that the mechanism of wage formation is postulated exogenously rather than derived from optimal individual behaviour.

*Would you agree that rational voters will make their voting decision based on information relating to both the past performance of a political party as well as expected future performance?*
Past information has to be used to form expectations about the future. Even voters who are forward-looking have to look backward to form expectations. The question 'are voters backward or forward-looking?' is very misleading. Furthermore, I find the research on this point often both confused and confusing. A different, more useful, question is whether the voters use 'efficiently' the past information that they have to form expectations about the future. In other words, the question is whether voters use 'rationally' their past information. This is a difficult but well-posed question, which is similar to questions raised in finance.

*To what extent do opportunistic behaviour and partisan behaviour depend on the confidence of an incumbent administration that it will be re-elected? Is it the case that the more confident an administration is of re-election, the more likely it is to behave ideologically?*
Possibly, perhaps likely. I have not seen a 'rational' model making this point. Bruno Frey and Friedrich Schneider back in 1978 made this point in their 'non-rational' models.

## General Macroeconomic Issues

*How influential has the literature relating to time inconsistency, credibility and reputation been to the development of politico-economic models?*
In my case these contributions have been very influential. I think that this literature has been an important driving force behind the new wave of politico-economic models in the 1990s, although it is fair to say that now this literature has a life of its own.

*Why do governments create inflation?*
One important reason is to try to reduce unemployment. A second reason relates to the financing of budget deficits. Also, when inflation becomes entrenched in the system it is costly to reduce it. These reasons may apply differently to different countries, and at different points in time.

*What is the relationship between political and economic instability? How has the UK managed to combine political stability with a relatively poor economic performance in the post-war period? How does this compare to the Italian experience?*
The UK has been 'stable' but very polarized. Conservative and Labour governments have had very different programmes. On the other hand Italy has had the opposite problem, namely frequent government changes but with always the same people ending up in office. The result for Italy has been a lack of fiscal discipline. However, concepts such as political stability and polarization are difficult to measure in practice.

*Should central banks have goal independence as well as instrument independence? What is your view of the contracting approach suggested by Carl Walsh?*
Legislatures should set, once and for all, price stability (defined as low inflation, between 0 and 3 per cent) as the sole goal of monetary policy. Central banks should do whatever they want to achieve that goal. I do not know whether you want to call this instrument or goal independence. Carl Walsh [1995a] has produced a good paper but I would like to see further work in a more political direction. For example, how does Walsh's contracting approach deal with the fact that in the real world we have partisan and opportunistic politicians, rather than benevolent social planners?

*Are you in favour of monetary and fiscal rules?*
My answer to the previous question covers my views on monetary rules. Personally I am against balanced budget rules for national governments but in favour of such rules for sub-national governments.

*Does reducing inflation from moderate rates, say from 10 per cent to 5 per cent, bring any significant real economic benefits in the form of improved performance with respect to employment and economic growth?*

If inflation remained stable forever at say 10 per cent, with perfect certainty and everything adjusted, it wouldn't matter very much. But higher inflation results in more variable and less predictable inflation, which is costly. Thus, on balance I believe that there are benefits in reducing inflation.

*Where do you stand on the issue of European Monetary Union? For countries like Italy and the UK do the costs of Monetary Union not outweigh the benefits?*

The benefits of Monetary Union have been oversold. There are clearly both pros and cons to such an arrangement. Italy has benefited from the Maastricht target, otherwise it would have done even less to put its 'house in order'. However, this is not sufficient reason to join a monetary union. Although a full answer to this question would require a whole article, my feeling is that the economic arguments in favour of European Monetary Union are quite weak.

*In your view what are the most important lessons and policy implications to arise from recent research into the interaction of politics and the macro-economy?*

First procedures, namely how policies are determined. This matters for the outcome. Second, when thinking about 'optimal institution building' one should not ignore conflicts of interests. Third, models based on 'social planners' cannot completely explain the empirical evidence and may be misleading or useless if used for policy prescriptives.

*What kind of political system is most conducive to macroeconomic stability?*

For an OECD economy I would choose an electoral system with a majoritarian emphasis. The American system of presidential–legislative checks and balances has also worked quite well. Different electoral systems imply different choices in the trade-off between moderation and gridlock. An English system is probably at the extreme of the 'no moderation but no gridlock' scale. The current Italian system is at the opposite end. Perhaps the US system is a happy medium.

*At the moment what research are you currently engaged in and what in your opinion are the important areas of research which macroeconomists should concentrate on in the future?*

I am working on three main areas. The first area is the issue of the political economy of major fiscal adjustments where I have already published several papers with Roberto Perotti. I am also interested in what determines the number and shapes of countries, that is, economic theories of secessions and mergers and their relationship with factors such as geography and trade and so on. For example, see my paper with Enrico Spolare [1997]. Third, I am also researching into the effect of socio-ethnic fragmentation on the choice of fiscal policy in US cities and localities. Personally, I find issues relating to fiscal policy more intriguing than those associated with monetary policy, especially as we know less about the former than the latter. I think that the political economy of social security reforms and, more generally, reforms of the welfare state will be the number one item in the policy agenda of OECD countries during the next decade. The research of economists needs to keep up with important events.

# 11. The renaissance of economic growth research

> No previous episode of enrichment approaches modern economic growth – not China or Egypt in their primes, not the glory of Greece or the grandeur of Rome. (McCloskey, 1994)

> Of all the policy questions concerning growth, the most fundamental is whether there are any policies that an omniscient, omnipotent, benevolent social planner could implement to raise the welfare of all individuals in an economy. (P. Romer, 1989)

## 11.1  Introduction

In 2002 there were 192 internationally recognized independent countries in the world that included the 191 members of the United Nations plus Taiwan (Alesina and Spolare, 2003). Among these countries are some that by historical standards are extremely rich and many more that are relatively poor. Their size, measured by geographical area, by total population, or by total GDP, varies enormously. Measured by geographical and population size we observe large poor countries (India) and large rich countries (USA) as well as small rich countries (Switzerland) and small poor countries (Sierra Leone). We also see every other possible combination in between. When we examine the economic growth performance of these countries we also see a wide variety of experience, from the high positive rates observed during the last four decades of the twentieth century among the Asian Tigers (Hong Kong, South Korea, Singapore, Taiwan) to the negative growth rates experienced in many sub-Saharan countries during the last couple of decades. Since sustained economic growth is the most important determinant of living standards, there is no more important issue challenging the research efforts of economists than to understand the causes of economic growth. In reviewing the differential growth performances of countries such as India, Egypt, the 'Asian Tigers', Japan and the USA, and the consequences of these differentials for living standards, Lucas (1988) observed that 'the consequences for human welfare involved in questions like these are simply staggering. Once one starts to think about them, it is hard to think about anything else'.

In this chapter we review many of the important theoretical, empirical and political-economy issues relating to modern economic growth and the determinants of living standards that have captivated the research interests of both economists, economic historians and other social scientists during the twentieth century.

## 11.2 The 'Great Divergence'

Nothing in human history compares with the impact that the Industrial Revolution has had on the living conditions for the world's population. Sustained growth of both total GDP and GDP per capita date from the great transformation unleashed by this event. While economic historians continue to debate the origins, timing and quantitative aspects of the Industrial Revolution, there is no doubt that during the last 250 years the main consequence of this event has been a distinctive regime change as the world economy began to experience a new epoch of what Kuznets (1966) called 'modern economic growth'. It should also be noted that modern economic growth and capitalism are synonymous, for as Baumol (2002) writes:

> what is clear to historians and laypersons alike is that capitalism is unique in the extraordinary growth record is has been able to achieve in its recurring industrial revolutions that have produced an outpouring of material wealth unlike anything previously seen in human history.

Baumol's point had been recognized by Karl Marx and Friedrich Engels over 150 years earlier in their *Communist Manifesto* of 1847 when they observed that 'the bourgeoisie has created more massive and more colossal productive forces than have all preceding generations together'.

In contrast to most of human history, the modern epoch has been characterized by a population explosion, rising life expectancy, rapid urbanization, diversified patterns of employment and steadily rising income per capita for the world as a whole (Easterlin, 1996). However, because the Industrial Revolution and economic growth have spread unevenly across the world, the modern era of human history has also witnessed the emergence of unprecedented global inequality. Since the beginning of the nineteenth century the world economy has experienced what Pomeranz (2000) calls the 'Great Divergence' and Pritchett (1997) refers to as 'Divergence, Big Time'. International differences in living standards, measured by real income per capita, are enormous even after making adjustments to the estimates that take into account variations in purchasing power and household production.

The 'Great Divergence' of income per capita is a modern phenomenon. Before the nineteenth century, for the vast majority of the economies and peoples of the world, the process of economic growth was 'sporadic and inconsistent'. It was not until the second half of the twentieth century that growth spread to many living in the Third World. As Table 11.1 shows, living

*Table 11.1  Level[a] and rate of growth[b] of GDP per capita: world and major regions, 0–1998 AD*

| Region | 0[a] | 1000[a] | 1820[a] | 1998[a] | 0–1000[b] | 1000–1820[b] | 1820–1998[b] |
|---|---|---|---|---|---|---|---|
| Western Europe | 450 | 400 | 1 232 | 17 921 | −0.01 | 0.14 | 1.51 |
| Western off-shoots | 400 | 400 | 1 201 | 26 146 | 0.00 | 0.13 | 1.75 |
| Japan | 400 | 425 | 669 | 20 413 | 0.01 | 0.06 | 1.93 |
| Average, Group A | 443 | 405 | 1 130 | 21 470 | −0.01 | 0.13 | 1.67 |
| Latin America | 400 | 400 | 665 | 5 795 | 0.00 | 0.06 | 1.22 |
| Eastern Europe & former USSR | 400 | 400 | 667 | 4 354 | 0.00 | 0.06 | 1.06 |
| Asia | 450 | 450 | 575 | 2 936 | 0.00 | 0.03 | 0.92 |
| Africa | 425 | 416 | 418 | 1 368 | −0.00 | 0.00 | 0.67 |
| Average, Group B | 444 | 440 | 573 | 3 102 | −0.00 | 0.03 | 0.95 |
| World | 444 | 435 | 667 | 5 709 | −0.00 | 0.05 | 1.21 |

*Notes:*
[a]  Measured in 1990 international dollars.
[b]  Annual average compound growth.

*Source:*  Maddison (2001), Table 1.2.

581

standards across the world, as measured by GDP per capita, did not improve in any significant way during the first one thousand years AD. However, since about 1750, beginning in Great Britain, the phenomenon of sustained modern economic growth has become 'the defining feature of human history' and by 1950 embraced a third of the population of the earth.

Contemporary differences in living standards are themselves the product of differences in growth rates that have been observed during the last 200 years and are highlighted in Table 11.2. Three important commonly used measures of living standards are represented, namely gross national income (GNI) per capita measured in international dollars (PPP – purchasing power parity – $), life expectancy, and the Human Development Index (HDI). The HDI is a composite measure of three equally weighted basic components, namely, real income per capita (PPP US$ = $Ypc$) adjusted to reflect the assumption of rapidly diminishing marginal utility of income above the world average; longevity as measured by life expectancy at birth ($L$); and educational attainment ($E$) captured by the adult literacy rate (weighted 2/3) and the combined gross primary, secondary and tertiary enrolment ratio (weighted 1/3). Therefore, the HDI estimate for any economy ($j$) is a simple weighted average of $Ypcj + Lj + Ej$. Although there are serious index number problems in using the HDI as a measure of living standards and the HDI has come in for a considerable amount of criticism, it has nevertheless proved to be a useful additional development indicator, complementing, but not replacing, the traditional 'commodity'-based measures of progress such as income per capita. While there has been unprecedented divergence between the income per capita of the OECD economies and many developing countries, Crafts (1999, 2000) has argued that a more optimistic picture of the progress of human welfare emerges if we examine long-run trends in the HDI. For example, the HDI scores for many poor countries in 2002 are well ahead of the estimated 1870 HDI scores for the leading countries of that time (current G7 countries) as measured by their per capita income. Crafts concludes that by taking a broader view of progress, it is 'likely that the growth of living standards since 1870 as measured by real national income per capita is substantially underestimated' (Crafts, 2001; see also Becker et al., 2003; Crafts, 2003).

Data on total population for each country is also included in Table 11.2. The 40 countries included accounted for 4795.7 million (79 per cent) of the world's population of 6054 million in 2000. Important points to note include the close correlation between income per capita, life expectancy and the HDI; the underperformance of Botswana and South Africa on their life expectancy and HDI scores relative to their position in the income per capita ranking; the ratio of the USA's GNI per capita to Sierra Leone's is a staggering 72–1 (note, the highest GNI per capita recorded by the World Bank for 2002 was Luxembourg, with 51,160 PPP$).

*Table 11.2*    *Three indicators of living standards: 40 countries*

| Country | GNI per capita (PPP$), 2002[a] | Life expectancy in years, 2000[b] | HDI, 2000[b] | Total population (millions), 2000[c] |
|---|---|---|---|---|
| USA | 35 060 | 77.0 | 0.939 | 282 |
| Canada | 28 070 | 78.8 | 0.940 | 31 |
| Australia | 26 960 | 78.9 | 0.939 | 19 |
| Hong Kong | 26 810 | 79.5 | 0.888 | 4.4[d] |
| Germany | 26 220 | 77.7 | 0.925 | 82 |
| France | 26 180 | 78.6 | 0.928 | 59 |
| Japan | 26 070 | 81.0 | 0.933 | 127 |
| UK | 25 870 | 77.7 | 0.928 | 60 |
| Italy | 25 320 | 78.5 | 0.913 | 58 |
| Singapore | 23 090 | 77.6 | 0.885 | 2.3[d] |
| Korea, Rep. | 16 480 | 74.9 | 0.882 | 47 |
| Czech Rep. | 14 500 | 74.9 | 0.849 | 10 |
| Hungary | 12 810 | 71.3 | 0.835 | 10 |
| Saudi Arabia | 11 480 | 71.6 | 0.759 | 21 |
| Poland | 10 130 | 73.3 | 0.833 | 39 |
| Argentina | 9 930 | 73.4 | 0.844 | 37 |
| South Africa | 9 870 | 52.1 | 0.695 | 43 |
| Chile | 9 180 | 75.3 | 0.831 | 15 |
| Mexico | 8 540 | 72.6 | 0.796 | 98 |
| Malaysia | 8 280 | 72.5 | 0.782 | 23 |
| Russian Fed. | 7 820 | 66.1 | 0.781 | 146 |
| Botswana | 7 770 | 40.3 | 0.572 | 2 |
| Brazil | 7 250 | 67.7 | 0.757 | 170 |
| Thailand | 6 680 | 70.2 | 0.762 | 61 |
| Iran | 6 340 | 68.9 | 0.721 | 64 |
| Turkey | 6 210 | 69.8 | 0.742 | 65 |
| Ukraine | 4 650 | 68.1 | 0.748 | 50 |
| China | 4 390 | 70.5 | 0.726 | 1 261 |
| Egypt | 3 710 | 67.3 | 0.642 | 64 |
| Indonesia | 2 990 | 66.2 | 0.684 | 210 |
| India | 2 570 | 63.3 | 0.577 | 1 016 |
| Vietnam | 2 240 | 68.2 | 0.688 | 79 |
| Zimbabwe | 2 120 | 49.2 | 0.551 | 12 |
| Pakistan | 1 940 | 60.0 | 0.499 | 138 |
| Bangladesh | 1 720 | 59.4 | 0.478 | 130 |
| Kenya | 990 | 50.8 | 0.513 | 30 |
| Nigeria | 780 | 51.7 | 0.462 | 127 |
| Ethiopia | 720 | 43.9 | 0.327 | 64 |
| Tanzania | 550 | 51.1 | 0.440 | 34 |
| Sierra Leone | 490 | 38.9 | 0.275 | 5 |
| World[e] | 7 570 (A) | 66.9 (A) | 0.722 (A) | 4 795.7 (T) |

*Notes*:
[a] Gross national income per capita, PPP$, *World Development Indicators, 2003,* World Bank.
[b] Human Development Index and Life Expectancy, *Human Development Report 2002*, United Nations.
[c] Total population, *World Development Report 2002*, World Bank.
[d] Hong Kong and Singapore data from *Human Development Report 2002*.
[e] A = Average, T = Total.

### 11.3   In Praise of Economic History

It is our view that a knowledge of history in general, and economic history in particular, is important to understand how societies and economies change. Since contemporary economic historians are primarily interested in the long-run development of economies, they seek to understand the fundamental causes of economic growth, the determinants of technological progress, the evolution and impact of institutions, and the historical origins of current economic problems. With respect to the determination of technological progress, which is now at the forefront of endogenous growth theory, Wright (1997) argues that if economists wish to take technology seriously then economics 'will have to become a more historical discipline' (see also Mokyr, 2002, 2005). In his influential 1986 paper, William Baumol also advises economists interested in long-run growth to pay more attention to the 'brilliant insights' and 'powerful analysis' of economic historians.

Before the 1960s, even though large amounts of invaluable quantitative data were produced by economic historians, much of their analysis tended to be atheoretical. The traditional approach to the study of economic history was largely descriptive. This situation changed dramatically during the 1960s as formalization and analytical rigour spread from mainstream economics to the field of economic history. From the early 1960s scholars such as Nobel Memorial Laureates Robert Fogel and Douglass North pioneered the 'new' quantitative approach to economic history, or 'cliometrics', defined as 'the application of economic theory and quantitative methods to the study of history' (Goldin, 1995).

During the last four decades the 'cliometric revolution' has demonstrated that economic historians have much to gain from a knowledge of economic theory and methodology. The 'new' approach has emphasized the need for scholars to be precise and explicit about which hypotheses are being tested in order to connect the historical investigation with quantitative analysis. However, economists also have much to gain from a greater knowledge of history, in particular economic history (Snowdon, 2002c). Indeed, one of the main developments highlighted in this chapter is how in recent years economic theorists appear to have followed Goldin's (1995) advice that 'only the oblivious can ignore history in modern economics, and only the unenlightened would chose to do so'. Goldin's recommendation is especially relevant to those economists interested in the long-run issue of economic growth. Not only does the past provide a gigantic laboratory for testing various hypotheses in economics; history also contains many lessons that can provide useful information for contemporary policy makers, not least those in the developing countries and transition economies. Because the past shapes the present it must also influence the future. As Goldin argues, the 'remnants of the past, which shape the realm of the possible today, are always with us, norms, structures, institutions, and even people'. While history rarely repeats itself exactly, it does offer guidance, broadens our stock of knowledge, highlights what may be important in determining outcomes, and 'enables us to identify and read signals' (Horrell, 2003). It is worth noting that several prominent macroeconomists have, in recent years, made important contributions to growth analysis by engaging in quantitative economic history (see Lucas, 2000b, 2002; Hansen and Prescott, 2002; Parente and Prescott, 2005; and section 11.21).

## 11.4 Back to the Long Run

Following the stimulating and important contributions of Abramovitz (1986), Baumol (1986), P. Romer (1986) and Lucas (1988), the study of long-run economic growth once again became a very active research area. Increasingly, many economists accept that macroeconomic analysis and policies resting solely on the short view will be, to quote Viner, 'a structure built on shifting sands' (Baumol, 1986). This reorientation of research emphasis is regarded as long overdue by many economists. Although the revival of research into the elusive ingredients of growth began in the mid-1980s it was not until the 1990s that the literature really exploded. Two important surveys of macroeconomics bear witness to this fact. Mankiw's (1990) survey of macroeconomics makes no mention of economic growth whatsoever, while Fischer's (1988) survey devotes a mere four sentences to the 'Theory of Growth' and only refers to Paul Romer's 1986 paper in passing. However, by 1989 Robert Barro and Paul Romer were launching a major joint research project on economic growth through Harvard University and the National Bureau of Economic Research and, reflecting this development, in 1996 the first issue of the *Journal of Economic Growth* was published. After 1990 a constant flow of new books and journal survey articles also began to appear, indicating the much higher profile and new urgency given by economists to research on economic growth (see, for example, Grossman and Helpman, 1991; Fagerberg, 1994; P. Romer, 1994a; Mankiw, 1995; Crafts and Toniolo, 1996; Aghion and Howitt, 1998; Gylfason, 1999; Temple, 1999; Solow, 2000, 2001; Easterly, 2001a; Easterly and Levine, 2001; Jones, 2001a; Lucas, 2002; Barro and Sala-i-Martin, 2003; Rodrik, 2003; Aghion and Durlauf, 2005; see also Snowdon and Vane, 1997a; Snowdon, 2003a).

Given the significant adverse impact that poor growth performance has on economic welfare and the resultant importance attached to growth by economists, it is perhaps surprising that during the twentieth century the research effort in this field has been cyclical. Concern about the sustainability of economic growth was a major concern of the classical economists, with the pessimism of Thomas Malthus and David Ricardo contrasting with the optimism of Adam Smith (Rostow, 1990). However, during the period 1870–1929 economists' research was heavily influenced by the 'marginalist revolution' and was therefore predominantly micro oriented, being directed towards issues relating to the efficient allocation of given resources. For a quarter of a century after 1929–33, issues relating to the Great Depression and Keynes's response to that event dominated discussion as the new science of macroeconomics evolved. In the period 1939–56 growth theory was dominated by the neo-Keynesian contributions of Roy Harrod (1939, 1948) and Evsey Domar (1946, 1947, 1948), and in the period 1956–70 by the seminal contributions of Nobel Memorial Laureate Robert Solow (1956, 1957), who, along with Trevor Swan (1956), pioneered work on the neoclassical growth model. However, as Domar commented in 1957, 'in economic theory growth has occupied an odd place: always seen around but seldom invited in. It has either been taken for granted or treated as an afterthought'.

It is certainly the case that research on the theoretical front in this field ran into diminishing returns and 'effectively died' in the 1970–85 period. This was due mainly to its perceived lack of empirical relevance, the diversion of economists' research interests towards business cycle analysis in the wake of the aggregate instability experienced throughout the world in the 1970s, and the impact of the rational expectations 'revolution' within academia (see Chapter 5, and Barro and Sala-i-Martin, 2003). In a survey of the contents of three leading economics journals Laband and Wells (1998) found that

> during the first half of the twentieth century, there was increasing scholarly output of papers written about economic growth and development. This scholarly interest/production peaked in the 1950s and then declined markedly throughout the 1960s, 1970s, and 1980s. This trend reversed itself abruptly during the first half of the 1990s, with a surge in production of articles on economic growth.

How far this burgeoning literature has significantly progressed economists' knowledge of the causes of growth remains to be seen (see Nelson, 1997; Abramovitz, 1999; Kenny and Williams, 2001).

During the last 50 years there has been a shift of theoretical focus as neo-Keynesian growth models were replaced by neoclassical models as the dominant framework for analysis. Neoclassical theories have in turn been challenged by endogenous growth theory since the mid-1980s (Snowdon and Vane, 1997a; Solow, 2001). But what explains the high-profile resurgence of interest in growth analysis during the last couple of decades? We identify this resurgence of interest since the mid-1980s to have been stimulated by the following 12 factors, of which the first three played a crucial role:

1. New theoretical insights inspired by the research of Paul Romer (1986, 1987b, 1989, 1990, 1994a) and Robert Lucas (1988, 1990b, 1993, 2002); new theoretical tools have been of paramount importance.

2. The availability of a rich array of new data for a large number of countries (for example Summers and Heston, 1991; Maddison, 2001). Economists now have data for most countries which extend back to 1960. Recent empirical research has also focused on patterns of cross-country growth (Durlauf and Quah, 1999).

3. A growing realization that a large number of developing countries, particularly in sub-Saharan Africa, were not 'catching up' and converging with the levels of income per capita of the rich OECD economies (Abramovitz, 1986, Baumol, 1986, P. Romer, 1986, 1989; Lucas, 1988).

4. The sudden and unexpected collapse of the Soviet Union and other 'Eastern Bloc' economies at the end of the 1980s focused attention on the relationship between social, political and economic structures and an economy's capacity to sustain economic growth (Fukuyama, 1992; Snowdon, 2003b).

5. Increasing concern during the 1980s that the economic position of the USA relative to other major OECD economies, especially Japan and Germany, was being eroded (Thurow, 1992).

6. Concern relating to the causes of the productivity growth slowdown, beginning in the late 1960s/early 1970s, but not clearly recognized until the early 1980s (Fischer et al., 1988; Baumol et al., 1989). Writing in 1988, Fischer described this event as 'the most significant macroeconomic development of the last two decades'. More recently, in the late 1990s interest in the USA has focused on a productivity acceleration associated with the emergence of an information-technology-driven 'new economy' (see Gordon, 2000b; Jorgenson, 2001; Jorgenson and Stiroh, 2000).

7. Increasing awareness of problems relating to the measurement of economic growth and that the true rate of progress is likely to be 'substantially underestimated' using conventional estimation techniques (Fogel, 1999; Nordhaus, 2001). The findings of the Boskin Commission suggest that US GDP growth has been underestimated by about 0.9 per cent per annum in the period 1970–96 (Boskin, 1996). In addition, the rise of information technology and with it the 'knowledge' (or 'weightless') economy, and a potential reversion to non-market production further increased the need to refine national income accounting techniques (Stafford, 1999).

8. Increasing recognition of the spectacular growth performance displayed by the 'East Asian Tiger' economies as well as the 'growth disasters' and disappointments experienced in many developing economies, espe-

cially in sub-Saharan Africa, Latin America and Southern Asia (World Bank, 1993; Bhagwati, 1993; Bloom and Sachs, 1998; A. Taylor, 1998; Collier and Gunning, 1999a, 1999b).

9.   The increasing influence, during the 1980s, of the real business cycle approach to the study of economic fluctuations where the Solow neo-classical growth model is used as the benchmark for studying both fluctuations and growth (Kydland and Prescott, 1982). Real business cycle theorists argue that the growth process has a large random element and it is this that causes the 'short-run' fluctuations of output. Aggregate instability is simply the 'manifestation of the process of stochastic growth' (Ryan and Mullineux, 1997). Whereas mainstream macroeconomists treat business cycles and economic growth as largely independent phenomena, real business cycle theorists view aggregate fluctuations as the economy's optimal response to supply-side (productivity) shocks (see Chapter 6).

10.  A much-neglected factor in explaining the growth of interest in a particular branch of an academic discipline is the influence exerted by 'internal scientific characteristics'. Because the incentive structure in academia is related closely to publications, particularly in the USA, a new idea or research programme which is 'article-laden', with a rich vein of topics to mine, is highly contagious. An article-laden new theory supported by new data sets, which challenges the existing orthodoxy, will always prove to be a powerful force within academia (Snowdon and Vane, 1996).

11.  During the last decade there has been an increasing number of papers devoted to what we would label the 'new political macroeconomics of growth'. In addition to the work of Mancur Olson (1993, 2000), the innovative contributions of Daron Acemoglu and his co-authors have been particularly important in reawakening interest in the 'political barriers' to growth (see Acemoglu and Robinson, 2000a, 2000b, 2000c, 2001, 2003; Snowdon, 2004c).

12.  For some economists, such as Robert Lucas (1987, 2003) and Edward Prescott (1996), the renewed interest in growth stems from their belief that business cycle fluctuations 'are not costly to society' and that it is more important for economists to worry about 'increasing the rate of increase in economy-wide productivity and not smoothing business fluctuations' (Prescott, 1996). Indeed, attempts to stabilize the economy in the short term could adversely affect long-term growth prospects (Cooley and Ohanian, 1997; Blackburn, 1999).

## 11.5 Why is Economic Growth So Important?

Since the middle of the eighteenth century human history has been dominated by the phenomenon of modern economic growth. In the eighteenth and
nineteenth centuries economic growth had been largely confined to a small
number of countries (Bairoch, 1993; Easterlin, 1996; Maddison, 2001). Gradually, 'modern' economic growth spread from its origins in Great Britain to
Western Europe and initially to overseas areas settled by European migrants
(Landes, 1969, 1998). The dramatic improvement in living standards that has
taken place in the advanced industrial economies since the Industrial Revolution is now spreading to other parts of the world. However, this diffusion has
been highly uneven and in some cases negligible. The result of this long
period of uneven growth is a pattern of income per capita differentials between the richest and poorest countries of the world that almost defies
comprehension (see Tables 11.1 and 11.2). The importance of economic
growth as a basis for improvements in human welfare cannot be overstated
and is confirmed by numerous empirical studies (see, for example, Dollar and
Kraay, 2002a, 2002b). Even small inter-country differences in growth rates of
per capita income, if sustained over long periods of time, lead to significant
differences in relative living standards between nations. There is no better
demonstration of this fact than the impact on living standards of the growth
experiences of the 'miracle' East Asian economies compared with those of
the majority of sub-Saharan African economies since 1960 by which time the
decolonization process was well under way.

It is worth remembering throughout this discussion that the doubling time
for any variable growing exponentially at an annual rate of 1 per cent is
approximately 70 years. The so-called 'rule of seventy' says that if any
variable grows at $g$ per cent per annum, then it will take approximately $70/g$
years for that variable to double in value. More formally, this can be demonstrated as follows (Jones, 2001a). If $y_t$ is per capita income at time $t$, and $y_0$
some initial value of per capita income, then the value of $y_t$ is given by
equation (11.1):

$$y_t = y_0 e^{gt} \qquad (11.1)$$

Equation (11.1) says that if $y_0$ grows continuously and exponentially at a rate
$g$, its value at time $t$ will be $y_t$. Let the length of time that it will take for per
capita income to double (that is, for $y_t = 2y_0$) be $t^*$. Therefore $t^*$ will be the
solution to equations (11.2) and (11.3) below:

$$2y_0 = y_0 e^{gt^*} \qquad (11.2)$$

$$t^* = \log 2/g \tag{11.3}$$

Since $\log 2 \approx 0.7$, then for a growth rate of 1 per cent, $t^* \approx 0.7/0.01 \approx 70$ years. We can generalize this relationship and say, for example, that any country which has per capita income growth of $g = 5$ per cent will see its living standards double in $70/g = 14$ years. Thus the impact of even small differentials in growth rates, when compounded over time, are striking. David Romer (1996) has expressed this point succinctly as follows: 'the welfare implications of long-run growth swamp any possible effects of the short-run fluctuations that macroeconomics traditionally focuses on'. Barro and Sala-i-Martin (2003) also argue that 'economic growth ... is the part of macroeconomics that really matters', a view in large part endorsed by Mankiw (1995), who writes that 'long-run growth is as important – perhaps more important – than short-run fluctuations'.

Table 11.3 illustrates the compounding effect of sustained growth on the *absolute* living standards of five hypothetical countries, labelled A–E, each of which starts out with an income per capita of $1000.

*Table 11.3    The cumulative impact of differential growth rates*

| Period in years | A g = 1% | B g = 2% | C g = 3% | D g = 4% | E g = 5% |
|---|---|---|---|---|---|
| 0 | $1 000 | $1 000 | $1 000 | $1 000 | $1 000 |
| 10 | 1 100 | 1 220 | 1 340 | 1 480 | 1 630 |
| 20 | 1 220 | 1 490 | 1 800 | 2 190 | 2 650 |
| 30 | 1 350 | 1 810 | 2 430 | 3 240 | 4 320 |
| 40 | 1 490 | 2 210 | 3 260 | 4 800 | 7 040 |
| 50 | 1 640 | 2 690 | 4 380 | 7 110 | 11 470 |

The data show how, over a period of 50 years, variations in growth rates ($g\%$) between countries A–E, cause a substantial divergence of relative living standards.

The hypothetical data in Table 11.3 are replicated in Figure 11.1, which clearly highlights how diverging living standards can emerge over what is a relatively short historical time period of 50 years. Following Galor and Mountford (2003) in Figure 11.2 we also reproduce the actual growth experience of different regions of the world using Maddison's (2001) data.

Figures 11.1 and 11.2 illustrate how economic growth is the single most powerful mechanism for generating long-term increases in income per capita as well as divergence in living standards if growth rates differ across the

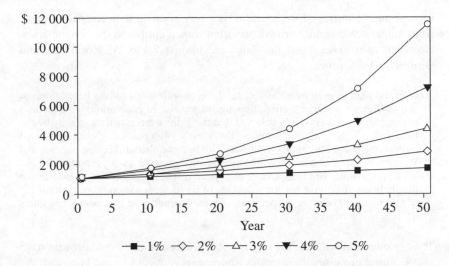

*Figure 11.1   The impact on per capita income of differential growth rates*

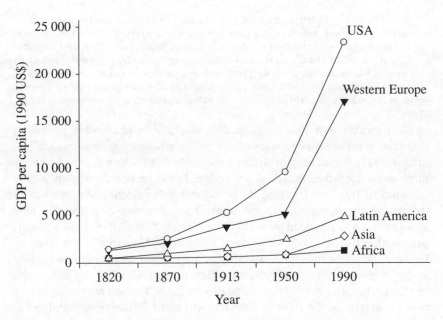

*Source:*   Galor and Mountford (2003).

*Figure 11.2   The great divergence*

regions and countries of the world. Over very short time horizons the gains from moderate economic growth are often imperceptible to the beneficiaries. However, over generations the gains are unmistakable. As Rosenberg and Birdzell (1986) argue:

> Over the year, or even over the decade, the economic gains (of the late eighteenth and nineteenth centuries), after allowing for the rise in population, were so little noticeable that it was widely believed that the gains were experienced only by the rich, and not by the poor. Only as the West's compounded growth continued through the twentieth century did its breadth become clear. It became obvious that Western working classes were prospering and growing as a proportion of the whole population. Not that poverty disappeared. The West's achievement was not the abolition of poverty but the reduction of its incidence from 90 per cent of the population to 30 per cent, 20 per cent, or less, depending on the country and one's definition of poverty.

These views, emphasizing the importance of long-run economic growth, have also featured prominently in policy statements in recent years. For example, in the concluding section of the introduction to the Council of Economic Advisers' (CEA) *Economic Report of the President* (2004, p. 27) we find the following statement:

> As the Founding Fathers signed the Declaration of Independence the great economist Adam Smith wrote: 'Little else is requisite to carry a state to the highest degree of opulence from the lowest barbarism but peace, easy taxes, and tolerable administration of justice: all the rest being brought about by the natural course of things'. The economic analysis presented in this *Report* builds on the ideas of Adam Smith and his intellectual descendants by discussing the role of government in creating an environment that promotes and sustains economic growth.

The importance of sustainable growth was also emphasized in providing justification for the change in monetary policy arrangements made in the UK in May 1997. Within days of winning the election, the 'New Labour' government announced that the Bank of England was to operate within a new institutional framework giving it operational independence with respect to the setting of short-term interest rates. The economic case for this new arrangement was provided on 6 May 1997 by the Chancellor of the Exchequer, Gordon Brown, when, in an open letter to the Governor of the Bank of England, he stated that 'price stability is a precondition for high and stable levels of growth and employment, which in turn will help to create the conditions for price stability on a sustainable basis. To that end, the monetary policy objective of the Bank of England will be to deliver price stability (as defined by the Government's inflation target) and, without prejudice to this objective, to support the Government's economic policy, including its objectives for growth and employment' (Brown, 1997; see also Brown, 2001).

The power of economic growth to raise living standards is perhaps best illustrated by the history of the twentieth century. Despite two devastating world wars, the Great Depression and collapse of international integration during the interwar period, and the rise and fall of the socialist experiment, the majority of the world's population are better off than their parents and grandparents in terms of income per capita (PPP$). If life expectancy is taken into account there has been a remarkable improvement in welfare (see Crafts, 2003).

## 11.6 Modern Economic Growth in Historical Perspective

In addition to the 'Great Depression' of the 1930s, and the 'Great Inflation' of the 1970s, the third phenomenon that has dominated the macroeconomic history of the twentieth century has been the spread of economic growth among the economies of the world. Indeed, Robert Lucas (see interview at the end of Chapter 5) believes 'that economic growth, and particularly the diffusion of economic growth to what we used to call the Third World, is *the* major macroeconomic event of the twentieth century'. As Maddison's (2001) data show, before the modern era living standards for the vast majority of the world's population progressed at a glacial pace. In reflecting on the 'Economic Possibilities of Our Grandchildren', Keynes (1930b) commented that 'From the earliest times of which we have record ... there was no very great change in the standard of life of the average man living in the civilised centres of the earth ... This slow rate of progress, or lack of progress, was due to two reasons – to the remarkable absence of important technical improvements and to the failure of capital to accumulate.'

Since an increase in the capacity to produce can either be absorbed by an increase in population or lead to an increase in per capita income, it is important at the outset to distinguish between extensive and intensive growth. Reynolds (1985) defines extensive growth as a situation where an increase in GDP is fully absorbed by population increase with no upward trend in per capita income. The pre-modern world economy was not characterized by persistent stagnation. The fact that for thousands of years the world's population increased, even if 'glacially slowly', is evidence of extensive growth. If we assume that for the vast majority of people, subsistence living was the norm, then a larger population is only possible if total output also rises (Kremer, 1993). So extensive growth has been 'fairly common' throughout human history (Lal, 1999).

In contrast, intensive growth is where GDP growth exceeds population growth, allowing a sustained rise in living standards as measured by real income per capita. As Reynolds shows, periods of intensive growth have usually been preceded by a long period of extensive growth, often lasting several centuries, and the significant 'turning point' for any economy is the period of transition from extensive to intensive growth. The 'turning point is actually a period of a decade or two around the cited year, during which one observes a significant and continuing rise in *per capita* income' (Reynolds, 1994). In the past, in predominantly agrarian (organic) economies, the possibilities for sustained intensive growth were extremely limited. The availability and productivity of land determined the amount of extensive growth, but once the supply of suitable agricultural land was exhausted, diminishing returns set in. When these forces are combined with Malthusian population dynamics it is hardly surprising to find that many classical economists predicted the inevitability of a long-run stationary state involving subsistence standards of living for the vast majority of humanity.

It is also useful to make a further distinction when discussing intensive growth. Eric Jones (1988) distinguishes between two forms of intensive growth, namely, 'Smithian growth' and 'Promethian growth'. Smithian intensive growth relies on the gains to productivity that can be made from the division of labour, specialization and trade. Such growth must eventually run into diminishing returns as there are limits to the gains from resource reallocation. In contrast, Promethian intensive growth is sustainable, being driven by technological progress and innovation. It was in the latter part of the eighteenth century that we began to see the emergence of Promethian growth in Britain as during the Industrial Revolution a predominantly organic economy was replaced by a mineral-based one. Of course, the billion-dollar question that many economists and economic historians have tried to answer is: why did Promethian growth begin in a specific geographical location (that is, Britain) and why at a specific time in history? (See Landes, 1969, 1990, 1998; Crafts, 1983, 1985; E. Jones, 1988; Wrigley, 1988; Mokyr, 1990, 1993, 2005; Diamond, 1997; Lal, 1999; Jay, 2000; Pomeranz, 2000, Jones, 2001b.)

The phenomenon of intensive Promethian growth represents, in Easterlin's (1996) view, a distinctive 'regime change'. Easterlin divides world economic history into three epochs, each of which possess distinctive characteristics in terms of the main form of occupation, principal type of population settlement, and the growth rates of population and real GDP per capita. Easterlin's epochs consist of first, a prehistoric epoch ending about 8000 BC; second, an epoch of settled agriculture, initiated by the Neolithic agricultural revolution, which lasted until the middle of the eighteenth century; and third, an epoch of modern economic growth involving an enormous transformation in the structure and character of economic activity. In the modern growth regime, initially, the positive Malthusian relationship between income per capita and population growth persists, leading to a population explosion. Eventually, however, the modern growth regime 'is characterised by steady growth in both income per capita and the level of technology' and this leads to 'a negative relationship between the level of output and the growth rate of population' as the demographic transition kicks in (Galor and Weil, 2000). Several economists have recently argued that any story of the growth process, in addition to accounting for the modern experience of sustained growth, should also be able to account for the long period of Malthusian stagnation (see Galor and Weil, 1999, 2000; Galor and Moav, 2002; Hansen and Prescott, 2002; Parente and Prescott, 2005; see also section 11.21).

## 11.7  The Stylized Facts of Growth

A convincing theory of economic growth obviously needs to be consistent with the stylized facts of growth that have emerged from historical experience. It was Kaldor (1961) who first set out what he considered to be the main empirical observations with which any growth theory needed to be consistent. Kaldor's six stylized facts, or broad tendencies, are set out below (K1–K6), together with the additional 'facts' (R7–R11) noted by P. Romer (1989) and (J12–J14) noted by Jones (2001a).

K1    Output per worker grows continuously, with no secular tendency for the rate of growth of productivity to decline.

K2    The capital–labour ratio shows continuous growth.

K3    The rate of return on capital is stable.

K4    The capital–output ratio is stable.

K5    The shares of labour and capital in GDP remain stable.

K6    We observe significant variation in the rate of growth of productivity across countries.

R7    In a broad cross-section of countries the average growth rate is uncorrelated with the level of per capita income.

R8    Growth is positively correlated with the volume of international trade.

R.9    Growth rates are negatively correlated with population growth.

R10   Growth accounting research always finds a 'residual'; that is, accumulation of factor inputs alone cannot account for growth.

R11   High-income countries attract both skilled and unskilled workers.

J12    There is enormous variation in income per capita across countries.

J13    Growth rates for the world as a whole, and for individual countries, vary substantially over time.

J14    The relative position of any country in the world distribution of income can change.

Of course not all of these stylized facts are independent. As Romer (1989) points out, fact K2 results from facts K1 and K4. Facts K4 and K5 imply fact K3. Romer also questions the validity of K5 (see also Jones, 2004). With respect to fact J13, economists have only recently attempted to provide a comprehensive theory that can explain the evolution of growth rates from Malthusian stagnation to 'modern economic growth' (see Galor and Weil, 1999, 2000; Hansen and Prescott, 2002).

## 11.8 Proximate v. Fundamental Sources of Growth

In Temple's (1999) survey of growth empirics he highlights the fact that one of the important history lessons since 1960 has been that while some countries have succeeded in 'making a miracle', other countries have been 'growth disasters'. When analysing the experience of the miracle economies, economists need to 'use these events to help in assessing economic policies that may affect growth rates in other countries' (Lucas, 1993). However, this cannot be done without having theoretical structures in place that help researchers make sense of the 'mass' of data that is now available to economists. As Lucas argues, to be able to glean valuable lessons from the East Asian experience, 'One needs, in short, a theory'. Echoing this theme, Temple (1999) reminds economists of what is perhaps the key issue: 'Why have some countries grown rich while others remain poor? It is hard to think of a more fundamental question for economists to answer.'

In analysing developments in growth theory it is useful to begin by distinguishing between proximate and fundamental causes of growth. The proximate causes relate to the accumulation of factor inputs such as capital and labour, and also to variables which influence the productivity of these inputs, such as scale economies and technological change. The research of growth accountants such as Denison (1967, 1974, 1985), Jorgensen (1996, 2001) and Maddison (1972, 1987, 1995) has produced a useful taxonomy of the various proximate sources of growth, and the neo-Keynesian, neoclassical and endogenous growth theories tend to concentrate on modelling these proximate variables. However, once we have considered the impact of these proximate determinants of growth we are left with the deeper question: 'Why are some countries so much better than others at accumulating human and physical capital and producing or adopting new ideas and knowledge?' That is, we need to investigate the fundamental determinants of growth (see Rodrik, 2003).

The fundamental or deep sources of growth relate to those variables that have an important influence on a country's ability and capacity to accumulate factors of production and invest in the production of knowledge. For example, Temple (1999) considers the following 'wider' influences on growth: population growth, the influence of the financial sector, the general macroeconomic environment, trade regimes, the size of government, income distribution and the political and social environment. To this list Gallup et al.

(1998) would add the neglected influence of geography. Moving from the proximate to the fundamental causes of growth also shifts the focus of attention to the institutional framework of an economy, to its 'social capability' (Abramovitz, 1986), 'social infrastructure' (Hall and Jones, 1997, 1999) or 'ancillary variables' (Baumol et al., 1994). There is now widespread acceptance of the idea that 'good' governance and institutions and incentive structures are an important precondition for successful growth and development (World Bank, 1997, 2002).

In his historical survey of economic growth analysis, Rostow (1990) put forward a central proposition that 'from the eighteenth century to the present, growth theories have been based on one formulation or another of a universal equation or production function'. As formulated by Adelman (1958), this can be expressed as equation (11.4):

$$Y_t = f(K_t, N_t, L_t, A_t, S_t) \qquad (11.4)$$

where $K_t$, $N_t$ and $L_t$ represent the services flowing from the capital stock, natural resources (geography) and labour resources respectively, $A_t$ denotes an economy's stock of applied knowledge, and $S_t$ represents what Adelman calls the 'sociocultural milieu', and Abramovitz (1986) more recently has called 'social capability', within which the economy functions. More sophisticated models distinguish between human and physical capital. Indeed, many authors regard human capital as the key ingredient of economic growth (Lucas, 1988; Galor and Moav, 2003). Heckman (2003), for example, argues that China's below average spending on investment in education compared to physical capital accumulation is 'a serious distortion' of policy that is likely to retard progress in China. Goldin (2001) has also attributed much of the US economic success in the twentieth century to the accumulation of human capital.

According to Rostow (1990), 'something like the basic equation is embedded equally in Hume's economic essays, Adam Smith's *The Wealth of Nations*, the latest neoclassical growth model, and virtually every formulation in between'. This universal equation encompasses both proximate and fundamental causes of economic growth and Abramovitz drew attention to the importance of these factors 50 years ago (see Nelson, 1997). Clearly, $S_t$ contains the influence of non-economic as well as economic variables which can influence the growth potential and performance of an economy including the institutions, incentives, rules and regulations that determine the allocation of entrepreneurial talent (Baumol, 1990). Hence in recent years economists' research into the 'deeper' determinants of growth has led some to stress the importance of institutions and incentive structures (North, 1990; Olson, 2000), trade and openness (Krueger, 1997; Dollar and Kraay, 2003) and the much-neglected impact of geography (Bloom and Sachs, 1998). It is important to note that Adam Smith had highlighted all three of these 'deeper' determinants of growth over 200 years ago!

In sections 11.17–11.20 we will examine the 'deeper' determinants of economic growth in more detail, but first, in sections 11.8–11.10, we survey the three main waves of growth theory that have been influential in the second half of the twentieth century to date. All three approaches emphasize the proximate determinants of growth, namely:

1. the neo-Keynesian Harrod–Domar model;
2. the Solow–Swan neoclassical model; and
3. the Romer–Lucas-inspired endogenous growth models.

In each case the ideas developed represent interesting examples of multiple discovery. The first wave of interest focused on the neo-Keynesian work of Roy Harrod (1939, 1948) and Evsey Domar (1946, 1947). In the mid-1950s the development of the neoclassical growth model by Robert Solow (1956) and Trevor Swan (1956) stimulated a second, more lasting and substantial, wave of interest, which, after a period of relative neglect between 1970 and 1986, has been reignited (Mankiw et al., 1992; Mankiw, 1995; Klenow and Rodriguez-Clare, 1997a, 1997b). The third and most recent wave, initiated by the research of Paul Romer (1986) and Robert Lucas (1988), led to the development of endogenous growth theory, which emerged in response to perceived theoretical and empirical deficiencies associated with the neoclassical model (P. Romer, 1994a; Crafts, 1996; Blaug, 2002).

## 11.9   The Harrod–Domar Model

Following the publication of Keynes's *General Theory* in 1936, some economists sought to dynamize Keynes's static short-run theory in order to investigate the long-run dynamics of capitalist market economies. Roy Harrod (1939, 1948) and Evsey Domar (1946, 1947) independently developed theories that relate an economy's rate of growth to its capital stock. While Keynes emphasized the impact of investment on aggregate demand, Harrod and Domar emphasized how investment spending also increased an economy's productive capacity (a supply-side effect). While Harrod's theory is more ambitious than Domar's, building on Keynesian short-run macroeconomics in order to identify the necessary conditions for equilibrium in a dynamic setting, hereafter we will refer only to the 'Harrod–Domar model', ignoring the subtle differences between the respective contributions of these two outstanding economists.

A major strength of the Harrod–Domar model is its simplicity. The model assumes an exogenous rate of labour force growth ($n$), a given technology exhibiting fixed factor proportions (constant capital–labour ratio, $K/L$) and a fixed capital–output ratio ($K/Y$). Assuming a two-sector economy (households and firms), we can write the simple national income equation as (11.5):

$$Y_t = C_t + S_t \tag{11.5}$$

where $Y_t = GDP$, $C_t =$ consumption and $S_t =$ saving.

Equilibrium in this simple economy requires (11.6):

$$I_t = S_t \tag{11.6}$$

Substituting (11.6) into (11.5) yields (11.7):

$$Y_t = C_t + I_t \tag{11.7}$$

Within the Harrod–Domar framework the growth of real GDP is assumed to be proportional to the share of investment spending ($I$) in GDP and for an economy to grow, net additions to the capital stock are required. The evolution of the capital stock over time is given in equation (11.8):

$$K_{t+1} = (1-\delta)K_t + I_t \tag{11.8}$$

where $\delta$ is the rate of depreciation of the capital stock. The relationship between the size of the total capital stock ($K$) and total GDP ($Y$) is known as the capital–output ratio ($K/Y = v$) and is assumed fixed. Given that we have defined $v = K/Y$, it also follows that $v = \Delta K/\Delta Y$ (where $\Delta K/\Delta Y$ is the incremental capital–output ratio, or ICOR). If we assume that total new investment is determined by total savings, then the essence of the Harrod–Domar model can be set out as follows. Assume that total saving is some proportion ($s$) of GDP ($Y$), as shown in equation (11.9):

$$S_t = sY_t \tag{11.9}$$

Since $K = vY$ and $I_t = S_t$, it follows that we can rewrite equation (11.8) as equation (11.10):

$$vY_{t+1} = (1-\delta)vY_t + sY_t \tag{11.10}$$

Dividing through by $v$, simplifying, and subtracting $Y_t$ from both sides of equation (11.10) yields equation (11.11):

$$Y_{t+1} - Y_t = [s/v - \delta]Y_t \tag{11.11}$$

Dividing through by $Y_t$ gives us equation (11.12):

$$[Y_{t+1} - Y_t]/Y_t = (s/v) - \delta \qquad (11.12)$$

Here $[Y_{t+1} - Y_t]/Y_t$ is the growth rate of GDP. Letting $G = [Y_{t+1} - Y_t]/Y_t$, we can write the Harrod–Domar growth equation as (11.13):

$$G = s/v - \delta \qquad (11.13)$$

This simply states that the growth rate $(G)$ of GDP is jointly determined by the savings ratio $(s)$ divided by the capital–output ratio $(v)$. The higher the savings ratio and the lower the capital–output ratio and depreciation rate, the faster will an economy grow. In the discussion that follows we will ignore the depreciation rate and consider the Harrod–Domar model as being represented by the equation (11.14):

$$G = s/v \qquad (11.14)$$

Thus it is evident from (11.14) that the Harrod–Domar model 'sanctioned the overriding importance of capital accumulation in the quest for enhanced growth' (Shaw, 1992).

The Harrod–Domar model, as Bhagwati recalls, became tremendously influential in the development economics literature during the third quarter of the twentieth century, and was a key component within the framework of economic planning. 'The implications of this popular model were dramatic and reassuring. It suggested that the central developmental problem was simply to increase resources devoted to investment' (Bhagwati, 1984). For example, if a developing country desired to achieve a growth rate of per capita income of 2 per cent per annum (that is, living standards double every 35 years), and population is estimated to be growing at 2 per cent, then economic planners would need to set a target rate of GDP growth $(G^*)$ equal to 4 per cent. If $v = 4$, this implies that $G^*$ can only be achieved with a desired savings ratio $(s^*)$ of 0.16, or 16 per cent of GDP. If $s^* > s$, there is a 'savings gap', and planners needed to devise policies for plugging this gap.

Since the rate of growth in the Harrod–Domar model is positively related to the savings ratio, development economists during the 1950s concentrated their research effort on understanding how to raise private savings ratios in order to enable less developed economies to 'take off' into 'self-sustained growth' (Lewis, 1954, 1955; Rostow, 1960; Easterly, 1999). Reflecting the contemporary development ideas of the 1950s, government fiscal policy was also seen to have a prominent role to play since budgetary surpluses could (in theory) substitute for private domestic savings. If domestic sources of finance were inadequate to achieve the desired growth target, then foreign aid could fill the 'savings gap' (Riddell, 1987). Aid requirements ($Ar$) would simply be calculated as $s^* - s = Ar$ (Chenery and Strout, 1966). However, a major weakness of the Harrod–Domar approach is the assumption of a fixed capital–output ratio. Since the inverse of $v$ ($1/v$) is the productivity of investment ($\phi$), we can rewrite equation (11.14) as follows:

$$G = s\phi \tag{11.15}$$

Unfortunately, as Bhagwati (1993) observes, the productivity of investment is not a given, but reflects the efficiency of the policy framework and the incentive structures within which investment decisions are taken. The weak growth performance of India before the 1980s reflects, 'not a disappointing savings performance, but rather a disappointing productivity performance' (Bhagwati, 1993). Hence the growth–investment relationship turned out to be 'loose and unstable' due to the multiple factors that influence growth (Easterly, 2001a). Furthermore, economists soon became aware of a second major flaw in the 'aid requirements' or 'financing gap' model. The model assumed that aid inflows would go into investment one to one. But it soon became apparent that inflows of foreign aid, with the objective of closing the savings gap, did not necessarily boost total savings. Aid does not go into investment one to one. Indeed, in many cases inflows of aid led to a reduction of domestic savings together with a decline in the productivity of investment (Griffin, 1970; White, 1992). The research of Boone (1996) confirms that inflows of foreign aid have not raised growth rates in most recipient developing countries. A further problem is that in many developing countries the 'soft budget constraints' operating within the public sector created a climate for what Bhagwati calls 'goofing off'. It is therefore hardly surprising that public sector enterprises frequently failed to generate profits intended to add to government saving. In short, 'capital fundamentalism' and the 'aid-financed investment fetish', which dominated development thinking for much of the period after 1950, led economists up the wrong path in their 'elusive quest for growth' (King and Levine, 1994; Easterly, 2001a, 2003; Easterly et al., 2003; Snowdon, 2003a). Indeed, William Easterly (1999), a former World Bank economist, argues that the Harrod–Domar model is far from dead and still continues to exercise considerable influence on economists working within the major international financial institutions even if it died long ago in the academic literature. Easterly shows that economists working at the World Bank, International Monetary Fund, Inter-American Bank, European Bank for Reconstruction and Development, and the International Labour Organization still frequently employ the Harrod–Domar–Chenery–Strout methodology to calculate the investment and aid requirements needed in order for specific countries to achieve their growth targets. However, as Easterly convincingly demonstrates, the evidence that aid flows into investment on a one-for-one basis, and that there is a fixed linear relationship between growth and investment in the short run, is 'soundly rejected'.

A further weakness of the Harrod–Domar framework is the assumption of zero substitutability between capital and labour (that is, a fixed factor proportions production function). This is a 'crucial' but inappropriate assumption for a model concerned with long-run growth. This assumption of the Harrod–Domar model also leads to the renowned instability property that 'even for the long run an economic system is at best balanced on a knife-edge equilibrium growth' (Solow, 1956). In Harrod's model the possibility of achieving steady growth with full employment was remote. Only in very special circumstances will an economy remain in equilibrium with full employment of both labour and capital. As Solow (1988) noted in his Nobel Memorial lecture, to achieve steady growth in a Harrod–Domar world would be 'a miraculous stroke of luck'. The problem arises from the assumption of a production function with an inflexible technology. In the Harrod–Domar model the capital–output ratio ($K/Y$) and the capital–labour ratio ($K/L$) are assumed constant. In a growth setting this means that $K$ and $Y$ must always grow at the same rate to maintain equilibrium. However, because the model also assumes a constant capital–labour ratio ($K/L$), $K$ and $L$ must also grow at the same rate. Therefore, if we assume that the labour force ($L$) grows at the same rate as the rate of growth of population ($n$), then we can conclude that the only way that equilibrium can be maintained in the model is for $n = G = s/v$. It would only be by pure coincidence that $n = G$. If $n > G$, the result will be continually rising unemployment. If $G > n$, the capital stock will become increasingly idle and the growth rate of output will slow down to $G = n$. Thus, whenever $K$ and $L$ do not grow at the same rate, the economy falls off its equilibrium 'knife-edge' growth path. However, the evidence is overwhelming that this property does not fit well with the actual experience of growth (for a more detailed discussion of the Harrod–Domar model see Hahn and Matthews, 1964; H. Jones, 1975).

## 11.10  The Solow Neoclassical Growth Model

Following the seminal contributions of Solow (1956, 1957) and Swan (1956), the neoclassical model became the dominant approach to the analysis of growth, at least within academia. Between 1956 and 1970 economists refined 'old growth theory', better known as the Solow neoclassical model of economic growth (Solow, 2000, 2002). Building on a neoclassical production function framework, the Solow model highlights the impact on growth of saving, population growth and technolgical progress in a closed economy setting without a government sector. Despite recent developments in endogenous growth theory, the Solow model remains the essential starting point to any discussion of economic growth. As Mankiw (1995, 2003) notes, whenever practical macroeconomists have to answer questions about long-run growth they usually begin with a simple neoclassical growth model (see also Abel and Bernanke, 2001; Jones, 2001a; Barro and Sala-i-Martin, 2003).

The key assumptions of the Solow model are: (i) for simplicity it is assumed that the economy consists of one sector producing one type of commodity that can be used for either investment or consumption purposes; (ii) the economy is closed to international transactions and the government sector is ignored; (iii) all output that is saved is invested; that is, in the Solow model the absence of a separate investment function implies that Keynesian difficulties are eliminated since *ex ante* saving and *ex ante* investment are always equivalent; (iv) since the model is concerned with the long run there are no Keynesian stability problems; that is, the assumptions of full price flexibility and monetary neutrality apply and the economy is always producing its potential (natural) level of total output; (v) Solow abandons the Harrod–Domar assumptions of a fixed capital–output ratio ($K/Y$) and fixed capital–labour ratio ($K/L$); (vi) the rate of technological progress, population growth and the depreciation rate of the capital stock are all determined exogenously.

Given these assumptions we can concentrate on developing the three key relationships in the Solow model, namely, the production function, the consumption function and the capital accumulation process.

**The production function**
The Solow growth model is built around the neoclassical aggregate production function (11.16) and focuses on the *proximate* causes of growth:

$$Y = A_t F(K, L) \qquad\qquad (11.16)$$

where $Y$ is real output, $K$ is capital, $L$ is the labour input and $A_t$ is a measure of technology (that is, the way that inputs to the production function can be transformed into output) which is exogenous and taken simply to depend on time. Sometimes, $A_t$ is called 'total factor productivity'. It is important to be clear about what the assumption of exogenous technology means in the Solow model. In the neoclassical theory of growth, technology is assumed to be a public good. Applied to the world economy this means that every country is assumed to share the same stock of knowledge which is freely available; that is, all countries have access to the same production function. In his defence of the neoclassical assumption of treating technology as if it were a public good, Mankiw (1995) puts his case as follows:

The production function should not be viewed literally as a description of a specific production process, but as a mapping from quantities of inputs into a quantity of output. To say that different countries have the same production function is merely to say that if they had the same inputs, they would produce the same output. Different countries with different levels of inputs need not rely on exactly the same processes for producing goods and services. When a country doubles its capital stock, it does not give each worker twice as many shovels. Instead, it replaces shovels with bulldozers. For the purposes of modelling economic growth, this change should be viewed as a movement along the same production function, rather than a shift to a completely new production function.

As we shall see later (section 11.15), many economists disagree with this approach and insist that there are significant technology gaps between nations (see Fagerberg, 1994; P. Romer, 1995). However, to progress with our examination of the Solow model we will continue to treat technology as a public good.

For simplicity, let us begin by first assuming a situation where there is no technological progress. Making this assumption of a given state of technology will allow us to concentrate on the relationship between output per worker and capital per worker. We can therefore rewrite (11.16) as:

$$Y = F(K, L) \tag{11.17}$$

The aggregate production function given by (11.17) is assumed to be 'well behaved'; that is, it satisfies the following three conditions (see Inada, 1963; D. Romer, 2001; Barro and Sala-i-Martin, 2003; Mankiw, 2003). First, for all values of $K > 0$ and $L > 0$, $F(\cdot)$ exhibits positive but diminishing marginal returns with respect to both capital and labour; that is, $\partial F/\partial K > 0$, $\partial^2 F/\partial K^2 < 0$, $\partial F/\partial L > 0$, and $\partial^2 F/\partial L^2 < 0$. Second, the production function exhibits constant returns to scale such that $F(\lambda K, \lambda L) = \lambda Y$; that is, raising inputs by $\lambda$ will also increase aggregate output by $\lambda$. Letting $\lambda = 1/L$ yields $Y/L = F(K/L)$. This assumption allows (11.17) to be written down in intensive form as (11.18), where $y$ = output per worker ($Y/L$) and $k$ = capital per worker ($K/L$):

$$y = f(k), \text{ where } f'(k) > 0, \text{ and } f''(k) < 0 \text{ for all } k \tag{11.18}$$

Equation (11.18) states that output per worker is a positive function of the capital–labour ratio and exhibits diminishing returns. The key assumption of constant returns to scale implies that the economy is sufficiently large that any Smithian gains from further division of labour and specialization have already been exhausted, so that the size of the economy, in terms of the labour force, has no influence on output per worker. Third, as the capital–labour ratio approaches infinity ($k \rightarrow \infty$) the marginal product of capital ($MPK$)

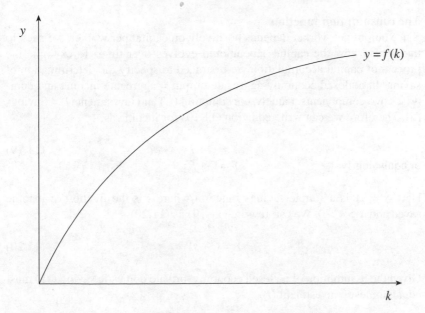

*Figure 11.3    The neoclassical aggregate production function*

approaches zero; as the capital–labour ratio approaches zero the marginal product of capital tends towards infinity ($MPK \to \infty$).

Figure 11.3 shows an intensive form of the neoclassical aggregate production function that satisfies the above conditions. As the diagram illustrates, for a given technology, any country that increases its capital–labour ratio (more equipment per worker) will have a higher output per worker. However, because of diminishing returns, the impact on output per worker resulting from capital accumulation per worker (capital deepening) will continuously decline. Thus for a given increase in $k$, the impact on $y$ will be much greater where capital is relatively scarce than in economies where capital is relatively abundant. That is, the accumulation of capital should have a much more dramatic impact on labour productivity in developing countries compared to developed countries.

The slope of the production function measures the marginal product of capital, where $MPK = f(k + 1) - f(k)$. In the Solow model the $MPK$ should be much higher in developing economies compared to developed economies. In an open economy setting with no restrictions on capital mobility, we should therefore expect to see, *ceteris paribus*, capital flowing from rich to poor countries, attracted by higher potential returns, thereby accelerating the process of capital accumulation.

### The consumption function

Since output per worker depends positively on capital per worker, we need to understand how the capital–labour ratio evolves over time. To examine the process of capital accumulation we first need to specify the determination of saving. In a closed economy aggregate output = aggregate income and comprises two components, namely, consumption ($C$) and investment ($I$) = Savings ($S$). Therefore we can write equation (11.19) for income as:

$$Y = C + I \tag{11.19}$$

or equivalently
$$Y = C + S$$

Here $S = sY$ is a simple savings function where $s$ is the fraction of income saved and $1 > s > 0$. We can rewrite (11.19) as (11.20):

$$Y = C + sY \tag{11.20}$$

Given the assumption of a closed economy, private domestic saving ($sY$) must equal domestic investment ($I$).

### The capital accumulation process

A country's capital stock ($K_t$) at a point in time consists of plant, machinery and infrastructure. Each year a proportion of the capital stock wears out. The parameter $\delta$ represents this process of depreciation. Countering this tendency for the capital stock to decline is a flow of investment spending each year ($I_t$) that adds to the capital stock. Therefore, given these two forces, we can write an equation for the evolution of the capital stock of the following form:

$$K_{t+1} = I_t + (1 - \delta)K_t = sY_t + K_t - \delta K_t \tag{11.21}$$

Rewriting (11.21) in per worker terms yields equation (11.22):

$$K_{t+1}/L = sY_t/L + K_t/L - \delta K_t/L \tag{11.22}$$

Deducting $K_t/L$ from both sides of (11.22) gives us (11.23):

$$K_{t+1}/L - K_t/L = sY_t/L - \delta K_t/L \tag{11.23}$$

In the neoclassical theory of growth the accumulation of capital evolves according to (11.24), which is the fundamental differential equation of the Solow model:

$$\dot{k} = sf(k) - \delta k \tag{11.24}$$

where $\dot{k} = K_{t+1}/L - K_t/L$ is the change of the capital input per worker, and $sf(k) = sy = sY_t/L$ is saving (investment) per worker. The $\delta k = \delta K_t/L$ term represents the 'investment requirements' per worker in order to keep the capital–labour ratio constant. The steady-state condition in the Solow model is given in equation (11.25):

$$sf(k^*) - \delta k^* = 0 \qquad (11.25)$$

Thus, in the steady state $sf(k^*) = \delta k^*$; that is, investment per worker is just sufficient to cover depreciation per worker, leaving capital per worker constant.

Extending the model to allow for growth of the labour force is relatively straightforward. In the Solow model it is assumed that the participation rate is constant, so that the labour force grows at a constant proportionate rate equal to the exogenously determined rate of growth of population $= n$. Because $k = K/L$, population growth, by increasing the supply of labour, will reduce $k$. Therefore population growth has the same impact on $k$ as depreciation. We need to modify (11.24) to reflect the influence of population growth. The fundamental differential equation now becomes:

$$\dot{k} = sf(k) - (n+\delta)k \qquad (11.26)$$

We can think of the expression $(n + \delta)k$ as the 'required' or 'break-even' investment necessary to keep the capital stock per unit of labour $(k)$ constant. In order to prevent $k$ from falling, some investment is required to offset depreciation. This is the $(\delta)k$ term in (11.26). Some investment is also required because the quantity of labour is growing at a rate $= n$. This is the $(n)k$ term in (11.26). Hence the capital stock must grow at rate $(n + \delta)$ just to hold $k$ steady. When investment per unit of labour is greater than required for break-even investment, then $k$ will be rising and in this case the economy is experiencing 'capital deepening'. Given the structure of the Solow model the economy will, in time, approach a steady state where actual investment per worker, $sf(k)$, equals break-even investment per worker, $(n + \delta)k$. In the steady state the change in capital per worker $\dot{k} = 0$, although the economy continues to experience 'capital widening', the extension of existing capital per worker to additional workers. Using $^*$ to indicate steady-state values, we can define the steady state as (11.27):

$$sf(k^*) = (n+\delta)k^* \qquad (11.27)$$

Figure 11.4 captures the essential features of the Solow model outlined by equations (11.18) to (11.27). In the top panel of Figure 11.4 the curve $f(k)$

graphs a well-behaved intensive production function; $sf(k)$ shows the level of savings per worker at different levels of the capital–labour ratio $(k)$; the linear relationship $(n + \delta)k$ shows that break-even investment is proportional to $k$. At the capital–labour ratio $k_1$, savings (investment) per worker $(b)$ exceed required investment $(c)$ and so the economy experiences capital deepening and $k$ rises. At $k_1$ consumption per worker is indicated by $d - b$ and output per worker is $y_1$. At $k_2$, because $(n + \delta)k > sf(k)$ the capital–labour ratio falls, capital becomes 'shallower' (Jones, 1975). The steady state balanced growth path occurs at $k^*$, where investment per worker equals break-even investment. Output per worker is $y^*$ and consumption per worker is $e - a$. In the bottom panel of Figure 11.4 the relationship between $\dot{k}$ (the change of the capital–labour ratio) and $k$ is shown with a phase diagram. When $\dot{k} > 0$, $k$ is rising; when $\dot{k} < 0$, $k$ is falling.

In the steady state equilibrium, shown as point $a$ in the top panel of Figure 11.4, output per worker $(y^*)$ and capital per worker $(k^*)$ are constant. However, although there is no intensive growth in the steady state, there is extensive growth because population (and hence the labour input $= L$) is growing at a rate of $n$ per cent per annum. Thus, in order for $y^* = Y/L$ and $k^* = K/L$ to remain constant, both $Y$ and $K$ must also grow at the same rate as population.

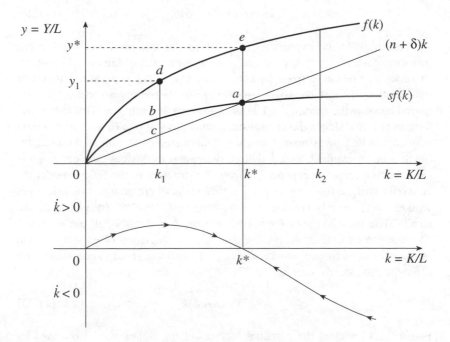

*Figure 11.4   The Solow growth model*

It can be seen from Figure 11.4 that the steady state level of output per worker will increase (*ceteris paribus*) if the rate of population growth and/or the depreciation rate are reduced (a downward pivot of the $(n + \delta)k$ function), and vice versa. The steady state level of output per worker will also increase (*ceteris paribus*) if the savings rate increases (an upward shift of the $sf(k)$ function), and vice versa. Of particular importance is the prediction from the Solow model that an increase in the savings ratio cannot permanently increase the long-run rate of growth. A higher savings ratio does temporarily increase the growth rate during the period of transitional dynamics to the new steady state and it also permanently increases the level of output per worker. Of course the period of transitional dynamics may be a long historical time period and level effects are important and should not be undervalued (see Solow, 2000; Temple, 2003).

So far we have assumed zero technological progress. Given the fact that output per worker has shown a continuous tendency to increase, at least since the onset of the Industrial Revolution in the now developed economies, a model that predicts a constant steady state output per worker is clearly unsatisfactory. A surprising conclusion of the neoclassical growth model is that without technological progress the ability of an economy to raise output per worker via capital accumulation is limited by the interaction of diminishing returns, the willingness of people to save, the rate of population growth, and the rate of depreciation of the capital stock. In order to explain continuous growth of output per worker in the long run the Solow model must incorporate the influence of sustained technological progress.

The production function (11.16), in its Cobb–Douglas form, can be written as (11.28):

$$Y = A_t K^\alpha L^{1-\alpha} \tag{11.28}$$

where $\alpha$ and $1 - \alpha$ are weights reflecting the share of capital and labour in the national income. Assuming constant returns to scale, output per worker ($Y/L$) is not affected by the scale of output, and, for a given technology, $A_{t0}$, output per worker is positively related to the capital–labour ratio ($K/L$). We can therefore rewrite the production function equation (11.28) in terms of output per worker as shown by equation (11.29):

$$Y/L = A(t_0)(K/L) = A(t_0)K^\alpha L^{1-\alpha}/L = A(t_0)(K/L)^\alpha \tag{11.29}$$

Letting $y = Y/L$ and $k = K/L$, we finally arrive at the 'intensive form' of the aggregate production function shown in equation (11.30):

$$y = A(t_0)k^\alpha \tag{11.30}$$

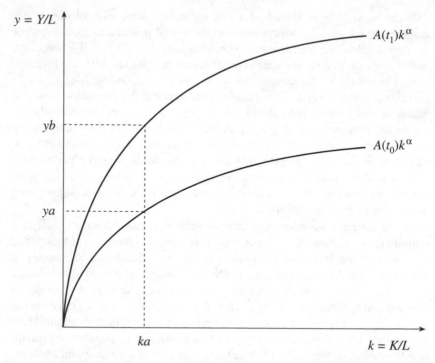

*Figure 11.5   Technological progress*

For a given technology, equation (11.30) tells us that increasing the amount of capital per worker (capital deepening) will lead to an increase in output per worker. The impact of exogenous technological progress is illustrated in Figure 11.5 by a shift of the production function between two time periods ($t_0 \Rightarrow t_1$) from $A(t_0)k^\alpha$ to $A(t_1)k^\alpha$, raising output per worker from *ya* to *yb* for a given capital–labour ratio of *ka*. Continuous upward shifts of the production function, induced by an exogenously determined growth of knowledge, provide the only mechanism for 'explaining' steady state growth of output per worker in the neoclassical model.

Therefore, although it was not Solow's original intention, it was his neoclassical theory of growth that brought technological progress to prominence as a major explanatory factor in the analysis of economic growth. But, somewhat paradoxically, in Solow's theory technological progress is exogenous, that is, not explained by the model! Solow admits that he made technological progress exogenous in his model in order to simplify it and also because he did not 'pretend to understand' it (see Solow interview at the end of this chapter) and, as Abramovitz (1956) observed, the Solow residual turned out to be 'a measure of our ignorance' (see also Abramovitz, 1999). While Barro and Sala-i-Martin (1995) conclude that this was 'an obviously unsatisfactory situation', David Romer (1996) comments that the Solow model 'takes as given the behaviour of the variable that it identifies as the main driving force of growth'. Furthermore, although the Solow model attributes no role to capital accumulation in achieving long-run sustainable growth, it should be noted that productivity growth may not be independent of capital accumulation if technical progress is embodied in new capital equipment. Unlike disembodied technical progress, which can raise the productivity of the existing inputs, embodied technical progress does not benefit older capital equipment. It should also be noted that DeLong and Summers (1991, 1992) find a strong association between equipment investment and economic growth in the period 1960–85 for a sample of over 60 countries.

Remarkably, while economists have long recognized the crucial importance of technological change as a major source of dynamism in capitalist economies (especially Karl Marx and Joseph Schumpeter), the analysis of technological change and innovation by economists has, until recently, been an area of relative neglect (see Freeman, 1994; Baumol, 2002).

Leaving aside these controversies for the moment, it is important to note that the Solow model allows us to make several important predictions about the growth process (see Mankiw, 1995, 2003; Solow, 2002):

1. in the long run an economy will gradually approach a steady state equilibrium with $y^*$ and $k^*$ independent of initial conditions;
2. the steady state balanced rate of growth of aggregate output depends on the rate of population growth ($n$) and the rate of technological progress ($A$);
3. in the steady state balanced growth path the rate of growth of output per worker depends solely on the rate of technological progress. As illustrated in Figure 11.5, without technological progress the growth of output per worker will eventually cease;
4. the steady state rate of growth of the capital stock equals the rate of income growth, so the $K/Y$ ratio is constant;
5. for a given depreciation rate ($\delta$) the steady state level of output per worker depends on the savings rate ($s$) and the population growth rate ($n$). A higher rate of saving will increase $y^*$, a higher population growth rate will reduce $y^*$;
6. the impact of an increase in the savings (investment) rate on the growth of output per worker is temporary. An economy experiences a period of higher growth as the new steady state is approached. A higher rate of saving has no effect on the long-run sustainable rate of growth, although it will increase the level of output per worker. To Solow this finding was a 'real shocker';

7.  the Solow model has particular 'convergence properties'. In particular, 'if countries are similar with respect to structural parameters for preferences and technology, then poor countries tend to grow faster than rich countries' (Barro, 1991).

The result in the Solow model that an increase in the saving rate has no impact on the long-run rate of economic growth contains 'more than a touch of irony' (Cesaratto, 1999). As Hamberg (1971) pointed out, the neo-Keynesian Harrod–Domar model highlights the importance of increasing the saving rate to increase long-run growth, while in Keynes's (1936) *General Theory* an increase in the saving rate leads to a fall in output in the short run through its negative impact on aggregate demand (the so-called 'paradox of thrift' effect). In contrast, the long tradition within classical–neoclassical economics of highlighting the virtues of thrift come a little unstuck with the Solow model since it is technological progress, not thrift, that drives long-run growth of output per worker (see Cesaratto, 1999)!

## 11.11   Accounting for the Sources of Economic Growth

Economists not only need a theoretical framework for understanding the causes of growth; they also require a simple method of calculating the relative importance of capital, labour and technology in the growth experience of actual economies. The established framework, following Solow's (1957) seminal contribution, is called 'growth accounting' (see Abel and Bernanke, 2001. Some economists remain highly sceptical about the whole methodology and theoretical basis of growth accounting, for example Nelson, 1973). As far as the proximate causes of growth are concerned we can see by referring back to equation (11.28) that increases in total GDP ($Y$) come from the combined weighted impact of capital accumulation, labour supply growth and technological progress. Economists can measure changes in the amount of capital and labour that occur in an economy over time, but changes in technology (total factor productivity = TFP) are not directly observable. However, it is possible to measure changes in TFP as a 'residual' after taking into account the contributions to growth made by changes in the capital and labour inputs. Solow's (1957) technique was to define technological change as changes in aggregate output minus the sum of the weighted contributions of the labour and capital inputs. In short, the Solow residual measures that part of a change in aggregate output which cannot be explained by changes in the measurable quantities of capital and labour inputs. The derivation of the Solow residual can be shown as follows. The aggregate production function in equation (11.28) shows that output ($Y$) is dependent on the inputs of capital ($K$), labour ($L$) and the currently available technology ($A$), which acts as an index of total factor productivity. Output will change if $A$, $K$ or $L$ change. In equation (11.28) the exponent on the capital shock $\alpha$ measures the elasticity of output with respect to capital and the exponent on the labour input $(1 - \alpha)$ measures the elasticity of output with respect to labour. The weights $\alpha$ and $1 - \alpha$ are estimated from national income statistics and reflect the income shares of capital and labour respectively. Since these weights sum to unity, this indicates that (11.28) is a constant returns to scale production function. Hence an equal percentage increase in both factor inputs ($K$ and $L$) will increase $Y$ by the same percentage. Since the growth rate of the product of the inputs will be the growth rate of $A$ plus the growth rate of $K^{\alpha}$ plus the growth rate of $L^{1-\alpha}$, equation (11.28) can be rewritten as (11.31), which is the basic growth accounting equation used in numerous empirical studies of the sources of economic growth (see Maddison, 1972, 1987; Denison, 1985; Young, 1995, Crafts, 2000; Jorgenson, 2001).

$$\Delta Y/Y = \Delta A/A + \alpha \Delta K/K + (1-\alpha)\Delta L/L \qquad (11.31)$$

Equation (11.31) is simply the Cobb–Douglas production function written in a form representing rates of change. It shows that the growth of aggregate output $(\Delta Y/Y)$ depends on the contribution of changes in total factor productivity $(\Delta A/A)$, changes in the weighted contribution of capital, $\alpha \Delta K/K$, and changes in the weighted contribution of labour $(1 - \alpha)\Delta L/L$. By rearranging equation (11.28) we can represent the productivity index (TFP) which we need to measure as equation (11.32):

$$TFP = A = Y / K^{\alpha} L^{1-\alpha} \qquad (11.32)$$

As already noted, because there is no direct way of measuring TFP it has to be estimated as a residual. By writing down equation (11.32) in terms of rates of change we can obtain an equation from which the growth of TFP (technological change) can be estimated as a residual. This is shown in equation (11.33):

$$\Delta A/A = \Delta Y/Y - [\alpha \Delta K/K + (1-\alpha)\Delta L/L] \qquad (11.33)$$

Data relating to output and the capital and labour inputs are available. Estimates of $\alpha$ and hence $1 - \alpha$ can be acquired from historical national income data. For example, in Solow's original paper covering the US economy for the period 1909–49 he estimated that the rate of growth of total output $(\Delta Y/Y)$ had averaged 2.9 per cent per year, of which 0.32 percentage points could be attributed to capital $(\alpha \Delta K/K)$, 1.09 percentage points could be attributed to labour $(1 - \alpha \Delta L/L)$, leaving a 'Solow residual' $(\Delta A/A)$ of 1.49 percentage points. In other words, almost half of the growth experienced in the USA during this period was due to unexplained technological progress! In Denison's (1985) later work he found that for the period 1929–82, $\Delta Y/Y = 2.92$ per cent, of which 1.02 percentage points were be attributed to $\Delta A/A$. More recent controversial research by Alwyn Young (1992, 1994, 1995) on the sources of growth in the East Asian Tiger economies has suggested estimates of rates of growth of TFP for Taiwan of 2.6 per cent, for South Korea of 1.7 per cent, for Hong Kong of 1.7 per cent and for Singapore a meagre 0.2 per cent! So although these economies have experienced unprecedented growth rates of GDP since the early 1960s, Young's research suggests that these economies are examples of miracles of accumulation. Once we account for the growth of labour and physical and human capital there is little left to explain, especially in the case of Singapore (see Krugman, 1994b; Hsieh, 1999; Bhagwati, 2000). Going further back in history, Nick Crafts (1994, 1995) has provided estimates of the sources of growth for the British economy during the period 1760–1913. Crafts's estimates suggest that 'by twentieth century standards both the output growth rates and the TFP rates are quite modest' (Crafts, 1995).

The most obvious feature of the post-1973 growth accounting data is the well-known puzzle of the 'productivity slowdown'. This slowdown has been attributed to many possible causes, including the adverse impact on investment and existing capital stocks of the 1970s oil price shocks, a slowdown in the rate of innovation, adverse demographic trends, an increasingly regulatory environment and problems associated with measurement such as accounting for quality changes (Fischer et al., 1988).

In a recent survey of the growth accounting literature Bosworth and Collins (2003) reaffirm their belief that growth accounting techniques can yield useful and consistent results. In the debate over the relative importance of capital accumulation v. TFP in accounting for growth Bosworth and Collins conclude that 'both are important' and that 'some of the earlier research understates the role of capital accumulation because of inadequate measurement of the capital input'.

## 11.12   The Convergence Debate

Since 1945 the economies of what used to known as the Third World have been viewed as participating in an attempt to achieve economic development and thereby begin to 'catch up' the rich countries of the world in terms of per capita income. The growing awareness of the wide variety of experiences observed among developing countries in this attempt has been a major factor in motivating renewed research into the important issue of economic growth.

It is generally accepted that the Third World's efforts to join the ranks of the so-called 'mature industrial countries' represent one of the major social, economic and political phenomena of the second half of the twentieth century. This attempted transition to modern economic growth will rank with the taming of the atom as the most important event of this period. (Fei and Ranis, 1997)

Modern discussion of the convergence issue began with the contribution of Gerschenkron (1962), who argued that poor countries could benefit from the advantages of 'relative backwardness' since the possibilities of technological transfer from the developed countries could vastly speed up the pace of industrialization. However, this debate has much earlier origins, dating back to 1750, when Hume put forward the view that the growth process would eventually generate convergence because economic growth in the rich countries would exhibit a natural tendency to slow through a process of 'endogenous decay' (Elmslie and Criss, 1999). Oswald and Tucker (see Elmslie and Criss, 1999) rejected Hume's arguments, putting forward an endogenous growth view that 'increasing, or at least non-decreasing, returns in both scientific and economic activity will keep poor countries from naturally converging towards their rich neighbours'. Elsewhere, Elmslie has also argued that in the *Wealth of Nations*, Smith (1776) took up an endogenous growth position since societal extensions to the division of labour will allow the rich countries to continuously maintain or extend their technological lead over poorer countries (see Elmslie and Criss, 1999). This argument also lies at the heart of Babbage's 1835 thesis that the perpetual advances in science provide the foundation for further advancement and economic progress. Elmslie and Criss argue that Babbage's case against the restrictive laws on the export of machines is 'the best statement of endogenous growth in the classical period'. For, as Babbage argued, the growth of other countries does not pose an economic threat because 'the sun of science has yet penetrated but through the outer fold of Nature's majestic robe'.

In more recent times the issue of convergence began to receive a great deal of attention from the mid-1980s and this growth of research interest stems mainly from the growing recognition that many poor economies were failing to exhibit a tendency to close the per capita incomes gap with rich countries (see Islam, 2003). The conundrum of non-convergence of per capita incomes across the world's economies was first clearly articulated by Paul Romer (1986). The convergence property in the Solow model stems from the key assumption of diminishing returns to reproducible capital. With constant returns to scale, a proportional increase in the inputs of labour and capital leads to a proportional increase in output. By increasing the capital–labour ratio an economy will experience diminishing marginal productivity of capital. Hence poor countries with low capital-to-labour ratios have high marginal products of capital and consequently high growth rates for a given rate of investment. In contrast, rich countries have high capital-to-labour ratios, low marginal products of capital and hence low growth rates (see the aggregate production function $A(t_0)k^\alpha$ in Figure 11.5). The severity of diminishing returns depends on the relative importance of capital in the production process and hence the size of the capital share ($\alpha$) determines the curvature of the production function and the speed at which diminishing returns set in (see DeLong, 2001). With a small capital share (typically $\alpha = 1/3$), the average and marginal product of labour declines rapidly as capital deepening takes place. It is obvious from an inspection of the production function in Figures 11.3–11.5 that in the Solow model capital accumulation has a much bigger impact on output per worker when capita per worker ratios are low compared to when they are high. In a risk-free world with international capital mobility this tendency for convergence will be reinforced (Lucas, 1990b). In the long run the neoclassical model also predicts convergence of growth rates for economies which have reached their steady state. However, as pointed out by Romer, the neoclassical hypothesis that low income per capita economies will tend to grow faster than high income per capita economies appears to be inconsistent with the cross-country evidence.

In his seminal 1986 paper Romer raised important doubts about the preference economists display for a growth model which exhibits diminishing returns to capital accumulation, falling rates of growth over time, and convergence of per capita income levels and growth rates across countries. Evidence relating to falling rates of growth can be found by examining the historical growth record of 'leader' economies compared to other economies (where leader is defined in terms of the highest level of productivity). Maddison (1982) has identified three leader economies since 1700, namely: the Netherlands, 1700–85; the UK, 1785–1890; and the USA, 1890–1979. As the twenty-first century begins, the USA remains the leader economy. But, as Romer notes, the rate of growth has been increasing for the leader economies from essentially zero in eighteenth-century Netherlands to 2.3 per cent per annum for the USA in the period 1890–1979. Historical data for industrial countries also indicate a positive rather than negative trend for growth rates. Hence, rather than modify the neoclassical growth model, Romer introduced an alternative endogenous theory of growth where there is no steady state level of income, where growth rates can increase over time, and where income per capita differentials between countries can persist indefinitely.

The general property of convergence is often presented as a tendency of poor countries to have higher rates of growth than the average and for rich countries to grow more slowly than average. In the world as a whole 'no such tendency is found' (Sachs and Warner, 1995). However, there is strong evidence of convergence among the OECD economies as well as between US states, Japanese prefectures and European regions within the European Community (Baumol, 1986; DeLong, 1988; Dowrick, 1992; Barro and Sala-i-Martin, 2003). The conflicting evidence led Baumol to suggest that there may be a 'convergence club' whereby only those countries with an adequate human capital base and favourable institutions can hope to participate in convergent growth. More recently, DeLong and Dowrick (2002) have shown that 'what convergence there has been has been limited in geography and time' and, as a result, to use Pritchett's (1997) words, there has been 'Divergence, Big Time' (see Jones, 1997a, 1997b; Melchior, 2001).

The research inspired by Barro (1991) has shown how the prediction of convergence in the neoclassical model needs considerable qualification. If all economies had identical savings rates, population growth rates and unlimited access to the same technology, then relative capital intensities would determine output per capita differentials between countries. Poor countries with low capital intensities are predicted to grow faster than rich countries in the period of transitional dynamics en route to the common steady state equilibrium. In this situation there will be unconditional or absolute convergence. Clearly, given the restrictive requirements, this outcome is only likely to be observed among a group of relatively homogeneous countries or regions that share similar characteristics, such as the OECD economies and US states. In reality, many economies differ considerably with respect to key variables (such as saving propensities, government policies and population growth) and are moving towards different steady states. Therefore the general convergence property of the Solow model is conditional. 'Each economy converges to its own steady state, which in turn is determined by its saving and population growth rates' (Mankiw, 1995). This property of conditional convergence implies that growth rates will be rapid during transitional dynamics if a country's initial output per capita is low relative to its long-run steady state value. When countries reach their respective steady states, growth rates will then equalize in line with the rate of technological progress. Clearly, if rich countries have higher steady state values of $k^*$ than poor countries, there will be no possibility of convergence in an absolute sense. As Barro (1997) notes, 'a poor country that also has a low long-term position, possibly because its public policies are harmful or its saving rate is low, would not tend to grow rapidly'. Conditional convergence therefore allows for the possibility that rich countries may grow faster than poor countries, leading to income per capita divergence! Since countries do not have the same steady state per capita income, each country will have a tendency to grow more rapidly the bigger the gap between its initial level of income per capita and its own long-run steady state per capita income.

This can be illustrated as follows. Abstracting from technological progress, we have the intensive form of the production function written as (11.34):

$$y = k^\alpha \qquad (11.34)$$

Expressing (11.34) in terms of growth rates gives (11.35):

$$\dot{y}/y = \alpha \dot{k}/k \qquad (11.35)$$

Dividing both sides of Solow's fundamental equation (11.26) by $k$ gives equation (11.36):

$$\dot{k}/k = sf(k)/k - (n+\delta) \qquad (11.36)$$

Therefore, substituting (11.35) into (11.36), we derive an expression for the growth rate of output per worker given by equation (11.37):

$$\dot{y}/y = \alpha[sf(k)/k - (n+\delta)] \qquad (11.37)$$

In Figure 11.6 the growth rate of the capital–labour ratio $(\dot{k}/k)$ is shown by the vertical distance between the $sf(k)/k$ function and the effective deprecia-tion line, $n + \delta$ (see Jones, 2001a; Barro and Sala-i-Martin, 2003). The intersection of the savings curve and effective depreciation line determines the steady state capital per worker, $k^*$. In Figure 11.7 we compare a rich

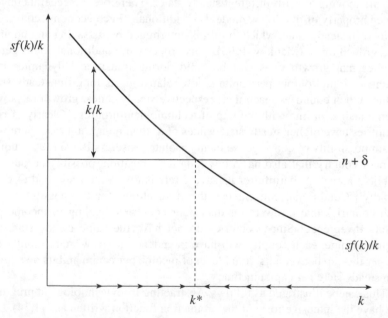

*Figure 11.6   Transition dynamics*

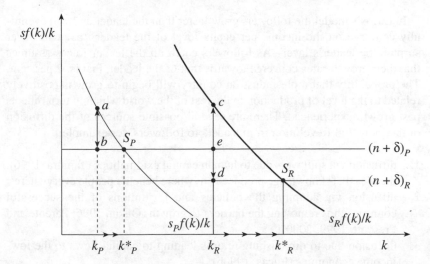

*Figure 11.7 Conditional convergence*

developed country with a poor developing country. Here we assume (realistically) that the developing country has a higher rate of population growth than
the developed country, that is, $(n + \delta)_P > (n + \delta)_R$, and also that the developed
country has a higher savings rate than the developing country. The steady
state for the developing country is indicated by point $S_P$, with a steady state
capital–labour ratio of $k_P^*$. Similarly, the steady state for the developed country is indicated by points $S_R$ and $k_R^*$. Suppose the current location of these
economies is given by $k_P$ and $k_R$. It is clear that the developed economy will
be growing faster than the developing country because the rate of growth of
the capital–labour ratio is greater in the developed economy (distance $c$–$d$)
than the developing country ($a$–$b$). Figure 11.7 also shows that even if the
developed country had the same population growth rate as the developing
country it would still have a faster rate of growth since the gap between the
savings curve and the effective depreciation line is still greater than that for
the developing country, that is, $a$–$b < c$–$e$.

Robert Lucas (2000b) has recently presented a numerical simulation of
world income dynamics in a model which captures certain features of the
diffusion of the Industrial Revolution across the world's economies (see
Snowdon, 2002a). In discussing prospects for the twenty-first century Lucas
concludes from his simulation exercise that 'the restoration of inter-society
income equality will be one of the major economic events of the century to
come'. In the twenty-first century we will witness 'Convergence, Big Time'!
In short, we will witness an ever-growing 'convergence club' as sooner or
later 'everyone will join the Industrial Revolution'.

In Lucas's model the followers grow faster than the leader and will eventually converge on the income per capita level of the leader, 'but will never surpass the leader's level'. As followers catch up the leader Lucas assumes that their growth rates converge towards that of the leader, that is, 2 per cent. The probability that a pre-industrial country will begin to grow is positively related to the level of production in the rest of the world which in turn reflects past growth experienced. There are several possible sources of the diffusion of the Industrial Revolution from leaders to followers, for example:

1. diffusion via spillovers due to human capital externalities (Tamura, 1996), the idea that 'knowledge produced anywhere benefits people everywhere';
2. diffusion via adopting the policies and institutions of the successful countries thus removing the barriers to growth (Olson, 1996; Parente and Prescott, 1999, 2000);
3. diffusion due to diminishing returns leading to capital flows to the low-income economies (Lucas, 1990b).

Lucas's simulations predict that the diffusion of the Industrial Revolution was relatively slow for the nineteenth century but accelerated 'dramatically' in the twentieth century, finally slowing down towards the year 2000 'because there are so few people left in stagnant, pre-industrial economies'. In Lucas's simulation, by the year 2000, 90 per cent of the world is growing. Given the rate of diffusion, world income inequality at first increases, peaking some time in the 1970s, and then declines, 'ultimately to zero'. According to Lucas, the long phase of increasing world income inequality, discussed by Pritchett (1997), has passed. The growth rate of world production is predicted by the model to peak 'around 1970' and thereafter decline towards a rate of 2 per cent sometime just beyond the year 2100. The predictions of Lucas's model appear 'consistent with what we know about the behaviour of per capita incomes in the last two centuries' (Lucas, 2000). However, Crafts and Venables (2002) do not share the optimism of Lucas. Taking into account geographical and agglomeration factors, they conclude that the playing field is not level and therefore the convergence possibilities among the poor countries are much more limited than is suggested by Lucas. Rather, we are likely to observe the rapid convergence of a selected group of countries (for detailed and contrasting views on the evolution of global income distribution see Sala-i-Martin, 2002a, 2002b; Bourguignon and Morrisson, 2002; Milanovic, 2002).

While Solow's model predicts conditional convergence and explains growth differences in terms of 'transitional dynamics', an alternative 'catch-up' hypothesis emphasizes technological gaps between those economies behind the innovation frontier and the technologically advanced leader economies (Gerschenkron, 1962; Abramovitz, 1986, 1989, 1990, 1993). The 'catch-up' literature also places more emphasis on historical analysis, social capability and institutional factors (see Fagerberg, 1995).

Whereas in the Solow model the main mechanism leading to differential growth rates relates to rates of capital accumulation, in the catch-up model it is the potential for low income per capita countries to adopt the technology of the more advanced countries that establishes the potential for poor countries to grow more rapidly than rich countries. In other words, there appear to be three potential (proximate) sources of growth of labour productivity, namely:

1. growth through physical and human capital accumulation;
2. growth through technological change reflecting shifts in the world production frontier;
3. growth through technological catch-up involving movement toward the world production frontier.

In other words, poor countries have the additional opportunity to grow faster by moving toward the technological frontier representing 'best practice' technology, or as P. Romer (1993) puts it, poor countries need to reduce their 'idea gaps' rather than 'object gaps'. Kumar and Russell (2002) find that there is 'substantial evidence of technological catch-up' while Parente and Prescott (2000) have emphasized that in many countries the failure to adopt 'best practice' technology is due to barriers that have been erected to protect specific groups who will be adversely affected (at least in the short run) by the changes that would result from technological change. Both the neoclassical and catch-up arguments imply that economic growth rates are likely to be closely related to per capita GDP, with poor economies benefiting in terms of economic growth from their relative backwardness. There is also accumulating evidence that more open economies converge faster than closed economies (Sachs and Warner, 1995; Krueger, 1997, 1998; Edwards, 1993, 1998; Parente and Prescott, 2000). While this appears to be true in the modern era, Baldwin et al. (2001) argue that during the Industrial Revolution international trade initially contributed to the divergence between rich and poor countries. However, they also suggest that in the modern era, the huge reduction in the transaction costs of trading ideas 'can be the key to southern industrialisation' (see also Galor and Mountford, 2003).

Finally, we should note that while there has been 'Divergence, Big Time' with respect to per capita GDP, this is in 'stark contrast' to what has been happening across the globe with respect to life expectancy, where there has been considerable convergence. Becker et al. (2003) compute a 'full income' measure for 49 developed and developing countries for the period 1965–95 that includes estimates of the monetized gains from increased longevity. By estimating economic welfare in terms of the quantity of life, as well as the quality of life, Becker et al. show that the absence of income convergence is reversed. 'Countries starting with lower income grew more in terms of this "full income" measure. Growth rates of "full income" for the period average 140% for developed countries, and 192% for developing countries' (see also Crafts, 2003).

## 11.13  Beyond the Solow Model

Although the lack of a theory of technological change is a clear weakness of the basic neoclassical growth model, Mankiw (1995) argues that many general predictions from the theory are 'broadly consistent with experience'. For example, cross-country data indicate a strong negative correlation between population growth and income per capita and a strong positive correlation between income per capita and savings/investment rates (Jones, 2001a). As predicted by the model, rates of growth in the rich OECD economies are relatively low while rapid growth rates have been observed in countries moving from an initial position of relatively low income per capita and low capital intensity. There is also strong evidence of convergence among relatively homogeneous economies such as the OECD and between regions and states within the USA, Europe and Japan (Baumol, 1986; Barro and Sala-i-Martin, 1995). In larger, more diverse data sets there is little evidence of the expected negative relationship between growth rates and some initial (for example 1960) level of income per capita, that is, absolute convergence (P. Romer, 1986, 1989; DeLong, 1988). However, 'the central idea of conditional convergence receives strong support from the data' (Barro, 1991, 1997) and has considerable explanatory power for both countries and regions. The growth accounting research of Alwyn Young (1992, 1994, 1995) has shown that the rapid growth of the Asian Tiger economies is easily explicable and can be attributed mainly to rapid accumulation of factor inputs rather than unusually high total factor productivity growth. As Paul Krugman (1994b) argues, an implication of this research is that this rapid growth can therefore be expected to slow down considerably in the future, as it has already done in Japan. The Solow model has also been used to provide a plausible 'reconstruction' account of the 'miracles' of Japanese and German post-1945 growth, and also the relatively good growth performance of France and Italy, in terms of the transitional dynamics towards a high income per capita steady state. It seems plausible that these economies grew rapidly in the post-war period because they were 'reconstructing' their capital stock following the destruction resulting from the Second World War.

However, there are a number of important deficiencies and puzzles which the Solow model finds difficult to overcome and explain. First, in the Solow model, while economic policy can permanently influence the level of per capita output (for example by raising the savings ratio via tax inducements), it cannot alter the path of long-run growth. Growth rates can only be increased temporarily during the transitional dynamics en route to the new steady state. Cross-country growth differentials are also explained in terms of the transitional dynamics which allow countries to grow faster than their long-run sustainable growth rates. Sustained growth in the Solow model is only possible if there is technological progress, since without it per capita income growth will eventually cease due to the impact of diminishing returns to capital accumulation. Given that per capita incomes have been rising for over 100 years in a large number of countries, and growth rates have displayed no overall tendency to decline, the role of technological progress in the Solow model in explaining sustainable growth becomes crucial. But herein lies the obvious shortcoming of the neoclassical model since 'the long-run per capita growth rate is determined entirely by an element – the rate of technological progress – that is outside the model ... Thus we end up with a model of growth that explains everything but long-run growth, an obviously unsatisfactory situation' (Barro and Sala-i-Martin, 1995). Furthermore, as P. Romer (1989) highlights, in terms of policy advice for long-term growth the neoclassical model has little to offer!

A second problem relates to the evidence, which clearly shows that income per capita differentials across the world are much greater than predicted by the model. Differences across countries in capital intensities are too small to account for the observed disparities in real incomes. Using a Cobb–Douglas production function framework it is possible to allocate differences in the level of per capita incomes between countries to variations in levels of total factor productivity growth and the accumulation of factor inputs. In particular it is possible to estimate how much of the income disparities witnessed between rich and poor countries can be attributed to different capital intensities since total factor productivity is common across all countries. Substituting from equation (11.34) to equation (11.26) gives equation (11.38):

$$\dot{k} = sk^{\alpha} - (n+\delta)k \qquad (11.38)$$

Setting this equation equal to zero (the steady state condition) and substituting into the production function yields (11.39):

$$y^* = [s/(n+\delta)]^{\alpha/(1-\alpha)} \qquad (11.39)$$

Equation (11.39) is now in a form that enables a solution to be found for the steady state output per worker ($y^*$). As Jones (2001a) highlights, we can see from equation (11.39) why some countries are so rich and some are so poor. Assuming exogenous technology and a similar value for the capital exponent

($\alpha$), countries that sustain high rates of saving, and low rates of population growth and depreciation, will be rich. According to the neoclassical growth model the high-income economies have achieved their high living standards because they have accumulated large per worker stocks of capital. However, although the model correctly predicts the directions of the effects of saving and population growth on output per worker, it does not correctly predict the magnitudes. As Mankiw et al. (1992) and Mankiw (1995) argue, the gaps in output per worker (living standards) between rich and poor countries are much larger than plausible estimates of savings rates and population growth predict using equation (11.39). The crux of the problem is that with $\alpha = 1/3$ there are sharply diminishing returns to capital. This implies that a tenfold gap in output per worker between the USA and India would require a thousandfold difference in the capital–labour ratios between these countries! (It should be noted that this result is highly sensitive to the choice of $\alpha = 1/3$ for the share of capital in GDP.)

A third problem with the Solow model is that given a common production function (that is, exogenous technology) the marginal product of capital should be much higher in poor countries than in rich countries. Given the parameters of the Solow model, the observed tenfold differential in output per worker between rich and poor countries implies a hundredfold difference in the marginal product of capital if output gaps are entirely due to variations in capital intensities. Such differentials in the rate of return to capital are simply not observed between rich and poor countries. As David Romer (1996) observes, such differences in rates of return 'would swamp such considerations as capital market imperfections, government tax policies, fear of expropriation and so on and we would observe immense flows of capital from rich to poor countries. We do not see such flows.' But the rate of return to capital in poor countries is less than expected and the anticipated massive flows of capital from rich to poor countries have not been observed across poor countries as a whole (Lucas, 1990b).

A fourth difficulty relates to the rate of convergence, which is only about half that predicted by the model. The economy's initial conditions influence the outcome for much longer than the model says it should (Mankiw, 1995).

In conclusion, it appears that within the Solow growth framework, physical capital accumulation alone cannot account for either continuous growth of per capita income over long periods of time or the enormous geographical disparities in living standards that we observe. In terms of Figure 11.3, the data on output per worker (or income per capita) that we actually observe across the world reveal much greater disparities than those predicted by the Solow model based on differences in capital per worker.

The new growth models emerging after 1986 depart from the Solow model in three main ways. One group of models generates continuous growth by abandoning the assumption of diminishing returns to capital accumulation. To achieve this, Paul Romer (1986) introduced positive externalities from capital accumulation so that the creation of economy-wide knowledge emerges as a by-product of the investment activity of individual firms, a case of 'learning by investing' (Barro and Sala-i-Martin, 2003). A second approach models the accumulation of knowledge as the outcome of purposeful acts by entrepreneurs seeking to maximize private profits; that is, technological progress is endogenized (P. Romer, 1990). A third class of model claims that the role of capital is much more important than is suggested by the $\alpha$ term in the conventional Cobb–Douglas production function shown in equations (11.28)–(11.30). In their 'augmented' Solow model, Mankiw et al. (1992) broaden the concept of capital to include 'human capital'. The first two classes of model constitute the core of endogenous growth theory whereas the Mankiw, Romer and Weil (MRW) model constitutes what Klenow and Rodriguez-Clare (1997a, 1997b) call a 'neoclassical revival'. The central proposition of endogenous growth theory is that broad capital accumulation (physical and human capital) does not experience diminishing returns. The growth process is driven by the accumulation of broad capital together with the production of new knowledge created through research and development.

## 11.14 Endogenous Growth: Constant Returns to Capital Accumulation

During the mid-1980s several economists, most notably Paul Romer (1986, 1987b) and Robert Lucas (1988), sought to construct alternative models of growth where the long-run growth of income per capita depends on 'investment' decisions rather than unexplained technological progress. However, as Crafts (1996) notes, the term investment in the context of these new models refers to a broader concept than the physical capital accumulation reported in the national accounts; research and development (R&D) expenditures and human capital formation may also be included. 'The key to endogenous steady state growth is that there should be constant returns to broad capital accumulation'. Hence in order to construct a simple theory of endogenous growth, the long-run tendency for capital to run into diminishing returns needs to be modified to account for the extraordinary and continuous increases in observed per capita incomes across the world's economies. In the early versions of the new endogenous growth theory the accumulation of capital plays a much greater role in the growth process than in the traditional neoclassical model. In many ways the work of Romer revives the earlier seminal contribution of Arrow (1962) on 'learning by doing'. Arrow had shown how the productivity of labour increases with experience, and experience is a function of cumulative investment expenditures that alter the work environment. That is, a firm's accumulation of capital produces external effects on learning. However, as Blaug (2002) argues, 'it strains credulity to believe that this could account, not just for a once-and-for-all increase in output, but also for a *constant* rate of increase in total factor productivity year in year out'.

Building on Arrow's insight, Romer broadened the concept of capital to include investment in knowledge as well as the accumulation of physical capital goods. Since the knowledge gained by workers in one firm has public good characteristics and is at best only partially excludable, then knowledge spillovers occur such that investment in knowledge (R&D) by one firm increases the production potential of other firms. No individual firm can completely internalize the positive impact that their investment in physical and human capital has on the economy-wide stock of knowledge.

Paul Romer's 1986 model can be illustrated by modifying the production function. In equation (11.40) the production function includes technology ($A$) as an endogenous input:

$$Y = F(K, L, A) \tag{11.40}$$

At the micro level, the output of an individual firm ($j$) depends on its own inputs of capital ($Kj$), labour ($Lj$) and the economy-wide state of knowledge ($A$), as indicated in equation (11.41):

$$Yj = F(Kj, Lj, A) \tag{11.41}$$

In this formulation the growth of knowledge (technology) is assumed to depend on the growth of capital because capital deepening fosters technological spillovers that raise the marginal productivity of capital across the economy as a whole. Therefore any increase in aggregate $K$ will improve $A$ and hence the productivity of all firms. In Romer's (1986) endogenous growth model the expansion of aggregate knowledge results from learning externalities among firms. In effect, the higher the level of the capital stock in an economy, the more productive each firm will be via a process of 'learning by doing'. So while a firm's production function exhibits constant returns to scale and diminishing returns to capital accumulation, the aggregate production function will exhibit increasing, rather than constant, returns to scale.

One of the simplest models of endogenous growth is the $AK^*$ model shown in equation (11.42) below (Rebelo, 1991):

$$Y = K^{\alpha} H^{\beta} = AK^* \tag{11.42}$$

Here $A$ is a constant, $K^*$ represents a broad measure of capital ($K^{\alpha} H^{\beta}$), and $\alpha + \beta = 1$. As Crafts (1995) points out, 'models of this kind put investment centre stage and see growth as an investment-driven process. There is no role for the Solow residual.' Therefore there is a close similarity between the *AK* model and the Harrod–Domar model. In both models there are no diminishing returns and hence no reason for growth to slow down as capital deepening occurs. If one group of countries has higher average savings rates, lower depreciation rates and lower capital–output ratios than some other group of countries, then the first group will grow faster than the second group permanently and 'divergence, big time' will be the rule.

The *AK* class of endogenous growth models has been subject to heavy criticism, mainly on account of their key assumption of an absence of diminishing returns to the capital input. The *AK* model predicts a permanent increase in the growth rate following an increase in the investment/GDP ratio of an economy. However, Jones (1995), in a time series analysis of 15 OECD countries in the post-1945 period, argues that the *AK* models are inconsistent with the empirical evidence. Although the investment/GDP ratios increased significantly in the 1950–89 period, growth rates of GDP per worker remained stable or have fallen. This finding has been challenged by McGrattan (1998). By considering time series evidence from a larger sample of countries over a longer time period McGrattan finds the main predictions of *AK* theory to be confirmed by the data. Using data from Maddison (1995) for the period 1870–1989, McGratton finds that 'higher investment rates correspond to higher growth rates, with the exception of the US economy where there is little variation in the growth rate of GDP per capita'. Extending the analysis to cross-sectional data for 125 economies in the period 1960–85 also reveals 'a definite positive correlation between investment rates and growth rates'.

## 11.15 Endogenous Growth: The Economics of Ideas

The issue of convergence has raised as an important question the possible importance of differences in technology (knowledge) across the economies of the world. The Solow model attempts to explain per capita income level and growth differences assuming that technology is a pure public good and is therefore freely available to all countries irrespective of their level of development. An increasing number of economists, and most economic historians and development economists see significant technology gaps as the crucial problem facing poor countries. Such an approach emphasizes the need for policies to be adopted that will close 'idea gaps' between nations (P. Romer, 1993).

Paul Romer's 1986 model explains technological progress as an unintentional by-product of capital accumulation by individual firms. Subsequently, Romer (1990), dissatisfied with his initial approach, proceeded to develop a second strand of new growth theory. Endogenous innovation models embrace a neo-Schumpeterian framework of endogenous technological change based on three premises (Grossman and Helpman, 1991, 1994; Crafts, 1996; Aghion and Howitt, 1998). First, as in the Solow model, the basic driving force behind economic growth is technological change, that is, improvements in knowledge about how we transform inputs into outputs in the production process. Second, technological change is endogenous, being determined by the deliberate activities of economic agents acting largely in response to financial incentives. Third, the defining characteristic of ideas/knowledge is that 'once the cost of creating a new set of instructions has been incurred, the instructions can be used over and over again at no additional cost' (Romer, 1990). Therefore ideas are non-rivalrous outputs and their use by one firm or person does not in any way reduce their availability to other firms or persons. Ideas are also 'partially excludable', where excludability is defined as the ability of the owners of a good to prevent other economic agents from using it without payment. As Romer (1990) notes, 'excludability is a function of the technology and the legal system'. Given Romer's second premise that technological change results from the purposeful actions of self-interested economic agents, improvements in technology (new ideas) must generate benefits to individuals that are at least 'partially excludable', for example by having patent laws.

Romer's insights have led to a burgeoning of research into the economics of ideas (Jones, 2002, 2005). The three premises discussed above have two important implications for the theory of economic growth. First, because ideas are non-rivalrous, they can be accumulated without limit on a per capita basis. Second, because of incomplete excludability (appropriability), knowledge creation involves substantial spillovers of benefits (externalities) which cannot be entirely captured by the economic agents who produce the ideas. The 'unbounded' growth and 'incomplete appropriability' features of the economics of ideas imply that 'output cannot be a constant-returns-to-scale function of all its inputs taken together'. Romer's analysis implies increasing returns to scale and by implication microfoundations based on the presence of imperfect competition (see Romer, 1994a).

While a non-rivalrous good such as a new idea involves a fixed cost of production, which is often substantial, once the new knowledge has been created there is zero marginal cost involved with any further use of the new idea. A new design is costly to produce but once in existence it can be used as often as desired and in as many contexts as desired. It is for this reason that legal mechanisms such as patents and copyrights exist in order to grant investors monopoly rights over a new idea, at least for a time, so that they can earn a reward for their new ideas (Kremer, 1998; Mazzoleni and Nelson, 1998). The importance of this issue has been illustrated by North (1990), who argues that the economic development of Western Europe did not seriously begin until the development of property rights ensured that individuals could reap some of the benefits of their 'ideas' and helped to speed up the pace of technological change (Crafts, 1995). The era of modern economic growth, beginning with the Industrial Revolution in Britain,

> occurred when the institutions protecting intellectual property rights were sufficiently well developed that entrepreneurs could capture as a private return some of the enormous social returns their innovations would create ... history suggests that it is only when the market incentives were sufficient that widespread innovation and growth took hold. (Jones, 2001a)

In the case of the USA the framers of the US Constitution were eager to 'promote the progress of science and useful arts'. Therefore an intellectual property clause providing for copyright and patent rights appears in the first article of the Constitution and by 1810 the USA 'far surpassed Britain in patenting per capita' (Khan and Sokoloff, 2001). The failure of China to lead the first Industrial Revolution has also been attributed to that country's inability to establish a free market, institutionalize property rights, provide an environment conducive to emulation and innovation, and to absorb foreign technology (Landes, 1998). Thus according to the new breed of endogenous growth models, 'the government has great potential for good or ill through its influence on the long-term rate of growth' (Barro, 1997). Economic growth can be influenced not only by policies that affect trade regimes, technology transfer, the provision of infrastructure and financial markets, but also by policies that affect taxation and incentives, the protection of intellectual property rights and the maintenance of law and order.

By developing an endogenous theory of technological change Romer has challenged both the traditional and augmented versions of the Solow neoclassical growth model (see below, section 11.16). In the neoclassical model technology is assumed to be exogenous and hence available without limitation everywhere across the globe. Romer (1995) rejects this assumption on the basis of 'overwhelming evidence' that technology is not a pure public good. The neoclassical model emphasizes 'object gaps', differences in physical and human capital, in explaining income per capita differentials across nations. While Mankiw (1995) believes that much of the variation in living standards can be explained by differences in the quantities of human and physical capital, in contrast Romer (1993) emphasizes 'idea gaps', productivity differences resulting from technology gaps, as the main source of divergent living standards.

Parente and Prescott (1994, 1999, 2000) also attribute differences in international incomes to technology gaps. In their research they have found evidence to suggest that these productivity gaps are not caused by fundamental differences in the stock of available knowledge that developing countries have access to. Instead, Parente and Prescott argue that there exist barriers in the form of society-imposed constraints which prevent firms in many developing countries from adopting better production methods, and many of these constraints 'are put in place to protect the interests of groups vested in current production processes'. As a result they conclude that most differences in international incomes 'are the result of differences in total factor productivity'. Parente and Prescott (2005) conclude that 'changes in a country's institutions that result in large increases in the efficiency with which resources can be used in production give rise to growth miracles'.

Romer's position has received recent support from the research of Easterly and Levine (2001), who find that the 'residual' (total factor productivity) rather than factor accumulation can explain most of the cross-country income and growth differentials. Their data show that while factor accumulation is persistent, growth is not. Nelson and Pack (1999), in their discussion of the Asian miracle and modern growth theory, also stress the importance of the entrepreneurship, innovation and learning that these economies had to undertake before they could successfully assimilate new technologies. In their view the accumulation of human and physical capital is a necessary but far from sufficient part of this process. What is crucial for success is the establishment of a policy environment that nurtures learning, and for economists to better understand the learning process taking place during the assimilation of new ideas and technologies they need 'a better theory of firm behaviour in such situations'.

Historical experience demonstrates that the creation and transmission of ideas has undoubtedly been an important determinant of current living standards (Rosenberg, 1994; Mokyr, 2005). If Romer is correct and the poor countries do suffer from idea gaps rather than object gaps, then a significant part of worldwide poverty can be eliminated 'at relatively low cost' via technological 'catch-up'. A clear implication of this analysis is that nations which isolate themselves from the free flow of ideas, or erect barriers to the adoption of new technologies, will suffer relative stagnation since trade policies and openness affect innovation and growth. Foreign direct investment can act as a significant channel for the diffusion of new innovations and ideas, thereby enhancing the growth process (Grossman and Helpman, 1990; Romer, 1994b; Sachs and Warner, 1995; Proudman and Redding, 1997; Edwards, 1998; Parente and Prescott, 2000). Therefore, at least potentially, poor economies have the most to gain from reducing restrictions to international trade, encouraging inward FDI flows and investing in human capital because by doing so they can gain access to the stock of world knowledge (World Bank, 1998/9). While in the neoclassical model the removal of inefficiencies caused by trade barriers will produce level effects on production possibilities but no sustained growth effects, in endogenous growth models the growth effects of increasing economic integration are likely to be much more important.

A further implication of Paul Romer's research is that for the USA to maintain its leadership position, government policies must continue to support a high level of R&D activities in both private and public institutions. Given the well-documented large divergence between social and private rates of return from R&D expenditures, the government has a vital role to play in preventing underinvestment in this activity. In a recent investigation of the optimal rate of R&D investment in the USA Jones and Williams (1998) conclude that the private rate of return to R&D in the USA is of the order of 7–14 per cent, while a 'conservative estimate' of the social rate of return is 30 per cent. Therefore Jones and Williams conclude that optimal R&D spending as a share of GDP is 'more than two to four times larger than actual spending' (see also Jones and Williams, 2000).

In contrast to the supply-side view of the growth of knowledge, ideas and technological change, Schmookler (1966) argues that technological change is primarily demand-induced. Unlike Romer's model, where a key input to the development of new technology is the supply of previous innovations (see Jones, 2005), Schmookler sees the stimulus to technological change and innovation as the need to solve current technological problems; that is, technological change is demand-driven and dependent on the usefulness of new ideas. In a recent discussion of Schmookler's work, Kelly (2002) concludes that the supply- and demand-side influences on technology are complementary.

An important deficiency of recent endogenous growth theories is that they lose the prediction of conditional convergence, a prediction which Barro (1997) argues has a 'strong empirical regularity in the data for countries and regions'. To rectify this flaw Barro and Sala-i-Martin (1997) have developed a model that combines elements of endogenous growth with the convergence implications of the Solow model. Their model has the following elements:

1. in the long run the rate of growth in the world economy is driven by technological discoveries in the leading economies;
2. follower economies share in the new innovations via a process of imitation;
3. since imitation is generally cheaper than innovation, 'most countries prefer to copy rather than invent';
4. the relatively low cost of imitation implies that the follower economies will grow relatively faster than the leader economies and converge, at least part way, towards the leaders;
5. as the amount of uncopied innovations decreases, the costs of imitation will tend to rise and therefore the follower's growth rate will tend to slow down;

6.    therefore, the Barro/Sala-i-Martin model generates a form of conditional convergence based on the diffusion of technology across countries and resembles the predictions of the Solow model;
7.    in the long run 'all economies grow at the rate of discovery in the leading places'.

The Barro/Sala-i-Martin hybrid model therefore establishes a framework where long-run growth is driven endogenously by the discovery of new ideas in the 'leading-edge' economies, but also retains the convergence properties of the neoclassical growth model via the impact of the imitation behaviour of follower countries.

## 11.16   An Augmented Solow Model: A Neoclassical Revival?

As it stands, the neoclassical growth model, relying as it does on differences in capital–labour ratios across countries to explain the wide disparities in levels of per capita output, cannot satisfactorily explain world income differentials. In response to this deficiency Mankiw et al. (1992) 'augment' the Solow model by including the accumulation of human capital as well as physical capital. The key to their approach is the argument that the conventional estimate of $\alpha$, capital's income share, may not be a good indicator of the overall contribution of capital. By adding human capital to the model the production function becomes (11.43):

$$Y = K^{\alpha} H^{\beta} (AL)^{1-\alpha-\beta} \text{ and } \alpha + \beta < 1 \tag{11.43}$$

Here we now have four factors of production combining to produce output where $H$ is the stock of human capital and $AL$ is the labour input measured in efficiency units, which captures both the quantity of labour and the productivity of labour determined by available technology (see Mankiw, 2003). The production function exhibits constant returns to scale and with $\alpha + \beta < 1$ there are diminishing returns to 'broad capital'. But with a larger capital share ($\alpha + \beta = 2/3$) the average product of labour declines more slowly as accumulation takes place since the size of the capital share determines the curvature of the production function and hence the speed at which diminishing returns set in. Diminishing returns to the broader concept of capital will be much less severe than in the traditional Solow model where $\alpha = 1/3$. When $\alpha$ is small, the curvature of the production function in Figure 11.3 is large. But by augmenting the model with human capital, the transition to the steady state is much slower and 80 per cent of international differences in living standards can be explained by differences in the rate of population growth and the accumulation of both human and physical capital (Mankiw et al., 1992;

Mankiw, 1995). The transitory impact of any increase in the rate of investment in the MRW model will have prolonged effects. However, because the exponents on $K$ and $H$ sum to less than one, this 'neoclassical revival' in growth theory does not provide a model of endogenous growth. Per capita income will eventually settle down in a steady state and grow at the exogenously determined rate of technological progress.

For some critics the MRW model, by taking the public-good view of technology, has failed to address the crucial issue of variations in total factor productivity growth and technical efficiency across nations (Klenow amd Rodriguez-Clare, 1997a; 1997b). While the augmented Solow model better explains international differences in living standards, it cannot account for the persistence of economic growth. Endogenous growth theory attempts to show how persistent growth may take place without having to resort to exogenous technological progress (Bernanke and Gurkaynak, 2001).

## 11.17 Focusing on the Fundamental Causes of Growth

The research of economists shows that successful economies are those with high rates of accumulation of human and physical capital together with sustained technological progress. But this conclusion then raises the crucial question: why do some nations successfully achieve this outcome while others fail? Olson (1996) has highlighted the fact that high rates of growth seem to occur in a subset of poor countries rather than in all low-income countries as the transitional dynamics of the Solow neoclassical growth model imply. Given that capital and technology can migrate across political boundaries, the persistence of significant differences in the level of output per worker suggests the presence of persistent barriers to growth and development (Parente and Prescott, 2000). An obvious deterrent to the free flow of capital from rich to poor countries arises from the greater risk involved in investing in countries characterized by macroeconomic instability, trade barriers, inadequate infrastructure, poor education, ethnic diversity, widespread corruption, political instability, disadvantageous geography and frequent policy reversals. To understand why some countries have performed so much better than others with respect to growth it is therefore necessary to go beyond the proximate causes of growth and delve into the wider fundamental determinants. This implies that we cannot hope to find the key determinants of economic growth by using narrow economic analysis alone. To explain growth 'miracles' and 'disasters' requires an understanding of the history of the countries being investigated as well as how policy choices are made within an institutional structure involving political distortions.

Dani Rodrik (2003) has provided a useful framework for highlighting the distinction between the proximate and fundamental determinants of eco-

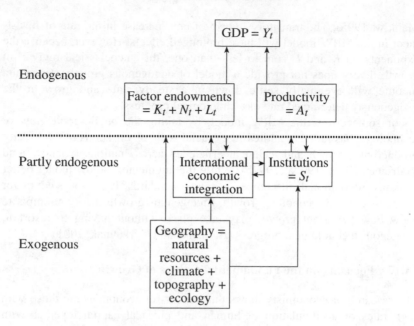

*Figure 11.8   Proximate and fundamental sources of growth*

nomic growth. Figure 11.8, adapted from Rodrik, captures the main factors
that determine the size and growth of any economy. Referring back to equation (11.4), in the upper part of Figure 11.8 we can see the influence of the
proximate determinants of growth, with output being directly influenced by
an economy's endowments of labour ($L_t$), physical capital ($K_t$), natural resources ($N_t$) and the productivity of these resources ($A_t$). The impact of both
technical and allocative efficiency is captured within the productivity variable. In the lower portion of Figure 11.8 we observe the major fundamental
determinants of economic growth, including social capability ($S_t$). Rodrik
provides a threefold taxonomy of the fundamental determinants of growth,
namely geography, integration and institutions. These categories highlight
three major research areas, within a voluminous and rapidly expanding literature, that have dominated growth analysis in recent years. Many social scientists
would argue forcefully that the influence of culture should be added to the list
of important deeper determinants of economic performance. It is certainly the
case that economic historians have given much greater consideration to culture as a determinant of economic performance than economists. For example,
David Landes argues that 'Culture Makes Almost All the Difference' (Harrison
and Huntington, 2000). For other interesting discussions of the influence of
culture on economic growth and development the reader should consult

Huntington, 1996; Temin, 1997; Landes, 1998; Lal, 1999; Dasgupta and Serageldin, 2000; Barro and McCleary, 2003; Grief, 2003.

As Rodrik points out, the central question in growth analysis is: which of the causal relationships in Figure 11.8 matters most? However, Rodrik also notes that geography is the only exogenous factor in his threefold taxonomy, with integration and institutions 'co-evolving with economic performance'. The causal interrelationships between the variables in Figure 11.8, indicated by the two-way direction of some of the arrows, suggest that there are complex feedback effects at work. Therefore empirical work, in the form of endless cross-country regressions, that attempts to establish clear lines of causality must be treated with 'extreme care'.

## 11.18 Institutions and Economic Growth

While poor countries have enormous potential for catch-up and convergence, these advantages will fail to generate positive results on growth in countries with an inadequate political, legal and regulatory framework. The notion that institutions profoundly influence the wealth of nations is of course an old idea first eloquently expressed by Adam Smith. Ever since the publication of Adam Smith's *Wealth of Nations* in 1776 economists have been aware that security of property rights against expropriation by fellow citizens or the state is an important condition for encouraging individuals to invest and accumulate capital. Given this pedigree, economists have tended to centre their analysis of the deeper determinants of growth on the role of institutions. Emphasis here is placed on factors such as the role of property rights, the effectiveness of the legal system, corruption, regulatory structures and the quality of governance (North, 1990; World Bank, 1997; Olson, 2000; Acemoglu et al., 2001, 2002a; Glaeser and Shleifer, 2002). From an institutionalist perspective the search for the deeper determinants of growth has led to what Hibbs (2001) has called 'the politicisation of growth theory'. By 'politicisation' Hibbs is referring to the increasing emphasis given by many growth researchers, in particular the seminal contributions of Douglass North, to the importance of 'politics, policy and institutional arrangements'. These factors ultimately determine the structure of incentives, the ability and willingness of people to save and invest productively, the security of property rights and the incentive to innovate and participate in entrepreneurial activity. Political–institutional factors also appear to be robust determinants of growth in many cross-country regression studies (Knack and Keefer, 1995, 1997a, 1997b; Sala-i-Martin, 1997; Dawson, 1998; Durlauf and Quah, 1999; Easterly and Levine, 2003; Rodrik, 2003; Rodrik et al., 2004).

While the presence of technological backwardness and income per capita gaps creates the potential for catch-up and convergence, Abramovitz (1986) has highlighted the importance of 'social capability' without which countries will not be able to realize their potential. Social capability refers to the various institutional arrangements which set the framework for the conduct of productive economic activities and without which market economies cannot function efficiently. Temple and Johnson (1998) suggest that indexes of social development developed in the 1960s by Adelman and Morris (1967) have 'considerable predictive power' (see also Temple, 1998). Temple and Johnson (1998) show that these measures, after allowing for initial income, are 'very useful in predicting subsequent growth' and 'if observers in the early 1960s had given more emphasis to these indexes of social capability, they might have been rather more successful in predicting the fast growth of East Asia, and underperformance of sub-Saharan Africa'.

**Developing effective institutions**
Clearly the major income differentials that we observe around the world have a lot to do with differences in the quality of countries' institutions and economic policies as well as the quality of political leadership. This explains the rapid growth witnessed in a subset of East Asian developing countries since around 1960 and the relative stagnation of most of sub-Saharan Africa over that same period. Many economists believe that the main reasons why some countries progress and grow rapidly while others stagnate cannot be found in the area of geography and factor endowments. Countries with poor natural resources such as Japan, Taiwan and South Korea have experienced 'miracle' growth while many natural resource-abundant economies in sub-Saharan Africa, such as Zaire (from 1997 the Democratic Republic of Congo), have been growth 'disasters'. Reynolds (1985) concludes that the single most important explanatory variable of economic progress is the political organization and the administrative competence of government (see Herbst, 2000). Gray and McPherson (2001), in their analysis of the leadership factor in African policy reform, conclude that 'a large number of African countries, perhaps the majority, have been ruled by individuals who had sufficient power to implement reforms had they been so motivated. However, their motivation led them in different directions.' It is also the case that the political and economic losers from the changes that economic development requires will often act as barriers to progress (Acemoglu and Robinson, 2000a; Parente and Prescott, 2000).

Given the importance of these issues, the recent political economy of growth literature has focused on such factors as the relationship between economic freedom, democracy and growth (for example Barro, 1996, 1999; Clague et al., 1996; Minier, 1998; Benson Durham, 1999; Landman, 1999; Olson, 2000); property rights and growth (for example North and Weingast, 1989; North, 1990; DeLong and Shleifer, 1993; Acemoglu and Johnson, 2003); ethnic heterogeneity, political conflict and growth (for example Easterly and Levine, 1997; Acemoglu and Robinson, 2000a, 2000b, 2000c, 2001, 2003; Collier, 2001; Easterly, 2001b); the impact of inequality and political instability on growth (for example Alesina and Rodrik, 1994; Alesina et al., 1996; Lee and Roemer, 1998; Barro, 2000; Glaeser et al., 2003; see also Chapter 10); and various measures of social capability/social infrastructure/ social capital and growth, including trust (for example Knack and Keefer, 1995, 1997a, 1997b; Abramovitz and David, 1996; Landau et al., 1996; Hall and Jones, 1997, 1999; Temple, 1998; Temple and Johnson, 1998; Paldam, 2000; Rose-Ackerman, 2001; Zak and Knack, 2001).

According to the World Bank (2002), there is a growing body of evidence linking the quality of institutional development to economic growth and efficiency across both time and space and there is now widespread acceptance of the idea that 'good' institutions and incentive structures are an important precondition for successful growth and development. Because economic history is essentially about the performance of economies over long periods of time, it has a significant contribution to make in helping growth theorists improve their ability to develop a better analytical framework for understanding long-run economic change (North and Thomas, 1973; North, 1981, 1989, 1990, 1994; Myles, 2000).

The story that emerges from economic history is one which shows that the unsuccessful economies, in terms of achieving sustained growth of living standards, are those that fail to produce a set of enforceable economic rules of the game that promote economic progress. As North (1991) argues, the 'central issue of economic history and of economic development is to account for the evolution of political and economic institutions that create an economic environment that induces increasing productivity'.

North (1991) defines institutions as 'the humanly devised constraints that structure political, economic and social interaction'. The constraining institutions may be informal (customs, traditions, taboos, conventions, self-imposed codes of conduct involving guilt and shame) and/or formal (laws, contract enforcement, rules, constitutions, property rights). In an ideal world the informal and formal institutions will complement each other. These institutions provide a structure within which repeated human interaction can take place, they support market transactions, they help to transmit information between economic agents and they give people the incentives necessary to engage in productive activities. History is 'largely a story of institutional evolution' and effective institutions 'raise the benefit of co-operative solutions or the costs of defection' (North, 1991).

A good example demonstrating the importance of institutions for sustained economic growth is provided by the post-Second World War reconstruction of Europe. As DeLong and Eichengreen (1993) argue, 'the Marshall Plan significantly sped western European growth by altering the environment in which economic policy was made' and by providing support to a recovery strategy based on the restoration of a market-based economic system, together with the necessary supporting institutions. In retrospect we now know that the period 1950–73 turned out to be a 'Golden Age' of economic growth in the 'mixed' economies of Western Europe, and DeLong and Eichengreen conclude that the Marshall plan was 'history's most successful structural adjustment programme'. Eichengreen (1996) also extends the institutional based explanation of why Europe was able to enjoy a 'Golden Age' of economic growth in the 25-year period following the implementation of the Marshall Plan. European economic growth during this quarter-century was faster than any period either before or since (Maddison, 2001). According to Eichengreen, the foundation for this 'Golden Age' was a set of domestic (the social market economy) and international institutions (GATT, the development of free intra-European trade, the Bretton Woods institutions) that 'solved problems of commitment and co-operation that would have otherwise hindered the resumption of growth'.

For individuals living in a typical rich OECD economy in the twenty-first century it is easy to take most of these market-based institutions for granted because they have evolved over such a long historical period. But the 'trials of transition' witnessed in the former communist economies remind us just how difficult it is to make market economies operate effectively without having the necessary institutional infrastructure in place.

### Evidence from 'natural experiments'
One very important source of divergence in per capita incomes emphasized by Fukuyama (1989, 1992), Olson (1996, 2000) and DeLong (2001) has arisen because of political developments which have influenced the choice of economic system and policies. Those countries which attempted to 'develop' behind the 'Iron Curtain' now have much lower income per capita than countries which had a comparable income per capita in 1950 and followed the capitalist path.

> The fact that a large part of the globe was under communist rule in the twentieth century is one major reason for the world's divergence ... depending on how you count and how unlucky you are, 40 to 94 per cent of the potential material prosperity of a country was annihilated if it happened to fall under communist rule in the twentieth century. (DeLong, 2001)

The most obvious examples involve the comparative development experiences of East and West Germany, North and South Korea, and China with Taiwan/Singapore/Hong Kong. But comparisons between other neighbouring countries seems reasonable, for example, comparisons between Russia and Finland, Hungary and Austria, Greece and Bulgaria, Slovenia and Italy, and Cambodia and Thailand reveal significant differences in living standards.

Of the examples mentioned above, the most dramatic 'natural experiment' has occurred in the Korean peninsula during the second half of the twentieth century. Following the surrender of Japan in August 1945, Korea was divided at the 38th parallel into two zones of occupation, with armed forces from the Soviet Union occupying the 'North' and American armed forces occupying the 'South'. In the summer of 1948, following the May elections, the American zone of occupation became the Republic of Korea, and in September 1948 the northern zone became formally known as the Democratic People's Republic of North Korea. Both 'Koreas' claimed full political jurisdiction over the entire Korean peninsula and this disagreement led to the Korean War, which lasted from June 1950 until the armistice of July 1953. Since then the 38th parallel has remained the dividing line between the two Koreas, with the 'communist North' adopting a centrally planned economic strategy and the 'capitalist South' putting its faith in a capitalist mixed economy. As the data in Tables 11.4 and 11.5 make clear, the impact of these choices on living standards in the two Koreas, made some 50 years ago, could not have been more dramatic. As Acemoglu (2003b) notes, 'a distinguishing feature of Korea before separation was its ethnic, linguistic and economic homogeneity. The north and south are inhabited by essentially the same people with the

*Table 11.4    A tale of two Koreas*

| Indicator | Population ('000) | GDP PPP $ millions | GDP per capita PPP $ | Population ('000) | GDP PPP $ millions | GDP per capita PPP $ |
|---|---|---|---|---|---|---|
| Year | North Korea | North Korea | North Korea | South Korea | South Korea | South Korea |
| 1950 | 9 471 | 7 293 | 770 | 20 846 | 16 045 | 770 |
| 1955 | 8 839 | 9 361 | 1 054 | 21 552 | 22 708 | 1 054 |
| 1960 | 10 392 | 11 483 | 1 105 | 24 784 | 27 398 | 1 105 |
| 1965 | 11 869 | 15 370 | 1 295 | 28 705 | 37 166 | 1 295 |
| 1970 | 13 912 | 27 184 | 1 954 | 32 241 | 62 988 | 1 954 |
| 1975 | 15 801 | 44 891 | 2 841 | 35 281 | 111 548 | 3 162 |
| 1980 | 17 114 | 48 621 | 2 841 | 38 124 | 156 846 | 4 114 |
| 1985 | 18 481 | 52 505 | 2 841 | 40 806 | 231 386 | 5 670 |
| 1990 | 20 019 | 56 874 | 2 841 | 42 869 | 373 150 | 8 704 |
| 1995 | 21 553 | 32 758 | 1 520 | 45 081 | 534 517 | 11 873 |
| 1998 | 21 234 | 25 131 | 1 183 | 46 430 | 564 211 | 12 152 |

*Source*:    Adapted from Maddison (2001).

*Table 11.5    Growth rates of per capita GDP (%): the two Koreas*

|             | 1950–73 | 1973–98 |
|-------------|---------|---------|
| North Korea | 5.84    | –3.44   |
| South Korea | 5.84    | 5.99    |

*Source*:   Adapted from Maddison (2001).

same culture, and there were only minor differences between the two areas.' Therefore, this natural experiment, of dividing the Korean peninsula into two countries, each distinguished by very different policies and institutions, 'gives a clear example of how, despite the very similar economic conditions, political leaders often chose very different policies with very different outcomes'.

As Maddison's (2001) data indicate, per capita GDP in North Korea in 1950 was $770 (at 1990 international prices). By 1998 this had only risen to $1183. In sharp contrast, although per capita income in South Korea in 1950 was also $770, by 1998 it had risen to $12 152! This again demonstrates the powerful effect that differential growth rates can have on the relative living standards of two countries. While North Korean per capita economic growth during the 1950–73 period was initially impressive (5.84 per cent per annum), during the 1973–98 period the rate of growth collapsed to minus 3.44 per cent. During the 1950–73 period South Korea's growth rate was also 5.84 per cent. However, during the years 1973–98 South Korea's per capita growth rate increased to 5.99 per cent. By 1999, World Bank (2002) data indicate that the 47 million people living in the South had a life expectancy of 73 whereas for the 23.6 million people living in the North, life expectancy was 60 and in recent years North Korea has been experiencing a famine (Noland et al., 2001).

These 'natural experiments' show that where national borders also mark the boundaries of public policies and institutions, easily observable differentials in economic performance emerge (Fukuyama, 1992; Olson, 1996). In DeLong's (1992) view, 'over the course of the twentieth century communism has been a major factor making for divergence: making nations that were relatively poor poorer even as rich industrial economies have grown richer'.

**Democracy, the quality of governance and growth**
Does growth promote democracy or does democracy promote growth? Recent research into the link between democracy, dictatorship and growth has produced support for both of the above linkages. Barro (1996, 1997, 1999) provides evidence in support of the Lipset (1959) hypothesis which suggests that prosperity promotes democracy. Barro's research confirms this hypoth-

esis as a 'strong empirical regularity'. Since the empirical evidence also supports the hypothesis that economic freedom promotes prosperity, Barro concludes that policies that promote economic freedom will also promote greater democracy through the Lipset prosperity effect. It is certainly indisputable that there has never been a liberal democracy (free and regular competitive elections) where there is an absence of economic freedom (see Friedman, 1962; Kornai, 2000; Snowdon 2003b).

Bhagwati's (1995) essay on democracy rejects an earlier popular view highlighted in his 1966 book on *The Economics of Underdeveloped Countries* that developing countries may face a 'cruel dilemma' in that they must somehow choose between economic development or democracy. During the 1960s democracy was often portrayed as a luxury that poor countries could not afford. It was often argued that to achieve rapid growth requires tough decisions and that in turn necessitates firm political leadership free from democratic constraints. The balance of opinion has now moved away from accepting as inevitable this 'Cruel Dilemma Thesis'.

While prosperity undoubtedly sows the seeds of democracy, the idea that a stable democracy is good for sustained growth has also been receiving increasing support in the literature. If property rights are the key to reducing transaction costs and the promotion of specialization and trade, then it should be no surprise to observe that 'almost all of the countries that have enjoyed good economic performance across generations are countries that have stable democratic governments' (Olson, 2000; Rodrik, 2000). Whereas good governance and economic prosperity are good bedfellows, autocrats, who are also invariably kleptomaniacs, are a high-risk form of investment. As Easterly (2001a) notes, 'governments can kill growth'.

For most of human history the vast majority of the peoples of the world have been governed by what Mancur Olson (1993, 2000) calls 'roving bandits' and 'stationary bandits'. History provides incontrovertible evidence that benevolent despots are a rare breed. Roving bandits (warlords) have little interest in promoting the well-being of the people living within their domain. A territory dominated by competing roving bandits represents a situation of pure anarchy and any form of sustainable economic development is impossible. With no secure property rights there is little incentive for people to produce any more than is necessary for their survival since any surplus will be expropriated by force. Stationary bandits, however, can extract more tax revenue from the territory they dominate if a stable and productive economy can be encouraged and maintained. In this situation despots have an incentive to provide key public goods such as law and order. But property rights can never be fully secure under autocratic forms of governance because the discretionary powers of the autocrat create a time-inconsistency problem. That is, the autocrat will always have a credibility problem. History shows that absolutist princes always find it difficult to establish stable dynasties, and this uncertainty relating to succession prevents autocrats from taking a longer-term view of the economy. For example, the monarchy in England between the rule of William the Conqueror (1066) and the 'Glorious Revolution' (1688) was plagued by repeated crises of succession (for example the 'Wars of the Roses'). Only in a secure democracy, where representative government is accountable and respectful of individual rights, can we expect to observe an environment created that is conducive to lasting property rights (Fukuyama, 1989, 1992).

Acemoglu's recent research highlights the importance of 'political barriers to development'. This work focuses on attitudes to change in hierarchical societies. Economists recognize that economic growth is a necessary condition for the elimination of poverty and sustainable increases in living standards. Furthermore, technological change and innovation are key factors in promoting growth. So why do political élites deliberately block the adoption of institutions and policies that would help to eliminate economic backwardness? Acemoglu and Robinson (2000a, 2000b, 2000c, 2001, 2003, 2005) argue that superior institutions and technologies are resisted because they may reduce the political power of the elite. Moreover, the absence of a 'strong institution' allows autocratic rulers to 'adopt political strategies which are highly effective at diffusing any opposition to their regime ... the kleptocratic ruler intensifies the collective action problem and destroys the coalition against him by bribing the pivotal groups' (Acemoglu et al., 2003b). Often financed by natural resource abundance and foreign aid, kleptocrats follow an effective power sustaining strategy of 'divide and rule'. In the case of Zaire, with over 200 ethnic groups, Mobutu was able to follow such a strategy from 1965 until he was overthrown in 1997. Acemoglu's research reinforces the conclusions of Easterly and Levine (1997), who find that ethnic diversity in Africa reduces the rate of economic growth (see next section).

The general thesis advocated by North and Olson is also confirmed by DeLong and Shleifer (1993), who show that those cities in medieval Europe that were under more democratic forms of government were much more productive than those under the autocratic rule of 'princes'. The incompatibility of despotism with sustainable economic development arises because of the insecurity of property rights in environments where there are no constitutional restrictions on an autocratic ruler. DeLong and Shleifer assume that the size of urban populations is a useful proxy for commercial prosperity and 'use the number and sizes of large pre-industrial cities as an index of economic activity, and changes in the number of cities and the sizes of urban population as indicators of economic growth'. Their city data show how between the years 1000 and 1500, the centre of economic gravity in Europe moved steadily northward. Although in the year 1000 Western Europe was a 'backwater' in terms of urban development, by 1800 it was established as the most prosperous and economically advanced region of the world. While London is ranked as the 25th largest European city at the beginning of the thirteenth century, by 1650 it had risen to second place (after Paris), and by 1800 London was first. DeLong and Shleifer argue that security of property can be thought of as a form of lower taxation, with the difference between absolutist and non-absolutist governments showing up as different tax rates on private property. It has also been argued by Douglass North that the establishment of a credible and sustainable commitment to the security of property rights in England required the establishment of parliamentary supremacy over the crown. This was achieved following the 'Glorious Revolution' of 1688 which facilitated the gradual establishment of economic institutions conducive to increasing security in property rights (North and Weingast, 1989; North, 1990). The contrasting economic fortunes of the North and South American continents also bear testimony to the consequences of divergent institutional paths for political and economic performance (Sokoloff and Engerman, 2000; Acemoglu et al., 2001, 2002a; Khan and Sokoloff, 2001).

The failure in many countries to develop good governance has had serious, often drastic, economic and political consequences. The case for democracy rests very much on how regular elections and a free press and media act as important mechanisms that increase the accountability of politicians. In a principal–agent model, the scope for rent-seeking activities by politicians, who have potential access to huge resources, is greatly increased if the citizens of a country lack information and are denied the opportunity to hold politicians accountable via regular and guaranteed competitive elections (see Adsera et al., 2003).

In sum, we think that Winston Churchill had it right when he made his famous statement defending democracy in the House of Commons (11 November 1947):

> No one pretends that democracy is perfect or all wise. Indeed it has been said that democracy is the worst form of government except for all those other forms that have been tried from time to time.

### Rent seeking, trust, corruption and growth
In order to foster high levels of output per worker, social institutions must be developed which protect the output of individual productive units from diversion. Countries with perverse infrastructure, such as a corrupt bureaucracy, generate rent-seeking activities devoted to the diversion of resources rather than productive activities such as capital accumulation, skills acquisition, and the development of new goods and production techniques (Murphy et al.,

1993; Mauro, 1995). In an environment of weak law and contract enforcement, poor protection of property rights, confiscatory taxation and widespread corruption, unproductive profit- (rent-) seeking activities will become endemic and cause immense damage to innovation and other growth-enhancing activities (Tanzi, 1998).

There is abundant evidence that economic incentives can influence the productivity and interests of talented individuals who potentially can make a huge contribution to the accumulation of wealth. For individuals or groups of individuals to have an incentive to adopt more advanced technology or engage in the creation of new ideas requires an institutional framework which allows for an adequate rate of return. In an interesting development of Schumpeter's theory of entrepreneurship Baumol (1990) has shown that by extending the model, so that it encompasses the 'allocation' of entrepreneurial skills, the power of the model to yield policy insights is greatly enhanced. In Schumpeter's (1934) analysis he identifies five forms of entrepreneurial activity in addition to those related to fostering improvements in technology, namely:

1.   the introduction of new goods and/or new quality of an existing good;
2.   the introduction of a new production method;
3.   the opening of a new market;
4.   the 'conquest' of a new source of supply of raw materials;
5.   the new organization of any industry.

Baumol (1990) argues that Schumpeter's list is deficient and in need of extension to include:

6.   'innovative acts of technology transfer that take advantage of opportunities to introduce already available technology to geographical locales whose suitability for the purpose had previously gone unrecognised or at least unused';
7.   'innovations in rent seeking procedures'.

This last category is of crucial importance because it includes what Baumol calls 'acts of unproductive entrepreneurship'. Given that Baumol defines entrepreneurs as 'persons who are ingenious and creative in finding ways that add to their own wealth, power, and prestige', it follows that one of the main determinants of the allocation of entrepreneurial talent at a particular time and place will be the 'prevailing rules of the game that govern the payoff of one entrepreneurial activity relative to another'. Talented individuals are naturally attracted to activities with the highest private returns. There is no guarantee that such activities will always have the highest social rate of return. Therefore entrepreneurs can be 'unproductive', even 'destructive', as well as pro-ductive from society's point of view. While in some economies talented people become conventional business entrepreneurs, in others talent is at-tracted to the government bureaucracy, the armed forces, religion, crime and other rent-seeking activities. Since the 'rules of the game' can and do change, we can expect to see a reallocation of entrepreneurial talent appropriate to any new environment. The forms of entrepreneurial behaviour that we ob-serve will obviously change over historical time and across geographical space. Therefore the allocation of entrepreneurship between productive, un-productive and destructive activities cannot but have a 'profound effect' on the innovativeness, and hence growth, of any economy. For example, Landes (1969) suggests that the reason why the Industrial Revolution began in Eng-land rather than in France is linked to the allocation of talent. Any country interested in growth must ensure that its most able people are allocated to the productive sectors of the economy. Murphy et al. (1991) argue that a possible reason for the productivity growth slowdown in the US economy during the 1970s could be the misallocation of human capital because talented individu-als have increasingly become rent seekers (for example lawyers) rather than producers (for example engineers). They conclude that the 'allocation of talented people to entrepreneurship is good for growth and their allocation to rent seeking is bad for growth'. In Baumol's view the predominant form of unproductive entrepreneurship in economies today is rent seeking, and the prevailing laws, regulations and structure of financial incentives will inevita-bly have a major effect on the 'allocation of talent'.

These insights suggest that a fruitful line of research is to focus on cross-country differences in incentive structures facing entrepreneurs with respect to encouragement to create new enterprises, adopt new technologies and thereby increase growth. If barriers to productive entrepreneurship are delib-erately created by specific groups who have a clear vested interest in the *status quo*, then the task of economists is to offer policy advice about how to design and establish institutions that minimize this 'unproductive' behaviour. When an environment is created that is conducive to the adoption of new ideas by entrepreneurs, a type of capital is generated which economists have referred to as 'organizational' or 'business' capital, which exists independ-ently of the entrepreneur. Countries that lack organizational capital will remain unattractive to foreign direct investment.

Trust between economic agents is a crucial determinant of the cost of transactions. This idea has a long pedigree (Fukuyama, 1995). For example, John Stuart Mill (1848) noted that there are counties in Europe

where the most serious impediment to conducting business concerns on a large scale, is the rarity of persons who are supposed fit to be trusted with the receipt and expenditure of large sums of money … The advantage to mankind of being able to trust one another, penetrates into every crevice and cranny of human life: the economical is perhaps the smallest part of it, yet even this is incalculable.

In a recent paper, Zak and Knack (2001) have taken up this insight and show that the extent of trust in an economy 'significantly' influences growth rates, and that 'high trust societies produce more output than low trust societies'. In economies where there is a high level of trust between transactors, the rate of investment and economic growth is likely to be higher than in low-trust environments. This finding supports the earlier empirical research of Knack and Keefer (1995, 1997a, 1997b), who find a positive relationship between trust and growth for a sample of 29 market economies. Zak and Knack argue that trust is lower in countries where: (i) there is an absence of formal (laws, contract enforcement) and informal (ostracism, guilt, loss of reputation) mechanisms and institutions which deter and punish cheaters and constrain opportunistic behaviour; (ii) population heterogeneity (ethnic diversity) is greater; and (iii) inequalities are more pervasive. Easterly and Levine (1997) find that ethnic diversity in Africa reduces the rate of economic growth since diverse groups find it more difficult to reach cooperative solutions and scarce resources are wasted because of continuous distributional struggles, of which civil war, 'ethnic cleansing' and genocide are the most extreme manifestations (Bosnia, Rwanda, Kosovo, Afghanistan). Collier's (2001) research suggests that ethnically diverse societies are 'peculiarly ill suited to dictatorship' and that providing there is not 'ethnic dominance' in the political system, then democratic institutions can greatly reduce the potential adverse economic impact of ethnic diversity and the wars of attrition that can take place between competing groups. Easterly (2001b) argues that formal institutions that protect minorities and guarantee freedom from expropriation and contract repudiation can 'constrain the amount of damage that one ethnic group could do to another'. In Easterly's framework of analysis the following relationship holds:

$$\text{Ethnic conflict} = f(\text{ethnic diversity, institutional quality})$$

Easterly's research findings show that ethnic diversity does not lower growth or result in worse economic policies providing that good institutions are in place (Snowdon, 2003a). Good institutions also 'lower the risk of wars and genocides that might otherwise result from ethnic fractionalisation'. Rodrik (1999a, 1999b, 2000) has also shown how societies with deep social divisions and a lack of democratic institutions of conflict management are highly vulnerable to exogenous economic shocks (see also Alesina and Rodrik, 1994). The adverse effect of an external shock ($S$) on economic growth is the bigger the greater the latent social conflict (*LSC*) and the weaker are a society's institutions of conflict management (*ICM*). Rodrik's hypothesis can be captured by the following relationship:

$$\Delta \text{ growth} = - S(LSC/ICM)$$

Rodrik (1999a) uses this framework to explain the numerous 'growth collapses' that occurred across the world economy after the economic shocks of the 1970s. In his empirical analysis countries with democratic and high-quality government institutions demonstrated better macroeconomic management and as a result experienced less volatility in their growth rates than countries with weak institutions of conflict management.

## 11.19  Trade and Economic Growth

Another important strand of the growth literature points to the importance of increasing international economic integration ('globalization') as a major fundamental determinant of economic growth. It is argued that there are sound theoretical reasons for believing that more open economies grow faster than more closed economies. In a recent survey of the literature, Lewer and Van den Berg (2003) conclude that the 'impact of trade on economic growth appears to be very important for human welfare'. Moreover, the proponents of this view support their case with numerous empirical studies and conclude that, overall, 'globalization' has had a positive effect on economic growth (Sachs and Warner, 1995; Krueger, 1997; Edwards, 1998; Frankel and Romer, 1999; O'Rourke and Williamsom, 1999; Baldwin, 2000; Bhagwati and Srinivasan, 2002; Dollar and Kraay, 2003, 2004; Bordo et al., 2002b; Bhagwati, 2004; Winters, 2004; see also Snowdon, 2001c, 2003c).

While economists recognize that freer trade will have a 'level effect' in raising a country's output once and for all, the likely impact on the rate of growth of output is much more controversial. For example, Lucas (1988) suggests that the removal of barriers to trade may induce a series of boosts to output which are level effects disguised as growth effects. In the standard open economy version of the Solow growth model, trade liberalization can have a temporary, but no permanent, effect on the long-run rate of growth. As Rivera-Batiz and Romer (1991) note, the main problem is that economists do not have a 'rigorous model' to justify their belief that increased economic integration will tend to increase the long-run rate of growth. Rodriguez and Rodrik (2000) have claimed that little evidence can be found 'that open trade policies – in the sense of lower tariff and non-tariff barriers to trade – are significantly associated with economic growth'. In response, Bhagwati and Srinivasan (2001) argue that an open trading regime not only allows the

beneficial level effects to be gained from comparative advantage but also has
a positive influence on growth. But rather than relying on 'endless' (and
'mindless') cross-county regression evidence, Bhagwati and Srinivasan appeal to the numerous in-depth country case studies which support the
growth-inducing effects of greater openness (Bhagwati, 1978; Krueger, 1978;
Balassa, 1989; Edwards, 1998). Krueger (1997, 1998) is in no doubt that the
developing countries that followed more outward-oriented strategies have
grown faster on a sustained basis than those who 'blithely abandoned' the
principle of comparative advantage and adopted, and maintained for long
periods, import substitution (ISI) policies. Krueger links the initial hostility
to outward-oriented strategies after 1945 to the powerful influence of *dirigiste*
ideas which in turn were a legacy of the Great Depression and the apparent
success of state-led development in the Soviet Union. Bhagwati (1993) recalls how India was propelled towards a 'harmful' ISI strategy because many
of India's influential economists during the 1950s, including P.C. Mahalanobis,
took the idea of 'elasticity pessimism' with respect to exports too seriously.
In contrast to India, the experience of over four decades of outstanding
economic growth performance achieved by the East Asian 'miracle' economies is also positively linked to their choice of open trade regime. The
empirical work of Sachs and Warner (1995), Ben-David (1996), Edwards
(1993, 1998), and Ben-David and Loewy (1998) adds support to the mainstream view that there is a strong link between free trade and income
convergence among nations. Lawrence and Weinstein (2001), while providing support to those who advocate more liberal trade policies, reject the
'export fetishism' of some earlier studies and emphasize instead the growth-
enhancing effects of an increasing share of imports in GDP via its effect on
innovation and learning (see Rodrik, 1995). What is certain is that a more
open economy will have access to cheaper imported capital goods from the
world market (see DeLong and Summers, 1993; Jones, 1994).

An important factor influencing convergence identified by Sachs and Warner
(1995) is the degree of openness of an economy:

> We suggest that the most parsimonious reading of the evidence is that conver-
> gence can be achieved by all countries, even those with low initial level of skills,
> as long as they are open and integrated in the world economy ... the convergence
> club is the club of economies linked together by international trade ... In terms of
> the conditional convergence hypothesis, we argue that the apparent differences in
> long-term income levels are not differences due to fundamental tastes and tech-
> nologies, but rather to policies regarding economic integration.

Sachs and Warner identify a 'closed' trading regime as one that has at least
one of the following characteristics: (i) non tariff barriers covering 40 per
cent or more of trade; (ii) average tariff rates of 40 per cent or more; (iii) a

black market exchange rate that is depreciated by 20 per cent or more relative to the official exchange rate, on average, during the 1970s and 1980s; (iv) a socialist economic system (as defined by Kornai, 1992); and (v) a state monopoly on major exports. An open economy is one where none of the above conditions hold. The case of China is the only real puzzle. However, as Sachs and Warner explain, with respect to international trade, the Chinese economy was essentially liberalized for non-state firms, especially those operating in the Special Economic Zones in the coastal areas. And the fastest-growing areas in China in the period 1978–94 were all coastal provinces with the exception of Xinjiang (Ying, 1999).

The research findings of Sachs and Warner lead them to four important conclusions: first, 'there is strong evidence of unconditional convergence for open countries, and no evidence of unconditional convergence for closed countries'; second, 'closed countries systematically grow more slowly than do open countries, showing that "good" policies matter'; third, 'the role of trade policy continues after controlling for other growth factors'; and fourth, 'poor trade policies seem to affect growth directly, controlling for other factors, and to affect the rate of accumulation of physical capital'. Therefore, Sachs and Warner's reading of the evidence suggests that trade policy should be viewed as 'the primary instrument of reform' where trade policy serves as a proxy for an entire array of market reforms.

At the theoretical level, work in the endogenous growth literature has emphasized the importance of the flow of ideas in stimulating technological innovation (P. Romer, 1990, 1993, 1994b). In this context the greater a country's exposure to the world outside the more it is likely to gain from the research and development activities of other countries, including new ideas relating to organizational methods. As Paul Romer argues, 'The key role for trade is that it lets developing countries get access to ideas that exist in the rest of the world'. This view also receives support from Robert Solow, who suggests that 'The only way you can make sense of trade having an effect on the long-run growth rate is not so much whether the country is export led, but whether the country is in contact with the rest of the world' (see Solow interview at the end of this chapter). Edwards (1998) provides a simple framework for considering the relationship between TFP growth and openness. This framework is summarized in equations (11.44) and (11.45).

$$Y_t = A_t f(K_t, L_t) \qquad (11.44)$$

$$\dot{A}/A = \theta + \omega(W - A)/A \qquad (11.45)$$

Here $Y_t$ is GDP, $A_t$ is the stock of knowledge, or TFP, $K_t$ is physical capital and $L_t$ is labour measured in efficiency units. Growth will depend on the rate of change of $A_t$, $K_t$ and $L_t$. Edwards assumes that there are two sources of TFP growth: first, a domestic source fuelled by innovation and dependent on domestic human capital (education); and second, an international source 'related to the rate at which the country is able to absorb (or imitate) technological progress originating in the leading nations'. Imitation depends on a 'catch-up' term. Those countries furthest from the technological frontier have the greatest potential for imitation. In equation (11.45) $\dot{A}/A$ is the rate of growth of TFP, $\theta$ is the domestic rate of innovation, $\omega$ is the speed at which a country is able to close its knowledge gap and is influenced by trade policies, $W$ is the world stock of knowledge assumed to grow at a rate $g$ (where $g \geq \theta$). For the world's technological leader (the USA since the 1890s) $g = \theta$ and $W = A$. Edwards argues that, in keeping with many ideas-based models of growth, more open economies 'have a greater ability to absorb ideas from the rest of the world and, thus, have a higher $\omega$' and 'an important property of this simple model is that countries that liberalise trade will experience transitional productivity growth that exceeds that of countries that maintain their trade distortions'. Because trade between nations is likely to act as a conduit for the dissemination of ideas, inward-looking trade and development strategies which erect barriers to trade will therefore inhibit the transmission of knowledge.

The extent of North–South R&D spillovers has been investigated by Coe et al. (1997). Given that almost all R&D activity is carried out in the developed countries, there are clearly opportunities for developing countries to benefit from knowledge spillovers, especially from the USA. The empirical evidence presented by Coe et al. indicates that the total factor productivity of developing countries is 'positively and significantly related to R & D in their industrial country trade partners and to their imports of machinery and equipment from the industrial countries'.

In the model developed by Ben-David and Loewy (1998) openness creates greater competitive pressure on domestic firms which, in response, seek to acquire foreign knowledge relating to production processes and techniques (see also Parente and Prescott, 2000; Baumol, 2002). Hence trade flows facilitate the transfer of ideas and stimulate the growth of the economy. Because many poor countries have adopted protectionist strategies, their trade barriers act as a 'buffer that limits knowledge spillovers'. Ben-David and Loewy argue that so long as such barriers persist, the income gap between countries will continue to exist.

Remarkably, Adam Smith (1776) anticipated the argument that free trade facilitated the flow of ideas and knowledge:

> Nothing seems more likely to establish this equality of force than the mutual
> communication of knowledge and of all sorts of improvements which an extensive

commerce from all countries to all countries naturally, or rather necessarily, carries with it.

In Irwin's (1996) view, these insights of Smith, relating to technology transfer and the dynamic benefits of openness, 'were outstanding for the period in which he was writing'.

While the majority view of economists leans towards the Bhagwati position on trade and growth, Rodrik (1995, 1999a) remains critical of those who place too much emphasis on 'globalization' and exports as the easy road to economic development. He continues to emphasize that policy makers in developing countries need to formulate a growth strategy that recognizes the importance of domestic institutions (including democracy) and domestic investors rather than one that is built solely around a 'hazardous obsession with global integration'. Unlike Bhagwati and Krueger, who have provided a sustained critique of ISI policies, Rodrik (1999a, 1999b) argues that the wrong lessons have been learned about the growth experiences of countries that adopted ISI policies. According to Rodrik, ISI policies worked very well for about twenty years before the late 1970s, and the subsequent growth collapses and disappointing economic performance of many ISI-adopting countries 'had little to do with ISI policies'. The developing countries that successfully weathered the economic shocks of the 1970s and 1980s were those that quickly and decisively made the appropriate macroeconomic adjustments and also had effective domestic institutions of conflict management. So the reason that the East Asian economies have been better equipped to cope with economic turbulence compared to Latin America and sub-Saharan Africa is not that they were outward-oriented and the others remained closed; rather it was because Latin America and sub-Saharan Africa 'did a much worse job' in managing and absorbing the shocks. Rodrik does not deny the potential benefits of openness, but he warns policy makers and fellow economists that for openness to be a successful component of any development strategy, it must not be regarded as a substitute for a domestic strategy. The 'knee-jerk' globalizers among policy makers mistakenly seem to imply that globalization, by itself, can work miracles for a developing country's economy. Therefore Rodrik remains a strong advocate of the importance of domestic investment, human and physical capital formation, as the fundamental determinant of economic growth. While empirically the relationship between investment and growth 'tends to be erratic in the short run ... cross-national studies have shown that investment is one of the few robust correlates of economic growth over horizons spanning decades' (see Rodrik, 1995, 1999a; see also Vamvakidis, 2002).

A reasonable conclusion from the above discussion is that it appears to be openness rather than exports *per se* which seems to matter for enhanced economic performance, but also that to fully benefit from the potential benefits of openness developing counties need a complementary domestic strategy that includes building 'institutions for high-quality growth' (Rodrik, 2000, 2003, 2005) . Openness is a means to an end, not an end in itself. Interestingly, as the research of Alesina and Spolare (2003) shows, as the world economy becomes more open, the size of a country's domestic market becomes less important as a positive influence on the level and growth of productivity. As globalization spreads, the benefits of size diminish. Predictably the number of countries in the world has increased from 74 in 1945 to 192 in 2004.

## 11.20   Geography and Growth

In recent years several scholars have revived the idea that geography has an important influence on economic performance. There have been two strands in this literature. The first, represented by the work of economists such as Paul Krugman, Anthony Venables and Michael Porter, highlights the role of increasing returns, agglomeration, size, clusters and location in the productivity performance of nations and regions (see Krugman, 1991a, 1991b, 1997; Krugman and Venables, 1995; Martin, 1999; Crafts and Venables, 2002; Porter, 2003; Yang, 2003). With intellectual roots in the work of Alwyn Young, Gunnar Myrdal and Nicholas Kaldor, the 'new economic geography' models highlight the impact of cumulative causation effects whereby success breeds success. In these models globalization can initiate cumulative processes that lead to the persistence of uneven spatial (urban, regional, and international) development. As Crafts and Venables (2002) point out, in a world dominated by increasing returns, cumulative causation, agglomerations effects and path dependency, the prospects that increasing international integration will lead to convergence are much less certain.

A second strand in the literature emphasizes the direct impact that geography can have through climate, natural resources and topography. Such factors obviously influence the health of a population, agricultural productivity, the economic structure of an economy, transport costs and the diffusion of information and knowledge. Geography, it is argued, plays an important role in determining the level and growth of income per capita (see Diamond, 1997; Bloom and Sachs, 1998; Gallup et al., 1998; Bloom et al., 2003). For a critique of this literature see Acemoglu et al., 2001, 2002a).

An important stimulus to the revival of interest in the impact of geography on economic performance comes from the increasing recognition that income per capita and latitude are closely related. Countries nearer to the equator, with a few exceptions (such as Singapore), have lower income per capita and HDI scores than countries located in more temperate zones. The strong negative empirical association between living standards and proximity to the tropical latitudes is strongly influenced by the 'dismal growth performance of the African continent' which has produced the 'worst economic disaster of the twentieth century' (Artadi and Sala-i-Martin, 2003; see also Easterly and Levine, 1997; Collier and Gunning, 1999a, 1999b; Herbst, 2000). What accounts for the extraordinarily poor economic performance of sub-Saharan African economies during the second half of the twentieth century, particularly since decolonization?

Bloom and Sachs (1998) have argued that six sets of factors have featured in various accounts of the poor economic performance of sub-Saharan African economies, namely explanations based on:

1. unfavourable external factors related to colonial and cold war legacies;
2. volatility in primary exports terms of trade;
3. internal politics conducive to authoritarianism and corruption;
4. *dirigiste* economic policies emphasizing import substitution and fiscal profligacy;
5. demographic trends involving rapid population growth and a 'stalled demographic transition'; and
6. ethnic diversity and low levels of social capital (trust).

However, in addition to these factors, which have all played some role, Bloom and Sachs believe that economists ought to 'lift their gaze above macroeconomic policies and market liberalisation' and recognize the constraining influence on sub-Saharan Africa development of its 'extraordinarily disadvantageous geography'. By having the highest proportion of land area (93 per cent) and population (659 million, in 2000) of all the world's tropical regions, sub-Saharan Africa, by virtue of its climate, soils, topography and disease ecology, suffers from low agricultural productivity, poor integration with the international economy and poor health and high disease burdens now boosted with the onset of an AIDS epidemic. According to the World Bank Development Report (2002), sub-Saharan Africa has the lowest per capita income of all the major regions of the world ($480, and PPP$1560). In 1999 sub-Saharan Africa's life expectancy of 47 years was also the lowest, and sub-Saharan Africa's under-5 mortality rate of 159 per 1000 births the highest, in the world. Certainly, the evidence supports a positive link between the health of nations and their ability to accumulate wealth (Bloom et al., 2004).

The influence of geographical factors on economic growth and development was not lost on Adam Smith (1776), who recognized that success in trade was greatly enhanced by having easy access to water transportation. Smith (1776) noted that it is upon the sea-coast, and along the river banks of navigable rivers, that industry of every kind naturally begins to subdivide and improve itself ... All the inland parts of Africa, and all that part of Asia which lies any considerable way north of the Black and Caspian seas ... seem in all ages of the world to have been in the same barbarous and uncivilised state in which we find them at present.

Recently, Rappaport and Sachs (2003) have shown that economic activity in the USA is overwhelmingly concentrated along or near its ocean and Great Lakes coastal regions. As Adam Smith recognized, proximity to coastal regions greatly enhances productivity performance and the quality of life.

Whilst not arguing a new case of geographical determinism, and also recognizing the crucial role played by economic policies, Bloom and Sachs believe that 'good policies must be tailored to geographical realities'. They conclude that Africa will be well served if economists take advantage in their research of 'much greater cross-fertilisation' from the accumulated knowledge in other fields such as demography, epidemiology, agronomy, ecology and geography. Thus an important divide in the world does exist, but it is not between North and South; rather it is between countries located in temperate latitudes compared to those in the tropics (see also Sachs and Warner, 1997; Diamond, 1997; Hall and Jones, 1999; Landes, 1990, 1998; Sachs, 2003).

Finally in this section we draw attention to the recent research on the 'natural resource curse', that is, the tendency of some countries that possess abundant natural resources to grow more slowly than natural resource-poor countries. While democracies such as the USA, Canada and Norway tend to manage oil and other natural resources well, this is far from the case in countries governed by predatory kleptocratic autocrats where the presence of 'black gold' stimulates rent-seeking behaviour, political instability and, in the extreme, civil war (see Sachs and Warner, 2001; Eifert et al., 2003). As Sala-i-Martin and Subramanian (2003) document, 'Nigeria has been a disastrous development experience' despite having large oil resources. Successive corrupt military dictatorships have simply plundered the oil revenues. In contrast to Nigeria, the experience of Botswana, with its lucrative diamond resources, has been completely different. The economic success of Botswana is mainly due to the quality of its governance and institutions (see Acemoglu et al., 2003).

## 11.21   Growth in History: In Search of a Unified Theory

Before considering the 'ideal conditions' for economic growth we will briefly survey the new and exciting literature that attempts to provide a unified account of the 'Great Escape' of leading world economies from 'Malthusian stagnation' to a regime of 'modern economic growth'. Prominent here has been the research of scholars such as Daron Acemoglu, Gregory Clark, Richard Easterlin, Oded Galor, Martin Goodfriend, Gary Hansen, Simon Johnson,

Charles Jones, Eric Jones, Michael Kremer, David Landes, Robert Lucas, Angus Maddison, John McDermott, Omer Moav, Joel Mokyr, Douglass North, Stephen Parente, Kenneth Pomeranz, Edward Prescott, James Robinson and David Weil. The main puzzles to explain are these:

1. Why did no country or region of the world, before the eighteenth century (the Malthusian era), experience lasting intensive growth, that is, sustained increases in per capita GDP?
2. What led to the 'Industrial Revolution', and was this 'Revolution' inevitable?
3. What caused the 'Great Divergence' in living standards across the world that has taken place during the last 250 years?

It is difficult to imagine that there are any bigger or more difficult questions for economists to answer! At the moment, scholars working on providing answers to these questions are at the frontiers of growth theory and empirics. Increasingly, in order to provide plausible answers to such questions, growth theorists have begun to appreciate the value of economic history and the previous research carried out by economic historians. Indeed, there has recently emerged a growing synergy between growth theory, economic history and development economics that has been long overdue. While the Solow and Romer models may provide convincing explanations of the modern experience of economic growth in developed economies, they do not account for the major growth transition that occurred with the onset of the Industrial Revolution. What is needed is a unified theory that can account for the major features of the Malthusian era as well as the modern growth regime as documented in Table 11.1. Currently there are several plausible accounts or 'stories' of the evolution of world living standards.

**The natural selection, evolution story**
Galor and Moav (2001, 2002) highlight the interplay between Darwinian and Malthusian forces. The struggle for survival during the epoch of Malthusian stagnation gradually leads to an evolutionary improvement in the quality of human capital, which in turn stimulates an increase in the rate of technological progress. This eventually creates the conditions conducive to a 'take-off' of sustained economic growth. Galor and Weil (1999, 2000) carry this story forward and explain how an endogenous transition takes place with an economy moving from a 'Malthusian Regime' to a 'Post-Mathusian Regime' before finally entering the 'Modern Growth Regime'. The first two regimes are separated by an acceleration of technological progress while the latter two are separated by the demographic transition which is driven by utility-maximizing fertility behaviour (see Lee, 2003).

**The population, ideas and property rights story**
Michael Kremer (1993), building on the work of Paul Romer, constructs a model where technological progress is driven by ideas. In turn the number of ideas depends on the size of the population. Therefore, during the Malthusian era, while improvements in living standards are negligible, technological progress causes the size of the population to increase, which further stimulates technological progress through the creation of more ideas. Kremer's model predicts that, historically, the growth rate of population will be proportional to its level, at least before the worldwide spread of the demographic transition in the latter part of the twentieth century (see Lee, 2003). Charles Jones (2001b) adds to this story a key requirement that in order for technological progress to win the race against Malthusian diminishing returns, not only do there need to be increasing returns to accumulable factors; there also need to develop 'innovation-promoting institutions' as emphasized by North (1990).

**The Mathus to Solow story**
Hansen and Prescott (2002) and Parente and Prescott (2005) build models where an economy is initially dominated by a land-intensive, low-productivity 'Malthus technology' with low knowledge input. Eventually, as knowledge grows, driven by the profit motive, the economy gradually switches to one that is dominated by a much more productive 'Solow technology'. An earlier model of Goodfriend and McDermott (1995) emphasizes the transition from household to market production driven by the increasing returns to specialization made possible by a growing population.

**The institutions and property rights story**
North and Weingast (1989) highlight the positive impact that the establishment of more secure property rights had on innovation and entrepreneurship in Britain before the Industrial Revolution. Acemoglu et al. (2002b), building on this idea, trace the rise of the colonial 'Atlantic trader' economies after 1500 and link their subsequent growth success to the influence of the commercial bourgeoisie who demanded and obtained changes in institutions that led to greater protection of property rights. This is turn provided a foundation for the Industrial Revolution to take place in Britain.

**The 'Gifts of Athena' story**
Mokyr (1990, 2002, 2005) surveys the history of technological change and traces the intellectual roots of the Industrial Revolution to important changes in the method and culture involved with the creation and dissemination of new knowledge. 'The Scientific method that evolved in seventeenth century Western Europe meant that observation and experience were placed in the

public domain' (Mokyr, 2005) and scientific knowledge became a public good. 'Open science' and verification, rewarded by fame and recognition, became part of what Mokyr calls the 'Industrial Enlightenment'. The notion that economic progress was possible dominated this new enlightenment. The wave of 'macroinventions' and 'microinventions' (the 'wave of gadgets') that characterized the Industrial Revolution would not have been possible without these intellectual roots. As Mokyr notes, 'knowledge creates opportunities, but it does not guarantee action' (2005). Moreover, the 'emphasis on the Enlightenment illustrates how economists should think about culture and cultural beliefs'.

These are just some of the recent stories that attempt to provide a unified account of the evolution of world income over the very long run. The interested reader should also consult Jones (1988), Easterlin (1996), Landes (1998), Lucas (2002), Maddison (2001) and Clark (2003).

## 11.22 The Ideal Conditions for Growth and Development: Rediscovering Old Truths

Given our extended discussion of economic growth, it seems appropriate to conclude by asking the question, 'what are the ideal conditions likely to foster significant improvements in living standards?' In order to generate the 'ideal conditions' for material progress, Landes (1998) has argued that the lessons of history imply the following prerequisites:

1. an environment which fosters initiative, competition and emulation;
2. that job selection be based on merit, competence and performance;
3. financial rewards should relate to effort/enterprise;
4. the economy must be fully exposed to existing technological knowledge;
5. that education be widespread amongst the population.

These prerequisites in turn imply:

6. an absence of discrimination based on irrelevant criteria (race, religion, gender);
7. an expressed preference for scientific rationality over 'magic and superstition'.

The political and social institutions conducive to achieving these goals will involve:

8. providing laws protecting the security of property, personal liberty and secure rights of contract;
9. reducing rent-seeking behaviour;
10. providing for a more stable, moderate, honest, efficient and responsive (democratic) government operating within a framework of publicly known rules (Tanzi, 1999).

The importance of these preconditions for sustainable growth has been increasingly recognized, although frequently deliberately ignored, since the publication of Adam Smith's *Wealth of Nations* in 1776. While no economy in the world meets Landes's 'ideal' conditions for material progress, it is obvious that some come much closer to meeting the above criteria than others.

Along similar lines, Rodrik (2005) identifies certain desirable 'meta principles' that seem to apply across the globe regardless of history, geography and stage of development. They include the importance of: incentives; security of property rights; contract enforcement and the rule of law; the power of competition; hard budget constraints; macroeconomic and financial stability (low inflation, prudent regulation and fiscal sustainability); and targeted redistribution that minimizes distortions to incentives.

To a large extent these 'meta principles' are 'institution free' in the sense that they do not imply any fixed set of ideas about appropriate institutional arrangements. In other words, there are many possible models of a mixed economy and in practice the capitalist market-oriented economies that we observe across the world exhibit a 'diverse range of institutional arrangements'. Every capitalist system consists of an amalgam of public and private institutions and, as the 'new comparative economics' recognizes, European, Japanese, East Asian and American forms of capitalism differ. However, as Rodrik argues, in each case there are firmly in place 'market-sustaining institutions' which he divides into four categories:

1. market-creating institutions (property rights and contract enforcement);
2. market-regulating institutions (regulatory authorities);
3. market-stabilizing institutions (monetary, fiscal and financial authorities);
4. market-legitimizing institutions ( democracy and social protection).

Given this framework, Rodrik concludes that there is 'no unique correspondence between the *functions* that good institutions perform and the *form* that such institutions take'. There is plenty of room for 'institutional diversity' consistent with meeting the broad 'meta principles' (see Snowdon, 2002d).

On the basis of the above discussion many developing and transition economies have a long way to go before they can hope to transform their economies into systems that are capable of generating sustained improvements in living standards. Without a significant change of direction what hope is there for the citizens of countries such as North Korea? Thus while growth theory and empirical research show that poor countries have enormous potential for catch-up and convergence, these advantages will fail to generate positive results on growth in countries with an inadequate political, legal and regulatory framework. Research also indicates that economic growth does in general benefit the poorest groups in society, so anyone who claims to care about the poor should also favour 'the growth-enhancing policies of good rule of law, fiscal discipline, and openness to international trade' (Dollar and Kraay, 2002b).

As we enter the new millennium liberal democracy is on the increase across the nations of the world (Barro, 1997; World Bank, 1997). Whether this 'world-wide liberal revolution' constitutes the 'end point of mankind's ideological evolution', as argued by Fukuyama (1989, 1992), is debatable. Huntington (1996) offers a more pessimistic scenario with his controversial argument that the twenty-first century will be characterized by 'The Clash of Civilisations' based on cultural–religious divides! However, if the trend towards increasing democratization continues, and the pessimistic predictions of Huntington turn out to be wrong, the prospects for peace and 'spreading the wealth' in the twenty-first century are greatly increased. Research indicates that while democracies are just as likely to fight wars in general, and are also more likely to prevail in conflicts with autocratic regimes, they are also much less likely to wage war with one another. Compared to dictatorships, democratic governments are more accountable to their electorates and have better institutional means of conflict management and resolution (Lake, 1992; Dixon, 1994). If the twenty-first century turns out to be more democratic and peaceful than the twentieth century, then we can be much more optimistic about the prospects for growth and poverty reduction across all the world's economies. As suggested by Minier (1998), a useful motto for the twenty-first century is '*liberté, egalité, fraternité and prosperité*'. In such a world 'Convergence, Big Time' is not impossible.

# ROBERT M. SOLOW

Copyright: Donna Coveney

Robert Solow was born in 1924 in Brooklyn, New York and obtained his BA, MA and PhD from Harvard University in 1947, 1949 and 1951 respectively. He began his academic career as an Assistant Professor of Statistics (1950–54) at the Massachusetts Institute of Technology (MIT), before becoming Assistant Professor of Economics (1954–8), Professor of Economics (1958–73) and Institute Professor of Economics (1973–95) at MIT. Since 1995 he has been Institute Professor Emeritus of Economics at MIT.

Professor Solow is best known for his seminal work on growth theory and capital theory, and for his development and championing of neo-Keynesian economics. In 1987 he was awarded the Nobel Memorial Prize in Economics 'for his contributions to the theory of economic growth'. Among his best-known books are: *Linear Programming and Economic Analysis* (McGraw-Hill, 1958), co-authored with Robert Dorfman and Paul Samuelson; *Capital Theory and the Rate of Return* (North-Holland, 1963); *Inflation, Unemployment and Monetary Policy* (MIT Press, 1998), co-authored with John Taylor; and *Growth Theory: An Exposition* (2nd edn, Oxford University Press, 2000). His most widely read articles include: 'A Contribution to the Theory of Economic Growth', *Quarterly Journal of Economics* (1956); 'Technical Change and the Aggregate Production Function', *Review of Economics and Statistics* (1957); 'Analytical Aspects of Anti-Inflation Policy', *American Economic Review* (1960), co-authored with Paul Samuelson; 'Does Fiscal Policy Matter?' *Jour-*

*nal of Public Economics* (1973), co-authored with Alan Blinder; and 'On Theories of Unemployment', *American Economic Review* (1980).

We interviewed Professor Solow in Chicago, in his hotel room, on 4 January 1998, while attending the annual conference of the American Economic Association. In what follows we present an abridged version of the interview, which focuses on Professor Solow's views on economic growth. The full text of the interview, including Professor Solow's views on the development of modern macroeconomics, can be found in Snowdon and Vane (1999b).

## Background information

*When did you first decide to study economics?*
Well, there is a story to that. I came to Harvard College in 1940 as a 16-year-old freshman with no intention of studying economics; I did not even know what economics was. At that point I thought I might be a biologist but I proved to be no good at that so I started off as a major in general social science. I studied subjects like elementary economics, psychology, sociology and anthropology. The reason I was interested in social science was just the circumstances of the time. Remember it was 1940, the Depression was just over, and the war had just begun. In 1942, after two years, I quit Harvard College and joined the army, which seemed more important to me then. In 1945 I returned to education and I said to the girl I left behind and who has been my wife ever since, 'You majored in economics; was it interesting?' When she said yes I decided to give it a try. At the time I was under pressure to choose something to study because I was discharged in August and the school term was due to start in September. I was still an undergraduate. Anyway, it turned out all right. So the reason I studied economics was related both to my general interest in what was happening – why society was not working so well in the 1930s and 1940s – and to sheer desperation because I had to do something in a hurry.

*As a student, which of your teachers inspired your interest in economics?*
Mainly Wassily Leontief, who taught me for one course, even before I joined the army. In those days Harvard College had a tutorial system and every student majoring in economics had a member of the faculty assigned to him as a tutor. We met once a week and it was obviously an imitation of the Oxford and Cambridge system. Wassily was my tutor and I really learnt my economics from him; he was undoubtedly the main person who inspired my interest in economics. The only other teacher in those days who really caught my imagination was Dick Goodwin, who had been my teacher in the elementary economics course that I had taken in 1940–41. I hit it off with

him very well. After the war when I came back I studied more economics with him.

*Which economists have had the greatest influence on the direction that your own work has taken?*
Since I completed my PhD degree, Paul Samuelson and Jim Tobin – both very good friends – are the people whose way of doing economics I admired and still admire. They were representatives of what I now (I did not see it then) think of as the new style of doing economics after the war. Economics went from being a sort of cultural subject to a model-building subject, and I liked that. Paul Samuelson and Jim Tobin were the people who for me exemplified that new approach. The other name I would mention, but not from a personal contact point of view, only from his work, was Lloyd Metzler. I read Metzler's work after I had read Samuelson's [1939] multiplier–accelerator papers. Metzler's [1941, 1947] papers on inventory cycles and 'Wealth, Saving and the Rate of Interest' [1951] were absolutely splendid. I did not know Lloyd Metzler very well because he had gone off to Chicago by then and later he suffered a terrible brain tumour. After that he was no longer the real Lloyd Metzler.

## Economic growth

*The whole issue of economic growth has seen a regeneration of interest in recent years and many prominent economists like Robert Barro and Xavier Sala-i-Martin [1995] regard it as the part of macroeconomics that really matters. There seems to have been a neglect of Nobel Prize awards in this area, so do you anticipate that this relative neglect will be rectified in the future given the importance of growth for human welfare?*
Well, I would not describe it as a relative neglect. I think that what looks like neglect is actually something quite different. They started the Nobel Prize awards in Economics in 1969, and, unlike Physics or Chemistry, which had been going for years, there was a long backlog of people who were clearly of that calibre, if you have that kind of prize. Therefore it was only natural to start picking them up in turn. There are exceptions. Some people came out of order; for example Ken Arrow (deservedly) came early in the awards but even he was paired with John Hicks who was old by then. In 1987 when I got the award nobody born later than me had yet been given the prize, so in a way it is still just rolling up the carpet from the old end. My view is that if growth theory, the empirical analysis of growth, and ideas connected with them, continue to be popular, the subject will attract the best people in the profession. And yes, there surely will be more awards in this area. By the way, I do not know how you count Arthur Lewis and Ted Schultz, who were interested

in economic development – Ted Schultz in a very different way – but Arthur Lewis contributed that famous 1954 paper on 'Economic Development with Unlimited Supplies of Labour'. So I would not say that there has been a neglect; I would say the timing has been natural. There are likely to be more surprises, coming at a slightly greater rate than the past, because we are now getting up to contemporary people, to economists who were doing their work fairly recently. Since 1987 there has been a real outburst of work on growth so there will be more awards in that area.

*Your 1956 and 1957 papers have clearly had a profound impact on the direction of research in the area of economic growth. Can you tell us what were the main influences which led you into that research and which generated those papers?*
Yes, I do recall what led me to that research. I became interested in growth for three main reasons. First, in the early 1950s everybody was interested in economic development, for the obvious reason that most of the population of the world was living in poor economies. I was passively interested in economic development, but I have never been actively interested – in a research way – in what happens in underdeveloped countries. But I got to thinking about development issues and I had read Arthur Lewis. I knew I was not going to work on development issues, but it did get me interested in the general area of economic growth. Then Paul Samuelson and I had started thinking about what later became Dorfman, Samuelson and Solow [1958], the book on *Linear Programming*. That was the second factor. In the course of that research we thought about the Von Neumann and Ramsey models. So from the optimization and linear programming end and the idea of using programming theory to deal with intertemporal optimization, I also got interested in growth. The third influence was my reading of the work of Harrod and Domar; but I guess my reaction to their ideas was a little different from some other economists. I was suspicious of the Harrod–Domar model for reasons which I have occasionally explained. It occurred to me that if the world works in the way suggested by their model, then the history of capitalism would have been much more erratic than it has been. If Harrod–Domar was a good macro model for the long run, then it is impossible to explain, to my mind, how contained economic fluctuations have been, how you can draw a trend and look at fluctuations around that trend, and how those fluctuations stay 3–4 per cent either side of trend, except for a few major depressions. I thought that there must be a way of modelling growth that does not have the knife-edge property of the Harrod–Domar model. Those were the influences which led me to the 1956 paper.

*You mentioned Arthur Lewis in your answer. His model was described as a classical rather than neoclassical model. Do you think that the classical*

*economists made any important lasting insights on the issue of economic growth?*
When you say classical economists do you mean Smith, Ricardo and Mill and so on?

*Yes.*
If so, that is not where I got any intellectual help, for a number of reasons. First, I am not very well read in the history of economic thought. I know the potted versions of Smith, Ricardo and Mill, but I would never trust myself to have a deep thought about classical economics. I have looked back to see if there was anything that I missed, and I would say that apart from Mill on the stationary state, and Ricardo to a certain extent as Mill's predecessor, I did not find much there other than vague ideas. They were obviously interested in the long run but that does not butter any parsnips really. The relationship of diminishing returns to the stationary state, especially in Mill, obviously has some relationship to the work I was doing in the mid-1950s. That paid off a lot. On the other hand the obvious thing on the negative side is that Ricardo at the beginning, and Mill a little later on in the course of the Industrial Revolution, were thinking about the long run and yet the notion that growth can be maintained by technological improvements did not seem to occur seriously to either of them.

*Was your 1956 paper accepted for publication straight away?*
Yes. I can pinpoint when I was working on it; it was in 1955. I sent it to the *Quarterly Journal of Economics* and they accepted it right away. Writing papers is very hard for me; and so throughout my whole career I have only written papers when I thought that either I had something really serious to say, or I had to produce a paper for a *Festschrift* or something like that. In the latter case anything intellectually respectable would do. But the papers that I write of my own free will are usually pretty serious, otherwise it is not worth the effort, because I really do not like doing it.

*Earlier you mentioned the growth of interest in development economics which took off as a research area during the 1950s. Why did development economics emerge during this period as a separate branch of economics from growth theory?*
Why did it happen that way? Well, I am going to offer a suggestion but it is not original to me. I guess it comes originally from Paul Krugman of MIT. On the whole the personality types in the profession who became interested in economic development were not model builders. They were collectors of data and generalizers from rough empirical data, like Simon Kuznets; or they were like Ted Schultz, really deeply into underdeveloped agriculture, or they

were people interested in history and backwardness for its own sake. That sort of temperament is not suited to model building. Growth theory, *par excellence*, yielded to model building. So even Arthur Lewis, whom I mentioned earlier, thought of his 1954 paper as a minor sideline to his book *The Theory of Economic Growth* [1955]. The people who got interested in the theory of economic growth were interested in model building.

*When we talked to James Tobin in 1993 he remarked that the really good papers in economics always contain a surprise. Were you surprised to find that the steady state rate of growth is independent of the saving rate?*
Oh yes. I wrote that up right away and wanted to publish it in spite of my dislike of writing papers. I thought it was a real shocker. It is not what I expected at all, and by the way, when I did the 1957 paper on technical change I also expected a different answer from the one that I found. I expected that the main source of growth would be capital accumulation because that is what everyone talked about and I had heard that all my life as a student. Those were both real surprises.

*That 1957 paper inspired a vast literature on growth accounting, with contributions from economists such as Denison, Kendrick, Jorgenson, Maddison and others. After 40 years of work, what have we learned about the sources of economic growth?*
I think we have learned a great deal, not compared with what might be learned, but compared to what we have learned in other areas of macroeconomics. The notion that technical change or the residual accounts for much more of growth than you would expect, much more of productivity increase than capital accumulation, has stood up. Where it has not stood up – as in the work of Alwyn Young [1995], Jong Il Kim and Larry Lau [1994], Sue Collins and Barry Bosworth [1996] on the four Asian Tigers – it has been fascinating and you actually learn a great deal (assuming it is all true, of course); they have recorded staggeringly rapid growth but not in the same way as the historical capitalist economies. That basic distinction between capital accumulation and the residual has proved to be very informative. We have also learned a lot about the importance of human capital, as distinct from tangible capital, but the relative importance of each is still not settled. You still find what look like perfectly sound empirical papers which come up with conflicting results about the importance of human capital, depending on the time period, the model and other factors, especially the way 'human capital' is measured. I was delighted to learn after the fact that in my 1957 paper, at the very beginning, I said that what I called technical change included a lot of things such as human capital, although I did not have that language then. But the work on growth accounting, beginning

with Edward Denison and then continuing on, has taught us a great deal about the nature of growth. I would say that the fact that the growth of the current advanced industrial economies only owes a little to the exploitation of natural resources is very interesting and this too has come out of growth accounting methods.

*In 1970 the first edition of your book,* Growth Theory: An Exposition, *was published. Following that, for the next 16 years, the interest of macroeconomists in the issue of economic growth, or more accurately growth theory, went into relative decline. Why do you think that happened?*
I think it happened because the profession ran out of ideas and you cannot maintain interest in any subject simply on the basis of looking more and more closely into the existing ideas. Edward Denison was still writing his books during this period, all of which I read and admired. But there were no new ideas. The merit of the contributions from Paul Romer [1986] and Bob Lucas [1988] – I do not know how to divide it up between them – is that they renewed interest in the subject by bringing in new ideas. That always attracts people to any branch of economics, and I presume the same thing is true of chemistry. So it was just a case of intellectual diminishing returns. Around 1970 we simply ran out of new ideas.

*The first paper on endogenous growth in the new phase of interest in economic growth was Paul Romer's [1986] 'Increasing Returns and Long-Run Growth'. What do you think inspired the new research? Was it the convergence controversy issue which also emerged about the same time with the contributions of Abramovitz [1986] and Baumol [1986]?*
Well, you are going to have to ask Lucas and Romer that question.

*OK, we will ask Paul Romer that question when we interview him tomorrow.*
I would have said, just from the second-hand evidence of reading their papers, that the convergence issue was more of a stimulus to Bob Lucas than it was to Paul Romer. It may have influenced Paul Romer as well, but I do not remember anything in that 1986 paper which suggests that, though I could easily have forgotten. I am inclined to think that Paul Romer had an idea, found it exciting and followed it. But Lucas gave more signs of having been fascinated by the international comparisons.

*What are your views on the convergence issue? Your 1956 model predicts conditional convergence and this prediction seems to fit reasonably well to a group of countries, a 'convergence club'. Yet there are other poor countries which are showing little sign of catching up with the rich industrialized countries.*

I have no independent thoughts on this at all. I just read the literature, not all of it because there is so much. But I read enough of it to develop opinions and these go roughly like this. First of all I am at heart very suspicious of all this international cross-section research. I read it, sometimes it is interesting and sometimes it is not, but in the back of my mind there is always a question as to whether I should believe it. The fundamental reason why I am dubious about it is that there is no solution to the inverse causation issue. The more right-hand-side variables that go into those regressions, the more they seem to me to be just as likely the consequences of success or failure of long-term economic growth as the cause. The second reason I am suspicious is that I learned from Ross Levine at the World Bank a long time ago that most of those results are not robust. They do not stand up if you make minor variations. The third reason I am suspicious is that I keep asking myself, do I really believe that there is a surface out there in space whose axes are labelled with all the things Robert Barro and company put on them? Do I believe that there is such a surface, and countries or points on that surface could in principle move from one place to another on it and then move back to where they began by changing their form of government or by having more or fewer assassinations? A small voice says maybe, but I would not bet anything on the existence of that surface. So I am dubious about that whole line of research. If you look at it as a pure time series problem, the way Danny Quah (1993) does, if you look at conditional convergence – and conditional convergence is the only version of this that makes sense – then the evidence does look more or less as if there really is something to the distinction between growth and development. There is a group of countries, which for one reason or another do not catch on to the railroad train as it goes by and I am inclined to attribute that to their lacking some institutional infrastructure, some sociological infrastructure, whatever. If I had to throw in my lot with one camp or the other I would support the convergence club.

*Another factor which has contributed to the reawakening of interest in the growth issue has been the so-called productivity slowdown which began in the late 1960s/early 1970s. Do you believe there was a productivity slowdown and, if so, what were the possible causes?*

Yes, I do believe that there was a productivity slowdown. All the debate about price indices does not seem to me to produce a convincing case against the observation that there has been a productivity slowdown. There is no reason to suppose that if you made the same corrections on price indices before 1970 you would not have at least as much overstatement of inflation. So I think there was a productivity slowdown, I think it had an international character, it happened as much in Japan as it did in the USA, and I think that as far as anyone can tell at least half or more of it is a

mystery still. But when I say mystery I think we should distinguish between two senses of the word inexplicable (or mystery, for that matter).
When I say something is inexplicable or a mystery I could mean that I
cannot pin down in detail the causes of the phenomenon. But inexplicable
may also mean that it is utterly shocking! How could such a thing happen? I
think the productivity slowdown is inexplicable only in the first of those
two senses. There is nothing in any piece of growth economics, theoretical
or empirical, which says that the rate of growth of the residual is an
invariant, that it cannot change from one period of time to the next. We
know by the usual backward extrapolation that there cannot have been
productivity growth at 1 or 2 per cent a year forever or else Oliver Cromwell
would have been crawling around in skins. By the way, this goes back to a
significant analytical issue. When I say that in my work in the 1950s I
treated technical change as exogenous, that does not mean that I really
believed at the time that it had no internal economic causes. In the very
same papers I always treated population growth as exogenous, but I did
know about Malthus, and there is clearly a connection between economic
development and demographic patterns. What I meant by saying something
is exogenous was that I do not pretend to understand this; I have nothing
worthwhile to say on this so I might as well take technical change as given
for reasons which are inexplicable in the first sense I mentioned before. I do
not know what the determinants of technical change are in any useful
detail. But technical change is not inexplicable in the second sense. I am
not shocked to learn that productivity growth after 1973 is slower than
before 1973, nor would I have been shocked in this sense if it had been
higher.

*If we take a longer-term view, going back a hundred years or so, perhaps the
bigger puzzle is the above trend productivity performance of the post-war
period up until the 1970s.*
Exactly. I do believe that. It is a hypothesis that makes sense to me; and I can
even tell a story that makes sense to explain it. But keep in mind that I am, so
to speak, estimating one parameter with one degree of freedom, so there is no
real test being made. The story I tell myself is as follows: from 1930 to 1947
or so, a certain amount of technological change and other improvements in
productive knowledge were taking place, but could not be incorporated into
the real economy, first because of the Great Depression and then because of
the war. So beginning around 1950 the world had a 20-year backlog of
technological improvements to incorporate into practice. After 1950 this
began to happen. That seems to make perfectly good sense; but I do not
believe that it is possible to test the hypothesis because there is nothing to
compare it with.

*Are there any strong theoretical or empirical reasons for believing that moderate inflations of less than 10 per cent have any significant adverse effects on economic growth?*

I am not up on all the literature on this topic. But what I have gathered is that, at least empirically, the evidence is that rapid inflation is unconditionally bad for economic growth, but relatively slow inflation, even perhaps averaging 10 per cent annually, has no visible correlation with economic performance. I doubt that theory compels that view; but I can easily imagine that theory would be compatible with that view.

*The modern phase of endogenous growth theory has now been with us for just over ten years. What do you think have been the most important developments or insights which have emerged from this research programme? Have we learned anything useful?*

Less than I had hoped. My own opinion, which I think is now shared by Paul Romer, is that the early developments – the so-called *AK* models which simply amounted to saying let us assume that there are exactly constant returns to the collection of accumulatable factors of production, human and physical – all that led nowhere because it was not robust theory. It is very unlikely that growth could happen that way. If you adopt the *AK* view, it is the simplest thing in the world to say: I can show you how reducing a tax on capital will increase the growth rate, or I can show you how making leisure less attractive will increase the growth rate. But that sort of stuff went nowhere and added no real insights because it rested entirely on a linearity which is so unlikely to be true. But then when you start asking questions about what *does* govern the accumulation of technical knowledge, how could you model the accumulation of human capital, then you begin to get into really interesting issues. That is what I like about all that literature.

*The current crisis involving the so-called 'Asian Tiger' economies is making big news. Their success in the past has been identified with, among other factors, export performance. What in your view is the relationship between foreign trade and growth? Has the East Asian growth 'miracle' been export-led?*

Well, I am uncertain about the relationship between trade and growth. Empirically there does seem to be a relationship. I have lots of friends who have worked on this empirically and while their results differ, and some of them come up empty-handed, it appears that openness to trade favours economic performance. It is a bit less clear, at least in the literature I have read, what the source of that relationship is. The very important distinction needs to be made between factors that have growth effects and factors that have level effects. Imagine exponential growth as a linear trend on semi-log paper. You can ask: are there forces that take a country's trend line and lift it without changing its slope, a level effect, shifting the trend roughly parallel? It is clear that anything that improves economic efficiency can do that. So trade which increases economic efficiency can almost certainly do that. If what you are looking for is something that will change the slope of the trend line, the rate of growth, then sheer efficiency gains from trade cannot do that except temporarily, not over a very long period of time. The only way you can make sense of trade having an effect on the long-term growth rate is not so much whether the country is export-led, but whether the country is in contact with the rest of the world.

*So the important factor for growth is the degree of openness of an economy?*
Yes, openness in general and especially the will and the capacity to pick up new technology and new ideas from the rest of the world. I am absolutely clear that a positive impact from trade on efficiency and the level of output happens, and that those countries that went in for export-led growth rather than import substitution integrated themselves with the world economy and learned things. Some of it they learned from transplants, from direct foreign investment and multinationals. But whether or not there are any cases of really long-term changes in growth rates as a consequence of trade is I think very uncertain. I can easily imagine a country breaking out from being an underdeveloped stagnant economy and getting on the growth train as a result of trade. That I can easily see. But whether a country that is already growing at the same sort of rate as the OECD economies can improve its *growth rate* over a period of many decades by virtue of openness or trade, that seems to me to be unproved.

*There were some interesting papers published in the first issue of the* Journal of Economic Growth *[1996] by Robert Barro, Alberto Alesina and others on the relationship between democracy and economic growth, and political instability and economic growth. Barro, for example, suggests that the best way we can help poor countries is to export our economic system to them and if, as a result, their economies improve, they will tend to become more democratic. In other words economic freedom, by promoting economic growth, will eventually lead to more democratic outcomes in today's poor countries. Have you looked at this literature and developed any ideas on these issues?*
That gets into questions that are too big for little old me [*laughter*]. But my reaction to that kind of literature has always been as follows. I can easily see that if you compare a democratically organized country with a country which is really tightly oligarchically organized, then the democratically organized economy is going to tap the bigger store of entrepreneurship, whereas the oligarchs in the non-democratic countries pretty soon give up any entrepre-

neurial pretensions they ever had in favour of wine, women and song or whatever [*laughter*]. There is also the question of whether you can run a modern economy in a tightly authoritarian regime or whether these are incompatible. What happens next in China is going to be the big example of this dilemma. I can understand this kind of difference. But the notion that if you could take roughly democratic countries and order them on a scale from zero to one, that going from 0.5 to 0.6 on a measure of democracy gets you a big or detectable difference in growth rate or even the level of output, that seems to be much less likely.

*The greens and environmentalists are always warning everyone that the costs of economic growth will eventually outweigh the benefits. Do you ever worry about the environmental consequences of growth? Can the world sustain OECD levels of output per capita for China, South Asia, Africa and Latin America?*
Yes, I worry first of all that rapid population growth will begin to encroach on the possibilities of improving productivity and on the environment. Furthermore, one of my sons is interested in these issues professionally; he likes to say that China is made of coal, that China is just one large coal deposit. Now if they were simply to burn that coal, while it might not have any effect on the growth rate of GDP as we measure GDP, it would certainly have a big effect on the growth of some rough welfare equivalent of GDP. Yes, of course I worry about these things. I worry more about that than I do about resource exhaustion, simply because we seem to be a lot further from resource exhaustion. By the way, I do think that the issue of the relationship between economic growth and the environment is, to put it crudely, probably going to boil down to a race between technology and pollution. We do not have much of a grip on the likely outcome of that issue and possibly cannot get much of a grip on it. It is foolish to be a fatuous optimist on these issues, but it is equally foolish to believe that we have come to the end of our capacity to overcome resource limitations technologically.

*What sort of issues are you currently working on?*
Well, not much. I am going on 74 years old and travelling a lot, as you have noticed. I do not have a long, active research agenda at the moment, although I would like to get back to one if I can. I still intend to do work in macroeconomics. The main thing that I want to work further on is what macroeconomics looks like when it takes imperfect competition seriously. Frank Hahn and I wrote an approximately unreadable book [1995] which was published a couple of years ago. There we made an attempt to outline how you might make a macro model that takes imperfect competition seriously, and possibly also takes increasing returns seriously, because increasing returns to scale are

a standard reason why competition is imperfect. We might have done reasonably well in that particular chapter, but we did not carry the model nearly far enough. In particular we did not develop it to the point where you could sensibly ask what the appropriate values are for the main parameters, if the model is to be roughly in the ball park for the US, British or German economy. I would like to go back and develop that model further. I also have a couple of ideas on growth theory, but that is another story.

# PAUL M. ROMER

Paul Romer was born in 1955 in Denver, Colorado and obtained his BS (Maths, 1977) and his PhD (1983) from the University of Chicago. His main past posts have included: Assistant Professor at the University of Rochester, 1982–8; Professor at the University of Chicago, 1988–90; and Professor at the University of California, Berkeley, 1990–96. Since 1996 he has been Professor in the Graduate School of Business at Stanford University.

Professor Romer is best known for his influential contributions to the field of economic growth, which have led to the renaissance of economic growth analysis and, in particular, the development of endogenous growth models which highlight the importance of ideas in driving economic growth. His most widely read articles include: 'Increasing Returns and Long-Run Growth', *Journal of Political Economy* [1986]; 'Growth Based on Increasing Returns Due to Specialization', *American Economic Review* [1987]; 'Endogenous Technological Change', *Journal of Political Economy* [1990]; 'Idea Gaps and Object Gaps in Economic Development', *Journal of Monetary Economics* [1993]; 'The Origins of Endogenous Growth', *Journal of Economic Perspectives* [1994] and 'Why, Indeed, in America? Theory, History, and the Origins of Modern Economic Growth', *American Economic Review* [1996].

We interviewed Professor Romer in Chicago, in his hotel room, on 5 January 1998 while attending the annual conference of the American Economic Association.

## Background Information

*Where and when did you first begin to study economics?*
I was a math and physics major at the University of Chicago. I took my first economics course in my senior year because I was planning to go to law school. I did well in the class and the professor encouraged me to go on to graduate school to study economics. Economics offered some of the same intellectual appeal as physics – it uses simple mathematical models to understand how the world works – and in contrast to physics, it was an area of academic study where I could actually get a job.

In some ways staying at the University of Chicago was attractive because it had a very exciting economics department but I had already been there for four years. Even though I had had very little Chicago economics training I did not think it was a good idea to spend my whole career as a student in one place, so I started in the PhD programme at MIT. There I met my wife, who was just visiting for a year from Queens University in Canada. After two years at MIT we went back to Queens to finish her final year of training in medicine. That was when I started working on growth. At the end of that year I transferred to Chicago, where my wife had a fellowship position, and completed my PhD. I finished my PhD and entered the job market in 1982 – my thesis is actually dated 1983 because it took me a year to polish it up.

*As a student did you find any of your teachers to be particularly influential or inspirational?*
Well, Sam Peltzman was the professor who encouraged me to switch my career path from law to economics. I shudder to think what my life would have been like if he hadn't asked to talk with me after the mid-term and I had gone on to law school. It is an episode that I try to keep in mind – that professors can be very influential, and a little bit of attention to your students as people can make a big difference in their lives.

Besides having saved me from a life in the law, Sam was also an excellent teacher. He was the first person to show me that you could take very simple tools – demand curves or indifference curves – and derive surprising insights about how the world works. Having mentioned Sam, I should also mention some other very good teachers that I had. Donald McCloskey, now Deirdre McCloskey, was the second person I had for economics. Donald, like Sam, took economics very seriously. Together, they gave me an excellent introduction to the subject. I should also mention that at Chicago, they did not offer what is known as a 'principles' course, the watered-down, mind-numbing survey course that most universities offer as a first course in economics. At Chicago, they started right off at the intermediate microeconomics level. So I had the enormous advantage of starting off with challenging, intellectually coherent material and first-rate teachers. I was very fortunate.

Later in graduate school, when I was back at Chicago, Bob Lucas and Jose Scheinkman had a big influence on my style and the way I look at the world. They set a standard for rigour and discipline – zero tolerance for intellectual sloppiness – that I have aspired to ever since. But probably the best year of graduate school was the year I spent at Queens University because I had a lot of interaction with the faculty there. Normally as a graduate student you do not really get that much time to sit and talk with members of the faculty as colleagues. At Queens I had more of that kind of experience. Some of the people I talked with intensively during that year – Russell Davidson and James McKinnon – are terrific economists and had a big effect on my career.

## Development of Macroeconomics

*Are there any particular papers or books that you would identify as having a major influence on the development of macroeconomics?*
For me that's too broad a question. I could list all the usual suspects, people like Keynes, and so on. I'd be more comfortable describing the contributions that have influenced my own work.

*Tell us about the influences on your own research interests.*
Bob Lucas brought a style to macroeconomics that had a big impact on a whole generation of people, including me. There are several papers that exemplify this style. One is his 1972 *Journal of Economic Theory* paper on 'Expectations and the Neutrality of Money'. Another would be his 1978 *Econometrica* paper 'Asset Prices in an Exchange Economy'. But his 1971 *Econometrica* paper, 'Investment under Uncertainty,' written with Edward Prescott, is probably the best example because it really brought to the fore-front and crystallized for macroeconomists the connection between what we did in macroeconomics and what the rest of the profession had been doing in general equilibrium theory. In that paper Lucas and Prescott used the connection between solving optimization problems and equilibria that has become such a powerful tool in modern macroeconomics. That 1971 paper builds on the work of people like Cass [1965] and Koopmans [1965], who had been working in growth theory, and this basic approach for characterizing dynamic equilibria can be traced all the way back to Frank Ramsey's [1928] paper. Still, Lucas and Prescott took this approach much further into the core of macroeconomics. If all you have seen is the theory of investment as devel-

oped by the macro modellers and presented by the macro textbook writers, this paper is like a flash of lighting in the night that suddenly shows you where you are in a much bigger landscape.

*You mentioned the influence of Bob Lucas's work. What do you think has been the lasting impact of his work, particularly the work he carried out in the 1970s for which he was awarded the Nobel Prize?*

I think the deeper impact of Lucas's contributions has been on the methodology of the profession. He took general equilibrium theory and operationalized it so that macroeconomists could calculate and characterize the behaviour of the whole economy. Just as Peltzman and McCloskey took intermediate microeconomics seriously, Lucas took general equilibrium theory seriously. Many of the people doing general equilibrium theory for a living did not really seem to believe in what they were doing. They gave the impression that it was a kind of mathematical game. Economists working in trade and growth had shown us how we could use general equilibrium models, but they were not ready to bring dynamics and uncertainty into the analysis. It was economists working first in finance, then in macroeconomics, who took the theory seriously and showed economists that fully specified dynamic models with uncertainty had real implications about the world. A very important result of that methodological shift was a much greater focus on, and a much deeper understanding of, the role of expectations. But this is only part of the deeper methodological innovation. You still wouldn't know it from reading textbooks, but to research professionals, it finally is clear that you can't think about the aggregate economy using a big supply curve and a big demand curve.

One of the ironies in this revolution in thinking is that the two people who did the most to bring it about, Lucas and Robert Solow, ended up at swords' points about the substantive conclusions that this methodology had for macroeconomic policy. Solow's work has also had a huge impact on the profession, pushing us in the same direction. His work on growth also persuaded economists to take simple general equilibrium models seriously. Many people recognize the differences between Lucas and Solow over macro policy questions, but fail to appreciate the strong complementarity between their work at the methodological level. If Joan Robinson had won the day and banished the concept of a production function from professional discourse, Lucas and Prescott could never have written 'Investment under Uncertainty'.

*During the 1980s, the real business cycle approach to aggregate fluctuations developed in parallel with new growth theory. How do you view that work, in particular the way it has sought to integrate the analysis of fluctuations and growth?*

A lot of the progress in economics still comes from building new tools that help us understand very complicated systems. As a formal or mathematical science, economics is still very young. You might say it is still in early adolescence. Remember, at the same time that Einstein was working out the theory of general relativity in physics, economists were still talking to each other using ambiguous words and crude diagrams.

To see where real business cycle theory fits in, you have to look not just at its substance and conclusions but also at how it affected the methodological trajectory I was talking about before. You can think of a hierarchy of general equilibrium models – that is, models of the whole economy. At the top you have models of perfect competition, which are Pareto-optimal so that you can solve a maximization problem and immediately calculate the behaviour of the economy. Then, at the next level down, you have a variety of models with some kind of imperfection – external effects, taxes, nominal money, or some kind of non-convexity. In many cases you can find a way to use some of the same maximization tools to study those dynamic models even though their equilibria are not Pareto-optimal. This is what Lucas did in his 1972 paper 'Expectations and the Neutrality of Money'. Formally it is like an external effect in that model. It is also what I did in my first paper on growth.

The real business cycle guys went one step further than Lucas or I did in trying to simplify the analysis of aggregate economies. They said, 'We can go all the way with pure perfect competition and pure Pareto optimality. We can even model business cycles this way. Doing so simplifies the analysis tremendously and we can learn a lot when we do it.' My personal view – and increasingly the view of many of the people like Bob King, who worked in this area – is that at a substantive level real business cycle theory simplifies too much. It excludes too many elements that you need to understand business cycles. This doesn't mean that the initial work was bad. It just means that we are now ready to go on to the next stage and bring back in things like predetermined nominal prices. Methodologically this work helped us refine our tools so we'll do a better job of understanding predetermined prices when we bring them back into the model.

We frequently make progress in economics by seeming to take a step backwards. We assume away real problems that people have been working on in vague and confused ways, strip things down to their bare essentials, and get a better handle on the essentials using some new tools. Then we bring the complications back in. This is what Solow was doing, and what drove Robinson to distraction, when he modelled the production structure of an economy using an aggregate production function. Later we brought back many of those complications – irreversible investment, limited *ex post* substitution possibilities, and so on – back into the model. The real business cycle theorists did the same kind of thing, and during the simplification phase, they also made people mad.

## Economic Growth

*In Lucas's [1988] paper 'On the Mechanics of Economic Development' he comments that once you start to think about growth it is hard to think about anything else. In the introduction of their textbook* Economic Growth *Robert Barro and Xavier Sala-i-Martin [1995] argue that economic growth is the part of macroeconomics that really matters. In the light of these comments by very influential macroeconomists, do you think that, on reflection, economists have in the past spent too much time trying to understand business cycles?*

That is almost right. Remember that we experienced major macroeconomic calamities in the interwar period. These depressions were sufficient to wipe out 30 to 40 years' worth of growth. Economists who grew up during this era certainly didn't have any trouble thinking about something else besides long-run growth. They naturally focused on avoiding those calamities.

So I don't think that you can make the statement that focusing on growth is more important in some absolute sense than focusing on stabilization. What I think is correct is that we now know how to avoid the kind of catastrophic events that we saw in the UK in the 1920s and in the USA in the 1930s. Those were both major mistakes in monetary policy and we now know how to avoid them. We also know how to avoid the disruptive hyperinflations of the interwar era. Recently, we have even developed better monetary rules for avoiding the less disruptive but still costly inflation of the 1970s. Once you have learnt to avoid those kinds of problems, growth stands out as the most important remaining issue on the agenda.

I do believe that there was a period in the 1960s and 1970s when macroeconomists were spending too much time looking at business cycles – the smaller cycles and fluctuations which characterized the post-war period – and too little time on growth. We should have kept working on stabilization policy, but we should also have worked on the determinants of long-run growth. Adjusting the balance is what my career has been all about.

When I teach students I try very hard to get them to get this balance right. I give them an analogy about a runner who is trying to train for a marathon. Asking whether growth is more important than stabilization is like asking whether conditioning is more important than putting on a tourniquet when the runner starts bleeding. In a sense the training and the technique of running really are what wins races. But if the runner is bleeding to death, it is pretty silly to lecture her about getting in better shape.

But now, when we look at the allocation of the profession's intellectual resources today, we are in a situation where we can learn more about how to make minor adjustments in the amplitude of cycles or in the trend rate of growth. Faced with that trade-off, it is very clear that small improvements in the trend rate of growth can have far greater effects on the quality of life, and this area has been understudied.

Looking back, one of the reasons why economists avoided questions about growth was that our tools were not sufficiently well developed. Purely technical or mathematical issues about the existence of a solution to an infinite horizon maximization problem, transversality conditions, knife-edge behaviour and explosive growth deterred economists from asking the right kind of substantive questions about long-run growth. Now that our tools are better, we have been able to set those issues aside and make progress on the substantive questions.

*The classical economists were very concerned with long-run issues such as growth. Did you find any inspiration for your work by going back and looking at the contributions of the classical economists and other early work on growth?*
I did spend some time thinking about that, reading Adam Smith and Alfred Marshall. For example, I read the 1928 paper by Allyn Young, which builds on Marshall's work. I think it is in the same issue of the *Economic Journal* as Ramsey's paper. So there was a period where I spent a couple of years trying to sort out the connections between what Young and Smith were saying and what I was trying to say. I did that for a while and enjoyed it, then I stopped doing it. I am not sure I would recommend it as a research strategy for a young person, but it can be interesting and instructive.

When I started working on growth I had read almost none of the previous literature. I started very much from a clean sheet of paper and only later went back to try to figure out what other people had said. I think that in a lot of cases that is the right way to do it. If you devote too much attention to ancestor worship, you can get trapped and lose the chance to see things from a new perspective. Of course, in economics, your ancestors are still around, occupying positions of power in the profession, and they are not always happy when someone comes along and tries to take a fresh look at things.

*During the whole period from the marginalist revolution in the 1870s through to the mid-1950s economists were mainly concerned with microeconomic developments and managing the birth of macroeconomics during the Great Depression. Then the issue of economic growth came back on to the scene during the 1950s. One of the puzzles is that during the period when growth theory made great advances, with the contributions of Solow in 1956 and 1957, the field of development economics seemed to evolve as an almost separate area of interest. Why did that dichotomy happen?*
I am probably going to sound like a broken record here, repeating my message over and over, but the divide was methodological. The growth guys

talked math; the development guys still talked words. They diverged further and further because they could not understand each other. It was less the differences in the substantive questions they were asking than the tools they were selecting to try to address them.

*Wasn't it more the case that development economists actually wanted and needed to say something about policy issues?*
There was an element of that. As I said about the real business cycle theorists, sometimes you have to take a step back and simplify to make progress developing new formal tools. This is hard to do when you are in the thick of the process of trying to offer policy advice.

If you go back and read Smith, Marshall or Young, you have to be struck by what an incredibly wrenching transformation the economics profession has gone through, from operating as a purely verbal science to becoming a purely mathematical one. Remember that Allyn Young's paper came out at the same time, even in the same issue, as Frank Ramsey's. Ramsey was using tools like the calculus of variations that physicists had been using for decades. But economists were still having trouble with basic calculus. Jacob Viner needed help from his draughtsman to get the connection right between long-run and short-run average cost curves. Nowadays economists use math that is as sophisticated and as formal as the math that physicists use. So we went through a very sharp transition in a relatively short period of time. As we learned how to use mathematics we made some trade-offs. You could think of a kind of production possibility frontier, where one axis is tools and the other axis is results. When you shift effort towards the direction of building tools you are going to produce less in the way of results. So the development guys would look at Solow and say, 'What you are producing has no useful content for policy makers in the development world; you guys are just off in mathematical space wasting time while we are out here in the real world making a difference.' The tool builders should have responded by explaining the intertemporal trade-off between results and tool building and that as a result of this work we can give better policy advice in the future. Overall the right stance for the profession as a whole is one where we approve of the division of labour, where the people who specialize in those different activities can each contribute and where we do not try to force the whole profession into one branch or the other. Ideally we should keep the lines of communication open between the two branches.

*Let us turn to Robert Solow's contributions. What do you see as being the main strengths and weaknesses of the Solow growth model? Some economists like Greg Mankiw [1995] would prefer to modify the Solow model rather than follow the endogenous growth path.*

When it was introduced, the Solow model made several very important contributions to economics and progress in this tool-building direction. It was a very important demonstration of how you could take general equilibrium theory and apply it and say things about the real world. As I suggested before, Solow helped persuade us that there are ways to think about the equilibrium for the whole economy, using simple functional forms and simplifying assumptions, and get some important conclusions out of that. It is a very different style of general equilibrium theory from that of Arrow and Debreu and their more abstract work that was going on at the same time. Remember that Solow and Samuelson had to engage in vicious trench warfare about this time with Cambridge, England, to make the world safe for those of us who wanted to use the concept of a production function.

At the substantive level – which I think is where your question was directed – the strength of Solow's model was that he brought technology explicitly into the analysis in both his empirical paper and his theoretical paper. He had an explicit representation for technology, capital and labour. Those are the three elements that you have to think about if you want to think about growth. That was the good part. The downside was that because of the constraints imposed on him by the existing toolkit, the only way for him to talk about technology was to make it a public good. That is the real weakness of the Solow model. What endogenous growth theory is all about is that it took technology and reclassified it, not as a public good, but as a good which is subject to private control. It has at least some degree of appropriability or excludability associated with it, so that incentives matter for its production and use. But endogenous growth theory also retains the notion of non-rivalry that Solow captured. As he suggested, technology is a very different kind of good from capital and labour because it can be used over and over again, at zero marginal cost. The Solow theory was a very important first step. The natural next step beyond was to break down the public-good characterization of technology into this richer characterization – a partially excludable non-rival good. To do that you have to move away from perfect competition and that is what the recent round of growth theory has done. We needed all of the tools that were developed between the late 1950s and the 1980s to make that step.

Let me place the other strand of growth in context, the so-called *AK* versions of endogenous growth. In these models, technology is just like any other good – we might put another label on it and call it human capital or we can call it generalized capital – but technology is treated as being completely analogous with physical capital. I think that approach represented a substantive step backwards compared to the Solow model. The *AK* models are less sophisticated than the Solow model because those models do not recognize that technology is a very different kind of input. As I suggested earlier, I also disagree with the real business cycle methodology that says 'Let us do everything with perfect competition'. Before, you could argue that there was no alternative, but that's no longer true. We have perfectly serviceable dynamic general equilibrium models with monopolistic competition and there is no reason not to use them if they capture important features of the world.

There is still a group that says 'Let's just treat technology as pure private good and preserve perfect competition'. Then there is another group of economists who, like Mankiw, say that technology is different, but we can treat it as a pure public good just as Solow did. I think that both of these positions are mistaken. There are incredibly important policy issues where the pure private-good characterization and the pure public good characterization of technology are just completely off the mark.

*Wasn't your earlier work, as exemplified in your 1986 paper, more concerned with increasing returns than the determinants of technology change?*
You have to look between the lines of that paper at what was going on at the methodological level, because remember, methodological and formal issues had been holding everything up. The logical sequence in my 1986 paper was to say that as soon as you think about growth, you have to think about technology. As soon as you think about technology, you have to confront the fact that there is a built-in form of increasing returns – technically, a non-convexity. Notice that is all there in Solow's model. If you look at $AF(K, L)$ you have got increasing returns in all the relevant inputs $A$, $K$ and $L$. So up to this point, Solow and I are on the same track. You have to think of technology as a key input and one that is fundamentally different from traditional inputs. As soon as you think about that, you face increasing returns or non-convexities. Then you have to decide how to model this from a methodological point of view. Solow said treat it as a public good. There are two variants of that. One is that it comes from the sky and is just a function of time. The other is that the government could publicly provide it. I think Solow had both of those in mind and it does not really matter which you specify. What I wanted was a way to have something where there are some increasing returns but also some private provision. I wanted to capture the fact that private individuals and firms made intentional investments in the production of new technologies. So in this sense, the paper was very much about technological change. To allow for private provision, I used the concept of Marshallian external increasing returns. This lets you describe an equilibrium with price taking but still allows you to have non-convexities present in the model. That was a first provisional step. It was a way to capture the facts: there is some private control over technology, there are incentives that matter, and there are increasing returns in the background. What happened between 1986 and 1990 was that I worked hard at the mathematics of this and persuaded myself

that the external increasing returns characterization was not right either – just as the public-good assumption of Solow was not right.

Whenever you write down theories you make approximations, you take short cuts. You are always trading off the gains from simplicity against the losses in our ability to describe the world. The public-good approximation was a reasonable first step, but we needed to keep working and improve on it. The external increasing returns approximation was something of an improvement but the later monopolistic competition version [Romer, 1990] was the one that gets about the right trade-off between simplicity and relevance.

*Since Solow's [1957] paper there has been a huge literature on growth accounting. What do you think have been the main substantive findings from this research?*
The general progression in that area has been to attribute a smaller fraction of observed growth to the residual and a higher fraction to the accumulation of inputs. The way that literature started out was a statement that technology is extremely important because it explains the bulk of growth. Where we are now is that technology does not explain, all by itself, the majority of growth. Initially, we overstated its importance when we claimed that technological change explained 70 per cent of growth all by itself. But there are some people who would like to push this further and say there is really no need to understand technology, because it is such a small part of the contribution to growth. They argue that we can just ignore it. That is a *non sequitur*. It does not follow logically. We know from Solow, and this observation has withstood the test of time, that even if investment in capital contributes directly to growth, it is technology that causes the investment in the capital and indirectly causes all the growth. Without technological change, growth would come to a stop.

*When we spoke to Bob Solow yesterday he explained why he made technology exogenous in his model. It was simply due to his lack of understanding of the causes of technological change.*
That is a reasonable provisional strategy when you are dealing with a complicated world.

*A great deal of attention during the past decade or so has been focused on the so-called convergence issue. At the same time as your first important endogenous growth paper was published in 1986, Moses Abramovitz and William Baumol also had papers published that drew attention to this catch-up and convergence debate. This controversy continues to draw research interest, for example, in a recent issue of the* Journal of Economic Perspectives *Lant Pritchett [summer 1997] has a paper entitled 'Divergence, Big Time'.*

*When we talked to Edward Prescott two days ago he was reasonably confi-*
*dent that convergence would eventually occur. Did this important debate*
*influence your own thinking about growth and what are your views on this*
*area of research?*

It is very important to keep clear what the facts are. The facts are that over the
time horizon that people have looked at the data, say from 1950 to the
present, there is very little evidence of overall convergence. Everybody agrees
about this, even if it is not always stated up front. People who describe this
tendency for countries to converge are saying that if everything else were the
same – if you hold all the right variables constant – then there would be a
tendency for countries to converge. For example, this is one of the key results
in Robert Barro's work. This is really just a refined statement of the convergence club interpretation articulated by Baumol. If you look at countries that
have the same values for these variables, then they tend to converge. But it is
also true that in the background, the overall progress towards reduced dispersion in per capita incomes has been very modest. Pritchett was making a
useful background point. If you go back before 1950, it must be the case that
there was a period where incomes diverged quite a bit – some countries
moved very rapidly ahead as others were left behind. At that time, the overall
distribution of income widened for a period of time. More recently, in the
post-war years, the overall distribution has been roughly constant.

So why do we care about this issue? First you might care about it from a
human welfare point of view, or an income distribution point of view. On those
grounds there is some reason for pessimism – we really have not made that
much progress in the last 30 or 40 years. You might also care about it because
you think it might help you discriminate between different theories of growth –
which ones are right and which are wrong. Many people have asserted that this
process of conditional convergence – everything else equal, incomes converge
– is consistent with a pure Solow style model, that is, one where knowledge is a
public good, all technology is a public good. So they say the evidence is
consistent with the public-good model of technology. That statement is correct
but the evidence is also completely consistent with a model where technology
is not a public good. In this interpretation, the technology gap model, flows of
technology between countries are what drive the convergence process. In this
explanation, the convergence you see is catching up with technology, not just
catching up in the stock of capital per worker. Under the Solow model as
interpreted by Mankiw and others, technology is already the same everywhere
in the world. It is a public good that is in the air like a short-wave radio
broadcast, so under this model there is no room for technological catch-up. It
still mystifies me that people try to justify this model in the face of direct
evidence about the importance of technology flows. But they certainly use the
conditional convergence evidence to back up their position.

So I do not think that the convergence controversy has helped us discriminate between the different models. As a result, I think a great deal of the attention that the convergence controversy has generated has been misplaced. Prescott's assertion is that he does not think that we are going to see continued divergence. I think he is probably right about that. I personally think that these flows of technology between countries are very important forces in the big convergence episodes that we have seen. If you look at a country like Japan and ask what lies behind its very rapid convergence with the leading nations of the world, then the transfer of technology was a critical part of the process. There are grounds for optimism, looking ahead. If we can get the right institutions in place in these developing countries, the same process of flows of technologies could be unleashed and we really could see some narrowing of worldwide income inequality. If you weight it by countries the situation looks worse than if you weight it by people, at least during the last ten years. This is because the process of catching up in China will make a huge difference to the overall picture. And China is a good illustration of what is wrong with the public-good model. China had a high savings rate before the reform era. What's most different now in the sectors of manufacturing where China has been so successful has been the flow of technology into China via direct foreign investment – reforms that changed the incentives that foreign firms faced to bring technology and put it to work in China.

*Did you ever look at the work of economists such as Gunnar Myrdal (1957) and Nicholas Kaldor [1970b], who tended to reject the equilibrating properties of the neoclassical model in favour of the forces of cumulative causation? In their models a lack of convergence is no surprise.*
It interested me in the same way that Allyn Young interested me. I wanted to see how much there was in common between what I and what they were thinking. But it is very hard to tell, quite frankly, when you go back and read economics that is stated in purely verbal terms. There is always the danger that you read between the lines and say, oh, they had it exactly right – here is this mathematical model which shows what they were thinking. But that is usually based on a charitable reading and one that ignores some of the ambiguities and confusions. I wrote a paper like that at one point interpreting Allyn Young's paper, so one could probably do that for some of the other economists in this area. For example the big push paper by Murphy, Shleifer and Vishny [1989a] did this for some of this literature. So the right conclusion to make is that these were very smart people and they did have some good ideas, but they were working with very crude tools. I guess I would describe ancestor worship as a research strategy as probably an unproductive one [*laughter*]. But as a consumption activity it is something that can be fun.

*Well, we want to keep you on the topic of ancestors for a moment. Given that your research has concentrated heavily on the influence and determinants of technological change and the importance of R&D, has the work of Joseph Schumpeter ever influenced your ideas?*
No, I can honestly say that it has not. Schumpeter coined some wonderful phrases like 'creative destruction' but I did not read any of Schumpeter's work when I was creating my model. As I said, I really worked that model out from a clean sheet of paper. To be honest, the times when I have gone to try to read Schumpeter I have found it tough going. It is really hard to tell what guys like Schumpeter are talking about [*laughter*].

*Too many words and not enough math?*
Yes, and words are often ambiguous.

*That problem has also been the source of confusion and the various conflicting interpretations of Keynes's* General Theory.
Yes, right. Paul Krugman [1994c] has a nice article talking about the big push idea in development economics. When you state it now in mathematical terms, the way Murphy, Shleifer and Vishny did, you see how clearly the idea can be expressed and you wonder why someone had not done it before. I think that what it shows is that economists now are the beneficiaries of a lot of development of mathematical modes of thinking and analysis and it seems very easy to us now because we have those tools to work with. Before these techniques were available it was really very tough.

*Let us go back to the issue of non-rivalry and excludability with reference to the growth of knowledge and technological change. How do you get the balance right between encouraging technological change by using incentives and yet making the new ideas and discoveries available to the rest of society? There is a trade-off problem here with respect to patent rights.*
Sure. What's interesting about this question is that it is not resolved. If you take traditional private goods that are excludable and rival, we know what the best institutional arrangement is: strong property rights and anonymous markets. That's all you need. This is a remarkably important insight that economists must still communicate to the rest of the world. If people understood it, there would not be so much resistance to pricing roads, pollution or water in agriculture. Non-economists are still slow to understand how powerful the price mechanism is for allocating and producing rival goods.

But when you come to non-rival goods, we do not know what the right institutions are. It is an area that I think is very exciting because there is a lot of room for institutional innovation. One strategy is to work out a rough trade-off where you allow patent rights but you make them be narrow and have a finite duration. You would allow partial excludability – less than full but stronger than zero excludability. We often talk as if that is the general solution. But in fact, this is not the general solution. You have to break the question down by type of non-rival good. There are some non-rival goods like the quadratic formula or pure mathematical algorithms that traditionally have been given no property rights whatsoever. There are other forms of non-rival goods like books. You will get a copyright for this book of interviews, which is a very strong form of protection. The text that you write and my words – you can take them and put a copyright on them so that nobody else can reuse them. I can not even reuse my own words without getting permission from you [*laughter*]. So that is a very strong form of intellectual property protection. What we need is a much more careful differentiation of different types of non-rival goods and an analysis of why different institutional structures and degrees of property protection are appropriate for different kinds of goods.

Patent rights or legal property rights are only a part of the story. We create other mechanisms, like subsidies for R&D. We create whole institutions like universities which are generally non-profit and government supported, that are designed to try to encourage the production of ideas. The analysis of institutions for non-rival goods is more subtle than many people realize.

For example, I have argued that it is very important to distinguish human capital from ideas – they are very different types of economic goods. Human capital is just like capital or land. It is an ordinary private good. I agree with Gary Becker on this. I think a lot of claims about human capital externalities are wrong. Nevertheless, when people conclude that we should not have any government subsidies for the production of human capital, I disagree. Why is that? It is because human capital is the crucial input into producing ideas. If you want to encourage the production of ideas, one way is to subsidize the ideas themselves. But another way is to subsidize the inputs that go into the production of ideas. In a typical form of second-best analysis, you may want to introduce an additional distortion – subsidies for scientists and engineers – to offset another – the fact that the social returns from new ideas are higher than the private returns. You create a much larger pool of scientists and engineers. This lowers the price of scientists and engineers to anybody who wants to hire their services to produce new ideas.

So in general, the optimal design of institutions is an unresolved problem. We have seen a lot of experimentation during the last 100 years. I have made the claim that the economies that will really do well in the next 100 years will be the ones that come up with the best institutions for simultaneously achieving the production of new ideas and their widespread use. I am quite confident that we will see new societal or institutional mechanisms that will get put in place for encouraging new ideas.

*Research into economic growth has extended into a large number of other interesting areas in recent years. For example Alberto Alesina and Dani Rodrik [1994] have explored the relationship between inequality and growth, Robert Barro [1996], Alberto Alesina and others [1996] have explored the relationships between democracy, political stability and growth. How do you view this work? Can we help poor countries more by exporting our economic systems than our political systems, as Barro has suggested?*

Let me back up a little here. One of the disciplines that formal economic theory forces on you is that you must start with an explicit conceptual framework. For example, Marshallian analysis makes us think about supply v. demand when we look at the world. General equilibrium theory forces us to split the world into preferences and the physical opportunities available to us. That split is really important and I always try to get my students to think about it when they approach a question. What do people in your model want? What are the production possibilities that are available to them?

All of growth theory has been operating under the physical opportunities question side of the model. We describe the physical opportunities as physical objects like raw materials and then start to think about ideas as recipes for rearranging these objects. When you start to think about democracy and politics, you have to start addressing the other side of the model. What is it that people want? What drives their behaviour? If you expand the concept of preferences and say that it is everything that is inside of people's heads, it includes all kinds of things that sociologists and psychologists talk about: tastes, values and norms, and so on. When you start to talk about the connections between economic growth and democracy you really have to start enquiring into these issues. Barro's assertions are based on some empirical generalizations and they are fine as far as they go, but what is missing there is any kind of theoretical understanding of the connection between economic development and political structures. This is not just a problem in economics. It is also a deep problem in political science. There are many fundamental issues that have not been addressed in political science. To begin with, why does anybody bother to vote? The standard theory that political scientists have is that people go and vote because they have a stake in the outcome and they want to influence the outcome so it goes their way – fewer taxes and more transfers, and so on. That theory contradicts itself as soon as you state it because the probability that any one voter will be decisive in an election is so trivial that the cost of going to the polls just dwarfs any possible expected gain that anyone could get from going to the polls.

So I would just assert a cautionary note here. There is a little bit of empirical evidence that suggests a connection between the level of income and democracy, but we really face an almost total theoretical vacuum in studying this question. We are unlikely to make much progress until we have some theoretical foundations that force us to think clearly about the issues involved.

*Another controversial area that has received much attention in the economic development literature is the relationship between foreign trade and growth. This is especially topical given the current crisis, which has spread throughout the 'Asian Tiger' economies that are often held up as prime examples of export-driven growth. As economists we can easily envisage an effect on the level of GDP coming from trade, but can trade influence the rate of growth?*
There are two mechanisms here. From a development point of view the main thing you want to think about is this process of catching up. The key role for trade is that it lets developing countries get access to ideas that exist in the rest of the world. I tell my students that in the advanced countries of the world, we already know everything that we need to know to provide a very high standard of living for everybody in the world. It is not that we lack physical resources; it is not a lack of mass or matter that makes people in India and China poor. What makes them poor is that they do not have access to the knowledge and ideas that we have already worked out in North America, Europe and Japan for doing all the things that we do in the modern economy. The trick to make them better off is just to get that knowledge flowing into those countries. Much of it is very basic knowledge – like how to operate a distribution system so that clothes get from a factory to a store shelf so that someone can buy a shirt when they want one. How do you make sure that food does not spoil and is distributed to the right locations at the right times? How do you implement quality control systems in a manufacturing process? This is all basic knowledge but it is the stuff that raises living standards. A lot of that knowledge can be put to work in poor countries if they allow the right kinds of trade. Direct foreign investment from multinationals, in particular, is important for getting quick access to these kinds of ideas.

There is also a second issue. If you take the rich economies, OECD countries for example, the larger the market the bigger the incentives are to develop new ideas. So free trade in very large market areas creates greater incentives for innovation and therefore leads to more technological progress. If you don't think that this is true, just ask yourself how much innovation would be taking place in Silicon Valley if products made there had to be sold just in the USA, or just in California, or just in Santa Clara County? Some, to be sure, but a lot less than we see right now.

So trade matters for catching up. It also matters for sustaining growth in the leading countries.

*Since growth is so important to the improvement of living standards, it is inevitable that governments will try to influence the growth rate. What should*

*the role of government be with respect to growth? In particular, what role do
you see for monetary and fiscal policy here?*

On monetary policy it is a bit like the distinction I talked about before –
stopping the bleeding v. getting in shape. There is a certain amount of
emergency medicine that governments have to be prepared to engage in. A lot
of that amounts to an injunction to do no harm. It helps enormously if policy
makers just keep from screwing up the way they did in the interwar period.
But a sensible monetary policy only creates the opportunity for growth to
happen; it does not make it happen. On the fiscal side, a government has to be
able to pay its bills and it must keep from taxing income at such high rates
that it severely distorts incentives.

There are other policies that also matter. Some of those involve creating a
legal framework. What kind of institutions matter if you are in the USA?
Venture capital, fluid capital markets – think of all the things that help a
company like Intel come into existence and grow into a huge force. The
government did not have to do anything very active but it did have to put in
place structures that permitted venture capital, a new-issue stock market and
so forth. Beyond that there are measures related to human capital. There is a
role for government there. The modern university, as it emerged in the USA
in the last century, is one that is very focused on training and practical
problem solving. It is subsidized by the government. As I said before, subsidizing human capital is a very important way to indirectly subsidize
technological change. So the modern university is an example of the kind of
institution that the government can support.

I should add the caveat that many of the direct roles that people articulate
for the government are not justified. A lot of people see endogenous growth
theory as a blanket seal of approval for all of their favourite government
interventions, many of which are very wrong-headed. For example, much of
the discussion about infrastructure is just wrong. Infrastructure is to a very
large extent a traditional physical good and should be provided in the same
way that we provide other physical goods, with market incentives and strong
property rights. A move towards privatization of infrastructure provision is
exactly the right way to go. The government should be much less involved in
infrastructure provision. So that is one area where I disagree with some of the
wild-eyed interventionists. Another is the notion that the government should
directly subsidize particular research programmes to produce particular kinds
of ideas. If you compare that mechanism with the mechanism of subsidizing
human capital and letting the market mechanism allocate where the human
capital goes and what ideas get developed, the human-capital-based approach
works better. Selecting a few firms and giving them money has obvious
problems. How do bureaucrats get access to all the decentralized information
they need if they are to decide which projects should be supported? How do

you keep rent seeking and pork barrel politics from dominating the allocation process?

*A great deal of thought has been given to the design of institutions to avoid non-trivial rates of inflation. However, the relationship between inflation performance and growth performance is far from clear, especially at low rates of inflation. How do you read the evidence on this issue?*
Inflation is somewhat damaging and it is probably a non-linear relationship, so the higher the rate of inflation gets the more damaging it is likely to be.

*Is this due to the greater variability of inflation at higher rates?*
At least partly. The variability and the higher rates both make the damage grow more than linearly. There is no trade-off, fundamentally, between growth and inflation and therefore no reason not to aim at very low levels of inflation from a growth perspective. The best place to be is at a very low level of inflation and there is no reason to accept, say, 10 per cent inflation because we think we can get some benefit in terms of long-run growth. So if you are trying to do the best job you can on growth, you basically want to aim for whatever the consensus is on minimal inflation. That will vary between zero and 2 or 3 per cent at the moment. It may not be too harmful to be up at 6 per cent instead of 2 or 3, but if it is harmful at all, why accept even that?

*During the early 1970s a great deal of interest was stirred up by the book* Limits to Growth *[Meadows et al., 1972]. Since then the environmental movement has become increasingly influential. Do you ever think or worry about the environmental impact of growth or the possibility of resource limitations on growth? Can the rest of the world expect to enjoy the same living standards currently enjoyed in the OECD economies without generating an environmental catastrophe?*
Environmental problems are real problems. They are cases where our current institutional structures do not put prices on physical objects that should have prices on them. When you do not have prices on fish in the sea, market incentives cause fishermen to overfish. We know that we need to institute either a price mechanism or some regulatory system that has the same effect as a price mechanism. We will face a big challenge if, for example, human sources of carbon dioxide prove to be too much for the carrying capacity of the atmosphere. We are going to have trouble implementing a worldwide price or a regulatory system to deal with this, but we will need to do it.

However, all this is very different from saying that there are long-run limits to growth. The way to think about limits is to ask, 'What does it mean to say that our standards of living are higher now or that we have more income now than we had 100 years ago?' It does not mean that we have more mass, more pounds or kilos of material. What it means is that we took the finite resources that are available here on earth and just rearranged them in ways that made them more valuable. For example, we now take abundant silicon and we rearrange it into microchips that are much more valuable. So the question is: how much scope is there for us to take the finite amount of mass here on earth and rearrange it in ways that people will find more valuable? Here, you can make a strong case that the potential is virtually unlimited. There is absolutely no reason why we cannot have persistent growth as far into the future as you can imagine. If you implement the right institutions, the type of growth might take a slightly different form from what we anticipated. If carbon dioxide turns out to be a really big problem and we implement institutions which raise the price of carbon emissions, then cars will get smaller. Or we might drive cars somewhat less frequently, or we might rely on video conferencing, instead of driving automobiles, to meet with family and so on. We could shift to much greater reliance on renewable biomass or photovoltaics as a primary source of energy. We have the technology to do this right now. It's a more expensive way to generate electricity than burning oil and coal, but if income per capita is five to ten times higher 100 years from now, paying a bit more for energy will be a minor issue.

The bottom line is that there are pollution and other environmental problems that we will need to address. But these problems will not stop microchips from getting faster, hard disc storage densities from continuing to get higher, new pharmaceuticals from being introduced, new communications technologies from emerging, new methods for distributing goods like overnight delivery and discount retailing from emerging. All those processes will continue in the rich countries and will spread to the poor countries. In the process, the standards of living will go up for everyone.

*In looking at the post-war economic growth performances of Germany and Japan compared to the UK, do you think there is anything in Mancur Olson's [1982] argument, developed in his book* The Rise and Decline of Nations, *that societies which have been stable for a long time such as the UK develop organizations for collective action which are harmful to economic efficiency and dynamism?*
His conjecture is interesting, but to evaluate it we have to come back to the discussion we had earlier about production possibilities versus preferences. What Mancur tried to do was bring back into the discussion some theory about what is going on inside someone's head. He wanted to do this so he could understand the political dynamics that influence policy decisions about universities, regulations, rent seeking and so on. Those are important questions both from a development perspective and from a long-run growth perspective for advanced countries like the UK. These are important issues,

but when we think about them it is important to distinguish between assertions about the physical world and assertions about what goes on inside someone's head. Anytime you bring politics into the discussion you are crossing that divide. At that point it is always important to remind oneself that we know very little about this area. Mancur is relying on a few empirical generalizations. He looks at historical episodes where something like a revolution or a war frees things up and then you see rapid growth. He has also looked at the general process of the growth slowdown. History is never a completely reliable guide for these kinds of questions because we do not have very many observations and the current circumstances are always different from the past. I always caution someone like Mancur to be honest about the extent of our ignorance in this area, although I encourage economists to think about these questions. Just saying that the physical world presents us with enormous opportunities for growth does not mean that we will necessarily organize ourselves and take advantage of them as rapidly as we could.

*Moses Abramovitz [1986], your colleague at Stanford University, has stressed the importance of what he calls 'social capability' in the catch-up process. Differences among countries' productivity levels create a potential for catch-up providing the follower countries have the appropriate institutions and technical competence. Can we operationalize a concept like social capability?*
Social capability is one of those vague terms like social capital that I think would benefit from the kind of clarification that you are forced to engage in when you write down a mathematical model. It could be something that you understand in this physical opportunity side of the theoretical framework. For example, you can think of human capital as a key complementary input for technology. So just as physical capital by itself cannot explain much – neither land nor labour can themselves produce corn, but the two of them together can – it could be that human capital is the key complement for ideas or knowledge just as land is complementary to labour. Just bringing in physical capital from the rest of the world will not work if you do not have the human capital there to work with it.

You could also interpret social capability in a broader sense. You could ask whether a country has a political or social ethic or a set of norms that lets markets operate, that encourages risk taking, that supports the rule of law as opposed to either corruption or purely discretionary negotiations. You can interpret social capability in that broader sense and there are some important issues there. But when you do this, you have to recognize that you are theorizing about what goes on in someone's head.

*A great deal of research and effort has been put into investigating the existence, causes and consequences of the productivity slowdown in the USA and*

*other advanced industrial countries. What is your personal interpretation of the findings from this research?*
When I talk to students and with people from outside the university, I try to be honest about our ignorance. It is always very tempting for economists to claim more than they know. We do not know what happened with the productivity slowdown in two senses. First, I don't think we know for sure what the basic facts are. The quality of the data is such that we cannot speak with authority and answer the question about what has happened over time to the rate of growth of productivity. Second, even if there was a slowdown we do not know the reasons with any confidence. In a recent paper with Kevin Murphy and Craig Riddell [Murphy et al., 1998] I have started looking at the labour market evidence which suggests to me that technological change has proceeded at a pretty rapid but steady pace for the last three or four decades, neither slowing down nor speeding up. This calls into question some of the interpretation of the output data that we have, which does suggest that there has been a big slowdown. But all of the inferences here have to be quite tentative. You have to be realistic about what you can expect. It could be that when we get the hard numbers we will conclude that there was a productivity slowdown and we may never completely understand why it happened. I have never claimed that endogenous growth theory is necessarily going to be able to predict or explain precisely all the things that we observe. The economy is a very complicated beast and the goal for us should not be to predict within a few tenths of a percentage point the rate of growth, prospectively or retrospectively. The real test is, does the theory give us some guidance in constructing institutions that will encourage growth? Does it help us understand what kinds of things led to difference between the growth performance of the UK and the USA in the last 100 years? If the theory gives us that kind of guidance, then it has been successful and can help us design policies to improve the quality of people's lives and that is an extremely important contribution.

*Where do you think the direction of research into economic growth is likely to go next or where should it go next?*
I have referred a couple of times to the process of crossing the divide from thinking only about the physical opportunities to thinking about what goes on in someone's head. Once we do that more systematically, we can begin to understand the choices that individuals and societies make about growth. I believe that we already know the policies that would speed up growth in a country like India. What we need to know is why individual and collective decision procedures in India keep them from implementing these policies. This should be the next item on the research agenda.

# 12. Conclusions and reflections

> I have never been able to grasp how one can understand any idea without knowing where it came from, how it evolved out of previous ideas ... Great theories, in economics as in other subjects, are path dependent ... that is, it is not possible to explain their occurrence without considering the corpus of received ideas which led to the development of that particular new theory; had the body of received ideas been different we would have arrived at a different theory at the culmination of that development. In other words, without the history of economics, economic theories just drop from the sky; you have to take them on faith. The moment you wish to judge a theory, you have to ask how they came to be produced in the first place and that is a question that can only be answered by the history of ideas. (Blaug, 1994)

## 12.1 Introduction

In this book we have sought to shed light on the origins, development and current state of modern macroeconomics. In doing so our chosen approach has been to discuss in Chapters 3–9 the central tenets underlying, and the policy implications of, seven main competing schools of thought in macroeconomics as they evolved in historical perspective. In addition, in Chapters 10–11 we have discussed important developments associated with the 'new political macroeconomics' and the renaissance of research into the area of 'economic growth'. From the discussion of the preceding chapters we hope to have conveyed to the reader that modern macroeconomics is both an exciting and controversial subject. This is most forcefully demonstrated by the contrasting answers given in the interviews with leading economists who have made such a profound contribution to the ever-changing and ongoing debates witnessed in the field of macroeconomic theory and policy, and the history and methodology of macroeconomics research. The purpose of this concluding chapter is to briefly reflect on the broad sweep of those twentieth-century developments in macroeconomics, which we have surveyed in more detail in individual chapters in this book.

Before engaging on this task it is interesting to consider the approach taken by two eminent macroeconomists – Olivier Blanchard, Professor of Economics at MIT, and Michael Woodford, Professor of Economics at Columbia University – who have both produced reflective surveys of the development of short-run macroeconomics (excluding discussion of the new political macroeconomics and economic growth) during the twentieth century.

**12.2    Twentieth-Century Developments in Macroeconomics: Evolution or Revolution?**

In his survey Blanchard (2000) acknowledges that:

> on the surface, this history of macroeconomics in the twentieth century appears as a series of battles, revolutions, and counterrevolutions, from the Keynesian revolution of the 1930s and 1940s, to the battles between Monetarists and Keynesians of the 1950s and 1960s, to the Rational Expectations revolution of the 1970s, and the battles between New Keynesians and New Classicals of the 1980s.

However, Blanchard argues that viewing progress in macroeconomics in this way creates the 'wrong image' and that instead 'the right one is of a surprisingly steady accumulation of knowledge'. In surveying the development of macroeconomics over the course of the twentieth century he identifies three epochs, namely:

1.   pre-1940, an epoch of exploration;
2.   1940–80, an epoch of consolidation; and
3.   post-1980, a new epoch of exploration.

Pre-1940, research into what we now call short-run macroeconomics centred on the two 'largely disconnected' fields of monetary theory and business cycle theory. In the former case, monetary theory was dominated by the quantity theory of money and concentrated on issues relating to the short-run non-neutrality, and long-run neutrality, of money. In the latter case, business cycle theory consisted of a 'collection of explanations, each with its own rich dynamics', as evidenced for example by Haberler's (1937) survey of pre-Keynesian views contained in his book *Prosperity and Depression*. According to Blanchard, the methodological contributions of Keynes's (1936) *General Theory* made a 'crucial difference' to integrating the two fields by pulling together all the relevant factors previously used in their study. By analysing the interplay between the goods, labour and money markets, Keynes provided a coherent framework that had been missing in earlier work.

The epoch 1940–80 Blanchard refers to as a period of consolidation. The foundation for this prolonged period of consolidation was provided by Keynes's (1936) integrated framework and Hicks's (1937) IS–LM interpretation of the *General Theory*. This framework was built upon and extended. Among the 'steady accumulation of knowledge' that took place over this period it is possible to identify a number of examples, which include:

1.   improvements in the availability of economic data, for example follow-

ing the work of James Meade and Richard Stone (1944) in developing a system of national accounts;

2. the development of, and improvements in, econometric methods (see Hoover, 1995a, 2001a, 2001b);
3. more detailed modelling of the behavioural relationships of consumption (for example Modigliani and Brumberg, 1954; Friedman, 1957), investment (for example Jorgenson, 1963) and the demand for money (for example Baumol, 1952; Tobin, 1958);
4. the construction of macroeconometric models of the economy, for example Klein and Goldberger (1955);
5. the incorporation of the expectations-augmented Phillips curve analysis into macroeconomic models and an examination of the implications for stabilization policy, for example Friedman (1968a);
6. more careful modelling of how expectations are formed, for example Cagan (1956); Muth (1961); and
7. an examination of the implications of rational expectations for the analysis of policy changes, for example Lucas (1976).

This list is far from being exhaustive and merely illustrates a number of important developments and breakthroughs achieved during this period, some of which were recognized by the award of the Nobel Memorial Prize in Economics (see Blaug and Vane, 2003; Vane and Mulhearn, 2004). However, by the end of the 1970s Blanchard argues that 'too casual a treatment of imperfections' led to a 'crisis' in macroeconomics, which initially resulted in two different routes of enquiry. In the ensuing post-1980 epoch of new exploration one group of economists labelled new Keynesians (see for example Gordon, 1990; Mankiw and Romer, 1991) concentrated their attention on market imperfections in goods, labour and credit markets, and their implications for macroeconomics. Another group referred to as real business cycle theorists (see for example Kydland and Prescott, 1982; Long and Plosser, 1983; Prescott, 1986) adopted new classical methodology and assumptions and initially explored how far equilibrium theorizing could go in explaining aggregate fluctuations without resorting to monetary shocks and without introducing imperfections in their analysis.

In contrast, in his survey Woodford (2000) agues that the 'degree to which there has been progress over the course of the century is sufficiently far from transparent' and that macroeconomics 'has been famously controversial'. Acknowledging that 'discussions of twentieth-century developments in macroeconomics make frequent references to revolutions and counter revolutions' (see for example the titles adopted by Klein, 1947; Clower, 1965; Brunner, 1970; Friedman, 1970c; Johnson, 1971; Tobin, 1981; Begg, 1982; Barro, 1984; Tomlinson, 1984; Booth, 1985; Dimand, 1988; Blaug, 1991b), he traces the development of macroeconomics in historical perspective. Starting from Keynes's (1936) *General Theory* he tracks progress in macroeconomics from the Keynesian revolution, the neoclassical synthesis, the Great Inflation and the crisis in Keynesian economics, monetarism, rational expectations and the new classical economics, real business cycle theory to a new neoclassical synthesis. From Woodford's historical perspective the evolution of economists' thinking on macroeconomics has been far from smooth.

It should be immediately apparent that the approach we have taken in this book more closely parallels that taken by Woodford. There is no dissent that the birth of modern macroeconomics can be traced back to the publication of Keynes's (1936) *General Theory* or that macroeconomics is a 'quintessentially twentieth-century development' (Woodford, 2000). Indeed, Blanchard (2000) notes that the term 'macroeconomic' does not appear in the economics literature until it formed part of the title of an article by De Wolff which was published in 1941, while the term 'macroeconomics' first appeared in the title of an article by Klein published in 1946. The central belief which underpinned the ensuing Keynesian revolution in macroeconomic thought is the need for stabilization, the view that the authorities can, and therefore should use discretionary fiscal and monetary policy to stabilize output and employment at their full employment levels (see Modigliani, 1977). According to Gerrard (1996), a unifying theme in the evolution of modern macroeconomics thereafter has been an 'ever-evolving classical-Keynesian debate' involving contributions from various schools of thought that can be differentiated and classified as being orthodox (the orthodox Keynesian and orthodox monetarist schools), new (the new classical, real business cycle and new Keynesian schools) or radical (the Austrian and Post Keynesian schools).

The rise and fall of orthodox Keynesian economics owed a great deal to its problem-solving effectiveness. It appeared to provide a robust explanation of a severe empirical problem, namely mass unemployment, which had persisted long enough not to be easily explained away as a minor anomaly. In addition it offered an attractive political action programme for the resolution of the diagnosed problem. Whilst it contained a number of serious conceptual problems, for example inconsistencies and ambiguities of presentation alongside more radical elements, these were effectively submerged by the neoclassical synthesis process. This synthesis of classical and Keynesian ideas, captured by the IS–LM AD–AS framework, represented the consensus view before the 1970s and was the standard approach to macroeconomic analysis both in textbooks and in professional discussion.

The demise of orthodox Keynesianism was in large part the result of its failure to deal adequately with the major new empirical problem posed by stagflation in the 1970s. Conceptually much of its 'heuristic power' had 'petered out' and 'run dry' (Leijonhufvud, 1968). As Klamer (1984) concedes, 'the 70s were a decade of retreat, defence, and frustration' for Keynesian economics. During periods of consensus in macroeconomics divisions among economists naturally become less intense and less visible in the literature. The inherent weaknesses and practical failings of both Keynesianism and economic positivism highlighted in the late 1960s and early 1970s led to the demise of much of the old orthodoxy without its replacement by any single dominant new approach. Any continuing 'submerged' competition between rival macroeconomic explanations became more open and pronounced. The revival of much of the 'old economics', in a traditional (Austrian) or new form (monetarist, new classical and real business cycle approaches), under-mined much of the 'new economics' of orthodox Keynesianism, which in turn encouraged the development of new Keynesian accounts. The more radical Post Keynesian interpretation of Keynes's (1936) *General Theory* also continues to offer an alternative vision of how the macroeconomic sys-tem operates.

Keynesianism was initially faced by a potent rival, monetarism, which was better able to explain the empirical anomaly of stagflation in a more consist-ent fashion. As we have discussed, in the orthodox monetarist view (and the new classical approach) there is no need for stabilization policy, the authori-ties can't, and therefore shouldn't, attempt to stabilize fluctuations in output and employment through the use of activist aggregate demand management policies. Monetarism, in turn, experienced a period of progress before being faced with problems of its own, not least as noted earlier in Chapter 4 the sharp decline in trend velocity in the 1980s in the USA and elsewhere. The collapse of a stable demand for money function in the early 1980s was to seriously undermine monetarism. During the early 1970s a second counter-revolution took place associated with new classical school which cast further doubt on whether traditional Keynesian aggregate demand management poli-cies can be used to stabilize the economy. While new classical macroeconomics evolved out of the monetarist approach, it in fact provided a sustained chal-lenge to the monetarist as well as the Keynesian orthodoxies. As we have seen, the new classical case against discretionary policy activism and in favour of rules is based on a different set of arguments (most notably the policy ineffectiveness proposition, the Lucas critique and time inconsistency) to those advanced by orthodox monetarists.

New classical macroeconomics displayed important conceptual progress both by nurturing a rational expectations revolution, which was subsequently widely incorporated into the macroeconomic mainstream, and by highlight-ing the role of aggregate supply. However, important criticisms were increasingly directed at new classical macroeconomics concerning certain conceptual, empirical and policy deficiencies. Its empirical results have been, at best, somewhat mixed and inconclusive. Contrary to its early claims, both unanticipated and anticipated policy changes appear to affect output and employment, while several economies have experienced real costs of announced disinflation. New classical macroeconomics has certainly left its mark, and both real business cycle theory and new Keynesian economics can be viewed as a response to issues raised by Robert E. Lucas Jr and other prominent new classicists.

During the 1980s a considerable divide emerged between the flexi-price competitive equilibrium real business cycle models and the sticky-price new Keynesian models, where monetary influences are viewed as central to any explanation of the path of real variables in the short run. In the real business cycle approach there is no need for stabilization policy. Furthermore, as monetary factors are irrelevant in explaining such fluctuations, monetary policy can't be used to influence output and employment even in the short run. In these circumstances governments shouldn't attempt to reduce fluctuations in output and employment, which are Pareto-efficient responses to shocks to the production function. In contrast, new Keynesians argue that there is a need for stabilization policy as capitalist economies are subjected to shocks from both the demand and supply side of the economy, which cause inefficient fluctuations in output and employment. Furthermore, since governments can improve macroeconomic performance, they should pursue stabilization policy. Although there is no unified view among new Keynesians with respect to the rules versus discretion debate, new Keynesians do not advocate 'fine-tuning' the economy, but have instead championed the case for 'rough-tuning' in response to large divergences in output and employment from their natural levels. Today the new Keynesian stance can best be characterized as one which supports the case for some kind of constrained discretion in the form of an activist rule, along the lines, for example, of a flexible Taylor-type rule.

As an aside, it is interesting to note that new Keynesian economics could have been named new monetarist economics (Mankiw and Romer, 1991) in that it represents a synthesis of certain key foundations of monetarism and new classical macroeconomics. For example, the new Keynesian school has absorbed what it regards as valid components of the monetarist and new classical counter-revolutions, most notably the natural rate hypothesis and the rational expectations hypothesis. However, responding to the challenge of new classical macroeconomists, the new Keynesian school has provided rigorous microfoundations to explain why markets may fail to clear due to wage and price stickiness. In so doing it has been able to account for involuntary unemployment as an equilibrium phenomenon and provide a rationale to justify interventionist policies to stabilize the economy.

Of course the demise of orthodox Keynesianism also permitted the revival of interest in such non-mainstream accounts as that of the Austrians and the salvaging of Keynes's fundamental ideas by the Post Keynesians.

In Chapters 4–9 we examined the nature and extent of disagreement within macroeconomics resulting from the dismantling of the Keynesian orthodoxy. Over the decades macroeconomists have largely been engaged in emphasizing their differences rather than their similarities. They have often been more concerned with differentiating their intellectual products in the academic arena alongside a willingness to display conflicts over policy advice in the public arena. In short, there has been a tendency to emphasize uniqueness of identity, which, in turn, has led to both diversity and labelling.

Table 12.1 highlights some of the important features of the schools of macroeconomic thought explored in Chapters 3–9 of this book. The mainstream development of macroeconomics can be read from top to bottom, that is, from orthodox Keynesian to new Keynesian. The Austrian and Post Keynesian approaches represent the most important non-mainstream approaches. Two points should be borne in mind when consulting this table. First, within each school identified, there are differences of opinion and emphasis: the table merely characterizes the view most commonly held on particular issues. Second, as is evident from a close scrutiny of the table, there is a considerable degree of overlap between the various schools on a number of issues. This suggests that, in practice, the dividing line between schools is becoming increasingly blurred on many issues. With the benefit of hindsight, differences between schools have often been exaggerated. Take, for example, the debate between Tobin and Friedman concerning the transmission mechanism of monetary policy. In commenting on the debate Stanley Fischer (1994) suggests that:

> you can read Friedman's and Tobin's statement of the transmission mechanism and you can't tell who wrote which. The analogy I use is that when I was a kid I could tell cars apart coming down the road. Then the differences between say a Chev and a Ford were enormous. Now if you look at an old car I know it's a 1950s model but I don't have any idea whether it's a Ford or a Chev because they look practically identical. In that sense the methods and models they used and the issues they looked at were very similar.

Ten years ago in the concluding chapter to our book *A Modern Guide to Macroeconomics* (Snowdon, Vane and Wynarczyk, 1994), we noted that 'at the present moment macroeconomics lacks the degree of consensus it once had under orthodox Keynesianism' and that 'while there does not appear to be any clearly emerging consensus on the horizon we should not be surprised if a synthesis develops in the future, possibly even from disparate schools'. According to Marvin Goodfriend and Robert King (1997), the intellectual currents of recent years are moving modern macroeconomics towards a 'New Neoclassical Synthesis'. The new synthesis 'inherits the spirit of the old in that it combines Keynesian and classical elements'. This can be seen by

Table 12.1 Some areas of agreement and disagreement in macroeconomics

| Schools in macroeconomics | Dominant source of instability | Expectations | Price/wage adjustment | Market adjustment | Notion of equilibrium | Dominant time frame | Rules v. discretion |
|---|---|---|---|---|---|---|---|
| Orthodox Keynesian | Fluctuations in autonomous expenditure | Adaptive | Emphasis on nominal wage rigidity | Weak | State of rest probably below full employment | Short | Discretion |
| Orthodox monetarist | Monetary disturbances | Adaptive | Flexible | Strong | Market clearing at natural rate | Short and long | Rules |
| New classical | Monetary disturbances | Rational | Perfectly flexible | Very strong | Market clearing at natural rate | Long = short | Rules |
| Real business cycle | Supply shocks (mainly technological) | Rational | Perfectly flexible | Very strong | Market clearing at moving natural rate | Long = short | Rules |
| New Keynesian | Demand and supply shocks (eclectic) | Rational | Emphasis on price rigidities | Slow | Consistent with involuntary unemployment | Predominantly short | Constrained discretion |
| Austrian | Monetary disturbances | Reasonable | Flexible | Strong | Tendency towards | Short and long | Rules |
| Post Keynesian | Fluctuations in autonomous expenditure | Reasonable | Sticky | Very weak | State of rest probably below full employment | Short | Discretion |

noting that the key elements in the new synthesis comprise: intertemporal optimization; rational expectations; imperfect competition in goods, labour and credit markets; and nominal rigiditics and costly price adjustment. In their analysis Goodfriend and King conclude that the new neoclassical synthesis suggests several important conclusions about the role of monetary policy. First, monetary policy has real effects in the short run. Second, there is little by way of a long-run trade-off between inflation and real activity. Third, inflation is costly and it is important to eliminate it. Fourth, the credibility of policy actions has an important impact on monetary policy outcomes. Goodfriend and King argue that these conclusions point the way to a rules-based monetary policy framework with inflation targeting acting as the nominal anchor.

### 12.3 Is There a Consensus on Key Macroeconomic Issues?

Our discussion has highlighted some of the major trends in the development of modern macroeconomics and has inevitably focused on areas of controversy and disagreement. However, it would be wrong to conclude that there is no consensus on a number of key macroeconomics issues. In this final section we summarize six main areas on which there now appears to be widespread though by no means unanimous agreement, noting that in some instances this agreement has only been reached after intense debate and controversy. The present consensus view among macroeconomists can be characterized as follows:

1.  The trend movement of real GDP is primarily driven by supply-side factors. As such, in the long run, the growth of real GDP depends upon increases in the supply of factor inputs and improvements in the state of technology (Solow, 1997). While there are various policies governments can adopt to influence economic growth – including encouraging education and training, capital formation, and research and development – there is continuing debate over what is the best way to increase the economy's productive capacity and what role the government can and should play in encouraging growth. Economists now are also much more aware of the importance of undertaking research into the deeper determinants of economic growth and the need for growth theories to account for the growth experiences of both the Malthusian era and the era of modern growth.
2.  Real GDP fluctuates around a rising long-term trend and short-run fluctuations in real GDP are primarily caused by aggregate demand shocks. As we have seen, real business cycle theorists, such as Prescott, challenge this consensus view, arguing that fluctuations in real GDP

are driven predominantly by persistent supply-side shocks and are fluctuations in the natural rate of output, not deviations of output from a smooth deterministic trend. The reason why movements in aggregate demand can influence real output is linked to the presence of nominal rigidities. Macroeconomists also debate whether governments cause instability and what policies they can and should pursue to reduce short-run fluctuations in economic activity. In attempting to identify the main cause of cycles emphasis is placed on various sources of aggregate demand shocks, including fluctuations in autonomous expenditures (for example Keynesians and Post Keynesians); monetary shocks (for example monetarists, new classicists and Austrians); and political distortions to macroeconomic policy (for example political business cycle theorists). Interestingly, compared with the experience of the Great Depression, fluctuations in real GDP in the post-Second World War period have been relatively minor – the main exceptions being the periods following the two adverse OPEC oil price (supply) shocks and the period of disinflation in the early 1980s in the USA and Europe. As Solow (1997) comments, 'fluctuations around trend are contained within a moderately narrow corridor'.

3.    While the authorities face a short-run trade-off between inflation and unemployment, in the long run the trade-off disappears. As Blinder (1997a) argues, the expectations-augmented Phillips curve 'has worked very well' and along with 'Okun's Law' represents a 'sturdy empirical relationship'. In the short run it is widely accepted that the authorities can reduce unemployment below the natural rate by engaging in expansionary aggregate demand policies. Reducing unemployment involves a short-run trade-off as inflation increases. Alternatively, enacting contractionary aggregate demand policies which reduce inflation involves a short-run trade-off as unemployment increases. In the long run, however, there is no trade-off between inflation and unemployment. A corollary is that in the long run the authorities can achieve a lower rate of inflation with no change in the natural rate of unemployment, and that to reduce the natural rate, which is held to be independent of the level of aggregate demand, requires microeconomic (aggregate supply management) policies which improve the structure and functioning of the labour market. Some new Keynesians would add one important qualification to this consensus view, namely that in circumstances where the actual rate of unemployment remains above the natural rate for a prolonged period, the natural rate (or what new Keynesians would prefer to refer to as NAIRU) will tend to increase due to hysteresis effects. In other words, some new Keynesians argue that the natural rate (or NAIRU) can be affected by the level of aggregate demand (Blanchard, 1997b).

4. In the long run the rate of growth of the money supply determines the rate of inflation. Friedman has convinced the majority of the profession and policy makers that sustained inflation is a monetary phenomenon and that the main aim of monetary policy should be the pursuit of a low and stable rate of inflation. Indeed, many countries now have a long-run inflation target with monetary policy directed to keep the growth of aggregate demand stable in order to create macroeconomic stability.

5. In contrast to the dominant Keynesian view held in the 1950s and early 1960s, it is now widely accepted that governments should not attempt to 'fine-tune' their economies in order to keep output and employment close to, or at, their full employment or natural levels using discretionary aggregate demand policies. Most economists now accept that the stabilizing potential of activist discretionary fiscal policy is at best limited and that the stabilizing role of fiscal policy lies embedded in automatic stabilizers. Furthermore, there has been a marked change of focus away from fiscal policy towards monetary policy as the main tool of stabilization policy. The modern discussion over rules versus discretion involves that between advocates of flexible Taylor-type rules versus those who favour rough-tuning. With respect to monetary policy there are few remaining advocates of Friedman's hard core monetarist prescription for a $k$ per cent rule for money growth. The empirical evidence also indicates that in the short run monetary policy has real effects, so both the 'classic Keynesian and vintage RBC view about the cyclical ineffectiveness of monetary policy has been buried' (Eichenbaum, 1997).

6. Again, in contrast to the 1950s and 1960s when stabilization was regarded as a control-theory problem, it is now viewed as a game-theoretic problem. The insight that the policy regime adopted by the authorities affects people's expectations and behaviour is now widely accepted. So too is the importance given to establishing the credibility of policy and the design of institutions to conduct credible policy, as evidenced by the increasing attention given to the issue of central bank independence. Furthermore, most economists agree that the short-run output/employment costs of disinflation will be less if policy is credible. While Taylor (1997b) includes the rational expectations hypothesis in his core of practical macroeconomics, Solow (1997) remains a sceptic.

To sum up, 'the good news for policymakers is that there is indeed a core of usable macroeconomics; the good news for macroeconomic researchers is that there is a lot of work still to be done' (Blanchard, 1997b).

As to the future course of macroeconomics, two main pathways immediately stand out. First, real business cycle models are likely to be integrated more into the mainstream (Danthine, 1997). Certainly over recent years a number of real business cycle models have introduced nominal rigidities which allow for the short-run effects of money on output and employment. Second, there is likely to be continuing interest shown in new growth theory and empirics, and especially the now burgeoning research into the deeper determinants of growth (Temple, 1999; Rodrik, 2003). By providing a better understanding of the growth process, the renaissance of growth analysis holds out the prospect of providing insights which may prove invaluable in helping design policies which could make a significant difference to long-term growth rates and living standards. In particular, research that integrates important ideas from economic history, development economics, new political economy and modern growth theory literature is likely to provide important new insights into the growth process (see, for example, Galor and Weil, 2000; Acemoglu and Robinson, 2003).

David Romer (2003) argues that in many cases the adoption of inefficient policies that reduce welfare has been due to individuals and policy makers having biased or irrational beliefs ('misconceptions') about how the economy works. This implies that economists need to ensure that those individuals who are engaged in making important policy decisions are at least aware of the major research findings of economists. In turn, economists need to appreciate how strategic interaction among individuals and groups that represent different interests can distort policy making.

In our broad survey of the development of macroeconomics we have shown that while the objectives of macroeconomic policy have remained largely unchanged, there have been significant shifts in policy makers' views about how the economy works which in turn have led to major changes in the conduct of macroeconomic policy. These changes have occurred largely as a result of improvements in economic understanding driven by the research of economists. The evolution of thinking on the Phillips curve trade-off between inflation and unemployment provides an excellent example of how developments in economic theory and empirical evidence have led to a change in policy makers' views concerning the feasibility and sustainability of achieving low unemployment targets using aggregate demand expansion (see Romer and Romer, 2002, 2004). Another good example is provided by the decision in May 1997 to give greater independence to the Bank of England. This move can be directly traced to the research findings of economists.

However, while there has been progress in macroeconomic analysis, our existing knowledge will always remain incomplete, for, as Alan Greenspan (2004) notes:

> despite extensive efforts to capture and quantify what we perceive as the key macroeconomic relationships, our knowledge about many of the important linkages is far from complete and, in all likelihood, will always remain so. Every

model, no matter how detailed or how well designed, conceptually and empirically, is a vastly simplified representation of the world that we experience with all its intricacies on a day-to-day basis.

While it remains to be seen what the next significant development will be in macroeconomics, it is clear that macroeconomics will continue to change and progress by a process of evolution and/or revolution. One thing we can be sure about, with regard to the future direction of macroeconomics, is that it will continue to surprise us just as much as it has done in the past. As Lucas commented in our interview with him:

> when a macroeconomic consensus is reached on an issue (as it has been, say, on the monetary sources of inflation), the issue passes off the stage of professional debate, and we argue about something else. Professional economists are primarily scholars, not policy managers. Our responsibility is to create new knowledge by pushing research into new, and hence necessarily controversial, territory. Consensus can be reached on specific issues, but consensus for a research area as a whole is equivalent to stagnation, irrelevance and death.

# Bibliography

Titles marked with an asterisk are particularly recommended for student reading.

*Abel, A.B. and Bernanke, B.S. (2001), *Macroeconomics*, 4th edn, New York: Addison-Wesley.

Abraham, K.G. and Haltiwanger, J.C. (1995), 'Real Wages and the Business Cycle', *Journal of Economic Literature*, September.

Abramovitz, M. (1956), 'Resource and Output Trends in the US Since 1870', *American Economic Review*, May.

*Abramovitz, M. (1986), 'Catching Up, Forging Ahead, and Falling Behind', *Journal of Economic History*, June.

Abramovitz, M. (1989), *Thinking About Economic Growth*, Cambridge: Cambridge University Press.

Abramovitz, M. (1990), 'The Catch-Up Factor in Post-War Economic Growth', *Economic Inquiry*, January.

Abramovitz, M. (1993), 'The Search for the Sources of Growth: Areas of Ignorance, Old and New', *Journal of Economic History*, June.

Abramovitz, M. (1999), 'What Economists Don't Know About Growth', *Challenge*, January/February.

*Abramovitz, M. and David, P. (1996), 'Convergence and Deferred Catch-Up: Productivity Leadership and the Waning of American Exceptionalism', in R. Landau, T. Taylor and G. Wright (eds), *The Mosaic of Economic Growth*, Stanford: Stanford University Press.

*Acemoglu, D. (2003a), 'A Historical Approach to Assessing the Role of Institutions in Economic Development', *Finance and Development*, June.

Acemoglu, D. (2003b), 'Why Not a Political Coase Theorem?', *Journal of Comparative Economics*, December.

Acemoglu, D. and Johnson, S. (2003), 'Unbundling Institutions', NBER Working Paper, No. 9934, September.

Acemoglu, D. and Robinson, J.A. (2000a), 'Political Losers as a Barrier to Development', *American Economic Review*, May.

Acemoglu, D. and Robinson, J.A. (2000b), 'Why Did the West Extend the Franchise? Democracy, Inequality and Growth in Historical Perspective', *Quarterly Journal of Economics*, November.

Acemoglu, D. and Robinson, J.A. (2000c), 'Democratisation or Repression?', *European Economic Review*, May.

Acemoglu, D. and Robinson, J.A. (2001), 'A Theory of Political Transitions', *American Economic Review*, March.

Acemoglu, D. and Robinson, J.A. (2003), 'Economic Backwardness in Political Perspective', NBER Working Paper, No. 8831, March.

Acemoglu, D. and Robinson, J.A. (2005), *Economic Origins of Dictatorship and Democracy* (forthcoming).

*Acemoglu, D., Johnson, S. and Robinson, J.A. (2001), 'The Colonial Origins of Comparative Development: An Empirical Investigation', *American Economic Review*, September.

*Acemoglu, D., Johnson. S. and Robinson, J.A. (2002a), 'Reversal of Fortune: Geography and Institutions in the Making of the Modern World Income Distribution', *Quarterly Journal of Economics*, November.

Acemoglu, D., Johnson. S. and Robinson, J. A. (2002b), 'The Rise of Europe: Atlantic Trade, Institutional Change and Growth', NBER Working Paper, No. 9378, November.

Acemoglu, D., Johnson. S. and Robinson, J. A. (2003a), 'An African Success Story: Botswana?', in D. Rodrik (ed.), *In Search of Prosperity: Analytic Narratives on Economic Growth*, Princeton: Princeton University Press.

Acemoglu, D., Robinson, J.A. and Verdier, T. (2003b), 'Kleptocracy and Divide and Rule: A Model of Personal Rule', Working Paper, July, http://econ-www.mit.edu/faculty/index.htm

Ackley, G. (1966), *Macroeconomic Theory*, New York: Collier-Macmillan.

Adelman, I. (1958), *Theories of Economic Growth and Development*, Stanford: Stanford University Press.

Adelman, I. and Morris, C.T. (1967), *Society, Politics and Economic Development*, Baltimore: Johns Hopkins University Press.

Adsera, A., Boix, C. and Payne, M. (2003), 'Are You Being Served? Political Accountability and Quality of Government', *Journal of Law, Economics and Organisation*, October.

Aghion, P. and Durlauf, S. (eds) (2005), *Handbook of Economic Growth*, Amsterdam: Elsevier.

Aghion, P. and Howitt, P. (1998), *Endogenous Growth Theory*, Cambridge, MA: MIT Press.

Aghion, P., Caroli, E. and Garcia-Penalosa, C. (1999), 'Inequality and Economic Growth: The Perspective of the New Growth Theories', *Journal of Economic Literature*, December.

Aidt, T.S. (2003), 'Economic Analysis of Corruption: A Survey', *Economic Journal*, November.

Akerlof, G.A. (1979), 'The Case Against Conservative Macroeconomics', *Economics*, August.

Akerlof, G.A. (1982), 'Labour Contracts as Partial Gift Exchange', *Quarterly Journal of Economics*, November.

Akerlof, G.A. (1984), 'Gift Exchange and Efficiency Wage Theory: Four Views', *American Economic Review*, May.

*Akerlof, G.A. (2002), 'Behavioural Macroeconomics and Macroeconomic Behaviour', *American Economic Review*, June.

Akerlof, G.A. and Yellen, J.L. (1985a), 'A Near-Rational Model of the Business Cycle, with Wage and Price Inertia', *Quarterly Journal of Economics*, Supplement.

Akerlof, G.A. and Yellen, J.L. (1985b), 'Can Small Deviations from Rationality Make Significant Differences to Economic Equilibria?', *American Economic Review*, September.

Akerlof, G.A. and Yellen, J.L. (eds) (1986), *Efficiency Wage Models of the Labour Market*, Cambridge: Cambridge University Press.

Akerlof, G.A. and Yellen, J.L. (1987), 'Rational Models of Irrational Behavior', *American Economic Review*, May.

Akerlof, G.A. and Yellen, J.L. (1988), 'Fairness and Unemployment', *American Economic Review*, May.

*Akerlof, G.A. and Yellen, J.L. (1990), 'The Fair Wage–Effort Hypothesis and Unemployment', *Quarterly Journal of Economics*, May.

Akerlof, G.A., Dickens, W.T. and Perry, G.L. (1996), 'The Macroeconomics of Low Inflation', *Brookings Papers on Economic Activity*.

Akerman, J. (1947), 'Political Economic Cycles', *Kyklos*.

Akhtar, M.A. (1995), 'Monetary Policy Goals and Central Bank Independence', *Banca Nationale Del Lavoro Quarterly Review*, December.

Aldcroft, D.H. (1993), *The European Economy, 1914–1990*, 3rd edn, London: Routledge.

Alesina, A. (1987), 'Macroeconomic Policy in a Two-Party System as a Repeated Game', *Quarterly Journal of Economics*, August.

Alesina, A. (1988), 'Macroeconomics and Politics', *NBER Macroeconomics Annual*.

*Alesina, A. (1989), 'Politics and Business Cycles in Industrial Democracies', *Economic Policy*, April.

Alesina, A. (1994), 'Political Models of Macroeconomic Policy and Fiscal Reforms', in S. Haggard and S. Webb (eds), *Voting for Reform*, Oxford: Oxford University Press.

Alesina, A. (1995), 'Elections, Party Structure, and the Economy', in J.S. Banks and E.A. Hanushek (eds), *Modern Political Economy: Old Topics, New Directions*, Cambridge: Cambridge University Press.

*Alesina, A. (2000), 'The Political Economy of the Budget Surplus in the United States', *Journal of Economic Perspectives*, Summer.

Alesina, A. and Barro, R.J. (2002), 'Currency Unions', *Quarterly Journal of Economics*, May.

Alesina, A. and Drazen, A. (1991), 'Why are Stabilisations Delayed?', *American Economic Review*, December.

Alesina, A. and Gatti, R. (1995), 'Independent Central Banks: Low Inflation at No Cost?' *American Economic Review*, May.

*Alesina, A. and Perotti, R. (1994), 'The Political Economy of Growth: A Critical Survey of the Recent Literature', *World Bank Economic Review*, September.

*Alesina, A. and Perotti, R. (1995a), 'The Political Economy of Budget Deficits', *IMF Staff Papers*, March.

Alesina, A. and Perotti, R. (1995b), 'Fiscal Experiences and Adjustments in OECD Economies', *Economic Policy*, October.

Alesina, A. and Perotti, R. (1996a), 'Fiscal Discipline and the Budget Process', *American Economic Review*, May.

Alesina, A. and Perotti, R. (1996b), 'Reducing Budget Deficits', *Swedish Economic Policy Review*, Spring.

Alesina, A. and Perotti, R. (1996c), 'Income Distribution, Political Instability and Investment', *European Economic Review*, June.

Alesina, A. and Perotti, R. (1997a), 'Fiscal Adjustments in OECD Countries: Composition and Macroeconomic Effects', *IMF Staff Papers*.

Alesina, A. and Perotti, R. (1997b), 'The Welfare State and Competitiveness', *American Economic Review*, December.

Alesina, A. and Perotti, R. (1998), 'Economic Risk and Political Risk in Fiscal Unions', *Economic Journal*, July.

Alesina, A. and Rodrik, D. (1994), 'Distributive Politics and Economic Growth', *Quarterly Journal of Economics*, May.

Alesina, A. and Rosenthal, H. (1995), *Partisan Politics, Divided Government and the Economy*, Cambridge: Cambridge University Press.

Alesina, A. and Roubini, N. (1992), 'Political Cycles in OECD Economies', *Review of Economic Studies*, October.

*Alesina, A. and Roubini, N. with Cohen, G.D. (1997), *Political Cycles and the Macroeconomy: Theory and Evidence*, Cambridge, MA: MIT Press.

Alesina, A. and Sachs, J. (1988), 'Political Parties and the Business Cycle in the United States, 1914–1984', *Journal of Money, Credit, and Banking*, February.

Alesina, A. and Spolare, E. (1997), 'On the Number and Size of Nations', *Quarterly Journal of Economics*, November.

Alesina, A. and Spolare, E. (2003), *The Size of Nations*, Cambridge, MA: MIT Press.

*Alesina, A. and Summers, L.H. (1993), 'Central Bank Independence and

Macroeconomic Performance: Some Comparative Evidence', *Journal of Money, Credit, and Banking*, May.

Alesina, A. and Tabellini, G. (1988), 'Credibility and Politics', *European Economic Review*, March.

Alesina, A., Barro, R.J. and Tenyero, S. (2002), 'Optimal Currency Area', *NBER Macroeconomics Annual*.

Alesina, A., Cohen , G. D. and Roubini, N. (1993), 'Electoral Business Cycles in Industrial Democracies', *European Journal of Political Economy*, March.

Alesina, A., Spolare, E. and Wacziarg, R. (2000), 'Economic Integration and Political Disintegration', *American Economic Review*, December.

Alesina, A., Spolare, E. and Wacziarg, R. (2005), 'Trade, Growth and the Size of Nations', in P. Aghion and S. Durlauf (eds), *Handbook of Economic Growth*, Amsterdam: Elsevier.

*Alesina, A. et al. (1996), 'Political Instability and Growth', *Journal of Economic Growth*, June.

Alesina, A. et al. (2003), 'Fractionalisation', *Journal of Economic Growth*, June.

Allsopp, C. and Vines, D. (2000), 'The Assessment: Macroeconomic Policy', *Oxford Review of Economic Policy*, Winter.

Alogoskoufis, G.S., Lockwood, B. and Philippopoulos, A. (1992), 'Wage Inflation, Electoral Uncertainty and the Exchange Rate Regime: Theory and UK Evidence', *Economic Journal*, November.

Alston, R., Kearl, J.R. and Vaughan, M.B. (1992), 'Is There a Consensus Among Economists in the 1990s?' *American Economic Review*, May.

Alt, J.E. (1985), 'Political Parties, World Demand and Unemployment: Domestic and International Sources of Economic Activity', *American Political Science Review*.

Alt, J.E. and Alesina, A. (1996), 'Political Economy: An Overview', in R.E. Goodin and H.D. Klingerman (eds), *A New Handbook of Political Science*, Oxford: Oxford University Press.

Alt, J.E. and Chrystal, A. (1983), *Political Economics*, Brighton, UK: Wheatsheaf.

Altonji, J.G. (1986), 'Intertemporal Substitution in Labour Supply: Evidence from Micro Data', *Journal of Political Economy*, June.

Alvi, E. (1993), 'Near Rationality/Menu Costs, Strategic Complementarity and Real Rigidity: An Integration', *Journal of Macroeconomics*, Fall.

Andersen, T.M. (1994), *Price Rigidity*, Oxford: Clarendon Press.

Ando, A. and Modigliani, F. (1965), 'The Relative Stability of Monetary Velocity and the Investment Multiplier', *American Economic Review*, September.

Arestis, P. (1996), 'Post Keynesian Economics: Towards Coherence', *Cambridge Journal of Economics*, January.

Arestis, P. (1997), *Money, Pricing, Distribution and Investment*, London: Macmillan.

*Arestis, P. and Sawyer, M. (1998), 'Keynesian Economic Policies for the New Millennium', *Economic Journal*, January.

Arnold, L.G. (2002), *Business Cycle Theory*, Oxford: Oxford University Press.

Arrow, K.J. (1962), 'The Economic Implications of Learning By Doing', *Review of Economic Studies*, June.

Arrow, K.J. and Hahn, F.H. (1971), *General Equilibrium Analysis*, San Francisco: Holden-Day.

*Artadi, E. and Sala-i-Martin, X. (2003), 'The Economic Tragedy of the Twentieth Century: Growth in Africa', NBER Working Paper, No. 9865, July.

Artis, M., Mizen, P. and Kontolemis, Z. (1998), 'Inflation Targeting: What Can the ECB Learn From the Recent Experience of the Bank of England?', *Economic Journal*, November.

Atkinson, A.B. and Micklewright, J. (1991), 'Unemployment Compensation and Labour Market Transitions: A Critical Review', *Journal of Economic Literature*, December.

Attfield, C.L.F., Demery, D. and Duck, N.W. (1985), *Rational Expectations in Macroeconomics: An Introduction to Theory and Evidence*, Oxford: Basil Blackwell.

Azariadis, C. (1975), 'Implicit Contracts and Underemployment Equilibria', *Journal of Political Economy*, December.

*Backhouse, R.E. (1995), *Interpreting Macroeconomics: Explorations in the History of Macroeconomic Thought*, London: Routledge.

*Backhouse, R.E. (1997a), 'The Rhetoric and Methodology of Modern Macroeconomics', in B. Snowdon and H.R. Vane (eds), *Reflections on the Development of Modern Macroeconomics*, Cheltenham, UK and Lyme, USA: Edward Elgar.

Backhouse, R.E. (1997b), *Truth and Progress in Economic Knowledge*, Cheltenham, UK and Lyme, USA: Edward Elgar.

Backhouse, R.E. (2002), 'Say's Law', in B. Snowdon and H.R. Vane (eds), *An Encyclopedia of Macroeconomics*, Cheltenham, UK and Northampton, MA, USA: Edward Elgar.

Backhouse, R.E. (2004), 'What was Lost with IS-LM', in M. De Vroey and K.D. Hoover (eds), *The IS–LM Model: Its Rise, Fall and Strange Persistence*, Durham, NC: Duke University Press.

Backus, D. and Driffill, J. (1985), 'Inflation and Reputation', *American Economic Review*, June.

Backus, D.K. and Kehoe, P.J. (1992), 'International Evidence on the Historical Properties of Business Cycles', *American Economic Review*, September.

Backus, D.K., Kehoe, P.J. and Kydland, F.E. (1992), 'International Real Business Cycles', *Journal of Political Economy*, August.

Bailey, M.N. (1974), 'Wages and Unemployment under Uncertain Demand', *Review of Economic Studies*, January.

Bailey, M.N. (1978), 'Stabilisation Policy and Private Economic Behaviour', *Brookings Papers on Economic Activity*.

Bain, K. and Howells, P. (2003), *Monetary Economics: Policy and Its Theoretical Basis*, Basingstoke: Palgrave.

Bairoch, P. (1993), *Economics and World History: Myths and Paradoxes*, Hemel Hempstead: Harvester Wheatsheaf.

Balassa, B. (1989), 'Outward Orientation', in H. Chenery and T.N. Srinivasan (eds), *Handbook of Development Economics Vol. II*, Amsterdam: North-Holland.

*Baldwin, R.E. (2000), 'Trade and Growth: Still Disagreement About the Relationships', OECD Economics Department Working Paper, No. 264, www.oecd.org/eco/eco

Baldwin, R.E., Martin, P. and Ottaviano, G.P. (2001), 'Global Income Divergence, Trade, and Industrialisation: The Geography of Growth Take-offs', *Journal of Economic Growth*, March.

Ball, L. (1990), 'Insiders and Outsiders: A Review Essay', *Journal of Monetary Economics*, December.

Ball, L. (1991), 'The Genesis of Inflation and the Costs of Disinflation', *Journal of Money, Credit, and Banking*, August.

Ball, L. (1994), 'What Determines the Sacrifice Ratio?', in N.G. Mankiw (ed.), *Monetary Policy*, Chicago: University of Chicago Press.

Ball, L. (1995), 'Time-consistent Policy and Persistent Changes in Inflation', *Journal of Monetary Economics*, November.

*Ball, L. (1999), 'Aggregate Demand and Long-Run Unemployment', *Brookings Papers on Economic Activity*.

Ball, L. and Cecchetti, S.G. (1988), 'Imperfect Information and Staggered Price Setting', *American Economic Review*, December.

*Ball, L. and Mankiw, N.G. (2002), 'The NAIRU in Theory and Practice', *Journal of Economic Perspectives*, Fall.

Ball, L. and Romer, D. (1990), 'Real Rigidities and the Non-Neutrality of Money', *Review of Economic Studies*, April.

Ball, L. and Romer, D. (1991), 'Sticky Prices as Coordination Failure', *American Economic Review*, June.

Ball, L. and Sheridan, N. (2003), 'Does Inflation Targeting Matter?', NBER Working Paper, No. 9577, March.

Ball, L., Mankiw, N.G. and Romer, D. (1988), 'The New Keynesian Economics and the Output–Inflation Trade-off', *Brookings Papers on Economic Activity*.

Balls, E. and O'Donnell, G. (eds) (2002), *Reforming Britain's Economic and Financial Policy*, Basingstoke: Palgrave.

Bank of England (1999), *Economic Models at the Bank of England*, London: Bank of England.

Bank of England (2003), 'Expectations of Inflation in the UK', *Bank of England Quarterly Bulletin*, Autumn.

Bardhan, P. (1993), 'Economics of Development and the Development of Economics', *Journal of Economic Perspectives*, Spring.

Barens, I. and Caspari, V. (1999), 'Old Views and New Perspectives: On Rereading Hicks's "Mr. Keynes and the Classics"', *European Journal of the History of Economic Thought*, Summer.

Barro, R.J. (1974), 'Are Government Bonds Net Wealth?', *Journal of Political Economy*, November/December.

Barro, R.J. (1977a), 'Unanticipated Money Growth and Unemployment in the United States', *American Economic Review*, March.

Barro, R.J. (1977b), 'Long-Term Contracting, Sticky Prices and Monetary Policy', *Journal of Monetary Economics*, July.

Barro, R.J. (1978), 'Unanticipated Money, Output and the Price Level in the United States', *Journal of Political Economy*, August.

*Barro, R.J. (1979), 'Second Thoughts on Keynesian Economics', *American Economic Review*, May.

Barro, R.J. (1981), 'Output Effects of Government Purchases', *Journal of Political Economy*, December.

*Barro, R.J. (1984), 'What Survives of the Rational Expectations Revolution? Rational Expectations and Macroeconomics in 1984', *American Economic Review*, May.

*Barro, R.J. (1986), 'Recent Developments in the Theory of Rules Versus Discretion', *Economic Journal*, Supplement.

*Barro, R.J. (1989a), 'New Classicals and Keynesians, or the Good Guys and the Bad Guys', *Schweizerische Zeitschrift für Volkswirtschaft und Statistik*.

*Barro, R.J. (1989b), 'The Ricardian Approach to Budget Deficits', *Journal of Economic Perspectives*, Spring.

Barro, R.J. (ed.) (1989c), *Modern Business Cycle Theory*, Cambridge, MA: Harvard University Press.

Barro, R.J. (1991), 'Economic Growth in a Cross Section of Countries', *Quarterly Journal of Economics*, May.

Barro, R.J. (1993), *Macroeconomics*, 4th edn, New York: John Wiley.

Barro, R.J. (1994), 'Interview with Robert Barro', in B. Snowdon, H.R. Vane and P. Wynarczyk, *A Modern Guide to Macroeconomics: An Introduction to Competing Schools of Thought*, Aldershot, UK and Brookfield, USA: Edward Elgar.

*Barro, R.J. (1995), 'Inflation and Economic Growth', *Bank of England Quarterly Bulletin*, May.

Barro, R.J. (1996), 'Democracy and Growth', *Journal of Economic Growth*, March.

*Barro, R.J. (1997), *Determinants of Economic Growth*, Cambridge, MA: MIT Press.

Barro, R.J. (1999), 'Determinants of Democracy', *Journal of Political Economy*, December.

Barro, R.J. (2000), 'Inequality and Growth in a Panel of Countries', *Journal of Economic Growth*, March.

Barro, R.J. and Gordon, D.B. (1983a), 'Rules, Discretion and Reputation in a Model of Monetary Policy', *Journal of Monetary Economics*, July.

Barro, R.J. and Gordon, D.B. (1983b), 'A Positive Theory of Monetary Policy in a Natural Rate Model', *Journal of Political Economy*, July.

Barro, R.J. and Grossman, H. (1976), *Money, Employment and Inflation*, New York: Cambridge University Press.

Barro, R.J. and McCleary, R.M. (2003), 'Religion and Economic Growth', *American Sociological Review*, October.

Barro, R.J. and Rush, M. (1980), 'Unanticipated Money and Economic Activity', in S. Fischer (ed.), *Rational Expectations and Economic Policy*, Chicago: University of Chicago Press.

Barro, R.J. and Sala-i-Martin, X. (1995), *Economic Growth*, New York: McGraw-Hill.

Barro, R.J. and Sala-i-Martin, X. (1997), 'Technological Diffusion and Convergence', *Journal of Economic Growth*, March.

Barro, R.J. and Sala-i-Martin, X. (2003), *Economic Growth*, 2nd edn, Cambridge, MA: MIT Press.

Barsky, R.B. and Kilian, L. (2001), 'Do We Really Know that Oil Caused the Great Stagflation?', *NBER Macroeconomics Annual*.

Bartels, L.M. and Brady, H.E. (2003), 'Economic Behaviour in Political Context', *American Economic Review*, May.

Bates, R.H. (1981), *Markets and States in Tropical Africa*, Berkeley, CA: University of California Press.

Bates, R.H. (2001), *Prosperity and Violence: The Political Economy of Development*, New York: W.W. Norton.

Baumol, W.J. (1952), 'The Transactions Demand for Cash: An Inventory Theoretic Approach', *Quarterly Journal of Economics*, November.

Baumol, W.J. (1977), 'Say's (at least) Eight Laws, or What Say and James Mill May Really Have Meant', *Economica*, May.

*Baumol, W.J. (1986), 'Productivity Growth, Convergence and Welfare: What the Long-Run Data Show', *American Economic Review*, December.

*Baumol, W.J. (1990), 'Entrepreneurship: Productive, Unproductive and Destructive', *Journal of Political Economy*, October.

Baumol, W.J. (1999), 'Say's Law', *Journal of Economic Perspectives*, Winter.

Baumol, W.J. (2002), *The Free-market Innovation Machine: Analysing the Growth Miracle of Capitalism*, Princeton: Princeton University Press.

Baumol, W.J., Blackman, S.A.B. and Wolfe, E.N. (1989), *Productivity and American Leadership*, Cambridge, MA: MIT Press.

Baumol, W.J., Nelson, R.R. and Wolfe, E.N. (1994), *The Convergence of Productivity: Cross National Studies and Historical Evidence*, Oxford: Oxford University Press.

*Bean, C.R. (1994), 'European Unemployment: A Survey', *Journal of Economic Literature*, June.

*Bean, C. (1998), 'The New UK Monetary Arrangements: A View From the Literature', *Economic Journal*, November.

Bean, C.R., Layard, R. and Nickell, S.J. (eds) (1986), *The Rise in Unemployment*, Oxford: Basil Blackwell.

*Beaud, M. and Dostaler, G. (1997), *Economic Thought Since Keynes: A History and Dictionary of Major Economists*, London: Routledge.

Becker, G.S., Philipson, T.J. and Soares, R.R. (2003), 'The Quantity and Quality of Life and the Evolution of World Inequality', NBER Working Paper, No. 9765.

Begg, D.K.H. (1982), *The Rational Expectations Revolution in Macroeconomics: Theories and Evidence*, Oxford: Philip Allan.

Begg, D.K.H., Dornbusch, R. and Fischer, S. (2003), *Economics*, 7th edn, Maidenhead: McGraw-Hill.

Benabou, R. (1996), 'Inequality and Growth', *NBER Macroeconomics Annual*.

Bénassy, J.P. (1993), 'Nonclearing Markets: Microeconomic Concepts and Macroeconomic Applications', *Journal of Economic Literature*, June.

Ben-David, D. (1996), 'Trade and Convergence Among Countries', *Journal of International Economics*, May.

Ben-David, D. and Loewy, M.B. (1998), 'Free Trade, Growth and Convergence', *Journal of Economic Growth*, June.

Benjamin, D.K. and Kochin, L.A. (1979), 'Searching for an Explanation of Unemployment in Inter-war Britain', *Journal of Political Economy*, June.

Benson Durham, J. (1999), 'Economic Growth and Political Regimes', *Journal of Economic Growth*, March.

Berger, H., de Hahn, J. and Eijffinger, S.C.W. (2001), 'Central Bank Independence: An Update of Theory and Evidence', *Journal of Economic Surveys*, February.

Bernanke, B.S. (1983), 'Non-Monetary Effects of the Financial Crisis in the Propagation of the Great Depression', *American Economic Review*, June.

Bernanke, B.S. (1993), 'The World on a Cross of Gold: A Review of "Golden Fetters", the Gold Standard and the Great Depression', *Journal of Monetary Economics*, April.

Bernanke, B.S. (1995), 'The Macroeconomics of the Great Depression: A Comparative Approach', *Journal of Money, Credit, and Banking*, February.

*Bernanke, B.S. (2000), *Essays on the Great Depression*, Princeton: Princeton University Press.

Bernanke, B.S. and Carey, K. (1996), 'Nominal Wage Stickiness and Aggregate Supply in the Great Depression', *Quarterly Journal of Economics*, August.

Bernanke, B.S. and Gertler, M. (1989), 'Agency Costs, Net Worth and Business Fluctuations', *American Economic Review*, March.

Bernanke, B.S. and Gertler, M. (1995), 'Inside the Black Box: The Credit Channel of Monetary Policy Transmission', *Journal of Economic Perspectives*, Fall.

Bernanke, B.S. and Gurkaynak, R. (2001), 'Is Growth Endogenous? Taking Mankiw, Romer and Weil Seriously', *NBER Macroeconomics Annual*.

Bernanke, B.S. and James, H. (1991), 'The Gold Standard, Deflation and Financial Crisis in the Great Depression: An International Comparison', in R.G. Hubbard (ed.), *Financial Markets and Financial Crisis*, Chicago: University of Chicago Press.

Bernanke, B.S. and Mishkin, F.S. (1992), 'Central Bank Behaviour and the Strategy of Monetary Policy: Observations From Six Industrialised Countries', *NBER Macroeconomics Annual*.

*Bernanke, B.S. and Mishkin, F.S. (1997), 'Inflation Targeting: A New Framework for Monetary Policy', *Journal of Economic Perspectives*, Spring.

Bernanke, B.S. and Parkinson, M.L. (1991), 'Procyclical Labour Productivity and Competing Theories of the Business Cycle: Some Evidence from Interwar US Manufacturing Industries', *Journal of Political Economy*, June.

Bernanke, B.S. and Woodford, M. (1997), 'Inflation Forecasts and Monetary Policy', *Journal of Money, Credit, and Banking*, November.

*Bernanke, B.S. and Woodford, M. (eds) (2004), *Inflation Targeting*, Chicago: University of Chicago Press.

Bernanke, B.S., Gertler, M. and Watson, M. (1997), 'Systematic Monetary Policy and the Effects of Oil Price Shocks', *Brookings Papers on Economic Activity*.

*Bernanke, B.S., Laubach, T., Mishkin, F.S. and Posen, A.S. (1999), *Inflation Targeting: Lessons from the International Experience*, Princeton: Princeton University Press.

Besley, T. and Case, A. (2003), 'Political Institutions and Policy Choices: Evidence From the United States', *Journal of Economic Literature*, March.

Bhagwati, J. (1966), *The Economics of Underdeveloped Countries*, London: Weidenfeld and Nicolson.

Bhagwati, J. (1978), *Foreign Trade Regimes and Economic Development: Anatomy and Consequences of Exchange Control Regimes*, Cambridge, MA: Ballinger.

Bhagwati, J. (1984), 'Development Economics: What Have We Learned?', *Asian Development Review*.

Bhagwati, J. (1988), 'Poverty and Public Policy', *World Development*, May.

Bhagwati, J. (1993), *India in Transition: Freeing the Economy*, Oxford: Clarendon Press.

Bhagwati, J. (1995), 'Democracy and Development: New Thinking on an Old Question', *Journal of Democracy*, October.

Bhagwati, J. (2000), *The Wind of the Hundred Days: How Washington Mismanaged Globalisation*, Cambridge, MA: MIT Press.

*Bhagwati, J. (2004), *In Defence of Globalisation*, Oxford: Oxford University Press.

Bhagwati, J. and Srinivasan, T.N. (2001), 'Outward Orientation and Development: Are the Revisions Right?', in D. Lall and R. Snape (eds), *Essays in Honour of Anne A. Krueger*, Basingstoke: Palgrave.

*Bhagwati, J. and Srinivasan, T.N. (2002), 'Trade and Poverty in Poor Countries', *American Economic Review*, May.

Bhaskar, V., Machin, S. and Reid, G.C. (1993), 'Price and Quantity Adjustment Over the Business Cycle: Evidence From Survey Data', *Oxford Economic Papers*, April.

Black, F. (1987), *Business Cycles and Equilibrium*, Oxford: Basil Blackwell.

Blackburn, K. (1987), 'Macroeconomic Policy Evaluation and Optimal Control Theory: A Critical Review of Some Recent Developments', *Journal of Economic Surveys*.

*Blackburn, K. (1992), 'Credibility and Time-Consistency in Monetary Policy', in K. Dowd and M.K. Lewis (eds), *Current Issues in Financial and Monetary Economics*, Basingstoke: Macmillan.

Blackburn, K. (1999), 'Can Stabilisation Policy Reduce Long-Run Growth?', *Economic Journal*, January.

*Blackburn, K. and Christensen, M. (1989), 'Monetary Policy and Policy Credibility', *Journal of Economic Literature*, March.

Blackburn, K. and Ravn, M.O. (1992), 'Business Cycles in the UK: Facts and Fictions', *Economica*, November.

Blanchard, O.J. (1984), 'The Lucas Critique and the Volcker Deflation', *American Economic Review*, May.

Blanchard, O.J. (1986), 'Reagonomics', *Economic Policy*, October.

Blanchard, O.J. (1990a), 'Why Does Money Affect Output? A Survey', in B.M. Friedman and F.H. Hahn (eds), *Handbook of Monetary Economics*, New York: North-Holland.

Blanchard, O.J. (1990b), 'Comment on B.T. McCallum, New Classical Macroeconomics: A Sympathetic Account' in S. Honkapohja (ed.), *The State of Macroeconomics*, Oxford: Basil Blackwell.

Blanchard, O.J. (1992), 'For a Return to Pragmatism', in M. Belongia and M. Garfinkel (eds), *The Business Cycle: Theories and Evidence*, London: Kluwer Academic Publishers.

Blanchard, O.J. (1997a), *Macroeconomics*, New Jersey: Prentice-Hall.

*Blanchard, O.J. (1997b), 'Is There a Core of Usable Macroeconomics?', *American Economic Review*, May.

*Blanchard, O.J. (2000), 'What Do We Know About Macroeconomics that Fisher and Wicksell Did Not?', *Quarterly Journal of Economics*, November.

*Blanchard, O.J. (2003), *Macroeconomics*, 3rd edn, New Jersey: Prentice-Hall.

Blanchard, O.J. and Fischer, S. (1989), *Lectures on Macroeconomics*, Cambridge, MA: MIT Press.

Blanchard, O.J. and Katz, L.F. (1997), 'What We Know and Do Not Know About the Natural Rate of Unemployment', *Journal of Economic Perspectives*, Winter.

Blanchard, O.J. and Kiyotaki, N. (1987), 'Monopolistic Competition and the Effects of Aggregate Demand', *American Economic Review*, September.

Blanchard, O.J. and Quah, D. (1989), 'The Dynamic Effects of Aggregate Demand and Supply Disturbances', *American Economic Review*, September.

Blanchard, O.J. and Summers, L.H. (1986), 'Hysteresis and the European Unemployment Problem', *NBER Macroeconomics Annual*.

Blanchard, O.J. and Summers, L.H. (1988), 'Beyond the Natural Rate Hypothesis', *American Economic Review*, May.

Blanchard, O.J. and Wolfers, J. (2000), 'The Role of Shocks and Institutions in the Rise of European Unemployment: The Aggregate Evidence', *Economic Journal*, March.

Blaug, M. (1991a), *The Historiography of Economics*, Aldershot, UK and Brookfield, USA: Edward Elgar.

*Blaug, M. (1991b), 'Second Thoughts on the Keynesian Revolution', *History of Political Economy*, Summer.

Blaug, M. (1992), *The Methodology of Economics: Or, How Economists Explain*, 2nd edn, Cambridge: Cambridge University Press.

Blaug, M. (1994), 'Not Only an Economist – Autobiographical Reflections of a Historian of Economic Thought', *American Economist*, Fall.

Blaug, M. (1997), *Economic Theory in Retrospect*, 5th edn, Cambridge: Cambridge University Press.

*Blaug, M. (2002), 'Endogenous Growth Theory', in B. Snowdon and H.R. Vane (eds), *An Encyclopedia of Macroeconomics*, Cheltenham, UK and Northampton, MA, USA: Edward Elgar.

*Blaug, M. and Vane, H.R. (2003), *Who's Who in Economics*, 4th edn, Cheltenham, UK and Northampton, MA, USA: Edward Elgar.

Blaug, M. et al. (1995), *The Quantity Theory of Money: From Locke to Keynes and Friedman*, Aldershot, UK and Brookfield, USA: Edward Elgar.

Bleaney, M. (1985), *The Rise and Fall of Keynesian Economics*, London: Macmillan.

Bleaney, M. (1996), 'Central Bank Independence, Wage Bargaining Structure and Macroeconomic Performance in OECD Countries', *Oxford Economic Papers*, January.

Blinder, A.S. (1979), *Economic Policy and the Great Stagflation*, London: Academic Press.

Blinder, A.S. (1986), 'Keynes after Lucas', *Eastern Economic Journal*, July/September.

Blinder, A.S. (1987a), *Hard Heads, Soft Hearts: Tough-Minded Economics for a Just Society*, New York: Addison-Wesley.

*Blinder, A.S. (1987b), 'Keynes, Lucas and Scientific Progress', *American Economic Review*, May.

Blinder, A.S. (1988a), 'The Challenge of High Unemployment', *American Economic Review*, May.

*Blinder, A.S. (1988b), 'The Fall and Rise of Keynesian Economics', *Economic Record*, December.

Blinder, A.S. (1991), 'Why Are Prices Sticky? Preliminary Results From An Interview Study', *American Economic Review*, May.

Blinder, A.S. (1992a), 'Déjà Vu All Over Again', in M. Belongia and M. Garfinkel (eds), *The Business Cycle: Theories and Evidence*, London: Kluwer Academic Publishers.

Blinder, A.S. (1992b), 'A Keynesian Restoration is Here', *Challenge*, September/October.

Blinder, A.S. (1994), 'On Sticky Prices: Academic Theories Meet the Real World', in N.G. Mankiw (ed.), *Monetary Policy*, Chicago: University of Chicago Press.

*Blinder, A.S. (1997a), 'Is There a Core of Practical Macroeconomics That We Should All Believe?', *American Economic Review*, May.

*Blinder, A.S. (1997b), 'What Central Bankers Can Learn From Academics and Vice Versa', *Journal of Economic Perspectives*, Spring.

Blinder, A.S. (1998), *Central Banking in Theory and Practice*, Cambridge, MA: MIT Press.

Blinder, A.S. and Solow, R.M. (1973), 'Does Fiscal Policy Matter?', *Journal of Public Economics*, November.

*Bloom, D.E and Sachs, J. (1998), 'Geography, Demography and Economic Growth in Africa', *Brookings Papers on Economic Activity*.

Bloom, D.E., Canning, D. and Jamison, D.T. (2004), 'Health, Wealth and Welfare', *Finance and Development*, March.

Bloom, D.E., Canning, D. and Sevilla, J. (2003), 'Geography and Poverty Traps', *Journal of Economic Growth*, December.

Böhm-Bawerk, E. v. (1959 [1884;1889;1909]), *Capital and Interest*, 3 vols, South Holland, IL: Libertarian Press.

Bolton, P. and Roland, G. (1997), 'The Breakup of Nations: A Political Economy Analysis', *Quarterly Journal of Economics*, November.

Boone, P. (1996), 'Politics and the Effectiveness of Aid', *European Economic Review*, February.

Booth, A. (1985), 'The Keynesian Revolution and Economic Policy-making – A Reply', *Economic History Review*, February.

Bordo, M.D. and Schwartz, A.J. (2003), 'IS-LM and Monetarism', NBER Working Paper, No.9713, May.

Bordo, M.D., Choudhri, E.U. and Schwartz, A.J. (2002a), 'Was Expansionary Monetary Policy Feasible During the Great Contraction? An Exploration of the Gold Standard', *Explorations in Economic History*, January.

*Bordo, M.D., Goldin, C. and White, E.N. (1998), *The Defining Moment: the Great Depression and the American Economy in the Twentieth Century*, Chicago: University of Chicago Press.

*Bordo, M.D., Taylor, A. and Williamson, J.G. (eds) (2002b), *Globalisation in Historical Perspective*, Chicago: University of Chicago Press.

Boskin, M.J. (1996), *Towards a More Accurate Measure of the Cost of Living*, Final Report to the Committee on Finance of the US Senate.

*Bosworth, B.P. and Collins, S.M. (2003), 'The Empirics of Growth: An Update', *Brookings Papers on Economic Activity*.

*Bourguignon, F. and Morrisson, C. (2002), 'Inequality Among World Citizens: 1820–1992', *American Economic Review*, September.

Brandolini, A. (1995), 'In Search of a Stylised Fact: Do Real Wages Exhibit a Consistent Pattern of Cyclical Variability?', *Journal of Economic Surveys*, June.

Braun, R.A. and Evans, C.L. (1998), 'Seasonal Solow Residuals and Christmas: A Case for Labour Hoarding and Increasing Returns', *Journal of Money, Credit, and Banking*, August.

Brendon, P. (2000), *The Dark Valley: A Panorama of the 1930s*, London: Jonathan Cape.

Bridel, P. (1987), *Cambridge Monetary Thought*, New York: St Martin's Press.

Brimmer, A.F. (1983), 'Monetary Policy and Economic Activity: Benefits and Costs of Monetarism', *American Economic Review*, May.

*Britton, A. (2002), 'Macrocconomics and History', *National Institute Economic Review*, January.

Bronfenbrenner, M. (ed.) (1969), *Is the Business Cycle Obsolete?*, New York: Wiley.

Broughton, J.M. (2003), 'On the Origins of the Fleming–Mundell Model', *IMF Staff Papers*, April.

Brown, G. (1997), 'Letter from the Chancellor to the Governor: 6th May 1997', *Bank of England Quarterly Bulletin*, August.

Brown, G. (2001), 'The Conditions for High and Stable Growth and Employment', *Economic Journal*, May.

Bruno, M. and Sachs, J.D. (1985), *The Economics of Worldwide Stagflation*, Cambridge, MA: Harvard University Press.

Brunner, K. (1968), 'The Role of Money and Monetary Policy', *Federal Reserve Bank of St. Louis Review*, July.

Brunner, K. (1970), 'The Monetarist Revolution in Monetary Theory', *Weltwirtschaftliches Archiv*, March.

Buchanan, J.M. (1976), 'Barro on the Ricardian Equivalence Theorem', *Journal of Political Economy*, April.

Buchanan, J.M. and Wagner, R.E. (1978), 'Democracy and Keynesian Contributions: Political Biases and Economic Consequences', in J.M. Buchanan, J. Burton and R.E. Wagner, *The Consequences of Mr Keynes*, London: Institute of Economic Affairs.

*Buchanan, J.M., Burton, J. and Wagner, R.E. (1978), *The Consequences of Mr Keynes*, London: Institute of Economic Affairs.

*Budd, A. (1998), 'The Role and Operations of the Bank of England Monetary Policy Committee', *Economic Journal*, November.

Buiter, W.H. (1980), 'The Macroeconomics of Dr. Pangloss: A Critical Survey of the New Classical Macroeconomics', *Economic Journal*, March.

*Buiter, W.H. (2003a), 'James Tobin: An Appreciation of His Contribution to Economics', *Economic Journal*, November.

Buiter, W.H. (2003b), 'Deflation: Prevention and Cure', NBER Working Paper, No. 9623, April.

Burns, A. (1959), 'Progress Towards Economic Stability', *American Economic Review*, May.

Burns, A.F. and Mitchell, W.C. (1946), *Measuring Business Cycles*, New York: NBER.

Burnside, C., Eichenbaum, M. and Rebelo, S. (1995), 'Capital Utilization and Returns to Scale', *NBER Macroeconomics Annual*.

Burton, J. (1981), 'Positively Milton Friedman', in J.R. Shackleton and G. Locksley (eds), *Twelve Contemporary Economists*, London: Macmillan.

Cagan, P. (1956), 'The Monetary Dynamics of Hyperinflation', in M. Friedman (ed.), *Studies in the Quantity Theory of Money*, Chicago: University of Chicago Press.

Cagan, P. (1993), 'Does Endogeneity of the Money Supply Disprove Monetary Effects on Economic Activity?', *Journal of Macroeconomics*, Summer.

Cairncross, F. and Cairncross, A. (eds) (1992), *The Legacy of the Golden Age: The 1960s and their Economic Consequences*, London: Routledge.

Campbell, J.Y. and Mankiw, N.G. (1987), 'Are Output Fluctuations Transitory?', *Quarterly Journal of Economics*, November.

Campbell, J.Y. and Mankiw, N.G. (1989), 'International Evidence on the Persistence of Economic Fluctuations', *Journal of Monetary Economics*, March.

Capelli, P. and Chauvin, K. (1991), 'An Interplant Test of the Efficiency Wage Hypothesis', *Quarterly Journal of Economics*, August.

Capie, F.H. (ed.) (1991), *Major Inflations in History*, Aldershot, UK and Brookfield, USA: Edward Elgar.

Caplin, A.S. and Spulber, D.F. (1987), 'Menu Costs and the Neutrality of Money', *Quarterly Journal of Economics*, November.

Caporale, T. (1993), 'Knut Wicksell: Real Business Cycle Theorist', *Scottish Journal of Political Economy*, November.

Caporale, G.M. (1993), 'Productivity Shocks and Business Cycles', *Applied Economics*, August.

Carabelli, A.M. (1988), *On Keynes's Method*, New York: St Martin's Press.

Carlin, W. and Soskice, D. (1990), *Macroeconomics and the Wage Bargain*, Oxford: Oxford University Press.

Carmignani, F. (2003), 'Political Instability, Uncertainty and Economics', *Journal of Economic Surveys*, February.

Carlson, K.M. and Spencer, R.W. (1975), 'Crowding Out and Its Critics', *Federal Reserve Bank of St. Louis Monthly Review*, December.

Carlton, D.W. (1986), 'The Rigidity of Prices', *American Economic Review*, September.

Carter, M. and Maddock, R. (1984), *Rational Expectations: Macroeconomics for the 1980s?*, London: Macmillan.

Carvalho, F.J.C.D. (1995/6), 'The Independence of Central Banks: A Critical Assessment of the Arguments', *Journal of Post Keynesian Economics*, Winter.

Cass, D. (1965), 'Optimum Growth in an Aggregative Model of Capital Accumulation', *Review of Economic Studies*, July.

Cecchetti, S.G. (1998), 'Understanding the Great Depression: Lessons for Current Policy', in M. Wheeler (ed.), *The Economics of the Great Depression*, Kalamazoo, MI: W.E. Upjohn Institute for Employment Research.

Cecchetti, S.G. (2000), 'Making Monetary Policy: Objectives and Rules', *Oxford Review of Economic Policy*, Winter.

Cesaratto, S. (1999), 'Savings and Economic Growth in Neoclassical Theory', *Cambridge Journal of Economics*.

Chadha, B. and Prasad, E. (1993), 'Interpreting the Cyclical Behavior of Prices', *IMF Staff Papers*, June.

Chadha, B., Masson, P.R. and Meredith, G. (1992), 'Models of Inflation and the Costs of Disinflation', *IMF Staff Papers*, June.

Chamberlin, E.H. (1933), *The Theory of Monopolistic Competition*, Cambridge, MA: Harvard University Press.

Chappell, H.W. with Havrilesky, T.M. and McGregor, R.R. (1993), 'Partisan Monetary Policies: Presidential Influence through the Power of Appointment', *Quarterly Journal of Economics*, February.

*Chari, V. (1998), 'Nobel Laureate Robert E. Lucas Jr: Architect of Modern Macroeconomics', *Journal of Economic Perspectives*, Winter.

Chari, V.V., Kehoe, P.J. and McGrattan, E.R. (2002), 'Accounting for the Great Depression', *American Economic Review*, May.

Chatterjee, S. (1999), 'Real Business Cycles: A Legacy of Countercyclical Policies', *Federal Reserve Bank of Philadelphia Business Review*, January/February.

Chenery, H.B. and Strout, A.M. (1966), 'Foreign Assistance and Economic Development', *American Economic Review*, September.

Chick, V. (1983), *Macroeconomics After Keynes: A Reconsideration of the General Theory*, Oxford: Philip Allan.

*Chick, V. (1995), 'Is There a Case for Post Keynesian Economics?', *Scottish Journal of Political Economy*, February.

Cho, J.O. and Cooley, T.F. (1995), 'The Business Cycle with Nominal Contracts', *Economic Theory*, June.

Choudri, E.U. and Kochin, L.A. (1980), 'The Exchange Rate and the International Transmission of Business Cycle Disturbances', *Journal of Money, Credit, and Banking*, November.

Chow, G.C. (1975), *Analysis and Control of Dynamic Economic Systems*, New York: John Wiley.

Christiano, L.J., Motto, R. and Rostagno, M. (2004), 'The Great Depression and the Friedman–Schwartz Hypothesis', NBER Working Paper, No. 10255, January.

Chrystal, K.A. (ed.) (1990), *Monetarism: Vols I and II*, Aldershot, UK and Brookfield, USA: Edward Elgar.

Clague, C., Keefer, P., Knack, S. and Olson, M. (1996), 'Property and Contract Rights in Autocracies and Democracies', *Journal of Economic Growth*, June.

Clarida, R., Gali, J. and Gertler, M. (1999), 'The Science of Monetary Policy:

A New Keynesian Perspective', *Journal of Economic Literature*, December.

Clarida, R., Gali, J. and Gertler, M. (2000), 'Monetary Policy Rules and Macroeconomic Stability: Some Evidence and Some Theory', *Quarterly Journal of Economics*, February.

Clark, G. (2003), 'The Great Escape: The Industrial Revolution in Theory and History', University of California, Davis, Working Paper, September.

Clower, R.W. (1965), 'The Keynesian Counter-Revolution: A Theoretical Appraisal', in F.H. Hahn and F.P.R. Brechling (eds), *The Theory of Interest Rates*, London: Macmillan.

Clower, R.W. and Howitt, P. (1996), 'Taking Markets Seriously: Groundwork for a Post Walrasian Macroeconomics' in D. Colander (ed.), *Beyond Microfoundations: Post Walrasian Macroeconomics*, New York: Cambridge University Press.

Cochran, J.P. (2001), 'Capital-Based Macroeconomics: Recent Developments and Extensions of Austrian Business Cycle Theory', *Quarterly Journal of Austrian Economics*.

Coddington, A. (1976), 'Keynesian Economics: The Search for First Principles', *Journal of Economic Literature*, December.

*Coddington, A. (1983), *Keynesian Economics: The Search For First Principles*, London: Allen and Unwin.

Coe, D.T., Helpman, E. and Hoffmaisler, A.W. (1997), 'North–South R and D Spillovers', *Economic Journal*, March.

Colander, D.C. (ed.) (1984), *Neoclassical Political Economy*, Cambridge, MA: Ballinger.

Colander, D.C. (1988), 'The Evolution of Keynesian Economics: From Keynesian to New Classical to New Keynesian', in O.F. Hamouda and J.N. Smithin (eds), *Keynes and Public Policy After Fifty Years, Vol 1: Economics and Policy*, Aldershot, UK and Brookfield, USA: Edward Elgar.

Colander, D.C. (ed.) (1996), *Beyond Microfoundations: Post Walrasian Macroeconomics*, New York: Cambridge University Press.

Colander, D.C. (2004), 'The Strange Persistence of the IS–LM Model', in M. De Vroey and K.D. Hoover (eds), *The IS–LM Model: Its Rise, Fall and Strange Persistence*, Durham, NC: Duke University Press.

*Colander, D.C. et al. (1992), 'Symposium on New Keynesian Macroeconomics: The Emergence of the Microfoundations of Macroeconomics', *Eastern Economic Journal*, Fall.

Cole, H. and Ohanian, L.E. (1999), 'The Great Depression in the United States From a Neoclassical Perspective', *Federal Reserve Bank of Minneapolis Quarterly Review*, Winter.

Cole, H. and Ohanian, L.E. (2002a), 'The Great UK Depression: A Puzzle and Possible Resolution', *Review of Economic Dynamics*, January.

Cole, H. and Ohanian, L.E. (2002b), 'The US and UK Great Depressions Through the Lens of Neoclassical Growth Theory', *American Economic Review*, May.

*Collier, P. (2001), 'Implications of Ethnic Diversity', *Economic Policy*, April.

*Collier, P. and Gunning, J. (1999a), 'Explaining African Economic Performance', *Journal of Economic Literature*, March.

*Collier, P. and Gunning, J. (1999b), 'Why has Africa Grown So Slowly?', *Journal of Economic Perspectives*, Summer.

Collins, S.M. and Bosworth, B.P. (1996), 'Economic Growth in East Asia: Accumulation Versus Assimilation', *Brookings Papers on Economic Activity*.

Cooley, T.F. (ed.) (1995), *Frontiers of Business Cycle Research*, Princeton: Princeton University Press.

Cooley, T.F. (1997), 'Calibrated Models', *Oxford Review of Economic Policy*, Autumn.

Cooley, T.F. and Ohanian, L.E. (1991), 'The Cyclical Behaviour of Prices', *Journal of Monetary Economics*, August.

Cooley, T.F. and Ohanian, L.E. (1997), 'Postwar British Economic Growth and the Legacy of Keynes', *Journal of Political Economy*, June.

Cooley, T.F. and Prescott, E.C. (1995), 'Economic Growth and Business Cycles', in T.F. Cooley (ed.) *Frontiers of Business Cycle Research*, Princeton: Princeton University Press.

Cornwall, J. (ed.) (1984), *After Stagflation*, Oxford: Basil Blackwell.

Corry, B.A. (1962), *Money, Saving and Investment in English Economics, 1800–1850*, London: Macmillan.

Crafts, N.F.R. (1983), 'British Economic Growth, 1700–1831: A Review of the Evidence', *Economic History Review*, May.

Crafts, N.F.R. (1985), *British Economic Growth During the Industrial Revolution*, Oxford: Clarendon Press.

Crafts, N.F.R. (1994), 'The Industrial Revolution', in R. Floud and D. McCloskey (eds), *The Economic History of Britain Since 1700: Volume 1*, 2nd edn, Cambridge: Cambridge University Press.

Crafts, N.F.R. (1995), 'Exogenous or Endogenous Growth? The Industrial Revolution Reconsidered', *Journal of Economic History*, December.

*Crafts, N.F.R. (1996), 'Post-Neoclassical Endogenous Growth Theory: What are the Policy Implications?', *Oxford Review of Economic Policy*, Summer.

*Crafts, N.F.R. (1999), 'Economic Growth in the Twentieth Century', *Oxford Review of Economic Policy*, December.

Crafts, N.F.R. (2000), 'Globalisation and Growth', IMF Working Paper, No. 00/44, March.

Crafts, N.F.R. (2001), 'Historical Perspectives on Development', in G. Meier and J.E. Stiglitz (eds), *Frontiers of Development Economics: The Future in Perspective*, Oxford: Oxford University Press.

Crafts, N.F.R. (2003), 'Is Economic Growth Good for Us?', *World Economics*, July–September.

*Crafts, N.F.R. and Toniolo, G. (eds) (1996), *Economic Growth in Postwar Europe*, Cambridge: Cambridge University Press.

Crafts, N.F.R. and Venables, T. (2002), 'Globalisation and Geography: An Historical Perspective', in M. Bordo, A. Taylor and J.G. Williamson (eds), *Globalisation in Historical Perspective*, Chicago: University of Chicago Press.

Cross, R. (1982a), *Economic Theory and Policy in the U.K.: An Outline and Assessment of the Controversies*, Oxford: Martin Robertson.

Cross, R. (1982b), 'The Duhem–Quine Thesis, Lakatos and the Appraisal of Theories in Macroeconomics', *Economic Journal*, June.

Cross, R. (ed.) (1988), *Unemployment, Hysteresis and the Natural Rate Hypothesis*, Oxford: Basil Blackwell.

*Cross, R. (ed.) (1995), *The Natural Rate of Unemployment: Reflections on 25 Years of the Hypothesis*, Cambridge: Cambridge University Press.

Cross, R. (2002), 'Hysteresis', in B. Snowdon and H.R. Vane (eds), *An Encyclopedia of Macroeconomics*, Cheltenham, UK and Northampton, MA, USA: Edward Elgar.

Cross, R. et al. (1993), 'The NAIRU', *Journal of Economic Studies*.

Crucini, M.J. and Kahn, J. (1996), 'Tariffs and Aggregate Economic Activity: Lessons from the Great Depression', *Journal of Monetary Economics*, December.

Cukierman, A. (1992), *Central Bank Strategy, Credibility and Independence*, Cambridge, MA: MIT Press.

Cukierman, A. (1994), 'Central Bank Independence and Monetary Control', *Economic Journal*, November.

Cukierman, A. and Meltzer, A.H. (1986), 'A Positive Theory of Discretionary Policy, the Cost of a Democratic Government, and the Benefits of a Constitution', *Economic Inquiry*, July.

Cukierman, A., Edwards, S. and Tabellini, G. (1992), 'Seigniorage and Political Instability', *American Economic Review*, June.

Culbertson, J.M. (1960), 'Friedman on the Lag in Effect of Monetary Policy', *Journal of Political Economy*, December.

Culbertson, J.M. (1961), 'The Lag in Effect on Monetary Policy: Reply', *Journal of Political Economy*, October.

Cunningham Wood, J. (1983), *John Maynard Keynes: Critical Assessments*, Vols 1–4, Beckenham: Croom Helm.

Dalziel, P.C. (1991), 'Theoretical Approaches to Monetary Disinflation', *Journal of Economic Surveys*.

Danthine, J. P. ( 1997), 'In Search of a Successor to IS–LM', *Oxford Review of Economic Policy*, Autumn.

Danthine, J.P. and Donaldson, J.B. (1993), 'Methodological and Empirical Issues in Real Business Cycle Theory', *European Economic Review*, January.

Danziger, S., Van der Gaag, J., Smolensky, E. and Taussig, M. (1982–3), 'The Life Cycle Hypothesis and the Consumption Behaviour of the Elderly', *Journal of Post Keynesian Economics*, Winter.

Dasgupta, P. and Serageldin, I. (eds) (2000), *Social Capital: A Multifaceted Perspective*, Washington, DC: World Bank.

Davidson, G. and Davidson, P. (1988), *Economics for a Civilised World*, London: Macmillan.

Davidson, P. (1972), *Money and the Real World*, London: Macmillan.

Davidson, P. (1977), 'Money and General Equilibrium', *Economie Appliquée*.

*Davidson, P. (1978), *Money and the Real World*, 2nd edn, London: Macmillan.

Davidson, P. (1980), 'Post Keynesian Economics: Solving the Crisis in Economic Theory', *Public Interest*, Special Issue; reprinted in D. Bell and I. Kristol (eds) (1981), *The Crisis in Economic Theory*, New York: Basic Books.

Davidson, P. (1982), *International Money and the Real World*, London: Macmillan.

Davidson, P. (1982–3), 'Rational Expectations: A Fallacious Foundation for Studying Crucial Decision-Making Processes', *Journal of Post Keynesian Economics*, Winter.

Davidson, P. (1984), 'Reviving Keynes's Revolution', *Journal of Post Keynesian Economics*, Fall.

*Davidson, P. (1991), 'Is Probability Theory Relevant for Uncertainty? A Post Keynesian Perspective', *Journal of Economic Perspectives*, Winter.

*Davidson, P. (1994), *Post Keynesian Macroeconomic Theory: A Foundation for Successful Economic Policies for the Twenty-First Century*, Aldershot, UK and Brookfield, USA: Edward Elgar.

Davidson, P. (1996), 'What Revolution?: The Legacy of Keynes', *Journal of Post Keynesian Economics*, Fall.

Davidson, P. (2002), 'Restating the Purpose of the Journal of Post Keynesian Economics After 25 Years', *Journal of Post Keynesian Economics*, Fall.

Davidson, P. and Weintraub, S. (1973), 'Money As Cause or Effect', *Economic Journal*, March.

Davis, M.D. (1983), *Game Theory: A Non Technical Introduction*, New York: Basic Books.

Dawson, J.W. (1998), 'Institutions, Investment, and Growth: New Cross-Country and Panel Data Evidence', *Economic Inquiry*, October.

Deane, P. (1983), 'The Scope and Method of Economic Science', *Economic Journal*, March.

Deininger, K. and Squire, L. (1996), 'A New Dataset Measuring Income Inequality', *World Bank Economic Review*, September.

*DeLong, J.B. (1988), 'Productivity Growth, Convergence and Welfare: Comment', *American Economic Review*, December.

DeLong, J.B. (1992), 'Growth in the World Economy, ca. 1870–1990', in H. Siebert (ed.), *Economic Growth in the World Economy*, Tübingen: Mohr/ Siebeck.

*DeLong, J.B. (1996), 'Keynesianism, Pennsylvania Avenue Style: Some Economic Consequences of the Employment Act of 1946', *Journal of Economic Perspectives*, Summer.

*DeLong, J.B. (1997), 'America's Only Peacetime Inflation: The 1970s', in C. Romer and D. Romer (eds), *Reducing Inflation: Motivation and Strategy*, Chicago: University of Chicago Press.

DeLong, J.B. (1998), 'America's Fiscal Policy in the Shadow of the Great Depression', in M. Bordo, C. Goldin and E. White (eds), *The Defining Moment: The Great Depression and the American Economy in the Twentieth Century*, Chicago: University of Chicago Press.

DeLong, J.B. (1999a), 'Introduction to the Symposium on Business Cycles', *Journal of Economic Perspectives*, Spring.

DeLong, J.B. (1999b), 'Why we Should Fear Deflation', *Brookings Papers on Economic Activity*.

DeLong, J.B. (1999c), 'Financial Crises in the 1890s and 1990s: Must History Repeat Itself?', *Brookings Papers on Economic Activity*.

*DeLong, J.B. (2000), 'The Triumph of Monetarism?', *Journal of Economic Perspectives*, Winter.

DeLong, J.B. (2001), *Macroeconomics*, Burr Ridge: McGraw-Hill Higher Education.

DeLong, J.B. and Dowrick, S. (2002), 'Globalisation and Convergence', in M. Bordo, A. Taylor and J.G. Williamson (eds), *Globalisation in Historical Perspective*, Chicago: University of Chicago Press.

DeLong, J.B. and Eichengreen, B. (1993), 'The Marshall Plan: History's Most Successful Structural Adjustment Programme', in R. Dornbusch, W. Nolling and R. Layard (eds), *Post-War Reconstruction and Lessons for the East Today*, Cambridge, MA: MIT Press.

*DeLong, J.B. and Shleifer, A. (1993), 'Princes and Merchants: City Growth Before the Industrial Revolution', *Journal of Law and Economics*, October.

DeLong, J.B. and Summers, L.H. (1986), 'The Changing Cyclical Variability of Economic Activity in the United States', in R.J. Gordon (ed.), *The American Business Cycle*, Chicago: University of Chicago Press.

DeLong, J.B. and Summers, L.H. (1991), 'Equipment Investment and Economic Growth', *Quarterly Journal of Economics*, May.

DeLong, J.B. and Summers, L.H. (1992), 'Equipment Investment and Economic Growth: How Strong is the Nexus?', *Brookings Papers on Economic Activity*.

DeLong, J.B. and Summers, L.H. (1993), 'How Strongly Do Developing Countries Benefit from Equipment Investment?', *Journal of Monetary Economics*, December.

Denison, E.F. (1967), *Why Growth Rates Differ: Post-War Experience in Nine Western Countries*, Washington, DC: The Brookings Institution.

Denison, E.F. (1974), *Accounting for United States Growth, 1929–1969*, Washington, DC: The Brookings Institution.

Denison, E.F. (1985), *Trends in American Economic Growth*, Washington, DC: The Brookings Institution.

De Prano, M. and Mayer, T. (1965), 'Tests of the Relative Importance of Autonomous Expenditure and Money', *American Economic Review*, September.

Deutscher, P. (1990), *R.G. Hawtrey and the Development of Macroeconomics*, Basingstoke: Macmillan.

De Vanssay (2002), 'Marshall–Lerner Condition', in B. Snowdon and H.R. Vane (eds), *An Encyclopedia of Macroeconomics*, Cheltenham, UK and Northampton, MA, USA: Edward Elgar.

De Vroey, M. (2000), 'IS–LM à la Hicks Versus IS–LM à la Modigliani', *History of Political Economy*, Summer.

*De Vroey, M. (2001), 'Friedman and Lucas on the Phillips Curve: From a Disequilibrium to an Equilibrium Approach', *Eastern Economic Journal*, Spring.

De Wolff, P. (1941), 'Income Elasticity of Demand: A Microeconomic and a Macroeconomic Interpretation', *Economic Journal*, April.

*Diamond, J. (1997), *Guns, Germs and Steel*, New York: W.W. Norton.

Diamond, P.A. (1982), 'Aggregate Demand Management in Search Equilibrium', *Journal of Political Economy*, October.

Diamond, P., Shafir, E. and Tversky, A. (1997), 'Money Illusion', *Quarterly Journal of Economics*, May.

*Dimand, R.W. (1988), *The Origins of the Keynesian Revolution*, Aldershot, UK and Brookfield, USA: Edward Elgar.

*Dimand, R.W. (2002a), 'Ricardian Equivalence', in B. Snowdon and H.R. Vane (eds), *An Encyclopedia of Macroeconomics*, Cheltenham, UK and Northampton, MA, USA: Edward Elgar.

*Dimand, R.W. (2002b), 'Real Balance Effect', in B. Snowdon and H.R. Vane (eds), *An Encyclopedia of Macroeconomics*, Cheltenham, UK and Northampton, MA, USA: Edward Elgar.

*Dimand, R.W. (2002c), 'Balance of Payments: Keynesian Approach', in B. Snowdon and H.R. Vane (eds), *An Encyclopedia of Macroeconomics*, Cheltenham, UK and Northampton, MA, USA: Edward Elgar.

Dimand, R. (2004), 'James Tobin and the Transformation of the IS–LM Model', in M. De Vroey and K.D. Hoover (eds), *The IS–LM Model: Its Rise, Fall and Strange Persistence*, Durham, NC: Duke University Press.

Dixon, H. (1995), 'Of Coconuts, Decomposition and a Jackass: The Genealogy of the Natural Rate', in R. Cross (ed.), *The Natural Rate of Unemployment: Reflections on 25 Years of the Hypothesis*, Cambridge: Cambridge University Press.

*Dixon, H. (1997), 'The Role of Imperfect Competition in Keynesian Economics', in B. Snowdon and H.R. Vane (eds), *Reflections on the Development of Modern Macroeconomics*, Cheltenham, UK and Lyme, USA: Edward Elgar.

Dixon, H. and Rankin, N. (1994), 'Imperfect Competition and Macroeconomics: A Survey', *Oxford Economic Papers*, April.

Dixon, W. (1994), 'Democracy and the Peaceful Settlement of International Conflict', *American Political Science Review*, March.

*Dollar, D. and Kraay, A. (2002a), 'Spreading the Wealth', *Foreign Affairs*, February.

*Dollar, D. and Kraay, A. (2002b), 'Growth is Good for the Poor', *Journal of Economic Growth*, September.

Dollar, D. and Kraay, A. (2003), 'Institutions, Trade and Growth', *Journal of Monetary Economics*, January.

*Dollar, D. and Kraay, A. (2004), 'Trade, Growth, and Poverty', *Economic Journal*, February.

Domar, E.D. (1946), 'Capital Expansion, Rate of Growth and Employment', *Econometrica*, April.

Domar, E.D. (1947), 'Expansion and Employment', *American Economic Review*, March.

Domar, E.D. (1948), 'The Problem of Capital Accumulation', *American Economic Review*, December.

Domar, E.D. (1957), *Essays on the Theory of Economic Growth*, New York: Oxford University Press.

Dore, M. (1993), *The Macrodynamics of Business Cycles*, Oxford: Blackwell.

Dorfman, R. (1989), 'Thomas Robert Malthus and David Ricardo', *Journal of Economic Perspectives*, Summer.

Dorfman, R., Samuelson, P.A. and Solow, R.M. (1958), *Linear Programming and Economic Analysis*, New York: McGraw-Hill.

Dornbusch, R. (1976), 'Expectations and Exchange Rate Dynamics', *Journal of Political Economy*, December.

*Dornbusch, R., Fischer, S. and Startz, R. (2004), *Macroeconomics*, 9th edn, New York: McGraw-Hill.

Dow, C. (1998), *Major Recessions: Britain and the World 1920–95*, Oxford: Oxford University Press.

Downs, A. (1957), *An Economic Theory of Democracy*, New York: Harper and Row.

Dowrick, S. (1992), 'Technological Catch-Up and Diverging Incomes', *Economic Journal*, May.

Doyle, C. and Weale, M. (1994), 'Do We Really Want an Independent Central Bank?', *Oxford Review of Economic Policy*, Autumn.

Drago, R. and Heywood, J.S. (1992), 'Is Worker Behaviour Consistent with Efficiency Wages?', *Scottish Journal of Political Economy*, May.

Drazen, A. (2000a), *Political Economy in Macroeconomics*, Princeton: Princeton University Press.

*Drazen, A. (2000b), 'The Political Business Cycle After Twenty Five Years', *National Bureau of Economics Research Macroeconomics Annual*.

Driffill, J. (1988), 'Macroeconomic Policy Games with Incomplete Information: A Survey', *European Economic Review*, March.

Dunlop, J.G. (1938), 'The Movement of Real and Money Wages', *Economic Journal*, September.

Durlauf, S.N. (1989), 'Output Persistence, Economic Structure, and the Choice of Stabilisation Policy', *Brookings Papers on Economic Activity*.

Durlauf, S. and Quah, D. (1999), 'The New Empirics of Economic Growth', in J.B. Taylor and M. Woodford (eds), *Handbook of Macroeconomics, Vol. IA*, Amsterdam: Elsevier.

*Easterlin, R.A. (1996), *Growth Triumphant: The Twenty-First Century in Perspective*, Ann Arbor: University of Michigan Press.

Easterly, W. (1999), 'The Ghost of the Financing Gap: Testing the Growth Model Used in International Financial Institutions', *Journal of Development Economics*, December.

*Easterly, W. (2001a), *The Elusive Quest for Growth: Economists' Adventures and Misadventures in the Tropics*, Cambridge, MA: MIT Press.

Easterly, W. (2001b), 'Can Institutions Resolve Ethnic Conflict?', *Economic Development and Cultural Change*, July.

Easterly, W. (2003), 'Can Foreign Aid Buy Growth?', *Journal of Economic Perspectives*, Summer.

Easterly, W. and Fischer, S. (2001), 'Inflation and the Poor', *Journal of Money, Credit, and Banking*, May.

*Easterly, W. and Levine, R. (1997), 'Africa's Growth Tragedy: Policies and Ethnic Divisions', *Quarterly Journal of Economics*, November.

Easterly, W. and Levine, R. (2001), 'It's Not Factor Accumulation: Stylised Facts and Growth Models', www.worldbank.org.

Easterly, W. and Levine, R. (2003), 'Tropics, Germs and Crops: How Endowments Influence Economic Development', *Journal of Monetary Economics*, January.

Easterly, W., Devarajan, S. and Pack, H. (2003), 'Low Investment is Not the Constraint on African Development', *Economic Development and Cultural Change*, April.

Edwards, S. (1993), 'Openness, Trade Liberalisation and Growth in Developing Countries', *Journal of Economic Literature*, September.

Edwards, S. (1994), 'The Political Economy of Inflation and Stabilization in Developing Countries', *Economic Development and Cultural Change*, January.

*Edwards, S. (1998), 'Openness, Productivity and Growth: What Do We Really Know?', *Economic Journal*, March.

Eggertsson, G. B. and Woodford, M. (2003), 'The Zero Bound on Interest Rates and Optimal Monetary Policy', *Brookings Papers on Economic Activity*.

Eichenbaum, M. (1991), 'Real Business Cycle Theory: Wisdom or Whimsy?', *Journal of Economic Dynamics and Control*, October.

*Eichenbaum, M. (1997), 'Some Thoughts on Practical Stabilization Policy', *American Economic Review*, May.

Eichenbaum, M. and Singleton, K.J. (1986), 'Do Equilibrium Real Business Cycle Theories Explain Postwar US Business Cycles?', *NBER Macroeconomics Annual*.

*Eichengreen, B. (1992a), 'The Origins and Nature of the Great Slump Revisited', *Economic History Review*, May.

*Eichengreen, B. (1992b), *Golden Fetters: The Gold Standard and the Great Depression, 1919–1939*, New York: Oxford University Press.

Eichengreen, B. (1996), 'Institutions and Economic Growth: Europe After World War II', in N.F.R. Crafts and G. Toniolo (eds), *Economic Growth in Europe Since 1945*, Cambridge: Cambridge University Press.

Eichengreen, B. and Sachs, J.D. (1985), 'Exchange Rates and Economic Recovery in the 1930s', *Journal of Economic History*, December.

Eichengreen, B. and Temin, P. (2000), 'The Gold Standard and the Great Depression', *Contemporary European History*, July.

*Eichengreen, B. and Temin, P. (2002), 'Counterfactual Histories of the Great Depression', in T. Balderston (ed.), *The World Economy and National Economies Between the Wars*, London: Macmillan.

*Eichner, A.S. and Kregel, J.A. (1975), 'An Essay on Post Keynesian Theory: A New Paradigm in Economics', *Journal of Economic Literature*, December.

Eifert, B., Gelb, A. and Tallroth, N.B. (2003), 'Managing Oil Wealth', *Finance and Development*, March.

*Eijffinger, S.C.W. (2002a), 'Central Bank Independence', in B. Snowdon and H.R. Vane (eds), *An Encyclopedia of Macroeconomics*, Cheltenham, UK and Northampton, MA, USA: Edward Elgar.

*Eijffinger, S.C.W. (2002b), 'Central Bank Accountability and Transparency', in B. Snowdon and H.R. Vane (eds), *An Encyclopedia of Macroeconomics*, Cheltenham, UK and Northampton, MA, USA: Edward Elgar.

Eijffinger, S.C.W. and Keulen, M.V. (1995), 'Central Bank Independencies in Another Eleven Countries', *Banca Nazionale del Lavoro Quarterly Review*, March.

Eijffinger, S.C.W. and Schaling, E. (1993), 'Central Bank Independence in Twelve Industrial Countries', *Banca Nazionale del Lavaro Quarterly Review*, March.

Elmslie, B. and Criss, A.J. (1999), 'Theories of Convergence and Growth in the Classical Period: The Role of Science, Technology and Trade', *Economica*, February.

Els, van P.J.A. (1995), 'Real Business Cycle Models and Money: A Survey of Theories and Facts', *Weltwirtschaftliches Archiv*.

Eltis, W. (1995), 'John Locke, the Quantity Theory of Money and Establishment of a Sound Currency', in M. Blaug et al., *The Quantity Theory of Money: From Locke to Keynes and Friedman*, Aldershot, UK and Brookfield, USA: Edward Elgar.

Evans, G.W. and Honkapohja, S. (1999), 'Learning Dynamics', in J.B. Taylor and M. Woodford (eds), *Handbook of Macroeconomics*, Amsterdam: North-Holland.

Evans, G.W. and Honkapohja, S. (2001), *Learning and Expectations Macroeconomics*, Princeton: Princeton University Press.

Fackler, J.S. and Parker, R.E. (1994), 'Accounting for the Great Depression: A Historical Decomposition', *Journal of Macroeconomics*, Spring.

*Fagerberg, J. (1994), 'Technology and International Differences in Growth Rates', *Journal of Economic Literature*, September.

*Fagerberg, J. (1995), 'Convergence or Divergence? The Impact of Technology on Why Growth Rates Differ', *Journal of Evolutionary Economics*, Spring.

Fair, R. (1988), 'The Effect of Economic Events on Votes for President: 1984 Update', *Political Behaviour*.

Fair, R. (1992), 'The Cowles Commission Approach, Real Business Cycle Theories and New Keynesian Economics', in M. Belongia and M. Garfinkel (eds), *The Business Cycle: Theories and Evidence*, London: Kluwer Academic Publishers.

Fajnzylber, P., Lederman, D. and Loayza, N. (2002), 'Inequality and Violent Crime', *Journal of Law and Economics*, April.

Fama, E. (1980), 'Banking in the Theory of Finance', *Journal of Monetary Economics*, January.

Fay, J.A. and Medoff, J.L. (1985), 'Labour and Output Over the Business Cycle', *American Economic Review*, September.

Fei, J. and Ranis, G. (1997), *Growth and Development From an Evolutionary Perspective*, Oxford: Basil Blackwell.

Feiwel, G.R. (1974), 'Reflections on Kalecki's Theory of Political Business Cycle', *Kyklos*.

Feldstein, M. (1982), 'Government Deficits and Aggregate Demand', *Journal of Monetary Economics*, February.

Feldstein, M. (1986), 'Supply-Side Economics: Old Truths and New Claims', *American Economic Review*, May.

*Feldstein, M. (1992), 'The Council of Economic Advisers and Economic Advising in the United States', *Economic Journal*, September.

Feldstein, M. (ed.) (1999), *The Costs and Benefits of Price Stability*, Chicago: University of Chicago Press.

Fellner, W. (1976), 'Towards a Reconstruction of Macroeconomics – Problems of Theory and Policy', *American Enterprise Institute*.

Fellner, W. (1979), 'The Credibility Effect and Rational Expectations: Implications of the Gramlich Study', *Brookings Papers on Economic Activity*.

Fischer, S. (1977), 'Long-Term Contracts, Rational Expectations, and the Optimal Money Supply Rule', *Journal of Political Economy*, February.

Fischer, S. (1988), 'Recent Developments in Macroeconomics', *Economic Journal*, June.

Fischer, S. (1990), 'Rules Versus Discretion in Monetary Policy', in B.M. Friedman and F.H. Hahn (eds), *Handbook of Monetary Economics Vol. II*, Amsterdam: North-Holland.

Fischer, S. (1993), 'The Role of Macroeconomic Factors in Growth', *Journal of Monetary Economics*, December.

Fischer, S. (1994), 'Interview with Stanley Fischer', in B. Snowdon, H.R. Vane and P. Wynarczyk, *A Modern Guide to Macroeconomics: An Introduction to Competing Schools of Thought*, Aldershot, UK and Brookfield, USA: Edward Elgar.

*Fischer, S. (1995a), 'Central Bank Independence Revisited', *American Economic Review*, May.

Fischer, S. (1995b), 'The Unending Search for Monetary Salvation', *NBER Macroeconomics Annual*.

*Fischer, S. (1996a), 'Robert Lucas's Nobel Memorial Prize', *Scandinavian Journal of Economics*, March.

Fischer, S. (1996b), 'Why are Central Banks Pursuing Long-Run Price Stability?, in *Achieving Price Stability*, Federal Reserve Bank of Kansas.

*Fischer, S., Sahay, R. and Vegh, C. (2002), 'Modern Hyper- and High Inflations', *Journal of Economic Literature*, September.

Fischer, S. et al. (1988), 'Symposium on the Slowdown in Productivity Growth', *Journal of Economic Perspectives*, Fall.

Fisher, I. (1907), *The Rate of Interest*, New York: Macmillan.

Fisher, I. (1911), *The Purchasing Power of Money*, New York: Macmillan.

Fisher, I. (1933a), 'The Debt-Deflation Theory of Great Depressions', *Econometrica*, October.

Fisher, I. (1933b), *Booms and Depressions*, London: Allen and Unwin.

Fisher, I. (1973), 'I Discovered the Phillips Curve', *Journal of Political Economy*, March/April.

Fitoussi, J.P. and Phelps, E.S. (1988), *The Slump in Europe: Open Economy Theory Reconstructed*, Oxford: Blackwell.

Fitoussi, J.P., Jestaz, D., Phelps, E.S. and Zoega, G. (2000), 'Roots of the Recent Recoveries: Labour Reforms or Private Sector Forces', *Brookings Papers on Economic Activity*.

Fitzgibbons, A. (1988), *Keynes's Vision*, Oxford: Oxford University Press.

*Fleming, J.M. (1962), 'Domestic Financial Policies under Fixed and under Floating Exchange Rates', *IMF Staff Papers*, November.

Fletcher, G. (2002), 'Neoclassical Synthesis', in B. Snowdon and H.R. Vane (eds), *An Encyclopedia of Macroeconomics*, Cheltenham, UK and Northampton, MA, USA: Edward Elgar.

Fogel, R.W. (1999), 'Catching Up With the Economy', *American Economic Review*, March.

Forbes, K. (2000), 'A Reassessment of the Relationship Between Inequality and Growth', *American Economic Review*, September.

Forder, J. (1998), 'Central Bank Independencies – Conceptual Clarifications and Interim Assessment', *Oxford Economic Papers*, July.

Frankel, J.A. and Romer, D. (1999), 'Does Trade Cause Growth?', *American Economic Review*, June.

Freeman, C. (1994), 'The Economics of Technical Change', *Cambridge Journal of Economics*.

Frenkel, J.A. and Johnson, H.G. (eds) (1976), *The Monetary Approach to the Balance of Payments*, London: Allen and Unwin.

Frenkel, J.A. and Johnson, H.G. (eds) (1978), *The Economics of Exchange Rates*, Reading, MA: Addison-Wesley.

Frenkel, J.A. and Razin, A. (1987), 'The Mundell–Fleming Model a Quarter Century Later: A Unified Exposition', *IMF Staff Papers*, December.

Frey, B.S. (1978), *Modern Political Economy*, London: Martin Robertson.

Frey, B.S. and Schneider, F. (1978a), 'A Politico-Economic Model of the United Kingdom', *Economic Journal*, June.

Frey, B.S. and Schneider, F. (1978b), 'An Empirical Study of Politico-

Economic Interaction in the United States', *Review of Economics and Statistics*, May.

Frey, B.S. and Schneider, F. (1988), 'Politico-Economic Models of Macroeconomic Policy: A Review of the Empirical Evidence', in T.D. Willett (ed.), *Political Business Cycles*, Durham, NC: Duke University Press.

Friedman, B.M. (1988), 'Lessons of Monetary Policy from the 1980s', *Journal of Economic Perspectives*, Summer.

Friedman, B.M. (1992), 'How Does It Matter?', in M. Belongia and M. Garfinkel (eds), *The Business Cycle: Theories and Evidence*, London: Kluwer Academic Publishers.

Friedman, B.M. and Kuttner, K.N. (1996), 'A Price Target for U.S. Monetary Policy? Lessons from the Experience with Money Growth Targets', *Brookings Papers on Economic Activity*.

Friedman, M. (1948), 'A Monetary and Fiscal Framework for Economic Stability', *American Economic Review*, June.

*Friedman, M. (1953a), 'The Methodology of Positive Economics', in M. Friedman, *Essays in Positive Economics*, Chicago: University of Chicago Press.

*Friedman, M. (1953b), 'The Case for Flexible Exchange Rates', in M. Friedman, *Essays in Positive Economics*, Chicago: University of Chicago Press.

Friedman, M. (1956), 'The Quantity Theory of Money, A Restatement', in M. Friedman (ed.), *Studies in the Quantity Theory of Money*, Chicago: University of Chicago Press.

Friedman, M. (1957), *A Theory of the Consumption Function*, Princeton: Princeton University Press.

Friedman, M. (1958), 'The Supply of Money and Changes in Prices and Output', reprinted in *The Optimum Quantity of Money and Other Essays*, Chicago: Aldine, 1969.

Friedman, M. (1959), 'The Demand for Money – Some Theoretical and Empirical Results', *Journal of Political Economy*, June.

Friedman, M. (1960), *A Program for Monetary Stability*, New York: Fordham University Press.

Friedman, M. (1962), *Capitalism and Freedom*, Chicago: University of Chicago Press.

Friedman, M. (1966), 'Interest Rates and the Demand for Money', *Journal of Law and Economics*, October.

*Friedman, M. (1968a), 'The Role of Monetary Policy', *American Economic Review*, March.

Friedman, M. (1968b), 'Money: Quantity Theory', in D. Sills (ed.), *The International Encyclopedia of the Social Sciences*, New York: Macmillan Free Press.

Friedman, M. (1969), *The Optimum Quantity of Money and Other Essays*, Chicago: Aldine.

*Friedman, M. (1970a), 'A Theoretical Framework for Monetary Analysis', *Journal of Political Economy*, March/April.

Friedman, M. (1970b), 'Comment on Tobin', *Quarterly Journal of Economics*, May.

*Friedman, M. (1970c), *The Counter-Revolution in Monetary Theory*, IEA Occasional Paper No. 33, London: Institute of Economic Affairs.

Friedman, M. (1972), 'Comments on the Critics', *Journal of Political Economy*, September/October.

Friedman, M. (1974), *Monetary Correction*, IEA Occasional Paper No. 41, London: Institute of Economic Affairs.

*Friedman, M. (1975), *Unemployment Versus Inflation? An Evaluation of the Phillips Curve*, IEA Occasional Paper No. 44, London: Institute of Economic Affairs.

*Friedman, M. (1977), 'Nobel Lecture: Inflation and Unemployment', *Journal of Political Economy*, June.

Friedman, M. (1983), 'A Monetarist Reflects', *The Economist*, 4 June.

Friedman, M. (1984), 'Lessons from the 1979–82 Monetary Policy Experiment', *American Economic Review*, May.

Friedman, M. (1991), 'Old Wine in New Bottles', *Economic Journal*, January.

Friedman, M. (1992), *Money Mischief: Episodes in Monetary History*, New York: Harcourt Brace Jovanovich.

Friedman, M. (1993), 'The Plucking Model of Business Fluctuations Revisited', *Economic Inquiry*, April.

Friedman, M. and Meiselman, D. (1963), 'The Relative Stability of Monetary Velocity and the Investment Multiplier in the United States, 1897–1958', in *Commission on Money and Credit: Stabilization Policies*, Englewood Cliffs, NJ: Prentice-Hall.

Friedman, M. and Schwartz, A.J. (1963), *A Monetary History of the United States, 1867–1960*, Princeton: Princeton University Press.

Friedman, M. and Schwartz, A.J. (1982), *Monetary Trends in the United States and the United Kingdom: Their Relation to Income, Prices and Interest Rates*, Chicago: University of Chicago Press.

*Frisch, H. (1977), 'Inflation Theory 1963–1975: A Second Generation Survey', *Journal of Economic Literature*, Deember.

Frisch, R. (1933), 'Propagation Problems and Impulse Problems in Dynamic Economics', in *Essays in Honour of Gustav Cassel*, London: Allen and Unwin.

Frydman, R. and Phelps, E.S. (eds) (1983), *Individual Forecasting and Ag-

*gregate Outcomes: 'Rational Expectations' Examined*, Cambridge: Cambridge University Press.

Fukuyama, F. (1989), 'The End of History', *The National Interest*, Summer.

Fukuyama, F. (1992), *The End of History and the Last Man*, New York: The Free Press.

Fukuyama, F. (1995), *Trust: The Social Virtues and the Creation of Prosperity*, New York: The Free Press.

Galbraith, J. (1997), 'Time to Ditch the NAIRU', *Journal of Economic Perspectives*, Winter.

Galbraith, J.K. (1967), *The New Industrial State*, Boston, MA: Houghton Mifflin.

Galbraith, J.K. (1977), *The Age of Uncertainty*, Boston, MA: Houghton Mifflin.

Gali, J. (2002), 'New Perspectives on Monetary Policy and the Business Cycle', NBER Working Paper, No. 8767, February.

Gallup, J., Sachs, J.D. and Mellinger, A. (1998), 'Geography and Economic Development', NBER Working Paper, No. 6849, December.

*Galor, O. and Moav, O. (2001), 'Evolution and Growth', *European Economic Review*, May.

Galor, O. and Moav, O. (2002), 'Natural Selection and the Origin of Economic Growth', *Quarterly Journal of Economics*, November.

Galor, O. and Moav, O. (2003), 'Das Human Capital: A Theory of the Demise of Class Structure', Brown University Working Paper, July.

Galor, O. and Mountford, A. (2003), 'Trade, Demographic Transition and the Great Divergence: Why are a Third of People Indian or Chinese?', Brown University Working Paper, January.

*Galor, O. and Weil, D.N. (1999), 'From Malthusian Stagnation to Modern Growth', *American Economic Review*, May.

Galor, O. and Weil, D.N. (2000), 'Population, Technology, and Growth: From Malthusian Stagnation to the Demographic Transition and Beyond', *American Economic Review*, September.

*Garrison, R.W. (1989), 'The Austrian Theory of the Business Cycle in the Light of Modern Macroeconomics', *Review of Austrian Economics*.

Garrison, R.W. (1991), 'New Classical and Old Austrian Economics: Equilibrium Business Cycle Theory in Perspective', *Review of Austrian Economics*.

Garrison, R.W. (1992), 'Is Milton Friedman a Keynesian?', in M. Skousen (ed.), *Dissent on Keynes: A Critical Appraisal of Keynesian Economics*, New York: Praeger.

*Garrison, R.W. (2001), *Time and Money: The Macroeconomics of Capital Structure*, London: Routledge.

*Garrison, R.W. (2002), 'Business Cycles: Austrian Approach', in B. Snowdon and H.R. Vane (eds), *An Encyclopedia of Macroeconomics*, Cheltenham, UK and Northampton, MA, USA: Edward Elgar.

*Garrison, R.W. (2004), 'Overconsumption and Forced Saving in the Mises–Hayek Theory of the Business Cycle', *History of Political Economy*, Summer.

Gartner, M. (1996), 'Political Business Cycles When Real Activity is Persistent', *Journal of Macroeconomics*, Fall.

Gartner, M. (2000), 'Political Macroeconomics: A Survey of Recent Developments', *Journal of Economic Surveys*, December.

Geraats, P.M. (2002), 'Central Bank Transparency', *Economic Journal*, November.

Gerrard, B. (1988), 'Keynesian Economics: The Road to Nowhere', in J. Hillard (ed.), *J. M. Keynes in Retrospect*, Aldershot, UK and Brookfield, USA: Edward Elgar.

*Gerrard, B. (1991), 'Keynes's General Theory: Interpreting the Interpretations', *Economic Journal*, March.

Gerrard, B. (1996), 'Review Article: Competing Schools of Thought in Macroeconomics – An Ever-Changing Consensus? *Journal of Economic Studies*.

Gerschenkron, A. (1962), 'Economic Backwardness in Historical Perspective', in B.F. Hoselitz (ed.), *The Progress of Underdeveloped Areas*, Chicago: University of Chicago Press.

Ghosh, A. and Phillips, S. (1998), 'Warning: Inflation May be Harmful to Your Growth', *IMF Staff Papers*, December.

Glaescr, E. and Shleifer, A. (2002), 'Legal Origins', *Quarterly Journal of Economics*, November.

Glaeser, E., Scheinkman, J. and Shleifer, A. (2003), 'The Injustice of Inequality', *Journal of Monetary Economics*, January.

Glahe, F.R. (1973), *Macroeconomics: Theory and Policy*, New York: Harcourt Brace Jovanovich.

Goldin, C. (1995), 'Cliometrics and the Nobel', *Journal of Economic Perspectives*, Spring.

*Goldin, C. (2001), 'The Human Capital Century and American Leadership: Virtues of the Past', *Journal of Economic History*, June.

Golosov, M. and Lucas, R.E. Jr (2003), 'Menu Costs and Phillips Curves', NBER Working Paper, No. 10187, December.

*Goodfriend, M. (2004), 'Inflation Targeting in the US?', in B.S. Bernanke and M. Woodford (eds), *Inflation Targeting*, Chicago: University of Chicago Press.

*Goodfriend, M. and King, R.G. (1997), 'The New Neoclassical Synthesis and the Role of Monetary Policy', *NBER Macroeconomics Annual*.

Goodfriend, M. and McDermott, J. (1995), 'Early Development', *American Economic Review*, March.

*Goodhart, C.A.E. (1994a), 'Game Theory for Central Bankers: A Report to the Governor of the Bank of England', *Journal of Economic Literature*, March.

*Goodhart, C.A.E. (1994b), 'What Should Central Bankers Do? What Should be Their Macroeconomic Objectives and Operations?', *Economic Journal*, November.

Goodhart, C. and Presley, J. (1991), 'Real Business Cycle Theory: A Restatement of Robertsonian Economics?', Economic Research Paper, Loughborough University.

Gordon, D.F. (1974), 'A Neoclassical Theory of Keynesian Unemployment', *Economic Inquiry*, December.

Gordon, R.J. (1972), 'Wage Price Controls and the Shifting Phillips Curve', *Brookings Papers on Economic Activity*.

Gordon, R.J. (ed.) (1974), *Milton Friedman's Monetary Framework: A Debate With His Critics*, Chicago: University of Chicago Press.

Gordon, R.J. (1975), 'Alternative Responses to External Supply Shocks', *Brookings Papers on Economic Activity*.

Gordon, R.J. (1976), 'Recent Developments in the Theory of Inflation and Unemployment', *Journal of Monetary Economics*, April.

Gordon, R.J. (1978), 'What Can Stabilisation Policy Achieve?', *American Economic Review*, May.

*Gordon, R.J. (1981), 'Output Fluctuations and Gradual Price Adjustment', *Journal of Economic Literature*, June.

Gordon, R.J. (1982a), 'Price Inertia and Policy Ineffectiveness in the United States, 1890–1980', *Journal of Political Economy*, December.

Gordon, R.J. (1982b), 'Why US Wage and Employment Behaviour Differs From That in Britain and Japan', *Economic Journal*, March.

Gordon, R.J. (ed.) (1986), *The American Business Cycle: Continuity and Change*, Chicago: University of Chicago Press.

Gordon, R.J. (1988), 'Hysteresis in History: Was There Ever a Phillips Curve?', *American Economic Review*, May.

Gordon, R.J. (1989), 'Fresh Water, Salt Water, and Other Macroeconomic Elixirs', *Economic Record*, June.

*Gordon, R.J. (1990), 'What Is New-Keynesian Economics?', *Journal of Economic Literature*, September.

Gordon, R.J. (1993), *Macroeconomics*, 6th edn, New York: HarperCollins.

*Gordon, R.J. (1997), 'The Time-Varying NAIRU and its Implications for Economic Policy', *Journal of Economic Perspectives*, Winter.

*Gordon, R.J. (1998), 'Foundations of the Goldilocks Economy: Supply Shocks and the Time-Varying NAIRU', *Brookings Papers on Economic Activity*.

Gordon, R.J. (2000a), *Macroeconomics*, 8th edn, New York: Addison-Wesley.

Gordon, R.J. (2000b), 'Does the New Economy Measure Up to the Great Inventions of the Past?', *Journal of Economic Perspectives*, Fall.

*Gordon, R.J. (2003), *Macroeconomics*, 9th edn, New York: Addison-Wesley.

Grandmont, J.M. and Laroque, G. (1976), 'On Temporary Keynesian Equilibrium', *Review of Economic Studies*, February.

Gray, C. and McPherson, M. (2001), 'The Leadership Factor in African Policy Reform and Growth', *Economic Development and Cultural Change*, July.

Green, J. (1996), 'Inflation Targeting: Theory and Policy Implications', *IMF Staff Papers*, December.

*Greenspan, A. (2004), 'Risk and Uncertainty in Monetary Policy', *American Economic Review*, May.

*Greenwald, B.C. and Stiglitz, J.E. (1987), 'Keynesian, New Keynesian and New Classical Economics', *Oxford Economic Papers*, March.

Greenwald, B.C. and Stiglitz, J.E. (1988), 'Examining Alternative Macroeconomic Theories', *Brookings Papers on Economic Activity*.

*Greenwald, B.C. and Stiglitz, J.E. (1993a), 'New and Old Keynesians', *Journal of Economic Perspectives*, Winter.

Greenwald, B.C. and Stiglitz, J.E. (1993b), 'Financial Market Imperfections and Business Cycles', *Quarterly Journal of Economics*, February.

Grief, A. (2003), *Comparative and Historical Institutional Analysis: A Game Theoretic Perspective*, Cambridge: Cambridge University Press.

Griffin, K. (1970), 'Foreign Capital, Domestic Savings and Economic Development', *Oxford Bulletin of Economics and Statistics*, May.

Grilli, V., Masciandaro, D. and Tabellini, G. (1991), 'Political and Monetary Institutions and Public Finance Policies in the Industrialised Countries', *Economic Policy*, October.

Grossman, G. and Helpman, E. (1990), 'Trade, Innovation and Growth', *American Economic Review*, May.

Grossman, G. and Helpman, E. (1991), *Innovation and Growth in the Global Economy*, Cambridge, MA: MIT Press.

*Grossman, G. and Helpman, E. (1994), 'Endogenous Innovation in the Theory of Growth', *Journal of Economic Perspectives*, Winter.

Gujarati, D. (1972), 'The Behaviour of Unemployment and Unfilled Vacancies: Great Britain, 1958–71', *Economic Journal*, March.

Gyimah-Brempong, K. (2002), 'Corruption, Economic Growth and Income Inequality in Africa', *Economics of Governance*, November.

Gylfason, T. (1999), *Principles of Economic Growth*, Oxford: Oxford University Press.

Haberler, G. (1937), *Prosperity and Depression*, Cambridge, MA: Harvard University Press.

Haberler, G. (1963), *Prosperity and Depression*, 4th edn, New York: Atheneum.

Hahn, F.H. (1977), 'Keynesian Economics and General Equilibrium Theory', in G.C. Harcourt (ed.), *The Microfoundations of Macroeconomics*, London: Macmillan.

Hahn, F. (1982), *Money and Inflation*, Oxford: Basil Blackwell.

Hahn, F.H. (1987), 'On Involuntary Unemployment', *Economic Journal*, Supplement.

Hahn, F.H. and Matthews, R.C.O. (1964), 'The Theory of Economic Growth: A Survey', *Economic Journal*, December.

Hahn, F.H. and Solow, R.M. (1995), *A Critical Essay on Modern Macroeconomic Theory*, Cambridge, MA: MIT Press.

Haldane, A. (1998), 'On Inflation Targeting in the United Kingdom', *Scottish Journal of Political Economy*, February.

Haley, J. (1990), 'Theoretical Foundations of Sticky Wages', *Journal of Economic Surveys*.

Hall, R.E. (1991), 'Labour Demand, Labour Supply and Employment Volatility', *NBER Macroeconomics Annual*.

*Hall, R.E. (1996), 'Robert Lucas, Recipient of the 1995 Nobel Memorial Prize in Economics', *Scandinavian Journal of Economics*, March.

Hall, R.E. (2003), 'Modern Theory of Unemployment Fluctuations: Empirics and Policy Applications', *American Economic Review*, May.

Hall, R.E. and Jones, C.I. (1997), 'Levels of Economic Activity Across Countries', *American Economic Review*, May.

Hall, R.E. and Jones, C.I. (1999), 'Why Do Some Countries Produce So Much More Output Per Worker Than Others?', *Quarterly Journal of Economics*, February.

Hall, R.E. and Taylor, J.B. (1997), *Macroeconomics*, 5th edn, New York: W.W. Norton.

*Hall, T.E. and Ferguson, J.D. (1998), *The Great Depression: An International Disaster of Perverse Economic Policies*, Ann Arbor: University of Michigan Press.

Hamberg, D. (1971), *Models of Economic Growth*, New York: Harper and Row.

Hamilton, J.D. (1983), 'Oil and the Macroeconomy Since World War II', *Journal of Political Economy*, April.

Hamilton, J.D. (1988), 'The Role of the Gold Standard in Propagating the Great Depression', *Contemporary Policy Issues*, April.

Hamilton, J.D. (1996), 'This is What Happened to the Oil Price–Macroeconomic Relationship', *Journal of Monetary Economics*, October.

*Hammond, J.D. (1996), *Theory and Measurement: Causality Issues in Milton Friedman's Monetary Economics*, Cambridge: Cambridge University Press.

Hamouda, O.F. and Harcourt, G.C. (1988), 'Post Keynesianism: From Criticism to Coherence', *Bulletin of Economic Research*, January.

Hansen, A.H. (1949), *Monetary Theory and Fiscal Policy*, New York: McGraw-Hill.

Hansen, A.H. (1953), *A Guide to Keynes*, New York: McGraw-Hill.

Hansen, B. (1970), 'Excess Demand, Unemployment, Vacancies and Wages', *Quarterly Journal of Economics*, February.

Hansen, G.D. (1985), 'Indivisible Labour and the Business Cycle', *Journal of Monetary Economics*, November.

Hansen, G.D. and Prescott, E.C. (1993), 'Did Technology Cause the 1990–1991 Recession?', *American Economic Review*, May.

Hansen, G.D. and Prescott, E.C. (2002), 'Malthus to Solow', *American Economic Review*, September.

Hansen, L.P. and Heckman, J.J. (1996), 'The Empirical Foundations of Calibration', *Journal of Economic Perspectives*, Winter.

Harcourt, G.C. (1972), *Some Cambridge Controversies in the Theory of Capital*, Cambridge: Cambridge University Press.

Hargreaves-Heap, S.P. (1980), 'Choosing the Wrong Natural Rate: Accelerating Inflation or Decelerating Employment and Growth?', *Economic Journal*, September.

Hargreaves-Heap, S.P. (1992), *The New Keynesian Macroeconomics: Time Belief and Social Interdependence*, Aldershot, UK and Brookfield, USA: Edward Elgar.

Hargreaves-Heap, S.P. (2002), 'New Keynesian Economics', in B. Snowdon and H.R. Vane (eds), *An Encyclopedia of Macroeconomics*, Cheltenham, UK and Northampton, MA, USA: Edward Elgar.

*Harrison, L.E. and Huntington, S.P. (eds) (2000), *Culture Matters: How Values Shape Human Progress*, New York: Basic Books.

Harrod, R. (1939), 'An Essay in Dynamic Theory', *Economic Journal*, March.

Harrod, R.F. (1948), *Towards a Dynamic Economics*, London: Macmillan.

Harrod, R. (1951), *The Life of John Maynard Keynes*, London: Macmillan.

Hartley, J.E. (1997), *The Representative Agent in Macroeconomics*, London: Routledge.

*Hartley, J.E., Hoover, K.D. and Salyer, K.D. (1997), 'The Limits of Business Cycle Research: Assessing the Real Business Cycle Model', *Oxford Review of Economic Policy*, Autumn.

Hartley, J.E., Hoover, K.D. and Salyer, K.D. (eds) (1998), *Real Business Cycles: A Reader*, London: Routledge.

Havrilesky, T.M. (1993), *The Pressures on Monetary Policy*, Norwell: Kluwer Academic Publishers.

Hayek, F.A. (1931), 'Reflections on the Pure Theory of Money of Mr. J.M. Keynes', *Economica*, August.

Hayek, F.A. (1933), *Monetary Theory and the Trade Cycle*, London: Jonathan Cape.

Hayek, F.A. (1945), 'The Use of Knowledge in Society', *American Economic Review*, September.

*Hayek, F.A. (1948), *Individualism and Economic Order*, London: Routledge and Kegan Paul.

Hayek, F.A. (1967[1935]), *Prices and Production*, 2nd edn, New York: Augustus M. Kelley.

Hayek, F.A. (1976), *Denationalisation of Money: An Analysis of the Theory and Practice of Concurrent Currencies*, London: Institute of Economic Affairs.

*Hayek, F.A. (1978), *A Tiger By the Tail: The Keynesian Legacy of Inflation*, 2nd edn, London: Institute of Economic Affairs.

Hayek, F.A. (1983), 'The Austrian Critique', *The Economist*, 11 June.

Haynes, S.E. and Stone, J.A. (1990), 'Political Models of the Business Cycle Should be Revived', *Economic Inquiry*, July.

Heckman, J.J. (2003), 'China's Investment in Human Capital', *Economic Development and Cultural Change*, July.

Healey, N. (1996), 'What Price Central Bank Independence?', *Review of Policy Issues*, Spring.

Heilbroner, R.L. (1989), *The Making of Economic Society*, 8th edn, Englewood Cliffs, NJ: Prentice-Hall.

Heinlein, R. (1966), *The Moon is a Harsh Mistress*, New York: Putnam.

Hennings, K.H. (1997), *The Austrian Theory of Value and Capital: Studies in the Life and Work of Eugen von Böhm-Bawerk*, Cheltenham, UK and Lyme, USA: Edward Elgar.

Henry, S.G.B. and Ormerod, P.A. (1978), 'Incomes Policy and Wage Inflation: Empirical Evidence for the U.K. 1961–1977', *National Institute Economic Review*, August.

Herbst, J. (2000), *States and Power in Africa: Comparative Lessons in Authority and Control*, Princeton: Princeton University Press.

Hess, G.D. and Shin, K. (1997), 'International and Intranational Business Cycles', *Oxford Review of Economic Policy*, Autumn.

Heymann, D. and Leijonhufvud, A. (1995), *High Inflation*, Oxford: Oxford University Press.

Hibbs, D.A. (1977), 'Political Parties and Macroeconomic Policy', *American Political Science Review*, December.

Hibbs, D.A. (1987), *The American Political Economy: Electoral Policy and Macroeconomics in Contemporary America*, Cambridge, MA: Harvard University Press.

*Hibbs, D.A. (2001), 'The Politicisation of Growth Theory', *Kyklos*.

Hicks, J.R. (1937), 'Mr. Keynes and the "Classics": A Suggested Interpretation', *Econometrica*, April.

Hicks, J.R. (1950), *A Contribution to the Theory of the Trade Cycle*, Oxford: Oxford University Press.

Hicks, J.R. (1974), *The Crisis in Keynesian Economics*, Oxford: Basil Blackwell.

Hicks, J.R. (1977), *Economic Perspectives*, Oxford: Oxford University Press.

Hicks, J.R. (1979), *Causality in Economics*, New York: Basic Books.

Hirschman, A. (1973), 'The Changing Tolerance for Income Inequality in the Course of Economic Development', *Quarterly Journal of Economics*, November.

Holt, R.P.F. (1997), 'Post Keynesian School of Economics', in T. Cate (ed.), *An Encyclopedia of Keynesian Economics*, Cheltenham, UK and Lyme, USA: Edward Elgar.

*Hoover, K.D. (1984), 'Two Types of Monetarism', *Journal of Economic Literature*, March.

*Hoover, K.D. (1988), *The New Classical Macroeconomics: A Sceptical Inquiry*, Oxford: Basil Blackwell.

Hoover, K.D. (1991), 'The Causal Direction Between Money and Prices', *Journal of Monetary Economics*, June.

Hoover, K.D. (ed.) (1992), *The New Classical Macroeconomics*, Aldershot, UK and Brookfield, USA: Edward Elgar.

Hoover, K.D. (ed.) (1995a), *Macroeconometrics: Developments, Tensions and Prospects*, Boston, MA: Kluwer Academic Publishers.

Hoover, K.D. (1995b), 'Facts and Artifacts: Calibration and the Empirical Assessment of Real-Business Cycle Models', *Oxford Economic Papers*, January.

Hoover, K.D. (1995c), 'Relative Wages, Rationality and Involuntary Unemployment in Keynes's Labour Market', *History of Political Economy*, Winter.

Hoover, K.D. (ed.) (1999), *The Legacy of Robert E. Lucas Jr.*, Cheltenham, UK and Northampton, MA, USA: Edward Elgar.

*Hoover, K.D. (2001a), *Causality in Macroeconomics*, Cambridge: Cambridge University Press.

*Hoover, K.D. (2001b), *The Methodology of Empirical Macroeconomics*, Cambridge: Cambridge University Press.

Hoover, K.D. and Perez, S.J. (1994), 'Post Hoc Ergo Propter Once More: An Evaluation of "Does Monetary Policy Matter?" in the Spirit of James Tobin', *Journal of Monetary Economics*, August.

Horrell, S. (2003), 'The Wonderful Usefulness of History', *Economic Journal*, February.

*Horwitz, S.G. (2000), *Microfoundations and Macroeconomics: An Austrian Perspective*, London: Routledge.

Howitt, P.W. (1986), 'The Keynesian Recovery', *Canadian Journal of Economics*, November.

Howitt, P.W. (1990), *The Keynesian Recovery*, Oxford: Philip Allan.

Hsieh, C. (1999), 'Productivity Growth and Factor Prices in East Asia', *American Economic Review*, May.

Hume, D. (1752), 'Of Money', reprinted in A.A. Walters (ed.), *Money and Banking*, Harmondsworth: Penguin.

Huntington, S.P. (1996), *The Clash of Civilisations and the Remaking of the World Order*, London: Simon Schuster.

Hutchison, M.M. and Walsh, C.E. (1998), 'The Output–Inflation Tradeoff and Central Bank Reform: Evidence from New Zealand', *Economic Journal*, May.

Hutchison, T.W. (1977), *Keynes v The Keynesians*, London: Institute of Economic Affairs.

Inada, K. (1963), 'On a Two-Sector Model of Economic Growth: Comments and Generalisations', *Review of Economic Studies*, June.

Ireland, P.N. (2004), 'Technology Shocks in the New Keynesian Model', NBER Working Paper, No. 10309, February.

Irwin, D. (1996), *Against the Tide: An Intellectual History of Free Trade*, Princeton: Princeton University Press.

*Islam, N. (2003), 'What Have We Learned From the Convergence Debate?', *Journal of Economic Surveys*, July.

Jackson, D., Turner, H.A. and Wilkinson, F. (1972), *Do Trade Unions Cause Inflation?*, Cambridge: Cambridge University Press.

Jaffe, D. and Stiglitz, J.E. (1990), 'Credit Rationing', in B.M. Friedman and F.H. Hahn (eds), *Handbook of Monetary Economics*, Vol. II, Amsterdam: North-Holland.

James, H. (2001), *The End of Globalisation: Lessons from the Great Depression*, Cambridge, MA: Harvard University Press.

Jansen, D.W., Delorme, C.D and Ekelund, R.E. (1994), *Intermediate Macroeconomics*, New York: West Publishing Co.

Jay, P. (2000), *Road to Riches or the Wealth of Man*, London: Weidenfeld and Nicolson.

Jenkins, M.A. (1996), 'Central Bank Independence and Inflation Performance: Panacea or Placebo?', *Banca Nazionale del Lavoro Quarterly Review*, June.

Johnson, E.S. (1978), 'Keynes as a Literary Craftsman', in E.S. Johnson and H.G. Johnson (eds), *The Shadow of Keynes*, Oxford: Basil Blackwell.

Johnson, H.G. (1958), 'Planning and the Market in Economic Development', *Pakistan Economic Journal*, June.

Johnson, H.G. (1964), *Money, Trade and Economic Growth*, London: Allen and Unwin; excerpt from Chapter 5 reprinted in R.W. Clower (ed.), *Monetary Theory*, Harmondsworth: Penguin (1969) – page reference in text refers to reprint.

Johnson, H.G. (1969), 'Inside Money, Outside Money, Income, Wealth and Welfare in Monetary Theory', *Journal of Money, Credit, and Banking*, February.

*Johnson, H.G. (1971), 'The Keynesian Revolution and the Monetarist Counter-Revolution', *American Economic Review*, May.

Johnson, H.G. (1972a), 'The Monetary Approach to Balance of Payments Theory', in H.G. Johnson (ed.), *Further Essays in Monetary Economics*, London: Macmillan.

Johnson, H.G. (1972b), 'Inflation: A Monetarist View', in H.G. Johnson (ed.), *Further Essays in Monetary Economics*, London: Macmillan.

Jones, C.I. (1994), 'Economic Growth and the Relative Price of Capital', *Journal of Monetary Economics*, December.

Jones, C.I. (1995), 'Time Series Tests of Endogenous Growth Models', *Quarterly Journal of Economics*, May.

*Jones, C.I. (1997a), 'On the Evolution of World Income Distribution', *Journal of Economic Perspectives*, Summer.

Jones, C.I. (1997b), 'Convergence Revisited', *Journal of Economic Growth*, July.

*Jones, C.I. (2001a), *Introduction to Economic Growth*, 2nd edn, New York: W.W. Norton.

Jones, C.I. (2001b), 'Was an Industrial Revolution Inevitable? Economic Growth Over the Very Long Run', *Advances in Macroeconomics*, August.

Jones, C.I. (2002), 'Sources of US Economic Growth in a World of Ideas', *American Economic Review*, March.

Jones, C.I. (2004), 'The Shape of Production Functions and the Direction of Technical Change', Department of Economics, University of California, Berkeley, Working Paper.

Jones, C.I. (2005), 'Growth and Ideas', in P. Aghion and S. Durlauf (eds), *Handbook of Economic Growth*, Amsterdam: Elsevier.

Jones, C.I. and Williams, J.C. (1998), 'Measuring the Social Return to R and D', *Quarterly Journal of Economics*, November.

Jones, C.I. and Williams, J.C. (2000), 'Too Much of a Good Thing? The Economics of Investment in R and D', *Journal of Economic Growth*, March.

*Jones, E.L. (1988), *Growth Recurring: Economic Change in World History*, Ann Arbor: University of Michigan Press.

Jones, H.G. (1975), *An Introduction to Modern Theories of Economic Growth*, Sunbury-on-Thames: Nelson.

Jorgenson, D.W. (1963), 'Capital Theory and Investment Behaviour', *American Economic Review*, May.

Jorgenson, D.W. (1996), *Postwar US Economic Growth*, Cambridge, MA: MIT Press.

*Jorgenson, D.W. (2001), 'Information Technology and the US Economy', *American Economic Review*, March.

Jorgenson, D.W. and Stiroh, K. (2000), 'Raising the Speed Limit: US Economic Growth in the Information Age', *Brookings Papers on Economic Activity*.

Judd, J.P and Trehan, B. (1995), 'The Cyclical Behaviour of Prices: Interpreting the Evidence', *Journal of Money, Credit, and Banking*, August.

Kahn, R.F. (1929), 'The Economics of the Short Period', unpublished Fellowship Dissertation, Cambridge; published in 1989, London: Macmillan.

Kahn, R.F. (1931), 'The Relation of Home Investment to Unemployment', *Economic Journal*, June.

Kahn, R.F. (1984), *The Making of Keynes's General Theory*, Cambridge: Cambridge University Press.

Kaldor, N. (1955), 'Alternative Theories of Distribution', *Review of Economic Studies*, January.

Kaldor, N. (1961), 'Capital Accumulation and Economic Growth', in F.A. Lutz and D.C. Hague (eds), *The Theory of Capital*, New York: St Martin's Press.

Kaldor, N. (1970a), 'The New Monetarism', *Lloyds Bank Review*, July.

Kaldor, N. (1970b), 'The Case for Regional Policies', *Scottish Journal of Political Economy*, November.

*Kalecki, M. (1943), 'Political Aspects of Full Employment', *Political Quarterly*, October/December.

Kareken, J. and Solow, R.N. (1963), 'Monetary Policy: Lags versus Simultaneity', in *Commission on Money and Credit: Stabilization Policies*, Englewood Cliffs, NJ: Prentice-Hall.

*Kasper, S.D. (2002), *The Revival of Laissez-Faire in American Macroeconomic Theory,* Cheltenham, UK and Northampton, MA, USA: Edward Elgar.

Katz, L.F. (1986), 'Efficiency Wage Theories: A Partial Evaluation', *NBER Macroeconomics Annual*.

Katz, L.F. (1988), 'Some Recent Developments in Labour Economics and Their Implications for Macroeconomics', *Journal of Money, Credit, and Banking*, August.

Katz, L.F. and Krueger, A.B. (1999), 'The High-Pressure Labour Market', *Brookings Papers on Economic Activity*.

*Keech, W. (1995), *Economic Politics: The Costs of Democracy*, Cambridge: Cambridge University Press.

Keegan, W. (1984), *Mrs Thatcher's Economic Experiment*, Harmondsworth: Penguin.

Kehoe, T.J. and Prescott, E.C. (2002), 'Great Depressions of the Twentieth Century', *Economic Dynamics*, January.

Kelly, L.C. (2002), 'Pursuing Problems in Economic Growth', *Journal of Economic Growth*, September.

Kenny, C. and Williams, D. (2001), 'What Do We Know About Economic Growth? Or Why Don't We Know Very Much?', *World Development*, January.

Keuzenkamp, H.A. (1991), 'A Precursor to Muth: Tinbergen's 1932 Model of Rational Expectations', *Economic Journal*, September.

Keynes, J.M. (1913), *Indian Currency and Finance*, London: Macmillan.

Keynes, J.M. (1919), *The Economic Consequences of the Peace*, London: Macmillan.

Keynes, J.M. (1921), *A Treatise on Probability*, London: Macmillan.

Keynes, J.M. (1923), *A Tract on Monetary Reform*, London: Macmillan.

Keynes, J.M. (1925), *The Economic Consequences of Mr. Churchill*, London: Hogarth Press.

Keynes, J.M. (1926), *The End of Laissez-Faire*, London: Hogarth Press.

Keynes, J.M. (1929), 'A Programme of Expansion'; reprinted in *Essays in Persuasion* (1972), London: Macmillan.

Keynes, J.M. (1930a), *A Treatise on Money*, London: Macmillan.

Keynes, J.M. (1930b), 'The Economic Possibilities of Our Grandchildren', *Nation and Athenaeum*, October; reprinted in *Essays in Persuasion* (1963), New York: W.W. Norton.

Keynes, J.M. (1933), 'A Monetary Theory of Production', reprinted in D. Moggridge (ed.) (1973a), *The Collected Writings of John Maynard Keynes, XIII*, London: Macmillan.

*Keynes, J.M. (1936), *The General Theory of Employment, Interest and Money*, London: Macmillan.

*Keynes, J.M. (1937), 'The General Theory of Employment', *Quarterly Journal of Economics*, February; reprinted in D. Moggridge (ed.) (1973b), *The Collected Writings of John Maynard Keynes, XIV*, London: Macmillan.

Keynes, J.M. (1939a), 'Relative Movements in Real Wages and Output', *Economic Journal*, March.

Keynes, J.M. (1939b), 'Professor Tinbergen's Method', *Economic Journal*; reprinted in D. Moggridge (ed.) (1973b), *The Collected Writings of John Maynard Keynes, XIV*, London: Macmillan.

Keynes, J.M. (1940), *How to Pay for the War*, London: Macmillan.

*Keynes, J.M. (1972), Vol. IX, *Essays in Persuasion*, London: Macmillan.

Keynes, J.M. (1973a), *The Collected Writings of John Maynard Keynes, XIII*, edited by D. Moggridge, London: Macmillan.

Keynes, J.M. (1973b), *The Collected Writings of John Maynard Keynes, XIV*, edited by D. Moggridge, London: Macmillan.

Keynes, J.M. (1979), *The Collected Writings of John Maynard Keynes, XXIX*, edited by D. Moggridge, London: Macmillan.

Keynes, J.M. and Henderson, H. (1929), *Can Lloyd George Do It?*, London: Hogarth Press.

Khan, Z. and Sokoloff, K.L. (2001), 'The Early Development of Intellectual Property Institutions in the United States', *Journal of Economic Perspectives*, Summer.

Killick, T. (1976), 'The Possibilities of Development Planning', *Oxford Economic Papers*, July.

Kim, J.-I. and Lau, L.J. (1994), 'The Sources of Economic Growth of the Asian Newly Industrialized Countries', *Journal of the Japanese and International Economies*.

Kim, K. (1988), *Equilibrium Business Cycle Theory in Historical Perspective*, Cambridge: Cambridge University Press.

*King, M. (1997a), 'The Inflation Target Five Years On', *Bank of England Quarterly Bulletin*, November.

King, M. (1997b), 'Changes in UK Monetary Policy: Rules and Discretion in Practice', *Journal of Monetary Economics*, June.

King, M. (1999), 'Monetary Policy and the Labour Market', *Bank of England Quarterly Bulletin*, February.

*King, M. (2004), 'The Institutions of Monetary Policy', *American Economic Review*, May.

King, R.G. (1993), 'Will the New Keynesian Macroeconomics Resurrect the IS–LM Model?', *Journal of Economic Perspectives*, Winter.

King, R.G. and Levine, R. (1994), 'Capital Fundamentalism, Economic Development and Economic Growth', *Carnegie-Rochester Conference Series on Public Policy*, Vol. 40.

King, R.G. and Plosser, C.I. (1984), 'Money, Credit and Prices in a Real Business Cycle', *American Economic Review*, June.

King, R.G., Plosser, C.I. and Rebelo, S.T. (1988a), 'Production Growth and Business Cycles: I. The Basic Neoclassical Model', *Journal of Monetary Economics*, March.

King, R.G., Plosser, C.I. and Rebelo, S.T. (1988b), 'Production Growth and Business Cycles: II. New Directions', *Journal of Monetary Economics*, May.

Kirman, A.P. (1992), 'Whom or What Does the Representative Individual Represent?', *Journal of Economic Perspectives*, Spring.

Kirschner, D. and Rhee, W. (1996), 'Predicting the Pattern of Economics Research: The Case of Real Business Cycle Theory', *Journal of Macroeconomics*, Spring.

*Kirshner, J. (2001), 'The Political Economy of Low Inflation', *Journal of Economic Surveys*, January.

*Klamer, A. (1984), *The New Classical Macroeconomics*, Brighton: Wheatsheaf.

Klein, L.R. (1946), 'Macroeconomics and the Theory of Rational Behaviour', *Econometrica*, April.

Klein, L.R. (1947), *The Keynesian Revolution*, New York: Macmillan.

Klein, L.R. (1968), *The Keynesian Revolution*, 2nd edn, London: Macmillan.

Klein, L.R. and Goldberger, A.S. (1955), *An Econometric Model of the United States, 1929–1952*, Amsterdam: North-Holland.

*Klenow, P.J. and Rodriguez-Clare, A. (1997a), 'Economic Growth: A Review Essay', *Journal of Monetary Economics*, December.

*Klenow, P.J. and Rodriguez-Clare, A. (1997b), 'The Neoclassical Revival in Growth Economics: Has it Gone Too Far?', *NBER Macroeconomics Annual*.

Knack, S. and Keefer, P. (1995), 'Institutions and Economic Performance: Cross Country Tests Using Alternative Institutional Measures', *Economics and Politics*, November.

Knack, S. and Keefer, P. (1997a), 'Why Don't Poor Countries Catch Up? A Cross-National Test of an Institutional Explanation', *Economic Inquiry*, July.

Knack, S. and Keefer, P. (1997b), 'Does Social Capital Have an Economic Payoff? A Cross Country Investigation', *Quarterly Journal of Economics*, November.

Knight, F.H. (1933), *Risk, Uncertainty and Profit*, London: London School of Economics, reprint; first published in 1921.

Koopmans, T.C. (1949), 'The Econometric Approach to Business Fluctuations', *American Economic Review*, May.

Koopmans, T.C. (1965), 'On the Concept of Optimal Economic Growth', in *The Econometric Approach to Development Planning*, Amsterdam: North-Holland.

Kornai, J. (1992), *The Socialist System: The Political Economy of Communism*, Oxford: Clarendon Press.

*Kornai, J. (2000), 'What the Change of System from Socialism to Capitalism Does and Does Not Mean', *Journal of Economic Perspectives*, Winter.

Kramer, G.H. (1971), 'Short-term Fluctuations in US Voting Behaviour, 1896–1964', *American Political Science Review*, March.

Kremer, M. (1993), 'Population Growth and Technological Change: One Million B.C. to 1990', *Quarterly Journal of Economics*, August.

Kremer, M. (1998), 'Patent Buyouts: A Mechanism for Encouraging Innovation', *Quarterly Journal of Economics*, November.

Kreps, D.M. (1988), *Notes on the Theory of Choice*, Boulder: Westview Press.

Krueger, A.O. (1978), *Foreign Trade Regimes and Economic Development: Liberalisation Attempts and Consequences*, Cambridge, MA: Ballinger.

*Krueger, A.O. (1997), 'Trade Policy and Economic Development: How We Learn', *American Economic Review*, March.

*Krueger, A.O. (1998), 'Why Trade Liberalisation is Good for Growth', *Economic Journal*, September.

Krugman, P. (1991a), *Geography and Trade*, Cambridge, MA: MIT Press.

Krugman, P. (1991b), 'Increasing Returns and Economic Geography', *Journal of Political Economy*, June.

Krugman, P. (1994a), *Peddling Prosperity: Economic Sense and Nonsense in the Age of Diminished Expectations*, New York: W.W. Norton.

Krugman, P. (1994b), 'The Myth of Asia's Miracle', *Foreign Affairs*, November/December.

Krugman, P. (1994c), 'The Fall and Rise of Development Economics', in L. Rodwin and D.A. Schon (eds), *Rethinking the Development Experience: Essays Provoked by the Work of O. Hirschman*, Washington, DC: Brookings Institution; Cambridge, MA: Lincoln Institute of Land Policy.

Krugman, P. (1997), *Development, Geography and Economic Theory*, Cambridge, MA: MIT Press.

Krugman, P. (1998), 'Its Baaack! Japan's Slump and the Return of the Liquidity Trap', *Brookings Papers on Economic Activity*.

*Krugman, P. (1999), *The Return of Depression Economics*, New York: W.W. Norton.

Krugman, P. and Venables, A.J. (1995), 'Globalisation and the Inequality of Nations', *Quarterly Journal of Economics*, November.

Kumar, S. and Russell, R.R. (2002), 'Technological Change, Technological Catch-Up, and Capital Deepening: Relative Contributions to Growth and Convergence', *American Economic Review*, June.

Kuznets, S. (1955), 'Economic Growth and Income Inequality', *American Economic Review*, March.

Kuznets, S. (1966), *Modern Economic Growth*, New Haven: Yale University Press.

*Kydland, F.E. and Prescott, E.C. (1977), 'Rules Rather Than Discretion: The Inconsistency of Optimal Plans', *Journal of Political Economy*, June.

Kydland, F.E. and Prescott, E.C. (1982), 'Time to Build and Aggregate Fluctuations', *Econometrica*, November.

Kydland, F.E. and Prescott, E.C. (1990), 'Business Cycles: Real Facts and the Monetary Myth', *Federal Reserve Bank of Minneapolis Quarterly Review*, Spring.

Kydland, F.E. and Prescott, E.C. (1991), 'Hours and Employment Variation in Business Cycle Theory', *Economic Theory*.

*Kydland, F.E. and Prescott, E.C. (1996), 'The Computational Experiment: An Econometric Tool', *Journal of Economic Perspectives*, Winter.

Laband, D. and Wells, J. (1998), 'The Scholarly Journal Literature of Economics: An Historical Profile of the AER, JPE and QJE', *American Economist*, Fall.

Laidler, D.E.W. (1976), 'Inflation in Britain: A Monetarist Perspective', *American Economic Review*, September.

*Laidler, D.E.W. (1981), 'Monetarism: An Interpretation and an Assessment', *Economic Journal*, March.

Laidler, D.E.W. (1982), *Monetarist Perspectives*, Oxford: Philip Allan.

*Laidler, D.E.W. (1986), 'The New Classical Contribution to Macroeconomics', *Banca Nazionale del Lavoro Quarterly Review*, March.

Laidler, D.E.W. (1991), *The Golden Age of the Quantity Theory: The Development of Neoclassical Monetary Economies 1870–1914*, Oxford: Philip Allan.

Laidler, D.E.W. (1992a), 'The Cycle Before New Classical Economics', in M. Belongia and M. Garfinkel (eds), *The Business Cycle: Theories and Evidence*, London: Kluwer Academic Publishers.

Laidler, D.E.W. (1992b), 'Issues in Contemporary Macroeconomies', in A. Vercelli and N. Dimitri (eds), *Macroeconomies: A Survey of Research Strategies*, Oxford: Oxford University Press.

Laidler, D.E.W. (1993), *The Demand for Money: Theories, Evidence and Problems*, 4th edn, New York: HarperCollins.

*Laidler, D.E.W. (1999), *Fabricating the Keynesian Revolution: Studies of the Inter-War Literature on Money, the Cycle, and Unemployment*, Cambridge: Cambridge University Press.

Laing, D. (1993), 'A Signalling Theory of Nominal Wage Inflexibility', *Economic Journal*, November.

Lakatos, I. (1978), *The Methodology of Scientific Research Programmes*, Cambridge: Cambridge University Press.

Lake, D. (1992), 'Powerful Pacifists: Democratic States and War', *American Political Science Review*, March.

Lal, D. (1999), *Unintended Consequences: The Impact of Factor Endowments, Culture and Politics on Long-Run Economic Performance*, Cambridge, MA: MIT Press.

*Landau, R., Taylor, T. and Wright, G. (eds) (1996), *The Mosaic of Economic Growth*, Stanford: Stanford University Press.

Landes, D.S. (1969), *The Unbound Prometheus: Technological Change and Development in Western Europe from 1750 to the Present*, Cambridge: Cambridge University Press.

Landes, D.S. (1990), 'Why Are We So Rich and They So Poor?', *American Economic Review*, May.

*Landes, D.S. (1998), *The Wealth and Poverty of Nations: Why Some Are So Rich and Some So Poor*, New York: W.W. Norton.

Landman, T. (1999), 'Economic Development and Democracy: The View from Latin America', *Political Studies*, September.

Lawrence, R. and Weinstein, D. (2001), 'Trade and Growth: Import-Led or Export-Led? Evidence from Japan and Korea', in J.E. Stiglitz and S. Yusuf (eds), *Rethinking the East Asian Miracle*, Oxford: Oxford University Press.

Lawson, T. and Pesaran, H. (eds) (1985), *Keynes's Economics: Methodological Issues*, London: Croom Helm.

Layard, R. and Nickell, S.J. (1998), 'Labour Market Institutions and Economic Performance', Centre for Economic Performance (LSE) Discussion Paper, No. 407.

Layard, R., Nickell, S.J. and Jackman, R. (1991), *Unemployment, Macroeconomic Performance and the Labour Market*, Oxford: Oxford University Press.

Layard, R., Nickell, S.J. and Jackman, R. (1994), *The Unemployment Crisis*, Oxford: Oxford University Press.

*Lee, R. (2003), 'The Demographic Transition: Three Centuries of Fundamental Change', *Journal of Economic Perspectives*, Fall.

Lee, S.P. and Passell, P. (1979), *The New Economic View of American History*, New York: W.W. Norton.

Lee, W. and Roemer, J. (1998), 'Income Distribution, Redistributive Politics, and Economic Growth', *Journal of Economic Growth*, September.

Leeson, R. (1994a), 'A. W. H. Phillips M.B.E. (Military Division)', *Economic Journal*, May.

Leeson, R. (1994b), 'A. W. H. Phillips, Inflationary Expectations and the Operating Characteristics of the Macroeconomy', *Economic Journal*, November.

*Leeson, R. (1997a), 'The Trade-off Interpretation of Phillips's Dynamic Stabilisation Exercise', *Economica*, February.

*Leeson, R. (1997b), 'The Political Economy of the Inflation–Unemployment Trade-off', *History of Political Economy*, Spring.

Leeson, R. (1997c), 'The Eclipse of the Goal of Zero Inflation', *History of Political Economy*, Fall.

Leeson, R. (ed.) (1999), *A. W. H. Phillips: Collected Works in Contemporary Perspective*, Cambridge: Cambridge University Press.

Leibenstein, H. (1957), *Economic Backwardness and Economic Growth*, New York: Wiley.

Leibenstein, H. (1979), 'A Branch of Economics Is Missing: Micro–Micro Theory', *Journal of Economic Literature*, June.

Leijonhufvud, A. (1968), *On Keynesian Economics and the Economics of Keynes*, London: Oxford University Press.

Leijonhufvud, A. (1973), 'Effective Demand Failures', *Swedish Journal of Economics*, March.

*Leijonhufvud, A. (1981), *Information and Co-ordination: Essays in Macroeconomic Theory*, Oxford: Oxford University Press.

*Leijonhufvud, A. (1992), 'Keynesian Economics: Past Confusions, Future Prospects', in A. Vercelli and N. Dimitri (eds), *Macroeconomics: A Survey of Research Strategies*, Oxford: Oxford University Press.

Leijonhufvud, A. (1993), 'Towards a Not-too-Rational Macroeconomics', *Southern Economic Journal*, July.

Leijonhufvud, A. (1998a), 'Three Items for the Macroeconomic Agenda', *Kyklos*.

Leijonhufvud, A. (1998b), 'Mr. Keynes and the Moderns', *European Journal of the History of Economic Thought*, Spring.

Lerner, A. (1944), *The Economics of Control*, New York: Macmillan.

Leslie, D. (1993), *Advanced Macroeconomics Beyond IS–LM*, Maidenhead: McGraw-Hill.

Levacic, R. (1988), *Supply Side Economics*, London: Heinemann.

Lewer, J.J. and Van den Berg, H. (2003), 'How Large is International Trade's Effect on Economic Growth?', *Journal of Economic Surveys*, July.

Lewis, W.A. (1954), 'Economic Development with Unlimited Supplies of Labour', *Manchester School of Economic and Social Studies*, May.

Lewis, W.A. (1955), *The Theory of Economic Growth*, London: Allen and Unwin.

Lilien, D.M. (1982), 'Sectoral Shifts and Cyclical Unemployment', *Journal of Political Economy*, August.

Lindbeck, A. (1976), 'Stabilization Policies in Open Economies With Endogenous Politicians', *American Economic Review*, May.

Lindbeck, A. (1992), 'Macroeconomic Theory and the Labour Market', *European Economic Review*, April.

*Lindbeck, A. (1998), 'New Keynesianism and Aggregate Economic Activity', *Economic Journal*, January.

Lindbeck, A. and Snower, D.J. (1985), 'Explanations of Unemployment', *Oxford Review of Economic Policy*, Spring.

Lindbeck, A. and Snower, D.J. (1986), 'Wage Setting, Unemployment, and Insider–Outsider Relations', *American Economic Review*, May.

Lindbeck, A. and Snower, D.J. (1988a), 'Cooperation, Harassment and Involuntary Unemployment: An Insider–Outsider Approach', *American Economic Review*, March.

Lindbeck, A. and Snower, D.J. (1988b), *The Insider–Outsider Theory of Employment and Unemployment*, Cambridge, MA: MIT Press.

Lipset, S.M. (1959), 'Some Social Requisites of Democracy: Economic Development and Political Legitimacy', *American Political Science Review*.

Lipsey, R.G. (1960), 'The Relationship Between Unemployment and the

Rate of Change of Money Wage Rates in the U.K. 1862–1957: A Further Analysis', *Economica*, February.

*Lipsey, R.G. (1978), 'The Place of the Phillips Curve in Macroeconomic Models', in A.R. Bergstrom (ed.), *Stability and Inflation*, Chichester: John Wiley.

Lipsey, R.G. (1981), 'The Understanding and Control of Inflation: Is There a Crisis in Macroeconomics?', *Canadian Journal of Economics*, November.

Littleboy, B. and Mehta, G. (1983), 'The Scientific Method of Keynes', *Journal of Economic Studies*, Special Issue.

Littlechild, S. (1990), *Austrian Economics, vol. 2*, Aldershot, UK and Brookfield, USA: Edward Elgar.

Litterman, B. and Weiss, L. (1985), 'Money, Real Interest Rates and Output: A Reinterpretation of Postwar U.S. Data', *Econometrica*, January.

Ljungqvist, L. and Sargent, T.J. (1998), 'The European Unemployment Dilemma', *Journal of Political Economy*, June.

Lohmann, S. (1992), 'Optimal Commitment in Monetary Policy: Credibility Versus Flexibility', *American Economic Review*, March.

Long, J.B. and Plosser, C.I. (1983), 'Real Business Cycles', *Journal of Political Economy*, February.

Lovell, M.C. (1986), 'Tests of the Rational Expectations Hypothesis', *American Economic Review*, March.

Lucas, R.E. Jr (1972a), 'Expectations and the Neutrality of Money', *Journal of Economic Theory*, April.

Lucas, R.E. Jr (1972b), 'Econometric Testing of the Natural Rate Hypothesis', in O. Eckstein (ed.), *The Econometrics of Price Determination Conference*, Washington Board of Governors: Federal Reserve System.

*Lucas, R.E. Jr (1973), 'Some International Evidence on Output–Inflation Tradeoffs', *American Economic Review*, June.

Lucas, R.E. Jr (1975), 'An Equilibrium Model of the Business Cycle', *Journal of Political Economy*, December.

Lucas, R.E. Jr (1976), 'Econometric Policy Evaluation: A Critique', in K. Brunner and A. Meltzer (eds), *The Phillips Curve and Labor Markets*, Amsterdam: North-Holland, Carnegie-Rochester Series on Public Policy.

*Lucas, R.E. Jr (1977), 'Understanding Business Cycles', in K. Brunner and A.H. Meltzer (eds), *Stabilization of the Domestic and International Economy*, Amsterdam and New York: North-Holland.

*Lucas, R.E. Jr (1978a), 'Unemployment Policy', *American Economic Review*, May.

Lucas, R.E. Jr (1978b), 'Asset Prices in an Exchange Economy', *Econometrica*, November.

*Lucas, R.E. Jr (1980a), 'Methods and Problems in Business Cycle Theory', *Journal of Money, Credit, and Banking*, November.

Lucas, R.E. Jr (1980b), 'The Death of Keynesian Economics: Issues and Ideas', University of Chicago, Winter.

*Lucas, R.E. Jr (1981a), *Studies in Business Cycle Theory*, Oxford: Basil Blackwell.

Lucas, R.E. Jr (1981b), 'Tobin and Monetarism: A Review Article', *Journal of Economic Literature*, June.

Lucas, R.E. Jr (1981c), 'Rules, Discretion and the Role of the Economic Adviser', in R.E. Lucas Jr, *Studies in Business Cycle Theory*, Oxford: Basil Blackwell.

Lucas, R.E. Jr (1987), *Models of Business Cycles*, Oxford: Basil Blackwell.

Lucas, R.E. Jr (1988), 'On the Mechanics of Economic Development', *Journal of Monetary Economics*, July.

Lucas, R.E. Jr (1990a), 'Supply-side Economics: An Analytical Review', *Oxford Economic Papers*.

Lucas, R.E. Jr (1990b), 'Why Doesn't Capital Flow From Rich to Poor Countries?', *American Economic Review*, May.

Lucas, R.E. Jr (1993), 'Making a Miracle', *Econometrica*, March.

Lucas, R.E. Jr (1994a), 'Interview with Robert Lucas', in B. Snowdon, H.R. Vane and P. Wynarczyk, *A Modern Guide to Macroeconomics: An Introduction to Competing Schools of Thought*, Aldershot, UK and Brookfield, USA: Edward Elgar.

Lucas, R.E. Jr (1994b), 'Review of Milton Friedman and Anna J. Schwartz's *A Monetary History of the United States, 1867–1960*', *Journal of Monetary Economics*, August.

*Lucas, R.E. Jr (1996), 'Nobel Lecture: Monetary Neutrality', *Journal of Political Economy*, August.

Lucas, R.E. Jr (2000a), 'Inflation and Welfare', *Econometrica*, March.

*Lucas, R.E. Jr (2000b), 'Some Macroeconomics for the 21st Century', *Journal of Economic Perspectives*, Winter.

Lucas, R.E. Jr (2002), *Lectures on Economic Growth*, Cambridge, MA: Harvard University Press.

Lucas, R.E. Jr (2003), 'Macroeconomic Priorities', *American Economic Review*, March.

Lucas, R.E. Jr and Prescott, E.C. (1971), 'Investment under Uncertainty', *Econometrica*, September.

Lucas, R.E. Jr and Rapping, L.A. (1969), 'Real Wages, Employment and Inflation', *Journal of Political Economy*, September/October.

*Lucas, R.E. Jr and Sargent, T.J. (1978), 'After Keynesian Macroeconomics', in *After the Phillips Curve: Persistence of High Inflation and High Unemployment*, Boston, MA: Federal Reserve Bank of Boston.

Lucas, R.E. Jr and Sargent, T.J. (1981), *Rational Expectations and Econometric Practices*, Minneapolis: University of Minnesota Press.

Lundberg, M. and Squire, L. (2003), 'The Simultaneous Evolution of Growth and Inequality', *Economic Journal*, April.

MacRae, C.D. (1977), 'A Political Model of the Business Cycle', *Journal of Political Economy*, April.

Maddison, A. (1972), 'Explaining Economic Growth', *Banca Nazionale del Lavoro Quarterly Review*, September.

Maddison, A. (1979), 'Long-Run Dynamics of Productivity Growth', *Banca Nazionale del Lavoro Quarterly Review*, March.

Maddison, A. (1980), 'Western Economic Performance in the 1970s: A Perspective and Assessment', *Banca Nazionale Del Lavoro Quarterly Review*, September.

Maddison, A. (1982), *Phases of Capitalist Development*, Oxford: Oxford University Press.

*Maddison, A. (1987), 'Growth and Slowdown in Advanced Capitalist Economies: Techniques of Quantitative Assessment', *Journal of Economic Literature*, June.

Maddison, A. (1995), *Explaining the Economic Performance of Nations*, Aldershot, UK and Brookfield, USA: Edward Elgar.

*Maddison, A. (2001), *The World Economy in Millennial Perspective*, Paris: OECD.

Madsen, J.B. (1998), 'General Equilibrium Macroeconomic Models of Unemployment: Can They Explain the Unemployment Path in the OECD?', *Economic Journal*, May.

Malinvaud, E. (1977), *The Theory of Unemployment Reconsidered*, Oxford: Basil Blackwell.

Maloney, J., Pickering, A.C. and Hadri, K. (2003), 'Political Business Cycles and Central Bank Independence', *Economic Journal*, March.

Mankiw, N.G. (1985), 'Small Menu Costs and Large Business Cycles: A Macroeconomic Model of Monopoly', *Quarterly Journal of Economics*, May.

*Mankiw, N.G. (1989), 'Real Business Cycles: A New Keynesian Perspective', *Journal of Economic Perspectives*, Summer.

*Mankiw, N.G. (1990), 'A Quick Refresher Course in Macroeconomics', *Journal of Economic Literature*, December.

Mankiw, N.G. (1991), 'Comment on J.J. Rotemberg and M. Woodford: Markups and the Business Cycle', *NBER Macroeconomics Annual*.

*Mankiw, N.G. (1992), 'The Reincarnation of Keynesian Economics', *European Economic Review*, April.

*Mankiw, N.G. (1995), 'The Growth of Nations', *Brookings Papers on Economic Activity*.

Mankiw, N.G. (1997), *Principles of Economics*, New York: Dryden Press.

Mankiw, N.G. (2001), 'The Inexorable and Mysterious Trade-off Between Inflation and Unemployment', *Economic Journal*, May.

Mankiw, N.G. (2002), 'US Monetary Policy in the 1990s', in J.A. Frenkel and P.R. Orszag (eds), *American Economic Policy in the 1990s*, Cambridge, MA: MIT Press.

*Mankiw, N.G. (2003), *Macroeconomics*, 5th edn, New York: Worth.

Mankiw, N.G. and Reis, R. (2002), 'Sticky Information versus Sticky Prices: A Proposal to Replace the New Keynesian Phillips Curve', *Quarterly Journal of Economics*, November.

Mankiw, N.G. and Romer, D. (eds) (1991), *New Keynesian Economics*, Cambridge, MA: MIT Press.

Mankiw, N.G., Romer, D. and Weil, D.N. (1992), 'A Contribution to the Empirics of Economic Growth', *Quarterly Journal of Economics*, May.

Mankiw, N.G., Rotemberg, J.J. and Summers, L.H. (1985), 'Intertemporal Substitution in Macroeconomics', *Quarterly Journal of Economics*, February.

Manning, A. (1995), 'Developments in Labour Market Theory and Their Implications for Macro Policy', *Journal of Political Economy*, August.

Marris, R. (1991), *Reconstructing Keynesian Economics with Imperfect Competition*, Aldershot, UK and Brookfield, USA: Edward Elgar.

Marshall, A. (1890), *Principles of Economics*, 1st edn, 8th edn 1929, London: Macmillan.

Marshall, A. (1920), *Principles of Economics*, London: Macmillan.

*Martin, R. (1999), 'The New Geographical Turn in Economics: Some Critical Reflections', *Cambridge Journal of Economics*, January.

Mas, I. (1995), 'Central Bank Independence: A Critical View from a Developing Country Perspective', *World Development*, October.

Matthews, K. and Minford, P. (1987), 'Mrs Thatcher's Economic Policies 1979–87', *Economic Policy*.

Matthews, R.C.O. (1968), 'Why has Britain had Full Employment Since the War?', *Economic Journal*, September.

*Mauro, P. (1995), 'Corruption and Growth', *Quarterly Journal of Economics*, August.

Mayer, T. (1978), *The Structure of Monetarism*, New York: W.W. Norton.

Mayer, T. (1980), 'David Hume and Monetarism', *Quarterly Journal of Economics*, August.

Mayer, T. (1990), *The Political Economy of American Monetary Policy*, New York: Cambridge University Press.

Mayer, T. (1994), 'Why is There So Much Disagreement Among Economists?', *Journal of Economic Methodology*, June.

*Mayer, T. (1997), 'What Remains of the Monetarist Counter-Revolution?', in B. Snowdon and H.R. Vane (eds), *Reflections on the Development of Modern Macroeconomics*, Cheltenham, UK and Lyme, USA: Edward Elgar.

Mayer, T. (1999), *Monetary Policy and the Great Inflation in the United States*, Cheltenham, UK and Northampton, MA, USA: Edward Elgar.

Mazower, M. (1998), *Dark Continent: Europe's Twentieth Century*, London: Penguin.

Mazzoleni, R. and Nelson, R.R. (1998), 'Economic Theories About the Benefits and Costs of Patents', *Journal of Economic Issues*, December.

McCallum, B.T. (1978), 'The Political Business Cycle: An Empirical Test', *Southern Economic Journal*, January.

McCallum, B.T. (1986), 'On Real and Sticky-Price Theories of the Business Cycle', *Journal of Money, Credit, and Banking*, November.

McCallum, B.T. (1989), 'Real Business Cycle Models', in R.J. Barro (ed.), *Modern Business Cycle Theory*, Cambridge, MA: Harvard University Press.

McCallum, B.T. (1992), 'Real Business Cycle Theories', in A. Vercelli and N. Dimitri (eds), *Macroeconomics: A Survey of Research Strategies*, Oxford: Oxford University Press.

McCloskey, D.N. (1994), '1780–1860: A Survey', in R. Floud and D.N. McCloskey (eds), *The Economic History of Britain Since 1700, Vol. I*, 2nd edn, Cambridge: Cambridge University Press.

McDonald, I.M. (1992), *Macroeconomics*, New York: John Wiley.

McDonald, I.M. and Solow, R.M. (1981), 'Wage Bargaining and Employment', *American Economic Review*, December.

McGrattan, E.R. (1998), 'A Defence of AK Growth Models', *Federal Reserve Bank of Minneapolis Quarterly Review*, Fall.

Meade, J.E. and Stone, J.R.N. (1944), *National Income and Expenditure*, London: Oxford University Press.

Meadows, D.H. et al. (1972), *The Limits to Growth*, London: Earth Island.

Mehra, R. and Prescott, E.C. (1985), 'The Equity Premium: A Puzzle', *Journal of Monetary Economics*, March.

Meier, G.M. (ed.) (1995), *Leading Issues in Economic Development*, 6th edn, Oxford: Oxford University Press.

*Melchior, A. (2001), 'Beliefs vs Facts in the Global Inequality Debate', *World Economics*, July–September.

*Meltzer, A.H. (1988), *Keynes's Monetary Theory: A Different Interpretation*, Cambridge: Cambridge University Press.

Mendoza, E.G. (1991), 'Real Business Cycles in a Small Open Economy', *American Economic Review*, September.

Menger, C. (1981[1871]), *Principles of Economics*, New York: New York University Press.

Metzler, L.A. (1941), 'The Nature and Stability of Inventory Cycles', *Review of Economics and Statistics*, August.

Metzler, L.A. (1947), 'Factors Governing the Length of Inventory Cycles', *Review of Economics and Statistics*, February.

Metzler, L.A. (1951), 'Wealth, Saving and the Rate of Interest', *Journal of Political Economy*, April.

Meyer, S. (1981), *The Five Dollar Day, Labour Management and Social Control in Ford Motor Company, 1908–21*, Albany: State University of New York Press.

Milanovic, B. (2002), *Worlds Apart: Inter-National and World Inequality, 1950–2000*, Washington, DC: World Bank.

Mill, J.S. (1848), *Principles of Political Economy*, Harmondsworth: Pelican, 1970.

Mill, J.S. (1982), *On Liberty*, Harmondsworth: Penguin English Library.

Millard, S., Scott, A. and Sensier, M. (1997), 'The Labour Market Over the Business Cycle: Can Theory Fit the Facts?', *Oxford Review of Economic Policy*, Autumn.

Minford, A.P.L. (1991), *The Supply Side Revolution in Britain*, Aldershot, UK and Brookfield, USA: Edward Elgar.

*Minford, A.P.L. (1997), 'Macroeconomics: Before and After Rational Expectations', in B. Snowdon and H.R. Vane (eds), *Reflections on the Development of Modern Macroeconomics*, Cheltenham, UK and Lyme, USA: Edward Elgar.

Minford, A.P.L. and Peel, D.A. (1982), 'The Political Theory of the Business Cycle', *European Economic Review*.

Minford, A.P.L. and Peel, D.A. (1983), *Rational Expectations and the New Macroeconomics*, Oxford: Martin Robertson.

Minford, A.P.L., Brech, M. and Matthews, K.G.P. (1980), 'A Rational Expectations Model of the UK Under Floating Exchange Rates', *European Economic Review*, September.

Minford, A.P.L., Ashton, P., Peel, M., Davies, D. and Sprague, A. (1985), *Unemployment: Cause and Cure*, 2nd edn, Oxford: Basil Blackwell.

Minier, J. (1998), 'Democracy and Growth: Alternative Approaches', *Journal of Economic Growth*, September.

Miron, J.A. (1994), 'Empirical Methodology in Macroeconomics: Explaining the Success of Friedman and Schwartz's *A Monetary History of the United States, 1867–1960*', *Journal of Monetary Economics*, August.

Mises, L. v. (1953[1912]), *The Theory of Money and Credit*, New Haven, CT: Yale University Press.

Mises, L. v. (1966), *Human Action: A Treatise on Economics*, 3rd edn, Chicago: Henry Regnery.

Mishkin, F.S (1982), 'Does Anticipated Monetary Policy Matter? An Econometric Investigation', *Journal of Political Economy*, February.

*Mishkin, F.S. (1999), 'International Experiences with Different Monetary Regimes', *Journal of Monetary Economics*, June.

Mishkin, F.S. (2000a), 'Inflation Targeting in Emerging-Market Economies', *American Economic Review*, May.

Mishkin, F.S. (2000b), 'What Should Central Banks Do?', *Federal Reserve Bank of St. Louis Review*, November/December.

*Mishkin, F.S. (2002), 'Inflation Targeting', in B. Snowdon and H.R. Vane (eds), *An Encyclopedia of Macroeconomics*, Cheltenham, UK and Northampton, MA, USA: Edward Elgar.

Modigliani, F. (1944), 'Liquidity Preference and the Theory of Interest and Money', *Econometrica*, January.

Modigliani, F. (1977), 'The Monetarist Controversy, or Should We Forsake Stabilization Policies?', *American Economic Review*, March.

Modigliani, F. (1986), *The Debate Over Stabilisation Policy*, Cambridge: Cambridge University Press.

Modigliani, F. (1988a), 'The Monetarist Controversy Revisited', *Contemporary Policy Issues*, October.

Modigliani, F. (1988b), 'Reagan's Economic Policies: A Critique', *Oxford Economic Papers*, September.

Modigliani, F. (1996), 'The Shameful Rate of Unemployment in the EMS: Causes and Cures', *De Economist*, October.

*Modigliani, F. (2003), 'The Keynesian Gospel According to Modigliani', *American Economist*, Spring.

Modigliani, F. and Brumberg, R. (1954), 'Utility Analysis and the Consumption Function: An Interpretation of Cross-Section Data' in K.K. Kurihara (ed.), *Post-Keynesian Economics*, New Brunswick, NJ: Rutgers University Press.

Modigliani, F. and Papademos, L.D. (1975), 'Targets for Monetary Policy', *Brookings Papers on Economic Activity*.

Moggridge, D. (1992), *John Maynard Keynes: An Economist's Biography*, London: Routledge.

Mokyr, J. (1990), *The Lever of Riches: Technological Creativity and Economic Change*, Oxford: Oxford University Press.

*Mokyr, J. (1993), *The British Industrial Revolution: An Economic Perspective*, Boulder, CO: Westview Press.

Mokyr, J. (2002), *The Gifts of Athena*, Princeton: Princeton University Press.

*Mokyr, J. (2005), 'Long-Term Economic Growth and the History of Technology', in P. Aghion and S. Durlauf (eds), *Handbook of Economic Growth*, Amsterdam: Elsevier.

Morgan, B. (1978), *Monetarists and Keynesians: Their Contribution to Monetary Theory*, London: Macmillan.

Mosley, P. (1978), 'Images of the Floating Voter: Or, the Political Business Cycle Revisited', *Political Studies*, February.

Muellbauer, J. (1997), 'The Assessment: Business Cycles', *Oxford Review of Economic Policy*, Autumn.

Mullineux, A.W. (1984), *The Business Cycle After Keynes*, Brighton: Wheatsheaf.

Mullineux, A.W. and Dickinson, D.G. (1992), 'Equilibrium Business Cycles: Theory and Evidence', *Journal of Economic Surveys*.

Mullineux, A.W., Dickinson, D.G. and Peng, W. (1993), *Business Cycles*, Oxford: Basil Blackwell.

Mundell, R.A. (1960), 'The Monetary Dynamics of International Adjustment under Fixed and Flexible Rates', *Quarterly Journal of Economics*, May.

*Mundell, R.A. (1962), 'The Appropriate Use of Monetary and Fiscal Policy for Internal and External Stability', *IMF Staff Papers*, March.

*Mundell, R.A. (1963), 'Capital Mobility and Stabilisation Policy under Fixed and Flexible Exchange Rates', *Canadian Journal of Economics and Political Science*, November.

*Mundell, R.A. (2000), 'A Reconsideration of the Twentieth Century', *American Economic Review*, March.

Mundell, R.A. (2001), 'On the History of the Mundell–Fleming Model', *IMF Staff Papers*, Special Issue.

Murphy, K., Riddell, C. and Romer, P.M. (1998), 'Wages, Skills and Technology in the United States and Canada', in E. Helpman (ed.), *General Purpose Technologies*, Cambridge, MA: MIT Press.

Murphy, K.M., Shleifer, A. and Vishny, R.W. (1989a), 'Industrialisation and the Big Push', *Quarterly Journal of Economics*, May.

Murphy, K.M., Shleifer, A. and Vishny, R.W. (1989b), 'Income Distribution, Market Size and Industrialisation', *Quarterly Journal of Economics*, August.

Murphy, K.M., Shleifer, A. and Vishny, R.W. (1991), 'The Allocation of Talent: Implications for Growth', *Quarterly Journal of Economics*, May.

Murphy, K.M., Shleifer, A. and Vishny, R.W. (1993), 'Why is Rent-Seeking So Costly to Growth?', *American Economic Review*, May.

Muscatelli, A. (1998), 'Optimal Inflation Contracts and Inflation Targets with Uncertain Central Bank Preferences: Accountability Through Independence?', *Economic Journal*, March.

Muscatelli, A. and Trecroci, C. (2000), 'Monetary Policy Rules, Policy Preferences, and Uncertainty: Recent Empirical Evidence', *Journal of Economic Surveys*, December.

Mussa, M. (1976), 'The Exchange Rate, The Balance of Payments and Monetary and Fiscal Policy under a Regime of Controlled Floating', *Scandinavian Journal of Economics*.

Muth, J.F. (1961), 'Rational Expectations and the Theory of Price Movements', *Econometrica*, July.

Myles, G.D. (2000), 'Taxation and Economic Growth', *Fiscal Studies*, March.

Myrdal, K.G. (1957), *Rich Lands and Poor: The Road to World Prosperity*, New York: Harper and Row.

Myrdal, K.G. (1973), 'Equity, Growth and Social Justice', *World Development*, March–April.

Naish, H.F. (1993), 'Imperfect Competition as a Micro Foundation for Keynesian Economics: A Graphical Analysis', *Journal of Macroeconomics*, Spring.

Ndulu, B.J. and O'Connell, S.A. (1999), 'Governance and Growth in Sub-Saharan Africa', *Journal of Economic Perspectives*, Summer.

Nelson, C.R. and Plosser, C.I. (1982), 'Trends and Random Walks in Macroeconomic Time Series: Some Evidence and Implications', *Journal of Monetary Economics*, September.

Nelson, R.R. (1956), 'A Theory of the Low Level Equilibrium Trap', *American Economic Review*, December.

Nelson, R.R. (1973), 'Recent Exercises in Growth Accounting: New Understanding or Dead End?', *American Economic Review*, June.

Nelson, R.R. (1997), 'How New is New Growth Theory?', *Challenge*, September–October.

*Nelson, R.R. and Pack, H. (1999), 'The Asian Miracle and Modern Economic Growth Theory', *Economic Journal*, July.

Nickell, S. (1990), 'Unemployment: A Survey', *Economic Journal*, June.

*Nickell, S. (1997), 'Unemployment and Labour Market Rigidities: Europe Versus North America', *Journal of Economic Perspectives*, Summer.

Nickell, S. (1998), 'Unemployment: Questions and Some Answers', *Economic Journal*, May.

Noland, M., Robinson, S. and Wang, T. (2001), 'Famine in North Korea: Causes and Cures', *Economic Development and Cultural Change*, July.

Nordhaus, W.D. (1975), 'The Political Business Cycle', *Review of Economic Studies*, April.

Nordhaus, W.D. (1989), 'Alternative Approaches to the Political Business Cycle', *Brookings Papers on Economic Activity*.

Nordhaus, W.D. (1994), 'Policy Games: Co-ordination and Independence in Monetary and Fiscal Policy', *Brookings Papers on Economic Activity*.

Nordhaus, W.D. (2001), 'New Directions in National Economic Accounting', *American Economic Review*, May.

North, D.C. (1981), *Structure and Change in Economic History*, New York: W.W. Norton.

North, D.C. (1989), 'Institutions and Economic Growth: An Historical Approach', *World Development*, September.

*North, D.C. (1990), *Institutions, Institutional Change and Economic Performance*, Cambridge: Cambridge University Press.

North, D.C. (1991), 'Institutions', *Journal of Economic Perspectives*, Winter.

*North, D.C. (1994), 'Economic Performance Through Time', *American Economic Review*, June.

North, D.C. and Thomas, R. (1973), *The Rise of the Western World: A New Economic History*, Cambridge: Cambridge University Press.

North, D.C. and Weingast, B.R. (1989), 'Constitutions and Commitment: The Evolution of Institutions Governing Public Choice in Seventeenth-Century England', *Journal of Economic History*, December.

O'Brien, D.P. (1975), *The Classical Economists*, Oxford: Clarendon Press.

Obstfeld, M. (1998), 'The Global Capital Market: Benefactor or Menace', *Journal of Economic Perspectives*, Fall.

Obstfeld, M. (2001), 'International Macreconomics: Beyond the Mundell–Fleming Model', *IMF Staff Papers*, Special Issue.

Obstfeld, M. and Taylor, A. (1998), 'The Great Depression as a Watershed: International Capital Mobility over the Long Run', in M. Bordo, C. Goldin and E. White (eds), *The Defining Moment: The Great Depression and the American Economy in the Twentieth Century*, Chicago: University of Chicago Press.

O'Donnell, R.M. (1982), 'Keynes: Philosophy and Economics', unpublished PhD, University of Cambridge.

O'Donnell, R.M. (1989), *Keynes: Philosophy, Economics and Politics*, London: Macmillan.

Okun, A. (1962), 'Potential GNP: Its Measurement and Significance', *Proceedings of the Business and Economics Statistics Section of the American Statistical Association*, Washington, DC: ASA.

Okun, A. (1975), 'Inflation: Its Mechanics and Welfare Cost', *Brookings Papers on Economic Activity*.

Okun, A. (1980), 'Rational Expectations with Misperceptions as a Theory of the Business Cycle', *Journal of Money, Credit, and Banking*, November.

Okun, A. (1981), *Prices and Quantities: a Macroeconomic Analysis*, Oxford: Basil Blackwell.

Olson, M. (1982), *The Rise and Decline of Nations*, New Haven, CT: Yale University Press.

Olson, M. (1993), 'Dictatorship, Democracy and Development', *American Political Science Review*, September.

*Olson, M. (1996), 'Distinguished Lecture on Economics in Government: Big Bills Left on the Sidewalk: Why Some Nations are Rich, and Others Poor', *Journal of Economic Perspectives*, Spring.

Olson, M. (2000), *Power and Prosperity: Outgrowing Communist and Capitalist Dictatorships*, New York: Basic Books.

O'Rourke, K.H. and Williamson, J.G. (1999), *Globalisation and History: Evolution of the Nineteenth Century Atlantic Economy*, Cambridge, MA: MIT Press.

Paish, F.W. (1968), 'The Limits of Incomes Policies', in F.W. Paish and J. Hennessey, *Policy for Incomes*, London: Institute of Economic Affairs.

Paldam, M. (1979), 'Is There an Electoral Cycle? A Comparative Study of National Accounts', *Scandinavian Journal of Economics*.

Paldam, M. (2000), 'Social Capital: One or Many? Definition and Measurement', *Journal of Economic Surveys*, December.

Parente, S.L. and Prescott, E.C. (1994), 'Barriers to Technology Adoption and Development', *Journal of Political Economy*, April.

Parente, S.L. and Prescott, E.C. (1997), 'Monopoly Rights: A Barrier to Riches', Federal Reserve Bank of Minneapolis Staff Report 236, July.

Parente, S.L. and Prescott, E.C. (1999), 'Monopoly Rights: A Barrier to Riches', *American Economic Review*, December.

*Parente, S.L. and Prescott, E.C. (2000), *Barriers to Riches*, Cambridge, MA: MIT Press.

Parente, S.L. and Prescott, E.C. (2005), 'A Unified Theory of the Evolution of International Income Levels', in P. Aghion and S. Durlauf (eds), *Handbook of Economic Growth*, Amsterdam: Elsevier.

*Parker, R. (2002), *Reflections on the Great Depression*, Cheltenham, UK and Northampton, MA, USA: Edward Elgar.

Parkin, M. (1986), 'The Output–Inflation Tradeoff When Prices Are Costly to Change', *Journal of Political Economy*, February.

Parkin, M. (1992), 'Where Do We Stand?', in M. Belongia and M. Garfinkel (eds), *The Business Cycle: Theories and Evidence*, London: Kluwer Academic Publishers.

Parkin, M. and Bade, R. (1982a), 'Central Bank Laws and Monetary Policy', unpublished, University of Western Ontario.

Parkin, M. and Bade, R. (1982b), *Modern Macroeconomics*, Oxford: Philip Allan.

*Patinkin, D. (1948), 'Price Flexibility and Full Employment' *American Economic Review*, September.

Patinkin, D. (1956), *Money, Interest and Prices: An Integration of Monetary and Value Theory*, Evanston, IL: Row Peterson.

Patinkin, D. (1969), 'The Chicago Tradition, the Quantity Theory, and Friedman', *Journal of Money, Credit, and Banking*, February.

Patinkin, D. (1976), *Keynes's Monetary Thought: A Study of its Development*, Durham, NC: Duke University Press.

Patinkin, D. (1982), *Anticipations of the General Theory?* Oxford: Blackwell.

Patinkin, D. (1990a), 'In Defence of IS–LM', *Banca Nazionale del Lavoro Quarterly Review*, March.

*Patinkin, D. (1990b), 'On Different Interpretations of the General Theory', *Journal of Monetary Economics*, October.

Patinkin, D. (1993), 'On the Chronology of the General Theory', *Economic Journal*, May.

Pearce, K.A. and Hoover, K.D. (1995), 'After the Revolution: Paul Samuelson and the Textbook Keynesian Model', in A.F. Cottrel and M.S. Lawlor (eds), *New Perspectives on Keynes*, Durham, NC: Duke University Press.

Perry, G.L. and Tobin, J. (eds) (2000), *Economic Events, Ideas, and Policies: The 1960s and After*, Washington, DC: The Brookings Institution.

Persson, T. (1988), 'Credibility of Macroeconomic Policy: An Introduction and a Broad Survey', *European Economic Review*, March.

Persson, T. and Tabellini, G. (1990), *Macroeconomic Policy, Credibility and Politics*, London: Harwood.

Persson, T. and Tabellini, G. (1994), 'Is Inequality Harmful to Growth?', *American Economic Review*, June.

Persson, T. and Tabellini, G. (2004), 'Constitutional Rules and Fiscal Policy Outcomes', *American Economic Review*, March.

Pesek, B. and Saving, T.R. (1967), *Money, Wealth and Economic Theory*, London: Macmillan.

Phelps, E.S. (1967), 'Phillips Curves, Expectations of Inflation and Optimal Unemployment Over Time', *Economica*, August.

Phelps, E.S. (1968), 'Money Wage Dynamics and Labour Market Equilibrium', *Journal of Political Economy*, August.

Phelps, E.S. (1972), *Inflation Policy and Unemployment Theory: The Cost–Benefit Approach to Monetary Planning*, New York: W.W. Norton.

Phelps, E.S. (1978), 'Commodity-Supply Shock and Full Employment Monetary Policy', *Journal of Money, Credit, and Banking*, May.

Phelps, E.S. (1985), *Political Economy: An Introductory Text*, New York: W.W. Norton.

*Phelps, E.S. (1990), *Seven Schools of Macroeconomic Thought*, Oxford: Oxford University Press.

Phelps, E.S. (1992), 'Expectations in Macroeconomics and the Rational Expectations Debate', in A. Vercelli and N. Dimitri (eds), *Macroeconomics: A Survey of Research Strategies*, Oxford: Oxford University Press.

Phelps, E.S. (1994), *Structural Slumps: The Modern Equilibrium Theory of Unemployment, Interest and Assets*, Cambridge, MA: Harvard University Press.

Phelps, E.S. (2000), 'Lessons in Natural Rate Dynamics', *Oxford Economic Papers*, January.

Phelps, E.S. and Taylor, J.B. (1977), 'Stabilizing Powers of Monetary Policy Under Rational Expectations', *Journal of Political Economy*, February.

Phelps, E.S. and Zoega, G. (1998), 'Natural Rate Theory and OECD Unemployment', *Economic Journal*, May.

Phelps, E.S. et al. (1970), *Microeconomic Foundations of Employment and Inflation Theory*, New York: W.W. Norton.

*Phillips, A.W. (1958), 'The Relation Between Unemployment and the Rate of Change of Money Wage Rates in the United Kingdom, 1861–1957', *Economica*, November.

Pierce, J.L. (1995), 'Monetarism: The Good, the Bad and the Ugly', in K.D. Hoover and S.M. Sheffrin (eds), *Monetarism and the Methodology of Economics: Essays in Honour of Thomas Mayer*, Aldershot, UK and Brookfield, USA: Edward Elgar.

Piga, G. (2000), 'Dependent and Accountable: Evidence from the Modern Theory of Central Banking', *Journal of Economic Surveys*, December.

Pigou, A.C. (1941), *Employment and Equilibrium*, London: Macmillan.

Pigou, A.C. (1943), 'The Classical Stationary State', *Economic Journal*, December.

Pigou, A.C. (1947), 'Economic Progress in a Stable Environment', *Economica*, August.

Pindyck, R. and Rubinfeld, D.L. (1998), *Microeconomics*, 4th edn, Englewood Cliffs, NJ: Prentice-Hall.

*Plosser, C.I. (1989), 'Understanding Real Business Cycles', *Journal of Economic Perspectives*, Summer.

Plosser, C.I. (1994), 'Interview with Charles Plosser', in B. Snowdon, H.R. Vane and P. Wynarczyk, *A Modern Guide to Macroeconomics: An Introduction to Competing Schools of Thought*, Aldershot, UK and Brookfield, USA: Edward Elgar.

Pomeranz, K. (2000), *The Great Divergence: China, Europe and the Making of the Modern World Economy*, Princeton: Princeton University Press.

Poole, W. (1988), 'Monetary Policy Lessons of Recent Inflation and Disinflation', *Journal of Economic Perspectives*, Summer.

Porter, M. (2003), 'The Economic Performance of Regions', *Regional Studies*, August/October.

Posen, A.S. (1995), 'Declarations Are Not Enough: Financial Sector Sources of Central Bank Independence', *NBER Macroeconomics Annual*.

Posen, A. (1998), 'Central Bank Independence and Disinflationary Credibility: A Missing Link', *Oxford Economic Papers*, July.

*Prescott, E.C. (1986), 'Theory Ahead of Business Cycle Measurement', *Federal Reserve Bank of Minneapolis Quarterly Review*, Fall.

Prescott, E.C. (1996), 'Interview with Edward C. Prescott', *The Region*, September.

Prescott, E.C. (1998), 'Needed: A Theory of Total Factor Productivity', *International Economic Review*, August.

Prescott, E.C. (1999), 'Some Observations on the Great Depression', *Federal Reserve Bank of Minneapolis Quarterly Review*, Winter.

*Prescott, E.C. (2002), 'Prosperity and Depression', *American Economic Review*, May.

Presley, J.R. (1986), 'J.M. Keynes and the Real Balance Effect', *The Manchester School*, March.

*Pritchett, L. (1997), 'Divergence, Big Time', *Journal of Economic Perspectives*, Summer.

Proudman, J. and Redding, S. (1997), 'The Relationship Between Openness and Growth in the United Kingdom: A Summary of the Bank of England Growth Project', *Bank of England Quarterly Bulletin*, November.

Purvis, D.D. (1980), 'Monetarism: A Review', *Canadian Journal of Economics*, February.

Quah, D. (1993), 'Galton's Fallacy and Tests of the Convergence Hypothesis', *Scandinavian Journal of Economics*, December.

Quah, D.T. (1995), 'Business Cycle Empirics: Calibration and Estimation', *Economic Journal*, November.

Radcliffe Committee on the Working of the Monetary System (1959), *Report*, Cmnd 827, London: HMSO.

Raff, D.M.G. and Summers, L.H. (1987), 'Did Henry Ford Pay Efficiency Wages?', *Journal of Labour Economics*, October.

Ramey, G. and Ramey, V.A. (1995), 'Cross-Country Evidence on the Link Between Volatility and Growth', *American Economic Review*, December.

Ramsey, F. (1928), 'A Mathematical Theory of Saving', *Economic Journal*, December.

Rappaport, J. and Sachs, J.D. (2003), 'The United States as a Coastal Region', *Journal of Economic Growth*, March.

Ravn, M.O. and Sola, M. (1995), 'Stylised Facts and Regime Change: Are Prices Procyclical?', *Journal of Monetary Economics*.

Rebelo, S. (1991), 'Long-Run Policy Analysis and Long-Run Growth', *Journal of Political Economy*, June.

Redman, D.A. (1992), *A Readers Guide to Rational Expectations*, Aldershot, UK and Brookfield, USA: Edward Elgar.

Reynolds, L.G. (1985), *Economic Growth in the Third World, 1850–1980*, New Haven: Yale University Press.

Reynolds, L.G. (1994), 'Government and Economic Growth', in G.M. Meier (ed.), *From Classical Economics to Development Economics*, New York: St Martin's Press.

Riddell, R. (1987), *Foreign Aid Reconsidered*, Baltimore: Johns Hopkins University Press.

Rivera-Batiz, L. and Romer, P.M. (1991), 'Economic Integration and Endogenous Growth', *Quarterly Journal of Economics*, May.

Robbins, L. (1971[1934]), *The Great Depression*, Freeport, NY: Books for Libraries Press.

Roberts, P.C. (1989), 'Supply-Side Economics: An Assessment of the American Experience', *National Westminster Bank Quarterly Review*, February.

Robertson, D.H. (1926), *Banking Policy and the Price Level*, London: P.S. King.

Robertson, D.H. (1956), *Economic Commentaries*, London: Macmillan.

Robinson, J. (1933), *The Economics of Imperfect Competition*, London: Macmillan.

Robinson, J. (1962), *Economic Philosophy*, Harmondsworth: Penguin.

Robinson, J. (1971), *Economic Heresies*, London: Macmillan.

Robinson, J. (1972), 'The Second Crisis in Economic Theory', *American Economic Review*, May.

Robinson, J. (1975), 'What Has Become of the Keynesian Revolution?', in M. Keynes (ed.), *Essays on John Maynard Keynes*, Cambridge: Cambridge University Press.

Robinson, J. (1998), 'Theories of "Bad" Policy', *Journal of Policy Reform*.

Rodriguez, F. and Rodrik, D. (2000), 'Trade Policy and Economic Growth: A Sceptics Guide to Cross-National Data', *NBER Macroeconomics Annual*.

*Rodrik, D. (1995), 'Getting Interventions Right: How South Korea and Taiwan Grew Rich', *Economic Policy*, April.

*Rodrik, D. (1996), 'Understanding Economic Policy Reform', *Journal of Economic Literature*, March.

Rodrik, D. (1999a), *The New Global Economy and Developing Countries: Making Openness Work*, Washington, DC: Overseas Development Council.

Rodrik, D. (1999b), 'Where Did All the Growth Go? External Shocks, Social Conflict and Growth Collapses', *Journal of Economic Growth*, December.

Rodrik, D. (2000), 'Institutions for High-Quality Growth: What Are They and How to Acquire Them', *Studies in International Development*, Fall.

Rodrik, D. (ed.) (2003), *In Search of Prosperity: Analytic Narratives on Economic Growth*, Princeton: Princeton University Press.

*Rodrik, D. (2005), 'Growth Strategies' in P. Aghion and S. Durlauf (eds), *Handbook of Economic Growth*, Amsterdam: Elsevier.

Rodrik, D., Subramanian, A. and Trebbi, F. (2004), 'Institutions Rule: The Primacy of Institutions Over Geography and Integration in Economic Development', *Journal of Economic Growth*, June.

Roed, K. and Zhang, T. (2003), 'Does Unemployment Compensation Affect Unemployment Duration?', *Economic Journal*, January.

Rogerson, R. (1988), 'Indivisible Labour, Lotteries and Equilibrium', *Journal of Monetary Economics*, January.

Rogerson, R. (1997), 'Theory Ahead of Language in the Economics of Unemployment', *Journal of Economic Perspectives*, Winter.

Rogoff, K. (1985), 'The Optimal Degree of Commitment to an Intermediate Monetary Target', *Quarterly Journal of Economics*, November.

Rogoff, K. (1988), 'Comment on Macroeconomics and Politics', *NBER Macroeconomics Annual*.

Rogoff, K. (1990), 'Equilibrium Political Budget Cycles', *American Economic Review*, March.

Rogoff, K. (2002), 'Dornbusch's Overshooting Model After Twenty-Five Years', *IMF Staff Papers*, Special Issue.

Rogoff, K. (2003), 'Disinflation: An Unsung Benefit of Globalisation', *Finance and Development*, December.

Rogoff, K. and Sibert, A. (1988), 'Equilibrium Political Business Cycles', *Review of Economic Studies*, January.

Romer, C.D. (1986a), 'Spurious Volatility in Historical Unemployment Data', *Journal of Political Economy*, March.

Romer, C.D. (1986b), 'New Estimates of GNP and Unemployment', *Journal of Economic History*, June.

Romer, C.D. (1986c), 'Is the Stabilisation of the Postwar Economy a Figment of the Data?', *American Economic Review*, June.

Romer, C.D. (1989), 'The Pre-war Business Cycle Reconsidered: New Estimates of GNP, 1869–1908', *Journal of Political Economy*, February.

Romer, C.D. (1990), 'The Great Crash and the Onset of the Great Depression', *Quarterly Journal of Economics*, August.

Romer, C.D. (1992), 'What Ended the Great Depression?', *Journal of Economic History*, December.

*Romer, C.D. (1993), 'The Nation in Depression', *Journal of Economic Perspectives*, Spring.

Romer, C.D. (1994), 'Re-Measuring Business Cycles', *Journal of Economic History*, September.

*Romer, C.D. (1999), 'Changes in Business Cycles: Evidence and Explanations', *Journal of Economic Perspectives*, Spring.

Romer, C.D. (2004), 'The Great Depression', in *Encyclopedia Britannica*, Upper Saddle River, NJ: Pearson Education.

Romer, C.D. and Romer, D.H. (1989), 'Does Monetary Policy Matter? A New Test in the Spirit of Friedman and Schwartz', *NBER Macroeconomics Annual*.

Romer, C.D. and Romer, D.H. (1994a), 'Monetary Policy Matters', *Journal of Monetary Economics*, August.

Romer, C.D. and Romer, D.H. (1994b), 'What Ends Recessions?', *NBER Macroeconomics Annual*.

Romer, C.D. and Romer, D.H. (eds) (1997), *Reducing Inflation: Motivation and Strategy*, Chicago: University of Chicago Press.

Romer, C.D. and Romer, D.H. (1999), 'Monetary Policy and the Well-Being of the Poor', *Federal Reserve Bank of Kansas City Economic Review*.
*Romer, C.D. and Romer, D.H. (2002), 'The Evolution of Economic Understanding and Postwar Stabilisation Policy', Department of Economics, University of California, Berkeley, Working Paper.
Romer, C.D. and Romer, D.H. (2004), 'Choosing the Federal Reserve Chair: Lessons from History', *Journal of Economic Perspectives*, Winter
*Romer, D. (1993), 'The New Keynesian Synthesis', *Journal of Economic Perspectives*, Winter.
Romer, D. (1996), *Advanced Macroeconomics*, New York: McGraw-Hill.
*Romer, D. (2000), 'Keynesian Macroeconomics Without the LM Curve', *Journal of Economic Perspectives*, Spring.
Romer, D. (2001), *Advanced Macroeconomics*, 2nd edn, New York: McGraw-Hill.
Romer, D. (2003), 'Misconceptions and Political Outcomes', *Economic Journal*, January.
Romer, P.M. (1986), 'Increasing Returns and Long-Run Growth', *Journal of Political Economy*, October.
Romer, P.M. (1987a), 'Crazy Explanations for the Productivity Slowdown', *NBER Macroeconomics Annual*.
Romer, P.M. (1987b), 'Growth Based on Increasing Returns Due to Specialisation', *American Economic Review*, May.
Romer, P.M. (1989), 'Capital Accumulation in the Theory of Long-Run Growth', in R.J. Barro (ed.), *Modern Business Cycle Theory*, Cambridge, MA: Harvard University Press.
Romer, P.M. (1990), 'Endogenous Technological Change', *Journal of Political Economy*, October.
Romer, P.M. (1993), 'Idea Gaps and Object Gaps in Economic Development', *Journal of Monetary Economics*, December.
*Romer, P.M. (1994a), 'The Origins of Endogenous Growth', *Journal of Economic Perspectives*, Winter.
Romer, P.M. (1994b), 'New Goods, Old Theory, and the Welfare Costs of Trade Restrictions', *Journal of Development Economics*, February.
*Romer, P.M. (1995), 'The Growth of Nations: A Comment on Mankiw', *Brookings Papers on Economic Activity*.
Rose-Ackerman, S. (2001), 'Trust and Honesty in Post-Socialist Societies', *Kyklos*.
Rosen, S. (1985), 'Implicit Contracts: A Survey', *Journal of Economic Literature*, September.
Rosenberg, N. (1994), *Exploring the Black Box: Technology, Economics and History*, Cambridge: Cambridge University Press.

Rosenberg, N. and Birdzell, L.E. (1986), *How the West Grew Rich*, New York: Basic Books.

Rostow, W.W. (1960), *The Stages of Economic Growth*, Cambridge: Cambridge University Press.

Rostow, W.W. (1990), *Theories of Economic Growth from David Hume to the Present*, Oxford: Oxford University Press.

Rotemberg, J.J. (1987), 'The New Keynesian Microfoundations', *NBER Macroeconomics Annual*.

Rotemberg, J.J. and Summers, L.H. (1990), 'Inflexible Prices and Procyclical Productivity', *Quarterly Journal of Economics*, November.

Rotemberg, J.J. and Woodford, M. (1991), 'Markups and the Business Cycle', *NBER Macroeconomics Annual*.

Rothbard, M.N. (1963), *America's Great Depression*, Los Angeles: Nash Publishing.

Rothschild, K.W. (1971), 'The Phillips Curve and All That', *Scottish Journal of Political Economy*, November.

Rush, M. (1987), 'Real Business Cycles', *Federal Reserve Bank of Kansas City Economic Review*, February.

Ryan, C. (2002), 'Business Cycles: Stylised Facts', in B. Snowdon and H.R. Vane (eds), *An Encyclopedia of Macroeconomics*, Cheltenham, UK and Northampton, MA, USA: Edward Elgar.

*Ryan, C. and Mullineux, A.W. (1997), 'The Ups and Downs of Modern Business Cycle Theory', in B. Snowdon and H.R. Vane (eds), *Reflections on the Development of Modern Macroeconomics*, Cheltenham, UK and Lyme, USA: Edward Elgar.

Rymes, T.K. (ed.) (1989), *Keynes's Lectures, 1932–35: Notes from a Representative Student*, London: Macmillan.

*Sachs, J.D. (1999), 'Twentieth-Century Political Economy: A Brief History of Global Capitalism', *Oxford Review of Economic Policy*, December.

*Sachs, J.D. (2003), 'Institutions Matter, But Not For Everything', *Finance and Development*, June.

*Sachs, J.D. and Warner, A.M. (1995), 'Economic Reform and the Process of Global Integration', *Brookings Papers on Economic Activity*.

Sachs, J.D. and Warner, A.M. (1997), 'Fundamental Sources of Long-Run Growth', *American Economic Review*, May.

Sachs, J.D. and Warner, A.M. (2001), 'The Curse of Natural Resources', *European Economic Review*, May.

Sala-i-Martin, X. (1997), 'I Just Ran 2 Million Regressions', *American Economic Review*, May.

Sala-i-Martin, X. (2002a), 'The Disturbing "Rise" of Global Inequality', NBER Working Paper, No. 8904, April.

Sala-i-Martin, X. (2002b), 'The World Distribution of Income', NBER Working Paper, No. 8933, May.

*Sala-i-Martin, X. and Subramanian, A. (2003), 'Addressing the Natural Resource Curse: An Illustration From Nigeria', NBER Working Paper, No. 9804, June.

Salant, W.S. (1988), 'The Spread of Keynesian Doctrines and Practices in the United States', in O.F. Hamouda and J.N. Smithin (eds), *Keynes and Public Policy After Fifty Years, Vol 1: Economics and Policy*, Aldershot, UK and Brookfield, USA: Edward Elgar.

Salop, S.C. (1979), 'A Model of the Natural Rate of Unemployment', *American Economic Review*, March.

Samuelson, P.A. (1939), 'Interactions Between the Multiplier Analysis and the Principle of Acceleration', *Review of Economics and Statistics*, May.

Samuelson, P.A. (1946), 'Lord Keynes and the General Theory', *Econometrica*, July.

Samuelson, P.A. (1948), *Economics*, New York: McGraw-Hill.

Samuelson, P.A. (1955), *Economics*, 3rd edn, New York: McGraw-Hill.

Samuelson, P.A. (1983), 'The Keynes Centenary: Sympathy From the Other Cambridge', *The Economist*, 25 June.

Samuelson, P.A. (1984), 'Evaluating Reagonomics', *Challenge*, November/December.

Samuelson, P.A. (1988), 'In the Beginning', *Challenge*, July/August.

*Samuelson, P.A. and Solow, R.M. (1960), 'Analytical Aspects of Anti-Inflationary Policy', *American Economic Review*, May.

Sandilands, R. (2002), 'Great Depression', in B. Snowdon and H.R. Vane (eds), *An Encyclopedia of Macroeconomics*, Cheltenham, UK and Northampton, MA, USA: Edward Elgar.

Sanfey, P.J. (1995), 'Insiders and Outsiders in Union Models', *Journal of Economic Surveys*.

*Santomero, A.M. and Seater, J.J. (1978), 'The Inflation–Unemployment Trade-Off: A Critique of the Literature', *Journal of Economic Literature*, June.

Sargent, T.J. (1979), *Macroeconomic Theory*, New York: Academic Press.

Sargent, T.J. (1982), 'The End of Four Big Inflations', in R.H. Hall (ed.), *Inflation: Causes and Effects*, Chicago: University of Chicago Press.

Sargent, T.J. (1993), *Rational Expectations and Inflation*, 2nd edn, New York: HarperCollins.

Sargent, T.J. (1999), *The Conquest of American Inflation*, Princeton: Princeton University Press.

Sargent, T.J. and Wallace, N. (1975), 'Rational Expectations, the Optimal Monetary Instrument and the Optimal Money Supply Rule', *Journal of Political Economy*, April.

Sargent, T.J. and Wallace, N. (1976), 'Rational Expectations and the Theory of Economic Policy', *Journal of Monetary Economics*, April.

Sargent, T.J. and Wallace, N. (1981), 'Some Unpleasant Monetarist Arithmetic', *Federal Reserve Bank of Minneapolis Quarterly Review*, Autumn.

Savage, L. (1954), *The Foundations of Statistics*, New York: John Wiley.

Say, J.B. (1821), *A Treatise on Political Economy*, London: Longmans.

Schmookler, J. (1966), *Invention and Economic Growth*, Cambridge, MA: Harvard University Press.

Schneider, F. and Frey, B. (1988), 'Politico-Economic Models of Macroeconomics Policy: A Review of the Empirical Evidence', in T.D. Willet (ed.), *Political Business Cycles: The Political Economy of Money, Inflation and Unemployment*, Durham, NC: Duke University Press.

Schuknecht, L. (1996), 'Political Business Cycles and Fiscal Policies in Developing Countries', *Kyklos*.

Schultz, K. (1995), 'The Politics of the Political Business Cycle', *British Journal of Political Science*.

Schumpeter, J.A. (1934), *The Theory of Economic Development*, Cambridge, MA: Harvard University Press.

Schumpeter, J.A. (1939), *Business Cycles*, New York: McGraw-Hill.

Schumpeter, J.A. (1942), *Capitalism, Socialism and Democracy*, London: Allen and Unwin.

Schwartz, A.J. (1992), *Monetarism and Monetary Policy*, IEA Occasional Paper No. 86, London: Institute of Economic Affairs.

Selgin, G.A. (1988), *The Theory of Free Banking: Money Supply Under Competitive Note Issue*, Totowa, NJ: Roman and Littlefield.

Shackle, G.L.S. (1967), *The Years of High Theory*, Cambridge: Cambridge University Press.

*Shackle, G.L.S. (1974), *Keynesian Kaleidics*, Edinburgh: Edinburgh University Press.

Shapiro, C. and Stiglitz, J. (1984), 'Equilibrium Unemployment as a Worker Discipline Device', *American Economic Review*, June.

Shaw, G.K. (1984), *Rational Expectations: An Elementary Exposition*, Brighton: Wheatsheaf.

Shaw, G.K. (1988), *Keynesian Economics: The Permanent Revolution*, Aldershot, UK and Brookfield, USA: Edward Elgar.

Shaw, G.K. (1992), 'Policy Implications of Endogenous Growth Theory', *Economic Journal*, May.

Shaw, G.K. (2002), 'Balanced Budget Multiplier', in B. Snowdon and H.R. Vane (eds), *An Encyclopedia of Macroeconomics*, Cheltenham, UK and Northampton, MA, USA: Edward Elgar.

Sheffrin, S. (1989), *The Making of Economic Policy*, Oxford: Basil Blackwell.

Sheffrin, S.M. (1996), *Rational Expectations*, 2nd edn, Cambridge: Cambridge University Press.

Shiller, R.J. (1997), 'Why Do People Dislike Inflation?', in C.D. Romer and D.H. Romer (eds), *Reducing Inflation: Motivation and Strategy*, Chicago: University of Chicago Press.

*Siebert, H. (1997), 'Labour Market Rigidities: At the Root of Unemployment in Europe', *Journal of Economic Perspectives*, Summer.

Siklos, P.L. (ed.) (1995), *Great Inflations of the Twentieth Century: Theories, Policies and Evidence*, Aldershot, UK and Brookfield, USA: Edward Elgar.

Simkins, S.P. (1994), 'Do Real Business Cycle Models Really Exhibit Business Cycle Behaviour?', *Journal of Monetary Economics*, April.

Sims, C.A. (1972), 'Money, Income, and Causality', *American Economic Review*, September.

Sims, C.A. (1980), 'Comparisons of Interwar and Postwar Business Cycles: Monetarism Reconsidered', *American Economic Review*, May.

Sims, C.A. (1983), 'Is There a Monetary Business Cycle?', *American Economic Review*, May.

Sims, C.A. (1996), 'Macroeconomics and Methodology', *Journal of Economic Perspectives*, Winter.

*Skidelsky, R. (1983), *John Maynard Keynes, Vol. 1: Hopes Betrayed 1883–1920*, London: Macmillan.

*Skidelsky, R. (1992), *John Maynard Keynes, Vol. 2: The Economist as Saviour 1920–1937*, London: Macmillan.

Skidelsky, R. (1996a), 'The Influence of the Great Depression on Keynes's *General Theory*', *History of Economics Review*, Winter–Summer.

Skidelsky, R. (1996b), *Keynes*, Oxford: Oxford University Press.

*Skidelsky, R. (2000), *John Maynard Keynes, Vol. 3: Fighting for Britain, 1937–46*, London: Macmillan.

Skousen, M. (1990), *The Structure of Production*, New York: New York University Press.

Smith, A. (1776), *An Inquiry Into the Nature and Causes of the Wealth of Nations*, R.H. Campbell and A.S. Skinner (eds) (1976), Oxford: Clarendon Press.

Smith, D. (1987), *The Rise and Fall of Monetarism: The Theory and Politics of an Economic Experiment*, Harmondsworth: Penguin.

Smith, R.T. (1992), 'The Cyclical Behaviour of Prices', *Journal of Money, Credit, and Banking*, November.

Smithin, J. (2002), 'Phillips Curve', in B. Snowdon and H.R. Vane (eds), *An Encyclopedia of Macroeconomics*, Cheltenham, UK and Northampton, MA, USA: Edward Elgar.

Snowdon, B. (1997), 'Politics and the Business Cycle', *Political Quarterly*, July.

Snowdon, B. (2001a), 'Keeping the Keynesian Faith: Alan Blinder on the Evolution of Macroeconomics', *World Economics*, April–June.

Snowdon, B. (2001b), 'Redefining the Role of the State: Stiglitz on Building a Post-Washington Consensus', *World Economics*, July–September.

Snowdon, B. (2001c), 'Bhagwati on Growth, Trade and Development in the Second Age of Globalisation', *World Economics*, October–December.

*Snowdon, B. (2002a), *Conversations on Growth, Stability and Trade*, Cheltenham, UK and Northampton, MA, USA: Edward Elgar.

Snowdon, B. (2002b), 'The Ups and Downs of Capitalism: Ben Bernanke on the "Great Depression" and the "Great Inflation" ', *World Economics*, April–June.

Snowdon, B. (2002c), 'In Praise of Historical Economics: Bradford DeLong on Growth, Development and Instability', *World Economics*, January–March.

Snowdon, B. (2002d), 'Should We Be Globaphobic About Globalisation? Dani Rodrik on the Economic and Political Implications of Increasing International Economic Integration', *World Economics*, October–December.

Snowdon, B. (2003a), 'In Search of the Holy Grail: William Easterly on the Elusive Quest for Growth and Development', *World Economics*, July–September.

Snowdon, B. (2003b), 'From Socialism to Capitalism and Democracy: Janos Kornai on the Trials of Socialism and Transition', *World Economics*, January–March.

Snowdon, B. (2003c), 'Back to the Future: Jeffrey Williamson on Globalisation in History', *World Economics*, October–December.

Snowdon, B. (2004a), 'Outside the Mainstream: Axel Leijonhufvud on Twentieth Century Macroeconomics', *Macroeconomic Dynamics*, February.

Snowdon, B. (2004b), 'Beyond the "Ivory Tower": Stanley Fischer on the Economics of Contemporary Global Issues', *World Economics*, January–March.

Snowdon, B. (2004c), 'Explaining the "Great Divergence": Daron Acemoglu on How Growth Theorists Rediscovered History and the Importance of Institutions', *World Economics*, April–June.

Snowdon, B. and Vane, H.R. (1995), 'New Keynesian Economics Today: The Empire Strikes Back', *American Economist*, Spring.

Snowdon, B. and Vane, H.R. (1996), 'The Development of Modern Macroeconomics: Reflections in the Light of Johnson's Analysis After Twenty-Five Years', *Journal of Macroeconomics*, Summer.

*Snowdon, B. and Vane, H.R. (eds) (1997a), *A Macroeconomics Reader*, London: Routledge.

Snowdon, B. and Vane, H.R. (1997b), 'Modern Macroeconomics and Its

Evolution from a Monetarist Perspective: An Interview with Professor Milton Friedman', *Journal of Economic Studies*.

Snowdon, B. and Vane, H.R. (1998), 'Transforming Macroeconomics: An Interview with Robert E. Lucas Jr.', *Journal of Economic Methodology*, June.

Snowdon, B. and Vane, H.R. (1999a), 'The New Political Macroeconomics', *American Economist*, Spring.

Snowdon, B. and Vane, H.R. (1999b), *Conversations with Leading Economists: Interpreting Modern Macroeconomics*, Cheltenham, UK and Northampton, MA, USA: Edward Elgar.

Snowdon, B. and Vane, H.R. (2002a), 'James Tobin, 1918–2002: An "Unreconstructed Old Keynesian" Who Wouldn't Quit', *World Economics*, July–September.

*Snowdon, B. and Vane, H.R. (2002b), *An Encyclopedia of Macroeconomics*, Cheltenham, UK and Northampton, MA, USA: Edward Elgar.

Snowdon, B., Vane, H.R. and Wynarczyk, P. (1994), *A Modern Guide to Macroeconomics: An Introduction to Competing Schools of Thought*, Aldershot, UK and Brookfield, USA: Edward Elgar.

Soh, B.H. (1986), 'Political Business Cycles in Industrialized Democratic Countries', *Kyklos*.

*Sokoloff, K. and Engerman, S. (2000), 'Institutions, Factor Endowments and Paths of Development in the New World', *Journal of Economic Perspectives*, Summer.

Solomou, S. (1996), *Themes in Macroeconomic History: The UK Economy, 1919–39*, Cambridge: Cambridge University Press.

Solow, R.M. (1956), 'A Contribution to the Theory of Economic Growth', *Quarterly Journal of Economics*, February.

Solow, R.M. (1957), 'Technical Change and the Aggregate Production Function', *Review of Economics and Statistics*, August.

Solow, R.M. (1966), 'The Case Against the Case Against the Guideposts' in G.P. Schultz and R.Z. Aliber (eds), *Guidelines, Informal Controls and the Market Place: Policy in a Full Employment Economy*, Chicago: University of Chicago Press.

Solow, R.M. (1979), 'Another Possible Source of Wage Stickiness', *Journal of Macroeconomics*, Winter.

Solow, R.M. (1980), 'On Theories of Unemployment', *American Economic Review*, March.

Solow, R.M. (1985), 'Economic History and Economics', *American Economic Review*.

Solow, R.M. (1986), 'What is a Nice Girl Like You Doing in a Place Like This? Macroeconomics After Fifty Years', *Eastern Economic Journal*, July–September.

Solow, R.M. (1988), 'Growth Theory and After', *American Economic Review*, June.

Solow, R.M. (1990), *The Labour Market as a Social Institution*, Oxford: Basil Blackwell.

Solow, R.M. (1994), 'Perspectives on Growth Theory', *Journal of Economic Perspectives*, Winter.

*Solow, R.M. (1997), 'Is There a Core of Usable Macroeconomics That We Should All Believe In?', *American Economic Review*, May.

Solow, R.M. (1998), 'How Cautious Must the Fed Be?', in R.M. Solow and J.B. Taylor, *Inflation, Unemployment and Monetary Policy*, Cambridge, MA: MIT Press.

*Solow, R.M. (2000), *Growth Theory: An Exposition*, 2nd edn, Oxford: Oxford University Press.

Solow, R.M. (ed.) (2001), *Landmark Papers in Economic Growth*, Cheltenham, UK and Northampton, MA, USA: Edward Elgar.

*Solow, R.M. (2002), 'Neoclassical Growth Model' in B. Snowdon and H.R. Vane (eds), An *Encyclopedia of Macroeconomics*, Cheltenham, UK and Northampton, MA, USA: Edward Elgar.

*Solow, R.M. and Taylor, J.B. (1998), *Inflation, Unemployment and Monetary Policy*, Cambridge, MA: MIT Press.

Solow, R.M. and Tobin, J. (1988), 'Introduction to the Kennedy Reports', in J. Tobin and M. Weidenbaum (eds), *Two Revolutions in Economic Policy: The First Economic Reports of Presidents Kennedy and Reagan*, Cambridge, MA: MIT Press.

Sowell, T. (1972), *Say's Law: An Historical Analysis*, Princeton: Princeton University Press.

Spence, M. (1974), *Market Signalling*, Cambridge, MA: Harvard University Press.

Sraffa, P. (1926), 'The Law of Returns Under Competitive Conditions', *Economic Journal*, December.

Stadler, G.W. (1990), 'Business Cycle Models with Endogenous Technology', *American Economic Review*, September.

*Stadler, G.W. (1994), 'Real Business Cycle Theory: A Survey', *Journal of Economic Literature*, December.

Stafford, G. (1999), 'Economic Growth: How Good Can it Get?, *American Economic Review*, May.

Staiger, D., Stock, J.H. and Watson, M.W. (1997), 'The NAIRU, Unemployment and Monetary Policy', *Journal of Economic Perspectives*, Winter.

Stein, H. (1969), *The Fiscal Revolution in America*, Chicago: University of Chicago Press.

Stewart, M. (1986), *Keynes and After*, 3rd edn, Harmondsworth: Penguin.

Stiglitz, J.E. (1984), 'Price Rigidities and Market Structure', *American Economic Review*, May.

*Stiglitz, J.E. (1987), 'The Causes and Consequences of the Dependency of Quality on Prices', *Journal of Economic Literature*, March.

*Stiglitz, J.E. (1992), 'Methodological Issues and the New Keynesian Economics', in A. Vercelli and N. Dimitri (eds), *Macroeconomics: A Survey of Research Strategies*, Oxford: Oxford University Press.

Stiglitz, J.E. (1993), *Economics*, New York: W.W. Norton.

*Stiglitz, J.E. (1997), 'Reflections on the Natural Rate Hypothesis', *Journal of Economic Perspectives*, Winter.

Stiglitz, J.E. (1999a), 'Central Banking in a Democratic Society', *De Economist*.

Stiglitz, J.E. (1999b), 'Towards a General Theory of Wage and Price Rigidities and Economic Fluctuations', *American Economic Review*, May.

*Stiglitz, J.E. (2000), 'The Contribution of the New Economics of Information to Twentieth Century Economics', *Quarterly Journal of Economics*, November.

*Stiglitz, J.E. (2002), 'Information and Change in the Paradigm in Economics', *American Economic Review*, June.

Stiglitz, J.E. and Greenwald, B. (2003), *Towards a New Paradigm in Monetary Economics*, Cambridge: Cambridge University Press.

Stock, J.H. and Watson, M.W. (1988), 'Variable Trends in Economic Time Series', *Journal of Economic Perspectives*, Summer.

Strigl, R. (2000 [1934]), *Capital and Production*, Auburn, AL: The Ludwig von Mises Institute.

Sugden, R. (1987), 'New Developments in the Theory of Choice Under Uncertainty', in J.D. Hey and P.J. Lambert (eds), *Surveys in the Economics of Uncertainty*, Oxford: Basil Blackwell.

Summers, L.H. (1986), 'Some Sceptical Observations on Real Business Cycle Theory', *Federal Reserve Bank of Minneapolis Quarterly Review*, Fall.

Summers, L.H. (1988), 'Relative Wages, Efficiency Wages, and Keynesian Unemployment', *American Economic Review*, May.

Summers, L.H. (1990), *Understanding Unemployment*, Cambridge, MA: MIT Press.

Summers, L.H. (1991a), 'The Scientific Illusion in Empirical Macroeconomics', *Scandinavian Journal of Economics*.

Summers, L.H. (1991b), 'How Should Long-Term Monetary Policy be Determined?', *Journal of Money, Credit, and Banking*, August.

Summers, L.H. (1996), 'Why are Central Banks Pursuing Price Stability? A Comment', *Achieving Price Stability: A Symposium*, sponsored by the Federal Reserve Banks of Kansas City, Kansas City, MO: The Bank.

Summers, R. and Heston, A. (1991), 'The Penn World Table (Mark 5): An

Expanded Set of International Comparisons, 1950–88', *Quarterly Journal of Economics*, May.

*Svensson, L.E.O. (1996), 'The Scientific Contributions of Robert E. Lucas Jr.', *Scandinavian Journal of Economics*, March.

Svensson, L.E.O. (1997a), 'Optimal Inflation Targets, "Conservative" Central Banks and Linear Inflation Contracts', *American Economic Review*, March.

Svensson, L.E.O. (1997b), 'Inflation Forecast Targeting: Implementing and Monitoring Inflation Targets', *European Economic Review*, June.

Svensson, L.E.O. (1999), 'Inflation Targeting as a Monetary Policy Rule', *Journal of Monetary Economics*, June.

Svensson, L.E.O. (2000), 'The First Year of the Euro-System: Inflation Targeting or Not', *American Economic Review*, May.

Svensson, L.E.O. (2003a), 'Escaping From the Liquidity Trap: The Foolproof Way and Others', *Journal of Economic Perspectives*, Fall.

Svensson, L.E.O. (2003b), 'What is Wrong With Taylor Rules? Using Judgement in Monetary Policy Through Targeting Rules', *Journal of Economic Literature*, June.

Swan, T.W. (1956), 'Economic Growth and Capital Accumulation', *Economic Record*, November.

Tamura, R. (1996), 'From Decay to Growth: A Demographic Transition to Economic Growth', *Journal of Economic Dynamics and Control*, June–July.

*Tanzi, V. (1998), 'Corruption Around the World: Cause, Consequences, Scope and Cures, *IMF Staff Papers*, December.

Tanzi, V. (1999), 'Transition and the Changing Role of Government', *Finance and Development*, June.

Tanzi, V. and Schuknecht, L. (2000), *Public Spending in the Twentieth Century: A Global Perspective*, Cambridge: Cambridge University Press.

Tarshis, L. (1939), 'Changes in Real and Money Wages', *Economic Journal*, March.

Tavelli, H., Tullio, G. and Spinelli, F. (1998), 'The Evolution of European Central Bank Independence: An Updating of the Masciandaro and Spinelli Index', *Scottish Journal of Political Economy*, August.

Taylor, A.M. (1998), 'On the Costs of Inward-Looking Development: Price Distortions, Growth, and Divergence in Latin America', *Journal of Economic History*, March.

Taylor, H. (1985), 'Time Inconsistency: A Potential Problem for Policymakers', *Federal Reserve Bank of Philadelphia Business Review*, March/April.

Taylor, J. (1972), 'The Behaviour of Unemployment and Unfilled Vacancies: Great Britain, 1958–71, An Alternative View', *Economic Journal*, December.

Taylor, J.B. (1980), 'Aggregate Dynamics and Staggered Contracts', *Journal of Political Economy*, February.
Taylor, J.B. (1989), 'The Evolution of Ideas in Macroeconomics', *Economic Record*, June.
Taylor, J.B. (1992a), 'The Great Inflation, the Great Disinflation, and Policies for Future Price Stability' in A. Blundell-Wignall (ed.), *Inflation, Disinflation and Monetary Policy*, Sydney: Ambassador Press.
Taylor, J.B. (1992b), 'Synchronised Wage Determination and Macroeconomic Performance in Seven Large Countries', in A. Vercelli and N. Dimitri (eds), *Macroeconomics: A Survey of Research Strategies*, Oxford: Oxford University Press.
*Taylor, J.B. (1993), 'Discretion Versus Policy Rules in Practice', *Carnegie-Rochester Conference Series on Public Policy*, Amsterdam: North-Holland.
*Taylor, J.B. (1996), 'Stabilisation Policy and Long-Term Growth', in R. Landau, T. Taylor and G. Wright (eds), *The Mosaic of Economic Growth*, Stanford: Stanford University Press.
Taylor, J.B. (1997a), 'Comment', in C.D. Romer and D.H. Romer (eds), *Reducing Inflation: Motivation and Strategy*, Chicago: University of Chicago Press.
*Taylor, J.B. (1997b), 'A Core of Practical Macroeconomics', *American Economic Review*, May.
Taylor, J.B. (1998a), 'Monetary Policy Guidelines for Employment and Inflation Stability', in R.M. Solow and J.B. Taylor, *Inflation, Unemployment and Monetary Policy*, Cambridge, MA: MIT Press.
Taylor, J.B. (1998b), 'Monetary Policy and the Long Boom', *Federal Reserve Bank of St. Louis Review*, December.
Taylor, J.B. (1999), 'A Historical Analysis of Monetary Policy Rules', in J.B. Taylor (ed.), *Monetary Policy Rules*, Chicago: University of Chicago Press.
*Taylor, J.B. (2000a), 'Reassessing Discretionary Fiscal Policy', *Journal of Economic Perspectives*, Summer.
*Taylor, J.B. (2000b), 'Teaching Modern Macroeconomics at the Principles Level', *American Economic Review*, May.
Taylor, J.B. (2001), *Economics*, 3rd edn, New York: Houghton Mifflin.
Temin, P. (1976), *Did Monetary Forces Cause the Great Depression?*, New York: W.W. Norton.
*Temin, P. (1989), *Lessons From the Great Depression*, Cambridge, MA: MIT Press.
Temin, P. (1993), 'Transmission of the Great Depression', *Journal of Economic Perspectives*, Spring.
Temin, P. (1997), 'Is it Kosher to Talk About Culture?' *Journal of Economic History*, June.
Temin, P. (1998), 'The Causes of the American Business Cycle: An Essay in

Economic Historiography', in J.C. Fuhrer and S. Schuh (eds), *Beyond Shocks*, Boston, MA: Boston Federal Reserve Bank.

Temple, J. (1998), 'Initial Conditions, Social Capital and Growth in Africa', *Journal of African Economies*, October.

*Temple, J. (1999), 'The New Growth Evidence', *Journal of Economic Literature*, March.

Temple, J. (2000), 'Inflation and Growth: Stories Short and Tall', *Journal of Economic Surveys*, September.

*Temple, J. (2003), 'The Long-Run Implications of Growth Theories', *Journal of Economic Surveys*, July.

Temple, J. and Johnson, P. (1998), 'Social Capital and Economic Growth', *Quarterly Journal of Economics*, August.

Theil, H. (1956), 'On the Theory of Economic Policy', *American Economic Review*, May.

Thirlwall, A.P. (1993), 'The Renaissance of Keynesian Economics', *Banca Nazionale del Lavoro Quarterly Review*, September.

Thurow, L.C. (1983), *Dangerous Currents: The State of Economics*, New York: Random House.

Thurow, L. (1992), *Head to Head*, New York: Morrow.

Timbrell, M. (1989), 'Contracts and Market Clearing in the Labour Market', in D. Greenaway (ed.), *Current Issues in Macroeconomics*, Basingstoke: Macmillan.

Tinbergen, J. (1952), *On The Theory of Economic Policy*, Amsterdam: North-Holland.

Tobin, J. (1958), 'Liquidity Preference as Behaviour Towards Risk', *Review of Economic Studies*, February.

Tobin, J. (1970), 'Money and Income: Post Hoc Ergo Propter Hoc', *Quarterly Journal of Economics*, May.

*Tobin, J. (1972a), 'Inflation and Unemployment', *American Economic Review*, March.

Tobin, J. (1972b), 'Friedman's Theoretical Framework', *Journal of Political Economy*, September/October.

Tobin, J. (1975), 'Keynesian Models of Recession and Depression', *American Economic Review*, May.

*Tobin, J. (1977), 'How Dead is Keynes?', *Economic Inquiry*, October.

Tobin, J. (1980a), *Asset Accumulation and Economic Activity: Reflections on Contemporary Macroeconomic Theory*, Oxford: Basil Blackwell.

*Tobin, J. (1980b), 'Are New Classical Models Plausible Enough to Guide Policy?', *Journal of Money, Credit, and Banking*, November.

Tobin, J. (1980c) 'Stabilisation Policy Ten Years After', *Brookings Papers on Economic Activity*.

*Tobin, J. (1981), 'The Monetarist Counter-Revolution Today – An Appraisal', *Economic Journal*, March.

Tobin, J. (1985), 'Theoretical Issues in Macroeconomics', in G.R. Feiwel (ed.), *Issues in Contemporary Macroeconomics and Distribution*, Albany: State University of New York Press.

*Tobin, J. (1987), *Policies For Prosperity: Essays in a Keynesian Mode*, P.M. Jackson (ed.), Brighton: Wheatsheaf.

Tobin, J. (1988), '"Comment" on David Romer's paper "What are the Costs of Excessive Deficits?"', *NBER Macroeconomics Annual*.

Tobin, J. (1989), 'Keynesian Theory: Is It Still a Useful Tool in the Economic Reality of Today?', *Revista di Politica Economica*, April.

*Tobin, J. (1993), 'Price Flexibility and Output Stability: An Old Keynesian View', *Journal of Economic Perspectives*, Winter.

Tobin, J. (1995), 'The Natural Rate as New Classical Economics', in R. Cross (ed.), *The Natural Rate of Unemployment: Reflections on 25 Years of the Hypothesis*, Cambridge: Cambridge University Press.

*Tobin, J. (1996), *Full Employment and Growth: Further Essays on Policy*, Cheltenham, UK and Brookfield, USA: Edward Elgar.

Tobin, J. (1997), 'An Overview of *The General Theory*', Cowles Foundation Paper, No. 947.

Tobin, J. (1998), 'Monetary Policy: Recent Theory and Practice', Cowles Foundation Discussion Paper, No. 1187.

Tobin, J. (2001), 'Fiscal Policy: Its Macroeconomics in Perspective', Cowles Foundation Discussion Paper, No. 1301, May.

Tocqueville, A. de (1835), *Democracy in America*, New York: Random House, 1954.

Tomlinson, J.D. (1984), 'A Keynesian Revolution in Economic Policy-Making?', *Economic History Review*, May.

Townshend, H. (1937), 'Liquidity-Premium and the Theory of Value', *Economic Journal*, March.

Treasury (1999), *The New Monetary Policy Framework*, London: H.M. Treasury.

Trevithick, J.A. (1975), 'Keynes, Inflation and Money Illusion', *Economic Journal*, March.

Trevithick, J.A. (1992), *Involuntary Unemployment: Macroeconomics from a Keynesian Perspective*, London: Harvester-Wheatsheaf.

Trevithick, J.A. and Stevenson, A. (1977), 'The Complementarity of Monetary Policy and Incomes Policy', *Scottish Journal of Political Economy*, February.

Trigg, A. (2002), 'Business Cycles: Keynesian Approach', in B. Snowdon and H.R. Vane (eds), *An Encyclopedia of Macroeconomics*, Cheltenham, UK and Northampton, MA, USA: Edward Elgar.

Tufte, E.R. (1975), 'Determinants of the Outcomes of Midterm Congressional Elections', *American Political Science Review*, September.

Tufte, E.R. (1978), *Political Control of the Economy*, Princeton, NJ: Princeton University Press.

Ugur, M. (ed.) (2002), *An Open Economy Macroeconomics Reader*, London: Routledge.

Vamvakidis, A. (2002), 'How Robust is the Growth–Openness Connection? Historical Evidence', *Journal of Economic Growth*, March.

Vane, H.R. (1992), 'The Thatcher Years: Macroeconomic Policy and Performance of the UK Economy, 1979–1988', *National Westminster Bank Quarterly Review*, May.

*Vane, H.R. and Mulhearn, C. (2004), 'The Nobel Memorial Prize in Economics: A Biographical Guide to Potential Future Winners', *World Economics*, January–March.

Vane, H.R. and Thompson, J.L. (1979), *Monetarism: Theory, Evidence and Policy*, Oxford: Martin Robertson.

Vercelli, A. (1991), *Methodological Foundations of Macroeconomics: Keynes and Lucas*, Cambridge: Cambridge University Press.

Vetter, H. and Andersen, T.M. (1994), 'Do Turnover Costs Protect Insiders?', *Economic Journal*, January.

Vickers, J. (1998), 'Inflation Targeting in Practice: The UK Experience', *Bank of England Quarterly Bulletin*, November.

*Vines, D. (2003), 'John Maynard Keynes 1937–46: The Creation of International Macroeconomics', *Economic Journal*, June.

Von Neumann, J. and Morgenstern, O. (1953), *The Theory of Games and Economic Behaviour*, 3rd edn, Princeton: Princeton University Press.

Wagner, R. (1977), 'Economic Manipulation For Political Profit: Macroeconomic Consequences and Constitutional Implications', *Kyklos*.

Waller, C.J. and Walsh, C.E. (1996), 'Central Bank Independence, Economic Behaviour and Optimal Term Lengths', *American Economic Review*, December.

Walsh, C.E. (1986), 'New Views of the Business Cycle: Has the Past Emphasis on Money Been Misplaced?', *Federal Reserve Bank of Philadelphia Business Review*, February.

Walsh, C.E. (1993), 'Central Bank Strategies, Credibility and Independence: A Review Essay', *Journal of Monetary Economics*, November.

Walsh, C.E. (1995a), 'Optimal Contracts for Central Bankers', *American Economic Review*, March.

Walsh, Carl (1995b), 'Recent Central-Bank Reforms and the Role of Price Stability as the Sole Objective of Monetary Policy', *NBER Macroeconomics Annual*.

Walsh, C.E. (1998), *Monetary Theory and Policy*, Cambridge, MA: MIT Press.

Walters, A.A. (1971), 'Consistent Expectations, Distributed Lags and the Quantity Theory', *Economic Journal*, June.

Walters, B. and Young, D. (1997), 'On the Coherence of Post Keynesian Economics', *Scottish Journal of Political Economy*, August.

Warming, J. (1932), 'International Difficulties Arising Out of the Financing of Public Works During a Depression', *Economic Journal*, June.

Weber, S. (1997), 'The End of the Business Cycle?', *Foreign Affairs*, July/August.

Weintraub, E.R. (1979), *Microfoundations*, Cambridge: Cambridge University Press.

Weiss, A. (1980), 'Job Queues and Layoffs in Labour Markets with Flexible Wages', *Journal of Political Economy*, June.

Weiss, A. (1991), *Efficiency Wages: Models of Unemployment, Layoffs and Wage Dispersion*, Oxford: Clarendon Press.

Weitzman, M.L. (1985), 'Profit Sharing as Macroeconomic Policy', *American Economic Review*, May.

Wheeler, M. (ed.) (1998), *The Economics of the Great Depression*, Kalamazoo, MI: W.E. Upjohn Institute for Employment Research.

White, H. (1992), 'The Macroeconomic Impact of Development Aid: A Critical Survey', *Journal of Development Studies*, January.

White, L.H. (1989), *Competition and Currency: Essays on Free Banking and Money*, New York: New York University Press.

Wickens, M. (1995), 'Real Business Cycle Analysis: A Needed Revolution in Macroeconometrics', *Economic Journal*, November.

Wicksell, K. (1958), 'Ends and Means in Economics', in his *Selected Papers on Economic Theory* (ed. E. Lindahl), London: Allen and Unwin.

*Willet, T.D. (ed.) (1988), *Political Business Cycles: The Political Economy of Money, Inflation and Unemployment*, Durham, NC: Duke University Press.

Williamson, S.D. (1996), 'Real Business Cycle Research Comes of Age: A Review Essay', *Journal of Monetary Economics*, August.

Wilson, T. (1980), 'Robertson, Money and Monetarism', *Journal of Economic Literature*, December.

Winters, A. (2004), 'Trade Performance and Economic Performance: An Overview', *Economic Journal*, February.

Wittman, D.A. (1977), 'Candidates with Policy Preferences: A Dynamic Model', *Journal of Economic Theory*, February.

*Woodford, M. (2000), 'Revolution and Evolution in Twentieth-Century Macroeconomics', in P. Gifford (ed.), *Frontiers of the Mind in the Twenty-First Century*, Cambridge, MA: Harvard University Press.

Woolley, J.T. (1994), 'The Politics of Monetary Policy: A Critical Review', *Journal of Public Policy*.

World Bank (1993), *The East Asian Miracle: Economic Growth and Public Policy*, Oxford: Oxford University Press.

*World Bank (1997), *The State in a Changing World*, Oxford: Oxford University Press.

World Bank (1998/9), *Knowledge for Development*, Oxford: Oxford University Press.

*World Bank (2002), *Building Institutions for Markets*, Oxford: Oxford University Press.

Wright, G. (1997), 'Towards a More Historical Approach to Technological Change', *Economic Journal*, September.

Wrigley, E. (1988), *Continuity, Chance and Change: The Character of the Industrial Revolution in England*, Cambridge: Cambridge University Press.

Yang, X. (2003), *Economic Development and the Division of Labour*, Oxford: Blackwell.

*Yellen, J.L. (1984), 'Efficiency Wage Models of Unemployment', *American Economic Review*, May.

*Yergin, D. and Stanislaw, J. (1999), *The Commanding Heights: The Battle Between Government and the Marketplace That is Remaking the Modern World*, New York: Touchstone.

Ying, L.G. (1999), 'China's Changing Regional Disparities During the Reform Period', *Economic Geography*, January.

Young, A. (1928), 'Increasing Returns and Economic Progress', *Economic Journal*, December.

Young, A. (1992), 'A Tale of Two Cities: Factor Accumulation and Technical Change in Hong Kong and Singapore', *NBER Macroeconomics Annual*.

Young, A. (1994), 'Lessons from the East Asian NICs: A Contrarian View', *European Economic Review*, April.

*Young, A. (1995), 'The Tyranny of Numbers: Confronting the Statistical Realities of the East Asian Growth Experience', *Quarterly Journal of Economics*, August.

Young, W. (1987), *Interpreting Mr. Keynes: The IS–LM Enigma*, Cambridge: Polity Press.

Young, W. and Darity, W. Jr (2004), 'IS–LM–BP', in M. De Vroey and K.D. Hoover (eds), *The IS–LM Model: Its Rise, Fall and Strange Persistence*, Durham, NC: Duke University Press.

Young W. and Zilberfarb, B.Z. (eds) (2000), *IS–LM and Modern Macroeconomics*, Boston, MA: Kluwer Academic Publishers.

Zak, P.J. and Knack, S. (2001), 'Trust and Growth', *Economic Journal*, April.

Zarnowitz, V. (1985), 'Recent Work on Business Cycles in Historical Perspective', *Journal of Economic Literature*, June.

*Zarnowitz, V. (1992a), 'What is a Business Cycle?', in M. Belongia and M. Garfinkel (eds), *The Business Cycle: Theories and Evidence*, London: Kluwer Academic Publishers.

Zarnowitz, V. (1992b), *Business Cycles: Theory, History, Indicators and Forecasting*, Chicago: University of Chicago Press.

*Zijp, R. (1993), *Austrian and New Classical Business Cycle Theories: A Comparative Study Through the Method of Rational Reconstruction*, Aldershot, UK and Brookfield, USA: Edward Elgar.

# Author index

Abel, A.B. xiv, 237, 301, 305, 306, 307, 321, 333, 378, 387, 408, 603, 612
Abraham, K.G. 328
Abramovitz, M. 34, 88, 585, 586, 587, 597, 610, 620, 635, 666, 693
Acemoglu, D. 31, 32, 517, 562, 563, 588, 635, 636, 637, 639, 642, 643, 652, 654, 656, 706
Ackley, G. 37, 38
Adelman, I. 597, 636
Adsera, A. 643
Aghion, P. 34, 556, 557, 585, 628
Aidt, T.S. 562
Akerlof, G.A. 57, 74, 160, 187, 247, 336, 372, 374, 384, 385, 388, 391, 392, 393, 432, 441
Akerman, J. 518
Akhtar, M.A. 262
Aldcroft, D.H. 12
Alesina, A. 2, 29, 30, 31, 195, 259, 260, 261, 262, 279, 413, 517, 519, 525, 526, 532, 535, 536, 537, 539, 542, 543, 544, 545, 547, 548, 549, 550, 551, 553, 554, 555, 556, 557, 558, 560, 564, 566, 567, 569, 572, 579, 637, 646, 652, 688
Allsopp, C. 416
Alogoskoufis, G.S. 261
Alston, R. 6
Alt, J.E. 30, 536, 565
Altonji, J.G. 328
Alvi, E. 398
Andersen, T.M. 371, 395
Ando, A. 171
Arestis, P. 187, 359, 376, 452
Arnold, L.G. 240, 297
Arrow, K.J. 336, 460, 625
Artadi, E. 653
Artis, M. 413
Ashton, P. 263, 285
Atkinson, A.B. 423

Attfield, C.L.F. 230
Azariadis, C. 384

Backhouse, R.E. 13, 46, 72, 113, 182, 230, 321
Backus, D.K. 257, 329, 341, 548
Bade, R. 260, 361
Bailey, M.N. 16, 384
Bain, K. 196
Bairoch, P. 589
Balassa, B. 648
Baldwin, R.E. 621, 647
Ball, L. 249, 250, 335, 363, 370, 378, 379, 394, 398, 403, 411, 429, 430, 437
Balls, E. 416, 419
Bardhan, P. 388
Barens, I. 113
Barro, R.J. 22, 32, 34, 72, 112, 156, 162, 163, 230, 231, 246, 268, 269, 288, 296, 297, 312, 317, 318, 320, 323, 346, 358, 360, 363, 371, 412, 430, 431, 440, 550, 556, 557, 564, 585, 586, 590, 603, 604, 610, 612, 617, 618, 622, 623, 625, 629, 631, 635, 636, 637, 640, 659, 662, 678, 688, 697
Barsky, R.B. 358
Bartels, L.M. 534
Bates, R.H. 563
Baumol, W.J. 13, 34, 46, 580, 584, 585, 587, 597, 611, 617, 622, 644, 650, 666, 697
Bean, C.R. 258, 401, 418
Beaud, M. 113, 223
Becker, G.S. 582, 621
Begg, D.K.H. 44, 230, 697
Benabou, R. 556
Bénassy, J.P. 362
Ben-David, D. 648, 650
Benjamin, D.K. 337

Benson Durham, J. 636
Berger, H. 414
Bernanke, B.S. xiv, 9, 11, 27, 76, 77, 79,
    80, 81, 170, 237, 260, 262, 301,
    305, 306, 307, 321, 333, 334, 378,
    382, 387, 400, 408, 413, 414, 415,
    416, 552, 603, 612, 633
Besley, T. 517
Bhagwati, J. 588, 600, 601, 614, 641,
    647, 648
Bhaskar, V. 429
Birdzell, L.E. 592
Black, F. 323
Blackburn, K. 251, 256, 257, 262, 327,
    548, 549, 588
Blackman, S.A.B. 587
Blanchard, O.J. xiv, 5, 6, 9, 29, 85, 113,
    220, 262, 267, 269, 300, 301, 307,
    335, 341, 360, 362, 365, 374, 401,
    406, 408, 429, 696, 698, 704, 705
Blaug, M. 1, 5, 33, 113, 163, 164, 175,
    182, 598, 626, 695, 697
Bleaney, M. 23, 260
Blinder, A.S. 29, 56, 110, 145, 179, 196,
    197, 262, 267, 279, 299, 330, 335,
    340, 341, 357, 358, 364, 365, 383,
    428, 429, 430, 439, 442, 443, 536,
    704
Bloom, D.E. 587, 598, 652, 653
Böhm-Bawerk, E. v. 474, 475
Boix, C. 643
Bolton, P. 564
Boone, P. 601
Booth, A. 17, 697
Bordo, M.D. 76, 77, 82, 113, 647
Boskin, M.J. 587
Bosworth, B.P. 614, 665
Bourguignon, F. 620
Brady, H.E. 534
Brandolini, A. 328
Braun, R.A. 334
Brech, M. 249
Brendon, P. 10
Bridel, P. 122
Brimmer, A.F. 185, 249
Britton, A. 2, 3, 5, 413
Bronfenbrenner, M. 299
Broughton, J.M. 135
Brown, G. 411, 414, 549, 592
Brumberg, R. 113, 697

Brunner, K. 50, 193, 697
Bruno, M. 21
Buchanan, J.M. 23, 90, 111, 195, 519
Budd, A. 258, 418
Buiter, W.H. 23, 145, 168, 196, 247,
    270, 367, 410, 416
Burns, A. 16
Burns, A.F. 305
Burnside, C. 334
Burton, J. 23, 218, 519

Cagan, P. 205, 324, 697
Cairncross, A. 21
Cairncross, F. 21
Campbell, J.Y. 335
Canning, D. 652, 653
Capelli, P. 429
Capie, F.H. 556
Caplin, A.S. 430
Caporale, G.M. 342
Caporale, T. 298
Carabelli, A.M. 75
Carey, K. 77, 80, 81
Carlin, W. 334, 362, 403, 409
Carlson, K.M. 110
Carlton, D.W. 429
Carmignani, F. 544, 555
Caroli, E. 556, 557
Carter, M. 225, 230
Carvalho, F.J.C.D. 262
Case, A. 517
Caspari, V. 113
Cass, D. 675
Cecchetti, S.G. 370, 415, 416
Cesaratto, S. 612
Chadha, B. 249, 329
Chamberlin, E.H. 364
Chappell, H.W. 551
Chari, V.V. 220, 337
Chatterjee, S. 332
Chauvin, K. 429
Chenery, H.B. 601
Chick, V. 57, 452
Cho, J.O. 350
Choudri, E.U. 80, 82
Chow, G.C. 250
Christensen, M. 257, 548
Christiano, L.J. 337
Chrystal, K.A. 193, 565
Clague, C. 636

Clarida, R. 27, 419, 421, 423, 427
Clark, G. 657
Clower, R.W. 71, 72, 697
Cochran, J.P. 497
Coddington, A. 57, 70, 71, 277, 451, 452
Coe, D.T. 650
Cohen, G.D. 2, 30, 31, 195, 262, 525, 536, 572
Colander, D.C. 23, 56, 72, 113, 361, 365, 519
Cole, H. 15, 76, 79, 336, 337
Collier, P. 564, 588, 637, 646, 653
Collins, S.M. 614, 665
Cooley, T.F. 26, 307, 321, 322, 329, 350, 588
Cornwall, J. 248
Corry, B.A. 54
Crafts, N.F.R. 17, 582, 585, 593, 594, 598, 613, 614, 620, 622, 625, 626, 628, 629, 652
Criss, A.J. 615
Cross, R. 28, 175, 187, 192, 247, 401, 403, 405, 406, 411
Crucini, M.J. 79
Cukierman, A. 258, 538, 550, 551, 556
Culbertson, J.M. 169
Cunningham Wood, J. 57

Dalziel, P.C. 249
Danthine, J.P. 297, 307, 326, 705
Danziger, S. 459, 471
Darity, W. Jr. 113
Dasgupta, P. 635
David, P. 637
Davidson, G. 473
Davidson, P. 55, 57, 76, 113, 170, 324, 361, 431, 452, 453, 455, 458, 463, 469, 470, 473
Davies, D. 263, 285
Davis, M.D. 253
Dawson, J.W. 635
De Hahn, J. 414
De Prano, M. 171
De Vanssay, X. 124
De Vroey, M. 113, 222
De Wolff, P. 85, 698
Deane, P. 6
Deininger, K. 556
DeLong, J.B. 3, 17, 21, 77, 88, 142, 147, 195, 197, 358, 364, 421, 611, 616,

617, 622, 636, 637, 638, 640, 642, 648
Delorme, C.D. 329
Demery, D. 230
Denison, E.F. 34, 326, 596, 613, 614
Deutscher, P. 54, 69, 86, 87, 298
Devarajan, S. 601
Diamond, J. 594, 697
Diamond, P. 380, 412, 652, 654
Dickens, W.T. 160, 416
Dickinson, D.G. 297, 536
Dimand, R.W. 62, 111, 113, 120, 124
Dixon, H. 175, 231, 361, 364, 365, 376, 494
Dixon, W. 659
Dollar, D. 589, 597, 647, 659
Domar, E.D. 33, 586, 598
Donaldson, J.B. 297, 307, 327
Dore, M. 240
Dorfman, R. 49, 663
Dornbusch, R. 11, 44, 103, 113, 270, 325, 376, 377
Dostaler, G. 113, 223
Dow, C. 342
Downs, A. 523, 527, 539
Dowrick, S. 617
Doyle, C. 262, 553
Drago, R. 429
Drazen, A. 2, 30, 262, 517, 525, 536, 544, 546, 548, 554, 556
Driffill, J. 256, 257, 548
Duck, N.W. 230
Dunlop, J.G. 328
Durlauf, S.N. 335, 585, 587, 635

Easterlin, R.A. 580, 589, 594, 657
Easterly, W. 412, 536, 557, 563, 564, 585, 600, 601, 630, 635, 637, 641, 642, 646, 653
Edwards, S. 547, 556, 621, 630, 647, 648, 649
Eggertsson, G.B. 416
Eichenbaum, M. 29, 323, 332, 334, 336, 350, 705
Eichengreen, B. 10, 76, 79, 80, 81, 82, 637, 638
Eichner, A.S. 452
Eifert, B. 654
Eijffinger, S.C.W. 260, 414, 418, 551, 553

*Modern macroeconomics*

Ekelund, R.E. 329
Elmslie, B. 615
Els, van P.J.A. 307
Eltis, W. 164
Engerman, S. 643
Evans, C.L. 334
Evans, G.W. 228, 430

Fackler, J.S. 77
Fagerberg, J. 585, 604, 621
Fair, R. 336, 428, 525
Fajnzylber, P. 558
Fama, E. 323
Fay, J.A. 334
Fei, J. 615
Feiwel, G.R. 518
Feldstein, M. 23, 112, 300, 412, 416
Fellner, W. 249, 269
Ferguson, J.D. 76
Fischer, S. 6, 8, 11, 44, 103, 113, 220,
    247, 257, 258, 268, 301, 307, 325,
    328, 360, 363, 367, 368, 376, 409,
    411, 412, 413, 416, 442, 536, 540,
    551, 552, 556, 573, 585, 587, 614,
    701
Fisher, I. 53, 79, 121, 135, 216
Fitoussi, J.P. 401, 404, 407
Fitzgibbons, A. 75
Fleming, J.M. 123
Fletcher, G. 122
Fogel, R.W. 587
Forbes, K. 556
Forder, J. 262
Frankel, J.A. 647
Freeman, C. 611
Frenkel, J.A. 135, 164, 188, 191
Frey, B.S. 2, 30, 521, 523, 525, 526,
    544, 545, 547
Friedman, B.M. 196, 249, 409, 414
Friedman, M. 7, 21, 23, 25, 44, 79, 82,
    89, 144, 160, 163, 164, 165, 166,
    168, 169, 170, 171, 174, 175, 176,
    179, 182, 184, 186, 193, 194, 195,
    198, 202, 221, 236, 238, 249, 278,
    285, 294, 300, 322, 323, 342, 354,
    384, 410, 413, 454, 528, 550, 641,
    697
Frisch, H. 140
Frisch, R. 223, 308
Frydman, R. 228

Fukuyama, F. 587, 638, 640, 642, 645,
    659

Galbraith, J. 142, 187, 364, 423
Galbraith, J.K. 14, 56, 95
Gali, J. 27, 411, 419, 421, 423, 427, 431
Gallup, J. 596, 652
Galor, O. 34, 590, 591, 595, 596, 597,
    621, 655, 706
Garcia-Penalosa, C. 556, 557
Garrison, R.W. 475, 491, 497, 504, 508
Gartner, M. 413, 517, 544
Gatti, R. 31, 553, 554, 574
Gelb, A. 654
Geraats, P.M. 413
Gerrard, B. 28, 57, 451, 698
Gerschenkron, A. 615, 620
Gertler, M. 27, 358, 382, 400, 419, 421,
    423, 427
Ghosh, A. 412
Glaeser, E. 558, 635, 637
Glahe, F.R. 122
Goldberger, A.S. 697
Goldin, C. 76, 77, 584, 597
Golosov, M. 430
Goodfriend, M. 29, 269, 410, 411, 413,
    427, 656, 701
Goodhart, C.A.E. 258, 262, 298, 550,
    551
Gordon, D.B. 256, 269, 550
Gordon, D.F. 384
Gordon, R.J. 9, 11, 27, 78, 113, 174,
    244, 246, 247, 248, 268, 269, 278,
    296, 330, 357, 358, 360, 361, 364,
    366, 369, 370, 373, 375, 379, 381,
    384, 401, 406, 421, 426, 429, 536,
    537, 587, 697
Grandmont, J.M. 470
Gray, C. 636
Green, J. 413
Greenspan, A. 415, 706
Greenwald, B.C. 21, 305, 327, 336, 360,
    398, 399, 400, 409, 430
Grief, A. 635
Griffin, K. 601
Grilli, V. 260, 551
Grossman, G. 585, 628, 630
Grossman, H. 72, 363
Gujarati, D. 140
Gunning, J. 588, 653

Gurkaynak, R. 633
Gyimah-Brempong, K. 558
Gylfason, T. 585

Haberler, G. 37, 54, 236, 298, 696
Hadri, K. 541
Hahn, F.H. 247, 383, 458, 459, 460,
    602, 671
Haldane, A. 413
Haley, J. 385
Hall, R.E. 220, 369, 370, 380, 401, 597,
    637, 652
Hall, T.E. 76
Haltiwanger, J.C. 328
Hamberg, D. 612
Hamilton, J.D. 80, 304
Hammond, J.D. 170, 171, 174, 180
Hamouda, O.F. 452
Hansen, A.H. 70, 102, 113, 201
Hansen, B. 140
Hansen, G.D. 334, 348, 585, 595, 596,
    656
Hansen, L.P. 322
Harcourt, G.C. 452, 478
Hargreaves-Heap, S.P. 361, 362, 405
Harrison, L.E. 634
Harrod, R. 33, 57, 455, 518, 569, 586,
    598
Hartley, J.E. 27, 294, 297, 309, 322,
    332, 336, 343
Havrilesky, T.M. 535, 551
Hayek, F.A. 23, 55, 89, 180, 237, 474,
    475, 488, 503, 504, 508, 516
Haynes, S.E. 536
Healey, N. 551
Heckman, J.J. 322, 597
Heilbroner, R.L. 11
Heinlein, R. 480
Helpman, E. 585, 628, 630, 650
Henderson, H. 58
Hennings, K.H. 475
Henry, S.G.B. 185
Herbst, J. 636, 653
Hess, G.D. 341
Heston, A. 355, 587
Heymann, D. 412
Heywood, J.S. 429
Hibbs, D.A. 30, 31, 517, 525, 526, 532,
    534, 536, 538, 539, 541, 547, 548,
    570, 635

Hicks, J.R. 22, 37, 57, 70, 102, 113,
    298, 366, 465, 466, 467, 696
Hirschman, A. 558
Hoffmaisler, A.W. 650
Holt, R.P.F. 452
Honkapohja, S. 228, 430
Hoover, K.D. 25, 27, 28, 61, 170, 208,
    220, 222, 230, 236, 237, 238, 267,
    268, 283, 290, 294, 297, 322, 327,
    332, 335, 336, 343, 353, 697
Horrell, S. 585
Horwitz, S.G. 475
Howells, P. 196
Howitt, P.W. 34, 72, 359, 442, 585, 628
Hsieh, C. 614
Hume, D. 54, 164
Huntington, S.P. 4, 634, 635, 659
Hutchison, M.M. 259
Hutchison, T.W. 15

Inada, K. 604
Ireland, P.N. 400, 431
Irwin, D. 651
Islam, N. 615

Jackman, R. 362, 395, 401, 403, 406, 423
Jackson, D. 193
Jaffe, D. 400
James, H. 76, 79, 80
Jamison, D.T. 653
Jansen, D.W. 329
Jay, P. 594
Jenkins, M.A. 551
Jestaz, D. 401, 404, 407
Johnson, E.S. 174
Johnson, H.G. 5, 9, 23, 24, 121, 164,
    165, 188, 191, 339, 557, 697
Johnson, P. 636, 637
Johnson, S. 635, 643, 652, 654, 656
Jones, C.I. 34, 585, 589, 594, 595, 597,
    603, 617, 618, 622, 623, 627, 628,
    629, 631, 637, 648, 654, 656
Jones, E.L. 594, 657
Jones, H.G. 602, 608
Jorgenson, D.W. 587, 596, 613, 697
Judd, J.P. 327, 330

Kahn, J. 79
Kahn, R.F. 57, 61, 376
Kaldor, N. 169, 324, 557, 595, 685

Kalecki, M. 518, 570
Kareken, J. 169
Kasper, S.D. 8
Katz, L.F. 384, 385, 401, 406, 429
Kearl, J.R. 6
Keech, W. 517
Keefer, P. 635, 636, 637, 646
Keegan, W. 185
Kehoe, P.J. 297, 329, 337, 341
Kelly, L.C. 631
Kenny, C. 586
Keulen, M.V. 551
Keuzenkamp, H.A. 225
Keynes, J.M. 8, 9, 14, 22, 36, 45, 49, 54,
    55, 56, 58, 59, 60, 61, 62, 63, 65,
    66, 68, 69, 70, 71, 73, 77, 79, 83,
    84, 88, 101, 201, 202, 206, 225,
    229, 236, 298, 327, 328, 396, 430,
    451, 453, 455, 456, 457, 459, 460,
    461, 462, 464, 465, 468, 470, 471,
    484, 493, 503, 510, 512, 518, 593,
    612, 696, 698, 699
Khan, Z. 629, 643
Kilian, L. 358
Killick, T. 521
Kim, J.-I. 665
Kim, K. 236, 238, 297
King, M. 403, 413, 415, 416, 418
King, R.G. 29, 113, 269, 298, 303, 323,
    361, 410, 411, 427, 431, 601, 701
Kirman, A.P. 336
Kirschner, D. 341
Kirshner, J. 412
Kiyotaki, N. 374
Klamer, A. 56, 165, 698
Klein, L.R. 57, 70, 108, 451, 697, 698
Klenow, P.J. 34, 598, 625, 633
Knack, S. 635, 636, 637, 646
Knight, F.H. 229
Kochin, L.A. 80, 82
Kontolemis, Z. 413
Koopmans, T.C. 264, 675
Kornai, J. 641, 649
Kraay, A. 589, 597, 647, 659
Kramer, G.H. 525
Kregel, J.A. 452
Kremer, M. 593, 628, 656
Kreps, D.M. 471
Krueger, A.B. 401
Krueger, A.O. 597, 621, 647, 648

Krugman, P. 76, 147, 175, 360, 410,
    614, 622, 652, 686
Kumar, S. 621
Kuttner, K.N. 414
Kuznets, S. 557, 580
Kydland, F.E. 26, 221, 249, 250, 251,
    263, 269, 283, 294, 307, 309, 317,
    320, 321, 322, 323, 324, 326, 327,
    328, 331, 341, 351, 409, 413, 546,
    550, 588, 697

Laband, D. 586
Laidler, D.E.W. 9, 17, 50, 51, 99, 165,
    169, 173, 174, 191, 193, 222, 274,
    299, 336, 357, 363, 365, 428, 536
Laing, D. 367
Lakatos, I. 182
Lake, D. 659
Lal, D. 593, 594, 635
Landau, R. 637
Landes, D.S. 589, 594, 629, 635, 645,
    654, 657
Landman, T. 636
Laroque, G. 470
Lau, L.J. 665
Laubach, T. 27, 413, 416
Lawrence, R. 648
Lawson, T. 75
Layard, R. 362, 395, 401, 403, 406, 408,
    423
Lederman, D. 558
Lee, R. 655, 656
Lee, S.P. 12
Lee, W. 637
Leeson, R. 142, 144, 146, 176, 180
Leibenstein, H. 388, 389, 392
Leijonhufvud, A. 37, 57, 71, 72, 73, 74,
    75, 99, 113, 230, 336, 359, 391,
    398, 410, 412, 446, 484, 494, 513,
    698
Lerner, A. 519
Leslie, D. 365
Levacic, R. 300
Levine, R. 564, 585, 601, 630, 635, 637,
    642, 646, 653
Lewer, J.J. 647
Lewis, W.A. 556, 600, 665
Lilien, D.M. 335
Lindbeck, A. 357, 360, 361, 394, 395,
    396, 410, 422, 431, 432, 526, 535

Lipset, S.M. 640
Lipsey, R.G. 23, 137, 139, 140, 142, 248
Litterman, B. 323
Littleboy, B. 75
Littlechild, S. 475
Ljungqvist, L. 214, 263, 285, 352, 404
Loayza, N. 558
Lockwood, B. 261
Loewy, M.B. 648, 650
Lohmann, S. 259
Long, J.B. 26, 295, 323, 331, 697
Lovell, M.C. 228
Lucas, R.E. Jr. 22, 23, 24, 25, 26, 33, 34, 89, 145, 157, 162, 165, 182, 203, 211, 219, 221, 222, 224, 232, 233, 234, 235, 236, 237, 238, 239, 240, 241, 250, 263, 264, 265, 266, 267, 269, 272, 294, 295, 296, 297, 305, 306, 307, 308, 311, 328, 348, 353, 354, 358, 383, 430, 441, 472, 540, 550, 579, 585, 587, 588, 596, 597, 598, 616, 619, 620, 624, 625, 647, 657, 666, 675, 678, 697
Lundberg, M. 556

Machin, S. 429
MacRae, C.D. 526, 535
Maddison, A. 17, 18, 34, 326, 581, 587, 589, 590, 593, 596, 613, 616, 627, 638, 639, 640, 657
Maddock, R. 225, 230
Madsen, J.B. 408
Malinvaud, E. 72
Maloney, J. 541
Mankiw, N.G. xiv, 7, 24, 27, 33, 36, 175, 194, 197, 242, 284, 313, 332, 334, 335, 348, 358, 359, 361, 363, 364, 371, 372, 378, 379, 398, 409, 431, 433, 442, 449, 450, 585, 590, 598, 603, 604, 611, 617, 622, 624, 625, 629, 632, 633, 680, 697, 700
Manning, A. 384, 422
Marris, R. 376
Marshall, A. 388
Martin, P. 621
Martin, R. 652
Mas, I. 551
Masciandaro, D. 260, 551
Masson, P.R. 249

Matthews, K. 248, 249
Matthews, R.C.O. 17, 602
Mauro, P. 563, 644
Mayer, T. 6, 50, 164, 171, 173, 193, 197, 358, 422, 551
Mazower, M. 10
Mazzoleni, R. 628
McCallum, B.T. 297, 332, 360, 536
McCleary, R.M. 635
McCloskey, D.N. 579
McDermott, J. 656
McDonald, I.M. 381, 395
McGrattan, E.R. 337, 627
McGregor, R.R. 551
McPherson, M. 626
Meade, J.E. 697
Meadows, D.H. 691
Medoff, J.L. 334
Mehra, R. 281, 348
Mehta, G. 75
Meier, G.M. 520
Meiselman, D. 171
Melchior, A. 617
Mellinger, A. 596, 652
Meltzer, A.H. 57, 62, 65, 538
Mendoza, E.G. 341
Menger, C. 474
Meredith, G. 249
Metzler, L.A. 662
Meyer, S. 394
Micklewright, J. 423
Milanovic, B. 620
Mill, J.S. 5, 645
Millard, S. 334
Minford, A.P.L. 89, 230, 248, 249, 262, 263, 285, 300, 404, 539
Minier, J. 636, 659
Miron, J.A. 204
Mises, L. v. 475, 508
Mishkin, F.S. 27, 197, 246, 260, 262, 269, 413, 414, 415, 416, 552
Mitchell, W.C. 305
Mizen, P. 413
Moav, O. 595, 597, 655
Modigliani, F. 22, 57, 68, 70, 73, 101, 102, 113, 145, 171, 187, 196, 262, 264, 300, 331, 402, 518, 697, 698
Moggridge, D. 57
Mokyr, J. 584, 594, 630, 656, 657
Morgan, B. 122

Morgenstern, O. 466
Morris, C.T. 636
Morrisson, C. 620
Mosley, P. 525
Motto, R. 337
Mountford, A. 590, 591, 621
Muellbauer, J. 333, 334
Mulhearn, C. 697
Mullineux, A.W. 236, 269, 297, 307,
    327, 536, 588
Mundell, R.A. 10, 123, 130, 135
Murphy, K.M. 560, 643, 645, 685, 694
Muscatelli, A. 259, 411, 413
Mussa, M. 191
Muth, J.F. 207, 219, 221, 224, 225, 226,
    230, 238, 697
Myles, G.D. 637
Myrdal, K.G. 557, 685

Naish, H.F. 382
Nelson, C.R. 299, 300, 301, 303, 309,
    331, 335
Nelson, R.R. 556, 586, 597, 612, 628,
    630
Nickell, S. 263, 328, 362, 395, 401, 403,
    404, 406, 408, 422, 423
Noland, M. 640
Nordhaus, W.D. 30, 262, 331, 525, 526,
    527, 529, 530, 532, 535, 536, 537,
    542, 547, 553, 565, 570, 587
North, D.C. 597, 628, 635, 636, 637,
    643, 656

O'Brien, D.P. 37
O'Donnell, G. 416, 419
O'Donnell, R.M. 57, 75, 76
O'Rourke, K.H. 647
Obstfeld, M. 135, 414
Ohanian, L.E. 15, 76, 79, 329, 336, 337,
    588
Okun, A. 235, 268, 376, 381, 429
Olson, M. 517, 558, 588, 597, 620, 633,
    635, 636, 638, 640, 641, 692
Ormerod, P.A. 185
Ottaviano, G.P. 621

Pack, H. 601, 630
Paish, F.W. 146
Paldam, M. 536, 637
Papademos, L.D. 187, 402

Parente, S.L. 355, 562, 585, 595, 620,
    621, 629, 630, 633, 636, 650, 656
Parker, R.E. 9, 13, 77
Parkin, M. 220, 260, 361, 372
Parkinson, M.L. 334
Passell, P. 12
Patinkin, D. 14, 22, 23, 56, 57, 62, 71,
    72, 73, 113, 120, 166, 167, 452
Payne, M. 643
Pearce, K.A. 61
Peel, D.A. 89, 263, 285, 539
Peng, W. 536
Perez, S.J. 170
Perotti, R. 31, 519, 550, 554, 555, 556,
    557, 558, 560, 569
Perry, G.L. 23, 160, 416
Persson, T. 257, 517, 538, 554, 556,
    558
Pesaran, H. 75
Pesek, B. 121
Phelps, E.S. 28, 57, 144, 174, 205, 221,
    223, 228, 247, 268, 328, 330, 332,
    357, 361, 363, 364, 367, 370, 376,
    381, 383, 384, 389, 401, 404, 405,
    407, 408, 409, 413
Philippopoulos, A. 261
Philipson, T.J. 582, 621
Phillips, A.W. 23, 113, 136, 140
Phillips, S. 412
Pickering, A.C. 541
Pierce, J.L. 196
Piga, G. 413, 414
Pigou, A.C. 120, 122
Pindyck, R. 379
Plosser, C.I. 26, 41, 89, 201, 295, 297,
    298, 299, 300, 301, 303, 309, 311,
    317, 321, 323, 324, 326, 327, 331,
    335, 697
Pomeranz, K. 34, 580, 594
Poole, W. 196, 249
Porter, M. 652
Posen, A.S. 27, 262, 413, 416, 554
Prasad, E. 329
Prescott, E.C. 26, 27, 33, 76, 79, 80,
    221, 249, 250, 251, 263, 269, 281,
    283, 294, 297, 298, 307, 309, 317,
    320, 321, 322, 323, 324, 325, 326,
    327, 328, 331, 334, 337, 338, 344,
    348, 351, 355, 356, 409, 413, 546,
    550, 562, 585, 588, 595, 596, 620,

621, 629, 630, 633, 636, 650, 656, 675, 697
Presley, J.R. 97, 122, 298
Pritchett, L. 34, 580, 617, 620, 683
Proudman, J. 630
Purvis, D.D. 173, 193

Quah, D.T. 322, 341, 365, 587, 635, 667

Raff, D.M.G. 394
Ramey, G. 412
Ramey, V.A. 412
Ramsey, F. 675, 679
Ranis, G. 615
Rankin, N. 365
Rappaport, J. 654
Rapping, L.A. 220, 224, 233, 240, 311
Ravn, M.O. 327
Razin, A. 135
Rebelo, S.T. 303, 334, 626
Redding, S. 630
Redman, D.A. 226, 230
Reid, G.C. 429
Reis, R. 364
Reynolds, L.G. 593, 594, 636
Rhee, W. 341
Riddell, C. 694
Riddell, R. 601
Rivera-Batiz, L. 647
Robbins, L. 475
Roberts, P.C. 300
Robertson, D.H. 97, 357
Robinson, J.A. 31, 32, 517, 562, 563, 588, 635, 636, 637, 642, 643, 652, 654, 656, 706
Robinson, J. 17, 55, 71, 93, 113, 324, 364, 452
Robinson, S. 640
Rodriguez, F. 647
Rodriguez-Clare, A. 34, 598, 625, 633
Rodrik, D. 517, 556, 558, 585, 596, 633, 635, 637, 641, 646, 647, 648, 651, 652, 658, 706
Roed, K. 404
Roemer, J. 637
Rogerson, R. 187, 348
Rogoff, K. 30, 135, 257, 258, 376, 419, 525, 526, 532, 538, 547, 552, 553, 572

Roland, G. 564
Romer, C.D. 12, 16, 23, 79, 82, 170, 171, 197, 238, 335, 412, 413, 419, 422, 706
Romer, D. 23, 27, 32, 33, 170, 171, 197, 238, 335, 363, 364, 373, 378, 379, 380, 382, 398, 412, 413, 419, 422, 423, 424, 426, 427, 429, 430, 431, 442, 450, 590, 598, 604, 611, 624, 625, 632, 647, 697, 700, 706
Romer, P.M. 34, 354, 579, 585, 587, 595, 598, 604, 615, 616, 621, 622, 623, 625, 626, 627, 628, 629, 630, 647, 649, 666, 673, 683, 694
Rose-Ackerman, S. 637
Rosen, S. 383
Rosenberg, N. 394, 592, 630
Rosenthal, H. 30, 517, 539, 542, 545
Rostagno, M. 337
Rostow, W.W. 10, 586, 597, 600
Rotemberg, J.J. 328, 334, 360, 371, 372, 380, 430
Rothbard, M.N. 475
Rothschild, K.W. 140
Roubini, N. 2, 30, 31, 195, 262, 517, 525, 536, 542, 572
Rubinfeld, D.L. 379
Rush, M. 268, 297
Russell, R.R. 621
Ryan, C. 269, 297, 307, 327, 588
Rymes, T.K. 113

Sachs, J.D. 21, 31, 80, 82, 88, 219, 542, 587, 596, 598, 616, 621, 630, 647, 648, 652, 653, 654
Sahay, R. 556
Sala-i-Martin, X. 32, 162, 288, 297, 563, 585, 586, 590, 603, 604, 611, 617, 618, 620, 622, 623, 625, 631, 635, 653, 654, 662, 678
Salant, W.S. 17
Salop, S.C. 388, 389
Salyer, K.D. 27, 294, 297, 322, 332, 336, 343
Samuelson, P.A. 22, 54, 56, 70, 101, 142, 144, 174, 201, 277, 298, 300, 358, 662, 663
Sandilands, R. 77
Sanfey, P.J. 394
Santomero, A.M. 136, 179

Sargent, T.J. 22, 23, 24, 26, 89, 205, 214, 219, 242, 249, 263, 265, 266, 267, 269, 281, 285, 352, 353, 404, 472, 540
Savage, L. 464, 466, 467, 468
Saving, T.R. 121
Sawyer, M. 359, 452
Say, J.B. 46
Schaling, E. 260
Scheinkman, J. 558, 637
Schmookler, J. 631
Schneider, F. 2, 30, 525, 526, 544, 545, 547
Schuknecht, L. 522, 538
Schultz, K. 544, 545, 546
Schumpeter, J.A. 298, 519, 644
Schwartz, A.J. 25, 79, 82, 113, 164, 165, 170, 202, 236, 238, 322, 323, 324, 354
Scott, A. 334
Seater, J.J. 136, 179
Selgin, G.A. 516
Sensier, M. 334
Serageldin, I. 635
Sevilla, J. 652
Shackle, G.L.S. 71, 76, 229
Shafir, E. 412
Shapiro, C. 388, 390, 409, 423
Shaw, G.K. 112, 230, 431, 600
Sheffrin, S.M. 230, 332, 398
Sheridan, N. 419
Shiller, R.J. 412
Shin, K. 341
Shleifer, A. 558, 560, 635, 636, 637, 642, 643, 645, 685
Sibert, A. 30, 525, 526, 538, 547, 572
Siebert, H. 263, 401, 404
Siklos, P.L. 556
Simkins, S.P. 307
Sims, C.A. 169, 268, 322, 323
Singleton, K.J. 323
Skidelsky, R. 8, 14, 56, 57, 62, 75, 77, 82, 83, 86, 89, 90, 91, 150, 175
Skousen, M. 507
Smith, A. 7, 13, 615, 635, 650, 653
Smith, D. 185
Smith, R.T. 327, 329
Smithin, J. 135
Smolensky, E. 459, 471
Snowdon, B. 5, 10, 17, 23, 25, 30, 31, 32, 57, 68, 70, 73, 74, 75, 77, 113, 145, 165, 175, 220, 221, 222, 229, 230, 235, 267, 284, 292, 295, 297, 304, 328, 336, 339, 342, 348, 357, 360, 361, 362, 412, 413, 414, 429, 430, 452, 523, 536, 537, 549, 560, 564, 584, 585, 586, 587, 588, 601, 619, 641, 646, 647, 658, 661, 701
Snower, D.J. 394, 395, 396, 422
Soares, R.R. 582, 621
Soh, B.H. 536
Sokoloff, K. 629, 643
Sola, M. 329
Solomou, S. 301
Solow, R.M. 29, 33, 110, 142, 144, 145, 146, 169, 176, 187, 262, 264, 267, 275, 300, 325, 383, 385, 391, 392, 395, 410, 441, 466, 585, 586, 598, 602, 609, 611, 612, 613, 660, 663, 683, 703, 704, 705
Soskice, D. 334, 362, 403, 409
Sowell, T. 46
Spence, M. 388
Spencer, R.W. 110
Spinelli, F. 258
Spolare, E. 31, 564, 565, 578, 579, 652
Sprague, A. 263, 285
Spulber, D.F. 430
Squire, L. 556
Sraffa, P. 93
Srinivasan, T.N. 647
Stadler, G.W. 268, 297, 308, 332, 335
Stafford, G. 587
Stanislaw, J. 523
Startz, R. 11, 103, 113, 325
Stein, H. 17
Stevenson, A. 184
Stewart, M. 16
Stiglitz, J.E. 21, 122, 187, 262, 305, 327, 336, 360, 361, 364, 380, 382, 383, 385, 388, 390, 398, 399, 400, 409, 422, 423, 430, 432, 522, 553
Stiroh, K. 587
Stock, J.H. 335
Stone, J.A. 536
Stone, J.R.N. 697
Strigl, R. 508
Strout, A.M. 601
Subramanian, A. 563, 635, 654
Sugden, R. 467

Summers, L.H. 17, 31, 259, 260, 261, 294, 322, 328, 332, 333, 334, 336, 348, 354, 394, 401, 406, 413, 416, 549, 551, 553, 554, 611, 648
Summers, R. 355, 587
Svensson, L.E.O. 220, 257, 258, 413, 414, 416, 420
Swan, T.W. 33, 586, 598, 602

Tabellini, G. 260, 517, 538, 548, 551, 554, 556, 558
Tallroth, N.B. 654
Tamura, R. 620
Tanzi, V. 522, 644, 658
Tarshis, L. 328
Taussig, M. 459, 471
Tavelli, H. 258
Taylor, A. 414, 647
Taylor, A.M. 588
Taylor, H. 255
Taylor, J.B. 3, 29, 229, 247, 268, 270, 328, 363, 367, 369, 370, 376, 409, 410, 411, 412, 420, 422, 423, 424, 426, 427, 705
Taylor, J. 140
Taylor, T. 637
Temin, P. 10, 76, 79, 80, 81, 82, 171, 342, 635
Temple, J. 412, 585, 596, 609, 636, 637, 706
Tenyero, S. 564
Theil, H. 520
Thirlwall, A.P. 359
Thomas, R. 637
Thompson, J.L. 173, 193
Thurow, L.C. 391, 587
Timbrell, M. 383
Tinbergen, J. 250, 520
Tobin, J. 5, 14, 16, 22, 23, 32, 55, 112, 113, 121, 146, 147, 148, 156, 169, 174, 175, 184, 187, 220, 222, 223, 232, 262, 268, 278, 295, 300, 313, 324, 331, 334, 338, 358, 359, 360, 361, 396, 398, 402, 430, 442, 469, 518, 697
Tocqueville, A. de 519
Tomlinson, J.D. 17, 697
Toniolo, G. 17, 585
Townshend, H. 71
Trebbi, F. 635

Trecroci, C. 411, 413
Trehan, B. 327, 330
Trevithick, J.A. 46, 66, 184
Trigg, A. 298
Tufte, E.R. 525, 532, 536
Tullio, G. 258
Turner, H.A. 193
Tversky, A. 412

Ugur, M. 135

Vamvakidis, A. 651
Van den Berg, H. 647
Van der Gaag, J. 459, 471
Vane, H.R. 5, 23, 25, 30, 68, 70, 73, 75, 145, 165, 173, 175, 187, 193, 220, 221, 222, 229, 235, 267, 284, 292, 295, 297, 304, 328, 339, 348, 360, 361, 362, 452, 585, 586, 588, 661, 697, 701
Vaughan, M.B. 6
Vegh, C. 556
Venables, A.J. 652
Venables, T. 620, 652
Vercelli, A. 29
Verdier, T. 563, 642
Vetter, H. 395
Vickers, J. 413
Vines, D. 83, 84, 85, 416
Vishny, R.W. 560, 643, 645, 685
Von Neumann, J. 466

Wacziarg, R. 564, 565
Wagner, R. 23, 90, 195, 519
Wallace, N. 26, 242, 249, 269, 540
Waller, C.J. 259
Walsh, C.E. 257, 258, 259, 297, 550, 552, 576
Walters, A.A. 225
Walters, B. 452
Wang, T. 640
Warming, J. 61
Warner, A.M. 616, 621, 630, 647, 648, 654
Watson, M.W. 335, 358
Weale, M. 262, 553
Weber, S. 299
Weil, D.N. 33, 34, 450, 595, 596, 598, 624, 625, 632, 655, 706
Weingast, B.R. 636, 643, 656

Weinstein, D. 648
Weintraub, E.R. 57, 170
Weiss, A. 385, 388, 429
Weiss, L. 323
Weitzman, M.L. 423
Wells, J. 586
Wheeler, M. 76
White, E.N. 76, 77
White, H. 601
White, L.H. 516
Wickens, M. 322, 338, 341
Wicksell, K. 6
Wilkinson, F. 193
Willet, T.D. 517, 537
Williams, D. 586
Williams, J.C. 631
Williamson, J.G. 647
Williamson, S.D. 296, 297, 343
Wilson, T. 122
Winters, A. 647
Wittman, D.A. 539
Wolfe, E.N. 587, 597
Wolfers, J. 401, 408

Woodford, M. 4, 85, 220, 380, 413, 416, 697, 698
Woolley, J.T. 535, 551
Wright, G. 584, 637
Wrigley, E. 594
Wynarczyk, P. 25, 75, 221, 229, 295, 701

Yang, X. 652
Yellen, J.L. 372, 374, 384, 385, 388, 391, 393, 441
Yergin, D. 523
Ying, L.G. 649
Young, A. 679
Young, A. 613, 614, 622, 655
Young, D. 452
Young, W. 113

Zak, P.J. 637, 646
Zarnowitz, V. 305, 307, 327, 537
Zhang, T. 404
Zijp, R. 223, 224, 238, 241
Zilberfarb, B.Z. 113
Zoega, G. 364, 401, 404, 407, 408

# Subject index

accelerationist hypothesis 62
adaptive expectations 227, 528, 535
aggregate demand externality 374
aggregate supply
  models of 53, 67, 78, 233, 243,
    315–19, 397, 400
aggregate supply hypothesis 233–5
agreement/disagreement in
  macroeconomics 3–6, 695–707
AK growth model 626–7
animal spirits 102, 225, 463, 468, 512
asymmetric information 388, 537
augmented Solow growth model 625,
  632–3
Austrian approach 15, 28, 89, 238, 298,
  474–516

balance of payments 124–35
  automatic adjustment of 189
  monetary approach to 187–92
Bank of England 414–17, 549, 553, 706
bonds and net wealth 110–12, 121–2
Bretton Woods 84, 187, 191, 638
business cycle 1, 3, 9–13, 16, 33, 76–82,
  170, 236–42, 300–320, 396–401,
  503–9, 525–46
business cycle stylised facts 304–7

capital accumulation 606–9
capital deepening 607, 626
capital fundamentalism 556–7, 601
capital widening 607
calibration 320–22
capital market imperfections 382,
  398–400
catch-up hypothesis 88, 614, 620–21,
  630, 650, 659
central bank independence 257–62, 532,
  549–54, 592, 705
classical approach 7, 8, 13, 14, 22,
  37–54

classical model
  output and employment determination
    in 38–45
  Say's law and the 45–50
  quantity theory of money and the
    50–54
Cobb–Douglas production function 609,
  613, 623
comparative advantage 648
constant returns to scale 604, 625
consumption function 59, 62, 265,
  510–12, 606
convergence
  conditional 617, 631, 648
  unconditional 617, 649
convergence club 617, 619
convergence debate 614–22, 659
coordination failure 73, 74, 230, 336,
  359, 398
corruption 523, 558, 643–6
Council of Economic Advisers 23, 146
Cowles Commission 22
credibility 248–9, 262, 546, 548–9
credit rationing 400
crowding out 61, 69, 107, 110, 132
customer markets 381

deflation 77, 120, 416, 513–15
demand for money 51, 62, 104
  and the modern quantity theory
    166–74
  empirical evidence 168–73
  Keynesian approach 70, 104–6
democracy 10, 636, 640–43, 658–9
dictatorship 10, 562–3, 641–3
disinflation 247–9, 267, 334, 421, 705
Dornbusch's overshooting model
  376–8

economic growth 1, 18, 32–4, 479–83,
  556–64, 579–659, 706

economic history and 580–82, 593–5,
        654–7
fundamental causes 596–8, 633–54
geography and 652–4
ideal conditions for 657–9
importance of 589–93
inequality and 556–62, 637
institutions and 562–4, 635–47,
        651–2, 658
intensive 593–4
natural experiments and 638–40
political barriers and 642
Promethean 594
proximate causes 596–8, 603, 612
renaissance of research in 585–8
Smithian 594
stylized facts and 595–6
trade and 647–52
effective demand 14, 58, 63, 69, 70, 102,
        410, 453–5
efficiency wage theories
    and adverse selection 388–9
    and fairness 391–3
    and labour turnover 389
    and shirking 389–91, 423
    generalized 384–8
endogeneity of money 190, 298, 323
Employment Act, US 15
entrepreneur economy 461–3, 644
ethnic diversity 563–5, 635, 642, 646
exchange rates 123–35
    fixed 187–91
    flexible 191–2, 416
expectations
    adaptive 180–81, 227
    rational 29, 181, 225–30
expenditure switching policies 189–90

Federal Reserve 79, 81–2, 170, 415,
        505, 515
First World War 80, 81
fiscal policy 17, 106–14, 705
    power of 107, 109–10, 118, 130, 132,
        194–5
Fisher effect 54
Fisher equation 52
foreign aid 601–2, 642
Friedman, Milton 7, 25, 163, 175, 194,
        222
    interview with 198–218

Friedman–Meiselman debate 171–3
functional finance 519
fundamentalist Keynesianism 71

General Agreement on Tariffs and Trade
        84
game theory 250, 252–6, 297, 546, 705
    non-cooperative 254–5
    repeated 256
globalization 647, 651–2
Golden Age 17, 18, 21, 88, 535, 638
Gold Standard 79–82, 258, 337
government budget constraint 110–11
government failure 27, 55, 300, 522–3
government, role of 7–8, 55, 65, 77,
        473, 521–3
gradualism versus cold turkey 183
Great Depression 2, 8–16, 33, 76–82,
        88, 170–71, 334, 336–8, 421, 515,
        518, 586, 703
Great Divergence 34, 580–83, 655
Great Inflation 3, 142, 219
growth accounting 612–14

Harrod–Domar model 33, 557, 598–603,
        627
human capital 597, 620–21, 625, 632–3,
        650
hysteresis effects 247, 335, 405–8, 544,
        704

imperfect/monopolistic competition 362,
        364, 371–6, 382, 411
imperfect information 224, 238, 308,
        331
implicit contract models 384
incomes policy 247–8, 423
indexation 184, 382
Industrial Revolution 34, 580, 589, 594,
        609, 619, 620–21, 629, 655–7
inflation 3, 83, 513–14, 549–54
    and unemployment 135–44, 175–85
    causes of 181–2, 191
    costs of 411–13
    costs of reducing 182–5
    cure for 413–22
    in the G7 economies 20
    in the UK economy 3, 182
    in the US economy 3, 182, 191
    targeting 257, 411, 413–19, 703

inside money 323
insider–outsider theories 394–6
International Monetary Fund 84
intertemporal capital restructuring
  475–9
intertemporal labour substitution 233,
  308, 311–13, 328, 332
intertemporal structure of production
  475–83
investment trap 118–20
invisible-hand theorem 22, 55
IS–LM model 23, 61, 70, 171–4, 423–4,
  431, 696, 698
  closed economy 102–23,
  open economy 85, 123–35
  with flexible prices 116–22, 315

Keynes effect 115–16, 118
Keynes's
  analysis of the labour market 65–9
  analysis of the quantity theory of
    money 69–71
  legacy and the classical revival 85–90
  main propositions 59–65, 144–7
  paradox of thrift 49, 485, 501–3
  rejection of Say's law 69
Keynes's *General Theory* 8, 13, 29,
  54–76, 696
  and the 'new scholarship' 75–6
  interpretations of 57, 70–75, 101–46
Keynesian approach 7–8, 24–5, 101–47,
  324, 484, 501–13
Keynesian consensus 15–24
Keynesian model
  underemployment equilibrium in the
    68, 114–22

labour hoarding 333
learning by doing 336, 625
liquidity preference 62, 64, 104,
  468–70, 491
liquidity trap 68, 74, 104, 106–8,
  116–18, 120, 147, 410
loanable funds market 47–8, 489–92,
  498, 512
Lucas critique 26, 264–7, 297, 340, 699
Lucas, Robert E. Jr. 25, 220–23, 707
  interview with 272–93
Lucas 'surprise' supply function 224,
  234, 340

macroeconometric models 26, 195,
  264–6
Mankiw, N. Gregory 27
  interview with 433–50
market clearing 224, 230–32, 238, 367
mark-up pricing 379–80
Marshall–Lerner condition 124
Marshall Plan 637–8
menu costs 371–5, 428, 430
microfoundations of macroeconomics
  27, 71, 72, 223, 299, 340, 360, 371,
  403, 431, 700
monetarist approach 25, 50, 89, 163–97,
  324, 483, 515
monetary policy 25, 26, 106–14, 705
  power of 107–9, 133, 190, 244–7
  role and conduct of 185–7, 196,
    413–22
monetary rule 196, 246, 420
money and business cycles 25, 170,
  236–42, 322–4, 503–9
  empirical evidence on 170, 246, 268
money illusion 38, 66, 175, 177, 223,
  236, 412, 460–61
multiplier 58, 60–62, 73, 103, 298
Mundell–Fleming model 123–35, 377
  fiscal expansion within 128, 131
  monetary expansion within 129, 134

NAIRU 27, 187, 401–8
Nash equilibrium 254
natural rate of unemployment 25, 44,
  401, 403–7, 494
natural resource curse 642, 654
near rationality 374–5
neoclassical growth theory 313, 321,
  602–12
neoclassical synthesis 21–4, 70, 74,
  101,122, 146, 698
neutrality of money 38, 63, 70, 308, 315,
  322–4, 335, 398, 454, 458, 469
  long-run 236, 696
  short-run 223–4, 235, 696
new classical approach 25–6, 89,
  219–71, 294–7
New Deal 337
new Keynesian approach 21, 27, 268,
  340, 357–432
new neoclassical synthesis 29, 410–11,
  427, 701, 703

new political macroeconomics 29–32,
  517–66
Nobel Memorial Prize in Economics 24,
  148, 165, 198, 272, 344, 660, 697
nominal anchor 413, 416, 703
nominal rigidity 361, 363, 365, 419, 428
  of prices 371–6
  of wages 65–7, 121, 366–71
non-neutrality of money 238–9, 247,
  330, 363, 369, 419, 459–61, 463,
  468, 472, 550

OPEC 299, 401, 407, 543, 703
open economy policy trilemma 414
optimal control theory 250
Okun's law 235, 540, 703
outside money 121

patents 628–9
Phillips curve 23, 25, 30, 113, 235–8,
  254, 266, 358, 419, 424, 426, 514,
  527–36, 550, 703, 706
  expectations-augmented 174–87, 697
  original 135–44
Pigou effect 120–22
policy ineffectiveness proposition
  242–7, 268, 699
political business cycle models 30, 195,
  261–2, 517–54
  Hibbs partisan model 532–5
  Nordhaus opportunistic model 30,
    526–32
  rational opportunistic model 537–8
  rational partisan model 259, 538–44
  synthesis model 545–6
political economy
  of debts and deficits 554–5
  of economic growth 32, 556–64,
    635–47
Post Keynesian approach 28, 228–9,
  248, 324, 376, 451–73
Prescott, Edward C. 25, 26
  interview with 344–56
principal agent problem 389, 411, 523,
  552, 643
procyclical prices 328–30
production function 39–41, 309,
  315–16, 325, 333–4, 603–6, 626,
  632
production possibilities frontier 492–6

productivity slowdown 587
propagation mechanism 240, 308, 311
property rights 629, 636, 641–3, 656
Public Choice school 519

quantity theory of money 483, 696
  Cambridge approach 51
  modern version of 163–74
  traditional 50–54

random walk 299–303, 309, 335
rational expectations 29, 219, 225–30,
  252, 268, 270, 297, 365, 367, 411,
  430, 464–5, 535, 539–41, 705
rationing models 362
Reaganomics 300
real business cycle approach 26–7,
  267–9, 294–343, 588
real business cycle model 307–20
real rigidity 365, 378–96
  of prices 378–83
  of wages 383–96
real wages
  countercyclical v. procyclical 327–8,
    368, 371, 544
reinterpretation of Keynes 70–75
rent seeking 304, 523, 643–5, 654, 658
representative agent 309–11, 336
reputation 248, 256–7, 546
research and development 336, 625–6,
  631, 650
Ricardian equivalence 111–12
Romer, Paul M. 587, 625–31
  interview with 673–94
rules v. discretion 26, 196–7, 249–57,
  546, 548–9, 700

sacrifice ratio 247–8, 257–8, 267, 406
Say's law 13, 15, 23, 455–8, 471
schools of thought 6, 24–9
Second World War 1, 8, 10, 15, 16, 17,
  22, 76, 83
secular stagnation 88
seigniorage 556
signal extraction problem 233, 239, 308
size of nations 564–5
Skidelsky, Robert
  interview with 91–100
social capability 597, 634–6
Solow growth model 602–12

Solow residual 34, 325–8, 333–4, 612–13
Solow, Robert M. 23, 24, 598, 602
  interview with 660–72
stagflation 23, 698–9
steady state 607–8
strategic complementarity 398
stylised facts 304–7, 309, 317, 321–2, 324, 326–30, 371, 408–9, 429, 544, 595–6
supply-side 15, 299
supply-side school 300
supply-side policies 33, 186–7, 263–4, 338
supply-side shocks 26, 303–4, 311

Taylor rule 196, 420, 700, 705
technological change 594, 603, 609–12, 625, 627–32, 649–51, 655–7
  endogenous 625–31
  shocks 304, 308, 309, 313–14, 317–18, 333
theory, role of 4
thick market externality 380
time inconsistency 26, 249–57, 546, 641, 699
Tobin, James 23, 24, 174
  interview with 148–62
transitional dynamics 617–19, 620, 623
Treasury view 58, 69, 107

trend reverting 301
trend stationary 301
tunnel effect 559–60

uncertainty 463–72, 512
unemployment 2, 11, 78, 135–44, 176–87, 235, 244–5, 253, 260, 334, 383–96, 401–8, 527–42
  frictional and structural 44, 140, 493–4
  involuntary unemployment 8–9, 45, 58, 65, 66–7, 71, 73, 145, 232, 267, 328, 334, 365, 383, 387, 390–91, 393, 396, 398–9, 409, 432, 453, 457–8, 462, 493
  in the G7 economies 19
  in the UK economy 2, 408
  in the US economy 2, 11, 408
unit root 303, 335

wage contracts
  implicit 384
  staggering of 368–9
Wall Street crash 10
Walrasian auctioneer 38
Walrasian general equilibrium theory 21, 72–3, 222–3, 238
wealth effect 319
World Bank 84
World Trade Organisation 84